LIFE AFTER DEATH

THE ANCHOR BIBLE REFERENCE LIBRARY is designed to be a third major component of the Anchor Bible Group, which includes the Anchor Bible commentaries on the books of the Old Testament, the New Testament, and the Apocrypha, and the Anchor Bible Dictionary. While the Anchor Bible commentaries and the Anchor Bible Dictionary are structurally defined by their subject matter, the Anchor Bible Reference Library will serve as a supplement on the cutting edge of the most recent scholarship. The series is open-ended; its scope and reach are nothing less than the biblical world in its totality, and its methods and techniques the most up-to-date available or devisable. Separate volumes will deal with one or more of the following topics relating to the Bible: anthropology, archaeology, ecology, economy, geography, history, languages and literatures, philosophy, religion(s), theology.

As with the Anchor Bible commentaries and the Anchor Bible Dictionary, the philosophy underlying the Anchor Bible Reference Library finds expression in the following: the approach is scholarly, the perspective is balanced and fair-minded, the methods are scientific, and the goal is to inform and enlighten. Contributors are chosen on the basis of their scholarly skills and achievements, and they come from a variety of religious backgrounds and communities. The books in the Anchor Bible Reference Library are intended for the broadest possible readership, ranging from world-class scholars, whose qualifications match those of the authors, to general readers, who may not have special training or skill in studying the Bible but are as enthusiastic as any dedicated professional in expanding their knowledge of the Bible and its world.

David Noel Freedman
GENERAL EDITOR

LIFE AFTER DEATH

A History of the Afterlife in the

Religions of the West

ALAN F. SEGAL

DOUBLEDAY
New York   London   Toronto   Sydney   Auckland

PUBLISHED BY DOUBLEDAY
a division of Random House, Inc.
1745 Broadway, New York, New York 10019

DOUBLEDAY and the portrayal of an anchor with a dolphin
are trademarks of Doubleday, a division of Random House, Inc.

Scripture quotations contained herein are from the New Revised Standard Version
Bible, copyright © 1989 by the Division of Christian Education of the National Council
of Churches of Christ in the U.S.A., and are used by permission. All rights reserved.

Book design by Leslie Phillips

Library of Congress Cataloging-in-Publication Data
Segal, Alan F., 1945–
Life after death : a history of the afterlife in western religion / Alan F. Segal.
p. cm.
Includes bibliographical references and index.
ISBN 0-385-42299-7 (alk. paper)
1. Future life. I. Title.
BL535.S438 2004
202'.3—dc22   2004052775

Printed in the United States of America
August 2004
First Edition

3   5   7   9   10   8   6   4   2

Dedicated to

from whom I learned wisdom about life

CONTENTS

*

PART FOUR. The Path to Modern Views of the Afterlife

*

ACKNOWLEDGMENTS

In ten years of living with this project, I sought help from many persons, first in writing the constantly expanding scope of the work, then in condensing the material to a more readable text. I want to thank Jim Charlesworth, who suggested I work on this project, and Andrew Corbin for his advice on how to defeat my own obsessiveness and compulsivity to finish the book—he was an invaluable aid at every stage of the book's creation.

I especially want to cite Will Oxtoby, who offered his critique at several important junctures and his practiced eye as an editor. My graduate students helped by reading and commenting on the text, especially in the early phases. In particular, I would like to thank Adam Gregerman, who served as a research assistant and helped me edit the first draft. Asha Moorthy, Lillian Larsen, Nick Witkowski, Jason Yorgason, Ethan Segal, Jordan Segal, Jodi Eichler, and Delman Coates were very helpful in reading through the early drafts of the manuscript and helping me see some of the issues more clearly. Innumerable undergraduate students helped me with various aspects of the study, and they are thanked in the appropriate place. I would like to thank Darcy Hirsh especially; she served as research assistant and helped me focus my discussion on gender issues.

When this project was done, it was hard to impose on a friend so much to read this huge manuscript. But John Gottsch, André Unger Carol Zaleski, and David Ulansey each offered to help in extraordinary ways by reading the whole thing through and offering their expert opinions on the subject and flow of the argument. Larry Hurtado read through several New Testament chapters and offered expert opinion, as well as his critique. Ben Sommers did the same with the Hebrew Bible chapters and suggested areas where my graduate studies in Ancient Near Eastern Studies needed to be renovated. Although none took my point of view on the manuscript, they helped me make my arguments more cogent, and I am grateful to all of them. I would especially like to thank David N. Freedman who read the manuscript very carefully and offered extensive suggestions.

Over the last dozen years I have received several grants that allowed me to spend time on this manuscript. I would especially like to thank Barnard College, which supported my research in countless ways over the last decade, and to my students there—both from Columbia and Barnard—who asked fundamental questions and so helped develop the book. Teaching graduate courses at Columbia University and participation in the graduate program allowed me to concentrate on the scholarly aspects of the book. The Annenberg Institute for Advanced Jewish Studies provided a semester of support and a group of concerned scholars with whom to consult. Williams College appointed me a Croghan Scholar that allowed me to try out my ideas in the wider community through lectures and discussions. I would also like to thank the Mellon Foundation for a semester grant to pursue Islam and diaspora religion and the ACIS and NITLE for providing a summer seminar with extraordinarily interesting colleagues for the development of a Web site on Islam. This helped me resurrect my earlier studies in Arabic and Islam and reach a new level of comfort in dealing with Muslim texts and concepts.

I would like to acknowledge work published elsewhere in different form: "Text Translation as a Prelude for Soul Translation" in *Translation and Anthropology* (Ed. Paula G. Rubel and Abraham Rosman, New York: Berg, 2003), *Jesus at 2000*, and some parts of *Paul the Convert*.

I would like to thank Steve Siebert and the staff at Nota Bene Associates, first for designing a word processing program like Nota Bene, which is perfect for scholarly studies in Western religions, and second for helping me to produce this manuscript.

A. F. SEGAL
New York, 2003

ABBREVIATIONS

Abbreviations in the notes and parenthetically in the text for the books of the Bible; Old and New Testament Apocrypha; Old and New Testament Pseudepigrapha; Dead Sea Scrolls and other texts from the Judean Desert; versions of the Taludic tractates; Targumic texts and other Rabbinic works; and Ancient and Classical Christian writings are those given in the SBL Handbook of Style (Ed. Alexander, Kutsko, Ernest, and Decker-Lucke, Hendrickson, 1999). Abbreviations for secondary sources are listed below.

AB	Anchor Bible
AGJU	Arbeiten zur Geschichte des antiken Judenthums und des Urchristentums
ANET	*Ancient Near Eastern Texts Relating to the Old Testament.* Ed. J. B. Pritchard. 3d ed. Princeton, 1969.
ANRW	*Aufstieg und Niedergang der römischen Welt: Geschichte und Kultur Roms im Spiegel der neueren Forschung.* 1972– .
BJS	Brown Judaic Studies
CAH	Cambridge Ancient History
CANE	*Civilizations of the Ancient Near East.* Ed. J. Sasson. 4 vols. New York, 1995.
CBQ	*Catholic Biblical Quarterly*
DJD	Discoveries in the Judaean Desert
EncJud	*Encyclopedia Judaic.* 16 vols. Jerusalem, 1972.
EPRO	Etudes préliminaries aux religions orientales dans l'empire romain
ER	*The Encyclopedia of Religion.* Ed. M. Eliade. 16 vols. New York.
HR	*History of Religions*
HTR	*Harvard Theological Review*
HUCA	*Hebrew Union College Annual*
IDB	*The Interpreter's Dictionary of the Bible.* Ed. G. A. Buttrick. 4 vols. Nashville, 1962.

JAOS	*Journal of American Oriental Studies*
JBL	*Journal of Biblical Literature*
JE	*The Jewish Encyclopedia.* Ed. I. Singer. 12 vols. New York, 1925.
JJS	*Journal of Jewish Studies*
JQR	*Jewish Quarterly Review*
JSJ	*Journal for the Study of Judaism in the Persian, Hellenistic, and Roman Periods*
JSNT	*Journal for the Study of the New Testament*
JSOT	*Journal for the Study of the Old Testament*
JSPSup	Journal for the Study of the Pseudepigrapha, Supplement Series
JSS	*Journal of Semitic Studies*
JTS	*Journal of Theological Studies*
KTU	*Die keilalphabetischen Texten aus Ugarit.* Ed. M. Dietrich, O. Loretz, and J. Sanmartin. AOAT 24:1. Neukirchen-Vluyn, 1976.
NHL	*Nag Hammadi Library in English.* Ed. J. M. Robinson. 4th rev. ed. Leiden, 1996.
NovT	*Novum Testamentum*
NRSV	New Revised Standard Version
NTS	*New Testament Studies*
PGM	*Papyri graecae magicae: Die griechischen Zauberpapyri.* Ed. K. Priesendanz. Berlin, 1928.
RB	*Revue Biblique*
RHR	*Revue de l'histoire des religions*
RSV	Revised Standard Version
SBL	Society of Biblical Literature
SBLSCS	Society of Biblical Literature Septuagint Cognate Studies
SRSup	*Studies in Religion,* Supplement
TDNT	*Theological Dictionary of the New Testament.* Ed. G. Kittel and G. Friedrich. Trans. G. W. Bromiley. 10 vols. Grand Rapids, 1964–1976.
TWNT	*Theologische Wörterbuch zum Neuen Testament.* Ed. G. Kittel and G. Friedrich. Stuttgart, 1932–1979.
VC	*Vigliae christianae*
VTSup	Supplement to *Vetus Testamentum*
WUNT	Wissenschaftliche Untersuchungen zum Neuen Testament

LIFE AFTER
DEATH

Introduction

The Undiscover'd Country

THE DREAD of something after death,
The undiscover'd country, from whose bourn
No traveller returns, puzzles the will . . .
     (*Hamlet*, Act 3, Scene 1, lines 78–80)

Shakespeare, Suicide, and Martyrdom

FEW OF US contemplate revenge or suicide as seriously as Hamlet did. Yet, Hamlet's words go far beyond his own predicament. They speak eloquently to us about the human situation, which seems as adamantine now as it was in 1602 when the play appeared. For good reason, it has become the most famous speech in the English language. To mention that the soliloquy begins with the words: "To be or not to be" is to identify it worldwide.

Hamlet ponders life at its hardest moments. But for the dread of death and fear of what may come afterwards, he would end his life, avoiding the troubles he has inherited. His decision against suicide, and for revenge, is made reluctantly, in full knowledge of the terrors of death that his ghostly father has intimated for him. He now has a supernatural reason to believe the spirit's message, both about posthumous punishment and about his father's murderer.

Hamlet's solitary revenge has been sharpened to a fine point by the World Trade Center disaster of September 11, 2001, a mass murder evidently also motivated out of revenge and driven by supernatural justifications. Nineteen extremist Muslims, indoctrinated with a caricature of

Muslim martyrdom, perpetrated one of the most callous slaughters of innocent civilians in human history, not in spite of divine retribution but convinced that their deed would ensure their resurrection and bring them additional eternal rewards before the Day Of Judgment. The horrible waste of more than 2,800 innocent lives was directly driven by notions of sexual felicity after death: A group of virgin, dark-eyed beauties awaited each of the suicidal murderers. "You cannot kill large numbers of people without a claim to virtue."[1] Surely such desperate men, intelligent, sophisticated, and coordinated enough to have planned a global outrage, would not be persuaded by such a naive and adolescent vision of heaven? Every significant public commentator has stressed that there were more important political, economic, social, and personal motivations for the attack. But, in the end, the visions of an afterlife quite different from our own have awakened us to the original meaning for our phrase "holy terror."

In the minds of Israeli settlers, those religiously motivated few among the Israelis who want to live in the land designated for a projected Palestinian state, pious Jews who have died at the hands of Arabs are also martyrs whose special reward will commence in heaven. To their loved ones, these Jewish martyrs look down on their surviving families from the heavenly Talmudic academy (the *Yeshiva shel Ma'ala*), encouraging the pioneers of a new nation to continue to settle and live in the occupied territories. While these Jewish views of the afterlife are considerably less sensual than the Muslim ones, the faith of the religious settlers is no less intense. Like the Islamic extremists in this respect, the settlers have innovated on traditional views of the afterlife to give meaning to their own political purposes.[2]

This book will attempt to put these modern tragedies into historical context. I had already researched the sociology of the afterlife for a decade when the World Trade Center disaster focused our national attention on *jihad*. The tragedy convinced me that this study of the relationship between heaven and social agendas had an importance beyond the scholarly community. This book has become a study of Western Religions.

Shakespeare called death and the afterlife "the undiscover'd country" from which no one returns, a sensible metaphor to Shakespeare's own "Age of Discovery," as the New World, still largely unexplored, was not yet completely mapped. Taking my cue from Hamlet, this study will attempt to see the relationship between "being" and "not being," between "sleeping" and "dreaming perchance," between the undiscovered land of the afterlife and those who imagine what lies within it.

This book is not a study of death, how to cope with it, what the process of dying is, nor how we may best accomplish the work of grieving. A great many books have recently focused on these ultimate moments of life, and, where relevant, I will rely on their conclusions with a reference. What I propose to do is sign on for "the long voyage," just as a ship's crew did in Shakespeare's "Age of Discovery," to penetrate the darkness of death and map the new day of the afterlife as it is depicted in western culture. I want to show the connection between visions of the afterlife and the early scriptural communities who produced them. I want to study the early, traditional maps of the afterlife that we find in our foundational Western religious texts and the territory they inscribe in the religious life of the vibrant societies that produced them. I want to not only ask what was believed, but to ask why people wanted an afterlife of a particular kind and how those beliefs changed over time. It will be a long and arduous trip, mostly through strange, half familiar, and fascinating landscapes. We will return with treasure, knowledge, and understanding of beliefs quite different from our own, yet reassurance that religious visions are not inexplicably beyond our abilities to mediate or change. This book is the logbook of that voyage.

We can easily answer the question of why Shakespeare used an explorer's metaphor to describe the afterlife: The discovery of the Americas was the great news of his day. But, why did the Egyptians insist on an afterlife in heaven while the body was embalmed in a pyramid on earth? Why did the Babylonians view the dead as living underground in a prison? Why did the Hebrews refuse to talk about the afterlife in First Temple times (1000–586 BCE) and then begin to do so in Second Temple times (539 BCE–70 CE)? Why did the Persians envision the afterlife as bodily resurrection while many Greeks narrated the flight of a soul back to heaven? How can a single culture contain different and conflicting views of the afterlife at the same time? Since all these cultures told stories of people who went to heaven, what did people find when they went there while yet alive, and why was it important to make the journey? These questions are much more complicated and more interesting than understanding the use of a casual metaphor, even by an author as gifted as Shakespeare. However, they can be investigated in the same way, through the study of texts and contexts as well as the religions and societies that produced them.

Intimations of Immortality

WE SURELY KNOW instinctively that every religious tradition uses the afterlife to speak of the ultimate reward of the good, just as we instinctively

3

know that stories of "heaven" will describe the most wonderful perfections imaginable in any one time and place, even as stories of "hell" will describe the most terrible and fearful punishments imaginable. A book that catalogues the history of surfeit in each culture would be an interesting cultural history in itself, but it would avoid the hard questions.

Jerry L. Walls begins his serious and quite sophisticated inquiry into heaven in *Heaven: The Logic of Eternal Joy*[3] with a crucial incident in the life of St. Augustine, as narrated in his *Confessions*. Augustine is with his famous mother, Monica, who is but a few days from her death. She has just convinced Augustine to be baptized as a Christian. At this tender and intimate moment, the two have a conversation that leads to the conclusion that no bodily pleasure can compare with the happiness of the martyred saints in heaven. For a moment, they feel that heaven is so close to them in life that they can almost touch it. Walls uses this scene as the starting point for his philosophical inquiry into the validity of notions of heaven. I would ask, instead, how the martyrs came to be envisioned as living eternally in heaven, why this discourse was so closely associated with the nearing death of Monica, and how closely it cohered with Christian doctrines of proselytization and mission. For Walls, it is the beginning of a description of what awaits us; for me, it is an example of how we as humans symbolize what of us is stronger than death in ways that are congruent with our lives in culture and society. The hardest questions are part of a historian's task. This book will attempt to outline a social history. We will not ask theological questions so much as the basic question of a historian: *"cui bono"?* To whose benefit is this belief in the afterlife?

American Afterlife:
Resurrection Versus Immortality of the Soul

WE WILL HAVE to take a very hard look at some cherished aspects of Judaism and Christianity. The church father Tertullian equated Christianity with a belief in the resurrection: "By believing in resurrection, we are what we claim to be."[4] By "resurrection," he opined, "orthodox" Christians should believe in literal, fleshly resurrection, with its attendant end-of-time and judgment of sinners. Even though Tertullian was a churchman, his opinion was not unchallenged. Many Christians of his day believed with the Platonists that the soul was immortal but the body perished forever. It will become clear to us later that Tertullian's view of this phenomenon is itself governed by his personal dispositions and the historical context in which he lived. For now, it should be important

4

for us to know that in the Christianity that Tertullian prescribed, bodily resurrection was something he devoutly wished for, nay prayed for, preached, and held other Christians heretical because they did not believe it literally.

Today, most American Christians of all denominations continue to assent to a belief in resurrection. But closer scrutiny shows that many do not believe that the physical body will be resurrected, as Tertullian preached, but that the soul will dwell in heaven after death. What they call "resurrection of the body" actually refers technically to "immortality of the soul." The notion of resurrection is only strongly characteristic of a sizeable minority of Americans. A traditional, strong, and literal view in a resurrection of the body is, in fact, a very strong indicator that the person is on the evangelical, fundamentalist, or Orthodox Jewish side of the line.[5]

Religious belief is a gradient. But that distinct line three-quarters of the way toward the right of the religious spectrum is the big story in American religion at the beginning of the twenty-first century. Americans on the left of that line—let us call them the liberal, mainline religions for lack of a better term—have more in common with each other than they do with their coreligionists across the line. Liberal Jews, Protestants, Catholics, Muslims, and the great Asian faiths actually have more in common with each other, in terms of attitudes towards politics and economic and moral questions, than they do with their own coreligionists in the fundamentalist camp. Fundamentalists of all religions in the United States also have more in common with each other in terms of moral, political, and economic views, than they do with their coreligionists in the liberal camp.[6]

Gallup Poll Findings

IN THEIR EXTREMELY interesting and provocative book, George Gallup Jr. and James Castelli note that there is a fundamental difference between the liberal and mainline churches in the United States on the one hand and the fundamentalist and evangelical churches on the other. Asking people whether they believe in immortality of the soul or resurrection of the body (when the terms have been clarified) is probably the simplest way to discover this basic rift in American life, even in our secular society.

We already know that religion is much more significant on average to Americans than it is to Europeans or even to Canadians, our closest neighbors. Since the time of De Tocqueville, Europeans have noted Americans' special interest in religion.[7] More recently, Gerhard Lenski showed that our religious choices are statistically as important for predicting our other attitudes as is anything else that can be measured or named in our lives.[8] We know a great deal about what a person is likely to think politically, how she will spend money or vote, what kind of occupations she will seek, what kind of recipes he will bake, what kind of organizations she will join, what kind of child-rearing practices they will practice and advocate, and a myriad of other things, when we have some specificity about that person's religious beliefs and community. The very notion of which pronouns are appropriate to each of these activities is governed as significantly by religious values as by anything else.

Asking about an afterlife still defines a crucial and very conflicted battlefield in American life, one that challenges our political as well as religious convictions. It separates liberal from conservative, Republican from Democrat, northerner from southerner, rich from poor, educated from uneducated, and pious from impious. But it is more fundamental than any of these. It cuts to the very quick of what we Americans think is important in life. Americans still answer "yes" to the question: "Do you believe in God?" far more often and more enthusiastically than most other western countries, upwards to a level of 94 percent in one poll,[9] on a level equal to Ireland and India and far higher than Scandinavia, England, France, Spain, or Italy.

Competition in the Religious Marketplace

ONE INTERESTING result of that history is enshrined in the First Amendment, absolutely forbidding the establishment of any state religion, and arguably guaranteeing the separation of church and state. Not only does every other country previously named sponsor a religion as an instrument of the state, but by doing so, they also provide a protected market for one religion to live. Our society, on the contrary, encourages competition among religions within the marketplace of ideas, though fundamentalist Christianity continues to lobby the government for more support while criticizing Jews and Catholics for trying to subvert the government. Although we accuse ourselves of being unfair to religious organizations and superficial in our beliefs,[10] we have also inadvertently created a competitive environment for healthy religious life. Competition in the marketplace of religious ideas has produced a very important set of religious organizations in our society. Like anything else that has been mass-marketed, our religion comes to us in sound-bites and slogans, making it seem trivial and superficial by comparison to religious discussions in the past. But it is designed to be marketed.

6

Our religious vibrancy, then, is a double-edged sword. Whatever we think of religion, we must admit that religion is still an important part of our lives, in spite of the once-touted, enormous secularization of American society after the Vietnam War. By the seventies, the opinion polls indicated that we were growing more secular. By the early nineties these numbers had decisively turned around. We forgot that when the baby boomers all entered young adulthood together, their numbers would skew our statistics toward the secular, unless we also controlled for age. Adolescents and young adults are very much less likely to take doctrines of religion or fear of mortality seriously in American life. Questions of career and family predominate in the early adult years. But, as we age, we Americans apparently still return to these more perennial and more ultimate human questions.

The effect of age on interest in the afterlife is easy enough to see. I once had the experience of giving a series of classes on the Bible to a group made up of adolescents and retirees exclusively, a classic "bimodal distribution." When it came time to study the Bible's doctrines of the afterlife, I asked them if they believed in one. All the retirees in the audience answered affirmatively—no surprise given their age and that the course was being held in front of children in a Conservative synagogue. (What they would have said more privately is anyone's guess.) But even in that context none of the twenty or so teenagers would answer "yes" to the question. Age is an important factor in the articulation and interest in beliefs in an afterlife. Older people characteristically show more recognition of mortality and, at the same time, lower anxiety about death. Church membership and high commitment also correlates with low death anxiety. Conventional religiosity—church membership with low commitment— has so far not shown any measurable effects on fear of death.[11]

Religion Returns When the Afterlife Beckons

WHEN THE BABY BOOMERS began to return to religion and church membership in the eighties, their return dramatically corresponded to an upswing in the political action of conservative religious groups. As a result, no one today would question the importance of religion as an indicator of political and economic values in American life. The correlation is much higher in international affairs where Islam led the way into the political arena. After the Iranian revolution of 1979, we realized we had to factor religion into the our international political policies; after 9/11, we realized that we are no longer an island fortress. Being part of the globalization process means that we are deeply affected by extremist religious beliefs and movements brewing elsewhere in the world.

Because of all these reasons, our stated beliefs in the afterlife are increasing significantly, according to studies done by Andrew M. Greeley and Michael Hout.[12] A significantly greater fraction of American adults believe in life after death in the 1990s than in the 1970s. According to data from the General Social Survey (hereafter GSS) there has been a marked change in some groups' beliefs in life after death. Although Protestants who say that they believe in life after death have remained stable at about 85 percent (very high to begin with, anyway), Catholics, Jews, and people of no religious affiliation have become more likely to report beliefs in the afterlife. For instance, the percentage of Catholics believing in an afterlife rose from 67 percent to 85 percent for those born between 1900 and 1970. When the variables were analyzed, one important factor to Greely and Hout was their contact with Irish clergy, who communicated their commitment to the Catholic population in general.

Among Jews the percentage was even more interesting but puzzling. Jews who report important and stable notions of life after death have always been significantly fewer statistically than Christians, presumably due to the lower emphasis on afterlife in most varieties of American Judaism. Nevertheless, Jewish belief in the afterlife rose from 17 percent amongst the cohort born in 1900–1910 to 74 percent amongst the 1970 cohort, a very significant jump. Perhaps Jews have understood that our culture asks us to answer "yes" to that question but not to spend much time thinking about it. In any event, Jews are still twice as likely as Christians to say that they don't know if there is life after death.

The reasons for this change are not as easy to discern. Contact with Protestants was not a measurable factor (among those Jews who did not later convert). Immigrant status seems to be an important factor in rejecting notions of the afterlife for both Catholics and Jews. Perhaps the experience of immigration is itself so disruptive that it seriously affects notions of afterlife felicity for the immigrant generation. Among Jews this may be because those most likely to leave Europe at the turn of the century were the ones least impressed with Rabbinic exhortations to stay within the European religious community and not go the United States, which they called "the *treyfer* (non-kosher) land." Those who immigrated to the United States, and later Canada, called it *"der goldener Land,"* the Golden Land, showing that the Jews who came to the United States came more to better their economic opportunities than to gain religious freedom. Reform Jews are only about 10 percent less likely to report beliefs in life after death than Orthodox Jews. What differs is the kind of afterlife they envision. Mainline Jews are close to Protestants in their adoption of a spiritual afterlife; Orthodox Jews report a belief in bodily resurrection. In the second and third generation of immigrants, perhaps acculturation itself accounts for the higher correlation with Protestant views of heaven.

Greeley and Hout did not systematically test the hypothesis that American First Amendment rights promote competition in religion and thus are more successful at raising people's religious consciousness, but their findings are in consonance with this "supply-side" theory of American religious life. They strongly endorse a "supply-side" notion of American religious life, and it does make a certain amount of sense.

Nearly all Christians think that union with God, peace and tranquility, and reunion with relatives are likely to await them as well as many of the other descriptions of the afterlife previously mentioned. Yet, few are explicitly part of the official Christian doctrine of resurrection. Many of these beliefs correlate highly with immortality of the soul, which has been synthesized with resurrection in Christianity since the fourth century but is not a significant New Testament doctrine. Americans do seem to agree more or less about these criteria, but some differences do exist: Jews are slightly more likely than Christians to imagine a nonpersonal existence; one half of Jews, but only one fifth of Christians, see a "vague" existence as likely. This finding seems intriguingly tied to Jewish ethnicity. It would be interesting to compare other groups segregated by ethnicity and questioned in an "ethnically aware" environment.

The Demise of the Devil[13]

ANOTHER INTERESTING phenomenon in American life is the gradual disappearance of any notion of hell in the liberal and mainline churches.[14] Many have seen this "demise of the devil" as a sign that we are losing our moral bearings—our sense of evil. On the other hand, one might just as easily argue that the demise of the devil is an indication that the United States is coming to terms with itself as a culturally-plural country, and as a result many of us have lost our desire to carry religious vengeance out on our fellow-countrymen in the next world, ironically just at the moment when so many fundamentalist extremists around the world are preaching our damnation.[15]

Jonathan Edwards, one of the founders of the Great Awakening and

President of Princeton University, several times described the horrors of hell for Americans in his justly famous sermons. The one quoted below is from "Sinners in the Hands of an Angry God":

> That world of misery, that lake of burning brimstone, is extended abroad under you. There is the dreadful pit of the glowing flames of the wrath of God; there is Hell's wide gaping mouth open; and you have nothing to stand upon, nor anything to take hold of; there is nothing between you and Hell but air; 'tis only the power and mere pleasure of God that holds you up.[16]

Eighteenth-century Americans were impressed with these images and motivated to strive even more fervently towards the good and eschew evil, though Edwards' own theology was based on the premise that God's will for each of us individually was unknowable. His Great Awakening was enormously successful. This vision of hell affected American's social behavior just as much as the desire for a just society stimulated Edwards to this vision. Visions of heaven and hell serve evangelization.

Indeed, there is some evidence that the spike of interest in "gothic" or "supernatural" worldviews (for example, "vampires and vampire slayers," the "occult," and "space aliens") among teenagers is not so much lack of religious guidance as rebellion against previously strict fundamentalist or evangelical upbringing. These phenomena are common enough among teenagers and frequent subjects of teen-oriented entertainment. But they appear especially often among teens rejecting their own family's fundamentalism and evangelicalism.[17] There are even attempts by evangelical churches to capitalize on this teenage interest for evangelization and confirmation of teen faith with such evangelical tools as a "Hellhouse," a Halloween walk-through depiction of the evils of non-evangelical moral codes, presenting evangelical religion as the solution to demonically controlled lives.[18]

Whatever the cause, there is a palpable change in American notions of the afterlife: very few of us think we are going to hell or even that we are in danger of going to hell. In fact, very few of us outside of the right wing conservatives take hell's existence seriously at all. We must never forget that the lines of causation between our current lives and our hopes for the future are bidirectional. Our current lives affect our notions of the afterlife; our notions of the afterlife affect our behavior in this one. In most of our permissive society, a vision of hell would probably be greeted with disbelief by most Americans and even by derisive laughter by some. Our desire to do away with hell is natural enough, but it may not be because we want to sin with impunity. It may just as easily be due to our loss of a sure sense that our individual religions are the only right ones. Because we feel our society's notions of equality are divinely endowed, we may be losing the easy surety that any American whose religion differs from us is automatically damned. That could be indicative that an incipiently multicultural society is forming in the United States as old parochialisms fade.

What Americans Actually Think about Heaven

FOR THE MAJORITY of Americans, heaven has become a virtual democratic entitlement. Surely we tend to project on our view of a happy afterlife those things that we think are best, most lasting, virtuous, and meaningful in this life while eliminating those things we think are the most difficult, frustrating, evil, and inessential. The data are mostly from Christians, but the description of heaven is in some ways a projective test for all Americans, with adjustment for the specifically Christian doctrines. Here is a basic list of talking points, taken from Gallup and Castelli:

- The afterlife will be a *better life and a good life.*
- There will be *no more problems or troubles.* "No trials and tribulations . . . worries and cares will vanish . . . no worries, no cares, no sorrows. I think to be worried all the time would really be awful."
- There will be *no more sickness or pain.*
- The afterlife will be a *spiritual, not a physical realm.* "Totally spiritual . . . lack of physical limitations . . . there's not going to be a three dimensional experience."
- It will be *peaceful.* "I think we'll be more peaceful because you really live your hell on earth."
- The afterlife will be *happy and joyful, no sorrow.*
- Those who make it to heaven will be happy.
- They will be in the presence of God or Jesus Christ.
- There will be love between people.
- God's love will be the center of life after death.
- Crippled people will be whole.
- People in heaven will grow spiritually.
- They will see friends, relatives, or spouses.
- They will live forever.

- There will be humor. . . .
- People in heaven will grow intellectually.
- They will have responsibilities.
- They will minister to the spiritual needs of others.
- Those in heaven will be recognizable as the same people that they were on earth.
- There will be angels in heaven.[19]

It is significant that few of the descriptions of heaven contain depictions of explicitly Christian doctrines. We see in these descriptions a significant ranking of values in American life this side of eternity. The first series of points deal with personal and familial happiness. The second express the importance of work, accomplishment, and looking after others, some of which would be very unusual priorities in past European visions of heaven and incomprehensible in ancient ones. Significantly among Americans, humor is often cited as an important component of heavenly life, arguably because we use humor to dispel tension over ethnic and regional differences. Indeed, our American notions of a competitive economy—positive growth, positive development, continuous education—are deeply enshrined in our contemporary notions of heaven.

These points are a litmus test of American goals and values, "transcendent" and ultimate values as seen from our perspective in the early twenty-first century, even as it is a filter to leave out those things that most keep us from achieving them.[20] If we also had a description of hell then we could see more clearly all the things which Americans feel are contrary to these values, and how given a heavenly economy, they should be punished. It is just as significant that we no longer excel in descriptions of hell or damnation. If we look at earlier conceptions of heaven and hell, we may be able to perceive similar correlations with earlier social structures and policy. Dealing with other cultures' concepts of the afterlife historically will yield the same important information, but will involve historical attention to details that are not nearly so well known or easy to discover.

We have seen that Americans—liberal or conservative, mainline church, sectarian or even unchurched—have significant beliefs about an afterlife. Indeed, more Americans believe in an afterlife than believe in God. These beliefs range from literal resurrection of the body to immortality of the soul, to deathless existence with flying saucers in the stars, to nothing specific beyond the confidence that we will have something to enjoy. Immortality of the soul, as opposed to the resurrection of the body, is inherent in most of our descriptions. Individuals within the mainline churches believe in an afterlife but they tend to feel comfortable with a range of individual opinions. They normally feel that their more conservative confrères have mistaken the literal Biblical formulations for the underlying truths behind it. Conservative churches believe in immortality of the soul in addition to belief in the literal resurrection of the body. They report that they believe it with certainty and that their liberal coreligionists are dangerously incorrect.

So in spite of our sophistication, pragmatism, and economic dominance of the world, American culture is full of significant depictions of an afterlife everywhere. We seem to live with these depictions and the attendant contradictions that come with them without difficulty, as have cultures everywhere in the past. Although some of us forcefully maintain that there is no afterlife, most of us take at least an agnostic and, more likely, a positive view towards our survival of death.

Is fear the source of contemplation of the end? Even the elderly see that the saying, "There are no atheists in foxholes," is not true. Approaching death sometimes makes some people more convinced of the falsity of religious teaching about the afterlife. What seems to be universally true is that atheists are likely to keep their beliefs quiet at religious funerals. Their comments might appear impolite and cruel to the mourners. Even the doubtful or disbelieving bereaved can find comfort in the rites of the occasion. Most people find the familiar language and ritual of funerals to be themselves consoling, if not immediately, then after their grief has receded. In general, we have a good social understanding of where we should use the language of departed souls, of resurrection and millennial expectations, of ghosts and goblins, or of nothing at all. Society teaches us to keep these notions from contradicting each other.

Our mass media culture has only made these differing beliefs more available to us and has given us pictorial representations of them that would have been impossible only a few years ago. In my seminar on afterlife, we annually list all the recent films which have been significantly concerned with afterlife or depicted it in some graphic way. We usually fill the board with over a hundred movie titles in minutes. Children's cartoons are full of violence as well as depictions of ghosts and spirits, together with visual images of cartoon characters surviving their comic and very frequent deaths. Books, films, and TV talk shows are replete with depictions of Near Death Experiences (hereafter NDEs) and endlessly discuss whether or not they are demonstrations of the truths of the afterlife, as they appear to be. Sincere and seemingly sane persons of impeccable credibility relate them to us with conviction. Popular TV programs like

The X-Files or *Touched by an Angel* and popular films like *Ghost* or *The Sixth Sense* so successfully affected teenage as well as adult markets that these productions have spawned many imitators and have had a significant effect on American teen identity concepts, whether the teens reported that they were "Conservative," "mystical," "experimenters," "resisters," "marginal," or "irreligious." [21]

Near Death Experiences

NO TOPIC HAS occupied American discussions of the afterlife as much as Near Death Experiences (NDEs), which have a number of common themes beyond the fearful emergencies that cause them—bright light, a feeling of warmth, a long tunnel, possibly a meeting with deceased family members, a reluctant return to painful existence. Those who have experienced them usually find their faith strengthened or confirmed, and have left the American public significantly impressed.[22] The gift of their faith confirmed is also a revelation to us all because the survivors seem to demonstrate life after death in a scientific setting. Even non-Christians have taken a significant interest in them.[23]

But can these NDEs really tell us scientifically what we want to know? Can there be any true scientific confirmation of a life after death if no one can actually visit the abode of the dead and come back with a verifiable traveler's report? This book will take the position that the important issues about God and the afterlife are beyond confirmation or disconfirmation in the scientific sense. The questions posed here are more like: "What makes an action just or a sunset beautiful?" than they are like the question: "Is there sodium in table salt?" The presence of an afterlife, like the existence of God, is not amenable to scientific analysis. Nevertheless, we are still required by science and by use of our reason to eliminate unlikelihoods or impossibilities from our faith discourse. Because we cannot prove the existence of God scientifically, we are not thereby empowered to believe that the earth is flat or that the moon is made out of green cheese. Nor are we free to ignore the question because a great many of the most important questions in life are impossible to confirm or refute.

Some of us have achieved certainty about these issues. Those who have evangelical faith and many who have experienced an NDE have consequently received an additional gift of confidence in the face of universal and ultimate fears. But, given the enormous amount of discussion and literature that exists on these experiences, one unexpected finding that George Gallup has disclosed in his book, *Adventures in Immortality,* is how rare they actually are, compared to the population at large and how rare is the typical experience of "confirmation" among the relatively rare NDE itself.[24] Even the argument that the occasional NDE in children proves that it is a real experience and not just a mirror of our social beliefs in a natural experience or hallucination of some sort cannot be maintained.[25] Once one looks at a selection of cartoon depictions of the afterlife and their presence in movies and books of all types, there can be no doubt about how the young can be socialized to expect an NDE so easily.

Although we cannot take just any report as proof of the afterlife, we should take these experiences seriously. Throughout this book, the authenticity of confirming religious experiences will be championed, especially in the chapters concerning religious experience in ancient Israel. Belief in life after death is virtually universal in human experience. Very often, these notions come together with symbols of rebirth or regeneration.[26] Though a relatively small percentage of Americans experience NDEs, a mere fraction of one percent, this yields a rather large number in absolute terms—more than a million Americans. Furthermore, the notion that we can visit the dead or cause them to visit us, that we can go to heaven and see what is there, the notion that this visit will confirm our cherished earthly beliefs, is an extremely important and constant theme in world literature. In one sense all these experiences seem to promise verification but so far they have not met scientific criteria. Ultimately, we need to study why people undertake these trips and how their means—whether they be NDEs travel or altered states of consciousness—affect the meaning discovered from the trip itself. Which afterlife do they validate? There are many different views of the afterlife available to us as Americans and citizens of the world.

What History Can Tell Us

A BELIEF IN an afterlife is older than the human race if Neanderthal burials are to be trusted. We see many pieces of evidence of Neanderthal religion in sites of Mousterian culture. In particular, the Mousterians left flowers, grain, and other grave goods in their interments, suggesting that they believed the departed could use the implements they provided for them.[27] Assuming for a moment that we are justified in concluding that the Neanderthals were not our species exactly but a closely associated one (an assumption that is still hotly debated), the notion of an afterlife would precede humanity. Belief in spirits, both benevolent (as in departed ancestors, for example) and malicious (as in ghosts) are virtually omnipresent in human culture, though they sometimes share the stage with more so-phisticated notions of a beatific afterlife.

"Sharing the stage" is an appropriate phrase for how we reconcile our impressions of an afterlife. We have only to look at Shakespeare's *Hamlet* to realize how easily we accept the combination of traditional Christian-ity with belief in spirits and ghosts. The New Testament itself contains the belief in spirits and demons. The belief in spirits and ghosts functions in a number of ways in a society—including enforcing moral standards, upholding various institutions, and guaranteeing appropriate burial of corpses.

The Bible, viewed historically, shows us how varied our views are, even within Western traditions. These variations are made even more evident by studying the Quran as scripture. Even if we look at only one tradi-tion—either Judaism, Christianity, or Islam—we find that the view of the afterlife is fascinatingly varied. For example, we will see that the Bible it-self at first zealously ignores the afterlife. When the Bible does discuss the afterlife, it does so to resolve very specific questions within its own cul-ture. In fact, all the notions of life after death in the Hebrew Bible as well as those formed afterward seem to be borrowed to some degree or an-other. None of these notions were borrowed early nor without prejudice.

Previous, shorter studies of the subject have shown the dichotomy be-tween resurrection of the body and immortality of the soul. Scholarship clearly understands immortality of the soul to be a Platonic Greek notion. Opinion about where the notion of resurrection of the body comes from is mixed. Many scholars, as we shall see, think it comes from Persia. Oth-ers think that it is a native Israelite belief, derived from specific experi-ences of tragedy. Many have thought that the two beliefs—resurrection of the body and immortality of the soul—are logically mutually exclusive. More recently scholars have shown they combine easily and quite thor-oughly rendering the old distinctions obsolete. This study, which exam-ines the data a bit more carefully, will show that there is partial evidence for each of these opinions and evidence of the converse as well. The im-portant factor for understanding the belief in the hereafter is not so much the origin of the notions but how the notions are used within a specific so-ciety at a specific time—what the metaphors are being used to express about our human predicament. Biblical notions of the afterlife in Biblical times were just as changeable, conflicting, and revealing as our own in this time. They existed in an exceptionally rich and very complex mythi-cal polemic and equilibrium with their neighboring cultures.

First of all, study of notions of afterlife in the Bible will demonstrate the goals and interests of the culture that produced them, just as it shows us something about the origin of North American values. Secondly, this study will give us a very important clue as to the value of religion in our lives. The function, structure, role, and solace of religion are problems almost as puzzling as death itself, but unlike what awaits us after death, they are phenomena that can be verified with a variety of ordinary data. However we must be careful not to equate religion with the notion of life after death. It is logical for us in the West to assume that a belief in life after death, if not the explicit Christian one, is close to the essence of religion because a specific notion of the afterlife is so central to Christianity's master narrative. We must therefore examine whether that perception holds across all the world's religions.

Afterlife: The Essence of Religion?

PRIMARY INTEREST in the afterlife simply does not hold true across all human culture. Many religions—such as contemporary Judaism and Confucianism—give far less attention to notions of the afterlife than does Christianity. In what must surely be a parody of Jewish views, David Sloan Wilson reported in the *New York Times:* "A scholar at a religious conference told me that what little Judaism has to say about the afterlife is only there because Christians asked them." [28] The point David Sloan Wilson was making is that an afterlife belief is not necessarily the essence of religion. That seems correct.

But his statement about Judaism is entirely wrong. We shall discover that Judaism did indeed have quite vibrant views of the hereafter and those views flow quite naturally into Christianity where they are featured much more strongly. At a certain point, Jews began to desensitize themselves to discussions of the afterlife. The fact that mainline denominations of Judaism today de-emphasize notions of the afterlife has as much to do with their strategy for modern life—emphasizing that Judaism is a "religion of reason." Some mainline American Protestant denominations do not give much attention to afterlife either, emphasizing social action and spiritual experience instead.

Every religion has an answer to the inquiry of an afterlife, even though it may borrow that answer from another source and adherents to that particular religion may want to criticize or correct it from within. Although not all religions put afterlife in the center of their beliefs, as does Christianity (at least in Tertullian's estimation), the afterlife is one of the fundamental building blocks of religion. If we look at how the West constructed its notion of life after death, we shall gain some notion of the historical stages that conceptions of heaven went through, as well as the reasons for those conceptions and how they have changed. In looking at a particular religion's afterlife belief, we will be looking at a society's notion of transcendence, its ideas about what is most important in human life.

Scholars of religion have become skeptical of any of the suggested "essences" of religion—even such an obvious one as a doctrine of the continuity of life beyond the grave. It would be unwise to adopt as the essence of religion the very thing that most characterizes Christianity—the very religion that has most ruled the consciousness of the West for two millennia. Yet, if the net is thrown wide enough, if any kind of belief in the survival of personality is included in our search, all human societies contain at least the rudiments of a belief in life after death.

The Pygmies of Africa were once held up as a religionless culture because they have few dogmas, and they think that religion is a kind of intellectual slavery to their putative political masters. But even they hold certain beliefs about pygmy survival in a life after death that is much at one with the forest. Or take another example: Although some Chinese religions may easily be categorized philosophies (for example, contemporary Neo-Confucianists on the island of Taiwan), the Chinese continue to perform rituals, build temples, and venerate ancestors, assuming they survive to become close watchers and protectors of life in the family. Although notions of the afterlife are present in Chinese religion, they are not always central to its doctrines. Sometimes it is evidenced primarily in ritual.

We must also consider the history of European misperceptions about the religions of the world. Europeans misperceived the religion of native Africans in South Africa for centuries, thinking that the Hottentots, Bechuana, and Besuto, for example, had no religion because they had no churches, religious hierarchy, liturgy, nor exact dogmas about salvation and the afterlife.[29] They often felt these cultures practiced a degraded form of Islam or Judaism because they circumcised and followed food laws. This gave the Europeans an excuse to impose their own religion upon the Africans. The European standard for religion was deeply involved in notions of afterlife and tended to judge all others by their own notions.

Most, if not all, of the world's cultures maintain some sort of belief in life after death. Perhaps this is simply because no one can escape the difficult question of what happens to our loved ones when they die. However strong religious faith is, it can never fully overcome the feeling of loss of those who loved the departed. In some societies these beliefs have a guardian and intercessary role. In other societies the ancestors, ghosts, and spirits of the dead are malevolent creatures. But almost every society uses these practices as a way of enforcing proper funeral and postmortem proprieties. The rites must not be left undone, lest the children prove unworthy of the love the parents and grandparents bore them when they were young. The transformed dead may support a system of justice; they may help support a particular priesthood, class of prophets, healers, or kingship; or the dead may help support the integrity of the family.

Because notions of life after death help us conquer our ultimate fears of mortality in important ways, they also help society or culture organize and maintain itself. The same results can be attained whether the dead are malevolent or benevolent, though the kind of rite necessary and the kind of offices to perform them will differ markedly. We all know that notions of life after death differ widely from culture to culture and from major religion to major religion. Indeed, even a quick study of the major religions of the world reveals differing and sometimes conflicting or contradictory notions of life after death. But the fact that these views differ radically does not mean that they are invalid or ridiculous. Behind these notions lie a limited number of functions and structures. Beneath the visions of paradise expressed in countless different cultural idioms, there are a certain number of universal functions: Primary among them are the reification and legitimation of a society's moral and social system; but one could just as easily argue that there is something fundamental to human life in them and that without them we would be totally lost in the world.

The Afterlife Is Sacred

THERE IS ONE more issue that needs to be addressed. That is the sensitivity many people feel when their notions of the afterlife are challenged. Professor Krister Stendahl reflects on his earlier work on resurrection and immortality, stating that he received more unhappy letters on this subject than on any other subject that he has ever undertaken.[30] If his edited and circumspect work—an admirable volume created under the supervision of both a well-educated, rational man and a man of faith—was subject to unfair and sometimes hateful criticism, perhaps I should expect a torrent for my more unorthodox treatment of the subject. But I will not broach the issue of religious truth and certainty until the very end of this project and hope the reader will have the patience to wait until then for my conclusions.

We are in a field where both the faithful and the disbelieving legitimately have their doubts and where strong argumentation is often used as a goad to dispel them. Ferocious emotional tirades on both sides are nothing but bad faith. We must be careful to allow ourselves to live with the ambiguity, not to try to impress ourselves with the rationality of our faith because of the strength of our emotions, when there are no sure claims to make. The justification for this is not just to preserve dispassionate or disinterested inquiry. We live in a marketplace of ideas, where people are constantly trying to sell something expensive to us with extravagent claims. The American critical stance should be: "Let the buyer beware." We have frequent recent examples of televangelists convicted of preying on our innocence and our legitimate religious hopes and fears for their own enormous financial gain. Some of our recent films are, without doubt, just as surely pandering to our hopes. We have witnessed firsthand the scurrilous use of Muslim notions of the afterlife to motivate murder, resulting in a national tragedy of unprecedented proportions.

Even academic research has fallen victim to this temptation, for far less reward, if far less damage. I think of the example of Elizabeth Kübler-Ross, who wrote *On Death and Dying*, as a salutary example.[31] This famous and justly praised book on the grieving process was a passionate defense of giving the dying the opportunity to face their own deaths in a constructive way. The book came out of a clinical setting, the result of a study of persons dying of cancer, and concluded that our medical procedures were designed to protect the feelings of doctors and caregivers rather than to allow the dying the dignity to deal with their impending deaths. The study maintained that when those who know that they will die soon are given the opportunity to grieve for themselves, some experienced more honest, meaningful, and less painful deaths. Kübler-Ross described the grieving process as a healing one, going from anger and denial through depression to somber acceptance. Her observations struck a chord with everyone. Her analysis of the treatment of the dying in hospitals, with the attendant later techniques to encourage the dying through the grieving process, significantly changed hospital attitudes and therapeutic techniques, among both physicians and other caregivers. Kübler-Ross's first book concerned only the process of dying and grieving; quite soon, however, her books began to propound that she had found sure evidence of life after death in her clinical settings, mostly in Near Death Experiences.

Then Kübler-Ross personally experienced yet another turn of events: a series of strokes, the last being as late as 1995, which left her facing the prospect of her own slow and debilitating death. Don Lattin in a report for the *San Francisco Chronicle* interviewed her in 1997 and found her very unhappy about her situation, recanting her previous, more religious, philosophy. She described her current state: "It's neither living nor dying. It's stuck in the middle. My only regret is that for 40 years I spoke of a good God who helps people, who knows what you need and how all you have to do is ask for it. Well that's baloney. I want to tell the world that it's a bunch of bull. Don't believe a word of it."[32]

It is bad enough that the person who had done most in the twentieth century to define the successful grieving process should herself fall victim to one of its most obvious pitfalls: "stage 2: anger" as she called it. Kübler-Ross was widely reported to have recanted her observations about the afterlife, and worse still, to have admitted that she cynically invented her surety both to enrich herself and to benefit her clinical work. Some say her religious belief was a kind of "stage 1: denial." Others say that her cynicism and admissions of fraud were the result of her depression, from which she has now recovered. Maybe so, but what does it say of her later reaffirmations? Perhaps Kübler-Ross's experience means that we all harbor affirmations as well as doubts in our mind about an afterlife and that both can be helpful as well as destructive.

But wherever the truth lies—if indeed, it can be put into the simple sentences that journalists require—the story is a clear example of both our collective need for surety where none obtains and for individuals' ability to hold a series of conflicting ideas simultaneously. Let's be frank: Both the faithful and disbelieving rightfully have doubts and should have them. Faith without doubt is merely intolerance, ultimately fanaticism. Without doubt, faith turns to rabid zealotry and inspires tragedies such as the World Trade Center attack. Death anxiety is a strong and important reality with important adaptive uses in human life. Doubt is the one thing that helps keep faith from becoming fanaticism.

Death Anxiety

SHAKESPEARE himself portrays death anxiety in *Measure for Measure*:

'Tis too horrible!
The weariest and most loathed worldly life
That age, ache, penury, and imprisonment
Can lay on nature is a paradise
To what we fear of death.
(*Measure for Measure*, Act 3, Scene 1, lines 127–131)

Poor Claudio says these abject lines in the same scene that he begins with heroic words about sacrificing himself to save his sister's honor: "If I must die, / I will encounter darkness as a bride, And hug it in mine arms" (lines 81–83). In this briefest moment, Shakespeare risks our respect by portraying his character suddenly turn cowardly in contemplating the horrors of death and hell. The greater risk provides us with a deeper truth about our humanity.

Modern idiom is much poorer than Shakespeare's. He shows us that death anxiety infects everything we do as humans, even when we are trying to be brave. It is part of the human condition; indeed it seems a consequence of self-consciousness itself. It is a price we pay for being aware of ourselves as beings. Whether it is better to face this cold end without the benefit of religious understanding or to adopt religious views of the afterlife is still very much an open question, which is where Shakespeare leaves it. Which is the true denial of death? This book will attempt to answer that question by looking at the development of our notions of the afterlife. We shall also see that notions of life after death are themselves important and helpful tools in the development of our self-consciousness.

An Outline of the Study

FIRST, WE WILL look at the concept of afterlife in Egypt, a considerable amount of data. We can use the opportunity of studying a culture with such elaborate notions of the afterlife and heavy use of social resources to defend them to ask some general questions about human notions of the afterlife.

Then we will research the notions of Mesopotamia and Canaan, more and more important respectively for the study of Israel. In contrast to Mesopotamia, Canaan, and Egypt, the Hebrew Bible is almost entirely silent about life after death. This silence is in pointed opposition to the rich description of the afterlife of Egypt and the surrounding cultures. Israelite First Temple religion, which is highly independent and highly polemical against these three cultures in the form we have in the Bible, is also deeply dependent upon them for its more basic concepts. We shall have to ask how characteristic of Israelite culture is the Bible's perspective. Is it the dominant ancient position or a small minority imposing a "YHWH only" perspective on the culture?

We then turn to ancient Iran, Persia, which is crucially important for the rise of notions of bodily resurrection in Second Temple Judaism but next to impossible at this juncture to evaluate historically. Then, we will look at Greek culture, whose notion of the immortality of the soul was also to change Israelite culture and Western notions of afterlife forever. We will next look at the Biblical literary productions of the Persian and Hellenistic periods, ending with the book of Daniel, in which resurrection is predicted for the first time unambiguously and the equally important Greek notion of immortality of the soul, which enters Judaism by another means and with another social background. In addition we will look at the reports of the various sects and forces in Judea and Diaspora from the point of view of the major historians of the day. We will also review the issue of religiously altered and religiously interpreted states of consciousness.

Armed with these social and methodological tools, we will investigate the Jesus movement, the apostle Paul, and the Gospels. Then we will move on to the noncanonical gospels, the apocrypha of the Jewish and Christian communities, the Church Fathers and their major opponents, the Gnostics. Subsequently, we will consider the notions of life after death in the Mishnah, Talmud, and Rabbinic Judaism generally. The final chapter will explore Islam. The order of chapters is therefore roughly chronological throughout, although the chronology in each chapter will necessarily overlap with the others. It will be necessary to synchronize them from time to time so we can be aware of parallel beliefs in different religious traditions. At the end, after we have examined these early and foundational traditions in detail, we will look at later Jewish, Christian, and Muslim views.

To conclude, we will return to the issue of the matter of meaning and truth in the notion of afterlife. The enormous quantity of material does not yield easily either to a strictly historical or to a strictly topical approach. Our study will at least attempt to show that there are organic, historical relationships between the texts of the various literary genres and communities of belief. In every case, I try to ask the questions we have so far asked—what do these notions of the afterlife suggest about the ultimate meaning of life to these people? Why do they change over time? What social and historical issues lie behind these changes? How do the doctrines themselves condition further discussion and conflict within the various communities as they relate to other communities who value the same traditions? Why do we insist that life continues beyond the grave and why do we give credence to those who have experienced it and return to tell us about it?

PART ONE

THE CLIMATE OF

IMMORTALITY

1

Egypt

DESERVEDLY OR NOT, ancient Egypt is known as a culture obsessed by the afterlife. Even the Egyptian cultures of the Neolithic era buried their dead with grave goods, suggesting a continuation of life in the grave. The Hebrews may have been deeply influenced by the Egyptians. When the Hebrews finally arrived in the land of Canaan to stay, by 1200 BCE, they arrived from Egypt. During the Egyptian captivity of the Hebrews, the major beliefs of Egyptian afterlife had already been developed and practiced for a millennium. According to the Biblical account, Egypt had been the home of the Israelites, who were sojourners there for four hundred years. Canaan itself was nominally under the influence of Egypt, as the Canaanites were Egyptian vassals. The material culture of Canaan shows innumerable Egyptian influences. Egypt was the strongest political force in the area until the Middle Iron Age, and Egyptian influences appear frequently in Canaanite and Israelite religious, political, and decorative motifs until the rise of Assyria.[1] Nevertheless, the Hebrews were not overly impressed with Egyptian religion.

Egyptian Geography and
Its Effect on Egyptian Myths

THE GREEKS, on the other hand, were impressed. For the Greeks, Egypt was an ancient, mysterious, and mystical world. The pyramids were already two millennia old in the sixth century BCE, when Herodotus visited

Egypt. He stood at a comparable distance to the pyramid's builders as we do to Jesus's followers and so he stood in appropriate awe of Egypt's antiquity. He also singled out Egyptian science, in particular its effective use of geometry, as worthy of great veneration.

Ancient Egypt gives us the longest continuous history in the ancient world. It was a fabulously wealthy and stable culture. Egypt's stability depended on its wealth and its insulation from the rest of the ancient world by oceans, deserts, and mountain ranges. The Nile river gave it a rich agriculture and an easy means of transportation, while the mountains and deserts gave it unprecedented security for vast periods of time. These blessings combined to yield a deeply conservative political and religious culture of enormous longevity, all based on its uniquely favored geography.

In Egypt, geography is destiny. Egyptian religion is a meditation in narrative form on the significance of the unique geographical and climatic features of the country. The warm Nile flows northward out of Africa like a languorous cobra: Its tail starts in African lakes, carrying the rich volcanic soil northward to Egypt. Its body is contained between twin, almost impenetrable desert mountain ranges of the Upper Kingdom. Its hood is stretched out in broad fertile swamps of Lower Egypt's delta, it jaws biting at the underbelly of the Mediterranean. No wonder the Egyptians depicted the cobra so often as the symbol of kingship.

The desert and the mountains make the country virtually invulnerable on the east and west, disciplining the Nile into a long, thin valley. Through the middle of this long, oval basin runs a pronounced but very narrow, green stripe of alluvial fertility, on either side of the river. The border of green represents the furthest reach of the Nile's flood; in many places that border is so distinct that one can stand with one foot on the desert sand and one on cultivated land. Indeed, one ancient Egyptian word for Egypt is *Khemet*—the Black (i.e., fertile) Land.

In ancient Egypt, the most practical movement throughout the country was up the Nile or down the Nile, greatly aided by the prevailing wind originating from the north or northwest and blowing southward on many, fortunate days. For the ancient Egyptian, upstream therefore meant south, a direction navigated by sailing with the wind, or by tacking across it, which explains the invention of the lateen-rigged, triangular sail of the Egyptian *faluka* (pl. *fala'ik*). Travel north was simpler still, as it was downstream, running with the current. The Nile Valley as a climatic and geographical system is unique among the world's great river basins, leaving a mark on the Egyptian sensibility in culture and religion. Egypt is virtually a self-enclosed system.

Given the poverty and overpopulation of modern Egypt, it is hard to remember that, in ancient times, Egypt was synonymous with both wealth and wisdom. Since the ancient world's wealth depended on agriculture, Egypt was a paradise on earth. It could harvest three crops a year. The regular annual flooding of the Nile deposited a constantly renewing layer of fertile soil, carried down river from Africa, producing an unparalleled agricultural opportunity, which was exploited for millennia for grains, fruits, and vegetables. In the Delta, this dark stripe spread out into wide green marshes; along the banks to the south, the arable land was extended east and west by cleverly designed irrigation pumps and canals. The river itself was richly populated with tasty animal life—including game, fowl, and fish.

Rightly did Herodotus call Egypt "the gift of the Nile." No one since has proclaimed a more apt or heroic epithet for this country. As there is virtually no rain in the country, the Nile river is the only practical source of water. Flooding of the Nile is not a catastrophe but a great divine blessing— the source of Egypt's very existence. In a sense, the Nile has a cycle of birth and death on an annual basis. By summer, the river lies quietly and moves slowly, while the fields beside it gradually parch, turn to dust, erode, and blow away into the desert with the sandstorms. After that, the only available water for agriculture comes from a few wells, likely fed by the Nile too, as the winter rains of the Near East almost entirely bypass Egypt.

The cycle starts in August as the sun ends its eclipse of the Dog Star, Sirius, giving the month one of its oldest epithets, "the dog days of summer." In Egypt Sirius was known as the goddess Sothis, who was the harbinger of the Nile's flooding. At the start of autumn the Nile begins visibly to stir, responding to rain falling in Central Africa. Increasing in momentum, it floods in fall and winter over the miles of flat land on either side, creating at its northern end an enormously broad, triangular delta. Consequently it is often called in modern Egyptian Arabic *Baḥar An-Nil,* the Nile Sea. When it recedes, it leaves a layer of fertile mud in which crops can be planted, almost seeming to seed themselves and grow magically, without help from man. This process continued yearly for millennia until the building of the High Dam at Aswan in the 1960s prevented the soil from reaching the farmlands and thus breaking Egypt's ancient connection with the Nile's annual flood cycle.

The Egyptian sun is incessant. Summer and winter, it is like a great broiler-oven. Every day it is ignited in the east, burns furiously all day, and is not extinguished until it mercifully falls below the horizon in the west, only to roar into flame again the next day. Plants, birds, and animals all respond to its rhythms. Even the winds seem to emanate from its disk. The path of the sun down the western mountains and under the earth, where the dead were buried, followed by its daily reascent from behind the Eastern mountains, was a source of wonder for ancient Egyptians as it was for all peoples. The notched, eastern and western mountain ranges let the Egyptians calibrate the sun's movements exactly, designating seasons and festivals. The sun made an evident, diurnal journey under the earth, followed by a regular rebirth, slowly moving north then south annually along the mountain ranges. With the Nile, this movement was used as both a timepiece and a metaphor for the rebirth of the dead in eternity.

All of this imagery manifested itself in the ancient Egyptians' view of the universe, which not only described their world but defined their place within it. The flood of the Nile, human reproduction, and the sun were the three obvious symbols for life in Egypt, and they also served as the basis for the Egyptians' notions of the afterlife. To appreciate the influence of these symbols, we shall first have to look at the *mesocosm,* the social system, from the ancient Egyptian point of view. Like many other societies, Egyptians applied the term "humanity" to themselves only, sometimes using the words for "foreigner" and "subhuman" interchangeably. The Greeks called non-Greeks *barbarians* (from the word for bearded), because they were not civilized enough to shave. The Egyptian royalty and priesthood too shaved their hair off, but unlike the Greeks who shaved their faces, the Egyptian nobility shaved off all their body hair, wore perfumed wigs, and painted their eyes. Hairy outsiders were therefore seen more as animals than humans. Foreigners, having hair, were also infested with lice and vermin, like animals.

Foreigners were associated with disorder. Geography gave the Egyptians ways to describe foreigners as well as avoid them. The words for desert or mountain were synonymous with chaos, as they were characterized by inconstant rains and other irregular occurrences. The Egyptians hated chaos and praised the regularity of the Nile.[2] For them, the capricious rain could only be understood as an imperfect example of the benefits available to them from the Nile.

Aten was so good he even gave the uncivilized, foreignors in strange lands an approximation of the Nile—rain—poor and unreliable though that may be in comparison to the regularity of the Nile floods. Exceptional as their life was, to them it was natural and everyone else lived in imperfect imitation of it. Inside the sheltered land of Egypt, however, all was blissfully ordered, regular, and patterned for well-being; anxiety came from the disruption of the plan. The word that the Egyptians used to express this well-being and truth was "life," *Ankh,* symbolized by the famous *Ankh* sign, a cross with a loop at the apse. The Egyptians also personified order as justice, *ma'at,* which was depicted as a fragile feather or a lovely young goddess wearing a single feather in her headdress who often spread her multicolored wings to protect her charges, as she does at the entrance to the sarcophagus chamber in the tomb of Nefertari, principal wife of Rameses II.[3]

The Egyptians were not foolish enough to think that all this well-being, order, and justice were given naturally and without effort. No, these benefits could not be achieved without constant human attention to the details of life. For instance, though reliable enough to make the Egyptians complacent, the river could be mischievous. The annual flood could fail or be insufficient to meet the needs of the people. The river had to be carefully and painstakingly controlled by elaborate irrigation channels. In addition the Nile was filled with terrible dangers: snakes, vermin, disease, hippopotami, and crocodiles. These dangers had to be controlled by force or appeased with various exorcisms and offerings. Agricultural advantages could best be maximized by strong authority to supervise irrigation, dike and canal building, and city planning. *Ankh* had to be earned by appeasement of the gods and by regulation. Consequently leaders served in both sacral and military roles. "Good order" or "justice," again called *ma'at,* was both a gift from the gods and the result of good government. It had to be earned by each Egyptian, by upholding justice and right dealing, thus putting oneself in perfect harmony with the forces of nature.

Ma'at was preeminently the responsibility of the pharaoh, the king of Egypt as well as its god on earth. The title "pharaoh" is a kind of polite euphemism, to avoid saying anything directly to the king, much as we say "Your Majesty." It literally means "the great house"; the term was a synecdoche, like "the White House," used today to stand for the executive branch of the American government.

Another way of describing the pharaoh was as the shepherd of his people. The concept of the king as a benevolent herdsman made it necessary for him to dispense *ma'at,* good order, which was related to the proper conduct of life. If *ma'at* were interrupted, it was a sure sign that the divinity was displeased. So the king had to make sure that the administration of his country was properly done, just as herds had to be properly maintained. The pharaoh was the feeder of the people, just as the shepherd was feeder of his flock.

Physically and culturally, the Valley of the Nile breaks into the narrow trough of the Nile Valley—Upper Egypt—and the spreading delta of Lower Egypt. Upper Egypt has ties to the desert and to Africa; Lower Egypt faces out toward the Mediterranean Sea and Asia. Separated from the rest of the world by protective mountain ranges to the east and west, these two kingdoms are also separated from each other very effectively by rapids or cataracts. The name for Egypt in Hebrew is *Mitzrayim*— literally, "the two Egypts." In fact, the two Egyptian dialects were different enough to produce the constant refrain: "It was confusing, as if a man of the Delta were suddenly to speak to a man from Elephantine." [4] This saying reflects that the first and most important of the five cataracts separates the two kingdoms near Elephantine, though all of them are serious boundaries, forcing portages and delaying trade, communication, and military control. The earliest kings, of which Pharaoh Narmer is the most famous, were responsible for unifying the country. The so-called Narmer Palette displays many symbolic representations of the unification of the two countries, including the depiction of two snakes intertwined, perhaps engendering offspring.

Thereafter, the unification of the two kingdoms is seen in virtually every aspect of the pharaoh's symbology. Pharaoh united in his person both Upper and Lower Egypt as stable dynastic kingship in Egypt was achieved with the union of the two parts of the valley. This uniting was a creative force for Egypt. Pharaoh was the descendant and holder of the military force that united the two kingdoms. Pharaoh's bureaucracy and the cults he supported kept that unity strong.

Pharaoh's life was also symbolic of his role in guaranteeing *ma'at*. Like the Nile, everything about his life was ordered and symbolic. Diodorus Siculus, a Greco-Roman writer of the first century CE, painted a picture of the king of Egypt as the actor of a lifelong symbolic drama, in which rituals controlled the King's every hour and every act. Like *Le Roi Soleil* of eighteenth century France, the hours of his day and night were laid out according to the strictest plan. The king was directed by law and tradition to do what was politically and ritually required. Diodorus goes on to state that these regulations covered not only the king's administrative actions but also his personal freedom to take a walk, bath, or even enjoy his wives and concubines. He was allowed no personal initiative in his governmental actions but was required to act in conformity with established laws. There is good evidence that this was not always so. But Diodorus insists that the pharaohs of his time were quite happy in this obsessive schedule because they believed that those who followed their natural emotions fell into error, whereas pharaohs, by compulsively following the ancient laws, were personally freed from responsibility for wrongdoing and thus guaranteed a beatific afterlife.[5]

The ritual drama was a national representation of the forces that made Egypt possible: The king's person was thought divine, united with the sun in various ways. The pharaoh was reborn, as it were, with every new generation just as the sun was reborn every day and the Nile renewed agriculture every year. Thus, the king of Egypt issued out of the body of the sun god and, on death, returned to him, or, just as frequently, was seen as the falcon-headed sun god Horus of Upper Egypt and became Horus' father Osiris, the god of embalming, upon his death.

The same might have been said of any king, in various ways, from the beginning of Egyptian history to the end. As long as the dynasty was secure and prospering, so was the country. The converse was just as true. The relationship between geography and religion begins with cosmology, the study of creation, moves through the order of the state, and ends with the famous Egyptian views about the afterlife. As their geography is unique, so too the Egyptians were virtually unique in depicting the sky as a goddess, the earth a god. In almost all nations, it is the sky god, with his warlike thunder and his fertilizing rain who naturally becomes the masculine principle in the sexual drama of cosmic creation. However Egypt's rainfall is too sparse to support agriculture. For the Egyptians, the sky, Nut, was a woman, while Earth, Geb, was a man, since the earth carried the Nile flood. The mud that came in the flood brought fertility to the land. Hence some Egyptian myths picture the first creation as an act of male masturbation. Corresponding to this solitary sexual act, the Nile itself appears to bring fertility by a surge of creative fluid, without the help of anyone or anything else but itself.[6]

But myth is never content to symbolize a process only once. Whether or not the myths that we have are combinations of countless local myths, the end effect is that the crucial aspects of life are symbolized again and again, in various related ways, as if, in Levi-Strauss's words, two people were trying to communicate across a raging waterfall. The message is repeated and repeated in many different ways and with many different symbols because, in Levi-Strauss's estimation, the interference level in cultural communication is very high.

The complexity of Egypt's religion is sometimes dizzying. The various gods of the Nile had their own animal emblems and could be depicted in animal, human, or mixed animal-human form, seemingly related to the local fauna. In fact, depictions of gods varied widely across the country.

Possible contradictions between local versions of stories did not seem to bother the Egyptians overly much. Animals animated the Egyptian pantheon. For instance the lion was associated with Ra at Heliopolis. The dog and jackal were animals of Anubis, whose cult was centered at Sekhem. The vulture was connected to Neith at Sais. The black boar was the symbol of Seth at Avaris. At Hermopolis, Thoth had the form of the ibis and the ape. Amun of the Libyan desert, like Khnum the wind god, was sometimes depicted with the horns of a ram. So also was Arsaphes, sometimes called "son of Isis," worshiped at Fayyum, where Ichneumon was equally sacred. The crocodile divinity was Sobek, in whose city, Crocodilopolis for the Greeks and now called Kom Ombo, was a temple with a lake where tame crocodiles were kept and mummified after death. The wolf-headed deity was Wepwawet, like Anubis, a lieutenant of Osiris. His name, which literally means "the wolf of North Nubia (Wawet)," displays his geographic origins and his appearance in one myth is a way of tying far-flung localities to a national, master myth. The great sky goddess was Hathor, the celestial cow of Dendera. Horus, offspring of Isis, was portrayed as a falcon and associated with the sun, worshiped at Edfu. To Osiris the special bulls known as Apis and Mnevis were consecrated at Memphis. Bastet was a cat who was worshiped both nationally and locally. Just as the local deities were connected to national myths, so the narrative of that myth connected the local rites to those of the nation.

According to Diodorus, the deification of these animals was introduced (at the bidding of Isis) throughout the land of Egypt because of their special help in the discovery of wheat and all the labors of tilling the ground. But we can also see them being swept up into a "master narrative" to unify an originally disunified country. Each of these animal sanctuaries accrued its own rituals and purity regulations, which were constant and quite stringent. The Egyptian pantheon was thought strange to foreigners even in antiquity, and not by Hebrews alone, with their uniquely monotheistic sensibilities. The Greeks made fun of the Egyptians for deifying their pets and, seemingly, anything that grew in their gardens.

On each of these local icons, the name of Ra would be grafted, with a conventional vowel change, in an act of priestly imperialism in honor of the sun god. Thus the sun was Atum-Re, the creator god, at Heliopolis (*'Iwnu*). He was Re-Harakhte, Re-Horus of the Horizon. He became Montu-Re a falcon god, Sobek-Re, a crocodile god, and Khnum-Re, a ram god. He became Amon-Re, king of the gods at imperial Thebes.[7] The earliest texts, the *Pyramid Texts,* are associated with the solar Ennead

34

(group of nine) of Heliopolis. Many of the early kings constructed solar temples in association with their tombs, an association that continues into the pyramid-building period.[8] At Heliopolis, the sun god took the name Atum "the All." Thus, the sun could even be Atum-re, explicitly combining two different names for the sun god. In this guise, he was often represented as pharaoh in human form, wearing the double crown of Egypt.

Although gods have been depicted as the authors of our lives as far back as the time of the Egyptians, depicting them with the forms of political power that are indigenous to the people worshiping them suggests that the causation of who caused whom to be runs in both directions at once. Consequently, Atum engenders Shu, the dry air and light, and Tefnut, the power of moisture. This creation can be depicted as an act of magical power *(heka)* or by an act of masturbation. A third generation of gods comes from Shu and Tefnut, now more tangible in the form of the earth, Geb, and the sky, Nut. Geb and Nut engender two further pairs of gods before they are separated by Shu. The latest pair are Osiris and his brother Seth, with their respective sisters/spouses, Isis and Nephthys. The gods married their sisters and so did the pharaohs. These nine, the Heliopolitan Ennead (or the Nine of Heliopolis), are predominate in the religious literature of Egypt. But there are also other groups of gods to consider, including prominently, the Ogdoad (the group of eight) of the city of Khnum (later called Hermopolis) in Middle Egypt. These gods were Nun and Nunet (primeval waters), Heh and Hehet (eternity), Kek and Keket (darkness), and Tenem and Tenemet (twilight).

Instead of seeking simple analogies among the various pantheons, we should attempt to understand the symbolic nature of Egyptian religion. Sometimes a myth was created by the interaction between the ideographic hieroglyph and the Egyptian word. For instance, in the Middle Kingdom, humanity was created out of the tears of the creator sun god. The myth, like the rebus-like system of hieroglyphics itself, is based on wordplay, because humans *(rmt)* and tears *(rmit)* have the same consonantal structure.[9] Consistency seems to be more important to us than it was for the Egyptians; or else they were unable to achieve it right away. For the ancient Egyptian, the sky could be supported by posts or held up by a god. It could rest on walls or be a cow or a goddess whose arms and feet touch the earth. The process of slowly unifying many local traditions encompassed a much larger degree of ambiguity than would appeal to us. Each of the major accounts of creation in ancient Eyptian documents, namely those found in the *Pyramid Texts, The Book of the Dead,* and *The Memphis Theology,* suggest several incongruent ways that the creation took place. These ambiguities reflect underlying different geographical origins for many creation stories.

Pyramids and Mummies

MUMMIFICATION was practiced in Egypt as early as the Old Kingdom. In burial sites dating millennia before the historical period, we have evidence that the Egyptians purposely took advantage of the natural preservation of bodies in the desert. Mummification, artificially aiding natural preservation of the body in dry sand, evolved into a science quite early. Because of the dry climate, the Egyptian interest in stability could be technologically applied to mortuary practice. Once the dessicating properties of *natron* (a naturally-occurring mixture of salts and carbonates) were discovered, the technology developed rapidly. The mummified body was also eviscerated, presumably because the internal organs are more apt to decay, and the organs were separately interred in what Egyptologists now call canopic jars. The body was dipped in various other unguents and preservatives, then carefully, ritually, and symmetrically wrapped in yards of linen ribbon, which also enclosed various charms, amulets, and talismans. Finally, it could be covered with a mask made of costly materials, as it was in early days, or, later in Hellenistic times, with a very realistic, encaustic (beeswax and honey-based) painted image of the deceased encased in cartonnage or papier-mâché.[10] Then it was placed in a series of coffins.

Our word "mummy" derives from the Arabic word for bitumen because the desiccated mummies develop a characteristic dark pitchlike hue and bitumen was, in fact, sometimes used in the preservation process. Since the desiccating process virtually destroyed all tissue except the skin and bones, mortuary priests began to pad the skin with various substances so as to conserve a more natural look. Artificial eyes were often placed on top of the eyelids and the eye socket filled with marbles or onions.[11] All this contributed to a more naturally appearing mummy. No one fully understands what mummification meant to the Egyptians but its meaning seems to adhere to the process of preserving the body for eternity. In early Egyptian society, the body itself could stand for the "self." Transforming the body somehow symbolized or paralleled the transformation of the self into its afterlife form.

The mummies were originally placed in *masteba* tombs, an Arabic word which simply means "bench" and refers to their trapezoidal shape. Pyramids (Egyptian *m'r*) were constructed, in some sense, by placing mastebas on top of each other, in ever decreasing size like a wedding cake, as the famous step pyramid of Saqqara shows. As the form developed, the steps between them were then filled in. Many texts suggest pyramids represent the primal mountain emerging from the sea at creation. Over a hundred pyramids were built, of which more than eighty survive today. After several failures, the Egyptians found the ideal proportions for their pyramids, the ratio of base to height being exactly 2π. This occasions a mystery, as the early Egyptians are otherwise unaware of the value and importance of π. Tabloid television programs regularly attribute this ratio to the arrival of visitors from outer space.

The mystery is solved, however, when one posits that the Egyptians laid out their pyramids with a measuring wheel with a known radius, which also served as the basic unit of height. Since the measuring wheel's circumference automatically measured one unit of π for each unit of height, it automatically built π into the equation. So, if the construction engineers laid out the pyramid with each half of the base measuring the same number of revolutions of the wheel as they planned for the units of the height, the ratio of base to height would be exactly 2π, even if the architects themselves had no knowledge of how to calculate the constant. In any case, the result is an exceptionally massive and stable building, the equivalent of a man-made mountain of stone. Indeed they have survived like mountains.

The person credited with the invention of the pyramid is Imhotep, the great architect of King Djoser (2630–2611 BCE) of the Third Dynasty. He designed the famous step-pyramid as the pharaoh's tomb, which soon evolved into the smooth-walled pyramidal form. Pyramids were exclusively used for royal tombs during this period. The steps suggest a ladder or staircase for the king to ascend to his heavenly abode, as in one of the depictions of the ascent of the pharaoh in the tomb of Unas. The first true pyramid was the one constructed for Sneferu near Saqqara and was quickly joined by the one built for his son Khufu (Cheops) and, finally, by those of their successors, Kaphren and Merikare, completing the great pyramid complex at Saqqara, which tourists visit daily by the thousands. The pyramid was also associated with the famous pyramidal *benben* (perhaps meaning "shining") stone of Ra, attesting to the importance of the priests of Heliopolis in the development of the form, as the shape appears to be a depiction of the spreading out of the sun's rays. The pyramidal capstone made of shining *electrum* (a natural alloy of gold and silver), reflecting light in all directions at the top of pyramids and obelisks, was known as the *benbenet,* a term also derived from the base meaning of "shine" or "reflect." The king's ladder to heaven and the rays of the sun become architecturally wedded together by the Fourth Dynasty. Many of the spells in the *Pyramid Texts* suggest that the pharaoh rises to heaven by means of a ladder:

N. ascends on the ladder which his father Ra made for him.[12]

or

Atum brought to N. the gods belonging to heaven, he assembled to him the gods belonging to earth. They put their arms under him. They made a ladder for N. that he might ascend to heaven on it.[13]

Indeed many pyramids made use of a spiral ascending staircase, later filled in to achieve the pyramidal shape, as both a construction necessity and a religious symbol.[14] The ladder, the staircase, was part of the magic of the pyramid itself.

In the first pyramid inscriptions, found in the pyramid of King Unas, we see a variety of methods for achieving this ascent. After the first inscriptions in pyramids, the pyramid symbol itself became the determinative in hieroglyphic writing to indicate that the next word was a tomb; that connection continues long after the Egyptians stopped building pyramids. It is quite important for the later history of Western notions of afterlife that the Egyptian pharaoh achieved immortality by stepping into the heavens. The association of heaven with immortality is uniquely an Egyptian invention, occurring many millennia before it becomes part of Biblical or Greek tradition.

The ancient pharaohs were at first the only ones to climb to heaven with the sun because they were the only ones who could organize the community and pay to construct the great pyramids, the great stone machines that propelled the dead pharaoh to heaven. The great pyramids of Giza are laid out according to the compass directions and also line up exactly with important stars, suggesting the location of the pharaoh's *akh* (transformed spirit) or the direction of his journey.[15]

Two different sets of stars were important to Egyptian burials. Up until the Twelfth Dynasty, the Egyptians were interested in stars above the ecliptic, hence stars which never set. Like the North Star, they were the "indestructible" stars (Ikhemu-Seku, the stars that never fail), representing astral immortality in a direct and important way. Until the Twelfth

Dynasty, the entrances to the pyramids and tombs were aligned with these stars, likely so as to enable the *ba*-soul of the pharaoh to ascend directly to them. The Middle Kingdom focused on the stars that set and rose in the sky periodically, some of which were planets (Ikhemu-Weredu, "never resting stars"). They sank into the netherworld only to rise again at regular intervals (which were often noted in the tomb) and so became a potent symbol for regeneration, especially important for the Osiris cult.[16] The stars known to the Greeks as the "decans" because they helped keep time in the night were also used by the Egyptians.

These exact parallels with geographical and astral features were designed to aid the dead directly in their flight to immortality. Very quickly too, the tombs were filled with spells for the same purpose. Unfortunately pyramids were very expensive and vulnerable to looting. When Thebes, with its central location, became more important as a capital, burial was thence moved to the Valley of the Kings, where the tombs were carved out of the foot of a very obvious and prominently pyramidal-shaped mountain. So, in a sense, the pharaohs never did leave behind the notion of resting in pyramids; they merely moved their final resting places to a much greater pyramid, closer to their new capital, and one where their costly possessions could be more easily protected.

The Osiris Myth

THE OSIRIS-ISIS mythology was central to Egyptian notions of the afterlife. It also functioned to help unify the countries of Upper and Lower Egypt into one single political and religious unit. A complete text of the story of Osiris was not obtained until the first century when Plutarch wrote *de Iside et Osiride,* probably conflating several versions of the story to a single consistent text. Before that, we have but fragments of the same myth. The legend runs thus: Just as the Nile flows again after its deathly ebb in summer and yearly restores the land of Egypt, so the divine Osiris, both husband and brother of Isis, undergoes many periodic trials for the salvation he brings through the funerary cult. Osiris is a beneficent king, teaching Egypt how to grow crops, establish laws, and worship the gods. Isis and Osiris, sister and brother, are also perfect lovers. They even mated in the womb of Nut, the sky goddess. Isis is invoked as the one who made her brother Osiris endure and live. She, the Great One, burns incense for her young child, the new-born god Horus; so Egyptian mothers did in imitation of her. Isis is figured in the Hellenistic period as an especially kind warm-hearted wife, sister and mother, nursing her child and keeping a good home, indeed later serving as the sculpture-model for the Christian figure of the Madonna and child. It is Isis's tears that make the Nile rise and bring back life to the dead earth.

Life is never perfect, in myth or reality. Osiris is victimized by his evil brother Seth. Seth tricks Osiris into entering a chest, prefiguring the mummy case, where he is slain and set afloat. Isis discovers that Seth has killed and cruelly dismembered the body of Osiris. With this event, the story begins to take on its characteristic emphasis on the process of disposal of bodies and their transformation into new life.

Since Osiris and Isis are the divinities most associated with the mortuary rites, this story is quintessentially a justification and legitimation of that science. According to the tale recounted by Plurarch, Isis casts about looking for ways to bring her brother back to life. She visits Byblos in Phoenicia to make the cedar ark in which the body is to be buried, as indeed one of the pharaoh's sarcophagi was usually made from cedar, a wood whose preservative properties were here given mythical justification. In fact this is the same place Solomon goes to find cedar paneling for the Temple of YHWH.

Isis finds Osiris near Byblos and frees him from the chest but then Seth chops Osiris's body into fourteen parts and scatters them over Egypt. After a long search, Isis finds all the missing parts save one—the phallus. Indeed, many Egyptian spells are dedicated to reanimating the phallus.[17] Then, grief-stricken Isis, wife and sister of Osiris, reconstitutes the body and restores it to life with the help of Anubis, by means of the mummification process:

> Look: I have found you lying on your side, O completely inert one! My sister, said Isis to Nephthys, it is our brother, this. Come, that we may lift up his head! Come that we may reassemble his bones! Come that we may erect a protective barrier before him! Let this not remain inert in our hands! Flow, lymph that comes from this blessed one! Fill the canals, form the names of the watercourses! Osiris, live, Osiris! May the completely inert one who is on his side rise. I am Isis.[18]

Isis buries all the body parts but, since she is not able to find Osiris's penis (it has been thrown into the Nile), she makes him an artificial one.[19] As is clear here, this action somehow refers yet again to the Nile's flood and its perceived creativity while also symbolizing that even the funerary cult cannot bring back the power of generation to the dead king. Isis then impregnates herself magically with the relics of Osiris and gives birth to

Horus (or Harpocrates, as he was known in Greek), sired by her brother and husband Osiris.

While Osiris becomes lord of the underworld, his son Horus, the falcon-headed sun god of Upper Egypt, stays permanently on earth, fighting continuously with his uncle Seth, the ruler of chaos, until he succeeds both in battle and in the courtroom. The pharaoh is both Osiris and Horus, in two different sequential "avatars," attempting to live up to the divine symbol systems of the Upper and Lower Egypts, as well as this world and the next. The reigning pharaoh is identified with Horus, so these battles are mythologically equivalent with the battle to keep civilization safe in war and to rule wisely in court, the two great venues of the pharaoh on earth. The dead pharaoh is transformed by mortuary ritual into Osiris, where his responsibilities change to the good government of the dead. A stable and intact tomb was a symbol of prosperity and harmony between this world and the next. But the physical intactness of the tomb certainly also provided the launching pad that allowed its inhabitant to ascend to heaven. As Morenz says,

> Logically, and as a rule, ascent to heaven and existence there are linked with the heliopolitan doctrine and are counterpart to the dominion of Osiris over the dead. This is expressed most distinctly in an address of the sky-goddess Nut to the dead king: "Open up your place in the sky among the stars of the sky for you are the Lone Star . . . ; look down upon Osiris when he governs the spirits, for you stand far from him, you are not among them and you shall not be among them." Accordingly, the desire is voiced that the king should not die, or his death is simply denied: "Rise up . . . for you have not died;" or: "My father has not died the death, for my father possesses a spirit [in] the horizon." [20]

Meanwhile, back on earth, the strife between Seth and Horus continues into the next generation. Finally, Atum-Re intervenes, telling Seth and Horus to stop quarreling. Seth invites Horus to his house for a banquet. During the night, Seth inserts his penis between Horus's thighs in an act of homosexual frottage, seemingly establishing his dominance over him, but Horus catches Seth's semen in his hands, afterwards delivering it to his mother Isis. Isis cuts off Horus's hands, throws them in the water, and then makes him a new pair of hands. Since the water now has the hands of Horus, it gains the powers of Horus. Furthermore, the constant substitution of artificial limbs for dead or polluted natural ones seems to be another reference to the magic of the priests in restoring fertility.

The writer Diodorus Siculus gives us some further hints about the meanings of this perplexing myth, by telling us some details about how the story was institutionalized in temples and ritual. From him, as well as Plutarch and Herodotus, we learn that since Isis wishes Osiris to be honored by all the inhabitants of Egypt, she fashions over each of his cut-up fragments the figure of a human body. Then, she calls the priests of each locality together and asks them to bury the artificial body, made out of spices and wax, in the various districts and to honor Osiris as a god. At each supposed burial place, a temple or shrine was dedicated. This story also legitimates the spread of the funerary cult and the primacy of the Osiris priesthood in its performance, as well as giving each locality a specific role in the cult and hence a narrative place in a united Egypt.

Besides enacting the story of the flood of the Nile and the annual return of life of the land, Diodorus shows us that each of the local temples of Osiris became part of an organization of central religion through this myth and, in effect, the unity of the state is brought about through the combination of local cults and deities into a central religious procession. The myth, among other things, narrates this unity in story form. Such a story is not what we would call a constitution but it is certainly part of what unified the state into a conceptual whole that could apprehended by the ancient Egyptian.

Rituals of the Osiris cult associate the annual story of the god with the fertility of the land, as well as with the death of kings. The "Great Procession" at Abydos, the place where the early kings were buried, took place at the first rise of Nile (late summer) and involved bringing the statue of Osiris to a designated tomb area, where he stayed overnight, followed by his triumphal and jubillant return to the temple. Since Osiris was identified with the dead king, logic suggests the continuity of the pharaonic succession, going from the death of the old king to the birth of the new one, just at the time when the Nile was about to renew Egypt's fertility. In Ptolemaic temples, there was often a room called the "tomb of Osiris."

The connection between Osiris—strictly, a god of the dead—with fertility was seen in his other major festival, which took place at the end of the inundation *(3ḥt)*, in the month of Khoiak (approximately December), known from a long Ptolemaic inscription at Denderah. In this ceremony, which resembled a funeral because it signified the end of the flood and the start of Spring (i.e., *prt*, "the coming out" of the seeds), Osiris was identified with the erection of the Djed pillar, a commonly occuring Egyptian symbol which somewhat resembles a modern high-tension tower. The pillar itself seems to to symbolize the power of Osiris. Two important rituals firmly associate Osiris with new vegetation. The first was the central role of "Osiris Gardens" and the second was the ritual of "the grain mummy" or Osiris effigy. The grain Osiris was an effigy made of soil and seeds, which was publicly paraded and then displayed as it germinated, which could then be placed in a trough called a garden *(ḥspt)*. These grain effigies also represented the reunification of the body of Osiris. These aspects of the dead Osiris were depicted in temple art as a reclining mummified body of Osiris with rows of grain growing out of the length of his body.

This festival's liturgy featured what Jan Assman calls "raise yourself litanies" (in German: Erhebe-dich Litaneien).[21] These are prayers beginning with the words "Raise yourself" *(ṭs ṭw),* suggesting the imagery of "resurrection," except that Osiris never returned to the world of the living. Only the grain, which was fertilized and raised by his presence, did. Significantly, these litanies are well known from the *Pyramid Texts* and became more and more important to mortuary literature.[22] The festival securely linked the two different worlds of Osiris, his mastery of the arts of mummification and the king's burial with his ascribed role as a vegetative god linked to the Nile flood. The depiction of the death and rebirth of vegetation in the natural world has become crucial for cultural descriptions of the afterlife world over.

Egyptian Conceptions of the Afterlife

IN HIS JUSTLY-FAMOUS book, *Before Philosophy,* John Wilson points out that there are two different kinds of responses to death among the Egyptians.[23] We can see them illustrated in different tomb paintings and inscriptions. Near the Step Pyramid in Saqqara, there is a tomb of a vizier of the Old Kingdom, a man who lived around 2400 BCE, which I have seen myself on two different occasions. His rooms were crammed with scenes of life and the lust for it. He is shown spearing fish while his servants trap a ferocious hippopotamus. He is depicted presiding over the judgment of tax delinquents. There are pictures of him listening to his wife playing the harp and watching his children play.

On the other hand, there is another tomb painting from the Late Period, the tomb of a man who lived about 600 BCE. Here we see no joie de vivre, no exuberance, no bellowing hippopotamus, no playful children. The walls were covered with ritual and magical texts. The purpose of the texts was to provide the dead person with a map and the techniques for traveling through the realm of Osiris to find eternal rest there. Successful accomplishment of the journey made the person an *akh* or transformed dead.[24]

The temptation, against which Wilson warns us, is to take this stark contrast to indicate a change in Egyptian sensibility. That is an unwarranted conclusion; these two faces of life are two sides of the same Egyptian sensibility, as they are of European and American sensibilities. It may only be the personality of the tomb's occupant, the predilection of the painter, or merely just a question of the taste or prevailing style in interior tomb decorating. There is no way to tell how characteristic this was of the age in which they lived. Christian cemetery art too alternates between figuration of death and symbols of resurrection. In many New England colonial burying grounds, there is scarce indication of the Christian faith in the resurrection. The inscriptions tend to concentrate on death and decay rather than transfiguration and resurrection. Distinctly Egyptian symbols are also prominent in the Christian burying ground on the property of Yale University for example, which I walked by almost daily for several years. The gate to the cemetery carries Egyptian motifs and is surmounted by an Egyptian, winged sun disk. All we can tell for sure about funerary art worldwide is that the contrasting symbols are part of the complete story.

For Egyptians, the hearty pleasures of life and the grim procedures for maintaining one's existence in the afterlife were both appropriate to tomb decorations. Yet, the many engravings that picture the dead being revivified by the prayers and spells offered by the living were meant in a more literal way than we can imagine. The ritual texts, the living doing their ritual tasks, the processions and commemorations of the living in the forecourts of the tombs, and the dead cavorting around in their tombs in the sweet Egyptian afterlife, are all part of the same Egyptian conception of our ultimate demise. They all had a part in the life of the Egyptian people; all were happening simultaneously.

Similarly, Egyptian culture seems to contain radically different evaluations of life of this world. Sometimes life was optimistic and sometimes it was shockingly pessimistic. Pessimism is a long-standing tradition in the Ancient Near East, literarily in the same genre as the Bible's Proverbs, Job, Ecclesiastes, and some Psalms, as well as many famous Mesopotamian Wisdom works. Some of their literary works contemplate suicide suggesting that death is better than life, as does the book of Job here and there.

Because of the legacy of the pyramids and the invention and preservation of hieroglyphs, almost everything that we know about ancient Egyptian religion has to do with the ultimate fate of the dead. The hieroglyphs were invented by the priesthood largely for the purpose of recording and glorifying their role in making pharaohs immortal, and keeping track of the riches which that role brought them. Hieroglyphs are, as the name certainly states, sacred script, prominently displayed in pyramids and tombs; other styles of writing, hieratic and later demotic, were reserved for more secular purposes, although even these had some religious uses. In the earliest period, hieroglyphs were carved and painted in tombs, temples, and religious pillars in grand houses. The purpose of the script, as is clear from every place we find it, was to cast spells to immortalize the dead, giving them by invocation a life for eternity.[25]

Instead of being "damned" or "saved," the Egyptians distinguished between the *akh,* a transfigured person in the afterlife, and the only other alternative, to be *mut,* a corpse. One might, quite simply, die forever, or be "resurrected" for the pleasures of the afterlife.

On the other hand, the Egyptians sometimes depicted this process as a journey through an underworld fraught with danger. Only those who had the protection of the appropriate spells and had lived a moral life could safely maneuver avoiding the pitfalls. With the benefit of the prayers and/or spells, recited by priests, one's corpse was embalmed and transformed, becoming *akh,* a word connoting light and everlasting and radiance, and illustrating again how many aspects of Egyptian religion were affected by solar imagery. *Akhet,* for instance, means "horizon" but can be factored into two parts, the home of light, at least for the transfigured ones, and the sun, the author of all life. *Mut,* on the other hand, derives from a Semitic root meaning "death," frequently appearing in both Arabic and Hebrew.[26]

The *Pyramid Texts* are found in the tombs of the Old Kingdom pharaohs starting with Unas (or Wenis or Unis; the vowel patterns in Ancient Egyptian are educated guesses), the last king of the Fifth Dynasty (c. 2350 BCE). At first, they were found only on the walls but later also on the sacrophagus. Still later they are found on the *hr tp,* or the *hypokephalos,* as the Greeks would call it. Shaped variously, it was often a small disk-shaped object made of papyrus, cartonnage, or some other material, which the Egyptians placed under the head of the dead, to serve as a kind of pillow. They believed it would magically cause the head and body to be enveloped in flames, thus adding to the divinization process. It served as a kind of "prompter," reminding the head of the mummy of its ritual lines, in case he forgot them at the crucial moment. The *hypokephalos* itself symbolized the eye of Re or Horus, and the scenes portrayed on it related to notions of resurrection and life after death. The *hypokephalos* represented the entire world, all that the sun encircles, both the upper sky and the nether world. Writing spells on *hypokephaloi* and other objects were symbolic of the importance of knowing these correct spells at the correct moment on the journey to the afterlife.

Spells were also found on the tombs of queens and, by the end of the Old Kingdom, on tomb walls and coffins of court officials. They represented the spells necessary to bring the body to its final resting place and are believed to mirror the ritual of the royal funeral, though precisely how the service began and ended is still debated.[27] The pyramid of Unas contained 227 spells, which were widely copied into later tombs.

The description of the afterlife, known in Egyptian as the *Duat,* is somewhat vague in the early period but it does contain a "field of reeds," a "field of offerings," a "lake of the jackal," and a "winding waterway," which became much more prominent later.[28] It is hardly a surprise that the sky was envisioned as needing to be traversed by boat, given Egyptian geography, consequently the dead were dependent upon the services of various ferrymen and servants to accomplish the journey.

The myth of Osiris's dismemberment by Seth, his evil brother and god of disorder, served as a narrative structure on which to base the transformation to eternal life, but like writing itself, its ritual observances were largely confined to the aristocracy. For one thing, mummification itself was very expensive. When a deceased was properly embalmed by the priesthood of Osiris, his (or her) everlasting life was symbolized by putting the hieroglyphic symbol of Osiris before the proper name. At first, this symbol was reserved for the pharaoh only. As we have seen, the pharaoh was considered to be Horus on earth and Osiris when he rose into the heavens. The victory of Osiris's son Horus against Seth was declared "true of voice," and the same term followed the cartouche of the immortalized mortal. Indeed, each of the utensils or statues in temples had to receive a special rite of consecration, an "opening of the mouth," in which a sword symbolically opened the nostrils or mouth of the deceased to enable breathing in the afterlife. Again, we see that the intervention of the living was necessary as an act of piety for the immortality of the dead.

Thus, the great funerary rituals of ancient Egypt were not simple acts of piety for the corpse but performative utterances, processes of actual revivification in the afterlife. The artist who created the sacred objects was called *sankh,* "giver of life," and the ritual of bringing the corpse life was called *heka,* a great cosmic power to make rituals effective. The term *heka* itself is often translated as "magic" but in fact it overlaps quite fully with what we would call "religion" as well, there being no need in Egypt to separate religion and magic. *Heka* depicts a creative and protective power, a precondition for all life.[29] It is probably most profitably translated into English as "power." *Heka* was often depicted as the *Werethekau,* the cobra, who also appears as *Wadjyt,* the symbol of Lower (northern) Egypt on the brow of the pharaoh.

All we today have left of these ritual observances are the huge monuments of this religion but it is clear that each pyramid and tomb was but the solid remains of a vast social drama of remembrance and ritual transformation and that the immortalization service was carried on for the benefit of the person entombed. The religious duties and rituals performed by the priests ensured the immortality of the dead as much as the tomb and the mummification itself.

As with most cultures, the Egyptian view of the afterlife contained many different and often conflicting opinions at the same time. The Heliopolitan priesthood promoted the identification of its local god Amon-Re, the sun, with the pharaoh. The pharaoh, identified with this divinity, was believed to return to his immortal status after death, from which he surveyed the earth from the heavens each day. King Unas was the first "to make the walls of his tomb speak." Compared to the bare walls of previous dynasties, Unas's richly inscribed pyramid burial chamber has a programmatic sequence including formulas against serpents and others that might invade the extremities of the tomb. A complete menu of offerings was provided to sustain the body of the departed on its way to the afterlife. Next declarations of the continued life of the pharaoh were delivered.[30] One extract from the pyramid of Unas declared:

> There is no word against Unas on earth among men.
> There is no misdeed against Unas in the sky among gods.
> Unas has removed the word against himself, he has erased it,
>   in order to rise up to the sky.
> Wepwawet (the 'opener of ways') has let Unas fly to the sky
>   among his brothers the gods.
> Unas has moved his arms as a god, has beaten his wings as a
>   kite, and flies up, the flyer O men! Unas flies up away
>   from you.[31]

Following these declarations, Unas was said to have ascended directly to heaven.

In *Pyramid Text* 306, this conception of ascent was transformed into Unas's ride in the solar boat. Just as the pharaoh visited his kingdom by means of a boat, so the sun god sails across the skies to his more exalted destinations. As the sun went to rest every night and was gloriously re-born every morning, so also the pharaoh was reborn for eternal happiness in the other world. The eastern horizon of heaven becomes the analogue for entry into paradise:

> Going in and out of the eastern doors of heaven among the followers of Re. I know the Eastern souls.
>
> . . .
>
> I know that central door from which Re issues in the East. Its south is the pool of *Kha*-birds, in the place where Re sails with the breeze; its north is the waters of *Ro*-fowl, in the place where Re sails with rowing. I am the keeper of the halyard on the boat of god; I am the oarsman who does not weary in the barque of Re. (*ANET,* 33)

There is a suggestion of a test to prove the pharaoh's divine birth as he ascends heavenward. Although originally used for the pharaoh only, the texts were extended eventually to the pharaoh's queens by the end of the Sixth Dynasty and by the Eleventh and Twelfth Dynasties (twenty-first century BCE and later) they were being used by the elite nonroyal class. By the First Intermediate period, the imagery was being used beyond the pharaoh's family and palace, suggesting that the chaos of the Interme-diate period which brought wider and more diffuse political control also brought with it a correspondingly wider access to the benefits of the afterlife.

The Ka, *the* Akh *and the* Ba

THE EMBALMING process was a ritual enactment of the myth of Isis and Osiris. It preserved the body for the afterlife, and the techniques of em-balming were a secret of the priesthoods. The name of Osiris was affixed to the dead pharaoh, completing the identification of the king with the god. As everyone knows, if only from the tomb of King Tutankhamun in the Eighteenth Dynasty, during the first dynasty of the New Kingdom, the Egyptian pharaohs expected life in the world to come to be physical and pleasurable, just as this life had been. Thus, they saved their possessions for their future life.

So too even in the early period. The tombs of private citizens, not kings, provide the best evidence about the state of belief in life after death dur-ing this early period. Persons of high station adorned the walls of their tombs with scenes of everyday life, possibly indicating their conception of life after death. The *ka* was the most ritually important of all the Egyptian words for a person's afterlife. The tomb was the "house of the *ka*," which could physically dwell in it. The *ka* was often understood as something like a "twin" or "double." Thus, the *ka* was an image of the living person, which after death could be viewed as living on in the tomb, requiring regular food offerings.[32] The *ka* could just as well dwell in a statue, a portrait of the living person, while the deceased's embalmed body lay below in a sarcophagus.[33]

But the *ka* was not just at the tomb. The *ka* could also dwell in the sky, as this example shows:

> He that flieth flieth! He flieth away from you, ye men. He is no longer on earth, he is in the sky. Thou his city-god, his *ka* is at his side (?). He rusheth at the sky as a heron, he hath kissed the sky as a hawk, he hath leapt skyward as a grasshopper.[34]

The relationship between Horus and Osiris can be expressed through the agency of the *ka*. The hieroglyph for *ka* is two arms raised in adoration or embrace. Thus Horus, as the son of Osiris, can be seen as his worshiper and embracer, sharing his *ka*. The present pharaoh was then the embracer, the worshiper, the adorer, and the sacred sharer in the essence of his father, Osiris, who was his *ka*. As Jan Assmann writes:

> This constellation of father and son, one in the hereafter, one in the world of the living, is one of the most fundamental elements of ancient Egyptian culture. The funerary cult is based on the idea that only the son is capable of reaching into the world of the dead and of entering a constellation with his dead father that bridges the threshold of death and that is mutually supportive and life-giving. This is what is meant by the Egyptian word *akh*. A widespread sentence says: *Akh* is a father for his son, *akh* is a son for his father.[35]

When the pharaoh died, he returned to his father Osiris, tracing the way to the afterlife. Ascent could be effected in any number of ways—by bird or beetle, for instance—but a favorite image was of a passenger on the boat of the sun, which appeared close to earth at dawn and dusk and mounted high in the sky the next day. The person, or his *ka*, survived death in the sky but his image remained on earth to receive the rites and rituals which were due the departed.

This image made of the departed was as close a likeness as possible, considered to be a physical embodiment of the individual, so that the *ka* could take up residence and receive offerings. The common word for statue, *shesep,* probably originally means "a receiver," and when used in the phrase *shesep-r-ankh* (a receiver in order to live, a receiver of life), it denotes the capacity of the image to serve as a "receptacle" for the vital image of the deceased.[36] The Sphynx, the famous human-headed lion at Giza, was originally one such *shesep-r-ankh* on a grand scale and originally supported a mortuary temple for a cult to the *ka* of the king at its base. Attention to the image as the receptacle of life-giving spirit may explain the meticulous attention given to producing a lifelike mummy. Like a hieroglyph, a lifelike mummy conveyed the essence, or identity, of the dead person. This conception of the image possibly also lies behind the entire hieroglyphic writing system of ancient Egypt and is mirrored in the commemorative cult, where the priestly establishment dramatized the process of immortalization in ritual. In a way, the pharaoh's mummy becomes his hieroglyphic spell generating his immortality.

The grave was also visited by the *ba,* another and in some ways more important Egyptian soul concept, which was often represented as a human-headed bird.[37] Like the *ka,* the *ba* was a complex and diverse phenomenon, whose use changed through time and depended on the referent as well.[38] Proving that even the iconography was not stable, the *ba* was also designated as a ram or a ram's-headed divinity, as the nocturnal sun god was sometimes understood to be a ram, probably because the syllable *ba* also could mean "ram." His barque traveled on a watercourse that was the otherworldly mirror image of the earthly Nile, returning him to the place where he was to rise each morning in the East. At first, only the pharaoh was described as having a *ba,* so it may function as the pharaoh's divinity in this context. Gradually, however, first the court and then, by the New Kingdom, the nobility and royal bureaucracy were described as having a *ba,* which seems to parallel their participation in the afterlife.[39] Especially from the New Kingdom onwards, the focus of Egyptian interest in the afterlife appears to have concentrated more and more on the realm of Osiris underground.

No one knows precisely how the *ka, ba,* and *akh* interact, were synthesized, or how all of these related to "spirits," "ghosts," or "demons." It sometimes seems as if the transformed dead successfully reunite the three aspects of life.[40] Probably, these words, like the complicated pantheon itself, reflect local differences brought into a national system. Very likely there were different explanations for the three major types of soul even in antiquity.[41] The word "shadow," *shut* or *showt,* could also have the force of what we call "soul" in a general sense.[42] But all these different words occurred in different rituals performed at the tomb, in the presence of the departed, and yet the departed was also enjoying the afterlife in the *Duat,* the Egyptian name for the afterlife land. The fact that these several aspects of the person could remain separate after death, to be reunited at night with special ceremonies—and indeed did not congeal into a single notion of soul until the Hellenistic period—may suggest that the Egyptians did not reify the concept of the self as strongly as did other cultures that superseded them, as we shall see later. Furthermore, the ancient Egyptian could speak of his *djet*-body, his *haʿu*-body, his "belly," or his "soul" and mean his body proper. The *sah,* another word for "body," was not itself expected to rise up physically after death.[43]

Indeed, there is good evidence that ancient Egyptians did not normally understand themselves as a single "self" at all but rather as a kind of harmony among forces. For example, the chagrin of love can be described in terms of dissociation of heart and self:

My heart quickly scurries away
when I think of your love (= my love of you).
It lets me not act sensibly,
It leaps up from its place.
It lets me not put on a dress,
nor wrap my scarf around me;
I put no paint upon my eyes,
I'm even not anointed. (Chester Beaty Papyrus: C 2.9; C 3.1)[44]

Great fear is likewise understood as a dissociation. Here is quoted Sinuhe, the main character of a famous Egyptian story, before pharaoh:

Stretched out on my belly I did not know myself before him
while this god greeted me pleasantly.
I was like a man seized by darkness.
My Ba was gone, my limbs trembled,
My heart was not in my body,
I did not know life from death. (Sinuhe B 252–56)[45]

Thus, the coherence of "the self" in ancient Egypt is problematic. One of the most famous wisdom pieces in Egyptian literature is the *Dialogue of a Man and his Ba* (sometimes called *The Dialogue of the Self and the Soul*). The "self" addresses the *ba* and is answered by it. Since this dissociation did not happen in ordinary circumstances, it was an important and extraordinary condition, symbolizing great emotional distress. The subject of this important internal dialogue was whether to "go away" (*šmj*) or not, a conventional way to express "to die." In this context, we see a man contemplating suicide, asking Hamlet's famous question: "To be or not to be?"

It is unclear whether the self says that there is no afterlife or there is no earthly remembrance of those who have gone on. The moral of the story is that what is worse than death is never to have been born.[46] It is life that provides us with enjoyment. But just as important to notice is that Egyptian anthropology had not quite unified "the self" into a single, cognizant being. We also notice this contemplation in early Greek thought, but there we can trace a gradual rise of a single concept of a thinking, transcendent self. Here all three conceptions continue in use. In both cultures—early Greek and early Egyptian—the separation of the self into several different parts is correlated with the various social situations in which a person was expected to participate in the afterlife: present at the tomb as *ka* with the mummified body, in the heavens with the divine *ba* or *akh* residing in the house of Osiris, while enjoying the *Duat* in the "field of rushes," receiving gifts at the "field of offerings," riding the "barque of millions," and many more. There was no need to posit a single experiencing self as long as the person appeared in all the contexts that society determined. A great many of the aspects of the self specifically have to do with the ways in which the dead were expected to participate in the institutions of social life in Egypt, either within religious rituals or in the journey to the afterlife, in which such scenes as judgment recapitulated the values of Egyptian culture. So, in important ways, the notion of a consistent self was a product of human speculation about the nature of the afterlife. We shall see this point repeated again and again in various ancient cultures.

Returning to the plight of the supplicant in the *Dialogue of a Man with his Ba*, we see that the condition of the soul got worse before it got better. The third stanza contains the widely quoted ode on the comforts of death:

Death is before me today
Like a sick man's recovery,
Like going outdoors after confinement.

Death is before me today
Like the fragrance of myrrh,
Like sitting under a sail on a day of breeze.

Death is before me today
like the fragrance of lotus
Like sitting on the shore of drunkenness.

The repetition emphasizes that death can be a release from the troubles of life. This is not the standard notion of life in Egypt, where death is avoided and life is loved, but an exploration of doubt, anomie, and depression; and that accounts for its remarkable power. All the Egyptian love lyrics and exuberant scenes of life in Egyptian wall painting show how strange this dialogue was. It was an eloquent paean to the end of an unhappy life. The promise was for greater felicity in the next life.

Jan Assman finishes his discussion of this articulate and sad poem by saying that it is extraordinary and perhaps characteristic of a particular moment in Egyptian history:

The basic problem is what an individual does with his or her own solitariness in the context of a culture that constructs the person in terms of plurality. How can a person built on communication and constellation persist when communication fails and constellations break? It is the same question that underlies Whitehead's famous definition: "Religion is what an individual does with his own solitariness."[47]

The answer that the *Dialogue of the Man with his Ba* provides is the answer of religion.[48]

Akh: *Felicity on the Other Side and Its Attainment*

ASSMANN SUGGESTS further, in another work, that the notion of a consistent "self" was reached in parallel fashion with the development of the notion of a transcendent *akh,* the glorified body of the afterlife.[49] It was, he professes, the development of the notion of *ma'at,* justice, right order, that allowed this consistency to develop.[50] If *ma'at* could be achieved in this life, could it not be achieved in parallel fashion in the next life? The same notions of justice and equity, which followed good behavior in this life, ought also to obtain in the life to come. For this to develop, one needed to bring the notion of a courtroom from this life to the next. One had to develop a more sophisticated notion of the principle of identity between the person in this life and the next, a notion of "person" who could be punished and rewarded for behavior in this life. I would suggest that it is the glorified self, the *akh*, which is in some ways the completed form of the *Ba*, the "transcendent self" after death that provides the key, as it were, for knitting together a unified notion of the self in Egyptian culture, making the imaginative exercise of an afterlife indispensable for coming to full terms with ourselves as persons.

The condition of an Egyptian in the afterlife was first of all dependent upon correct behavior in this life but also apparently dependent upon amassing enough possessions to use in the next world, and more importantly on completing the correct funeral rituals, at least in the eyes of the priests, who wrote the texts. When the dead achieved *akh* status, usually translated "glorified being," he had evidently completed all necessary steps for reaching the afterlife. This, no doubt, implied the attainment of priestly ritual purification, mummification, and burial. To achieve this status was to achieve the balanced and enduring order of justice, or *ma'at*, as it was known in Egyptian. This implied right order in the cosmos and right order on earth, brought by the power and authority of the pharaoh but maintained by the Osiris priests, who had the primary responsibilities for mummification.

By the Middle Kingdom, the tombs also depict star charts and figures quite clearly, presumably to help the dead navigate their trip, thus adding the starry heaven to the vocabulary of images of immortality available to the Egyptians for decorating tombs. In particular, the north star was invoked as "the star that cannot perish" a proof from nature that the pharaoh was immortal, since this star is at the top of the heavens, just where the pharaohs should go.

Burial was the beginning of this upward-bound process. The continued survival and well-being of the royal and aristocratic dead also depended on the establishment and maintenance of a mortuary cult. The cult might have been performed by the relatives of the deceased in ordinary families or by priests for the more aristocratic dead. An organized priestly cult was normally endowed by a grant of cultivated land, from which profits the offerings and ministrations of the priests were financed. Consequently the mortuary temples were the province of the very powerful and wealthy but employed a large number of caretakers and priests who reaped the benefits of the aristocracy's piety.

The Social Sources of Egyptian Afterlife

TO WHOSE benefit was this religious system? The social implications of this system are obvious. Immortality was the prerogative, first of the pharaoh, and only afterwards of his most trusted and intimate retinue.[51] It was essentially provided by the Osiris priests who knew how to embalm the body of the pharaoh and hence how to benefit from royal patronage. Since they dispensed salvation, in sacred spheres they were more powerful than the pharaoh himself. The priests and the pharaoh thus cooperated in the earthly power whose purpose was to provide the land with stability and peace, the pharaoh with eternal life, symbolized by ensuring the state of continuity between Osiris and Horus. At first, the attainment of immortality was closely associated with the state cults, controlled by powerful priesthoods. Even as the attainment of life after death became more and more democratic, more and more individual entrepreneurs of the afterlife sprang up, led by more and more needed priesthoods, embalmers, and funeral directors.

Essentially, the state cults and their entrepreneurial imitators were supported by those who could pay to have embalming done. They, in turn, benefited from the stability of political power which the pharaoh enforced, further implying that service to the gods brought natural stability as well as political stability and completed the circle by promising an eternal afterlife for anyone who respected *ma'at*.[52]

A number of histories of Egypt trace the continuing "democratization" or popularization of the immortalitization process through the succeeding dynasties.[53] The *Coffin Texts,* collections of inscriptions taken from funerary stelae of the Middle Kingdom (c. 2160–1580 BCE), and *The Egyptian Book of the Dead,* succeeding Egyptian religious documents compiled in the New Kingdom (c. 1539–1075 BCE), both attest to the expanding clientele of persons who applied for and attained the *akh* state. Whether this represents a real democratization or merely an expansion of the literary record to nonroyal persons cannot be clearly distinguished. But the *Coffin Texts* allowed a wider circle of people the immortalitization of the pharaoh by a union with the gods.

Along with this seeming expansion of divine membership came an increasing "Osirification" of the mortuary ritual. The dead person was seen as an *avatar* of Osiris, with the ritual surrounding the Osiris myth coming to predominate in funerary practices. Finally, this seems to parallel the weakening of kingship during The First Intermediate Period, followed by the strengthening of kingship again under the Theban rule of the early Middle Kingdom.

A number of scholars see this progressive identification of the dead with Osiris as a backwards step in religious evolution because it seemed to make the success of the process more and more dependent upon correct

Osirian ritual practices alone. This is a bold, modern, Western, value judgment. As S. G. F. Brandon noted, it is particularly interesting that concomitant with the wider clientele of persons eligible for eternal life came the scene of the judgment of the soul in the underworld.[54] The judgment of the "soul" was what allowed nonroyal persons into the afterlife.

An Egyptian word for the self-conscious self is the "heart," as it is in Israel. In contrast to the Old Kingdom, where the heart played no role at all, the heart became a central topic in the tomb inscriptions starting in the Intermediate Period and the Early Middle Kingdom. With the coming of personal judgment comes a confession of the self's purity also, as the following inscription demonstrates.[55]

> I am truly an official of great heart, a sweet lovable plant.
> I am no drunkard, I was not forgetful;
> I was not sluggish at my task.
> It was my heart that furthered my rank,
> It was my character that kept me in front.[56]

In the earliest Egyptian period, the pharaoh himself was described as attaining his immortal state upon the successful completion of the funerary rites, presumably because the pharaoh himself served as judge in this world. As more and more people were able to attain to *akh* state, however, a judgment scene developed in Egyptian literature. Prior to the *Instruction for King Merikare* (found in wisdom texts dated around 2100 BCE) the idea appeared that a person's destiny depends upon the absence of complaints made against him or his ability to refute them in the heavenly court. In this particular wisdom text, the emphasis of the judgment shifts to the person's own moral achievement. The person's deeds were pictured as heaps of good and ill to be laid in front of the court. Furthermore, the striking image of the balance of the god Re, in which he weighed *ma'at*, became a major theme of the judgment scene.

A major new theme, found in the *Coffin Texts,* was the depiction of the dangers of the journey through the earth. The earth should not have kept the dead king imprisoned in its depths when he must always strive for the sky. The *Coffin Texts* fairly swarm with chthonic demons and other obstructing forces. Perhaps this dates from the growing practice of burying the court officials of the king around his pyramid in *mastaba* tombs, most of which have not survived the ravages of the ages.

In the *Amduat,* the pharaoh traveled to his final reward through the hours of the night. He undergoes several adventures. Initially, he begins in his boat but must also navigate through the desert where the boat transforms into a snake. He encounters trials at almost every hour of the night. He finally was reborn in the East in the morning. Egyptian descriptions of beings of the underworld, the enemies of Osiris are represented in either human form or by hieroglyphs denoting "shadows" or "souls." They were drawn in pits of fire. The damned were condemned to a "second death," which was evidently equivalent to consignment to a "hell" in the afterlife. Brandon suggests that Egyptian mortuary cults were essentially magical techniques for the acquisition of immortality.[57] So, there were other aspects of Egyptian religion as well, aspects in which moral behavior was not emphasized and monitored, especially when the epic adventures of the pharaoh in the afterlife were narrated. Pharaoh's subjects, on the other hand, needed to demonstrate moral behavior to gain a glorified afterlife.

Akhenaten and The Egyptian Book of the Dead

THE REIGN OF Amenhotep IV, the famous Akhenaten, provided a brief respite in the process. A member of the Eighteenth Dynasty, and possibly the father of King Tutankhamon (born Tutankhnaten), Akhenaten briefly changed the religious culture of New Kingdom Egypt. As his name change suggests, he stopped patronizing the traditional gods of Egypt in favor of the single cult of Aten, the sun disk itself, with the result being that the traditional cults fell into disfavor. He even changed the capital to a newly constructed city, Akhetaten, where he and his wife Nefertiti were free to develop the new cult.[58] Erik Hornung suggests that his religious reform, worshiping the religion of light, totally stopped the mortuary practices of the Osiris priesthood.[59] As Hornung says:

> The wakening of the dead to new life was no longer accomplished nocturnally in the netherworld, but in the morning, in the light of the rising sun and at the same time as those still alive. All was now oriented toward the east, and indeed, even the tombs lay in the eastern mountain of Akhetaten—in the text of the earlier boundary stelae Akhenaten gave directions to prepare his tomb there, "where the sun rises"; the "West," previously the mortuary realm on whose "beautiful ways" the blessed dead had walked, disappeared from the concept of the world.[60]

Whatever actually happened in this interesting period in Egyptian history, after Akhenaten's death, the religion of Egypt returned to its traditional gods and its traditional interests. The change of this young heir's name to the now familiar Tutankhamon suggests that he was early put in the tutelage of the Osiris priesthood, while the religion of his predecessor, whatever it was exactly, was zealously erased. After Akhenaten we find *The Egyptian Book of the Dead,* which seems to signal the orthodox renaissance after its brief interregnum.

Beyond the brief religious reform, we might wonder how many other religious reformations were tried and defeated in Egyptian religion. Considering how important the mortuary cult was and how few people had access to it because of its expense, it is a wonder that more revolutions are not recorded. The Egyptian penchant for wiping out the memory of history's losers is, no doubt, part of the issue. Another part is the likelihood that some way for ordinary people to share in the ultimate felicity was present but that it did not reach historical remembrance.

Whatever the reason, the failure of Akhenaten's reform brought with it a new creative stage in Egyptian religion. The centerpiece of the restoration was a new book: *The Egyptian Book of the Dead.* By itself it is not an innovation. *The Egyptian Book of the Dead* is a compilation and anthologization of similar sorts of material found in the *Coffin Texts,* under the further influence of Osirification. There is no telling whether the texts were brought together in this way in the early copies. Our extant books are a kind of expanded anthology, evidently without too much editorial activity, in which every text known at the time was included in some way. It first appears on the interior walls of the coffin of Queen Mentuhotep, who ruled in the Middle Kingdom. The text was not written in either the classic, very educated and formal hieroglyphics or the less formal cursive hieroglyphics but in a yet easier script, known as hieratic. Sometime after the text was deciphered, the coffin itself disappeared, so no new research can be done on it.

In *The Egyptian Book of the Dead,* quintessentially the work of the New Kingdom, which is historically parallel with the Exodus of the Israelites from Egypt, it is the heart of the deceased that is balanced against *ma'at,* symbolized by a single feather. The title, *The Egyptian Book of the Dead,* is a Western invention, just as inaccurate as our title for the *Bardo Chodol,* the so-called *Tibetan Book of the Dead.* The Egyptian work's actual title is "The Book of Going Forth by Day," meaning that the spells contained within the book gave its benefactors the power to live during the day instead of just existing at night, like ghosts and spirits. Chapters 30 and 125 of *The Egyptian Book of the Dead* are especially concerned with the judgment scene. In chapter 125, we find this famous negative confession:

> I have not done that which the gods abominate.
> I have not defamed a slave to his superior
> I have not made (anyone) sick.
> I have not made (anyone) weep.
> I have not killed.
> I have given no order to a killer.
> I have not caused anyone suffering.
> I have not cut down on the food-(income) in the temples,
> I have not damaged the bread of the gods.
> I have not taken the loaves of the blessed (dead).
> I have not had sexual relations with a boy.
> I have not defiled myself. (*ANET*, 34)

Here, we find the values that were expected of the Egyptians who could read this text. The list in the later chapter is even more complete. Besides noting that pederasty, murder, and profanation of religious objects was forbidden, so too was valorized and rewarded the generous treatment of servants and all the behaviors valuable to the Egyptian state. Since the scrolls were richly illustrated, it was probably read out to those who could not read, with effective use of the accompanying pictures.

Of the many depictions of this interesting scene, perhaps the most complete, is to be found in *The Papyrus of Ani*. In this fine papyrus, dating from the Nineteenth Dynasty (ca. 1320 BCE), Ani, an important ecclesiastical official at Thebes and Abydos, was depicted together with his wife, in festal attire watching the judgment scene in the "Hall of the Two Truths" *(ma'ati)*.

The center of the picture depicts a great suspension scale with two balance cups suspended. The hieroglyph for heart is engraved on one side and a feather, the symbol of *ma'at,* on the other. The weighing of the heart was obviously a depiction of its worth against the standard of justice, bringing the invention of interchangeable measurement into the science of the soul. This, in itself, helps us understand what democratization of the afterlife must have meant because people with different deeds and occupations were measured against a fixed standard. The point of the scene was that Ani's heart had to be found lighter than the feather of *ma'at.* Since the heart was the seat of intelligence, it was the part of the person answerable for moral behavior. It was commonly associated with the *ba*. As a result of this trial, Ani became, in effect, an *akh* in the afterlife and achieved in death a kind of complete personal reintegration in his exalted and transcendent state. The obvious representation of this would be depictions of the deceased among the stars, and indeed such illustrations exist. Ani apparently preferred to think of himself as savoring the joys of life. One vision of beatific existence did not contradict or prevent him from enjoying the other as well.

Heka, *or Power*

TO BE SURE, many of the rituals were supposed to work merely by the power of the ritual itself, the *heka*. But the underlying tone of moral character assumed in this scene is found explicitly in chapter 125 of *The Egyptian Book of the Dead*. Here was a profession of moral innocence. In the first section, addressed to Osiris, the reciter protests innocence of a long list of impieties and immoralities. In the second section, addressed to forty-two tutelary divinities, is a second list of protestations of innocence. This is followed by a prayer:

> Hail to you, O gods of this place! I know you, I know your names. I shall not fall under your blows. You will not report that I am evil to this god in whose retinue you are. My case shall not come through you. My case shall not come through you. You shall say that *ma'at* returns me, in the presence of the Universal Lord; for I have practiced *ma'at* in Egypt. I have not offended the god. My case shall not be reported as evil. . . .[61]

Power over the tutelary divinities depended on knowing their correct names, apparently so that one could address a spell or report on them in the event that they did not behave as instructed. In the afterlife, as in this life, the bureaucrats and administrators could not be expected to automatically represent one's case impartially. Special spells were like divine *bakshish* (the contemporary Arabic word for small "tips" or "bribes"), necessary at every turn to insure performance.[62] This procedure looks to us like magic, but it is a commonplace even in the modern Middle East. One wonders whether it should not be considered high religion in Egypt because the effect of the spells is to change one's immortal status, not change one's life on earth. And, as I said above, Egypt did not make any distinction between magic and religion, so probably we should not in our attempt to distinguish various facets of their religious life.

But besides what seems to us to be an obvious magical response to an anxious life, we recognize that moral values are present as well. The pharaoh may have achieved immortality because the gods loved him so much they gave him the correct spells or prayers, or he may have successfully passed all the ordeals he faced in his journey to the afterlife. But the "the middle classes" (i.e., the client retainers and workmen of the pharaoh) definitely had to lead moral lives, as the judgment scene shows, in order to receive their just reward. The history of Egyptian religion, at first blush so stable and conventional, like most Egyptian inscriptions, by its very steadiness underlines important moves forward in the history of religion. We have now moved squarely into a moral universe, governed by a final ordeal of guilt or innocence. The result is a new sense of self.

Once more Egyptians made the trip to the underworld, more moral values crept into the narrative. There can be no doubt of the moral functions of *The Egyptian Book of the Dead*. It instructed the reader on how to live one's life so as to gain "acquittal" of charges that might prevent life in the hereafter. In a bureacratic world, which was just as given to lying and political intrigue as our own, the tale illustrated by example the rewards for truth-telling and moral behavior. It is particularly interesting that the demonstration of the moral basis of the afterlife was concomitant with the expansion of that reward to a wider clientele of persons. It is as if to say that the worth of the pharaoh for life ever after goes without saying. His role was to represent the state and the Egyptian people in all dealings with humans and gods. But when the process of sharing the benefits of the afterlife with pharaoh's loyal supporters began, the standards for worthiness were specified with more exactness. The virtues explicitly discussed were those that served the pharaoh's and the priests' state, but they were also personal virtues. The attainment of life in the hereafter was therefore dependent upon piety and a life of use and service to the Egyptian state. Furthermore, like most cultures, the Egyptians did not abandon previous notions when new ones came along. Instead, they just added the new ones so that sometimes the ritual and literature appears to contradict each other. Yet, it is more likely that Egyptians saw all the various notions as additive, describing a complex reality.

During The Third Intermediary period and thereafter, the capital and hence the royal tombs, were moved to Tanis, in the reedy areas of Lower Egypt. The preservation of the tombs in this area is poor, due to subterranean moisture. In addition the government unraveled, and Egypt began a rare period of feudalism. Power was restored by the Kushite kings of the Sudan in the south, beginning a foreigner-dominated period. But at the same time, they were the saviors of Egypt from certain political degeneration. The Kushites obeyed the degenerated conventions of The Third Intermediate Period, putting few hieroglyphs on the wooden coffins.

At the same time, they renewed interest in monuments, first, by imitating the stone coffins of the past out of wood and, second, by reviving texts such as *The Egyptian Book of the Dead* of the Ramesside period—in particular, formulas for breathing air to power over water in the afterlife. When the Tanite or Kushite dynasty took over, the process accelerated. Stone was reintroduced by Tarhaqa (the Tirhakah of the Bible) who constructed a tomb complex deep in the Sudan at Nuri. The Ushabtis (servant figures for the tomb) are among the finest carved in Egypt. An Ushabti text promoted *The Egyptian Book of the Dead* into its rightful place at the center of Egyptian rites of life after death. What followed was the beginning of a large temple and tomb complex. The vast scale was due to the efforts of Padiamenipet's assuming the title of chief-lector priest, which had more or less gone into desuetude for a millennium. His tomb complex contains many themes of the late Old Kingdom, as well as friezes of objects and the *Coffin Texts* from the early Middle Kingdom and *The Egyptian Book of the Dead* as well as the full range of underworld books of the New Kingdom.[63]

Egypt in Late Antiquity

CAMBYSES OF PERSIA, the Shah of Iran, ended the renaissance in 525 BCE when he invaded and conquered Egypt. This corresponds to the early Second Temple period of Israelite history and marks the period in which the Jewish colony of Elephantine at Aswan was founded. Like the Egyptians, the Israelites were ruled by the Persians. The Persians ruled Egypt for far longer than the brief Assyrian conquest under Esarhaddon in 671 BCE. The Persian kings and governors were styled as pharaohs after the Egyptian fashion, but they must have needed ambitious native talent to rule as some Egyptian administrators rose very high in the Persian bureaucracy. Egypt was turned into a regular province of the Persian Empire, with the priesthood protecting the rights of the Persian ruler, the King of Kings or *Shahan-Shah*, just as elsewhere in the Persian Empire. Ezra and Nehemiah in Israel, as well, ruled at the pleasure of the Shah of Iran.

Two centuries later, in 332 BCE, Alexander the Great conquered Egypt, styling himself as the savior of Egypt by assuming the title of Horus, the son of the sun god, and putting an end to Iranian rule over all of Western Asia. Yet, he retained the Persian administrative units, the *satrapies,* and their governors the *satraps,* even as he restored the hieroglyphic texts and temples. Alexander commanded the building of a fine new port city, to be named Alexandria, but left before construction began and did not live to see the city built.

Alexander died a mere decade later, leaving his general Ptolemy in charge of Egypt. His successors, the Ptolemaic dynasty, in effect, became the Greek pharaohs of the whole country. Although Ptolemy declared himself pharaoh and king (305 BCE), he did not aggressively meld cultures, as Alexander legendarily wanted. Though they often styled themselves in Egyptian fashion, the Ptolemaic rulers spoke educated, Attic Greek, not Macedonian Greek or Egyptian. The aristocracy supported them, making the Greeks a ruling class apart from the previous Egyptian culture. Cleopatra VII, the last ruler of the Ptolemaic dynasty, just as purebred Greek as the first Ptolemy, was the first to claim to understand demotic Egyptian. But, so far as we know, there was not a single Egyptian document in the famous library at Alexandria and all government correspondence was in Greek, thus excluding most native Egyptians from controlling their own country or even understanding what the government was doing much of the time.

Instead, the rulers continued the ancient cults as a way of communicating with the people. The Ptolemies kept the good order of the people, as the Persians did, by patronizing the Egyptian temples and religious cults of the people, building many huge new edifices, styling themselves in the traditional roles of the pharaohs. The Egyptian priests, for their part, cooperated. But they went far beyond cooperation. They began the process of explaining their religion to a classical audience and later developed hellenized forms of their cults which became popular all around the Roman world.

The Romans continued this two-tiered system of social stratification on the basis of language for a thousand years, until the Arab conquest. A brief revival of Egyptian texts and funerary beliefs surfaced during the reign of Cleopatra VII. But Egypt did not regain its independence until the twentieth century. The Romans offered not nearly the same kind of support to the Egyptian cults as the Ptolemies did, setting the stage for the arrival of a new religion, Christianity, to replace the weakened old one.[64]

Diodorus Siculus, who wrote about the Egypt of 56 BCE when he visited it, describes funeral ceremonies that suggest a parallel between the supernatural judgment in the afterlife and the social judgment placed on the person in this life. Before the burial, there was a public evaluation of the deceased, with an attendant verdict, he tells us. When the judgment was negative, the person was denied a proper burial, unless it was a crime for which the family was able to make restitution. When the burial was not done properly, the deceased's way to the afterlife was blocked.[65] In general, then, Diodorus was extraordinarily impressed with the level of Egyptian morality. (212)

This late report is one of our clearest views of popular religion in Egypt. How far back this practice goes, we cannot speculate. But it certainly would explain why ordinary people were able to put up with the conspicuous consumption of the aristocracy. And it shows how religious beliefs can function in social situations as well as how much of religion is a social discourse where the prescribed script interacts with all the actors to produce socially acceptable rewards.

During the Greco-Roman period, the cult of Isis spread throughout the Greek- and Latin-speaking world. This was facilitated by the visit of Manetho, chief priest of Isis, to the mysteries of Demeter celebrated at Eleusis. Upon his return, he reformulated Isis worship into a "mystery cult," from whence it became easily understandable throughout the Roman Empire. In spite of the Roman aristocracy's resistance to foreign religions, the Mysteries of Isis were soon found virtually everywhere in the Empire, including Rome itself.

Roman Egyptians also began to adopt new forms. For instance, a new secular document, the passport, was paralleled in religious documents when magical texts began giving safe-conduct to the dead. This clearly bears on the Gnostic gems and the later Jewish magical spells to be found in the Hekhalot texts (early Jewish mysticism), all of which detail how inscribed amulets operate as passports throughout the perilous journey up to the highest heavens where the angels or, alternatively, the gods of salvation reside. It is as if Roman bureaucracy formed the basis of the description of the evil world. The Egyptian had to rise to an area of joy above it, where the true high gods of Egypt were still powerful, though the demons now controlled the earth.

In the second century CE, the funerary tradition was still alive and well, though almost entirely transferred into the demotic language. The priesthoods certainly were employed to gain the favor of the Roman emperors, whom they styled as immortal gods. Yet in the third century not one text produced showed any innovative signs, which corresponds to a period of bleak military tensions and bloodthirsty revolts and suppressions. After that, Rome actively suppressed Egyptian religious forms, just as they suppressed Jewish symbols of independence. The last known hieroglyphic text is datable to August 24, 394 CE at Philae near Aswan while the last demotic text was two graffiti, again from Philae, datable to 452 CE. In Kush, Egyptian forms continued for a while, especially as Kushites had never completely given up pyramid building. They also continued to place judgment scenes on tomb-temple walls.[66] The final blow came when Christianity arrived as a Roman protest movement, soon becoming quite popular throughout the Empire.

In the Christian period, little can be said to have survived intact from the Pharaonic period. As telling as may be the relationship between early Egyptian religion and some of the forms of Christianity, we lack any proof for the channel of transmission. Maybe the connection is through the religion of Isis and Serapis (a Greek contraction of Osiris-Apis) which had already entered Roman life. And again the sign for life *ankh,* seems to be the predecessor for the crucifix, which was not an early Christian symbol and appears to evolve out of contact with Egyptian culture through the monasteries of Pachomius, the founder of Christian monasticism in Egypt.[67]

Some Relationships with Israel

EGYPT WAS ONE of the two birthplaces of the Israelite people, according to Biblical legend. We find archeological evidence in the First Temple period, that at Kuntillet ‘Ajrud, Israelites could figure YHWH as a calf-headed deity in much the same way as Osiris-Apis of Egypt.[68] It is likely to have been influenced by Canaanite tradition as well, but the imagery of Egypt is much in evidence. Especially the West Semitic pantheon has been influenced by Egyptian religion.[69]

Because of the close historical contact at the origin of Israelite history, it is also possible that Egyptian beliefs in life after death had some effect on Israelite culture. One would expect a relationship to emerge. Israelites did in fact develop a notion of bodily resurrection returning to a perfected life, though no such ideas made any inroad in Israelite texts during the First Temple period (1000 BCE–586 BCE). No specifically Egyptian imagery can be seen in it, however, and had any putative Egyptian origin been known, it would have been sufficient to condemn it in Israelite eyes.[70]

Freud popularized the notion that Israelite monotheism came originally from the Egyptian heresy of Pharaoh Amenhotep IV, Akhenaten, but

Freud's chronology was off by centuries. As Akhenaten worshiped the disk of the sun and the cult that he founded was all but erased afterwards, it seems unlikely that it could have converted the Hebrews centuries later, when even Hebrew imagery about God is so different. There is a certain amount of evidence that Hebrew psalms occasionally borrowed from Egyptian sources. For instance, Psalm 104 seems to incorporate aspects of *The Hymn to Aten,* but the specific traces of Egyptian religion were removed, leaving only the suspicion that some Hebrew intellectual admired the turn of phrase of the heretical "monotheistic" Egyptian priesthood.

So, in general, if Egyptian thought is present in some attenuated way in Jewish or Christian thinking, it is hard to demonstrate. The Egyptians spoke an afterlife far away in another place, sometimes in the stars, and accompanied by a long and dangerous journey, with a postmortem judgment scene. The Biblical Israelites of the First Temple period spoke hardly at all of an afterlife. In the Hellenistic period, Jews living in the land of Israel most often spoke about a reconstructed earth at the end of time, with a judgment scene there and no resurrection until then, and no embalming or mummification.[71]

It is true that the Exodus narrative says that Joseph's body was mummified but that is specific to his adventures in Egypt, a little historicizing detail inserted into the narrative, not a pattern that Israelites followed. Egyptian religion was based on the hieroglyphic script and was always very graphic, while Israelite thought was, in general, aniconic. It is worth noting that Egyptian imagery has little in common with Israelite notions. The only exception to this would be the obvious borrowing of the figure of the Madonna and child from the Mysteries of Isis (Isis with Horus on her lap) into Christianity, which is as likely to have taken place first in Rome as in Egypt. This illustrates the phenomenon that images sometimes move where sense might more easily forbid their entry. This phenomenon will be more obvious in the relationship between Israel and its close Canaanite neighbors.

Instead, what most strikes any reading of the vast Egyptian traditions on the subject is not just the complete lack of parallel in Israelite thought but Israel's opposition to Egyptian religion, and vice versa. The Egyptian figuration of Seth is in important ways a caricature of the gods of the Semitic Shepherd Kings, the Hyksos, evincing a polemical edge to Egyptian mythology, as happens in every culture. Israelite tolerance of Egyptian religion can hardly be expected to be any better, considering how widely Egyptian religion was itself satirized. The story of the golden calf is a satire on religious practices amongst the Canaanites and the Egyptians but is also likely to be a product of the civil war between the North and South in dynastic Israel.[72] Here, one sees clearly, the victory of the Judean version of monotheism, which predominates in the Bible, over the Northern cult is extremely important. For the Hebrews, the sky could not contain Osiris, as it already contained YHWH, and the dead, who were at best spirits, could not travel there.

Egyptian notions of the preservation of the body may at first seem related to the Second Temple period Jewish notion of resurrection. But this connection too becomes a contrast when one considers the differences in the treatment of the body. The Egyptians considered the preservation of the body necessary for the journey to heaven, as life would continue there in much the same way as here. But they did not envision the afterlife in the physical body. The Hebrews held no such notion that the body had to be embalmed. Indeed, they forbade it. But they later affirmed the notion that the afterlife would be on this earth, perfected, and it would arguably take place in the physical body (or at least a perfected physical body). There is a strong tradition in Jewish mysticism that the dead will achieve a transformed angelic state. It is quite possible that Egypt helped Israel come to these conclusions, as we shall see. In this respect, it is likely to be the general mystical synthesis of the Hellenistic world, in which Egypt had an important part, that affected Jewish mystical views, and not a specifically national Egyptian tradition. In other words, Egyptian ideas affected Jewish mysticism but the Egyptian tag had to be removed first.

In earlier times the evidence is much more tenuous. YHWH does not specifically share any of Osiris's characteristics. The dead do not go to heaven in ancient Israelite thought, rather if anything they remain underground. Israelite tradition does, of course, show the rudiments of a belief in spirits and ghosts, though worship of them is proscribed by the party that produced the Bible. So does every culture known to us. Yet, there is almost nothing in Israelite thought that allows us to directly link any of the concepts of heavenly afterlife with the very vibrant traditions that we see in Egypt, at least until the Hellenistic period.

Canaanite religion certainly did influence Israelite conceptions of the deity and Canaanite religion is clearly influenced by Egypt. The difficulty with this theory is not the conceptualization of the influence but the demonstration of the relationship. In the Hellenistic period too, Egyptian thought was popularized by the religion of Isis, which spread everywhere. In this guise, these notions had important consequences in Jewish and Christian thought; indeed, Egyptian ideas may still be influencing our thought today. But, if this can be granted, then it was an already very denatured and denuded Egyptian thought that served as the basis of the influence. The Egyptian tradition of Late Antiquity was taken over by philosophers and mystics and other independent religious practitioners. It will be one basis, as we shall see, for a rarified astral immortality that became very popular among the privileged pagans of Late Antiquity. In the process, it lost any organic relationship it had to the situation-in-life *(Sitz-im-Leben)* in Egypt.

Summary

EGYPTIAN NOTIONS of the afterlife can yet be appreciated for the touching beauty they contain. Throughout antiquity, from the Sixth Dynasty on, Egyptian literature produced magnificent, affecting, vibrant, personal prayers in the form of letters to the dead:

> A communication by Merirtyfy to Nebetiotef: How are you? Is the West taking care of you according to your desire? Now since I am your beloved upon earth, fight on my behalf and intercede on behalf of my name. I did not garble a spell in your presence when I perpetuated your name upon earth. Remove the infirmity of my body! Please become a spirit for me before my eyes so that I may see you in a dream fighting on my behalf. I will then deposit offerings for you as soon as the sun has risen and outfit your offering slab for you.[73]

Egyptian culture is one of great antiquity and also great conservatism and stability. Yet, we can see definite and important developments in Egyptian religion. From our vantage point, we see from the immensely long history of Egypt that even heaven has a history. Such a perspective was not available to people living in ancient Egypt. They naturally connected their views of the afterlife with those of the first pharaohs, seeing mostly the continuity. Such perceptions ought, at the very least, make us aware of the limitations of our own perceptions of stability in our culture. We too have undergone vast changes since the birth of Rabbinic Judaism and Christianity. We may not blithely conclude that we believe the same things as did our coreligionists at the origins of our traditions. Consequently we may not conclude that the afterlife is a fixed place with fixed characteristics, a geographical location which never changes. We must face the obvious conclusion that even our afterlife is suited to our interests in this world. It is a projection of our own desires and goals, as we shall see. But we have a long story ahead of us yet.

Secondly, we have seen that this development has a great deal to do with the social forces that dominate Egyptian society over a long period of time. The democratization of admission to the afterlife seems to be related to the breakup of the Old Kingdom and subsequent affluence of the retainers and bureaucracy of the Middle Kingdom. Thus we see in the depiction of the afterlife important social, economic, and political goals as well as personal ones.

Thirdly, the afterlife is an important factor in defining personal goals. In Egypt we see that a notion of a person became inherent in the speculation about fate and disposition after death. Presumably, Egyptians preserved the body because it was more easily effected than in other places in the world. It may itself have been a *shesep rankh,* a receiver of life like the consecreated statues of the pharaohs. But with the development of more democratic notions of the afterlife, a more sophisticated notion of identity had to develop. There had to be a principle of identity linking the *akh,* the glorified person, with the person on earth whose moral behavior determined the final outcome. It may be that it was the developing barter economy that forced *ma'at* to accommodate these new ideas, as it depended on a notion of balance and worth, a concept that came out of the development of a market economy. It is scarcely possible to define exactly how it came about. But whatever factors combined to bring about the scene of the judgment of the soul, it had the effect of validating a notion of individual personhood on earth. Eventually this relationship has the effect of helping to define internal human conscious life in our own religions.

In Egypt, finally, we can see the correlation between the climate of the Nile Valley and the national myths of the ancient Egyptians. Not only does this correlation explain the climate in usable ways, it also gives the Pharaoh the role of the hero, who conquers death as the immortal sun. Eventually, ordinary Egyptians understood themselves, defined themselves and the transcendent part of their lives, by imitating the Pharaoh's path through the underworld. The afterlife became the mirror of the self.

2

Mesopotamia and Canaan

Egypt Compared to Canaan and Mesopotamia

EGYPT CERTAINLY developed significant traditions of life after death; Egyptian styles and influences are found throughout Canaan. Whatever the influence, Mesopotamia and Canaan were more closely related to each other and also to ancient Israel than any of them were to Egypt. The intimate relationship starts linguistically. Whether ancient Hebrew is considered closer to Canaanite or Aramaic, it is a semitic language and, hence, much more closely related to Syrian, Mesopotamian, and Canaanite dialects than to Egyptian ones. This closer relationship applies not only to language but also to mythology and culture as well.

Mesopotamian and Canaanite views of life after death were significantly more pessimistic than Egyptian ones. The Egyptian vision of ultimate felicity with the sun god in the sky vanished. Instead, the dead lived underground in estrangement from humans and gods. This more Stoic vision of the afterlife seen in *The Gilgamesh Epic*—the great Mesopotamian epic of loss and bereavement—was even found at Megiddo in the land of Israel. Hebrew tradition seems more closely influenced by Mesopotamian and Canaanite traditions but the presence of other semitic mythologies in the Bible is hotly debated. For one thing, it is hard to know precisely which Bible motifs are Canaanite or Mesopotamian and how deeply they affected Israel. This issue will dog every parallel that we examine.

Mesopotamia lacked the unity of Egypt. It had once been ruled by the

Sumerians, whose culture and language is still something of a mystery to us. Even they do not appear to be the original inhabitants of the land, an honor which currently goes to a group known as the Ubaidians (after Tel al-Ubaid where their archeological remains were found), who established village life in Mesopotamia. The Sumerians arrived in the last quarter of the fourth millennium BCE (ca 3300–3000 BCE). They spoke an agglutinative language which has defied any and all attempts at classification; it is now considered a language isolate.

Etana, King of Kish, is the first king whose deeds were recorded; he probably ruled at the beginning of the third millennium BCE. He is described in a later document as the person who stabilized all the lands, probably meaning that he was the first empire-builder. Shortly thereafter, the city of Uruk took over the rulership of the area under a man named Lugalbanda, ancestor of Gilgamesh. The deeds of the kings of Uruk occupied the epic imagination of the Sumerians and their descendants. The Sumerians were surpassed in turn by the city of Kish, returned to power to be surpassed by Ur, and finally again by Lagash. They were conquered by semitic groups and then Sumerian rule revived for a final time (2100–1720 BCE), when Gudea of Lagash ruled and produced a famous, pious statue of himself, now synonymous with Sumerian art in the modern world. So the most famous Sumerian face comes from the very last era of Sumerian rule. Mesopotamia was indeed noticeably different from Egypt in that it was impossible to create the kind of stability and freedom from attack that the Nile River system gave the Egyptians.[1]

Long before the Hebrews' entrance on the world stage, the Sumerians were supplanted by many groups of semitic-language speakers, who partly inherited the culture of their forebears and partly innovated it into their culture (ca 2300–2100 BCE). These groups sometimes use a word cognate with the Biblical word "Amorite" to describe themselves. Although they seem to have been forced out of the Arabian peninsula, the continuous change of political fortunes in Mesopotamia insured a thorough mixture of cultures. Though the semites (that is, the people who spoke semitic languages, not a race of people) inherited the writing of their forebears, they used it to express their own language. The texts of the classical period in Mesopotamia were written in a semitic language which we call "Akkadian" (after Akkad, the city of the first great semitic king, Sargon), the language name signifying the family of dialects which include most prominently Babylonian and Assyrian. These closely related tongues each became imperial languages as the political and military role of Babylonia and Assyria expanded, one at the expense of the other. As a result even the semitic texts of the area show, in their enormous variation, the development of the long history of the ancient Near East.

Climate, Geography, and the Babylonian Creation Stories

As IN EGYPT, the geography of Mesopotamia had an effect on its religious life. Civilization in the Tigris-Euphrates valleys also depended upon rivers but less on floods than it did in Egypt. We think of these areas as arid, desert Arab locations, and much of the countryside is empty waste now. But the Tigris and Euphrates river deltas are marshy and swampy, full of reeds growing in brackish water. In Mesopotamia, floods were normally seen as evil. Good order depended upon the effective use of canals to drain swamps, irrigate crops, and avoid floods, which destroyed rather than replenished fields, as in Egypt.

As in Egypt, many creation stories developed, stressing different factors, which seemed to coexist without much logical difficulty. Most understood creation as based on the sexual reproduction of animals and humans. Others used the notion of separation and distinction to talk about creation. The most famous creation story, *Enuma Elish* (literally "When on high . . ."), combines these same factors, using more ancient traditions to produce yet another variation on the themes.[2] Indeed, because this myth parallels the Canaanite and the Israelite stories of creation, it is often thought to have West Semitic origins and therefore is especially important to Biblical studies.

The Babylonian creation story parallels the arrival of civilization (i.e., city life) in the area. It depicts the universe's beginning as a split between the god of sweet water, Apsu (the cosmic ocean above and below the earth), and the goddess of saltwater (sea), Tiamat (related to the Hebrew *tehom*, meaning "deep" in Gen 1:1), who were originally locked in sexual embrace.

> When on high, the heaven had not been named,
> Firm ground below had not been called by name,
> Naught but primordial Apsu, their begetter,
> (And) Mummu-Tiamat, she who bore them all,
> Their waters comingling as a single body;
> No reed hut had been matted, no marsh land had appeared,

When no gods, whatever had been brought into being,
Uncalled by name, their destinies undetermined—
Then it was that the gods were formed within them.

(Tablet 1.1–8, *ANET*, 61)[3]

Eventually Marduk, god of Babylon, destroys Tiamat, who is brutally killed while bound, then split and refashioned into the cosmos. Warfare was part of the fabric of life in this contentious river valley, producing new order and new government. From each piece of the goddess, Marduk fashions part of the known world and from the divine blood of Tiamat's general Kingu, Marduk makes the human race: "Out of his blood, they fashioned mankind" (Tablet 6.32, *ANET*, 68). The importance of blood in the Babylonian creation story mirrors the Biblical concept of blood as the location of life (See, e.g., Gen 4:10; 9:4). The Babylonian creation story concerns many important conceptions for the Mesopotamian peoples. Among them is the prominence of Mesopotamian accomplishments in civil engineering—canals, for example—in separating brackish, chaotic swamp into farmland and estuary. Central political rule produced land reclamation and expanded agriculture through irrigation but depended upon the dominance of one city-state over another. The long and incomplete history of Mesopotamian creation stories mirrors the often incomplete dominance of one group of allies over the others in the area. Certainly, the primacy of Marduk in this version was meant to demonstrate the destined role of the city of Babylon to rule by military force in the area.

More often, the Mesopotamian versions of creation included clay with the liquid that creates humanity. Fabrication out of clay is so omnipresent in Babylonian creation stories that *Enuma Elish* may have assumed it and simply neglected to mention clay explicitly. Made from clay, a living being is possessed of a breath-life-force (*napištu*, cognate with the Hebrew word *nefesh*). It might also contain another wind-like component, the *zaqiqu*. This latter was sometimes viewed in bird form and associated with dreaming because it was able to flit about and depart the body when it was asleep.[4]

In the Atramḥasis epic, which contains both a creation and a flood, a very interesting new aspect is developed; the nascent human is fused with an *eṭemmu*. *Eṭemmu* is the standard word for ghost in Mesopotamia. In this case, however, the text does not indicate that we have a divine spirit or an immortal soul. Rather, it almost seems to imply the opposite, the human who possesses *eṭemmu* now must die. When the human dies, the *eṭemmu* takes up residence underground while the *esemtu* or the *pagru* (two words signifying "corpse") rests in the earth.[5] Thus, as in the Biblical story, the forces that combine to keep us mortal were evident in the creation story itself. Because the word *eṭemmu* comes from *ṭemum* (report, instruction, wisdom), we see that mortality and wisdom are related from the first.[6] Cosmology, the story of our beginnings, is a very common way to address the issue of whom we are and what our "self" is. But that is not the only way in which the Mesopotamians reflected on human identity and mortality.

Adapa

IN MESOPOTAMIA, most of the gods lived in the sky, though one powerful goddess, Ereshkigal, and her consort ruled the underworld, sometimes named *Cutha,* while demons and fearful monsters lived in between, populating the oceans and the underground. Several stories describe trips to visit the abodes of the gods. Each exists in a variety of texts found in different locations and in different languages, and often emphasize different, indeed opposing notions.[7] These stories share some characteristics of modern travel narratives, meant to tell of the fantastic sights in the world; they then move on effortlessly to reveal the structure of the universe and the afterlife.

The oldest known ritual text mentioning Adapa was actually written in the first person, with Adapa as the persona adopted by the exorcist for expelling demons. Throughout the history of Mesopotamian exorcism texts, Adapa is compared to the king in his powers and abilities.[8] Furthermore, he is related to the mythical *apkallu* figures, who are semidivinities associated with scribal guilds and easy to spot in Mesopotamian art: They are figured as anomalous creatures who combine human and fish elements, or alternatively, human and bird elements. This makes them the masters of two environments, and they are known throughout Mesopotamian literature as the sages of old. Wise Adapa, the first human being and priest of Eridu, is both an admirable man and a trustworthy guide to the afterlife as he has visited heaven and knows what is there:

> Wide understanding he had perfected for him
> to disclose the designs of the land.
> To him he had given wisdom;
> eternal life he had not given him. (*ANET,* 101.)

While Adapa is fishing, the south wind overturns his boat. In a fit of pique, Adapa breaks the wings of the wind. This strange locution appears to refer to a technique of exorcism, specially related to defeating the demons who cause diseases. Thus, Adapa and the "good demon" Pazuzu are called upon to defeat disease-bearing demons, whose powers are depicted as winds.[9]

Unfortunately every therapy has a cost. The god Anu is furious at Adapa for his impious action and instructs his gerent Ilabrat to bring Adapa before him. Adapa has the protection of Ea, who suggests to Adapa how best to dress for the occasion. Ea instructs Adapa to leave his hair unkempt and to generally signify his deep mourning, telling the heavenly gatekeepers, Tammuz and Gizida, that he is grieving for them. Furthermore, in a detail that ironically anticipates the Demeter/Persephone legend as well as Genesis, Adapa is told by Ea not to eat anything put before him while there. However, if they offer garments or oil, he may use them.

Adapa proceeds to climb the road to heaven. At the gate of the heavenly realm, Tammuz and Gizida are pleased to discover that someone commemorates them on earth. As a result, they send forward a good report to Anu, who listens to Adapa's story and is apparently won over, at least to the point of extending the courtesies of heaven to this worthless mortal. Good manners oblige Anu to give Adapa clothes and oil, as well as the bread and water of life, which will make him immortal. Significantly these are exactly the same gifts given to the dead to keep them domesticated within the family and working for the family's interests in the afterlife. In this context, the proffered gifts are what hospitality demands.[10] Unfortunately for us humans, Adapa refuses to eat or drink, exactly as Ea has advised him. By not eating, he forgoes the chance for immortality. Adapa has inadvertently accepted rites associated with burying the dead as well as insulting the god's hospitality in a kind of ritual double entendre, which results in humanity losing its chance for immortality, to gain funeral rites, only afterwards gaining wisdom.[11]

The themes of knowledge and eating fabulous elixirs of immortality are parallel to the Biblical Adam and Eve story. In the Mesopotamian story, the food of everlasting life is water and bread, obvious symbols of basic human sustenance, as are good clothing and oil. The wisdom that Adapa gains refers to his exorcistic powers. Comparably in the Biblical story wisdom is depicted as a fabulous but forbidden fruit while clothes are a later gift of God after the primal couple loses their innocence. Adam and Eve receive the power of moral discernment, which is a very great good in the Biblical story; but the result appears the same: Humans cannot live forever like gods. We cannot tell if this is so in Adapa's case because the ancient text breaks off before the denouement of the story.

Shlomo Izre'el recently completed a full-scale study of the Adapa myth.[12] For him, the relationship between gods and humans is easily understood in the myth. While animals, humans, and gods have life, only humans and gods can have wisdom and only gods can have eternal life. What humans get, instead, are divinely sanctioned rites. Perhaps wisdom serves as a consolation, which might even be understandable as a theme of the garden of Eden story in the Bible. On the other hand, the Adapa story provides us with a convincing etiology for a particular group of ritual exorcisms.

Etana

THE ETANA EPIC though even more fragmentary and inconclusive than the Adapa legend should also be explored. Etana was the famous King of Kish, described in the Sumerian King List as: "A shepherd, the one who ascended to heaven."[13] He resorts to undertaking a heavenly journey in order to find the plant of birth, hoping to remedy his childlessness. Unfortunately, the remedy is difficult to obtain because it belongs to the beautiful but dreaded goddess Inanna (Akkadian: Ishtar). Progeny was a significant way to gain "immortality" in Mesopotamian culture, as it is in ours, and miraculous plants are now seen as the stock-in-trade of Near Eastern myth and fable. Perhaps this myth makes reference to some real plant with a reputation for medicinal properties in augmenting fertility. Regardless Etana's adventure begins with an act of compassion: He saves an eagle from imprisonment by a serpent in a pit and, in return, Etana is allowed to hitchhike a ride with the eagle to heaven. But the eagle offends Shamash, the sun god, by traversing his realm with a mortal. The Annunaki, who now serve as a council of fifty "Fates," eat the snake's offspring in their bird-like form.

The Etana text becomes fragmentary just as Etana becomes too heavy a burden for the eagle. Doubting that he can make the journey, Etana begins to fall. At this point, we are unable to decipher what happens to our much beset hero. Heaven is not for mortals, either alive or dead. Like Icarus, Etana is a person dangerously out of his native environment whose punishment, a fall from a great height, was tragic. Unlike the fate of Icarus, Etana's end does not appear to be disastrous. Whatever happens next, Etana appears to have accomplished his mission, since other texts list Etana's son and heir among the kings of Kish and no existing text reports a premature demise (*ANET*, p. 114).

We can perhaps interpolate some of the missing data: The eagle probably returns the favor that Etana has done for him saving Etana from his fall. Furthermore, Etana's name has long been connected with wisdom. And it is in Wisdom Literature, the literary advice of scribes together with their knowledge of divination and exorcism, that we find the most references to heaven and hell.

Wisdom, Ascent to Heaven, and Mortality

SOME OF THE references to heaven appear in technical contexts as well. In the *Assyrian Dream Book,* there are also a few short references to ascensions. The most famous one can be found in Column IV of the *Susa tablet:*

> If a man ascends and the go[ds bless him:
> this man] will die.
>
> If a man ascends and the gods [curse him:
> this man will live long.] [14]

The Assyrian texts follow the standard reversal pattern for these dream manuals, interpreting positive dream happenings with negative outcomes in life and vice versa. Nevertheless, we should not overlook the implication that these short texts evidently associate dying with a heavenly journey. A person who dreams of ascending to heaven will die, whereas one who is cursed in the dream will live long. However early death does not mean that the dying one will ascend to heaven; actually it means the opposite. Life in this world was believed to be cursed by the gods. The call to heaven was not the result of a normal journey after death for, in this culture, the dead went below ground. An ascent to heaven in dreams, privileged though it might have been, presaged death in real life. One sees this dilemma even in the conventions of writing in Mesopotamia and Canaan. The determinative *dingir,* which indicates that the word which follows was the name of a god or a theophoric name (one in which the name of the god appears), was a depiction of a star. This scribal convention only underlines this society's notion that the heavens were where the gods were; they were the stars.[15] Humans were believed to inhabit the earth until their deaths and then, even if they had visited heaven, they went below ground.

In the famous Wisdom lament, *Ludlul Bel Nemeqi* ("I Will Praise the God of Wisdom,") one sees other casual references to the afterlife, heaven and hell, in a context that reiterates the limitations of life on earth. The writer of the poem, Shubshi-Meshre-Shakkan, observes that one can never divine the will of the gods:

> Who can know the will of the gods in heaven?
> Who can understand the plans of the underworld gods?
> Where have humans learned the way of a god?
> He who was alive yesterday is dead today.
> One moment he is worried, the next he is boisterous.
> One moment he is singing a joyful song,
> A moment later he wails like a professional mourner.
> Their condition changes (as quickly as) opening and shutting
>   (the eyes).
> When starving they become like corpses,
> When full they oppose their god.
> In good times they speak of scaling heaven,
> When they are troubled they talk of going down to hell.
> I am perplexed at these things; I have not been able to
>   understand their significance. (2.35–47; *ANET,* 597)

This entire poem is one of praise, as the first line tells us. But in the middle of the poem, the author tells of his terrible *anomie,* especially when his luck was down. Indeed, his description of the meaninglessness of life seems more convincing than his affirmation. He believes that we are silly creatures, expansive in good fortune yet heedless of the gods' wills and depressed in bad times. The wise course, therefore, is to realize our limitations and keep a good will towards the divinity. Sickness and bad fortune are described as a kind of death itself, a motif that appears regularly in the Bible. Good fortune is salvation from the bad. In this context, Shubshi-Meshre-Shakkan uses the image of scaling heaven and going down to hell. But the phrases do not mean what they normally mean to us: All the dead go below, while only the great heroes like Etana are given a glimpse of heaven, where the gods dwell. Thus "heaven" and "hell" have no moral meaning as they do for us; they may simply be addresses. The heroes return with great wisdom because they have seen sights normally reserved for the gods. Like Etana, their wisdom was realized in the acceptance of their mortality. The themes of wisdom and mortality are unconditionally wed in the ancient Near East.

Seeing the God

IN ONE RITE, however, all cultures in the ancient Near East are united. Both Egypt and Mesopotamia, as well as Canaan and later Israel, attach great importance to seeing a god face-to-face. Indeed, seeing a god seems to be the most basic purpose of a heavenly ascent. Although the gods did not usually appear to humans in Mesopotamia, rather they made their wills known by divination, the myths frequently depict men speaking to gods face-to-face. In Mesopotamia, statues of worshipers were dedicated by rich patrons at the altars of gods, so that they could eternally gaze on the divinity in statue form, give them obeisance, and bask in their presence. The large eyes of the worshipers' statues expressed the religious importance of the cultic viewing, just as the large noses of the statues of the gods emphasized their pleasure at smelling the sacrifices humans gave them. Even as early as Sumer, wide-eyed Gudea was depicted before the goddess of Lagash:

> When thou turnest thy gaze upon thy people, plenty comes to
> them of itself;
> The pious young man whom thou guardest lives long thereby.[16]

So too in Ugarit, a Canaanite city on the Syrian coast, the meeting between the god and a human hero was emphasized. There were, and in some religions there still are, important rituals in which humans and gods supposedly meet on various occasions. In Israel, the populace was expected to appear before God in Jerusalem as often as three times a year. In addition the priesthood and the king also participated in various rituals of ascent to the temple at these times. On the Day of Atonement, the high priest entered the holy of holies. He pronounced the name of God according to its letters and only the smoke of the incense prevented him from a full view of the deity. Even so, many Israelite heroes saw God. Adam and Eve and a variety of figures in Biblical history saw God face-to-face and lived because God spared them, though the penalty for this vision was explicitly death: "But," He said, "you cannot see My face; for man shall not see Me and live" (Exodus 33:20).[17]

Inanna

THE HEAVENS or the high mountains were believed to be the domain of the gods. Some of the heavenly gods visited the underworld as well; when they went, like Adapa and Etana, they were out of place. The underworld was considered the domain of death. Sometimes not even the gods could escape death. That is what happened to Inanna when she visited the realm of the dead underground. The most spectacular of the journey stories is *The Descent of Inanna* (Akkadian: Ishtar) to the underworld. Inanna decides to visit her older sister Ereshkigal, the ruler of the underworld ("From the great above, she set her mind to the great below" [line 1]). Fearing that she might come to some harm in the netherworld, Inanna instructs Ninshubur, her messenger, to wait three days and, failing any report from her, to go for help to Nippur, the city of Enlil, and plead with him not to let her remain in the underworld. If Enlil refuses to help her, Ninshubur was to go to Ur, the city of the moon god Nanna, and repeat his plea. Failing there, he was to go to Eridu, the city of Enki, the god of wisdom, who would not fail to come to her aid. The story traces not just a succession of cities but, likely as well, a ritual journey of the cult statue of the goddess. Again, wisdom is linked to the issue of mortality and immortality.

Inanna then heads off, dressed in her seven *mi* or "attributes," which are objects of adornment, tools, and implements of war: the crown of the plain, the wig of her forehead, the measuring rod of lapis lazuli, the lapis necklace, the gold ring, the breastplate, the *pala*-garment. She decorates herself in *kohl,* a luxurious, blue eye makeup.[18] In current parlance, we would call them her "signature fashion statements." Then, as she descends to the underworld, she must progressively take off each of her seven *mi,* until she appears naked in front of the throne of her sister. Ereshkigal promptly condemns her to death. At once, Inanna becomes a corpse, hanged from a peg to decay and fester. Simultaneously, famine and infertility strike the earth, clarifying the climatological dimension of the story.

It looks as if the Mesopotamian poets anticipated our saying: "You can't take it with you" by millennia. We might suppose that this truism would not need stating but the ancient world knew of the wonders of Egypt, where the rulers did take it with them—everything from their possessions to their body immortalized by enbalming. And they all placed grave goods in tombs.

After three days, Ninshubur, as instructed earlier, alerts the gods; but as expected, only Enki stands by Inanna. He makes two fly-like creatures, the *kurgarru* and the *kalaturru,* instructing them to sprinkle the meat with the grass and water of life sixty times so that Inanna's body will be preserved enough that it can rise, perhaps a reference to a specific funeral custom in Mesopotamia. Ereshkigal does lament the dead, as part of her regal functions. When the two mourners join her in lamentation, she is pleased and grants them a boon. The mourners then ask for the moldy meat hanging on the peg. When they sprinkle the meat, Inanna is resurrected.

However the Anunnaki, the group of scholarly ancestors who act like grim fates in assisting Ereshkigal, will not let her leave unless she arranges a hostage. She appoints Dummuzi (Akkadian: Tammuz), her husband, as a substitute for her. Dummuzi's sister Geshtinanna (literally: wine maiden), in turn, offers to sacrifice her freedom for Dummuzi for half the year. So the two alternate time in the underworld, sharing the hostage responsibility for Inanna's freedom. The trading of positions between Tammuz and Geshtinanna depicted the alternation of crops in the Middle East—grain (Tammuz) in the winter and spring rainy season and fruits (Geshtinanna) in the dry, summer and early fall seasons, before the rains started the cycle over again.[19] Rather like the Demeter-Persephone story of Greece, this story provides a narrative that explains the agricultural year, in this case, why grain grows at a different season (winter and spring) then fruit (summer and fall). Like the Greek example too, the annual alternation of seasons and the change in flora suggest that death is a natural part of life and will surely be followed by a rebirth and reawakening.[20]

Inanna was a goddess but her death and return to the living were real, just as the grief for her loss was real. This suggests something about human finitude and how the continuous rhythms of nature, especially as domesticated in agriculture, overcome our limited human existence. Unlike the Greek version in the Eleusinian Mysteries of Demeter (which we will investigate later), there is no explicit evidence that the Mesopotamians thought that religious rites could make us come back to life after our deaths. However, there may have been rituals of immortalization which have been lost.

In this case, the explicit resurrection is directly correlated with Inanna's astronomical counterpart. Sumerian Inanna was identified with Akkadian Ishtar. They were both identified with the planet Venus, which in turn was personified as the Greek Aphrodite and the Roman goddess of love, Venus. These mythological identifications are even older than classical antiquity. They all refer to the planet Venus, known as the morning or evening star, the third brightest object in our heavens. Unlike other stars, however, Venus did not behave in a regular and easily understandable way. Today, we know that Venus is a planet not a star. But this observable behavior made Venus an object of veneration and marvel, best explained by positing a divinity which motivated the star. In Old Assyrian texts, for example, Venus was called the star *(kakkubum)* and invoked as "the god of our fathers" *(i-li a-ba-e-ni),* an epithet of the God of the patriarchs as well.[21]

Not only is Venus an easily visible and observable object in the dusk and dawn sky, its absence is just as noticeable. It falls below the horizon periodically, completing five settings in eight years and inscribing the exact same five-pointed star as it crosses the horizon in each cycle. Very likely this is what occasioned the story of the descent of Inanna. Her return above the horizon after a set period of time, to take on the role of the morning and evening star, is no doubt explained by Inanna's resurrection and reascent to her proper and glorious place in the heavens. Because of the vividness and regularity of the natural symbolism, the story also has repercussions about the possibility of resurrection and afterlife.

The Nineveh version of the Inanna text includes lines which suggest that the agricultural metaphor was being used to promise a kind of ritual revivification of the dead:

> When Dummuzi rises [*ellanni*], and when the lapis lazuli pipe
> and the carnelian ring rise with him,
> When male and female mourners rise with him,
> Then let the dead come up [*lilunimma*] and smell the incense.[22]

How the dead can rise and enjoy some of the goodness of this netherworld is not yet clear. For now, it is important to note that the myth, so far as we can tell, is ritually associated with commemoration of the dead rather than with any holiday of seasonal change. The notion of resurrection and afterlife is developed by analogy from the natural world, where death seems periodic and is followed by the annual rebirth of plant life. Perhaps it is fair to suggest that the pattern is an agricultural and even a feminine one, since the major characters are powerful women and the mode of continuity is cyclical. In any event, the language of "deathlessness" is taken from the cycles of agriculture rather than the concept of fame in battle. In addition the conceptions were capable of reenactment in ritual form, normally a sign that it has special significance within a society.

Nergal and Ereshkigal,
King and Queen of the Underworld

THE SAME architecture of heaven is reproduced in reverse in the fragmentary *Epic of Nergal and Ereshkigal*. Apparently, the drama begins when the gods seek to include Ereshkigal in their banqueting, though she cannot leave her subterranean realm. From here we learn that Nergal, who is her husband, was originally a sky god who was invited underground to become consort to the dread Queen, Ereshkigal. Just as Inanna did, Nergal has to remove his clothing when he goes through the various gates to the kingdom of the underworld. He was warned not to accept Ereshkigal's hospitality but he is crazy about her cooking, to say nothing of her considerable skills in lovemaking. Their orgy goes on for a marathon week without interruption.

At that point he tries to escape but it is too late; the other gods force him to return, at the request of Ereshkigal. Insatiable Ereshkigal is eager for more of Nergal's loving, so Nergal is forced to become her consort, which he does dutifully. It is she, however, who presides over the court of the Anunnaki, the "fates" who welcome and instruct each new arrival about the rules of the city. There is some evidence that this descent (and perhaps ritual return) is timed with the arrival of winter in the month of *Kislimu*.[23] In this story both sexuality and eating insure our mortality.

Gilgamesh

THE STORY OF Gilgamesh teaches lessons about the proper use and limitation of grief. Even with the hope suggested by the descent of Inanna, the dominant advice about death and afterlife in Mesopotamian society was resignation and acceptance. The oldest recorded story centering on human life after death in the West is the story of Gilgamesh, earliest versions probably dating back to 3000 BCE and the early history of the Sumerians. The text content is nearly complete and is certainly a most poignant story, one which remains incredibly vivid and engrossing even to modern readers.[24] The basic story of King Gilgamesh was gradually augmented over the millennia in Akkadian—specifically in the Babylonian and Assyrian dialects of Akkadian, as these two empires asserted power over the area. Semitic texts contain the most complete version of the epic. But the moral of the story changes radically between the various redactions of the epic.

The Epic of Gilgamesh, as we now have it, takes place on an earth situated between the world of the heavenly gods and the underworld. The hero, Gilgamesh (originally Bilgamesh), is astride two worlds: two-thirds divine, one-third human (however that could be!), ruler and king of the city of Uruk.[25] His behavior at the beginning of the epic can be characterized as wild, unruly, and clearly antisocial. Even the gods are concerned. From one perspective, the epic can be understood as Gilgamesh's education in the proper motivations and behaviors for a king.

The gods prepare Enkidu as a friend for Gilgamesh because Gilgamesh's behavior is so unacceptable. Enkidu is Gilgamesh's twin but also a kind of nature-child, clothed in his own hair, who can talk to the animals until a prostitute, appointed by the goddess Inanna, teaches him the secrets of human sexuality, in a weeklong pleasure orgy. But there are costs to this honeymoon dalliance. Enkidu loses his ability to live and talk with the animals, showing that skillful sexuality is a civilized, human art, not a natural one, in the eyes of the ancient Mesopotamians. After Enkidu cuts his animal hair and becomes properly educated in the ways of the civilized world, he becomes a worthy companion for Gilgamesh.

This episode is one of the few places in myth where female sexuality is associated with culture rather than nature. Inanna is portrayed as a provocative woman throughout but one who has powerful boons to give humanity.[26] Gilgamesh and Enkidu eventually become friends. The imagery suggesting marriage between them is so strong that many scholars see an explicit homosexual union to be part of their relationship, though no sexual act is explicitly described in the myth. At the very least, their relationship is homoerotic. But against the homosexual interpretation of the text is the unabashed explicitness of the depiction of heterosexual sex. Given the lack of embarrassment in describing heterosexual acts, the silence of the text about any explicit homosexual relationship between them probably means us to understand that the relationship was a deep, male-bonded, homoerotic friendship, which gives way to Gilgamesh's heterosexual duties as king.[27]

At first, Enkidu provides Gilgamesh with heroic diversions and quests. The epic narrates several of these adventures binding their friendship, but their pillaging also incurs the powerful wrath of Inanna, after Gilgamesh spurns her flirtatious advances and the two kill her protected bull. Gilgamesh's spurning of Inanna's advances is a puzzling narrative in which Ishtar proposes marriage to the hero. At first he demurs, saying he could not possibly afford the bride price (6.22–28). But then, he launches into a long insulting harangue of the goddess, listing the many lovers whom she has loved, abandoned, and worse (6.58–63). He details the various punishments that befell her various lovers when she tired of them.

There may have been something more sinister involved as well. To have accepted the marriage proposal may have trapped Gilgamesh in the same situation of Nergal, the god of the underworld, Geshtinanna and Dummuzi (Tammuz), who must stay underground as substitute hostages for Inanna.[28] Inanna's proposal of marriage might very well result in Gilgamesh having permanent responsibilities underground. He would be hidden from human view and unable to complete his mission. In any event, it certainly valorizes the male realm of war and fame over against the realm of marriage and family and suggests that fame in battle is even better than immortality below ground, a theme that appears again in *The Odyssey*.[29]

Ironically, in later versions of the story, Gilgamesh becomes an underworld ruler himself, though that story is not included in the epic. However other versions do show that over the long history of stories about this hero, many contradictory sides of these themes were explored. Regardless at this point in the story, the goddess vows that one of our heroes will die and that hero turns out to be Enkidu.

After Enkidu dies, Gilgamesh sets out on a quest to find the remedy for death. Before his death, Enkidu has a dream in which his final destination is described. The place to which the dead go is "the House of Darkness," or "the House of Dust," a place of no return:

> He leads me to the House of Darkness,
>   The abode of Irkalla,
> To the house which none leave who have entered it,
> On the road from which there is no way back,
> To the house wherein the dwellers are bereft of light,
> Where dust is their fare and clay their food.
> They are clothed like birds, with wings for garments,
> And see no light, residing in darkness.
> In the House of Dust, which I entered,
> I looked at [rulers], their crowns put away;
> I [saw] princes, those (born to) the crown,
>   who had ruled the land from the days of yore.
>   (7.4.30–40)[30]

In the underworld, Enkidu is transformed into a bird-like creature, similar to some of the Apkallu, which we know means that he has become an *eṭemmu*, a ghost.

Gilgamesh's beloved friend Enkidu dies, not honorably in battle, but is struck down by disease. Through his death we learn the fate that the Mesopotamians believed awaits all of us in death. Gilgamesh laments his friend in a set piece which is probably a good example of a funeral lamentation, what the Mesopotamians referred to as "honoring the dead."

The grief-stricken were expected to lay aside their good garments, to remove their head-covering, and go about unkempt, unbathed, and ungroomed. Fasting also plays a role in public sorrow, as does flagellation and laceration. But after the end of the official mourning period, there were ceremonies of purification and return to normal dress and grooming.

With Enkidu's obsequies completed, Gilgamesh sets out to find immortality. The funeral has not really brought Gilgamesh peace of mind. Because he still grieves for the loss of his friend, his battle companion Enkidu, he frames a new quest, to find a way to restore him to life. But he also grieves for himself for he now knows and understands that his fate will be the same.

For Gilgamesh, his friend's demise is the beginning of wisdom. At the beginning of the epic he encouraged Enkidu with the brave words that we should all fight bravely for only the gods live forever. Since we all die, we must seek fame before we go to the grim kingdom. He had clearly known that death was a danger in their combats but had not understood exactly what death would mean. Now, with his friend gone, he begins to realize that life means eternal loss. By the end of the epic, he learns what he has already stated at the beginning but without full understanding: Only the gods live forever. Death is the lot of humanity. It is one thing to know about death in the abstract; it is another thing to affirm it after the death of a loved one with the parallel recognition that we too must die. Gilgamesh thus comes to knowledge of his state of mortality. For the ancient Near Eastern mind, wisdom and mortality were two fundamental aspects of the human predicament, two sides of the same coin. The Biblical story of Adam and Eve says the same.

Strangely enough, Gilgamesh learns this from the human Utnapishtim, who has been rewarded by the gods with immortality because of his conservation efforts. He is a Babylonian Noah who built an ark to protect humans and animals from the flood. Utnapishtim has avoided going to the underworld as an *eṭemmu*. But the epic does not thereby dissolve in a logical morass, because myth typically moves forward by playing with opposing forces. We must accept that the human Utnapishtim casually has attained what the whole epic is saying is impossible for humanity. We can sympathize with the frustrated Gilgamesh who cannot get what

Utnapishtim has—immortality. Thus, Utnapishtim belongs undeniably to the transcendent realm, though he started as a man, while Gilgamesh belongs to our realm, where age and death take their toll.

In a seemingly playful way, Utnapishtim challenges Gilgamesh to a trial by ordeal in which Gilgamesh can earn the immortality that he is seeking. Utnapishtim dares Gilgamesh to stay awake for a week. But Gilgamesh comically and miserably fails, falling asleep almost as soon as the suggestion is offered and sleeping an entire week away. So unconscious is he of the time that the week has to be measured for him in the moldy remains of his uneaten meals. Seven days of bread stand in front of him, each in a more decayed condition. Perhaps this is a reference to funeral offerings. Nevertheless the plot contains the observation that the need to sleep and eat are two things which make us mortal, an observation that will later fuel ascetic disciplines designed to mimic immortality in other cultures.

The Gilgamesh Epic, as myth and literature, served in its own day as the quintessential guide for grieving to the inhabitants of Mesopotamia. For us as well who can hardly be unmoved by its stark elegance, the epic illustrates one means of coping with the inherently human problem of moral meaning that always eludes us in grief—inevitably raising the question of one's own and others' mortality—and ending with quiet acceptance. With such a universal and longlasting theme, it is no wonder that the different recensions seem to put slightly different emphases on the story. Both the Sumerian and the Babylonian texts picture Gilgamesh seeking to immortalize his name as he goes out to fight. The Babylonian version concentrates on the problem of mortality in comparison to the immortality of the gods.[31]

The refrain of the barmaid goddess Sidduri, from the old Babylonian edition, expresses this resignation most clearly in her famous *carpe diem* speech:

> As for you, Gilgamesh, let your belly be full,
> Make merry day and night.
> Of each day make a feast of rejoicing,
> Day and night dance and play!
> Let your garments be sparkling fresh
> Your head be washed; bathe in water.
> Pay heed to a little one that holds on to your hand.
> Let a spouse delight in your bosom,
> For this is the task of a [woman.][32]

Sidduri tells Gilgamesh, in effect, to give up his life of adventuring, set-tle down, marry, and have children. Immortality is not achievable for hu-manity in this strict, three-tiered world. This version of the epic counsels its readers to appreciate life and not to hope for more of life's pleasures after death. It also says that although manly feats bring renown, maturity brings the steadiness of a householder. We find a quite similar sentiment expressed in Ecclesiastes 9:7–10.

Without the twelfth tablet, though, the story of Gilgamesh is framed with an *inclusio:* the beginning and end are an identical *paean* to glorious Uruk, the city Gilgamesh rules. The consolation for Gilgamesh is the city—the human accomplishments of city building, government, law, and sexuality (which is a civilized pleasure to be taken in great quantities in the story)—that is solace against the loss of friends and the knowledge of death. And that is what all who read the epic story in its various Sumer-ian, Babylonian, and Assyrian versions, were to learn as well. Both the be-ginning and the ending of the poem glorify the city of Uruk and, through this city, the major cultural achievement attained in the fertile crescent. It is from this achievement that we mark the beginning of civilization:

> Observe its walls, whose upper hem is like bronze;
> behold its inner wall, which no work can equal.
> Touch the stone threshold, which is ancient;
> draw near the Eanna, dwelling-place of the goddess Ishtar,
> a work no king among later kings can match.
> Ascend the walls of Uruk, walk around the top,
> inspect the base, view the brickwork.
> Is not the very core made of oven-fired bricks?
> As for its foundation, was it not laid down by the seven Sages?
> One part is city, one part orchard, and one part claypits.
> Three parts including the claypits make up Uruk.[33]

Implicit in the reactions of Gilgamesh to the death of his friend Enkidu are the same psychological stages of mourning which we perceive in our-selves. For instance, Gilgamesh goes through the stages of grief that Eliz-abeth Kübler-Ross notices in terminal cancer patients facing the prospect of their own death in her book *On Death and Dying.* It seems important to note then that this myth could well have served therapeutic functions for the society that read it, exemplifying both the fear and despair of los-ing friends and even a desperate attempt to get them back. Like the myth of Orpheus in the Greek world, our heroes and we ourselves fail to achieve immortality or to avoid loss. Stories like this teach its readers that, in the end, acceptance and resignation, followed by reattachment to life and enjoyment of its benefits, is the only proper outcome of grief.[34]

At the same time, the epic suffers from the Kübler-Ross dilemma we spoke of in the introduction. Just as Elizabeth Kübler-Ross herself eventually espouses both sides of the immortality debate, so does Mesopotamian culture when it makes Gilgamesh lord of the Underworld as well as the hero who learns to look at death soberly. It alternately asks us to live without denial and offers us Gilgamesh the god as an exemplar of helpful denial.

The Bible has deep affinities, both similarities and intriguing contrasts, with *The Gilgamesh Epic*. On the issue of life after death, the Bible is almost silent, yet the silence of the Hebrew Bible seems, like the Gilgamesh Epic, to imply a deep agreement that the proper concern of humanity is this life, not the next. The most intriguing affinities are hence found in Genesis 1–11, the prehistory of the Bible, the story of creation, Adam and Eve, and the events leading to the election of Abraham. And since the story of Adam and Eve is deeply important to the Biblical notion of mortality and afterlife in Judaism, when such concepts arise, we are compelled to look at the comparisons and contrasts between *The Gilgamesh Epic* and the Hebrew Bible. Both the Bible and *The Gilgamesh Epic* are highly glossed, palimpsest texts—that is, texts which have been written and overwritten through many different generations and versions to reach their present form. Indeed, the theory of the Bible's evolution from a series of different voices or documents seems most closely paralleled to the well-attested evolution of *The Gilgamesh Epic*.[35]

The Twelfth Tablet

THE NAGGING problem of *The Gilgamesh Epic* is the last tablet, Tablet 12, and associated individual legends of the two heroes. The eleventh tablet ends with the repetition of the first lines of the story, emphasizing the importance and beauty of the city of Ur. This *inclusio* has defined the length and breadth of the epic for the modern reader. Yet the ancient epic was originally separate incidents and even in its compiled form it contained a puzzling last tablet that has significant consequences for the notion of life after death. Tablet 12, however, seems to modern readers like an appendix to the epic, likely being translated into Akkadian directly from the far more ancient Sumerian.[36] It was appended to the epic because it describes conditions in the afterlife, where Gilgamesh goes to preside over the shades of the dead. Notice, however, that Gilgamesh does not go to heaven where the gods are, or to the ends of the earth, where Utnapishtim and his wife live.

In this final episode, Gilgamesh tries to retrieve two important magical gifts, a *pikku* and a *mikku,* which Inanna had given him for having protected the magical tree in her garden which she was saving to construct her bed and chair. The two objects have not been definitely identified, though they are sometimes assumed to be a drum and drumstick or a mallet and a ball. In any event, they are used in recreational play and get a good workout on their first day. On the second day, they fall into the underworld. Enkidu sets off to retrieve them and disappears, ignoring the advice that Gilgamesh has given him about the correct behavior as an interloper in the underworld. Enkidu sees an underworld quite consonant with the one already described to us. It is particularly important to notice the bird-like dead, who are there and who will be present in Canaan as well.

Gilgamesh petitions the gods for Enkidu's safe return. The god Enki agrees to seek the help of the sun god Utu, who returns at dawn bringing up Enkidu's shade. When he comes face-to-face with Enkidu, the two great friends embrace. But Enkidu warns Gilgamesh that he does not have good news. The afterlife is not pleasant; it is a gloomy and melancholy place where all the fine things of life rot. The most one can say is that there is justice in the next world.

A tablet from Ur provides even more information about the care of the dead, as this tablet continues beyond where the previous abruptly breaks off. Enkidu reports that the shades of Sumer and Akkad have been overrun by those of the Amorites, who have been persecuting them. According to George, this clearly alludes to the collapse of the Third Dynasty of Ur under pressure from the Amorite and Elamite invasions.[37] This particular development may well be a local variation of the larger story. When Gilgamesh finds out that his own ancestors are included in this persecution, he vows to correct the situation. He institutes mourning rites for his ancestors and fashions images of them. The strongest message of piety for the dead is being offered here. But the incident itself is out of chronological order for the epic as Enkidu is alive again and is trapped in the underworld. The lesson was considered more important than the chronology.

A further incident, the death of Gilgamesh, is much easier to understand with the newer, more complete text from Tell Haddad.[38] It continued to exist as a separate story, likely because it was used in funeral lamentations. Enlil tells us that Gilgamesh must die, even though he is partly divine. Though he will descend to the netherworld, he will be commemorated by annual funeral wrestling games. He will rule in the underworld. Then we witness the death of Gilgamesh, who suffers terribly from a disease before he succumbs. His deeds are recounted and the value of the knowledge he learned from Utnapishtim (Sumerian: Ziusudra) about mortality and the flood is emphasized. Then the lamentations are chanted, the funeral rituals are celebrated, the entombment is accomplished, and the memorial images are set up, followed by the first of the annual games.

The text is unfortunately too fragmentary to provide answers to the many questions we wish to ask. Gilgamesh witnesses the rewards for proper burial: He sees a scene in the underworld where all banquet together without rank or social privilege, which is also mentioned in several other texts. We shall return to the banqueting motif later, because it is an important ritual to commemorate the dead in Mesopotamia and Canaan. Many have assumed that the magical objects in the twelfth tablet also have a cultic importance in the preparation and disposition of the dead or in the funeral games thereafter. What is undeniable is that Gilgamesh, after his death, can be depicted as a judge of the underworld. And that is quite a contrast to the lesson he is taught by Sidduri in the old Babylonian version.

Motifs Compared

IN IMPORTANT ways, Gilgamesh and Enkidu are a couple, similar to the primal couple Adam and Eve in the Bible, ironically almost the "Adam and Steve" of televangelist polemics against homosexuality. But these similarities only underline the interesting contrasts. Enkidu was created covered with shaggy hair "like a woman" (1.2.36) and looks like Nisaba, the goddess of grain. He roams naked, like the primal couple in the Bible, paralleling their innocence by conversing with animals, with whom he enjoys enormous sympathy. Like Adam and Eve, he leads an idyllic, childlike existence, though he is more like a willful two-year-old than they are.

Enkidu's education is not exactly like the education of the Biblical primal couple. In order to tame his wildness, the shepherds and Gilgamesh send a prostitute to him. Innocence ends at puberty; it is time to learn the technology of civilization.

And the result is quite similar to Adam and Eve's temptation. After his first, weeklong, sexual encounter, Enkidu is described as wise and godlike: "You are wise, Enkidu, you have become like a god" (1.4.34). The conclusion is drawn that wisdom is divine, and we can share it with the gods. But, to it is melded the knowledge of our own mortality in both stories. In addition, Enkidu is saddened to discover that the animals now run from him. The lesson then is: When we are young, we are like animals in our innocence but we become wise when we recognize our own mortality. In the Bible, the original couple is innocent and free, though they become like gods, knowing good and evil, as a result of their disobedience. They evidently have sex in the garden in their innocent state (Gen 2:24), as marriage is validated before the fall. So sexuality is coupled with innocence here, part of nature not culture.

The parallels between the Gilgamesh story and the Adam and Eve story support the notion that the original intent of the Biblical story was just like the Gilgamesh story—to see the "fall" both as unfortunate, in the sense that innocence was lost, and as fortunate, at least in respect to the notion that humanity gains from it the knowledge of good and evil, which is godlike. In both accounts, we see a developmental psychology at work: Childhood is idyllic but maturity brings wisdom. On the other hand, the obvious and open sexuality of the Gilgamesh account is absent in the biblical account. The notion that a temple prostitute could be the medium of positive revelation is abhorent to the Bible. The specifics of the sexual act are also deleted from the Bible, leaving only the pale reference in Hebrew to carnal knowledge and marriage. However the motifs of the knowledge of mortality and the fall from natural innocence are strikingly similar, as scholar after scholar has pointed out.[39]

The most obvious comparison between the two stories is in the flood narrative. Even the motif of sending out birds to spy out dry ground is present in both. They are so similar as to leave little doubt that the Biblical account borrowed liberally from its Near Eastern milieu in presenting it, though possibly not directly from *The Gilgamesh Epic* itself. One striking difference between the two narratives is in the reason for the destruction of the world. In the Babylonian version, the reason seems to be overpopulation, as the gods grow discontented over the noise that humanity is making. In the Biblical account, God must destroy humanity because of the sin of *ḥamas,* violence, as it is called in Hebrew. The theme of a magical plant is also common to the two stories, as indeed it was in many of the previous ones. Through pharmacology, this plant links the themes of knowledge and eternal life. In the Bible, the plants are the tree of the knowlege of good and evil and the tree of life. In Gilgamesh, the plant is one that rejuvenates the old. Humanity is denied the full benefits of both in each case. In addition, the snake in both stories serves as the villain who prevents a totally happy outcome. In shedding his skin, he receives rejuvenation which Gilgamesh desires.

But the Bible and *The Gilgamesh Epic* part company radically in their mythical depiction of civilization. For the epic, civilization is truly comfort against mortality. But the Bible sees civilized life as the beginning of corruption. The temples of Mesopotamia with their ziggurat towers become in the Bible the tower of Babel. That tower is a sin against God, another example of humanity's trying to make itself like God. And the enterprise inevitably fails. So too, the victory of the agriculturalist Cain over the pastoralist Abel is seen as an act of murder. No doubt, we see in these stories a mythic portrayal of the original pastoral ideal with its freedom, sadly replaced by city life in the rise of civilized life, sedentary life as the destruction of the idolized Hebrew past of herding.

Both narratives deal with the human institution of marriage. In the Biblical version, the separation of Eve from Adam explains the institution of marriage ("Therefore a man leaves his father and his mother and cleaves to his wife, and they become one flesh," Gen 2:24). Furthermore, the punishments that God administers to Adam and Eve suggest that marriage is the normal state of postlapsarian humanity.[40]

The Gilgamesh Epic also represents a kind of developmental story of a hero who begins his career as a rebellious teenager acting out his hostility. Through various stages of his life, he learns how to behave in civilization. When he returns home after his failed quest, we know that he will fulfill his role as adult and father. But, while for the Hebrews marriage advances the claims of civilization, in Mesopotamia it is more ambiguous. Even more, marriage advances the counterclaims of human love and cultural innovations over against the divine realm. Inanna (Akkadian: Ishtar), the goddess of love and war is, in some ways, the protectress of human cultural life, in that the arts of love are civilizing and in other ways inimical to human cultural life. But she is "the goddess testosterone," governing lust and war. Inanna is everywhere depicted as both kindly and ferocious in demeanor, a terrible ambiguity that follows this goddess in every avatar, from the Indian goddess Kali-Durga through Babylonian Ishtar and Canaanite 'Anat.[41] This no doubt is meant to demonstrate the power of human emotion: Love and attraction are destructive as well as constructive, viewed as a natural and supernatural force as well as a human emotion. Love leads to romance, but when thwarted, it leads to jealousy and war. The same themes are emphasized in *The Iliad*.

Furthermore, Ishtar's immortality is no guarantee of her constancy; rather her open and aggressive sexuality is accompanied by an unacceptable inconstancy, which seems to be her most salient trait. Does that mean that this vibrant, sexually explicit culture also contained a rather large mythological warning against unbridled sexuality? Perhaps, though it is not clear what social realities lie behind this notion. It could be a story that maintains that arranged marriages are preferable to relationships dependent upon desire alone. But in any case, immortality with Ishtar was neither a permanent nor honorable position. In the end, one would be reduced to some animal existence, as when she tired of the shepherd husband and arranged for him to be killed by the wolf, or the gardener husband, who was transformed into a mole. This represents a return to a state before knowledge was achieved as an ironic punishment. Perhaps the Akkadian and Hebrew versions share a common male complaint that they are trapped into unwise unions or even marriage because of their sexual attraction to women, and that unbridled sexual attraction is foolishness, as the proverbs of all ancient Near Eastern nations make so clear. This is hardly what our culture would conclude but it seems to underlie the ancient mythological view of the institution of marriage.

Lastly, we review briefly the central issue of mortality in these two stories. We will have an occasion to compare Gilgamesh with Genesis and Homer's epics in more detail in following chapters. But, for the moment, we should note some additional similarities between Genesis and Gilgamesh which we need to unpack. Both *The Gilgamesh Epic* and the Genesis account of creation centrally involve the acquisition of knowledge and the explanation of death. The Gilgamesh Epic is concerned with the issue of death and the recognition that it is a constant in human life. Gilgamesh wearies himself greatly searching for a solution to the problem, only to realize that he knew it all along: Death must come to all. The narrative is really about his coming to understand what mortality means, a recognition that is the essence of the distinction between knowledge and wisdom. That wisdom makes him, finally, the king he ought to have been in the beginning.

The Bible too faces the issue of death, albeit obliquely, at the beginning of Genesis. The Bible, to be sure, notes that death is the consequence for disobedience. We could have lived innocently in the garden as intelligent animals, had we not disobeyed the command not to eat from the fruit of the tree of the knowledge of good and evil. But the emphasis of the story shifts. In the Biblical account, it is the coming to moral knowledge that takes up all the narrative space of the story. And the reason for this is simple to see. The Bible is primarily concerned with the depiction of a covenant between God and humanity. In order for the covenant to have any significance, humanity has to be divinely aware of the differences between good and evil and make a conscious choice for good. The moral vision of Genesis replaces the quest for immortality in *The Gilgamesh Epic* as the central concern of the narrative.

We do not wish to denigrate either *The Gilgamesh Epic* or the Genesis account. Each has a grandeur and a subtlety that come from its use of mythological motifs to arrange and order human life in a chaotic world. But the human worlds of culture which they create are quite different. *The Gilgamesh Epic* shows us a sophisticated and civilized world, at home in great urban centers, and proud of its own accomplishments. The Bible, which borrows and uses the motifs for its own purposes, shows us a world reluctantly civilized and aware of the dangers of civilization. The Biblical world is devoid of the competing powers that populate *The Gilgamesh Epic*. God rules everything; even the fall must somehow be according to His plan. The conflict then comes in God's constant struggle against chaos.

The Afterlife in Mesopotamia

THE SPIRITS OF the dead, the *etemmu,* after preparing themselves properly for their journey, set out towards the netherworld. As with all travelers in the ancient world, however, they are in for some adventures and dangers. They must pass through a demon-infested steppe and then cross the Khubur River. They may obtain help from Silushi (or Silulim) or Khumut-Tabal (literally: Quick, take [me] there!). The latter is a boatman somewhat like Charon of Greek mythology. When the *etemmu* reach the city of the dead, they must receive permission to enter from each of the seven gatekeepers, who guard seven walls, one inside each other, making the city invulnerable. Likely, however, it was just as important to keep the dead in, as to keep others out, because the dead were believed to cause enormous mischief on earth. The worst eventuality was to be denied entrance, the result of unatoned violent deaths or incomplete funeral arrangements. Evidently they must forfeit all their attributes, clothing, and possessions at the gates, as Inanna did. Sometimes the journey incorporated navigating the *apsu* (the sweet waters under the earth and the second of the three nether regions of Mesopotamian cosmology), and sometimes this was believed to be the path that babies take to be born. The dead supposedly travel back this way to visit their families for remembrance rites as well.

Alternatively, the netherworld which was so far to travel for the spirits, could be thought of as underground, just beneath our feet. A foundation trench might reach it, and in fact Gilgamesh is once pictured as almost touching it with the tips of his fingers. This detail may reflect Mesopotamian burial practices, which used below-ground family tombs for those who could afford them, joining an entire family in death. It also ensured, by proper care and rituals, that the ghosts who slept in the graves were never disturbed. If they were disturbed, trouble would befall the family members still on the earth.

Like Hades, the underworld was rather gloomy, a consequence of its belowground construction. But the sun god (Akkadian: Shamash; Sumerian: Utu) visited at night as he circled under the earth. The city of the dead was a well-ordered place, where the dead ate and drank at least sufficiently to their needs. Evidently, this was paradise enough for the ancient serfs, but sometimes they imagined the ranks reversed so the aristocracy waited on the serfs. This city was presided over by the now familiar Nergal and Ereshkigal, the king and queen of the Underworld, living in a marvelous lapis lazuli palace, and who dressed for every fine occasion. They had a great bureaucracy available to them when they held court, clearly a reflection of imperial political life on earth. The most famous of the royal retainers were the grim Annunaki. But there were others as well. Here is the account of the dream visit of Assyrian Prince Kummu:

> I saw Namtar, the vizier of the netherworld . . . and a man stood before him. He (Namtar) was grasping the hair of his head in his left hand and a dagger in his right . . . Namtartu, his wife, had the head of a *kuribu* [Hebrew: *cherub,* not a baby Eros figure as in Valentine's Day cards but a griffon-like creature, like the creatures depicted on the Ishtar Gate of Babylon]; the hands and the feet were human. Death had the head of a dragon; his hands were human . . . Khummut-Tabal, ferryman of the underworld, had the head of an anzu-bird; his four hands and feet . . . Bidu (Nedu), door-opener, had the head of a lion; his hands were human, his feet those of a bird. . . . There was a man—his body was black as pitch; his face resembled that of the anzu-bird (and) he was dressed in a red cloak. In his left hand he was carrying a bow; in his right hand, he was grasping a dagger (and) he trampled a snake [with] (his) left foot. When I raised my eyes, there was valiant Nergal sitting on a royal thone, crowned with the royal tiara, grasping in both his hands two grim maces, each with two . . . heads. . . . The Anunnaki, great gods, knelt to (his) right and left.[42]

The anzu-bird was a horrifying griffon-like creature that inhabited the underworld and sometimes served as a kind of angel of death. Also present below ground was Geshtinanna, the fruit maiden we met before as the sister of Dummuzi/Tammuz; she was also known in Akkadian as Belet-Seri and Dimpikug, the wife of Ningishzida (also called Gishzida or Gizzida, often the chair-bearer of the netherworld). His job was, typically, to check the names of the new arrivals against the roster so that uninvited guests like Prince Kummu or the dreaming Enkidu could be recognized and turned away. But some have crashed the party, usually by means of prophetic dreams, to report the details of the final disposition of the dead.

This scenario was not the only possibility, however, as we have already seen that Gilgamesh himself is sometimes pictured as holding court down below. Scurlock suggests that Gilgamesh's court may have been one of equity, where cases of civil damage were finally adjudicated in the afterlife.[43] Additionally, the sun god Shamash was also pictured as a judge in the underworld, as his daily circuit brings him there on his return trip. Shamash seems to confine his interest in ghosts who were pestering the living but also oversaw funeral offerings, making sure everyone received his proper due. None of these courts had the systematic role in rewarding good and punishing evil that we envision heaven and hell to hold in our culture.

Kispu: *The Mesopotamian Cult of the Dead*

ERESHIKIGAL'S kingdom offered a parsimonious sufficiency, but the welfare of the departed depended on the generosity of the survivors. Perhaps the Mesopotamian afterlife is best thought of as a kind of imprisonment, where the relatives are responsible for the care of the prisoner, as in many underdeveloped countries even today. A badly treated prisoner could be expected to escape and cause great harm to the living as evil spirits or ghosts. The dead, with the right treatment, would eat regularly, if frugally, from the *kispum* (from the verb *kasapu*, to share) offering and even occasionally banquet when their descendants held commemorative meals in their honor at the appropriate times.

The *kispu* offerings in Mesopotamia were monthly offerings of water and bread, but at special calendrical events, they might be more elaborate. The departed's first provisions—beer and honey as well as the bread and water—needed to more ample to sustain the long journey to the West, where the sun set, and where the great gates to the underworld were located.[44] The Adapa story supports the practice of ritual offerings, the same articles that Adapa needed to accept when he ascended to heaven, suggesting that the gods themselves sustain their immortality with these offerings.

The subsequent *kispu* offerings are models of interaction between the dead and the living, and also between the gods and the living to a certain extent. The dead were able to aid in bringing various benefits to society, like rain, protection against witchcraft, and increase to the herds. In return they needed to be fed, or they would be unable to perform their services and, indeed, themselves become malevolent. The *paterfamilias* was responsible for organizing the *kispu* events; the eldest son graduated to this responsibility on the death of his father. The eldest son's greater inheritance helped him shoulder the financial burden imposed by these responsibilities.

One way to think of these rituals was as a payoff to keep the dead happy. It was important to keep the dead inside the city except on these specified "visiting days"; otherwise they could possibly cause great mischief. Dead kings and aristocrats could expect a lavish banquet, indeed, as the offerings and feasts for them would be luxurious and profuse. The living also managed to eat quite well at these commemorative feasts. The same was true for dead heroes individually and stillborn children collectively, who were memorialized through shrines to their spirits.

Another way to think of the ritual was as a celebration of family integrity. Only intact families could organize themselves enough to carry out the ritual. In the *kispu* ritual, a communal meal was partaken with the dead, which valorized the community of those who ate in honor of a common ancestor.[45] This ritual was highly developed in Canaan, where it was called a *marziḥ,* apparently including sexual entertainments, and would prove a great moral test for the Israelites.

Enlil and Ninlil, Gilgamesh's Court, Evil Spirits

THE MYTH OF Enlil and Ninlil contains even more details of the underworld. The god Enlil was banished to the underworld as punishment for his rape of goddess Ninlil. But Ninlil evincing great loyalty to her abuser attempts to follow Enlil to the underworld. This action disrupts the order of the universe, since Ninlil's offspring is Nanna-Sin, the moon god, and therefore belongs in the heavens. Enlil, furthermore, does not want his offspring to live in the underworld. He devises a stratagem to create hostages to redeem Ninlil and their first offspring. As Ninlil leaves the city of Nippur and travels to the underworld, Enlil disguises himself on three separate occasions—as the gatekeeper to Nippur, the gatekeeper of the underworld, and the ferryman to the land of the dead. In each of these disguises, he impregnates Ninlil and fathers a child. Subsequently the three new offspring become important characters in Mesopotamian mythology. As a prison city, the afterlife will not free anyone without first taking a hostage, as we have already discovered from the story of the descent of Inanna. We suspect that Inanna was looking for a new hostage in her husband when she propositioned Gilgamesh. Even the gods had to pay a price for entering the underworld.

The deceased was called *mitu*—literally, simply a dead person or a ghost, in context. (The Hebrew equivalent is *mēt*). In the document known as "Gilgamesh, Enkidu, and the Netherworld," we learn the value of progeny:

> (Gilgamesh): "Have you seen him whose ghost has no one to
> care for him?"
> (Enkidu): "I have seen him. He eats what is scraped out of
> cooking pots (and) crusts of bread which are thrown
> into the street."
> "He who had one son—have you seen?"
> "I have seen. He weeps bitterly at the nail which was driven
> into his wall."
> "He who had two sons—have you seen him?"
> "I have seen. He sits on two bricks and eats bread."
>
> . . .
>
> He who had seven sons—have you seen?
> I have seen. As a companion of the gods he sits on a chair and
> listens to music." [46]

This society was saying that the more sons one had, the better, so it was in the afterlife that the father would be rewarded, just as one supposes that the family with many sons had a retirement fund waiting to be used when the *pater* and *mater familias* became too old to work the land. It also suggests that the social utility of rituals of filial piety are attendant upon the cult of the dead. We already know from the lament of Gilgamesh that statues of the deceased were often made in commemoration of the dead, the most elaborate were started even before death, to represent the patron's presence at rites of this type for which he was responsible. In the case of deceased royalty, offerings were made approximately every two weeks, at new and full moon. The offerings, which were foodstuffs, depended on the social class of the observers and might only be laid out, or they might actually be poured down a pipe laid in the earth. These feeding pipes also became very popular in Greco-Roman tombs. At Ebla, a royal cemetery was found that connected to a sanctuary to Rashaf, a god of the underworld, suggesting an organized funeral cult.

Untended graves, unburied corpses, or violent or unjust deaths all led to trouble from ghosts among the living. This created not only a *mitu,* a dead human being, but also an unpleasant spirit, a ghost, an *etemmu,* the two terms being used synonymously. *Etemmu* were often represented by a ram and otherwise depicted with many ramlike characteristics, hooves and horns. Especially annoying to ghosts was to have one's body left for predation by scavengers, a very dishonorable end, resulting in much mischief to any offending parties and the whole area generally. Thus, violent deaths or criminal mischief were apt to produce vengeful and troublesome ghosts. Two kinds of persons were not to be found among the hostile dead: suicides and those who died in childbirth. Suicide was an honorable way out of a dishonorable situation; while death in childbirth was a valorous death, like dying on a battlefield.

However, woe to those who could have married and had children, yet did not. Those who were marriageable and fertile but died childless were apt to become demons, called the *lilu* (female *lilitu;* Hebrew: *Lilith,* as in Adam's first wife in Rabbinic folklore, who becomes a demon). For Mesopotamia *lilu* and *lilitu* were classes of demons, not proper names. These creatures disguised themselves as seductive young people and entered into marriages with the living, apparently to fulfill their biological destiny posthumously. Failing that, they would sneak into houses at night to unite with hapless sleepers, causing noctural emissions, which in turn produced more demon succubi and incubi and, often, the early deaths of their unfortunate victims, who could even be carried off into demonic sexual bondage. When an adolescent young man had a nocturnal emission in Babylon, it was high time to get him married: His very life could depend on it! These stories do at least counteract the effect of protective mothers on their sons. Evidently these customs served as a kind of corrective to the many stories of sexual license told of unmarried men. Ghost stories underlined, by negative example, what the culture held dear. They were the negative reinforcers of family values.

Those who were infected with demons or haunted by ghosts of any sort could hire an exorcist to rid their person, house, or general area of these pests. Luckily, there was never a dearth of people who could perform these services. It was considered unsafe to talk of death openly, consequently there were a number of euphemisms available to the population to confuse the demons, who might be attracted by any open mention of death and cause someone's early demise. Death at the end of a long life was sad but expected; unexpected death or foreshortened life was, as everywhere, a tragedy. In Mesopotamian society, the tragedy of fatal or painful illness was explained as the work of demons, and there were a number of ritual undertakings to safeguard against them.

The Maqlu *Ritual*

TZVI ABUSCH and his student Seth Sanders have brought to the attention of the scholarly world a series of rituals which elaborate on how to prevent witches from overcoming a person in the course of life.[47] The texts, assembled from several different texts and known since the end of the nineteenth century, preserve a long complex of rituals, written on seven tablets. The *Maqlu* (burning) ritual was divided into three parts, the first two to be performed at night and the third the following morning. The primary participants were the exorcist or incantation-priest *(asipu)*, who was the ritual expert and his client, a bewitched man (who might be the king or some other wealthy person) who was the speaker and ritual actor. As in our society, the less well-to-do had to hire less expensive exorcists or do without the services of health professionals. The actor spoke for himself as well as for the whole community. The purpose of the ceremony was to judge and expel all witches, whether dead or alive. The result of the ritual was the utter destruction of these troublesome creatures, who were then banished from the cosmos altogether, including from the netherworld.

The beginning of the ritual was directed toward the night sky and the netherworld, including the divine inhabitants of each. According to the introduction, it seems as if the witches had disregarded a compact or covenant *(mamitu,* "oath") to which they were bound, and which was guaranteed by heaven and earth, a theme that is sometimes sounded in Biblical literature as well (see e.g., Joshua 24, where it is brought into the covenant between God and Israel). Therefore, the gods of heaven and earth became the enforcers of the oath. The speaker of the incantations attempted to gain the assistance of the heavens in support of his cause and to persuade the gods of the netherworld that the shades of the witches should be denied safe harbor. This ritual also gives us added background to stories of divination, necromancy, and exorcism in the Bible, such as the famous story of Saul and the witch of Endor in 1 Samuel 28.

Interestingly, Gilgamesh's name and reputation were invoked against the dead witches:

> Netherworld, netherworld, yea netherworld,
> Gilgamesh is the enforcer of your oath.
> Whatever you have done, I know,
> Whatever I do, you do not know,
> Whatever my witches do, there will be no one to overlook [it].

Gilgamesh made an appearance in his official capacity as a judge in the underworld. It was Gilgamesh himself who would enforce the oath. To make sure that Gilgamesh's aid did not go astray, the actor called upon another underworld goddess, *Belet-Seri,* the Akkadian name for Geshti-nanna, the co-hostage in the Inanna story. Probably this is connected to Gilgamesh's harsh refusal of marriage with Inanna. In order to visit her, he had to be appointed a messenger of the gods, an emissary of the heavenly court, someone like Adapa who ascended to heaven. Indeed, in the Old Babylonian texts, the exorcist claimed to be Adapa: "I am Adapa, exorcist of Eridu." [48] In order to be both on earth and in heaven, the speaker made several performative statements in the form of incantations and embarked on several purifying ritual actions.

The ritual was meant to protect the adept from witchcraft but also to provide the speaker with an incubated prophetic dream. It served as preparation for entering the world of the gods, which meant to ascend heavenwards, essentially to become a star or a god of the night sky and thus become inviolable (Maqlu 5.11–20 and 7.55–57). The identification is stated expressly in 7.50–57, where the actor asserts that the heavenly powers with whom he identifies, the stars, are "the great gods who are visible in the heavens" *(attunu ili rabuti ša ina šame naphnatunu).* The location of the experience, Zabban, was both a terrestrial place and a cosmic intersection between the world, the heavens, and the underworld. Evidently it was located at the horizon where the sun descended during the late summer season.

The *Maqlu* ceremony was performed during Abu (late July, approximately), at the season when ghosts came back to the world. The dead were awakened and, although not all became threats, some would become very dangerous indeed. The ritual actor took on his astral identity partly in order to stay awake through the first two ceremonial divisions but he rested between those parts and the morning rituals. In effect, he was asking for a dream, stimulated by incubation. If the dreams were evil, they could be nullified by Shamash, the sun, and the powers of water, Ea and Asalluhi.

Interestingly enough, these rites and rituals seem similar to the stories about Enmeduranki, another wise man who figures as the eponymous ancestor of the diviners just as Adapa is the ancestor of the exorcists. Diviners (*baru* priests) and exorcists (*asipu* priests) are separate functionaries, though many ancient practitioners were accredited to perform both rituals.[49] In both cases, human beings wish to convene the divine assembly, though humans are not authorized to command those with such high offices. In extispicy rituals, the diviner analogizes himself to the divine but in exorcism the agent becomes a divinity through a ritual transformation.

It is extremely relevant that these rituals are directly dependent upon the Gilgamesh epic, the Adapa myth, and the famous story of the Descent of Inanna, for they provide us with a window into some of the ways in which these stories were used ritually in the society that produced them. The myths were not just explanations, they were the "back story" for these technical manipulations for the benefit of the ritual organizers. Not only were they used in state monuments and present in libraries, they were the basis for various rituals of exorcism, purification, and healing. During the rituals, the adept ritually ascended to heaven in a shamanistic ceremony and brought back healing from disease and demons for the society. Thus, keeping the hostile dead away literally kept society healthy.

Adapa and the adept of the *Maqlu* ritual were even more closely linked by the end of Mesopotamian history. In Seleucid Uruk, these ritual priests presided at a large shrine dedicated to Adapa. By this period, the temple priesthood had already assumed the use of the *apkallu* depiction on their seals, which associated them with the scribal guilds as well. Furthermore, there was a distinct relationship between going to heaven, protecting society, being transformed into a star, and coming into the direct presence of the heavenly court. When Hebrew society finally affirmed a beatific afterlife, in the same Seleucid period, it also embraced these techniques of shamanistic heavenly journey for prophets, sages, and mystics. For the Israelites, the mediator was quintessentially Enoch, who occupied the same position in the Biblical genealogy as did Enmeduranki in the Babylonian King's list.[50]

Canaan: Climate and Pantheon

THE ISRAELITES lived in close contact with their Canaanite neighbors and picked up many religious practices from them, much to the dismay of some priests and prophets. But that was all we knew of Canaanite culture until the Amarna letters were found in Egypt (at Tel el-Amarna) and texts from the ruins of Ugarit (at Ras Shamra), a culturally Canaanite city near Latakia, were uncovered. Ugarit was far north and was destroyed by the sea peoples before the Israelites arrived in the land of Israel, consequently we cannot be sure that all the Canaanite customs we discovered would have still been in practice during Biblical times. Still later, we discovered a wealth of Phoenician inscriptions, which also represent Canaanite culture.

Nevertheless, from these sources, we have learned that Canaanite culture was both close to that of Mesopotamia and also heavily influenced by Egypt, which had been its feudal lord for centuries before the Israelites arrived in Canaan. We learn from these sites that the culture of Canaan was in close contact with Mesopotamia. Akkadian was the *lingua franca* of the Late Bronze Age. The Amarna texts contain copies of two important texts about the afterlife: "Adapa and the South Wind" and "Nergal and Ereshkigal." A fragment of *The Gilgamesh Epic* has been found at Megiddo, in the land of Israel.

But, we must expect that there were some individual aspects of the religious beliefs of the Canaanites that distinguish them from the Mesopotamians. The geography and climate of Canaan differed from both Mesopotamia and Egypt. There was no great river system upon which to depend for irrigation. The rainfall was plentiful only in the fall and winter rainy season, and only in the north, yielding very rich crops of grain and fruit, but fading off in the south to land usable only for animal husbandry, and finally to desert. Consequently, herding was far more important in Canaan than in either Mesopotamia or Egypt. Rain usually fell in two distinct patterns during the rainy season, which encompassed the winter. One rainy spell usually occured in the early fall, tending toward heavy but short downpours. A second period normally came later in winter, characterized by longer, gentler showers, which allowed for a winter wheat crop to ripen. The rain eventually failed in the late spring, though the dew was plentiful for a time. So it was still possible to grow a barley crop in spring, which tolerated dry weather and indeed rotted if it was too wet. The whole area is vulnerable to periodic droughts.

All these climatological features appear in Canaanite thought, transformed into myths about the gods. The effect of the climate can be seen in the myths of the major god of the Canaanite pantheon, Ba'al, the storm god, who brought fructifying rain and stud to the herd but who had septannual spells of weakness, in spite of his huge and awesome powers. In other words, the plenty given by the gods through rain was precarious.

East of the mountains was mostly desert, increasing from north to south, leaving little moisture for the deep valley of the Dead Sea and eastwards. In a good year, enough moisture fell on the eastern coastal mountain slopes to provide grass for spring grazing. In Canaanite mythology, desert and ocean were both gods whose demonic powers needed to be appeased or conquered. In any year, the rain might fail or come too late or last too long. The dew might not be adequate to the late crops. The late barley crop was especially worrisome, suffering both from too much moisture and too little. The counting of the omer (an ancient unit of measure) in Judaism, which traces the growing season of the barley crop, may be a reflection of this ancient agricultural anxiety. Geography as well as climate made life difficult in the area.

Canaan (and, hence, the land of Israel) was positioned on the narrow land bridge between Africa and Asia Minor. The narrow land was like a gate which opened to Europe, Africa, and Asia. He who controlled the gate had a lock on the access between the continents. It was the important strategic, military, and trade crossroads of three continents; whoever wished to dominate the area had to hold the three important roads—the royal road along the coast, the less easy and hot passage up and down the rift valley, and the difficult and treacherous passes between the mountains through Judea and Samaria.

Unfortunately, it was a gate all too easily opened. Israel gained control of all three roads at the height of its power, but that was only a brief period of time, when viewed against the history of the ancient Near East. Israel took up residence in the area as a group of mountain tribes, safe from the chariots of the great powers. It developed into a power when the great powers ceased to control the roads to the east and west of Israel's mountain stronghold. Israel's entire history as an independent state took place in a rare power vacuum when neither Egypt nor Mesopotamia was able to assert control of the roads. When the great empires reasserted themselves, the area became a constant battleground and the Israelite nation was doomed as an independent power; no local power could have resisted the huge military campaigns emanating alternatively out of Egypt or Mesopotamia and designed for world conquest. With such a climate and history, one can easily see why the gods were constantly battling to keep their positions.

El was the paramount god of the Canaanite pantheon. He held an august court of divinities, sometimes known as the *kokabê 'el*, the stars of 'El, who are the circumpolar, never-setting stars.[51] He holds court in the snow-capped mountains in the North. These are all epithets which are equally used by the God of Israel (see e.g. Ps 82). 'El was known as the Bull, symbolizing his strength and creative force of animal husbandry, though for most purposes he just sat on the sidelines like a white-bearded grandfather. His title "Father of Years," *abu shanima*, recalls the elderly man on the throne in Daniel 7:9, the *'atiq yomin*, the "Ancient of Days," and is no doubt one source of our image of God as an old man on a throne. But he often operated as what scholars call a *deus otiosus*, a distant and unconcerned god.

The most active god of the Canaanite hierarchy was Ba'al (or Haddad, Adad, Add, or Haddu) who was god of storms, rain, thunder, fertility to animals and people and, in general, all fertile, life-giving liquids.[52] What 'El's dignity prevented him from doing fell to his son Ba'al; so to him came the job of fighting off chaos, the sea, drought, death and, on the positive side, of bringing fertility to the land. He too was a bull when he took on his father's role as inseminator of the herd. The major epic of Ba'al from Ugarit involves Ba'al in a huge conflict with Yam (the sea), from a city by the seaside. Besides referring to the weather, and winter storms, the critical conflict with the sea perhaps also reflects similar interest in seafaring that we associate with the Phoenicians and Greeks. The Phoenicians and their colony of Carthage in North Africa were transplanted Canaanites.

Besides defeating Yam, Ba'al had to also defeat Mot (Death), who was the god of the underworld. Only after doing this could he claim the throne from his father 'El.[53] Ba'al's association with the Hebrew God was also clear. His epithets are: "Ba'al the Mighty" and "He Who Mounts The Clouds," the epithet that YHWH of the Hebrew Bible received (e.g. Ps 68:4; Heb). And, indeed, Ba'al was awarded the guidance of the vegetation, like Tammuz or Dummuzi. In this capacity he was known as "son of Dagan."[54] His dress was military and so reminds us of several depictions of YHWH as Lord of Hosts, though he was most often depicted with bull's horns, since he had himself taken on the power of the bull. In other words, the Hebrew God could alternatively pick up the epithets of Ba'al or 'El.

The consort of El was normally Asherah; but as the "Queen Mother" she too was deeply involved in the cult of her son Ba'al. She interceded with 'El to sanction a temple for Ba'al in token of his victory over Mot and Yam (literally "death" and "sea," cognates with the Hebrew *mawet*[55] and *yam*) and their allies Lothan (literally, the "writhing" animal, cognate with the Hebrew Leviathan). The first, Mot, was the god of death, chaos, and sterility, to whom Ba'al succumbed every seven years, causing famine. In Canaanite mythology, the building of a temple was divinely sanctioned and was the result of Ba'al's victory over all the forces of nature, succeeding to the throne of his father.

The story of Solomon's temple building, in turn, shares several themes and conventions with the Canaanite myth of the building of Ba'al's house. For instance, both were finished and dedicated at the beginning of the rainy season. In Isaiah 27 and Job 26:13, we hear of the LORD's famous conquest of the Leviathan, the Hebrew equivalent for Lothan. This ambivalence shows the great identity crisis of Israelite religion. Prophetically opposed to Canaanite religion, it nevertheless was suffused with Canaanite cultural forms and motifs and could hardly avoid them.

Asherah was a kind of "mother nature," often depicted as a tree of life. Her sacred tree was itself called an Asherah and symbolized her creative power. Thus, her role was suggestive both of the role Eve took in the Hebrew creation story and the Biblical tree of life. The Asherah was a potent symbol in Israelite agricultural life, as the Bible's opposition shows so powerfully: "You shall not plant any tree as a sacred pole *(Asherah)* beside the altar that you make for the LORD your God" (Deut 16:21).[56]

The consort of Ba'al was 'Anat, who was very much of a piece with the unforgettable Ishtar and Inanna in Mesopotamia. She was the goddess of love but also the gory goddess who went to battle, entertained, seduced, and slaughtered young men.[57] Along with Inanna and Ishtar, 'Anat should be thought of as the goddess testosterone, fostering sex and warfare. Like Ishtar's and Inanna's, 'Anat's cult animal was the lion. But she helped save Ba'al when he was weak and dying, until he was "resurrected."

Ishtar herself underwent a sex-change of sorts in migrating to Canaan, where she was transformed into her linguistic cognate, the god Athtar. Athtar was a god whose power was originally manifested in the planet Venus, bright star of dawn and dusk, worshiped by the ancestral Syrian tribesmen. Or she could keep her original gender in the person of the goddess Ashtoret or Athtoret. Ishtar and Inanna were identified as the planet Venus in Mesopotamia. The goddess Ashtoret, nemesis of the Hebrews in the Bible, like the god Athtar, was also identified with the planet Venus.

In settled agricultural life, Athtar became a god of irrigation. Even today in Arabic, the cognate word *'attara* means "to irrigate." While Ba'al was powerless, Athtar tried to take over the government of the cosmos but he was an inadequate substitute.[58] This reflects the periodic setting of the planet Venus under the horizon and also reflects on the sparse sufficiency of the dew for irrigation as the short, beautiful Canaanite spring turned into a long, hot, brutal summer.

There are some obvious relationships between this climatological pattern and the myth of the Descent of Inanna, the story of Ishtar and Tammuz and Gestinanna. They all start as ways of linking the periodic fall of Venus below the horizon with other, agricultural myths—here importantly with animal husbandry. When Ba'al conquers the sea, it is like Tiamat's loss to Marduk, resulting in sovereignty over it. Ba'al's return in the fall rains likewise symbolizes the renewal of fertility and brings restoration of the grain crops during the winter. He also importantly impregnates the herd, which induces the foaling season in the spring. And this cycle also has important ramifications for the cult of the dead, especially in relation to the New Year Festival in Babylon and Canaan.

The Hebrews knew more about Canaanite religion than Mesopotamian religion in the First Temple period. Babylonian religion made its strongest appearance after the Judeans were taken away to Babylonia in captivity (597–539 BCE).[59] But they were in constant contact with Canaanite culture throughout their inhabitation of Canaan; indeed, the prophets cautioned against the terrible immoralities of Canaanite religion, which they claim included human, infant sacrifice and sexual practices to insure fertility.

About the sexual practices, there seems little doubt, as ritual prostitution was practiced in the area. There is also evidence that Canaanite cults included human and infant sacrifice. The Roman claim against the Carthaginians—that they sacrificed their children—may not have been entirely propaganda: We have the skeletons of children in disturbing numbers in Punic temple sites. Since the Carthaginians were a Phoenician colony, they are representatives of Canaanite culture.[60] We also find children's bones buried at foundations and in large numbers near temples at Canaanite sites. But some scholars point out that, in a society with such high infant mortality, they need not have been sacrificed.

What seems more likely is that human sacrifice occurred in Canaanite culture. Besides the general accusation, the Bible gives us very specific references to occasional human sacrifice: For example, King Mesha of Moab sacrificed his eldest son on the walls of city to fend off the Israelite attack (2 Kgs 3:27). There are frequent reports and warnings against child sacrifice in the Bible (Gen 22:12; Exod 22:29–30; 34:20; Deut 18:10; Judg

11:30–31, 39; 1 Kgs 16:34), most of which suggest it was a regular feature of Canaanite life. But the Bible also describes human sacrifice as an extraordinary happening in Canaanite culture in time of crisis. One does not need to posit daily child offerings for sacrifice to be judged morally repugnant to the Hebrews.

Ba'al's Underworld Visit

BA'AL VISITED the underworld, as Inanna did. Exactly how he got there depends on the version of the story. The dominant version relates that after Ba'al built his palace, he sent messengers to Mot, the god of death. The messengers returned with an invitation to visit the underground. Ba'al expressed his submission with the phrase "Your servant I am, and yours forever" (1.5.II: 12), a clear oath of allegiance. Before leaving, Ba'al decided to mount a heifer and procure progeny. After a lacuna, we find that Ba'al's death was announced to his father 'El.

During that time, 'El, his priests, 'Anat, and the sun goddess Shapash mourn for Ba'al, contexting a ritual practice which continues into the Hellenistic period, using in Greek the equivalent names like Heracles or Adonis.[61] The Greek term is based on the Semitic *adon,* which like Ba'al, indicates dialectical equivalents of the terms for "master" and "husband." The mourning took place during the hot summer, in the month known as *Tammuz.* It may be related to Jephthah's daughter's mourning: "So she departed, she and her companions, and bewailed her virginity on the mountains" (Judg 11:38). In the Canaanite version, the mourner was usually 'Anat who followed 'El in mourning but even that makes an appearance in the Biblical record: " On that day the mourning in Jerusalem will be as great as the mourning for Hadad-Rimmon in the plain of Megiddo" (Zech 12:11). Hadad was another name for the storm god, Ba'al.

During the time of Ezekiel, we find pagan rites even in the Temple grounds: "Then he brought me to the entrance of the north gate of the house of the Lord; and behold, there sat women weeping for Tammuz" (Ezek 8:14). As the spring flowers bloom, so comes the end of the wheat and beginning of the barley harvests and the foaling of the animals, the rain stops and Ba'al goes underground, held in the sway of Mot (death), leaving his kingdom in the care of Athtar (dew). In summer comes the lamentation for his loss, which in turn, brings his return in the fall rains. The priesthood therefore protected and participated in the natural order in Canaan.

It is at the season of spring dew that Athtar is chosen a regent for Ba'al but is proven inadequate for the job. Finally, 'Anat confronts Mot, begs for his release, and then destroys him in a series of lines that seems to parallel the processing of the grain:

> With a sword she splits him,
> With a sieve she winnows him.
> With a fire she burns him,
> With millstones she grinds him,
> In a field she sows him (1.6.II:30–35)[62]

It is almost as if the passage is saying that the processing of grain into flour defeats death. Following this passage, we have a description of 'El's dream-vision, in which he discovers that Ba'al has returned to life.

Especially in the seventh year Mot challenged Ba'al in a critical conflict. This may parallel the sabbatical year in Israel; or, inversely, the sabbatical year may be a Yahwist answer to Canaanite customs. When Ba'al's returning presence was announced in dreams to his father 'El, we get the following ritual cry: "For Ba'al the Mighty is alive, / For the Prince Lord of the earth, exists." In this call of victory is perhaps the real meaning of Queen Jezebel's name, otherwise known to Bible readers as the idolatrous wife of King Ahab of Israel. It was the response to the phrase: *"'Iy zbl"* Canaanite (Ugaritic) for "Where is the Prince?" In a nasty little pun, the Hebrew *"'yzevel"* for the name Jezebel is taken to mean: "Without Dung." Likely it was just the Hebrew reaction to the cries of victory for the return of Ba'al.

As we have seen, this myth explains, among other things, the weather patterns of the Eastern Mediterranean. Ba'al was the god of rains; his disappearance meant that drought ruled: "The divine lamp, Shapash, grows hot,/the heavens are powerless by the power of divine Mot." This is a description of drought. The sun goddess Shapash waxed hot and no rain fructified the earth after the Spring foaling season was over. Like Inanna, Ba'al really died, and he really returned to life but, also like Inanna, he was always considered a god. There is no suggestion that this pattern in any way applied to humans. To the contrary, their return to life was through commemoration of the dead. No one expected them to leave their tombs. Instead, the purpose of the myth seemed originally to help keep the climate stable.

Aqhat *in the Canaanite Underworld*

CANAAN ALSO wrestled with matters of immortality and afterlife. There is another famous text, *The Epic of Aqhat,* which deals directly with death and loss, as well as, probably, commemoration and recovery. Aqhat was the son for whom the hero Dan'el had fervently prayed: to conceive a son, he presented generous offerings to the high gods, 'El and Ba'al. After he returned home, the Kotharat (conception and birth deities) visited him. He was a good host, feasting with them for six days. In return, they ensured offspring, a son Aqhat, to Dan'el and his wife, Danatay.

When Aqhat grew up, Dan'el received a bow and arrows from the god Kothar-wa-Ḥasis, after which more feasting ensued, showing Dan'el's gratitude and hospitality. Dan'el then transferred the prized weapons to his son with a blessing.

The plot thickened when the love and war goddess 'Anat coveted the weapons and attempted to bargain with Aqhat for the bow and arrows:

> Hear now, O hero Aqhat,
> Ask silver and I will give it thee,
> Even gold and I will freely bestow it on thee,
> But give me thy bow,
> Let the Sister of the Prince take thine arrows.

When this failed, she offered immortality. Evidently, 'Anat had promised something which everyone knew she could not deliver. She was depicted much like Inanna, with whom the savvy hero Gilgamesh refused marriage. Aqhat replied that he was not fooled by the offer:

> Fabricate not, O virgin;
> To a hero, thy lives are trash.
> As for mortal man, what does he get as his latter end?
> What does mortal man get as his inheritance?
> Glaze will be poured out on my head,
> Glaze will be poured out on my head,
> Even plaster on my pate,
> And the death of all men will I die,
> Yes, I will surely die.[63]

The story concentrates on the burial practice of glazing and plastering the head of the corpse, which we, indeed, find in excavated graves of the area, even as far south as Jericho.

'Anat received 'El's permission to punish Prince Aqhat. But the punishment got out of control. One of the divine thugs, Yatpan, disguised as a hunting falcon, actually killed Aqhat, instead of merely wounding him. As a result, the much envied bow was lost in the sea. As soon as Dan'el found out about the death, the crops failed and drought started. Most of the body was eaten by birds of prey. Dan'el gathered up the few remaining parts of Aqhat, buried them, beginning and completing a seven year period of mourning. Aqhat's sister Pagat then asked for a blessing from her father to complete the vengeance against Yatpan.

The scene for the vengeance visited upon Yatpan was a drinking feast, a *marzeaḥ* or *marziḥ*, which was the major rite of remembrance in this society and, in important ways, the equivalent of the *kispu* offerings of Mesopotamia. But the goddess 'Anat was also clearly depicted in the wrong for her behavior. So she was frequently depicted as the patroness of these feasts, in seeming compensation for her bad behavior. In some way, this long involved story of give-and-take underlies the script for the Canaanite *marziḥ* commemorative banquet.[64]

This entire episode is reminiscent of the death of Enkidu after Gilgamesh insulted Ishtar by refusing marriage and later killing Humbaba as well as the sacred bull of heaven. Here, as in many Canaanite myths, that death had climatic consequences. It also has within it the ancient Near East notion that when we seek immortality we risk offending the gods. We should not even think that we can achieve immortality because it will result in running afoul of the gods in horrendous ways. On the other hand, with the appropriate rituals, the dead could be commemorated and their status in the underworld improved. In these stories and in the rituals that dramatized them, are contained notions of misinvocation, equivocation, insult, and reversal.[65] The dead could be given relief from their status but never raised back to life in this world.

David P. Wright, in his study of the Aqhat epic, invokes the work of Mary Douglas with some justification, though perhaps he overplays the parallel with his analogy of dinner parties in Great Britain;[66] at least I have not attended any dinner parties that approximate the Canaanite example. The fact is that drinking parties and meals in general often do have a specific ritual character, with the etiquette representing a limited code, just as Mary Douglas pointed out for the cultures of Africa, ancient Israel, Australia, and Great Britain. If the different cultures do not send the same messages with their symbolic actions, that does not diminish the importance of the general perception.[67]

The *marzeaḥ* or *marziḥ* feasts did serve to define who the living kin were and hence who was included in family intimacy, by including the exalted ancestors with the invited guests. The mortals gave the offerings and libations at these feasts while the gods and exalted dead received them. Apparently they were raucous, even orgiastic, as well.[68]

It may be that the ending of the Aqhat myth provides us with the ultimate significance of the Ba'al myth for Canaanite notions of the afterlife. Aqhat refused 'Anat's promise of immortality because it was not actually a return to life:

Ask life, O hero Aqhat
Ask life and I will give it thee
Immortality and I will freely grant it thee,
I will make thee number years with Ba'al,
Even with the sons of 'El wilt thou tell months,
As Ba'al, even as he lives and is feted,
Lives and is feted and they give him to drink,
Singing and chanting before him
Even so will I give thee life, O Hero Aqhat.

What 'Anat apparently offers was the chance to be fêted at the *marziḥ,* not actual afterlife. He was like Ba'al, the head of the feast, but he was not a god and so he did not actually come back to life. Instead, he was fêted, toasted, praised with chanting and singing, and commemorated. This seems to mean that his "spirit" could be recalled from the afterlife to appear at the feast. Although he rejected this offer at the beginning of the story, this is probably what he got at the end.

The Canaanite Afterlife

WHEN THE CANAANITES died, their vital element, called a *npš* (like Hebrew: *nefesh,* usually translated as "soul," or "spirit") was thought to leave the body. Alternatively, Ugaritic texts speak of the going out of the "wind" or "breath" (*rḥ,* like Hebrew: *ruaḥ*). The word becomes *nbš* in Phoenician and is sometimes paralleled with the term *brlt.* Those scholars who maintain that Israel got its notion of a beatific afterlife from Canaan must come to terms with the fact that afterlife in these related groups of cultures was not particularly beatific or optimistic.[69] So we should not expect that Israel, in this early period of its existence, would concentrate on the pleasures of living with God after death. It is not hard to see that in envisioning the quality of a person that survives death, the Canaanites, like the Egyptians and the Mesopotamians, were also making judgments about what was important and transcendent in human life; they were finding ways of describing the meaning and final purpose of the earthly "self." Eventually, that would have to have consequences for the way they thought of their earthly existence. This will be the subject of a future chapter.

After the "soul" or "shade" left the body, life did not totally cease but continued on in another place—the kingdom of *Mot* ("Death," Hebrew: *mavet*), where it lived in the same kind of weak form that we saw in Mesopotamia. This is no surprise since the Canaanites practiced interment as well and it makes sense to think that people who bury the dead would have a tendency to view the dead as residing in the earth. In Canaan traditions, there is no proof of reward or punishment of the dead in any Jewish or Christian sense, though certain transformations of the dead could be effected ritually.

Only the gods were exempt from death and not all of them were, as most cultures have notions of older gods who were killed and supplanted by the present pantheon. Even the present gods were not entirely free of death, as Osiris, Inanna, and Ba'al and the other gods symbolizing some annual rhythm in nature have shown us. They form what is sometimes referred to as the "Dying and Rising gods" of the ancient Near East. This pattern may be more evident to Christians than it was to the ancients.[70] For one thing, no real resurrection is promised for their devotées. But there are definitely gods whose lives, deaths, and rebirths informed the ancients about the seasonal agricultural patterns in which they lived, linking them to the cycle of human birth and death.[71] Indeed, if any mythology is going to be relevant to the human tradition, the gods must be shown to suffer real loss and provide humanity with negative or positive models for dealing with it.

But, in most contexts, immortality was a key feature of a Mesopotamian and Canaanite god, even those who visited the underworld. They all survived their ordeals. But we do not; humans have to die. This is one of the lessons of yet another story, the Kirta legend, named for a legendary king of Khubar whose children thought him to be immortal because he was king.

That assumption prompted the king's children to ask their father: "Ah father! Should you die like mortal men? / Is not Kirta the son of 'El, the child of the Benevolent and Saint?" In spite of whatever may have been claimed in the enthronement rituals of Canaanite kings, it was still a naive question, even offensive to the gods. The irony is that we all die and only a child would think we are gods. But the story also parodies the pretensions of royalty and perhaps even specifically the Egyptian funerary cult.

It was the job of the children to care for the family's deceased and make sure that the proper rituals were maintained. It was the lineage that must survive, so a person's death was socialized into the memory of the lineage. As the Kirta legend tells us, among the duties a son owed to his father was that of supporting him in his drunkenness when returning from the commemorations of the dead. It turns out that this was a ritual concern because the dead were buried with a "wake" and later commemorated with a great drinking party called a *marziḥ* or a *marzeaḥ,* as the word would be pronounced in Hebrew.

Marziḥ *or* Marzeaḥ:
The Canaanite Cult of the Dead

As EVERYWHERE in the Middle East and many other places, the dead were buried with grave goods. The heads of the dead were often painted with glaze. Sometimes corpses were deliberately disfigured or dismembered; for instance, at Jericho not only do we find bright, colored head-painting, we also occasionally find that one or more arms or legs of the corpses were removed—ostensibly to render them harmless in any future hauntings. Many archeological remains show evidence of repeated offerings. Sometimes a large storage jar for this purpose stood at the entry to the tomb. In other places a jar was buried in such a way as to provide an underground depository and occasionally even a pipe was used for offerings to be accessed from the tomb below.

In Ugarit (Ras Shamra), family tombs were found connected to the house by a stone shaft, with evidence that they were used over long periods of time and reused with the prior remains pushed aside. Children were sometimes buried at the entrance to the tomb. There are even cultic halls above some great tombs, where offering jars could be filled and other rites to various gods could be performed. It was also the location of the grave-marker or stele, and evidently a herb garden for marjoram (*zaʿaṭar*) used in rituals for remembrance of the clan.[72]

Besides the funerary cult, there is considerable literary evidence in Canaan of the veneration, feeding, appeasing, and honoring of the transformed dead at regular intervals and whenever their help might be sought.[73] The basic goal of the cult of the dead seems to be to establish and continue a positive relationship between the dead and the living, in some sense to keep the dead part of the family.[74] At Ugarit, the dead evidently participated in the fall New Year festival, celebrating the return of Baʿal with the fall rains. This act of Baʿal is described in *KTU* 1.21:II.5–6. Although the text is damaged, it can be restored by supplying the conventional parallels: "Then he will heal you/the Shepherd will give life to you." The words were addressed to what seem to be a group of privileged, immortalized or specially commemorated dead, called *rpʾum* (cognate with Hebrew *refaʾim*), possibly vocalized as *rapiʾuma*. Many scholars find the Hebrew pronunciation the most convenient since pronunciation of Ugaritic words is speculative.

In any event, the connection between Ugaritic and Hebrew is crucial in this case because these words in Ugaritic (and others like them) for the dead and the ghosts come up again in Hebrew culture. Since the dead were to be "healed," perhaps the best explanation of the term *rpʾum* is that they were "the healed ones."

The identity of the *rpʾum* is heavily contested. The best guess links them with deified or transformed dead ancestors, similar to the *ilʾib*:

> Shapash, you rule the *rpʾum*, Shapash you rule the ghosts;
> Let the deities be your company, behold let the dead be your
>   company (*KTU* 1.6:VI.45–49)

The dead *(mtm)*, the deities *(ʾilm)*, the ghosts *(ʾilnym)* and the *rpʾum* are related to each other through parallel structure, as is conventional in Near Eastern poetry. Like Ra, Utu, Shamash and Baʿal, Shapash the sun goddess interceded between the living and the dead because at night she crossed the realm of the dead on her way back to the east for dawn. So it seems clear from the parallelism that the *rpʾum* participated in all the underworld categories—dead, gods, ancestors, ghosts. The identification is borne out in many other ways too.

The full context of *KTU* 1.21 shows how Baʿal would heal the dead:

> "Come into the house of my *marzeaḥ,* go into my house for
>   the *rpʾum*
> I invite you [into] my [hou]se, I call [you into] my [pa]lace.
> May the *rpʾum* flutter to the holy place, may the ghosts flutter
>   [to] the holy place, [May they come into the house of
>   my] *marzeaḥ.*
> Then he will he[al you], the shepherd will [give you life again],

Now I will go [one day and a second], [on the] third day I will
arrive   at the day I will arrive at the house, [I will
come in]to my   palace."
And Dan'el said: "[Come into the house of] my [*marzeah*], go
into my house for the *rp'um*.
[I invite you [into my house], I call you [into] my [pala]ce,
May the *rp'um* [flutter] to the holy place, may the gh[osts]
flutter [to the holy] place."

The best reconstruction of the scene is probably that Ba'al spoke the
first lines, to command the activity, and Dan'el made the full invitation to
the *rp'um*. This was Dan'el, the father of Aqhat, the Canaanite hero and
namesake of the prophet Daniel whose oracles attest to resurrection for
the first time in Israelite thought. The *rp'um* were invited to come to the
house of Dan'el's *marzeah*, also called "a house for the *rp'um*." We have
seen that *Marzeah* was a cultic meal and drinking party, defining an association of orgiasts, whose partying evidently included sexual entertainments, held in commemoration of the dead, as we see from several quite
explicit graffiti.[75] The source of the ritual may simply have been to provide lavish and royal entertainment for the arrival of dead, regarded as
distant and much beloved guests. But the excessive drinking may also
have stimulated altered states of consciousness.[76]

Whether or not a *marzeah* was a funeral wake, it could have been celebrated in remembrance of the honored dead. A god, Rapiu, evidently the
leader of the *rp'im* was described as "King of Eternity." [77] It may be that
Rapiu was often identified with 'El, who was depicted in another fragment as getting drunk at a *marzeah*. At other times, the god of the *rp'm*
seems closest to Ba'al. In any event, his strength, power, might and rule
were the qualities sought at the *marzeah*.

This is explicitly the sort of immortality that Ba'al offered his heroes
when he returned to take up rule in the fall. The participants in the meal
included human celebrants, and the divine who comprised, in the lowest
ranks, these transformed dead:

[   ] may the [*rp*]'*um* take part in the sacrifice, [   ] may the
ghosts [be str]engthened; [may they e]at like the dead
of the dead
[May they draw] near and enter the company; may they [   ]
on the day of the summer fruit.
May [the gho]sts eat, [yea,] may the [*rp'*]*um* drink.

117

[May they descend,] the god of the nut-trees, [the goddess]
    who is sitting on a twig.
[I have sacrifi]ced the sacrifice of Amurru, [   ] day [   ].

(*KTU* 1.20: I)

The day of the summer fruit suggests that this was part of the fall harvest New Year festival. The crops would include quintessentially nuts, which were said to need rain to ripen, as well as olives, fruits, and gourds.[78] There is also evidence that the *marzeaḥ* could have been held at other times of the year. But besides the fall festival, there was a clear connection with the Kotharot, the fertility goddesses emanating from the underworld, who here sat on twigs like birds. Indeed, it is quite probable that the *rp'um* were also pictured as birds (*KTU* 1.20: II.2), like the aviary transformation that Enkidu underwent and perhaps somewhat influenced by Egyptian conventions of iconography as well.

The transformed dead could also arrive in great chariots, as befitted gods, with their banners flying. The same mode of conveyance was available to YHWH. Psalm 68:18 speaks of God's myriads of chariots.[79] When God left Jerusalem to follow his people into exile, he arrived in Babylon in a luxurious, two-axle chariot-cart, witnessed by the prophet Ezekiel who was watching in prophetic trance (Ezek 1). Indeed, the name of the vehicle, a *mrkbt,* in Ugaritic, derived from the word for chariot, anticipates the Rabbinic name for the branch of Jewish mysticism arising from speculation of Ezekiel's vision, *Merkabah* mysticism.

Summary

EGYPT, MESOPOTAMIA, and Canaan all produced very sophisticated mythologies, which both acknowledged death and hoped for regeneration, and were known throughout the ancient world. It was mostly through Canaanite culture that Biblical religion received its knowledge of these wider traditions, at least in preexilic times. The Bible did not accept these mythological renditions of immortality uncritically, though the Biblical Israelites were certainly tempted by some of the promises it held. The prophets offer a long polemic against the horror of Canaanite religion, especially in its accusations of Canaanite child sacrifice and its ritual prostitution.

Nevertheless, a great many Canaanite images are to be found inside Israelite literature. It is in Canaanite religion that many of the literary images we normally understand as Israelite find their source. During the whole First Temple period (ca. 960–587 BCE) the battle raged, as we shall see, and the received Bible fought strongly against any articulate notion of an afterlife, beatific or not. The Bible, however, reaches its present form in the Second Temple period (515 BCE–70 CE). Just how much of the portrait of the First Temple period that we read in the Bible is actually historical is a moot point, as it is being filtered through the eyes of a much later and more sophisticated editor. It is quite possible to posit that the First Temple period was much closer to the culture of Canaan than the Bible paints it.[80] On the other hand, when it comes to issues of the afterlife, we cannot fail to miss that there is not much archeological evidence that the Israelites regularly offered food or drink to their dead, as was characteristic of the Canaanite cults.[81]

In the end, however, after notions of the afterlife entered Israel, it was not the notion of contact with the living that persisted as a beatific reward after death. On the contrary, the vision of the afterlife of the Mesopotamian and Canaanite cities became more the model of hell, not heaven, in the Bible.

3

The First Temple Period in Israel

THE YEARS of our life are threescore and ten,
    or even by reason of strength fourscore;
yet their span is but toil and trouble;
    they are soon gone, and we fly away.
Who considers the power of thy anger,
    and thy wrath according to the fear of thee?
So teach us to number our days
    that we may get a heart of wisdom. (Ps 90:10–12)

THIS PSALM OFFERS us sobering thoughts to ponder. The advice of the Bible is to value our fleeting time alive. Its advice is similar to Sidduri's advice to Gilgamesh, though it straightforwardly implores God for the wisdom to fear Him. In these few verses we can see the deep relationship between Biblical literature and Mesopotamian notions of the afterlife. Save for the monotheistic invocations, these verses might have served nicely as the moral to *The Gilgamesh Epic*. Furthermore, the Bible begins its discussion of the afterlife with the very same intuition we saw in Mesopotamia: Recognition of our mortality ought to lead directly to wisdom. The Mesopotamian version of this insight is, of course, much more ancient than the Bible and consequently couched in mythology, ritual, and polemic for the divination and exorcism guilds. The lyric poetry of Psalms expresses the relationship more privately, as does Wisdom Literature like

Ludlul Bel Nemeqi in Mesopotamia as well. The psalms allude to the mythical background of Mesopotamia.

We are used to reading the Bible as discursive literature, meant for us and our moral improvement. The Bible cannot be fully understood without seeing it in its historical context—Egypt, Mesopotamia, and Canaan for the First Israelite Commonwealth period (ca. 1200 BCE–586 BCE), Persia and Greece for the Second Temple period (515 BCE–70 CE). In this context, it is not the familiar guide to our moral lives but a strange and sometimes off-putting window into a culture that vanished long ago. In such an environment, it would be out of place to expect discursive arguments for or against the pagan world's notions of our ultimate ends. Instead, the Bible will rely on its own narratives and myths to express similarity and contrast with the environment in which it was written. Reading the Bible, we must be sensitive to both the constitutive and the polemical role of mythical narratives.

The Bible, as its name implies (*Ta Biblia* in Greek, meaning "the little books"), is not a single work but collective work, an anthology selected from a greater output of ancient Israelite literary works for a specific, theological purpose. One of those purposes was to show the sinfulness of Canaanite culture. Another was to narrate the covenant between God and his people Israel. Yet, when we look behind the voice of the redactor, or the editor, we often see a great deal of similarity between Israel and the cultures around it. For example, Psalm 29 seems equally at home in a Canaanite context, and Psalm 104 has an uncanny resemblance to Akhenaten's *Hymn to Aten,* so close, in fact, that several verses seem like direct borrowings.

That the Bible lacks a concrete narrative of the afterlife, as we have seen so often manifested in the pagan cultures around it, must, we suspect, not be just accidental or deficient; it must be part of the Biblical polemic against its environment. In contrast to the plethora of different ideas about life after death, in the great river cultures surrounding Israel, early Bible traditions seem uninterested in the notion of an afterlife. Practically every scholar who systematically surveys the oldest sections of the Biblical text is impressed with the lack of a beatific notion of the hereafter for anyone.

But that is not all that is missing: Virtually the entire mythological framework of cosmological discussion in the ancient world is lacking and the traces that remain are transformed. Everything—rain and dew, crops and increase of flocks, and historical events as well—is due to the Lord, the God of Israel. Gone is the exuberant pantheon of exalted, loving, quarreling, and warring gods. Gone too is most of the epic poetry, with its rich texture of myth glorifying the gods and ancient kings. Unlike the other ancients who reveled in the time of the gods, the *illud tempus* (Latin for "that time"), a mythical time at the beginning of the world when the gods and humans encountered each other directly, the Bible links the mythical past with the story of its historical figures by means of sturdy and understated prose. Everything seems to be part of the same story and narrative. The closest we get to *in illo tempore* ("in that time") in the Bible is the so-called "J" source of the Pentateuch where God manifests himself directly to a few well-chosen people, in charming literary tales.

In place of the booming *multi*verse ruled over by unpredictable gods of the nations around them, the writers of the Bible eventually offered, in their mythology, a *uni*verse under the direction of a single, moral God. One might say that they created the notion of a universe in proclaiming that one God created and ruled it. How carefully the rest of the Israelites listened to this message depended on the time period and the circumstances. And how long it took the Israelites to reach this stage is moot.

All the myths we discussed in previous chapters took place *in illo tempore,* in that other mythical time, set off by epic poetry in Egypt, Mesopotamia, and Canaan. The primeval history in the Bible is a mythical time too but it pretends, in contrast to the epic poetry we have surveyed, to be attached to our own time by unbroken genealogies and continuous prose narrative. In comparison to the cultures we have just reviewed, the first eleven chapters of Genesis are written in the same brief, concise prose narrative, designed to seem just as everyday as the events in the marketplaces of Israel.

Or, looked at another way, the events happening in the marketplaces and courts of Israel were meant to be just as important to history as the temptation of Adam and Eve in mythic time; they are all part of the same historical and moral drama.[1]

In the first instance this means that the rich geographical and climatic mythologies of Egypt, Mesopotamia, and Canaan, which link the natural world with death and regeneration, would take a backseat in Hebrew thought. We have no great epics that explain in narrative form why the rivers flood or the crops alternate or the dew suffices when the rains stop. Instead these are all due to the direct guidance of the one god, YHWH, the Holy One of Israel. YHWH is not so much present in the events of nature as He is the director of them. And He is present in an entirely new area of human endeavor which we have not seen before: He is the God of history. It is YHWH who directs the events which happen to Israel, as well as the fates of other nations.

The Bible suggests that the people Israel and its God, whose proper name is YHWH, usually designated by the word "LORD" in English Bibles, have entered into a specific agreement called a "covenant" (Hebrew: *Berîth*). The agreement says that YHWH will look after the people if they keep His laws, which include worshiping Him, Him alone, and observing a variety of laws for the religious, social, and moral benefit of the people, at least as those values were understood at that time. This covenant has a history; recounting the history of the covenant, in fact, is what creates the historical narrative of the Hebrew Bible. It also means that fortune and misfortune depend on controllable variables—the behavior of the people.

Not only does this make people responsible for their own fortunes in nature, it also has consequences for the conception of the self. In place of locating themselves geographically in the great forces of nature, the Israelites locate themselves in the unique history of Israel and, later, in the history of the dispersed Jewish people. That necessarily makes each individual more aware of the unique aspects of public and private moral experience. The Bible demythologizes nature and mythologizes history.

The Bible tells us that the Israelites found the path to the exclusive worship of YHWH difficult. Reading the Bible historically and in line with archeology shows us that it was even harder than it seems from the text alone. Archeology suggests that YHWH's cult really did not take hold completely until after the Israelites returned from Babylonian captivity in 539 BCE and that, indeed, much of the writing of Bible was edited or formulated then.

Why the Silence about the Afterlife?

IT COULD BE that Hebrew culture foresaw no significant afterlife for the dead, that the covenant had nothing to say about the afterlife except to warn against believing that another god could supply one. That belief would make the Hebrews absolutely unique among world cultures and especially strange in the ancient Near East, where elaborate ideas about postmortem existence and even more elaborate rituals were everywhere part of literature, myth, and social life.

We are not only faced with a huge silence, we are left without conclusive evidence for a sure explanation. How could the Bible have avoided discussing this issue? Since the reasons for the lack of information are obscure, the Bible presents us with the scholarly predicament of a classic argument from silence. The best we can offer is speculation, based on what clues we can find in the text and in archeological records. We know that the Bible's dislike of foreign cults and gods other than YHWH demytholo-gized all the gods, turning them into created objects. Presumably, any ex-tended discussion of life after death or the realm of the dead with its pantheon of divinities would open the door for idolatry or veneration of ghosts which the Bible, in its final and present form, has entirely for-bidden.

This hypothesis is given some credibility by the fact that most Biblical terms for the dead can be found in the book of Isaiah—predominently pos-itive terms like "souls," "divine ones," "healers," "holy ones," "knowing ones," and "those who pass over." A large number of scholars conclude from this usage that the dead had a powerful role in the lives of the living: They might even heal the sick and revive the dead for ordinary Israelites.[2] While some of these scholarly hypotheses may be exaggerated, it seems likely that the First Temple Israelites lived in a cultural continuum with the Canaanites and shared many beliefs with them. For instance, we find a cer-tain amount of archeological evidence that suggests the Hebrew God YHWH was sometimes viewed as having a female consort—as in the graf-fito to YHWH-ANAT at Kuntillet 'Ajrud and in later inscriptions at Ele-phantine in Egypt (Jer 44:7–8).[3]

We find nothing but vituperation against such an idea in the Bible, al-though we sometimes find figures like Wisdom taking on the conven-tional epithets of goddesses, as in Proverbs 1:20, as well as chapters 8 and 9. The Bible itself records that the Israelites and Judeans again and again went off to worship the fertility gods of Canaan and condemns this as sinning against the covenant with YHWH, for which natural disasters, in-vasions, and finally exile were the punishments. The prophets tell us re-peatedly of the crimes of Israelite commoners and kings.

The evidence suggests that the fight against ancestor worship was even more obvious and more dangerous, as it was actually a significant part of Israelite popular religion. In short, for all its honesty about the conflict, we shall see that the Bible gives us an idealized portrait of the battle be-tween Yahwism and Canaanite religion, largely as it was remembered after the Babylonian captivity.

The Séance at Endor

THERE ARE SOME passages that hint at a more complicated relationship between the Israelites and their Canaanite environment. For instance, Saul, when he feared God's disfavor, sought the services of a necromancer, following a practice that he himself had specifically forbidden, according to the narrative. Since exorcism and necromancing constituted a primary ritual supported by the myths of the afterlife in Egypt, Canaan, and Mesopotamia, it is worthwhile to look at this passage in some detail:

> When Saul inquired of the LORD, the LORD did not answer him, not by dreams, or by Urim, or by prophets. Then Saul said to his servants, "Seek out for me a woman who is a medium, so that I may go to her and inquire of her." His servants said to him, "There is a medium at Endor." So Saul disguised himself and put on other clothes and went there, he and two men with him. They came to the woman by night. And he said, "Consult a spirit for me, and bring up for me the one whom I name to you." The woman said to him, "Surely you know what Saul has done, how he has cut off the mediums and the wizards from the land. Why then are you laying a snare for my life to bring about my death?" But Saul swore to her by the LORD, "As the LORD lives, no punishment shall come upon you for this thing." Then the woman said, "Whom shall I bring up for you?" He answered, "Bring up Samuel for me." When the woman saw Samuel, she cried out with a loud voice; and the woman said to Saul, "Why have you deceived me? You are Saul!" The king said to her, "Have no fear; what do you see?" The woman said to Saul, "I see a *divine being* [emphasis added] coming up out of the ground." He said to her, "What is his appearance?" She said, "An old man is coming up; he is wrapped in a robe." (1 Sam 28:6–14a)

The most poignant part of this story is the way in which Saul must convince the woman to perform the ritual, which he has specifically forbidden and which she herself does not want to perform. Saul is so desperate to find out why the Lord is silent that he dares to use forbidden supernatural help. The entrepreneur he needs is described as a "medium," which he instructs his servants to seek out: "Seek out for me a woman who is a medium," literally a "mistress of ghosts." He wants to "inquire" of her, a word with prophetic and divinatory implications. Additionally, he uses the phrase "Consult a spirit for me," (literally, "enchant" a ghost for me).

In the eyes of the narrator, for Saul to have called upon the necromancer, traditionally the "witch of Endor" in English, is the last, most sinful act of a very desperate man. The woman's powers are real, not imaginary, for she accomplishes the task for Saul. The woman, seemingly in an act of kindness, slaughters a calf for the abandoned king Saul, who has not eaten all day, a detail which suggests the ritual preparations for a necromantic séance, something akin to the *marzeah* or *Marzih* (the Canaanite commemorative feast), where the presence of the ancestor was greeted with a feast.[4] So far as the Bible is concerned, then, the dead can be recalled, and there is a technology available for doing so; but it is sinful to do so, because they are "divine beings" and hence consulting them breaches the canons of Yahwism (1 Sam 28:13). As the book of Deuteronomy itself clarifies:

> When you come into the land that the LORD your God is giving you, you must not learn to imitate the abhorrent practices of those nations. No one shall be found among you who makes a son or daughter pass through fire, or who practices divination, or is a soothsayer, or an augur, or a sorcerer, or one who casts spells, or who consults ghosts or spirits, or who seeks oracles from the dead. For whoever does these things is abhorrent to the LORD; it is because of such abhorrent practices that the LORD your God is driving them out before you. You must remain completely loyal to the LORD your God. Although these nations that you are about to dispossess do give heed to soothsayers and diviners, as for you, the LORD your God does not permit you to do so. (Deut 18:9–14)

The word "witch," *(mekaŝŝepā)* used in English to describe the enchantress in Exodus 22:17, is the same word used to describe the "enchanter" *(Mekaŝŝēp)* in Deuteronomy (see also Lev 19:31, 20:6, 27), except that the gender in Deuteronomy is masculine (the common gender in Hebrew) instead of feminine. Both are strictly forbidden under pain of death. The female version comes from the earliest law code in Israelite history (JE law code = Exod 20:2–23:19), the general term is from the Deuteronomic law code (D law code = Deut 6–24), promulgated in the reform of Josiah in 621 BCE.

Necromancy Forbidden Is Necromancy Affirmed

ON THE OTHER hand, there is evidence of a strong Deuteronomistic editing in the material with careful attention given to the sin involved. When Josiah cleanses the witches from Judah, he also throws out the mediums and necromancers, using the very vocabulary used in the story in Samuel (2 Kgs 23:24).

It is suspicious that the idolatrous practices, forbidden so often, are mentioned in Deuteronomy as practices of the early Israelites. One might argue that they were introduced during the Assyrian period for there is good evidence that Assyrian cults were introduced into Judah by Kings Amon and Manasseh.[5] However, Saul's encounter with the necromancer is a popular, native, rural practice, not a cult introduced by royal patronage. There are times and places in Israelite life where the practices seem perfectly appropriate. For instance, Jeremiah and the other prophets seem to know about them.

Under the specific practices forbidden by legislation and at least once carried out in practice are exactly those which the medium of Endor performs. One cannot "enchant," "divine, intone, or cast spells," "consult or ask ghosts or familiar spirits," or "seek oracles from the dead." The vocabulary used by Saul to hire her services is explicitly the same vocabulary used to forbid the practice in Deuteronomy, so there is evidence of a literary relationship between the two pieces. Note too that in true ancient Near Eastern fashion, what Saul wants from this encounter is knowledge and the wisdom to make the best decision as king. It was normal for kings of nations to seek oracular advice. What is not clear is how much of the abhorence is due to the Deuteronomic reform and how much comes earlier. In spite of the Deuteronomistic narrative, the phenomenon and some opposition is historical, much earlier because it appears in the JE epic law code.

We learn something else from the law codes. These practices are grouped with the wicked idolatrous practices of the Canaanites—including child sacrifice. They are forbidden not only because they are immoral and abhorrent, but also because they violate monotheism—more exactly, they insult (the cult of) YHWH. This is, evidently, a new religious idea, as we have seen that gods usually act in concert in the area. While the gods may argue and oppose each other and while the priesthood of one site may dislike the priesthood of another area, one has to look far in this area to see the notion that no other cult may be practiced at all. It may have existed among the other tribal peoples, but we have little evidence of exclusivism in their religions. The Bible tells us in many ways that the Israelites did participate in the other religions, though it is careful to give us as little information as possible about what the practices were.

The Bible, as we have it, incorporates these ambiguities into an unambiguous *Kulturkampf*, a battle against a foreign culture. The Israelites were to owe everything to one God YHWH, the LORD, and one God alone. The reason the Israelites were given the land, which belonged to the Canaanites, is that they had sworn in the covenant not to participate in the practices of those who preceded them and who were dispossessed by the LORD for their sinfulness. That means, according to the law codes, that they were not to consult their own nor the ancestors of the Canaanites who were to be found in the land.

But at a certain earlier point there was more ambiguity. Another name for YHWH could be *El* or *Elohim*, who could also be seen as the god of the ancestor deities.[6] It is possible that the argument against invoking the dead was precisely against invoking the gods of the Canaanites, who were there first and who might have claimed credit for keeping the land and its inhabitants safe—or, at least, against not confusing the dead ancestors with YHWH.

Interestingly enough in 2 Kings 23, Josiah also throws out the *terafim,* ancestral spirits, known to be in the possession of Israelites in the patriarchal period and later. Since this occured in 621 BCE, not all the Israelites had hearkened to the law codes of earlier times. The ancestral spirits had altars and could be consulted and may have also been referred to as *elohim* (Gen 31:19, 30, 32; 35:2, 4; Judg 17:5; 18:14, 17, 18, 20; see Isa 8:19–20; Num 25:2; Ps 106:28). It seems quite likely that one of the meanings of the word *elohim* must also be "ancestral gods."[7] For instance, Laban's *teraphim* represent his ancestral deities—that is, his *elohim,* which were going to be outlawed as "foreign gods" in the eyes of the Biblical editors.[8]

From whence the divine being (literally: *elohim* or figuratively: "divine ghost ancestor") of Samuel comes in the Endor story is not specifically named, though he is pictured as "coming up," as if from under the earth, which is precisely where the dead go to and come from in the Mesopotamian and Canaanite traditions. When the ghost arrives and is identified as Samuel, his first question concerns why his rest has been so rudely interrupted. The dead in Hebrew thought are resting quietly; or at least, the righteous ones are. No doubt this is one reason why Isaiah is so angry with the necromancers:

> And when they say to you, "Consult the mediums and the wizards who chirp and mutter," should not a people consult their God? Should they consult the dead on behalf of the living for the teaching and for the testimony?[9] Surely for this word which they speak there is no dawn. They will pass through the land, greatly distressed and hungry; and when they are hungry, they will be enraged and will curse their king and their God, and turn their faces upward; and they will look to the earth, but behold, distress and darkness, the gloom of anguish; and they will be thrust into thick darkness. (Isa 8:19–22)

The necromancers are even described as "chirping" with a word that normally describes the sound of birds and further suggesting the birdlike character of the transformed ancestors in Egypt, Mesopotamia, and Canaan. If so, Isaiah was satirizing the practice by describing the necromancers and not the dead as "chirping," as if to say they are not contacting the dead, only making the sounds themselves.

Several laws in Israelite law codes prevented priests from serving actively in funerals. Leviticus ordains that priests can only attend the burials of their close kin (Lev 21:1–5). They should not indulge in ornate rituals of grief—appearing with dishevelled hair, rent garments, shaven heads, or gashed flesh (Lev 10:6; 19:27–28). The high priest is enjoined to even higher standards of abstention (Lev 21). These all seem designed to prevent the priesthood from serving in too prominent a way in rites for the dead or any cult divination. As Mary Douglas writes in her wise monograph on Leviticus:

> Mediumistic consultation with the dead was to be punished by stoning (Lev 19:26, 31; 20:6, 27). The dead could neither help nor be helped. Any form of spirit cult was rejected. Seers, sorcerers, witches, and diviners, any who cross the divide between living and dead, were denounced as evildoers. The Pentateuch did not just ignore its ancestors. It violently hated to be in communication with them. And this too is in line with the prophet Isaiah: 'O house of Jacob, come let us walk in the light of the Lord. For thou hast rejected thy people, the house of Jacob, because they are full of diviners from the east and of soothsayers like the Philistines. . . .' (Isa 2:5–6) The surrounding peoples in the Mediterranean and Aegean regions all had cults of the dead, Egypt, Assyria, and Babylonia, Ugaritic kings and commoners, and Canaan. But in the Pentateuch there is no sign of it. If it had been deliberately removed before the books were edited, why? [10]

This seems a true mystery until one considers the mind-set of the returning exiles. They see failure to heed to prophets as the cause of the disastrous end of the First Temple and the subsequent Babylonian exile. The main point is that YHWH does not allow necromancy, though there have been many Israelites who naturally think that their God not only allows it but sanctions it as a way to find out His will. Instead of finding food for the dead, the dead themselves, and the people who practice necromancy will themselves go hungry, for they have deeply offended the LORD. Furthermore, having dead around haunting the living would be even more disastrous.

The only question is: At what point in Israelite history does God actually forbid necromancy, and how many people hear the prohibition? There are precursors to the exilic campaign in Deuteronomy and Leviticus. For Mary Douglas, the radical change comes with the book of Leviticus, which she describes as "a totally reformed religion." [11] We have already seen that there were voices in the prophets and the earlier documents that strove for the surety which was achieved by the priestly redactors of Second Temple times (539 BCE–70 CE). Since both the books, Deuteronomy and Leviticus, have preexilic roots, it seems to me that the process begins there and equally with the literary prophets. Douglas' formulation of "a totally reformed religion" is the culmination of a process that had been developing in a variety of places throughout the First Temple period.

Back to the Witch of Endor

UNLIKE THE DEAD in Homer's Hades, who know no more of the earth than humans and who depend on new arrivals for the news, the dead Samuel is still a prophet and knows the outcome of the forthcoming battle. Likely, all the revivable dead have prophetic powers because Saul uses the technical term "inquire" *(dōrēš)* before he names the particular ghost to be raised, as well as the general term "ask" *(šō'ēl)* for the activity, as do the ordinances forbidding all necromantic activity.

Samuel tells Saul the most horrible news possible. Saul had suspected the worst anyway, ever since he had stopped receiving prophetic dreams. God had truly abandoned him for reasons that are not entirely specified in this text. Arguably, the reasons are a matter of speculation in Israelite society, as Saul himself was killed in battle, and David was successful where Saul was not.

The answers that the text provides seem a little contrived, at least as far as the themes of sin and punishment are concerned. Saul previously angered God by sacrificing before Samuel arrives at his war camp, thus usurping the privileges of the Shilonite priesthood, a social blunder that the Bible reflects with great candor. We can see in this incident a power struggle between the traditional priesthood and the newly-appointed king. And now that Samuel is dead, it is he who tells Saul that God has left him.

It is the historical record of Saul's defeat that the narrator must now explain. Saul's sin, necromancy, is retrojected backwards by the court historians to explain his unsuccessful military campaign as divine punishment. In the Israelite epic, Saul becomes a kind of Macbeth, whose willingness to consult with witches for his private ambition presages his end. David manifestly has God's favor because he succeeds where Saul failed and because he finally beats the Philistines to a standstill. Had Saul succeeded in battle we would never have had a story of the Witch of Endor and David would have remained a minor character in the narrative.

The entire Bible might have been edited so as to carefully keep out any reference to life after death, in line with its editorial biases. However it is a national literature, garnered from a variety of places under the scrutiny of an editor who evidently thought some traditions were too holy to leave out, even when they were scandalous. So we find many suggestions of a belief in ancestor cults as well as a life after death underneath the editorial suspicion of it. There were Israelites—a great many or there would not be such a polemic—who did precisely what the Bible warns them not to do. The Bible gives us sure evidence of a giant struggle against a religion like that practiced at Ugarit, a kind of "popular" debased religiosity in the eyes of the Bible. The creature that appears for our medium is not merely a ghost; it is a divine being *(elohim)*. *"Elohim"* is a word which is very commonly used specifically for the God of the Hebrews. Israelites too, we now know, were consulting a god by necromancy, not Saul only. Or, to put it another way, some Israelites must have interpreted the term *"elohim"* to mean their own ancestors in the land; they may have prayed to them and thought they were worshiping their god.[12]

The Marzeah *in the Mouth of the Prophets*

IT DOES NOT seem possible that the story of the Witch of Endor was a *marzeah* feast, rather a simpler, earlier ceremony of divination by necromancy. But there are two places where the preexilic prophets of the Bible explicitly mention the *marzeah*, as well as a few more references that refer to them, both before and after the exile.[13] The first is found in Amos:

> [Woe to those] who lie upon beds of ivory,
>> and stretch themselves upon their couches,
> and eat lambs from the flock,
>> and calves from the midst of the stall;
> who sing idle songs to the sound of the harp,
>> and, like David, improvised on musical instruments;

who drink wine in bowls,
>   and anoint themselves with the finest oils,
>   but are not grieved over the ruin of Joseph!
> Therefore they shall now be the first of those to go into exile,
>   and the revelry of those who stretch themselves shall pass
>   away. (Amos 6:4–7)

The last line, which includes the word *"mirzaḥ,"* has been difficult to translate. According to McLaughlin, this line is better understood as: "and the 'sprawler's' *marzeaḥ* shall cease," meaning that those who have "sprawled" on their couches (possibly, though not conclusively, implying intoxication, sexual excess, as well as idolatry) for this banqueting will be requited with exile.[14] The passage is an oracle of woe, promising destruction to the affluent of the northern state of Israel who lie on their ivory beds and neglect the needy and hence the commandments of the LORD. The description of their insensitivity to the needs of the poor, lying around drinking and eating all day, together with a word which could be vocalized *marzeaḥ,* suggests, rather than states, the kind of drinking feasts that we saw in Canaanite culture. Yet it is not idolatry itself which is their sin. They are secure and confident; however their luxuriousness is nothing but sin and will be punished. So the existence of an explicit, sinful *marzeaḥ,* as in Ugarit culture, is moot, unless there is other evidence to support it.[15]

There is some. There are hints of the practice in Hosea 9:1–6 and Hosea 7:3–7 of the *marzeaḥ,* though there are no direct references to it. The only other direct reference to the *marzeaḥ* occurs in Jeremiah 16:5–9:

> For thus says the LORD: Do not enter the house of mourning *(marzeaḥ),* or go to lament, or bemoan them; for I have taken away my peace from this people, says the LORD, my steadfast love and mercy. Both great and small shall die in this land; they shall not be buried, and no one shall lament for them or cut himself or make himself bald for them. No one shall break bread for the mourner, to comfort him for the dead; nor shall any one give him the cup of consolation to drink for his father or his mother.
>
> You shall not go into the house of feasting *(marzeaḥ)* to sit with them, to eat and drink. For thus says the LORD of hosts, the God of Israel: Behold, I will make to cease from this place, before your eyes and in your days, the voice of mirth and the voice of gladness, the voice of the bridegroom and the voice of the bride.

The passage explicitly mentions the *marzeaḥ* and explicilty clarifies the funeral context, even without the RSV translating the exact words in an identifiable way. John McLaughlin finds this reference insufficient for proving the existence of the Canaanite *marzeaḥ* here because the religious context is not clarified.[16] It may be that the term is being used ironically, and it may be that we do not adequately understand the context of this passage. But, contrary to McLaughlin, I find the relationship of the feast to the punishment convincing. Mourners are specifically mentioned, and the oracle of woe is promising death and destruction without proper burial to those who participate in the feasting. To me, this suggests a much more explicit funeral and ritual context than McLaughlin allows. It ironically states that the punishment for practicing such funeral rites will be the end of wedding joys.

So I conclude from these passages that there were a variety of funeral practices which offended the prophets, rites which resembled the funeral feasts of the Canaanites and Mesopotamians. Jeremiah 16:7 criticizes what appears to be banqueting: "No one shall break bread for the mourner, to comfort him for the dead; nor shall any one give him the cup of consolation to drink for his father or his mother." Ezekiel 24 suggests the same, as well as questions other kinds of mourning customs: "Sigh, but not aloud; make no mourning for the dead. Bind on your turban, and put your shoes on your feet; do not cover your lips, nor eat the bread of mourners" (v 17). Or again, "Your turbans shall be on your heads and your shoes on your feet; you shall not mourn or weep, but you shall pine away in your iniquities and groan to one another" (v 23). We may suspect that the bread of mourners is related to the meal of unleavened bread the witch of Endor fed Saul and related to Hebrew *marzeaḥ*, likely it is related to the offerings of bread in Mesopotamia and Canaan. Evidently, unleavened bread and ritual meals had a wide ritual context associated with the appearance of a god.[17] We have already seen that Israelites were indulging in necromancy. For me, this is adequate demonstration of a religious connection, though exactly what was forbidden in the Biblical texts remain elusive.

It seems clear that these customs are at least parallel to Canaanite culture and existed in significant strength in the Israelite state to warrant continuous and strong legislation as well as prophetic denunciation. The Bible maintains that the religion of the North was effectively Canaanite, though they pretend to worship the God of Israel, and thus they incur terrible punishment which eventually comes to Judah as well. These polemics serve as an explanation of the disastrous events that God allows to come upon Judah when they are conquered by the Babylonians (587 BCE).

Such is the meaning of the story of the golden calf in the Exodus narrative. Though it purports to be an event in the time of Moses, it actually indicts the northern cult with its calf symbol for the God of Israel, implicating the northern Levites for the sin.[18] That does not mean that Canaanite influence was absent in Judah, as we have already seen. Nor does it imply that idolatry was practiced by a small group of people, or that it was constantly diminishing. The Bible itself tells us that various kings were more open to Canaanite and Mespotamian religion and that the international diplomacy necessary to insure the survival of the Judean state brought with it detested religious practices, often through the agency of royal foreign wives. Archeology tells us that the culture of the Canaanites was widespread.[19]

Furthermore there are several exilic references (Ezek 8:7–13, 39:17–20) that may fit the *marzeaḥ* context, suggesting that it did not entirely cease with the destruction of the First Temple (587 BCE). The priestly source was not entirely successful in restricting it. The cult of the dead apparently continues to be an institution throughout the Hellenistic and Rabbinic periods as there are many suspicious references to *symposia* (Greek dinner parties, but a credible translation for *marzeaḥ*) in the LXX (the Greek translation of the Hebrew Bible) and associated literature. The word *"marzeaḥ"* appears in Rabbinic literature as well.

Israel's Sketchy Portrait of the Afterlife: Sheol and Gehenna

THE ISRAELITES grieved for the dead with the rest of humanity. We now know that grieving included cutting their clothes, wearing sackcloth, and invoking elaborate lamentations when they could be afforded, as in the other cultures of the ancient Near East. Israelites buried their dead with grave goods, though donating of the tithe or using it for grave goods is explicitly forbidden in the Bible: "I have not eaten of the tithe while I was mourning, or removed any of it while I was unclean, or offered any of it to the dead; I have obeyed the voice of the Lord my God, I have done according to all that thou hast commanded me" (Deut 26:14). The relationship between these rules and burial practices is not well understood. But it seems likely that giving the tithe to the dead is forbidden because it implies again that YHWH might be identified with the ancestral spirits. It also prevents the tithe from delivery to the priests of YHWH. On the other hand, providing food for the dead itself is not explicitly forbidden and was likely practiced.

Under such circumstances, we can understand the Bible's reticence to go into detail about the abode of the dead. The silence is not total, though the portrait of the final disposition of the dead is similar to the portrait of death in the Canaanite cities around them, not at all the optimistic notion of life after death which we find in Rabbinic Jewish and Christian writings.

In addition, there are not any notions of hell and heaven that we can identify in the Hebrew Bible, no obvious judgment and punishment for sinners nor beatific reward for the virtuous. Indeed, the most famous term for the abode of the dead in the Bible, *Gē' Hinnôm* (Josh 15:8; 18:16) or *Gê Ben-hinnôm* (*Gehenna*, as it was known in Greek), is not associated with hell or afterlife in the Hebrew Bible. It refers to a geographical locale on earth—literally, the Valley of Hinnom—a large ravine which can be seen today on the southwestern corner of the old city of Jerusalem. *Ge Ben Hinnom* remains this site's common name in modern Israel to this very day. In ancient times, it was apparently both a city garbage dump and the scene of an idolatrous cult where children were passed through fire (2 Kgs 23:10; 2 Chr 28:3; 33:6; Jer 7:31; 32:35).[20] In the Hellenistic period, and particularly in the New Testament, the location came to be used metaphorically for hell, full of fiery torment, which is probably why it is so familiar to us. But it does not yet have those connotations during the First Temple period.

To characterize the Biblical view of life after death, we must first investigate the use of the Biblical term "Sheol" (Hebrew: *še'ōl*). This is the term that is most often used in the Bible for the ultimate disposition of the dead (approximately 66 times and never to my knowledge in any other Semitic language) with its meaning clarified throughout the early period of Biblical history, although the terms "Abaddon" (perhaps forgetfulness or perdition), "pit," and "ditch," are used as well. It is likely that all these terms gather their implications from *qeber*, the more common term for "grave," with which they are often linked in apposition. In the story of Korah in Numbers 16:30–33, the earth opens to swallow some rebels whole, who then "go down alive into Sheol."[21]

No one completely understands the root meaning of the term "Sheol" but the best guess is that it comes from the widespread root *š-'-l*, meaning "to ask or inquire"—thus linking it with the story of the witch of Endor and the personal name "Saul" (Hebrew: *Sha'ul*), with which it shares the identical consonantal root. This immediately suggests a reason for Saul's name: He has attempted to "inquire" about his fate from the dead. There are some oblique parallel usages in other ancient Near Eastern roots. Arabic records these roots in many senses; the Akkadian term *"sa'ilu"* denotes "one who consults spirits"; and the Old South Arabic word *"m-s-'-l"* connotes an oracle.[22]

The other terminology seems less problematic. The abode of the dead is, as the various names imply, a region somewhere near the primal waters, under the earth (Num 16:30; Job 26:7), just as it was in Mesopotamia, as Hades was for the Greeks. Indeed, the Septuagint (hereafter LXX) routinely translates the Hebrew "Sheol" with the Greek, "Hades." And, like the Greek Hades, it was neither a place of reward nor of punishment inherently, merely the final destination where the dead go. It is dark and disordered (Job 10:20–21), a land of silence (Pss 94:17; 115:17), sometimes a grim city with gates (Job 38:17; Isa 38:10) and far from the presence of God, exactly as in Mesopotamian and Canaanite myth.

The abode of the dead is sometimes personified as an insatiable demon with wide open, gaping jaws (Prov 1:12; Isa 5:14; Hab 2:5). This is, no doubt, due to borrowing from the Canaanites, where the picture is far more common.[23] In Canaanite mythology, the pit *(ḫ-r)*, Arabic Ḥaur, and Akkadian Ḥurru all appear. In Ugarit the god Ḥauran appears, which no doubt contributes to the occasional Biblical personification. But nowhere in Hebrew society is the abode of the dead regarded as a place of special punishment. The notion of a fiery hell or place of punishment is a much later concept, likely due to Persian influence.

The Psalms and Hebrew Poetry about the Afterlife

THE BEST PLACE to see the importance of Sheol in Hebrew thought is in the book of Psalms. Unfortunately, Psalms is a composite work that does not easily yield up the date of each individual poem. Psalm 115 gives a short and very articulate view of the cosmos of the Hebrews:

> The heavens are the LORD's heavens, but the earth he has
> given to human beings.
> The dead do not praise the LORD, nor do any that go down
> into silence.
> But we will bless the LORD from this time on and
> forevermore. Praise the LORD! (Ps 115:16–18)

Sheol is the abode of the dead. The dead are not remembered and they are cut off both from the living and the presence of God:

> For Sheol cannot thank you,
> death cannot praise you;
> those who go down to the Pit cannot hope
> for your faithfulness.
> The living, the living, they thank you,
> as I do this day;
> fathers make known to children
> your faithfulness. (Isa 38:18–19)

This theme is repeated in Psalms 88 and 115:17 "The dead do not give praise to the LORD, nor do any who go down into silence." And this idea continues right into the Greek period. Sirach 17:27 also reflects this belief in the virtual nonexistence of the dead.

> Who will sing praises to the Most High in Hades,
> as those who are alive and give thanks?
> From the dead, as from one who does not exist,
> thanksgiving has ceased.

Were this a Canaanite document, one could easily assume that the kingdom of the grave is not part of one god's purview, being ceded to another power. Here one sees a similar thought expressed. But it is not openly stated; no opposing god could have any role under the watchful eye of the editor. In this touching petition, the Hebrew Bible recoils from discussing the kingdom of the dead.

Hidden Scriptural Evidence of the Polemic?

AS THE TEXTS from Ugarit have become more and more understandable and available, more and more possibilities for the relationship between cultures have emerged. The highwater mark was probably Mitchell Dahood's *Psalms* for the Anchor Bible series, which has been characterized with some justification as "parallelomania." [24] In it an enormous number of parallels between Ugarit and Israelite psalms were adduced.

Virtually every occurence of the word "land" in the Hebrew Bible has been claimed as a reference to the Canaanite underworld. Some claims have proved intriguing and others seem unlikely.[25] In like fashion, several interesting cruxes of Biblical statements that have heretofore been considered innocent are of interest to our inquiry into the Bible's notions of the afterlife.

Even the commandment to honor "your mother and father" that *"your"*[26] days may be long in the land may originally refer to ancestor worship, honoring parents after they have died, instead of through acts of filial piety while they are alive, as we interpret it today.[27] The insistence on "monotheism" in our parlance is therefore a philosophical shorthand way of expressing a much more complicated religious struggle. The prohibition against recognizing the ancestor gods as anyone else than YHWH, to practice or perform the cults of the Canaanites, yields the phenomenon we first noticed, the Bible's reticence to spell out notions of life after death. But, in spite of the reticence, there is no doubt that such practices were known to Hebrew culture, a notion that the editors of the Bible relied on but otherwise thought too dangerous (idolatrous) to include in their writings.

There are other places in the Bible where Sheol is depicted as not beyond the power of God (Job 26:6; Ps 139:8; Amos 9:12). Many of these passages again underline the constant Biblical refrain that God is the only God. They contradict the notion that Sheol contains no presence of God. It is hard to know whether this represents an evolutionary step in the development of monotheism or merely an alternative poetic trope which the psalmists and prophets could use. In any case, we should note that both statements occur in Biblical tradition. In many passages of the Bible, YHWH is God of the living and the dead, of this world and the next. These sentiments are most probably part of the Biblical polemic against other gods, in this case, against the notion that there is another god who is "Lord of the Underworld," as there was in every other culture surrounding the Hebrews.

More Optimistic Views of Death

IT IS SUGGESTED by L. R. Bailey that "within the Hebrew Bible, descriptions of biological death fall into two basic categories: An individual may experience either a 'good' or a 'bad' death."[28] Abraham's death at a ripe old age is an example of a good death, as he is "gathered to his ancestors" (literally: fathers). This suggests that death is, in some way, a family reunion. Eliphaz tells Job to seek the fate of the righteous: "You shall come to your grave in ripe old age, as a shock of grain comes up to the threshing floor" (Job 5:26).[29] Job does live to a ripe old age, seeing his children to the fourth generation, which is a rare privilege.

Wherever Sheol is mentioned, evil *(böse)*, untimely death is invariably at hand.[30] Jacob, distraught over the presumed death of Joseph, says: "I will go down to my son, mourning into Sheol" (Gen 37:35) and when the brothers tell him they must bring Benjamin back to Egypt he says: "You shall bring down my gray hairs with sorrow to Sheol" (Gen 42:38). The brothers say the same things about their father (Gen 44:31). Yet in the end, Jacob has a peaceful death: "And when Jacob had made an end of commanding his sons, he gathered up his feet unto the bed and expired, and he was gathered into his ancestors" (Gen 49:33). Perhaps this is indicative of the special use of language of the narrator of the E source in the Joseph legend. But it is shared by the narrator of the David/Solomon succession narrative.

In the succession narrative, David instructs Solomon not to allow Shimei ben Gera or Joab to live but to bring his gray hairs down to Sheol in blood (1 Kgs 2:9) and not in peace (1 Kgs 2:6). Afterward, David rests with his people and is buried in the city of David. The two deaths contrast with David's.

The phrase "being gathered to one's ancestors" (literally: fathers; i.e., forefathers, kin) appears to indicate proper burial and, if so, the term "fathers" is used as a common plural, including both genders as both men and women were buried in the same way and in the same places.[31] It is possible that the phrase originally indicated the practice of mixing the bones of the family in common for final disposition, which is an Iron Age innovation, evidenced throughout the Biblical period.[32]

A. Heidel and Philip S. Johnston have pointed out that the phrases "being gathered to one's ancestors" and "resting with one's ancestors" are not exactly equivalent with being buried, as Jacob is "gathered" several weeks before his body is buried in the land of Israel (Gen 50:1–13).[33] But it is possible that they merely anticipated the successful conclusion in the foreshortened narrative. If so, the expression outgrows its original context as immediate burial. It may even suggest that there was a ritual process of merging one's individuality with the collective ancestry of the people.[34]

This has yielded an interesting hypothesis from Eric Meyers that these phrases and practices indicate more firm Israelite control of the land.[35] It certainly seems to shed light on the language the Bible uses in describing the burials of the patriarchs: "Abraham breathed his last and died in a good old age, an old man and full of years, and was gathered to his ancestors" (Gen 25:8). We see the same phenomenon with regard to Jacob's death in Genesis 49:33. The Bible's description may well imply separate actions: "dying in a good old age," and being "gathered to his ancestors."

The phrase also refers to kings. To sleep "with one's ancestors" when describing the king evidently was meant to exclude death in battle, where the body could be lost. Peaceful burial with one's ancestors is itself seen as a reward for a good life. It is conceivable, therefore, that "being gathered to one's ancestors" refers to the whole primary inhumanation process, where the body is exposed in a tomb until only the bones remain and that "burial" proper referred to the secondary burial, the final disposition of the bones. This solution to the problem seems consistent with the text and the archeological evidence.

This may suggest that kings who died in battle were often buried where they fell, if their bodies could be recovered at all, whereas kings who died in "a good old age" were gathered to their ancestors, attaining the blessing of their bodies being available for proper burial near the capital. The burial of Josiah, arguably the best king that Judah enjoyed and the equal of David and Solomon, represents an interesting and more complicated case: Although he died in battle against the Egyptians at Megiddo (2 Kgs 23:29), the prophet Huldah had already prophesied that he would "be gathered to his fathers and be buried in peace" (2 Kgs 22:20). But there was nothing "peaceful" about his death, since he died in battle. After his death, his body was recovered and brought back to Jerusalem for burial in his own tomb (2 Kgs 23:30). And perhaps this is the sole consolation which the phrase "in peace" implies in this case.[36]

To make matters even more complicated, there is some evidence that "being gathered with one's ancestors" was a more generalized Canaanite conception as well. In Ugarit, the "gathered ones" (qabuṣi, KTU 1.161) represent the group of dead, divinized royal figures who are called upon with sacrifices to ensure peace for the land.[37] It may well be that the Ugaritic terminology sheds light on the later usage in the Hebrew narrative, especially as the patriarchs seem to have been especially remembered cultically in the various places where the narrative places them. The resulting conclusion about the Bible's turn of phrase is that we cannot entirely tell what the Bible means when it says that a person was "gathered to his ancestors." It is obvious that we will need to look at Israelite burial practices, but the archeological record contains enough variation to prevent many sure conclusions.

Material Evidence for the Disposition
of the Israelite Dead

THUS FAR, we have been investigating the texts of the Hebrew Bible until the Babylonian exile. But, as has been suggested all along, the texts are not the only way in which to study the religion of a people; there was a popular side in which Canaanite religious practices held more importance, in spite of the objection of Biblical writers and prophets. This side is not easy to find, as all our texts come down to us from the cult of YHWH, which viewed itself as victorious but only after terrible penalties of destruction and exile were paid.

Archeological evidence gives us a less tendentious view of ordinary Israelite life. Israelite burial locations and styles, as everywhere, depended on the deceased's station in life. There is also a great deal of variation in types of burial, including jar burials, individual burials in coffins (wood or ceramic) or without, cist tombs, pit burials, bench or niche burials, and communal or family tombs. Grave goods were very common. In the Late Bronze Age for Israel, during the settlement period (1200–1000 BCE), there is a distinct difference between lowland and highland patterns of burial, suggesting that the Israelite and Judahite patterns are more often seen in the hills, the strongholds of early Israelite tribal life.[38] The lowland patterns are considerably more sophisticated, as one would expect, since that is where the civilized Canaanite cities were.

Later on, Biblical cemeteries were often placed outside but near cities. In the Iron Age, they might contain fifty to one hundred tombs, with perhaps twice that many occupants, as tombs could be shared, often many times over. The tombs themselves ranged from rock-hewn to masonry-constructed to pits, and most commonly were composed of shafts with niche-like chambers, known to the Greeks as *arcosolia* (Hebrew: *Kukhim*). These niches were used for primary inhumation but afforded easy enough entry for collection of the bones afterwards. Quite often in the First Temple period (932–587 BCE), however, the bones were pushed to a stone groove at the back of the niche, which then allowed the niche to be reused. Secondary burial (collection of the bones in ossuaries) can be demonstrated in the First Temple period but became much more general in the Second Temple period (539 BCE–70 CE), when we have textual evidence and fine examples of ossuaries, as well as an occasional sarcophagus.[39]

Burials under floorboards were also common in the Iron Age. Perhaps those buried there were more in need of care or more closely associated with the household, such as women and children. Infants were often buried in storage jars there, close to an adult.[40] Twenty percent of the burials were not found either in cemeteries or settlements but in open fields. It is hard to interpret this datum. They may just have been the owners or tenants of the land. But they may also have been the community's leaders exclusively, who were perhaps understood to be the "guardians" of the crops. The practice of placing graves in fields was still common enough in the Talmudic period that it was mentioned without special legal comment in tractate Pe'ah.[41]

The poor could be buried in common graves (2 Kgs 23:6). Wealthy Israelites buried their dead in family tombs, like the Canaanites (Gen 23; 2 Sam 19:38; 1 Kgs 13:22). There are no obvious mortuary temples above the graves as in the royal houses of Ugarit, which is an important but inconclusive datum. Whether for the rich or the poor, the graves were often reused, especially in Iron Age times, with the bones being pushed aside or alternatively collected in pits where they were gathered for final disposition. In the Hebrew cases, we think that the bones were pushed aside more frequently than in the Canaanite cases. It is safe to say that in most respects the customs of the ordinary Israelites in burial scarcely differed from the Canaanites at all, and we often have difficulty distinguishing them in archeological sites, especially before the end of the eighth century BCE, when the effects of the prophets and finally the Deuteronomic Reform (621 BCE) began to enforce a purified religion.[42]

The Soul, or Nefesh, *and the Spirit, or* Ruaḥ

IF THE TERM "soul" *(nefesh, npš, nepeš)* in Hebrew means what it appears to mean, then there has to be something that survives death in the ancient Biblical world. Unlike the Canaanite cognate, the *"nefesh"* in Hebrew largely refers to a quality of a living person. Evidently, *"nefesh"* means what we would call a "soul," generally meaning a human being's personality or "personhood."

The word for what survives death in ancient Hebrew is *"refa'"* (*repa'*, plural, *refa'im*), which essentially means "ghost" or "spirit." Much has been made of these two word uses by scholars who question the consensus that the Hebrew Scriptures do not give us a doctrine of the afterlife.[43] John W. Cooper is especially anxious to impart the notion of "an ensouled afterlife," an intermediate state, to Hebrew thought. He is joined by James Barr who suggests in his provocative book on life after death that in Hebrew thought, the *nefesh* or *refa'* survives death in a significant and important way.[44]

Yet, there are not many grounds for optimism about what lies beyond the grave nor for thinking that this was the basis of later notions of immortal souls in a a beatific afterlife. The Bible does not describe an afterlife with anywhere near the intensity of the Mesopotamians or Canaanites, and if it existed in popular religion (as seems obvious), there is little reason to suspect that it would be any more beatific than the Canaanite notions.

True, *refa'* ("ghost") is logically a survival of the identity of the person. But to call *nefesh* an "intermediate state" is to assume that the ancient Israelites expected an amelioration in the afterlife or an intermediate state before the prophetic "end of days." There is no ancient evidence for an intermediate state; how the dead were to participate in "the day of the LORD," which the prophets sometimes predicted, is not evident. First, there are centuries of Hebrew thought before a "day of the LORD" in the sense of an eschatological end appears. Likely, it was to be enjoyed only by the living at first.

The real issue is not whether anything survives death but whether that something is punished for its sins or lives on in a beatific and desirable way. We must be careful of this distinction throughout: When *"refa',"* or *"nefesh,"* means nothing more than "shade," "ghost" or "spirit" in describing the afterlife, then it is no different from a host of other words for ghost throughout world religions. If there is no beatific afterlife and no judgment, then it does not matter much whether the "soul" is a "wraith," a "spirit," a "ghost," or a "shade." It is not an afterlife to be desired.[45]

Although *nefesh* occurs quite frequently in the Hebrew text, there is no evidence that the ancient Hebrews conceived of an "immortal" soul in our philosophical sense of the term. The notion of an immortal soul comes largely from Greek philosophers, especially Plato. We will discuss that concept when it is historically appropriate within Hebrew thought—that is, during the Hellenistic period, when Greek thought influenced Jewish thought deeply. The earlier, more native Hebrew notion was more inchoate and is tied to Canaanite notions; *nefesh* is even directly cognate with the Ugaritic term. It is important because it marks the identity of the person but not because it survives death for a beatific reward.

Besides the concept of soul, the Hebrews talked about the life principle as breath (rûaḥ, *ruaḥ*), which God shares with humans (Gen 1:1). The notions of *ruaḥ* and *nefesh* must be very similar, as is logical considering that "*nefesh*" is derived from one of the Hebrew words for "breathing." Basically, *nefesh* means something like "breath" or "life principle," which is evident in the first references to it in the Hebrew Bible, when the LORD God breathes into the man's nostrils the breath of life (*nishmat ḥayyim*, from *nešāmâ, nishamah*) and he became a living soul (*nefesh ḥayyah*, Gen 2:7). The word "*nishamah*," in this context, appears to signify "inhalation;" so a living soul is created by the inhalation of life. Probably, "*nefesh*" in this context means something like "living" or "breathing" creature, since it is also used frequently of animals, especially in the creation stories. It only means "soul" in a casual way, as when when we say that a ship went down with all souls lost, meaning all persons or lives lost. Indeed, the term "dead soul" actually occurs in Hebrew writing, where it means a corpse.[46] In short the problem is that we use the term differently from the Hebrews: We think we have a soul; the Hebrews thought they were a soul.

Consequently the Hebrews did not automatically or characteristically distinguish between body and soul as we may do. Instead, they thought of the two as a kind of unity, an animated body, where the *nefesh* served as the animator, or perhaps something more, like what we would call the "person" or even the "personality," rather than the life-breath, for which "*neshamah*" or "*ruaḥ*" served more explicitly. But it would be fruitless to seek exact understandings of these terms. Although the human person was thought of by the Hebrews to be a totality, as our term "person" implies, the Hebrews sometimes talked about the *nefesh* as departing or returning (Gen 35:18; 1 Kgs 17:21–22). Perhaps, at these particular times, it is better to think of it as a "self," noting that when the Hebrews use it they are discussing an individual in one way or another.

If we understand *nefesh* as meaning personhood or self, we must again be careful not to import modern notions of consciousness to a Hebrew notion. As personhood, the soul in Hebrew thought can undergo a kind of increase or decrease in strength, corresponding with a person's strength, character, or personality. To "pour out the soul" is to be faint, unconscious perhaps, or merely helpless (1 Sam 1:15; Ps 42:5). A strong soul can surpass human limitations by achieving a certain fortuitous grace, or "charisma" (Gen 23:8; 2 Kgs 9:15; Ps 33:20). Death is evidently the ultimate "soul-diminisher." When someone receives the "spirit of the LORD," it denotes a prophetic gift, not an ordinary quality of the personality, but a divine quality which gives the person an extraordinary strength, charisma, or skill.

In many ways, the ancient Hebrews thought of "soul" like "spirit," though "spirit" is something that a few chosen messengers explicitly share with the deity (i.e., "the spirit of God was upon me"), in creation, in life, and perhaps later after death, but only on specific occasions. The Bible does not tell us how the spirit manifested in humans in any explicit way. It was one of the many mysterious qualities in the life of the Hebrew. When discussing the meaning of a human life, the Bible always talks about life before the grave and usually concentrates on the issue of descendants, land, and the favor of the Lord. Life after death was not a significant part of the First Temple conversation about the meaning of life, but proper burial is.

In short, the ancient Hebrew notion of "soul" has no relationship to the Pythagorean and Platonic notion of an immortal soul, which is deathless by nature and capable of attaining bodiless felicity.[47] Later on, the Hebrews used the word *"nefesh,"* which they had been using for centuries, to do the work of the Greek notion of the word "soul" and when they wanted to express an intermediary step for the dead before they resurrected. Therefore, all these later examples will be ambiguous and difficult for us to parse because the same word can stand for either the Greek immortal soul, the intermediary state without a Greek sense of immortality, or both alternately, or even at once, in the same document. Yet, even in the Hellenistic period, many Jews spoke of the body/soul as the unity in a person.

Explicit Revivifications in the First Temple Period

THERE ARE several revivifications in the Hebrew Bible. In the Elijah-Elisha cycle, three different people are, at least, resuscitated from the dead: the son of the widow of Zarephath (1 Kgs 17:17–24), the son of the Shunamite woman (2 Kgs 4:18–37), and the man who was thrown into Elisha's grave (2 Kgs 13:20–21). These are all treated as resuscitations. They rise from the dead to live out their normal lives. They are miracles, nevertheless, extraordinary events which are worthy of special note and not the common fate of humanity. God is even praised as the author of miraculous resuscitations in Deuteronomy 32:39 and 1 Samuel 2:6 (see 2 Kgs 5:7).[48] None of them are specifically mentioned as the reward for a good life, though the mothers are praised. None are signs of a coming resurrection for all. They simply show the power of God over death and the extent of God's favor to the prophets.

The notion that God is the author of all life and death is found in several places in the Psalms and never more poignantly than in Psalm 104:29–30:

When you hide your face, they are dismayed;
> when you take away their breath[49] *(ruaḥ)*, they die and
>> return to their dust.

When you send forth your spirit,[50] they are created;
> and you renew the face of the ground.

According to Psalms, human being is purely a terrestrial creature who exists only at the pleasure of the deity.[51] In essence, when the Lord gives His breath to a person, that person lives. If He removes it, that person dies.

The Rewards of the Covenant

WHAT IS MOST obvious in the history of preexilic Israelite thought is that reward and punishment are certainties in this life. It is possession of the land, many offspring, length of days, and a favored life that is promised by God for obedience to his covenant. As God says to Abraham in Genesis: "As for you yourself, you shall go to your fathers in peace; you shall be buried in a good old age" (Gen 15:15).

Land, length of days, descendants, and a happy life is what the covenant promises to the Israelites. The prophets communicate the same concept, unlike Deuteronomy, in the technical language of treaties, but in the broader language of a covenantal agreement. Many prophets speak directly of covenant but do not envision it as a treaty. When the prophet Amos delivers the words of YHWH, "You only have I known of all the families on earth. Therefore I will punish you for all your iniquities" (Amos 3:2), he is not referring to a treaty. Rather, he is speaking the words of YHWH, who is publicly claiming a legal grievance. Amos reminds his hearers that Israel entered into a contract with YHWH, sealed by an oath, on which the people have defaulted. YHWH must therefore seek redress by covenantal means. He is describing what we might call a divine lawsuit, undertaken to preserve an arrangement foresworn by one partner.

Job

THE BOOK OF Job is a major Biblical voice on the issue of afterlife, a fact that has been noticed by many scholars. What is not so obvious is that it is, in a way, a development of the Israelite covenant metaphor. Many of the prophets take up this metaphor of the prophetic law-suit against Israel. Hosea himself uses the notion of a marriage gone sour, which is another obvious contractual obligation sworn by an oath. In so doing, he again and again uses images of marriage that were used by the Canaanites beforehand. Indeed, Ba'al's name itself literally means "husband" as well as "master." But God is not a contented partner; He periodically contemplates suing his adulterous spouse for divorce, invoking stringent penalties and threatening the ultimate penalty for his adulterous partner.

Only in the book of Job is the converse notion ever articulated, that human beings can justifiably sue God for nonperformance of His contractual duties. For that particular argument to be at all logically convincing, there cannot be a notion of life after death of any real consequence. If there were an afterlife of substantial consequence, then Job's suffering would not reach the level of a legally actionable suit against God. If there were an afterlife, Job could say that he is falsely accused by his friends, and that his predicament is painful. But he could not challenge God's justice because the score would not be complete in this life. That is why one finds the notion of Sheol present in the book of Job—not postmortem reward or punishment, merely the final disposition of souls. Indeed, it is the book of Job that shows us the very limits to which the older metaphor can go. It was the solace of *l'ancien regime*. The solace which the book of Job provides was not one which the majority of the people of Israel understood or accepted in the Second Temple period, where God was viewed as having made far better provision for rewards in the afterlife.

An enormous amount of research has been done on the book of Job. It is one of the most arresting, puzzling, and provocative pieces of ancient literature to have reached modern eyes.[52] Yet it is still not well understood. Part of our puzzlement is due to its composition, which is complex, layered, and not entirely consistent. The Job of the prose narrative at the beginning and end of the work finds an entirely different consolation and resolution to his plight—patience and acceptance—than the Job whose irascible words are part of the body of the text. Indeed, it is difficult to see where the notion of the patience of Job comes from at all, since he is irascible throughout the book. Then too, arguments which are discussed and dismissed are consistently brought up again by Job's friends and by Elihu, only to be shown irrelevant again at the end of the poetic section and yet receive a kind of limited validation in the prose conclusion. No doubt this was an issue over which the ancient culture itself was deeply conflicted.

To explain these phenomena, we must understand that the poetry within the book of Job, with its arguments about wisdom and justice, was characteristic of the entire ancient Near East. A large part of Job is merely an anthology of interesting poetry, which the editors preserved by including it in this pseudodrama. Consequently, we should not look for the kind of character or thought development that we associate with Western drama.

THE ABSENCE OF SATAN IN JOB

Many scholars have pointed to the character of Satan in the story of Job to explain evil, suffering, and death. Since Christianity, especially evangelical and fundamentalist Christianity, lives with a lively sense of Satan's kingdom in opposition to God, it naturally seeks confirmation for these beliefs in the book of Job. But the character of Satan, as he appears in Christianity and apocalyptic literature, is totally lacking in the book of Job. The character, who appears in the prose introduction, is not Satan but "the satan," a phrase which in Hebrew means only "the antagonist" or "the adversary," not a proper name of a character, and must be taken as a technical courtroom term such as "the prosecuting attorney." In any event, since "the antagonist" appears consistently with the definite article *(the),* no one with the proper name Satan appears here. Hebrew usage of the definite article is quite like English in this one respect. That means there is no consistent evil character in the drama of Job, only one of God's courtiers. The *hassaṭan* seems to designate the job description for a nameless member of God's divine council, the heavenly court whose responsibility it is to argue against proposals. The title designates something like our term the "Attorney General," referring to the office rather than the proper name of any particular attorney general, like John Ashcroft or Janet Reno.

THE LAWSUIT METAPHOR IN JOB

Some ideas in Job are surely developed by an editorial hand. A short but extremely suggestive article by J. J. M. Roberts gives us a significant suggestion about what that development is.[53] Roberts shows that a legal, courtroom metaphor is particularly important and relevant for Job 9. Actually I think the legal metaphor is even more important than Roberts suggests. It is one of the few themes that continues throughout the entire book. The book of Job is the only place in the Hebrew Bible that attempts to indict God for having failed at keeping a covenant.

Job begins his narrative by speculating on how to bring God into court. God is the judge; how can anyone enter into legal contention with Him, much less impeach him? God is quintessentially the person who is "wise in heart," with the heart serving as the organ of thought, not emotion, in Hebrew literature. Job complains that he cannot even see God, who is invisible. God continuously passes by him without being perceived. Job also knows that he cannot live long enough for a sufficient trial since God kills all, the just and the unjust. Here is confirmation that the notion of life after death in any meaningful sense must be absent from Job.

JOB'S SEARCH FOR AN ADEQUATE VENUE
AND LEGAL REPRESENTATION

Starting in Job 9:32, the issue of a trial is directly enjoined. Job complains that a trial between him and God is not possible. Who could bring Him into litigation? He designates an "umpire," an arbitrator, who will take his cause before God. But this proves to be impossible. There are no possible intermediaries who can intervene. These themes will come up again in future speeches and will end Job's words.

In Job 13, Job returns to these themes and decides that since there cannot be an "intermediary," he will plead his own case (Job 13:3, 6), though he feels certain that God will kill him.

He begins with a stinging indictment of the opinions of his so-called friends who challenge Job's innocence. He is innocent, he says, and so he will endeavor to do the impossible; he will plead his own case, though it kill him. He taunts God to show His face. He challenges Him to restrain Himself, so that Job himself can present his case and not be destroyed. He prays explicitly that God remove His terror. Then, Job proclaims his testimony (Job 13:20–22). He implies that he is being punished before his trial (13:26–28).

Showing His face is precisely what God eventually does. That is why the appearance of God, far from being an overwhelmingly authoritarian show of force, is actually meant to be an act of supererogatory grace on God's part. God actually does show Himself to Job; He owes Job an explanation, which is exactly what Job receives, even though neither he nor we can fully understand it.

Furthermore, that is exactly what Job expected. All he wanted was the legal attention—to know that his suffering was for a purpose. That is what God's appearance on the scene tells him. This episode of man visited by God is another example of a person who appeals to the heavenly court and receives wisdom as a solace for his suffering.

Job contends that he is too obedient a creature for God to bring before the court. In doing so, he states that there is no life after death worth having (14:1–2):

> A mortal, born of woman, few of days and full of trouble,
> comes up like a flower and withers, flees like a shadow and
>   does not last.

In chapter 14, Job provides a parable comparing trees to people. Job states that humans, unlike trees, have no chance for resuscitation. God allows trees to sprout new life even when their trunks are shrunken and their roots are dried up. At the scent of water, they freshen up and bring forth new shoots. But humans are different; when they grow old, they die. God changes their faces, allows them to age, then sends them away forever to a place where they cannot know even the honors that come to their children (Job 14:1–22). According to Job, a painful fate awaits us all. Nothing in the Bible tells us more clearly of the Hebrew notion of life and death. The notion was fatalistic in the sense that it understood life as a single, non-repeatable event, ending always in death, its natural finality.

THE HEAVENLY DEFENSE ATTORNEY TAKEN
FROM GOD'S DIVINE COUNCIL

The theme of a heavenly counselor is touched upon several more times in Job, although no specific person is designated; perhaps this means that one of God's angels could be appointed as a "court-appointed" attorney to bring Job's case to the heavenly court. God is depicted as having a large retinue as well as a divine council. The satan, the antagonist, is a divine counselor. Job is saying he is entitled to representation in the divine council as well to God. It is crucial to understanding the notion of afterlife in the Hebrew Bible, or more precisely, how the lack of one functions in the Hebrew sensibility. We have several examples in the Hebrew Bible where various divine courtiers serve in specific roles, seemingly in the course of ordinary deliberations. Legal representation is immaterial because in the end it is Job himself who presents his own case.

Job slowly comes to the conclusion that a counselor in the court of God will represent him: "Even now, in fact, my witness is in heaven, and he that vouches for me is on high" (Job 16:19) may imply that God Himself is his counselor or that he will find a special relationship with some other angelic creature. But the latter seems the most likely: "That he would maintain the right of a mortal with God, as one does for a neighbor" (Job 16:21). The issue which Job brings before a heavenly court cannot be resolved by ordinary courtroom procedure. It is an anomalous legal situation.

This situation puts the usual translation of Job 19:25 into sharp relief, which because of its relationship with Christianity has been seen as an affirmation of life after death. Actually the text has been garbled, and we cannot tell exactly what Job intended to say. But he is talking in legal vocabulary (*qum* of 19:25 has a legal context in Deut 19:15ff; Pss 27:12; 35:11; Isa 54:17; Mic 6:1; Job 30:28; 31:14). Verses 28 and 29 of Job 19 clarify that the setting is indeed a courtroom. The legal arbitrator *(go'al)*, who is not yet present will eventually prove Job right, even if it occurs years after his death. Other than this, it is very hard to make good sense out of the following famous lines: [54]

> "O that my words were written down! O that they were
>   inscribed in a book!
> O that with an iron pen and with lead they were engraved on
>   a rock forever!
> For I know that my Redeemer lives, and that at the last he will
>   stand upon the earth;
> and after my skin has been thus destroyed, then in my flesh I
>   shall see God,
> whom I shall see on my side, and my eyes shall behold, and
>   not another. My heart faints within me!
> If you say, 'How we will persecute him!' and, 'The root of the
>   matter is found in him';
> be afraid of the sword, for wrath brings the punishment of the
>   sword, so that you may know there is a judgment."
>   (Job 19:23–29)

Part of Job's predicament is, as he has said before, that he cannot find God nor see Him. Thus he asks for help from an appointed mediator. But it would be best if Job could present his case himself. He first considers sending a written deposition to the court. Then he says he would appear in person if he could. He would do so, even if his skin is seared off by his disease, by the presence of God, or by rotting in the grave.

The third party in this scenario, Job's attorney if you will, has now been variously referred to as an "umpire" (Job 9:33), "witness" (Job 16:19), "interpreter" (Job 16:19; 33:23), and "redeemer" (Job 19:25). The very variety of words used to describe the figure suggests that Job's savior is not a specific person but rather a "court-appointed attorney." However, from the prose narrative, we know that God does employ counselors. "The satan," the adversary, is an example of a member of the heavenly court whose function is to plead the negative side of causes.

Job fears that a hearing can never happen, even though simple justice demands that he have his day in court. And, of course, we understand from the beginning of the story what Job does not know: God already knows that Job's case is just and that the whole predicament is arranged as a test of Job's righteousness. It is, in a way, an exhibition of the contention that people can be good by nature and not merely good for the hope of reward.

However, an analysis of "self-justification" is an impossibility in the world Job inhabits. In Job's world Martin Luther's (1483–1546 CE) enormously influential Reformation arguments against self-justification make no sense at all. For in the end, God takes all our lives, sinner and saint and saves no one in the afterlife. Yet, the book of Job says that even in this world, there are people who are good purely for the sake of being good; Job is good and continues to be good, even though God is punishing him.

JOB'S CASE AGAINST GOD

Job's last speech is a veritable indictment against God. The language he uses clarifies that it is a formal, legal complaint or indictment, even if we do not know in detail precisely what legal or courtly rituals are being described. Job takes pen and ink and signs the indictment (Job 31:35), just as he had wanted to do (Job 19:23). Job 31 is very much the same kind of negative confession as an Egyptian's *Ba* could be expected to recite in the Court of the Two Justices. Note, though, that Job is asking for much more: He is asking for God's vindication in this life.

Job again seeks an indictment against God and we as readers serve as the grand jury. As readers, we are privileged because we know that Job is innocent. What we do not know is exactly what kind of rituals Job was performing to validate his ancient indictment: He would wear the charge on his shoulders or bind it into a crown so he could show that he has been punished with cause. Is this the description of a public indictment or a punishment? Is it a suit to get back the property and loved-ones which God has snatched? We do not know. His subsequent oaths may bear some unspecifiable relationship to exorcism texts; but then again, exorcisms may themselves be a kind of divine court trial. In any event, since Job cannot obtain an indictment in God's court, he will sign his own oath against God's justice and hope to bring God into court.

It is this background that makes sensible the seemingly very authoritarian answer which God gives. Modern Americans react very badly to the overpowering way that God appears and silences Job by citing Job's insignificance. We want a just, equitable, democratic answer with everyone having the same rights, powers, and possibility of redress. We demand an answer to God's callous treatment of Job's innocence. We want to know his family has not come to grief on his account. We want to know why God allows evil in the world. But Job has lesser goals. He merely wants to call God into court. We do not realize what an enormous request Job has asked—God's presence while Job is alive.

GOD WAIVES HIS "EXECUTIVE PRIVILEGE" AND APPEARS

And that enormous request is exactly what Job gets. The answer is precisely what Job hoped for but had no right to expect. The answer to Job is not that God's ways are inscrutable; Job already knows that. The answer is that God is so merciful that He even allows Himself to be taken into court and sued; indeed He willingly comes into His own court to give testimony. God is far more merciful than any ordinary ancient Near Eastern monarch. Job is allowed to see God, if not directly then out of a whirlwind, and he does not even have to ascend to heaven to do so. Unlike the other ancient Near Eastern heavenly voyagers, God comes to Job. And so, even though Job has been frightened and awed by God's power, he leaves court vindicated. And the text maintains that at least one innocent has been vindicated after his suffering, in this life. We expect so much more we miss the affirmation this text makes.

One may speculate as to what produced this timeless masterpiece. Was it the destruction of the Temple, or merely the considered suffering of a single individual? The text means the problem to be framed in the widest possible sense. Apparently, Job does not live in the land of Israel, rather the land of Uz. Although he fears God, he is obviously not an Israelite. So the text reaches a kind of universalism that is characteristic of some of the great prophets. Job is every righteous man asking questions of God. The text therefore asks its questions in the widest possible terms.

Nevertheless, the moral of the story is not only true of all righteous humanity, but is also just as true for the Israelites, those who have entered into a special covenant relationship with God. Ultimately Job was written for the people of Israel. In the end, the historian can go no further but the book stands as a monument to the furthest exploration that the Hebrew writer could go in understanding the covenant between God and his people. It tests the very extremity of the covenant metaphor, the very edge of what mythological thinking could express. Once one explores the notion that God himself could willfully break the covenant through his ations, the metaphor risks its own deconstruction.

Hints of a Beatific Afterlife and
the Consolation of Love

ENOCH AND ELIJAH

There are two great exceptions to the Biblical notion that all must eventually die. They are Enoch and Elijah. There is no doubt that they are meant to be exceptions; they prove the rule by violating it in such circumstances as to clarify that they are the only two exceptions. In a sense they prove the rule by violating it just as Utnapishtim and his wife proved humanity mortal by reaching immortality in Babylonian culture.

The name "Enoch" is mentioned in Genesis 4:17–18 as the son of Cain (J source) but the figure who is important to us is described in Genesis 5 (P source):[55]

> When Jared had lived a hundred and sixty-two years he became the father of Enoch. Jared lived after the birth of Enoch eight hundred years, and had other sons and daughters. Thus all the days of Jared were nine hundred and sixty-two years; and he died. When Enoch had lived sixty-five years, he became the father of Methuselah. Enoch walked with God after the birth of Methuselah three hundred years, and had other sons and daughters. Thus all the days of Enoch were three hundred and sixty-five years. Enoch walked with God; and he was not, for God took him. (Gen 5:18–24)

The name "Enoch" appears to come from the root which means "to train," "to educate," or "to become wise" in Hebrew. Thus a relationship with the Enmeduranki, Etana, and Adapa, seems quite reasonable from the start because they are also famous figures of wisdom who experience heavenly encounters. Furthermore, Enoch occupies the same place in the genealogy as does Enmeduranki in the Babylonian Kings list. Enmeduranki is king of Sippar, a city devoted to the sun god. Enmeduranki is the eponymous ancestor of the *baru* divinatory priests of Babylon, one of the great sources of Mesopotamian wisdom. He gives wisdom through his form of divination. The Biblical Enoch has a solar lifespan, living 365 years, a seemingly foreshortened life in Biblical days.

The text says twice that Enoch walked with God, a phrase that the Bible also only uses of Noah (Gen 6:9), though Adam is described as having walked with God in Eden at the cool of the day (Gen 3:8). Judaism in the time shortly before the time of Jesus develops many interesting traditions that link Enoch to Noah on this basis. They suggest that God walks with Enoch and Noah in paradise, perhaps based on the scene between God and Adam in the garden of Eden.

Afterward the Bible mysteriously omits any reference to Enoch's death. Instead, God "takes" him. Though we do not know the destination of this "taking," several parallels suggest that Enoch is taken to heaven. First, God "takes" Adam and puts him in paradise (Gen 2:15). Then in the parallel assumption story concerning Elijah, Elijah says he will be "taken" and then, when the time comes, he "ascends" by fiery chariot into heaven (2 Kgs 2:11, see excerpt below). Although "take" is a very common word in Hebrew, a few of the other occurrences of the word also suggest something like assumption into heaven. The best interpretation of this puzzling verse is that God assumes Enoch into heaven directly and bodily before death, as Elijah is later assumed into heaven.

Many things about this short report are important, but for now it is important that Enoch does not go to the place where the dead usually go, because his death is not mentioned. Perhaps, like Utnapishtim in Mesopotamia, Enoch will live forever. A similar fate awaits Noah according to several later Jewish traditions. Noah becomes a figure of special veneration at Qumran, for instance (4Q Mess Ar). In any event, an enormous literature builds up around Enoch's adventures in the cosmos. There will be a great deal more to say about the traditions that develop around Enoch in apocalypticism in future chapters.[56]

The same direct assumption into immortality is proffered to Elijah in the Hebrew Bible, but here the Bible goes out of its way to describe the assumption with more dramatic effects than the account of Enoch:

> When they had crossed, Elijah said to Elisha, "Ask what I shall do for you, before I am taken from you." And Elisha said, "I pray you, let me inherit a double share of your spirit." And he said, "You have asked a hard thing; yet, if you see me as I am being taken from you, it shall be so for you; but if you do not see me, it shall not be so." And as they still went on and talked, behold, a chariot of fire and horses of fire separated the two of them. And Elijah went up by a whirlwind into heaven. And Elisha saw it and he cried, "My father, my father! the chariots of Israel and its horsemen!" And he saw him no more. Then he took hold of his own clothes and rent them in two pieces. And he took up the mantle of Elijah that had fallen from him, and went back and stood on the bank of the Jordan. Then he took the mantle of Elijah that had fallen from him, and struck the water, saying, "Where is the LORD, the

God of Elijah?" And when he had struck the water, the water was parted to the one side and to the other; and Elisha went over. (2 Kgs 2:9–14)

Elijah is assumed into heaven in God's own chariot, a divine conveyance we have already seen in Canaan, but Elijah does not die. The fact that he joins the heavenly host in this way was not without implication in Canaanite religious life. But it is left totally unexpressed in the text we have. Instead, Elijah's assumption is understood as the justification for the miraculous powers given to his successor, Elisha, for whom this story functions as a great credential. Elijah's popularity in later Jewish folklore is based on this 2 Kings passage. He can visit Jews at Passover every year because he has not died and can travel back and forth between humanity and God's throne. These two stories represent special beatific afterlives which are not available to the rest of humanity in First Temple times.

THE SONG OF SONGS 8:6

In a different way a famous passage in the Song of Songs tells us an enormous amount about Hebrew views of the afterlife with an almost casual remark:

> Set me as a seal upon your heart,
>   as a seal upon your arm;
> for love is strong as death,
>   passion fierce as the grave.
> Its flashes are flashes of fire,
>   a raging flame. (Songs 8:6)

Marvin Pope, in his translation of The Song of Songs, has especially shown the Canaanite background to the love poetry in The Song of Songs.[57] The nut-garden and the two lovers, consolidating death with love, may be part of the ritual surrounding the memorialization of the *rpa'um*, in Hebrew the *"Refa'im."* Is this an explicit reference to presumed sexual license in the *marzeaḥ* ritual? Pope may well be right in his version; there are certainly many difficulties in understanding the passage. In addition, the poem contains marks of the presence of Canaanite gods (i.e., the word *"reshef,"* also the name of a Canaanite god, occurs twice in v 6b). But the basic meaning is also clear to all without positing a *marzeaḥ*. The Canaanite context is scarcely predominant even to those who have read the ancient Hebrew documents.

156

More important than the message the poem proclaims about love is the message it gives about mortality. We normally assume that love is stronger than death. But this passage says nothing of the sort. Certainly not a paean to undying love, the passage actually assumes a mortal world in which death holds sway. In that context, to say that it is love—embodied, passion included—which can, in a desperate contest, be the equal of death is not an optimistic statement for us in the Christian west. This is a striking contrast to European and American poetic tropes where love conquers all, even death. This sentiment is not so in Hebrew thought. Death is the strongest force on earth other than God Himself. Not even love can conquer death, though love can briefly make a beautiful and awesome conflagration. The references to seals in Song of Songs are obscure but the passage says that love and lovemaking can *equal* death in power by making life worthwhile. It is the statement, rather, of a person who has accepted a fatalistic world and found in it one thing which gives partial consolation to short, and often painful human lives.

The Garden of Eden as a Myth of Lost Immortality: Our Myth or Theirs?

THE ISRAELITES tried to banish the nature myths of Canaan and the native ancestor worship after a great deal of trouble. But the Israelites also valorized an historical myth of YHWH's covenant that bears investigating in the context of life after death. The creation stories in Genesis, indeed the first eleven chapters of Genesis totally, are nothing other than myths retold as if they were history. Ironically, however, the effect of the myth has been much stronger on our society than on that of the Israelites. The Israelites do not mention the garden of Eden often in subsequent literature. But we have so overlaid the story of the garden of Eden with commentary, so remythologized the story, that the Hebrews themselves would likely find it unrecognizable, if not embarrassing.

No story in history has had a more important effect on Western thought than the story of the garden of Eden. In its Christian version especially, it has been the source of the West's assumptions about life, death, immortality, and sexuality. But, a great deal of what we associate with the story is actually absent from the text. These associations have been supplied by various interpretive contexts over the centuries. To take a trivial example, the "apple" of Western iconography is entirely absent from the Hebrew text. So is Satan absent, just as he is absent in Job. This time not even the word "Satan" appears in the text. This has not stopped Western culture from seeing the snake as Satan because that interpretation is much easier to accept and less ambiguous. But, difficult as it may be to explain, the snake of Genesis 2 and 3 is merely a snake, albeit a wonderful snake with the power of speech. It may be similar to the mysterious snake that steals Gilgamesh's wonderful plant of rejuvenation, gaining the power to shed its skin. But it is not a god. Indeed, unlike the snake in *The Gilgamesh Epic*, it is punished.

Nor, as we shall see, is there any concept that can be remotely understood as "original sin." These pregnant words, so important to Christian theology, do not appear in the text; rather, they have been supplied long after, by pious believers seeking to make sense of this simple and rather naive story. Meanwhile, the original subtle meanings of the text have been washed away by our larger conceptualizations.[58]

THE FIRST IS THE LAST

To arrive at an approximation of what the story meant to those who told it orally and shaped its composition means that we must try to dismiss from our minds the accretions with which we are so familiar and whose resonances are so unwanted in our minds.

We must, first of all, separate the creation story of Genesis 1 from the creation story that begins at Genesis 2:3. The first story, the beginning of the Bible, is chosen to be a "Prologue in Heaven" to the story of Israel, a grand opening for the account of the history of Israel's beginnings in Mesopotamia and YHWH's gracious gift of the land of Canaan. The Hebrew editor's concern to eliminate polytheism is repeatedly seen in comparison with Babylonian creation myths. There is no mythological combat or conflict in Genesis's creation story. The gods of sky, earth, and heavenly bodies are merely reduced to objects of YHWH's creation.

Nevertheless, the first creation account in Genesis is trying to express the place of humanity within the world. That is why I call it "a mythological account" in *Rebecca's Children*.[59] Mythology is a narrative which attempts to get at the underlying assumptions of a society. It is not synonymous with fiction; indeed, it is the opposite. Only narratives believed to be true can function as myth. That means that the Eden story, the first 11 chapters of Genesis, and the entire account of the patriarchal period to the arrival of the children of Israel in Canaan, functioned as myth for the children of Israel settled in the land, no matter how much of it turns out to have a kernel of historicity.

So let us attempt to read the mythical code in the first chapter of Genesis. First of all, compare this story to the now familiar creation stories in

Egypt and Mesopotamia and note how the sun has been demoted. This is striking because the sun is almost always a deity in other cultures (often the most important one). The sun god or goddess is certainly the most important deity in understanding the concepts of the underworld because the sun seemingly goes underground every night, only to rise the next morning from the other side of the earth. All the ancient cultures viewed this as a journey through the underworld and made the sun an important carrier of messages to and from the next world.

The Biblical account of creation, on the other hand, portrays the sun as just another object in the heavens, not even a demigod. The sun is not the lord of the underworld; it is merely a creation of God. The same is true with the sea, the earth, and the whole content of the heavens. This not only contradicts the mythologies of the surrounding cultures; it also contradicts much of earlier Israelite thought in which the stars especially are seen as angels, messengers of God. The natural order is no longer filled with squabbling divinities; it is all one large kingdom with everything designed in perfect rule and subordinate to the God of all.[60]

Everything in Genesis is just as it appears in the normal, natural order. Indeed, that is the best clue for understanding the first creation story. What is created is the earth and heavens from our position as inhabitants of it. The whole story is told from the perspective of earth, where humanity lives. And the second obvious part of the story is its hierarchy. Everything is arranged according to an order imposed by the days of the week. The characters are ranked: first is God, the creator; that is evident. He creates by means of His word. Second in importance is the sabbath, the period of rest built right into the universe. And third is the human being, created at the last moment before the sabbath, the most important creature who was created male and female and in the image and likeness of God, whatever that may mean—looks, activities, and powers are all possible interpretations of the story. Every stage meets with God's approval. The whole is described as "very good."

Because human life is precariously dependent on sun and rain, crops and earth, and natural increase from herds, it is not trivial to say that these forces have godlike powers over us. Nevertheless, the Bible goes out of its way to debunk the idea that the natural world is filled with deities. Genesis demythologizes the natural world.

Absent in the Biblical account is special revelation—indeed, absent is the special revelation of the Exodus and the giving of the Law at Mount Sinai—human beings would naturally be led to the worship of the heavens. The Bible seeks to oppose and correct this perfectly natural human tendency from its first verse, by making the heavenly bodies creations of the one all-powerful God, thereby denying that the heavens or any other natural beings are worthy of human reverence. One God is better than many, according to this perspective, because it allows us to view the world as a unity and creation as a single, dynamic force.

In other words, the Bible is aware that nature is morally neutral. Not only is nature silent about right and justice, Genesis 1 goes on to say that no moral rules can be deduced from the fullest understanding of nature. Knowing even that humankind is the highest creature because we are free does not lead to any guidance about how this freedom is to be used. That is why there is an Eden story. The Eden story shows that moral discernment is a divine gift that comes from disobedience and has a cost: the price is our innocence.

ADAM AND EVE IN THE GARDEN OF EDEN:
AN EARLIER ACCOUNT OF CREATION

There are clearly two creation stories present in the Genesis narrative; one concludes at Genesis 2:4a, and the second begins immediately afterwards. The first story creates the man and woman together (Genesis 1:26); in the second, they are created separately, at different times. The first begins with the most famous beginning of all time, "In the beginning. . . ." The second has its own, less well known formula of initiation: "These are the generations. . . ." It is not nearly as dramatic but it is a convention for beginnings within the Bible; the first words of Genesis are not. The first account pictures the cosmos before creation as a watery chaos. The second pictures the world's beginning as a dry desert, waiting for water to allow it to bear fruit. The first account dates from rather late in Biblical history, a Mesopotamian context, where the separation of saltwater from fresh water with a system of canals brought the beginning of city life in the Tigris-Euphrates Delta; it also betrays certain knowledge of Babylonian mythology. Most likely it was written after the Babylonian exile (587–539 BCE).[61]

The second creation account betrays little of this sophisticated scientific, Mesopotamian view of life. Locked within it are the countless experiences of sojourners in the rocky rain shadow of the Judean hills, the leeside of the mountains where fog and dew as much as rain bring what little moisture nourishes the winter grass. Also locked within it is the experience of coming out of the Judean desert to see the verdant cities of the plain, stuck between the sea and the mountains, which coax the rain out of clouds onto the Shephelah and northern valleys every winter.

In the same way, the two stories end quite differently. Genesis 1:1–2:3 ends with the sabbath and a moment of peace and blessing. But the garden of Eden story ends with curses and with a sense both of gained potential and lost potential. The first story moves by means of its architectonic, repeated, high literary form, imposed by repeated phrases: "There was evening and morning, one day"; or "and God saw that it was good." We are led through a countdown of days, which imposes a tacit sense of evolution from good to better. The second story moves occasionally through the repetition of words but more often through dramatic presentation. In the first story, humanity is the most important piece of creation before the sabbath. In the second story, the man and his wife are part of the drama. The differences between the man and woman as thinking and interacting characters impels the whole narrative forward.

The garden of Eden story, which raises the issue of immortality even as it denies it, is by far the more complex story dramatically and is usually thought to be much older, being redacted in the monarchic period from traditions that go back several centuries to the northern and southern tribes. The first chapter of Genesis may be one of the last pieces to be added to the pentateuchal narrative, added by the final, priestly redactors, after having seen the great cities of Babylon, as an adequate prologue in heaven to the story they wanted to tell. The second story is merely a charming and amusing story, full of humor and irony, and also likely one of the earliest stories in the Bible.

The Eden story begins with a true moment of paradise. When the water wells up from the ground, creating what amounts to a desert oasis, the grasses begin to sprout and then the LORD God plants a garden for the man He has just made. Every tree grows pleasing to the sight and good for food with the tree of life in the middle of the garden. Here is the first reference to immortality, and this reference lets us know immediately that we are being transported into a fabulous imagined landscape, like the Mesopotamian myth of Enki and Ninhursag, which is the Sumerian myth of the loss of paradise. In Sumer, Eden was called Dilmun where Enki, the water god was allowed to eat eight plants. So there is a cultural context for the fabulous plants and the first of the two critical trees in Genesis, the tree of life.[62] The second tree, seemingly its polar opposite in terms of the story, is "the tree of the knowledge of good and evil." These two trees represent the two poles of movement in the story. The narrative moves us from paradisiacal amorality and immortality to awareness of good and evil within the limited, mortal world that we all know; the fantasy gives way to our familiar reality.

Indeed the Genesis description of paradise is a Middle Eastern pastoral landscape, familiar to us from the Arabian Nights as well as its ancient antecedents. The garden is filled with the great rivers of the world, including the Gihon, the spring that waters Jerusalem with the great river valleys of the fertile crescent.[63] The lyrical, pastoral tone continues uninterrupted with the first speech of God: "Of every tree of the garden you are free to eat; but as for the tree of knowledge of good and evil, you must not eat of it, for as soon as you eat of it, you shall die" (Gen 2:17). Though the fabulous description continues, the seeds of the drama are planted just as surely as the tree is.

The LORD God creates the man, as a potter might build a clay figure, but He breathes His spirit *(ruaḥ)* into him. The man needs companionship so God creates animals which the man names, showing his superiority over those who cannot name themselves. After creating the animals (again in contradistinction to the first story) the woman is created, supposedly to be one who is to be a helper—in Hebrew expressed much more mordantly as "a helper like/opposite him." Some of the problems inherent in the drama are already expressed in the term used of the woman's role. The institution of marriage is justified by the first speech of the man. It is very likely an oath of kin recognition:

> This one at last
> is bone of my bones
> And flesh of my flesh.
> This one shall be called Woman
> for from man she was taken. (Gen 2:23)

This language expresses a publicly ratified relationship, as it also seems to in 2 Samuel: "And say to Amasa, 'Are you not my bone and my flesh? God do so to me, and more also, if you are not commander of my army henceforth in place of Joab' " (2 Sam 19:13).

The mood of innocence is maintained even though the couple are married and may be functioning sexually. The man "tends the garden" rather than doing work for work proper would be a punishment for disobedience. Whoever is narrating is taking care to use words economically but exactly: "The two of them were naked but they were not ashamed" (Gen 2:25). In the Biblical description, the man and his wife are adult children—a fact brought out more strongly when we notice the Bible's frequent pairing of the images of children, nakedness, and not knowing good from evil (Isa 7:16, etc.). This is a dangerous, unstable state of innocence; it cannot last. Adam and Eve are as yet merely pets in a sheltered garden.

THE PLOT THICKENS, AND DRAMA IS
THE THICKENING AGENT

The inherent imbalance of the paradise is brought out by wordplay, placed exactly when the mood changes abruptly. Just as they are naked (*arumim*, Gen 2:25) so is the snake the most shrewd (*arum*, Gen 3:1) of all the animals. The words for "naked" and "shrewd" are homonymns but their meanings could not be more opposite. The snake is the antagonist in the drama. He asks the woman: "Did God really say: 'You shall not eat of any tree in the garden?' " (Gen 3:1). She answers bravely and articulately, beginning a dialogue of misprision: "We may eat of the fruit of the trees of the garden; but God said, 'You shall not eat of the fruit of the tree which is in the midst of the garden, neither shall you touch it, lest you die' " (Gen 3:2).

The story proceeds quickly to the snake's next statement, which is an ironic truth: He tells them that they will not die if they eat; rather their eyes will be opened and they will become like gods, knowing good and evil (Gen 3:4). Ironically, this was the exact truth. They do not die when they eat of the tree, and they do become like gods, knowing good and evil. As with the ancient Near East, wisdom and death are related. In Mesopotamia, wisdom is often the result of knowing our mortality. Death itself comes later.

The final damage comes when the woman sees how appealing the fruit is: "good for food," . . . "a delight to the eyes," . . . "and desirable to make one wise" (Gen 3:6). These are meant to underline the woman's sensuousness. Certainly she is the better equipped intellectually of the two characters. But she is also more sensuous, and that sensuality is her undoing. She eats and gives to her husband who eats as well.[64] She is a much better realized character than is Adam.

It may be that the story is blaming the woman for the sin of disobedience, but there is hardly anything in the story to clarify that interpretation. She is sensually attracted to the beautiful fruit, as well as clever enough to be outwitted by the cleverer snake. But is she any more to blame than her husband? After all, Adam is standing next to her throughout her conversation with the snake, and he can think of nothing to say. He just obeys his wife. If Eve is beguiled by the snake, Adam is beguiled by Eve's obvious intelligence and sensuousness. He is just as much to blame as she is. His inarticulateness and guilelessness has gotten him into this fix.

Not even the fruit makes Adam smart. What they get from the tree is not "intelligence"; their IQs are unaffected by the change. What they get is "knowledge of good and evil," which is meant to signify moral discernment, for they are now ashamed of their nakedness and so find leaves in which to dress. This is a development of the relationship between mortality and wisdom in the ancient Near East.

"Knowledge of good and evil" also has developmental implications in Hebrew, since often when it occurs in the text, it subsequently indicates the achievement of moral majority, as when a child becomes old enough to be responsible for its actions (e.g. Isa 7:15–16). These are culturally determined moral judgments which make more sense to the Hebrews than they would to, say, the Australian bushmen. But the story builds moral judgments into the fabric of God's promise. The moral discernment, newly won by Adam and Eve, also accounts for their guilt feelings, expressed by their hiding from the presence of the LORD God (Gen 3:10).

WHOSE IRONY IS IT?

More than a decade ago, the prolific literary critic, Harold Bloom, suggested that the author of this creation story was a woman. That was a sensational suggestion, very inspirational to the new women's movement and just what a professor of religion at a women's college (but part of a major university) would have liked to have happened. But the suggestion, upon reflection, seems far-fetched. It is always possible, but there is nothing inherent in the story to make a woman author or narrator necessary.

The ironies here are not that of a woman writer's having fun at a man's expense, as Harold Bloom has too blithely assumed but, unfortunately, another kind of not so innocent fun designed by men, men in a very male-dominated ancient, social world. Even when men are in charge, they reflect ironically on the power that women hold over them because of sexual attraction.

Though fabulous in wealth and fertility, Eden is meant to be a topsy-turvy world, emphasized for comic effect. When I say that it is a comic vision, I do not mean that it has no serious purpose. I mean that like good comedy, this story tells us something serious and deep about our nature as human beings. It picks humor to show us that truth.

However I do mean to say that to valorize Adam's position is to miss the point. Adam is duped, which makes him just as guilty of disobedience as Eve. I see no reason to think that the Hebrews blamed the woman any more than the man nor to think that human life was therefore considered depraved. Life, as we know it, is a punishment in this story. But there is no suggestion that there is a modicum of unatoned guilt in it. Indeed, if anything, the punishment for stealing fruit from the fruit bowl is already extreme, way beyond "measure for measure." The story merely explains how we got into this fix called mortal life and why we do not live in an Eden, though we can all imagine a paradise. In short, unlike Candide, the Bible thinks we do not live in the best of all possible worlds. Indeed, even God must fight continuously to preserve his initial act of creation. The Eden story was not written for us; it was written for the people who also understood the story of Adapa, where, for committing a minor culinary offense, humanity learned wisdom by losing immortality. The result of Adam and Eve's casual, childlike, disobedient credulity is terrible until we realize that this punishment merely defines life as we know it. Though sin is disobedience, the result is not the loss of immortality, which we can only imagine as an infantile fantasy, but the basic human predicament, as we all know it.

Now we see the effect of the comedy. The story comically implies that if the issue were native intelligence we would be living in a very different world, one in which women ruled. The reason that women are subject to men is that otherwise women would continuously lead unsuspecting men astray by their intelligence and seductiveness. Under the humor is a ferocious and discriminatory irony but it is as much a direct criticism of men as of women. The final effect of the story is to proof-text a world in which men are dominant; we could call this misogynistic after all (at least it must seem so to us, given our assumptions about the equality of women in work environments). But the story pokes fun at everyone and was written in a society that assumed that women were subject to the command of their fathers and husbands, not the society we live in.

In form, the story of the garden of Eden is quite like the story of Adapa, who followed Ea's bad advice about eating the bread of immortality and so was led astray innocently. In this case, we can have no other god, so we just have a snake. But he is just a snake; certainly he is not Satan. Our purpose in looking at the story is to see what (if anything) it implies about life in this world and the next. Some things are more obvious when we reflect on what we already know about Hebrew notions of the afterlife: It is this life that is important; even primal, naive immortality is but a childhood delusion.

Some overriding questions need to be addressed: First we need to ask about immortality and mortality. Were the man and his wife (now perhaps better Adam and Eve in their post-lapsarian identities, 3:20) immortal in the garden because that was their natural state or did they gain immortality temporarily in the garden because they were continuously eating from the tree of life? Is the fruit of the tree of life like a daily vitamin, conferring immortality but only for a period? This may actually have been the intention of the narrator. The verbs in the LORD God's banishment command support either interpretation: "Now that the man has become like one of us, knowing good and evil now he might stretch out his hand and take also from the tree of life and eat [continually?] and so live forever. . . ." The past tense of many of the verbs suggests that the act is to be a single one. Yet, the Hebrew present participle for "live" will support either the sense of present stative or present and future continuous action.

Eating from the tree of life was not forbidden until now. If the LORD God means that one bite of this fruit will make one immortal, then the real stupidity in the story is that Adam and Eve did not eat from it before God prevented them at the end of the story! Surely the story means for us to believe that we missed immortality by our own mistake; but this irony is a bit greater than the previous one, that our punishment is so much greater than our crime. I do not think that was the intent of the narrator. Everyone knows what the human condition really is; any other outcome would be seen merely as ridiculous and a waste of time. The narrator's job is only to explain how we got this way.

THE QUESTION OF EVIL IS BEST UNDERSTOOD
IN HISTORICAL CONTEXT

More intriguing still is the question of why the snake enticed the woman, if he is just a snake and not a cipher for Satan. The one thing that the identification with Satan does is to clarify all the motivations in the story: Satan's presence would say right from the beginning that we live in an eternal struggle between good and evil, present even in these childlike people. And it would say that Satan is stronger than God because he forces God to make people mortal, evidently opening up the rich possibility for a hell. That is the dominant interpretation of western Christianity. But it is enormously tendentious. When read properly, there is not a trace of this interpretation actually in the story with that doctrine in the background. Then why did the snake commit the crime?

A later text in the Bible sequentially, but perhaps one written around the same time, seems to suggest something rather more profound about the ways God picks His agents:

Then Micaiah said, "Therefore hear the word of the LORD: I saw the LORD sitting on his throne, with all the host of heaven standing beside him to the right and to the left of him. And the LORD said, "Who will entice Ahab, so that he may go up and fall at Ramoth-Giliad? Then one said one thing, and another said another, until a spirit came forward and stood before the LORD, saying: "I will entice him." "How?" the LORD asked him. He replied, "I will go out and be a lying spirit in the mouth of all his prophets. Then the LORD said, "You are to entice him, and you shall succeed; go out and do it. So you see, the LORD has put a lying spirit in the mouth of all these your prophets; the LORD has decreed disaster for you." (1 Kgs 22:19–23)

The scene is the court of the evil King Ahab where we hear the true prophecy of Micaiah ben-Imlah, a historical prophet who unfortunately has left us no writings. But his is a powerful, very effective, and very complicated prophecy. He reveals that God has deliberately misled all the other prophets in Ahab's court in order to accomplish the well-deserved death of Ahab. God has done so on the advice of one of His courtiers, a nameless spirit, who is then appointed "the lying spirit" for the specific purpose of misleading the prophets, just as "the satan" in Job apparently has the specific role of adversary in God's court. In that case, the existence of the satan implies nothing more than God used an angelic assistant to accomplish his plan. In the case of the garden of Eden, the same is implied about the snake.

All the prophets have told Ahab that he will win if he goes out to battle for Ramoth-Gilead. The Bible later tells us that he died there. The Bible offers an example of revelation as a flashback. God has previously set up the situation as a trap. The verb for what God's prophets do to Ahab is "entice" (1 Kgs 21, 22), not exactly the same "entice" which is used of the snake but a quite similar notion. Interestingly, the "enticement" of Eve has sexual connotations while the "enticement" of Ahab has the implication of being played for a fool. This is a particularly sharp irony against Ahab, who is portrayed as more stupid than Adam here, though he does not know it. In contrast the Judean king Jehoshaphat is a model of wise circumspection. Furthermore, the God of our Bible is quite capable of using both forms of enticement to refer to the foolishness of those who ignore His commandments.

The situation between Ahab and the primal couple is similar in that both are restrospective tellings of the facts of a situation in which God's actions seem equivocal. Ahab is a great sinner but he has the upper hand in this story; he is the powerful and successful king, while the wise Jehoshaphat is his ally. And the ironies in the latter case are far more savage. Ahab will be killed terribly and without mercy; both he and his queen, Jezebel, will be eaten by dogs, forbidden even a decent funeral. The Ahab story means to warn us of a death equally ugly to all those who would insult the majesty of YHWH by playing the harlot to other gods.

In this case, as in Eden, the LORD God must do something which appears wrong in our eyes in order to accomplish His greater plan. He must deliberately mislead His prophets in order to trick Ahab into going out into battle to die. If the same concept of enticement is being used in both cases, the next question must be, why it should be in God's interest for Adam and Eve to eat from the tree?

The answer appears quickly enough. Discernment of good and evil, the mark of mature human thought in the Bible, is a positive notion throughout. Had Ahab exercised his moral discernment, there would have been no need for a special emergency session in the divine throne room. He is rather like Eve but infinitely more demonic. He is a smart character who uses his intelligence rather than his moral discernment and winds up operating only for his own benefit.

The story says first of all that moral discernment gives us a divine nature, equal to YHWH in our ability to confront Him, though our intelligence operating without moral discernment is only a trap. In the case of Adam and Eve, the scene is played for laughs. In the case of Ahab, it is played as a revenge tragedy, an earnest moral tale. And though we think we have the upper hand, we are totally outclassed when we try to defeat YHWH using our intelligence. It also says that God favors the kingdom of Judah, at least sometimes, and he always hates the kingdom of Israel, even though they are far richer and more advanced.

And there is more to say than that. Not only does the ability to discern good from evil mark a mature human being, but there is a funny way in which the garden story is developmental in character. Like children, the primal pair learn right from wrong by being told to obey a rule, transgressing it, and receiving the punishment. The story is based on a simple observation about how we teach our children to make the same discernments. Such is the genius of myth worldwide.

The Covenant as the Reason
for Moral Discernment

SIMILAR STORIES of coming to knowledge are found in Gilgamesh. Enkidu is shown learning from the prostitute, who effects his estrangement from the animals. Adapa is even misled into giving up mortality by a different god's trick. The Bible has inherited a number of stories from Babylonia and elsewhere, tailoring them to its own task. The Bible, by comparison with Gilgamesh, is not interested nearly so much in the issue of immortality. Instead it emphasizes the issue of coming to moral discernment. It does so because its main themes—one God and covenant—are furthered by this treatment. Monotheism and protection against idolatry lead to the de-emphasizing of alternative religions and their possible opponent divinities. There can be no realm of the dead in a monotheistic system, unless that realm is squarely within the power of God.

Even more important, the covenant theme of the Hebrew Bible demands that humans have moral discernment. The covenant is a formal agreement between God and humanity. It demands that human beings enter into the agreement of their own choice. In order to enter the covenant one needs moral discernment. It is absolutely necessary for the task. Thus, the story of Adam and Eve, far from being just the story of how we lost immortality, is more aptly entitled "the story of how we can live well," having received the critical faculty of moral discernment and thus having evolved the aptitude to obey the covenant.

Notice that the covenant does not promise life after death beyond the commemoration of history and progeny to follow us afterwards. Life is the reward of the covenant, explicitly, not afterlife—certainly not the afterlife of Egypt, Mesopotamia, or Canaan. The Bible's intuition about life is that it should be lived heroically without illusions of fantasies afterwards and certainly without the disgusting rites that characterize its neighbors' views. The most obvious winners in this battle are the priests of YHWH who serve in Jerusalem. Their institution and their interpretation of Israelite history are what succeeds when this polemic is successful. The First Temple period may not have witnessed a pure Yahwism but, from the perspective of the later priests living in Second Temple times who redacted the Bible, this was the meaning of the conflicts between Israel and the Canaanites during the First Temple times.

Since we know that ultimately both Judaism and Christianity in its own way develop a notion of the hereafter which is moral and beatific, we need to ask ourselves a naive question: Could it really be that God spent so much time giving His prophets messages of antagonism to the notion of Canaanite afterlife only to reverse Himself later on? Changes in the concept of the afterlife over time argue against taking it literally. But reversals in the idea and existence of afterlife raise skeptical thoughts against the whole enterprise of describing heaven and hell as literal places where we literally go. Instead we must look to more sophisticated notions of the function and structure of the beliefs and defining the work they are designed to accomplish, both in society and in the development of our own consciousnesses.

PART TWO

FROM CLIMATE

TO THE SELF

4

Iranian Views of the Afterlife and Ascent to the Heavens

Reconstitution of the Jewish State and Borrowed Institutions

So FAR WE have traced Biblical traditions of the afterlife in the First Temple period, within its ancient Near Eastern cultural context: Egypt, Mesopotamia, and Canaan. Now we turn to the far more articulated and manifold notions of the afterlife in the Second Temple period. To do so, we must trace the afterlife notions of two more cultures—Persia and Greece—which had an important effect on Second Temple Israel (539 BCE–70 CE). In some sense, the material for the innovative Jewish notions of the afterlife come from Iran and Greece, though Jewish culture tailored the cloth to its own measurements. On the subject of the afterlife, Persian and Greek influence become the most important two factors in the development of Jewish conceptions, from which they entered Christianity, and hence became the most important factors in the description of the afterlife in the religions of the West.

With the destruction of the First Temple, the end came to the first Israelite state. After a sojourn in Babylon of more than a generation (597–539 BCE), where the Judeans encountered Babylonian religion directly, the Jews returned to the land of Judah, due to the beneficence of a new conquering people, the Persians, who vanquished the Neo-Babylonian Empire by pouring down into Mesopotamia on horseback from the eastern high plateau steppelands and who ruled from the area today known as Iran.

Some Israelites—not all, but some—returned from Babylon to rebuild their state on their ancient model; but they returned to a whole new world, where the old models of the state fit less and less and the previous unity of people and purpose was irrecoverable. They were no longer an independent nation, living on their own with only their own internal ideological battles to fight. Rather, they were confined to a smaller and subservient state, called the district of *Yehud* (Aramaic for Judah; Hebrew: *Yehudah*) or the province of "Across the River," in turn part of a larger Syrian satrapy whose official language was Aramaic, in turn part of a vast empire ruled by a people who spoke Persian. They were two languages away from their rulers who resided in faraway Iran at the other end of a well-developed imperial bureaucracy. Since they came from *Yehud*, a resident was a "*yehudi*"—a Judean, a term which eventually comes to mean "a Jew." [1] It took centuries before the religious implication of the name, which is so clear to us, became the primary meaning of the term. [2]

As member states of a large empire, they were aware of many different cultures with many different gods and many different ways of understanding our final ends. Ever wary of offending YHWH, especially after their terrible exile and punishment at His hands, they did not seek out the new ideologies: in fact, they tried, at first self-consciously, to reconstitute the previous state. But that proved impossible, as the Persians prefered to rule through the priests and not a king. The priests shortly became the ruling class in Judea while the kingship simply disappeared. In any event, their attempt imaginatively to reconstruct and record their past and their plans for the future is known to us today as the Bible, or at least the five books of Moses. The documents we understand as the core of the Bible were assembled in this period by the new aristocracy of Judea, the priests.

As the Jews heard about more attractive hereafters, they gradually revised their own conceptions of the afterlife in ways that give credit to their patient, long-suffering LORD. The result, which moved them toward a new Jewish synthesis of views of the afterlife, began as a group of tendentious and conflicted, but related, arguments about what the afterlife might be. The Jewish nation entertained, both accepting and rejecting, aspects of Persian and Greek thought. They did not accept these new notions uniformly but entertained them in various groups and classes of people. In a way, this shows that the reason for the polemic against Canaanite thought was not pure ethnocentrism but a reaction against something offensive in Canaanite culture itself, for the Jews readily accept notions of the resurrection of the body and the immortality of the soul, which came from Persian and Greek cultures respectively. This new synthesis would have far-reaching effects for our contemporary notions of the hereafter. At the beginning of the Hellenistic period (starting ca. 332 BCE), we have but hints of what the social and economic backgrounds of these concepts were. By the end of the period, we have very good ideas about the environment in which these notions grew and how they served society.

The Difficulty Studying Iran

IRAN'S INFLUENCE on Israel remains a true mystery. When the Iranian religious documents were first published in the West, in the nineteenth and early twentieth century, a wave of interest began in all things Zoroastrian (from the Greek spelling, "Zoroaster," of its principal figure Zarathushtra), not just because they were exotic and new expressions of wisdom, though that was certainly part of the attraction, but because Iranian imagery and especially its religious dualism seemed to mirror many things about Jewish and Christian thought in the first few centuries of our era. After a period of extravagent claims and intense polemical scrutiny, most of it hostile, the scholarly world has admitted almost nothing from Zoroastrianism as an influence on native Jewish tradition.[3]

But the counterreaction seems almost as mistaken as the prior enthusiasm.[4] In its two-hundred-year rule of Israel and subsequent five centuries-long influence in the Middle East, Iran and Zoroastrianism had many chances to influence Jewish thought. The problem is that there is no easy way to date Zoroastrian texts, leaving us no clear, unmistakable settings for cultural borrowing.

The general rules of borrowing seem easy enough. There is one important rule-of-thumb: An idea will be accepted only if it can be fully incorporated into the life of the second people. After all, neither lox nor bagels are Jewish in origin. It is the special use that is made of them in Jewish society which accounts for their special place in Jewish cuisine. Furthermore, lox and bagels become Jewish ethnic identifiers in the United States, which gives them their even more special status. In short, knowing the origin tells us something about a cultural item but it falls far short of an adequate description of its meaning in any particular culture. Knowing Zoroastrian or Greek origin of particular notions of the afterlife are important data. But, to get the full picture we must see how the idea functioned in Jewish thought.

The Antiquity of Iranian Religion and Its Undatability

WITH A HISTORY of some three thousand years, Zoroastrianism ranks with Judaism and Christianity as one of the ancient living Western religions. But Zoroastrianism has fared much worse even than Judaism in numbers. If Judaism currently has more than 14 million adherents worldwide, then Christianity with more than 1.4 billion members is certainly one hundred times larger. On the other hand, surviving Zoroastrians number more than one hundred times less than Jews, with considerably fewer than 140,000 contemporary believers.[5] One reason for the scarcity of Zoroastrians in the world is their hostility to intermarriage. Zoroastrians, except for a forward-thinking few, considered the children of all intermarriages non-Zoroastrians.

Zoroastrianism takes its name from that of its founder, Zarathushtra, who may have lived anytime between the eleventh and seventh century BCE but probably lived around the beginning of the eighth century BCE.[6] Zoroastrianism became the major religion of Iran, which took its name from its inhabitants, the Aryans. Their earliest Persian document, the *Avesta,* lends us the name of their earliest written language, Avestan, which seems to have separated from Sanskrit in the second millennium BCE.[7] The *Avesta* itself is made up of compositions, oral and written, from many different periods but started its process during this early period.

Earliest Zoroastrianism

THE ROOTS OF Zoroastrianism can be located in an eastern Iranian, tribal, pastoral society. Zoroastrianism should probably not be called a founded religion, as Zarathushtra was a prophetic reformer, who innovated in the original Mazdian Religion ("Wise" religion from the name of the supreme God *Ahura Mazda* "Wise Lord"). The religion developed yet further under the first Persian Empire, somewhat diluting Zarathustra's contribution.[8]

R. C. Zaehner established the usual chronologies and periodizations of Zoroastrianism in the very title of his work, *The Dawn and Twilight of Zoroastrianism.*[9] Even though we know little of Zarathushtra himself, we do know something of the "dawn" of Zoroastrianism under the Achaemenids, who are so famous for their fearsome invasions of Greece, ended by Alexander the Great. It was by conquering the Achaemenid Persian Empire that Alexander became the conqueror of the world. We also know something about the "twilight" Sassanian phase of Zoroastrianism, which began around 250 CE and continued to the seventh-century-CE Arab conquest. The Persian dialect of this period is known as Middle Persian or *Pahlavi,* the successor to Avestan.

But our information sundial is in total eclipse at the "high noon" of Zoroastrianism, the Arsacid or Parthian Empire, which ruled after freeing Persia from the successors of Alexander around 250 BCE until the rise of the Sassanians in the mid-third-century CE.[10] This largely unknown period is likely one of heavy influence of Persian and Greek culture on the land of Israel. Like the Jews, the Zoroastrians survived Alexander the Great's Macedonian regime and Seleucid Greek rule from Antioch. The Jews additionally were ruled by the Ptolemies of Egypt, and the Zoroastrians by a shortlived Greco-Bactrian state. The Persian state, with Zoroastrianism resurgent, indeed eventually with Zoroastrianism as the official religion, was the major enemy of Imperial Rome. It was also a significant host country to Jewish culture. The Babylonian Talmud was written under the Parthian and Sassanian Empires in the third through seventh centuries. It was Persia that gave the Jews an attractive place to live after the Roman Empire became Christian and began enacting prejudicial laws against Jewish life, worship, and culture.

Because the Persians had a written Scripture, their Muslim conquerors considered them a "people of the Book" *('ahl al-qitab),* just as Jews and Christians were, even though the Zoroastrians did not revere the Bible in any special way. So while they were called a "protected" *(dhimmi)* people like the Jews, they faced discrimination and heavy taxation as *dhimmis* under Islam, even as they were spared conversion to Islam. In this, they fared about as well as the Jews and Christians. Though Islamic tolerance might be judged imperfect by today's more multicultural standards, it was considerably more pluralistic than Medieval European Christianity and, like the Jews and Christians, Zoroastrians were far more fortunate than the minorities of Europe.

Unlike those of Judaism and Christianity, however, many of the sacred texts of Zoroastrianism were lost in their original form. Even when glossed by commentaries during the Greek and Arab conquests, the texts are incomplete, full of contemporary interpretations, and therefore hard to reconstruct or date. After the Arab conquest, Zoroastrianism continued to be handed down amongst priests and laity from generation to generation, through the rule of the Mongols, the Turks, and Persian Islamic rulers. The Zoroastrians continue even today, in small and poor communities in Iran, where they are subject to local prejudice and periodically to overt persecution.

Generations ago, many Zoroastrians emigrated to the west coast of India. In India, Zoroastrians were called by the Gujurati and Hindi word for Persian: "Parsi." They were also known as "fire-worshipers" because one of the major rites of the religion involves tending a sacred fire in the midst of a temple. The Parsis continue there today in small, sometimes affluent, endogamous, Indian-dialect communities in Gujarat, Bombay, the Deccan and in modern Pakistan.[11] After the British Raj they also migrated to some large English-speaking cities—principally London, Toronto, Los Angeles, and metropolitan New York City—where there are well-established communities with prayer halls, if not fully-functioning fire temples. Their reduced numbers can be explained partly because of their minority and often persecuted status, partly because there is no way to convert to Zoroastrianism, and partly because progeny of intermarriage are considered non-Zoroastrian.

Dualism Versus Monotheism in Zoroastrianism and Other Western Religions

THE PRINCIPAL holy book of the Zoroastrians is the *Avesta,* written in an early dialect of Persian, often so abstruse as to be understandable only through its Sanskrit cognates. Linguistically, the most archaic writings of the *Avesta* are the *Gathas* of the *Yasnas,* containing our only certain evidence of Zarathushtra's thinking and writing. The rest of the *Yasnas* and the *Yashts,* another hymnic part of the *Avesta,* are usually taken to be a bit later (perhaps as little as 200 years) in literary form, and may actually contain clues to the state of Indo-European religion in Persia before Zarathustra.

Zoroastrianism is famous for many beliefs and customs, but none more outstanding than its strong dualism. The high god is Ahura Mazda, who protects *asha* (wisdom and the good or truth, cognate with *ṛta* in Sanskrit) with his army of good *ashovans* but is opposed by a major opponent, Angra Mainyu, who advances the cause of *druj* (evil, perfidy, treachery, cognate with *betrüben* in German and "betray" in English) through his evil army of *Dregvans.* The good god, Ahura Mazda, is also the god of light, represented by fire, its purity and its light (ergo, the former trade-name of the GE lightbulb), while the bad god, Angra Mainyu, is the god of darkness. It is appropriate to pray to Ahura Mazda for guidance while

178

Angra Mainyu should be addressed only in curses and exorcisms, to expel his presence, and to keep him far away and powerless. The Zoroastrian priests venerate fire as representative of Ahura Mazda, of sanctity, and of purity. At first, fire altars were always outside, only in open and elevated places, as mentioned by Herodotus. Probably during the reign of Arta-xerxes II, the Zoroastrians began to pray in a fire temple (or *ateshgah*), in reaction to the building of temples to the Persian (but non-Zoroastrian) goddess Anahita throughout the empire.[12]

There are grounds for thinking that Zoroastrianism is also essentially monotheistic, as Zarathustra describes the good and evil forces as twin sons of Ahura Mazda (see Yasna 30, hereafter Y 30). In fact, several religions have taken to dualism as a way to explain how a good god could allow evil in the world. Though many think that dualism and monotheism are opposing phenomena, dualism actually seems to be a consequence of some difficulties with monotheism. From the perspective of ethics, monotheism is in opposition to polytheism, not to dualism. Once there is one god, he or she must be the author of all evil as well as all good. Indeed, one might argue that dualism is not a stage on the way to monotheism so much as a stage beyond it, a strategic retreat from monotheism governed by the recognition that monotheism makes the explanation of evil problematic.[13] In these dualisms, good will eventually conquer evil.

The problem is so pervasive that Judaism, Christianity, and Islam have episodically produced dualist solutions to the ethical problem. Apocalypticism, for instance, removes moral ambiguity in the character of God, both within Judaism and even more within Christianity, by externalizing evil as the demonic opponent to God. With a separate evil god who is the author of everything bad, sin and evil become easily understandable.

The dualistic, apocalyptic Jewish systems antecedent to Christianity are not well known, except for the Dead Sea Scroll community. Within apocalyptic Judaism, the satanic figure can be known by a variety of different names: Samael, Mastema, Belzebub, the Angel of Darkness, Malkirasha, and others. The power of the demonic opponent is temporary; after a time Satan's rule will be ended. It seems certain that the portrayal of Satan in Jewish apocalypticism, the New Testament, later Christian writings and Islam has been affected by Zoroastrian imagery and thinking about Angra Mainyu (e.g. Y 30:3–6; 45:2).[14] This influence came in several stages, including contact with Zoroastrianism, gnosticism, Manicheanism, and the Medieval dualist heresies. The same effect can be seen all along the silk road.[15]

There are other dualistic ways to resolve the problem of the high god's omniscience. Among the Greek philosophers, Plato especially opted for a body/soul or spirit/flesh dualism. Plato thought that there is one high god, the good or the beautiful, but he (or it) cannot mix into a corrupt world. Therefore, all that is bad in life is merely the product of the corrupted nature of matter and flesh. Our imperfect life is an unfortunate result of the deterioration of material objects, not from divinity, which is pure and good. The kind of dualism that Zoroastrianism developed—a cosmic battle below a high god who determines its ultimate outcome—looks a great deal like apocalypticism in Judaism and not at all like Platonism. It has a certain formal similarity to the Qumran community too, and has a certain effect on the developing Christian church. In late antiquity one might say both types of dualism could be found in gnosticism (see Ch. 15). Gnosticism is characterized by the revelation of secret knowledge *(gnōsis)* that can lead to salvation from an irredeemable world by personal transformation.

The Social Background of Dualism

SOME SOCIAL scientists have been interested in defining the social conditions that produce dualism but it is hard to maintain that there is anything more than a correlation between some social situations and dualism. Dualism sometimes emanates from a relatively small group that feels in some way beset with difficulties. Quite often, some kind of dualism is related to a group's feeling that their society is hostile towards them. Whether such dualism expresses itself in a generalized feeling of hostility against the larger group, as say fundamentalism in the United States, or a pariah cult like the Branch Davidians, depends on any number of historical factors, the moral schemes of the host and the sect, to say nothing of the unique historical circumstances. It seems unlikely that such a general explanation, developed out of studying minority groups in the modern world, could explain the development of dualism in Zoroastrianism, which becomes the state religion of the Persian Empire.

Unfortunately, we have virtually no knowledge of the social conditions that may have encouraged the Indo-European Persians to turn to dualism, to listen to Zarathustra. Since we know nothing of Zarathustra's biography, we know nothing of the time in which he lived. Whatever else Zoroastrian dualism may signify and wherever it may have come from, Zoroastrian dualism promotes a sense of the community of the redeemed. The Zoroastrians are those who seek the good and form a community of those who are protected by the high god Ahura Mazda. The evil forces will not participate in the heavenly community; they will be in hell being punished until the final consummation. Ultimately, credit must surely be given to the genius of Zarathustra himself and his intuition about how the universe and moral behavior were in dualistic congruence.[16]

The communal basis of the afterlife fits not only Zoroastrianism but strikes a particularly sympathetic chord with Judaism, as an ethnic and often a diaspora community, and with Christianity, as a growing sect after it, as well as with Manichaenism and Islam. We should look for the importance of a communal afterlife, with its implications for the community of the saved on earth, in all those communities who stress bodily resurrection, just like the Zoroastrians. Life in community was life with a body, it seems, at least in these historical instances; dualism was correlated with bodily resurrection. This seems so characteristic of Zoroastrianism and Jewish sectarianism that it is hard not to admit some kind of relationship. In Greco-Roman platonic dualism, on the other hand, matter itself is evil. Resurrection is therefore not desirable.

It is difficult to conclude more than this from the fragmentary evidence about Zoroastrian beginnings. There are no clear lines of causation between Zoroastrian dualism and the dualisms that grew up in Israel. On the other hand, several images taken from Zoroastrianism can be seen to influence Hebrew society. In Zoroastrianism, a notion of an apocalyptic end, the *frasho kereti*, was strongly articulated. Perhaps it is a specialized form of the Hindu concept of the many cosmic eras, the *Yugas*. But whatever the source, Zoroastrians believe that the world will come to an end and be reconstituted in a *Frasho Kereti*. This has certain affinities with the notion of apocalypse in Hellenistic Jewish thought as well as the *ekpyrosis* (cosmic conflagration) in Stoicism. In Israel there was already a notion that the Day of the LORD, originally just a national holiday, would not be joyful yet full of woe for the wicked. God was going to visit vengeance not joy on his sinful people.

Later apocalypses were influenced by Manichaeanism in its medieval period. Fairly quickly though, the influences can be seen going both ways: Were the crucial Christian and apocalyptic Jewish materials influenced by Zoroastrianism, or perhaps even the opposite, since we cannot date many Zoroastrian texts very well?[17] The Christian imagery in the depiction of Satan certainly derives partly from the various portraits of Angra Mainyu. But the Christian Satan develops independently and very formidably on his own, perhaps giving back to Zoroastrianism a well-developed demonology and an apocalyptic chronology. And, of course, the depiction of individuals judged each for his or her own sin seems clearly in line with parallel movements in Zoroastrianism and the Hebrew movement towards otherworldly judgment, which we see in Jeremiah, Ezekiel and Second Isaiah, as well as the later prophets. So is it possible to say that one influenced the other exclusively? Probably not. On the other hand, if there has to be a standard-bearer for this kind of dualism, I would expect that Zoroastrianism would fit the bill best, even if we cannot demonstrate crucial stages in the dialogue.

The Early Traditions: Gathas and Yasnas

IN THE ZOROASTRIAN case, the Gathas allow for a God above all, Ahura Mazda, as well as his two twin offspring, Angra Mainyu (the evil spirit) and Spenta Mainyu (the good spirit). The choices made by the two spirits (Y 30.5) lie at the root of Zoroastrian dualism, and they act as a prototype (Y 30.2; 49.3) of the choices that face each of us as we decide whether to follow the path of truth or that of untruth.[18]

Though there may be an original unity, dualism pervades Zoroastrianism at several levels at once. There is a cosmic dualism between truth and deceit (or the lie), coupled with the opposition of day against night, light against darkness. On the human level, there are "the truthful" who must battle against "the deceitful," which we can easily see as the social payoff of the cosmology and its expected parallel in the social world. One other convenient aspect of ethical dualism is that it makes for a clear-cut social system. In the divine realm, there are the *ahuras* and the *daevas,* the good and bad divinities. Between the divine and the human, there must be commerce through sacrifices; but there are good sacrifices and bad sacrifices.

The cosmic battle will end with the good triumphant. A final "turning point" is described as early as Yasna 43 and 51, but it is greatly elaborated in later writings.

> May Lord Mazda, ruling at will, grant wishes to him whosoever has wishes. I wish that enduring strength should come, in order to uphold Truth. Grant this to me through Devotion: recompenses of riches, a life of good purpose. . . . And may that man attain the better than good, he who would teach us the straight paths of salvation—those of the material world and of the mind, leading to the truth heights where dwells the Lord; a faithful man, of good lineage, holy like Thee, O Mazda! Then I shall recognise Thee as strong and holy, Mazda, when Thou wilt help me by the hand with which Thou holdest the recompenses that Thou wilt give, through the heat of Thy truth-strong fire, to the wicked

man and the just—and when the might of Good Purpose shall come to me. Then as holy I have recognised Thee, Lord Mazda, when I saw Thee as First at the birth of life, when Thou didst appoint rewards for acts and words, bad for the bad, a good recompense for the good, by Thy innate virtue, at the final turning point of creation. At which turning point Thou, O Mazda, hast come to the world with Thy Holy Spirit, with power through Good Purpose, by whose acts the people of Truth prosper. To them Devotion proclaims the judgments of Thy will—O Thou whom none deceives. (Y 43; Boyce 40)

In this passage a superior person is prophesied for the end of time. He will be the *saoshyant* (savior) of later Zoroastrian literature. It would be unreasonable to suppose that this figure is the basis for the Jewish messiah. "Messiah" is a Judean term used throughout the First Temple period. But nowhere in First Temple Hebrew Scripture does "messiah" refer to a future king, only the present one. A future king is addressed as "branch" or "scion of David." It is remarkable how infrequently the term is used even in intertestamental Judaism before the first century CE, and immediately after a short second Persian stint as rulers of Jerusalem. The expectation of a messiah in Judaism is understandable on its own terms as part of native Jewish religion. On the other hand, some of the cosmic imagery that is sometimes attached to the reign of the Messiah in the Greco-Roman period, especially his supernatural qualities, may well have been borrowed from Persia where they originally applied to the *saoshyant*.

The same source may explain the accelerated interest in an apocalyptic end in Israel. There was a "day of the LORD" in Israelite thought but it develops quickly into apocalypticism under the influence of Persian thought. In Persia, it underwent some development as well. In Yasna 43, that day is merely a hinted "turning point." It receives further development in Yasna 44:15–16 which alludes to the ultimate confrontation between Truth and Lie. Ahura Mazda is implored to "bring his impetuous weapon upon the deceitful and bring ill and harm over them." Two great opposing armies confront each other. Which side will be victorious? Obviously, tradition answers that it is the good, the light, and the moral.

The apocalyptic end will also be characterized by fleshly resurrection of the body. In Yasna 54 we have a description of the end of time: "The dead will rise in their lifeless bodies." [19] The vocabulary is consonant with the Jewish usage as well. This is the most important and interesting candidate for borrowing by the Hebrews, for resurrection does not truly enter Jewish life until after they have made contact with Persian society. It does not become explicit in Jewish life until after the contact has been firm for centuries, though the hints start almost immediately. The parallel vocabulary is not much to go on, but gives us ideas about one possible source of Jewish notions of the afterlife.

In the afterlife, the "soul" or "self" (Avestan: *uruuan;* Pahlavi: *urvan*) was to enjoy the fruits of its trials on earth. "Soul" is, of course, a very awkward way to translate this term. We can see here a parallel relationship between envisioning the afterlife and evaluating the notion of "self" in this world. As in all other cultures we have so far discussed, the narrative of the person's journey after death was a particular way of meditating on who we are, whether we are those who inhabit these bodies or whether we are these bodies, and what the meaning and process of our maturation is. By talking of the *urvan*'s final disposition and the way to attain it, the Persians were expressing that part of our lives on earth is transcendent, that part of our earthly life lives on after us. For the Zoroastrian, it is the ethically good part of a person's deeds and self. The person survived death as transformed into his *urvan* and achieved a happy afterlife through moral behavior.

An interesting subject for speculation is how the Zoroastrian notion of the resurrection of the earthly body affects notions of the "self." One obvious answer to the question comes from comparing the Zoroastrian notion of the resurrection of the body to its converse: the Greek notion of the immortality of the soul. The Greek philosophical notion functions in part to validate a battle against unbridled sexuality, making the freedom from our sexual urges one of the transcendent values of human life. Zoroastrianism contains no such ascetic impulses, though it does say that in the "fresh creation" people will naturally give up the corrupting process of eating, digesting, and excreting.

Thus, we can frame a hypothesis to be tested as we move into this period: The notion of resurrection, by comparison to immortality of the soul, tends to valorize and validate fully functioning sexual life in this and the next world, while immortality of the soul will valorize and validate intellectual life at the expense of sexuality. Our sexual lives are important and fulfilling to the Zoroastrians in ways that impressed Greek philosophers as decadent and distracting to intellectual life. We shall have to keep this in mind as we look at the various choices for afterlife in Jewish, Christian, and Muslim religious life.

The reward of the good person is transcendent because it will be with Ahura Mazda in the "House of Good Thought" (Y 32:15), whereas the deceitful will in the end come to the "House of the Lie" (Y 51:14) or even the "House of Worst Thought" (Y 32:13). To arrive in paradise, the truthful cross a famous bridge, the Chinvat bridge (Avestan: *cinnuuato peretush,* Y 46:10, lit. "the Account-Keeper's Bridge" also called "the Bridge of the Judge," or "the Bridge of the Mason.") The souls of the deceitful will be repulsed when they reach the bridge, from which they will be dispatched to the "House of the Lie" forever (Y 46:10–11):

> Whosoever, Lord, man, or woman, will grant me those things Thou knowest best for life—recompense for truth, power with good purpose—and those whom I shall bring to your worship, with all these shall I cross over the Chinvat Bridge. Karapans and Kavis by their powers yoke mankind with evil acts to destroy life. But their own soul and Inner Self tormented them when they reached the Chinvat Bridge—guests for ever in the House of the Lie!

An ordeal waiting to prove the righteous is hinted at in Yasna 51:9:[20]

> What reward Thou hast appointed to the two parties, O Wise One, through Thy bright fire and through the molten metal. Give a sign of it to the souls of men, to bring hurt to the wicked, benefit to the righteous.

Zarathushtra submits himself in advance and will survive the ordeal unharmed. However, not so those who are wicked. Furthermore, anyone who tries to destroy him will himself be destroyed.

The Yashts and the Younger Avesta

THE YASHTS are usually regarded as slightly younger than the Yasnas and of various ages but their date is hard to fix because they remained in constant flux; some may even be older than the Gathas, but many are considerably later than the Gathas. They were not canonized to the same degree as the Gathas so, over time, they evolved into a mixture of Avestan and Pahlavi. Other than noting the language glosses, it is hard to tell how many new notions from later times crept into the text. In this respect, they are quite like the Rabbinic literature of the Midrash, some of which developed under Persian auspices.

Yasht 19 gives a detailed description of resurrection. It says: "When the dead will rise, the one who restores life, the Undying (i.e., the *Saoshyant*) will come." Later in the same Yasht, we find: "When the dead rise, the

Living Incorruptible One (the *Saoshyant*) will come and life will be transfigured" (19.11). Note that the process is described very simply, with the verb "arise," which is parallel to the terminology which will come into use in the Jewish case as well.

The moral aspect of a person not only lives afterwards, it can be depicted in quite vivid terms, as a woman *psychopomp* ("leader of the soul"). In another part of the Younger Avestan writings, the *Videvdat* or *Vendidad* 19 ("Against the Demons"), we get a longer description of the *daena,* (lit. *vision* but, in context, the personification of conscience) of the just man. First, we see the same consistent story that the dead stay near the body until the dawn of the third day when, with the help of various gods, the dead start on their way to judgment.

After death, each *urvan* ("soul" or "person," later also identified with *fravashi* or *fravarti*), goes heavenward. It stays around the corpse for three days and then travels on to its reward.[21] It meets the *daena,* who is a comely maid for a righteous person, and who leads him over the Chinvat Bridge. The *daena* is explicitly the personification of a person's moral qualities, hence a representation of the person as well. The sinner, on the other hand, is led away by the Demon Vizaresha. In later tradition (but perhaps Zarathushtra himself suggested it), the soul *(urvan)* must stand on trial. The tribunal will be composed of Mithra, flanked by the two gods Sraosha and Rashnu.[22] Thus, these originally independent pre-Zoroastrian divinities are integrated into the pantheon of good gods supporting Ahura Mazda. The just "soul" is led before Vohu Mana on his golden throne and from there to an audience with Ahura Mazda and the Amesha Spentas, who also have their own golden thrones. A great many of these images recur in Jewish apocalypticism, and it is hard not to conclude that they are related. This story must have offered a very powerful tug on the imagination of the Zoroastrians. As time went by, the story became more and more elaborate. The next step came in the *Hadhokht Nask,* an Avestan liturgical piece, that, unfortunately, survives only in fragmentary form.

Some early texts discuss an ordeal at death and others at the end of time. But eventually, the story becomes completely symmetrical with both the good and the bad meeting their *daena.* The good pass on to paradise over the wide bridge with the *daena* as their guide or *"psychopomp"* (soul leader). But the sinners find that the bridge gets as thin as a knife blade and they fall into the abyss of hell, being grabbed by their *daena,* who has become a wraith. The Persians concentrated on the story of the soul's travels to its heavenly home. The Jews tell a similar story, though they invent their own details, so the influence will be limited to fairly small details.

The Disposition of the Body

THE EVENTS affecting the soul according to the Persians begin with the disposition of the body. In early Persian texts, there is a significant reference to the quite famous Zoroastrian practice of having a corpse rent by birds of prey and other scavengers as the preferred mode of disposition of the dead. Originally the Persian tribes appear to have practiced cremation, as the Indians did, but after the rise of Zoroastrianism, with its strict rules about keeping fire pure, the custom changed to exposure of the dead (usually for a week to a month), sometimes by gathering the large bones of the leg and skull afterwards, which were often put in special ossuaries, called *dakhma* and preferrably placing them high in the mountains.[23]

Exposure of the dead is a relatively rare practice in world religion, the most obvious analogy being Tibetan Buddhism, where the explanation is not hard to find. Since many Tibetans live in a treeless, permafrosted land, where neither cremation nor inhumation is easy, having bodies eaten by birds of prey seems the most efficient way to dispose of the deceased. No similar, simple cause suggests itself as a parallel explanation of Persian customs.

However there is another explanation. The parallel comes again from looking at Hindu practice. The reason the Zoroastrians expose their dead seems quite close to the ancient Indian practice of purifying the bodies of the dead on funeral pyres. Fire and light are both agents of purification and compare quite closely as formal operations. It seems as if the Hindus and the Iranians used two different technologies of burial to accomplish the same religious end, the purification of the final remains of the dead. Zoroastrian views of the purity of fire contribute to their abandonment of cremation. Perhaps also the lack of trees on the high Iranian plateau contributed to the Persian practice, but the explicit reason was to avoid polluting the fire or earth with a corpse.

There are also clues in Sanskrit and Avestan which point to a deeper structural parallel of Indian and Persian ritual. Paradise is considered a place of light and knowledge in both religions. Indeed, it appears as if many surrounding cultures thought that Ahura Mazda was the sun because in Assyrian inscriptions, Ahura Mazda appears, identified with the sun.[24] It appears, therefore, that the original reason the Persians layed out their dead on *dakhmas* (an open air walled enclosure) was to expose the corpses to the purificatory powers of the sun, in the same way as fire purifies the corpses in Indian thought. Furthermore, one wonders whether the very obvious and visible rending of the body did not itself stimulate a notion of bodily resurrection in Zoroastrianism, as a way of expressing a renewed wholeness in the apocalyptic end of time. In any event, after a year, the Persian texts declare that the body was resurrected.[25]

The rending of the dead eventually took a more refined form. At first, the Zoroastrians exposed the dead on a stony outcropping. But when they were conquered by Islam, the place of exposure was walled around and called a "tower of silence."[26] This too, Zoroastrians have termed a *dakhma*—a high enclosure, inside of which corpses are exposed to be dismembered by vultures. *Dakhmas* were impressive features to all travelers to Persia in Muslim times and continue to attract attention to Parsi communities in Gujurat in modern times. Indian sensibilities, however, are shocked at this practice and the Indian government has been pressuring the Parsis to stop it.[27]

In some crude way, burial practices themselves parallel the direction that the soul or self takes after death. The Egyptians entombed their mummified dead but the apex of their pyramidal tombs were meant to point the way to the stars. Usually cultures that practice inhumation tend to depict the dead as going underground, as we have seen in the Mesopotamian, Canaanite, and Israelite burials. They usually retain an image of the body when they imagine the posthumous self. The cultures that practice cremation seem to prefer the notion that the dead go to the sky. They may or may not retain a notion of the image of the body of the individual. Zoroastrians (and Tibetans), who have a rather unique way of disposing the dead, should be seen as practicing a variation of cremation. Exposure becomes, in effect, a slower form of cremation.[28]

Particularly revealing in this regard is the Zoroastrian sense that one should keep a corpse from being buried in the ground. We get the following interesting ruling in the *Videvdat* (Law against the Demons), a compendium of religious ordinance roughly contemporary with and resembling the Talmud:

> Let no man alone by himself carry a corpse. If a man alone by himself carry a corpse, the *Nasu* [corpse-demon] rushes upon him, to defile him, from the nose of the dead, from the eye, from the tongue, from the jaws, from the sexual organ, from the hinder parts. This *Druj* [false-

hood or disorder], this *Nasu*, falls upon him, stains him even to the end of the nails, and he is unclean, thenceforth, for ever and ever.[29]

The correct place for the body is not the ground, with its connections to *druj*, but the air, with its connection with *asha*. People who bury the dead (who include virtually all the Zoroastrians' significant enemies) are perpetually cursed with demons.

Later Zoroastrian Texts

LATER ZOROASTRIAN texts give a much more detailed view of the final events of history than the earlier texts do. The *Bundahishn* text is said to be *zend*, a Pahlavi gloss and commentary on an earlier text. Some *zend* commentaries are quite close translations while others are far-reaching commentaries. The *Bundahishn* bears some relationship to the *Bahman Yasht*, one of the hymnic texts which, in turn, takes its form from the *Avesta*. It captured the imagination of the Zoroastrians and continuously needed revision in view of new events. It outlines a terrible apocalyptic end constantly forecasted and constantly being reforecasted based on the latest current events, just as we can hear a new interpretations of Daniel and the Revelation of Saint John every week by televangelists who constantly read the newspaper as confirming prophecies.[30] The journey of the soul, or *urvan*, after death has a long and special place in Zoroastrian tradition. The apocalyptic end, the *frashkart*, or *frasho kereti* in Avestan, is a final "rehabilitation" rather than the end of the world because it takes place on earth and earth continues eternally: "non-aging, immortal, non-fading, forever living, forever prospering" (Yt 19:89).

In the Zoroastrian tradition, as humanity progresses, it loses interest in food and other earthly things. The gradual abandonment of eating becomes symbolic of the ascending path to immortality. Eating was paired with dying among the Zoroastrians, since everything that lives and dies needs to eat and digest. As humanity progressively gives up food, it gives up digestion and corruption, becoming perfected. This in turn deprives Āz (concupiscence), a bad goddess or demon, of her normal sustenance so she threatens to devour the other demons. In the *Zātspram*, she threatens to to eat up Ahriman but this version may have been influenced by a Zoroastrian monistic heresy known as "Zurvanism." At any rate, in the *Bundahishn*, Ahriman survives long enough to see Āz's weapons smashed, whereupon they both go hurtling into the deep darkness.

The Resurrection

ZOROASTRIANS begin with the bones when speaking of the resurrection. Since they practice exposure of the corpse, only the bones are left after the disposition of the dead. The same would be true had the body been buried and the flesh decayed in a sarcophagus, so we may expect that this imagery can be borrowed or reinvented in Judaism and Christianity in Hellenistic times when they both practice this form of burial.

The great day of general resurrection is called in "Pahlavi," *Ristaxez* ("raising of the dead"), just as it is in Judaism and Christianity. Notice that the Zoroastrian text says that resurrection is not nearly so difficult for God as creation itself, which is accomplished ex nihilo, from nothing. In chapters 6 and 9, we shall run into the same argument in 2 Maccabees, where it is argued in the converse way: The mother exhorts her children to keep the faith in resurrection in the face of their martyrdom because God, who made heaven and earth from nothing, can surely resurrect the martyrs. This is a most important parallel between Persian and Jewish notions of resurrection and suggests that the Jews could have been influenced by their Persian overlords, though we have no direct evidence of borrowing and no hint at what could have been the channel of transmission. On the other hand, Zoroastrian and Muslim heaven is bodily, as sexual congress is one of the joys that continues into the next world. Christian heaven is not sexual (though eventually sex comes back during Renaissance),[31] and Jewish notions are equivocal.

The resurrection body for Zoroastrians, however, is not exactly the body of this life, but a body which has entered a more perfected, spiritual state, called "the future body" *(tan i pasen)*. It is somewhat like the spiritual body *(soma pneumatikon)* that Paul describes in 1 Corinthians Ch. 10, as we shall see. Gayomart, the primal man in Zoroastrianism, will be the first to be resurrected, followed by the primal couple, Mashye and Mashyane (the Zoroastrian Adam and Eve), then everyone else, every righteous person and every sinner having already been punished sufficiently in the interim. Zoroastrians are not unitarians, but they are universalists: Everyone will be saved.

Rudolph Bultmann and his students expressed the idea that a Persian myth of a "redeemed redeemer" is the background for Christianity, especially in the Gospel of John. For Bultmann, Jesus was fit into the story of an original man who becomes the final savior. Here, that notion can be shown to be quite mistaken. Gayomart and the Sayoshyant are two different characters and so there is no single myth of a "redeemed redeemer" in Iranian thought at all. It is even dubious that the notion that the primal man, Adam, is Christ can be found in Christianity; 1 Corinthians 15:21–22 expresses an antithetical relation but not an identity. In the Gospel of John, it is the logos and the savior who are united for the first time in the incarnation of Jesus. These are Hellenistic Jewish and later Christian notions, explainable and understandable because of the special constraints of Hellenized Judaism and later of Christian conceptualizations of Jesus' role. The logos of the Gospel of John is best understood as a Greco-Jewish notion Christianized, not a Persian one Judaized.[32] On the other hand, many motifs from the Persian notion of resurrection have entered Judaism, to be domesticated in a slightly different way. Furthermore, the cosmic battle and the description of the demonic forces has had an enormous influence on Christian apocalypses, even on The Revelation according to John, as well as on Christian iconography.

The hero of the final battle is *Sōshyans,* or *Saoshyant,* sometimes called "the Savior," with which our English word it is cognate. It is hard not to interpret this name in a Christian context, but in Persia, the kind of "salvation" meant is "benefit" or "profit," not a remedy to our fallen sinful state. The *Saoshyant* is the last of Zarathusthra's posthumous children, arising in the last three millennia to bring about the "rehabilitation," the "fresh creation," the *frasho kereti.* The *Saoshyant's* function is to raise human bodies and separate them from the constituent elements into which they have decayed and reunite them with their "souls." After this they have to endure three days of molten metal to refine them. In historical tradition, there are actually reports that Zoroastrians underwent similar ordeals on earth to demonstrate their religious integrity or their honesty. Zoroastrians have walked between fiery piles of wood or had molten metal poured on them as a way of showing their faith would allow them to triumph.[33]

In the imaginative eye of *Bundahishn,* this future ordeal will be safely and easily passed by the righteous. They will feel as though they are in a warm, milk bath. Not so with the sinners, of course, who will undergo excruciating pain. But after the ordeal is over, everyone is purged of sins and malfeasances and everyone enters the newly reconstituted earth. *Sōshyans* himself brings one last vicarious sacrifice in behalf of humanity and then all enter the newly recreated world, in which eating has no more use and so contains a complete and unthreatened complement of animals. The one exception is that one last bull sacrifice is necessary for preparing the drink *haoma,*[34] the sacred and sacramental drink of the Zoroastrians, which here becomes like drinking from the grail to gain immortality. This *haoma* will be white, rather than the usual yellow (as it is purified from bulls' urine), suggesting that it will be higher and purer material. The ritual of taking this psychotropic drug is one of the central features of early Zoroastrianism, though precisely what *haoma* was has been lost. It seems, however, linguistically related to the Soma of the *Vedas*.

Orthodoxy in Sasanian Iran and Ascent

SHAUL SHAKED suggests some of the religious effects of the establishment of orthodoxy in Sasanian Iran (225 CE until the Muslim conquest).[35] The Sasanian period is usually represented as a period of great cultural stability, as it is the period in which Zoroastrianism becomes not just the personal religion of the rulers but the established religion of the whole Sasanian Empire. The Arsacid or Parthian period (ca. 225 BCE–ca. 225 CE) had featured great religious and cultural pluralism, matching a period of great Persian conquest and rule. The empire not only contained a host of indigenous, local cults, it also contained several rival religions to Zoroastrianism—Judaism, Christianity, and Manichaeanism, all offering a significant cosmology and alternative route to salvation. They were all mobile and identifiable by their particular rituals. To make matters worse for Zoroastrians, Christianity and its stepchild Manichaeanism, which had been founded by Mani out of a Syrian Christian ascetic movement, were explicitly missionary religions and were making considerable headway in the late Arsacid Empire.

A great innovation of this period, in the Roman Empire as well as its arch-enemy the Persian Empire, was the possibility of individual choice in matters of religion. Everyone participated in the cult of his own city in times past and was theoretically free to give such other worship as time and pocketbook allowed. But the choices were greatly limited by the local nature of village life. All that changed in imperial cities. And the bigger the empire, the more available choices. Cosmopolitanism was greatly stimulated by the conquest of Alexander the Great, who conquered the Persia as well as the Eastern Mediterranean Basin. By enforcing the spread of Greek language, Alexander and his successors brought everyone into communication in an unprecedented way. This was a tremendous opportunity as well as a tremendous threat to ancient religions. All over the known world, religions, including Egyptian religion, Judaism, Babylonian religion, as well as Christianity, Manichaeanism, and the philosophical schools of Greece, became open and attractive to people who lived far from the original home of the religion due to the ease of communication and travel. Each religion developed a "diaspora," or portable form, that first helped its own adherents while they lived far from home and later could and did attract people from all over the empire. Christianity and Manichaeanism had particularly formidable missionizers.

The early Sasanian Empire took action against this rampant multiculturalism. The result was the emergence of a Zoroastrian orthodoxy and suppression of a variety of alternative Zoroastrianisms. Competing religions were targeted even more for suppression. The first Sasanian kings, with their famous chief priests, Kartir and Tansar, began a systematic repression of the missionary religions within their empire. Judaism suffered from this persecution but perhaps, in retrospect, it was sheltered by its small numbers, restricted ethnicity, and lack of missionary zeal.

The results were more catastrophic for Christianity and Manichaeanism. They were immediately perceived as threats and persecuted severely, as Zoroastrian, Jewish, Manichaean, and Christian sources all attest. Zoroastrian orthodoxy emerged therefore partly as a defense against the perceived threat of Christian and Manichaean missionizing. Within the Zoroastrianism of the period, philosophical literature, which had already taken on the characteristics of a quest, began to treat other religions with skepticism. The *Dâstân-i Mēnōk-i Krat,* "the Law of the Spirit of Wisdom," begins in the following way:

> He went forth in the world in search of wisdom, from kingdom to kingdom and from province to province, and enquired, examined and comprehended concerning the several faiths and beliefs of those people whom he considered foremost in knowledge. . . . [36]

The start is a concession to open-mindedness and cultural pluralism, which is part of the history of Zoroastrianism. It subjects many faiths to scrutiny with a standard perhaps a bit too Zoroastrian for current tastes in comparative religion, but it expresses the hope that faiths will teach the relationship between wisdom and the moral achievements of every person. This kind of writing would be impossible in a missionizing faith.

At the same time, we find Zoroastrian tracts explicitly designed to defeat the thought of other religions, as in the *Škand gumānig-wizār* ("A Trenchant Resolver of Doubts"), a tractate against Manichaeanism written by Mardan Farouk. It makes instructive reading when compared and contrasted with Augustine's tractate against the Manichaeans. Augustine disliked Manichaean dualism, which Mardan Farouk found tolerable if impaired, while Augustine liked Manichaean asceticism, though he found it extreme, while Mardan Farouk found insufferable any ascetic practices at all. No wonder Manichaeanism disappeared, leaving us the silhouette of orthodox intolerance in the symmetrical tractates of opposition it left behind. In spite of this, Augustine was himself accused of having absorbed too much Manichaean asceticism, with some justification, for Augustine had been a Manichaean in his youth. Mardan Farouk, no doubt (had we the documents to prove it), would have been criticized for absorbing too much Manichaean-style asceticism. Such is the fate of heresiologists: They are invariably tarred with the same mixture they mix up for use against the heresies.

During this period, we find a new method for gaining religious surety in the ambiguous Sasanian world of religious competition. That was a heavenly journey, undertaken ritually and by means of psychotropic drugs to help the adept travel to the next world for the purpose of gaining firm faith. These were not undertaken casually but were well prepared ritual experiences in which visions were deliberately sought in a public context. For instance, the high priest Kartir (third century CE) left us a report concerning the existence of heaven and hell. Since this document was carved into monumental rocks on a public highway, we can be sure that it represents an official demonstration of the truth of Zoroastrianism. Unfortunately, the inscription is fragmentary, leaving us in doubt about many of its most important details. In the course of his ecstatic journey, Kartir was represented by his "likeness," accompanied by a woman, who seems to represent his *daena* (Pahlavi: *dēn*). His spirit-self "likeness" journeyed up to the throne of judgment, undergoing adventures with "deadly ones" and helpers. Kartir invoked *humata, hukhta,* and *hvarshta* to ward off the dangers of the journey. There is in the "Zoroastrian book of common prayer" a text called the *Vispa Humata,* which concerns this triad and which is praised as having the power of salvation from hell.[37] This ritual mantra resembles the prayers which the rabbis and hermetists used to protect themselves in their heavenly journeys. It seems likely that Persian religion influenced these Rabbinic traditions. There was apparently a cup in the throne of some of these rulers, a "pit" or "cave" in front of another one, and scales in front of a third ruler. The account was promulgated in a public place, obviously because it demonstrated the truth of the Zoroastrian religion though some of the details are very peculiar to this vision.

Arda Viraf Nama

EVEN MORE graphic is the *Arda Viraf Nama* (*The Book of Arda Viraf* or alternatively, his name can be figured Arda Wiraz), a ninth-century text, written after the Muslim invasion. It takes as its subject the arrival of Alexander the Great, the previous great crisis in Mazdayasnianism (based on the Pahlavi word for the religion of the followers of Ahura Mazda, essentially Zoroastrianism). After a great ceremony of lot-casting, Arda Viraf ("Truthful" Viraf) was elected to travel to heaven to find out how to resolve the crisis. He was given a special potion, evidently a dose of *mang,* the drug that the prophet legendarily gave to Vishtaspa to enable him to behold his future victory over the Hyaonas, probably hensbane. From this point onward in our study, the heavenly journey can in itself indicate that the subject has achieved a certain altered state of consciousness. That is not always important to the narrative but it is sometimes the most important aspect of the story, especially when prophetic authority is claimed for religious innovation. When the experience itself is emphasized in this way, we should look for explicit statements about the validity and composition of the self. In this case, as the Persian story of the soul's journey develops, we see a more and more consistent view of the self emerging. The Zoroastrian notion of the transcendant self is the one that carries the moral deeds of the individual, the *daena,* the *urvan,* and the *tan i pasen.*

Furthermore, Arda Viraf's travels through the hells and heavens of Ahura Mazda show that the heavenly journey is undertaken because that is where the righteous dead were believed to go. This is the first time we have seen the ultimate destination of the righteous and sinful dead differ. Along the way, Arda Viraf saw terrible punishments waiting for sinners and unimaginable bliss awaiting the righteous. He saw horrors of hell in detail, raising the possibility that his readers just liked to hear about the terrible punishments awaiting sinners. Thus, the trip to heaven to visit the gods to find wisdom and truth is the same journey undertaken by the dead at the end of life. According to Viraf, when living people do it, they are practicing for the final flight after death and, at the same time, confirming that the world assumed by their religion was real and actual. It was travel narrative used as a proof-text for the cosmos.

In form the *Arda Viraf Namah* is quite a bit like the parts of Jewish *hekhaloth* literature and the Christian apocalypses, also containing heavenly journeys which function in the same way to confirm the religious universe of the participant. The *hekhaloth texts* also contain instructions on how to meditate (rather than rely on a drug) and how to make certain rituals magically operant *(theurgy)*. Like the Persian document, the Jewish material also begins with a crisis, usually the famous martyrdom of ten prominent Jewish rabbis, called "The Ten Martyrs," a Midrashic tradition based on an historical tragedy perpetrated by the Romans at the end of the Second revolt or Bar Kokhba revolt (135 CE). The story always raises the issue of theodicy: Why whould God require martyrdom? But it does not face the possible destruction of the whole people and thus lacks the fearful emphasis on the specific and terrible punishments of hell that *Arda Viraf Namah* has. In content, the *Arda Viraf Namah* resembles Dante's descriptions of hell in *The Divine Comedy* and is likely one of the remote sources of Dante's work.

Besides the final disposition of the sinners and the righteous, Arda Viraf tells us that there are a whole class of people who are neither good nor bad but equally balanced in their good and evil deeds. These people will remain in a kind of limbo called the Hammistagan (place of the Motionless Ones) until the moment that they get their future body *(tan i pasen)*:

> I came to a place and saw the souls of a number of people who were in Hammistagan. And I asked the victorious, just Srosh and Adar Yazad, "Who are these and why are they here?" Just Srosh and Adar Yazad said: "This is called Hammistagan, "The Place of the Motionless Ones;" and until the *future body* these souls will remain in this place. They are the souls of those people whose goodness and evildoing were equal. Say to the people of the world: "Do not consider the most trifling good act to be 'trouble' or 'vexation,' for everyone whose good acts outweigh his bad ones goes to heaven, and everyone whose bad ones weigh more, to hell, even if the difference is only three tiny acts of wrongdoing; and those in whom both are equal remain until the *future body* in this hammistagan. Their punishment is cold or heat from changes in the atmosphere. And they have no other affliction." (Boyce, 86)

The Soul's Journey, the Whole Story, in Later Zoroastrianism

AFTER GIVING some of the early traditions, it is appropriate to acknowledge that the full story comes only from a much later source. The complete story of the soul's journey from death to the afterlife is most easily seen in the Middle Persian, or Pahlavi text, *Dâstân-i Mēnōk-i Krat*, probably datable to the ninth century, which contains the most complete narrative of the soul's journey to the afterlife but also contains a great many traditions that we have seen as early as the Gathas.[38]

While there was considerable development in Zoroastrian thinking, unfortunately this development is not yet entirely datable in any easy or convincing way. Any time we assert Persian influence we must understand that we have few agreed-upon ways of distinguishing the most sophisticated, medieval traditions from the earlier traditions which are more important for our purposes. The core of the tradition, the rising of the dead, however, was documented early enough to have affected Jewish thought directly in the second century BCE.

Since the Zoroastrian view of the end of time is paralleled by similar notions in the apocalyptic Jewish and Christian traditions, it is tempting to see Zoroastrianism as the source of them. But the dating is too problematic for surety. It may even be that Zoroastrian ideas were influenced by Hellenistic Jewish and Christian ones, as there were both Jews and Christians living in the Persian Empire. One can even find modern Zoroastrians who want to reestablish the connection between Iranian and Indian thought, and who feel that the notion of resurrection itself was borrowed from Judaism, rather than the other way around.[39]

The *Dâstân-i Mēnōk-i Krat* contains the final judgment awaiting all in the *Frasho kereti, frashkart* or *frashgird*. There, everyone will be forgiven, much like the later Rabbinic view of God's grace at the end of time. And they will be resurrected, yet not into physical bodies, rather into newly prepared "spiritual" or "future" bodies. It seems safest to say that during the Parthian and Sasanian periods all three religions—Zoroastrianism, Judaism, and Christianity—cross-fertilize each other. But it also seems likely that the kernel notion of resurrection was a Zoroastrian notion first, since it appears to be there right at the beginning of Zoroastrian literature. The Persian Empire, with all its far-flung satrapies, would not have borrowed such a major notion, which is, or becomes a critical notion in their religion from an otherwise almost unknown, insignificant little district in the far western parts of their empire, especially when it is first witnessed surely in Judaism and only in the second century BCE, when both the land of Israel and the Persian Empire had already been conquered by Alexander and was enjoying rapid Hellenization. If the end of the world is characterized by a cosmic battle, and there is a historical development, which all three religions admit, then there should be an end when good prevails over the threatening evil of the days of the writer. No one needs to borrow that notion from the other, but all three seem to trade motifs and details freely back and forth.

Still there are important differences between Jewish, Christian, and Zoroastrian apocalypses. In the earlier Jewish sectarian material and Christianity, the world ends with the certain destruction of the evil people. Zoroastrianism (and Rabbinic Judaism) find such lack of mercy impossible for God. For Zoroastrians, hell becomes a kind of purgatory, as not even dead sinners are condemned there for all eternity. Only the demons have bought property there; the others are merely renters. Perhaps the Rabbinic notion comes from the long association between the Rabbinic academies and Sasanian Zoroastrianism. However, later in our study, we will have adduced enough information to show social and political reasons why Rabbinic Judaism would imagine a heavenly world of forgiveness of sinners when the two host cultures in which it lived in the medieval world—Christianity and Islam—continued to believe in a heaven exclusively for believers. Briefly, to anticipate the argument: Intolerance is the luxury of victors while tolerance is characteristic of minorities who hope for toleration in a country that someone else controls.

Second Isaiah and Early Influence on the People of Israel

THERE ARE FEW certainties in the story of Zoroastrian-Jewish interaction, but it looks as if 2 Isaiah (or Deutero-Isaiah), especially Isaiah 44–47, polemicizes against Zoroastrianism and some of the claims of the *Shahan-Shah*, the King of Kings, as well as welcoming him as the savior of Israel.

> Thus says the LORD to his anointed, to Cyrus,
>> whose right hand I have grasped
> to subdue nations before him
>> and strip kings of their robes,
>>> . . .
> so that you may know that it is I, the LORD,
>> the God of Israel, who call you by your name.
> For the sake of my servant Jacob,
>> and Israel my chosen,
> I call you by your name,
>> I surname you, though you do not know me.
> I am the LORD, and there is no other;
>> besides me there is no god.
>> I arm you, though you do not know me,

> so that they may know, from the rising of the sun
>> and from the west, that there is no one besides me;
>> I am the LORD, and there is no other.
> I form light and create darkness,
>> I make weal and create woe;
>> I the LORD do all these things. (Isa 45:1a, 36–7)

Notice that 2 Isaiah declares Cyrus to be *Mashiah*—the anointed of God, messiah. This is the first time the term has been used to designate anyone other than a Jew. And it is the last time within Scripture. It demonstrates that the term was not nearly as well fixed as some today think; indeed, "messiah" could describe not just Judean kings, prophets, and priests, but Saul's shield and a number of other objects set up for an official purpose by the rite of anointing. But 2 Isaiah clearly means it in the political sense—appointment by God for a holy purpose which in turn, demonstrates his support for the new Persian regime that has just overthrown the Babylonians, who carried the Israelites away into exile. Second Isaiah's support will turn out to be well placed, because the Persians allowed the Israelites to return home from exile. Second Isaiah goes out of his way to show that Cyrus was appointed by God, even though Cyrus does not know Him. When the return actually takes place, the book of Ezra reads as if Cyrus were actually a worshipper of Israel's God:

> In the first year of King Cyrus of Persia, in order that the word of the LORD by the mouth of Jeremiah might be accomplished, the LORD stirred up the spirit of King Cyrus of Persia so that he sent a herald throughout all his kingdom, and also in a written edict declared: "Thus says King Cyrus of Persia: The LORD, the God of heaven, has given me all the kingdoms of the earth, and he has charged me to build him a house at Jerusalem in Judah. Any of those among you who are of his people—may their God be with them!—are now permitted to go up to Jerusalem in Judah, and rebuild the house of the LORD, the God of Israel—he is the God who is in Jerusalem; and let all survivors, in whatever place they reside, be assisted by the people of their place with silver and gold, with goods and with animals, besides freewill offerings for the house of God in Jerusalem." (Ezra 1:1–4)

This is an exaggeration; the Persians had their own gods (even if they appeared not to be fully Zoroastrians yet) and there were good political reasons why they let exiles return and granted religious freedom to their subjects. They wished to run their empire through priestly rather than royal bureaucracies. Israel was no exception.

However, the vision of the religious life described is not necessarily inaccurate for Cyrus's time.[40] Cyrus's new regime wanted to be known as a restorer of the old order so he supported the priesthoods of a number of peoples who had been subjugated by the Babylonians. Israel was not alone. Also under Cyrus began the Israelite priestly rule that we associate with the redaction of the Pentateuch. Native Israelite Messianic candidates—that is, royal descendants of the Davidic Dynasty, Sheshbezzar and Zerubbabel—are mentioned in the early Second Commonwealth records. But they do not assume kingly power. Shortly afterward we stop hearing of a legitimate heir to David.[41] Meanwhile, the priests took over the government in earnest.

On the other hand Isaiah 45 does not give Cyrus absolute free rein. Isaiah does polemicize against Cyrus in the first few verses and against dualism in the last few verses. At the beginning of the quotation we note that Isaiah clarifies that God is doing all these things, not Cyrus. And these great world events are not random clashes of armies; they are part of a divine plan for the purpose of rescuing YHWH's tiny people, Israel.

When Isaiah says that God makes darkness and light (v 7), he is actually risking a contradiction with Genesis 1, in which God makes light but not darkness. This merely begs the question as to whether Genesis ch. 1, the P prologue in heaven, was in existence at this period. It is quite possible that it was written later, whereas Genesis 2–4, the J epic was certainly in existence and may have served as the only creation story. This clarifies that the Hebrew God is not merely Spenta Mainyu, the good god of Zoroastrianism, for instance, who is inferior to Ahura Mazda. The whole passage makes most sense as a polemic against the newly arriving Zoroastrianism. Does this suggest a time when Zoroastrianism was rising in Persia but before it became a state supported religion? Yes, that would be the best bet but, as with many things chronological in the study of Zoroastrianism, we cannot be sure from these few clues alone.

The Sociology of the Return from Exile

A FASCINATING summary of sociological models for exile and return are to be found in Daniel L. Smith's, *The Religion of the Landless*.[42] We should particularly pay attention to the development of a concept of ethnicity in diaspora and its subsequent utility for this small, separate people in the world empire. Both the exile and the return to the land of Israel can in some ways be compared to the forced marches of a number of other peoples in world history, though the return of the Israelites was voluntary.

The need for people to return to devastated Israel was shortly to bring new prophets to the fore, prophets whom we know only because their prophecies have been appended to the book of Isaiah, perhaps merely to give it a happier ending. The very last chapter of Isaiah provides us with the beginnings of an apocalypse which will right a world where infidels appear to have gotten the upper-hand forever. The remnant of God did, however, have a task. They would return to the land of Israel and worship God there, even before the Temple was reconstructed, because He did not need a Temple: "The heaven is His throne; the earth his footstool" (Isa 66:1). And they would have the "Glory of the Lord" at their head, a warrior God who, like Ba'al, would protect them. The people would conceive and bring forth a new child, a new commonwealth. It would be a miracle, born in a day, testifying to the power and the "Glory of the Lord."

The exiled in Israel would return and even some of the nations would arrive as well. Even the old priesthood would be constituted from those who came back, a new unity from the old remnants. Those who ate swine and otherwise violated the ancient commandments would die terrible deaths for the "Glory of the Lord" himself would even arrive there with his heavenly hosts, all in their chariots. By such events God's miracles would be made manifest to the entire world. He would even make a new heaven and new earth so that the covenant could be reconstituted, as they were the witnesses to the breaking of the previous ones. The world would come to worship YHWH in Jerusalem, and the corpses of the dead would testify to the evil that overcomes those who disobey Him. His faithful remnant, Israel, however, would see His Temple, even though it could not and did not need to contain His Glory. All it needed was patience. Those who were faithful would see even Israelite bones flourish. These images became extremely important when the resurrection of the dead was prophesied in Daniel.

> Thus says the Lord:
> "Heaven is my throne
>   and the earth is my footstool;
> what is the house which you would build for me,
>   and what is the place of my rest?
>   . . .

For thus says the LORD:
"Behold, I will extend prosperity to her like a river,
    and the wealth of the nations
    like an overflowing stream;
and you shall suck, you shall be carried upon her hip,
    and dandled upon her knees.
As one whom his mother comforts,
    so I will comfort you;
    you shall be comforted in Jerusalem.
You shall see, and your heart shall rejoice;
    your bones shall flourish like the grass;
and it shall be known that the hand of the LORD
    is with his servants,
    and his indignation is against his enemies.
"For behold, the LORD will come in fire,
    and his chariots like the stormwind,
to render his anger in fury,
    and his rebuke with flames of fire.
For by fire will the LORD execute judgment,
    and by his sword, upon all flesh;
    and those slain by the LORD shall be many.

       . . .

"For as the new heavens and the new earth
    which I will make
shall remain before me, says the LORD;
    so shall your descendants and your name remain.
From new moon to new moon,
    and from sabbath to sabbath,
all flesh shall come to worship before me,
says the LORD. (Isa 66:1, 12–16, 22–23)

This prophecy begins with God reminding the Jews that he does not need a Temple. Then, it prophesies that Israel will regain its prosperity. God will be like a woman nursing her children, giving Israel suck, a very daring metaphor. Then he will "make their bones flourish like the grass," an extraordinarily portentious phrase for the notion of resurrection, whose importance has been all but ignored in scholarship. Immediately thereafter, the prophet saw the end of the world; God would protect his righteous and deliver the sinners to perdition. He would come in fiery chariotry with his angelic hosts to accomplish it. Then would come the new heaven and the new earth. Within this passage is the scriptural root of Israelite notions of the resurrection of the dead, though the atmosphere in which it developed was Persian. It took centuries before the root produced a plant—the book of Daniel, in which the concept of bodily resurrection finally flowers.

If there are further Babylonian, Canaanite, and Persian elements to this vision of judgment, they have been so well-incorporated into the historical description of the plight of Israel and the special providence of its God as to be inseparable. This vision serves as the basis for the apocalyptic end of time in which resurrection is promised. But that interpretation developed only in 168 BCE. In that vision, we shall see that the remnant of those who returned, as well as those who remained true to the covenant with YHWH, will serve as the community of those who are saved, just as in the paradisial vision of the Persian Empire.

5

Greek and Classical Views of Life After Death and Ascent to the Heavens

IN CONTRAST TO our investigations of previous cultures, there is no dearth of evidence about the Greek afterlife. Unlike our records of the fertile crescent, we have a vast body of extant Greek literature. There are, to be sure, important and nagging *lacunae* in our knowledge, especially at the beginnings, and there is a great deal more about ordinary life that we would like to know. But by comparison to the textual evidence of ancient Near Eastern cultures, we have ample amounts of information about Greek thinking on life after death as well as important information about customs and changes in Greek sensibilites over the centuries.

When it comes to Greek notions of the afterlife, we have whole categories of evidence: not the least of which are drama and epic, travel narratives, essays, philosophy, and religious writings, not to forget our considerable archeological remains. Any plan of attack in dealing with Greco-Roman evidence must be even more selective: to look briefly at the most important phenomena in Greek culture and then pick those things which most affect the citizens of Judea. Foremost among this will be Plato's notions of the afterlife, which penetrated Jewish culture deeply. Other aspects of Greek culture are also important because they form part of the great multicultural Hellenistic syncretism in which Judaism lived.

Greek culture and the religious texts it produced continued over millennia and spread to many different lands. Greek views of life after death underwent considerable evolution and variation. But even from the beginning, the Greeks had several different and conflicting views of death and the final disposition of the soul. After the development of the philosophical schools, varied and often conflicting conceptions of life after death continued within the culture, forming a not altogether logical amalgamation of different views. These broad views have been surveyed by an imposing number of different scholars; their very good and thorough work does not have to be rehearsed here.[1] We need to emphasize that not all Greek views agreed with the notion that the immortal soul separates from the body, though that is the innovation normally attributed to Greek authorship. Then too, we have already seen that in Egypt, Mesopotamia, Canaan, and Israel there is a "shade" or "shadow" that separates from the body at death, sometimes several different formulations of that continuing identity. So the concept that the soul can survive death is not precisely an innovation of Greek thought. What is an innovation is a radical dualism in which the immortality of the soul was seen to be provable, beatific, and the natural goal of existence. That was an innovation of Plato's philosophy.

It is an innovation with a history. Throughout Greek history there are reports of people of unusual religious talent, whom we might want to call shamans (after their counterparts in Central Asia) or sorcerers, who were able to leave their bodies while still alive and perform various services— like earthly or heavenly travel, healings, or divinations. Greeks who were supposed to have these talents included: Orpheus (mythical), Trophonius (mythical), Aristeas of Proconessus (early seventh century BCE), Hermotimus of Clazomenae (seventh century BCE?), Epimenides of Cnossus or Phaestus (ca. 600 BCE), Pythagoras of Samos (530s–520s BCE), Abaris the Hyperborean (sixth century BCE), Zalmoxis of the Thracian Getae (sixth century BCE), and Empedocles of Acragas (ca. 485–435 BCE).[2] The figures are legendary and often cannot be dated accurately. Furthermore, Greek myth also contains cautionary tales against heavenly journeys as the famous stories of Phaethon and Icarus demonstrate.

Here is the cautionary tale of Hermotimus of Clazomenae from the report of Apollonius' *Historiae Mirabiles* 3:

They say his [Hermotimus'] soul would wander from his body and stay away for many years. Visiting places, it would predict what was going to happen—for example, torrential rains or droughts, and in addition earthquakes and pestilences and the suchlike. His body would just lie there, and after an interval his soul would return to it, as if to its shell, and arouse it. He did this frequently, and whenever he was about to go on his travels he gave his wife the order that no one, citizen or anyone, should touch his body. But some people came into the house, prevailed upon his wife and observed Hermotimus lying on the floor, naked and motionless. They brought fire and burned him, in the belief that, when the soul came back and no longer had anything to reenter, he would be completely deprived of life. This is exactly what happened. The people of Clazomenae honor Hermotimus even to this day and have [built] a temple to him. Women may not enter it for the reason above [i.e., the wife's betrayal].[3]

The story is legendary, serving as the foundation story of a temple. But many Greeks believed that the soul could naturally depart from its body, not just in death, but also in life. This property of the soul, which could be exploited by religious entrepreneurs, demonstrated that the soul traveled to the afterlife at death. Eventually, these stories were taken as evidence for the immortality of the soul and the desirability of religiously altered states of consciousness.

Early Greek Beliefs and Burial Practices

WE MUST FOLLOW the story as chronologically as possible so we will begin with the Homeric epics. The texts of the Homeric Greeks and the archeological evidence of the earliest periods suggest that there was no strict reward for a heroic or moral life. The Isles of the Blessed (e.g., Hesiod ca. 730 BCE, *Works and Days*) and Elysian fields (*Odyssey* 4.561ff.) were occasionally open to the most valiant heroes in the ancient period. Menelaus is told that he will go to the Elysian Plain, as much because of the loss of honor he suffered in the rape of his wife Helen as for his stature as King of Sparta. Interestingly, neither "Elysion" nor "Radamanthys" (the ruler of the dead), appear to be native Greek terms.

As every student who still studies the traditional Western canon knows, the *Iliad* ends with the funeral games for the opposing dead heroes, Hector and Patroklus. The sworn enemies are united in a momentary fellowship of mourning. Achilles, who has killed Hector in single combat, counsels Priam to accept the death of his son:

> Bear up, and do not unceasingly lament away your heart.
> For you will not accomplish anything grieving for your son.
> Nor will you raise him up, and sooner will you suffer another
> evil. (24.549–51)[4]

Achilles tells Priam that nothing will ever bring Hector back. We find an interesting comparison with Israel here: At approximately the same time in quite another corner of the globe, David legendarily says about his dead son that the living go to the dead, not the dead to the living: "Can I bring him back again? I shall go to him, but he will not return to me" (2 Sam 12:23). The dead, then, did not cease to exist in either culture. Rather they remained in a shadowy underworld, as insubstantial shades, without strength or pleasure. The dead head off to their final resting place although they can return to bring messages to the living:

. . .

and there appeared to him the ghost of unhappy Patroklus
all in his likeness for stature, and the lovely eyes, and voice,
and wore such clothing as Patroklus had worn on his body.
The ghost came and stood over his head and spoke a word
     to him:
'You sleep, Achilles, you have forgotten me; but you
     were not
careless of me when I lived, but only in death. Bury me
as quickly as may be, let me pass through the gates of Hades.
The souls, the images of dead men, hold me at a distance,
and will not let me cross the river and mingle among them,
but I wander as I am by Hades' house of the wide gates.
     (23.65–74)

. . .

Oh wonder! Even in the house of Hades there is left
     something,
a soul and an image, but there is no real heart of life in it.
     (23.103–104)

Achilles is describing the appearance of his dead companion Patroklus. His phantasm, his image *(eidolon)* has appeared in a dream but Patroklus has not yet taken up eternal residence in Hades.[5] First, as Patroklus reminds him, he needs proper burial. Not to complete the proper burial would be the highest of moral breaches. He then utters a dire prophecy, that Achilles himself will fall before the walls of Troy (lines 80–81).

As in all ancient cultures, dreams, visions, and other religiously interpreted states of consciousness both gave the power to foretell the future and confirmed the culture's depiction of the afterlife. In *The Epic of Gilgamesh,* for instance, Enkidu foresaw his own death in a dream. In this case, the soul and image which Achilles dreams is a visible but not a tangible likeness of the dead warrior, his comrade Patroklus. Patroklus dissolves into mist, slipping through Achilles' arms when he tries to embrace him (lines 99–100). It is this visible likeness that is the religious background for the later philosophical understanding of soul *(psyche)* or the Latin *animus* (literally: wind)—that is, cognate with the Greek word for "wind," *anemos* (ἄνεμος). Indeed, the root meaning of psyche is derived from the idea of breathing (cf. *psychō,* "I breathe, blow").[6] In its early usage, there does not seem to be any relationship between *psyche* and thinking or feeling, but at this poignant moment we see that the emotional relationship between the heroic duo has survived Patroklus' death.[7]

Besides the aforementioned *psyche* and *anemos,* primary words which could point to parts of the "self" in the ancient Greek tradition would be *phrenes, noos,* and *thymos* but there were several others as well.[8] One of the most popular is the use of the word "shadows" or "shades" to refer to the dead: *skiai,* as that was expressed in Greek; but another would be *eidolon,* "image" or "phantom." The latter two have the advantage of referring to a likeness of the departed, even though it is an imperfect one. A unified concept of "self" was apparently won after a long battle which led to a notion of consciousness, then, to Socrates' notion of a transcendent self, and finally to the Aristotelian notion of a soul's body of knowledge which survives death but leaves behind individuality. The achievement of a single conception of the soul is crucial to the notion of reason and moral theory, and it is the beginning of our modern understanding of the "self."[9] From here, it was further developed by Plotinus and Augustine (see chap. 14).

According to Bruno Snell, the first writer to talk systematically of a "soul" as anything recognizable to us was the philosopher Heraclitus, who called the soul "psyche," distinguished it from the body, and said that the soul is endowed with a "logos," a rational plan, which was common to humanity and amenable to education. These concepts, according to Snell and Rohde, Heraclitus got from the lyric poets, who described our mental states in much more detail than did Homer.

As in the other ancient cultures, the Greeks faced questions of personal identity not only directly but often obliquely by asking the question: "What will become of me?" The soul, the shade, the *anemos,* the *thymos* all helped Greeks understand not only what remained after death but who it was that was doing the thinking and speaking and how to describe these internal processes. The ancient Greeks were sure that the soul separated from the body in dreams and trances; it left the body behind at death. The sophisticated notion of a consistent self in Greek philosophy is the product of a long process of visualization of the next life as well as this one, a meditation on what is the lasting outcome of a life, what is its transcendent meaning.

In fact, like the ancient Egyptian documents, the most early Greek documents could envision a person in several different ways, without a necessary unified view of the "self." What is different, however, is that through the early lyric poets, they also took an interest in how the self grew and progressed, emotionally and intellectually. They could discuss perception as "taking something in," or "learning," with the term *daena*, cognate to one of the Persian words for the moral self, the *daena*. There were several words to describe seeing and thinking. Also, forgetting *(lanthanesthai)* and remembering *(mimneskesthai)* were extremely important to notions of the "self." Memory itself played a crucial part in Plato's proof for the transcendent immortality of the soul.

The early Greeks burned their dead heroes near the battlefield. Perhaps this ritual too is congruent with the notion that the soul separates from the body. But, in more normal circumstances, as when someone died in peacetime, the dead might equally well be entombed or buried. What is unchangeable is that not to be properly cared for through funeral rites was a great disgrace, for soldier or civilian, as Patroklus reminds Achilles. Improper care could bring the ghost back to haunt the perpetrators, as an unburied person was not allowed to enter Hades.[10] Sometimes the ghosts could actually become vampires.[11] The rite was just more difficult to perform in wartime, therefore more appreciated. Several epitaphs make clear that normally the Greeks assumed that proper rites were effective in keeping the ancestor well-behaved after death, and that proper commemoration at specific intervals kept the memory of the departed alive and socialized within the community and, simultaneously, vindictive ghosts at bay.

Burial Practices

THE FIRST OF these rites was the funeral. The funeral *(kedeia)* had three distinct phases. They were (1) laying out the body *(prothesis)*, (2) its conveyance to the place of cremation or interment *(ekphora)*, and (3) the disposition proper which was the deposition of the cremated or inhumated remains. Prayers were offered for the chthonic deities to receive the dead kindly; texts of them are sometimes found on tombstones. From the eighth to the fourth century BCE, inhumation and cremation were practiced concurrently, though the popularity of each waxed and waned.[12] In Rome, once the correct funeral rituals were performed, the deceased officially belonged to the *Di Manes,* the communal, sainted ancestors.[13]

Later in Greco-Roman culture, corpses were buried in tombs in a sarcophagos (literally: "flesh-eater") until their flesh decayed. Then, the bones could be collected and placed in an ossuary, often of exquisite design. This process is called "secondary burial" and was practiced in Israel as well. Secondary burial in the form of disinterrment can still be found in England today, where charnel houses are used for depositing the collected bones of the dead. This makes possible the reuse of valuable churchyard plots. So too, in ancient Greece and in Hellenistic Israel, sarcophagi would be reused after the bones were gathered.

Personal depictions of the dead were quite frequent in affluent memorials, some with evocative poses of the person's characteristic habits. For example, a girl could be pictured with her pet dove, as in the beautiful memorial stone on display at the Metropolitan Museum in New York City.

Some possible hints of more pleasures awaiting the dead can be found in sarcophagus art. In certain Mycenaean tombs one finds depictions of a judgment scene with a scale, a *psychostasia* (weighing of souls), as well as butterflies, a symbol of the goddess Psyche and who is, in turn, the emblem and namesake of the soul.[14] But it is hard to know exactly how to evaluate these depictions since, in the *Iliad,* Zeus is represented as weighing the fates of Achilles and Hector at their earthly combat.[15] The parallel between the two actions—judgment during life and after death—suggests that we grow to understand our roles in life not only directly but also indirectly, by considering our ultimate ends and what our lives will be like when continued beyond the grave.

Graves and tombs were also the location of offerings to the dead. Like those of the Mesopotamians and Canaanites, tombs and graves, especially in the Hellenistic period, could be fitted with sophisticated plumbing pipes for periodic libations delivered to the remains.[16] When the bones or ashes were laid to rest in buried urns, the pipes conveyed the gifts into the urns.

Hades: The Location of the Dead

THE DOMINANT explanation for the location of the dead in the Homeric period was already the dark, underground kingdom of the god variously called Hades, Pluto, or Radamanthys. Later, the picture became more detailed: The dead were depicted as migrating, with Hermes as a guide, on a journey in which they encounter Cerberus the three-headed watchdog and pay their coins to Charon the ferryman to cross the river Styx. Small coins called obols were frequently placed in the corpse's mouth before the funeral to cover the ferry costs. The Homeric view of Hades was less articulated than these later familiar portraits but it was certainly part of later Greek notions and, what is more, quite close to the many other ancient views of the abode of the dead that we have seen in the ancient Near East.

In Homer's writing, Hades is merely where a soul *(psychē)* goes when its body dies. Besides the famous cases of Tantalus, Tityus, and Sisyphos and a handful of others, there are no real attempts to make Hades into a place of punishment or reward for a life deficient in happiness or virtue. Retributive justice was not the real function of Hades. Possibly, Hades was seen as punishment for all the dead for reckless behavior, as John Garland suggests.[17] But the Greeks apparently concluded that since death comes to all, Hades was the final destination for all.

One sure thing is, except for the specially treated mythical characters like Tantalus and Sisyphus, the virtuous and the sinners all lead the same life in Hades. The dead are weak and very much in the dark. Hades is a gloomy and very remote place, even though the sun visits it at night. As Odysseus' journey underground shows, souls need the living to provide blood libations in order to even materialize partially and, most of all, for information about the world of the living. Unlike Patroklus and the dead in the ancient Near East, who are prescient and can be consulted for divination, the Greek shades live in "that distant country," receiving information in the same way that anyone would in a remote place, through the newly arrived journeyers. The prophecy of Patroklus that Achilles will die at Troy is an exception, not the rule. We do not know whether Samuel's prophecies in the Bible were typical of Israelite visitations or not.

Fame Is Better than Immortality in the Odyssey

WHEN WE MEET Odysseus in the *Odyssey* Book 5, he is not the person we remember from the *Iliad*. He is weeping on the beach of the magical island of Ogygia, seemingly at his wits' end. But he is hardly in dire straits. He is the guest of the tall, beautiful, blonde, goddess Calypso, who has granted him immortality, an ever-new wardrobe, and her considerable sexual favors.

Tempted as we might be by this invitation, it was not satisfactory to

Odysseus, though he certainly enjoyed his temporary lodgings.[18] We know from the first books of the Odyssey that his kingdom of Ithaca was in grave danger. The suitors were conspiring to murder his son Telemachus and force Penelope to marry one of them. We learn from this incident that, for an Achaian hero, even immortality, fabulous sex with a beautiful blonde goddess, and an ever new wardrobe is not worth the price of family honor and fame. The island was a trap for Odysseus, preventing him from reentering the world to gain fame by protecting his kingdom. Ogygia—like Calypso herself, whose name means "covered up"—was hidden from human life, an unmanly temptation, and thus beneath the dignity of a hero. This epic functions as a moral exhortation to the ancient Greek to stop dallying on raids and return home, just as the *Iliad* was equally a moral example towards heroism in battle.

The cost of Odysseus's proper decision to eschew nameless, hidden immortality with Calypso is further emphasized by the *Odyssey* Book 11. Book 11 is a set-piece describing Odysseus' most daring journey, into Hades itself. Known as a *Nekyia* (literally: a séance), this chapter also resembles a warrior's raid into the underworld. After performing the expected libations, Odysseus set out on his journey, meeting the deceased among his crew, including Elpinor who cannot actually enter because he was not buried properly (11.50–54). As Odysseus enters, he finds many of his other dear departed ones there, beginning with his mother (11.84) Tiresius (1.90ff.), and, most importantly for our purposes, the greatest hero of the Greeks, Achilles (11.467ff.).

Although some Greek concepts of the afterlife were eventually inimical both to personal and to bodily resurrection, this depiction of spirits again shows that they retained an image of their physical selves. Everyone was recognizable by his or her bodily features; indeed, recognition was a major honor to the dead. The recently dead even retained their death wounds.[19] Although not physically embodied, they gain a modicum of physicality by drinking the blood of the sacrifice which Odysseus brings (e.g., 11.94–95). Embodiment was therefore part of the "revivication" process which Odysseus had learned how to accomplish ritually. But the "shades of the dead" are still intangible, dispersing like mist when Odysseus tries to embrace them. This is certainly not a concept of resurrection of the body, which we find in later Hebrew thought. But it is not yet the mature Platonic concept of bodiless souls either. It is more like our conception of ghosts.

One point of this description is to underline the value of honor. Odysseus had given up considerable pleasures and benefits to rescue his name and his honor. Needless to say, this book tells us that being dead, which will be his ultimate fate as well, is no fun either. Achilles says that he would rather be the poorest migrant worker or hireling on earth *(thēs)* than be the king of the dead (lines 489–91):

> Nay, seek not to speak soothingly to me of death, glorious Odysseus. I should choose, so I might live on earth, to serve as the hireling of another, of some portionless man whose livelihood was but small, rather than to be lord over all the dead that have perished.[20]

The cost of heroism is evident in Achilles' envy of the living. Even the greatest hero on earth, in the world of the Odyssey, becomes nothing more than an ephemeral shade after death. And so now we know the enormous price of Odysseus' decision to return to Ithaca and understand fully for the first time in the epic the enormous value of an Homeric hero's honor. Returning home means giving up any chance of immortality and subjects the hero to the challenges of homecoming *(nostos)*. The dangers of homecoming are symbolized by the fate of Agamemnon, who was murdered by his wife and her lover (see 11.385; 24.15–204 and elsewhere). However homecoming means that he will have the fame of having successfully defeated the Trojans and then return his kingdom to health, after rescuing his wife and assuring his son's succession.

Unlike *The Epic of Gilgamesh,* the *Odyssey* is not really about immortality, or even about not having it. Immortality is only used as a way to underline the real subjects: heroism and fame. The *Odyssey* begins with immortality refused rather than immortality sought (as in *The Gilgamesh Epic*) so it is the binary opposite of *The Gilgamesh Epic*. But binary oppositions eventually tell the same story. The *Odyssey* is about heroically battling against political and domestic disorder, which in some wider sense is the point of *The Gilgamesh Epic* as well, because Gilgamesh was not a good king until he had been made human by the knowledge of his own inevitable death. Both dramas are played out on a stage in which the hero's various possibilities for mortality and immortality are set against fame and explored.

There were other stories that valorized immortality in Greek culture. From one perspective, the *Odyssey* may be viewed as the lay of Telemachus' maturation or even the epic of Penelope's trial of patient waiting. But, for the Greeks, the title role goes to Odysseus, the fighting man. Both the stories of Gilgamesh and Odysseus center on male behavior, involving the idealization of male heroic, warlike values.

Demeter and Persephone,
the Eleusinian Mysteries

JUST AS IN Mesopotamia, there was another mythic pattern in the Homeric world, which we can see in the *Homeric Hymn to Demeter*. This hymn is written in the same heroic verse as the *Iliad* and the *Odyssey* but it tells another story: the familiar story of the rape of Persephone by the god of the underworld, Pluto. It serves the same purpose in Greek literature that the myth of "the Descent of Inanna" serves in ancient Sumerian literature. In some way, we keep coming upon the same naked narrative structures, each time newly dressed in the interests of a new culture.

Persephone is abducted by Pluto, the Lord of the underworld, while she is gathering spring flowers, which come with the rains. Persephone's mother Demeter wanders the world looking for her daughter; while she looks she neglects her duties and the natural world languishes throughout the summer, growing no grains or wheat, of which Demeter is the patron goddess. After she locates Persephone, she appeals to her Olympian siblings to release her, for none can actually enter the kingdom of death except Hermes, the messenger. The gods prevail on Pluto to allow her to leave. However, they discover that Persephone has eaten six pomegranate seeds. Because of this lapse, Persephone is forced to return to Pluto every year for six months. Again and again, we find that what keeps humanity from immortality is lack of circumspection while eating in front of the gods. Alimentation is definitely part of our mortal natures. The gods eat too (they like to eat sacrifices and *embrosia*), although they do not need to eat. Conversely, divinity can be achieved in the ascetic refusal of the pleasures of eating and generation, or at least, this will be the response of Christian monastics (see ch. 14).

During Persephone's forced annual sojourn underground, Demeter mourns again for her daughter, and the earth is not fertile. When Persephone is back above ground, Demeter is happy to be reunited with her daughter so she causes the grain to grow, probably the winter months when grain grows in Greece and the Near East, though the *Homeric Hymn to Demeter* sometimes uses ambiguous language. When the grain grows, the flowers return as well (lines 450–55; 471–3).[21] The grain harvest is in the spring, at the height of the flowering of plants and trees. In this respect, it is quite close to the story of the *Descent of Inanna,* which links her descent, not only with the periodic setting of the planet Venus, but also with the hot summer, when no grain grows but fruits ripen.

On one level the message is obvious enough. The story explains the change of seasons and the yearly harvest of grain. It also demonstrates the ritual efficacy of grief, libations, and sacrifices for the dead. It states that eating and drinking while in the underworld is what keeps the dead there, which is where they belong and should be. Those who bring the proper sacrifices and libations for the dead, allowing them to eat, never have troublesome ghosts around to torment them. It enforces that notion by telling the story of its polar opposite—a live person who wants to leave but cannot because she has eaten while there.

In its current literary form, the story explains the change of seasons by referring to marriage customs of the Hellenic world. Since marriages were arranged and daughters of the aristocracy were married quite young, they faced a parallel situation to Persephone, being forced to live with their husband's family. If, as was often true, the husband lived at some distance, it was quite normal for them to see their own mothers only at long intervals.[22]

Even once the social custom had been forgotten, the emotions within were rendered so effectively as to still touch readers. Both gods and humans know what it is to suffer the loss of loved ones. The motherly feelings which Demeter shows for her daughter are described in great detail. Repetition of the terminology "whether for deathless gods or mortal men" throughout the hymn emphasizes that although the story concerns the gods, the same grief for those underground unites us with Demeter. In this way, the imagined heavenly realm is made directly relevant to the human predicament. Even though they are both gods, and hence immortal, Demeter's loss of her daughter is poignant because it is the same grief humans feel at death, to whose kingdom Persephone is abducted.

In the ancient world, the story was not only charming but tremendously portentious. It not only told the story of the annual wheat crop, especially important to the farm lands in the areas around Athens and the small city of Eleusis on the other side of the Gulf. It was also the basis of a very significant, secret religious rite at Eleusis, the so-called Eleusinian mysteries, to which first the most noble Athenians and then the aristocracy of the Hellenistic-Roman world sought admission. The imagery of the cult was dominated by notes of immortalization and rebirth.[23]

Linked with the story is a subplot of how Demeter is prevented from making the mortal child Demophoön (other versions call him Triptolemus, a grain god) immortal because the mother Metaneira interrupted her while she was immersing the boy in a purifying fire. The mother seeing the child immersed in the fire and, falsely concluding that Demeter was killing her son, screamed her protest until the rite was prevented. This story may have important parallels to the Near Eastern cults in which a child was passed through fire, presumably as a human sacrifice. Of course, Israelite thought was outraged by such practices. If there was any hint of human sacrifice in the story, Homer ignores it. He only relates the possibility of immortalization.[24] This myth also may obliquely refer to the immolation of a corpse on the funeral pyre, one of the alternative ancient Greek customs for laying the dead to rest, so perhaps both originally linked proper burial with proper planting of crops, with similar results.

The Greek story of Demophoön's failed magic-fire rite of immortalization also supports a religious cult. It presumably took place at Eleusis, providing an etiology for the great mystery rites enacted there in the fall, which linked the continuity of the cycle of sowing and reaping with human mortality and immortality.[25] There were also lesser rites celebrated in the spring, when trees were tended for their fruits. The connections between the agricultural rites and the story are suggestive, allowing us to conclude that the stories which we have are somehow the script for rites of immortalization that are still largely mysterious to us.

Since the Eleusinian mysteries were held in express secrecy and also held in the highest regard, no ancient initiate openly spoke of them and, consequently, no one today knows exactly what happened in the Eleusinian temple. Of the external rites and the pilgrimage from Athens to Eleusis, we have a great many details. But the secret rites—which were enacted within the *telesterion,* a giant rectangular, windowless building near a cave thought to be an entrance to the underworld—have still remained what they were designed to be, a mystery.

We do know that the the temple was completely unlike any other Greek temple that we recognize. There were no graceful columned facades with friezes, triglyphs, metopes, or pediments, no forest of columns enclosing the god's sacred room and cult statue. In fact, there was only one opening of note in the walled structure, its door. The *telesterion* was designed for a secret, dark show, with a floor plan that suggests nothing so much as a contemporary movie theater.

There is some evidence that the initiation was a kind of "rave," complete with rampant drug experiences. As part of the evening's service, the initiates drank a barley brew called the *kykeon,* which might have been ritually prepared in such a way as to deliver a controlled dose of ergot poisoning and hence a significant psychedelic experience.[26]

Aristotle emphasized that the initate does not learn *(mathein)* anything but is made to experience *(pathein)* the mysteries that change his or her state of mind.[27] There was a representation of the myth in some form and also the details of the episode of Demeter's attempt to immortalize Demophoön at Eleusis. But exactly how the yearly return of the wheat and human immortality were related by the rite is unknown. On the other hand, those who had been initiated felt that they had conquered death and been reborn in some way. The mysteries guaranteed a better life and a different and probably better fate after death.[28] The *Hymn to Demeter* asserts that initiates were fortunate *(olbioi)* but that non-initiates did not have the same lot after death (lines 480–82):

> Happy is he among men upon earth who has seen these mysteries; but he who is unitiate and who has no part in them never has a lot of good things once he is dead, down in the darkness and gloom.

Plutarch, drawing on the mysteries, describes the soul at the moment of death:

> The soul suffers an experience similar to those who celebrate great initiations. . . . Wandering astray in the beginning, tiresome walkings in circles, some frightening paths in darkness that lead nowhere; then immediately before the end all the terrible things, panic and shivering and sweat, and amazement. And then some wonderful light comes to meet you, pure regions and meadows are there to greet you, with sounds and dances and solemn, sacred words and holy views; and there the initiate, perfect by now, set free and loose from all bondage, walks about, crowned with a wreath, celebrating the festival together with the other sacred and pure people, and he looks down on the uninitiated, unpurified crowd in this world in mud and fog beneath his feet.[29]

For Plutarch, then, the mystery religions anticipated death itself, transforming the initiate and turning death into a kind of rebirth. The mystery religion presents the soul with the opportunity to train for the trip to the afterlife and hence to defeat death.

M. L. Lord points out some interesting relationships between *The Hymn to Demeter* and the epics of Homer.[30] The hero Odysseus and the goddess Demeter undertake a journey in which they must encounter the world of death, to which they are strangers. In some versions of the myth, Demeter actually descends to Hades. In both cases, an absence causes disruption and near disaster. Both major figures must disguise themselves. Both succeed in their goals but both must accommodate to new circumstances. Demeter must accept her inability to immortalize humans and the partial loss of her daughter, compensated by the new rites at Eleusis which somehow transcend death, just as Odysseus must give up immortality and lose his crew in order to regain his family and kingdom.

But there surely is also a major contrast between the two stories. Odysseus gives up immortality for fame. On the other hand, the story of Demeter is linked to a seasonal, repeating pattern, in which immortality of some sort inheres to the proper initiation into the natural cycle of seasonal variation. It is an immortality that comes from instruction, from agrarian rhythm, from householding, and from the Greeks' traditionally female-gendered values of natural repetition and continuity. In the end, however, immorality is available to a much wider group of humans, men and women, than is the older heroic ideal represented by Odysseus. Only a few men could hope for the fame which Odysseus and his compatriots received. But a much wider group of people (men and women) could take advantage of the initiation into the Eleusinian mysteries.

It is worth digressing for a few moments to see how broad the pattern provided by Demeter and Persephone is. In Greek myth, Persephone's plight helps explain the alternation of seasons in Greece. A number of divinities in other societies are said to die or revive for similar reasons.[31] The Norse pantheon was viewed as immortal for a time until the "twilight of the gods" when they will all die. "The Green Knight" of English courtly romance survives decapitation by Sir Gawain. The story suggests that this resurrection represents the agricultural year itself, with its repeated patterns of growth and decay. It is worthwhile emphasizing that the Eleusinian mysteries were only the most famous of this kind of cult. There were several others of great antiquity in Greece, including Orphic and Bacchic mysteries. In the Hellenistic period, a number of national religions of non-Greek countries package themselves for diaspora and become popular mysteries throughout the Roman world—Isis, Mithras, the great mother Cybele, Adonis, and many others. The religion of Christianity starts in a Jewish milieu but picks up the language of mystery religions when it enters the Hellenistic and Roman world in the second and third centuries.

Other Myths of Heroes

AFTER THE Homeric period, many different notions of immortality coexisted with the older notions remembered in legend and epic. The Greeks told stories of heroes like Hercules, Perseus, or Castor and Pollux who, after dying, mounted to heaven. One other exception to the universal call of Hades was the cult of heroes. Every culture has its heroes but Greek culture listed them among the gods, not among humans. They were, in a sense, humans who had been *apotheosized*, deified, changed into gods. They were immortalized not just by fame and legend but also by ascent to the stars and memorialized, most of all, by their hero cult.

Great heroes had ascended to become astral constellations: Herakles, Orion, Perseus, and many of the other characters named in their dramas. But there were many, many more heroes in ancient Greece. Much like saints, the heroes each had their shrine *(herōon)*, or at least their own altar *(bomos)*. They were powerful enough to be rewarded with sacrifices *(enagizein)*, begged for their benefices, and worshiped as patron saints by an entire locality. It is on the basis of the hero cults as much as on the basis of "oriental notions of divine kingship" that the Roman Emperors sought out the title *divus*.

The Greek world also boasted of a number of renowned characters who were revived from death. The noble Alcestis, a paradigm for self-sacrificing wives, died for her husband and was offered resurrection to finish out her natural life. She was the subject of Euripedes's famous drama. The first Greek casuality of the Trojan War, Protesilaus, was revivified to give a good example both to soldiers and good hope for loyal soldiers' wives. All of these are legends turned to literature and more like resuscitations than actual resurrections because they do not live longer than their natural lives.

Both in the Hellenistic and Roman world, rulers eventually began to identify themselves with the gods, in some sense saying that their lives would emulate those of the heroes and achieve transcendent importance. We see this in the architecture of the great tombs, which came more and more to be modelled on temples, devoted to narrating the great deeds of the deceased as a hero. The Mausoleum, which enclosed the body of King Maussollos (ruled Caria from 377–353 BCE) of Halicarnassus (near Bodrum) and was accounted one of the Seven Wonders of the Ancient World, is the most famous of these structures. It may not be the clearest example of a tomb emulating the architecture of a temple, except in its size and prominence in the city; but it may serve as the parade example of an ordinary ruler claiming heroic honors in death by erecting a monumental building to his memory.

The Afterlife in Orphic Myth
and Pythagorean Philosophy

ARISTOTLE tells us (*De anima,* 410b, 28) that the Orphics taught that the soul enters the body from "the whole or the all" *(to holon)* as one breathes. After one dies, the soul abides in the upper atmosphere, as we learn from an inscription concerning the Athenians who perished at Potidea in 432 BCE: "The aether has received their souls, but their bo[dies the earth.]" [32] The Orphics are still a very complex, scholarly mystery. Some doubt that Orphism is a real religion, considering it something of an ancient fraud. Others say it was early and profoundly influential. [33] There are evidences of *thiasoi,* voluntary associations, which were devoted to Orphism. Still, that term may be misleading, as both Jewish synagogues and Christian churches were perceived as *thiasoi* in the Roman Empire because they neither met in temples nor sacrificed but instead met for instruction, discussion, and common meals. Evidently, Orphism could be construed as the latter, rather like Judaism and Christianity.

The Orphics took their cue from the famous story of Orpheus, the lyre player of Thrace, who went down to Hades to bring back his dead wife Eurydice. He lost her again because he turned to look at her just before he exited Hades, whereupon she vanished forever. Originally the story was about human being's inability to defeat death, and so we must be satisfied with beautiful lamentation, perhaps yet again reminding us of the value of commemoration for the expression of grief and its conclusion. The Orphics appear to have believed that they were to live in the moral purities taught by the group, and that there were special techniques for climbing to heaven after death, even if it had to be after many reincarnations.

The Orphics apparently believed that human beings were punished for each life before being reincarnated. [34] They placed gold leaves in the graves of the departed to help them through the various parts of the process:

> Out of the pure I come, pure queen of them below,
> And Eukles and Eubouleus, and other Gods and Daemons:
> For I also avow me that I am of your blessed race
> And I have paid the penalty for deeds unrighteous,
> Whether it be that fate laid me low or the Gods immortal
>
> . . .
>
> I have flown out of the sorrowful weary Wheel;
> I have passed with eager feet to the circle desired;

> I have sunk beneath the bosom of Despoina, Queen of the
>   Underworld.
>
> And now I come a suppliant of Holy Phersephoneia
> That of her grace she receive me to the seats of the
>   Hallowed—
> Happy and Blessed One, thou shalt be God instead of
>   mortal.[35]

The end of the poem promises that the deceased will be deified. The progress of the apotheosis suggests that they ascended to heaven to claim their divine status, unlike the Eleusinian mystery which sought its victory in Hades.

The Pythagoreans were also a group said to have conquered death. Pythagoreanism was founded by Pythagoras, a figure who lived somewhere between 750–500 BCE in Samos, an Island off the coast of Turkey, and then in Croton, a Greek colony in Calabria. Though he is the author of the famous theorem about the right triangle, little is known of Pythagoras himself; those who followed his teachings were encouraged to become mystics, not mathematicians. Pythagoreans developed an advanced religious doctrine combining theories of music, mathematics, diet, and ascetic practices. They too believed in the reincarnation and transmigration of souls and are often cited as the source of the Platonic doctrines. In Late Antiquity reports of Orphism and Pythagoreanism tend to coalesce. Scholars speak of the phenomenon as Neo-Pythagoreanism.

Stoics and Epicureans

MANY PHILOSOPHERS, and particularly the Epicureans, eschewed the doctrines of immortality preached by the Orphics and Pythagoreans. Epicurus based his philosophy on the atomic theory of Democritus. There was only one substance in the universe, matter, which was composed of unbreakable primal units—atoms. The opposite of matter was the void, vacuum. This corresponds with modern physics in a remarkable way, but the effects of the doctrine for the Greeks were religious and ethical.

"Void" is literally *asomatos,* or incorporeal. The soul was an atomic body or it was nothing, which even fits the Homeric evidence as well as any other theory does. It cannot be incorporeal, says Epicurus, in obvious direct contradiction to Plato.[36] The direct consequence of such a theory is that the person's body and soul both, like all other material bodies, are destroyed with death. So Epicurus could deny the Homeric depiction of the afterlife as truth but give it credence as an allegory. The same evaluation met any doctrine of immortality of the soul preached by Platonists. He suggests that the fear of death is fruitless:

> The most terrifying of evils, death, is nothing to us, since when we exist, death is not present. But when death is present, then we do not exist. It is nothing, then, either to the living or to the dead, since concerning the former it does not exist, and concerning the latter, they no longer exist (10.125)

Thus, the whole Epicurean tradition eschewed immortality. Lucretius, the Roman Epicurean, could comfort his followers by repeating that "death is nothing to us":[37]

> Therefore death is nothing to us, it matters not one bit, since the nature of souls (or minds, *animi*) is understood to be mortal; and as in time past we felt no distress . . . so, when we shall no longer be . . . nothing at all will be able to happen to us. . . . (*de rerum natura,* 3.830)

Although the notion of retribution was not prominent in Greek thought, evidently it had a following, enough for Lucretius to take the time to dispute it. There is no punishment after death, he says, in good Epicurean fashion, because there is no afterlife at all. We are not sentient beings after death, since we do not exist at all; therefore, we cannot suffer or be punished. He further says that funerary practice is absurd. There is no reason to take care of the corpse, he says, since there is no sensory perception of it. It does not matter whether it is buried or not. Or, running the argument the other way around: were there any "consciousness" left in the corpse, it would feel just as bad by being roasted on a pyre or being suffocated with burial or being embalmed with pitch. He obviously ignores the health problems avoided by disposing of the dead. What he was interested in was notoriety for the extremity of his opinion in a world that universally felt denial of funeral rites to be an unconscionable insult and humiliation both to the grieving family and the departed.

In the same vein, Cicero makes his character Scipio affirm: *sic habeto non esse te mortalem sed corpus hoc*—"hold this to be true, not you are mortal but [you are] this body" (*de re publica*, 6, 26). Seneca too was simply unconcerned with death: *mors est aut finis aut transitus* "death is either the end or a transition" [hence it is of no importance to us] (*Ep.*, 24, 65). These higher philosophical notions must have existed side by side with the more popular notions which Cicero, Lucretius, and Seneca wanted to dispute.

The Epicurean perspective on life was popular enough to be copied onto gravestones. The following Epicurean epitaph was so popular that it was often abbreviated: *non fui, fui, non sum, non curo* (I was not, I was, I am not, I don't care [or: suffer]; sometimes also *non eram, eram, non sum, non curo*) or in its Greek form: I was not, and I came into being; I am not, and I do not suffer.[38] This attitude only emphasized the Epicureans' defiance of all conventions, breaking with all civilities. But what they preached was serious: Death was a total end, the cessation of all thinking or feeling, therefore not to be feared.

The Stoics broke only with the Academy—Socrates, Plato, and Aristotle—in rejecting the value of meditation. They often found positions at court and in the homes of the wealthy. Although they believed that humanity was rational, for them reason was purely practical, showing us what the good life is. A vicious person is ruled by his passions, but a wise and virtuous person lives by reason and, hence, is free of slavery of the passions, a doctrine which Plato also emphasized strongly. As for life after death, the Stoics took an intermediary position between the strong denial of afterlife among the Epicureans and the complete acceptance of it among the Platonists. The stoics based their notion of the material cosmos on a divine fire called *logos*. This material suffused the universe with a reasoning power. Diogenes Laertius says that the Stoics believed:

[the soul] is both corporeal and survives death; but it is perishable, while that of the universe is imperishable, of which the [souls] of living beings are parts. . . . Cleanthes [believes] that all [souls] exist until the Conflagration, but Crysippus that only the souls of the wise [remain]. (7.156–7)

The Stoics did not decide the question; those who also inclined toward Platonism tended to accept that all souls would eventually be redeemed while the others did not. They did believe that the universe would be consumed in a conflagration, called the *ekpyrosis*. Panaetius in the second century BCE seems to have denied any survival at all while Posidonius, strongly influenced by Plato, accepted the preexistence of the soul and a postmortem ascent into the aether.[39]

Plato

PLATO STOOD with the aristocracy, though he never tired of caricaturing their hypocrisies in socratic dialogue. The writings of Plato (430?–347 BCE), which originated during the period that Greece was the arch-enemy of Persia, settled the issue of the immortality of the soul by philosophical demonstration for the Platonists and for an enormous number of admirers afterward. Plato's is the most influential philosophical system for religion in the West until the modern period. After an inital and telling phase of rejection, Platonism became the cornerstone of the Christian doctrine of immortality of the soul. Those pagans who followed his philosophy accepted the immortality of the soul in one form or another, though not necessarily its personal or individual survival. The most important documents in this context are Plato's *Phaedo* and *Apology*. In the *Apology*, we have Socrates' final defense and, in the *Phaedo,* we witness Socrates' execution. Plato uses his literary invention of the figure of Socrates, based on his real-life teacher, to speak Platonic philosophy. In the *Symposium,* Plato gives us a picture of Socrates standing still in a trance for a day and a night (220c). This kind of behavior—as well as his penetrating glance, his quick wit, his constant presence in the marketplace, and his incisive mind—help explain why Socrates had the effect that he did on his contemporaries. What Platonism provided was a theory by which the soul could soar free of the body by contemplation and thus demonstrate that the soul survives its life in the body. How closely Plato's Socrates resembles the Socrates of history, we cannot entirely tell.

In the final section of the *Apology,* Socrates asks what death is. His answer is that it is either annihilation or transmigration. If the former, then it is not to be feared because it will be a dreamless sleep. If the latter, then we shall go on to another life. In this he seems at one with the Epicureans and Stoics, except that he adds reincarnation of Pythagoras and Orpheus to the mix. But implicit in this statement is the realization that life is struggle and difficulty; dreamless sleep is preferable to a life of troubles and pain. If accurate, this can hardly be called a healthy agnosticism; it is in fact an evasion, showing unwillingness to discuss the topic seriously.

Plato's Socrates goes much further in his affirmation of the transmigration of souls. Both in the *Apology* and in the *Crito,* Socrates has deliberately refused several chances to escape (an escape route planned with the tacit approval of his captors) to a disgraced life in exile rather than drink poison hemlock, which is the sentence decreed upon him by the court. By refusing the invitation to save himself, he becomes a kind of philosophical martyr to his own truth. The dialogue, then, is not just a discourse on the issue of the immortality of the soul but a disquisition on martyrdom and justice. Socrates' behavior demonstrates his confidence in the demonstration. In some ways, Plato has already conceded the battle for the preservation of his body by refusing the ignominious choice of escape and discredit; in the *Apology,* he argues that one should concentrate all one's efforts on the improvement of the soul over against the body (*Apol.* 30a–b). Likewise, in the *Laws,* Socrates states that the soul is completely superior to the body because the soul is the principle of life while the body merely a resemblance of it. In the *Symposium,* Diotima gives a clear presentation of the way to achieve postmortem survival. The mortal body seeks the immortal by reproduction or imitation *(mimesis),* a vain and impossible effort, though a necessary one; but the soul is already immortal (*Symp.* 207d, 208a–b). To become immortal one only needs realize one's soul's divine potential for ascent.

In the *Phaedo,* Socrates undertakes to demonstrate that the soul is immortal so that his execution is but a momentary inconvenience that will allow him to soon join the company of superior humans and gods. In some ways, he is just trying to prove what many Greeks must have thought was self-evident. The proof is so important to the history of the afterlife in the West that it is worth reviewing in more detail. Socrates begins his conversation with the observation that opposites seem to be related—like the pain of his bonds and the pleasure of their removal. No one can have both at once (60b). (This seemingly casual observation becomes the assumption on which all further arguments are built.) This leads to further musings on the relationship between life and death, and that ordinary persons are afraid of death because they are going from life to an unknown end. Actually, continues Socrates, when viewed properly, a philosopher should not be afraid of death because it is the opportunity to live as a soul without a body:

> They are not aware of the way true philosophers are nearly dead, nor of the way they deserve to be, nor of the sort of death they deserve. (64b–c)[40]

Indeed, a great deal can be learned by thinking about death. Philosophers are encouraged to spend their lives doing it. For Socrates, death itself is the separation of the body from the soul:

Is it anything else than the separation of the soul from the body? Do we believe that death is this, namely, that the body comes to be separated by itself apart from the soul, and the soul comes to be separated by itself apart from the body? Is death anything else than that? (64c)

At the same time, philosophers should, in this life, seek something very similar to death: separation from the bondage of the body and passions. A philosopher's life is a kind of preparation for death because it teaches us to separate our selves from the desires of the body. Death, therefore, is part of the goal of philosophy because it removes us from the biggest source of distraction to the philosophical enterprise. Furthermore, a good philosopher has in some way already achieved his death, by totally subordinating his body to his soul, and, therefore, will never fear death:

> In fact, Simmias, he said, those who practise philosophy in the right way are in training for dying and they fear death least of all men. Consider it from this point of view: if they are altogether estranged from the body and desire to have their soul by itself, would it not be quite absurd for them to be afraid and resentful when this happens? If they did not gladly set out for a place, where, on arrival, they may hope to attain that for which they had yearned during their lifetime, that is wisdom, and where they would be rid of the presence of that from which they are estranged? (*Phaed.* 67e–68a)

For Platonic philosophy, asceticism—eschewing of the extremes of pleasure—among the aristocracy is what trains the mind to philosophy and to a noble death. Socrates then tries to demonstrate that these observations taken from experience are accurate to the truths of existence but that behind them are several *a priori* assumptions about the soul. Socrates tries to demonstrate that these assumptions are provable. But the proofs are interwoven with a number of arguments taken from religious tradition and observation. Throughout the centuries there has been a noticeable lack of consensus about what his argument actually is. I will try one way to unpack the arguments.

Socrates begins by setting up a series of forced decisions. Life and death are opposites, just as sleep and waking are opposites. Just as waking comes from sleep and vice versa; so life comes from death and vice versa. This takes us back to Socrates' original observation that pain and pleasure are opposites that come from each other. It will also become important in his last argument that the soul is the very thing which defines life;

therefore, it cannot be its opposite. Furthermore, as he has said previously, living comes from death in the way wakefulness comes from sleep. Socrates posits as a fact of life, observed closely, that opposites come one from another.

Since life comes from non-life, Plato tries to show that there is something more basic than either, a substance that underlies the change in status, a "person" as it were, who can come awake and go to sleep, a "soul" who can be alive or dead. He posits this "person" or "self" or "soul" existed previously to our birth by suggesting that we know things that we have not learned. To demonstrate that the soul preexists individual lives, Socrates uses our notion of recollection, suggesting that the basic categories of space, time, equality and inequality and other values are innate, not learned, so that the soul must precede the body.

Throughout the middle dialogues and particularly in the *Meno* (81d–86b), Plato talks about the importance of recollection. We all have had the experience of remembering something that we have previously learned and forgotten. This experience Plato closely identifies with learning. To reason something out is the same as recollecting it for Philo. In the *Meno*, Socrates asks a slave boy to reason out a problem and repeatedly insists that he is not teaching him. The learning process comes from within himself. For this reason, Plato seems to feel that all learning is closely akin to recollecting. Since it is recollecting, we must have known it before. Thus recollecting is a far broader intellectual process for Plato than it usually is for us. In the *Phaedo*, this statement is allowed to stand for itself.

Let us move on to the crucial religious (and usually unnoticed) aspect of this proof: Plato grounds the immortality of the soul on intellectual activity. Plato says that memory of the basic categories of comparison—qualities like: "more than," "less than," and "equal to"—demonstrates that we have knowledge before our births and thus our soul precedes our body. Memory, an aspect of thinking, proves the preexistence of the soul.

We may doubt the validity of the argument. Aristotle, Plato's own pupil, did, proclaiming that our intelligence is at birth a *tabula rasa*, to use the familiar Medieval, Aristotelian technical term. After all, Jean Piaget shows that we learn these categories, and not all that very early in our lives.[41] Piaget holds that there is an age at which children think that there is "more" milk in the tall, thin glass than in the short, fat glass, even after they have been explicitly shown the milk pouring from one to another, making it perfectly obvious to any adult that the glasses contain the same amount of milk. Then, after a certain age, children do realize that the milk is "the same." So it looks as though this is a learned quality, not an innate one. And Aristotle would certainly have brought this up, had he been privy to Piaget's experiments. Of course, Plato might object by claiming that younger children really did know that the milk in the two containers were equal, they just did not have the vocabulary yet to express it, using "more" when they meant "taller."

The point is not whether Plato was correct in his logical steps or his epistemology. The point is that the proof of immortality of the soul depends, right at this crucial point very pregnantly, on an act of thinking. It is a particular mentition—"recollection," *anamnesis,* in Greek—which indissolubly links immortality of the soul with our internal psychological "selves." This has the effect of turning thinking into a transcendent act.

Why Plato included so many thinking processes under the topic of "recollection" is not entirely clear but he was followed in some ways by his brightest student, Aristotle. Perhaps it is because the Greek word *anamimneskesthai,* translated as "to recollect," is the passive form of the verb "to remind" modified with the prepositional prefix *ana-,* meaning "again." "To recollect," *anamimneskesthai,* literally means "to be reminded again" in Greek, though neither "to remember" nor "to recollect" in English contain this connotation. Recollection, Plato says, involves "one thing putting you in mind of another" (*Phaed.* 73c–74d), which is understandable if the connotation of the verb is "to be reminded again" but relatively distant from the simple meaning of the English verbs "remember" or "recollect." [42]

Plato included many different mental faculties in his terminology for recollection. He was not just offering a proof of immortality. He was, at the same time, describing a whole new way to define the self, as a consistent, recollecting person with a personal history of memories. In the end, Plato essentially linked thinking with our selves and used it to demonstrate that the act of thinking is what grounds the immortality of the soul.

This is a quite different notion than any idea of immortality we have so far investigated. Immortality or the lack of it in myth was always linked to the performance of heroic, cultic, or ritual actions in society. It was sought or denied as part of a hero's quest. Immortality was linked to the body by the Persians, as it is by apocalyptic Jews who articulate resurrection of the body. But this is the first time in history that it is explicitly linked with a mental act. What Plato called "recollection" includes a great many mental processes which we in English might call discovery, reasoning, and logical analysis. [43]

Plato's argument is even more striking when we realize that he surely knew the Greek myth that the soul forgets everything upon crossing the river Lethe on its way to be born. Indeed, the word for "truth" *(alētheia)* in Greek was frequently glossed as "without forgetting" (as a folk etymology). Plato did not feel that the soul forgot everything as that would destroy his demonstration of its preexistence of the body. Plato was essentially saying that it is our mentation which survives death, no matter how many other faculties the soul may be said to have.

Plato was not exactly saying that our consciousness (in the modern sense of the word) makes us immortal or even that consciousness itself is worth preserving. The focus on consciousness in the West is a peculiarly modern, philosophical issue. Plato himself was not so impressed with the ordinary sense of consciousness as a continuous mental monitoring, at least as compared with other kinds of mental actions. He thought of consciousness as just the background noise of our significant mental life, just the awareness that our souls are combined with matter, the awareness that we are "awake" or the monitor is "on," so to speak. That was not a high-order process for Plato. Rather it is something everyone has with or without education or training or virtue, something to be left behind gladly when our souls escape from their bodily imprisonment. Plato rather connected rationality with meditation (both in the sense of concentration and in the sense of entering an altered state of consciousness) as well as with practical reason and suggested that there was a philosophical value in meditation and high-order mentation.

The act of "recollecting," a necessary predecessor to abstract thinking, was part of the process of forming ideas and gaining knowledge according to Plato. That was a symptom of the soul's immortality, the very process that underlined why the soul had to be immortal. Thus, the soul's education was what made for personal completion; it needed to be developed to its most refined potential. We might think of the process of thinking as one of conceiving ideas. Of all the possible ideas, the idea of conceiving the self was the most important. In this sense we can define the goal of thinking, finally, to be critical "self-consciousness." This is a high-order mentation both for Plato and for Aristotle. Indeed, it was Aristotle who first talked about the mind thinking itself and thinking of the Good, and the Good, in turn, as a mind thinking of all things, to which our own minds are analogous in their limited and passive way. Furthermore, Plato felt that personal deportment should be governed by what made the intellectual life easiest to accomplish.

This new definition of immortality is an enormous change from Greek tradition. Odysseus' goal was to build fame for himself as a military hero and ruler. To this end, he could fight, lie, cheat, womanize, murder, and otherwise carry on—all for the purpose of achieving a good homecoming and a balanced state. But Plato's immortality could be sought and won by anyone who developed his or her powers of thought, not just the heroic man of arms. In order to achieve the goal, the intellectual adventurer would have to promote moderation in behavior, deportment, and ethics— an enormous change from the life that Odysseus lived.

Plato's immortality was open to all but it was not democratic in the sense that everyone had an equal right to achieve it. Plato's notion was, in fact, elitist because it valorized intellectual life above every other kind of human activity as far as achieving the soul's ultimate purpose. Not everyone could achieve an intellectual life; one needed leisure and long years of education to follow the philosophical life which Plato recommended. Yet, by comparison to the goals outlined by Homer, the life of the intellectual was available to many. Though Plato took the immortality of the soul seriously, we can turn his perception around and note that to make the higher faculties of the soul immortal was also to make an important claim about the intellectual elite in the society, to valorize intellectuality as transcendently important. It was certainly a first step in defining the "self" in Western philosophy and altogether necessary for understanding the orgy of self-consciousness that has dominated Western philosophy in the modern period.

Plato's Forms

THE NEXT STEP in the proof of the immortality of the soul depends on Plato's notion that there are entities called the "forms" or "ideas" of all the material bodies on earth:

> If those realities we are always talking about exist, the Beautiful and the Good and all that kind of reality, and we refer all the things we perceive to that reality, discovering that it existed before and is ours, and we compare these things with it, then, just as they exist, so our soul must exist before we are born. If these realities do not exist, then this argument is altogether futile. Is this the position, that there is an equal necessity for those realities to exist, and for our souls to exist before we were born? If the former do not exist, neither do the latter? (*Phaed.* 77d–e)

Socrates does not try to demonstrate the forms here. He merely suggests that if the soul exists, it must be one of the forms or ideas. It would follow that what Socrates attempted to demonstrate for the soul would be true for all of the forms, though that is not explicitly discussed. But Socrates was not purposely excluding arguments. He attempted to address a further, plaguing issue: Perhaps souls do exist but although they preexist our bodies, they do not continue to exist after death or after a series of lives. It is also possible that the soul is a harmony, not a being in itself but a relationship between the parts, what we would today call an emergent property, which would die with the body and even devolve prior to demise. This latter possibility, refuted by Socrates, comes rather close to modern notions of the self.

Socrates still needed to demonstrate that the soul does not dissolve after death or, stranger yet, wear out after having inhabited several bodies. To demonstrate that the soul is indissoluble at death, just as he previously demonstrated that it preexists birth, Socrates again had to return to the issue of the forms—the good, the beautiful, and so forth (*Phaed.* 100b). Socrates distinguishes between the properties and the form of a thing by showing that "cold" is not the same as the "snow," nor "heat" as the "fire." He then defined the soul as the thing that brings life to a person, in total opposition of death (*Phaed.* 105d).

Socrates then took the next step, based on an observation accepted at the very beginning of the dialogue: He states that life and death come from the same thing and follow each other but cannot exist in the same object at the same time. He then suggested the solution to the conundrum: What makes something alive is the presence of a soul; what kills it is the departure of the soul. This is precisely analogous to claiming that snow is cold because it contains a substance called cold and fire is hot because it contains a substance called heat, and that these substances are separable from the objects that host them. Soul and life are different names for the same essence. The soul itself remains alive, indeed must remain alive by definition, because it *is* the life and has already been proven both to precede the body and outlive it.

This was not so much a logical proof as an analogy, the mental realization of a kind of symmetry. If Plato's analysis of objects and attributes was wrong, then his proof fails. Following this logic, we wind up with a definition of soul as the form or idea of life, something which is immortal by definition and depends on the prior assumption that the forms or ideas of everything on earth are the immortal plans for producing them.

The Platonic soul that survives death is not a "personal" soul in our modern sense of the word. Aristotle seemed even less sure that the immortal aspects of the soul contain our "personality." The personalization of the soul is a hypothesis for a later period—for Plotinus and especially Augustine (see ch. 14). Imperfect though the proof may be, it was on this demonstration that Plato's Socrates staked his life. In a way, he was a martyr for the notion of the immortal soul. And, indeed, the Western notion of the soul, even as mediated by Christianity, eventually depended on this dialogue of Plato, with all its attendant strengths and weaknesses.

There are, however, some aspects of the proof, which Christianity has understandably repressed. Socrates suggested that we do not live but once; instead, we have several "incarnations" to learn how to behave in such a way as to perfect our mental processes. Only when we successfully learn how to perfect the faculties of the soul so that we understand the separation of the soul from the body are we granted rest from reincarnation—a notion that sounds very much like the ideas of karma, samsara, and *moksha,* religious insights of another great Indo-European civilization, India.

For Socrates, humans can even be reincarnated as animals: "Those, for example, who have carelessly practiced gluttony, violence, and drunkenness are likely to join the company of donkeys or of similar animals" (81e). Surely Apuleius' *Metamorphosis,* which relates such a transformation in detail, was partly inspired by these lines. Almost all Church Fathers (excepting Origen and Gregory of Nyssa) denied that the soul has more than one earthly life to live because it seemed to blunt individual moral responsibility for any specific action.

The issue of justice is very much the central concern of the last part of the *Phaedo.* For Socrates, proper thinking and behavior creates its own reward; improper thinking and behavior creates its own punishment. Only by proper thinking can one gain the reward—which is stopping the chain of the soul's continual rebirths into this world. In a sense, life was considered punishment, full of pain and suffering, compared eternally to living as a disembodied soul (which can suffer no pain) in the afterlife. So the process of self-perfection implies a justice that operates as a pure mechanism of nature—a moral universe, in which human reward and punishment are built in, very like karma. "Metempsychosis," the doctrine of the transmigration of the soul from body to body, is obviously the result of penalties in past lives which must be reconciled for the soul to find rest in the Elysian fields. It does not imply suffering after death. Indeed, Plato appeared to be somewhat ambivalent on the notion of retribution. In the *Republic,* Plato represents a kind of Orphic doctrine of retribution by means of Adeimantus:

Musaeus and his son (Eumolpus) endow the just with gifts from heaven of an even more spirited sort. They take the righteous to another world and provide them with a banquet of the saints, where they sit for all time drinking with garlands on their heads, as if virtue could not be more nobly rewarded than by an eternity of intoxication. . . . When they have sung the praises of justice in that strain, with more to the same effect, they proceed to plunge the sinners and unrighteous men into a sort of mud-pool in the other world, and they set them to carry water in a sieve. (2.363 c–d) [44]

Although this is a satire on the teaching of Musaeus and Eumolpus, who were the legendary teachers of Orphism, one must not think that Plato completely denied any rewards and punishments after death. To the contrary, he suggests that justice and retribution do exist, though he can not demonstrate it with the same self-assurance as he achieves in proving the immortality of the soul. The process of the soul's perfection is itself a reward while reincarnation is punishment enough. Rather, the particularly graphic notion of being immersed in mud seems to be more like what Plato thought about life in this world.

At the end of the *Phaedo,* Socrates narrates his own understanding of how humans can come to this wider perspective on life, through a heavenly ascent to the outer limit of our world:

Our experience is the same: living in a certain hollow of the earth, we believe that we live upon its surface; the air we call the heaven, as if the stars made their way through it; this too is the same; because of our weakness and slowness we are not able to make our way to the upper limit of the air; if anyone got to this upper limit, if anyone came to it or reached it on wings and his head rose above it, then just as fish on rising from the sea see things in our region, he would see things there and, if his nature could endure to contemplate them, he would know that there is the true heaven, the true light and the true earth, for the earth here, these stones and the whole region, are spoiled and eaten away, just as things in the sea are by the salt water. (109d–e)

His description is more apt than he could possibly have imagined, as we would be like fish out of water if we were to but stick our heads above the tiny precious oxygenated atmosphere in which we live. We would see worlds that were until lately beyond our imaginings; but they would impress us with the value of our endangered, tiny environment in which we live our precarious existence, no bigger than a speck of dust when placed in astronomical distances that characterize our universe. This was not what Plato saw when he rose to these heights. From the perspective of the eternal heavens where the ideas reside, the corruptible earth is a puny failure and deserves nothing but our fond farewell. Indeed, the Hellenistic world was convinced that the hereafter would be far happier than the world we live in. In this, it was rather closer to what the mass of humanity has believed about our short and painful lives over the millennia.

Actually many Greeks came to believe that life was not worth the effort, a sentiment more poignant when we realize it was the aristocracy with their rare and exquisite leisure who said this, not the poor serf or slave whose life was constant drudgery. Only the privileged have the privilege of being bored. Sophocles proclaimed that it is best never to have lived:

> Never to have been born at all:
> None can conceive a loftier thought!
> And second-best is this: Once born,
> Quickly to return to the dust. (*Oedipus at Colonus,* 1218ff.)

Though this was a cynical statement of a man whose life had been a terrible trial, it was not his final thoughts on mortality, it came to fit the mood of late antiquity more and more. Plato felt that the soul would be better off in the realm of the ideas than on this imperfect earth, with all its tribulation. In the *Phaedrus,* Plato suggested that humans are reincarnated for the purposes of discipline, *askesis,* in order to purify the soul by affliction. In the *Symposium,* Plato described the process of ascent as one of intellection, learning by progressive stages of abstraction, to appreciate abstract good, in and of itself. By this process of intellection, and the ascetic processes necessary to perfect it, the soul ascends to heaven again and, with luck, never has to be reincarnated again. All of this presumes that life is a vale of tears to be transcended. Even in the most comfortable life we are still confronted with death, separation from loved ones, unhappiness, and unfulfillment.

After Plato, the Greek world took the notion that the isles of the blessed are in the sky seriously. If the soul is immortal, it must return to the immortal realm. When Socrates says his famous last words: "Crito, we owe a cock to Asclepius, make this offering to him and do not forget," he was stating that he was healed from the sickness of life; he needed to give a thank-offering to the god of health for having been healed. True health lies in correctly grooming the deathless soul, not in overly coddling the hapless body. Physical education was important only to maintain a neat house for the soul.

According to Plato, there is a kind of judgment of the dead, as he relates in the *Phaedrus*. Souls are first incarnated, and:

> . . . on the termination of their first life, brought to trial; and, according to their sentence, some go to the prison-houses beneath the earth, to suffer for their sins, while others, by virtue of their trial, are borne lightly upwards to some celestial spot, where they pass their days in the manner worthy of the life they have lived in their mortal form. But in the thousandth year both divisions come back again to share and choose their second life, and they select that which they severally please. And then it is that a human soul passes into the life of a beast, and from a beast who was once a man the soul comes back into a man again. For the soul which has never seen the truth at all can never enter into the human form; it being a necessary condition of a man that he should apprehend according to that which is called the generic form, which, proceeding from a variety of perceptions, is by reflection combined into unity. And this is nothing more or less than a recollection of those things which in time past our soul beheld when it travelled in the company of the gods, and looking high over what we now can see, lifted up its head into the region of eternal essence. (249)

Plato gives the notion of judgment after death an enormous boost. Evidently, Plato was more positively impressed with Orphism than he suggests in his satire in the *Republic*. But note how much the issue of theodicy underlies his imaginative reconstruction. Just as the Persians used dualism to moralize their social universe into a cosmic ethical struggle, so too Plato moralized the universe by coding matter and form as antithetical opposites. However, by valorizing the body as the principle of identity, the Persians were affirming that sexuality and other bodily pleasures were of primary importance in this world, as well as the next. The Platonists, for their part, took the converse perspective. They said that sexuality is something to be left behind in death and ignored as much as was prudent during life, as a way of perfecting the mind for its higher purposes. Perhaps Plato said this as a corrective to the immense sexuality in which Plato's world was drenched, as if to say that Plato only stressed "the golden mean." Later Platonists became sure that all contact with sexuality was bad for the meditative life. Sexuality's negative effects on ethics became more and more palpable until asceticism was the only intelligent lifestyle. But that was long after Plato.

Plato was no democrat, but ironically the Platonic innovation on the conception of afterlife tended to democratize the afterlife even more. Instead of the rare heroic term of short mortal fame, followed by eternal exile in Hades, as was sought by Odysseus, each person has immortality in his grasp by intellectual development. Everyone's soul is, by following the intellectual life, making progress toward the goal of remaining in Elysium, and can take several lifetimes to do it if necessary. Each life contributes to that progress. As we have seen, certain philosophically enlightened individuals could reduce the cycle of rebirths by living well as philosophers. But we all must take the same road to arrive at the same heavenly bliss. This, no doubt, would have surprised Socrates somewhat, as he had nothing but contempt for Athenian democracy. Evidently, they were opposed to the educated elite that he favored. Ultimately, this opposition may have cost him his life, though it was something he donated willingly.

It is precisely the problem of theodicy that occupies first place in the story of Er, the Pamphylian, mentioned in the *Republic*. Er proves the truth of Socrates' reasoning by personal experience because he returned alive after twelve days of death and reports on the fortunes of souls in the hereafter.

> "It is not, let me tell you," said I, "The tale to Alcinous told that I shall unfold, but the tale of a warrior bold, Er, the son of Armenius, by race a Pamphylian. He once upon a time was slain in battle and when the corpses were taken up on the tenth day already decayed, was found intact, and having been brought home, at the moment of his funeral, on the twelfth day, as he lay upon the pyre, revived, and after coming to life related what, he said he had seen in the world beyond." (*Resp.* 10.614 Bff.)[45]

Er then relates how he was chosen to be the messenger *(angelos)* to humanity to tell us what awaits in the other world. The story which he relates is one of punishments and rewards for those unrequited during their own life—those who had committed great wrongs were condemned to ten times the punishment in measures of one hundred years. The structure of this heavenly journey is clear. Those punished go into the earth. Those rewarded go to heaven, just as we have come to believe in the West. The central figure, Er, crossed from the lower realm to the higher one and returned to tell us that the universe conforms to just, equable rules. It is almost like an urban renewal project. Having been moved out of Hades and relocated in the heavens, the previous location of the afterlife is renovated as the abode of the sinful.

The story confirms that justice exists in the universe by claiming that the voyage is parallel to the one which the soul will take at death. Its purpose is to warn men of the implications of their actions upon the earth and exhort them to righteousness. One of the dominant motifs is that of the *agōn,* the athletic contest. The soul struggles in life as in athletic games and thereafter receives the trophy of astral afterlife as a reward for its victory. Plato seemingly had his doubts about the details of such tales but ended with this gentle correction:

> But if we are guided by me we shall believe that the soul is immortal and capable of enduring all extremes of good and evil, and so we shall hold ever to the upward way and pursue righteousness with wisdom always and ever." (*Resp.* 10.620e)

The soul's salvation for Plato was quintessentially an individual process. The soul is on an individual mission to purify itself. It travels through many bodies and cleanses itself from the impurities it gathers in human society. The intellectual achievement of the redemption of the soul is an individual process, though it may find what little solace adheres to life in a community of like-minded individuals. This contrasts quite strongly with the communal and sectarian nature of resurrection of the body in its Iranian and Jewish versions.

Aristotle on the Afterlife

ALTHOUGH Aristotle accepted Plato's valorization of *nous,* mind, he subjected Plato's thought to the most penetrating criticism. For Aristotle all philosophical problems could be best understood from the point of view of epistemology, the science of thinking. "All men by nature desire to know" is the first sentence of *Metaphysics;* everything flows from this perception. Like Plato, Aristotle believed the real is the intelligble, the intelligible real. But he offered an important qualification. The rational soul, Aristotle noted, does not discover an alien world when it apprehends anything. Rather it comes into possession of itself. Knowledge comes to us, first of all, from our own observations, from our senses. The process of thinking *(noesis)*, and even more so scientific thinking *(epistēmē)*, is nothing more than perceiving the form of the object from the object itself.

The mind *(nous)*, then, must be extracting the form of an object from the mind's sense perceptions of the object. If that is so, there need not be a separate world of forms to explain our thinking. The form is the principle or underlying order that we perceive in something. For Aristotle, Plato had separated the forms from sensible things too sharply, giving rise to a dubious sense of a separate metaphysical world of ideas. Though our souls know (as opposed to perceive) only ideas, the world in which the ideas subsist is logically the mind. Aristotle therefore could say that the soul is a perfect receptivity; the later Latin is *tabula rasa,* an empty slate. If so, there is nothing in the soul originally to recollect.

> It remains to speak about recollecting. First, then, one must take as being the case all that is true in the essays. For recollection is neither the recovery nor the acquisition of memory. For when someone first learns or experiences something, he does not recover any memory, since none has preceded. Nor does he acquire memory from the start, for once the state or affection has been produced within a person, then there is memory. *(Mem. rem.* 451a, 18)[46]

Aristotelian philosophy, then, does not support Plato's proof for the immortality of the soul.

Aristotle directly criticized the theory that "learning" is "recollection" in the *Prior Analytics* (67a, 8–27) and the *Posterior Analytics* (71a, 30–71b, 8). His understanding of recollection is confined to the special case of learning, namely relearning (*Mem. rem.* 451a, 21–5). For Aristotle this mental operation is closer to associating one idea with another, as when one idea reminds us of another, which is exactly what we would expect, given the implication of the word in Greek.[47]

To a certain extent Aristotle continued Plato's dualism. In his *De Anima,* for example, Aristotle assents to a number of Plato's notions. The body is to the mind as matter is to form. The soul is still the principle of life. It is, however, inseparable from the body as bodies are primary and their forms or ideas are secondary, to be perceived by us by our senses. The body provides a context for the intellect to develop. The mind has the potentiality of thought, and perception turns it to actuality. The *nous,* the intelligence, is therefore the process of turning the potentiality of the mind into actuality. Aristotle's notion of potentiality and actuality is another innovation.

The object also has primary actuality in the world. This, for Aristotle, was the same as saying that the principle of the perceived thing comes to subsist in the person's intellect because it existed elsewhere initially. The idea of the object is the same as the object as it resides in the mind; it is the same as the essence of the object, which only exists in the object itself. Since actuality is ranked higher than potentiality, actual knowledge must first subsist in an active intellect, which is a divine not a human quality.

As a result, Aristotle had a clearer idea of what individuality is but, by the same token, a healthier skepticism about what immortality could mean for any specific individual. We participate in divine processes when we think, so thinking demonstrates that there is intellect in the world. But that does not mean we are immortal. And thus, Aristotle's philosophy is easier for demonstrating the existence of a God; but Plato is easier for demonstrating the immortality of the soul.

That virtually assures that later religious commentators would combine Aristotelian with Platonic thinking and come up with a system that was friendly to the notions of God and immortality. The meaning of "Active Intellect" puzzled Aristotelian commentators for a millennium. Aristotle did not offer a precise definition. Many commentators, such as Alexander of Aphrodisias (flor. ca. 220 CE), thought that the Active Intellect was God. If not God, it would have to be one of a series of God's emanations. Other religious, medieval commentators—Al-Farabi, Ibn Sina, and Maimonides—thought that the Active Intellect was the angelic intelligence that governed the sublunar sphere from the moon, and that, therefore, it was the Active Intellect which also conveyed prophecy (now an intellectual process) to the true prophets. But, for Aristotle, the Unmoved Mover was named god. The *nous* remained divine in a more extended sense.

For one thing, how the extra-mental Active Intellect could relate to the active aspect of thinking is not clear. Aristotle, for instance, seems to have thought that memory and loving and hating perish at death. Although a person's acquired intellect survives death, memory does not (it inheres to the body), and therefore the soul retains nothing personal of its existence in matter. Immortality is a property of the Active Intellect, mind *(nous)* itself, which is a transcendant value. Perhaps then, Aristotle regarded the Active Intellect as a principle which is identical in all humanity, an Intelligence that enters into an individual and functions within him or her, and that survives the death of the individual. The individual soul does not survive in personal form.[48]

Nous had a kind of divinity for Aristotle and, perhaps, it is equivalent to the Unmoved Mover, as it is a perfect, active, actual intelligence, in contrast to our purely personal, receptive, imperfect one. While the soul and its intelligence are immortal and transcendent and while we can return to our divine source in the *nous*, personal immortality is even less possible in the Aristotelian system than in the Platonic one. It is probably this coldness with regard to our individual chances for a beatific afterlife that explains the relative unpopularity of the Aristotelian system in Hellenistic philosophy. It was hard for it to compete with the florid metaphysical world of middle and late Platonism, which found its way into a variety of religious systems in late Antiquity and to a considerable degree served as the basis of the philosophical account of religion in the West until the Enlightenment.

At first all the West knew of Aristotle was what had been absorbed into Middle and Neoplatonism. When finally, Western philosophy encountered Aristotelianism, it first took from it the intellectually more complete physics of Aristotle, with its geocentric view of the world. It was science (and as it turns out incorrect science), not religion, that could not do without Aristotle's sharp powers of observation and his account of the thinking process. As the indigestible parts of Aristotelianism belatedly entered religion, religion itself had to find a way to adjust. But that adjustment did not actively begin until the ninth century with the great medieval philosophers: Al-Farabi (870–950 CE), Ibn Sina (980–1037 CE), followed by Ibn Rushd (1126–98 CE), Maimonides (1135–1204 CE), and Aquinas (1225–1274 CE).

From Ascent to Instrument of the State

IN THE DREAM OF SCIPIO,[49] Cicero reflects on the values of the Republic and its defenders. Scipio the Elder (Africanus) returns to tell his younger namesake the future and ultimate rewards of the state. In his dream, Scipio is lifted high above the earth, where he finds out about the cosmos and the ultimate disposition of souls. Just as Socrates suggested, the dead are surely alive. It is we on earth who are really dead (*Resp.* 6.14). Platonism had thoroughly penetrated the philosophy of late Antiquity. And so had patriotism for the Republic. Those who support the state have special rewards. The narration continues with a description of the organization of the universe in its spheres and constellations. The purpose of the heavenly trip was not merely the revelation of the structure of the universe, now clearly described as spheres within spheres, but the inculcation of values that preserved the Republic:

And the noblest concerns are those assumed for the safety of your country; a soul stirred and trained by these pursuits will have a quicker flight to this abode, its own home; and this will be the faster, if even now, while imprisoned in the body, it reaches out and by contemplating what is beyond itself, detaches itself as much as possible from the body. (6.26)

Even as Cicero strove to preserve the values and government that had made a Republic possible, so too, the ascension and heavenly journey motif was brought into the debate about the correct government of the empire.

Before the emperors could arrogate for themselves the complete trappings of divinity, the story of the ascension of Romulus, a lawgiver and sole ruler, had to be refashioned to serve as a model for Julius, the second founder of Rome—thus both honoring Caesar and forming the mythical basis of the emperor's right to rule:

> There, Romulus was giving his friendly laws to the citizens, and Mars caught Ilia's son up. His mortal body became thin, dissolving in the air, as a lead pellet shot by a broad sling will melt in the sky. Suddenly a beautiful form more worthy of the high couches (of the gods), is the form of Quirinus, who is now wearing a sacred robe.[50]

Livy discusses Romulus' death and the rumors of it in terms reminiscent of the death of Julius Caesar:

> Then at first a few, then all, joyfully declared Romulus, the king and father of the city of Rome, to be a god, the son of god. They asked him with prayers for peace; so that he would always be pleased to wish favor for his children. I believe there were some even then who argued secretly that the king had been torn apart by the hands of the senators. Indeed, this rumor spread also, but very obscurely; the other version was enchanced by men's admiration for Romulus and their panic. (bk. 1, 16)[51]

This is a veiled reference to the assassination of Julius Caesar. But the rumors are calmed by the ascension story:

> Further, the stratagem of one man is said to have added to the credibility of the story. For, when the citizens were disturbed by the loss of the

king and were hostile toward the senators, Julius Proculus as it is told, a man of repute, (at least he was the author of this important thing) addressed the assembly. 'Romulus, Quirites,' he said, 'the father of this city, at the first light of this day, descended from the sky and clearly showed himself to me. While I was awed with holy fright, I stood reverently before him asking in prayer that I might look at him without sin.' 'Go,' he said, 'announce to the Romans that Heaven wishes that my Rome shall be the capital of the earth; therefore, they shall cultivate the military; they and their descendants shall know that no human might can resist Roman arms.' He said this and went on high. It is a great marvel what credence was generated by the man's tale, and how the loss of Romulus, for which the common people and the army grieved, was assuaged by the belief in his immortality. (1.16)

Livy's ironic attitude points out the value of the heavenly journey as a proof of immortality and as mythical underpinning of the developing Roman imperial system.

Vergil

VERGIL EXPLICITLY copies the form of the *Odyssey*, but it is a Platonic universe that he describes in his *Nekyia*, his séance to the underworld. In Book 6 of the *Aeneid*, pious Aeneas visits the dead, just as crafty Odysseus had before him in book 11 of the *Odyssey*. The major events of Odysseus' journey are reenacted in Aeneas' own journey. The readers were obviously familiar with what Odysseus saw in the land of the dead, but on the issue of life after death, and many other things, Vergil has made some revealing improvements on Homer.

Vergil's depiction of the underworld is remarkable in that it involves the kind of reward and punishment characteristic of the Platonic worldview. Under the tutelage of the Cumean Sibyl, the equivalent of Odysseus' Circe, Aeneas sets out on a guided tour of Hades. In front of him is the golden bough which Proserpine (Greek: Persephone) favors. Vergil's reference to Proserpine is appropriate, given the topic which he intends to pursue: death and its transcendence.

In Vergil's underworld, dead infants must stay outside the gates, constantly raising their shrill and plaintive cries; but they are not subject to any special torments. Inside the gates, by contrast, Minos presides over a court of the silent *(silentum concilliumque vocat),* ostensibly dispensing final justice (*Aen.* 6.432). Vergil's version of the realms of Hades are divided by ethical categories and are completely missing from Homer.

Phoenician Dido, whom Aeneas had to abandon in order to fulfill his Roman destiny, is but one of the tragic horde of the indolent and unmanly whom unyielding love has consumed to cruel wasting (*quos durus amor crudeli tabe peredit,* 6.442). The parallel with Odysseus' dalliance with Calypso and Circe is clearly the model for this incident. This is why Dante, literally as well as figuratively following the poet Vergil in his *Divine Comedy,* compassionately puts Paolo and Francesca at the highest rank of the "inferno." But compassion is not necessarily why Vergil has placed Dido where she is. As the fate of Dido shows, not Plato's transcendent love but stern Roman duty to the state is the highest good in this Roman vision of heaven. Dido represents both Rome's ancient enemy, Carthage, and a more recent one, Egypt.

No doubt Vergil had Antony and Cleopatra's recent bad example in mind when he wrote that Aeneas must forsake the beautiful African temptress to build the city of Rome. That is what Antony and Cleopatra's enemy Octavius Augustus would have had Antony do. In Octavius' estimation, Antony should have left his Egyptian whore and return to his rightful wife, Octavius' own sister. After Octavius defeated Antony and Cleopatra to secure the Roman republic for himself in 31 BCE, he assumed the title Augustus and became Vergil's patron. Likewise, in this Roman view of heaven, the heroes of the Roman state postpone present rewards to become the inhabitants of the Elysian fields (6.630ff.).

Cleopatra does not appear by name in Vergil's *Aeneid.* On the other hand, Vergil's benefactor Octavius Augustus Caesar, the most important person who opposed Cleopatra's designs, can hardly have been more pleased at Vergil's depiction of Dido's fiery torture in the *Aeneid.* It neutralized Cleopatra's victory by suicide over Octavius. Unlike Antony, after Aeneas enjoys the pleasures of Dido's North African realm, he returns to his pious duties to help found Rome, leaving Dido to perish out of love: "and for you my honor is gone and that good name that once was mine, my only claim to reach the stars" (4.430–32; see also 620–25).[52] The reference would have been clear as day to Vergil's contemporaries: Dido is a stand-in for Cleopatra; Aeneas provides the good Roman example that Antony should have followed. Shakespeare follows suit, with his own twist, as we shall see.

Aeneas plants the golden bough in the Elysian Fields, having come through the underworld to a land of green pastures and brighter light:

"Here an ampler ether clothes the meads with purple light, and they know their own sun and stars" *(largior hic campos aether et lumine vestit purpureo, solemque suum, sua sidera norunt, 6.637)* This is, first of all, an aristocratic place where the great soldiers of the Roman state continue their practice of arms, while the priests, bards, and others who ennobled Roman life are rewarded with eternal leisure. Just as in first-century Rome, it is service to the state more than good birth that brings with it ultimate felicity. Yet, we do not have strictly individual rewards and punishments; Romans, according to Vergil's representation, spend eternity with their peers and fellow heroes. The social utility of this doctrine in an empire that more and more depended on a new class of common soldiers and bureaucrats does not need any further emphasis. The state can find proper motivation for service by imagining a more perfect heaven with greater access for industrious Romans, who need rewards for earthly service.

Earlier, we see what happens to the villains of Vergil's world. Rhadamanthys holds sway over a particular part of hell in which the great sinners stay. Ranging from those who have put off atonement until the day of their death (6.565–70), a sin of omission, to perpetrators of much more serious sins of commission, Tartarus yawns twice as far down as Olympus is high (6.579). Entirely gone is the Homeric notion that the hero joins the common lot of shades underground, after a brief turn on earthly life, where everything depends on earthly fame.

Intellectually, Vergil's justification for adding judgment to Homer's Hades is Platonic thought. Once there is a self-conscious self who must achieve the beatific vision through its own actions, there can be a place of punishment as well as a place of reward. We have seen this pattern previously in Egyptian culture too. In Vergil's Hades, no one speaks Homeric Achilles' lines of envy for the living.

As in Plato's world, Vergillian souls do return to earth to complete their rehabilitation. Thus, Aeneas is given a vision of the glorious future which will be Rome's. Caesar is pointed out and then Augustus, his heir, scion of a god (*Divi genus*, 792). All that remains for us to recognize this as the familiar heaven of childhood's religion today is for this realm to be transferred to the unchangeable stars from the realms under the earth. But for it to be the Christian heaven, we need to substitute the religious and ethical values of the Judeo-Christian heritage for the values of the Roman republic.

Plutarch's Discussions of the
Judgment of the Dead

THE SAME new-found function of enforcing justice can be seen in Plutarch's *Moralia,* in his essay "On Those Who Are Punished by the Deity Late." In Plutarch's estimate, the abode of the souls had shifted to the heavens. Plutarch wanted to correct some details of the story while confirming the idea of the heavenly journey of the soul. After first making the point that the cruelest punishment is to see our loved ones and offspring suffering on account of our own misdeeds, Plutarch relates the story of one Aridaeus (renamed Thespesius after the adventure) who lived as a reprobate until one day he had a complete change of heart. The reason for his conversion to an ethical life was a heavenly journey that took the form of a Near Death Experience.

Several mysteries are revealed to Thespesius, including the ultimate destination of souls and the well-deserved punishment of Nero. Whatever else the author may relate, the tale functions as a theodicy, precisely because it parallels the journey of the soul after death. The heavenly journey itself is the basis of a personal, religious conversion, a new phenomenon of late antiquity but certainly not the only example of it.[53]

A complete ascent-descent myth can be found already in Vergil's *Fourth Ecologue.* Apollo's descent and return was not the self-conscious theme of the writer; rather, the birth of Augustus is viewed as the redemptive act in the cycle:

The last age of Sibyl's poem is now come. . . . Now a new offspring is sent down from high heaven. Do thou, chaste Lucina, favour the birth of the child under whom the iron breed will first cease and a golden race arise throughout the world. Now shall thine own Apollo bear sway.[54]

In the cult of the Emperor the ascension of the dead ruler was viewed in very literal terms. A quick look through the descriptions of the cult and the collections of iconography will verify that. The emperor could ascend in a chariot or on the back of an eagle. A shooting star signaled his demise.[55] The eagle was especially linked to the imperial cult. The practice arose of releasing a caged eagle from the top of the funeral pyre of the emperor.[56] Dio notes that centurions lit the pyre from below as an eagle was released, encouraging the belief that the soul was carried to heaven.[57] Beginning with Nero, coinage represents the motion of ascension with an eagle flying upwards.[58]

A remarkable diptych in the British museum depicts various symbols of *apotheosis,* deification, which had become part of the cult.[59] There are several intricate scenes. But the most relevant is the funeral scene with a pyre in the center from which a *quadriga* (the conveyance of Apollo or Helios), a chariot with four horses, is about to take off for heaven. The chariot is driven by a youth (probably Helios) whose pose and garment suggest great speed. To the right of the funeral pyre are two soaring eagles, probably symbolizing the divinized Emperor and Empress together. The *divus* is represented at the top, being born aloft by two winged beings. Looking down are the previously divinized ancestors and the signs of the Zodiac.

The figure of the charioteer in his *quadriga* had already achieved a stable and conventional form in the depictions of the zodiac. The sun is in the center, depicted by Helios in his *quadriga.* That the charioteer and *psychopomp* is Helios is supported by other archeological evidence—this time a pyre recovered at Rome, which even bears the inscription: *Sol me rapuit,* "The Sun has seized me".[60]

On his death-bed the emperor Vespasian quipped that he was becoming a god.[61] In the literary sources, the concept of the journey normally involved the soul of the deceased, while bodily ascension was limited to heroes, great men, and demigods like Romulus. Indeed, while Plato himself only suggested that souls come to live among the stars, the physics of the Romans insisted that the stars and souls were the same substance.[62] Pliny attributed this discovery to Hipparchus:

> Hipparchus will never receive all the praise he deserves since no one has better established the relation between man and the stars, or shown more clearly that our souls are particles of divine fire. (*Nat.* 2.26.95)

The use (and abuse) of divinization in the imperial cult is well known. A century after the Imperial system took hold, Hadrian decreed that the soul of his deceased lover, Antinous, had ascended to heaven and become a divinity.[63] But, by then, Caligula had made his horse a senator; the deification of the Emperor's lover seemed reasonable by comparison.

If it is true that both Greek and Roman societies from Plato to Plutarch, practically from one end of Greco-Roman philosophy to the other, know of the journey to the heavens, it is also true that the Romans adapted the motif and structure to express some enduring and important thoughts about their government and their rule. It was during the Hellenistic and Roman periods that the fundamental shift of ultimate human reward took place. The shift was only partly based on the notion that the heavens contained the ultimate reward for the righteous, while the underworld contained the punishment for the evil. Along with this moralizing of the pagan afterlife came also a great deal of astronomy, astrology, and cosmology, all of which helped to make plausible a human destiny in the stars.

It is quite possible that Hebrew and oriental thought influenced this pagan synthesis. Eastern astronomy and astrology certainly influenced the cosmology. The earth became the center of an onion of heavenly spheres, usually seen as seven in number, corresponding to the number of respective powers. Whenever Platonic notions are emphasized, the ultimate home of humans can be seen as the realm where the stars and ideas dwell, in the unchanging heavens. So although earthly life is still valued as important for civic duty, some interest applies to the afterlife for the first time in pagan intellectual life. In some way, voyage to the unchanging stars can be seen as a viable alternative to earthly existence. The heavens become the realm of ultimate salvation *(soteria, salvatio)* in the later Roman world.[64]

6

Second Temple Judaism

The Rise of a Beatific Afterlife in the Bible

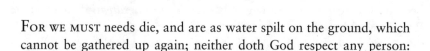

FOR WE MUST needs die, and are as water spilt on the ground, which cannot be gathered up again; neither doth God respect any person: yet doth he devise means, that his banished be not expelled from him. (2 Sam 14:14)

Here is the classic King James Version of the advice of the wise woman of Tekoa to David. The first part of the verse is clear and poignant. Our lives are like water spilt on the ground. Life is lost as it is lived; it cannot be recovered. Yet the second phrase of the passage seems more portentous and has been translated, as here, to say something more about God's rescue of the righteous from the abandonment of death. The word *nefesh* (soul) occurs in the text in a way that can be capitalized upon by later thinkers. The Hebrew is, in fact, not so much uncertain as part of a difficult argument. In context, it is part of a ruse, planned by Joab, to convince David to allow Absalom to return from exile. The woman seems to mean that King David should be just as lenient as God since, as David has himself judged, God desires the survival of a sole surviving son. Because the situation is parallel to the banishment of Absalom, it is equally an argument for allowing Absalom to return from exile without further punishment, a point which the wise woman immediately presses upon David.

The original meaning is not likely to go beyond the sad realization that everyone passes from God's sight, mitigated by the comfort that God mercifully can preserve the seed of a family for the next generation. Indeed, the Septuagint (the Greek translation of the Bible) points out that God will take the exiled as well. Yet the King James Version, basing itself partly on the Vulgate, translates the passage in a more generalized and a very much more hopeful way. The Vulgate is certainly one major step in the direction of the hereafter. A beatific afterlife is so powerful an incentive in life that once it has entered Christian life, it is hard to imagine that it was not always present in the Hebrew text.[1] But it was not.

Furthermore, life after death did not enter Jewish thought immediately after the Jews met the Persians and the Greeks. The right social and historical situation had to arise before a beatific afterlife was expressed in Jewish thought.

The Book of Ecclesiastes (Qoheleth)

THE BOOK OF Ecclesiastes was written during the Persian period (539–332 BCE) or, a bit later, during the early Hellenistic period (332 BCE–65 BCE). Along with Job, it is an articulate denial of life after death. It is so pointed a denial that one is forced to the conclusion that the Jews were aware of notions of afterlife in Persian and Greek culture.

Interestingly, the "stoicism" in Ecclesiastes might have come from almost any period of Israelite thinking, as a certain fatalism has been part of Near Eastern Wisdom literature since its inception.[2] But the grammar, word usage, and syntax indicate that the book was written in Second Temple times. Ecclesiastes is traditionally thought to date from the time of Solomon, who is identified as the narrator, *Qoheleth,* on the grounds that the narrator describes himself as "a scion of David, king in Jerusalem" (Eccles 1:1). There are no strong grounds for the identification with Solomon. The English title "Ecclesiastes" comes from the Latin transcription of the Greek translation of the term *qoheleth,* which was taken to mean something like "a member of the assembly." The rabbis, noting the fatalistic tone in it, said that although it was written by Solomon, it was written during his declining, more cynical years—the product of an old, worldly-wise and pessimistic man, who despite his greatness was also guilty of a number of very worldly sins. And so a remarkable document has come down to us by ascription to an undisputedly great, though tarnished, Judean king.

The most recent, full treatment of the book, *Ecclesiastes* by Choon-Leong Seow for the Anchor Bible, is a sober and almost convincing argument for its Persian provenance. To begin with, there are two widely recognized Persian loanwords in Ecclesiastes: *pardes* (2:5) meaning "garden, orchard" (cognate with Greek *paradeisos* and English "paradise") and *pitgam* (8:11) meaning "proverb, aphorism" (cognate with Greek *apophthegma* and English "apothegm"). The word "paradise" is, of course, crucial for the development of notions of the afterlife. But it has not yet been put to the purpose of describing our ultimate disposition.

These words are important because there is no clear evidence of any Persianism in Israelite documents prior to the Achaemenid period. Yet, we should be careful about concluding too much from these terms. Both these early Persian words—"paradise" and "apothegm"—are also found in Greek, either by cognation or by borrowing; they may just as well be an argument for Hellenization.

More importantly for the Persian dating, there are a great number of Aramaic phrases in Ecclesiastes. Aramaic was the lingua franca of the Persian Empire in its western provinces. Because of its closeness to Hebrew, Aramaic words were accepted readily into Hebrew, far more easily than Persian or Greek words. Indeed, many ancient writers seem unaware of the distinction. By the Roman and Byzantine periods, Aramaic had virtually replaced Hebrew as the common tongue. At the same time, many Greek and even Latin words were accepted into general parlance but the rate of absorption was much slower by comparison to Aramaic.[3] Persian words also creep in here and there, especially in the Talmudic period, where the major Jewish community was found in Babylonia. All of this makes certain that the book of Ecclesiastes dates to the end of the Persian or to the beginning of the Greek period in Israelite history. No other explanation seems realistic, but neither is there adequate grounds for more specificity.

One of the most obvious changes in Israelite life by the end of the Persian period was the rise of a commercial and monetary economy. The change to a moneyed economy can be seen in the epigraphy of the period and it can be seen here in Ecclesiastes. Seow notes that the effects of the new economic system on the wisdom literature in Ecclesiastes: "One who loves money will not be satisfied with money, nor whoever loves abundance with yield" (5:10). This statement recognizes that both barter and monetary exchange are economic realities. There are also a number of statements about interest and capital building. Ecclesiastes notes what every moneyed economy has thereafter noted: Money does not bring happiness. The worker sleeps well while the rich have no rest in their surfeit (5:12): "While Qohelet clearly draws on timeless wisdom teachings, he also addresses people facing a new world of money and finance."[4] Ecclesiastes reflects a very different social reality than the subsistence agriculture of preexilic Judah.

Even if Qoheleth was not himself a king and merely adopting that role as a literary conceit, he belonged to a class of people who were both working hard and benefiting from the newfound affluence:

> Behold, what I have seen to be good and to be fitting is to eat and drink and find enjoyment in all the toil with which one toils under the sun the few days of his life which God has given him, for this is his lot. Every man also to whom God has given wealth and possessions and power to enjoy them, and to accept his lot and find enjoyment in his toil—this is the gift of God. For he will not much remember the days of his life because God keeps him occupied with joy in his heart. (Eccles 5:18–20)

On the other hand, he is quite upset with a number of aspects of this new moneyed economy. He sees oppression of the poor, economic injustice, and even sudden ruin:

> No man has power to retain the spirit, or authority over the day of death; there is no discharge from war, nor will wickedness deliver those who are given to it. (Eccles 8:8)

He advises that investment and assumption of risk are profitable activities but should be balanced by charity for the less fortunate:

> Cast your bread upon the waters,
> for you will find it after many days.
> Give a portion to seven, or even to eight,
> for you know not what evil may happen on earth.
>   (Eccles 11:1–2)

Qoheleth admits that the newfound economic affluence is good but then critiques the accompanying greed. His message, that all is vanity, is meant to put this affluence in the correct perspective. Life is not just a race to accumulate the most goods, as it is full of terrible misfortunes and upheavals, and it always ends in death.

It is quite possible that this perception took place during the Persian period, as Seow suggests. It is also possible that the setting is the beginning of the Greek period, after the conquest of Alexander in 332 BCE. Indeed, as Seow himself has shown, and as a number of other people have suggested, the economic characteristics of the Hellenistic period were already well established during the Persian period.[5] If the Persians presided over the "takeoff" period of the economy, the Hellenists brought the development of true international trade, which Judea was well positioned geographically to exploit. In fact, the Jews complained bitterly of the lack of prosperity and affluence in the early Persian period (Neh 9:32–39). But Greek documents show a very comfortable, new urban class, the very ones who can appreciate the value of the new Hellenistic culture. To distinguish between the the cultural conditions of the end of the Persian period and the beginning of the Ptolemaic one may be impossible in Ecclesiastes.

Ecclesiastes is important for the history of the development of the notion of the afterlife, especially because it emphasizes that the idea does not develop early among Jewish aristocrats living in the land of Israel. If he were so disposed, Qoheleth could have appealed to either of two, well-developed foreign notions of beatific afterlife. He might have used either to encourage people to be honest and lead moral lives. But, evidently, he came to the opposite conclusion, and thus the book can be seen as a companion piece to the book of Job:

> Moreover I saw under the sun that in the place of justice, wickedness was there, and in the place of righteousness, wickedness was there as well. I said in my heart, God will judge the righteous and the wicked, for he has appointed a time for every matter, and for every work. I said in my heart with regard to human beings that God is testing them to show that they are but animals. For the fate of humans and the fate of animals is the same; as one dies, so dies the other. They all have the same breath, and humans have no advantage over the animals; for all is vanity. All go to one place; all are from the dust, and all turn to dust again. Who knows whether the human spirit goes upward and the spirit of animals goes downward to the earth? So I saw that there is nothing better than that all should enjoy their work, for that is their lot; who can bring them to see what will be after them? (Eccles 3:16–22)

The context for these observations by Qoheleth is the seeming injustice and hypocrisy in the world. Ecclesiastes does not rely on a concept of life after death to guarantee justice. Instead, it makes a different observation: God is testing humanity by showing them how close they are to animals, suggesting that the wisdom to perceive the situation will itself permit humanity to regain the proper path. The only afterlife Qoheleth suggests is that we return to dust, just as Genesis 3 says. Qoheleth is reasserting traditional Hebrew values but he valorizes them in a very affecting personal voice, a self-possessed personal sensibility that we have not heard before in Jewish society.

Qoheleth goes out of his way to say that the fate of both animals and humans is the same: They all die. But he then asks a rhetorical question, querying whether anyone knows for sure whether human spirit goes up while animals go down into the earth? This is a most astonishing question, since until now the Israelites and the Jews after them have articulated clearly that humans normally go down to Sheol when they die. Qoheleth was aware of new ideas percolating in the area, ideas which suggested that we ascend to the heavens when we die. He denies their validity.

His opposition may even be influenced by the foreignness of the ideas. It may be the very fact that the *Fravashi* is Persian and the immortal soul is Greek that bothers him. In any event it looks as if some unstated and uncharacterized notions of a beatific afterlife were already known in Jewish Hebrew culture that Ecclesiastes is going out of its way to question it. Even though Ecclesiastes denies a beatific afterlife, or says that we should never count on reward after death, merely asking the question and suggesting that our spirits can go up rather than down to the grave suggests that we have entered another phase in Hebrew thought.

Qoheleth himself counts on observation of the world to defeat the notion. He suggests that any such traditions of human spirit heading upwards after death is counterintuitive:

This is an evil in all that happens under the sun, that the same fate comes to everyone. Moreover, the hearts of all are full of evil; madness is in their hearts while they live, and after that they go to the dead. But whoever is joined with all the living has hope, for a living dog is better than a dead lion. The living know that they will die, but the dead know nothing; they have no more reward, and even the memory of them is lost. Their love and their hate and their envy have already perished; never again will they have any share in all that happens under the sun. Go, eat your bread with enjoyment, and drink your wine with a merry heart; for God has long ago approved what you do. Let your garments always be white; do not let oil be lacking on your head. Enjoy life with the wife whom you love, all the days of your vain life that are given you under the sun, because that is your portion in life and in your toil at which you toil under the sun. Whatever your hand finds to do, do with your might; for there is no work or thought or knowledge or wisdom in Sheol, to which you are going. (Eccles 9:3–10)

In this passage, Qoheleth accepts the notion of Sheol. He reproduces the solace of the Old Babylonian version of *The Gilgamesh Epic*. He explicitly denies resurrection and return to this world after death. Logically, he is also sceptical of the prophetic notion that God will Himself intervene to set the world right. He goes beyond pessimism and agnosticism about the life after death.

Instead, he states positively that there is no reward or punishment in the life after death. It is the same reward for all. But his reaction is not despair; rather it is closer to stoic *apatheia,* stoic indifference. Like Sidduri in the old Babylonian version of *The Gilgamesh Epic,* he suggests a carpe diem (literally: "seize the day") theme. Enjoy life. Eat and drink with enjoyment; let your family give you pleasure; dress well. This life is all that we can know. Don't count on anything more.

Here, in Ecclesiastes, is the beginning of the position that Josephus and the New Testament associate with the Sadducees. This class comes from the highest level of the society but, by the first century CE, Josephus calls them boorish and too indifferent to the needs of their inferiors. Whatever their manners, their rejection of life after death is grounded in Scripture, particularly in the book of Ecclesiastes.

The Wisdom of Jesus Ben Sira (Ecclesiasticus)

EVEN IN THE later book of the Wisdom of Jesus Ben Sira, also known as Sirach, Siracides or Ecclesiasticus, we find similar notions which stand heroically against any doctrine of beatific afterlife. All rewards and punishments are experienced in this life. Adversity is a test of one's faith: "Opt not for the success of pride; remember it will not reach death unpunished" (Sir 9:12). Even more important is his famous discussion of death:

> Give, take, and treat yourself well,
>   for in the netherworld there are no joys to seek.
> All flesh grows old, like a garment;
>   the age-old law is: all must die. (Sir 14:16–17)

This text merely says that all die. But in Ben Sira there is no remedy for death on the other side of the grave. There are two principal ways in which a person outlasts death. The first is through children (Sir 30:4–5). They will represent their parents after death. The other way is by means of lasting reputation (Sir 41:11–13). For Ben Sira, they are both the most admirable and worthwhile life occupations.

The Hebrew text is actually more pessimistic on the issue of afterlife than is the Greek. In the Greek translation, several possible allusions to retribution in the hereafter are mentioned, especially Sirach 7:17b and 48:11b. The reasons for this may be that the translation was written after the publication of the visions of Daniel while the original certainly precedes them. The Greek version was likely glossed to contain the ever more popular notions of life after death.

The Arrival of the Notion of Resurrection

EVIDENCE OF the gradual imposition of the idea of beatific afterlife surfaces in the later prophets and psalms. One of the most famous passages occurs in Ezekiel 37, dated sometime around the victory of Cyrus over the Neo-Babylonian empire in 539 BCE. But it actually means less than has been attributed to it:

> The hand of the Lord came upon me, and he brought me out by the spirit of the Lord and set me down in the middle of a valley; it was full of bones. He led me all around them; there were very many lying in the valley, and they were very dry. He said to me, "Mortal, can these bones live?" I answered, "O LORD God, you know." Then he said to me, "Prophesy to these bones, and say to them: O dry bones, hear the word of the LORD. Thus says the LORD God to these bones: I will cause breath to enter you, and you shall live. I will lay sinews on you, and will cause flesh to come upon you, and cover you with skin, and put breath in you, and you shall live; and you shall know that I am the LORD." So I prophesied as I had been commanded; and as I prophesied, suddenly there was a noise, a rattling, and the bones came together, bone to its bone. I looked, and there were sinews on them, and flesh had come upon them, and skin had covered them; but there was no breath in them. Then he said to me, "Prophesy to the breath, prophesy, mortal, and say to the breath: Thus says the Lord God: Come from the four winds, O breath, and breathe upon these slain, that they may live." I prophesied as he commanded me, and the breath came into them, and they lived, and stood on their feet, a vast multitude. (Ezek 37:1–10)

No passage in the Hebrew Bible appears to be more a discussion of bodily resurrection. It actually describes the physical process by which the bones of the dead are re-covered with flesh and built into human beings again. The passage has affected ever after the imagery and depiction of the resurrection promised by the Bible. Zoroastrian notions of the resurrection, starting with the bones of the dead, seems naturally to be implicated; but this parallel raises a whole host of chronological and historical problems.[6] The beginning of Ezekiel's career was far too early and too far west for Zoroastrian influence. Even if these images had been borrowed, they have been well adapted into Israelite thought. If the ultimate source is Zoroastrianism, gone is the notion of battle between good and evil at the end of time and gone is the importance of the saving drink of Haoma.

Instead, it looks to be the authentic and independent vision of the Israelite prophet. But the issue is not resurrection. There is no evidence that this passage is meant to be a prophecy of resurrection at all. It uses the imagery of resurrection in a very important and reassuring way. But it does not promise resurrection to the Judeans. Rather, it uses the metaphor of resurrection to promise national regeneration. There is no suggestion that resurrection is supposed to happen to anyone personally or individually. It is only the striking vehicle of the metaphor for the message of the prophecy. The very next words in the passage clarify that the vision is a symbolic depiction of the effect of prophecy on the exiles and not meant to be literal at all:

> Then he said to me, "Mortal, these bones are the whole house of Israel. They say, 'Our bones are dried up, and our hope is lost; we are cut off completely.' Therefore prophesy, and say to them, Thus says the LORD God: I am going to open your graves, and bring you up from your graves, O my people; and I will bring you back to the land of Israel. And you shall know that I am the LORD, when I open your graves, and bring you up from your graves, O my people. I will put my spirit within you, and you shall live, and I will place you on your own soil; then you shall know that I, the LORD, have spoken and will act," says the Lord. (Ezek 37:11–14)

The verses immediately following the description of bodily resurrection make clear that this is a prophetic vision, with a symbolic meaning for the present, not a literal prophecy of the end of time. The interpretation of the vision is to be found starting in verse 11, which states that the people are metaphorically dead, lacking in spirit and morale. The prophet's burden is to infuse them with a new spirit, which comes from his prophetic visions of restoration and his prophetic utterances of encouragement. The grave is clearly understood as low morale, exile, and cultic pollution. Those who return from exile are as though they have been restored to life. They again hear the prophetic voice. The kingdoms of Judah and Israel will be restored to life but they will be united under the aegis of the Davidic king. They will be one branch (vv 21ff.). And idolatry will cease to exist in the land and so will all the pollutions of idolatry and the dead bodies. They will all know the LORD.

The prophet also seems to be answering a question generated by a real issue of what to do about the bones of corpses strewn about the land of Israel a half century previously when the Babylonians devastated the land. For returning exiles, the question of the impurity of the land, impurity created by the unburied corpses, and impurity created by the sins of the forefathers, would have been significant. Perhaps the vision of the resurrection is one reflection on how God will resolve it.

Even if the passage is not meant to be a literal description of and promise of life after death, it can certainly furnish a new vocabulary of images of resurrection directly into Israelite thought and thus provide the language for belief in life after death in future generations. That, it has done extremely well. After the cultural situation to which the prophet speaks faded into history, his striking imagery of a personal life after death retains its prophetic immediacy. The Targum interprets this passage as the prophecy of the resurrection of the ten lost tribes of Israel (not all of Israel). The Dura Europos fresco paintings depict this scene vividly as a literal resurrection. The Church Fathers—especially Justin Martyr (*Apol.* 2.87), Irenaeus (*Haer.* 5.1) and Tertullian (*Res.* 30)—used this scene as a Biblical demonstration of the resurrection. Tertullian even refuted the Gnostic opinion that this passage referred only to the restoration of Israel and not to personal resurrection.

The rabbis interpreted the passages in various ways, including as a literal future resurrection scene, but were reluctant to use it as proof for the general doctrine of resurrection because it did not appear in the first five books of Moses and thus could not offer the best support and precedent for the doctrine. One rabbi even suggested imaginatively that the dead were actually resurrected as a sign of the end, that they sang their song of praise to the LORD, and then they died immediately again to await the final consummation.[7]

The Isaianic Apocalypse: Isaiah 24–27

THE LANGUAGE in chapters 24 through 27 of Isaiah is visionary; it describes life after death, and, again, it is not likely to be meant literally. But in this passage there is a good deal of ambiguity. While it is scarcely true that the imagery of life after death automatically assumes a mature belief in resurrection, it is quite true that this very concrete resurrection imagery suggests that the belief was present in Israelite society. Yet, the report that a prophet saw this vision is no guarantee that the imagery was not borrowed from Canaanite or Persian thought either.[8]

If notions of resurrection or beatific life after death were already present in Israelite thought, they had not been emphasized in any significant way. One would expect that a belief like resurrection of the body would enter with a bold statement, not sneak in the back door. One such place is Isaiah 25:8–9 where the prophet envisions a day in which God will destroy death:

> He will swallow up death for ever, and the LORD GOD will wipe away tears from all faces, and the reproach of his people he will take away from all the earth; for the LORD has spoken. It will be said on that day, "Lo, this is our God; we have waited for him, that he might save us. This is the LORD; we have waited for him; let us be glad and rejoice in his salvation."

This prophecy is a vision of a perfected future. It would be surprising if death were present in a perfected future. The vision is an example of the prophetic "Day of the LORD." The question is only how the prophet will articulate the remedy to death. Here, he picks a Canaanite motif of Ba'al's victory over Mot. Why the prophet has chosen a mythological Canaanite image is not clear—perhaps only because it was a known story or even partly out of a polemical concern to assert YHWH's, not Ba'al's, authorship of life and death.

In Canaanite mythology it was Ba'al who conquered death, but he has to renew the battle periodically. Save for Ba'al, whom death regurgitates, death itself swallows all. The prophet reverses the metaphor by applying it to YHWH as the savior of Israel and LORD of life and death. It is a brave and striking metaphor but not as much of a religious innovation as it first seems, even in Israel. What is striking about the image is that YHWH will defeat death historically, once and for all and forever, not defeat death every-so-often at the turn of seasons. Indeed, the whole point of the image is that death is still very much part of the world. God's action is awaited in the future. The vision is for the future, just as it is for the faithful to YHWH alone.

Another place where notions of eternal life enter the Isaianic apocalypse is Isaiah 26:19. This passage is much more complicated and much more difficult to understand:

> Your dead shall live, their corpses shall rise.[9] O dwellers in the dust, awake and sing for joy! For your dew is a radiant dew, and the earth will give birth to those long dead.
>
> Come, my people, enter your chambers, and shut your doors behind you; hide yourselves for a little while until the wrath is past.
>
> For the LORD comes out from his place to punish the inhabitants of the earth for their iniquity; the earth will disclose the blood shed on it, and will no longer cover its slain. (Isa 26:19–21)

This passage has been quoted throughout Western history, having donated its words to prayers and thanksgivings, as well as to titles of plays and poems, to inspire faith and religious vision, and promise salvation to every Abrahamic faith. Out of context, it seems much more clearly a reference to resurrection than it actually is, when read in its confusing and somewhat ambiguous literary context. Furthermore, making the passage's interpretation even more difficult, this Isaianic passage has not yielded much to historical analysis: nobody agrees when it was written or to what it refers.

Basing their views as much on its subject matter as anything else, many scholars suspect that chapters 24–27 of Isaiah, the so-called "Isaianic Apocalypse," are from a much later time than the original Isaiah of chapters 1–39.[10] Most of Isaiah 1–39 is from the First Temple period, from the eighth century BCE, written by a Judahite prophet during the Syro-Ephraimite War with the specter of a resurgent Assyria. But chapters 24–27 are in many ways like Isaiah 40–66, which discuss the return from exile (538–515 BCE), though they are angrier and more vehement. We call the nameless prophet of Isaiah 40–66 Second Isaiah (also called Deutero–Isaiah) since his prophecies were combined with the earlier one. There is also a third writer in the later parts of Isaiah 56–66, who can be called, conventionally, Third Isaiah.

But no one is sure who is the author of Isaiah 24–27 nor when he lived; no one can even satisfactorily identify the voice with any of the other authors in the book of Isaiah. Identifying the "Isaianic apocalypse" as contemporary with 2 or 3 Isaiah is only a guess made on the basis of the known composite nature of the volume.

Before speculating on the situation which produced the lines of Isaiah 26:19–21, we should analyze what they say in context. The lines are analogous to the Ezekiel 37. As in Ezekiel 37, there is an underlying ambiguity as to whether the prophet meant us to understand a literal resurrection. Unlike Ezekiel 37, where the prophecy is clearly intended to be metaphorical, here it is quite difficult to tell.

On the one hand, the context suggests a symbolic rather than a literal message. Obviously the writer does not mean that the people will literally give birth. It is again the people and their political, social regeneration that is the subject of the passage, just as it is in Ezekiel 37. The prophet points out the previous failures of the people. They have already tried to return to the LORD. But, unlike in Ezekiel 37, their endeavors are in vain. Like Ezekiel 37, the prophet promises that the people will be renewed with the help of the prophetic spirit, provided by the prophet. So far, the message is similar to Ezekiel, except ritual purity is not the issue, and the historical time and the imagery is unstated.

Unlike Ezekiel 37, whether or not we are dealing with a metaphor or the literal resurrection, the exact event that the prophet describes is obscure. The prophet may in fact be saying that the righteous dead will be the agents of God's punishment, that the righteous will arise to punish the sinners. If so, the prophet was using Canaanite language in a very ironic way, to say the dead will punish God's enemies who have ignored His words.

If I had to guess (and I do have to guess, since there are no completely convincing previous analyses of the passage for me to rely on), I would say that the author is actually 1 Isaiah, and that he is using the terminology of Canaanite myth and ritual ironically to talk about the terrible destruction brought to Jerusalem by the Assyrians, followed by their even more terrible and awesome retreat in 701 BCE. Since it has not been suggested before, let us explore the possibility that Isaiah 26 was written by the original Isaiah, and that the event he describes is the great Assyrian siege of Jerusalem, which was lifted when the Assyrian army was struck with a plague (2 Kgs 18–20, especially 19:35). Hezekiah himself became sick immediately afterwards (2 Kgs 20:1–21). And his recovery was seen as divine intervention to save the Judahite kingdom yet again. But this suggestion demands further explanation.

So far there is nothing that demands a literal reading of resurrection. Indeed, Psalms shows us that a terrible sickness like Hezekiah's might certainly be treated as if the king had already been in Sheol, only to recover to normal life with God's help, as we have seen so often in the conventional language of Psalms. It may also be the dominant metaphor for the recovery of the people after the siege. That means that the second, parallel line in Isaiah 26:19, which sounds so literal, may only be a restatement of the metaphor of regeneration: "For your dew is a radiant dew, and the earth will give birth to those long dead" (Isa 26:19b). Then the description of closing doors until the malevolence has gone by might be a literal reference to the siege with the Assyrian corpses still lying on the field of battle, like the firstborn dead of Egypt in the Exodus story.

That is speculation but so are all the other explanations of this passage. Even if unsubstantiated, this hypothesis shows that the passage does not have to be about the literal resurrection of the dead. Whatever else is true, in context, it is not a clear and impressive prophecy of literal future bodily resurrection.

So let us explore it further for a moment. The salvation of Jerusalem from the Assyrian menace in 701 BCE would have been seen as a mighty intervention from God, as is described in 2 Kings. The prophet would be explaining Israel's deliverance as a miraculous intervention from God, balanced by punishment for the enemies of God. The Israelites who participated in the cult of the dead, perhaps also other idolaters, are included in the punishment, reasoning "measure for measure": God will give these worshipers of the dead punishment from the dead. The dead will be His agents. Then the righteous, who were thought dead because they were surrounded by the Assyrians and truly given up for dead, will reemerge from the siege: "Your dead shall live, their corpses shall rise. O dwellers in the dust, awake and sing for joy!" (Isa 26:19). This also follows Hezekiah's reemergence from his sickness, after being considered dead, even by the prophet Isaiah himself.

Whatever else this speculation shows, it demonstrates that the Isaiah and Ezekiel passages need not be discussions of literal resurrection. However, even if both these passages are taken as references to literal resurrection, they hardly affect the general tenor of Israelite religion, which emphasized life on this earth and behavior in the world. That much is unaffected by the outcome of an analysis of Ezekiel 37 and Isaiah 26. But these two passages are absolutely crucial for understanding whence the language of resurrection comes. Metaphorical here, resurrection becomes absolutely literal in Daniel 12. Therefore these passages become the reservoir of images that illustrate what resurrection means.

Daniel 12: The Dead Arise at Long Last

THE FIRST CLEAR reference to resurrection can be defined exactly; both its date and circumstances can be fixed accurately:

> "At that time Michael, the great prince, the protector of your people, shall arise. There shall be a time of anguish, such as has never occurred since nations first came into existence. But at that time your people shall be delivered, everyone who is found written in the book. Many of those who sleep in the dust of the earth shall awake, some to everlasting life, and some to shame and everlasting contempt. Those who are wise shall shine like the brightness of the sky, and those who lead many to righteousness, like the stars forever and ever. But you, Daniel, keep the words secret and the book sealed until the time of the end. Many shall be running back and forth, and evil shall increase." (Dan 12:1–3)

The sign of the resurrection will be the arrival of the great prince, the archangel Michael. It will be a time of unprecedented, terrible tribulation. But the people whose names are written in the book shall be rescued. This book, which the prophet mentions in such a portentous way, had an ambiguous past in the Bible, though it quickly became part of standard Jewish lore (See e.g., ascension of Isaiah 9:21–22), eventually providing the central metaphor of the Jewish New Year (m. Rosh Hashanah 1:1). Even in the contemporary Jewish service of the New Year, "the Book of Life" has a major role. The book is, likely, to be identified with the mysterious book Moses mentions in Exodus 32:32: "But now, if thou wilt forgive their sin—and if not, blot me, I pray thee, out of thy book which thou hast written." Whatever the book, the metaphor dramatizes God's clear and predestined plan for vindication of the earth. Daniel 12:2 promises resurrection to some of Israel, not to all, not even to all those who are righteous, as would be true if Isaiah 26 or Ezekiel 37 were to be understood literally. The presence of the book suggests that God has indicated his intentions in advance, completed an inevitable plan, will hold to it, and that this knowledge is available to prophets like Moses who can read it ahead of time. The writer is, in effect, claiming the credentials of a prophet—not an oral one like the prophets of old, but a new wisdom prophet who can read God's plan when God choses to show it.

This writer is claiming prophecy and literary tradition at the same time. Besides the revelation of God's secret plan, he is aware of the previous writing on the subject, primarily the writing we have just reviewed, because his language is based on the metaphors in the prophets Isaiah and Ezekiel. Some of the language in Daniel 12:1–3 is taken directly from Isaiah 26:19, which says that the dead will "awaken." The writer of Daniel has taken the ambiguous prophecy of Isaiah in a literal sense, saying that "the sleepers in the dust" will literally arise.[11] But he did not take the writing literally in every respect because he has some innovative notions about the identity of the resurrected and the process of resurrection.

Strangely, he goes on to say that resurrection will not be reserved for the righteous alone. Also some whose behavior was reprehensible will be resurrected for eternal contempt and shame. This is totally missing from any of previous references in the Hebrew Bible but it is not totally out of keeping with Zoroastrian notions of resurrection, that promised it eventually to all. However, Zoroastrian influence is unlikely here. The Zoroastrians believed that the time in the grave would absolve all sinners from their sins. In this case, the resurrection promised to evildoers is not to forgive them but to punish them the more. Discussions of resurrection in Judaism only rewarded the righteous until the rise of Rabbinic Judaism which took seriously that all Israel will be saved, as does Paul: "And so all Israel will be saved; as it is written, 'The Deliverer will come from Zion, he will banish ungodliness from Jacob' " (Rom 11:26). Even in this case, the rabbis maintained that all Israel will be righteous.

Another passage that was particularly important to the seer is Isaiah 66. The only other place in the Hebrew Bible where the perplexing word *dera'on* (*lĕdor'ōn 'olām*, "eternal abhorance") of Daniel 12:2 appears is in Isaiah 66:24: "And they shall go forth and look on the dead bodies of the men that have rebelled against me; for their worm shall not die, their fire shall not be quenched, and they shall be an abhorrence to all flesh." The Septuagint translates the passage slightly differently, as "spectacle": "a spectacle for all flesh," I suppose meaning a spectacle of derision, showing that although the word was somewhat puzzling even in ancient times, a consensus about its meaning had already arisen.

But the connection with Isaiah 66 is not merely adventitious; it is a major clue to the composition of the passage. We are fortunate that the words only appear in these two places because they underline how much the seer in Daniel is actually dependent on Isaiah 66. Daniel's vision is prophecy and confirmation that the last part of Isaiah 66 is to come true in a surprising way with the resurrection of the righteous remnant:

And they shall go forth and look on the dead bodies of the men that have rebelled against me; for their worm shall not die, their fire shall

not be quenched, and they shall be an abhorrence to all flesh. (Isa 66:
23–24)

The term "abhorrence," used only twice in the Hebrew Bible, is like a
tracer bullet, showing that the vision of Isaiah 66 is being interpreted by
the seer in Daniel as a prophecy that will shortly come true. The imagery
of Isaiah 24–27 is itself interpreted in Isaiah 66.[12]

The nations will soon know of the Lord's power because He himself
will show them His Glory. Quite possibly, Daniel interpreted this passage
to mean that the "son of man," the manlike figure of Daniel 7:13 is appointed the Glory of the Lord. Daniel probably had the archangel Michael in mind for the position of "Glory of the Lord," because his name
means "he who is like God."

It looks like the resurrection prophecy of Daniel 12:1–2 is based on a
visionary understanding of Isaiah 66:14 "Your bones will flower like
grass." To establish a consistent picture, the seer must also combine Isaiah 66:14 with the imagery of Ezekiel 37, "the vision of the dry bones," in
which the bones lying dry in the valley come together with tendons, flesh,
and skin to form human beings again. The purpose of the resurrection in
Daniel 12, according to the seer Daniel's inspired exegesis of Isaiah 66:14,
was to show the plan of the Lord, that the Lord's hand would be known:
"that the hand of the LORD is with his servants and his indignation
against his enemies" (Isa 66:14). The medium of this combination of passages is a prophetic, revelatory vision, which combines passages from all
over the Bible, not in a casual fashion but in a very complex and sophisticated manner. But it is not exegesis; it is a visionary revelation, as the Daniel text explicitly says. It is a vision that the seer has received after avid
study of the text. This writing could not have been produced merely by an
intellectual exegesis of the text, but rather by a religiously altered state of
consciousness (see ch. 8). No exegete would have mixed all the motifs of
all these passages without seeking a methodological justification or calling attention to the way in which the passages should be combined; after
his study of Isaiah 66, the prophet experienced a dream or vision, in
which all the passages were combined into one.

Of particular interest is the following vision of judgment in Isaiah 66.[13]
In the vision the sinners are those who eat swine's flesh; God arrives in his
chariotry in his warrior ("Ba'al") form as the "Glory," easily the best interpretation of the human figure in Daniel 7:13–14.[14] God makes a new
heaven and a new earth, he brings judgment against his enemies. In this
vision of the end, Israel and the nations stream to Jerusalem to worship

together, and the dead bodies of those who have rebelled against God are to be an example to all flesh (presumably those who have come to Jerusalem). The seer of Daniel 12 has re-imbued the vision of Isaiah 66 with new life because the vision of the end of time in Isaiah 66 seems to him to fit the historical circumstances of Daniel 12.

This earliest undoubted reference to literal resurrection in the Hebrew Bible suggests that both the righteous and the very evil need to be resurrected for the purposes of giving them their valid and well-deserved deserts. This hope comes not just from the study of Scripture but from observation of historical events. The prophet understood a particular historical circumstance by visionary experience in which he saw the events of Isaiah 66 (itself an interpretation of Isaiah 24–27, together with Ezekiel 37 as well). As a result, he produces Daniel 12. The new Scripture describes a particular historical and social situation which can be characterized and, ultimately, identified. First of all, it was a time when there were gentiles near Jerusalem, possibly the suggestion of a foreign army. It comes, no doubt, from the observation that the pious had been suffering, not for forgetting God's law but precisely because they observed it. It comes from a time when some were eating pork and others, trembling for the fear of God, forbeared from the sin. If God was letting his faithful suffer, the very promises of the Bible are brought into doubt. The context for this observation must surely be persecution and martyrdom. The passage obviously describes the Maccabean revolt.

Astral Transformation for the Maskilim and the "Holy Ones"

BESIDES THE general resurrection and punishment, a very interesting special reward is promised to those who make others wise (hamaskilim). They shall shine like the brightness of the heaven, like (or, more exactly: as) stars forever. Given the mythological past of wisdom in the ancient Near East, it is probable that the author means here not just a literary figure but a literal identification of the knowledge-givers with the stars. They shall be luminous beings, transformed into shining stars, which can only mean to the Jews that they shall become angels. For stars had been identified as angelic creatures from earliest times (e.g., Judg 5:20; also Job 38:7).

One should also note that the term for brightness here is zohar, not accidentally also the name of the principal work of Kabbalah, the Zohar. Since we shall shortly see that the "Son of Man" is enthroned next to God in Daniel 7:13–14, it is quite possible, in fact likely, that this is meant to depict how God will exalt those "wisdom-givers" who become "angels." Several different figures are actually identified with the "Son of Man" in later literature: Jesus is identified with the "Son of Man" in the Gospels; Enoch is identified with the "Son of Man" in *1 Enoch* 70–71; Metatron is identified with Enoch in *3 Enoch*. These passages demonstrate that the leaders will gain the heavenly reward of divine enthronement as angels and stars have. Thus, inherent in this short notice is the basis for Jewish ascent mysticism in all the later mystic literatures: apocalypticism, Merkabah, and especially Kabbalah, which takes one of its primary intuitions into reality from this passage.

But what kind of leaders will be given such an exalted reward? The best answer appears to be those who are faithful enough to undergo martyrdom. Many scholars note the relationship between this passage and a possible martyrdom in Isaiah 53, especially verses 8 and 10. We do not know which specific events may have occasioned this prophetic utterance in Isaiah 53. It must have been something which 2 Isaiah's listeners easily recognized. Though there is a clear reference to a righteous sufferer, there is no discussion of life after death in 2 Isaiah. It is not even clear that the righteous sufferer is a martyr, as his death is not clearly stated. The most we can say with surety is that the sufferer is brought close to death and then saved by God's will to see his offspring, though he had suffered terribly.

The Social and Historical Situation: The Maccabean Wars

WE KNOW THE specific events that produced the literal prophecy of a bodily resurrection in Daniel. It was the persecution of Antiochus in the Maccabean Wars, in which forced eating of pork served as the test of faith. Although the story purports to be from the Persian Period, scholarly opinion has surmised that the events producing the visions in Daniel are from a much later time, from the terrible events in the Maccabean war. During this period, as all Jewish children know from the story of Hannukah, righteous Jews were martyred "for their faith," probably for the first time in Jewish history.[15]

Some stories of this period actually illustrate the importance that statements of life after death could achieve in this dark period of Jewish history. First, we note that stories of resurrection are not necessary for a martyr's death to be meaningful, even in this period. The martyr Eleazar, described in 2 Maccabees 6:18, refused to eat pork, or even to eat acceptable food if the crowd had been told it was swine's flesh.

> "Such pretense is not worthy of our time of life," he said, "for many of the young might suppose that Eleazar in his ninetieth year had gone over to an alien religion, and through my pretense, for the sake of living a brief moment longer, they would be led astray because of me, while I defile and disgrace my old age. Even if for the present I would avoid the punishment of mortals, yet whether I live or die I shall not escape the hands of the Almighty. Therefore, by bravely giving up my life now, I will show myself worthy of my old age and leave to the young a noble example of how to die a good death willingly and nobly for the revered and holy laws." When he had said this, he went at once to the rack. (2 Macc 6:21–31)

The old man Eleazar died a martyr's death, even though he was offered what the persecutors think was a merciful and respectful way out; he accepted martyrdom rather than compromise his faith, because in his last remaining few moments, he did not want to make a mockery of the divine rules by which he had lived his entire life. Not insignificantly, he points out that there are punishments for sinners, either before or after death.

Soon (2 Macc 7) seven brothers and their mother are put to the same torture. In later versions this story became the story of "Hannah and her Seven Sons," though she was not yet named in this early version. The story is one of such unmitigated horror that the savagery of the days of the Judges pales by comparison. The barbarity of this scene must have struck everyone with fear and doubt about the promises which God had made.

Although the subject of the story is the time of the Maccabean revolt, very few scholars would actually date the composition of this passage to the time of the evil edicts of Antiochus. Second Maccabees was seemingly written in Greek and some years after the events narrated in them had passed. The passages in 2 Maccabees 6 and 7 could easily have been a separate source, which was added into the text by the editors. So we must be careful to note that we do not have a record of actual events but the literary creation of a new genre, a "martyrology." Although the term "martyr" is not found in pre-Christian acounts, we already see the existence of a pattern of celebration of the death of these heroes. When the text says that they leave behind a pattern or model (*hypodeigma*, 2 Macc 6:31) of nobility and a memory of virtue *(mnemosyne),* the major theme was of the righteous persecuted and then rewarded by God. That is the master narrative of martyrdom before the term arose in later Christianity.[16]

The purpose of this writing is to celebrate the "martyr" as a brave sacrifice for the truth and authenticity of the religion. Martyrdom is a complex social process in which the death of an innocent victim is taken as a proof of the truth of the religion by the audience, be it literary or actual.[17] We see a similar method in effect at the beginning of Maccabees, where the editor has included several letters, which may even be authentic, in order to set the scene for the coming problems. On the other hand, he does not here tell the reader that he is relying on an external source so there is some attempt to present the literary creation as fact. The purpose is probably, among other things, to provide a model of martyrdom for present and future martyrs to follow.

This gruesome story differs in several important ways from the story of Eleazar which preceded it. Although the youths are as valliant as the old man, their reasons for allowing themselves to be martyred are quite different. Several of the sons make brave statements of the afterlife:

> "You accursed wretch, you dismiss us from this present life, but the King of the universe will raise us up to an everlasting renewal of life, because we have died for his laws."
>
> . . .
>
> "I got these from Heaven, and because of his laws I disdain them, and from him I hope to get them back again."
>
> . . .
>
> "One cannot but choose to die at the hands of mortals and to cherish the hope God gives of being raised again by him. But for you there will be no resurrection to life!" (2 Macc 6:9, 11, 14)

All of this seems to be a way of spelling out what the first brother says:

> "The Lord God is watching over us and in truth has compassion on us, as Moses declared in his song that bore witness against the people to their faces, when he said, 'And he will have compassion on his servants.' " (2 Macc 7:6)

The mercy of God, which makes the whole notion of resurrection necessary in the case of martyrdom, is a way of spelling out the prophecy that we have already seen in Daniel 12. Resurrection shows God's continuing mercy in vindicating those who suffer marytrdom. The resurrection will be bodily, in fact, very bodily, as the third son's remarks make clear. It is much more physical than the resurrection described in Daniel. The effect of this extreme attention to the body in the restoration of this world shows that the tradition of resurrection was not at all obligated to Platonic or any other Greek philosophical thought, although 2 Maccabees was written first in Greek using Greek cultural norms in a variety of ways.

The palpability of the bodily resurrection, wherever it comes from, has become a quintessentially Jewish idea because, when it distinguishes the oppressed from the oppressors, it speaks to the reward which a pious Israelite must obtain through the covenant and, if necessary, through martyrdom. It was the remedy given by God to the Jews because of the cruelty and oppression of foreign domination, a notion which carried on directly into the Roman period. And it is easy to see why it was stressed at this particular moment. The persecutors have destroyed the bodies of these young martyrs, though Deuteronomy promised length of days to those who kept God's law. But God's mercy guaranteed that they would have their youth back and have the pleasures of their bodily existence again when God raises them.

In the Greek epitomist's comments in 2 Maccabees 12:43,[18] we also see a similar interest in resurrection:

> He also took up a collection, man by man, to the amount of two thousand drachmas of silver, and sent it to Jerusalem to provide for a sin offering. In doing this he acted very well and honorably, taking account of the resurrection (ἀνάστασις). For if he were not expecting that those who had fallen would rise again (ἀναστῆναι), it would have been superfluous to pray for the dead.

Creatio ex Nihilo *Is Born to Bolster Resurrection*

ONE OTHER important aspect of this passage is often overlooked. The mother encouraged her martyr sons in several ways, but nowhere more importantly than when she exalted God's creative powers:

> "I do not know how you came into being in my womb. It was not I who gave you life and breath, nor I who set in order the elements within each of you. Therefore the Creator of the world, who shaped the beginning of humankind and devised the origin of all things, will in his mercy give life and breath back to you again, since you now forget yourselves for the sake of his laws." (2 Macc 7:22–23)

And this can be seen even more clearly in 2 Maccabees 7:28: "I beseech you, my child, to look at the heaven and the earth and see everything that is in them, and recognize that God did not make them out of things that existed. Thus also mankind comes into being."

This is the first clear statement of *creatio ex nihilo,* the first time God is clearly praised as creating the world from nothing.[19] In Genesis 1, God does not actually create everything—darkness and the deep precede creation. God creates man from dust of the earth in Genesis 2. The writers of the great prologue in heaven of Genesis 1 were not sensitive to the theological principles which we have inherited from Aristotelianism. Even Isaiah 45, which we looked at briefly above, only praises God as the creator of good and evil, light and darkness, not everything. Perhaps Isaiah's prophecy meant, therefore, to include everything. Explicitly one might argue that the oppositions—good and evil, light and darkness—implies that God is the author of everything. Now, in the face of the Persians, it is necessary to stress that point explicitly.

In the previous examples where resurrection was discussed, some bodily residuum remains: The dry bones knit together in Ezekiel, the corpses of those who rest in the dust become the basis of the awakened and resurrected saints in Daniel. Here, the text is impelled to stress that God creates from nothing. The martyrs will be resurrected from nothing—even if the bodies of the martyrs are burned and their dust scattered—just as all humans come originally from nothing and the universe itself was created from nothing.

Although the innovation in 2 Maccabees is "creation from nothing," it is not being used to teach a philosophical doctine. Rather what is being stressed is God's power to do anything, even the seemingly improbable task of reconstituting a human being when there is nothing left of the corpse. The result of this assertion is the reassurance that God can certainly resurrect the righteous from dust, even from nothing, if nothing remains. There is no gainsaying the absolute innovations which the sudden importation of ideas of life after death found in Hebrew thought and the effect that it immediately had. The argument that the original creation was from nothing is of secondary interest.

One normally thinks that Aristotelian principles suggest the necessity that God create out of nothing, else anything that is coterminous with God can be also thought of as equal with Him. But this passage shows that the motivation for developing a notion of *creatio ex nihilo* is actually the necessity of clarifying what bodily resurrection means. God needs to not just to preserve the souls of the righteous alive. Now, God needs to be praised for the power to create their bodies again. Previously, the creation testified to God's power and the Sabbath was the ritual celebration of His power. Now, the creation is also the demonstration of God's power to resurrect. That was a total innovation in Jewish thought.

Even more interesting is the extent to which this passage mirrors the argument of Zoroastrianism in the Bundahishn (see ch. 4, p. 190). Unfortunately, the Bundahishn is normally thought to be redacted later than 2 Maccabees, though certain traditions in it may be early and this argument would have to be one of the early parts. We must be careful about this parallel, as credibility about God's ability to effect resurrection is a natural enough question anywhere resurrection is propounded. It may equally be an independent argument adduced out of necessity in each place. Creation from nothing is not an obvious necessity based on the reality of resurrection. It seems to be a borrowing from Zoroastrianism.

But that is hardly proven. It is merely an interesting parallel. The parallel, whatever else it may show, does emphasize Zoroastrian thought can be one context, one contributing factor, in which the notion of Jewish bodily resurrection arose. The second century BCE leaves plenty of time for Zoroastrianism to have influenced Judaism. If there was influence, it also shows that religious ideologies only borrow where they have serious need to adapt. It is not exactly the same doctrine which was developed in Zoroastrianism. It is not less Jewish for being more Zoroastrian. For the Jews, it is the issue of martyrdom that brought resurrection to the fore and that is its Jewish meaning.

One more interesting passage in 2 Maccabees (14:37–46), dealing with the martyrdom of Razis, further illustrates the ideas already discussed. The text tells how Razis attempts to commit suicide but shows instead that his act is actually a kind of martyrdom. Even though the wound is self-inflicted, everyone understands that Razis' death was a result of Nicanor's persecution. As a result, Razis dies spewing his own innards but praying that God will return them to him. The terrible pain that he suffers is taken as a token of his enormous faith. The resurrection envisioned seems purely physical, and very bodily, just as are the other resurrection hopes in the book. It appears to come at the end of time. Immortality of the soul is never mentioned in this case nor anywhere else in the book.[20]

The notion of life after death developed in the land of Israel to explain the martyrdom of the righteous for their religious views. The original idea of resurrection was possibly borrowed from Zoroastrianism. But that hardly describes its essence, structure, or function in Israelite life. The point is: The doctrine of judgment and rewards and punishments in the afterlife was first articulated because it was necessary that the doctrine develop to help people understand the implications of their faith. Wherever the idea comes from, it was tailored to Jewish sensibilities by the time it appeared in Jewish culture. It was there to resolve an important moral, political, and social issue in the time period of Daniel. We will need to return to these texts many times in coming chapters, to fully explore the implications of these short and puzzling texts.

Babylonian Influence, the Enoch Legends, and the Son of Man

BESIDES ZOROASTRIAN and continuing Canaanite influences, ancient Mesopotamian influences are also much in evidence in Second Temple times. First exiled to Babylon by force and then returned to the land of Israel as a part of a great Persian world empire, the Jews were as able as anyone on earth to appreciate the importance of Babylonian wisdom. Babylonian traditions are absorbed in many different parts of the Bible and in various extrabiblical works. Like all the other traditions that were borrowed into Judaism, they were adapted specifically to Hebrew purposes. The reason that these traditions show up in the Enoch literature is apparently due to the Maccabees themselves. They caused a schism in the priesthood. When they took over the role of high priest as well as king, they alienated a group of priests who retreated to the desert and eventually set up the community which used the Dead Sea Scrolls as its library. The displaced or separatist priests, the Zadokites who were actually the founding priesthood of the Second Temple, developed their own traditions, which we see in the Enoch literature.[21]

The Biblical figure of Enoch in Genesis 4 and 5 seems to parallel the Mesopotamian traditions of Enmeduranki and Adapa, wise men who traveled to heaven and founded divinatory priesthoods and ecstatic prophetic guilds, as we have seen in previous chapters. The receipt of these notions in Israel appears in a few verses about Enoch in Genesis, the visions in Daniel 7–13, the enormous pseudepigraphical literature we know as *1 Enoch, 2 Enoch, 3 Enoch,* and many of the new pseudepigraphical works we find in the Dead Sea Scrolls. The Enoch literature itself evinces sure signs of composite authorship, with each book sometimes containing five or six different independent blocks of traditions, which can often be shown to have circulated separately. The enormous variety in this Jewish material can be shown to be based on the Mesopotamian traditions which we surveyed earlier. All this suggests a long and fruitful period of interaction between Israel and Mesopotamian religion, in a variety of different contexts, rather than one confined only to the Second Temple period:[22]

> When Jared had lived a hundred and sixty-two years he became the father of Enoch. Jared lived after the birth of Enoch eight hundred years, and had other sons and daughters. Thus all the days of Jared were nine hundred and sixty-two years; and he died. When Enoch had lived sixty-five years, he became the father of Methuselah. Enoch walked with God after the birth of Methuselah three hundred years, and had other sons and daughters. Thus all the days of Enoch were three hundred and sixty-five years. Enoch walked with God; and he was not, for God took him. (Gen 5:18–24)

The report of this Biblical Enoch is contained within the genealogy leading up to the flood. Enoch often occupies the same position in this genealogy as Enmeduranki (sometimes Enmeduranna) does in the Babylonian King List, arguing that there is a much longer ancient Near Eastern background to the Biblical story. For instance, Enoch's 365-year life is paralleled by Enmeduranki's association with the sun god. Enmeduranki was also summoned to the divine council chamber. Enmeduranki was also given heavenly and underworld secrets and enthroned by the gods and finally given secret techniques of divination.[23] These themes are prominent in the Enoch material; the most likely explanation is that they were borrowed into it because they were so well known and this short puzzling statement provided a way to make Enoch part of Hebrew prehistory as well. It is the same kind of borrowing we saw in the flood narrative and other events of Biblical prehistory—details from the Wisdom tradition of the known world, which were blended into Israel's story after having received a distinctive Israelite stamp.

There are several other anomalous parts to the Biblical story. First and most importantly for any study of immortality in the Bible, Enoch's story is notable in that he alone, of all the members of this genealogy, has no death notice. Instead, the text twice says that Enoch "walked with God," (Gen 5:22; 5:24) and, at the end of the second, the text states "he was not, for God took him." This gives the writer the ability to talk about Enoch's heavenly journey and also about his final disposition in heaven. In doing so, he brought into the narrative all the various notions of translation, heavenly transformation, angelification, and even Messianic redemption. And along the way he describes the mechanisms of solar regularity and weather.

If the terse report in the Bible was a way of "burying" Enoch in the heavens, as it were, it did not work. This surprising violation of the conventional genealogical story stimulates an enormous explanatory novelistic literature. It is likely responsible for the earliest known, extra-canonical Hebrew literature. The Enoch literature assumes that Enoch was transported to heaven at the end of his relatively short, earthly life (his immediate relatives live far longer), presumably cutting his life short for the ultimate reward: astral transformation and enthronement in heaven.

Enoch's journey to heaven and his transformation there validates the ecstatic and mystical experience of those who stay on earth. It quite nicely fills in the Hebrew Bible's otherwise puzzling reference to those who in the psalms dwell "with God." It also confirms by eyewitness report that God intends to reward the righteous after their suffering and punish the oppressors. Furthermore, Enoch's heavenly journey represents the human transcendence of our material situation to the deathless realm. All of these aspects of the Enoch story become part of the story of Jesus' resurrection and ascension as well.

Enoch is supposed by this literature to have been commissioned specially by God as a "court-appointed" defense attorney for the rebellious angels. Though he "lost his first case" because the sin of the rebellious angels was so great, Enoch tried his level best and is rewarded for his efforts. The divine edict was that the evil angels must be punished by damnation yet God rewards Enoch for his righteous efforts. The narrative has obvious correlatives with those righteous sufferers on earth who stay true to God's word. One may pray for the sinners but God will punish them anyway.

Enmeduranki's relationship to the ecstatic *baru* priests and Babylon is significant. The Enoch material too is deeply related to the wisdom of the priestly tradition as we find it among the Dead Sea Scroll sectarians who were disenfranchised priests. They boasted of secret wisdom which allowed them knowledge of the heavenly world and gave them access to the presence of God.

Along the way we who are not yet initiated into the secret wisdom but who read the story of Enoch are treated to a narrative demonstrating that God is running the universe well and fairly, explaining all the magnificent machinery of the heavenly economy, and revealing in detail how God's justice rewards the dead in heaven and punishes the wicked. It also warns us to be prepared for the sudden breakthrough of the apocalyptic end, which will devour the evil powers who have oppressed God's saints and turn the earth over to the righteous for the peaceful reign of God forever. So besides giving us a short course on the heavenly economy, it develops the standard apocalyptic themes that evil may be in control on earth, but God has plans for the world which will very soon even the score.

The solar calendar is evidently one of the secrets which Enoch imparted to the Qumran community. Qumran observes a solar calendar made up of twelve months of thirty days, divided up into priestly courses, and supplemented by the appropriate number of intercalated days fit between the weeks. These intercalated days stand outside the normal week; as a result the holidays always fall on the same day of the week; no other sect observed such a symmetrical calendar. And since the other sects in Judea figured their calendars by the phase of the moon, it also gives an extra dimension to the apocalyptic work, "The War of the Sons of Light Against the Sons of Darkness," found for the first time at Qumran in the Dead Sea Scrolls. It seems likely that the title refers to the calendar and designates the group as the "sons of light" marking them off from the rest of the Jews as well as the gentiles.[24] In short, it is an independent witness to the sectarian nature of the Enoch literature.

The Enoch literature has been known for many centuries in Greek, but also in more obscure languages like Ethiopic, Armenian, Slavonic, Mandaean, Arabic and even Turkic dialects in Central Asia. From this varied literature it becomes clear that there are at least five separate compositions present in the contemporary version of *1 Enoch*. The various versions of *1 Enoch* come to us in Aramaic (from Qumran), Greek, and the major text, as it is received from the Ethiopian Christian church. The Aramaic versions at Qumran seem to be the earliest editions but from the variety of different versions and a variety of secondary texts that existed in the first century, it is also evident that the tradition was much more fluid than the received Ethiopic version. Different communities may have picked those parts of the tradition that most suited them.

When Aramaic fragments of *1 Enoch* were found at Qumran Cave 4, it became clear that the story was very ancient—some of it going back to the third century BCE. In some sense, the Enoch literature is the link between the prophecies in Daniel and the Qumran community.[25] Some of the Jewish version of the tradition, then, may be earlier than the visionary material in Daniel. In fact, a number of scholars have assumed that the material in *1 Enoch* is older than the story in Genesis 5, Genesis forming a *précis* of yet older material. The idea that Enoch literature is older than

Genesis which is therefore dependent on it, and not the other way around, is still shocking and not established.[26] It is more likely both Genesis and Enoch drew on earlier sages.

Luckily, to look at the afterlife material, we do not have to solve these thorny problems. For our purposes all three documents, *1 Enoch* (in its primary Ethiopic, Greek, and Aramaic versions), *2 Enoch* (Slavonic) and *3 Enoch* (Hebrew) are relevant but in very different ways. We will look at the latter two books in future chapters. *1 Enoch* or, *The Ethiopic Book of Enoch*, is the first of many books based on the terse Biblical report. It provides us with a reservoir of information about life after death, scenes of judgment and apocalyptic ideology. In chapter 14, Enoch begins his journey to heaven to intercede for the fallen angels:

> And behold I saw the clouds: And they were calling me in a vision and the fogs were calling me; and the course of the stars and the lightnings were rushing at me and causing me to desire; and in the vision, the winds were causing me to fly and rushing me high up into heaven. And I kept coming (into heaven) until I approached a wall which was built of white marble and surrounded by tongues of fire; and it began to frighten me. And I came into the tongues of the fire and drew near to a great house which was built of white marble, and the inner wall(s) were like mosaics of white marble, the floor of crystal, the ceiling like the path of the stars and the lightnings between which (stood) fiery cherubim and their heaven of water; and flaming fire surrounded the wall(s), and its gates were burning with fire. (*1 En* 14:8–12, Charlesworth, I, 20)

In back of this description is the blueprint for the heavenly Temple, on which the earthly Temple in Jerusalem was patterned. Apparently, even before the Second Temple was destroyed during the war with the Romans, religious Jews fretted over the condition of the earthly Temple, either because of the behavior of the priests or the plan of the building itself, which differed from the original plan and also from the visionary rebuilt temple described in Ezekiel.[27]

As we have already seen in Isaiah 66, the visible presence of God in His Temple is often called "God's Glory," linking it with the vocabulary in Exodus 24:16–17 (also see LXX), other significant places in the Hebrew Bible, and preeminently in Ezekiel. The Greek term *doxa* has little to do with "opinion" or "praise" in standard Greek but rather it is translation Greek and became the technical Hebrew term *Kābôd,* which is translated by *doxa* in the LXX and which thereafter can indicate God's principal angelic mediator, who carries the divine name, or even God's human manifestation.[28]

Besides the major transformation motif, which parallels Daniel 12, Enoch also reports on the final disposition of the dead. Such a report has the immediate effect of confirming the Bible's presumed promise that the righteous will be rewarded, the sinners punished. This, we find elaborated in *1 Enoch* 22, the first (and in many ways the most instructive) of many, many tours of heaven, confirming heaven as the realm of the transformed dead. It is included in a part of the work known as *The Book of the Watchers*:

Then I went to another place, and he showed me on the west side a great and high mountain of hard rock and inside it four beautiful corners; it had [in it] a deep, wide, and smooth (thing) which was rolling over; and it (the place) was deep and dark to look at. At that moment, Raphael, one of the holy angels, who was with me responded to me; and he said to me, "These beautiful corners (are here) in order that the spirits of the souls of the dead should assemble into them—they are created so that the souls of the children of the people should gather here. They prepared these places in order to put them (i.e., the souls of the people) there until the day of their judgment and the appointed time of the great judgment upon them. I saw the spirits of the children of the people who were dead and their voices were reaching unto heaven until this very moment." I asked Raphael, the angel who was with me, and said to him, "This spirit, the voice of which is reaching (into heaven) like this and is making suit, whose (spirit) is it?" And he answered me saying, "This is the spirit which had left Abel, whom Cain, his brother, had killed; it (continues to) pursue him until all of (Cain's) seed is exterminated from the face of the earth, and his seed has disintegrated from among the seed of the people." At that moment, I raised a question regarding him and regarding the judgment of all, "For what reason is one separated from the other?" And he replied and said to me, "These three have been made in order that the spirits of the dead might be separated. And in the manner which the souls of the righteous are separated (by) this spring of water with light upon it, in like manner, the sinners are set apart when they die and are buried in the earth and judgment has not been executed upon them in their lifetime, upon this great pain, until the great day of judgment—and to those who curse (there will be) plague and pain forever, and the retribution of their spirits. They will bind them there forever—even if from the beginning of the world. And in this manner is a separation made for the souls of those who make the suit (and) those who disclose concerning destruction, as they were killed in the days of the sinners. Such has been made for the souls of the people who are not righteous, but sinners and perfect criminals; they shall be together with (other) criminals who are like them, (whose) souls will not be killed on the day of judgment but will not rise from there." At that moment I blessed the Lord of Glory and I said, "Blessed be my Lord, the Lord of righteousness who rules forever. (1 *En* 22, Charlesworth I, 25–26)

In this depiction, Enoch sees to the farthest west, where the sun goes down. The West is where the dead were located in Egyptian lore and the sun is the messenger to the dead in all the nations surrounding Israel. But in this depiction, in the far West, Enoch finds a great pit in which four different categories of dead are awaiting judgment. These are therefore temporary holding pens for the dead, not a permanent prison, as the judgment is still in the future. The dead are in a kind of intermediary state. Yet we already know their final disposition by the kinds of conditions in which they wait. It looks like a kind of heavenly, judicial bureacracy.

The writer of this passage was well acquainted with how ancient empires disposed of their war captives. The scene resembles nothing so much as a Mesopotamian frieze of the taking of a city after a siege, an image that the Assyrians especially valued because it demonstrated their overwhelming power. The inhabitants, those who are not killed outright, are divided up into various groups for their final disposal. Because this is a narrative journey and not merely a prophecy like Daniel, we are treated to a horrifying scene, meant to instill repentance in any who might hear it.

In back of it seems to be real experience with foreign ruling powers. Truly, the taking of a city would have been one of the most horrifying scenes of war that anyone of that time could have imagined. In any event, the heavenly scene then represents compensation for the indignities which the Jews and especially the pious among them had to endure, with God figured as the ultimate conqueror and bringer of justice. The Israelites of Second Temple times lived in a big empire or a complex of client states rather than as a completely independant country. But they lived on the border where skirmishes between empires sometimes happened. In fact, colonial and post colonial theory will help us understand the varieties of religious and social movements that arose in Second Temple times. Those responses will be outlined in the next few chapters. But one thing is clear: Unlike most of the Greek examples already discussed, this afterlife definitely contains punishments for sinners and rewards for the righteous, with no equivocation.

The presence of Abel in this Enoch vision is very important. He has become more than the first murder victim. In this context, Abel was the prototype of martyrs. Finally, there is the compartment for those who will remain in death forever, not being either good enough to be resurrected nor bad enough to be punished eternally. These categories seem to be dictated by the features of Israelite culture and law, as well as a reflection of the prophecy of Daniel 12 itself, which discusses the very good and the very bad but seemingly leaves the ordinary people dead forever. The Greek version of v 13b makes this clear when it says: "They shall not be punished on the day of judgment and they shall not be raised hence." The Zoroastrians also exercised their imaginations on this intermediate group. They are not the persecutors nor the zealously pious. They are merely the ordinary folk, probably disdained for their lack of interest in the religious life.

Since this is a tour, conducted at a specific moment in time, we do not see the future restoration when the righteous will inherit the earth. But we are given several clear indications of the eventual judgment. In *1 Enoch* 25, we see the tree of life (Gen 3:22), which the righteous will inherit at the final judgment when God descends to earth. As a result, the elect will receive the fruit of the tree and will achieve "long life"—this is obviously the Tree of Life from Eden.

Lastly, we should note that the issue of the principle of identity in the afterlife is addressed in a new way in this extended Enoch passage. The spirits are called "souls" but they are eventually resurrected bodily. The fact that they exist in an intermediary state has suggested to many that Platonic dualism was already present here.[29] But it seems doubtful to me that these are the immortal souls of Platonism. Rather they seem more like any number of souled beings in the ancient Near East.

The soul is the equivalent of ghost or spirit, as it is throughout Hebrew culture. In other words, there is, in this passage, no explicit new, philosophical speculation about what exactly immortality of the soul would entail in terms of the identity of the person, other than it means that the person will be resurrected. This passage seems to reflect the ancient Hebrew notion of "soul" as a person, which can be alive or dead in the Bible. Quite clearly here, they are the "shades," a person who continues to live in the intermediary state. It is but an unsubstantial state, which retains the identity of the person until the resurrection for the just alone. But there is no specific notion of an immortal soul as in Platonic thought.

In fact, to pay too much attention to the influence of Platonism here is to mistake what is important about the passage: This narrative picture of the afterlife demands a new reification of a soul, similar to the explanations we have seen in Egypt, Mesopotamia, and Canaan. One can hardly have a system of postmortem punishment and reward after death if there is no vehicle to pass on the moral identity of the person.

Conversely, this has ramifications for the definition of person in these passages. What applies to the afterlife also applies to life itself. The word *nepeš*, "soul," is ancient. But here it is explicitly being used as a moral principle of postmortem identity and hence that identity is reified in life, which is a more complicated affair for people living both in a Jewish religious context and a wider imperial one. It is no longer possible for a person to have more or less of the quantity of soul, explaining his charisma or effectiveness. Instead, one's moral identity, implicit in Hebrew thought throughout, needs to carry into the postmortem state.

Because the writers of the First Temple period were so adamantly opposed to the culture of the Canaanites, this Second Temple openness to the religious insights of other cultures seems an innovation. During the First Temple period, from the perspective of the editors of the Bible, the Israelites were involved in a desperate *Kulturkampf* with an abhorrent religion, which practiced idolatry, ritual prostitution, and infant sacrifice. We know that this is the projection backwards of Jews in the Persian period, who wished to warn their brothers against the dangers of acculturation. Even so, and in spite of the sensibilities of the YHWH-alone party in Hellenistic Jewish society, much imagery and sometimes even the religious practices of the other nations did enter Jewish culture.

Zoroastrianism was one source of interest to the Jews. The Zoroastrians had a prophetic religion, based on the revelations of a prophet, who preached the importance of staying away from evil and emulating the good. They had conquered the evil oppressors of the Israelites and their Shah, Cyrus, had even been proclaimed "Messiah" by Isaiah. The Jews were subsumed into the far-flung Persian Empire and their religion treated with respect. The Jews must have noticed that Zoroastrians, in many ways, lived a moral life from a Jewish perspective.

The same is true for Greek culture. We know about far more variation in Greek culture than we know about Persian culture and we know that not everything in Greek culture pleased Jewish sensibilities, just as not everything in Persian culture would have met their approval. But especially the Greek philosophical schools lived morally and abstemiously. There were issues of idolatry to face with both foreign cultures. The Zoroastrians venerated fire while the Greeks reverenced images. Both were suspicious but neither was in the same category as the immorality attributed to the Canaanites: human sacrifice and ritual prostitution. There may have been other Jewish issues with Zoroastrian purity laws and practices. There were certainly many, well-attested, moral issues which Jews raised about Hellenistic culture. But, even so, religious ideas from both flowed more freely into Jewish culture.

Part of the reason is surely the establishment of large empires with good communication. Life in large empires brought with it more cultural mixing than was possible for a small, embattled state in First Temple times. In some important way, the sect that produced Daniel stood over against acculturation to Greek ideas. It is, therefore, surprising that the book of Daniel would even broach using Canaanite imagery in the enthronement of the "Son of Man" and "ancient of days." The Canaanite roots of the imagery of "the Son of Man" was likely not recognized by the sectarians.

The revelations of Daniel were delivered as prophecy and demanded acceptance on that ground. Evidently, large sections of Jewish society, including the Rabbinic community eventually, were willing to grant it legitimacy, though there is every reason to think that the Sadducees would never have allowed the book of Daniel in their canon because they opposed the whole idea of an afterlife. To see in detail how different parts of Jewish society reacted to these influences, we have to study their texts. It is to that task that we now turn.

PART THREE

VISIONS OF RESURRECTION

AND THE IMMORTALITY

OF THE SOUL

7

Apocalypticism and Millenarianism

The Social Backgrounds to the Martyrdoms
in Daniel and Qumran

The Visions in the Book of Daniel

THE IMPLICATIONS of Daniel 12 are so crucial to understanding the conception of the afterlife in Judea and so important for the rise of Rabbinic Judaism, Christianity, and Islam that we must delve into its secrets more completely. The comparative, social-historical technique which we have been using to analyze other cultures' views of the afterlife can be used to understand the development of Biblical views of the afterlife. Set in the context of the wider world, Biblical traditions about the afterlife show the same correlation with social institutions that we have seen in other cultures.

"Apocalypticism," whatever else is implied, has meant the revelation of the secret of the coming end of time, the violent end of the world, and the establishment of God's kingdom.[1] Apocalypses are often pseudepigraphical, that is, fictitiously ascribed to an earlier hero or patriarch. Many apocalyptic books—notably Daniel and Revelation, the only two Biblical books in the genre—also have arcane symbolism, strict dualism of evil against good, and puzzling visions, the meaning of which is hardly clear from a first reading. Second Maccabees, with its martyrology, establishes a conventional story of religious martyrdom, whether or not the events happened in just the way the text describes, but, by comparison with Daniel, it is a book of critical history.

Apocalypticism has a long history. Possibly, some of the noncanonical books, especially *1 Enoch* and related material, preceded the Biblical book of Daniel. We cannot be sure. History gives us many examples of movements arising full-blown in response to certain events, while others seem to simmer for a long while and focus into a movement after a previously existing literature of apocalypticism suddenly galvanizes a new sect, due to specific events. The best we can do is distinguish between apocalyptic literature and apocalyptic movements, while realizing that each is dependent upon the other.[2]

With Daniel, we are on the cusp of understanding the details of the social circumstances that produced this apocalyptic notion of resurrection. We have already seen that apocalypticism is one response to persecution, or to take a larger perspective, one possible response to colonial domination. We shall see others in future chapters. But before we came to understand the relationship between apocalypticism and social circumstances, we could only surmise how the Jews developed a religious form of apocalypticism. Daniel's direct statements on astral immortality, promising a starry future to those who turn many to righteousness and resurrection for some of the good, was such an innovation in Hebrew thought that we must pause to investigate the circumstances that produced it.

The Form of the Book

THE BOOK OF Daniel contains two distinct content sections and two distinct languages: Hebrew and Aramaic. But the contents do not parallel the languages. Evidently the current, received book is composed of fragments from two different copies, one in Hebrew, the other in Aramaic, but the contents had already each assumed more or less in the form which we have today and the language break does not follow the change in subject matter. Why the current book came to be passed on in this form is anyone's guess. We may be grateful for the quandary because it is possible that the book would not have been canonized if it had not contained some Hebrew. Certainly, no book written in Greek was ever allowed into the Masoretic Text by the rabbis.

Behind the seam produced by the change of language, we note another seam, almost as obvious, based on a change of content, which must underlie both the Hebrew and Aramaic versions. The first part of the book of Daniel consists of several miracle stories about the seer Daniel, purported to have lived during the reigns of Nebuchadnezzar, Darius the Mede, and Cyrus, a miraculously long lifespan. Nor do these reigns easily correspond with the historical personages. These stories make more sense as popular tales. They are stories that preach constancy to the laws of Moses, to the benefits of dietary regulations, and to the other special rules of Judaism, even though the penalty for keeping them may be martyrdom. They are almost the same kind of martyrdom stories we saw in the last chapter with one major innovation: The narrator depicts God as actually saving his righteous martyrs from the threatened martyrdom, thus miraculously preventing them from being martyred at all.[3]

The famous stories of Daniel in the lion's den and the fiery furnace impress the readers with God's special regard for those who follow his laws, as they portray God's repeated deliverance of Daniel from the threatened martyrdoms. It is important that the heroes are in actual and real danger of death but preserved alive by divine intervention. It is, from this point of view, an important variation of the martyrology genre, showing the value of righteousness, steadfastness, and wisdom, even in the face of oppression. So although no explicit martyrdom appears, we have, in effect, a martyr tradition defined by the innocent sufferer delivered by God's intervention. Although they are fictional, they teach real lessons in martyrdom, as well as promise salvation for the wise, persevering, and courageous.

Daniel is the name of a famous Canaanite hero, the father of Aqhat, the subject of an ancient epic. Furthermore, the name Daniel is a combined form of the word for judge (Hebrew: *dan*) with the suffix *'el* which is a divinity name, usually translated as "great" when appended to another term. In form, it literally means " 'El is my Judge." Daniel was a wise ruler in the past, and Daniel's wisdom, special skills, and revelatory knowledge are prominent aspects of the story. In this period, names ending with the suffix "-el" come to indicate angels in Hebrew—like Gabriel, Michael, Uriel, Raphael, and a myriad of others.

The Date of the Book

THE TALES MAY not be from the Babylonian (587–539 BCE) or the Persian period (539–333 BCE) but they are certainly more ancient than the visions which follow, starting in chapter 7, which were produced around 165 BCE. The visions purport to be prophecies from the Babylonian and Persian period, we have already seen that they are actually the product of the Maccabean period (168–165 BCE), as every recent historical analysis has found.[4] As interesting as the tales of Daniel may be, the visions that follow them must interest us more for their concrete and detailed revelation of a beatific afterlife. These fantastic visions gain credibility by their linkage to the stories of the rescue of the righteous seers that precede them. They predict that the martyrs and saints of the future who, unlike Daniel and his friends, actually undergo torture and death, will yet be returned to life by resurrection, just as the previous martyrs had been preserved by direct divine intervention. Together these two different genres of literature, connected by the theme of the preservation of the saints, are connected to become the literary output of the seer Daniel. The persecutions of Antiochus Epiphanes in the life of Judea, which produced the holiday of Hanukkah are the stimulus for these speculations into the nature of the afterlife.

While the visions purport to be prophecies, the writer already knows that many of the events related in the visions have already come to pass; he need only predict a relatively short span of time before the final consummation. The events of the Maccabean period can be established by the prophecies in Daniel 7:8 and its interpretation in 8:9. "The little horn speaking great things" must be Antiochus IV Epiphanes, the Seleucid king of Syria and ruler of Judea during the first half of the second century BCE. His evil reign is described as "a time, two times, and a half a time of the little horn," which is an allusion to the three and one-half years when Antiochus persecuted the Jews during the Maccabean revolt. The mention of "the abomination of desolation," a parody of the epithet of Haddad, is a reference to the stationing of Syrian troops in the Temple and the subsequent desecration of Temple purity (Dan 11:31; 12:11).[5] The Syrian troops probably worshipped Haddad in the Jerusalem Temple.

The author's skill in describing the events of the Maccabean revolt is so good that when the story goes awry, it reveals the likely date of composition for the visions. The major prediction of Daniel, which actually did not come true, is that Antiochus would die in Egypt before his return to Jerusalem after the war with Egypt (Dan 11:40–45). In fact, Antiochus did not die in Egypt. His attack was cut short by the intervention of the Romans, who forced him into an embarrassing peace with an expensive tribute. On his return, he stopped in Jerusalem and punished the city mightily for its rebelliousness, presumably using the vessels of the Temple to help pay his bill to Rome.

Daniel 7 and Canaanite Imagery

THE VISIONS ARE not imagined or written merely as history, however; instead the deliberate change in perspective to the fictional narrator in the past signals the birth of a new form of prophetic consolation, which we have already labeled "apocalypticism"—the secret revelation or uncovering of God's plan. The visions predict that, after the present arrogant dominion has had its short day of dominance, God will intervene and destroy the hateful oppressors who also arrogantly oppose God's will. From this point of view, the apocalypticist is prophesying revenge against the hated oppressor just as surely as he is predicting the promised remedy for its injustice. As opposed to prophecy, where repentance can avert any of God's threats, in this vision, the predicted end will come, regardless of human behavior. No one expects Antiochus to repent and become a believer in God. His fate is sealed. But there are many in Israel who did not favor the program of the apocalyptic prophet. Their only recourse was to join the virtuous by conversion to the prophet's group or sect. This is an important new social phenomenon that we will have to investigate to understand what resurrection means.

The end will come in the following way: A divine figure characterized by the term "ancient of days" (Dan 7:9) presides over the divine council at the last judgment and sentences this last, fourth kingdom to destruction. Then there appears in the clouds of heaven "one like a Son of Man" (Dan 7:13, *kebar 'enash*), an expression in Biblical Aramaic that means only "like a human figure." His human appearance contrasts with the monstrous figures that have preceded him in the vision so we may further conclude that his human shape, so emphasized by this puzzling designation, is meant to distinguish him as the good figure from the bizarre animals who are the evil figures. An angel interprets the figure as symbolizing "the holy community, the saints of the most high" (Dan 7:27), who are the sect of the righteous who expect to be saved at the consummation.

The imagery in this passage comes directly out of Canaanite mythology.[6] The enthronement of the two figures and the names used for them correspond rather closely to the Canaanite description of 'El, the older, father god, sometimes known in Ugaritic as "the father of years" *(abu shanima)* rather like the Aramaic term used here, "an ancient of days" (*'atiq yamin*, Dan 7:9) or "the ancient of days" (*'atiq yamaya*, Dan 7:13). The indefinite noun in Daniel 7:9 suggests that it is a description of the figure rather than its proper name or title. The Biblical character with his white, woolly beard parallels the description of the Canaanite divinity. The "Son of Man" must therefore be closer to the Canaanite divinity Ba'al, the son of 'El, who supersedes his father in the regulation of the cosmos.[7] In parallel fashion, it too is likely to be a description rather than a title. Probably then, in its present context, the figure like a "Son of Man" or, more idiomatically, "the manlike figure" is meant to be understood as an unnamed, principal, heavenly figure in God's retinue, probably the functional equivalent of the so-called "Prince of the Presence" in later Jewish mysticism, since he is enthroned next to the ancient of days, the grandfatherly figure.

It is unlikely that the figure is a mortal human because the text would have said that it was a human being, not a figure shaped like one. Hence, the figure is likely to be a specific archangel—perhaps Michael but possibly Gabriel—who are mentioned in other visions. The human figure in heaven is more or less what we would call an angel, a person shaped like a human but obviously part of the divine court. Since it is the "primary" angel, we might consider calling it God's *Kavod* or "Glory" or, even in later Jewish terminology, his *Shekhinah* (though that figure is usually gendered feminine in Midrash). Instead of the transient evil kingdom of Antiochus, he establishes a permanent, everlasting, and universal kingdom, which brings salvation from the sufferings in the present, transient, and evil kingdom of Antiochus Epiphanes.

This author must be writing very close to the events of the Maccabean revolt. By framing his predictions as prophecy, he is saying that God has known about this particularly heinous villainy from the beginning and planned for its short duration. The vision is prophecy because it reveals God's plans for the immediate downfall of this terrible kingdom. This, no doubt, consoled the disheartened and persecuted members of Israel who were being martyred and killed, not for having abandoned God's word but specifically because they were keeping it: God has vengeance in mind for the oppressors and felicity for those who stay true to God's word. After Daniel admits his anxiety about the vision, the angel explains what the plan is, and after that, the final judgment quickly follows, being shared by "the Son of Man" and the "saints of the most high," who are the beneficiaries of the war and succeed to an everlasting kingdom.

It is not clear exactly who the "Saints of the Most High" are. They appear to be humans as they are described as "the people." But they also have a name that suggests angels: "The Holy Ones of the Most High," an alternate translation of the same term. It also suggests martyrdom, as "sanctification of the name" is the standard term for martyrdom in Rabbinic Hebrew. These possible implications all turn out to be true when we look at the fuller context, including the Dead Sea Scrolls.

The saints cannot be all the people, as we know that not all the people will be saved or resurrected in the afterlife (Dan 12:1–3). Furthermore,

Daniel 11:32 distinguishes between the "those who violate the covenant" and the "people who know their God":

> Forces from him shall appear and profane the Temple and fortress, and shall take away the continual burnt offering. And they shall set up the abomination that makes desolate. He shall seduce with flattery those who violate the covenant; but the people who know their God shall stand firm and take action. And those among the people who are wise shall make many understand, though they shall fall by sword and flame, by captivity and plunder, for some days. When they fall, they shall receive a little help. And many shall join themselves to them with flattery. (Dan 11:34)

These verses narrate that the evil oppressors profane the Temple and they set up an "abomination that makes desolate." We do not know exactly what this means but it is a severe insult to the purity of the Temple. The best guess is that they set up a pagan altar in the Temple. "They" are evidently the Greek Syrians, soldiers of Antiochus Epiphanes, who occupied the land and persecuted the Jews for their religion, at least in the eyes of 1 Maccabees and Daniel. It may be that their very presence inside the inner Temple precincts was the crucial action which stimulated this prophecy, but the very ferocity of the argument suggests that they also committed other acts of desecration. The violators of the covenant are those parts of the society who were allies of the Greeks, whom both Maccabees and Daniel understand as apostates. There were evidently a good many people who just passively ignored the events. Daniel 12 suggests that there will be those who just live and die, experiencing no resurrection. In the distinct minority are those few who know God. They teach the people the truth and fight against oppressors. They must be the group that produced this book, and they had a sectarian organization and identity.[8]

The party of the faithful are also specified as "those among the people who are wise" who "make many understand," which probably means "give instruction to the many" in Daniel 11:33. They pay dearly for this service as they fall "by sword and flame, by captivity and plunder for some days." They became martyrs by combat and captivity. And they are the group that will, at the end of days, become angels (stars) in Daniel 12:3. The story suggests that the faithful have been martyred and that, for their supreme sacrifice, they will not only be resurrected but "they who have made the many righteous will shine as stars forever." This is the equivalent of becoming angels and so can be called *angelomorphism*.[9] The events are just about to happen, nearly upon us.

The angelic army is quite possibly related to the *rapiuma,* the royal dead war heroes of Canaan, as the imagery in Daniel 7 has Canaanite roots as well. Sometimes Canaanite gods were described as stars. But it is clear that these heroes had human rather than birdlike forms. Unlike the Canaanite story, which explained where the dead were and established regular feasts to keep them happy in the afterlife, this story functions to punish those who have opposed Israel, especially those who have dared to murder God's most wise and sacred saints. It describes the final reward not of kings but of martyrs.

There are also analogies with Greek thinking, where great heroes become the heavenly constellations. The point is, however, that it is not exactly Greek nor Canaanite nor Persian, though it is generally parallel to all of them, using the native Hebrew vocabulary for resurrection together with martyrdom, as reunderstood from the ambiguous Scripture appearing in the prophets. Possibly this can be seen as part of the general process in the Hellenistic period of transferring the abode of the dead from under the earth to the heavens. But no one in the group that produced this text would have been aware of that perspective. In a sense then, the death of the saints, their "martyrdom" as the church would call its fallen heroes, has sharpened the age-old question of why the righteous suffer to the point that the writers of Daniel adapted a very popular idea in the ancient Near East, until this moment missing in the history of Israel: the notion of resurrection as a reward for saints and martyrs.

The conception of life after death that it outlines is not exactly like anything else we have seen thus far. Although it is resurrection, which might put it into the same camp as Zoroastrianism, it is not at all what Persian resurrection was. For one thing, it is not at first guaranteed to all the good. Nor does it eventually extend to the evil once they have purged themselves of their evildoing. In this text, reward is only promised to some of the good and punishment only to some of the evil. The evil will also be resurrected but they ought not to be glad of their resurrection because they regain their bodies only to be punished. Furthermore, there is a large group of ordinary Israelites who receive neither resurrection nor special punishment, who just die and are no more.

As we have seen, it is a picture of life after death adapted to the circumstances of this particular group. It is derived, as we saw in the last chapter, from putting together a number of Biblical passages in a new, inspired way and narrating a consistent new story about it. It promises punishment for the evil ones, a restored life for those who have been cut off before their natural span, and astral immortality, eternal life as an angel, to those who make others wise, evidently the principal teachers or leaders of the group, or at least those among them who were martyred. As opposed to the majority of the Persians, who saw the end of the world as an eventuality, and resurrection as the privilege of the whole human race eventually, this group expected it to happen momentarily, as the final consummation is the very next event narrated. They also think that only the very righteous—themselves—will ever attain resurrection. This is a sectarian stance, which gives us important information about the kind of group that created these documents.

The Sociology of the Daniel Group

OTTO PLÖGER argued in his now classic *Theocracy and Eschatology*[10] that the group of people who produced this vision can be characterized as a "conventicle-spirit of deliberate separatism in that membership of the 'true' Israel is made to depend on the acknowledgment of a certain dogma, namely the eschatological interpretation of historical events, which meant, in effect, membership in a particular group" (Plöger, p 19). Plöger struggled to find words to express what he saw. He said that the afterlife described in Daniel is limited to those people who join the group and come to share its assumptions. Plöger wrote before sociology became more readily utilized in Biblical studies, so his description requires a further explanation.

Plöger means that the group that produced Daniel was a small group of committed religious fighters and teachers. They expected God to reward them for their suffering and for the injustices that were done to the rest of the faithful. We already know a great deal more about them: The members of the group illuminated by it are called "those who are wise" or "the wise men of the people" and help many to insight, or suffer martyrdom (Dan 11:33, 35) "but will one day shine like the stars" (Dan 12:3). And there is some suggestion that they have priestly functions.

This surprising religious ideology is not very close to the position of the Maccabees, even though the Maccabees had a priestly lineage. In 1 Maccabees, the events that founded the Hasmonean house, the dynasty of the Maccabees, are expressed in activist and political terms. While God's sovereignty is acknowledged, what we would call ordinary causation is the immediate source of history. In 1 Maccabees there are but few references to God's miraculous intervention in history.

On the other hand, the book of Daniel is full of supernatural interventions directly in history, all prophesied or divined ahead of time by special dreams and revelations. In fact, the military action of the Maccabees appears to be directly addressed in the book of Daniel—as another group allied to the sect and called the "little help" (Dan 11:34), evidently belittled out of disappointment and frustration. The group that produced Daniel cannot be the Maccabees but it may be something like the group of people called the *Hasidim* ("pious ones," Hasideans in Greek) in 1 Maccabees 2.[11] In 2:42, a group of *Hasidim* or Hasideans is described as joining the Maccabean cause, but some are subsequently martyred because they offer no resistance to military action on the Sabbath. They made a common cause with the more practical Maccabean soldiers but evidently gave up hostilities once the Temple was purified.

But trouble resumes, this time between the Maccabees and some priests, as the Maccabees get more and more ambitious when they become rulers. Evidently a priestly group broke decisively with the Maccabees in 142 BCE when Simon Maccabee was proclaimed "high priest forever, until a faithful prophet should arise" (1 Macc 14:41). The Maccabees came from a rural priestly family but they were not of the high priestly family. They were not eligible for the high priestly office so they took it by force. By 142 BCE they were very Hellenized themselves. Possibly they produced the short paean in Psalm 110, so important to later Christianity, which proclaims a new high priestly line forever, from the order of Melchizedek (literally: the righteous king). The Maccabees may propose Melchizedek as an alternative lineage to the high priestly lineage through Zadok which they usurped because they had become the kings of the country. If so, the sectarian group that produced Daniel may have assumed that the Maccabean high priest was actually Malkirasha (the sinful king) and that they themselves were the righteous ones. This is later characteristic of the Dead Sea Scroll community. There must be a relationship.

The Dead Sea Scrolls and Daniel

THE DEAD SEA SCROLLS give a totally unexpected glimpse of Jewish sectarian life, for they are concerned with the nature of the actual community as well as its apocalyptic expectations about the end of time. Since the Dead Sea Scrolls reflect an Essene-like group, they make possible for the first time a view of the workings of an actual apocalyptic community, comparing the social organization described in the Dead Sea Scrolls with known and newly-found apocalyptic writings, and even, with some care, the descriptions which Josephus and Philo give us concerning the Essenes.

It is the Dead Sea Scrolls that give us the most hints as to the importance of the events described in Daniel for the millennialist sect. In the scrolls we find a number of different materials, some of which were important only to the sect while others were of more general interest to Judaism. Among the sectarian writings were a series of *pesherim* (*pĕšărîm*, "solutions," "interpretations"), which purport to give the full meaning of various prophetic texts. The full meanings tend to be hidden references to historical events which happened to the sect and which they then recognized as prophesied in the Bible. None would have been obvious to anyone outside the group and show how readily scripturally centered groups can reread texts so long as they serve as prophecies for events critical to sectarian history.

This underlies the constant use of Scripture to produce political ideology. In this respect, their interpretation of Scripture could function as myth. The ideological content of myth and religious story has been the subject of many recent continental intellectuals, producing a garden of ideas, a few of whose blooms will decorate this portrait of the Dead Sea community.[12] The Qumran group itself was founded as a rebellion of priests to the Maccabees' usurpation of the high priesthood, as well as the kingship. Evidently, the Dead Sea Scroll community, whose antecedents may have fought with the Maccabees against the Syrian Greeks, were later abandoned by them and summarily thrown out of the Temple.

Eventually, after a period of chaos, a person emerged, called by the sect "The Teacher of Righteousness," who was persecuted by one of the Maccabean kings. Most likely, the persecutor, known as the "Wicked Priest" in the Dead Sea Scrolls, is the same Simon who proclaimed himself high priest, but it may have been any of his successors. This may well identify the Hasideans as the forefathers of the Qumran or Dead Sea Scroll sectarians; but, if not, it certainly marks the group as another quite similar, dissident and isolated group of purists who had a special and secret view of divine providence. We have ample examples of the views of the Dead Sea Scroll community, who were certainly "a special conventicle" of apocalypticist Jews who expected God to intervene on their behalf and return them to rightful power. If the authors of Daniel were not the exact forebears of the Qumran community, they appear to be another closely associated group with relatively similar goals, expectations, and sociology.[13] The Qumran group, however one identifies them, is defined by its priestly character and revolutionary social apocalypticism.

One thing they had in common was millenarianism. Just as Daniel is a millenarian text, so the Dead Sea Scrolls reveal to us a millenarian community living in expectation of the immediate end of the world. It is important to note therefore that the Danielic group may have been revolutionaries, but they were not necessarily from an underclass yearning to be free of economic domination, as we would normally assume in the modern period. Instead they were aristocrats, priests, who have been dispossessed of their traditional sacerdotal roles. The Judaism they evince is priestly in character.

The Dead Sea Scrolls and the "Essenes:" From Literary Apocalypse to an Actual Apocalyptic Group

THE DEAD SEA SCROLLS are now normally identified as Essene writings. But we cannot be absolutely sure that the Dead Sea Scrolls were exactly the group whom various writers called in Greek the "Essenes." (We have no satisfactory equivalent for the Greek term in Hebrew or Aramaic. Thus, they appear to us to be mentioned neither in the New Testament nor in Rabbinic literature.) For one thing, there are apparently a number of groups with slightly different habits who called themselves or were called by the name "Essene" and they may, in turn, be related to the still different group which Philo called the *Therapeutai* ("Healers"). "Healer" is one possibility for the meaning of the term "Essene" in Aramaic, as it could easily come from the root *'-s-y,* meaning "to heal." Josephus calls them the *essaioi* frequently, which could be a more exact Greek transliteration of "Healers," *Assai'in.*

On the other hand, another possibility seems more likely in view of the ascent traditions which we see there. The word "Essene" may indeed come from the root *ḥ-s-y* meaning to be pious and it connects them with the *Hasidim* of the time of the Maccabees. This also has the advantage that it can account for both Greek forms, *Essaioi* and *Essenoi* as the absolute form "pious one" is *ḥesin,* while the construct emphatic form "the pious ones" is *ḥesaia.* Philo also connects the name of the community with the Greek word *hosiotēs,* "piety," "holiness." The community, as we shall see, frequently called itself, "Holy Ones" or *kedošim* in Hebrew.[14]

According to Philo, who gives us the only description of the *therapeutai,* they lived in Egypt, where they founded a communal settlement. They were the model community for Jewish mystics who sought to ascend and gain a vision of God: "But it is well that the Therapeutai, a people always taught from the first to use their sight, should desire the vision of the Existent and soar above the sun of our senses (*Contempl.* 11). They were severely ascetic in their diet and their primary concern was "self-control" *(egkrateia, continence);* they gave little thought for their physical appearance, taking care only to dress in white for their religious observances. Furthermore, they preferred chaste marriage to carnal marriage (*Contemp.* 68). Philo says that on account of this, they live "in the soul alone" and can be called "citizens of heaven." Quite possibly, they believed themselves transformed into angelic beings, even while on earth, as a result of their mystical ascents and ascetic behavior.[15]

In Palestine these sects had an added, political dimension. The Dead Sea Scrolls found at Qumran were the product of a cloistered group that closely resembled the Essenes of Philo's and Josephus' description:

> The doctrine of the Essenes is wont to leave everything in the hands of God. They regard the soul as immortal and believe that they ought to strive especially to draw near to righteousness. They send votive offerings to the Temple but perform their sacrifices with a different ritual of purification. For this reason they are barred from those precincts of the Temple that are frequented by all the people and perform their rites by themselves. Otherwise, they are of the highest character, devoting themselves solely to agricultural labor. . . . Moreover, they hold their possessions in common, and the wealthy man receives no more enjoyment from his property than the man who possesses nothing. The men who practice this way of life number more than four thousand. They neither bring wives into the community nor do they own slaves, since they believe that the latter practice contributes to injustice and that the former opens the way to a source of dissension. Instead they live by themselves and perform menial tasks for one another. They elect by show of hands good men to receive their revenues and the produce of earth and priests to prepare bread and other food. (*Ant.* 18.18–22).

As we have seen, the Essenes probably formed a separate priestly group when a high priest not to their liking was appointed in Jerusalem. They eventually supported an alternate leader who taught righteously and was therefore called the "Teacher of Righteousness." They had previously retired to the desert but with him they established their own center of priestly purity away from the center of priestly power in Jerusalem. Though they did not set up a Temple in the desert, they interpreted their communal body as the Temple of the LORD, an idea that was to be paralleled in Christianity. The Essenes were distinguishable from other protest groups of their day by their priestly character.

Resurrection at Qumran

FOR THE LONGEST time, nothing showed up in the scrolls to demonstrate that the Dead Sea Scrolls supported resurrection or immortality. This was a great problem for scholarship. Some even asserted for a while that these people were Sadducees because Josephus reports that the Sadducees believed in no afterlife, which is also confirmed by the New Testament in Acts 23:6–9.[16]

Immortality, as distinct from resurrection, is better attested in discussing the Essenes, but not in the scrolls themselves, only in Josephus' and Philo's description of them. Whether the substance of Josephus' account is confirmed in the Dead Sea Scroll texts depended entirely on each scholar's opinion about how much poetic license Josephus should be allowed in his descriptions. Josephus describes Essenic "immortality of the soul." But he is translating the concept of resurrection, a notion totally foreign to pagan Romans, into immortality of the soul, which his Hellenistic audience could understand more readily.

In fact, Josephus described the Essenes in terms completely appropriate to a Neo-Pythagorean sect, with their notion of the immortality of the soul. We know that Josephus' description of the Essenes concentrated on their "mystic" meditations and abilities, to make them understandable and less dangerous to the pagan audience, while the texts we have from the Dead Sea show them to be a deeply apocalyptic community, fully expecting to fight against the sinner, Jews and gentiles.

It seems likely that Philo was writing in the same tendentious way. And so it is safer to describe apocalypticism and mysticism as Siamese twins, joined at the hip, unless there is some specific need to distinguish between these two notions. Or, they are like magnetism and electricity; two different effects of the same electromagnetic wave. In this Judean society at this particular time, we always find mysticism and apocalypticism together. The reasons for this have to do with the positions of Philo and Josephus as subaltern clients of the Roman order, people whose education and culture puts them in a very good position to mediate Jewish values to a Roman world. Rather than refer to the Essenes in terms that accurately depict their beliefs, they both described the Essenes in ways likely to interest their audience, which was cultured and Hellenistic (see ch. 8, on mystical experience).

What the scrolls themselves showed was far more like resurrection, when looked at very closely. There were a few hints that these Dead Sea Scroll sectarians were not the Sadducees of Josephan description. The earliest published scrolls themselves were not particularly helpful because they never confront the issue as such. We encounter statements such as, "Hoist a banner, O, you who lie in the dust, O bodies gnawed by worms, raise up an ensign" (1QH 6:34–35; cf. 11:10–14), which may connote bodily resurrection. On the other hand, the poet's language may just be symbolic.

The community rule, discussing the reward of the righteous and the wicked, assures the just of "eternal joy in life without end, a crown of glory and a garment of majesty in unending light" (1QS 4:7–8), and the sinners of "eternal torment and endless disgrace together with shameful extinction in the fire of the dark regions" (1QS 4:12–13). This seems like resurrection but it is hard to be sure. If so, it is interesting to observe that resurrection was not conceived of as an entirely new state of being, but rather as a direct continuation of the position attained on entry into the Community.

From that moment, the sectarian was raised to an "everlasting height" and joined to the "everlasting council" and "congregation of the sons of heaven" (1QH 3:20–22). Salvation was coterminous with membership in the group in a strongly apocalyptic model. But they could not be ordinary Sadducees if one gives any credence to the New Testament, since it says the Sadducees believe in no afterlife, neither as a spirit or an angel (especially Acts 23:7; but also Matt 22:23; Mark 12:18; Luke 4:1, 20:27). It must be true that their traditions were priestly because the core of the movement was priestly in heritage, with lay-persons being grafted to it.

In the 1990s a scholarly revolt took place against the few professors who controlled the texts. Some of the texts had been published promptly, but the flow of publication had slowed considerably. The revolt was based on impatience that many important texts, which deserved to be in the public domain, remained unpublished and were seemingly delayed by personal problems, idiosyncrasies, and academic politics. Acting boldly, perhaps too boldly, a number of scholars published the remaining texts without permission.[17] When the full Qumran hoard was finally published, there were many demonstrations that the Qumranites believed in resurrection of the dead and many more examples of their apocalyptic and mystical beliefs. In the new batch of publications was a passage in which resurrection was clearly promised and several more places that supported it.

The lines themselves almost echo the lines of the current Jewish prayer-book: "And the Lord will perform marvelous acts such as have not existed, just as He said, for He will heal the fallen and will make the dead live for he will proclaim good news to the meek" (4Q 521, lines 11–12). In this passage, Psalm 146 is reinterpreted in order to bring in a reference to resurrection. The canonical Psalm 146 warns not to trust humans, even princes (because, among other things, they die) but to trust God who performs marvelous things.

These motifs of earthly salvation and deliverance occur in a number of other Jewish Scriptures, including Isaiah 61:1–4, which explains the prophet's vocation to bring good tidings and proclaim liberty to the captives. Thus, the prophet took on the role of announcing the good tidings which God will bring (see also Ps 145:14; Isa 35:5; 42:7; as well as many places in apocalyptic literature). In the Qumran community God is pictured, not only as doing all this but also as raising the dead, certainly the most miraculous of all the "good news." It affirms resurrection, even though the original psalm actually emphasized that men die, implying that only God lives forever.

In the Qumran passage it is the LORD who does these wonderful things, which now include resurrection, in a way that is reminiscent of the contemporary Jewish prayerbook. In Matthew 11:4–6, a similar group of signs fulfilled is understood to foretell the coming end time and, from the context, it turns out to be Jesus who fulfills them, not God directly. The newly published passage puts the Dead Sea Scrolls clearly in line with those in the first century who accepted resurrection, including Christianity and Rabbinic Judaism. It caused considerable scholarly stir and readjustment of theories about the Dead Sea sectarians. For instance, it completely undermines any theory that the Dead Sea Scroll sectarians could have been Sadducees, although still priestly in their approach to Judaism. The Sadducees, in fact, stood with the Hellenistic world in a number of ways as clients of the Romans when possible. The Qumranites were clearly very critical of the behavior of the Sadducees (as well as the Pharisees).

Even more interesting, these new scrolls tell us something very important about Josephus, something that we had strongly suspected for a long time. It confirms the suspicion that Josephus was writing very tendentiously on this topic, figuring the beliefs of the Essenes in Hellenistic form. Josephus does not stress resurrection because his Hellenized Roman community would not have understood resurrection of the body and certainly would not have perceived resurrection of the body as worth attaining. They may even have known it as the belief of their arch-enemies the Persians, and so would have been even more contemptuous of it. Josephus would certainly not want to stress a belief which the Jews had in common with the enemies of the Roman order. Instead, Josephus says that they believe the soul to be imprisoned in the body for life but once released from the bonds of the flesh, they rejoice and are borne aloft (*J.W.* 2.155), suggesting a heavenly journey like the Romans' and not unlike that found in the Enoch books, which were represented at Qumran. Good souls receive a reward in an abode beyond the ocean, a kind of paradise, says Josephus, not unlike the Greek notion of the Isles of the Blessed. Evil persons are sent to never-ending punishment in the murky dungeon of the world.

When the passages on resurrection were published, Josephus' strategy as a writer became clearer. All of this research was synthesized in an enormous and prescient, two-volume French work by Émile Puech.[18] Puech actually published long before all the scrolls came out, anticipating the direct evidence of resurrection, so his book is a masterpiece of scholarly reconstruction. He probably had access to all the scrolls from the Dead Sea but he did not find any overt notions of resurrection, as we know exist today. Instead, through a series of very astute inferences, Puech demonstrated in detail that the Dead Sea Scrolls sectarians believed in resurrection of the dead, that it was combined with ascension to heaven, and that Josephus was translating his descriptions into a Hellenistic medium.[19]

Puech also assumes that the dualism and the apocalyptic imagery in the Dead Sea Scrolls community come, not only from Canaanite imagery like Daniel, but from Persian culture. On the other hand, we know that not every text found at the Dead Sea was produced by the group. They collected a library of like-minded but not necessarily sectarian literature. Lastly, we cannot be entirely sure that the archeological remains found at Qumran belonged to the Essene group. But, despite other possibilities, right now they seem to be in the right place for the community of Essenes described by Pliny the Elder. And the contents of the sectarian writings of the Dead Sea Scrolls appear to correspond generally (though not in every respect) to the description which Josephus gives us of the Essenes.

The Essene Community

THE ESSENES lived a communal, monastic life at a time when such practices were rare but attested in some of the Greco-Roman philosophical sects as well. The extent to which the Essenes were willing to go in their asceticism and celibacy was unknown elsewhere. Josephus as well as Philo was much impressed by this abstemious lifestyle. To the ancients, this behavior was judged philosophical, as philosophers were identifiable by their strange, garb, ungroomed appearance, and often by their communal lifestyles. Josephus takes pains to describe the details of their life as if they were a philosophical school: They elected special officers and lived a rigorous life under their supervision. They kept all their property in common and dressed very simply, except when they changed into white garments for meals and prayer services. They were up before sunrise for prayer and work. Then they purified themselves by daily baptism in cold water and ate their noon meal. During the meal they sat quietly and only spoke in an orderly fashion. The spectacle of their quiet eating was so unusual that the silence appears like a mystery (*J.W.* 2.132). Then they worked until evening and ate in the same manner.

Their Sabbath observances were equally impressive. They kept the rules very strictly and did not allow themselves to defecate at all on that day so as not to profane the purity of the camp with their excrement. Probably this was because they also expected angelic visitations and heavenly ascent on that day and therefore could not risk offending the angels with bodily pollutions. All their judicial procedings were by vote and by leadership from the elders. This is in general consonance with the materials we find in the Dead Sea Scrolls.

The Essenes "immortalize" *(athanatizousin)* the soul (*Ant.* 18.18); but we know that they actually believed in resurrection of the body and in apocalyptic fatalism. Josephus was strictly correct but he did not translate the more colorful parts of their beliefs, which would have meant nothing to the Romans who had no familiarity with Jewish Scripture. It seems more likely that he was suggesting that they believed in a ritual process by which the elect are translated to heaven and become part of the angelic host, a ritual process by which the "soul" is "apotheosized." It is very hard to know to what this may actually correspond, as Josephus was trying to characterize a basically Semitic group to a pagan, philosophically trained readership, who were the only practical readers of his work.

The Qumran community's library contains many writings which generally verify this description, but not at all in the Greek style that Josephus employs. It stands to reason that not all the books in the collection belonged to the group exclusively. The Enoch literature seems to be one of that category of literature which actually precedes the Qumran community and helped form it.[20] Josephus' account of providence, fate and foreknowledge is framed in terms proper to Greek philosophy, not the religious life of Judea. But many, many of his observations appear to hold true for the group of texts found at Qumran.

Still there are some surprises and, indeed, some striking ones: For one thing, the Qumran texts contain some extraordinarily warlike themes, especially in the apocalyptic documents. There, it seems clear, the group will become divine fighters of the last judgment. The angels, however, will provide the most powerful weapons against the enemies of truth and they will do most of the fighting. This small group could not expect to beat the armed Temple priests or the Herodians, much less the Roman oppressors, without massive divine aid. The Qumranites would uniquely be able to fight on the side of the angels because they keep the strictest possible purity rules and so are fit to remain in community with them. One supposes that Josephus left this part out because it would have made the Essenes seem like a revolutionary group when they were religious revolutionaries, not political ones.

To us, however, the Essenes are beginning to look like extremist, apocalypticist groups today who have sometimes taken up arms to further their cause. We do not have direct evidence of their active militancy but we do find their works at Masada where the violent and militaristic Zealots went for their last stand.

The most impressive aspect of the Qumran finds is that they show us how a first-century apocalyptic community actually lived and worked. We must not get the impression that the Qumran group was the only apocalyptic group; they were but one of many, starting with those who produced Daniel and before. But in Qumran we have the outlines of their actual communal structure, a datum that gives a more three dimensional view of apocalypticism, changing it from a literary genre to a social phenomenon. Here was a group of persons who expect the end of the world very soon, a major apocalyptic theme which is entirely missing from Josephus' description. Their notion of life after death, which has just emerged from the texts, was closely associated with the life of the group. It was hard to understand how anyone else except themselves would share in the life to come.

Angelomorphism at Qumran

QUMRAN'S FELLOWSHIP with angels and their use of Daniel pointedly raises a new question, implied by Josephus' description: Did the Qumran elite expect to be transformed into angels? If so, did they think they were already angels on earth? Israeli scholars Rachel Elior and Bilhah Nitzan concluded that there was a harmonic and mystical relationship between the angels and the Qumranites. The members of the community wanted to approach God's throne and their hymnic texts demonstrate this relationship.[21] Other scholars see only their desire to ascend; others only the presence of the angels amongst them at the end of days. Scholars disagree vehemently about the correct definition of mysticism in Judaism; yet the solution seems in sight.[22] New monographs of Crispin H. T. Fletcher-Louis and Rachel Elior convincingly argue that the purpose of the language of mystical participation at Qumran was angelification.[23]

Since its publication, "The Angelic Liturgy" (11QShirshab, and the various other fragments found in cave 4) have been interpreted as a cycle of psalms which the angels in heaven sing for the thirteen Sabbaths that make up each of the four seasons of the year.[24] The publication of these documents was a much awaited, carefully edited, and very well-received scholarly enterprise. In the years since its publication, a number of anomalies have suggested that perhaps the cycle of liturgy shows us something even more spectacular than an angelic liturgy, the liturgy of the human priests of Qumran who were actually undergoing transformation into angelic creatures, worshiping in the heavenly Temple. The liturgy seems to map a seven-stage ascent to heaven to view God's throne and glory. As a result they antecede the more developed mystical journeys of the Hekhalot literature and show what was at stake in mystical ascent in Judaism.

Angelomorphism can be found in at least one very important place, 1QSb 4:24–28, in the blessings on the group members:

> May you be as an Angel of the Presence in the Abode of Holiness to the Glory of the God of [hosts]
>
> May you attend upon the service in the Temple of the kingdom and decree destiny in company with the Angels of the presence, in common council [with the Holy Ones] for everlasting ages and time without end; for [all] His judgments are [truth]!
>
> May He make you holy among His people, and an [eternal] light [to illumine] the world with knowledge and to enlighten the face of the Congregation [with Wisdom].
>
> [May He] consecrate you to the Holy of Holies! for [you are made] holy for Him and you shall glorify His Name and his Holiness.

There are several ways in which a person can resemble an angel in this passage, and the text betrays the same ambiguous use of the word "like" that is also implicit in Daniel 12:2. Does it imply likeness to the brightness of the heavens or identity and melding with the heavenly figure? Should "*k*" be translated as "like" or "as"?[25] In favor of transformation are several other passages. As early as 1972, Milik noted that the fragment of 4QAmram calls Aaron (brother of Moses but in this context, founder of the priesthood) an angel of God.[26] Furthermore, S. F. Noll has drawn attention to the similarity of description between angels and the sectarians.[27] The sect uses the term "prince" *(sar)* for some members of the sect as well as for angels (CD 6:6; 4QpPsa 3:5; cf. 1QH 6:14). It also likens the privilege of these believers to that of ministering angels (cf. Josh 5:14; Dan 10:13, 20; 12:1; 1QS 3:20; CD 5:18; 1QM 13:10). The ministering angels were commonly depicted as those angels who served as priests in God's heavenly Temple. This terminology is also commonplace in other Jewish mystical texts. When it is placed in the context of Daniel, more interesting implications emerge. The group prays to be made "holy among His people," language which suggests both angelic as well as priestly ministration and, especially, martyrdom in Daniel. It also prays to illumine the world with knowledge and wisdom, the job of the *maskilim* in Daniel.

At the climax of the liturgy (the twelfth and thirteenth songs), there is both a vision of God's chariot (twelfth song) and his Glory (thirteenth song). The thirteenth song is the climax of the liturgy, according to this interpretation. In it, the human form seated on the throne in Ezekiel 1 first comes into view. The human high priesthood makes manifest the anthropomorphic appearance of the likeness of the Glory of the Lord. Rather than crowned angels in heaven, the exalted creatures of the thirteenth song are the human saints in heaven, who have received their crowns as result of their transformed status. The Glory of Ezekiel 1 is visible but it appears to be embodied as the community's high priest, especially in his high priestly garments, miter and breastplate.

Everyone agrees that the final vision of the divine throneroom is the climax of the vision. It is the angelification that is still debated. But angelification seems to be demonstrated in the more recent publications of the texts. Two fragments from cave 4 published in DJD 7 (1982) have shed further light on this phenomenon. The first (4Q491) has been discussed by scholars hotly since Baillet considered it the self-description of Israel's archangel Michael. But Morton Smith pointed out in 1990 that the speaker is more appropriately described as a mortal human being who has been raised into heaven.[28] The figure is given a "mighty throne in the congregation of the gods" (line 12) and will be "reckoned" with the gods (line 14). This suggests that a community member was being transformed into an angel, as both *Elim* (gods) and *Bene ha-Elohim* (the sons of gods) were angelic designations.

The second fragment is included in *The Sons of the Sage* (4Q510–511). The relevant part reads:

> Some of those who are seven times refined and the holy ones God shall sancti[fy] as an everlasting sanctuary for Himself and purity amongst the cleansed. They shall be priests, His righteous people, his host and servants, the angels of his glory. They shall praise Him with marvelous prodigies.

Most commentators have understood the passage to refer to human ministers to the angels, but Fletcher-Louis and Elior make a cogent case that there are other distinct possibilities. Furthermore, "holy ones" and "ministering angels" are regular angelic designations, even in this period. We have already seen the connection between these terms and martyrdom in Daniel.

More interesting and more difficult to adjudicate is the question of whether the process of angelification is to take place only with martyrdom, at the end of time, some combination of both, or in the presence of the community. Some texts suggest that the process has already begun or, even, been completed in the community. The future tense suggests an action that will be complete in the future but, as everyone familiar with Semitic tenses knows, the verb form itself does not prevent the process from having started already in the past or present, as the Hebrew future is actually an imperfect tense.

Fletcher-Louis and Elior also demonstrate that there are gradations of "the holy ones" in the community. The angelomorphic priesthood seems to have been the elite of the total population of Qumran. This is consistent with the evidence that the movement was split into two groups—those who maintained stricter laws, probably being priests, and those who maintained the lesser laws, probably being laity. In the document known as 4QMMT we find a distinction drawn between Israel, who are the "holy ones" and Aaron, who is the "holy of holy ones." The existence of the "holy of the holy ones" corresponds to the promise in 4Q511 frag. 35 that God will make holy some of the holy ones (line 2). This suggests some special heavenly holiness otherwise not attained on earth.

These texts, in turn, lead to the possibility that there was a ritual connection between the celibacy of some Essenes and their angelomorphic identity. According to Josephus, some Essenes were celibate and others were not (*J.W.* 2.119–21, 160–61). Joseph Baumgarten and Elisha Qimron have argued that one passage in the Damascus Document (CD 6:11–7:8) clarifies this Josephan report. Qimron especially has reconciled the two reports by saying that they designate the intentional community of celibate priests and the rest of the movement who live in "the camps of Israel." [29] Certainly, this agrees with Josephus' report that the Essenes "renounced pleasure as an evil and regarded self-control *(continence)* and resistance to passions as a virtue" (*J.W.* 2:120). This purity is quite similar to that required for the eschatological war, presumably because angelic hosts were involved (1QM 7:3–6).

In other words, in Fletcher-Louis's estimation, the elite at Qumran adopted a celibate life because they attempted to live in a permanent state of Temple purity, which they understood as tantamount to and anticipatory to full angelic existence. As such, all sexual expression was inappropriate for Temple purity, but it must also have seemed unnecesary because the community had transcended earthly relations and had been transformed into the priests serving forever in the heavenly Temple. Celibacy was itself equivalent to martyrdom as a qualification for status as a "holy one." The topics of asceticism, celibacy, and the issues of gender which it raises will be treated in a later chapter.[30] For now we must note only that the leaders in the Qumran community were regarded as angels, that they mediated between heaven and earth, that they were exemplars of the perfection which the group emulated and revered, and were actually revered as semi-divinities, probably in a similar fashion to the martyrs of Maccabean times.

The Dead Sea Scrolls, in sum, give us a totally unexpected glimpse of Jewish sectarian apocalyptic life, describing the rules of an ancient apocalyptic community and allowing us to match their social organization with their apocalyptic writings. Even more exciting is the extent to which the Dead Sea Scroll community illustrates the relationship between apocalyptic notions of the end and mystical notions of resurrection and angelomorphism. The Qumran community felt itself to be so closely connected to the angelic realm that it appears to have viewed itself or at least the leaders of the community as the *maskilim*, "those who are wise" of the famous Daniel 12:2 passage: "Those who are wise will shine with the brightness *(Zohar)* of the heaven, like the stars forever." The phrase, conventionally translated "those who are wise," is actually more causative and intensive in Hebrew, implying "those who make others wise," such as teachers or prophets. In the *Hodayot*, 1QS, *The Song of the Sabbath Sacrifice*, 4Q181, and many other texts, the members have been raised from normal human existence to the heavenly heights, seemingly to live as angels, which is functionally what transformation into a star would mean. It is not clear whether the forebears of the Qumran group wrote the apocalyptic sections of the book of Daniel or not. But the Qumran sectarians certainly used the prophecies in it to explain their exalted state.

The Native American Evidence

IN ORDER TO understand the sociology of the Qumran community and various conceptions of the afterlife, we must make a very large jump from ancient Israel; we must move into the modern period and see what millenarianism looks like in our own time, when we can study it in more detail.

One modern case is that of the Shawnee Prophet and his brother, who led a messianic movement that eventuated in the Battles of Tippecanoe and the Thames. This movement and its leaders, Tecumseh and Tenkswatana, have been described by R. David Edmunds in his classic work, *The Shawnee Prophet*.[31] Edmunds shows that Tenkswatana's religious leadership in reviving the Shawnee tribes' fading power and cohesion was strengthened by Tecumseh's secular leadership abilities. It was the charisma and religiously framed exhortation of the leaders of this movement that united the tribes behind them to try to halt their increasing deprivation. And, as happened later in the case of the Ghost Dance, their religious activities, their "dances" and other rituals, were misunderstood and viewed as hostile by the whites, who felt they needed to put the Indians down forcefully.

We find a similar story among the Seneca tribes when we consider their prophet, Handsome Lake.[32] His visions, and the resulting religious and moral revitalization of this particular Native American community, began around 1800 with newly arriving settlers in what was then the American frontier, western New York State near Lake Erie.

In the spring of 1799, it is reported, some friends found Handsome Lake seemingly dead on his bed. As they began to lay him out for burial, they discerned a warm spot on his body. After two hours he miraculously began breathing again. When he fully recovered consciousness, he recounted the story of his vision. In that and subsequent visions, he suggested a new moral code, called *Gaiwiio,* for the Iroquois Confederacy, to which the Seneca belonged. The code preached self-respect in terms coming from both Native American and the Western European religion of the white man, in particular, from Quakerism. The Iroquois were to give up alcohol, witchcraft, love magic, and abortion, all of which, the prophecy said, had contributed to their great troubles and their unhappy history living near white settlers. The reward promised by the prophecy was the resurgence and restoration of the Iroquois religion and society to the state it had been in before the predations of the white settlers.

The troubles, the visions, and Handsome Lake's preaching had a great effect on those who heard him. This was a Messianic movement that can be called, in Wallace's term, a "revitalization movement," an attempt to renovate the old ways, with some changes, in a time of great crisis.[33] In some sense, Handsome Lake was showing his people that there was a new way in which the old language and culture could help the tribal people cope with the crisis of white invasion.

Some common social and psychological conditions seem to underlie the attraction of individuals to Messianic, millennial, and apocalyptic movements. People who join these movements feel deprived of something meaningful in their society. Marxist interpretations of millennialism stress the appeal of millennial hopes to colonized people who have minimum access to the rewards of their own labor. Normally, Marxist interpreters also note that the millennialist movements are but "symbol manipulation," a first, pre-political step on the road to a more significant political revolutionary movement.[34]

But the economic forms of deprivation which help motivate these movements are not the only kind of deficiency which the movements address. In the case of the Senecas, economic troubles were only part of a whole set of evils: powerlessness, illness, social deviance and immorality, decline of cultural integrity, meaninglessness. Every aspect of the social structure and culture of the Native American society was weakened and threatened with destruction by the steady deprivations of white culture. The deprivation (if deprivation can be used to cover a variety of anomic situations) was brought on by white settlement that started in the eastern frontier and soon spread, with the westward movement of the whites, to the Great Plains and beyond.

In this situation there emerged yet another Messianic leader, a Paiute from western Nevada, to preach what became known among the whites as the Ghost Dance religion. Wovoka lived all his life in a rather small geographical area, the Mason Valley of western Nevada, about forty miles northwest of the Walker Lake Indian reservation but his influence was felt a great deal further. As was the custom in those days, he also took an "Anglo" name, John. Since he occasionally worked at the ranch of David

Wilson, he was known by the name Jack Wilson. Wovoka was a classic apocalyptic prophet preaching nativism to culturally deprived people. He experienced his first revelation about 1887, after which he began to teach new dances and rituals to his people.

Wovoka's principal vision came on January 1, 1889, during a solar eclipse. He was taken up into the spirit world where he was given a message for his people. He taught that the whites would be supernaturally destroyed and dead Native Americans would return to earth. So too, the buffalo and other game, then in grave danger of extinction as were the Indians themselves, would return and the old way of life would flourish on a reconstituted earth where sickness and old age would disappear. (This looks like a great many Jewish apocalypses too.) Thus, Wovoka promised not only an end to the tribes' worldly troubles but a complete restoration here on earth of the Indians' traditional life as it was before the white settlers and the soldiers came. Such a promise meant, as well, the elimination of the whites. The whites, learning of these promises and seeing a threat in the recommended dances and rituals, began a campaign against him. They called the transcendent spirit in whose name the Messianic leader claimed to speak by the denigrating name of "ghost." Since the principal ritual of the believing community was dancing, the movement became known to the whites as the "Ghost Dance Religion."

The Ghost Dance movement was an expression of an unrealistic hope, a fantasy for the Indians. Yet that is but one side of the drama. It always takes opposition to galvanize the movement. The whites took the prophecy as a potentially violent attack on them but they did not wait for further provocation or to find out whether the movement might turn out to call for nonviolent confrontation. They killed those they thought believed in it, a response that culminated in the massacre of Chief Big Foot and his entire band at Wounded Knee on December 29, 1890, about a year after Wovoka's revelation. As a movement, the Ghost Dance Religion probably would have had a stabilizing effect on the endangered society of the tribes, helping them to adjust to their miserable and deteriorating situation. And it is far from clear that it had an activist military aspect until the whites attacked. But it is almost impossible for this dominant group not to feel threatened by the massing of peoples and the heightened feelings that movements of this type often engender. And the ignorant fear and violence of the whites did not allow a nonviolent or passively aggressive solace to develop.[35]

The underlying hostility and fear separating the Indian and white communities is clearly the reason that the whites made the judgment and took the action about the Ghost Dance religion that they did. This case reveals how ambiguous the character and effects of different millennial movements can be. Sometimes they can be seen and treated as pure symbol manipulation—that is, changing the language but not changing the material situation of the deprived. Other times they may be seen as the precursors to political action and violence. The reasons that one movement remains quietistic, in the realm of hope and fantasy, while another takes an activistic path to political action and violence, can only be discerned in the individual histories of each movement. Those reasons are complicated, involving the reactions not only of the sectarians, but also the reactions of colonial powers.

Melanesian Millennialism

KENELM BURRIDGE and Peter Worsley have studied the various revitalization movements that came into being in Melanesia after the Second World War.[36] Millennialism has been largely ignored in studies of Biblical religion and Christian origins, though the titles of both anthropological works are quotations from the Bible.[37] Few if any scholars of religion have successfully put their work to use in understanding Islamic apocalypticism. But there are important common elements uniting Hellenistic Jews with Native Americans in the nineteenth century, contemporary Melanesia and even militant Islam. All had to deal with problems of acculturation and disorganization brought on by the domination of an imperial colonial power. The two modern sets of revitalization movements—native American and recent Islamic—attempted to restore meaning and integrity to the society in the same ways that ancient Jewish society dealt with Greek culture and Roman domination: by following a prophet announcing that God or the Great Spirit would restore their society, if only they would follow special rules of moral order and religious belief.

If the causes of such movements are similar, often the movements exhibit similar characteristics. The most important similarity, perhaps, between ancient and modern apocalypticism is that both characterize time as a linear process which leads to the destruction of the evil world order that has made them suffer. For both, also, there will be an "end of days," a decisive consummation of history. As opposed to holding an optimistic view of social and cultural progress, members of apocalyptic communities are impatient with the corrupt present, seeing it as a series of unprecedented calamities. The "end of days" is seen as a sudden, revolutionary leap into an idealized future state, when believers will finally be rewarded for their years of suffering and believing, while their oppressors and other evil infidels will be duly and justly punished.[38] Consequently, these movements tend to be brief episodes in religious history. Normally the end does not occur as predicted or the hostility of the surrounding society is so great that the movements are relatively short-lived.

Deprivation

SOCIAL AND cultural "deprivation" is a common source of Messianic movements.[39] But deprivation is not a simple phenomenon. Nor does deprivation itself "cause" millennialism. Severely deprived people may themselves react in different ways. And very severe crises may actually inhibit or prevent a society from producing any new ideological reaction. In seventeenth-century Jewry, when Shabbatai Zevi's Messianic cult became so popular, it did not originate in the lands terrorized by pogroms but in lands nearby where Jews were not personally affected by the slaughters. On the other hand, they were deeply worried about the tragedies happening to Jews elsewhere, which were viewed as imperiling their security. It is not only the actual victims of persecution, but also the nearby survivors who see themselves equally vulnerable to the threat.

Besides deprivation of some sort, there must be a willingness to interpret one's lot in explicit religious terms. This is usually supplied by millenarianism or fundamentalism and, when fundamentalism has done its educating job thoroughly, it may itself foster the birth of a millenarian cult or an extremist cult. There must also be an ideology of apocalypticism, which can be supplied by the traditional religion or invented by a new prophet's innovative revelations or both. But there must be a leader whose life and behavior exemplifies the piety of the group (like Osama bin Laden). There is often a practical leader who organizes the movement.

Although the sociological picture of ancient apocalypticism is incomplete, apocalyptic movements in the modern period, particularly those in Melanesian and Native American religions (with all the dangers inherent in analogies between ancient and modern movements), evidence clear sociological commonalities. The modern data also have limitations, but because they are complete by comparison to data in the ancient period, they serve as a practical guide.

Melanesian and Native American societies during the last century, though far removed from the world of Maccabean Judaism in history, geography, and material culture, exhibited some of the same social forces. They, too, had to deal with the problems of acculturation and disorganization brought on by European domination, similar to ancient Jewish society's need to deal with the problem of Greek culture—whether it be defined as Egyptian Greek, Syrian Greek, or later Roman domination—as well as their own oppressive leadership in the Hasmonean dynasty. The colonial relationship between the subject group producing the religious movement and the imperial power seems significant in every case.

In Messianic movements, the leader's individual skills and talents, the way he or she communicates the new messianic beliefs, values, and ideals, have a key effect on the movement. The leader comes to be revered by the community of believers, not primarily as a strong political leader but as a person who exemplifies the moral values of the group.[40] This is an important perception for understanding the rise of the Qumran sect, whose organizer and possible founder was the Teacher of Righteousness. The perception is crucial for the rise of Christianity as well.

What Modern Apocalypticism Can Tell Us about Martyrdom, Resurrection, and Deprivation in Daniel

IN RECENT years we have seen several other American examples of the violent history of millenarian sects, as well as a surprising relationship with martyrdom and notions of life after death. In the case of Jonestown in Guyana in 1979, the movement ended in a mass suicide, in which hundreds of people apparently willingly drank cyanide-laced punch, though they were not in any danger. Those who knew what was happening thought they were escaping persecution by commiting suicide. It is interesting to note that there were constant rehearsals of this mass suicide, in which the initial horror of the suicide was dissipated by habituation. It is a dramatic and terrible illustration of the process of building mythological patterns for martyrdom.

In the somewhat similar case of the Branch Davidians in 1993, the movement ended in a suicidal conflagration in Waco Texas, which was partly due to the sect's own hostility to authority, partly due to the justifiable suspicions of their neighbors, partly due to the rash and inept initial attempt by law-enforcement officials to disarm them. After the initial battle lines were drawn, with heavily armed sectarians facing off against heavily armed authorities, the whole situation resembled nothing so much as a ticking bomb, scheduled to go off at some unknown time, despite the best efforts of many people who sought to defuse it.

There is also the equally sad example of the members of "Heaven's Gate," who inexplicably all committed suicide to join the spaceship hiding behind Comet Hale-Bopp, which was coming to save them from this life. These incidents have illustrated to the people of the world how powerful is religious faith in motivating people's actions towards martyrdom.

These people were not necessarily conscious martyrs to their cause in the Christian, Jewish, or Muslim tradition, but they are bizarre variations of them. Many were martyrs by their own definition. In the case of the Heaven's Gate group, they simply thought they had found the door to a better existence. But this is a common claim of willing martyrs.

Martyrdom, we can see already, is an oblique attack by the powerless against the power of oppressors. It is a way of canceling the power of an oppressor through moral claims to higher ground and to a resolute claim to the afterlife, as the better, permanent reward, giving the oppressors only a temporary advantage. The sinister aspects of this inversion of authority were only fully revealed when used by the power structure to encourage martyrdom of their soldiers—in short, to encourage martyrdom as a motivation for an army. This is not usually an apocalyptic notion but it can be a key power of the powerful over the naively religious, as in Islamicist political extremism when martyrdom was turned into an offensive weapon. We shall turn to the Islamicist version of suicide soldiering in the last chapter.

Let us review. From modern examples, we can see that what produces martyrdom and exaltation of the afterlife is, first of all, a colonial and imperial situation, a conquering power, and a subject people whose religion does not easily account for the conquest. There must also be a society that is predisposed to understand events in a religious context. This can be provided by either an apocalyptic cult or a fundamentalist movement within the society, as well as ordinary religious life. "Deprivation" of some sort is another important ingredient. The word "deprivation" has been highlighted with quotation marks because the nature of the "deprivation" will be our next topic of attention. We shall see that "deprivation" is not necessarily or even primarily political or economic. Those dominated believe the "deprivation" is not just political but also a religious challenge. It may merely be the superiority of an imperial class over a group of the pious who consider the imperial class sinful.

For this imperial situation to be an active motivator, the political, social, or economic oppression of the disadvantaged must be perceived as a religious as well as a political and social threat. The oppression must be an event that is seen as a possible disconfirmation of the religious views of the society: The death of saints was a seeming disconfirmation of the covenant of Israel or the salvation of Christ. The existence of the State of Israel as a Jewish state in the midst of the traditional *Dar Es-salam*, the habitation of Islam, is not just a political threat but a disconfirmation of the continued progress Islam should be making in its pacification of the world. So it serves as one motivation for the terrorist acts of extremists groups like *Ḥamas* and *Hizballah*. (There is far more to this story, which we will discuss in detail in ch. 15.)

From here we must face the thorny problem of the motivation of the society that supports martyrdom as an option. There is no modern consensus on what constitutes the exact motivation of the oppressed in the book of Daniel and the associated ancient literatures. Indeed very few scholars have even tried to link the ancient events to the modern world.

Dissonance and Status Ambiguity as Deprivation

THE MOST RECENT searching challenge to the notion that deprivation and disconfirmation are motivators to apocalypticism and martyrdom has been tendered in the interesting book by Stephen L. Cook, *Prophecy and Apocalypticism*.[41] In the end, I disagree with the main point of his book, but he reviews the issues in a suggestive and interesting way. So it is useful to bring up the issues in the book directly. The book surveys the later prophets as well as much of anthropological discussion of the last half century. Cook's hypothesis is that, for Israel,

> [P]roto-apocalyptic texts are *not* products of groups that are alienated, marginalized, or even relatively deprived. Rather, they stem from groups allied with or identical to the priests at the center of restoration society. First, the proto-apocalyptic description of the end-time assault of "Gog of Magog" in Ezekiel 38–39 expresses the same central-priestly motifs and concerns as the rest of the book of Ezekiel. Second, proto-apocalyptic texts in Zechariah 1–8 appear to have been written in support of the Second Temple establishment.[42]

Cook forgets that the societies that produce these movements are ones in which religon is the dominant language, not politics or economics. The nature of the deprivation is likely to be expressed in religious rather than economic or political terms. As well, Cook takes no account of the issues of colonial and imperial oppression and the reactions of the various subgroups that form in this situation. But, there is an important sense in which Cook's hypothesis is true. The suicide hijackers of 9/11/01 were not the most materially deprived of the Arab world. On the contrary, they were quite privileged. One needs education and economic power to accomplish such ends. This is why Cook says that it is not deprivation that causes these groups.

But his notion of deprivation is just too narrow. The young Arab terrorists' very willingness to pursue Western occupations and their failure to gain jobs equal to their achievement was apparently a motive in their movement into Islamist extremism. They were also educated in strongly Muslim schools where the reasons for this disparity were sought in religious terms. So we need some more subtle notions of what deprivation is, to understand religious impulses towards martyrdom and the way notions of the afterlife feed it.

Terrorists are often members of both the dominant and the subdominant groups but failures in their own aspirations. Having been educated in radical fundamentalist Madrassas (religious schools) that Islam is the highest and most perfect religion, they then take their technical training to Europe and the United States where they see that Islamic countries rank far behind the European and American world in political rights, economic development, and social freedoms. Or, they remain in Muslim societies in which they have no real opportunity to practice their technical skills. The only freedom and opportunity which presented itself in the 90s was to fight as a *mujahid* against the Russians, where the young warriors were brought under the influence of extremist thinkers like Osama bin Laden and also witnessed the defeat of the Russian invaders and the diffidence of American aid.

This dissonant situation can be explained basically by either one of two different tacks: Either the Islamic world is not as perfect as they previously had been taught or the Western world had stolen these technical treasures from its rightful owners, the pious Muslims, and, with it, stolen Muslim dignity. Of course, the real culprits here are the failed and repressive Muslim states in which they were raised and the almost magical notion of the success of Islam which they were taught in fundamentalist Madrassas.

But facing the fact that the naive Islam they were taught may itself have contributed to their wildly exaggerated self-perceptions is unthinkable to a person with that education. Because of the immoral ways of the West, the violence of the Zionist interloper on Arab territory, and the constant exhortation to hatred of people whose lives are different, the way of violence against the outsider is both possible and satisfying. It gives vent to rage and personifies the evil as something outside the body of Islam, just as surely as the projection of personal impulses onto the world as Satan excuses the bad behavior of Christian fundamentalists. While the first realization might lead to political reform, the second avoids the indignity of the first and leads to Islamic extremism. What Israel and the West have stolen from these young Muslim men in their own estimation is their confidence and pride in their own moral superiority, their self-esteem, at least as they understand the dynamics of the world.

But both the perception of the problem and the perception of the solution are provided by a mythical Islamist ideology which so distorts the actual causes of distress in the Muslim world as to to make any impartial assessment or determination of amelioration impossible. Few other people in their situation would have explained it that way but the religious fundamentalist education they received limits their choices for analysis on this crucial topic. So in a real sense, they produce their own problematic, for which violence and terrorism against the West is the solution. One sees the same notion at work on the so-called Muslim street. By believing that Israel was the true culprit in the World Trade Center attack, they preserve their sense that all problems in the Muslim world are due to demonic outside attack and every Muslim attack on the West is essentially a well-deserved defense against aggressive and murderous Western intervention.

The Dead Sea Scrolls Again

So TOO ON THE world stage and even in ancient history: Fundamentalism and millenarianism both arise out of dissatisfaction and doubt of a colonial or even a scientific ideology overspreading a traditional culture, just as Hellenism was overspreading Judea. We have, for instance, seen that the Dead Sea Scrolls are millenarian and also deeply related to priestly tradition, so there can be no cogent argument with Cook's understanding of the source of the apocalypticism we have seen there. The question is only whether this excludes the Dead Sea Scrolls group from being "alienated," "marginalized," or "deprived," as Cook maintains.

Some traditional priests were in danger of being deprived of their independent rulership in Hasmonean Judea and the Roman Empire, and therefore they Hellenized to keep power. They themselves (the Sadducees) were active in the revolt against Rome in 66 CE, so they did have feelings of deprivation which they remedied by warfare. Another group of priests were so alienated by the claims of the Hasmoneans to both kingship and the high priesthood that they withdrew to the desert to found their own community. The Qumranites were doubly deprived, first by the Romans, and second by the Hellenized priesthood. They founded a mystical, martyr-oriented group that, nevertheless, considered themselves the most privileged, indeed angels already. But it was an ideology that reversed their very deprived state in the desert. Deprivation of both religious and material needs—in this case, deprivation from their traditional roles and lack of access to their traditional redemptive media—is a necessary precondition for millenarianism.

Other predisposing factors are also present. These frustrations may produce some of the literature that we find in the Enoch cycle. One extremely important factor is the presence of a leader (The Teacher of Righteousness) whose personal example and teachings help galvanize people's hopes toward a specific religious goal, with the attendant necessary means of achieving it. Furthermore, and this is most important, there must be a tendency to impose religious meaning on events and to be searching for a more satisfactory system of religious values.

Sometimes, it is the leader who provides this expectation; but normally the society has traditionally sought religious solutions to historical problems before the leader arises, though he or she may preach a new variation on the solutions available in the society. Thus, the factors of felt troubles and deprivation, anxiety, strong leadership, and promise of a better society under the aegis of religion, all affect the production of millennialist or Messianic movements. We see this clearly in the revelations of the seer who is known to us only as Daniel. This religious innovation, granted to Daniel as a prophetic dream, provides the basis for the new understanding of the cult. Its source was an irregular state of consciousness, which is not that unusual for the source of a religious innovation.

Another such figure was clearly the "Teacher of Righteousness" of the Qumran group. The texts of the Dead Sea Scrolls report that for a long time after they were forced from their appointed rounds they continued to be lost in the wilderness. Then the Teacher of Righteousness arose and showed them how to organize themselves into a cenobitic community, a monastic life where the community comes together for meals. They honored their founder figure but there is no evidence that they expected him to return. Instead, they expected a great war at the end of time when the angels in heaven would come down and fight against the vastly superior forces on the other side. This would be possible because they kept themselves in such a state of purification as to allow for angelic presence at any time. Likely, they thought that their own forebears in the movement were the angels who would return.

Some of these movements then, like the Dead Sea Scroll community itself, even arise out of ambiguities in the way a religion is interpreted by different classes in a colonial and imperial setting. As priests they are entitled to a certain status in society which has been taken away, not by the Syrian oppressors but, ironically, by the Maccabean kings. While the whole society understood the fight to be against the Syrian Greeks, there was concerted military action in Judea. But when the priests alone were deprived of their traditional meaning and "access to the redemptive media," the result was a religious innovation, a millenarian community of the Dead Sea Scrolls. This allowed them to divide the world into good and evil, identify themselves with only the good, and predict that God and his angelic minions (some of whom are the sainted dead of the group) will soon defeat the arrogant dominion of those who flout the law. This was a problem only for a small, well-defined group in the society.

Though all people require norms for orienting their lives, religious systems at times provide better norms for some parts of society than for others. When groups see themselves as cut off from the goals of society, in terms of power, ethics, or status, and from the feelings of self-worth that arise from achieving these goals, they may coalesce into antisocial movements of *communitas,* or communitarian idealism.[43]

Such movements, which stress an alternative social structure to that of the dominant majority, can appeal widely to one whose status is ambiguously defined by a society. Status ambiguities were common in Roman society because class was defined by law, not by occupation and buying power. Therefore, people who succeeded in a trade often achieved a status above their legal station in life. Reform of the basic social categories appeals to such people, and they are seeking to redress a deprivation, but one could hardly call them materially deprived in any normal sense. While deprivation of both material needs or spiritual status is necessary for the development of apocalypticism, it, too, is not sufficient to produce an apocalyptic movement.

To develop an apocalyptic cult, in contrast to a purely political movement, people must have a propensity to impose religious meanings upon events and must be searching for a more satisfactory system of religious values. The factors of need, deprivation, anxiety, leadership, and the propensity to interpret events in a religious framework all came together in first century Judea. The result over the next two centuries was the rise of a variety of apocalyptic cults, both religious and political.[44]

The Dead Sea Scrolls community is a very clear example of this latter kind of group. Because the Maccabees and their successors controlled the

Temple but were (in the eyes of the Dead Sea Scroll sect) usurpers, they prevented this group, and indeed the entire world in the eyes of the group, from enjoying the benefits of God's sacrificial service on earth. The service in heaven continued, however, and this group considered themselves not merely resurrected at the end of time but also exalted to angelic status, following the prophecy of Daniel 12:3, so that they could participate in the divine service.[45] They may even have been the source of the visionary sections of Daniel. Contrary to Cook's critique, then, the Qumran community was both priestly and apocalyptic, and their deprivation had nothing to do with their social class and present economic power. Rather it had to do with their estrangement from their traditional role as God's priests.

The apocalyptic element (revealing the "end of time") in Messianic movements is not explicitly political. But its vision of a future ideal state of societal affairs always implicitly involves the destruction of the current evil political order. The promised, new social order is always an idealization, a utopia, often an imagined and recaptured past state of perfection ("paradise," as the Western term often figures it) that will be recreated in the future.[46]

Deprivation is what fuels these movements. But the source of the deprivation is inherent in the colonial situation itself. The colonial or imperial power evinces a great many superiorities to the native culture, despite the imperium's distinct moral deficiencies from the native point of view. Yet, at the same time, the most religiously pious in the society, those who ought to be most favored by God, are materially and culturally disadvantaged in the imperial system. This creates cognitive dissonance, another kind of deprivation. In a way, though it is usually seen as a threatened disconfirmation of the native religion. When the goal cannot be achieved in this life, the rewards can be transferred to the next.

The Destiny of the Dead Sea Scroll Community

THE ESSENES had a mysterious ending. We do not know whether they remained quiescent or took an active, revolutionary role. The settlement at Qumran was destroyed by the Romans, as their arrowheads and the distinct evidence of catastrophic burning amply show. Was this because they fought the Romans after welcoming the revolt of 66 CE as the end they were expecting? We do not know. Certainly, their documents were warlike, though they themselves had no active role in the final battle, except to maintain their ritual purity. We have found Qumran writings including "The War of the Sons of Light against the Sons of Darkness" at Masada, the last stronghold of the zealots. This certainly argues that the Dead Sea Scrolls were a goad to revolt. Or did they remain in their passive, ascetic mode of resistance to Roman rule right to end? Were they just in the wrong place at the wrong time? At this moment, we do not know. We do know, however, that they were tortured and martyred by the Romans during the revolt against Rome, who must have thought them a threat. Josephus tells us as much.

One thing is not puzzling, though. The metaphor of resurrection as arising from sleep came from Isaiah 26:19 and the way it was instantiated came from the visions in Daniel. Not only does resurrection itself seem to be like arising from the sleep of death, but the knowledge that resurrection will take place also comes from sleep, from dream visions. That is, it comes from religiously interpreted states of consciousness. This raises the issue of how Scripture and altered states of consciousness interact in these sectarians. To find out how Scripture could effect later visions, we must investigate the nature of ecstatic experience itself.

8

Religiously Interpreted
States of Consciousness

*Prophecy, Self-Consciousness,
and Life After Death*

———— ◦◦◦◦ ————

Prophecy as Justification for Religious Innovation

THERE ARE hints of ancient Israelite popular views of the afterlife in the Hebrew Bible. But a detailed notion of a hereafter was banished for so long from Biblical literature that when it appeared for the first time, in the prophecy of Daniel, its belated presence required special revelatory authority:

> Many of those who sleep in the dust of the earth shall awake, some to everlasting life, and some to shame and everlasting contempt. Those who are wise shall shine like the brightness of the sky, and those who lead many to righteousness, like the stars forever and ever. (Dan 12:2–3)

We have dealt with this passage previously. Now however we need to look at the justification for this religious innovation and the implications of this passage for the study of consciousness. This passage is ostensibly set in Babylon, during the Medean Empire. It outlines a novel interpretation of resurrection which culminates in some of the leaders ("those who are wise") being transformed into angels, as the stars were conventionally understood as angels (see Judg 3:20; Job 38:7). The notion of astral immortality was not, however, out of place in the Hellenistic world of the writers of this text.

Such a major change in a scripturally based religion takes a very special justification. Starting in chapter 7, the book of Daniel represents its contents as having arrived in revelatory dream visions, not the usual method for the literary prophets, but certainly well known as a medium for God's word, since the story of Joseph: [1] "In the first year of Belshazzar king of Babylon, Daniel had a dream and visions of his head as he lay in his bed. Then he wrote down the dream, and told the sum of the matter." (Dan 7:1).

I take this to be an example of a religiously interpreted state of consciousness (RISC), since dreams, which are a commonplace in human experience, are being interpreted as prophetic, new revelations, which justifies the scriptural innovation. Related terms are "altered states of consciousness" (ASC) or "religiously altered states of consciousness" (RASC). The terms all refer to the same phenomenon but in different guises. [2] RASC stresses that an altered state of consciousness is claimed by the adept while RISC recognizes this claim but does not specify that any actual altered state needs to be achieved by the actor, only that the behavior is considered to be consonant with RASC, thus the behavior is being interpreted religiously. RASC can be used by actor and observer; RISC is an analytic term, giving recognition to the difficulty in measuring exactly what ecstasy or trance is.

The particular vision that produces the notion of resurrection in Daniel is not just a dream vision, it is a waking vision. Since it is a vision, it is clearly a religiously interpreted state of consciousness (RISC). If we grant that the narrator actually had such a vision, we could also consider it a RASC. RASC grants the native claim while RISC recognizes only that a special state of consciousness is being claimed:

At that time I, Daniel, had been mourning for three weeks. I had eaten no rich food, no meat or wine had entered my mouth, and I had not anointed myself at all, for the full three weeks. On the twenty-fourth day of the first month, as I was standing on the bank of the great river (that is, the Tigris), I looked up and saw a man clothed in linen, with a belt of gold from Uphaz around his waist. His body was like beryl, his face like lightning, his eyes like flaming torches, his arms and legs like the gleam of burnished bronze, and the sound of his words like the roar of a multitude. I, Daniel, alone saw the vision; the people who were with me did not see the vision, though a great trembling fell upon them, and they fled and hid themselves. So I was left alone to see this great vision. My strength left me, and my complexion grew deathly pale, and I retained no strength. Then I heard the sound of his words; and when I heard the sound of his words, I fell into a trance, face to the ground. But then a hand touched me and raised me to my hands and knees. (Dan 10:2–10)

Here Daniel sees an extraordinary vision but only after he has practiced ascetic discipline for three weeks. He says that it is a vision *(mâr'eh)*, which he alone saw, though the others were frightened. He is unable to move and falls into a trance *(nîrdâm)*, a RASC if we believe the report but, at any rate, a RISC. He interprets the state in terms of ancient Israelite prophetic categories, that the hand of the LORD is upon him as it was on the prophets of old, and interprets that phrase literally enough that the hand of the Lord can raise him to his hands and knees. By using RISC for the critical, most general category, we avoid having to decide what exactly is the state of consciousness being claimed, as well as whether it is real, imagined, hallucinatory, or faked.[3] We are just noting that it is the quality of the experience that justifies its truth for the actor. The specific characteristics of the RISC are interesting questions which can be explored in various contexts, depending on what the texts claim. But we do not need to address the issue of the truth of the RISC, if the report lacks sufficient evidence for us to decide.

A Plan of Attack in the Hellenistic World

JUDGING THE issue of consciousness in the ancient texts of the Hellenistic world is an intriguing question, and it is complicated further by changing notions of the value of that experience in different classes and over time. By the Second Temple period, historical prophecy was in the eyes of the central authorities either a phenomenon of the distant past or the eschatological future.[4] In other words, to the central authorities only fake prophets would claim it. But that is precisely what makes it so important to the understanding of groups like the sects that produced Daniel, the Dead Sea Scrolls, or the New Testament. They all felt that the end of time was upon them and therefore prophets would again speak authoritatively about the end. And they felt in some tension with the central authorities. What was most important was the conventions available for them to speak. Such an important doctrine as life after death and resurrection was not merely discussed as a philosophical option. It was a new dispensation revealed through revelation, which arrived through the medium of a dream to the seer whom we know only as Daniel, in approximately 165 BCE.

Elliot R. Wolfson, in his book on Merkabah mysticism, suggests how to get out of the trap of excessive reductionism:

> Bearing the inherently symbolic nature of the visionary experience in mind, we can now set out to answer another question that has been posed by scholars with regard to the visionary component of this literature. Did the Merkabah mystics actually ascend to the celestial realm and did they see something "out there," or should these visions be read as psychological accounts of what may be considered in Freudian language a type of self-hypnosis? Or, to suggest yet a third alternative, would it perhaps be most accurate to describe the heavenly journey in Jungian terms, as a descent into and discovery of the archetypal self?
>
> From a straight-forward reading of the extant sources it would appear that some texts assume a bodily ascent, a translation into the heavenly realm of the whole person with all the sensory faculties intact, whereas others assume an ascent of the soul or mind separated from the body as the result of a paranormal experience such as a trance-induced state. But even in the case of the latter explanation, typified most strikingly in *Hekhalot Rabbati* in the story concerning the recall of R. Nehuniah ben Ha-Qanah from his ecstatic trance, it is evident that the physical states are experienced in terms of tactile and kinesthetic gestures and functions appropriate to the body, such as the fiery gyrations of the eyeballs, ascending and descending, entering and exiting, standing and sitting, singing and uttering hymns, looking and hearing.[5]

Whatever one thinks of Jungian analysis, Wolfson must be correct in thinking that mystical ascents were really experienced and that they had a salutary effect for the mystic as well as for society or they would not have been practiced and supported. Jung suggests that these images are fundamental psychological processes that aid the quest for individuation. I would certainly agree that they are normal occurences and can be significant, meaningful, and salutary to human life in cultures that value them. Yet it may not be wrong to suggest, at the same time, that some of these ancient visions may appear to us today to be hallucinations, or self-hypnosis, in the sense that we believe that they must be wholly due to internal stimuli and could not take place outside the body. But there is an important difference in the case of a religious experience, where a socially acceptable and even admirable interpretation explains the RISC and no anti-social behavior results. Wolfson is further right in pointing out that there is a complex relationship between texts and RISC in Biblical communities. Experiences grow out of texts, and texts grow out of experiences. That will be key to our inquiry.

Wolfson refers to the famous story in the *Hekhaloth Rabbati* where R. Nehuniah ben Ha-Qanah is sitting on a marble dias, apparently in a RASC, describing the sights of his journey through the heavens to an assembled Sanhedrin. He says something puzzling, and the attendant rabbis wish to recall him to earth. The method is not entirely clear but appears as follows: allow ben Ha-Qanah to come into contact with an object that might be polluted enough to affect his ability to remain in heaven but not polluted enough to affect his status on earth. Since there are aspects of this story that seem historically improbable (e.g., the Sanhedrin) and others that seem illogical (e.g., Rabbi Hakkanah then proceeds on his way again), the literary quality of the tale cannot be ignored. On the other hand, it is generally consonant with the material which Hai Gaon reports that he knows about, in which the mystic sat on earth while his "soul" traveled through the palaces and progressed toward the highest heaven.

The Gaon was aware that the journey took place internally, while the adept was on the ground. It was a social occasion in which the whole Sanhedrin was gathered around him. This culture did not interpret the experience as a hallucination, rather a RASC. There is good evidence suggesting that the experience was a self-induced, altered state of consciousness. But that does not automatically make it hallucinatory or insane. Changes in states of consciousness are trainable, even under conscious control both in their trigger and ending mechanisms, and have meanings specific to the society that values them. The understanding of the events was positive, though the evaluation may differ as the text filters down through the ages. For example, Jewish scholars have not been reticent to voice their distaste for these phenomena because they do not meet the scholars' own definitions of Judaism.

The Heavenly Journey, Dreams, Visions, and the Soul's Journey after Death

MARY DEAN-OTTING, in her book *Heavenly Journeys*,[6] displays in convenient form many of the motifs of the heavenly journey. The notion that God communicates through dreams is part of the epic tradition in Israelite thought, being a special characteristic of the E source in the Pentateuch. Furthermore, the book of Daniel is probably the source for the notion that revelation could be sought by incubating dreams. Dean-Otting herself does not shy from the conclusion that these psychological states are characteristics of the ascent in Hebrew thought and vice versa, that ascent is characteristic of altered states of consciousness. Though her study does not stress the relationship between ascent and RISC, it seems to many scholars to be the most obvious interpretation of the evidence.

In a way, visions are no different from dreams. We all have dreams, several times a night. In the morning we find them strange and sometimes worthy of mention, but usually we dismiss them immediately. Without training, we remember very few for more than a couple of hours. Since most of us do not produce the hormones important for memory while we sleep, what we train ourselves to remember may not be the dream itself but a rationalized, faint recollection of it. If we lived in a different kind of culture, however, one in which dreams were thought revelations, we would be sensitive to their import in entirely different ways and, chances are, we would seek to remember them more devotedly.

Almost all aspects of our dream experience are sensitive to training. We can stimulate our remembrances of dreams directly by waking up during the dream and reciting or writing them down. Other techniques for remembering dreams include consciously or unconsciously creating conditions that disturb sleep indirectly—such as anxiety, mourning, eating too much or little, or praying.

Dreams, too, are very much related to daily experience, both in content and emotional tone. That would mean that anyone who spent his or her time in careful exegesis of the "ascent texts" which describe the heavens, the divine throne room, and the journey there, would likely eventually dream about the same details. Besides reflecting the "unconscious" issues of life, with training, people are sometimes consciously able to manipulate the content and even the progress of their dreams, a phenomenon known as "lucid dreaming." Lastly, oral reporting and literary processes are always available to subject the dream experience to correction when it goes far from the expected details.

We should note that a person who seeks out a dream and treats it as a revelation is relying, from our point of view, on ordinary human experience but is choosing to treat the experience as a revelation, in short, a RISC. Because of the value attached to the experience, we should expect that techniques for receiving and remembering dreams would easily enter religious life either directly or indirectly in various rituals. And since we should not privilege any sort of experience from what we normally expect in our modern world, that is all that we mean when we say that someone is receiving a dream-vision. We cannot say what the dream actually was before the person sets out to explain it. If the person does explain it, necessarily more cognitive issues will come into play, including difficulties in remembering it, and the natural tendency to edit the memory in transmitting it.

However, there are some times when sleep experience is evidently treated quite differently in our society, mostly because we do not understand all of the processes of sleep. For instance, a *New York Times* science article describes an unusual sleep phenomenon.[7] A physical condition, known as sleep paralysis, common in some people especially at the onset or subsidence of sleep, can be interpreted as a witch attack in Newfoundland, known as "the old hag," or even as an alien abduction in the United States. It can involve paralysis, pressure in the head, weight on the chest, struggle for breath, ringing in the ears—even a near death experience. In Japan, where there is both a predisposition and a regular name for "sleep paralysis" *(kanashibari)*, people recognize it as a particular medical complaint.

This seems to suggest that many phenomena that are common in our psychic lives are evaluated by whatever religious or cultural criteria are available. Culture imposes an etiology and explanation on a great variety of our experiences. If this is true of our sleep states, it must be equally true of our waking states. Altered waking states, such as visions, ecstasy, or out-of-body experiences, are explained in a culture by whatever mechanisms are available in religion and mythology. Depending on those explanations, the culture makes a decision about the "sanity" of the actor.

Furthermore, there is a perfectly normal reflex of dreaming which can appear as a waking vision; that is the phenomenon known variously as the "hypnagogic state" or the "hypnopompic state," depending on whether it is experienced upon entering sleep or upon reawakening. Some people, but evidently not all of us (at least not without training), can easily induce this state. As its name suggests, it is related to hypnosis and, though it occurs during sleep, is very susceptible to conscious suggestion. It can also happen during meditation or other kinds of deep thought and it is sometimes also a state in which out-of-body experiences take place.[8]

Dan Merkur has made this state the basis for his analysis of gnosticism.[9] Although we do not know everything about this state that we would like to know, and it is quite variable in different people, in terms of its existence, the pleasure with which it is greeted, and the insights gained from it, it is widely documented as a state in which the subject is sometimes unable to distinguish between waking and sleeping modes, confusing what we think is dream imagery with waking experience. What makes dreams such a good example of this process is that dreams are omnipresent and accepted as normal throughout the world.

Usually in cultures that posit a non-normal state of consciousness in prophecy, dreams are also specially marked as having a divine origin. We know that this was believed true in Hebrew society because of the famous dreams of Joseph and Daniel. So from the perspective of the actor or adept, these were religious experiences, clearly understood to have religious consequences. And, although Daniel and Joseph are pseudonymous characters in the Biblical narrative, there is no reason to believe that people did not have these experiences. When Daniel begins to speak, the first thing he says is that his night visions came to him as dreams. Prophetic dreams are virtually universal throughout the world; they were especially important media for revelation in the ancient world, including early Christianity and Judaism, and are commonly held to be revelatory or the equivalent in all cultures today.[10]

Dreams were expected and prepared for by the prophets and seers in late Hebrew prophecy and apocalypticism. They are well documented as well later in Jewish mysticism. Vigils, usually pious night vigils of lamentation for the destruction of the Temple, are characteristic of many of the same apocalypses and are also present in 2 *Enoch* as well as later Jewish apocrypha. Vigils are particularly prone to bringing on hypnagogic and hypnopompic states. Whether these preparations are isolated as specific techniques by the text is beside the point; dreams are peculiarly both within control and out of rational control, so that they can be seen as messages from a deity or not, depending on the culture.

The validity of dreams as divine communication was almost universally accepted in the Hellenistic world. In those texts with remarkable frequency, they are the medium for revelation. The point of bringing in this research is not to reduce all revelations to misunderstood ordinary experience but to show that religiously interpreted states of consciousness are neither exotic nor uninterpretable in our notions of ordinary possibility. We should not treat the claims as impossible or insane; rather they can be real experiences interpreted by another system of causation than we might usually choose today.

RISC Experiences, Shamanism, and Techniques for Achieving Them in Judea

WHAT WE KNOW about dreams can be applied analogously to visions. I do not think it is out of place to read the reports of non-normal states of consciousness as important, interesting, valid, and valorizing, even when the vision excludes a specific mention of ascent. But the presence of ascent may be taken as an indicator of RISC in many different contexts. The ascent motif is known to adhere to a number of observable cases of ecstatic religious experience in the contemporary world—especially in shamanism. Many different societies valorize shamanic ascent.[11]

Mircea Eliade, a famous Romanian comparativist who presided over the History of Religions program for many years at the University of Chicago, studied shamanism extensively and imprinted on it certain assumptions which consciously and unconsciously color our field even today.[12] We can appreciate the value of his work—especially in sensitizing us to the importance of religion in our lives—if not every one of his theories.

He suggested that ascent and possession/trance were united with healing in shamanism. The shaman normally ascends to heaven to heal a wayward "soul," whose misadventures had caused the illness in the first place. Eliade's well-known studies closely weld trance with ascension but there are so many different kinds of trances and possessions that any number of possible connections are possible.[13]

Eliade's work was based on reading various literary texts and field reports. Subsequent field work demonstrated that possession, trance, and ascent—as well as the other characteristics of shamanism—are independent variables, even though they correlate at various times and places. Though various techniques of shamanism diffuse historically, not all shamanism can be shown to be historically related.

Ascent as a Marker for ASC

AS EARLY AS Daniel, the theme of night visions becomes important. Daniel 7 announces itself as both a dream and a vision. This compares with the dream of Nebuchadnezzar in Daniel 2:1; 4:6–7 and the subsequent revelations which are called visions (ḥāzōn Dan 8:1; mâr'eh 10:1). Daniel receives "visions of his head on his bed," that he writes down. Most scholars have interpreted this usage to indicate a revelatory dream, which was written down afterwards.

This formulation also can be found in the early parts of Enoch:

This is the book of the words for righteousness and the chastisement of the eternal watchers, in accordance with how the Holy and Great One had commanded in this vision. *I saw in my sleep what I now speak with my tongue of flesh* (italics added) and the breath of the mouth which the Great One has given to man (so that) he (man) may speak with it—and (so that) he may have understanding with his heart as he (the Great One) has created and given it to man. (*1 En* 14:2–3)

Enoch too receives his ascent vision in his sleep and then communicates it afterwards. In the Testament of Levi, the first vision is accomplished with a spirit of understanding. Later, sleep falls upon the seer, perhaps as in Genesis 28:12, and he experiences ascent. *Third Enoch* begins with a scene of great mourning for the destruction of the Temple and continues to an experience of ascent. In the Apocalypse of Abraham, Genesis 15, where a deep sleep falls upon Abraham, forms the background to the story. The apocalypse retells the "covenant between the pieces." It interprets Abraham's sleep as a waking vision:

And it came to pass when I heard the voice pronouncing such words to me that I looked this way and that. And behold there was no breath of man. And my spirit was amazed, and my soul fled from me. And I became like a stone, and fell face down upon the earth, for there was no longer strength in me to stand upon the earth. And while I was still face down on the ground, I heard the voice speaking. . . . (*Apoc Ab* 10)

Here, the apocalypticist has interpreted the Hebrew word *tardemah* in Genesis 15, usually translated as "deep sleep," as purely a daytime trance. His body was completely incapacitated but he saw the arrival of the angel and then used the sacrificed birds to ascend. It is conceivable that an exegete would have found these connections but why would the exegete then translate the experience of Abraham into a first person narrative? He must be relating it to his own knowledge, either personally or from another adept. Although this state is described as a waking vision, we may understand these changes in the same way as dreams. Naturally occurring states of consciousness can be understood in religiously important ways in the correct context. Altered states of consciousness must be stimulated for most people while others just occur naturally.

The native understanding of the phenomenon in Jewish culture is not so much "rapture" as explicitly "ecstasy" in its technical sense (*ek* + *stasis*, meaning "standing outside"), as the narrator states that his soul fled. He means this to be understood as a non-normal and religiously altered state of consciousness. He further characterizes the physical trauma with a description of a seizure. The terminologies of dream vision, spirit possession, and soul flight are used interchangeably here to indicate that the experience was non-normal, a RASC. It would be realistic to consider that ecstasy and mysticism ascents were being practiced and that they were expressed as astral journeys.

In 4 *Ezra* there are three famous other techniques—fasting, eating flowers of the field, and drinking a fiery liquid. They can be understood as "triggering" techniques for achieving trance, as they are quite unusual behaviors otherwise in this society. The last item, drinking a fiery liquid, may even reflect the Persian tradition of imbibing psychedelic drugs, although it occurs inside a RISC, for the purposes of remembering Scripture, having the function of a magical memory potion.

Fasting is a well understood technique for achieving changes in consciousness and was practiced frequently by the heavenly journeyers; in some sense it does not matter whether the culture chooses to mark the activity as directly related to the vision or merely one of the preparations, like obtaining ritual purity. As a physical stimulus, fasting will not only bring on vivid dreams but can produce trance and other psychagogic states. While we do not know whether "the flowers of the field" ingested by the seer had any psychotropic properties, the description of the special diet may imply a specific agent and is, at the very least, a significant part of the fasting theme. Poppies, henbane, marijuana, and jimson weed, as well as other psychoactive plants, grow wild in profusion around the Mediterranean.

Hymn singing was the most important means of achieving ascent in the Merkabah texts.[14] The repetition of mantras is a well-known technique for meditation in Hinduism and Buddhism. Although Jewish texts do not valorize hymn singing as a technique, very intent and highly concentrated hymn singing occurs throughout the texts. *Hekhaloth Rabbati*, for example, explicitly starts the ascent by saying that a certain psalm is to be recited by the adept exactly 112 times.

Trance is itself a widely varying combination of various physical states—including pulse, breathing, a complex variety of different brain waves, as well as quite different reports about the nature of consciousness and remembrance while possessed. Therefore an enormous variety of physical phenomena can be trained and selected by the traditions within a society as meaningful for a RISC experience. There are gradients in spirit possession and meditation, everything from light or no trance to deep unconsciousness. Given the evidence, it would be foolish either to deny or affirm that prophets or apocalypticists could or could not produce their writings in an altered state. Furthermore, it would be difficult to judge on the basis of the texts whether any particular one or combination of the physical characteristics of trance were present during these revelations.

The important thing, in the end, is what the texts claim, because that is the record of at least part of what is prescribed in the society. Claiming that they are visions is, in terms of the society, tantamount to them being so, unless there is specific evidence from the society to suggest that they are being faked. There must be evidence trusting or distrusting each report.

We should not shy away from comparing these Israelite religious experiences with those narrated in Persian thought, where the vision is explicitly caused by a narcotic drink. Though the heavenly journeys of Kartir and Arda Viraf were somewhat later than *1 Enoch* and the *Apocalypse of Abraham,* for example, it would not be outrageous to think that the adept was sitting on earth while the spirit roamed the heavens in a RISC. This differs quite significantly from the older, mythological description, where the god or hero literally went to heaven. In these later, more mystical cases, we may posit that actual RISC experience is behind the accounts, though it cannot be ordinary experience, and it cannot be reconstructed in detail. Indeed, it may even be that the earlier mythological narratives mean to suggest RISC as well. Early literature is notoriously weak on experiential terminology. Frequently in Akkadian, for instance, dreaming is expressed by the phrase: "I slept and I saw."

The Neurological Background of the Heavenly Journey

THERE HAS BEEN a great deal of research on the various neurological states that may underlie religious and other anomalous experiences.[15] These books demonstrate that perfectly normally-functioning brains can spontaneously or by various techniques be stimulated to have anomalous or religious experiences. These experiences are quite different from the hallucinations produced by mental illness, derangement, and random acts of violence, although they are alike in that they all have an etiology in unusual processes in the brain.

Newberg, D'Aquili, and Rause conclude their book, *Why God Won't Go Away,* by positing that feelings of mystic unity are a characteristic of the brain in some of its rarest operations. Among other things, these rare states involve deafferentation or disinhibition, two names for a misfunction in the brain when nerve fibers fire erratically and stop sending meaningful signals to the central nervous system. This state is detectable by means of a variety of brain-imaging techniques (CAT, SPECT, or MRI).[16] When this happens, subjects report unusual experiences that can be interpreted religiously, if the context is right.

In a unitary mystical experience, in which Newberg, D'Aquili and Rause are particularly interested, both left and right parietal lobes are neutralized. The right lobe is very important to the way we experience physical space. It is in charge of proprioception, the body's knowledge of where its appendages are in space—a neurological process that, though important, normally goes on without conscious intervention. The left parietal lobe, conversely, seems to be quite important to the generation of the subjective sense of self. When both centers experience deafferentation, which essentially means "quieting" the specific lobes of the brain, either through mystical meditation or through wild and uncontrolled overstimulation, making the brain unable to decode its messages, the result may be a unitive mystical experience.[17]

But these unitive experiences have quite a different etiology than the shamanistic experience on the heavenly journey. Newberg, D'Aquili, and Rauss are interested in the disinhibition of both right and left parietal lobes, which cover various aspects of the body's sense that we exist in specific points in space and time.[18] The result may be a unitary, mystical experience. But when only the right center is involved, we can posit a different experience.[19] When the proprioception center is quiet (as determined by CAT scans, MRIs, SPECTs and other medical diagnostic means), subjects report that they can no longer perceive their bodily location, but have a distinct feeling of bodiless motion in space.

Some people are able to achieve these states spontaneously; others train to achieve the state in meditation; still others report the state after disease, trauma, or under the effects of various drugs. The drug Ketamine, known as "Special K" in the club circuit, is known often to produce out-of-body experiences in its abusers.[20]

These out-of-body experiences have been studied and normally differ quite markedly from shamanistic or heavenly journeys produced in religious contexts. But these drug experiences occur in quite different circumstances than shamanistic ones. There has been considerable study of the conditions that might predispose people to have out-of-body experiences, the aftereffects, and their relationship to other predispositions like epilepsy, seizures, hypnotizability, and a variety of other personality and neurological factors.[21] By no means are these mechanisms well understood or entirely mapped.[22] But it seems clear that there is, at the least, a physiological component of RISC and also culturally available narratives as explanations of it. It is reasonable to suppose that expectations and context count for a great deal in predisposing the content of the experience, especially where a religion provides detailed instruction through texts and lessons on how to achieve these states.

In other words, deafferentation or disinhibition experiences may be the physiological root of the experience, but the detailed ascent to heaven would be equally due to social and cultural expectations of the adept. Mystics usually train for years for their out-of-body experiences, while drug abusers normally do not even want them. There are still other people who seek to have these experiences quickly, without long training. For example, a quick check of self-help books in print will yield dozens of books that teach subjects how to "astrally project themselves" or have "out-of-body" experiences. This suggests to me that it is not that difficult for a motivated learner to achieve the experience. Mystics and shamans who have very detailed experiences must be predisposed by their years of practice and study to have specific kinds of experience while in disinhibition or deafferentation. Combined with that experience is whatever content is available in the culture for explaining such intense, mystical experiences. If the adept has been studying the texts of previous journeys in a specific mystic, apocalyptic, or shamanic tradition, chances are that the content of the experience will confirm the tradition.

There may well be similar physiological conditions behind the "Near Death Experience." When combined with trauma, people close to death may reach disinhibition. But they also experience the familiar, long dark tunnel, the bright light at the end, combined with the distinct feeling that they are floating or moving rapidly through the tunnel. The tunneling vision is likely due to malfunctioning of the optical centers of the brain. While we do not understand these states well, it already seems clear that in back of them are neurologically determined experiences that feel distinctly like being out-of-body.

If there is a biological basis for these experiences, there surely is also a broad vocabulary of images which the individual mind brings into the experience, based on personal history, training, and culture. I suggest that the difference between deafferentation or disinhibition and a detailed mystical ascent to heaven is the long mystical training of the adepts who learn both techniques for achieving the physical states and the culture's social and cultural lore about what the state means.[23]

Are Jewish Apocalyptic and Merkabah Texts Exegesis or the Record of a RISC?

APOCALYPTIC texts are not simply exegeses of previous texts but combine study with revelatory experience. The texts themselves may even be palimpsests of many adepts' experiences stretched over generations. It is sometimes impossible to separate the literary from the mystical experiences.

One way to adjudicate between RISC and exegesis is to look at the nature of the religious innovation and its expression. Is the innovation small enough to be considered within the realm of exegetical activity, or is it so great that only a vision could justify such a change? There are significant places in the book of Daniel where exegesis cannot explain the great innovations: For instance, in Daniel 7, the scene is a heavenly throne room with two manlike figures, one an "ancient of days" and the second a "Son of Man" (bar 'enash in Biblical Aramaic and in the postbiblical dialect barnasha'). "Son of Man" is not a title and can only mean the divine figure has a manlike form, because the phrase "son of man" usually means simply "a human being" in most Semitic languages. The exact phrase in Daniel is "one like a Son of Man" (kebar 'enash), signifying that the next figure in the vision was shaped like a man. The use of the preposition "like" also signifies that this is not Daniel's usual consciousness.

The best guess as to the identity of the figure shaped like a man is that he is a depiction of the Glory of the LORD, the Kabod YHWH, the same principal human manifestation of God—an angel or a principal angel in whose form God deigns to appear, for some angels were envisioned in human form. At his second appearance, Gabriel is described as "the man Gabriel whom I had seen in the vision at first" (Dan 9:21). Then in Daniel 10:5 "a man clothed in linen," probably an angel, is described in a way reminiscent of Ezekiel's description of God's glory. Again in Daniel 10:16, Daniel sees a human figure, probably as before, an angel "shaped in the likeness of men" (kidmût bĕnê 'ādām). These are characters who appear in other visions as well.

All this would be conventional except for one thing: there are two different manifestations of God, one old ("the ancient of days") and the other young ("the Son of Man"). God appearing in two different forms at once is very puzzling, a description that clearly innovates on the notion that God can appear in whatever form He wants. Behind this passage is originally a Canaanite mythologem describing 'El's enthronement of his son Ba'al, but no one knows how it could become a proper Jewish vision.[24] An obvious explanation for such an innovation is that someone was remembering an actual dream. In any event, revelatory authority was being claimed for the vision.

The Daniel passage is based upon the Ezekiel passage (Ezek 37) but no one would say that it is simple exegesis. Unlike Ezekiel, the prophet stayed on earth in his bed but he was transported to heaven at the same time as he translated the Ezekiel passage into his personal experience. Somehow the experience of the later prophet, writing under the pseudonym of Daniel, was translated and conditioned by the writings of Ezekiel. At the same time the prophet incorporates all kinds of new experience, including the Canaanite mythological image, into his scene. No obvious exegetical conventions are mentioned in the text. It is simply narrated as a story. If this was not a vision then it ought to be.

It cannot be merely exegesis of the Ezekiel passage because there is no attention at all to explaining the earlier text. Instead it is as if the previous descriptions of the heavenly throne room were experienced by the narrator. There is much manifestly new material in it, unique in the Biblical canon. In fact, in such a traditional culture no one could make up such a heretical scene as two divinities who are one without relying on some divine sanction. Novelistic imagination could not have done the trick for the ancients. So a narrative of real experience seems obvious. The big question is: "What kind of experience is it?"

The text tells us that it is a "dream vision." And it has all the qualities of a dream vision experienced after meditating and studying the earlier texts. At the same time it follows its own dreamlike plot and logic. It seems very much like what it is supposed to be—a dream. The hypothesis that we have a transcript of the dream-vision, with the attendant caveat that all language implies interpretation, is the best explanation for the event. We have no way of knowing how many changes may have entered the text before it is witnessed in the archeological record. But from early texts that we do have, we know that Biblical texts, thought to contain the word of God, was transcribed very conservatively.

We have already seen an important and interesting case in which the seer's vision was actually composed of a conflation of several different previous visions—that is the vision of Daniel 12. In previous chapters we have seen how Daniel 12:1–3 is actually a kind of inspired commentary on Isaiah 66, illumined by the visionary combination of images in Ezekiel 37 and Isaiah 26. When we discussed these passages earlier, it was clear that these were not exegeses but new revelatory interpretations of the Isaiah 66 passage. We may never know precisely which situations produced it. The adept whose vision we have in Daniel 12 was certainly reading Isaiah quite carefully before the dream. There is no doubt that it was a RISC. Daniel 7:9–14 is equally based on very similar images, combined with the passages above.

Many, many other religious texts in Scripture fit the same RISC pattern. Christopher Rowland describes the way apocalyptic material relates to its Biblical past.[25] He notes, for instance in 4 Ezra 12:11, that the man (vir perfectus) who rises from the sea is an allusion to Daniel 7 and, most especially, to verse 13, which describes the "Son of Man," who comes with the clouds of heaven (the passage that we just studied and that we discovered to have been itself the result of a vision).

Yet, allusions to figures rising from the sea come from earlier in the chapter in Daniel, where the beasts are said to arise from the sea. This kind of mélange of images is not the result of exegesis; indeed it is totally anathema to any educated Hebrew exegesis, which is quite exacting and governed by many technical terms, but actually the result of meditation on the whole chapter, reorganized by a free-ranging consciousness. As Rowland himself concludes: "It is most unlikely that a careful interpreter of Daniel 7 would have linked the divine envoy with the home of the beasts and thereby deliberately linked the divine with the demonic in the way in which we find it in this chapter."[26]

The specific details of the vision in 4 Ezra are brought about, according to the text, not just by dream visions but induced by fasting and mourning leading to a revelation. Regardless, the characteristics of the text remain the same. The writers do not comment on the text and produce a commentary. They seemingly combine the images at will and come up with a detailed new narrative which uses the fragmentary images of the Bible to forge a new story of consolation. The presence of RISC is undeniable.

These texts differ fundamentally from any of the accepted means of exegesis. They are not Midrash, not Rabbinic exegesis. Neither are they homilies, nor targums, all of which are clearly understood genres of exegesis, each with its own format and technical terms. Nor are they pesher, which is commonly believed itself to be an inspired exegesis. (So most scholars have no problem accepting even some exegesis as inspired.)[27]

Even more obvious is the relationship between the various ascent texts in Enoch and their Biblical forebears. Many of the traditions found in the Enoch cycle are excellent examples. The ascent texts appear to flesh out various Biblical texts into a vision of heavenly reward and punishment.

We are constantly given the details of Daniel 12 spelled out in many ways. The good are rewarded and the evil punished. We see the leaders rewarded with heavenly immortality as stars and the very worst of the sinners punished for having persecuted the righteous. A very interesting relationship between Biblical texts and those found in Enoch is formed by the elements from Ezekiel 1 and Isaiah 6. The theophany in *1 Enoch* 14:8 is clearly related to the theophany in Ezekiel, but there are very few precise contacts. Apart from the reference to the throne which is just as much influenced by Isaiah 6:1 (see *1 En* 14:18, "a lofty throne") the frequent mention of fire and certain key words like "lightning" and "crystal," as well as the reference to the wheels of the Merkabah (14:18), there are very few actual contacts. But the chapters from Ezekiel and Isaiah are clearly informing the Enoch texts.

We must not discount the idea that somewhere along the line, a literary copyist glossed some of the Biblical material. But the most obvious way to describe the relationships between the two sets of texts is that the Biblical quotations were read and understood by people who studied them carefully, and then they became parts of the dreams and visions which those same people experienced. The glossing came afterwards when the exegetes noticed inconsistencies. The reading is the process by which the seer assimilated details of the text into memory, which made them available later as the bits of experience out of which the ascensions were formulated.

Jews of the first centuries BCE and CE, like all preceding and succeeding centuries, took RISC very seriously.[28] They also valued ecstasy, or trance, as a medium for revelation and developed techniques for signaling that ecstasy or trance was occurring.[29] The same language also seemed to the ancients to suggest something very deep and mystical about the way in which humans resembled God and conversely how God could be figured in human form. These beliefs pervaded Jewish culture as well and enriched Jewish spirituality. In the Hellenistic period, these terms rightly became associated with the language of translation in two senses—in the translation of the texts and also in the sense of ascent, ascension, or theurgy, the magic use of shamanic techniques to stimulate these "out-of-body" experiences. This vocabulary in Greek was known to Paul and became a central aspect of Paul's explanation of the Christian message.[30]

RASC: *Apocalypticism and the Immortality of the Soul Compared*

IN APOCALYPTICISM, the heavenly journey accomplishes many things but it can be summarized as confirming that God's cosmos does indeed operate on moral principles, even though the enemies of God and the oppressors of the sect may appear to be powerful and arrogant. The expected end *will* arrive with its attendant resurrection of the dead and judgment of sinners, though there are no specific texts in the Hebrew Scripture until Daniel that describe resurrection in detail. The visionary himself in his altered state becomes a kind of eschatological verifier, going to heaven to see what is in it. We must not forget that the ecstatic journey to heaven is also a widely experienced and fully legitimate part of the classical heritage.[31]

The way in which altered states of consciousness verified the notion of the immortal soul was different, though the effect was similar. The notion of the "psyche" as the "essence" of a person was archaic in Greece, though we have seen that there were several competing notions for the location of life. In the philosophical tradition, it slowly and progressively took over as the religious formulation of human identity. For Plato and Aristotle the soul contained a number of faculties, including keeping the body from decomposing and serving as the seat of intellect. For us all these are properly corporeal faculties, explained by various faculties of the body, leaving us with a sense that the soul refers only to our psychic lives. But for the early philosophers there were much wider issues, as Erich Rohde makes clear:

> What the Ionic philosophers in connection with the rest of their cosmology had to say about the soul of man did not for all its striking novelty bring them into direct conflict with religious opinion. Philosophy and religion used the same words to denote totally different things; it could surprise no one if different things were said about quite different objects.
>
> According to the popular view, which finds expression in Homer, and with which, in spite of their very different estimate of the relative values of body and soul, the religious theory of the Orphics and other *theologi* also agreed—according to this view the "psyche" was regarded as a unique creature of combined spiritual and material nature that, whatever it may have come from, now dwells within man and there, as his second self, carries on its separate existence, making itself

felt when the visible self loses consciousness in dream, swoon, or ecstasy. . . . In the same way, the moon and stars become visible when no longer obscured by the brighter light of the sun. It was already implied in the conception itself that this double of mankind, which could be detached from him temporarily, had a separate existence of its own; it was no very great step from this to the idea that in death, which is simply the permanent separation of the visible man from the invisible, the latter did not perish, but only then became free and able to live by and for itself.[32]

Similar claims are made about the soul as are being made about apocalyptic ascent, though they provide evidence for a different view of the afterlife. There would have been no need to validate and justify new texts, which promise resurrection as resurrection was not a concept to be proven. Once the soul could be shown from experience to separate from the body and return, as in an ecstatic trance, then the rest of the Platonic theory also gained probability.

Our Accounts of Consciousness and the Soul

THE PLATONIC proof for the immortality of the soul depends on the mental qualities of memory and self recognition. For the ancients, the soul had many properties which are best explained by various neurological events. So the most interesting aspects of the soul adhere to its role in defining our interior lives, our consciousness. It is therefore worthwhile to digress for a moment more about the contemporary study of consciousness. Epistemology and the more recent search for an adequate description of and explanation of consciousness are such full and interesting fields of inquiry that even a survey would demand a whole book in itself.[33] The next few paragraphs merely will be a description of the working definitions that I have adopted.

We now have good physiological evidence that there is no single organ in the brain that corresponds to consciousness. Thus, consciousness is not a single unified phenomenon with a single origin; rather, it is a unitary experience which we effortlessly and unconsciously synthesize from various capacities operating more or less independently in our brains. Consciousness includes perception, cognition, and memory, but also proprioception and a variety of other functions. When organs in the brain are damaged in strokes and injuries, we observe the selective effects on our conscious processes. We may lose the faculty of speech temporarily or permanently, for instance. These are easily correlated with observable damage to areas in the brain. So we now know experimentally what various areas in the brain contribute to consciousness.

We also have the ability to selectively hone consciousness and to perform other tasks without conscious intervention. Almost everyone has had the experience of driving home from work, lost in thought, without being conscious of the process of driving at all and without being able to remember a single moment of it without the utmost concentration. By observation of hypnotic states we also know that consciousness is not continuous but the "breaks" are not always like a "black out" or "blue screen" on a television broadcast. We have breaks in consciousness when we are not aware that we have missed something.

This suggests that consciousness is an emergent property, not inherent to any one organ but something that emerges from the harmonious operation of a series of processes. Because consciousness is emergent and complex, and because consciousness itself can be the subject of thought, we have a feeling that I will call "self-consciousness." "Self-consciousness" is affected greatly by our cultural understandings of what our consciousness is. Buddhists may not only have different notions of selfhood than Christians; because of these differing religious definitions, their experience of self may well be different. That suggests that there cannot be a simple and single description of self-consciousness. Like RISC, it is partly a culturally mediated experience. The notion of the soul or the transformed body of apocalypticism really can and does effect how we understand ourselves.

It is not consciousness in itself which should be of interest to us right now. Many species of animals may be conscious. Anyone who has observed animals closely becomes convinced of it. But self-consciousness is a human, cultural phenomenon, though animals may have the rudiments of it. By experiment, we know that the higher apes are able to recognize themselves in a mirror, while dogs and cats and other animals usually show no recognition of the image as themselves. The most they can do is mistake their reflection for another animal.

Daniel Povinelli and John Cant speculate that the evolutionary explanation for our self-concept is that it is necessary to have a self-concept to swing through the trees with the kind of advanced skills which apes evince, making far more complicated judgments than, for instance, squirrels or bats do when they move through the canopy.[34] One supposes that proprioception, this sense that we know where we are in space, develops into culturally mediated notions of whom we are and how our internal states define us as individuals.

So self-consciousness is analogous to RISC but made up of yet more complex cultural conceptualizations. John D. Gottsch has shown that religions may themselves be a response to the further self-perception that not only are we unique, but we must all die.[35] This certainly does not explain all religious phenomena but it is surely a partial explanation of the development of notions of the afterlife. It is tempting to posit that the notion of the immortal soul is coterminous with the emergence of self-consciousness. But since self-consciousness is a complex and culturally determined phenomenon in and of itself, this is no easy task.

This, for instance, is the major problem with the cult classic of Julian Jaynes, *The Origin of Consciousness in the Breakdown of the Bicameral Mind*.[36] His bold thesis was, that originally, before the Odyssey was written, the Greeks could not distinguish between internal and external processes easily because they had not yet developed the phenomenon of the bicameral mind, with each hemisphere concentrating on one aspect of cognition. Because of this, they easily mistook their own internal voice and cognitions as the voices of gods. He also said that the change to a bicameral mind took place between the writing of the *Iliad* and the *Odyssey*, which seems to him to be a clearly definable moment in historical time. (Actually, it is not. He did not take into account that the two books were being created and edited simultaneously, over a long period of time.) Since then, only transitional or abnormal personality types have approximated this state. This is a bold, interesting, and wrong hypothesis in any number of important ways. But it is also fascinating speculation that anticipates more scientific experimentation.

A number of other scholars have traced the emergence of self-consciousness to a variety of other time periods, some as late as the Middle Ages, the romantic movement of the nineteenth century, or even the Victorian novel. It now seems clear that these scholars outlined instead some important cultural change in self-consciousness, not the basic phenomenon, which must be much older than historical time.[37] In the nineteenth century, many novelists—Henry James jumps to mind immediately—stressed the necessity of coming to more full consciousness, portraying the difficulties of characters who were insufficiently aware of themselves or the motives of their contemporaries. Psychological novels like those of Henry James are sometimes held up as the effect of the West's finally having achieved full self-consciousness. For the purposes of this study, we have seen that major milestones were passed in the philosophical writing of Plato. We shall see, in later chapters, more milestones in the writings of Plotinus, and Augustine respectively. None of them invented self-consciousness per se, but each changed or added an important aspect to the description of our self-consciousness so as to resolve various intellectual problems. Each valorized personal experience in a new way and keyed into our interior lives more completely than his predecessors to explain an intellectual problem that he had encountered in his philosophy.

What we need to take from this discussion is that only great conceptual changes in religious, social, philosophical, and artistic life—in short culture—do affect how we understand ourselves, an axiom that seems little in need of demonstration. Self-consciousness builds on our biological consciousness by explaining the self in a socially meaningful way. The notion of the immortality of the soul had just such an effect on how we value our own self-consciousness. The notion of the soul and its immortality helps us understand who we are and why we think we are important. By positing that the soul was immortal, the Greeks were also positing that self-consciousness—or, better, memory, our learning, experiencing and changing mind—is a transcendent and valuable phenomenon that outlasts our earthly existence. By defining the afterlife as a resurrection of the body, apocalypticists also suggested what the purpose of individual life was and also inscribed martyrdom as a fitting and sensible sacrifice to help bring about the coming of God's kingdom.

It follows that in investigating "the Undiscover'd Country" of the afterlife, we are actually investigating our own self-consciousness through the mirror of our culture. The words we use will be the words our culture gives to us for understanding these "peak experiences" in our consciousness. The journey to heaven is also a journey into the self. This conclusion becomes inescapable. Saying that, however, is saying a great deal more than that we build our afterlife out of our imaginations. It is saying that we then invest those imaginative constructions with the authority of reality through a very complicated social procedure. Whether we can say anything more about the afterlife and our conscious perception of it will have to wait until the conclusions of this book, if not the conclusion of our personal life!

Demonstrations of the Soul's Separation from the Body and Immortality

We have noted that neither for the Greeks nor for the Hebrews was the soul exactly equivalent with self-consciousness. Technically the soul contained a plethora of other functions. For both Greeks and Jews, soul was originally a rather vague way of describing human identity, including emotions and appetites. The Greeks seemed more willing to posit that the soul could separate from the body, but both admitted the possibilities of separated souls.

With the Greek philosophers, specifically with the Platonists, the soul began to be considered "the unique" seat of identity, and demonstrating that it was immortal was also demonstrating that we were transcendent creatures. The notion of psyche was given strong support by unusual states of consciousness like dreams, visions, and ecstasy, where the soul's presence could be more clearly studied, separated from the body and without the normal background of bodily processes like pain and proprioception. What needed to be proven was that the soul was immortal. Since part of the Platonic notion of immortality adhered to the notion that the soul was separable from the body, and every single heavenly ascent could be understood as the soul's separation from the body, the experience of heavenly journey itself became an experiential proof and confirmation of the truth of Socrates' (Plato's) reasoning. The separation of the soul from the body in sleep and in mystical ascent was the demonstration of the immortality of the soul. This is true not only in the magical papyri and the hermetic writings but also in the philosophical writings of the classical world.

Nor do we have to look very far to find this demonstration in Hellenistic Jewish literature as well. Philo himself tells us quite emphatically that he experienced ecstasy (he calls it corybantic frenzy) while studying philosophy. In short, he claims that his exegesis is the product of divine revelation through meditation and study. He describes what happens to him in intellectual journeys to heaven, ascribing the experience to a special gift of God:

> On other occasions, I have approached my work empty and suddenly become full, the ideas falling in a shower from above and being sown invisibly, so that under the influence of divine possession [hypo katochēs entheou], I have been filled with corybantic frenzy [korbantian] and have been unconscious of anything, place, persons, present, myself, words spoken, lines written. For I obtained language, ideas, an enjoyment of light, keenest vision, pellucid distinctness of objects, such as might be received through the eyes as the result of clearest showing. (Migr. 35; see Cher. 27)

> There was a time when I had leisure for philosophy and for the contemplation of the universe and its contents, when I made its spirit my

own in all its beauty and loveliness and true blessedness, when my constant companions were divine themes and verities, wherein I rejoiced with a joy that never cloyed or sated. I had no base or abject thoughts nor grovelled in search of reputation or of wealth or bodily comforts, but seemed always to be borne aloft into the heights with a soul possessed by some God-sent inspiration, a fellow-traveller with the sun and moon and the whole heaven and universe. Ah then I gazed down from the upper air, and straining the mind's eye beheld, as from some commanding peak, the multitudinous world-wide spectacles of earthly things, and blessed my lot in that I had escaped by main force from the plagues of mortal life. But, as it proved, my steps were dogged by the deadliest of mischiefs, the hater of the good, envy, which suddenly set upon me and ceased not to pull me down with violence until it had plunged me in the ocean of civil cares, in which I am swept away, unable even to raise my head above the water. Yet amid my groans I hold my own, for, planted in my soul from my earliest days I keep the yearning for culture which ever has pity and compassion for me, lifts me up and relieves my pain. To this I owe it that sometimes I raise my head and with soul's eyes—dimly indeed because the mist of extraneous affairs has clouded their clear vision—I yet make shift to look around me in my desire to inhale a breath of life pure and unmixed with evil. And if unexpectedly I obtain a spell of fine weather and a calm from civil turmoils, I get me wings and ride the waves and almost tread the lower air, wafted by the breezes of knowledge which often urges me to come to spend my days with her, a truant as it were from merciless masters in the shape not only of men but of affairs, which pour in upon me like a torrent from different sides. (*Spec.* 3.1–6)

Philo describes his own meditative experiences as heavenly journeys. He contrasts them with any number of ordinary thinking functions or the cares of a busy life, which detracts from the process of revelatory thinking. He virtually states that the meditative states are not only joyeous but also moments of the reception of divine revelations.

Hellenism itself made this religious form even more attractive as a mythic structure, much as the apocalypticists may have wanted to deny the pagan versions of it. Ecstatic religion was valued highly among the Greeks and all the countries they conquered or influenced, as it has been in many if not most societies. There were many metaphors and descriptions of these RISCs and just as many interpretations of them—from demonic spirit possession to a god taking up residence inside the person. But one important metaphor for the divine nature and importance of the phenomenon is again seen in the narration of the heavenly journey. This is not a casual trance phenomenon but, in some sense, the ultimate human experience of transformation or even immortalization.

The narrative of the pagan Paris Magical Papyrus makes this equally clear. In this "recipe for immortalization," a magical document from the third century CE, the practitioner ascends to heaven in a trance for the purpose of gaining divine knowledge of the future, for confirming the worldview of the participants and the spectators (in the Paris Magical Papyrus it is largely an Egyptian world view), and for becoming transformed into a divine being. The Greek word used is *anathanatismos*, the process of becoming deathless. But the beginning of the ascent is brought on through a RASC, which is brought on apparently through hyperventilation:

> Draw in breath from the rays, drawing up three times as much as you can, and you will see yourself being lifted up and / ascending to the height, so that you seem to be in mid-air. You will hear nothing either of man or of any other living thing, nor in that hour will you see anything of mortal affairs on earth, but rather you will see all immortal things. For in that day / and hour you will see the divine order of the skies: the presiding gods rising into heaven, and others setting. (*PGM* I.537–45)[38]

It is conventional in scholarly literature to treat this experience as inferior or faked because it appears in a magical papyrus. It should be seen, rather, as a valid religious experience and, hence an important clue to the fascinating relationship between magic and religion in the ancient world. Except in places where the two were radically distinguished—as, for instance, in some varieties of Judaism and Christianity where magic was seen as demonic—the ancient world saw magic as completely parallel with religion. It may have been practiced by independent practitioners instead of organized priesthoods. Indeed, as the late Hellenistic world became more impressed with the theosophic powers of independent practitioners and magicians, the importance of magicians increased in the intelligentsia, as well as in the lower classes.

Heavenly ascent can also be easily seen in the *Corpus Hermeticum*, which eschews other religions and practices to advocate its own communal theosophical variety of community. At the very beginning of the *Corpus,* the narrator makes clear that the truths contained therein were received by revelation in an altered state of consciousness or RASC:

> Once, when thought came to me of the things that are and my thinking soared high and my bodily senses were restrained, like someone heavy with sleep from too much eating or toil of the body, an enormous being completely unbounded in size seemed to appear to me and call my name and say to me: "What do you want to hear and see; what do you want to learn and know from your understanding?" [39]

This particular experience shares with apocalypticism a community of believers and a commitment to a particular religious lifestyle. But it makes use of the notion of the immortality and separability of the soul to make its point. The one word that best describes this new entrepreneurial spirituality of late antiquity is "theurgy." [40] Theurgy, more than anything else, represents the force that transformed "magical" and hermetic tracts and rituals into acceptable religion in the Roman Empire.

Theurgy is a Hellenistic neologism that pointed to a new kind of technique in religion, which we often consider to be magic. The theurgist, as opposed to a theologian, not only studied the divine arts but learned how to control and "work" the gods. [41] Indeed, since *"ergon"* (work) can easily refer to a ritual in Greek, theurgy implies a religious "praxis," a ritual. Theurgy itself had been brought into the Roman Empire through the agency of the Chaldeans.

As far as we know, the earliest person claiming this art was Julianus, a contemporary of Marcus Aurelius (d. 180 CE). [42] He, in turn, claimed an association with an earlier Julianus, who gave him the secrets of the *Chaldean Oracles.* The technique of theurgy became more and more associated with the late Neoplatonic school, to such an extent that Proclus could define theurgy grandly as "a power higher than all human wisdom, embracing the powers of divination, the purifying powers of initiation, and, in short, all the operations of divine possession." [43] This explains why the term "magic" and with it the notion of personal religious entrepreneurship became acceptable in some aristocratic circles. Simply, it became a consistent religion, appealing to philosophers as well as their aristocratic students because of its promises of spiritual power together with a kind of independence from organized cults, although theurgy tended itself to be practiced within philosophical schools or religious conventicles like the Hermetic community. Theurgy involved ecstatic trances and séances to unite with the God and to gain specific powers from the specific God.[44] Whether the phenomenon was judged to be religion or magic depended on a long social discourse of conflict and resolution in any number of different contexts.[45]

The Hekhaloth texts in Jewish mysticism and also the documents known as the Hermetic Literature[46] are very much part of the theurgic movement. They all involve the use of trance to ascend to the heavens and accomplish some religious end. By the end of the fourth century, whatever their diverse beginnings, these religious groups would have all been seen as similar phenomena. The relationship between theurgy and Hekhalot mysticism is especially interesting. For instance, one of the procedures noted by Leda Ciraolo to bring down a star or, in one case, the constellation Orion as a *parhedros* (a "familiar"), resembles to a great degree the kinds of procedures used in Merkabah mysticism to swear an angel to do one's bidding.[47]

Philosophers of the fourth century were not only the academics we expect them to be today but also members of philosophical communities which look very much like religious voluntary associations *(thiasoi)*. Certainly the Jews who performed the Hekhaloth ascensions were also members of a very highly defined religious community. Michael Swartz's book, *Scholastic Magic* suggests formal philological grounds for distinguishing between the ascent techniques and the *Sar Torah* ("Prince of Torah") material. The Poimandres, also known as *Corpus Hermeticum* I, as well as Tractate VII, make clear that the speaker belongs to a community of like-minded people with a mutually agreed ethics where there is a missionary impulse and perhaps even a kind of eschatology present. It would be hard to say which of these phenomena was earlier but the origin is not the issue. Hypothesizing an origin for a religious phenomenon is actually more like projecting a theory onto the past.

In any case, it is clear from the hermetic literature, from magic, and these writings that the separability of the soul from the body was confirmed in these ecstatic states—indeed, standing outside the body is exactly what "ecstasy" means in Greek. These RISC experiences naturally confirmed that the classical worldview was correct, just as they confirmed for the apocalypticist the notion that he was part of the elite who would soon be transformed into an angel as a reward for his patience and suffering in God's name. Both of these experiences were, with no difficulty at all, called prophecy in the ancient communities that produced them, though they could also be known by other names.

The long-standing consensus among Jewish scholars, based indeed on the Rabbinic proposition that prophecy had ceased centuries before the rise of Christianity, is challenged even by such a "rationalist" as Josephus. As Rebecca Gray shows in her provocative book on prophecy in Second Temple times, Josephus was capable not only of ascribing prophecy to ordinary people who were almost contemporaries but also understanding that the prophecy was for the purposes of disclosing notions of "immortality of the soul," as he always calls notions of life after death:[48]

> I do not consider such stories extraneous to my history, since they concern these royal persons, and in addition, they provide instances of something bearing on the *immortality of the soul* and of the way in which God's providence embraces human affairs; therefore I have thought it well to speak of this. (*Ant.* 17.354)

Josephus demonstrates his faith in life after death by the fact that a deceased person named Alexander, the husband of Glaphyra, appears to her in this prophetic dream, thus showing God's "providential care." Josephus understands that such an important aspect of God's special providence for the righteous is revealed through prophecy and that this further demonstrates that the soul is immortal. Josephus never questions the notion that the soul of a deceased husband can actually appear in a dream-vision. He illustrates that even Hellenistic intellectuals valued their dreams as divine proof that God would immortalize them after death.

Apocalypticists likewise held that the righteous would be absorbed into God's human form. Hellenistic intellectuals thought that the soul was separable from the body, that it remembered the basics of life from previous existences, that it was immortal and so would guarantee preservation of knowledge and consciousness into the infinite future. All of that was vouchsafed to the ancients through altered states of consciousness. At the same time, their descriptions of the presumed afterlife helped them define who they were in their own society.

9

Sectarian Life in New Testament Times

THE TWO DIFFERENT views of afterlife in Jewish society—resurrection of the body and immortality of the soul—begin to be blended together in various ways in the last centuries BCE and the first centuries CE. One great exception to this blending of doctrines of the afterlife is the nascent Christian movement, which at first eschews the notion of the immortality of the soul as hostile to its message. After a century, the church, as it spreads through the Hellenistic world, began to synthesize the resurrection of the body with the immortality of the soul in ways that made sense to its growing Hellenistic audience.

Tombstones and Epitaphs

DURING THE LATE Hellenistic period, we find a great many important epitaphs and graffiti. Not many mention resurrection or immortality explicitly but one should not conclude that views of the afterlife were equally rare. Even the few we have show that the idea was percolating through society. Especially by the third and fourth century CE and later, from whence most of them came, notions of afterlife were widespread within the Jewish and Christian communities.

The fact is that not everyone chooses to mention resurrection or immortality of the soul on a tombstone, where thoughts of mortality may be equally apposite. In New England cemeteries of the seventeenth and eighteenth centuries, one finds thoughts of mortality regularly, mentions of resurrection rarely. One should not from that distribution of evidence conclude that the American colonists were not Christians.

The evidence from tombs has been well collected in a variety of archeological publications and gathered in the handy summary of Pieter W. van der Horst.[1] The majority of tombstones from the Hellenistic period concentrated on the life and death of the occupant of the tomb; or else they cursed anyone who would desecrate the grave. For instance, this widely-quoted one:

> Here under the shelter of this stone, stranger, lies . . .
> Demas, deserting the old age of his very pitiable mother
> and his pitable little children and his mourning wife.
> He helped many men by his skill.
> Weep for the man who has left the most honourable . . .
> and his city, and the abodes and friendship of men.
> Demas, about thirty years old, in the fifty-fourth year,
>   the third of the month Hathyr.
> You too, Alexander, friend of all and without reproach,
>   excellent one, farewell.
>   (Leontopolis, 117 BCE, van der Horst, 154)[2]

There is no mention of the afterlife.

On the other hand, notions of afterlife are more frequent in the later centuries than the early ones. Sometimes they make an unusual appearance:

> I, Hesychios, lie here with my wife. May anyone who dares to open [the grave] above us not have a portion in the eternal life. (129)
> > or
> Whoever would change this lady's place [i.e. the woman buried in this grave], He who promised to resurrect the dead will Himself judge. (162)

This is certainly not the kind of appearance one would expect of a religious innovation as momentous as beatific afterlife. On the tombstone, it is the graverobber who is threatened with the lack of an afterlife rather than the pious dead who is lauded with its surety. It even leaves grounds for thinking that the writers were using the conception ironically, expecting that it would be effective in keeping the grave safe from the rabble. It, however, leaves no doubt that such a belief is to be found amongst the Jews by late Antique times.

Even more, the following short graffito is of uncertain tone: "Good Luck on your Resurrection!" (van der Horst, 194)[3] It is hard to know exactly how to understand this sentiment. One wants to think it is a pious wish, but a nagging feeling of facetiousness accompanies any modern reaction to the line. Perhaps it would be better to translate it as "Good fortune on your resurrection!" One thing is clear: Resurrection was clearly a well understood notion in the community by the fourth century. Exactly what happened earlier can only be resolved by looking at texts.

Prelude: The Book of Jubilees

JUBILEES IS centuries older than these epitaphs, though it is also hard to tell exactly what or how old the book of Jubilees is. It presents itself as a revelation given to Moses and rehearses all the history of Genesis down to the time of Moses, as a kind of Midrash. It has left its mark at Qumran and in many other documents like *The Genesis Apocryphon* and *The Temple Scroll*. It is a rehashing of the story, with new motifs added, including some apocalyptic ones like the division of all history into Jubilee periods of 49 years, but it is not an apocalyptic book in and of itself. The earliest copy of the text was found at Qumran in Hebrew but it is widely known elsewhere in Greek, Syriac, Latin, and Ethiopic. It is not known for sure whether the book was written at Qumran or just happened to be found in their library. In that book, right after the death of Abraham, there is an interesting report about the end of time:

And he lived three jubilees and four weeks of years, one hundred and seventy-five years. And he completed the days of his life, being old and full of days. For the days of the lives of the ancients were nineteen jubilees. And after the Flood they began to be less than nineteen jubilees and to grow old quickly and to shorten the days of their lives due to much suffering and through the evil of their ways—except Abraham. For Abraham was perfect in all of his actions with the LORD and was pleasing through righteousness all of the days of his life. And behold, he did not complete four jubilees in his life until he grew old in the presence of evil (and) his days were full.

And all of the generations which will arise henceforth and until the day of the great judgment will grow old quickly before they complete

353

two jubilees, and their knowledge will forsake them because of their old age. And all of their knowledge will be removed. And in those days if a man will live a jubilee and a half, they will say about him. "He prolonged his life, but the majority of his days were suffering and anxiety and affliction. And there was no peace, because plague (came) upon plague, and wound upon wound, and affliction upon affliction, and evil report upon evil report, and sickness upon sickness, and every evil judgment of this sort one with another: sickness, and downfall, and sleet, and hail, and frost, and fever, and chills, and stupor, and famine, and death, and sword, and captivity, and all plagues, and suffering. (*Jub.* 23:8–15)

But after all that, things will begin to reverse themselves:

> And in those days, children will begin to search the law,
> and to search the commandments
> and to return to the way of righteousness.
> And the days will begin to increase and grow longer
> among those sons of men, generation by generation,
> and year by year, until
> their days approach a thousand years,
> and to a great number of years than days.
> And there (will be) no old men and none who is full of days.
> Because all of them will be infants and children.
> And all of their days they will be complete
> and live in peace and rejoicing
> and there will be no Satan and no evil (one) who will destroy,
> because all of their days will be days of blessing and healing.
> (*Jub.* 23:26–29)

In the end of time, they shall regain those fabulous ages of the primeval heroes. *Jubilees* 23:30–31 even speaks of the healing of God's "servants" and "righteous ones." They will "rise up" and drive out their enemies, obviously on this earth. They will see and give great praise and rejoice forever and ever with joy. This much is clearly a national restoration.

This is as Isaiah 65:20–22 predicts but carried to more extreme limits. It is almost as if they will return to the garden of Eden. But it does give history a certain kind of symmetry. It also does something very much more interesting with regard to the issue of afterlife. It says that the apocalyptic end will approximate the incredibly long lives of the ancient heroes, an

354

eschatology fit for the Samaritans, as they base their entire religious future on the first five books of Moses. But it is not a Samaritan vision because it valorizes Jerusalem. Rather it is an exegetical exercise about how to read the beginning of the Bible as the key to the end of history, without relying on anything else. And the emphasis is on priests. It is based on the depiction of history in the five books of Moses and may just be an independent and native view of the future. But unlike the view of life in Daniel, it does not have an obvious evil end for the political overlords of the country. One supposes that they will merely lose their possessions and not gain the rewards of the faithful. The book of Jubilees illustrates a parallel that often exists between the original times and the end time, an *Urzeit* = *Endzeit* parallel (beginning of time = end of time), as German scholarship has aptly dubbed it.

It is, however, combined with the more traditional notion of resurrection as well:

> And then the Lord will heal his servants,
> and they will rise up and see great peace.
> And they will drive out their enemies,
> and the righteous ones will see and give praise,
> and rejoice forever and ever with joy;
> and they will see all of their judgments and all of their curses
>   among their enemies.
> And their bones will rest in the earth,
> and their spirits will increase joy,
> and they will know that the LORD is an executor of judgment,
> but he will show mercy to hundreds and thousands,
> to all who love him. (*Jub.* 23:30–31)

This passage in Jubilees is also found in Qumran MS 4Q176 21.[4] This is a very unusual passage in that there will be resurrection, but the bones of the righteous will remain in the earth while their spirits will increase in joy, at least at first. Thus, a sort of resurrection is blended with a sort of immortality of the soul, though neither one of them is a typical example of that belief. The "spirit" and "bone" motif is very reminiscent of Ezekiel 37. Immortality of the soul is not spelled out in any philosophically meaningful way. Indeed, what will increase joy is called "spirit" not soul, in the same way that Paul seems to favor "spirit" over the Greek "soul." Here, immortality is simply added into the narrative as another marvelous aspect of the coming redemption. Perhaps it suggests that the saints will be angels until the last days. In any event it shows a distinct predisposition to mix any of a range of afterlife possibilities and read them back into the five books of Moses. There is no particular reason why this passage could not illustrate the combination of the originally Greek notion of the immortality of the soul with the apocalyptic notion of the resurrection of the body; such a combination is found quite frequently in later literature. It is just unusual so early.[5]

The Parables of Enoch (1 En 37–71)

WE HAVE ALREADY studied the beginning of the book of 1 *Enoch*, material which is undoubtedly older than Christianity, probably by centuries. But in 1 *Enoch* 37–71 we are presented with a dating quandary. If the "manlike figure" was not necessarily an earthly figure whose identity was sought before Jesus, there may have been at least one other person who was assumed to fit the role and who clearly predates Jesus: Enoch, as portrayed in the Enochic literature, now known to be widespread in Judaism through the Dead Sea Scrolls.[6] We have also already surveyed the Enoch material generally and seen its relationship to priesthood, secret knowledge, heavenly transformation, and the Dead Sea Scroll community. Now let us look at it in more detail. It is also crucial for understanding the thought-world of early Christianity. Unfortunately, we do not know how to date the parables. They appear to be early but they are missing from the Enoch material at Qumran, raising the prospect that they may themselves be a later, even a Christian composition, since they appear most prominently in the version of 1 *Enoch* found in the Ethiopian Christian canon.

First, let us see what is in them. In *The Parables of Enoch* (1 En 37–71) comes the climax of angelification in the earliest Enoch material, though exactly where this passage falls in the development of the Enoch tradition is ambiguous. Enoch performs various Messianic functions. He is righteous and knows divine secrets (46:3). He is victorious over the mighty of the earth, whereupon he judges the wicked (46:4–8; 62:9; 63:11; 69:27–29). He is probably the same figure as "The Chosen One" or "The Elect One" and the "messiah," since virtually identical functions are attributed to all three figures (49:2–4; 51:3–5; 52:4–9; 55:4; 61:4–9; 62:2–16).[7] He judges "in the name of the LORD of Spirits" (55:4), sitting on the throne (51:3; 55:4; 61:8; 62:2–6; 70:27) and at the end of his life, he reascends to his enthroned status.

The Parables of Enoch contain several references to angelic transformation. In chapter 39, Enoch ascends to heaven while reciting hymns and blessings, where he is overcome with the splendor of the throne rooms. His face changes on account of the vision, which evidently reflects the experience of the prophecy that "those who are wise shall shine as the stars" (Dan 11:2), because *1 Enoch* 62:15 states that the elect shall shine as stars and be clothed with garments of glory.

The Parables of Enoch strongly emphasize the role of a Messianic figure called the "Son of Man" (46:1–4; 48:2–7; 49:2–4; 61:8–9; 62:1–7, 13–14; 69:26–29; 71:14–15). No doubt, these passages are meant to exegete and make clear who is the figure enthroned next to God in Daniel 7:13–14. For this literature, he is the messiah, an anointed ruler of Israel (42:4; 48:10). Daniel 7:13–14 concentrates not on the human attributes of this figure but his role in the final judgment. Any Messianic role is missing in the Daniel text. But for this part of the Enoch literature, the Son of Man was messiah, a heavenly ascender and heir to the divine realm. The Messianic expectation and the expectation that the evil oppressors will be punished are quite parallel.

This seems like a commonplace to us who are used to Christian claims for the role of the messiah. But it is an innovation here. No previous interpretation of Daniel 7 has specified that the second figure enthroned in heaven is the Messiah. Indeed, the heavenly location of the scene and the enormous stature of the figures argues strongly against any Messianic interpretation and for a divine or angelic interpretation. In other depictions of the end, it is sometimes a messiah who will punish the evil ones; but just as often there is no messiah in the plan. Sometimes the whole story of the end of the world is narrated with no mention of a Messianic figure, as is true of Daniel 7.

In *1 Enoch,* we are also treated to a description of the process by which humans are transformed into stars (more exactly, angels), just as Daniel 12 prophesies. The Daniel prophecy is discussed in chapter 39, where Enoch views the dwelling places of the elect, the righteous and the angels together, all as luminous creatures. In chapter 62, the righteous are described as rising from the earth with that "Son of Man." They will receive eternally new garments of glory, which will become garments of life for them, from the LORD of spirits. (This imagery often suggests a baptizing community since unclothing and reclothing are part of the baptismal ritual and are often exegeted in baptismal liturgies as a transformation of one's very essence.)

More importantly, at the end of *The Parables of Enoch* in chapters

70–71, Enoch is mystically transformed into the figure of the "Son of Man" on the throne: "My whole body [was] mollified and my spirit transformed" (*1 En* 71:11). This is an extraordinarily important event, as it describes a mystic transformation of the heavenly journeyer Enoch into the angelic vice-regent of God, giving a plausible explanation of how the sectarians that produced the visions in Daniel expected to be transformed into stars. *First Enoch* 71 gives us not just the fulfillment of the prophecy in Daniel 12 but a first-person, confessional report of the very experience of undergoing the astral transformation, albeit in the name of a pseudepigraphical hero. No doubt this process is not just a unique event but the archetypical event for the transformation of the saints to come. That means that Jesus' transformation into "the Son of Man" was not a single and unique event for the Ethiopian Christian church—rather the most important, if not the first, of a series of angelic transformations. Since it is a confessional report, it is likely to be the interpretation of someone's mystical RASC experience.

Where this material actually fits in the development of Enoch tradition is not clear. The received text, Ethiopic Enoch, is canonized by the Ethiopian Christian church and has a regular part in their Bible. But that is not the only extant version of this book. At Qumran, *1 Enoch* is present except chapters 37–71 are missing. In its place we find a "Book of the Giants" in Aramaic. Chapters 37–71, "The Parables," are therefore known to us primarily in a Christian edition, where the "Son of Man" has already been identified as the Christ. How it is possible for Enoch to be absorbed into the figure who will later be identified as the Christ in Ethiopian Christianity has never been fully explained. But it may be that the Christian community, like Jewish communities before and after it, interpreted "the manlike figure in heaven" ("Son of Man") not as a title but merely as "a human figure," as the archetype for the angelification of all the saints at the end of time. The *geʿez* (the ancient Ethiopic language) actually uses several closely related terms for the "Son of Man," suggesting that it is not a title. "Son of Man" does not seem like a title in the Gospels either, since it only occurs in the mouth of Jesus. Likely, "Son of Man" was not originally a title in Judaism either, merely one more reference to the unnamed, human figure in Daniel 7:13ff.[8]

Because the ecstatic ascent of the living parallels exactly the ascent of the dead after death, *Enoch* 70–71 may retell Enoch's previous earthly ascent. More likely, it refers to Enoch's ascent at the end of his short (only 365-year!) life. The number, of course, connects Enoch with the solar calendar, which the Qumran community used instead of the more usual lunar calendar of Semitic lands. The sun was also, as we have seen, an important symbol of regeneration and afterlife, since it visits the lands of the dead underground. And it was the basis of their 365-day solar calendar, which makes them "the children of light," in opposition to the "children of darkness," who are evidently everybody who observes the lunar calendar—or, essentially, everyone else.[9]

That would suggest even more that the path Enoch takes in mystical ascent is the path to secret knowledge and the same path that the righteous person takes at life's end. It is a path upward through the workings of the zodiac and the heavens, which is known because Enoch's journey there in primeval times was recorded in the secret literature of the group. The puzzling superscription to chapter 70, the composite nature of the text, and some possible imprecision in chronology prevent complete surety on this issue: "And it happened after this that his living name was raised up before that Son of Man and to the LORD from among those who dwell upon the earth" (1 En 70:1).

The journey was taken by Enoch's "name," not precisely his "soul," again reflecting a level of mystical speculation that predates the full effects of the importation Platonic notion of immortality of the soul into Jewish culture. Enoch's name is, in effect, an anomalous way to resolve the question of identity, another way to express the "self." What is the continuity between the earthly Enoch and his heavenly twin? It is his "name." Very likely, this is meant to be a unique expression of Enoch's identity and may refer to the tradition that the names of the righteous and the messiah were stored under God's throne at the beginning of time.

Ordinary folk have souls. There are "souls" in the holding pens; what exactly is implied by the term "souls" is not precisely explained. They could be equally pre-Platonic *psychai* or the more Biblical Hebrew *nefashot*. But they are not explicitly immortal in themselves, because not all of them will be resurrected in bodies at the end; nor are they explicitly the carriers and recipients of the consciousness of the person. They are not explicitly Platonic souls as there is no reference to consciousness or memory, which are defining issues for Platonic thinking. They merely mark the identity of the dead. On the other hand, they may show the beginning of the combination of the two conceptions in narrative (where it will be easier to accomplish than in philosophical literature).

359

The Apocalypses (1 En 72–90)
and the Epistle of Enoch (91–107)

OTHER ASPECTS of the prophecy in Daniel, or perhaps of Daniel together with *Jubilees* 23:30–31, can be seen in later Enochian interpretations. In *1 Enoch* 90:37–39, in the vision of the white bull (or cow),[10] believers are mystically transformed into white cattle, which in turn, appear to symbolize the messiah:

And I [Enoch] saw that a snow-white cow was born, with huge horns; all the beasts of the field and all the birds of the sky feared him and made petition to him all the time. I went on seeing until all their kindred were transformed, and became snow-white cows; and the first among them became something, and that something became a great beast with huge horns on its head. The Lord of the Sheep rejoiced over it and over all the cows. I myself became satiated in their midst. Then I woke up and saw everything.

After the transformation of the messiah, the believers also are transformed into white cows. Thus symbolically, the believers come to share the being of the messiah. The messiah not only saves but serves as the model for transformation of believers. In 91:10 there is an explicit statement that the righteous one shall arise from sleep and that prophecy is repeated in a somewhat longer statement in 92:3–4. In both cases the reference to sleep is an indication that the text is relying on Isaiah 26 and Daniel 12.

Enoch 102–104 does not explicitly mention a general resurrection of the dead, only a reward for those who have died in righteousness. The destinies of the righteous and the sinners are adumbrated in chapter 103 and following:

For all good things, and joy and honor are prepared for and written down for the souls of those who died in righteousness. Many and good things shall be given to you—the offshoot of your labors. Your lot exceeds even that of the living ones. The spirits of those who died in righteousness shall live and rejoice; their spirits shall not perish, nor their memorial from before the face of the Great One unto all the generations of the world. Therefore, do not worry about their humiliation. "Woe to you sinners who are dead! When you are dead in the wealth of your sins, those who are like you will say of you, 'Happy are you sinners! (The sinners) have seen all their days. They have died now in prosperity and wealth. They have not experienced struggle and battle in their lifetime. They have died in glory, and there was no judgment in their lifetime. You yourselves know that they will bring your souls down to Sheol; and they shall experience evil and great tribulation—in darkness, nets, and burning flame. Your souls shall enter into the great judgment; it shall be a great judgment in all the generations of the world. Woe unto you, for there is no peace for you! (*1 En* 103:3–8)

The souls are again important as narrative details but are not described as the immortal souls of Greek philosophy because there is no interest in continuity of consciousness for philosophical development in these documents. But unlike many other depictions, these souls go down to Sheol for judgment. While they are damned, they are the lucky ones among the damned for they will not have to experience judgment in this life, the fate of the evil of the days of the apocalypse. Surely, this is the punch line of the apocalypse: The evil ones alive today are going to experience the worst possible tortures. But we notice one more thing—having been emptied of the righteous, Sheol has now been fully refurbished as Hell, the place of punishment for the sinners.

One might say that there is some unacknowledged Greek influence in this anomalous vision. But it is more likely to be a kind of natural variation on a Hebrew notion, a variant of the native Israelite notion of the *nefesh,* the personality of the believer. One needs to have a carrier of identity so that a sinner is sentenced to special punishments. There is no attention to philosophical adequacy in these stories; only the necessity of making a narrative link between people on earth and the dead who are judged. These Jewish notions overlap with popular Greek notions of the "soul" and they do not imply anything more than "shades" or "ghosts" or "spirits." [11]

The righteous will find in the hereafter all the rewards that eluded them in this life. In chapter 104, the righteous are exhorted to remain faithful, even though they see the sinners benefitting from their evil actions in this unredeemed world:

But you shall shine like the lights of heaven, and you shall be seen; and the windows of heaven shall be opened for you. Your cry shall be heard. Cry for judgment, and it shall appear for you; for all your tribulations shall be (demanded) for investigation from the (responsible) authorities—from everyone who assisted those who plundered you. Be hopeful, and do not abandon your hope, because there shall be a fire for you. You are about to be making a great rejoicing like [or: as] the angels of heaven. You shall not have to hide on the day of the great judgment, and you shall not be found as the sinners; but the eternal judgment shall be (far) away from you for all the generations of the world. Now fear not, righteous ones, when you see the sinners waxing strong and flourishing; do not be partners with them, but keep far away from those who lean onto their own injustice; for you are to be partners with the good-hearted people of heaven. (*1 En* 104:2–7)

In the end, the reward will be theirs. They will appear as the stars in heaven and will shine "like the lights of the heavens," clearly an interpretation of Daniel 12. For the Biblical "windows of heaven" the Ethiopic translated closely, while the Greek translated according its more familiar classical idiom: "the gates of heaven." The Greek also clarified that the good hearted people in heaven are the angels.

The Epistle of Enoch and Resurrection

THERE IS ROOM to doubt whether the explicit raising of the dead is a teaching of the section of *1 Enoch* known as "the Epistle of Enoch" (*1 En* 91–105). Resurrection may be assumed but not mentioned, though there is no indication that it is assumed. Both Nickelsburg and Cavallin point out that resurrection of the dead is not explicitly affirmed in this section.[12] Yet chapters 102–4 speak of a retribution immediately after physical demise. Sinners scoff that righteousness has no reward since all die (*1 En* 102:7). But the writer affirms a mystery because he has been given a glimpse of heavenly books. Daniel promised resurrection to some, judgment to some, and transformation to some. While the text generally preseves the categories defined by Daniel 12, it does not describe them all in detail. The trip itself, the heavenly journey, offers first-person testimony that the scoffers are wrong.

Evident in Daniel and from the literature at Qumran, those people who believed in resurrection had little patience with the Greco-Roman overlords of the country. They may have been part of actively revolutionary sects, though determined, passive resistance was even more typical of Israelite sectarian life. The resurrection traditions encouraged martyrs against the dominant, imperialistic culture. Nor did they like the upper classes of Judaea, those who cooperated with the Romans and who gained their income from serving and aiding the foreign "occupiers."

The newly published texts at Qumran show that they believed in resurrection, no doubt as angels and as stars, as Josephus implies with his descriptions of Essenic afterlife beliefs. Although these promises of resurrection, ascension, and heavenly immortality as angels came from a sectarian background, the ideas were attractive enough to the culture as a whole that they spread out far more broadly than the sectarian conventicles of first-century CE Judaism. The ideas appeared in less defined form among the Pharisees, who were hardly a millenarian sect, though they apparently did have a distinct group identity. But to fully understand how these ideas filtered through the society, we must look at another notion of life after death, immortality of the soul, and the wider context of sectarian life in Judaism, including Christianity.

The Septuagint

THE SEPTUAGINT is the ancient translation of the Hebrew Bible into Greek. The *Letter of Aristeas* propounds that the Septuagint was produced by the royal *fiat* of Ptolemy Philadelphus, the Greek Ruler of Egypt, but it appears also to reflect the scriptural understandings of several generations of Hellenistic Jews, who themselves were progressively less able to understand the Hebrew text. The legendary beginnings of the book are that it was produced by seventy (hence the abbreviation LXX; Septuaginta means "seventy" in Latin) scholars working at Ptolemy's behest. Begun by the third century BCE and completed before 132 BCE, the Septuagint differs from the Hebrew Bible in both content and meaning. First it contains a number of interesting books that Rabbinic Judaism later excluded as noncanonical—for instance, the books of 1 and 2 Maccabees.

Even the order of the books of the Bible is different in the Septuagint; the Greek Bible has been reorganized in more complicated categories, including sections for historical books, wisdom, and prophecy, as well as the Torah (first five books of Moses). Although the translation sometimes is quite literal, in other places it is as much a commentary as a translation. Some scholars hold that the readings of the Septuagint reflect the actual meaning of the original Hebrew, while the received Jewish text, the so-called Masoretic Text (MT), is a departure from it. The Dead Sea Scrolls often present a Hebrew text closer to the LXX than the MT, giving some credence to its early witness of Bible readings, especially in Samuel and Jeremiah. Other passages, however, simply evidence Christian interpolations. However that problem may be resolved, the commentary on various passages gives us an inkling of how the Hellenistic Jewish community could understand its Bible. One of the most interesting things about the LXX is the way in which resurrection creeps into its pages. In this respect the LXX is clearly innovative over the MT.

Because the Hellenistic period does contain a notion of an immortal soul, as well as resurrection of the body, the translators of the Septuagint understood several Biblical passages in light of their own times. In some places, where the Hebrew is ambiguous in meaning, the later Greek translation resolves the ambiguity in the direction of the afterlife. Many of the passages in the Hebrew Bible that are used later to demonstrate life after death consequently meant considerably less in Hebrew than they are made to mean in Greek. Sometimes modern English translations side with the tendentious Greek translations instead of leaving the ambiguity intact. We have seen passages like this, which can imply resuscitation in the Hebrew Bible. For instance:

> See now that I, even I, am he, and there is no God beside me; I kill and make alive. (Deut 32:39)

> . . . the Lord kills and brings to life; he brings down to Sheol and raises up. . . . (1 Sam 2:6)

> "Am I God to kill and make alive?" (2 Kgs 5:7)

The first two passages are found in poetic portions in Hebrew, "The Song of Moses" (Deut 32:1–43) and Hannah's *Magnificat* at the birth of Samuel (1 Sam 2:1–10). Both "psalms" take as their most central theme praise for God's power in saving and preserving His people. The order of the verbs may say that God first kills and then brings to life, as the Septuagint appears to want to translate. But the poetry may only be saying that God has the power of life and death. He may kill one person and then bring another to life, conventional powers of YHWH which were also said of Ba'al, for instance. In other words, the word *meḥayyeh*, a *pi'el* intensive or causative form of the verb "live," perhaps ought more accurately to be translated as "preserve or keep alive," rather than "make alive" or "resurrect," as several translations prefer. It may also be hinting at something more, that God may kill and resuscitate the same person to finish out his normal life, though this interpretation seems a bit forced. The Greek, which reflects a much later time when such notions were more common, translates in a more tendentious fashion, in which resurrection is hinted at and which gives an excuse to tendentious Bible translators.

Like several other additions, this passage may show Christian tampering, as Christianity used the Greek text widely in their liturgical life.

In Deuteronomy 32:39, the Hebrew verbs for "I kill and I preserve" are rendered into Greek literally as "I [shall] kill and I [shall] make alive." All the verbs are placed in the future tense, which can easily translate the Hebrew imperfect, though the sense here would be better translated with a simple Greek present tense. Does the future suggest here that the Greek text is stressing judgment at the end of time or future life or resurrection? There really is no sure way to tell, though a great many grammatical arguments have forced this interpretation beyond credibility.

So too with Psalm 1:5 and Psalm 21 (22):30.[13] Psalm 49 (LXX:48):16 was an interesting crux for us (see chap. 3): "But God will ransom my soul from the power of Sheol, for he will receive me [Selah]." The Hebrew for "for" is *ki*, which is rendered into Greek as *hotan*, meaning "when," yielding a less ambiguous reading than the Hebrew: "God will ransom my soul from the power of Sheol when he shall receive me." Certainly, this interpretation makes immortality far more obvious in the Greek than in the Hebrew text. But the small change also results in the implication that a beatific afterlife comes directly after death.

Similarly Proverbs 12:28 is occasionally cited as an example of life after death. The verse in Hebrew reads, "In the path of righteousness is life, but the way of path (?) leads (*'al māvvet*). The Hebrew text is corrupt. *Netivah* ("path" or possibly "her path") is extremely hard to interpret and seems out of context. Consequently, there is no obvious translation of this phrase into English. The Septuagint (LXX), which was not slow to find immortality in the Hebrew Bible, translates the phrase as "In the roads of righteousness is life but the roads of those remembering evil is death." "Remembering evil" appears to refer to those fools who hold grudges or who spread libel. LXX does not pick up on any connotations of immortality in the book, in spite of its otherwise well noted proclivities to expound immortality.

Furthermore, the verse has another problem, the phrase, *'al mavvet*, which has traditionally been interpreted as "to death" can be interpreted as "immortality," since *'el* usually means "to," but can mean "not" in a few contexts. The later is usually thought to be a far-fetched and somewhat tendentious interpretation, as it is not an easily understandable translation grammatically at this spot in Hebrew. Mitchell Dahood, however, pointed out that there is a similar phrase in Ugaritic (*blmt*, perhaps to be vocalized *b'al mawwet*), which usually dos mean "immortality." This parallel has brought the previous translation into question and given great encouragement to those who would like to push the interpretation of "immortality." As a result, just five years later, R. B. Y. Scott, translated Proverbs 12:28, "On the road of righteousness there is life, and the treading of its path is deathlessness." [14] The translation is very well expressed in English, showing Scott to be a master translator. It is at the height of the scholarly enchantment with the texts from Ugarit. But several considerations argue against his rendering and suggest that we should allow the pendulum to swing back in the original direction. First, nowhere else in Hebrew do we find this phrase used in this way. Second, and more crucial, the stylistic context of this chapter of Proverbs is very easy to describe and is quite different from the "immortality" interpretation. This makes the whole translation dubious.

The stylistic context is this: Each couplet in this chapter and the next is made up of antithetical statements, expressing the familiar, two-path theme of righteousness and folly. Each couplet contrasts the wise person with the fool in an antithetic way. This translation would violate that almost invariable form; the more traditional translation leaves that antithetic scheme intact. Rather, it looks like this is a place where the Septuagint's translation is correct because it had an earlier reading, which had become corrupted and undecipherable by the time of the Masoretes. Thus, this is a case where the exact Hebrew text has been lost but the Greek LXX has preserved the basic meaning, that fits the context of these chapters. 'Al mavvet means "to death" and not "to immortality."

Psalm 65 (66):1, 9 receives "of the resurrection" in the Septuagint without any Hebrew equivalent in the Masoretic Text. This seems to be an early Christian gloss, as the psalm was used liturgically by Christians in the feast of the resurrection. The Greek rendering of verse 9a likewise has "for my soul" in place of the Hebrew "our soul" and "to life" in place of the Hebrew "in life." This suggest an innovative Greek interpretation of a deathless state for the individual soul, a personal immortality, whereas the Hebrew version speaks of deliverance for the whole person in this life. Like the previous example, it is likely a gloss inserted by Christians to make their own beliefs more obvious.

Job 14:14 has been rendered in such a way as to directly contradict the Hebrew text. Job asked whether a person shall live again. His answer was "No!" But the LXX answers "Yes." The Greek translates the answer: "I will wait until I exist again. Then You shall call and I will listen to You." All these clear departures from the Hebrew text add resurrection into the text. None unambiguously insert the immortality of the soul, though Psalm 49 may have hinted at it. If these interpretations were inserted by the Jewish community, one would expect a mixture of doctrines to occur because immortality of the soul was available and discussed frequently by Hellenistic Jews; but the early Christian community was only interested in the resurrection of the dead. Since the passages most likely imply resurrection of some sort; the nature of the change strongly suggests that they are Christian interpolations.[15]

The Immortality of the Soul in Israel

THE JEWISH community of the diaspora was familiar with Greek notions of immortality of the soul because some of them had studied Greek philosophy. In order to fill in the portrait of the afterlife in Second Temple Judaism, we have to leave the sectarian, religious revolutionary context of the doctrine of resurrection and visit with the aristocracy. The immortality of the soul was explicitly borrowed from Platonism. It tended to interest Jews who lived in quite different neighborhoods from those who cherished resurrection. The immortality of the soul was, at first, a very intellectual notion in Jewry; in this period, intellectuals mostly lived in the very best neighborhoods.

The vector for the innovation was a group of affluent Jews who had Greek educations and who valued Greek literacy, advancing far beyond use of serviceable Greek in pursuit of commerce and trade. Not even all the aristocracy adopted these notions and those who did, did so slowly over centuries. The classes of Judea and Jews in general who adopted the idea of the immortality of the soul, with its attendant assumptions about memory and consciousness, were not the same as those who adopted notions of resurrection.

Jews liked immortality of the soul for the same reason that Greeks did. Immortality of the soul appealed to the intellectual elite because it valorized their intellectual pursuits. It was mainly adopted by classes of people who were not only rich but beholden to Greek rule, deeply involved in Greek intellectual ideas, and who were attempting to combine Judaism with the Greek intellectual currents of their day. Immortality of the soul was the ideology of the rich.

One important group of aristocrats who lived in the land of Israel—the Sadducees—rejected all notions of life after death, even though they had Hellenized. This would include many of the Hasmonean dynasty, the descendants of the Maccabees. They had no need of Platonic afterlives to justify their social positions because the Torah gave them hereditary control of the Temple. In fact, as we have seen, they seem to have some considerable Greek education too but they were more interested in the Stoic and Epicurean schools because they best fit the attitude of the received books of the Hebrew Bible.

The intellectuals who adopted a Platonic afterlife from Greek culture were those who made a living in Greek society and needed Greek intellectual credibility for their support. They were part of the client class, those who worked for the upper class rulers, or even sometimes themselves part of the Greco-Roman elite. This would include the Alexandrian Philo Judaeus, Josephus, several other Jewish philosophical writers and the Pharisees, or more exactly, the rabbis, as they gave up their sectarian status and became the ruling body in Jewish life. In doing so, they eventually synthesized the notion of an immortal soul with the notion of bodily resurrection. Christianity also provided another meeting point for the two ideas but they did not blend so easily in Christianity, leaving us with centuries of interesting attempts to synthesize them.

Philo Judaeus (ca 20 BCE–ca 50 CE)

IT IS HARD to say that Philo was typical of anyone but himself. His enormous wealth and power would suggest that he represented the cynosure of Jewish Hellenism, rather than a typical example of it. We also have more of his work than any other Hellenistic Jewish philosopher and perhaps more than any other philosopher, with the exception of Plato and Aristotle. His enormous literary corpus was unique in the Hellenistic Jewish world. He was also unique in his attempt to synthesize Greek with Hebrew thought. His apologetic technique is very sophisticated. He repeatedly maintains that the Hebrew Bible not only illustrates Greek philosophical views through allegory (as do the *Iliad* and *Odyssey,* according to the Greek commentators) but morally surpasses them. For Philo, Greek philosophers and the Hebrew Bible told the same philosophical truth. The Bible is a better and more direct expression of the truth; the Greeks actually imitated the "oracles" of Moses!

Philo was mostly an exegete, writing commentaries on the Biblical works. He rarely indulged in systematic philosophical exposition. So it is difficult to find an epitome of his ideas on any subject. A synthesis of his work must be gleaned from reading many different treatises in concert rather than reading any one philosophical tractate. We have to be satisfied with a brief characterization of his writing on the afterlife rather than an extensive discussion of it.

Philo was born to a very wealthy Alexandrian family, a couple of decades before Jesus. He was a contemporary of both Jesus and Paul, outliving Jesus but probably predeceasing Paul by a few years. Unlike Jesus and like Paul, Philo was born in a major center of Hellenistic culture. But Alexandria was a far greater and more culturally privileged city than Tarsus and Philo's family was likely far richer than Paul's (about whom we know nothing other than Luke's often debated bibliographical summary), as Philo came from one of the wealthiest families in the city.

Strangely, for all his writing, we know little about Philo's personal life. We do not know how his family became rich, though they were well diversified by Philo's birth. As a wealthy boy, Philo presumably received private tutoring, presumably also a *gymnasion* education, that taught him the arts and sciences as well as physical education. Likely, he participated in Greek athletics, which were played naked. His writings give us a window into the wealthiest level of the Jewish aristocracy and the intellectual elite. He saw nothing in these activities per se to detract from his perfect observance of Jewish law, though he did not practice the Jewish law in conformity with the Pharisees. Pharisaism had not much penetrated Alexandria in this period. Philo's life and writing make clear that Jewish observance and Pharisaism were not equated in the first century, especially in the Diaspora. There were, in this period, many legitimate interpretations about how to carry out the commandments that God had given Israel.

Philo lived long enough to accompany the Jewish legation to Rome to intercede with Gaius Caligula (r. 37–41 CE) against various anti-Jewish actions in Alexandria. Philo described himself as an old man when he made this trip to Rome, which took place in the mid-first century CE. His interview with the emperor nearly cost the lives of the whole delegation. The Emperor's decision would certainly have been tragic for the Jews. Providentially, it was the emperor who died. Caligula was assassinated before he could rule on the matter, convincing the Jews of divine intervention in their favor. Claudius, who succeeded Caligula, promulgated the famous rescript that guaranteed the Jews of Alexandria rights enjoyed by the Greek citizenry *(isopoliteia)* though it did not grant citizenship proper.

In his beliefs about life after death, Philo was perhaps representative of the new Jewish intellectual class, well attuned to Greek philosophical traditions, able to understand the Bible and Judaism in the highest Greek philosophical tradition. This is a crucial mark of an acculturated person. Being a good Platonist, Philo discussed the immortality of the soul without ever broaching the resurrection of the body. Since we have previously seen that the Septuagint evinces a distinct interest in resurrection but no obvious clear statement of immortality of the soul, many of the resurrection texts were likely inserted later than Philo, by Christian interpolators.

Philo was an expert at allegorization. He believed that the perfection of the intellectual and moral faculties is what leads to immortality of the soul. We know that Philo had a keen appreciation of Greek athletics. But when thinking of eternal felicity, continuity of consciousness rather than bodily preservation most appealed to Philo's sensibilities.

Philo did not use the word *anastasis* or its derived verb forms which signify "resurrection" in the Septuagint and the New Testament. He did not use any forms derived from *egeiro* to signify postmortem existence, as Paul liked to do. He would not have liked the notion of flesh rising from the dead. Instead, he almost exclusively used the Greek term *athanasia*, immortality, to describe the afterlife. He scarcely mentioned any Messianic hopes about the Jews, hoping to defuse any political issue between pagans and Jews.

But he did valorize Jewish martyrdom, saying that Jews accepted death as if it were "immortality" (*Legat.* 117.2) and says that when threatened by death Jews were given "immortality" (*Legat.* 369.2). He said that Jewish youth sought liberty as eagerly as "immortality" (*Prob.* 117.4). Philo means to call our attention to martyrdom, which he admired, and rewarded with immortality, not resurrection. These are values which the intellectuals in the pagan world understood as well: It was admirable that a person might give his or her life to protect political freedom or to remain true to religious beliefs. Philo accessed his Jewish knowledge, explicitly explaining Jewish notions of martyrdom to his Hellenistic readership by dressing it in Platonic garb.

Philo also made central to his notion of the Bible's message an ascent to see God. In fact, for Philo, the name Israel was itself the designation for ascent of the soul through philosophical contemplation. The allegory was based on a presumed Hebrew etymology. For Philo "Israel" meant "person who saw God," *ish shera'ah el ('îš šerā'ah 'ēl)* in Hebrew. This refers both to Jacob's wrestling with the angel *('El)* and to the people's quest for God in their religious contemplations. It is also applicable to any who pursue philosophy to its correct conclusion, a vision of God. It therefore refers to "anyone" (not just Jews) who employs philosophy to find God. The allegory functions in a universal way in Philo's writing.[16] To support this notion of philosophical ascent as the goal of human life, Philo outlined a clear mystic allegory that culminates in the intellectual and spiritual ascent to heaven to the presence of God, who is the author both of prophecy in this life and immortalization in the next life.

Philo did not so much demonstrate that the soul was immortal as assume it. It is implicit in his anthropology, which is quite consistent throughout. Man is made of flesh and spirit: the body is dust, though it is animated by divine spirit, which is not created but originates directly from the Lord, the Father and Ruler of the Universe. The body is created mutable and impermanent. The soul is immutable, immortal, and permanant. Our lives are created because God directed our souls to be placed within our bodies. This "spirit" or "soul," He breathed into humanity, making him a composite, mutable, and dying creature who, because of his immortal soul, is also an immortal creature. So Philo called humanity the border between mortality and immortality.[17]

Philo would rather cede some of the LORD's power as creator than cede any of His immutability. Anything that the LORD directly created would imply change (and therefore imperfection) in Him; hence the soul, like all the ideas, must be uncreated, while the material creation is the product of an artisan angel, the *demiurge* (artisan, literally: people's worker). The mind is the soul of the soul (*Opif.* 66, *Her.* 55). In so doing, Philo indicated that the center of consciousness, the part that survives death, is the mind and thus valorized it as the transcendent part of humanity, a quite notable innovation on the biblical conception of the "soul." Philo's philosophical terms seem for the first time in Judaism to clearly designate the center of the personality, the personal and individual aspects of spiritual life. For Philo they must do so, as he believed strictly in individual reward and punishment for individual moral decisions. Thus, he tried to demonstrate that some of Plato's notions were not the full truth.

Philo was also the first philosopher to describe the world of ideas, the sum total of all ideas in the universe, with the name *kosmos noētos,* the intelligible world. This conception allowed him to clarify an important aspect of God's divinity (though its full nature is hidden from us). Philo identified this intelligible world with a *hypostasis* (separate manifestation) of God, which he called the *logos,* the rational pattern of the world. The Gospel of John 1:1 translates *logos* as "Word" but it never means "Word" in any lexical sense. It is this rational hypostasis of God which the Gospel of John proclaims as the creative agent in the world (1:3) and is incarnated in the person of Jesus (1:14). Philo would have agreed with the first statement but found the second illogical and impossible. This term already had a long history and a technical meaning in Stoicism but Philo found it advantageous for his own mixture of Stoicism and Platonism, so he developed new meanings and uses for it.

The stoic *logos,* which means rational principle or blueprint, not only functions like the platonic *nous,* reason or divine mind, it is also used by Philo to describe the way in which God acts in this world. Every place where an angel is mentioned in Scripture, Philo understood that the *logos* was present. He also used the word *logos* to refer to YHWH, the tetragrammaton (four-lettered) name of God. This is the name of God that is translated as "LORD" in English Bibles. In Greek, YHWH was already being pronounced *'Adonay* translated as *Kyrios* (meaning "Lord") in Philo's own time. Philo understood *logos* and *kyrios* to denote a divine presence, God's principal angel messenger to the world. Philo understood that God made the world through the *logos,* which in this context is probably best understood as a "blueprint," and is thus to be identified with the Platonic artisan of the material world, known as the *demiurge* (the people's worker). Philo saw Genesis 1 as the creation of the world of ideas, Genesis 2–3 as the creation of the material world. The world of ideas is eternal, even though the ideas were created by God. Philo was trying to synthesize the cosmogony of Plato, which featured an eternal and uncreated world of ideas, with the Biblical narrative of temporal creation. The *logos,* the same divine emanation which is called "Wisdom," can almost be understood as eternal in Proverbs 8 (especially in Greek). It will become a very important aspect of Christian and Jewish mysticism. Philo's identification of the *logos* with the intelligible world was also a crucial step towards the definition of the "self" in Neoplatonism.

For Plato, immortality must also be an attribute of the mind, which is part of the very nature of being human. Mortality, conversely, is directly related to our bodily nature. In direct opposition to Plato, Philo believed that the soul is immortalized by moral behavior so those who do not act morally are condemned to punishment or non-existence at death. Sin causes the soul to lose its immortality. This is the allegorical meaning of the story of the garden of Eden. For Philo the allegorical meaning of this tale was the only meaning; there was no literal, historical garden of Eden because it resorts to too many absurdly naive notions about God. So Genesis 2–3 has an allegorical, moral meaning but no literal truth. The Bible only yields its ultimate truths through allegory. For Philo, the Bible provided a critique of Plato: the immortality of the soul does not necessarily mean its indestructibility.

Although Philo adopted the notion of the immortal soul from Plato, he gave primacy to the kind of ethical behavior that is outlined by the

Bible, instead of the kind of ethical behavior implicit in the practice of Greek philosophy. Philo would not have objected to the practice of philosophy—true philosophy is exactly equal to the life outlined by the Bible—but the reasoning of the philosophers is less perfect than the commands of Scripture. For Philo then, the most important and transcendent value was not consciousness itself but the moral deeds that perfect consciousness. Thus, Philo bent up the Platonic transcendent mind to the portrayal of the Jewish notion of a moral individual. Indeed, true philosophy would coincide perfectly with Biblical morality:

> The souls of those who have given themselves to genuine philosophy
> . . . study to die to the life in the body, that a higher existence immortal and incorporeal in the presence of Him who is himself immortal and uncreated, may be their portion. (*Gig.* 14)

Some of this sounds just like Plato's Socrates, who said that the truly philosophical person lives as though already dead. But for Philo it was the process of moral education itself that brings us into the presence of God and transforms us into immortal creatures. There may be a hint of our previously discussed resurrection and transformation motifs in these doctrines but, if so, they are highly refined. Instead, Philo made clear that the soul enters immortality with all its faculties, including its memory, intact. This was an issue for Platonists but it was hardly an issue at all for Philo. If the soul retained no memory after it left the body, there would be scarce sense in punishing it. It was Philo who crafted the notion of the immortal soul which is so familiar to us in the West; he carved it out of the raw material that Plato bequeathed to him.

There are a few places where Philo even hinted that he knew the more native Jewish interpretation of afterlife, seemingly backing into a notion of resurrection. In the allegory of grief over a rebellious child, Israel, Philo hinted at other kinds of immortality but he did not take the description to the point of contradiction:

> Then like a fond mother she will pity the sons and daughters whom she has lost, who in death and still more when in life were a grief to their parents. Young once more, she will be fruitful and bear a blameless generation to redress the one that went before. (*Migr.* 35; see *Cher.* 27) [18]

Philo, in characteristic fashion, understood Isaiah 54 allegorically. Probably, Philo was not actually thinking of bodily resurrection per se, but the perfection of God's kingdom on earth, which suited his philosophical principles more exactly.

Because Philo thought of the soul as a perfected body, he sometimes described it as made out of the same stuff as stars. He was able to identify the righteous dead with the stars themselves, hence as angels, as we have seen in the apocalyptic literature:

> When Abraham left this mortal life, "he is added to the people of God" (Gen 25:8), in that he inherited incorruption and became equal to the angels, for angels—those unbodied and blessed souls—are the host and people of God. (*Sacr.* 5)

Some would suggest that "equal to angels" means only "like angels." But Philo explained exactly what he meant—they are the unbodied and blessed souls, who are "the people of God." "Equal to" in Greek means "equated with," not "something like angels." [19] Philo was giving us his own interpretation of by-now familiar apocalyptic traditions. But he styled them not in terms of resurrection (they are unincarnate souls) but in terms of incorporeal intelligences. We learn that the stars and the angels are both incorporeal and intelligences:

> The men of God are priests and prophets who have refused to accept membership in the commonwealth of the world and to become citizens therein, but have risen wholly above the sphere of sense-perception and have been translated into the world of the intelligible and dwell there registered as freemen of the commonwealth of ideas, which are imperishable and incorporeal. (*Gig.* 61)

Notice that Philo did not use the standard vocabulary for resurrection in these passages, rather made up his own vocabulary to distinguish his thinking from other Jewish writers. In most passages, however, Philo explicitly regarded death as the soul's liberation from the prison of the body. Here he seems to have tried to accommodate post-Biblical interpretations to his brand of Platonism.

Philo also coded his philosophy according to gender. Matter is feminine and passive to the masculine *logos* and *nous*. Unbridled sexuality is both a distraction and a detraction for both men and women. Unfortunately, it is the influence of women on men with which Philo seemed obsessed. Since women distract men, the influence of women must be limited by human rules and regulation for the good of both sexes. Women, though theoretically the equal of men and equally responsible for their actions, are simply not described as being as responsible as men, because they are prejudicially viewed as weaker in reason. Certainly their will is viewed as weaker; their sexuality must therefore be disciplined by reason. This was a typical judgment of Platonism but Philo seemed more zealous than most in his judgment. Philo highlighted the sexual abstinence and even celibacy of the *Therapeutai*, whom he admired and who were so similar to the Qumran group.[20]

Philo noted that philosophical meditation is transformative in itself. It does not need to end in a right vision of the Existent One:

> Therefore we sympathize in joy with those who love God and seek to understand the nature of the living, even if they fail to discover it; for the vague investigation of what is good is sufficient by itself to cheer the heart, even if it fail to attain the end that it desires. But we participate in indignation against that lover of himself, Cain; because he has left his soul without any conception whatever of the living God, having of deliberate purpose mutilated himself of that faculty by which alone he might have been able to see him. (*Post.* 21)

Philo thus was able to harmonize Judaism with Greek philosophy. For him, both said the same, when each is seen in its finest light.

Josephus as Sociologist of the Sects and Parties of Judaea

PHILO'S ATTEMPT to correct Platonism by means of Biblical truth is paralleled in a converse way by Josephus' description of the sectarian life of Judea in the first century. Josephus was saved from death by Vespacian and so became his client. All his writings were meant to explain Judaism to the educated Roman audience. As apologetic as Philo, Josephus used philosophical terminology in a more popular way to make Jewish notions of the afterlife understandable to his educated pagan Roman audience. In the process he also confirmed that notions of immortality of the soul emanate from the client classes of Judea while resurrection was featured among those opposed to Roman rule.

Josephus described the social classes of first-century CE Judea by mentioning the three most important sects and a "fourth philosophy." He called them "heresies" (*haireseis*) by which he meant only "sects." The Greek had no implication of unacceptable religious views. But neither did he mean "sects" in a technical sociological sense: the groups may have been anything from a technical religious sect to a denomination, even an occupation or voluntary society.

He tells us whom the sects were: There were Sadducees, Pharisees, and Essenes (*J. W.* 2.119; *Ant.* 18.11–12). The Sadducees were closer to an occupational group or a social class; the Pharisees were something like a voluntary association; and the Essenes were a sect in the technical sense. The "fourth philosophy" were the Zealots or political revolutionaries. Josephus considered them "bandits" or perhaps in our idiom, "terrorists."

The Sadducees appeared to be the traditional aristocracy, priestly in nature. On the other hand, their philosophy, which denied life after death, did not appeal to many, according to Josephus (*J. W.* 2.164–65). One doubts whether one could enter this group merely by adopting its philosophy because they were wealthy and priestly. For Josephus, the Sadducees were not merely a social and political grouping; they had clear religious views as well. Or, as we have been noticing throughout the ancient Near East and the classical world, their social position inclined them to a certain disposition toward life after death. "The Sadducees hold that the soul perishes along with body" (*Ant.* 18.16). The Sadducees did not believe in fate, feeling that God is distant from human beings and that we must take responsibility for what we will: "All things lie within our own power so that we ourselves are responsible for our well-being, while we suffer misfortune through our own thoughtlessness" (*Ant.* 13.173). Josephus clearly saw that such a doctrine favored the wealthy. The Sadducees suggested that their wealth was deserved and was just payment for their superior morality. Josephus likely was born into the group, as he was himself descended from a priestly family. But he called them "boorish." In Josephus' organization of the issues, belief in life after death and the issue of justice in this world are intimately connected.[21] Furthermore, Josephus' portrayal of Sadducees is paralleled in the Gospels, where Jesus and Sadducees argue over resurrection (Matt 22:23–33; Mark 12:18–27; Luke 20:27–40).

It was the Sadducees who raised the issue of afterlife because they did not accept it. Jesus demonstrated the concept of resurrection by quoting two different Scriptures and assuming that there can be no contradiction between them. Since Scripture says that YHWH is God of Abraham, Isaac, and Jacob and he is also called "the living God," (actually "God of the living" in Greek), then the patriarchs must still be alive. This was not only an effective argument in the first century CE, the Gospels are especially impressed with it.

The Sadducean Bible would not have contained the visions in Daniel that indubitably propound the notion of resurrection. Although we have no identifiably Sadducean text—that is, no writing that we can identify as specifically Sadducean in a sectarian sense—many Biblical and intertestamental books actually reflect their perspective. Ecclesiastes and Job would be favorite texts of the Sadducees. The Wisdom of Jesus Ben Sira (Ecclesiasticus as it it is called in Greek), which does not contain any concept of beatific immortality, would have been highly prized among them. It would not be too hard to claim it as a Sadducean text. They were an unusual combination of traditional Israelite culture and Hellenistic culture.

Access to Paradise in This Life and the Next

THERE IS A clear parallel between the explicit theology of the Sadducees and their social class. As lords of the land, they had a relatively privileged life. They appeared to need no other rewards than those they took in this world. One might have easily imagined exactly the opposite: the aristocrats took for themselves the rewards of the next world just as they took the rewards of this life. Such was the case in Egypt of the Pharaohs, for instance. Indeed as we have just seen, the great aristocratic Jewish philosopher of Alexandria, Philo Judaeus, adopted a very Platonic notion of the immortality of the soul, which gave primacy to those with the leisure to study.

No universal logic makes any particular correlation between social class and theology inevitable. All that one can claim is that social class remains an important variable in the way religious beliefs are apprehended in any society. What explains this particular correlation between stoic indifference to the afterlife and the traditional aristocracy is Biblical tradition itself. Although the Sadducees were Hellenists, they knew and understood what the Biblical tradition is and they honored it in their own priestly way. The Pharisees characterized the Sadducees as heretics but they were not. Instead of evincing a willful heresy to the tradition of the fathers, the Sadducean position actually reflected the converse. The Sadducees knew that when the Bible is interpreted literally there is scant evidence for any afterlife worth having.

An important architectural feature in the villas of the wealthy only emphasizes the logic of Sadducean religious belief. A number of very interesting studies have been completed on the usage of the word "paradise." [22] It is a loan word into Hebrew from Persian and Greek equally. The term is well known with the meaning of pleasure garden rather than orchard.

377

The late Hellenistic period saw different gardening styles in Persia and in the Hellenistic world. The Greeks preferred to take their leisure in walled gardens with water features but the Persians liked to hunt in enclosed gardens, which the Romans thought unmanly. The Romans also thought that wearing baggy pants like the Persians was effeminate; real men wore dresses, or togas, as they called them.

But a crucial religious corollary to ancient gardening practices has been missed by most scholars: The wealthy called their pleasure garden, with their ordered bowers and with pools and walks, a paradise (sing. *paradeisos*, pl. *paradeisoi*), as Ecclesiastes had called his gardens *pardesim* (sing. *pardes*, paradise): "I made myself gardens and parks, and planted in them all kinds of fruit trees" (Eccles 2:5). The wealthy had a paradise on earth in the back gardens of their estates. Access to a paradise was strictly confined to the wealthy and their guests. This lends an important social connotation to the use of the term "paradise" to designate the afterlife. For instance, the palaces of King Herod contain large architecturally designed gardens, complete with pools for refreshment and beauty.[23] This large architectural feature was called a "paradise" (*paradeisos* in Greek), a pleasure garden, even by the rulers of the Hellenistic world. So, in some sense, the Herodians and Sadducees needed no paradise in the afterlife because they enjoyed paradise daily while on earth. The lower classes envisioned their lives after death in the form that the wealthiest enjoyed in this life and, to complete God's justice, usually denied the aristocrats (whom they thought sinful) access to it.[24]

The Sadducees are not the faulty Bible interpreters that the rabbis wish to make of them. They needed no paradise after death because they found paradise in their backyards. They believed that is exactly what they deserved, as stated in the Bible. Indeed, they stayed closer to the text of the Bible than the rabbis. Their sin was that they were literalists. But Sadducean denial of life after death put them in an understandable and respectable Greek position as well. They were seen as closely related intellectually to the Epicureans of the early Hellenistic period. It takes no stretch of the imagination to see that Stoicism and Epicureanism, with their lack of a beatific afterlife, would have appealed to them. Indeed, Josephus compared them to the Epicureans. Because of this easy and natural connection with Epicureanism, the aristocrats of the land of Israel were able to assume that Greek and Hebrew thought were easily synthesized. Like the aristocratic Epicureans of Greek culture, the traditional "old money" aristocracy of Hellenistic Israel felt that life should be faced in the most steadfast and brave terms, without reference to any beatific afterlife. It was a heroic and noble tradition that came down directly from the Biblical Sheol and from the Greek Hades, which was so well described in the epics. There was no reason to believe that these two places were not synonymous.

The Paradox of the Pharisees and Josephus's Hermeneutics

It is the Pharisees who present us with a paradox. The Sadducees needed no notion of the afterlife. The millennialists need a strong notion of resurrection, which gives justice to those who suffer and heavenly transformation to some of those who fall as martyrs. The Pharisees had religious beliefs which are harder to understand if set parallel to their social position. Indeed, we will not entirely be able to understand Pharisaic beliefs until we study Paul the ex-Pharisee and then the rabbis. The rabbis are the heirs to the Pharisees and many of their ideas are to be found in their writings.

We know that the Sadducees had to share power with the Pharisees, who were apprently a skilled class of scribes and craftsmen who studied the laws in detail. Not only did Josephus describe them as the most accurate interpreters of the law, he did so in language that suggests that they already possessed the "oral law," which is characteristic of the rabbis. Josephus described their product as *nomima*, "legal enactments" (*Vita* 191), and said in several places that they handed down *(paredosan)* regulations not recorded in the Torah of Moses (*Ant.* 13.297; 17.41). The Greek terminology suggests oral transmission, as does the sentence structure, which contrasts the Pharisaic enterprise with the written law. Josephus described the Pharisees as more abstemious in their personal habits than the patrician Sadducees: "They simplify their standard of living" (*Ant.* 18.12). He said that they were not impressed by luxury nor sought it in this world. Rather they were respectful and deferential to elders and kept their word (*Ant.* 18.12). "The Pharisees are affectionate to each other and cultivate harmonious relationships within the community" (*J.W.* 2.166).

This is a standard description of the solace of philosophical communities in the Greco-Roman world. True philosophers not only read and meditate on the truths of the universe, they also translate their beliefs into communal life, living with their fellows in an ideal community. Josephus styles the Sadducees as an arrogant and powerful class (they had indeed fomented the war with Rome before political leadership was usurped by the Zealots), while he styled the Pharisees (with whom he had his differences) as a circumspect scribal client class of the Romans, sharing in the government and attempting to negotiate a peace with the Romans. The Pharisees seemed less impressed with Judaean military might, less interested in rebellion, and more willing to put up with the Romans, because they saw Roman power as overwhelming, though they can hardly be said to have liked them. In fact, Josephus was quite often annoyed with the Pharisees when he was military commander of the Galilee during the early days of the revolt because they constantly attempted to negotiate a cessation of hostilities and undermine his more militant position.

After Josephus was captured by the Romans, and indeed was accepted into the retinue of Vespasian and Titus, he began to change his opinion about the Pharisees. This makes a great deal of sense as he must have realized the futility of any hostility against the Romans. The Pharisees became his favorite candidates to take over the reins of government after the revolt in his later work the *Antiquities* for they are most in favor of peaceful co-existence with the Roman Empire.[25] It was the Pharisees who take over the role as mediators of the Roman rule and representative leaders of the native community.

Why then did they believe in resurrection, which is the mark of a revolutionary group? The Pharisees, who were expert at understanding the law, believed that there are rewards and punishments, as well as life after death. They were educated men, helpful in running the state. Though Josephus was from a priestly family himself and so heir to the Sadducee position, should he have desired it, he stated that he learned to govern his life according to the rules of the Pharisees, since he wanted a career in public life (*Vita* 10–12).

This is not to be interpreted as Josephus' conversion to Pharisaism.[26] In the *Jewish Wars*, Josephus often appears not to like Pharisees much, especially in his public career as a general during the war, when they were constantly trying to have him removed from office. His background made him suspicious of them and his attempt to style himself as a Pharisee was less than entirely convincing. In his later writing, *Jewish Antiquities*, Josephus suggested that the Pharisees were the class of people who Rome trusted best to govern Judea after the destruction of the Temple. That was decades after the war but that was Josephus' final position, after a great many twists and turns.

Yet, more religious persons than Josephus found the Pharisees' piety impressive. Jesus said that unless one's "righteousness surpasses even that of the Pharisees," one will not enter the kingdom of heaven (Matt 5:20). Jesus' admiration had limits, because, according to Mark, the Pharisees could be criticized for setting aside the commands of God in order to observe their own traditions (Mark 7:9). We do not have to accept these statements as the actual words of Jesus to understand the kind of praise and criticism that was being offered by ordinary Jews. In this respect, Christianity gave us invaluable evidence about the opinions of ordinary Jews. The Pharisees, like all the sects of first century Judaea, were a controversial group.

Josephus was like Philo in his almost complete avoidance of the term *anastasis* (literally, raising up, the Judaeo-Greek technical term for "resurrection") and related words for resurrection proper. He does not seem at all interested in the notion of resurrection of the body. "Immortality" is the term he used to describe life after death, and he quite often, like Philo, larded the description of life eternal with notions of heavenly journeys to the deathless stars.

Josephus said of the Pharisees: "Every soul, they maintain, is imperishable but the soul of the good alone passes into another body, while the souls of the wicked suffer eternal punishment" (*J. W.* 2.163). This has often been taken to mean that the Pharisees believed in fleshly resurrection in the same way as Christians do; but this is a very broad generalization. The Pharisees, we will see, had a less specific and more interesting view.

Nor does this mean that Josephus attributed to Pharisees the Platonic notion of metempsychosis, or reincarnation, though he certainly used exactly that language to describe Pharisaic beliefs. Rather, Josephus described the Pharisees as envisioning another, different kind of body for imperishable souls. Because Josephus was involved in a very tricky hermeneutical process in explaining Jewish beliefs for a sophisticated, philosophical pagan audience, whose notions of the afterlife were deeply affected by Greek philosophy, exactly what the Pharisees believed is not recoverable from him.

When Josephus said that "the soul of the good alone passes into another body," he meant that the earthly body is corruptible. Josephus probably meant that the Pharisees believed that righteous persons will receive a new, incorruptible body. This is exactly what Paul says in 1 Corinthians 15. Since Paul was an ex-Pharisee (as well as a Christian), Josephus may have been accurate in his own way, though it would hardly appear to us as the simplest way to describe their beliefs.[27]

The Pharisees' belief in life after death was entirely congruent with their Roman client status. The rabbis, the Pharisees' intellectual descendants, believed in an afterlife that could be figured flexibly in either Greek or more native apocalyptic terms, or even others terms, depending on the circumstances (see ch. 14).

This hypothesis preserves the symmetry between the Pharisees' middle social position and their afterlife beliefs. Judaea evinced a party system that expresses social, political, and religious differences. The afterlife, whether based on resurrection or immortality of the soul, was one of the crucial subjects that distinguished between them. This is not so surprising as it sounds since beliefs about the afterlife are also highly correlated with class and politics in the United States.

Martyrdom and the Fate of the Essenes

THE ESSENES are not mentioned in Rabbinic literature but were fully described by Josephus. They seem to be closely related to the group that secreted the texts we find in the caves around Qumran, though not all the texts found there need be Essenic, and the Dead Sea Scroll sectarians may not be the only kind of Essene that existed. Josephus had no doubt that these people believed in life after death, though he figured it as immortality of the soul. Resurrection of the body is more likely to have been their true belief, as their own texts tell us. Josephus again characterized Essene beliefs in a way that Romans would understand. Dead Sea Scroll texts tell us that it was resurrection of the body that preserved Essene faith, a faith that was tested by martyrdom[28] According to Josephus, the Romans tortured the Essenes for refusing to renounce their Jewish practices, especially the dietary laws:

> They were racked and twisted, burnt and broken, and made to pass through every instrument of torture in order to induce them to blaspheme their lawgiver and to eat some forbidden thing; yet they refused to yield to either demand, nor even once did they cringe to their persecutors or shed a tear. Smiling in their agonies, mildly deriding their tormentors, they cheerfully resigned their souls, confident that they would receive them back again. (*J. W.* 2.152–53)

Josephus explained the martyrdom of Essenes who, he said, believe in fate and the immortality of the souls and also believed that souls can ascend to be immortalized. He figured them in exactly the same terms as 4 Maccabees figured the woman and her seven children. Josephus also described the Essenes in terms that the Romans would understand. They respected the brave endurance of those tormented among the Jews just as they respected the same qualities of Christian martyrs afterwards. They expected to receive their souls back again. This seems very much like resurrection; it is hard to know what a Roman would have made out of that statement. Now that we know that the Dead Sea Scrolls do evince resurrection of the body, it makes special sense. The Essenes believed in fate only in the sense that they were apocalypticists who believed that God has already foreordained who will live and die when the end of days comes. As seems implicit here, Josephus used the term "soul" when he meant resurrection of the body, the doctrine most closely associated with martyrdom in Jewish culture. The phenomenon is quite widespread in Hellenistic Jewish literature but the connection with resurrection of the body comes clear only when Josephus discussed the suicide of the defenders of Masada.

Josephus's Account of the Martyrs at Masada

WHEN JOSEPHUS discussed the act of martyrdom that ended the First Jewish Revolt against Rome, he is at his most articulate. A good historian was expected to fill in stirring speeches where no words were left to us. The speech of Eleazar ben Yair, one of the leaders of the defenders of Masada against the Roman siege, is the work of Josephus himself. He described the hopeless situation of the defenders of Masada and then wrote the appropriately heroic speech for the leader of the defense.

Josephus' Eleazar first appealed to heroism. God determined that they should all die since the Romans were close to vanquishing them, although they enjoyed the best strategic position possible and an enormous cache of supplies and weapons. On the other hand, God graced them with information that many of their compatriots in revolt had not possessed—the knowledge of their imminent capture. He therefore urged "a noble death in liberty" (*J.W.* 7.326) rather than a life in slavery and dishonor.

Though some were convinced by this appeal, others were more compassionate for their wives and children. For this reason, Eleazar continued on to a discussion of the immortality of the soul (*J.W.* 7.341). Josephus reports that "Death truly gives liberty to the soul and permits it to depart to its own pure abode, there to be free of all calamity" (*J.W.* 7.344). Josephus continued by positing that the soul is the principle of life in the world: whatever it inhabits is alive and whatever it abandons immediately dies. He then tried to demonstrate that the soul is independent of the body in sleep and will be all the more independent after death.

We recognize immediately that this is Plato's proof of the immortality of the soul, if somewhat popularized. As an actual historical occurrence, this proof is unlikely to have occurred to Eleazar, leader of the Zealot defenders, at this momentous occasion. But it is sure to have impressed Josephus's readers deeply, especially his Greco-Roman audience, who would better understand the motivations of the Jews when phrased in this particular way; when possible, the Romans emphasized that they had vanquished worthy enemies, not overrun some group of ill-prepared peasants.

Thus, Josephus figured the zealot defenders of Masada as if they were Greek philosophers. But it is unlikely that the events or conceptions Josephus described were anything like the ideas of afterlife that the desperate defenders of Masada would have embraced. They, like all other Jewish sectarian groups of the day, would have been more attracted by the notion of bodily resurrection to enjoy the rest of the life which had been denied them by faith. We have noticed that all the nativist groups of the first century—all the groups that faced martyrdom, Christianity included—affirmed bodily resurrection, not the immortality of the soul.

Some More Information about Life after Death from Acts

JOSEPHUS'S DESCRIPTION of the afterlife beliefs of the sects of Judea is most dramatically confirmed by a story Luke tells us about Paul. Acts 23 illustrates that the issue of life after death was still being fiercely fought in first-century Judea:

> When Paul noticed that some were Sadducees and others were Pharisees, he called out in the council, "Brothers, I am a Pharisee, a son of Pharisees. I am on trial concerning the hope of the resurrection of the dead." When he said this, a dissension began between the Pharisees and the Sadducees, and the assembly was divided. (The Sadducees say that there is no resurrection, or angel, or spirit; but the Pharisees acknowledge all three.) Then a great clamor arose, and certain scribes of the Pharisees' group stood up and contended, "We find nothing wrong with this man. What if a spirit or an angel has spoken to him?" (Acts 23:6–9)[29]

This passage tells us that the Sadducees denied any resurrection, either as a soul (obviously as an immortal soul) or as an angel (angelomorphic resurrection). So far as Luke is concerned, there were two ways in which our immortal lives could be figured: as an immortal soul or as an angel. From everything we have seen, the latter description is another way to figure the resurrection of the body. This narrative also tells us that afterlife was a matter of great dispute in Jewish society and not tacitly assumed by all.

Immortality of the Soul Used to Justify Suffering and Martyrdom in Other Jewish Literatures

THE DEAD SEA SCROLLS, Enoch, and the Daniel tradition can be contrasted with Wisdom of Solomon, which uses a Greek notion of immortality, but also combines it with a more traditionally Jewish notion of resurrection:

> But the souls of the righteous are in the hand of God,
>   and no torment will ever touch them.
> In the eyes of the foolish they seemed to have died,
>   and their departure was thought to be an affliction,
> and their going from us to be their destruction;
>   but they are at peace.
> For though in the sight of men they were punished,
>   their hope is full of immortality. (Wis 3:1–4)

The occasion of the discussion is the death of the righteous. These may be the martyrs but the description is so general as to include any righteous person who dies early or childless. As with the apocalyptic sensibility, the writer of Wisdom claims that the righteous dead are immortal, with God. The wicked will be punished, both on earth, and by not sharing the immortality of the righteous. God will overturn the plans of the evil, and disasters will follow them. Yet, unlike in the apocalyptic works, there is no obvious resurrection at the end of time. In fact, the issue in Wisdom 1:15–2:24 is strictly one of theodicy. If there is a restoration on earth, it is accomplished in the subtlest ways: "They will govern nations and rule over peoples, / and the Lord will reign over them forever" (3:8). It is not clear that this means resurrection or restoration of the martyrs at all.[30]

The theme is developed through contrast. When reading through the passage, at first, we think we will see the theme of Ecclesiastes return, with its marvelous critique of Persian Jewish and Greek Jewish affluence with incipient stoicism. Since there is no earthly justice, Epicureanism is the rational choice: *Carpe diem!* Yet this passage shows by rational progression that such beliefs lead not only to disregard of God, they finally lead to the persecution of the righteous.

The stoicism and epicureanism of the beginning is overturned by a more traditional Jewish view of God's providence. This is an important, intellectual, and logical analysis of the eventual end of those who disregard God. In the end, it is the righteous who will triumph. The passage even ends with a reference to supernatural evil, created by the devil. Yet, how different is this from the analysis of the justification of the righteous in the Daniel and 2 Maccabees passage! It is much more like Philo's or Josephus' figuration of apocalypticism in terms of Platonism. There is no explicit discussion of the end of time and the world disruption which will reward the righteous with apocalyptic vengeance. Rather instead the work tries to show how divine Wisdom (as a separate hypostasis of God) has aided the righteous throughout Biblical history.

The Greek influence is a natural extension of explaining native Jewish notions of righteousness and the rewards of martyrdom to Greek audiences. The Greek influence is a hermeneutical processs, not just a translation of terms from one language to another but an attempt to translate notions of afterlife from one culture to another, where "resurrection" is better understood as "immortality." Even more important is the social context of these ideas, which place it squarely in the higher classes of Jewish life, who have seen fit to articulate the inchoate notion of afterlife in the Bible with the help of Greek philosophy. The people who wrote these passages are concerned with God's justice but they are not revolutionaries. They tell a story of those who deny life after death and wind up denying God. They stay as close as possible to the original Hebrew notions in the Psalms.

Similarly, we cannot tell from this passage whether the afterlife is immediately after death or at the end of time, whether it is experienced bodily in any way or is equivalent to immortality of the soul. The text seems deliberately to downplay any apocalyptic notion and concentrate on the immortal reward which God gives to martyrs. After the tradition ramifies in various ways, many more complicated combinations will be possible, but this beginning seems to preserve different origins for the different notions of life after death in Jewish thought.

Similarly, the trend which was foremost in the Maccabean literature was an interest in immortality. By the time of 4 Maccabees, the fashion in which immortality was expressed was as a synthesis of Greek and First Temple Israelite thought:

Although the ligaments joining his bones were already severed, the courageous youth, worthy of Abraham, did not groan, but as though transformed by fire into immortality he nobly endured the rackings. (4 Mac 9:21–22)

but all of them, as though running the course toward immortality, hastened to death by torture. (14:5)

but, as though having a mind like adamant and giving rebirth for immortality to the whole number of her sons, she implored them and urged them on to death for the sake of religion. (16:13)

for on that day virtue gave the awards and tested them for their endurance. The prize was immortality in endless life. (17:12)

As opposed to the corresponding passages in 2 Maccabees, there is no elaborate discussion of resurrection here, no corresponding cosmological argument that God made everything, no promise that He will recreate from nothing those whose bodies have been destroyed by the tyrant. There is no need to discuss the body at all. There is still a clear relationship between martyrdom and immortality, but the immortality is not resurrection. It is astral immortality (4 Mac 9:21–22), even with the torturers' fire serving to cleanse mortality from the martyrs.

By the first century, it is not enough to say that resurrection is a native Jewish notion while immortality of the soul is a Greek notion; they have both made their appearance in Jewish culture. What is particular to these passages is the notion that God will reward the righteous after their suffering by benefitting them with immortality (4 Mac 17:1). The particular kind of immortality depends entirely on the taste, or more exactly on the social position and predisposition of the writer. These ideas entered Jewish society in different ways; they also underscored the social fragmentation that accompanied the Greek conquest in the fourth century BCE. By the first centuries BCE and CE we have clearly differentiated social circumstances, which also showed up in the various understandings of life after death.[31]

The Jesus Movement and the Criterion of Dissimilarity

No SUBJECT in history has received more attention than the person of Jesus and the character of the movement he headed.[32] The Jesus movement is best understood as a millenarian movement. No theory is without detractors in this much discussed topic, but the apocalyptic hypothesis is the dominant approach of the twentieth century to the study of the movement that Jesus began. It was the perspective championed most successfully by one of the outstanding men of the twentieth century, Albert Schweitzer, who was an accomplished scholar of the New Testament, as well as a world renowned physician and a great humanitarian.[33] He pointed out that no one would have made up the stories of Jesus' forecasting the end of time on the basis of what happened in Christianity afterwards (e.g. Matt 4:17; Mark 1:15; Matt 16:28; Luke 4:19, as we shall see). Jesus was an apocalypticist, at least in some of his teaching, and that fact must be faced squarely.

There are some strong logical reasons why Jesus must have headed an apocalyptic movement. To see them one needs quickly to review the history of the New Testament scholarship on the subject. In the eighteenth and nineteenth centuries, the historicity of the Gospel stories was brought into doubt by the philosophers of the Enlightenment. They asked: "What makes the stories of the Old or New Testament any more historically probable than Aesop's fables or Grimm's fairy tales?" The historical truth of the New Testament depends entirely on one historical source, entirely written by people who previously accepted Jesus as their personal savior.[34]

As a way of combating this cultured critique of religion, a number of scholars throughout the nineteenth and twentieth centuries developed criteria that would apply to any historical source, such as the New Testament, which was written by people who had already accepted the truth of its major propositions. A number of important criteria were adduced—like Jewish background, multiple and early attestation, easy translation into Aramaic—but they can all be expressed as "the Criterion of Dissimilarity," especially if it is understood to include criteria of embarrassment and multiple attestation.[35] For a fact about Jesus to be accepted as unassailable, it must *not* be in the interest of the church to tell us.[36]

The historical question is more limited. How does Jesus fit into the Jewish world's notions of the afterlife? One must come at the problem indirectly. One must begin with several assured or virtually assured conclusions, many deduced by pure logic from the Gospel stories: Jesus lived as a Jew and died for his Judaism. His politics were seen as subversive to the Romans. He must have been an apocalypticist himself, otherwise there would have been no adequate reason for his movement to have expected his return immediately. He was the leading figure in a small movement of apocalyptic Jews who saw his death as a martyrdom, like many previous

Jewish martyrdoms. Whether he was actually a political danger is quite another question. Some apocalypticists have political ambitions; others do not. Some movements have political objectives and others remain inchoate. Jesus was an apocalyptic prophet. Whatever Jesus' Jewish and Roman politics were, they were not considered primary to his church, once the church understood his message as the salvation of the world.

Then we come to the mystery of the Resurrection, which we pass over for a moment. Jesus' earliest disciples saw a moral and apocalyptic victory in "the Easter event." They interpreted it not just as a sign that Jesus had been resurrected from the dead but had ascended to heaven to sit next to God, inaugurating the final consummation of history. The earliest Christians experienced the continued presence of Jesus in their lives, not in some attenuated form but exactly in the form of resurrected Messiah, angel of the Lord, the Son of Man (all at once) who was enthroned next to God.[37] This must be true though it does not pass the criterion of dissimilarity because it is simply what all the canonical New Testament documents say about the Christ of faith. Paul identified Jesus as risen savior and Messiah because he had visions that clarified that relationship for him.

The Gospels show that the identification of Jesus with the "Son of Man" in Daniel is early and important but it is a postresurrection doctrine. The evangelists preached that the man Jesus, crucified and resurrected, became the figure prophesied in Daniel 7:13-14, a figure the church calls "the Son of Man" but who is probably better understood as "a manlike figure in heaven" not a title at all (e.g. Matt 24:29-31; 25:31-46 and parallels). We know how they made this identification, that it was part of the *kerygma* (the core proclamation of the Early Church), and that it was consistent with Paul's ecstatic and visionary Christianity.

The Gospels make this identification on the basis of two other Hebrew Bible passages—Psalm 110 and Psalm 8, taken in conjunction with Daniel 7:13-14. The three passages together can almost be read as a narrative of the resurrection and ascension of Jesus as the figure enthroned next to God (cf. Mark 13:24-27; Luke 21:25-28). We do not know why the Gospels make this identification except that the figure was part of a very famous apocalyptic document—the visions of Daniel 7-12, the first place where resurrection is mentioned unambiguously in the Hebrew Bible and is part of the vision in which resurrection and the ascension and the angelic status of the saints is first described.

Whether or not we can take this known fact back a few years and posit that Daniel figured prominently in Jesus' own personal teachings is more speculative, just as it is difficult to tell even today, when a known figure is quoted by a newspaper, much less a well-meaning friend, what exactly the figure said. Jesus wrote nothing down so everything we know about him was reported by his hearers. We know that the identification of the Christ with Daniel 7:13 is an early and strong tradition and it is impossible to explain without an apocalyptic—not just eschatological—content in Jesus' preaching, a fact that also passes the criterion of dissimilarity. Jesus must have preached repentance for the coming end of the world and recommended a radical change of behavior as the only way to cope with these events. He was, in the words of my colleagues Markus Barth and John Dominic Crossan, an eschatological Jesus—but I think, given these beliefs he must have been even more, an apocalypticist.[38]

Relying on the method of the criterion of dissimilarity, the discoverable core of Jesus' message must have been apocalyptic and millennialist. The reasons for this are strong: First, some of Jesus' statements were predictions that imply that the end of time was coming soon. Second, they talked about an event that did not happen. None of those who heard Jesus' message actually witnessed the Son of Man coming in power:

> "For the Son of Man is to come with his angels in the glory of his Father, and then he will repay everyone for what has been done. Truly I tell you, there are some standing here who will not taste death before they see the Son of Man coming in his kingdom." (Matt 16:27–28; see also 10:23)

The passage seems to meet the criterion of dissimilarity. There is only one convenient way to explain why such sayings remain part of the corpus of Jesus' work: Jesus actually predicted the end fairly quickly. This prediction has a very clear context within Judaism and was understandable in the social world that Jesus inhabited.

But it is another thing to say that apocalypticism was the only content of Jesus' teaching. That is not necessarily so; indeed, what was core and secondary might depend entirely on the ancient or modern listener. Apocalypticism is only the central fact in our understanding of Jesus' historicity because of the scholarly filter that we have had to use to demonstrate the historicity of Jesus. No one who only teaches about the end would have garnered Jesus' following. Apocalyptic prophets are the stuff of comedy and *New Yorker* cartoons. Jesus must also have had a teaching and example which won converts. Jesus must have been a charismatic figure. From this apocalyptic core, we may suspect that resurrection of the faithful and their transformation could not be far behind.

Jesus spoke of the Son of Man and the resurrection of the dead, both apocalyptic prophecies found in the book of Daniel. Before the fateful events of Jesus' Passover pilgrimage to Jerusalem, these notions could hardly have been fully distinguished from more political expectations of the coming of God's kingdom, with the possible help of the Messiah. That is to say, although early Christianity was a religious revolution, its political aims were yet inchoate. Some of Jesus' followers seem to have had revolutionary expectations, though passive revolution (maintaining ethical and cultic purity so that God and His angels could bring about political change) was the stronger tradition in Judaism, as the Qumran community showed us.

We also know, by the criterion of dissimilarity, that Jesus was an apocalypticist who had strong feelings of scorn for the putative rulers of his country. The overturning of the moneylenders' tables at the Temple is an important datum for his feelings. The message of Jesus that, with repentance, all are equal before God was typical of most sectarian apocalypticism of the time. Christian practices of public repentance, baptism, and chaste communal living were likewise typical of other contemporary apocalyptic groups.

Yet the similarity only emphasizes the striking difference between the earliest Christians and the Qumran covenanters (the Dead Sea Scrolls), for example. The Jesus movement equated the purity laws with moral laws, just as the Qumran movement did. But the Jesus movement was not priestly in orientation; rather, it gave special attention to redeeming sinners who had violated the purity rules. Like the Dead Sea Scroll community, groups that eschew sexuality virtually equated purity laws with sin, as a great many of the purity laws dealt with sexuality. Through John the Baptist, baptism became the Christian rite uniquely demonstrating repentance from sin, though there is no good evidence that Jesus performed it (e.g., John 4:2). Its corresponding emphasis on converting the distressed or sinful began in the teaching of John the Baptist, became characteristically Christian, and probably reflected Jesus' strong charismatic influence.

But, contrary to what many New Testament scholars think, Jesus was not totally uninterested in purity either, as the rite of baptism itself shows. It is not, as many have supposed, that Jesus was opposed to purity rules while the Pharisees fostered them. It is rather that Jesus, something like the Qumran sectarians, interpreted purity obligations in the moral realm, therefore preached the ones that furthered avoidance of sin (not necessarily egalitarianism). The Pharisees and the rabbis after them, separated the two spheres; sin was sin for the Pharisees. But purity was an almost totally separate system that operated without any necessary sin in most cases.[39]

Although Jesus accepted the Jewish law, he occasionally indulged in symbolic actions designed to provoke questions about the purpose of the Torah, such as healing the chronically ill or picking grain on the Sabbath. These actions could have been directed at the Pharisees or other sectarian interpreters of the Torah without implying that the Torah itself was invalid.[40]

As the Christian movement developed, some Christians showed signs of a primitive communalism, implicit in their pooling of resources. Christianity did not adhere to the social code of the Essenes, yet it did contain the seeds of a radical criticism of private property and believed strongly in sharing all economic resources (Acts 2). "No man can serve two masters. . . . You cannot serve God and mammon (money)" (Luke 16:13). Jesus was suspicious of people of means: "It is easier for a camel to go through the eye of a needle than for a rich man to enter the Kingdom of God" (Mark 10:24). This statement does not prevent a rich man from becoming part of the movement but it suggested that the rich would not be much in evidence at Jesus' table. Jesus certainly established a higher price for the rich than the poor. Early Christianity thus exhibited a deep suspicion of property. Given the command to share all things with the poor, few confident and successful people would have entered the movement at first. At best, those whose wealth had brought with it no feelings of achievement or worth would have been better targets for evangelism—for instance, tax-collectors and prostitutes.

Of special interest is the frequency with which reports of religiously altered states of consciousness appear in early Christianity. Was Jesus a mystic? Not in the modern sense of the term as a person who studiously seeks out visions by disciplined contemplation. But, there is a possibility that he sought these experiences in the frequency with which reports of that type occured in early Christian texts. And it was very hard if not impossible to be an apocalypticist without being a visionary in Jesus' Jewish culture. If Jesus was a visionary, that means he experienced religiously altered states of consciousness. Three scholars have attempted recently to place Jesus within the mystical tradition and altered states of consciousness.[41] It is hard to imagine Jesus being an apocalypticist without also positing RISC and visions. Religious visions were also characteristic of Paul. Jesus, however, did not leave us with elaborate visions, like the literary apocalypses. He used his apocalyptic insight into life for prophetic aims, to critique the social order he saw. And this made him and his mission virtually unique in Jewish life.

This Jesus and his apocalypticism are still mostly mysterious and mostly distant from us. His apocalypticism is what most challenges us. Otherwise, he would have been just another preacher of return to Jewish piety. This portrait of Jesus is not very different from the one which the New Testament gives us of John the Baptist, who lived and died as an apocalyptic Jew in everyone's opinion. What changes the portrait is not Jesus' marytrdom alone, as John was also martyred. It is Jesus' followers' interpretation of the Easter event. After the Easter events and Jesus' presumed resurrection, the Jesus movement began experiencing his presence in their midst. Apparently, people anticipated that John the Baptist might come back, but no one actually experienced it. But Jesus' disciples experienced his resurrection. Consequently they began to work out a Christology of a crucified Messiah raised to angelic and divine status. The event of Jesus' resurrection also initiated the end of time, which they expected to come to conclusion very quickly. The fact that the end did not come as soon as it was expected has necessitated many changes in their thought structure, which evolved over centuries.

Jesus as Messiah

IN THE GOSPEL of Mark, Jesus denied himself the title "Messiah" whenever it was applied to him (Mark 8:27–31, for instance), except at his trial. But someone must have had Messianic expectations of him because that was recorded as the Roman charge against him on the cross: "King of the Jews."[42] This cannot be a Jewish charge because it was insulting and humiliating to Jews. The crucifixion extinguished any political Messianic expectation of some of Jesus' followers. But it was the very title "King of the Jews" that his followers felt had been vindicated by the resurrection. Though the Gospels are clear that no one actually saw the resurrection event, his followers became convinced of the reality of the resurrection because of his postresurrection appearances. Resurrection is exactly the reward that apocalypticism promises for martyrs, but resurrection does not come until the end is nigh.

Since the resurrection had already happened, the disciples of Jesus became convinced that the end of time must already be upon them. From this point onward, Christians have believed that they are living in the end of days which will soon see fulfilled with the coming of the Kingdom of

God. Jesus' resurrected body of Glory appeared several times to Paul, showing him that those who believe in the risen Christ will soon follow him into the Kingdom and into Christ *(en christo)* in a transformed, even angelic state. All of these beliefs are understandable as Jewish apocalyptic beliefs transformed by the events of the fateful Passover in which Jesus journeyed to Jerusalem to worship his God properly and warn those who did not that the kingdom would shortly arrive.

Immortality of the Soul Versus Resurrection of the Body with Regard to the Jesus Movement

THE EARLY BIBLE writings so effectively guarded against the danger of Canaanite cults of the dead that when the "high" religion needed a notion of life after death it naturally turned to the two great dominant cultures of the Second Temple period: Persia and Greece. The Jewish writers borrowed resurrection of the body from Persia and immortality of the soul from Greece. They did not simply borrow but adapted notions to their own situation so that it became just as much a native Israelite discussion held with native Israelite terms and traditions. Persian ideas were more helpful to the masses because they were subversive to the Hellenistic and Roman order.

Cultures as a whole do not borrow. They do not adopt customs or ideas uniformly. Nor do they borrow without radically changing and refitting the ideas. Resurrection of the body appealed to the activist groups. It evolved out of religious martyrdom because it gave martyrdom a transcendent justification; but behind it was often a political and religious struggle for Jewish independence. It is the same struggle that produced the independent kingdom of the Maccabees. The Maccabees themselves did not write the book of Daniel; they were too astute politically. It was written by a sectarian group, possibly the shadowy "Hasidean" sectarians, possibly the group who evolved into the Qumran sectarians. Resurrection of the body provided a way to balance the equation of divine retribution. Foreign invaders had killed the faithful saints of Israel. Resurrection of the body gave transcendent worth to the death of the martyrs by stating that God would make good on his covenantal promises to reward the righteous and punish the iniquitous. It also shows us what the young martyrs wanted and needed most: They deserved to get their bodies back and to live again on the earth. And they deserved to be transformed into immortal and unchangeable stars, to become God's avenging army of angels who would scourge the earth of persecutors and evildoers.

The immortality of the soul came from different circles and reflected entirely different social concerns. It was adopted by a very well educated, very acculturated Jewish elite, completely at home or nearly at home in Greco-Roman culture. This elite understood the intellectual heritage of Platonism but also wanted to express it in Jewish form. The rewards of immortality of the soul were precisely what an educated elite wanted most. Older scholars and intellectuals do not need or even want their old bodies back. What they want is a continuation of their well-schooled and well-studied consciousness, the knowledge and the wisdom that they have accumulated through a lifetime of meditation. It is an "intellectual's immortality," one in which the result of continuous study would never be lost. The Jewish version of immortality of the soul, with its sure sense of personal, conscious survival of death, was even better for an intellectual elite in Israel than the Platonic form of the proof once reincarnation was removed. The once-and-for-all nature of Philonic notions of the immortality of the soul could then more fully serve Jewish ethical interests. Philosophical meditation on the immortal soul also provided a way to allow that at least some of us could find immortality in the stars, just as resurrection of the body did. Both had individual traditions that provided for ascent and transformation to astral bodies in the heavens. This was also in keeping with Greek notions of the apotheosis of heroes and Egyptian notions of the proper destination of the righteous. Indeed, the notion that the soul ascended to the stars was the dominant religious notion of the Hellenistic world. It crossed many different religions and was the closest thing to a universal religious doctrine that the Roman world produced.

Expectations of resurrection and ascension can be assumed to be high in the events surrounding Jesus' death. Jesus died as a martyr, trying to protect and fulfill teachings of the Jewish law, especially as he had preached repentance and understanding for sinners. In the eyes of his followers, his martyrdom was seen as a symbol of the beginning of the promised recompense for the righteous' suffering, the apocalyptic consummation. Specifically, the events of Easter were seen by the first Christians as the beginning of the fulfillment of the events in Daniel. Daniel 7:9–14, Daniel 12:3, together with Psalm 110 (most often used to express Jesus' ascension and often his divine status), and Psalm 8 are the most commonly quoted Old Testament passages in the New Testament. (When the New Testament was being written, the Jewish Scriptures were the *only* Scriptures.)

The Christians were not the first group to speculate on the traditions in Daniel. Although it is doubtful that the "Son of Man" was a specific title before Christianity, the verses in Daniel assured that the identity of the "manlike figure" in Daniel was a secret that would be unraveled at the end of time. For the group that had formed around the charismatic wonder-worker and apocalyptic prophet named Jesus, the secret was now revealed and the end of time was now starting to come true: Jesus was the crucified and resurrected Messiah, the very Son of God (both a royal and an angelic title) who would shortly return to bring punishment to sinners and eternal life to his saints.

PART FOUR

THE PATH TO MODERN

VIEWS OF THE AFTERLIFE

10

Paul's Vision of the Afterlife

PAUL IS OUR first Christian writer. His writings present us with the first reflections on the faith that the man Jesus was both Christ and God and that, through Him, all who have faith will be resurrected. His writing not only presented the first witness to an important new vision of the afterlife in Judaism, it also gives us interesting evidence for the notions of afterlife among the Pharisees, which we found difficult to understand from Josephus' report alone. Our difficulties are compounded by the fact that the Rabbis, who claim the Pharisees as their forebears, did not redact their literature in canonical form before the beginning of the third century. When the first Rabbinic literature was finally produced, the Rabbis had already refined their notion of the afterlife in subtle ways. So Paul gives us good evidence for the history of Jewish ideas in the mid-first century, evidence which we cannot easily find elsewhere.

Paul offers us the same opportunity with regard to Christianity. He wrote in the mid-decades of the first century CE before the Gospels were compiled. He made very infrequent reference to any of the traditions found within them, although we believe that the Gospels were already in some stage of development. He rarely gives us any of Jesus' words. He quotes Jesus directly on only two subjects, divorce (1 Cor 7:10–12) and the Lord's Supper (1 Cor 11:23–27), indirectly only on a few more. Both categories have enormous significance for our understanding of Christian afterlife. Paul's testimony is consonant with later Gospel tradition about the Lord's Supper and divorce but does not agree with it in every word.

His understanding of the ritual parallels his notions of the resurrection body. Other than that, Paul gives us scant information about the man Jesus.[1] What Paul gives us is a record of his own spiritual life and his faith in the crucified messiah. To appreciate all the important data that Paul gives us regarding both Judaism and Christianity, we need to be able to distinguish between Paul's use of Jewish and Christian teaching and his innovations. This task is most difficult.

But we have some aid. When Paul quotes Scripture, it is the Hebrew Bible in Greek that he cites. For him, there was no other Scripture, no written New Testament Gospels and no Christian document with the authority of Scripture. Though he must have known something about the Gospel traditions, the *evangelion* was for him an oral message, which was a genre certainly familiar from his Pharisaic background. He even uses Rabbinic formulas of transmission when he quotes them (e.g., 1 Cor 11:23). Although the Gospel traditions fulfilled Scripture, they were not yet Scripture.

Most scholars agree that Paul's characteristic rhetoric and style have little in common with the language of the Gospels. Although he may have considered the actual words of Jesus part of an oral tradition, he quotes them only where a Pharisee would need to rely on exact formulations: for deciding legal issues. When dealing with apothegms and other traditions, Paul shows us the same willingness to paraphrase and even to encode for memory that a Pharisee might have utilized in learning Rabbinic tradition. In short, Paul is surprisingly free of the religious thought structures of the Gospels and, what is even more interesting, the Gospels (which are later than his writings) are surprisingly independent of Pauline thought. Considering the effect that we now automatically ascribe to Paul's career, this is a very important observation. It shows us that he was not nearly as influential in the first century as he appears to be now. This will give pause to all those who think that Paul invented Christianity. He did not. But his testimony is extraordinarily interesting because he tells us his inner Christian experience.

Paul understood the messiahship of Jesus through his resurrected appearances in Paul's own experience, while the Gospels understood the messiahship of Jesus through the events of Jesus' life and mission. This difference in perspective stamps each writing in unique and sometimes unreconcilable ways. This difference in perspective is extremely important in the history of Christian ideas about resurrection.

Commission and Conversion

PAUL'S MOST BASIC perspective is as a convert and a missionary. By "convert," we can mean what Christianity later will mean by "convert."[2] But Paul is not himself the best example of the later Christian model of conversion because he did not convert from paganism to Christianity, rather from a sophisticated and educated form of Judaism to a new, apocalyptic form of it. A minimum definition of "conversion," then, would be that Paul changes religious community—from the Pharisaic community to a group of sectarian, apocalyptic Jews who had unique and novel notions about the divinity and messiahship of their founder, Jesus of Nazareth. To understand Christianity one really needs to understand the effect of conversion and mission on the organization of the religion. The mission and expansion of Christianity was not just a historical accident but is also traceable to its internal dynamic, which put immense energy into the conversion of the world. Paul's understanding of conversion was not exactly the model that triumphed in Christianity, though Christians looked back at him as a model for how a missionary should behave.

In one respect, at least, Paul was completely unlike the later model of mission and expansion: Though Paul leaves Pharisaism, he never shows any recognition that his Christianity was different from his Judaism. He never felt that he left Judaism, so we should consider any departure from Judaism to be the opinion of his enemies and not his own opinion. By his own estimation, Paul remained a Jew throughout his life, changing from one kind of Jewish denomination to another.

Paul's Vision and the Power of the Spirit

PAUL'S REASONS for changing religious communities are plainly stated. He grew to know Christ, whom he took as his Lord:

> But whatever gain I had, I counted as loss for the sake of Christ. Indeed I count everything as loss because of the surpassing worth of knowing Christ Jesus my Lord. For his sake I have suffered the loss of all things, and count them as refuse, in order that I may gain Christ. (Philip 3:7–8)

There is reason to believe him, for revelations were common in his day. The only thing strange about Paul's further reflection on his conversion is that Paul did not know the man Jesus, or at least there is no evidence that he ever met him. So Paul's writing, though it is the first Christian writing, is the writing of a convert after the Easter events. Although Paul is not a disciple of Jesus, he is a Jew and he can also claim an important and prestigious pedigree in Pharisaism; in these crucial places, he does so. But he also says that all that is overthrown by his Christian commitment, so he offers himself as a demonstration of the power of the Spirit. This is not only a conversion but it is one that Paul himself ascribes to a religiously altered state of consciousness (RASC). He has received this conversion as a gift of the Spirit. His personal biography functions as a miraculous witness to the power of the Spirit in his life and in the world.

For instance, Paul reminded the Corinthians that they had already accepted his claim of legitimacy and that others too became evangelized because of them, his gentile converts; indeed they are his "letter from Christ" (2 Cor 3:3). His seemingly miraculous success in evangelizing the gentiles also is validation for his claims to special revelation and mission. This is, for Paul, proof of the operation of the Holy Spirit in the end-time and the validity of his RASC.

The Spirit and the Church's Apocalypticism

PAUL'S UNDERSTANDING of the end of time is apocalyptic. He imminently expects the end. His grasp of the resurrection is firmly mystical but in the Jewish tradition, not the Greek one.[3] He describes his spiritual experiences in terms appropriate to a Jewish apocalyptic-mystagogue of the first century. Even in his earliest preaching and writing, his discussions of resurrection depended directly on the apocalyptic end:

> For they themselves report concerning us what a welcome we had among you, and how you turned to God from idols, to serve a living and true God, and to wait for his Son from heaven, whom he raised from the dead, Jesus who delivers us from the wrath to come. (1 Thess 1:9–10)

This is not philosophy; it is missionizing. He reminds his readers what he has told them when he was there. Having been evangelized by the Spirit himself, Paul uses the language of spiritual transformation to evangelize others, in this case gentiles. Paul's use of kerygmatic formulas in missionary activity is evident. After turning from idols, Paul's gentile converts learn to wait for God's Son from heaven, who will rescue them from the coming wrath. This seems in some respects a violation of the passage in Daniel 7:13 where the role of the "Son of Man" was to bring judgment against sinners. But that is how an apocalyptic mission functions. It warns people that the only way to avoid punishment is to join the apocalyptic community. This is true in apocalyptic communities in Judaism. Here it has been transferred to the sinning of the gentiles themselves. The innocent Early Church was, conversely, part of the larger role of judgment against the mighty and the sinners; but even the new converts would be protected and rescued from the wrath which will soon overtake the whole earth.

The proof that all these things are about to happen is that Jesus, the Son, was raised from the dead. The resurrection was a sign that the end of time is upon us: "But in fact Christ has been raised from the dead, the firstfruits *(aparchē)* of those who have fallen asleep" (1 Cor 15:20). Paul uses two traditional Jewish metaphors at once in saying that the dead have only fallen asleep (Isa 26:19; Dan 12:2). He further suggests that Jesus was the special thank offering, the first fruits offered, following which the resurrected will soon awake and begin ripening in the fields or on the tree (Deut 26). This is not just what Paul proclaimed. It is also what the church proclaimed, as he again used the language of tradition transmission:

> Now I would remind you, brethren, in what terms I preached to you the gospel, which you received, in which you stand, by which you are saved, if you hold it fast—unless you believed in vain. For I delivered to you as of first importance what I also received, that Christ died for our sins in accordance with the scriptures, that he was buried, that he was raised on the third day in accordance with the scriptures, and that he appeared to Cephas, then to the twelve. Then he appeared to more than five hundred brethren at one time, most of whom are still alive, though some have fallen asleep. (1 Cor 15:1–6).

A similar formula of the kerygma, the basic proclamation of the church, can be found in the salutation of Paul's letter to the Romans where Jesus is mentioned as "seed of David" according to the flesh but, more importantly, "Son" according to spirit and power and from the resurrection of the dead, "Our Lord." Jesus' Lordship is inherent in his resurrection, the transformation from his earthly, fleshly, meek state to his heavenly, spiritual and powerful state as the Christ and Son from heaven. Thus, the relationship between flesh and spirit is homologous with the relationship between "son of David" and "son of God." Though the contrast is characteristic of Pauline thought, it may well have preceded Paul's use in his sermons and have been part of the primitive tradition. This is also visible in 1 Cor 15:45: "Thus it is written, 'The first man Adam became a living being'; the last Adam became a life-giving spirit.'" Spirit is not only what God gives man, it is the goal of human evolution to a higher state.

Spirit for Paul is seen within a Jewish context. In 1 Corinthians 15:45 he refered to the creative spirit of God which was hovering over the waters in Genesis 1:1. The spirit of the Lord resurrects the dead in Ezekiel 37:6. The spirit of the Lord gave Paul his prophetic visions. Christians will be changed into spiritual bodies in their resurrection state (1 Cor 15:44).

The very same Spirit of God which directs prophecy also directed Paul's sermons and also miraculously accounts for Paul's success and the success of the Gospel. In form, however, Paul's kerygmatic message appears to grow out of Jewish missionary literature, in which the promise of resurrection and the fear of the end of time feature prominently, as one would expect from a preacher. Thus Paul's own experience helped organize the early Christian church for expansion; conversely, it energized the group's commitment to the new religious sect.

Mission and Vision

THE SPECIFIC nature of Paul's personal vision of Christ changed the quality of that apocalyptic prophecy in a characteristically christological way. It is not so much that Paul affected Christian apocalypticism as he exemplified Jewish apocalypticism with a single and important change—Jesus had ascended to be the Messiah and heavenly Redeemer, a part of God. This would be characteristic of Christian preaching ever afterward.

Here is another Pauline version of the vision of the end, this time seemingly in answer to a crucial question for new converts:

But we would not have you ignorant, brethren, concerning those who are asleep, that you may not grieve as others do who have no hope. For since we believe that Jesus died and rose again, even so, through Jesus, God will bring with him those who have fallen asleep. For this we declare to you by the word of the Lord, that we who are alive, who are left until the coming of the Lord, shall not precede those who have fallen asleep. For the Lord himself will descend from heaven with a cry of command, with the archangel's call, and with the sound of the trumpet of God. And the dead in Christ will rise first; then we who are alive, who are left, shall be caught up together with them in the clouds to meet the Lord in the air; and so we shall always be with the Lord. Therefore comfort one another with these words. (1 Thess 4:13–18)

Some in the community died without the end having come. The resurrection of all Christians will follow closely upon the coming of the Lord, also explicitly called both Jesus and Christ. (This formula demonstrates Paul's transferral of the traditionally divine name YHWH to a designation of the Messiah [*Kyrios* = LORD].) It both shows Paul to be entirely within the Jewish mystical tradition, yet to have made important Christian modifications in it. But he did not go on in baroque detail about the nature of the apocalyptic end. Instead, he concentrated on the issue of resurrection in a way that was not necessarily characteristic of apocalypticism before.

But Paul was preaching the start of the period of resurrection based on the death and resurrection of the Christ, to gentiles at that, so the lack of apocalyptic detail is understandable. In 1 Thessalonians 4, the resurrection of all living Christians immediately follows upon the resurrection of the dead. Jesus will keep faith with the dead, again called "those who have fallen asleep" as in Daniel 12. Thus, Paul reproduced a typical apocalyptic pattern, though his apocalyptic pattern also had several unique and quite identifiably Christian characteristics. At the same time, the enormous value of sermons of this kind for the mission of the church are obvious.

The Chain of Vision and the Spirit

WE SEE THE same connection between Paul's apostolic authority and the resurrection of the Christ when Paul replied to accusations of antinomianism: "Paul an apostle—not from men nor through man, but through Jesus Christ and God the Father, who raised him from the dead" (Gal 1:1). The epistolary greeting emphasizes the connection, especially as Paul, otherwise, was fonder of simple salutation formulas in his correspondence (1 Cor 1:1; 2 Cor 1:1) and Romans 1:1.[4] In 1 Corinthians 9:1–11, Paul again responds to accusations that appear to have been leveled at his missionary activity. And once again, he emphasizes his personal vision of Christ: "Have I not seen Jesus our Lord?" (1 Cor 9:1).[5]

In 1 Corinthians 9, Paul used the perfect tense of the verb "to see" to describe his visionary experience ("Am I not free? Am I not an apostle? Have I not "seen" Jesus our Lord? Are not you my workmanship in the

Lord?" 1 Cor 9:1) Paul emphasized that his vision was equivalent to normal "seeing," just as you and I might see each other. But Paul actually did not want to stress the ordinariness of the seeing, only that he saw as clearly as the other apostles. He was aware of the special nature of his revelation.[6]

Paul also wanted to demonstrate that his vision of Christ was the same type and order as that of the other apostles, even though he experienced Christ in visions only, while they learned directly from Jesus. In 1 Corinthians 15 and elsewhere Paul used the Greek aorist passive *ophthei* (the passive voice of the simple past) to describe this kind of seeing:

> . . . and that he appeared to Cephas, then to the twelve. Then he appeared to more than five hundred brethren at one time, most of whom are still alive, though some have fallen asleep. Then he appeared to James, then to all the apostles. (1 Cor 15:5–7)

The visionary language works in several ways at once. First, it follows the tradition of the LXX for describing visions. In the Septuagint the aorist passive of the verb "to see" is used frequently with the sense either of "visionary seeing" or of "seeing a divine being." In short, it has the sense of the word "appear" in English, when that word is used to describe a visitation of a divine figure.

Secondly, Paul used the very same verb and form to describe his own seeing and that of the original apostles. This demonstrated that he was their equal in every way. Conversely, Paul assumed that he saw exactly the same person that the original apostles saw except that he saw the risen Christ. Just because Paul is using the technical language of vision, however, does not mean that he thought they were hallucinations. To the contrary, these were visions undertaken through the Spirit and were therefore spiritual depictions of what is soon to become actual.

Paul was essentially saying that he is among those few special prophets who received a vision of God—prophets like Abraham, Enoch, Noah, Job, Moses, Elijah, Isaiah, and Daniel, those same people who followed in the ancient Near Eastern tradition of Enmeduranki, Adapa, Etana, Gilgamesh, Dan'el and Aqhat. Implicit in this tradition is the conclusion that Jesus ascended to heaven to become the "Son of Man," just like the heroes of ancient Biblical tradition. When he returns, the end will come upon all and only those in Christ will be rescued.

He contrasted that with the experience of the disciples of Jesus, who saw merely the man Jesus. It is not their experience of the teacher Jesus which was important. And the reason for this is that it is not the earthly Jesus who preached and demonstrated that the resurrection had already started. Rather it is the *risen Christ* who has ascended to the Father. Because Paul had seen the Christ in his resurrected body, Paul knew that the resurrection had begun and that all who came to believe in him were the firstfruits of this resurrection. Paul and all those who saw him are the first apostles and prophets of this new epoch in human history. That his seeing was visionary means that it was of a higher order than ordinary seeing. What Paul said about the spiritual bodies is a direct result of that vision, a further description of that vision.

Paul's Own Mysticism

IN SECOND CORINTHIANS 12 Paul said even more—that he himself, like the Biblical and mythical Enoch, also traveled (*harpagenta*, "seized") to the heavens looking for the answer to cosmological problems. This is one of the highest spiritual gifts that Paul could imagine and it was meant to establish his credentials as a receiver of spiritual gifts (*pneumakia*, 1 Cor 9:11; 14:1; 2 Cor 2:13). Paul's references to apocalypses and visions, as well as heavenly ascent, put him squarely within apocalyptic tradition. Although the account of Paul's ecstatic conversion in Acts is a product of Luke's literary genius, Paul gave his own evidence for ecstatic experience in 2 Corinthians 12:1–10:

> I must boast; there is nothing to be gained by it, but I will go on to visions and revelations of the Lord. I know a man in Christ who fourteen years ago was caught up to the third heaven—whether in the body or out of the body I do not know, God knows. And I know that this man was caught up into Paradise—whether in the body or out of the body I do not know, God knows—and he heard things that cannot be told, which man may not utter. On behalf of this man I will boast, but on my own behalf I will not boast, except of my weaknesses. (2 Cor 12:1–5)

As in Galatians 1, Paul called this experience an *apokalypsis,* an apocalypse, a revelation. Just as in Acts and Galatians 1, the actual vision is not described. Unlike Luke's general description of Paul's conversion and Galatians 1, however, this passage contains hints of a heavenly vision or possibly two different ones, depending on whether the paradise visited in the ascension can be located in the third heaven.[7] The vision was both mystical and apocalyptic.[8] The Pauline passage is also deeply rooted in

Jewish ascension traditions, which imposed a certain structure of ascent on all reports of this period.[9] Similar ascensions can be seen in apocalyptic literature—for instance, *1 Enoch* 39:3; 52:1; 71:1–5 as well as *2 Enoch* 3; 7; 8; 11; *3 Baruch* 2.

The information contained in 2 Corinthians 12 is so abstruse and esoteric that it must be teased from context and combined with our meager knowledge of apocalypticism and Jewish mysticism. While techniques of theurgy and heavenly ascent were secret lore in Rabbinic literature (see b. *Hagiga* 13a–15b), Rabbinic literature starts in the third century, so without Paul we could not demonstrate that such traditions existed in Pharisaism as early as the first century.

Most people understand 2 Corinthians 12 as referring to Paul himself, but that the rhetoric demands he stress his modesty.[10] To identify himself as the heavenly traveler would be boasting, and it would have conceded the point that special revelatory experience grants special privileges, which is what he was fighting against in the passage. This would contradict his statement that charismatic gifts cannot themselves prove faith (1 Cor 12–13). Yet, if the dominant interpretation is correct, Paul was actually revealing some information about his own religious experience in this passage.

For one thing, Paul seems to be talking about himself. By the end of the passage, Paul undoubtedly spoke about himself, without specifying that he had changed the subject. He said that he had spoken three times with the Lord about "a thorn in the flesh" (2 Cor 12:7–10), which he called "a messenger from Satan," probably an infirmity; but "the Christ" decided that it perfected his power. As a sudden change in subject would be clumsy, most scholars affirm that Paul is speaking about himself throughout. Furthermore, Paul's admission that he had spoken to Christ about his infirmity three times in itself implies a communication greater than petitionary prayer.[11]

Some scholars, like Michael Goulder, see this passage essentially as Paul's satire on claims to heavenly knowledge. But in order to see the section as ironic, one needs to find a crux to warrant an ironic reading. Otherwise, anything in any passage could be used ironically.[12] Paul had no problem admitting to other visions and apocalypses so there is no problem in positing that he had an apocalyptic, mystic, ecstatic spiritual life. Although the passage can be understood in other ways, Paul revealed that he had several ecstatic meetings with Christ over the previous fourteen years.

Christopher Morray-Jones has very persuasively argued that Paul's experience in 2 Corinthians corresponds to the Temple vision of Acts 22:17.[13] He has also recently published a brilliant analysis of the famous "transparent illusion" in the Hekhaloth texts.[14] The conclusions seem reasonable. But, even if Morray-Jones's conclusion is not accepted, the evidence of 2 Corinthians is undoubtedly a first-century report of a heavenly ascent that Paul says is important for Christian experience.

We should not think of 2 Corinthians 12 as the verbatim recording of Paul's actual experience. Rather we should think of it as his mature reflections on the experience after many years of Christian learning. Converts learn the meanings of their experience in their new community. This is true of Paul's mysticism as well; even though he is our first Christian writer he is not the first Christian. He learned his Christianity from the community in Damascus and, in turn, became a spokesperson for it. His subsequent Christian experience cannot have failed to have affected his memories of these events as that is a quite common and widely verified aspect of conversions even today.[15] This implies a significant growth of his maturity of Christian thought in the years between his conversion and his writings which we cannot clearly delineate.

It is only surprising that a Pharisee would claim these visions, since we tend to think that the Rabbis were rationalists. The Rabbis, the successors to the Pharisees, keep a respectful silence about these spiritual experiences, even though we have certain evidence that they were not so rare. Yet Paul does not give us much description. Hence, we do not know whether Paul was unusual for a Pharisee in his reception of these visions or whether he was actually quite typical. If so, Rabbinism would then have expunged them from its purview after Paul and the rise of Christianity. We know that the Mishnah contains very many serious cautionary rules in the way of open discussion of such experiences (e.g., m. Hagigah 2). But Merkabah Mysticism continued to develop even after the Rabbinic rules were put into effect, as the hekhaloth literature and various haggadic and Talmudic stories are all later than these traditions. Jewish mysticism certainly, and perhaps apocalypticism as well, sought out visions and developed special practices to achieve them.[16] Thus, we may safely assume that Paul experienced a number of visions in his life, that his conversion may have been one such prophetic incident, though it need not have been one, and that the meaning of these ecstatic experiences was mediated by the gentile Christian community in which he lived.

Mysticism and apocalypticism were part of Jewish tradition before Paul converted; he may thus have learned about ecstatic experience as a Pharisee or merely known about them from his general Jewish past. He may also have learned them in Christianity. Ultimately someone Jewish must have brought them into Christianity since there was not very much time between the end of Jesus' ministry and the beginning of Paul's. From the Damascus Christian community and Paul's own protestations of his education "from the Lord," it is much more likely that Paul was educated in Jewish mysticism before his conversion, and hence brought this style of spiritual experience to bear on his Christian experience.

Paul's Christian interpretation of these apocalyptic mystical visions is also a mark of his long association with the Christian community.[17] The Christian nature of his vision is due to the experience itself as he interpreted it. We need not suppose that the divine nature of Paul's revelation precluded influence from his supporting Christian community as well. All converts naturally find the meaning of their conversions in the community that values them, and that meaning is revealed to them progressively after conversion.

Apocalypticism and Mysticism

APOCALYPTICISM and mysticism have rightly remained separate categories in scholarly parlance because they refer to two different, easily distinguishable types of literature. But they do not appear to be unrelated experiences. Jewish mystical texts are full of apocalypses; early apocalyptic literature is based on ecstatic visions with profound mystical implications. Normally in an apocalyptic text we get a description, often in the first person, of a vision and ascent. In the mysticism of the Rabbinic period we get the same kind of description, in the mouth of a famous Rabbi, equally as pseudonymous, together with some of the preparations necessary to receive the vision. They may just be two different ways of describing the same kind of experiences. This suggests that scholars have without sufficient warrant carried a distinction in literary genre into the realm of experience. It is likewise misleading always to distinguish between ecstatic, out-of-body visions (as found in mysticism) and literal bodily ascensions to heaven (as are more frequently found in apocalypticism).[18] They may all be RISCs described in different terms.

In Merkabah Mysticism loosely construed (traceable from composition of Enoch to the rise of Kabbalah in the twelfth century), the mysticism of the early Rabbinic movement which concentrated on ascents to heaven, magical chants and procedures, as well as spells and rituals to remember Torah, the voyager often spoke as though he was actually going from place to place in heaven; yet we know from the frame narratives that the adept's body was on earth, where his utterances were questioned and written down by a group of disciples.[19] Paul spoke at a time before these distinctions were clear or accepted by his community. He was not sure whether the ascent took place in the body or out of it.

We should note that Paul did not utilize the concept of a soul *(psyche)* to effect this heavenly travel. Not being sure of whether the ascent took place in the body or out of the body is the same as saying that one is not taking account of the Platonic concept of the soul. Had Paul been using the Platonic version, he certainly would have known quite well that the only way to go to heaven, to ascend beyond the sublunar sphere, was by leaving the body behind. Indeed, we shall see several important places, especially 1 Corinthians 15, where Paul's concept of "soul" was quite limited, unschooled by Platonic ideas of the soul's immortality.

Rather, as we have just seen, Paul used the term "spirit" *(pneuma)* more frequently. Paul's pneumatology derives from the traditional language of Biblical prophecy and it is also the way Paul understood resurrection to arrive. This suggests that Paul may have understood being "in Christ" as a literal exchange of earthly body for a new *pneumatic,* spiritual one to be shared with the resurrected Jesus at the eschaton, since "spirit" is the source of all Paul's knowledge gained in visions. For him it was not yet concrete reality because it was not fully present. On the other hand, the spiritual vision was not hallucination either. It was prophecy in process of becoming concrete.

Even if Paul was not sure of how a visionary journey could be taken, we are. The question of whether a heavenly journey could take place in or out of the body may be settled for us only by assuming that this was an ecstatic journey, a RASC. Modern science balks at the notion of physical transport to heaven, except in space ships, whereas a heavenly journey in vision or trance is credible and understandable. This only underlines Paul's interesting conflation of what to us seems two different categories. So we are not free to ignore that fact when we try to establish what actually happened. When a heavenly journey is described literally, the cause may be literary convention or the belief of the voyager; but when reconstructing the actual experience, only one type can pass modern standards of credibility.

Paul's confusion as to whether his ecstatic journey to heaven took place in the body is a rare insight into first-century thinking, since it demonstrates either a disagreement in the community or more likely a first-century mystic's inability to distinguish between bodily and spiritual journeys to heaven. In effect, then, Paul was merely saying that the ascender experienced a RASC. But our world no longer supports his quandary; nor did the ancient world shortly after Paul's time. They adopted the Platonic notion of the soul, which answered the question sufficiently for them. Indeed, the answer still informs religious life today. It seems likely, however, that the presence of a heavenly journey is itself a signifier that ecstatic experience is taking place.

The Spiritual Body and
Its Presence in Ascent Mysticism

WE MUST ASK how Paul conceived such a journey to take place without a developed concept of the soul. The first answer may just be that he thought it took place in the body. He had already told us that he was not sure whether the ascender was "in the body" or not. He was quite sure that resurrection would not be fleshly, though it may be bodily. Since it already seems clear that Christ's body, as it appeared to him in visions, and the body of the resurrected believer were parallel, it must be that the ascender's body and the body of the resurrection were analogous as well. The demonstration appears to be 1 Corinthians 15:44, where Paul described a mystical notion of a spiritual body *(soma pneumatikon)* which was received by the Christ, and Paul found residence in it in the same way that God inspired the prophets or Enoch became part of the Son of Man.

Paul used a prophetic anthropology to explain this spiritual body. God gave the prophet His spirit and the spiritual body participated in the resurrection. This put Paul in the same category as the apocalypticists who first recorded the notion of bodily resurrection. It also put him rather far from those classes of people who championed the notion of the immortality of the soul, though Paul, being an apostle to the gentiles, may have known of the doctrine. He certainly seemed familiar with Stoic and Cynic doctrines and methods of argumentation.[20]

With only the most general hints about Paul's conversion in his own writing, we must fill in how the Jewish cultural context informed his experience. Ezekiel 1 was one of the central chapters that Paul used to understand his own conversion. The vision of the throne chariot of God in Ezekiel 1, along with the attendant vocabulary of the Glory or *kavod* (*kābôd*) for the human figure described there as God's glory or form, has been recognized as one of the central themes of Jewish mysticism, which in turn is closely related to the apocalyptic tradition.[21] The very name *Merkabah*—that is, Throne chariot Mysticism, which is the usual Jewish designation for these mystical traditions even as early as the Mishnah (ca.

220 CE: See Mishnah Hagigah 2:1)—is the Rabbinic term for the heavenly conveyance described in Ezekiel 1.[22] The truly groundbreaking work of Hugo Odeberg, Gershom Scholem, Morton Smith, and Alexander Altmann[23] showing the Greco-Roman context for these texts in Jewish mysticism, has been followed up by a few scholars who have shown the relevance of these passages to the study of early Rabbinic literature,[24] as well as apocalypticism and Samaritanism, and Christianity.[25]

The entire collection of Hekhaloth texts has been published by Peter Schaefer[26] and translations of several of the works have already appeared.[27] Nevertheless, the results of this research have not yet been broadly discussed, nor are they yet well known.[28] The ten volume compendium known in English as *The Theological Dictionary of the New Testament*, edited by G. Kittel, has scarcely a dozen references to Ezekiel 1, although it is a crucial passage informing the Christology of the New Testament, as Gilles Quispel has so cogently pointed out.[29]

The Angelic Liturgy from Qumran (4QShirShab) confirms the same themes of Jewish mysticism which we can only date to the third century from mystical sources.[30] The "Angelic Liturgy" cannot be dated later than the first century CE and is very likely pre-Christian. In it there are many oblique references to the divine hierarchies, the seven heavens inside one another, and the appearance and movements of God's throne chariot familiar to scholars who study Merkabah Mysticism.[31] The adepts thought that they had ascended liturgically to the heavenly temple to worship on the Sabbath; they assumed that they achieved angelomorphic immortality. *First Enoch* and Ezekiel 1 seem to be the Scriptural passages informing these beliefs but the hierarchy of the heavens is best known to us from such Merkabah documents as the *Reuyoth Yehezkel* ("The Visions of Ezekiel"). Paul's ascension was parallel to the mystical experiences which apocalyptic Jews like the Qumran community were reporting and, hence, an important clue to the beginnings of Merkabah Mysticism.

Whatever the intention of the author of *1 Enoch*, which may be construed in any number of ways, the relationship of Paul's experience to the theme of the ascension of the great ones to heavenly figures is extremely important.[32] Like Enoch, Paul claimed to have gazed on the Glory, whom Paul identifies as the Christ. Like Enoch, Paul understood that he had been transformed into a more divine state, which would be fully realized after his death. Like Enoch, Paul claimed that this vision and transformation was somehow a mystical identification with the Son of Man figure. Like Enoch, Paul claimed to have received a calling, his special status as intermediary, which also came through the spirit. Paul specified the meaning of this calling for all believers, a concept absent in the Enoch texts that we have, although it may have been assumed within the original community. All of this is further confirmed by the angelomorphism of the Angelic Liturgy at Qumran.

Yet complete surety about the history of this tradition is elusive. Paul did not explicitly call the Christ "the Glory of the Lord."[33] And because the *Parables* (1 En 37–71) are missing from the Dead Sea Scrolls, we cannot date them accurately. As opposed to the earlier Enoch material, they may date to the first century or later and may have been influenced by Christianity, since they are extant only in the Ethiopic version of Enoch, the official canon of the Ethiopian Christian church. Yet, whatever the date of *1 Enoch* 70–71, there is no doubt that the stories of Enoch's ascensions in *1 Enoch* 14 antedated Paul and could have influenced any of his conceptions about the heavenly journey.[34]

Shortly before his death, Morton Smith reported that he had found a text which firmly anchors these experiences to the first century and to Qumran, thus necessarily to a long prehistory in that community. In 4QMa of the Dead Sea Scrolls found at Qumran, Morton Smith sees evidence to translate a passage:

> [El Elyon gave me a seat among] those perfect forever, a mighty throne in the congregation of the gods. None of the kings of the east shall sit in it and their nobles shall not [come near it.] No Edomite shall be like me in glory. And none shall be exalted save me, nor shall come against me. For I have taken my seat in the [congregation] in the heavens, and none [find fault with me.] I shall be reckoned with gods and established in the holy congregation.

Smith's translations are careful and his reconstructions conservative. Along with the Angelic Liturgy this is now persuasive evidence that the mystics at the Dead Sea understood themselves to be one company with the angels, whom they call the *b'nei Elohim (běně 'Ĕlōhîm)*, which they must have achieved through some Sabbath rite of translation and transmutation.[35]

As long as the date of *1 Enoch* 70–71 cannot be fixed exactly and as long as evidence of the Dead Sea Scrolls remains provocative and debatable, Paul himself remains the earliest author explicitly expressing this kind of angelic transformation in Judaism. But the transformation that Paul achieved is coterminous with achieving resurrection in the afterlife. If his discussion of transformation can be related to apocalyptic mysticism in Judaism, he also becomes the only Jewish mystic of this period to relate this personal experience confessionally. The difference between this experience and the other ancient Near Eastern journeys to heaven—Adapa, Etana, Enoch, etc—is that from this period onward, the journey is most often being made through RASC. In Paul's writing, we have an anomalous case where he is not sure whether it is made in the body or in the spirit. But it seems clear that spiritual bodies and angelic bodies must now be considered analogous. They are bodily but they are not flesh. Paul believed that they were bodies like the heavenly bodies but with distinctions to be made between heavenly bodies (1 Cor 15:41). This suggests that Paul would have ranked Christ higher than an ordinary angel but that he would have considered both divine in some general way.

There is adequate evidence, then, that many Jewish mystics and apocalypticists sensed a relationship between the angels and important figures in the life of their community. The roots of this tradition are pre-Christian, though the tradition was massively developed by Christianity. Furthermore, Jewish scholars have overlooked Christianity as evidence for the existence of these traditions in first-century Judaism. Paul did not have to be a religious innovator to posit an identification between a vindicated hero and the image of the *Kavod*, the manlike figure in heaven, although the identification of the figure with the risen Christ is a uniquely Christian development. If so, along with the mysterious, anonymous psalmist from Qumran, Paul was a rare Jewish mystic who reported his own personal, identifiably confessional mystical experiences in the fifteen hundred years that separate Ezekiel from the rise of Kabbalah.

Paul himself gives the best evidence for the existence of ecstatic journeys to heaven in first-century Judaism, with his report in 2 Corinthians.[36] His inability to decide whether the voyage took place in the body or out of the body is firm evidence of a mystical ascent and shows that the voyage had not been interiorized as a journey into the self, which later became common in Kabbalah. Since the Rabbis proscribed the discussion of these topics except singly, to mature disciples, and only provided they had experienced it on their own (M. Hag. 2.1), the Rabbinic stories interpreting the Merkabah experience often took place while traveling through the wilderness from city to city, when such doctrines could easily be discussed in private (b. Hag. 14b). This is precisely the scene that Luke picked for Paul's conversion.[37]

It is significant that in 2 Corinthians 12, when Paul talked about mystical journeys directly, he too adopted a pseudepigraphical stance. He did not admit to the ascent personally. Apart from the needs of his rhetoric,

Rabbinic rules also forbade public discussion of mystic phenomena. A first-century date for this rule would explain why Paul would not divulge his experience in his own name at that place. It would also suggest why Jewish mystics consistently picked pseudepigraphical literary conventions to discuss their religious experience, unlocking the mystery behind the entire phenomenon of pseudepigraphical writing. But none of the standard discussions of this incompletely understood phenomenon mention Paul's confession or the Mishnah here.[38] Again, Paul may be giving us hitherto unrecognized information about Jewish culture in the first century which is unavailable from anywhere else.

Transformation into the Christ

WHEN PAUL was not faced with a direct declaration of personal mystical experience, he revealed much about mystical religion as it was experienced in the first century. Paul himself designated Christ as "the image of the Lord" in a few places: 2 Corinthians 4:4, Colossians 1:15 (if it is Pauline), and he mentioned the *morphé* (form, shape) of God in Philippians 2:6.[39] More often he spoke of transforming believers into "the image of His son" in various ways (Rom 8:29; 2 Cor 3:18; Phil 3:21, and 1 Cor 15:49; also Col 3:9). These passages are critical to understanding what Paul's experience of conversion was. They must be seen in closer detail to understand the relationship to Jewish apocalypticism and mysticism, from which they derived their most complete significance for Paul. Paul's longest discussion of these themes occurs in 2 Corinthians 3:18–4:6. Here he assumes the context rather than explaining it completely:

> Now the Lord is the Spirit, and where the Spirit of the Lord is, there is freedom. And we all, with unveiled face, beholding the glory of the Lord, are being changed into his likeness from one degree of glory to another; for this comes from the Lord who is the Spirit. Therefore, having this ministry by the mercy of God, we do not lose heart. We have renounced disgraceful, underhanded ways; we refuse to practice cunning or to tamper with God's word, but by the open statement of the truth we would commend ourselves to every man's conscience in the sight of God. And even if our gospel is veiled, it is veiled only to those who are perishing. In their case the god of this world has blinded the minds of the unbelievers, to keep them from seeing the light of the gospel of the glory of Christ, who is the likeness of God. For what we preach is not ourselves, but Jesus Christ as Lord, with ourselves as your

servants for Jesus' sake. For it is the God who said, "Let light shine out of darkness," who has shone in our hearts to give the light of the knowledge of the Glory of God in the face of Christ.

Paul began this passage by reference to the spiritual nature of the Christ, calling him both "Lord" and "Spirit." He ended this passage by identifying "the Glory of God" with Christ. The question is, how literally did he mean it? There is reason to think that he was being fully literal and candid, since transformation was a sensible expectation of apocalyptic Jews in the first century. Paul used these terms in their Biblical technical sense to identify the Christ with the human manifestation of God and then suggested that this was the same as his spiritual visions of Christ. For now, the main point must be the usually unappreciated use of the spiritual language of transformation in Paul's works. Paul's entire description of resurrection is framed around his visionary experience, which in turn carried his argument that he was the equal of the fleshly disciples and apostles of Jesus.

In 2 Corinthians 3:18, Paul said that believers will be changed into Christ's likeness from one degree of glory to another. He refered to Exodus 33 and 34, where Moses' encounter with the angel of the Lord is narrated. Earlier in Exodus, the angel of the Lord was described as carrying the name of God (Exod 23:21). Moses sees the "Glory of the Lord," makes a covenant, receives the commandments upon the two tables of the law and, when he comes down from the mount, the skin of his face shines with light, as the Bible states (Exod 34:29–35). Moses thereafter must wear a veil except when he is in the presence of the Lord. Paul assumed that Moses made an ascension to the presence of the Lord, was transformed by that encounter and that his shining face was a reflection of the encounter, perhaps even as a foretaste of his angelic destiny. But Paul also made a polemical point about the fading of Moses' halo of light (2 Cor 3:13) that implied Christians have a more lasting glory (2 Cor 4:4) because they have accepted the Gospel.

Paul used strange and significant mystical language. But what is immediately striking about it is that Paul used that language to discuss his own and other Christians' experience "in Christ." Transformation becomes the possibility and goal of all believers. Paul even explicitly compared Moses' experience with his own and that of Christian believers. Their transformation is of the same sort, but the Christian transformation is greater and more permanent. Once the background of the vocabulary is pointed out, Paul's daring claims for Christian experience become clear.

The point, therefore, is that some Christian believers also make such an ascent somehow, also share in the divine spirit, and also experience more permanent spiritual effects than the vision Moses received. The church has witnessed a theophany as important as the one vouchsafed to Moses but the Christian theophany is greater still, as Paul himself experienced and testified. The Corinthians were said to be a message from Christ (2 Cor 3:2), who was equated with "the Glory of God." The new community of gentiles was not given a letter written on stone (Jer 31:33) but God's message was delivered by Paul as Moses delivered the Torah to Israel. The new dispensation was more splendid than the last, not needing the veil with which Moses hid his face. Paul's own experience proved to him and for Christianity that all will be transformed.

Paul's term, "the Glory of the Lord" must be taken both as a reference to Christ and as a technical term for the *Kavod*, the human form of God appearing in Biblical visions. In 2 Corinthians 3:18, Paul said that Christians behold the Glory of the Lord as in a mirror and are transformed into his image.[40] For Paul, as for the earliest Jewish mystics, to be privileged enough to see the *kavod* or Glory *(doxa)* of God was a prologue to transformation into His image *(eikon)*. Paul did not say that all Christians made the journey but compared the experience of knowing Christ to being allowed into the intimate presence of the Lord, to be given entrance to God's court. And he himself had made that journey.

The result of the journey (over several years of proselytizing) was to identify Christ as "the Glory of the Lord." When Paul said that he preached that Jesus was Lord and that God "has let this light shine out of darkness into our hearts to give the light of knowledge of the Glory of God in the face of Christ" (2 Cor 4:6), he seems clearly to have been describing his own conversion and ministry, just as he described it in Galatians 1, and just as he was explaining the experience to new converts for the purpose of furthering and strengthening their conversion.[41] His apostolate, which he expressed as a prophetic calling, was to proclaim that the face of Christ is the "Glory of God." It is very difficult not to read this passage in terms of Paul's description of the ascension of the man to the third heaven and conclude that Paul's conversion experience also involved his identification of Jesus as the "Image" and "Glory of God," as the human figure in heaven, and thereafter as Lord, Spirit, Christ, Son, and Savior.

The identification of Christ with the Glory of the Lord brings a transformation and sharing of the believer with the image as well. This is the same as regaining the image of God which Adam lost. This transformation is accomplished through death and rebirth in Christ, which can be experienced in direct visions as Paul apparently did, or by anyone through baptism. But the important thing is to note how completely the theophanic language from Greek and Jewish mystical piety has been appropriated for discussing what we today call conversion. It was Paul's primary language for describing the experience of conversion, because it gives a sense of the transformation and divinization (or angelification) that he felt was inherent in his encounter with the risen Christ. This transformation and angelification is authenticated in communal life, in social transactions (for instance, 1 Cor 12–14, also 1 Cor 5:1–5).

Concomitant with Paul's worship of the divine Christ is transformation. Paul said in Philippians 3:10: "that I may know him and the power of his resurrection and may share his sufferings, becoming like him in his death" *(symmorphizomenos toi thanatoi autou)*. Later, in Philippians 3:20–21, he said: "But our commonwealth is in heaven, and from it we await a Savior, the Lord Jesus Christ, who will change *(metaschematisei)* our lowly body to be conformed in shape *(symmorphon)* to his glorious body *(toi sōmati tēs doxes autou)* by the power that enables him even to subject all things to himself."

English does not allow us to build such a vivid image into one word. If we had an English word for it, it would be *symmorphosis,* like "metamorphosis" but with a more intimate and transformative meaning. The Greek verb means literally "to be morphed together with," what our word "metamorphosize" suggests, except that it states that the reformation will explicitly take place "together with" *(sym-)* his glorious body, suggesting the outcome is a new compound of both. The body of the believer eventually is to be transformed together with and combined into the body of Christ. The believer's body is to be changed into the same spiritual body of glory as that of the savior.

We need to coin another new word to understand the next part of this statement, where Paul talked about transformation in a slightly different way. Paul struggled with the expression of his mystic intution. He also said that the change will *metaschematize* (change the structure of) our lowly body so that it will become His glorious body (Phil 3:10). Again English does not easily allow us to appreciate this unusual feature of the Greek language. But Paul was suggesting that this transformation from our lowly body to His glorious body "metaschematizes," creates a new "metascheme," perhaps to be understood as a new master-narrative of the history of salvation in Israel. This vision, would, in effect, produce an entirely new understanding of what salvation meant. We know that a great deal of the story is not new. But the identification of the divine figure in heaven with the crucified Messiah on earth, with whose suffering one is to be identified, is entirely new. And it clearly came not from any preexistent prophecy but from the events of the end of Jesus' life.

Paul exhorted his followers to imitate him as he imitated Christ: "Brethren, join in imitating me, and mark those who so live as you have an example in us" (1 Cor 11:1). The followers were told to imitate Paul as he himself imitated Jesus. All of this suggests that the body of believers would be refashioned into the glorious body of Christ, a process which starts with conversion and faith but ends in the parousia, the shortly-expected culmination of history when Christ returns. It all depends on a notion of body that is a new spiritualized substance, a new body which is not flesh and blood, which cannot inherit the kingdom (1 Cor 15:42–50).

Paul's depiction of salvation and the transformation of the believer was based on his understanding of Christ's glorification, partaking of early Jewish apocalyptic mysticism for its expression. The basic notion of transformation into an angelic or astral form may even have survived from a pre-Christian setting because Paul did not mention resurrection here at all. Clearly glorification is doing the work of resurrection in this passage. Likewise, in Romans 12:2 Paul's listeners were exhorted to "be transformed *(metamorphousthe)* by renewing of your minds." In Galatians 4:19 Paul expressed another but very similar transformation: "My little children, with whom I am again in travail until Christ be formed *(morphed, morphōthēi)* in you!"

This transformation, surprisingly, was to be effected by being transformed into Christ in his death *(symmorphizomenos tou thanatou autou,* Phil 3:10). This identification with the death of Jesus is a crucial issue for understanding Paul's religious experience. Paul predicted that the believer would be transformed into the glorious body of Christ, through dying and being reborn in Christ. As we shall see, Paul saw the phenomenon as being related to baptism. Paul's central proclamation is: Jesus is Lord and all who have faith have already undergone a death like his, so will share in his resurrection by being transformed into his form, spirit, and shape. As we have seen, this proclamation reflects a baptismal liturgy, implying that baptism provides the moment whereby the believer comes to be "in Christ." Christianity may have been a unique Jewish sect in making baptism a central rather than a preparatory ritual, but some of the mystical imagery came from its Jewish past, probably through the teachings of John the Baptist.[42]

Paul's conception of the risen body of Christ as the spiritual body

(1 Cor 15:43–44) at the end of time and as the body of Glory (Phil 3:21) thus originates in Jewish apocalypticism and mysticism, modified by the unique events of early Christianity. Spirit is a synonym for the "Glory" and "form" which Christ has already received. The meaning of Romans 8:29 can be likewise clarified by Jewish esoteric tradition. There, as we have seen, Paul spoke of God as having "foreordained his elect to be conformed (*symmorphous* again) to the image of his Son." Paul used the genitive here rather than the dative as in Philippians 3:21, softening the identification between believer and savior. But when Paul stated that believers conform to the image of His Son, he was not speaking of an agreement of mind or ideas between Jesus and the believers. The word behind the English word "conformed" is *symmorphon* again. Appearing in an oblique case, the word *symmmorphous* itself still suggests a spiritual reformation of the believer's body into the form of the divine image. Paul's language for conversion—"being in Christ"—developed out of mystical Judaism.

This, it seems to me, is the reward that Paul expected Jews, and by extension gentiles, to gain when they had faith in Christ. They came to be "in Christ." It may be that Paul assumed all who were part of Israel were to be saved, as he says in Romans. What he was offering those who believed in Christ was not merely salvation but transformation. This was beyond the rewards offered by the Sadducees certainly, and by those usually understood to be righteous Jews in Pharisaism (i.e., mSanhedrin 10).[43] He was maintaining that those who believe in Christ, Jew or gentile alike, will join his heavenly body.

First Corinthians 15

PAUL'S MAIN discussion of resurrection is in 1 Corinthians 15. In that letter, he began by showing that those who understand real wisdom are truly initiated into the revelations of the Holy Spirit. The language sounds something like what may be imagined to have taken place in mystery cults, as many scholars have pointed out. But why guess as to its possible relationship to a hypothetical piety in this period when it is demonstrably close to the language of Jewish apocalyptic mysticism that we find at Qumran, for instance, 1 Corinthians 2:6–10:[44]

> Yet among the mature we do impart wisdom, although it is not a wisdom of this age or of the rulers of this age, who are doomed to pass away. But we impart a secret and hidden wisdom of God, which God

decreed before the ages for our glorification. None of the rulers of this age understood this; for if they had, they would not have crucified the Lord of glory.

But, as it is written,

> "What no eye has seen, nor ear heard,
> nor the heart of man conceived,
> what God has prepared for those who love him,"

[from Isa 64:4; 65:17]

God has revealed to us through the Spirit. For the Spirit searches everything, even the depths of God. (1 Cor 2:6–10)

Paul wrote in the context of considerable communal argumentation and factional dispute. His interpretation of the Gospel was called into question by his opponents. He averred that his only source was the risen Christ; his only proof was his success, which is supplied by the Spirit.[45]

In this context, Paul spoke of those who were qualified, the mature ones who evidently shared his perspective and, perhaps, to some extent his experience. This is a plausible extrapolation when the term refers so often to the initiated in the mystery religions. But quite close to home, at Qumran, knowledge and "perfection" were expected of the membership and only "the perfected ones" had access to the full secrets of the sect (1QS 1:8; 2:2; 3:3, 9; 5:24; 8:20ff.; 9:2, 8ff., 19).[46]

Mystery was one of the central tenets of Qumran. Paul also described the revelation of the crucified Messiah as a mystery (1 Cor 2:8). Even so, it also contrasts with mystery at Qumran. Paul's mystery was not secret in the way that mystery at Qumran was. Although it needed to be taught and it was not universally accepted, it did not itself need to be secret. Paul's mystery found its particular adherents. Unlike the Qumran community, Paul evidently thought all Christians will be transformed, whereas the issue was moot at Qumran but it looks like the transformation was restricted to the priests.

In 1 Corinthians, Paul discussed the issue of the final disposition of the body before he discussed the issue of resurrection and transformation itself. In this passage he may also have been responding to the Greek notion that the body decays while the soul lives on. A. J. Wedderburn has astutely observed that the issue in 1 Corinthians 6 is the normal conception of the afterlife in a Greek environment.[47] It is in this context that Paul took up the issue of the body:

> "All things are lawful for me," but not all things are beneficial. "All things are lawful for me," but I will not be dominated by anything. "Food is meant for the stomach and the stomach for food," and God will destroy both one and the other. The body is meant not for fornication but for the Lord, and the Lord for the body. And God raised the Lord and will also raise us by his power. (1 Cor 6:12–14)

The Greeks believed that the body was destined for destruction. But Paul did not follow through with a Platonic analysis of the immortality of the soul.[48] Instead, he stayed in the apocalyptic-mystical world of Judaism, defending and sharpening that notion in view of the Greek assumptions about the continuity of life after death. Paul immediately suggested that the body will survive death, for it belongs to the Lord. God will raise it in glory and perfection by means of the spirit, just as he raised up the body of Jesus, who is even now in his spiritual state.

This kind of talk will demand a clarification in a Greco-Roman context. But, as Paul was still discussing various moral issues within the community, he postponed his discussion until later in the letter, to 1 Corinthians 15. There Paul summed up his entire religious experience in an apocalyptic vision of the resurrection of believers. Paul began with a description of his previous preaching and suggested that if his listeners gave up belief in the resurrection then they believed in Christ in vain:

> Now if Christ is proclaimed as raised from the dead, how can some of you say there is no resurrection of the dead? If there is no resurrection of the dead, then Christ has not been raised; and if Christ has not been raised, then our proclamation has been in vain and your faith has been in vain. We are even found to be misrepresenting God, because we testified of God that he raised Christ—whom he did not raise if it is true that the dead are not raised. For if the dead are not raised, then Christ has not been raised. If Christ has not been raised, your faith is futile and you are still in your sins. Then those also who have died in Christ have perished. If for this life only we have hoped in Christ, we are of all people most to be pitied. (1 Cor 15:12–19)

Paul claimed to have given them, indeed emphasized as the first importance, the true teaching, as he had himself received it. And that teaching was simply that Christ died for sins in accordance with Scripture, that he was entombed and rose three days later, all in accordance with Scripture.

There is no doubt that this is the earliest Christian teaching with regard to the resurrection: It is part of the primitive *kerygma* or proclamation of the church.

MARTYRDOM AND TRANSFORMATION

For Paul the identification with Jesus mystically made everyone a martyr and, logically, made everyone qualified for the resurrection rewards of a martyr. Those who believe in Christ are worthy of the same rewards as the martyrs, who can expect not just a bodily existence at the final end of history, but who can also expect the further reward of the martyred few ("those who lead many to knowledge") as heavenly angels (stars) for having enlightened the world:

> We are afflicted in every way, but not crushed; perplexed, but not driven to despair; persecuted, but not forsaken; struck down, but not destroyed; always carrying in the body the death of Jesus, so that the life of Jesus may also be manifested in our bodies. (2 Cor 4:8–10)

Even more so for those who actually suffer for their faith. These spiritual experiences of transformation into the Christ form analogies to the life and death of Jesus. Those who suffer as the Christ suffered can expect identification with the exalted Christ *(symmorphosis)*. And more concretely it means that the believer must be ready to accept suffering as part of Christian discipleship.[49]

For Paul there was not much explicit recognition that a resurrection without the end was very strange. Paul apparently felt that the time was peculiarly out of joint because the first resurrection had happened but the end had not yet come about. Clearly, he thought the last stage would shortly arrive. And, as we know, the demonstration that the age had begun was the actual appearance of Jesus to him.

Paul—in contradistinction to some later Gnostic traditions—began from the supposition that the death and burial was real and hence the resurrection was actual and in accordance with Scripture (1 Cor 15:3). Paul then listed those to whom the postresurrection Jesus appeared. In Paul's understanding the postresurrection appearances rather than the physical presence of Jesus was primary. He included himself modestly in the list of those to whom Jesus had appeared. But if the list had been made up of those who knew Jesus in the flesh, Paul would have been left out and James would have been preeminent. The corruptible flesh of the earthly Jesus is not the point for Paul. He deliberately widened the concept of apostleship to include persons like himself who had a spiritual relationship with the Christ. For him, it is Jesus the heavenly redeemer who reveals himself to his chosen, who is the proof of faith, not merely those who may have heard Jesus's preaching.

In verses 12–19, Paul claimed that the deniers of the resurrection of the dead were denying the Gospel which they had received and initially believed. He began a series of arguments which ended in the *reductio ad absurdum* that "if Christ has not been raised, then our proclamation has been in vain and your faith has been in vain." The rhetoric depended on the hearers' understanding that the premise was wrong. This argument only made sense to believers; no one else would have seen the absurdity of the conclusion. A great number of scholars have speculated on what the Corinthians had been misled into believing. They could have been pre-Gnostics or proto-Gnostics, who denied that the body is raised.

But, in fact, they need not have been either; they could merely have been following ordinary Greek popular thought in a Platonic vein, thinking that the soul is immortal but that the body cannot be raised from the dead (nor would anyone want to be embodied, given the choice). That is to say, they may only have been ordinary Greeks for whom the Christian message of the resurrection of Jesus might naturally have been interpreted in a different context than the apocalyptic one out of which Paul originally spoke. A person might survive death through the immortality of the soul in Greek thought but a bodily resurrection was never any significant part in Greek thinking.[50]

It is not necessarily true, as Paul argued, that all those who died in Christ would have been thought by his listeners to have perished. They may merely receive their divine reward on the basis of their deeds, or knowledge, or the soul's natural inclination.[51] But, as Paul suggested, this notion, whoever the author is, denies the salvific nature of Christ's death in totality. It is the bodily resurrection of Jesus that guarantees that God's plan for the final destruction of the evil ones of the world is already set in place. For if the soul is immortal by nature and that is the highest form of immortality to be achieved, then the sacrifice of Christ is unnecessary.

In verses 20–28 Paul stopped arguing against enemies and began articulating his own notions. He showed that the resurrection of Christ entails the future resurrection of all the righteous dead as Christ is the "firstfruit of them who have fallen asleep" (vs 20), yet again using the term that is clearly dependent upon Daniel 12 and, in turn, Isaiah 26 (also see, e.g., LXX Ps 87:6). Probably then, the scriptural passage that Paul had in mind earlier (1 Cor 15:3) is none other than Daniel 12:2: "And many of those who sleep in the dust of the earth shall awake, some to everlasting life, and some to shame and everlasting contempt. And those who are wise shall shine like the brightness of the firmament; and those who turn many to righteousness, like the stars for ever and ever" (Dan 12:1–3).

Paul's argument was made on the basis of analogy from Adam. Just as death came from Adam, so eternal life comes from Christ. But Christ is the first, then those who belong to Christ. At the end, Christ will hand over the kingdom of God to the father, after he has destroyed every power. Paul was making clear reference to the "Son of Man" passage in Daniel 7:13 when he said that Christ must reign until he has put all his enemies under his feet. There are other enthronement passages in the Hebrew Bible but none others in which the reign of justice is made dependent upon the enthroned figure. Together with the transformation, Paul posited an apocalyptic end; the two are deeply connected.

Why Paul never actually used the term "Son of Man" is something of a mystery. It may be because he knew Hebrew and Aramaic too well. "Son of Man" is not a proper title or even a good translation for the original phrase. Whereas Mark 10:45 writes "The Son of Man came . . . to give his life as a ransom for many," Galatians 2:20 paraphrases the saying with "Son of God." Similar, possible paraphrases in the later Deutero-Pauline literature are translated with Greek word *anthropos* (human being), Jesus Christ (1 Tim 2:5–6) or "the Son of the Man" (Eph 5:2, Titus 2:13–14). This is important evidence suggesting that Paul intended to refer to the vision in Daniel 7:13–14 in his own writing, but that he did not recognize the phrase "Son of Man" as a title for the figure in heaven in Daniel. Although Paul never used the term "Son of Man" he clearly identified the Christ with the "Son of Man" figure on the throne in Daniel 7:13. Paul showed the antiquity of that position, without affirming to us that "Son of Man" was a title. In this, he seems rather to have been working in a Jewish context in which any Scripture can be read as prophecy, without relying on any preexistent titles for Jesus.

Heavenly man traditions are crucial to the development of the Christian meaning of Jesus' earthly mission.[52] They inform all the New Testament discussions of the "Son of Man" in ways that have been infrequently discussed by the leading scholars studying the term.[53] While it is quite likely that some of Jesus' followers thought of him as a messiah or a messianic candidate during his own lifetime, they were disabused of that idea by his arrest, trial, and death on the cross as "The King of the Jews," for no pre-Christian view of the messiah conceived of the possibility of the failure of the Messianic mission and his demise at the hands of the Romans.[54]

Instead, the disciples' experience of Jesus' resurrection and ascension to the right hand of God confirmed the originally discarded Messianic title retrospectively in a new, dynamic, and ironic way. Resurrection and ascension had already entered Jewish thought in the century previous to Jesus, as a reward for the righteous martyrs of the Maccabean wars. Thus, while Christianity represents a purely Jewish reaction to a tragic series of events in Jesus' life, the reaction was at the same time absolutely novel. The process should be of special interest to Jewish scholars as well as students of Christology, because it is the clearest evidence we have from the first century on as to how new religious groups were founded on historical events understood as fulfillment of Scripture. It shows how Jewish expectations derived from Biblical texts intersected with historical events, even quite anomalous historical events. The events were given meaning by creative interplay between the facts and a hermeneutic process of reading any passage in the Bible as prophecy that could be fulfilled in a new and surprising way. Given Paul's mysticism, it also links personal transformation with the end of the evil, unredeemed world.

The Christian innovation is to have identified the angelic or divine figure who brought judgment, the Son of Man of Daniel 7:13 and who could also be called "the Lord," with Jesus the Messiah or *Christos*. No other movement so far has shown any interest in conflating "Lord" with "the Messiah," though the Qumran community had already identified divine terms like 'El, with the principal angels of God (11QMelch). On the basis of Daniel 7:9–14 and Daniel 12, together with Psalms 8 and 110, the Christian community found the Scriptural support that clarified what God had in mind for the end of history.

We can now see this in better detail. Since Jesus died as a martyr, expectations of his resurrection would have been normal in some Jewish sects.[55] But the idea of a crucified messiah was unique. In such a situation, the Christians only did what other believing Jews did in similar circumstances: They turned to Biblical prophecy for elucidation. No Messianic text suggested itself as appropriate to the situation. But Psalm 110:1 was exactly apposite: The LORD says to my lord: "Sit at my right hand until I make your enemies your footstool." [56]

Here was a description of the enthronement of a Davidic descendant, now understood as a heavenly enthronement after death and resurrection. Yet nothing in the Bible text makes the death or resurrection part of the narrative inevitable. It must have come from the historical experience of the events of Jesus' life, not the other way around. The early Christian community, after they experienced these events, found the Scripture that explained the meaning of the events. Thereafter, Psalm 110:1 could be combined easily with Daniel 7:9–13, the description of the enthronement of the "Son of Man." Daniel 7:9–13 seemed to prophesy Christ's exaltation and ascension because Jesus could be identified with the Son of Man, an angelic figure, who is, in turn, identified with the second "Lord" in the quotation from Psalm 110. Daniel 12:2 had promised astral, angelic immortality to those who taught wisdom, confirming the entire set of expectations. The combination of Psalm 110 with Daniel 7:13 (possibly together with Psalm 8) gives us a good explanation for the difficult "spiritual body" phrase in Paul's writing. In short, the combination of these two passages, seen together with the martyrdom of Jesus as the Messiah of Israel, produced the *kerygma* of the Early Church. It was this as well that allowed Paul to come to the conclusions he did, though he also received revelations and visions which confirmed the teaching.

FIRST CORINTHIANS 15:37–50

First Corinthians 15:35–50 is one of the most systematic expositions of the Jewish mystical and apocalyptic tradition, which seems central to Paul's message of the meaning of Christ's resurrection. The coming end means transformation and resurrection for all who believe in him:

> But someone will ask, "How are the dead raised? With what kind of body do they come?" Fool! What you sow does not come to life unless it dies. And as for what you sow, you do not sow the body that is to be, but a bare seed, perhaps of wheat or of some other grain. But God gives it a body as he has chosen, and to each kind of seed its own body. Not all flesh is alike, but there is one flesh for human beings, another for animals, another for birds, and another for fish. There are both heavenly bodies and earthly bodies, but the glory of the heavenly is one thing, and that of the earthly is another. There is one glory of the sun, and another glory of the moon, and another glory of the stars; indeed, star differs from star in glory. So it is with the resurrection of the dead. What is sown is perishable, what is raised is imperishable. It is sown in dishonor, it is raised in glory. It is sown in weakness, it is raised in power. It is sown a physical body, it is raised a spiritual body. If there is a physical body, there is also a spiritual body. Thus it is written, "The first man, Adam, became a living being"; the last Adam became a life-giving

428

spirit. But it is not the spiritual that is first, but the physical, and then the spiritual. The first man was from the earth, a man of dust; the second man is from heaven. As was the man of dust, so are those who are of the dust; and as is the man of heaven, so are those who are of heaven. Just as we have borne the image of the man of dust, we will also bear the image of the man of heaven. What I am saying, brothers and sisters, is this: flesh and blood cannot inherit the kingdom of God, nor does the perishable inherit the imperishable. (1 Cor 15:37–50)

In 1 Corinthians 15:35 Paul began a brief exposition of the nature of the resurrection body. He was, in this passage, outlining a notion of afterlife which had nothing to do with immortality of the soul; it is an offshoot of Jewish apocalypticism, out of which the Christian kerygma grows. But he was also cognizant of the beliefs of the audience so he merely ignored and did not argue against the immortality of the soul. Instead, he fastened again on the notion of spirit to explicate how the physical body of believers would be transformed by the resurrection. His argument had nothing to do with what happened to Christ during the passion nor did he mention any empty tomb. His argument is by analogy with his own experience and, by expressing it this way, he was trying to keep faith with his own experience of the Spirit of God. His use of language of the body is entirely unique.

The term for "physical body" is not exactly what one might expect but this is due to an unfortunate English translation. Neither the term *soma sarkikon* (fleshly body) nor the term *soma physikon* (physical body) occurs; rather the term which occurs is *soma psychikon*, "ensouled body," a word which can mean "natural body" but is not the most obvious term for it. Since it combines the word for soul with the term for body, it is in a sense the totality of the Platonic ensouled-body as the Hellenistic world understood it. In a Platonic system that would only mean human bodies as we know them, with matter and soul both, therefore corruptible bodies. Because "psyche" could be taken to mean life in the physical sense in a non-Platonic setting, it is not necessarily a problem, strange though it may look; *soma psychikon* does occur in Hellenistic literature with that meaning.[57]

But the contrasting term, *soma pneumatikon* is a complete contradiction in terms for anyone in a Platonic system, especially when contrasted with the psychic body just mentioned: "It is sown a physical body, it is raised a spiritual body. If there is a physical body, there is also a spiritual body" (1 Cor 15:41).

There is no easy way to subsume this pair of statements into Platonism. What Paul was doing, however, was contrasting the Platonic view of humanity (the unredeemed body composed of soul and flesh) with his own view of the redeemed body, one that now had been transformed by the Spirit of God. One might say that Paul was trying to characterize his apocalyptic vision in a Hellenistic context, something like Josephus did for the speech of Eleazar ben Yair. But Paul's message only really makes sense within its Jewish, apocalyptic context. For Paul, life in its most basic sense, psychic life, was also bodily life. "Pneumatic," spiritual life is bodily as well, though Paul immediately reiterated that flesh and blood cannot inherit the kingdom of God (1 Cor 15:50). The psychic body is the ordinary body (flesh and soul); the *soma pneumatikon* is the ordinary body subsumed and transformed by the spirit.

This new, spiritual, glorious body, which is the redeemed, resurrected body, is equivalent to Christ's body. And so the new body that God gives His faithful in the resurrection will be a "pneumatic" or "spiritual" body augmented by the "Spirit" of God. Indeed, Paul had been given a foretaste of the redeemed body because the Spirit of God already lived in him. As the end approaches, the working of the Spirit will grow stronger and stronger until the final transformation, when we will share the image of the heavenly body.

This completely coheres with Paul's notion that the fleshly way to salvation is not through observances of times and rituals, not through Jewish or gentile rituals, for that matter. Fleshly rituals are not a spiritual, transforming way to salvation. He argued that the nature of the resurrection body is different from anything we know, just as the nature of various fleshly creatures is different. Paul, in fact, left the issue of the nature of immortality in a peculiarly intermediate position. He affirmed that those who believe will have an imperishable bodily nature but he suggested that the faithful will receive it by bodily resurrection. The body of the resurrection will not be flesh and blood. It will be a body created in a sudden change, by *symmorphosis*. He knew from his visions that the process of transformation into a glorified, spiritual body had already begun. The process will be completed at the last trumpet.

The eschaton and destiny of all believers will be a transformation that does not necessarily do away with the body but "transforms" it to a spiritual substance. Paul made an explicit analogy with the stars, which are both spiritual and bodies at the same time. And that analogy is not merely adventitious. It links the transformation process with the passage in Daniel 12 yet again, since Daniel 12 described the wise as transformed into stars. The transformed in Christ will have, in short, the same substance as the stars, which are luminous and spiritual in nature. This was, for Paul, the very fulfillment of the end of time, as promised by Daniel 12.

In 1 Corinthians 15:45, Paul turned his attention to the relationship between transformation within the believer and the coming end. When speaking of the resurrection, Paul described a reciprocal relationship between Adam and Christ: Just as Adam brought death into the world so Christ, the second Adam, would bring resurrection.

Paul, however, was not so much talking about the man Jesus as he was talking about Christ's exalted nature as *anthropos*. Since the imagery is so dependent upon the contrast between fallen and raised states, this passage may also imply a baptismal setting. It is also interesting that the alternation is conceived in bodily terms, not as a transmigration of souls.

But the image of man is also part of the process of inward transformation for Paul. A great many of his uses of *anthropos* (man) suggest that a transformation of "all" believers was his objective. For instance, Romans 6:6 reads: "We know that our old self was crucified with him so that the sinful body might be destroyed, and we might no longer be enslaved to sin." Or in another, equally provocative place, Paul said: "So we do not lose heart. Though our outer nature is wasting away, our inner nature is being renewed every day" (2 Cor 4:16). In both cases, the translation has obscured that the underlying Pauline word was *anthropos*, "human," used to designate the internal state of transformation within us. But this is likely the very term that Paul used to designate the "Son of Man" in Daniel 7:13. Paul was, in fact, giving us a new vocabulary of inwardness, a new mysticism, built on the apocalyptic vision of the end of time.[58] He connected the inward state with the outward state. The inward state is not necessarily causing the outward condition of the world, nor is the outward condition of the world causing the inward state. But both are being transformed by God's plan.

THE RETURN TO PRIMAL INNOCENCE

Instead of leaving the body entirely behind as in the case of the Greek soul, the body of glory or pneumatic body is the natural body augmented. It becomes properly androgynous, an added spiritual nature, as it was when God created it in Genesis. It regains its divine likeness, its angelic completeness, the primal combination of maleness and femaleness that it lost at the beginning. This appears to be a consequence of attaining angelic status:

Then God said, "Let us make man in our image, after our likeness; and let them have dominion over the fish of the sea, and over the birds of the air, and over the cattle, and over all the earth, and over every creeping thing that creeps upon the earth." (Gen 1:26)

Notice that the Bible uses the same vocabulary of image and likeness as does the Ezekiel theophany, when speaking of God's glory:

Like the appearance of the bow that is in the cloud on the day of rain, so was the appearance of the brightness round about. Such was the appearance of the likeness of the glory of the LORD. And when I saw it, I fell upon my face, and I heard the voice of one speaking. (Ezek 1:28)

Paul explicitly says that the body of Christ is arsenothelous, androgenous, bisexual (genetically), hermaphrodite:

for in Christ Jesus you are all sons of God, through faith. For as many of you as were baptized into Christ have put on Christ. There is neither Jew nor Greek, there is neither slave nor free, there is neither male nor female; for you are all one in Christ Jesus. (Gal 3:26–28)

The term "son of God" is without sexual implication, a common gender, and it has throughout Jewish tradition denoted angels. Through baptism, this passage says explicitly, the Christian overcomes the antinomies of ordinary life, including the gender distinction, to become children of God—angels. To be an angel in this context means to have transcended flesh and gender. This means for Paul that the transformation that is effected through faith in Christ is begun in the act of baptism. It will end at the eschaton with the transformation of the faithful, just as Matthew will later say: "For in the resurrection they neither marry nor are given in marriage, but are like angels [59] in heaven" (Matt 22:30).

FIRST CORINTHIANS 15:51–57

From this follows the apocalyptic end:

Listen, I will tell you a mystery! We will not all die [Gk: fall asleep], but we will all be changed in a moment, in the twinkling of an eye, at the last trumpet. For the trumpet will sound, and the dead will be raised imperishable, and we will be changed. For this perishable body must put on imperishability, and this mortal body must put on immortality. When this perishable body puts on imperishability, and this mortal body puts on immortality, then the saying that is written will be fulfilled. (1 Cor 15:51–54)

Here is a full accounting of the apocalyptic end. It does not have the bizarre imagery of some of the apocalypses but the crucial issue of the disposition of the dead is handled fully. The mortal body will not be destroyed, to be left behind by the soul. Instead, it will put on immortality as a garment and be transformed by it. This is clearly another baptismal image and it suggests that what the natural body puts on to be transformed is the Spirit of God. For Paul, the self that sees the resurrection is the same as the old self but transformed, leaving behind sexuality and gender and becoming a new creation. The new creation is, in fact, a recovery of the original innocence of the primal human. This is the principle of identity for the Christian in the resurrection. It is not just what we are now but what we can be with God's Spirit. It is a transformed body.

In an effort to understand the relationship between transformation and justification, we must turn briefly to a later part of the Corinthian correspondence, where Paul discussed the effect of the spiritual transformation. The relationship between transformation and community is clarified there, so we will have to ignore momentarily the differing social context between the two letters. In 2 Corinthians 5:15–6:1, Paul spoke of the Christian as a new creation.

The "human point of view" is literally "according to the flesh" *(kata sarka)*, whereas the believer is "a new creation" of spirit *(pneuma)*. Again it is hard for us to imagine a spiritual body. But that is what Paul was suggesting. The reformulation experience changes the believer from a physical body to a new spiritual creation. It makes him become the righteousness of God, although the final consummation has not yet occurred. Paul could refer to himself even as an ambassador and fellow worker with Christ before the final transformation, participating in his body with him as he works.

Because the verb is implied, the passage can also be understood as implying that "there is a new creation," giving the event a cosmic as well as an individual significance. Paul connected the inner process of salvation with the outer process of world redemption. Now he also clarifies the social world: The process takes place in community. Like many visionaries, Paul meant to suggest not just a personal transformation but a transformation of community, indeed the cosmos as well, since all this took place in a radically apocalyptic framework.

Apocalyptic End in Romans 8

IN ROMANS 8, Paul returned to his previous metaphor that the resurrection of Christ is the firstfruits of the coming end (Rom 8:23). Now, he brings personal transformation and the apocalyptic end of the world into the saving action of the Spirit, synthesizing them into a unity:

> I consider that the sufferings of this present time are not worth comparing with the glory that is to be revealed to us. For the creation waits with eager longing for the revealing of the sons of God; for the creation was subjected to futility, not of its own will but by the will of him who subjected it in hope; because the creation itself will be set free from its bondage to decay and obtain the glorious liberty of the children of God. We know that the whole creation has been groaning in travail together until now; and not only the creation, but we ourselves, who have the first fruits of the Spirit, groan inwardly as we wait for adoption as sons, the redemption of our bodies. For in this hope we were saved. Now hope that is seen is not hope. For who hopes for what he sees? But if we hope for what we do not see, we wait for it with patience. (Rom 8:18–25)

Creation itself is on the verge of a gigantic transformation into the perfected earth under the effects of the Spirit. And humans too are being transformed by the Spirit into a new creation. Paul has already described how those who believe have suffered with Christ to become adopted as sons (Rom 8:14–17). Paul speaks of adoption, becoming heirs of God and coheirs with Christ, a legal metaphor of adoption in Roman law. But sonship also has the implication of angelic status in the Jewish world. Paul parallels the groaning of the universe to bring forth a new birth with the redemption of the body, the personal transformation of believers into the image of the Son:

> We know that in everything God works for good with those who love him, who are called according to his purpose. For those whom he foreknew he also predestined to be conformed to the image of his Son, in order that he might be the firstborn among many brethren. And those

whom he predestined he also called; and those whom he called he also justified; and those whom he justified he also glorified. (Rom 8:28–30)

Now the eschatological implications of personal transformations are fully exposed. The material world and the persons will all be transformed together at the end of time. Creation will achieve its perfected state. This is truly an apocalyptic vision, even though it is not expressed with all the accoutrements of other apocalyptic thinkers. Together with the perfected world, the believers will achieve a new perfection too, not as souls but as fully embodied humanity. Under the Spirit they will be transformed into the Christ and achieve a new divine humanity in Christ. They will essentially become angels, retaining their bodies but leaving fleshly existence behind.

Paul spoke of the transformation being partly experienced by believers already in their pre-parousia existence. His use of the present tense in Romans 12:2 and 2 Corinthians 3:18 underscored that transformation is an ongoing event. In 1 Corinthians 15:49 and Romans 8 it culminates at Christ's return, the *parousia*. This suggests that for Paul transformation was both a single, definitive event yet also a process that continues until the second coming. Indeed it is parallel to the consummation. The redemptive and transformative processes appear to correspond exactly with the turning of the ages. This age is passing away, though it certainly remains a present evil reality (1 Cor 3:19; 5:9; 2 Cor 4:4; Gal 1:4; Rom 12:2). The Gospel, which is the power of God for salvation (Rom 1:16), was progressing through the world (Phil 1:12; also Rom 9–11). It would have been hard not to see the success of the mission as a sign that the end was growing closer and the efforts of the faithful were helping to bring it. Paul's mission was, by all accounts, more successful than anyone imagined, including himself. The mystical vision of Christ was combined with a new and quite innovative missionary force in history.

The Presence of Christ in the Liturgy

PAUL'S COMMUNITIES must have had access to the presence of Jesus. That access was in the liturgical life of the community. The way that ordinary converts participated in the process of historical culmination was through the liturgical life of the community—through baptism and the Lord's Supper. Larry Hurtado has just finished an exciting new study of Christ devotion in early Christianity which makes this point quite effectively.[60] As several generations of scholars have now clarified, Paul understood that the name of Jesus and the term "Lord" not only referred to Jesus in his newly achieved divine dimension but used the name devotionally within the newly converted Christian community.

Given our lack of information, it is hard to know exactly how. One obvious place, where we do have evidence, is in baptism. Christian baptism was at first a full body immersion, as in Judaism, and that practice continued into earliest Christianity. Many sources attest that baptism was performed in the name of Jesus: "And Peter said to them, 'Repent, and be baptized every one of you in the name of Jesus Christ for the forgiveness of your sins; and you shall receive the gift of the Holy Spirit' " (Acts 2:38; see also 8:16 and 10:48). In the Corinthian correspondence, Paul explained that the recipients of his letter had not been baptized into his (Paul's) name (1 Cor 1:15), rather into the name of Jesus. As he said later: "And such were some of you. But you were washed, you were sanctified, you were justified in the name of the Lord Jesus Christ and in the Spirit of our God" (1 Cor 6:11). Just as is implied here, Acts says in several places that the reception of the Holy Spirit followed immediately upon baptism, giving us a social context for the Gospels' depiction of Jesus' own baptism being followed immediately by the descent of the spirit. The narrative parallel reflects the Early Church's understanding of the meaning of the ritual.

This parallel strongly suggests a liturgical basis for the reception of the Spirit in the baptismal ceremony in the early Palestinian, Christian community. It also suggests that the emergence of baptism in Pauline Christianity comes not from any presumed and unprovable links with Hellenistic mystery cults but easily and directly out of the use of this rite apocalyptically by Jewish millennialist groups. We now have considerable evidence that the rite was used at Qumran to prepare the community for their contact with the holy angels and the heavenly temple. Hence, the most obvious connection between Christianity and ritual immersion in an apocalyptic community is surely from the story of Jesus' own baptism "of repentance for the forgiveness of sins" at the hands of the apocalypticist John the Baptist (Mark 1:4).

All this demonstrates what Paul meant when he stated that the name of Jesus was used liturgically in baptism. Hurtado says: "The ritual invocation of Jesus in baptism helps explain why Paul described those baptized as having 'put on Christ' (Gal 3:27), and as having been 'buried with him [Christ] into his death' through the rite (Romans 6:4)." [61] Baptism was one way in which the believer came to be "in Christ" and therefore became mystically heir to the reward of the martyr—resurrection.

The other obvious liturgical rite of the Early Church was "the Lord's Supper." Paul himself used this title when describing the rite (1 Cor 11:20). The title itself establishes the relationship of the rite with the name of Christ, as we already know that the designation of *kyrios* is part of the church's primitive proclamation of the risen Christ's divinity through association with Daniel 7:13, Daniel 12:3, Psalm 110, and probably Psalm 8. Likewise, in 1 Cor 11:27 and 10:21 Paul referred to the "cup of the Lord" and the "table of the Lord," which only underlines the same liturgical use of the name Lord in early Christianity.

When Paul described the tradition he knew about the eucharistic words of Jesus, he stated that the ritual was to be done in remembrance of the Lord until He returns: "For as often as you eat this bread and drink the cup, you proclaim the Lord's death until he comes" (1 Cor 11:26). The presence of the Lord in community was assumed by Paul to be liturgical.

At the Jewish passover, the Rabbis of the Mishnah instituted the practice that "each generation should think of itself as if it too was brought out of Egypt, as if it too stood at the sea, as if it too stood as Sinai." This involved an act of imagination, and an act of telling, "and you shall tell . . ." which turns the ritual from being merely a remembrance to being an reenactment, a liturgical act of remembrance.

For Paul, the purpose of the Lord's Supper liturgy is, quite similarly, an imaginative reenactment, through the wine and bread, an *anamnesis* for the Lord until he comes. Indeed, in 1 Corinthians 5:7, Paul alluded directly to Jesus' death as a Passover sacrifice. Again, it is the proclamation of the death of Christ in the Lord's Supper which Paul connected with remembrance of Him. So this rite confirmed the believer's coming to be "in Christ." This is a strikingly different view from that of the Synoptic Gospels.

The Transformation of All Believers in Suffering

OF COURSE, the mystical experience of conversion is not only with the risen Christ in liturgy but with the crucified Christ, as well. The most obvious relationship between the believer and Christ is suffering and death (Rom 7:24; 8:10, 13). By being transformed by Christ, one is not simply made immortal, given the power to remain deathless. Rather one still experiences death as the Christ did, and like him survives death for heavenly enthronement. This is a consequence of the Christian's divided state. Although part of the last Adam, living through Spirit, the Christian also belongs to the world of the flesh. As James Dunn has noted: "Suffering was something *all* believers experienced—an unavoidable part of the believer's lot—an aspect of experience as Christians which his converts shared with Paul: Rom 5:3 ('we'); 8:17 ('we'), 2 Cor. 1:16 ('you endure the same sufferings that we suffer'); 8:2; Phil. 1:29ff. ('the same conflict which you saw and now hear to be mine'); 1 Thess. 1:6 ('imitators of us and of the Lord'); 2:14 ('imitators of the churches of God in Judea: for you suffered the same things'); 3:3 ('our lot'); 2 Thess. 1:4–6." [62] And if the suffering were not actual, it was vicarious in the liturgy of baptism and the Lord's supper. If it was real, it was the price of bringing the end. The believers fully participate in the coming end, through their missionary efforts, through their personal transformation, and finally through their suffering.

Thus, the persecution and suffering of the believers were a sign that the transformation process had begun; it is the way to come to be "in Christ." Paul was convinced that being united with Christ's crucifixion meant not only immediate glorification but suffering for the believers in this interim period (2 Cor 4:8–10 again). The glorification follows upon the consummation of history. The connection between suffering and resurrection was clear in Jewish martyrology; indeed the connection between death and rebirth was even a prominent part of the mystery religions as well. But the particular way in which Paul made these connections was explicitly Christian.

Summary

PAUL'S OWN conversion experience and his mystical ascension form the basis of his theology. His language shows the marks of a man who has learned the vocabulary of the day for expressing a theophany when he was a Pharisee and then received several theophanies as he became a Christian. First and foremost, Paul's visionary life allowed him to develop a concept of the divinity of the Christ or Messiah in a way that was both a unique development within the Jewish mystical tradition, and at the same time, characteristically Christian. Second, he also used this Jewish mystical vocabulary to express the transformation that happens to believers. They warrant immortality because they have been transformed by becoming formed like *(symmorphous)* the savior. Next, he used the language of transformation, gained through contact with Jewish mystical-apocalypticism and presumably through ecstatic conversion, to discuss the ultimate salvation and fulfillment of the apocalypse, raising believers to immortality in a parallel process of redemption. Last, this tandem process was visible in the new community through it liturgical life, its missionary efforts, and its brave endurance of suffering.

Resurrection, especially in parenetic contexts, refers to the future life in which the believer will share the image that Christ now possesses.[63] Thus, Paul's resurrection language allowed the community of believers to describe their present experience. They were the community of those who would experience the resurrection which Jesus had already attained. Further, Paul believed that he was not only part of the community to achieve eternal life, as Daniel 12 predicted, but one of those who made others wise and who would shine as the stars in heaven. He and the community of the faithful would soon become angels in heaven at the last trumpet, perhaps even to share in the final judgment as angels, which was what the Qumran community thought.

For Paul the reward was not based on the empty tomb nor was it a belief in a proposition. It is the experience of transformation from mortality to immortality in the real presence of the Spirit of the risen Lord, which in turn, guaranteed his intercession in heaven and the coming transformation of those who believed in him. This is quite different from the narration that the Gospels offer us. In Paul's writings, we have a record of the Church's experience illuminated by his personal experience and continuing relationship with his savior. He was clear about the distinction between what was already evident inwardly although it was not yet evident outwardly, and why the inward and the outward processes are the same. The Gospels have no such distinction. His writing on this subject was close to that of mystic visionaries. The Gospels present no such separations. They rather present the story of Jesus' life from the point of view of an outside observer, though they are imbued with the perspective of a believer. They rather resemble apocalyptic writings.

This is an extraordinary picture of one man's religious affirmation of the transcendent nature of human life. It is also an enormous engine for conversion in the Hellenistic world. By connecting the internal process of transformation with the world's redemption Paul was able to suggest that faith had a material and spiritual effect upon the world. Paul was also able successfully to bridge and fuse the world of Jewish mysticism/apocalypticism with the world of pagan spirituality. To do so, he developed a notion of a self in transformation which attained transcendent status at the end of time but was continuously realizing it in the present. So while it was the body that is resurrected it was not merely the body; it was the body which included a divine consciousness, the Spirit, which was re-deeming the world. It was a picture of the self that said one could remake the world from what it is into what it should be, all by perfecting the self.

Previously we have seen that religious myth provides an analogy be-tween the self and divinity. In Paul's writing we have for the first time a record of the experience of mystic transformation of a limited human self into a transcendent divinity. But the question is: Could a personal trans-formation actually change the world? That answer is worked out by the Gospels.

11

The Gospels in Contrast
to Paul's Writings

WE HAVE SEEN that Paul, the earliest Christian writer, based his work on his spiritual visions. The Gospels are later than Paul. They reflect the religious needs of a later generation of Christians. Inherent within them is not just the story of Jesus's life from several different believers' points of view but also a further generation's reflections on the issues of faith, religious authority, and the afterlife. And, more than anything else, the Gospels are devices for the mission of the church, a different and broader mission than envisioned by Paul. Within the Gospels we see not only the synthesis of immortality and resurrection that Paul naturally provided but a battle to keep any extraneous notions of immortality of the soul out of the story of the Christ. It took centuries before Christianity could find an acceptable formula for incorporating it into the story of Christ's sacrificial death and resurrection. Neither body of writing gives us what actually happened. Each shows us a Christ who illustrated a unique and different view of the afterlife.

For Paul, faith meant belief in the validity of Paul's own personal revelations of the resurrected Christ. Paul's faith was based upon his own experience, his visionary revelations; so faith, vision, and knowledge were all deeply interwoven for him. His inward life was parallel to and indicative of the redemption of the world. Not so for those who worked within the apostolic tradition into which Paul fought so hard for inclusion. For them, the inward process became secondary and the redemption of the world primary. For them, faith meant belief in those who interpreted the story because they received their knowledge from those original apostles who sat at the feet of Jesus and witnessed the events in his life, death, and resurrection. Faith was trust that the traditions that came through the apostles was the correct teaching. It was a lineage of ministry and education but not visionary knowledge.

The earthly Jesus, conversely, had little to do with Paul's faith for he never met the man Jesus. Paul became a Christian because of his "vision of the risen Christ." For him, Jesus' resurrected body was a spiritual body *(soma pneumatikon)*. But for the evangelists, Jesus' resurrected body was a literal, physical body revivified. This exactly correlates with the approach of the apostolic succession, which is not based on visions of Christ (although it acknowledges their validity as a conversion experience) so much as on the personal testimony of those most trustworthy men who had witnessed the events of Jesus' life. There are, in fact, a variety of models for conversion in the Gospels (see e.g., Matt 12:38–42; Mark 1:16–20; 1:40–45; 2:13–17; 8:34–9:1; 19:46–52; Luke 5:1–11; 8:1–3; 13:1–5; 19:1–10). They involved men and some women who changed their lives radically to follow the teachings of Jesus, whose interpreters are the apostles. These stories take up a remarkable amount of space in the relatively compact narration of Jesus' ministry in Mark, for example. The importance of these stories as new and important models for conversion, as well as Luke's depiction of the conversion of Paul in Acts, cannot be underestimated.[1] The Gospels were edited for use in Christian mission.

The apostolic notion of resurrection is deeply affected by contrasts with Paul. Even the plain description of the events in Jesus' life came out altered from Paul's description. What Paul described in visionary terms, the evangelists describe literally. It is as if Paul represents the mystic dimension of Christian experience while the Gospels represent the apocalyptic dimension. In flat contradiction to Paul, the Gospels (when they discuss the process of resurrection at all) strongly assert a physical, fleshly notion of Jesus' bodily resurrection. It is this physical resurrection which most suits their mission of conversion. The Gospels were written for the conversion and maintenance of the community. Even the ritual life of the community reflected this missionary impulse.

The Eucharistic Words of Jesus

THE EUCHARIST words of Jesus in the Gospels are emblematic of the bodily resurrection of Jesus. In the Gospel of Mark, the Lord's Supper is described in the following manner:

And as they were eating, he took bread, and blessed, and broke it, and gave it to them, and said, "Take; this is my body." And he took a cup, and when he had given thanks he gave it to them, and they all drank of it. And he said to them, "This is my blood of the covenant, which is poured out for many. Truly, I say to you, I shall not drink again of the fruit of the vine until that day when I drink it new in the kingdom of God." (Mark 14:22–25)

This was a ritual in which the community, as well as the original disciples, could participate. The two other Synoptic Gospels hardly change the words of this passage. Matthew adds "When I drink it new *with you* in the kingdom of God" emphasizing the future liturgical role of the believer in the "Lord's Supper" (Matt 26:29). Luke adds a prophecy of the betrayal of Jesus (Luke 22:21–22). It stands to reason that if the church is going to become the body of Christ, then the primary ritual of that church's identity is going to have to display the literalness of the resurrection of the body. And it does, certainly here in the Gospels. Not only are the words constitutive of the community of those who believe in Christ, the bread and wine become the flesh and blood of Christ. The Gospel of John, often thought of as the most spiritual Gospel, is actually even more graphically literal in its depiction of the bread and wine as the body and blood of Christ: "Truly, truly, I say to you, unless you eat the flesh of the Son of Man and drink his blood, you have no life in you; he who eats my flesh and drinks my blood has eternal life" (John 6:53–54).

The eucharistic words of Jesus are rather close in every version. But there are some interesting additions to the Pauline version (1 Cor 11:23–32). In the first place, Paul sets the words at the Last Supper, which sides with the Synoptic Gospels as over against John. Paul's version used the modifier "which is for you" right after the "This is my body." This statement modifies the literal implication of the Gospels and emphasizes that the actions are set in a liturgy, an imaginative act of reenactment leaving open that the statement is itself a spiritual object of remembrance rather than a literal, physical action.

Paul also said that the ritual is to be enacted "in remembrance of me." Paul found remembrance *(anamnesis)* to be the basis of his spiritual life in Christ. But remembrance is something that takes place in the mind as part of a liturgical event. It is not the event alone which makes the ritual effective, because Paul described ways in which the liturgical moment could be violated by improper behavior. He said that one must "examine oneself" and "discern the body" in the ritual, meaning that the perception of the reality of the body of Christ is partly the responsibility of the participant. This process is one of intention and correct spiritual orientation. Luke also used the term *anamnesis* (Luke 22:19) to describe these events and perhaps he wished to bridge any gap between the other Gospel writers and Paul; he certainly shows this motivation in Acts. But Paul was far more acutely aware of the role of the participant using *anamnesis* and religious imagination in making the rite effective than are any of the Gospels.

To be sure, Paul and the Gospels present us with two different inscriptions of the same event. Persons holding these conflicting interpretataions of the event could have worshiped together. Both are constitutive for the Christian community, hence the body of Christ which is His church. But their understanding of resurrection, the body of Christ, and the role of the believer was quite different. Paul put more demands on the believer's consciousness. In short, in all the canonical Gospels, the Christ is physically present in the wine and bread. For Paul the sacrament was real but the discernment of the sacrament is in part mediated by the spiritual attitude of the participant. The nature of the resurrection in the Gospels will be parallel to this important distinction between them and Paul, the earliest Christian writer.

The Gospel of Mark

THE GOSPELS' assertions about Jesus' resurrection can be seen preeminently in the empty tomb tradition, which adumbrates in different ways in the different Gospels.[2] The tradition ramifies so as to emphasize that the resurrection was a physical event, that the resurrected body arose physically and was no longer to be found in the tomb. Part of this depiction is simply good storytelling. The Gospels present a narrative in ways that Paul never attempted. The transformation of this tradition to a literal bodily resurrection may also be polemical against the solipsistic dangers inherent in the Pauline testimony.

> And when evening had come, since it was the day of Preparation, that is, the day before the Sabbath, Joseph of Arimathea, a respected member of the council, who was also himself looking for the kingdom of God, took courage and went to Pilate, and asked for the body of Jesus. And Pilate wondered if he were already dead; and summoning the centurion, he asked him whether he was already dead. And when he learned from the centurion that he was dead, he granted the body to Joseph. And he bought a linen shroud, and taking him down, wrapped

him in the linen shroud, and laid him in a tomb which had been hewn out of the rock; and he rolled a stone against the door of the tomb. Mary Magdalene and Mary the mother of Jesus saw where he was laid. (Mark 15:42–47)

This report is the basis for the literary tradition concerning the resurrection of Jesus in the Gospels.[3] It contains all the details necessary for understanding the resurrection tradition, which follows next in Mark's Gospel and links the narrative with the crucifixion report, which immediately precedes it. It accounts for how Joseph of Arimathea is part of the tradition, without stating that the tomb in which Jesus was placed was Joseph's. It gives us a signficant reason why the two Marys are the first to visit the tomb after the resurrection and it suggests that ordinary Jews would have taken steps to make sure that any corpse was buried in accordance with Biblical law. What follows is the account of the discovery of the empty tomb:

When the Sabbath was over, Mary Magdalene, and Mary the mother of James, and Salome bought spices, so that they might go and anoint him. And very early on the first day of the week, when the sun had risen, they went to the tomb. They had been saying to one another "Who will roll away the stone for us from the entrance to the tomb?" When they looked up, they saw that the stone, which was very large, had already been rolled back. As they entered the tomb, they saw a young man, dressed in a white robe, sitting on the right side; and they were alarmed. But he said to them, "Do not be alarmed; you are looking for Jesus of Nazareth, who was crucified. He has been raised; he is not here. Look, there is the place they laid him. But go, tell his disciples and Peter that he is going ahead of you to Galilee; there you will see just him, as he told you." So they went out and fled from the tomb, for terror and amazement had seized them; and they said nothing to anyone, for they were afraid.[4] [The Shorter Ending of Mark v 8b] And all that had been commanded them they told briefly to those around Peter. And afterward Jesus himself sent out through them, from east to west, the sacred and imperishable proclamation of eternal salvation. (Mark 16:1–8b)

THE LONGER ENDING OF MARK

The longer ending in Mark is a historical problem entirely of itself. It is poorly attested in the ancient authorities, though it is part of the received text, hence also used in the Gospel reading for the Ascension Day and the Book of Common prayer. It seems to contain within it some of the traditional material of the later Gospels, which argues that it was written after the other Gospels were already written. Eusebius and Jerome (fourth-century, Church Fathers) both knew the tradition but raised doubts as to its authenticity by saying that it was missing in many Greek manuscripts known to them.[5] It surely represents another justification for the gentile mission: "And he said to them, 'Go into all the world and proclaim the good news [Gospel] to the whole creation' " (Mark 16:15). Perhaps it also represents the quickening of apocalyptic sentiment following the Second Jewish War against Rome:

> The one who believes and is baptized will be saved; but the one who does not believe will be condemned. And these signs will accompany those who believe: by using my name they will cast out demons; they will speak in new tongues; they will pick up snakes in their hands, and if they drink any deadly thing, it will not hurt them; they will lay their hands on the sick, and they will recover." (Mark 16:16–18)

It separates the ascension from the resurrection by three days and explicitly demonstrates that the risen Christ is the Son of Man enthroned next to God in Daniel 7:13 (v 19), invited to do so by Psalm 110:1:

> "So then the Lord Jesus, after he had spoken to them, was taken up into heaven and sat down at the right hand of God. And they went out and proclaimed the good news everywhere, while the Lord worked with them and confirmed the message by the signs that accompanied it.

It also shows that Christian proselytizers were healing and performing miracles in Jesus' name. Most of all, it provides a solution to some problems posed by the abrupt, shorter ending of Mark. It is a later reflection on the primitive Gospel tradition, demonstrating that we are dealing with important and deeply felt religious documents but ones that will hardly hold up to our contemporary notions of historiography.

THE SHORTER ENDING AND THE BURIAL

The shorter ending is more historically credible and far more enigmatic. Yet, one cannot demonstrate that even the sparse tradition of an empty tomb in the shorter ending is authentic to the time of Jesus. Paul gave us the earliest form of the resurrection tradition, and he was silent about the empty tomb. The shorter ending argues for a physical resurrection because the body was missing. Yet, the shorter ending does not necessarily contradict Paul because Paul believed in transformed flesh. In other words, the shorter ending did not of itself establish the physical resurrection of Jesus.

One might argue Paul's testimony that Jesus was buried implies an empty tomb and although his notion of resurrection is spiritual, it implies transformed flesh. In that case, one would argue it was the empty tomb itself that provided an alternative interpretation of a resurrection. That is very rational, but it does not correspond to the facts as I understand them. The early tradition is solid about the experiences of the women on the Easter morning, less solid on the antiquity of the empty tomb. So the issue hinges not on what might be the most logical hypothesis but on what evidence is the most ancient.

Religiously, we are confronted with a mystery, the source of the faith of a large section of the human race. The narrative itself is designed to stimulate that faith. The absence of the empty tomb in the writings of Paul suggests that he did not know about it, although it is always possible that the tradition existed already, that he knew it and merely did not mention it, or even that he did not like it. Lack of confidence in the empty tomb tradition might follow from Paul's silence. Furthermore, it calls into question the burial itself, on which it depends, which was neither a likely outcome of a Roman execution nor was it credible in its own right. It is so manifestly polemical as to raise the issue of credibility immediately. Dom Crossan has pointed this out in his characteristically dramatic way by suggesting that the body might have been tossed to the dogs.[6] This is a provocative suggestion and it does serve to emphasize the questionable nature of the Joseph of Arimathea story.[7] On the other hand, Jesus' burial is a stable part of the Gospel tradition and Paul explicitly said that Jesus was buried. Paul said in 1 Corinthians 15:3–4: "For I delivered to you as of first importance what I also received, that Christ died for our sins in accordance with the Scriptures, that he was buried, that he was raised on the third day in accordance with the Scriptures." Perhaps the reason the burial is mentioned is precisely because it was unusual for the Romans.

THE SCANDAL OF THE RESURRECTION

Crossan is certainly right that lack of burial would have been a scandal in the ancient world and that burial itself was somewhat unlikely for a political execution. But Christianity could have accommodated to that scandal if Jesus' body actually remained unburied. That does not end the issue of scandal in the resurrection narrative. Few commentators actually describe what seems to me to be the obvious scandal that the tradition of the empty tomb seeks to ameliorate. The fact is: No one actually saw Jesus arise.[8] This is a critical difficulty for the early mission of the church. The empty tomb tradition does face and then finesse the issue that no one saw Jesus rise. That does not firmly argue against its historicity but it tends to make a historian suspicious.

What can be demonstrated historically only is that no one actually saw Jesus's resurrection. Had there been witnesses they would not have been left out. I agree with Lüdemann that the original experience of the risen Christ must have been visionary appearances after death and that they must have started, as tradition has it, on the first day after the Sabbath, Easter Sunday. Paul gives us a good example of the intensity and purity and piety of those visions. If Paul is an example, believers would certainly have viewed visions as the actual presence of Christ and anticipatory of the end-times, which had already started and would soon be fully actualized. I suspect the visions of Peter and even James and the others were similar: They convinced Jesus' followers that he not only survived in a new spiritual state but that that state was as the manlike figure in heaven, "the Son of Man," whose reign inaugurated the millennium. Missionary work, however, demanded even more obvious proof. It demanded that Jesus himself, in the same body, walked among them.

This could hardly have been an issue for Paul, who had seen the risen Christ and was sure of Christ's presence in his life. For Paul the scandal of the new faith was the scandal of the cross, not the scandal of the resurrection. It was that: "We preach Christ crucified, a stumbling block to Jews and folly to Gentiles" (1 Cor 1:23). The notion of a crucified Messiah was an oxymoron, a contradiction-in-terms to Jews, who thought that the Messiah should be victorious, just as surely as it was folly to the gentiles, who thought an executed man was unworthy of veneration. Paul gives us the difficulty of the first generation of hearers of the Christian message in naked terms. The Gospels give us the developed missionary strategy for removing these doubts.

The Gospels, which go into the details of Jesus' life (which Paul never did) and so answer all such questions narratively, also provide cogent, historical answers, a missionary strategy to alleviate the doubts of the hearers to all historical problems, including why no one actually witnessed the resurrection. This raises the historical witness question to a crucial level. The empty tomb itself becomes the vehicle for alleviating that dearth of testimonial evidence for the resurrection, as well as the demonstration that the post-resurrection appearances were not hallucinations.

THE CORE OF THE EMPTY TOMB TRADITION

The core of the empty tomb tradition, at least in Mark, is simply that when some of the women (as we shall see, there is considerable confusion as to who went to the tomb in the various Gospels) came to anoint the body after the Sabbath, they found the tomb empty, and they left in a state of fear and perplexity (Mark 16:8). The Greek word for fear in Mark is *ekthambesthai* (fear, marvel), which is both the normal Biblical word for "fear" and consistently used in Mark and elsewhere to reflect a reaction to the awesome presence of the divine. It is better translated as "they were in awe." In fact, throughout the Hebrew Bible, the term "fear" was also used to express "awe" and associated religious emotions. Someone who "fears" God is a religious person, not a frightened person, for the Hebrew Bible.

The later Gospels describe the young man as an angel, though Mark did not. Yet, that was a safe inference for Mark's intention; even the most primitive tradition, here in Mark, must mean that the young man *(neaniskos)* in a white robe sitting on the right side was an angel.[9] But, if so, it is interesting to note the way in which Mark deliberately underplays his narrative, letting the reader make the reasonable conclusion.

The answer of the young man: "Do not fear!" also is typical of angelophanies. Significantly, the angelic message is a short statement of Christian kerygma: "Jesus . . . the crucified has been raised, he is not here." The presence of the angel, therefore, shows that the story is being treated as an apocalyptic angelophany and revelation. It was, as well, tailored for missionary purposes. Like Paul, this Christian variety of apocalypticism seems at first devoid of the florid imagery of visions that apocalypticism often produced. This simplicity is better suited for missionary purposes, as florid imagery was an intellectual, exegetical tradition, which would have confused ordinary gentile and Jew alike. Here, in a popular context among Jews and in the gentile mission, there would be little reason to propound complicated, symbolic visions based on Biblical models. The church needed, short, pithy statements of its core beliefs which could be used in mission and liturgy.[10]

In the narrative, the angel functions to defeat any criticism, which must have been early and serious, that the empty tomb was due to the theft of the cadaver or a resuscitation. Paul's discussion of this in 1 Corinthians 1 leaves us in no doubt about the early presence and seriousness of the criticism of the Christian proclamation. But, as historians, the issue is otherwise. It is neither clearly false nor clearly true. Scholars who look to this moment to confirm or deny faith are asking too much, historically, from this religious narrative.

Mark 16:8, which closes the shorter ending of the Gospel, is one of the most portentous endings in literature: "And, going out, they fled from the tomb, for trembling and astonishment seized them; and they said nothing to anyone, for they were afraid." Apparently, the word got out.

This is no way to end a Gospel! The ending is, however, the effect of artifice, for no Greek sentence can properly end with the word *gar*. It is even more difficult than ending a sentence with the word "furthermore" in English because grammatically *gar* should not be the last word in a sentence. Consequently, the current Gospel has been artifically separated from its true, original ending. In context, this phrase is followed by the commissioning of the disciples, in either the shorter or longer versions. There is no telling whether we have the original ending somewhere in the shorter ending, somewhere in the longer ending, or it simply disappeared. Possibly, the Gospel of Matthew preserves it, as it parallels Mark generally; but it is impossible to identify. The one sure thing is that the current critical text was not the Gospel's intended ending.

The empty tomb has considerable narrative value, even though it does not present us with an indubitable historical truth, like the lack of witness to the resurrection itself. It is always conceivable that, against our best logic, it actually happened. But, even if it did, the story of the empty tomb is not a particularly strong affirmation of the central events of Christianity, especially in comparison to the dramatic and life-changing personal visions of Paul.

One positive aspect of the empty tomb tradition, over against Paul, is that anyone there might have been able to verify it; unlike Paul's visions, the empty tomb is at least verifiable in principle. The empty tomb tradition objectifies the issue of confirmation by claiming that the events took place in normal, historical time. The Gospels' proclamation is different from the Christ preached by Paul in that they tell the story of Jesus' life, resolving a great many issues of Jesus' personality and intentions to the satisfaction of the second generation of Christians. The problem is that the solution was tried in different ways by a number of different narrators, creating a perplexing lack of agreement in the different Gospels, exactly at the moment when they should all agree. On the other hand, the diversity speaks to the importance and historicity of the Early Church's spiritual reactions.

The empty tomb also resolves another important problem: It denies the notion that Jesus' resurrection existence is merely as a "spirit," no different in theory than any other death.[11] Beliefs in ghosts or "shades" seem to be almost universal in the popular culture, then as now. The ancient Hebrew notion of *nefesh (nepeš)*, supported by its many ancient Near Eastern parallels, as well as the popular notion of ghosts and shades in Hellenistic culture, all suggest that the easiest explanation for what happens to the dead is that they become ghosts. Describing Jesus as a "spirit" unreasonably risked turning Jesus into a "ghost." More exactly, if Jesus were described as a "spiritual body," in ordinary historical time, instead of the Pauline "spiritual body" in a revelatory vision, the narrative would appear to be saying that Jesus was just another "disembodied soul," the same postmortem, ghostly form as is available potentially to everyone at death. To support the experience of Jesus' resurrection, his postmortem form needed to be more tangible than that.

It is probably too early in Christian tradition to sense a defense against a related problem for Christianity, the problem that the concept of the immortal soul of Platonism will cause. That is a thorny intellectual problem that vexed the Church Fathers. But we can anticipate the problem by noticing that it has something in common with figuring the postresurrection Christ as a "spirit" or a "ghost." In Platonism the soul is immortal by nature, so assuming that Jesus' immortal soul is what survived his death only says that his death was normal and without special import. As a result, it too totally undercuts any statement of Jesus' saving death. If one analyzes the death and presumed postmortem sightings of Jesus using the theory of an immortal soul, there is no necessity (or even possibility) of positing his saving death on the cross. If Jesus survived death as merely a ghost or spirit, then the only immortality is already available to all as a matter of the soul's nature. But the church maintains that Jesus' death is not ordinary. He died as a martyr and was resurrected as one, ascending to heaven to be exalted together with the "Son of Man" in Daniel 7:13, showing that the end-time had begun. Thus, his resurrection not only should be bodily, it *must* be bodily or it is not significant for the salvation of the world.

The Gospel of Matthew

BY THE TIME of Matthew, several further apologetic features have been added to the story. These appear to grow naturally out of difficulties in the Markan version of the story. The Matthean community evidently attempted to resolve some of the ambiguities in the Christian message created by Mark's story, issues that we have already enumerated. Part of the problem is the brevity of the narrative, even if some further short conclusion beyond "the shorter ending" can be assumed.

> After the sabbath, as the first day of the week was dawning, Mary Magdalene and the other Mary went to see the tomb. And suddenly there was a great earthquake; for an angel of the Lord, descending from heaven, came and rolled back the stone and sat on it. His appearance was like lightning, and his clothing white as snow. For fear of him the guards shook and became like dead men. But the angel said to the women, "Do not be afraid; I know that you are looking for Jesus who was crucified. He is not here; for he has been raised, as he said. Come, see the place where he lay. Then go quickly and tell his disciples, 'He has been raised from the dead, and indeed he is going ahead of you to Galilee; there you will see him.' This is my message for you." So they left the tomb quickly with fear and great joy, and ran to tell his disciples. Suddenly Jesus met them and said, "Greetings!" And they came to him, took hold of his feet, and worshiped him. Then Jesus said to them, "Do not be afraid; go and tell my brothers to go to Galilee; there they will see me." While they were going, some of the guard went into the city and told the chief priests everything that had happened. After the priests had assembled with the elders, they devised a plan to give a large sum of money to the soldiers, telling them, "You must say, 'His disciples came by night and stole him away while we were asleep.' If this comes to the governor's ears, we will satisfy him and keep you out of trouble." So they took the money and did as they were directed. And this story is still told among the Jews to this day. Now the eleven disciples went to Galilee, to the mountain to which Jesus had directed them. When they saw him, they worshiped him; but some doubted. And Jesus came and said to them, "All authority in heaven and on earth has been given to me. Go therefore and make disciples of all nations, baptizing them in the name of the Father and of the Son and of the Holy Spirit, and teaching them to obey everything that I have commanded you. And remember, I am with you always, to the end of the age." (Matt 28:1–20)

The Matthean evangelist demonstrates to us that by the time of this recension of the story, the wider community—probably both Jew and gentile—is aware of the empty tomb tradition. It can be assumed that some people, probably Jews because they would often be the first hearers, treat this story with some derision (Matt 27:62–66; 28:11–15). This suggests that after hearing the story of the resurrection, a skeptic's natural response was: "Someone has conveniently stolen the body." The Gospel's narrative defense against that attack is ingenious. According to Matthew, it's all due to the Jews. The Jews entered into a conspiracy by paying the Roman guard soldiers at the tomb to report that the disciples themselves stole the body. This enters the critical report of the detractors of Christianity—those encountered by the missionaries in the Matthean tradition in their daily work—into the historical record right where it can be defeated most easily. Since that important detail is absent in Mark, it must be a later gloss. It is a scurrilous detail, with anti-Semitic implications, which protects the bulwark of the empty tomb tradition.

To the Matthean narrator, it is easier to understand the criticism that the body could have been stolen as a calumny started by some unbelieving Jewish hearers of the Gospel who had bribed the pagan soldiers to lie, than to argue against the claim in some more theoretical way. The tradition probably reflects the existence of real, external, anti-resurrection polemic, whether Jewish or not would not matter, as we know from Paul that both gentiles and Jews had trouble believing in either the resurrection or the Messianic proclamations of Christianity.

The Gospel of Matthew also includes the additional famous calumny that the death of Jesus is the responsibility of the Jews forever: "And all the people answered, "His blood be on us and on our children!" (Matt 27:25). It is the Romans who execute Jesus, possibly in collusion with some of the priests. It is not the Jewish nation as a body who assented to it. But theologically, if some Jews were complicit in the death of Jesus, this could be seen as furthering God's plan for the world's redemption.

Why then are the Jews singled out for calumny? In view of the adumbration of the empty tomb tradition that we find in Matthew, it looks as if the real problem is that some Jews doubt the resurrection. But doubt is a universal phenomenon; believing Christians also have it and must deal with it, no matter how sincere their faith.[12] The writers of this document wanted to banish doubt. Doubt is potentially a problem in the missionary message of Christianity and equally a disquieting problem for the faith of any believing Christian. If doubt is present, it can always be exorcised by hatred of the Jews. Since it is the Jews who raise the doubt, scapegoating both defuses Jewish doubt but also quiets the nagging suspicion within. In this psychological fact of scapegoating, and not the passion narrative itself is the real dynamo of Christian anti-Judaism. The root of the problem is the inadequacy of the empty tomb tradition to serve as a positive demonstration of faith. Jews made the crucial mistake of being the first to point this out.

The Gospel of John

EVEN THOUGH the Johannine Gospel developed independently of the Synoptics, it likely had access to an early form of the Gospels of Mark and Luke for a number of important details, especially in the resurrection narratives. The Gospel of John also argues the physicality of the resurrection, possibly even earlier and more concretely than the received Markan version:

> Early on the first day of the week, while it was still dark, Mary Magdalene came to the tomb and saw that the stone had been removed from the tomb. So she ran and went to Simon Peter and the other disciple, the one whom Jesus loved, and said to them, "They have taken the Lord out of the tomb, and we do not know where they have laid him." Then Peter and the other disciple set out and went toward the tomb. The two were running together, but the other disciple outran Peter and reached the tomb first. He bent down to look in and saw the linen wrappings lying there, but he did not go in. Then Simon Peter came, following him, and went into the tomb. He saw the linen wrappings lying there, and the cloth that had been on Jesus' head, not lying with the linen wrappings but rolled up in a place by itself. Then the other disciple, who reached the tomb first, also went in, and he saw and believed; for as yet they did not understand the scripture, that he must rise from the dead. Then the disciples returned to their homes.
>
> But Mary stood weeping outside the tomb. As she wept, she bent over to look into the tomb; and she saw two angels in white, sitting where the body of Jesus had been lying, one at the head and the other at the feet. They said to her, "Woman, why are you weeping?" She said to them, "They have taken away my Lord, and I do not know where they have laid him." When she had said this, she turned around and saw Jesus standing there, but she did not know that it was Jesus. Jesus said to her, "Woman, why are you weeping? Whom are you looking for?" Supposing him to be the gardener, she said to him, "Sir, if you have carried him away, tell me where you have laid him, and I will take him away." Jesus said to her, "Mary!" She turned and said to him in Hebrew, "Rabbouni!" (which means Teacher). Jesus said to her, "Do not hold on to me, because I have not yet ascended to the Father. But

go to my brothers and say to them, 'I am ascending to my Father and your Father, to my God and your God.' " Mary Magdalene went and announced to the disciples, "I have seen the Lord"; and she told them that he had said these things to her.

When it was evening on that day, the first day of the week, and the doors of the house where the disciples had met were locked for fear of the Jews, Jesus came and stood among them and said, "Peace be with you." After he said this, he showed them his hands and his side. Then the disciples rejoiced when they saw the Lord. Jesus said to them again, "Peace be with you. As the Father has sent me, so I send you." When he had said this, he breathed on them and said to them, "Receive the Holy Spirit. If you forgive the sins of any, they are forgiven them; if you retain the sins of any, they are retained."

But Thomas (who was called the Twin), one of the twelve, was not with them when Jesus came. So the other disciples told him, "We have seen the Lord." But he said to them, "Unless I see the mark of the nails in his hands, and put my finger in the mark of the nails and my hand in his side, I will not believe." A week later, his disciples were again in the house and Thomas was with them. Although the doors were shut, Jesus came and stood among them and said, "Peace be with you." Then he said to Thomas, "Put your finger here and see my hands. Reach out your hand and put it in my side. Do not doubt but believe." Thomas answered him, "My Lord and my God!" Jesus said to him, "Have you believed because you have seen me? Blessed are those who have not seen and yet have come to believe."

Now Jesus did many other signs in the presence of his disciples, which are not written in this book. But these are written so that you may come to believe that Jesus is the Messiah, the Son of God, and that through believing you may have life in his name. (John 20:1–31)

The beginning of this Johannine passage may, in fact, evidence an earlier form of the empty tomb tradition than Mark 16, possibly enriched by contact with Matthew and Luke. But no scholarly consensus has emerged. It is even possible that the Johannine version helped Matthew with some of the details of his retelling. Furthermore, it stands in polemical relationship with the Gospel of Thomas.

The Johannine form simply notes that Mary Magdalene visited the tomb alone, and, finding it wide open and empty, suspected that someone had stolen the body, and she hurried to report the matter to the other disciples. She repeated this story until Jesus himself explained the events to her directly. Here is a version of the "stolen body" tradition which is not polemically fitted to the problem of Jewish scepticism. It rather looks as if we have found, in John's Gospel, the earliest nugget of the story of the "stolen body" motif. It is not necessarily a Jewish charge but just a logical conclusion from the empty tomb defined by a revelation.

The Gospel of John also has its own apologetic concerns to articulate, which it develops immediately afterwards. First, the importance of scriptural precedent for Jesus' resurrection is stressed, although, as is usual throughout, the specific Scripture is not mentioned: "For as yet they did not understand the Scripture, that he must rise from the dead." Second, various christological formulas are emphasized in showing that Jesus is now "Lord" and "God" (John 20:22–23). Jesus commissioned the disciples and actually breathed the Holy Spirit into them, demonstrating visually that his spirit is found within the church: "When he had said this, he breathed on them and said to them, 'Receive the Holy Spirit. If you forgive the sins of any, they are forgiven them; if you retain the sins of any, they are retained' " (John 20:28).

The church was given the power and legitimacy to forgive sins, as Jesus himself is said to have done during his ministry, a very powerful and important power that was more relevant to the post-Temple period of the Johannine church than it was to the initial disciples. The empty tomb tradition illustrates one reason that the church preserved different Gospels. To be sure, each Gospel's portrait of Jesus adds to the characterization of the others and helps produced a fuller portait. But the same is true of the polemical value of the Gospels. Just as important for the scrappy Early Church is that each Gospel polemicizes against different criticisms of the claims of the church. Since no Gospel contains all the arguments, and indeed a number of arguments are contradictory to each other, especially in narrative form, no one synthetic Gospel could be created.

The Gospel of John portrays Jesus' resurrection in very physical terms, though it is universally acknowledged to be the most "spiritual" Gospel. In spite of its spirituality (and its depiction of the glorious, victorious rather than a suffering Jesus), John's understanding of the resurrection was very material and fleshly: John's Jesus had been resurrected bodily and physically. Paul's prior notion of the apocalyptic significance of the progressive realization of spiritual bodies is not to be found in John.

The famous story of "Doubting Thomas" is often understood as John's endorsement of the "spiritual body." Careful analysis shows the opposite. Jesus appeared to the disciples in a locked room. Many claim that Jesus' entrance into a locked room demonstrates his spiritual nature. It may just as easily demonstrate that his appearance was not a cheap magic trick. While the motif of the locked room appeared for the purposes of showing the miraculous nature of Jesus' resurrection body, what happened after he materialized inside the room was a demonstration of the physicality of the resurrection body.

We think that a material or physical body cannot just appear in a locked room, so we conclude that the point of the story is that Jesus' body is spiritually present. The ancient world had fewer presuppositions about physical possibilities in nature, especially when the point of the story was that God's handiwork was being made miraculously manifest. If it were a science fiction story, say *Star-Trek,* which had said that Jesus was teleported to there from a spaceship we would have few problems accepting his physical and actual presence within the locked room. We understand that Jesus could be physically present if certain counterfactual, science fiction claims are accepted. The writers of this Gospel simply had different, counterfactural assumptions about the physical world. They wanted to stress the miracle that Jesus was a real body who miraculously appeared in a locked room. Thus, the story is in line with the other physical depictions of Jesus' bodily resurrection. Doubting Thomas' touching of Jesus' wounds only confirms the intention of the evangelist. It is the concreteness of the depiction, not its spiritual nature, which is the point of the story.

The miracle of Jesus' materialization led directly to Thomas's demonstration of Jesus' physicality. It also demonstrated, as the other stories did, that Jesus' appearance was not merely the appearance of a ghost or spirit. The story draws the further conclusion, which is the most important point, that those who believe and have not seen what Thomas saw are even more blessed for their greater faith. We shall see that the *Gospel of Thomas* does evince an overtly visionary view of Christ's resurrection.

In John 6, an explicit link between the resurrection and the eucharist is made. In John 6:35-50 we have one of John's feeding stories about the manna in the wilderness. In this context, the living bread is the lifegiving word of Jesus. Whoever believes in him will be resurrected on the last day (John 6:40, 44). As opposed to the Synoptic tradition, John did not emphasize that God was the author of these actions. For John it was Jesus himself who was manifesting his power.

> I am the living bread that came down from heaven. Whoever eats of this bread will live forever; and the bread that I will give for the life of the world is my flesh." The Jews then disputed among themselves, say-

ing, "How can this man give us his flesh to eat?" So Jesus said to them, "Very truly, I tell you, unless you eat the flesh of the Son of Man and drink his blood, you have no life in you. Those who eat my flesh and drink my blood have eternal life, and I will raise them up on the last day; for my flesh is true food and my blood is true drink. Those who eat my flesh and drink my blood abide in me, and I in them. Just as the living Father sent me, and I live because of the Father, so whoever eats me will live because of me. This is the bread that came down from heaven, not like that which your ancestors ate, and they died. But the one who eats this bread will live forever."

As we have previously seen, the physicality of the Eucharist is stressed in this passage. A number of readers have expressed almost a physical revulsion to the idea that Jesus could ordain his actual flesh and blood for consumption. But it is a symbolic statement. The evangelist's language is straining to express the physicality of the savior's resurrection, and his literal presence in the Lord's Supper, not the literalness of the believer's consumption. The resurrection of believers is linked to the physical ingestion of Jesus' body in the Eucharist. A further scriptural proof-text is brought through the mention of "bread from heaven," a typological reference to the Pentateuchal tradition of God's saving provision of manna to the children of Israel in the wilderness. The comparison provokes a contrast: God will preserve those who eat of His mass, as opposed to the children of Israel who had no such dispensation and died. This argument evinces a clear type/antitype form. But the main subject is the ritual effectiveness of the Lord's Supper. Verse 56 links the presence of Jesus in his resurrected state with the ritual itself. That is where and how he is physically present to the church of his believers, and not in visions.

The Gospel of Luke and The Acts of the Apostles

IT FALLS TO Luke to settle one important ambiguity left in John. Luke puts together an anthology of postresurrection appearances in chapter 24. In one of his postresurrection appearance stories the resurrected Jesus actually ate a meal:

While they were talking about this, Jesus himself stood among them and said to them, "Peace be with you." They were startled and terrified, and thought that they were seeing a *ghost* [or spirit]. He said to them, "Why are you frightened, and why do doubts arise in your hearts? Look at my hands and my feet; see that it is I myself. Touch me and see; for a *ghost* does not have flesh and bones as you see that I have." And when he had said this, he showed them his hands and his feet. While in their joy they were disbelieving and still wondering, he said to them, "Have you anything here to eat?" They gave him a piece of broiled fish, and he took it and ate in their presence. (Luke 24:36–43)

This is certainly another version of the "Doubting Thomas" story. Now the resurrected Jesus actually came in flesh and blood. He was not merely a ghost *(pneuma)* nor a "spirit," which Luke explicitly denies, although it is precisely the word that Paul used for the kind of body that the Christ had in 1 Corinthians 14:44, a "spiritual body" *(soma pneumatikon)*. The Gospel of Luke explicitly denies the very terms which Paul used to describe the resurrected presence of Christ.

Jesus not only showed his wounds and manipulated physical objects, as John portrays it, but he also ate. Jesus likely showed the apostles his hands and feet (Luke 24:40) because that is where he was wounded, as in the "Doubting Thomas" passage (John 24:20–29). Whatever traditions Luke may know, he certainly is the most articulate on the issue of the risen Jesus' physical presence. He adumbrates the story of the empty tomb and must, in fact, provide us with forty days between the resurrection and the ascension in order to fit in all the appearances of the postresurrection Jesus. The other Gospels seem, rather, to assume that the resurrection and the ascension happened coterminously. Thus, the resurrection appearances of Jesus are post-ascension appearances as well.

In Luke, we see other important and revealing variants of the empty tomb tradition. But none are more fascinating than the Emmaus story, that Jesus physically came to teach that the empty tomb was not an idle story:

But these words seemed to them an idle tale, and they did not believe them. But Peter got up and ran to the tomb; stooping and looking in, he saw the linen cloths by themselves; then he went home, amazed at what had happened. Now on that same day two of them were going to a village called Emmaus, about seven miles from Jerusalem, and talking with each other about all these things that had happened. While they were talking and discussing, Jesus himself came near and went with them, but their eyes were kept from recognizing him. And he said to them, "What are you discussing with each other while you walk along?" They stood still, looking sad. Then one of them, whose name was Cleopas, answered him, "Are you the only stranger in Jerusalem who does not know the things that have taken place there in these days?" He asked them, "What things?" They replied, "The things about Jesus of Nazareth, who was a prophet mighty in deed and word before God and all the people, and how our chief priests and leaders handed him over to be condemned to death and crucified him. But we had hoped that he was the one to redeem Israel. Yes, and besides all this, it is now the third day since these things took place. Moreover, some women of our group astounded us. They were at the tomb early this morning, and when they did not find his body there, they came back and told us that they had indeed seen a vision of angels who said that he was alive. Some of those who were with us went to the tomb and found it just as the women had said; but they did not see him." Then he said to them, "Oh, how foolish you are, and how slow of heart to believe all that the prophets have declared! Was it not necessary that the Messiah should suffer these things and then enter into his glory?" Then beginning with Moses and all the prophets, he interpreted to them the things about himself in all the Scriptures. As they came near the village to which they were going, he walked ahead as if he were going on. But they urged him strongly, saying, "Stay with us, because it is almost evening and the day is now nearly over." So he went in to stay with them. When he was at the table with them, he took bread, blessed and broke it, and gave it to them. Then their eyes were opened, and they recognized him; and he vanished from their sight. They said to each other, "Were not our hearts burning within us while he was talking to us on the road, while he was opening the Scriptures to us?" That same hour they got up and returned to Jerusalem; and they found the eleven and their companions gathered together. They were saying, "The Lord has risen indeed, and he has appeared to Simon!" Then they told what had happened on the road, and how he had been made known to them in the breaking of the bread. (Luke 24:11–35)

The story provides a precedent for a number of issues—including the Lord's Supper (Luke 24:30). Jesus' presence at the meal is parallel to his literal presence in the liturgical rite of the Lord's Supper. The story is also intended to demonstrate that the empty tomb tradition, at first thought to be an idle story worthy only of women within the community, was exactly what happened. The doubts raised by the "empty tomb" have nothing to do with the disbelief of the Jews; even the faithful have their doubts.

Conversely the Emmaus visitation provides yet another narrative argument for the credibility of the empty tomb. No less authority than Jesus himself demonstrated it (vv 25–26). This suggests quite strongly that the tradition of the empty tomb was not an effective argument. Nor were the advantages of a story of the empty tomb universally realized by the faithful within the church right away. Perhaps the implications of the long apologetic tradition of the empty tomb shows us more clearly why Paul did not mention it: He did not evidence a physically present Jesus and he did not involve himself in this kind of polemic. In Luke we have the final defense of the "empty tomb" both from within and without.

The ascension is then accomplished at the end of these appearances:

Then he led them out as far as Bethany, and, lifting up his hands, he blessed them. While he was blessing them, he withdrew from them and was carried up into heaven. And they worshiped him, and returned to Jerusalem with great joy; and they were continually in the temple blessing God. (Luke 24:50–53)

Luke's depiction of the ascension seems a little jarring because Luke is concerned with the physicality of Jesus' postresurrection appearance. In effect, Luke has resolved Paul's quandary as to whether the heavenly journey of 2 Corinthians 12 was corporeal or spiritual. For Luke, it was clearly a bodily ascension. What makes this even more interesting is that Luke was aware of the primitive kerygma, which he repeated in two key places:

The God of our ancestors raised up Jesus, whom you had killed by hanging him on a tree. God exalted him at his right hand as Leader and Savior that he might give repentance to Israel and forgiveness of sins. (Acts 5:30–31)

Being therefore exalted at the right hand of God, and having received from the Father the promise of the Holy Spirit, he has poured out this that you both see and hear. For David did not ascend into the heavens, but he himself says,

"The Lord said to my Lord,
'Sit at my right hand,
until I make your enemies your footstool.' "

Therefore let the entire house of Israel know with certainty that God has made him both Lord and Messiah, this Jesus whom you crucified." (Acts 2:33–36)

Evidently this ascension did not involve a process of *symmorphosis* as in Paul, or at least that is never made clear. Yet, like Paul, these short statements of *kerygma* (Christian missionary proclamation, the central doctrines of the church) were based on inspired reinterpretation of Scripture and were used as evangelical sermons. Like Paul, they talk of Jesus' passion and exaltation as part of the same process of salvation; passion and exaltation are two aspects of the death and resurrection of the Savior.

In any event, the identification of resurrection with enthronement is evident, and Psalm 110 is used as the proof-text. Enthronement is connected to Jesus' Messianic status as well in Acts 2:33–36, where Psalm 110 is used to demonstrate that Jesus is both Messianic and divine. The second "Lord" in Psalm 110 designates the Messiah, implicates him in divinity, but cannot be identified with David himself.

Very likely though, it was originally the inscription on the cross which made this Messianic connection obvious to the later interpreters of the events of Jesus' death.[13] The themes of Messianic candidacy and enthronement of the righteous martyr come together at the crucifixion. As Timo Eskola has said: "First Christians located the enthronement of the Messiah in the eschatological event of the resurrection of the dead."[14] And it is clear that these connections are made by preachers who are involved in the earliest Christian mission. Jesus was proclaimed as the enthroned Messiah whose resurrection and exaltation were proof of the coming eschaton. According to Luke, this is what the good news of the early Christian missionaries was. Indeed, it is very close to the message that Paul preached as well. In both cases, the message depended on the presence of the Christ in the community in baptism, in the Lord's Supper and in the gifts of the spirit which Luke links to the outpouring of the Spirit at Pentecost.

Both of these passages might have appeared in Paul but for two further elaborations that are characteristic of Luke and completely uncharacteristic of Paul. Although Paul is distrustful of his Jewish brethren, Paul did not usually pile on anti-Jewish phrases like Luke: "whom you had killed" and "this Jesus whom you crucified." These are characterics of a later time, when Jews and Christians are more at loggerheads. Whatever Jews were interested in Christianity had converted; the rest were skeptical, and many were hostile.

Between Paul and Luke's account of the resurrection, the theme of Jewish opposition to the Gospel has again and again entered Christian tradition. It is coterminous with the missionary impulse of Christianity. The opposition to the Christian mission was usually symbolized by the Jews who were therefore reviled. To explain away opposition, demonization of the Jews was undertaken.[15] Probably the Jews were used for this purpose because they were skeptical of the empty tomb tradition, to say nothing of the resurrection of Jesus, and many other claims of the church. The remarks of R. Abbahu in the Palestinian Talmud are later still but they are cogent and relevant:

> R. Abbahu said: "If a man says to you, 'I am God,' he is a liar. If he says, '(I am) the Son of Man,' in the end, people will laugh at him. If he says, 'I will go up to heaven,' he says so but he will not do it." (jTa'anith 65b)

There can be no doubt that Rabbi Abbahu was speaking against Christianity. It succinctly summarized the opposition of Jews: (1) no human is divine; (2) the Son of Man in heaven is not a human; (3) no one ascends to heaven. This skepticism took some time to grow. It entered Christian literature after the "empty tomb" story was circulated in Mark. It made its most obvious entrance in an anti-Jewish polemic in Matthew. But doubt about the empty tomb also surfaced in several places within the Christian community, where it charactized Christians and new converts alike. In ancient times, as in modern times, people hate most in others what they fear most within themselves.

The Transfiguration and the Martyrdom of Stephen

THESE RESURRECTION traditions do give us a sense of the way in which Jesus was remembered by the earliest church. He was first of all savior and only secondarily, if at all, a wise teacher and moral example. One other place may show how Jesus was experienced by the earliest community. That is the transfiguration, which can easily be understood as a RASC experience of the risen Jesus, recast as a precrucifixion theophany:[16]

> Now about eight days after these sayings Jesus took with him Peter and John and James, and went up on the mountain to pray. And while he was praying, the appearance of his face changed, and his clothes became dazzling white. Suddenly they saw two men, Moses and Elijah, talking to him. They appeared in glory and were speaking of his departure, which he was about to accomplish at Jerusalem. Now Peter

and his companions were weighed down with sleep; but since they had stayed awake, they saw his glory and the two men who stood with him. Just as they were leaving him, Peter said to Jesus, "Master, it is good for us to be here; let us make three dwellings, one for you, one for Moses, and one for Elijah"—not knowing what he said. While he was saying this, a cloud came and overshadowed them; and they were terrified as they entered the cloud. Then from the cloud came a voice that said, "This is my Son, my Chosen; listen to him!" When the voice had spoken, Jesus was found alone. And they kept silent and in those days told no one any of the things they had seen. (Luke 9:28–36)

Since the transfiguration (see also Mark 9:2–8 and Matt 17:1–8) is technically not a postresurrection appearance, we cannot study it here in detail. But it looks like an actual postresurrection experience of Jesus in the Early Church transferred back into the preresurrection narrative to serve as a foreshadowing of Christ's resurrection. It also suggests that Jesus' true nature was already perceptible in the preresurrection church. If so, it is not obvious to the participants. The disciples entirely mistake what is happening and behave in incomprehensible ways. The command to tell no one at the end of the Lukan version almost begs to be understood as an early recognition that many of the disciples did not know the transfiguration tradition until after the resurrection. It has many of the characteristics of an apocalyptic/mystical theophany: (1) The transfiguration takes place during prayer in the mountains, which is a significant convention for ecstatic experiences in Jewish apocalypticism. (2) The disciples' mental states are described as awake but heavy as if sleepy, which is often used as well in descriptions of ecstatic visions. (3) They are given a vision of Christ's glory, very close to the technical terminology in Jewish literature.

The details are even more suggestive. The cloud is a key characteristic of an appearance of the Glory of God. Most probably, it refers to the arrival of the "Son of Man" in Daniel 7:13: "As I watched in the night visions, / I saw one like a human being coming *with the clouds of heaven.* / And he came to the Ancient One / and was presented before him."

The voice in the cloud announces a message similar to the heavenly voice at the baptism: "This is my beloved Son, my chosen; listen to him." The differences between this announcement and the baptism are, however, important. First, the "well pleased" is missing from this announcement. Second, this time Jesus is announced as chosen *(eklektos),* terminology that is characteristic of Enoch and other candidates for angelification. The transfiguration is the mid-point in the story of Jesus' self-revelation. The heavens are torn open when Jesus is baptized. After the crucifixion, the veil of the Temple is torn open. The transfiguration takes points from each and packages them into an theophany.[17]

Last and most importantly, the voice commands the listeners to obey Jesus, just as the voice of God commands the Hebrews not to foresake the angel of the Lord in Exodus 23:21–22. This suggests strongly that Jesus is now being further announced not just as Son and Messiah but also as the angelomorphic messenger, the man-shaped divine creature enthroned in God's presence who can be identified with the angel who carries and, in some way, respresents the name of God, as in Exodus 23. The proper name for this figure in Jewish life contemporary with Jesus is the *Kavod,* the "Glory," who is pictured as a large and shining human figure (see Ezek 1:26). This is the capital announcement of early high Christology, especially in Mark where it functions as the only appearance of Jesus' resurrected body. Jesus is being acknowledged as human transformed into divinity—i.e., the principal angel of God, who partakes in God's name as Exodus 23 predicts.

To what does this correspond in the experience of the Early Church? One distinct possibility for interpretation, among the many that have been tried, has not been much discussed by scholars: The transfiguration is not only a misplaced resurrection appearance but also a narrative of the ecstatic, spiritual life of Christians in the Early Church period.[18] The transfiguration reflects visionary experience, not unlike Paul's; but it has been concretized by the Gospel tradition. Jesus continued to be experienced personally within the church after his death and resurrection, primarily within the ecstatic (RASC) experience of the Early Church. This transfiguration story may tell us something of the way in which he appeared to the early Christians, the form that Jesus' appearance took in the Early Church. It is certainly not very different from the kinds of visions of the Christ that Paul represents to us. It should be added to the other descriptions of ecstatic experiences, like speaking in tongues, in the Early Church.

Who is to say that Paul's experience was not in some ways typical of the early Christians? He was more articulate and more privileged in receiving spiritual gifts. But perhaps his experience was more typical than he admits. What makes Paul's experience so anomalous is that the Gospels, as opposed to Paul, assert the physicality of Jesus' resurrection—his resurrection in bodily form. But Paul's insistence on Christ's spiritual body becoming more and more manifest should be equally important to church tradition.

Nor is the resurrection tradition in Christianity ever very far from the issue of martyrdom, which is where it began in the books of Daniel and 2 Maccabees. Like Paul, who identified with Christ and who saw that identification with Christ to take place in suffering as well as in baptism, the Gospel tradition seeks to glorify the persecution that some of the faithful are undergoing. The obvious example is the stoning of Stephen, which is narrated in Acts 7. Most of the chapter is given over to a speech that appears to be a missionary speech against the Jews. After the trial, the transformative aspects of martyrdom are narrated in Stephen's execution scene:

> Now when they heard these things they were enraged, and they ground their teeth against him. But he, full of the Holy Spirit, gazed into heaven and saw the Glory of God, and Jesus standing at the right hand of God; and he said, "Behold, I see the heavens opened, and the "son of man" standing at the right hand of God." (Acts 7:54–56)

Stephen has a vision of the "Glory of God" which contrasts strongly with the Pauline view of the heavenly economy. Paul identified Christ with the "Glory of God." Luke describes the scene in terms given him by the early Christian tradition, directly from Daniel 7:9–14, so the "Glory of God" is identified with the Ancient of Days. The next verse identifies Jesus (not explicitly the Christ) with the "Son of Man" in the Gospels. But unlike the Daniel 7:9–14 scene in which the Son of Man is seated next to the Ancient of Days, Jesus as Son of Man is standing at the right hand of God. Likely, Jesus' standing (as opposed to the enthronement of the Son of Man in Daniel) is to greet the martyred Stephen as he is exalted into heaven after his martyrdom. Stephen's death is explicitly described as "falling asleep," linking it firmly with the promise of resurrection in Daniel 12. Without Daniel 12's prophecy of resurrection and exaltation, the Christian *kerygma* is incomprehensible. Conversely, Christianity is a specific figuration of Daniel's promise that those who make others wise shall shine like the stars. In effect, they are the angels. Here we see Stephen achieve that reward.

Certainly, Luke understood this vision as the fulfillment of Stephen's martyrdom, exaltation, and heavenly transformation, as his appearance at the trial makes clear: "And gazing at him, all who sat in the council saw that his face was like the face of an angel" (Acts 6:15). For Luke, martyrdom was certainly one path to angelic transformation. But it seemed clear that all who are believers in Christ will receive that title, even those who are still on earth.

An Anomalous Reference to the Afterlife in Luke

THERE IS ANOTHER anomalous reference to the afterlife in Luke which may imply yet other notions of the afterlife as well. Luke 23:42–43 implies an intermediary stage to the afterlife as a spirit or soul. Jesus said to one of the thieves crucified with him: "And he said, 'Jesus, remember me when you come into your kingdom.' And he said to him, 'Truly, I say to you, today you will be with me in Paradise.' " A number of theologians have used this passage to demonstrate that the notion of an immortal soul is antique within Christianity.[19] And it could mean that; indeed likely it was interpreted in this way when the notion of the immortal soul was strongly fixed in Christianity.

But it would be unwise to conclude too much from this one, anomalous saying. It only assumes the Jewish notion of *nefesh* or the apocalyptic notion of the righteous souls being held in heaven until the end-time began, as we have seen in the early Enoch material. It is similar to the apocalyptic statement in Revelations 2:7 that the righteous will eat from the Tree of Life in Paradise until the end comes. Note that the passage in Revelation, which contains a reference to eating, is so dramatically physical that it cannot support any notion of the immortality of the soul. None of this dissuades the Apocalypticist from his expectation of bodily resurrection; at best it explains that the dead remain in a privileged, intermediate state until the final resurrection.[20] They exist as bodies that can eat, "souls" in the ancient Hebrew sense of "ghosts," "spirits," or "shades," and can remain secreted in Paradise. It does not change the impression that the missionary thrust of the earliest church was for the physical resurrection of Jesus, his physical presence in the liturgical life of the church, and the physical resurrection of all who believe in him, and no more suggests immortality of the soul than did such details as the faithful's acquisition of crowns and thrones in apocalyptic literature.

The Gospel of Thomas *and* Q

Q IS THE NAME given to all the traditions that Luke and Matthew have in common but which are missing from Mark. (Q stands for *Quelle,* the

German word for source.) Some scholars believe that this represents a separate document equal to Mark in importance to the Early Church but now lost in its original form. Given the evidence, Q would have had to be a bare-bones "sayings source." This would explain how Matthew could put, for example, Jesus' famous sermon on a mount, while Luke placed the same sermon on a plain.

Many Q enthusiasts were heartened when *The Gospel of Thomas* was found, because this was a collection of 114 sayings of Jesus with a minimum of setting and narrative. It was, therefore, hailed as the first evidence that a "sayings source" actually existed. Although the parallels between Luke and Matthew can be understood as progressive copying of one manuscript by another under the influence of special traditions or oral influence of one Gospel on another in an intense but short history of its composition, the Q hypothesis is very vibrant today.

Resolving the existence or nature of Q is not critical to the history of the resurrection belief in Christianity.[21] What is necessary to study is *The Gospel of Thomas* itself, which contains very important traditions about resurrection, quite different from the canonical Gospels. *The Gospel of Thomas* shows definitively that there were early interpreters of resurrection who emphasized the converse of the canonical Gospels—namely, that Jesus' resurrection is entirely spiritual. *The Gospel of Thomas* presents us with a different trajectory of the resurrection tradition, like Paul's in its description of the spiritual nature of the resurrection event but far more extreme in its consequences. It is a second-century document although parts of it may have been written quite a bit earlier.

The most obvious example of spiritual resurrection is to be found in *The Gospel of Thomas,* where vision and knowledge *(gnōsis)* of the Lord can be sought and, when found, reveal the spiritual nature of one's own salvation. Although there are testimonies of its existence, it was first found in its entirety only in the Nag Hammadi corpus, a group of tiny codices discovered in a jar buried in antiquity at Nag Hammadi in Egypt and uncovered by an Egyptian *fellaḥ* (peasant, pl. *fellaḥin*) in 1947 while digging in the desert sand. Thirteen miniscule volumes, containing many different tractates, mostly written in Coptic, the last phase of ancient Egyptian and the holy language of the Coptic Christian church, were found within the jar. Though diminutive in physical size, some of the codices (i.e., books rather than scrolls) were quite long and all were jam-packed with writings. They contained much new information about early Egyptian Christianity. Letters in the binding of the covers of these books seem to date from the time period of Pachomius, the founder of Egyptian monasticism (second century). Historically, the group that collected this library were probably the disciples of Pachomius or persons communicating with him, as the letters stiffening the bindings are likely to be the autograph copies. But beyond that, we know less about them than we need to know.

Most of the documents are very strange, seemingly representatives of various stages in the evolution of a heresy we know as "Gnosticism." The group might not have recognized itself as heretical or even understood the name "Gnostic," as it is unclear when the term "Gnosticism" came into general usage. Some of the sayings in *The Gospel of Thomas* also closely resemble sayings of Jesus in the canonical Gospels. Scholars therefore consider it as an alternative version of the "orthodox" tradition.

The strange traditions found in *The Gospel of Thomas* describe a very spiritual, resurrected body. The strange traditions may explain the use of the disciple Thomas as the doubter in the Gospel of John. This Thomas tradition teaches a rarefied and spiritual Christianity that has little to do with fleshly wounds and literal resurrections. It is no wonder that Thomas became the one who recognized the physical presence of the Savior in the Gospel of John. How better for John to defeat this powerful, Thomasine interpretation of Jesus' mission, death, and resurrection than by having its author, Thomas, admit that his spiritual position was wrong? [22]

In *The Gospel of Thomas,* one sees no such appreciation for physical resurrection. In fact, one sees the other side of the argument:

Jesus said: "If they say to you, 'Where did you come from?' say to them, 'We came from the light,' (the place where the light came into being on its own accord and established [itself] and became manifest through their image). If they say to you, 'Is it you?' say 'We are its children, and we are the elect of the Living Father.' If they ask you, 'What is the sign of your Father in you?' say to them, 'It is movement and repose.' " His disciples said to him: "When will the repose of the dead occur? And when will the new cosmos come?" He said to them: "This thing which you expect has come, but you do not recognize it." (Logia 50–51)

Jesus in *The Gospel of Thomas* is the heavenly Savior and image of the Father who is not begotten. His resurrection had already happened and so had the resurrection of those who believe in him (Logia 50–51). But Jesus is never described as the messiah of Israel in *The Gospel of Thomas.* Instead, he is a revealer-savior who utters magnificently puzzling antinomies, paradoxes, and dilemmas. Unlike the parables in the Synoptic Gospels, which a few resemble outwardly, these Logia are genuinely puzzling; their purpose was apparently to demarcate those with Gnosis (knowledge) and, perhaps, those who had been taught or learned how to understand the parables from those who were outside the group and hence were totally puzzled by them.

The Logia seem to function somewhat like Zen koans, whose purpose is to bring the believer beyond the superficial antinomies of the world to greater hidden truths of vision and knowledge. No one Logion revealed the whole Thomasine tradition, but taken together and read together they slowly reveal a mystical whole, like the pieces of the puzzle. The experience of reading this gospel is very much like reading Jewish mystical literature like *Sefer Ha-Bahir* or *The Zohar*.[23] According to *The Gospel of Thomas,* then, humans come from the light and are destined to return to it if we but realize our heavenly origins. This interest in light as the source of saving knowledge is found in Philo and was characteristic of late pagan Neo-platonism as well as its stepfather Hermeticism, where light is the first created principle of the universe, synonymous with life, logos, and spirit. We also see similar notions in the Syriac *Odes of Solomon*.[24]

These mystical speculations about light can be made understandable in a Jewish context from the Genesis 1 creation account, which was possibly the catalyst that connected all these ideas.[25] As translated into Greek, this supernal light, the first light of all creation, which God called into being on the first day without use of stars or moon or sun, was *Phōs*, a double-entendre in Greek because it can mean either "light" or "man." Jesus therefore, also firstborn himself, could be equated with the human manifestation of the hidden light and truth in the universe. In other guises, this group of ideas is much like the Prologue to the Gospel of John where the creation is understood as having proceeded from the logos, which was divine in itself. But here, there is a further explicit step: those en*lightened* by Jesus became *Sons of Light* themselves. The notion is similar to the terms used by the Qumran community, who thought of themselves as the *běnē 'wr, the Sons of Light,* and felt that they were pure enough to be a single company with the angels.[26]

But the document did not retreat into a complete docetism (the doctrine that Jesus only "seemed" to be human). Logion 28 states this: "Jesus said: 'I took my stand in the midst of the world, and I *appeared* to them in *flesh.* . . .' " Yet it is not the fleshly appearance that is critical: "Jesus said, 'When you see the one who was not born of woman, prostrate yourselves on your faces and worship him. That one is your Father' " (Logion 15). Jesus showed the way to the spiritual Father.

So there is a deep ambiguity between actuality and the appearance of flesh. The Thomasine traditions parallel Paul in taking the spiritual nature of the resurrection body *(sōma pneumatikon)* very seriously indeed. Unlike Paul, however, this Gospel does not posit an apocalyptic end nor does it see the necessity of a material and physical resurrection: "This thing which you expect has come but you do not recognize it," says Logion 51, probably speaking of the resurrection. The theme of lack of recognition is mirrored throughout the work, becoming synonymous with the progress of each believer into more sophisticated Christianity:

His disciples said, "When will you become revealed to us and when shall we see you?" Jesus said, "When you disrobe without being ashamed and take up your garments and place them under your feet like little children and tread on them, then [you will see] the Son of the Living One, and you will not be afraid. (Logion 37)

When you see your likeness, you rejoice. But when you see your images which came into being before you, and which neither die nor become manifest, how much you will have to bear! (Logion 84)

Like all Thomasine Logia, they at first seem very strange until they are read in context with the rest of the document; they are meant to be read together and puzzled out. These Logia seem to imply a baptismal ceremony that is symbolic of removing the fleshly aspect of life entirely. The purpose of this removal is to shed one's body as children shed their clothes before a bath, evidently an image of innocence but also a symbol of rebirth and rejuvenation. The scene of shedding the body is accompanied by a heavenly ascent and preparation for a vision of the Savior, who will reveal Himself at the moment that the individual members of the group are worthy by their purity and discernment.

What social situation would account for this unusual and puzzling document? The community that valued this document was Egyptian, since the language of the document is Coptic, but the original language is likely to have been Greek, so there was a wider audience as well. It has been characterized as "Encratite" (ascetic, Jewish-Christian, and monastic) practically since the document was found. The document itself says its followers are *monachoi,* monks.

April D. deConick has profitably compared the religiosity in *The Gospel of Thomas* with Jewish mysticism as it advocates and prepares for a spiritual vision of the highest manifestation of God.[27] She makes a convincing case that Hermetic, Neoplatonic, and Jewish mystical communities had quite similar spiritual goals. This particular Gospel was valued by a highly ascetic community, probably of cenobitic monks. (They lived apart as hermits but they came together for meals and other rituals.) They were Christians but their Christianity was noticably lacking in Messianism. Their apocalypticism had been vitiated by the strength of the mystic vision that they sought. Why wait for the end of the world when visions give access to the Savior immediately?

They also were determined to do away with any material understanding of Jesus as Savior, viewing his resurrected form as entirely spiritual, essentially as a "very important soul" who ascended to the heaven and beckons to others to follow him (though they did not use that terminology). And their goal was to immortalize their beings by understanding the revelation offered them. They too seemed to feel that sexuality could be transcended in their attainment of divine or angelic status. Their language for attaining divine status was strikingly male-centered:

Simon Peter said to them, "Let Mary leave us, for women are not worthy of life." Jesus said, "I myself shall lead her in order to make her male, so that she too may become a living spirit resembling you males. For every woman who will make herself male will enter the kingdom of heaven." (Logion 114)

Presumably the saying was set in this community's equivalent to the Johannine resurrection story (e.g. John 20). There, Mary did not recognize Jesus at first. Simon Peter sought to have her taken away but Jesus spoke to her and she recognized the Savior after all. Logion 114 seems to have the same incident in mind. Evidently, the community symbolized transcending sexuality as "maleness" while it compared falling victim to sexuality as "femaleness." Simon Peter was represented as commanding Mary to leave, suggesting that females were not worthy of the [eternal] life, which was the goal of the community. But Jesus replied that he himself will show Mary the way to become male and thus also become a living spirit.

Through their maleness, all will enter the kingdom of heaven. The purpose of the Logion was to include women in the order if they too obeyed the monastic rules eschewing luxury and sexuality, on the model of Mary, who was after all, the first to see. But the language impresses us as so sexually biased as to make the message difficult for us to receive. In point of fact, the message also seems consonant with the angelic life expressed in Luke: Some of the privileged will live as angels while on earth and so become them when they are transformed into their eternal beings.

We must remember the perception of Crispin H. T. Fletcher-Louis of what angel Christology meant to the Gospel tradition.[28] Angelic status was a transcendence of sexuality. Here, in place of angelic life, we have a similar notion expressed with the language of the spirit. This ascetic behavior meant eschewing all sexual life. This career, in turn, also prohibited marriage and childbearing, which were crucial to what it meant to be a "woman" in ancient Greco-Roman society. Thus, ascetic life, meant an autonomous life, otherwise only available to men. If this is the type of asceticism represented in *The Gospel of Thomas,* and the ascetic behavior is a propaedeutic to receiving revelation through contemplation, then the text allows for women to access the means of spiritual enlightenment in ways that are not easily available elsewhere in society.[29] It just picks a way that seems strange to us to express it.

Another way in which Mary could become "male" was through a return to the Platonic myth of the andgrogyne. April D. deConick writes, "Since Eve was taken from Adam's side, so she must reenter him and become "male" in order to return to the prelapsarian state of Adam before the gender division.[30] Active creation as a prerequisite for salvation must be understood as a mandatory procedure while the disciple is still on earth. Jesus said, "During the days when you ate what is dead, you made it alive" (Logion 11). The substitution must come before bodily death. The fact that the disciples can turn dead matter into living substance indicates that a transformation from death to life is possible on the earthly level. "Jesus said, 'When you make the two one, you will become children of humanity, and then you say, "Mountain, move from here!' it will move" (Logion 106). In this version of Jesus' exploits, Jesus was not speaking of events to come in an eschatological future but stressing the disciples ability to transform the present miraculously by their meditation and faith.[31]

This "return" to the androgynous figure of Genesis is also characteristic of Valentinian Gnosticism and, to a lesser extent, to Jewish mysticism. Valentinian Gnostics and mystics believed that the very existence of two distinct and opposed sexes was caused by a tragic and unnecessary division for which humanity had suffered ever since.[32] This notion was evident early in the Thomasine tradition: "When you are in the light, what will you do? On the day when you were one, you became two. But when you become two, what will you do?" (Logion 11:3). The Valentinians as well believed that a redeemed person "radiated a vast serenity in which sexual desire had been swallowed up with all other signs of inner division."[33] The Gnostics believed that sexual temptation was a symbol of more deep-seated societal ills, and therefore the transcendence of desire was a "resurrection" of the self.[34] Many of Jesus' sayings in *The Gospel of Thomas* can be associated with encratism, an ascetic lifestyle characterized by abstinence, dietary restrictions, and voluntary poverty.

Finally, Mary's transformation can be interpreted as a movement from the physical and earthly to a realm that is spiritual and heavenly. The female represented the natural, material world, which must be thrown off and transformed into the male spirit who is transcendent and active. Elizabeth Castelli argues: "For progress is indeed nothing else than the giving up of the female by changing into the male, since the female is material, passive corporeal, and sense-perceptible, while the male is active, rational, incorporeal, and more akin to mind and thought.[35]

The belief in a progressive transformation into the male spirit is reminiscent of Neoplatonic notions of the order of the universe in which it is divided into a hierarchy of three levels of divine being: the One, the Divine Mind, and the Soul, under which resided the material world. In the *Enneads,* Plotinus suggested that in rising from the Divine Mind to the One, we leave behind the last shreds of division and separation, even the duality between the knower and the known. We do not see the One, nor even know it, but are made One with it.[36] Notions of this kind can be found throughout *The Gospel of Thomas:*

> When you make the two into one, and when you make the inner like the outer, and the outer like the inner, and the upper like the lower, and when you make male and female into a single one, so that the male will not be male nor the female be female . . . then you will enter [the kingdom.] (Logion 22:4–6)

The otherness of all that was not pure spirit would be healed. The female would be swallowed up in the male and would become male.

Wayne Meeks claims that the unification of opposites served in early Christianity as a prime symbol of salvation.[37] This notion is exemplified by a passage from *The Gospel of Philip* when read with Logion 18 of the *The Gospel of Thomas* about the necessary return to the beginning:

When Eve was in Adam, there was no death; but when she was separated from him, death came into being. Again if [she] go in, and take [her] to himself, death will be no longer. (*G. Philip* 166:22–26)

Have you discovered the beginning, then, that you are seeking after the end? For where the beginning is, the end will be. Blessed is the one who stands at the beginning: that one will know the end and not taste death. (Logion 18).

This comparison further emphasizes Jorunn Buckley's argument for the necessary return to Eden.[38] The "secret knowledge" necessary for eternal life can be intepreted as gaining self-knowledge through unification. Meeks explains, "The emphasis on salvation by self-knowledge suggests that the terms "male and female" are used metaphorically in the Thomas sayings to represent aspects of the individual personality.[39] Whether the dichotomy is taken literally or metaphorically, *The Gospel of Thomas* positions the female in the lowest initiatory stage. The female needs to be abolished in the male before the transformation into the spirit can occur.[40] A woman is twice removed from God, therefore making it more difficult, albeit possible, for women to gain salvation. In this text, Christ is not only seen as the revealer and teacher of salvific knowledge but also functions as a father and spouse for female followers.[41] Although *The Gospel of Thomas* maintains the patriarchal hierarchy, with the help of Jesus as their teacher or spouse, women do have the opportunity to transcend the material world and gain salvation through spiritual exercises leading to the gnosis or saving knowledge.

The apocalyptic ending, the characteristic that Paul and the Gospels have in common, is entirely missing. In its place is a spirit mysticism, which does not use the term "soul" but instead uses Jewish mystical terms like "image" and "form" and "shape," emphasizing that our human shape is a reflection of the divine, as in Genesis 1:26 and other places in the Bible. This seems as close as the resurrection tradition of Christianity can come to the Greek notion of the immortal soul without actually stating it. Jesus' resurrection body can be seen as merely one more spirit. Indeed, Greek dualism of soul and body deny the reality of fleshly resurrection, which by now was firmly ensconced in the canonical Gospel tradition.

On the other hand, *The Gospel of Thomas* includes within in it something that is hard to find in Greek philosophical notions of a soul—a myriad of Jewish and Christian rituals, including baptism, eucharist, and meditation—that served as a technique for receiving religious visions and from which the monastics received the gnosis that transforms them into immortal beings. The most famous logion is almost a command to enter psychoanalysis:

> Jesus said, "If you bring forth what is within you, what you have will save you. If you do not have that within you, what you do not have within you [will] kill you. (Logion 70)

We can see that this Logion, in context, is not exactly about the necessity of psychotherapy. It was a challenge to search for the truth in meditation. Those who found recognition within also recognized that they were the elect. Logion 70 is just as much about the group that recognized the truths contained in these arcane sayings—and only that group—because the "elect," the *maskilim,* those who knew of the Daniel 12 prophecy. It was those who will become the angels and the stars. And this means that the community that produced the Gospel of Thomas had an entirely different understanding of how to missionize the Gospel. There was no apostolic tradition; there was no physical presence; there was no empty tomb and no polemic of doubt with the Jews. Only those who really experienced Jesus in the spirit were converted. Instead of the physicality of the apostolic tradition, we had the ascetic and mystical exercises of a group of monks. The only goal of the Logia was to lead the mystical adept to the visionary presence of the Christ, which could be stimulated by studying and meditating on these gnomic and puzzling phrases of Jesus.

The notion of faith (which is critical to both the Gospels and Paul) has disappeared, and in its place gnosis, the vision, and subsequent transformation became paramount. For Paul, faith meant confidence that his visions would come true. For the Gospels, faith meant trust in the transmission of the canonical tradition through the apostles. Here, faith disappears and is replaced by gnosis (saving knowledge), attained by the mystic through visions. It is as if Paul's visionary Christianity, instead of being the mark of a special prophet, had become the explicit goal of all ascetics.[42] The spiritual process must be completed in this life: "Jesus said, 'Look for the Living One while you are alive, lest you die and then seek to see him and you will be unable to see (him)' " (Logion 59).

These early Christians set about to find the legitimate authority to become the successors to Jesus—namely, the authority of gnosis. We can contrast their spiritual authority with the other Christian understandings of authority. Paul suggested that the principle of authority was faith, but his understanding of faith in Christ meant faith that his vision was the key for understanding the meaning of Christ's resurrection. The Synoptic Gospels said, to the contrary, faith is primarily the acceptance of the authority and teachings of those of us who learned from those who learned at the feet of Jesus. It is a concrete, fleshly chain of tradition that was passed from teacher to pupil.

The community of *The Gospel of Thomas* may have started from the same assumptions as Paul's writing, but took their interpretation to the opposite extreme. Or they may have started from another, independent Thomasine interpretation of Christianity. We do not know. But we know what they thought: Only those who actually see the vision of the Savior will be transformed. It is not faith but the knowledge (gnosis) of God found in visions that brings salvation. It is to them that the true status of angels, stars, and elect is given. Like the intellectuals of a Greek philosophical school, they stressed the individual nature of salvation, the mind must figure it out for itself, with the help of the meditations that Jesus left. And the nature of the community appeared to have been very loose, a group of solitary, hermits who may have assembled only for special meals or rituals, and who will later be called cenobitic monks.

The nature of the transformed body of Christ and the location of that body on earth was a guide to the perfection of humanity. But it was, secondly, an argument that those who counted themselves the followers of Christ had no need to rule others; they knew that they shall rise to the heavens and become stars. The Synoptic Gospels, on the other hand, stress a tightly knit community whose salvation was based on accepting the legitimate apostolic authority of those who were physically taught by the master. They preached bodily resurrection and eschewed spiritual immortality of the soul. Both the Synoptic Gospels and *The Gospel of Thomas* seem to build on the revelation that Paul left. But they took it in completely different directions and they were each involved with a very different polemic with Paul.[43] Paul may not have been the earliest or most important Christian. But, in retrospect, his Christianity seems to have been the most controversial one. What actually happened at Easter is still an historical mystery as well as a mystery of faith. The one sure thing is that each Gospel interpreted the resurrection in a way consistent with its view of ultimate felicity and the rites necessary to achieve it.

12

The Pseudepigraphic Literature

So FAR WE have investigated a very important social aspect of the concept of afterlife: It coheres with the class structure of Hellenistic Israel. It is absent from the very traditional Sadducean classes, the old-guard agricultural aristocracy. The urban, Greek-literate aristocracy (I am thinking of Roman clients like Josephus and classically educated but longtime aristocrats like Philo) had the opportunity to adopt Platonic thought and synthesize it with Hebrew notions to come up with an immortality of the soul that suits Biblical ethics. Jewish intellectuals, like Greek ones, presumably found continuity of consciousness an attractive value, self-confirming of the value of their intellectual lives. So they were motivated to combine it with a more personal afterlife explicitly based on Biblical ethics.

Earliest Christianity, being an apocalyptic, charismatic, Jewish, nativist movement, strongly favored resurrection over immortality of the soul at its inception but was divided on whether the resurrection body is material or spiritual. Without resurrection it could not maintain that Jesus' death was unique, special, and redemptive. Very quickly though it became something quite a bit more, due to the missionary activities of Jewishly and Hellenistically educated people like Paul.

Paul had a very good Pharisaic education as well as a good command of Koine (Greek). Paul explained the ultimate Christian reward as resurrection but also affirmed that resurrection would take place in a spiritual body. The Gospels, by contrast, strongly affirmed that the resurrection body is our actual, physical, real body, as Jesus was really, actually, and physically present in the postresurrection appearances. He even ate and drank after his resurrection.

The contrast between them goes deep; it even shows up in their notions of the Eucharist. Whether the Gospels' point of view represents an anti-Pauline polemic or simply another "trajectory" in early Christianity is obscure. But the earliest varieties of Christianity can be classified as easily by the resurrection they preached as any other variable. For Paul, resurrection had started: It was a spiritual experience of transformation to a spiritual body that was in the process of becoming actual as he spoke. The Gospel writers, writing a generation later, also thought that the end-time had begun. But they stressed the physicality of that resurrection body at the end of time, soon to arrive. In the interim they preached themselves as the physical, actual, successors of Jesus. The apostolic succession was built on the faith that what Jesus taught his disciples was being physically and actually relayed through his apostles and successors, while Paul's notion of faith, rooted in his own visionary experience, meant trust that the visions he experienced were becoming actual.

The later hermits and Gnostics sought vision as well, stressing gnosis (knowledge) over Pauline *pistis* (faith) because it was through meditative states that one came to a vision of the Savior and realization of the spiritual nature of resurrection, while the church leadership could only offer faith in its teachings with a promise of later redemption. The Gnostics experienced the process of transformation as did Paul, seeing their resurrection as immortality of the soul. Like Philo, however, they did not see the immortality of the soul as an entitlement. The soul's immortality had to be awakened by the realization or knowledge *(gnōsis)* of its ultimate reward. The realization could only come about through asceticism and meditation, which imitated the angelic life and sacrificed the body in a kind of personally supervised self-martyrdom. After the birth of Christianity, the dichotomy between resurrection of the dead and immortality of the soul is more easily discussed in other varieties of Judaism than it is in Christianity.

For Paul, the reward of the martyrs came to be the reward of all Christians, who are united with the Christ and martyred with him. Furthermore, in all Christianity, life on this earth was supposed to be patterned on the life of the angels, a life in heavenly community, cleansed of sexuality. Especially those Christians, who could avoid sexual life and live purely like angels, were anticipating the state they would achieve at the expected end. The others were, in some sense, living a normal life in expectation of their later end. Given what Paul said about marriage and sexual fulfillment, it is hard to believe that his resurrection included any sexuality at all.

Martyrdom and Afterlife in Acts

THE ISSUE OF martyrdom was joined in the Gospels first, because Jesus was a martyr, but then in the various early Christian responses to persecution; the doctrine of resurrection itself was born out of persecution and martyrdom. In reflecting on martyrdom, Christians are also reflecting on the value of their earthly body through the mirror of their religious life. The converse—that in reflecting on the body, Christians are reflecting on the value of martyrdom—is also true. For the "orthodox," the endurance of the martyrs is often connected with the reality of the resurrection and, conversely, the unwillingness to undergo martyrdom is often connected with spiritual resurrection. One of the most frequent criticisms of the "Gnostics" was that they were unwilling to suffer martyrdom.

Stephen, the first Christian martyr, saw a vision of Daniel 7:13, the Son of Man, in the agony of his martyrdom. For Luke, Stephen's martyrdom took place in the second phase of church history, after the risen Jesus had ascended to heaven. Stephen and Paul saw the risen Jesus in visions as he existed in his heavenly, Son of Man, or "Glory of God" form. In this vision, contrary to New Testament and early Rabbinic tradition, the Glory of God is taken to refer to God himself, while Jesus is standing at the right hand of God and is identified quite explicitly with the Son of Man.

Stephen dies, forgiving his enemies, in imitation of Jesus and in stark contrast to the mad rabble who stoned him (Acts 7:54). But the term "martyr" had not yet acquired its technical meaning in Christianity. The bystanders, not Stephen himself, were called *"martyres"* (witnesses) in Acts 7:58. What Stephen witnessed is important; as readers, we see his vision of heaven with him. Equally important is the ironic way in which Paul was a "witness" at this *protomartyrium*.[1] According to the narrative, at the pre-conversion Paul was an accessory at the scene ("the young man Saul," Acts 7:58; "approved of their killing him," 8:1), which ironically presaged his own martyrdom by the sword according to later church tradition, as well as providing the transition into the story of Paul's conversion and mission which begin in earnest in Acts, chapter 9.

What made the crowd so angry was Stephen's scathing indictment of the stiff-neckedness of the Israelites, again and again choosing idolatry over the worship of the one, true God. Stephen's subsequent martyrdom confirms his indictment of Israel, for we see the true throneroom of God, with both figures present, as in Daniel, and demonstrating the accuracy of Isaiah 66, which Stephen actually quoted to the effect that the Lord is truly enthroned in heaven; hence worldly temples are but idolatry. The Christian position that the true body is the body of Christ, to which Stephen ascended, and which is also the church of the faithful, is implicit in the passage. As a result of the martyrdom, Stephen "falls asleep," a reference not only to his death but to the prophecy of the end-time (i.e., Isa 26:19 and Dan 12:3).

Instead of merely resting in the earth until the eschaton, Stephen's spirit enters heaven and is welcomed by the enthroned Son of Man. It is not possible to know exactly what is implied by this simple declarative narration. It does suggest that the martyrs will spend the time before the last trumpet in heaven; Stephen's martyrdom is meant to be a depiction of the fulfillment of the second part of the Daniel 12 prophecy, this time identifying the martyr with "those who are wise," who will "shine like the brightness of the heaven, like the stars forever." While the text does not tell us that Stephen became a star or an angel at this crucial point, it has previously said that "his face shone like the face of an angel" in Acts 6:15, before he began his polemical discourse. Evidently, the angelification process could begin even before the martyrdom proper. This further suggests that Stephen was engaged in the teaching that made people wise (*hammaskîlîm*, Dan 12:3b) before he was martyred, suggesting that the phrase was taken by Christians to mean that Stephen was engaging in missionary sermons, in which his indictment of the people of Israel is prominent. In Christianity, as in Judaism before it, the martyrs quintessentially received early transport to heaven before the end. Many later Jewish and Christian apocalypses follow this pattern, extending the reward of the martyr to all the faithful dead. These notions also form the basis of the Islamic belief that martyrs wait for the day of judgment in a garden of delights.

The Apocalypse of John

THE NEW TESTAMENT book of Revelation lent its name to the whole genre of literature (it is the Apocalypse of John in Greek) but it is not itself typical of the apocalyptic art. For one thing, it is the only totally apocalyptic book accepted as canonical in the Bible, though we have already seen that parts of Daniel, Isaiah, and Zechariah might also qualify as "canonical" apocalypses. Canonicity is an early vote of confidence, but only from the point of view of one particular, politically powerful interpretation of the Christian message.

The Apocalypse of John is not typical of apocalyptic literature. It is not pseudonymous, as it records the visions of one identifiable person, John the Apocalypticist (Rev 1:1), who was only later wrongly assumed to be John the Evangelist of the Fourth Gospel. The book differs greatly from the style of the Fourth Gospel and is not likely to have been written by John the Evangelist. The author clearly states that the visions were received on the island of Patmos (Rev 1:9). The book describes a time after the Fourth Evangelist and in an area of the world about which John the Evangelist seemed unconcerned—Anatolia, the Western part of modern Turkey, which was a bustling center of Hellenistic city life. All this suggests strongly that the Apocalypse testifies to a later time than the evangelist's lifetime and at least a generation after Paul, in an area of the world where Paul preached. The Apocalypse evidences considerably larger Christian communities than Paul knew, including many well-established, albeit small and struggling churches. The Apocalypse reports that Christians were being persecuted, praying for help, and looking for the end to come to save them, which the apocalypticist prophesied would soon come to pass, which will rescue the embattled community of the faithful. The revelations were entirely by visions; no dreams are mentioned. John's visions took him to the heavenly throneroom where he meets "the first and the last" (Rev 1:17), the risen Christ who dictates prophecies and revelations to him in angelic form.

There are other differences between this apocalypse and the Jewish apocalypses on which it is based. This is not just apocalypse, it is apocalypse on steroids. It does not, for example, contain the astronomical wisdom of the majority of the earlier Jewish apocalypses. On the other hand, it does prominently include divine throne visions and other elaborate visionary imagery reminiscent of Daniel. Unlike Daniel, these symbols have obvious Christian meanings, though there may also be Jewish meanings as the two terms were not yet mutually exclusive. This suggest that Revelation does not represent the interests of the priests who transmitted their astronomical science in their writings. But it does represent a tradition that was heavily influenced by reading Daniel 7 and 12, as one would expect of an early Christian community. It represents a different kind of disadvantaged group, a Christian group fighting for recognition among Jews and gentiles. And it is an important document for the study of the apocalyptic Christian environment, which was the seedbed of the church.[2]

The book begins with a circular letter to seven churches: "John to the seven churches that are in Asia: Grace to you and peace from him who is and who was and who is to come, and from the seven spirits who are before his throne" (Rev 1:4). The standard epistolary opening is followed by the direct claim to speak for the divine throne and seven spirits (pneumatōn) who are present there. It soon becomes evident that these seven spirits are the "guardian" angels of the seven churches; the message they bring from the throne is an exhortation to steadfastness: "As for the mystery of the seven stars which you saw in my right hand, and the seven golden lampstands, the seven stars are the angels of the seven churches and the seven lampstands are the seven churches" (Rev 1:20). This confirms that Revelation interprets angels and stars as equivalent.

There is good reason for the angels to appear before the divine throne: As we may already suspect, their churches were in crisis and danger. The danger can be understood as persecution and tribulation, which was also experienced by John while he was imprisoned on the island of Patmos (Rev 1:9–11).

"Patient endurance" had already become part of the martyrological tradition, as a description of the determined attitude of the martyr in the face of tribulation, as early as the Hellenistic treatments of the sacrifice of Isaac in 4 Maccabees.[3] But after a century of tribulation, patient endurance had become an art-form. The result of the crisis was the reception of visions of encouragement.

The revelation began as a prophecy from the risen Christ. The first and most important message of the Seer was simply that the Son of Man's resurrection is the promise that those who have been persecuted and martyred will not have died in vain:

> When I saw him, I fell at his feet as though dead. But he laid his right hand upon me, saying, "Fear not, I am the first and the last, and the living one; I died, and behold I am alive for evermore, and I have the keys of Death and Hades. Now write what you see, what is and what is to take place hereafter. (Rev 1:17–19)

Martyrdom was one important cause of the crisis of faith and confidence, as well as the principal reason for the need for ferocious revenge against the persecutors. Persecution is expressly mentioned in Rev 2:13

and martyrdom is strongly suggested. It is directly stated in Rev 20:4. The standard terms of the martyrdom tradition, developed in Judaism but perfected in Christian literature, appear with important emphasis: *thlipsis,* for the tribulation, and *hypomonē* for the steadfastness necessary to survive it (1:9; 2:3; 2:10, 13, 19, 25, 3:8; 10–11) or to gain the courage to face martyrdom.

As solace, the revelation simply and directly confirmed that the crucified messiah is still alive and so all who suffer death for his sake will also be resurrected. He will return and he will show his anger at the persecutors. The promise of resurrection and the defeat of death was a sure exhortation to steadfastness for those who witnessed the suffering and death of martyrs and who might be called upon themselves to suffer and die. The dynamic of the writing is very close to that of Daniel itself, though the Biblical sources contributing to the content of the revelation derived equally from church tradition.

Adela Yarbro Collins sums up the many reasons to adopt a political perspective in understanding this document, while John Collins concentrates on the significance of the fascinating imagery within it.[4] The letters to the churches make clear that there is a crisis of persecution in these communities. Although the opponents are sometimes called false Jews ("synagogue of Satan," Rev 2:9), the visions more often designate Rome as the persecutor and the major target for the coming divine vengeance, perhaps with Jews informing for the Roman overlords.

Even the number of the beast (666) is only the most famous among many indications that Rome was the major persecutor. Since numerological speculation is amazingly versatile and popular in Latin, Greek, and Hebrew (in all three languages letters can serve as numbers) and can be put to almost any purpose, any person might fit this puzzling description with a little arithmetic dexterity. But the most likely conjecture is that 666 refered to Nero, whose name can easily be written in Hebrew in such a way as to yield the number 666. If the emperor of the persecution was Domitian (90–96 CE) rather than Nero, the seer was understanding Domitian as the evil emperor Nero *redivivus,* a persistent popular belief at the time.

However difficult the situation, the faithful will eventually triumph because God is soon to wreak vengeance on the earth. The returning Christ brought fierce retribution to the persecutors, reward and consolation for the victims. Like the book of Daniel and the Jesus movement, the book of Revelation's basic model is nonviolent resistance for the community enforced with militant rhetoric of the punishments waiting for the enemies of God through the intervention of the Christ.[5] The Christ who returns is the agent of punishment. He will, for example, bring fearful conditions of disease, famine, war, and plague ("the four horsemen" of Rev 6), which the persecutors so richly deserved. In Revelation, the Christ appears as both the lamb, the gentle sacrificial animal identified with the martyrs, and the lion, the avenging fury against those who have opposed God's word.

One of the most intriguing aspects of the martyr visions is found in chapter 6, following the opening of the fifth seal:

> When he opened the fifth seal, I saw under the altar the souls of those who had been slain for the word of God and for the witness they had borne; they cried out with a loud voice, "O Sovereign Lord, holy and true, how long before thou wilt judge and avenge our blood on those who dwell upon the earth?" Then they were each given a white robe and told to rest a little longer, until the number of their fellow servants and their brethren should be complete, who were to be killed as they themselves had been. (Rev 6:9–11)

As in Acts, the afterlife is depicted with naive narrative simplicity; and it is all the more effective because of it. There is an implicit ambiguity in the word "soul." Though the "soul" terminology may suggest to us the Greek notion of immortal souls, it is more likely that the Hebrew word *nefesh* alone is understood here as the principle of identity for the martyrs in the intermediary state between their deaths and their resurrection. It seems no different from the word "spirit" used in Acts 7, referring to angels and exalted martyrs in heaven. It is however important that the "soul" language was developed to help serve the purpose of justifying the martyrs, explaining where they reside until the consummation.

The apocalyptic framework suggests an intermediate state and the final return of the righteous to the earth. The use of the word "soul" at this place may also have a social implication in that it refers to a specific group of Christians, those who had suffered and died and whose return will signal that God's justice is accomplished. One might also suggest that Hellenistic popular notions were being synthesized with the Hebrew ones to help combine notions of resurrection with immortality of the soul. The setting itself describes a much more Hellenized environment than the Gospels. Furthermore, the literature is a narrative rather than philosophical tractate, which facilitates the synthesis.

Christian resistance at this period, like Jewish martyr resistance before it, was predominantly passive resistance. That was what produced martyrs in this period and not political revolutionaries. We think that the group that produced Daniel was also politically passive in opposition to Syrian Greek rule; if the group was the "Hasideans" it was not militarily sophisticated. We cannot totally rule out active military action for all who revered the Dead Sea Scrolls, as some of the documents are extraordinarily militant, and who may have taken part in the First Jewish revolt against Rome (66–70 CE).

But, even they considered themselves the allies of the angels. It was God, not the human community, who was going to correct the situation. As in most religious millenarian movements, the role of the faithful is passive; they will wait while God and his divine agencies clear away the sinners. The faithful will even undergo martyrdom for their faith, suffering every torture with patient endurance. A number of scholars of millenarian movements point out that, in general, were there a reasonable chance of political or military action, the millenarian movement would likely have become a political revolutionary movement. In the early period, Christians followed the example of Jesus and were content to let God avenge the righteous because no one could militarily oppose Roman order and expect to win.

Apocalyptic Attempts to Handle Immortality of the Soul

BUT AN APOCALYPTIC expectation of the end of time could not be maintained forever without the arrival of the end. Eventually, Christianity would have to come to terms with the delay of the parousia or it would be abandoned as disconfirmed. Even Paul's notion of inward transformation depended on the arrival of the eschaton. As Christianity came to terms with the continued existence of the world, it incorporated two conceptions that were quite foreign to its original formulation—the immortality of the soul and an interim state in which the soul exists until the Savior arrives to judge the world. It also took an assumption of the corrupted, apocalyptic worldview and turned it into the doctrine of Original Sin, which builds human imperfectibility into the universe. In turn, it demands the rite of infant baptism to counteract it.[6]

We can find the attempt to come to terms with the delay of the parousia (the arrival of Jesus) in two primary literatures: the Church Fathers and the Apocrypha. As John Gager has cogently pointed out, Christianity had to deal with an enormous change in its religious life. In the first century, Christians were praying for the arrival of the apocalypse: "Thy Kingdom, come" (Matt 6:10). By the end of the second century, Tertullian tells us that Christians prayed "for the emperors, for their deputies, and all in authority, for the welfare of the world, and for the delay of the consummation."[7] The millenarian aspects of Christianity need to be jettisoned while keeping the motivations and energy of Christianity's proselytizing mission intact.

A similar problem existed within Judaism, in that the destruction of the Second Temple raised enormous apocalyptic expectations, which were first expressed, then disconfirmed, then explained further. But only a few Jews were millenarians, while the majority wanted to be good citizens of the Roman order. Both Judaism and Christianity needed to understand why God had not yet intervened to save the righteous and punish the sinners. In both traditions, the delay of the apocalypse meant a turn to immortality of the soul and an interim "waiting period" in which the souls were punished and rewarded in heaven before the end. For Christianity, being a heavily missionary movement, it also meant developing more articulate reasons for becoming Christian even if the end were not coming tomorrow.

This literature is vast so we will need to seek all the help we can. We will have to adopt a selective, topical approach. Richard Bauckham, who has analyzed many heavenly journey texts, developed his description of the genre of the "tour of hell." Some of his conclusions are so important as to be best presented by direct quotation:

(1) Cosmic tours, like those in *1 Enoch*, displayed from an early date an interest in the fate of the dead, among other cosmic secrets. With the emergence of belief in the punishment of the wicked after death, a tour of the punishments in hell was included in such apocalypses. *The Apocalypse of Elijah* was evidently an example of this development. It may even have been the earliest.

(2) Within the genre of tours of the seven heavens, there may have been apocalypses which included a tour of hell located (as in *2 Enoch*) within one of the heavens, but no such apocalypse has survived. Instead, we have apocalypses in which an ascent through the seven heavens is followed by a visits (sic!) to paradise and hell: *3 Baruch* (Slavonic) and *Gedulat Moshe*. (Since this pattern is also followed in the apocalypse in the Syriac *Transitus Mariae*, where hell, as in *2 Enoch*, is only reserved for the wicked in the future, the pattern probably predated its use in apocalypses which included a tour of hell.)

(3) Some cosmic tour apocalypses developed a particularly strong emphasis on the fate of the dead. Thus the *Gedulat Moshe*, while re-

taining a tour of the seven heavens with cosmological and angelological concerns independent of the fate of the dead, gives most space to the visits to hell and paradise, while even within the tour of the heavens Moses encounters the angel of death in the sixth heaven. The transition is then not great to apocalypses exclusively concerned with the fate of the dead, such as the *Apocalypse of Zephaniah* and the *Apocalypse of Paul*, which while they range quite widely over the heavens and the underworld and even the extremities of the earth, are interested only in matters concerned with the fate of the dead. In fact, the *Apocalypse of Paul* may well have developed from basically the same pattern as that of 3 *Baruch* and the *Gedulat Moshe:* ascent through the heavens, visit to paradise, visit to hell. . . . With the belief that the souls of the dead are first taken up to the throne of God for judgment before being taken to paradise or hell (ApPaul 14–18), this pattern became the way the seer could follow the path of souls after death and observe their fate.[8]

Bauckham looks at a series of later works, which we are not going to study in detail, because he has so aptly summed up their import. Even after Bauckham's detailed study, some interesting larger questions yet remain: Why, for instance, does the tradition ramify in the direction of postmortem judgment? Why do stories of the horrors of hell increase as time goes on? Answers to these questions must be somewhat general and speculative. But there is a certain, inescapable logic, which can be identified by meditating on Bauckham's observations.

One might begin with the observation that the purpose of these angelically guided tours of hell is basically to confirm the moral nature of the universe, in contrast to the obvious and undeserved rewards that too many sinners and oppressors receive on earth. If the end is not just around the corner, if the end has not arrived in centuries, then it is no longer enough to think that God will punish the sinners at the end and reward the righteous there. Reward and punishment needs to be closer to the events of earthly existence. In short, there needs to be a heaven and hell.

The predisposition of apocalyptic literature to imagine in horribly literal terms the just deserts of the sinners and enemies of the group compensates for the injustice on earth. But history tells us that life became easier for Christians as they progressed up the social ladder of the Roman Empire. Why then did they design even more ferocious punishments against the sinners?

It was the delay of the parousia. The more time that passed without the good being rewarded by the end of the world, the more vindictive the faithful became against the sinners. With no quickly arriving apocalypse, there would be no reason to convert to Christianity except to avoid more and more horrendous punishments for sinning. Hell was a convenient stick with which to whip the sinner and a great cautionary tale to encourage the faithful.[9] Under such circumstances, the details of hell depended on the writer's inventiveness against the persecutors of the faithful.

Yet there is one more, even stronger reason why hell became so important in apocalyptic literature. It is deeply connected to the process of synthesizing resurrection of the dead with immortality of the soul: The more clear the depiction of the immortal soul, the more terrible hell had to be. An immortal soul is not destructible at death. Once the soul's immortality is admitted (and therefore its universal and natural eternity acknowledged, as Plato taught), the more horrible must be the punishments for the badly behaved souls in hell. In the Daniel vision, the great sinners were resurrected for punishment. Most persons just remain dead, along with the ordinary righteous. But once the soul was immortal and all souls survived forever, then punishment had to be eternal as well, otherwise sinners would appear to get away with their dastardly deeds.

We already know that apocalyptic communities defined themselves (to a greater or lesser degree) as self-imposed pariahs, to avoid contamination ritually and morally from the surrounding society. They maintained their own ritual and moral purity, to their own specific and sectarian definition, and thus they constantly reminded themselves of their elect status: They will be the only persons to inherit God's coming kingdom. There was an inherent social dimension to resurrection of the body, a polemic against those who would not get it and a very clear definition of the saved. When the notion of resurrection was combined with immortality of the soul in a Jewish or Christian context, a number of adjustments needed to be made, one of which was that the role of hell had to be more fully emphasized; and the other is that the judgment needed logically to be relocated to the time of death so that the final disposition of the immortal soul could be made clear. The third is that compensatory doctrines like Original Sin would become more explicit to enforce the dualism.

Souls in the Apocalyptic End

SOULS IN an apocalyptic work might mean only the "personality" of the departed and not precisely what the Greek "immortal soul" implied. After all, *nefesh* was available as a word for "soul" from Genesis onwards. It is very hard to know when the implications of the Platonic notion began to be felt. Especially when there is a resurrection at the end of time, the issue is moot because the end settles all the scores. When souls achieve an intermediate state, it is only until the resurrection at the end of time when the virtuous regain the earth in one form or another. This is a stable feature of Christian understanding of the end-of-time. Yet, at a certain point, we note that no one expected the end immediately, so that the immortal soul began to have a place in thinking about the afterlife. Life in heaven became more than an intermediary state. Logically, this happened as apocalyptic notions diminished but the soul's intermediate state became more clearly defined. In other words, when the apocalyptic end receded, the intermediate state in heaven became more and more important. In this case, the doctrine of Original Sin began to function more strongly, and it was reinforced by the development of infant baptism.[10] It provided an additional reason to be among the faithful. Otherwise, mission fails and the church is not motivated to keep up the good works.

This is not the only logical way to combine the two traditions, not an inevitable outcome, but it does describe how the traditions were, in fact, combined in Christianity. We shall later note the interesting dissenting position that Origen and Gregory took in this dialogue.[11] But in the apocalypses there is little philosophical argumentation. Instead, the narrative developments pick obvious ways to cope with the idea of the immortality of the soul.

The result was a very powerful notion of hell, to cover great sinners and (mostly) infidels and which in turn eventually generated the need for less stringent places of punishment, purgatory and limbo, for the culpable within the church, since such horrendous punishments to innocent souls seemed to disconfirm statements of God's mercy. This theme, the generosity of communities imagining their victory in their imaginations, became quite common in later apocalyptic writing as well, especially as the notion of our ability to affect the status of the damned by our prayers and offerings gained popularity in Christian European life. Richard Bauckham also devoted considerable space to the conflict between justice and mercy. He noted the continuing theme of the earth giving back the dead.[12]

The Testament of Moses

MEANWHILE, the Jewish community was producing apocalypses as well. Like so many apocalyptic and pseudepigraphical documents, the *Testament of Moses* cannot be dated exactly. It has been credibly placed in

Maccabean times by some scholars. The crisis narrated in it is likely to be later, the destruction of the Temple (70 CE) or perhaps even the second revolt against Rome (132–135 CE). Martyrdom also figures in this document, as well as a tacit agreement that Jews can be buried anywhere: "The whole world is your sepulcher" (T. Mos 11:8). This is more than a cynical statement, rather a statement that the diaspora is of long duration already. The Levite *Taxo* is described as a martyr, along with his seven sons, as a sign that will bring on the final vengeance from the LORD:

> There let us die rather than transgress the commandments of the LORD of LORDS, the God of our fathers. For if we do this, and do die, our blood will be avenged before the Lord. (T. Mos 9:7)

The LORD's vengeance begins with Him leaving his throne and bringing chaos to the earth, in the same way that the warrior Ba'al or YHWH punished his enemies of old. But, as in the previous adaptation of these images for martyrdom, the righteous will be taken into heaven. The terminology for "raising" expresses a clear ascension, which as in earlier passages, probably assumed resurrection. In this case, it certainly promises astral immortality.

Fourth Ezra

THE BOOK OF 4 *Ezra* (also known as 2 *Esdras* in LXX nomenclature) is a first century CE book, with a great deal of Jewish material in it, resembling nothing so much as a primer about life after death. The central portion of the book (beginning with chap. 3) comprises the discussions and visions of the writer, living close to the destruction of the Second Jewish Temple in Jerusalem in 70 CE. It is, however, a typical pseudonymous book. It purports to be the religious discussions between an angel and Ezra, who is disconsolate about the destruction of the First Temple, in 587/586 BCE. The dominant English commentaries take the book to be a unity. Furthermore, the important commentary by Michael Stone in the *Hermeneia* series,[13] presupposes that the book contains the special visions of one person, whose religious questions are answered through RASC described throughout the book. This commentary is noteworthy for many felicities, not the least of which is that Stone faces the implications of the claimed revelatory quality of the narrative on the writer and reader. The material is somehow related to *Baruch* and the *Pseudo-Philo* literature.[14]

Regardless of the exact nature of the book's composition or its exact qualities as literature, the central issue of the book is theodicy, justifiying God's ways to humanity. As such, the issue of life after death comes up significantly throughout, both in apocalyptic terms of a world to come and the disposition of the soul after death.

The book begins in chapter 3, the first two chapters being a Christian addition usually designated as 5 Ezra.[15] Ezra begins by telling his spiritual difficulties. His spirit was greatly anxious and he prays for help in great agitation. Thus begins the dialogue which precedes the first of seven visions. Each vision is preceded by a strict regimen of fasting but visions three and six are also preceded by "eating of flowers," an obscure detail which reflects either asceticism or the ingestion of psychotropic substances. Either way, we can expect RISC will result. The first three visions are explicitly experienced at night while attempting to sleep (3:1; 6:17; cf. 6:30; 6:36; 9:27). Dream visions, we already know, are a distinct characteristic of Jewish RISC, especially in Daniel but also in 1 Enoch 14:2; 85:1; T. Levi 2:5; 8:1, 18 and Aramaic Levi 7–8. The visions in the book are meant to be understood as received in an altered state of consciousness.

In chapter 4 a dialogue begins between Ezra and the angel Uriel, who appears quite suddenly. But theophany per se is not the purpose of the meeting. The angel challenges Ezra to understand various of God's great unanswerable mysteries. In this respect, the meeting resembles the answer given to Job. But, unlike the book of Job where the appearance of God is enough to silence questions of theodicy, Ezra received the outlines of a longer answer from one of God's assistants. For example, in 4 Ezra, death is entirely the result of Adam's sin, rather like orthodox Christian doctrine of Original Sin, except that the sin is due to Adam alone. This answer enshrines the fallen state of humanity and makes salvation necessary for human perfection. It also preserves a kind of apocalyptic sociology, once the prediction of a coming end fades, because it suggests that only those within the group know how to escape Original Sin and attain salvation.

In probably the most famous vision, chapter 7, we see evidence of exegesis. But behind it is RISC, as the vision itself is repeatedly said to be a gift from God. In it, we have a reference to the entrances to the coming world, which are broad and safe and yield the fruit of immortality. Then the vision itself begins, in which Daniel 7 is one of the controlling texts. It is understood in an unusual way.

For my son the Messiah shall be revealed with those are with him, and those who remain shall rejoice four hundred years. And after these years my son the Messiah shall die, and all who draw human breath. And the world shall be turned back to primeval silence for seven days, as it was at the first beginnings; so that no one shall be left. And after seven days the world, which is not yet awake, shall be roused, and that which is corruptible shall perish. And the earth shall give up those who are asleep in it; and the chambers shall give up the souls which have been committed to them. And the Most High shall be revealed upon the seat of judgment, and compassion shall pass away, and patience shall be withdrawn; but judgment alone shall remain. Truth shall stand, and faithfulness shall grow strong. And recompense shall follow, and the reward shall be manifested; righteous deeds shall awake, and unrighteous deeds shall not sleep. Then the pit of torment shall appear, and opposite it the Paradise of delight. (4 *Ezra* 7:26–44)

This vision of the Messianic end is so different from Christianity's version that it bears special emphasis; it points out how fluid Messianic ideas were in the first century. Each vision of the end was closely correlated with each group's social position, ideals, and historical experiences. In this case, a group of people was trying to understand the suffering of the first revolt against Rome and the destruction of the Temple. Even so, the language is directly reminiscent of Daniel 12: "The earth shall give back those who are asleep in it, and the dust those who rest in it." This is the recompense that God owes to the righteous. These themes will become crucial to Islam.

The disposition of the nations is emphasized. They (obviously those who have oppressed Israel) will be resurrected to be shown the instruments of their final torture and then cast into perdition, though the text politely passes over the gruesome details with the phrase: "All shall see what has been determined for them" (v 43). Death is conceived of the body's separation from spirit, or soul (7:78, 100). As in most apocalyptic material, whether "the soul" means anything like the Greek immortal soul or merely the personality in a post-body existence is moot. The final consummation is a resurrection in refined bodily form (7:32).

After the description of the Messianic future, come a number of questions about the final disposition of souls, or spirits (7:75ff.). The classification of the condemned need not detain us, though it too is based on Daniel. But the categorization of the saved souls (7:91ff.) is based on the passage in Daniel 12, which prophesies that some will be given a special role as stars in the heaven.

The characterization is an interpretation of the passage in Daniel. The seer has introduced some new material which goes far beyond Daniel 12. The moral separation between the good and the evil has gotten more strict. There is to be no intercession by the righteous for the ungodly any more (v 102). In Daniel, the leaders ascend to stardom, most people are not resurrected and the very evil are resurrected for further punishment. Here, the resurrection of the good is still for the saved remnant but it is far more general, while the punishment of hell is reserved for most everyone else. In 4 Ezra 7:125, the faces of the abstinent are said to shine above the stars, confirming that the ascetic life leads to the angelic life, that cleanliness is next to godliness.

The Ezra apocalypticist inserted a higher category still, those who look upon God himself (Exod 24; 33:20–21, etc). Perhaps that was his understanding of the Danielic phrase "shine like the stars forever." In Revelation 1:16, we also see: "His face was like the sun, shining in full strength."

This vision, though based on Daniel, is not merely an exegesis of Daniel but is an interpretation of it, different and contradictory to it in many ways. This method of interpretation is quite unlike exegesis in that it can with impunity maintain as actual details that are inconsistent with the original vision. Pure exegesis would have had to explain any change of that magnitude. But it is quite like a visionary meditation. Abnormal states of consciousness, including prophetic dreams, are the easiest ways to explain the innovations and the seemingly contradictory information. These seers are prophetic dreamers, who study texts like Daniel during the day and seek interpretive dreams at night. The dreams are, as is natural, a combination of the texts and the contemporary problems of the seers, who are trying to come to terms with the destruction of Jerusalem.

The Baruch Literature

THE BARUCH literature is a treasure trove of interesting apocalyptic imagery and ascension traditions. This literature is based upon the figure of Jeremiah's *amanuensis* or secretary Baruch at the destruction of the First Temple. This historical character, already well known as the recorder and writer of Jeremiah's prophecies, became an important figure in his own right at the time of the destruction of the Second Temple. *First Baruch* (1 *Bar.* 1:1–38) may be dated as early as the second century BCE. After the destruction of the Second Temple, many different groups evidently speculated on the meaning of history through the person of Baruch, as the literature manifests many differing characteristics and cannot be attributed to a single person or school. During this period, 2 and 4 *Baruch* were written. *Third Baruch* is a vision of a heavenly journey like *The Apocalypse* and *Testament of Abraham, 1* and *2 Enoch*, the *Testament of Levi*, the *Martyrdom of Isaiah*, and the Merkabah literature. So the genre is very unusual and wide-ranging.

SECOND BARUCH

In *2 Baruch* (Syriac), the theme of angelic transformation receives enormous emphasis. It is set in the period of the destruction of the First Temple, though it is the destruction of the Second Temple that occasioned the text. This book has been influenced by Christianity and can be dated variously from the first to the third century CE. So it is hard to assess its exact social location. Besides the ascent and translation story, the book serves as a primer for the final disposition of the just and unjust in God's grand scheme, protected by the *imprimatur* of Baruch's revelatory experience.

Baruch follows several well-known techniques for achieving RASC, including fasting and lamentation, which are known to alter consciousness. *First Baruch* explicitly asks why one should remain righteous. The answer is clear: righteousness is God's goal for humans, therefore no person should indulge in self-destructive enterprises (12:5–20:4). After Baruch repeats the preparatory rites, he receives revelations of disasters that will shortly overtake the world, followed by the apocalypse, including the coming of the Messiah, the resurrection of the dead, and the final judgment (20:5–30:5).

In the final "balancing of the books," the righteous and the sinners both survived death so that the wicked could be punished. Not only was Baruch familiar with the texts in Daniel 12, which explicitly say that the evil and the good will be resurrected for the final judgment, he was also familiar with the visions in Ezra and relied on them to amplify his vision of the end (see particularly, *1 Enoch* 22 and *4 Ezra* 7:28ff.). Naturally, the details of the visionary literature itself were picked up in future visions. This is not necessarily the result of exegesis or literary allusion; it may just as easily be explained as the natural incorporation of known details into later visions because they appear in the visions of the apocalypticists after they have been studied.[16] The novel details may have come from visions or they might not. Further study is necessary in each case.

After a few more visions, which are also explained, Baruch repeats his preparation procedure yet again to ask specifically about the nature of the resurrection (49:1–52:7):

Listen, Baruch, to this word and write down in the memory of your heart all that you shall learn. For the earth will surely give back the dead at that time; it receives them now in order to keep them, not changing anything in their form. But as it has received them so it will give them back. And as I have delivered them to it so it will raise them. For then it will be necessary to show those who live that the dead are living again, and that those who went away have come back. And it will be that when they have recognized each other, those who know each other at this moment, then my judgment will be strong, and those things which have been spoken of before will come. (50:1–4, end of chapter)

The dead must be raised in their exact form so that God's justice will be evident to all. But then the righteous will be changed into a much more glorious form, as in 2 *Baruch* 51:3. This transformation conveniently solves the problem of identity in the afterlife before it goes on to the final consummation. In this further developed vision of the end, all the righteous share the rewards given by Daniel to "those who are wise." This represents a significantly different view of the meaning of that expectation.

Second Baruch 51:3–5 portrays a gradual transformation of all believers into angelic creatures, as the process of redemption is fulfilled:

Also, as for the glory of those who proved to be righteous on account of my law, those who possessed intelligence in their life, and those who planted the root of wisdom in their heart—their splendor will then be glorified by transformations, and the shape of their face will be changed into the light of their beauty so that they may acquire and receive the undying world which is promised to them. . . . When they therefore will see that those over whom they are exalted now will then be more exalted and glorified than they, then both these and those will be changed, these into the splendor of angels and those into startling visions and horrible shapes; . . . For they will live in the heights of that world and they will be like the angels and be equal to the stars. And they will be changed into any shape which they wished, for beauty to loveliness, and from light to the splendor of glory. . . . And the excellence of the righteous will then be greater than that of the angels.[17]

Here is an innovative interpretation of the visions of Daniel. The evil ones are transformed into the terrible beasts of the Daniel vision while the righteous are explicitly transformed into stars.

Cavallin points out that we may profitably compare this vision with Paul's discussion in 1 Corinthians 15.[18] He lists four important similarities between the two: (1) the general background of apology for the belief in resurrection; (2) reflection on the nature of the resurrection body; (3) the survival of some at the end; and (4) the idea of transformation and heavenly glorification of the righteous. This does not necessarily imply direct dependence, only a reworking of traditional material to answer similar questions. Since this is a revelation achieved in RASC, it does hint at the way in which texts inspire further visions.

THIRD BARUCH

Third Baruch is also relevant to our story. The work survives in two different forms—Slavonic and Greek—though there are good reasons for supposing that the Slavonic version represents a more original version of the text than the Greek, which shows considerable Christian reworking. In particular, the references to the disposition of the dead in the Slavonic version seem to be the more original. But, the Greek version retains the more common Jewish name of Samael for Satan while the Slavonic version has a more elaborate story of the fall of Satan-El,[19] who loses his angelic suffix *El* (like Michael, Gabriel, Raphael, Uriel, etc.) and becomes Satan after the fall. So both versions have undergone independent later development. But this and other characteristics make even the Slavonic version often seem more like a summary than the original narrative.[20]

Third Baruch is revelatory literature. As Baruch is crying over the destruction of the Temple, an angel appears to him. What happens thereafter is supposed to be a description of simple events yet the setting is one in which prophets often enter RASC. Lamentation is a regular occasion for the reception of altered states of consciousness in Jewish tradition, right into the modern period.

The Baruch literature ignores the Enoch tradition, although it resumes much of the information contained in Genesis 2–11. This inevitably leads to scholarly speculation that Baruch literature is polemical against Enochic material.[21] At any rate, it contains much expanded and sometimes bizarre notions of the punishment of sinners. The builders of the Tower of Babel are accorded special attention, as does punishment in hell. In the Greek version, Hades is placed in the third heaven (4:3, 4:6, 5:3), which seems to be an independent development. The Greek version interprets the birds that Baruch sees in the fourth heaven as the "souls of the righteous" (10:5), a motif which may reach back to Canaanite practice and which occasionally comes back in Islamic tradition. The notion of the immortality of the soul is well represented in the received version of this document, whatever the complicated origins of the tradition may have been.

Apocalyptic literature represents heavenly journeys as straight and ordinary narrative when, during this period at least, we know that they were achieved through RASC. There are documents that prefer to represent altered states in a dream context and others that prefer to ignore the issue of consciousness entirely. Many texts follow the same contrast we saw in the Gospels and Paul: Mystical texts describe RASC while apocalyptic ones describe the events as if they were happening in ordinary consciousness.

Second Enoch

SECOND ENOCH, extant in two Slavonic versions, is a further extension of the Enoch legend, most probably through a Christian recension, since the importance of Torah does not figure in the story. Yet, the possibility of a Semitic language, possibly even a Jewish *Vorlage* (original edition), especially in the shorter version, cannot be ruled out. Many Christians wrote in the Aramaic language as well, and there were Jewish Christians who claimed both Jewish and Christian identities at once, whatever their Christian and Jewish brothers may have thought of them. In 2 *Enoch* 22:7, Enoch is transformed during a face-to-face encounter with the LORD into "one of his glorious ones"—in short, an angel and a star. Note, however, the use of glorification language to characterize angelic status. God decrees: "Let Enoch join in and stand in front of My face forever," thus explaining for us the Rabbinic term "Prince of the Presence," which is normally applied to Metatron. It is the highest category of angel in 4 *Ezra*, and in this book it has become an official, titled position. Then, on the basis of this promotion, Enoch is transformed into his new angelic status:

> And the Lord said to Michael, "Go, and extract Enoch from [his] earthly clothing. And anoint him with my delightful oil, and put him into the clothes of my glory. And so Michael did, just as the Lord had said to him. He anointed me and he clothed me. And the appearance of that oil is greater than the greatest light, and its ointment is like sweet dew, and its fragrance myrrh; and it is like the rays of the glittering sun. And I looked at myself, and I had become like one of his glorious ones, and there was no observable difference. (2 *En* 22:8–10, recension A)

Here, the transformation is effected through a change of "clothing." The clothing represents Enoch's new transformed, immortal flesh as it is

immortal clothing. This is a significant parallel with Paul's future glorification of the mortal body in 2 Cor 5:1–10.[22] Enoch has been put "in" the
body of an angel, or he is "in" the manlike figure in *1 Enoch* 71. This may
all be a further explanation of Paul's use of the peculiar terminology "in
Christ."

The Testaments of the Twelve Patriarchs *and Daniel*

THE ORIGIN and date of the *Testaments of the Twelve Patriarchs* have
been much debated in recent years. It may either be a Jewish work composed as early as the second century BCE but to which a Christian editor
later added material, or it may instead be a Jewish Christian work dating
from the second century CE. The older notion that the text was composed
in Greek must now be reevaluated because of the Hebrew and Aramaic
fragments found at Qumran. These suggest that at least two of the testaments, the *Testaments of Naphtali and Levi,* were originally written in
Semitic languages. Even if others are later Christian compositions, the traditions inherent in the testaments have so many affinities to *1 Enoch, Jubilees,* and the Dead Sea Scrolls that the non-Christian material may be
assumed also to be pre-Christian.[23]

Like *Jubilees* and the Dead Sea Scrolls, the *Testaments* emphasize the
struggle between cosmological forces, which are typical of apocalypticism
and at the same time reflections on cataclysmic events in Judea during the
first centuries. The *Testaments* are particularly emphatic in their notion
that the patriarchs were resurrected. They use the word "raised," typical
for Hellenistic Judaism and Christianity, to express it in *T. Jud* 25:1;
T. Sim 6:7; *T. Zeb* 10:1–4; and *T. Ben* 10:6–10. In *T. Ben* 10, the patriarchs' resurrection, is combined with a universal resurrection: "All shall
rise, some to glory and some to shame" (10:8), just as in the general resurrection prophesied in Daniel 12. In *T. Simeon* 6:7, the patriarch prophesies his own resurrection: "Then I shall rise in joy and I shall bless the
Most High for His wonders." *Testament of Judah* 25:1 records a promise
of resurrection "to life" for all the patriarchs, which evokes Daniel 12:2.
In the *Testament of Judah* 25:4, the pattern of compensation for the faithful becomes clear: "And those who have finished in sorrow will rise, some
for glory, others for dishonor, and the Lord will judge Israel, first of all,
for their unrighteousness." *Testament of Benjamin* 10:6 includes Enoch
among the patriarchs.

Like the ascent vision in *1 Enoch,* the ascent in *Testament of Levi* interrupts the narrative.[24] It begins in a prophetic dream while Levi, the ancestor of the priestly line, is tending his flocks. An angelic guide brings him through the heavens, pointing out the cosmological features that most people of that time assumed to be there: the treasuries of rain, snow, fire, ice, and the brightness, placing the superior moral machinery higher than the merely meteorological machinery. At the beginning of chapter 5 the angel shows Levi God sitting on the throne and this exquisite sight is the sign that he will be given "the blessing of the priesthood until I shall come and dwell in the midst of Israel." It was the priests' job to see God. Theophany and priesthood go together because it was the priest who entered the holy of holies on the Day of Atonement.

The angel gives him a shield and sword to execute vengeance on Shechem, a key issue that may help understand the social location of the Testament. It seems to rely on the story of the destruction of Shechem and the sons of Ḥamor (Genesis 34) as a typology for some contemporary event (see also Josh 24:32, Judg 9:28, and Acts 7:16).

In chapter 8, we resume the vision narrative, suggesting that the story of Shechem was meant to have special import. When the vision continues, Levi is enthroned with all the honors of the high priesthood. But the writer is also seeking to legitimate his own community in his own day:

> "Levi, your posterity shall be divided into three offices as a sign of the glory of the Lord who is coming. The first lot shall be great; no other shall be greater than it. The second shall be the priestly role. But the third shall be granted a new name, because from Judah a king will arise and shall found a new priesthood in accord with the gentile model and for all nations. His presence is beloved, as a prophet of the Most High, a descendant of Abraham your father. To you and your posterity will be everything desired in Israel, and you shall eat everything attractive to behold, and your posterity will share among themselves the Lord's table. From among them will be priests, judges, and scribes, and by their word the sanctuary will be controlled." When I awoke, I understood that this was like the first dream. And I hid this in my heart as well, and I did not report it to any human being on the earth. (T. Levi 8:11–12)

Few have suggested how much this prophecy helped the gentile Christian church understand itself in contradistinction to the Jewish (and perhaps some in the Jewish-Christian) community. If the passage is using the story of Shechem as a typology, the vengeance taken against the circumcised might be a the result of a deliberate Biblical typology (symbolic reading of the Bible with a later incident in mind) predicting the lack of acceptance among the Jews of the Judaized Christians who thought to join the new Israel by circumcision through the story of Shechem. The narrator's point is that this replicates the pattern set in the Old Testament when the Israelites on one occasion unjustly attacked Canaan. Obviously, this was not the original interpretation of that story. The innovation emphasizes that one need not keep the special rules of Jewish diet. So this seems to be an explicitly gentile Christian revelation.

Daniel 5:11ff. was originally an independent apocalypse. The preserved are called "the souls of the saints."[25] The life to come is described as "rest" and "eternal peace" (v 11), probably attesting to contact with the book of Hebrews in the New Testament and as the definite liberation of Jerusalem and Israel. None of this allows any definite conclusion about the nature of souls or the bodies of those glorified in the rest. Eden is reestablished for the saints, along with a new Jerusalem and a new Israel. The Lord will himself reign together with humans.

In the *Testament of Asher,* the soul's continued existence rather than resurrection is emphasized. Nickelsburg has already pointed out the importance of 6:4–6 as a combination of the Greek and Jewish conceptions of afterlife, which we have previously seen:[26]

> For the ultimate end of human beings displays their righteousness, since they are made known to the angels of the Lord and of Beliar. For when the evil soul departs, it is harassed by the evil spirit which it served through its desires and evil works. But if anyone is peaceful with joy he comes to know the angel of peace and enters eternal life.

Nickelsburg sees in this text an example of "two-way-theology" as at Qumran, as well as many early Christian documents. "Two-way-theology" outlines the choice between a wicked and a righteous life as a clear and unambiguous choice, then demands that the reader choose righteously. This dualism is as much an indicator of the social position of the groups that produced the testament. We should not assume that the same group produced the entire *Testament of the Twelve Patriarchs,* as *Testament of Asher,* with its notion of separable souls and no resurrection, is quite different from the other material, where resurrection is the dominant metaphor for the afterlife.[27]

The Ascension of Isaiah

THE ASCENSION OF ISAIAH also focuses on ascent and heavenly transformation. We must not forget that the prophet Isaiah was assumed to be a martyr in later tradition, though the prophetic book gives us no definite evidence of it. In chapters 6 through 11, usually attributed to a Christian hand, the famous theophany of Biblical Isaiah 6 is understood as a heavenly journey where the prophet sees God. The prophet was taken through each of the seven heavens, stopping to view the glorious figure seated on the throne of each heaven.

Isaiah is told that his throne, garments, and crown await him in heaven (*Asc. Isa* 7:22). All those who love the Most High will at their end ascend by the angel of the Holy Spirit (7:23). In each heaven, Isaiah is glorified the more, emphasizing the transformation that occurs as a human travels closer and closer to God (7:24); effectively he becomes one of the angels. According to the other angels, Isaiah's vision is unprecedented; no one else who is to return to fleshly and bodily existence has been vouchsafed such a complete vision of the reward awaiting the good (8:11–13). But Isaiah must return to earth to complete his prophetic commission before he can enjoy the rest that awaits him in heaven.[28] The birth of the Messiah in Bethlehem through Joseph and Mary is related in some detail (11:1–21). The righteous dead and the martyrs and patriarchs are in the seventh heaven, including Abel (now the first martyr as well as the first murder victim) and Shem, while the damned are either no longer to be found or living in Sheol (11:22–24).

The climax of the story can be angelic transformation but the stated purpose of the journey in these early apocalyptic texts is usually theodicy—to understand God's justice. The journeys begin after a crisis of human confidence about God's intention to bring justice to the world, while the result of the journey is the discovery that the universe is indeed following God's moral plan. Thus the ancient Scriptures about God's providence are true and the evil ones who predominate on earth, even oppressing God's saints, will soon receive the punishment that they richly deserve.

The ascension story, especially if it was performed by an earthly hero before his death, also functions as justification for the suffering of the righteous, because it verifies what the community would like to believe— namely, that seeming injustices will be recompensed by their ascension to heavenly immortality after death, and that the evil ones will be condemned to hell. Although its narration describes exotic and amazing events, the purpose is pragmatic, to explain the structure of heaven and to provide an "eschatological verification" that God's plan will come to fruition. Immortalization is the explicit purpose of the text in the pagan ascensions. But in some of the Jewish material, where immortality is "automatically guaranteed" by moral living, more specific purposes are promulgated. Besides confirming God's plan in the face of the seeming victory of the ungodly or the slaughter of the righteous, the stories probably describe the mechanism by which immortality is achieved. Transformation to one's immortal state is pictured as becoming one with an angelic figure, perhaps illustrating the person's identification with a preexistent guardian angel.

The Apocalypse of Abraham *and the* Testament of Abraham

THE APOCALYPSE OF ABRAHAM narrates a heavenly journey placed at the covenant between the pieces in the life of Abraham (Gen. 15) and does not speak directly about the final disposition of the righteous and sinners at the last judgment. But the vestiture of Abraham and his glorification as an angel implies his and the righteous's final state of immortality. The imagery is, at the same time, baptismal. In chapter 21, paradise is depicted as on earth and, in chapter 31, the future rewards of the righteous and the destruction of the unclean are described. The use of Abraham as the role model for proselytes, a major theme in Jewish and Christian literature, is already clear in this document.

The *Testament of Abraham* is certainly Christian in several of its versions, but a Jewish version underlies it. It is difficult to know for sure what the original text would have been since the versions differ considerably from each other and certainly have had different histories.[29] The story concerns the events immediately preceding the death of the patriarch Abraham. In this regard, it is similar to a number of Midrashim that exist in Rabbinic literature. The archangel Michael is told by God to inform Abraham that the time of his death has arrived. He should put his affairs in order and make a will. The expectation is that the patriarch will voluntarily surrender his soul. Abraham, now reacting like any ordinary person, is loathe to do it. He tells Michael that he wants to see all the wonders of earth before he moves on to the next stage of existence. After consulting with God, who agrees to the plan, the archangel Michael takes Abraham on a tour that includes observing many people sinning and only a few acting morally. Since Abraham is saintly, he is given a tour of the heaven as well, so he is assumed bodily to heaven, while alive, but only for the period of the revelation, and we are the beneficiaries of his special privilege, since the entire voyage is reported in his testament.

Abraham sees many souls going to destruction but only a few being brought to heaven. We note possible Egyptian and Greek influences—at any rate, Hellenistic influence—as the souls are weighed by their deeds and judged against their "permanent records" in the divine hierarchy. There are three different ordeals—by fire, by record, and by balance, presided over in three stages by Abel, the twelve patriarchs, and by God himself. In this context, Abel was the first martyr as well as the first murder victim. Thus, the final synthesis of the two visions of the end is immortality of the soul immediately upon death, disposition of righteous and sinners by judgment, and an apocalypse at the end of time.

Abraham then intercedes on behalf of a soul that is judged neither wicked nor righteous. This provides an etiology for the Jewish doctrine of the *zekhut avoth*, the merit of the patriarchs, which allows them to intervene for sinners. The text both accepts the doctrine of the "merit of the patriarchs" and warns against abusing the privilege, since Abraham only intervenes in a very close case. On the other hand, Daniel 12 had promised a resurrection for only some, not all. The doctrine of the immortal soul makes clear that everyone gets an afterlife, though only some will enjoy it.

Pseudo-Philo

PRESERVED IN Latin under the name of Philo, the *Liber Antiquitatum Biblicarum* (abbreviated as *LAB*) is actually much closer to the Rabbinic genre of Midrash, a retelling of selected Biblical history from creation to the death of Saul. Its original language is probably Hebrew, though the traditions found in it have some relationship also to *4 Ezra* and *2 Baruch*. At the covenant given to Noah, the editor places a prophecy of the final resurrection:

> But when the years appointed for the world have been fulfilled, then the light will cease and the darkness will fade away. And I will bring the dead to life and raise up those who are sleeping in the earth. And hell will pay back its debt, and the place of perdition will return its deposit so that I may render to each according to his works and according to the fruits of his own devices, until I judge between soul and flesh. And the world will cease, and death will be abolished, and hell will shut its

mouth. And the earth will not be without progeny or sterile for those inhabiting it; and no one who has been pardoned by me will be tainted. And there will be another earth and another heaven, an everlasting dwelling place. (*LAB* 3:10)

The passage speaks of a universal resurrection of the righteous and wicked dead. The raising of those who "sleep in the earth" demonstrates that this is to be a resurrection of the body, though the mature Christian view of the judgment of the soul and the flesh *(iudicem inter animam et carnem)* also implies that the immortality of the soul has made a strong impression. Hell and the harrowing of hell are noted. Light and darkness cease and new heavens and earth are created. The righteous are also to be glorified in heaven, as Abraham "shall set his dwelling on high" (*super excelsa*, 4:11).

Even more striking is the prophecy inserted in the *Song of Deborah*, where the Bible equates angels and stars. Israel is now exalted in the same way: "He led you unto the height of the clouds and subdued angels under your feet" (*Sg. Deb.* 30:5). There, the people are told to imitate their forefathers: "Then your likeness shall be seen as the stars of the heaven, which have been manifested unto you at this time" (33:5). The soul also maintains an imprint of the physical: "Even though death may separate us, I know that our souls will recognize each other" (62:9), says Jonathan to David. The description of death and the afterlife is a bit more elaborated at the death of Moses: "You shall rest in that place until I visit the world *(saeculum)*. And I shall wake you and your fathers from the land where you sleep, and you shall find at the same time also an immortal habitation which is not occupied *(tenetur)* in time" (19:12).

Joseph and Aseneth

THE ROMANCE of *Joseph and Aseneth* is a Hellenistic Greek work which, in spite of its charm, has failed to garner a large audience over the centuries. It relates the story of the Biblical Joseph and his romance with Aseneth, the daughter of an Egyptian priest. Though there is little or no eschatology in the piece, Aseneth's conversion received a great deal of attention, including a prominent mystical transformation, with immortality as the result of conversion. In an important way, *Joseph and Aseneth* is meant to valorize conversion. The question is: "conversion to what?" Though on a simple narrative level, the conversion must be to Judaism, there are some reasons to believe that there may be typological layers of tradition in the book. Christianity may be the final goal of the typological drama in the final version of the work.[30]

The basic plot involves Aseneth's conversion from Egyptian religion to marry Joseph. On her journey, she receives a great many supernatural aids. Significant among them is the theophany of the angel Michael, introduced as "the chief captain of the Angel of the Lord" but also "the morning star," and "messenger of the light." After his departure by fiery chariot, Aseneth realizes that He is God but He also resembles Joseph exactly except that his entire being sparkles as brightly as fire, lightning, torches, and molten iron. Themes of heavenly doubles, angels who participate in the divinity of God, and the use of RISC aid the conversion process. In place of eschatology, the parable uses the distinction between Jew and gentile to enforce community boundaries. Inside of the group, symbols like the bread of life, the cup of immortality, and the oil of incorruptibility express the privileged status of those who have found religion acceptable to God.[31]

Outside the group, the bread of strangulation (non-kosher food?), the cup of apostasy, and the oil of corruption predominate. Aseneth receives an interesting revelation about a honeycomb and bees. The book is unusual in that it does not use the normal rhetoric of mission but rather celebrates the spiritual and mystic journey to the true faith. It could be an allegory for any Hellenistic faith but Christianity seems like the most obvious interpretation. It provides a very interesting intermediary case between apocalypticism and the later Jewish mysticism, but in a distinctly Hellenistic context

These apocalypses served to demonstrate the truth of the Christian message and also vividly dramatized what the faithful could expect. The steady progress of depictions of the immortality of the soul is evident. When immortality of the soul occurs, the judgment scene tends to center on the soul immediately after death, and the horrors of hell tend to be exaggerated. Frequently, the apocalyptic end can be left unemphasized and even dropped from consideration. Although Christianity and Judaism still maintain an apocalyptic end and lack of mention does not negate that belief, the emphasis on immortality of the soul certainly bespeaks a later time period when the apocalypse no longer occupies the Christian religious imagination. That seems to indicate that Christianity is no longer a sect and, perhaps, that Christianity is no longer as greatly concerned with fire-and-brimstone conversion sermons as it is in governing large numbers of Roman citizens in a peaceful and reliable manner.

But there are several other groups of literature which may profitably be compared with the Jewish and Christian apocalypses. Consider, first of all, the Jewish mystical literature as well as the pagan theosophical literature and magic. For all these literatures explicitly rely on notions of afterlife to increase their effectiveness and holiness. They all develop notions of apprenticeship to a heavenly power, who imparts secrets, and to whom it is sometimes necessary to journey. The heavenly secrets normally have to do directly with immortality and the moral, ethical, and ritual steps necessary to achieve it.[32]

Merkabah: Early Jewish Mysticism

THAT JEWISH mysticism has a history is due to Gershom Scholem. When many modern Jews were saying that Judaism was a religion of reason, more reasonable than Christianity, they thought, hence more able to deal with the modern world, Scholem pointed out that they were forgetting—trying desperately to forget—a lively tradition of Jewish mysticism. That history included Merkabah, Kabbalah, and Hasidism. The notion that mysticism is an analytic, cross-cultural concept itself is a modern phenomenon. Based on a Christian term, it has come to designate the knowledge of God by direct experience. From this point of view, prophecy may be thought of as a kind of mysticism. In the modern period, however, we tend to think of mysticism as quiet contemplation and the use of specific techniques of meditation, contemplation, and consciousness alteration. But it is important to note that if "mysticism" is an appropriate modern term to describe anything in the first century, it is mostly not quiet contemplation. Rather the apocalyptic mystics relied on the truth of ecstatic states, trances, dreams, visions, apocalypses, and other non-normal experiences to enrich their millenarian religious life.

Merkabah or "chariot vision literature," named after the vision of Ezekiel 1 of his prophetic book, was the first great movement in Jewish mysticism. What we shall call Jewish mysticism, for lack of a more descriptive term, especially that part of it which is concerned with resurrection and life after death, clearly grew out of apocalypticism, the tail end of the prophetic movement, which claimed the world is going to end abruptly.

Jewish mysticism, indeed even the doctrine of resurrection itself, depends on that very peculiar passage in Daniel 12:1–3, the only apocalyptic work accepted into the Hebrew Bible. This vision served as the basis for the doctrine of resurrection in Judaism. In the much later Jewish prayer for the dead, 'El Malay Rahamim, it is directly quoted. In that prayer, a regular part of Jewish interment and memorial services, the dead are said to be in heaven, shining with the brightness of the heavens, "under the wings of the Shekhina." The term "brightness" or "splendor" is zohar and is likely the basis for the title of the most famous book of Jewish mysticism, The Zohar, written in Spain in the High Middle Ages. So there is no question that this passage in Daniel was crucial to the later Jewish mystical tradition.

But this is only the prologue. Apocalypticism and Merkabah mysticism were not quiet contemplation. Instead they both witness to the active desire to journey to heaven and not merely out of curiosity about what was there. It was to verify that God's promises to the apocalypticists were true and reliable: Not only could one go to heaven at the end of one's life, some people actually went while alive, as Paul's report in 2 Corinthians 12 shows. The importance of going during life was to demonstrate to the community by eyewitness that humans go to heaven and receive their just reward after death. It was a kind of eschatological verificationism (pace Hick).[33]

But that is only part of the story. Ecstatic experience was self-validating and socially valuable because of its power in confirming the society's worldview. Since it was also RISC, it was also pleasurable, at least potentially, as an ecstatic experience. And going to heaven also conferred a number of other powers, as will be evident later. All this lies behind the mystic vocabulary for the goal of the journey: "to gaze on the King in His Beauty." This figure on the throne, already well known to us, was a sophisticated blending of all the notions of the Glory of the Lord, the Shekhina, and the Angel of the Lord.

This enigmatic human appearance of God, discussed with appropriate self-consciousness in the Bible, is related to the so-called "Son of Man." The preeminence of this angel is due primarily to the description of the angel of the Lord in Exodus. Exodus 23:20–21 states: "Behold, I send an angel before you, to guard you on the way and to bring you to the place which I have prepared. Give heed to him and hearken to his voice, do not rebel against him, for he will not pardon your transgression; for my name is in him." The Bible expresses the unique status of this angel by means of its participation in the divine name.[34] Thereafter in Exodus 33:18–23, Moses asks to see the Glory of God. In answer, God makes "his goodness" pass in front of him but He cautions, "You cannot see my face; for man shall not see me and live. . . . Behold, there is a place by me where you shall stand upon the rock; and while my glory passes by I will put you in a cleft of the rock, and I will cover you with my hand until I have passed by; then I will take away my hand and you shall see my back; but my face shall not be seen." Yahweh himself, the angel of God, and his Glory are melded together in a peculiar way, which suggested to its readers a deep secret about the ways God manifested himself to humanity.

The heavenly "Son of Man" appears in the vision in Daniel 7:13 in which an Ancient of Days appoints a human figure ("one like a Son of Man") to execute justice in the destruction of the evil ones. This human figure is best understood as an angel, though it is an unusual angel in that it can participate in divinity, as we will see.[35] Later on in Daniel, resurrection is promised both for the faithful dead and for the most heinous villains, who will be resurrected so that they may be sentenced to eternal perdition. *Hamaskilim,* or "those who are wise," apparently the elite of the apocalyptic group, will then shine as the stars in heaven (Daniel 12:3). This Scripture essentially states that the leaders will be transformed into angels, since the stars were identified with angels in Biblical tradition (e.g. Job 38:7).

In the Hellenistic period many new interpretations of Exodus 23–24, Ezekiel 1, and Daniel 7 grew up. The various descriptions of the angels were all melded into a single principal angelic mediator. The name "Yahoel" in the *Apocalypse of Abraham,* illustrates one interpretation of carrying the divine name, since it is a combination of the tetragrammaton and a suffix denoting angelic stature. Yahoel is described as the one: "in whom God's ineffable name dwells." Other titles for this figure included "Melchizedek," "Metatron," "Adoil," "Taxo," "Eremiel" and, preeminently in Christianity but also perhaps elsewhere, "the Son of Man," or "the manlike figure."

For instance, Melchizedek appears at Qumran, in the document called 11QMelch, where he is identified with the "Elohim" of Psalm 82:1, thus giving us yet another variation on the theme of carrying the name of God. This same exegesis is applied to Christ in Hebrews 1. Metatron is called YHWH haqqāṭôn, or YHWH junior, and sits on a throne equal to God's in 3 *Enoch* 10:1.[36] Typically, the name of the angel varies from tradition to tradition. Michael is God's "mediator" and general (*archistrategos,* 2 *Enoch* 33:10, *T. Dan* 6:1–5, *T. Abr* 1:4, cf. *The Life of Adam and Eve* 14.1–2). Eremiel appears in the *Apocalypse of Zephaniah* 6:1–15, where he is mistaken for God. In *The Ascension of Isaiah* 7:2–4, an angel appears whose name cannot be given.

Chief angelic mediators appear throughout the Jewish literature of the first several centuries.[37] The chief angelic mediator, which we may call by a number of terms—God's vice-regent, His *Vezir,* His *regent,* or other terms expressing his status as principal angel—is easily distinguished from the plethora of divine creatures, for the principal angel is not only head of the heavenly hosts but sometimes participates in God's own being or divinity: "My name is in him" (Exod 23:21). In dualistic contexts he is the angel who opposes Satan as "Prince of the World" (see e.g. *Apocalypse of Abraham* 13–14; 20; 22; 23; 29).

Alongside these traditions lies the stranger but more relevant notion in Christianity, in some apocalyptic-mystical groups, that certain heroes can be transformed into angels as part of their ascension. This may easily be the most puzzling part of the mystic traditions but, in view of Paul's mysticism and Christian notions of angelic transformation, it is the most important to summarize.[38] Amazingly, some patriarchs are also exalted as angels. In the *Testament of Abraham* 11 (Recension A), Adam is pictured with a terrifying appearance and adorned with Glory upon a golden throne. In chapters 12–13 Abel is similarly glorified, acting as judge over creation until the final judgment. *Second Enoch* 30:8–11 also states that Adam was an angel: "And on earth I assigned him to be a second angel, honored and great and glorious."[39] In the *Prayer of Joseph,* found in Origen's Commentary on John 2:31, with a further fragment in *Philocalia* 23:15, Jacob describes himself as "an angel of God and a ruling spirit," and claims to be the "firstborn of every living thing," "the first minister before the face of God," "the archangel of the power of the Lord," and "the chief captain among the sons of God."[40]

Enoch and Moses, however, are the most important non-Christian figures of divinization or angelic transformation. Philo describes Moses as divine, based upon the word God used of him in Exodus 4:16 and 7:1. Thus, *Sirach* 45:1–5 compares Moses to God in the Hebrew or "equal in glory to the holy ones," in the Greek version of the text. Philo and the Samaritans also expressed Moses' preeminence in Jewish tradition essentially by all but deifying him.[41] In the *Testament of Moses,* Moses is described as the mediator or "arbiter of his covenant" (*T. Mos* 1:14) and celebrated as "that sacred spirit, worthy of the Lord . . . the Lord of the Word . . . the divine prophet throughout the earth, the most perfect teacher in the world," the "advocate," and "the great messenger" (*T. Mos* 11:16–19). Indeed, Wayne Meeks concluded that "Moses was the most important figure in all Hellenistic Jewish apologetic."[42]

Another important and rarely mentioned piece of evidence of the antiquity of mystical speculation about the *Kabod* is from the fragment of the tragedy *Moses* written by Ezekiel the Tragedian.[43] There, in a document of the second century BCE or earlier, Moses is depicted as seeing a vision of the throne of God with a figure seated upon it. The figure on the throne is called *(phōs gennaios)*, "a venerable man" which is a double entendre in Greek, since *phōs* can mean either "light" or "man" depending on the gender of the noun.[44]

The surviving text of Ezekiel the Tragedian also hints at a transformation of an earthly hero into a divine figure when he relates that the venerable man *(phōs gennaios)* handed Moses his sceptre and summoned him to sit upon the throne, placing a diadem on his head. Although there is no explicit proof that Ezekiel meant this to be a starry or angelic existence, both notions are consonant with his description. The stars bow to Moses and parade for his inspection, suggesting that he is to be their ruler. Since throughout the Biblical period the stars are thought to be angels (Job 38:7), there is little doubt that Moses is here depicted as being leader of the angels, and hence above the angels. This enthronement scene with a human figure being exalted as a monarch or divinity in heaven resembles the enthronement of the "Son of Man"; the enthronement helps understand some of the traditions that later appeared in Jewish mysticism and may have informed Paul's ecstatic ascent. The identification of Jesus with the manlike appearance of God is both the central characteristic of Christianity and understandable within the context of Jewish mysticism and apocalypticism.[45]

Enoch is similarly esteemed as a heavenly voyager. According to *Jubilees,* Enoch undertakes a night vision in which he sees the entire future until the judgment day (*Jub.* 4:18–19). He spends six jubilees of years with the angels of God, learning everything about the earth and heavens, from their composition and motion to the locations of hell and heaven (4:21). When he finally ascends, he takes up residence in the garden of Eden "in majesty and honor," recording the deeds of humanity and serving in the sanctuary as priest (4:23–26); he writes many books (21:20), and there are indeed references to his writings in many other pseudepigrapha.[46]

The Hekhalot *Literature*

IN THE NINTH century, Hai Gaon recounts that a journey to view the divine figure was undertaken by mystics who put their heads between their knees (the posture Elijah assumed when praying for rain in 1 Kgs 18:42),[47] reciting repetitive psalms, glossolalic incantations, and mantralike prayers, which are recorded in abundance in the *Hekhalot* literature:[48]

When he seeks to behold the Merkabah and the palaces of the angels on high, he must follow a certain procedure. He must fast a number of days and place his head between his knees and whisper many hymns and songs whose texts are known from tradition. Then he perceives the chambers as if he saw the seven palaces with his own eyes, and it is as though he entered one palace after another and saw what is there. And there are two *mishnayoth* which the tannaim taught regarding this topic, called *Hekhaloth Rabbati* and *Hekhaloth Zutreti.*

The Gaon is aware of the mystical techniques for heavenly ascent and describes them as "out-of-body" experiences or "soul flight" where the adept ascends to heaven while his body stays on earth. Phrases like "as if he saw . . ." and "as though he entered . . ." suggest that he understands the entire journey as a RASC. The *Hekhaloth* texts themselves sometimes mention the transformation of the adept into a heavenly being, whose body becomes fire and whose eyes flash lightening, a theme which is repeated in the Paris Magical Papyrus.[49]

No one can prove that this kind of heavenly journey, which Ḥai Gaon describes, depicts pre-Christian Judea. But there is no harm in seeing what exactly happens to the tradition in a later time, in order to investigate what was happening in the first century. There is nothing unusual about claims to religiously interpreted states of consciousness (RISC) or religiously altered states of consciousness (RASC), and there are good reasons for thinking that the heavenly journey is itself a metaphor to express it. There are grounds for thinking that this particular variety of RISC was already vibrant in early Hellenistic times and may actually go back to the earliest myths in the ancient Near East.

The vision of the throne chariot of God in Ezekiel 1, along with the attendant vocabulary of glory or *kabod* for the human figure described there as God's glory or form, has also been recognized as one of the central themes of Jewish mysticism, which is closely related to the apocalyptic tradition.[50]

There is no doubt that this was an actual vision, received as a RISC. We have already seen how important the tradition of the heavenly journey is for verifying the truth of life after death. The very name "Merkabah"— that is, Throne-chariot mysticism, which is the usual Jewish designation for these mystical traditions even as early as the Mishnah (ca. 220 CE: See Mishnah Hagigah 2:1)—is the Rabbinic term for the heavenly conveyance described in Ezekiel 1.[51] The truly groundbreaking work of Hugo Odeberg, Gershom Scholem, Morton Smith, and Alexander Altmann,[52] showing the Greco-Roman context for these texts in Jewish mysticism, has been followed up by a few scholars who have shown the relevance of these passages to the study of early Rabbinic literature,[53] as well as of apocalypticism, Samaritanism, and Christianity.[54]

The entire collection of Hekhaloth texts has been published by Peter Schaefer[55] and translations of several of the works have appeared.[56] Nevertheless, the results of this research have not yet been broadly discussed, nor are they well known.[57] The Rabbis most often call God's principal angel Metatron. The term "Metatron" in Rabbinic literature and Jewish mysticism is probably not a proper name but a title adapted from the Greek word *Metathronos,* meaning "one who stands *after* or behind the throne." If so, it represents a Rabbinic softening of the more normal Hellenistic term, *synthronos,* meaning "one who is *with* the throne," sharing enthronement or acting for the properly throned authority. The Rabbis would have changed the preposition from one connoting equality (*syn-*, "with") to one connoting inferiority (*meta-*, "after or behind") in order to reduce the heretical implications of calling God's principal helping angel his *synthronos.*[58]

In *3 Enoch,* a Hebrew work that actually calls itself "The Book of Palaces," we enter immediately into an ascension discourse. It is introduced explicitly as a commentary on Genesis 5:24: "Enoch walked with God and he was no more for God took him." Rabbi Ishmael is introduced as the speaker and he explains the peculiar text. He reports his ascension through the six palaces and into the seventh, evidently the lower spheres, but depicted as fortified palaces with doors or gates.[59] Rabbi Ishmael has qualified for this honor because of his great piety and because he is high priest, though this tradition may in fact be conflating the Ishmael who was a contemporary of Rabbi Akiba in the second century with a previous first century Ishmael who was a priest. In any event this Rabbi Ishmael is the narrator of a number of other Merkabah texts, including *Hekhaloth Rabbati* and *Ma'aseh Merkabah.*

Essentially Ishmael becomes an ascender, a heavenly journeyer, who narrates his experience in the heavens and, at the same time, speaks from within the Rabbinic tradition. The heavens are divided into seven "palaces" or *hekhaloth,* which Scholem thought were all to be found in the last sphere of the heavens. They are stacked, one outside the other, like a heavily fortified city with fierce gatekeepers at each of the seven concentric defense walls. The adept shows a charm at each guardhouse, answers a question, and is conveyed into the next inner court until he reaches the throne room, just as he might be conveyed through a high-security fortress. There is some evidence that Arsacid Persian capital cities were laid out in this concentric form, with seven sets of walls. The Arsacid throne room was also based on a celestial model, containing in the center a fixed throne with depictions of heavenly bodies actually revolving around the it, some at relatively great distances, powered by animals treading on machinery hidden on the floor below.[60]

Scholem suggested that the palaces were all to be found in the highest sphere of the heavens because he could not find enough evidence to identify them with the later *sepherot* of Kabbalah. While this is an ingenious suggestion, more considered judgment suggests that the seven palaces are, indeed, the heavenly spheres themselves,[61] and the *sepherot* of Kabbalah are a later development, even though the name already exists in the early text *Sefer Ha-yetzirah*. The angel Metatron, The Prince of the Presence, becomes his angelic guide to the very throne of The Holy One. We have just seen that angels in the seventh heaven see the face of God in 4 *Ezra* 7. When Rabbi Ishmael recovers enough strength, he opens his mouth and sings the *Kedushah,* which is exactly the appropriate prayer to say in the presence of the divine throne. The text is obviously making a point about the origin of Jewish liturgy in the heavenly throne room, and conversely the attempt of the synagogue service (and the Temple service before it, no doubt) to pattern itself on the supposed heavenly service. The Dead Sea Scroll texts, particularly the Song of the Sabbath Sacrifice, make the same claim.

Sometimes the throne is empty and sometimes Metatron himself sits on it as God's regent. There are places in the text when the divine voice emanates from behind the *pargod,* the embroidered curtain in back of the throne. Other times the text states that God sits on the throne, though His presence is not described in any detail. Metatron or Zoharariel is God's regent, standing in for God himself, who is beyond figuration.

Metatron explains why he is called "Youth" or *Na'ar.* Though Metatron has seventy different names, the King of the King of Kings calls him "youth" because he is actually Enoch, the son of Jared and hence young in their eternal company (3 *En* 4:10). Here, a link with the Merkabah mystics and Enoch is established, a relationship that is furthered by the story of Enoch in the Bible: Enoch's father's name, Jared, means "he goes down," and is exactly the same verb used for the mystical ascent into the heavens, *yeridah Lamerkabah*. So when Enoch is listed as "ben Yarad," he is both "the son of Jared" and "a person who descends." At first blush, this seems a peculiar epithet for an exemplar of heavenly ascent. But this paradox is typical of the Merkabah mystics, who often said that they "went down" into the Merkabah.

This peculiar Rabbinic terminology has been the subject of a great deal of controversy. The best explanation for why an ascent to heaven should be called a "descent to the chariot" is to be found in the Biblical story of Elijah. In 1 Kings 18:42, Elijah prays by putting his head between his legs, the same posture which Merkabah mystics assume when they ascend to heaven.[62] Moreover, this body position is known to aid in achieving RASC, especially when combined with repetitious prayers and meditation, exactly as in the Hekhaloth literature. So whatever its origin, the parentage of Enoch (Jared) becomes a clue to the mystical techniques of ascent.

The "divinization" or "angelification" of Enoch serves as a human prototype for the ascenders who practice these techniques. The angels object to Enoch's elevation to no avail, as Enoch's new status meets with God's approval. The narrative of the angels' objection may easily be a mythological or literary attempt to handle objections to the notion of "angelification." Anyone who thought that these Jews ought not to be teaching that humans can be turned to angels would be defeated by the argument that the angels had already voiced this objection only to be silenced by God.

The same kind of story exists about the creation of man in Midrash and also in the pseudepigraphical book the *Vita Adae*. In chapter 14 of the *Vita Adae*, we find a very interesting tradition of the fall of Satan:

> And Michael went out and called all the angels, saying, "Worship the image of the Lord God, as the Lord God has instructed." And Michael himself worshiped first, and called me and said, "Worship the image of God, Yahweh." And I answered, "I do not worship Adam." And when Michael kept forcing me to worship, I said to him, "Why do you compel me? I will not worship one inferior and subsequent to me. I am prior to him in creation; before he was made, I was already made. He ought to worship me."

Satan refuses to worship Adam even though he is described as the "image of God." The "image of God" is one of the attributes of God's principal angel. Afterwards, Satan actually says the lines of "Day-Star, Son of Dawn" in Isaiah 14, the personage whom the Vulgate calls "Lucifer": "I will set my throne above the stars and I will be like the Most High" (*Vita Adae* 15). This passage is structurally parallel to the Merkabah story of Aḥer (Elisha b. Abuya) in front of Metatron in the heavenly throne room. Aḥer looks upon Metatron enthroned in heaven and concludes that there are "two powers in heaven," suggesting that the heresy he has in mind is Christianity or any other tradition with strong mediatorial figures. As a result, Metatron is punished with fiery whips. The Quran (Suras 2, 7, 15, 17, 18, 20, 38) also relates this legend of the fall of Satan, with a particularly strong parallel in Sura 7. Later Muslim tradition interprets Satan as God's most loyal subject because he refuses to bow down before anyone other than God. Different scriptural communities saw this heavenly scene in ways consistent with their understanding of God's relationship to his principal angelic mediator.

In this story, God (not the angel Michael as in *Vita Adae*) asks all the angels to bow down to the newly created Adam and they all agree except Satan (The Quran calls him 'Iblis), who refuses because no one but God deserves worship. This story makes Satan the most loyal rather than the least loyal of God's angels, thus tacitly giving approval to some kinds of seeming evil as really the greatest good, a very subversive doctrine which then justifies some antinomianism in Sufism and the extreme Shi'ite wing of Islam. 'Iblis is apparently an Arabicization of the Greek word *diabolos*.

Third Enoch handled these objections and returned to the narration. Rabbi Ishmael tells the story of Enoch's glorification and enlargement into Metatron, a parallel phenomenon to the transformation of Enoch into the "Son of Man" in *1 Enoch*.

Metatron also receives the heavenly secrets and gets a special robe, crown and name—YHWH *Hakaton*—all of which have special meaning within this mystic discipline, not only as the rewards for the righteous but as names for special spells and theurgic techniques. The term YHWH *Hakaton* ("the Lord, Jr.") suggests that transformed humans even become part of the divinity. Enoch receives the homage of the divine retinue and is finally transformed into a fiery being, the angel Metatron.[63]

Having witnessed the birth of a new angel, if not a new star, readers are now treated to a tour of the heavenly family, complete with ranks and officers. All the angels known in the Bible are described and fit into the master plan, with special attention to the angels described in Daniel, Isaiah, and Ezekiel. For example, a group of angels called "the Watchers" of Daniel 4 are singled out for special attention in chapter 28. They are also significant characters in the Enoch literature.

Next follows a description of the disposition of the good and the evil. The good souls *(neshamot)* of the righteous, both created and as yet uncreated, fly around the Throne of Glory. The basic scheme of Daniel is kept intact, however, even though we have some attention to immortal souls in the document, as souls in the intermediate state (after death but before resurrection) are also described, followed by the souls of those who are damned forever. These are probably the oppressors of the righteous community in the book of Daniel, reinterpreted as sinners generally. They are described as permanently stained black, like the bottom of a pot, while the intermediate souls only go down for a temporary cleansing, from which they emerge unstained.

In this passage, the immortality of the soul has been absorbed enough to compel the writer to describe judgment as an eternal process. But note that the enterprise of cleansing souls and reincarnating them mediates the stern judgment of the unrighteous that we find in the more apocalyptic texts. In Jewish mystical texts, the process of combining immortality of the soul with the resurrection of the body has yielded to a more merciful heavenly economy than was evident in Christian apocalypses.

Metatron also becomes the leader of innocent little souls who died studying Torah, as Jesus is described as the special Lord of little children in the Gospels (Mark 10:14). Here, the children play under the Throne of Glory, the same place that the souls of the martyred saints are stored in the book of Revelation.

Those who have died early must be accommodated in the divine hierarchy, so morning daycare has been arranged for the innocent souls who have been taken from life before they have had the opportunity to study the law and live their full span. Their education must be completed in heaven. Because they died in innocence they are treated in ways that were reserved for martyrs.

Hekhaloth, Iranian Religion, RASC, Magic, and Hermetism

MERKABAH MYSTICISM is later than some of the apocalypses we have studied, though the two corpora must certainly overlap and influence each other for a long time. At the same time, there are many facets of the literature which are undoubtedly from the early levels of Jewish tradition and which could, in fact, inform us about the mystical practices of the communities that produced apocalyptic literature. From the apocalyptic literature we can assume that many of the themes are early—including the notion of secrets and even the theurgy, the ascensions, angelic worship both as an object of speculation and an object of adoration. Indeed, the Dead Sea Scrolls contain an explicit angelic sabbath liturgy. All of these things, we see amply evidenced in the Dead Sea Scrolls and the New Testament.

The heavenly ascents of Kartir and Arda Viraf, reviewed in chapter 4, "Iran," are set in the third century CE. While the *Arda Viraf Nameh* is likely to be an early Islamic document in Zoroastrianism, the inscription of Kartir is much earlier. In Iranian religion, the use of psychedelic drugs has been firmly established and so the heavenly journey is also clearly a journey inwards into the psyche, replete with all the details of Zoroastrian heaven and hell.

The connection between these heavenly journeys and ecstatic experience is quite a bit earlier than the Arsacid period. The stories of Enmeduranki (equivalent with Enoch), Adapa, Etana, and others were cherished foundational stories among the divinatory priesthoods of ancient Mesopotamia. So the possibility exists that all these mystical techniques were already being practiced in the ancient prophetic and divinatory arts of ancient Mesopotamian culture.

If so, we should see their existence in the Hellenistic world as a secondary development to an entrepreneurial culture that developed under Greek rule. All over the world of late Antiquity traditional priesthoods were in decline and religious entrepreneurs of all types learned priestly traditions for personal spiritual and material benefit. In the process, they spread these ancient traditions far and wide.

There is little evidence for the use of drugs in Jewish and Christian texts, but there is considerable evidence of meditative techniques used to stimulate RASC, which are then understood as heavenly journeys. There are many hints that apocalyptic writings (which usually narrate the ascents as literal fact) and mystical writings (which specify the means for ascent in trance) are but choosing different literary conventions to describe the same phenomnea. By the same token, the techniques of Merkabah Mysticism were likely to be in use considerably earlier than the extant evidence shows. In particular, there is the well-known evidence of the New Testament: (1) Paul's report of a heavenly journey in 2 Corinthians 12; (2) The book of Revelation which contains similar notions of revealed secrets, apocalypses of "honor," "glory," "might," "power," and "wealth"; (3) God's heavenly retinue or house; and (4) the Colossians' heresy, which stressed the role of mediators between God and man.

It is crucial to define exactly how the two literatures, *Hekhaloth* texts and apocalyptic texts, relate; but that kind of exactitude is still impossible to achieve. *Hekhaloth* literature contains within it a great many apocalypses but it has much less—in fact, almost no—interest in spelling out the end of all oppressors. Rather like the later Christian apocalypses, the major emphasis of the texts is in explaining how God has balanced good and evil in the universe. This leads to the suspicion that its proponents were not especially subjected to persecution. They were rather secret esoteric groups of students within Rabbinic literature.[64] They were interested in all the goals of the Rabbinic movement including remembering as much of the holy law as they could. The difference between them and other Rabbis is that they used theurgy (special practices which look like magic) to achieve their goals where others may not have done so. This suggests that the *Hekhalot* literature was meant as a specific way of ensuring good citizenship and success within the Rabbinic movement. When the literature was transmitted and transformed by the medieval mystics known as *Haside-Ashkenaz,* it became even more obvious. But it is also evident from the reports of Hai Gaon at the end of the Talmudic period.[65]

Mystery Religions in Late Antiquity

WE HAVE ALREADY looked at the most famous mystery religion, the Mystery of Demeter at Eleusis or the Eleusinian Mysteries, based on the story told in the Homeric Hymn to Demeter.[66] In that religion, the story of Demeter and Persephone was explicitly interpreted in a way that spoke to issues of life and rebirth, this world and afterworld. During the Hellenistic and Roman periods, this cult grew enormously in wealth and international fame, so much so that a number of other religions explicitly remade themselves on the model of the *Eleusinian Mysteries.* The first and most famous of these is the *Mysteries of Isis.* Egyptian priests deliberately remade this cult of ancient Egypt, which was based on the myth of Isis and Osiris and was keyed to the level of the Nile. In the "diaspora" form of the religion, the Isis mystery centered in temples called *Isea* (plural of *Iseum*). Isis became a goddess of salvation for humanity. Her rituals were celebrated in parades and processions and were very well known throughout the Roman Empire. As a result, the mystery religion of Isis became a very popular religion within the Roman hegemony.

We know practically nothing about what exactly went on in the mystery religions because its initiated members were forbidden to reveal their secrets. And they mostly complied. They differed from each other but there must have been some uniformities. In his picaresque novel, *The Golden Ass,* Apuleius (second century CE) combines comedy with a very serious account of his hero Lucius' salvation through the intervention of Isis. Hapless Lucius has been turned into an ass as a result of his careless experimentation with magic with one of his amorous partners, the nimble Photis, who happens to be the servant of a witch as well as a sexual athlete. He is saved from this comic and very distressing condition by the intervention of Isis. The story resembles the story of "The Sorcerer's Apprentice." But the moral is wider than "a little bit of knowledge is a dangerous thing."

Apuleius conveys something about the behavior of young men by turning Lucius into an ass, as a result of his unbridled libido. The remedy to this condition is a very real religious conversion to the cult of the goddess Isis. In chapter 11 of the novella, a priest of Isis explains that the goddess has special care of her devotees, changing them from stupid creatures at the mercy of blind fate to mature people whose destiny is ruled by the goddess's providence. "For hostile fate has no power over those whose lives have been claimed by the majesty of our goddess. . . . Now you have been received into the protection of a Fortune who is not blind, but sees, and who illumines the other gods too with the radiance of her light."[67] The goddess promises her personal protection to the character Lucius as a remedy against blind fate. Initiation into her mysteries, described in only the most general way, eventually brings him across the threshold between life and death. The author Apuleius apparently underwent a similar experience of maturation as the character Lucius. Lucius says that he crossed the threshold of Proserpina and saw the sun at night (so he must be in the underworld). Some kind of immortalization ritual was part of his religious transformation. Exactly what, we do not know. But the original myth of Isis and Osiris was concerned with the immortality of the Pharaoh, linked with the flooding of the Nile, effected by means of the priesthood of Osiris.[68] The salvation of the goddess starts in this life because she saves Lucius from being blindly buffeted by fortune into a man with a destiny and significance as a devotee.

Another important mystery religion among the many was the religion of Mithras. It was named for the Persian god Mithra, the god of contracts. In its Roman form, however, Mithras was far more than that. In this secret underground cult, Mithras became a god who offered solar salvation. According to the myth, Mithras was born from a rock in a cave. His most famous feat was killing Taurus the bull in a famous *taurobolium* (bull-throwing) scene found in almost every Mithraeum. In the scene Mithras is shown quite realistically above the back of the bull, with a starry cape (depicting the milky way) billowing out behind him. He slays a bull with a dagger in the back of the neck while he turns away from the bull's head, normally with sheaves of wheat emerging where the bull's blood ought to be. The iconography is still somewhat mysterious to us, as it is rarely explained by any contemporary documents.

The mystery religion of Mithras was very widespread indeed, found in almost all of the major cities of the Roman Empire. It was very popular among the Roman legions for Mithraic *speleia* (caves, another name for the Temple) are found all along the borders of the Roman Empire and near major encampments of the army. Along with the *taurobolium* we often find representations of Mithras and Helios shaking hands, which allowed Dieterich to identify a famous Paris Magical Papyrus as a Mithras Liturgy. That identification was due, in the first instance, to the appearance of both divinities in the story of the heavenly journey found in a papyrus and the attempt of the ritual to produce an immortalization. But the identification has proven extremely controversial. On the other hand, the emperor was often identified with Sol Invictus or Helios, the sun. The clasped hands showing greeting and agreement between Mithras and Helios may well depict the importance of the army to the survival of the emperor; it would certainly explain the imperial patronage and the popularity in the army. Depictions from Mithraea also suggest the ranks of the initiates and the felicities that they found in the cult—transformation, heavenly journey, immortalization. The imagery of the *taurobolium* seems to have calendrical, astrological implications, just as the story of Isis and Osiris does in the *Isis Mysteries*.

David Ulansey, in his original and ingenious book, has shown that another famous depiction in the cult has implications for heavenly journeys. The lion-faced god is often shown with a snake entwining around him like a barber-pole stripe. The god somehow represents the power of the pole to turn the zodiac, as if the entire cosmos rotates around the polestar. In his hand, one often finds the orb of the cosmos, with the lines of the ecliptic and the equator crossed on the face of the globe. Both these lines and the signs of the zodiac are depicted backwards on the orb, showing that we are observing the cosmos from the outside looking in, from the view of someone who has transcended it, rather than from the inside out where we normally live. No doubt, this indicates a similar transcendence of fate and the zodiac that Lucius achieved in his salvation by the goddess Isis. But because there are no documents to explain the symbols for us, we do not know exactly how gaining the power to turn the pole brought about transcendence of earthly fate.

Late Antiquity relied on the originally agrarian and local religions of the past to depict a new kind of salvation, in which individual adepts could find immmortality through initiation and transformation, especially into stars. The famous early twentieth-century scholar Franz Cumont called this new form of religion "celestial immortality" or "sidereal eschatology." It can be found in Plato's *Timaeus* 41d, which connects each soul with its own star. The soul of each person begins as the intelligence of the star whence it returns after death. The *Empedotimus* of Heraclides Ponticus works out the story in detail, even identifying the Milky Way as the path on which souls ascend and descend and explaining its thick concentration of stars.[69]

The Magical Papyri and Theurgy

IN THE HELLENISTIC Greek and Coptic magical papyri there is a similar relationship between the stars and souls, the same relationship outlined by Plato. In a direct way, they approximate the stories of the angels that we find in the Christian and Jewish Apocalyptic literature and Merkabah mysticism. This time, however, the purpose was to achieve some material benefit for the adept through "magical" means. For instance, in the following magical papyrus, there is a rite for acquiring a "familiar" or assistant—in Greek, a *parhedros:*

At once there will be a sign for you like this: [A blazing star] will descend and come to stop in the middle / of the housetop, and when the star [has dissolved] before your eyes, you will behold the angel whom you have summoned and who has been sent [to you] and you will quickly learn the decisions of the gods. But do not be afraid: [approach] the god and, taking his right hand, kiss him and say these words to the angel, for he will quickly respond to you about whatever you want. But you / adjure him with this [oath] that he meet you and remain inseparable and that he not [keep silent or] disobey in any way. But when he has with certainty accepted this oath of yours, take the god by the hand, leap down, [and] after bringing him [into] the narrow room where you reside, [sit him] down. After first preparing the house / in a fitting manner and providing all types of foods and Mendesian wine, set these before the god, with an uncorrupted boy serving and maintaining silence until the [angel] departs. And you address preliminary (?) words to the god: "I shall have you as a friendly assistant, a beneficent god who serves me whenever I say, 'Quickly, by your / power now appear on earth to me, yea verily god!' " *(Cirado)*

Once the star descends, he becomes an angel, who is quickly bound by a spell to become an assistant *(parhedros)* to do the bidding of the adept. There are similar notions within some of the *Hekhaloth* tractates, in which an angel is sworn to do the bidding of the adept with an oath. Even in *3 Enoch,* Metatron and Enoch are said to be sworn to each other, or in one version "yoked together" (the word is: *nizdaweg,* which can even suggest the sex act).[70] Angels can be bound to do the bidding of the adept and then exorcised when that bidding is accomplished in *Hekhaloth* literature, just as the heavenly bodies can be charmed to earth in pagan magical papyri. There are many examples of charming down a star (or, alternatively, the moon, as they were all thought to be intermediary divine creatures) in the magical papyri.[71] The terms "angel," "daimon," and "god" change in particular contexts but may all be considered functional equivalents, subject to the special pleadings and vocabularies of each community.

The Mithras Liturgy is the record of a magical journey by a magician to visit the god, asking him to become a supporter.[72] It is the equivalent of an audience with an earthly ruler. It cannot be completely parallel to the process of appointing a *parhedros* because the divinity visited in *The Mithras Liturgy* is greater than an angel so the adept must go to heaven to visit him. Indeed, the boon he asks for is greater than that of the *parhedros.* He asks the god Helios Mithras to make him immortal and to give a prophecy. The request is granted, as the divinity takes up residence in the adept.

O Lord, while being born again *(palingenomenos),* I am passing away; while growing and having grown, I am dying; while being born from a life-generating birth, I am passing on, released to death—as you have founded, as you have decreed and have established the mystery. I am PHEROYRA MIOURI (lines 693–721)[73]

Though clearly not Jewish or Christian, these magical papyri stories have many, many formal similarities with the journeys that the *Hekhaloth* mystics made: trance (RISC), "magical" procedures, presentation of charms, strange and sometimes garbled and magical formulas, explanations or prophecies for the future. The pagans were reborn *(palingenomenos)* and then immortalized *(apanathanatismos)* by the procedure, just as Christians are "born again" by their faith. Jews already expected immortality so they concentrated on other benefits, like the ability to memorize more law or to receive material benefits, which were also asked for in the magical papyrus.

The Hermetic Corpus

SOMEWHAT similar notions can be seen in the Hermetic literature. In the *Poimandres*, the first tractate of the *Corpus Hermeticum*, the narrator, ostensibly Hermes (who is also identified with the Egyptian god Tat or Thoth), falls into a trance and sees a vision of a huge almost unlimited person, whose body seems to melt into light.[74] After a dialogue with this savior and an ascent to heaven, he learns that the secret of immortality is the knowledge of one's true nature:

> let him (who) is mindful recognize that he is immortal, that desire is the cause of death, and let him recognize all that exists.
>
> . . .
>
> "Those who lack knowledge, what great wrong have they done," I asked, "that they should be deprived of immortality." [75]

There is a clear message to realize the immortality that rests within us, normally discovered through ascent and heavenly revelation. The heavenly journey is coterminous with the RASC. In the Jewish and Hermetic literature there is also an ethical context. The magical papyri promise rewards only for the person who pays the magician for the rewards, though the magical papyri seem to be a *grimoire,* a magician's spell-book, which assumes that the possessor will at least observe the professional ethics of a member in good standing in the magical guild. One supposes, at the very least, that would entail not revealing the mysteries in the book.

Under the guise of theurgy these "magical" ascent procedures and many rites like them (which have been lost) gain a degree of respectability in the Late Antique world. To understand this we must investigate the entire phenomenon of theurgy—which means "working the gods" and is to be contrasted with theology, which means "studying the gods." As a phenomenon it is attributed to Julian the Chaldean and his son, also called Julian. Indeed, *ergon,* the second stem in the word "theurgy," is as good way to designate "ritual" in Greek, as there otherwise is no general, more universal term for "ritual" in Greek. So we should understand "theurgy" as working the gods by ritual means, something we usually call "magic." Theurgy would include bringing down angels, or "the moon," to do one's bidding. And the ritual that defined the theurgist more than any other was the *systasis,* a rite in which the soul of the theurgist was identified with the divine for various profane and holy purposes.[76]

The Pagan Revival and Theurgy

THE "SCIENCE" OF theurgy came into its own in the pagan revival of the mid-fourth century. After Constantine's vision of the cross at the battle for the Milvian Bridge, the process by which Christianity replaced the public, civic religion of the Empire continued apace—that is, until the short reign of Julian (later called "Julian the Apostate"), which began in 361 CE. Although many public sacrifices had already been abandoned in the progressive Christianization of the Empire, Julian the Apostate tried to restore them. He also turned to Iamblichus, the head of the Platonic academy, to help find an intellectual basis for paganism, which was refurbished to compete with, and hence, to parallel Christian practice.[77]

Iamblichus described theurgy in Platonic, intellectual terms, evidently also providing a number of religious rituals that paralleled those of the Christian church. This newly revitalized paganism, based as much on its rival Christianity as anything else, became a religion of personal piety and of salvation. With the foothold that Christianity had already made, it could hardly promise less. Under Julian's tutelage, pagan philosophy developed into a religion like Christianity. In the center of the new religion was a new ritual component, never before part of philosophical discourse. This ritual was called "theurgy."

In his essay, *On the Mysteries,* Iamblichus defends theurgy against Porphyry's more strictly philosophical skepticism. In the *Phaedo* (66b–c), Plato had outlined an immortal soul in such a way as to suggest that the body and the soul's moral journey through life affects its future rebirths or bliss in Elysium. But how anything corporeal could affect the soul is not completely clear in Plato's writing, and the question remained unsolved throughout antiquity, though many philosophers offered their own solutions. (In fact, lack of solution to this vexing problem remains today as one very significant reason not to accept the Cartesian formulation of the mind-body problem.)[78]

To see the importance of this topic for the religious life of the pagan philosophers, one has to return at least briefly to the most important ancient interpreter of Plato in Christian times, Plotinus. Plotinus interpreted the world of ideas of Plato in an even more determinedly intellectualist way than Plato had because Plotinus had read the works of Aristotle and the later Stoics. He also knew the terminology of *kosmos noetos,* the intelligible world, which is first witnessed in Philo and which referred to the logos, hence to the divine mind as an external force in the universe. Plotinus tried to bridge the gap between the body and soul from the other side—with human intellectual activities and meditations leading the way upward. Because intellect can turn inward and contemplate itself, he valorized the experience of self-consciousness in a way that was not discussed before.

Plotinus believed that the way to ascend was through self-conscious meditation and even suggested that nondiscursive thinking or an altered state of consciousness (ASC) was the way to overcome our materiality.[79] Plotinus was especially attuned to the feeling of living and experiencing in our mind. In the *Enneads* 5.8.9.1–3, Plotinus presents us with a thought-experiment by asking the reader to visualize a sphere. This, in turn, becomes the creative visualization to understand how "The One" can be formed of "the Many." What the experiment was for is not as important as the process of internal visualization to resolve issues.

In her recent book, Sara Rappe shows that this move begins what can only be called a meditation.[80] The visualization uses the active but directed powers of the imagination and the sustained presence of imaginative meditation as a way to change human self-awareness. By emphasizing this inwardness in a new, more dramatic form, Plotinus begins to fix on inward experience as the path to the ascent. He did not invent the notion that altered states of consciousness are a path to God. He systematically tried to incorporate ecstasy into his philosophical experience while Plato and Philo among others merely assumed that these experiences were part of their intellectual and religious lives. He tried to offer an adequate philosophical account of the flight of the soul toward God. Plotinus and his students, the pagan Neoplatonists, may not have been either Jewish or Christians but they were deeply religious people and their religion adhered to their philosophical praxis, especially with askesis or asceticism used to trigger these RISC states.

If Plotinus was the theorist of the soul's ascent, Iamblichus was the engineer and technician of the soul. According to Iamblichus, theurgic rituals and prayer were essential for the well-being of the soul and could even affect the disposition of the soul after death, as Plato himself had stated:

No operation, however, in sacred concerns, can succeed without the intervention of prayer. Lastly, the continual exercise of prayer nourishes the vigour of our intellect, and renders the receptacles of the soul far more capacious for the communications of the gods. It likewise is the divine key, which opens to men the penetralia of the Gods; accustoms us to the splendid rivers of supernatural light; in a short time perfects our inmost recesses, and disposes them for the ineffable embrace and contact of the Gods; and it does not desist till it raises us to the summit of all. It also gradually and silently draws upward the manners of our soul, by divesting them of every thing foreign to a divine nature, and clothes us with the perfections of the gods. (*On the Mysteries,* 272)[81]

Iamblichus explicitly contradicts Plotinus on this point for Plotinus explained the suffering of the soul as a product of its incomplete descent to the material world. Because the soul had descended, it could suffer but because it had not descended fully into matter, it could not totally be subsumed within materiality and destroyed. Iamblichus finds this doctrine of the soul to be both illogical and insufficiently spiritual. Instead, he posits the efficacy of specific rituals in effecting the soul's immortality, though they are done in material reality. The ritual is theurgy and the *systasis* is the primary example.

The Vehicle of the Soul

IN SO DOING, Iamblichus follows Porphyry in positing an entity known as the vehicle of the soul or the spirit-cart *(ochema-pneuma),* which partakes of both matter and soul without being essentially part of one or the other.[82] In the *Timaeus* (41e 1–2), Plato says that "the demiurge distributed each [soul] to each [star], and having mounted them [i.e., human souls] as if on a vehicle *(ochema),* he [i.e., the demiurge] showed them the nature of the universe." For the Neoplatonist the *ochema* or vehicle is not the star nor made of the star itself but the vehicle in which the star can subsist. It is the meeting ground of the spiritual and material. So once a star is situated in its own vehicle it may travel downward to become a human soul in our sublunar world of generation. Conversely, theurgy only has power over the vehicle, not the soul itself, but it has power to help the soul's reascension to the astral, immortal level because it can affect the soul's vehicle.

In this latter Neoplatonist philosophy, a star and a soul are two parts of an identical essence but in two different states of being. Further, each soul in some way has its own equivalent guardian star which governs its role on earth and in turn can reveal its earthly fortunes. The connection is made a unity on death. A knowledgeable person can therefore predict the future through *pronoia* (pre-knowledge or prophecy).

This is a further illustration of the Neoplatonic notion that the whole universe is a single, huge creature governed by its own "world-soul," within which each piece is related to another in regular ways. The material part of the universe, however, is subject to constant generation and degeneration while the pneumatic or spiritual aspect of the universe is, by nature, immortal and unchangeable. The Greek philosophic tradition tended to connect mental processes with the soul but not necessarily with consciousness itself because consciousness was merely the soul's recognition or feeling of having a body. All serious intellectual functions required a reflective and self-conscious soul, developed through training and theurgy.

The important thing to remember is not precisely how the Neoplatonists connected intellectual processes with the soul but that they did so in such a way as to develop a religious, sacramental life for philosophers. Whether this actually overcame the problem of the inability of matter to affect the soul is another question. Instead they developed a communal, religious life that centered around meditation and altered states of consciousness, the *askesis* for the salvation of the soul from material existence.

In opposition to Porphyry and Proclus, Iamblichus believed that the vehicle of the soul is immortal with the soul and that the rational soul is always attached to the vehicle, even in its astral state.[83] For him, this was the best description of the soul allowing for the efficacy of theurgy. The purpose of theurgy is to lead the soul upward to its rightful divine state, while magic, which deals with demons instead of gods, only sullies the soul further in its corporal body.[84] So, while Iamblichus believed in the efficacy of both theurgy and magic, he distinguished between them in terms of their purposes. Magic is secondary to theurgy because it deals with demons and egotistical, material betterment, making the soul impure, while theurgy, which deals with the gods, actually affects the salvation of the soul by tapping into the intellectual processes of the cosmos. The purpose of the soul's descent into the world is truly a religious one: It is to display the gods through our souls' lives here. In this way the soul's descent is the completion of the universe:[85]

Iamblichus synthesized the Chaldean, Hermetic, and Orphic writings into a consistent theory of occult ritual for immortalization. This was also meant to aggrandize theurgists so much from the common morality as to make them divinely powered and their ritual enactions divinely higher sacraments. He made them priests of an intellectual religion. Under Iamblichus' description, theurgists become pure souls, something like the *Bodhisattvas* of Mahayana Buddhism, special heroic beings who have been able to escape from the cycle of births and yet retain their purity (even in our impure realm) and use that enlightenment to help the rest of humanity rise out of imprisoned existence. Even more, theurgists provide a living example to counter the claims that Christians were making for the martyrs and saints.[86] It also means that with the help of the theurgists any mortal could rise above the material realm, escape from the body, and be united with the gods, through the sacraments of theurgy. Iamblichus was the intellectual who most clearly succeeded in inventing and justifying a ritual and religious side to late Neoplatonism, which was otherwise most inhospitable to such popular religious sentiments. The purpose of this philosophical inquiry was to arm pagan philosophy in every way for its last battle with Christianity.

The Last Battle between Christianity and Paganism

CHRISTIANITY HAD offered the Empire something that the previous religious and philosophical systems of paganism had been uninterested or unable to accomplish. It provided everyone with a religious goal of moral commitment and personal transcendence wrapped up in a tight package available to all through ritual actions. Neoplatonic philosophy offered a similar dispensation through abstruse philosophical contemplation, available only to those who had the disposition and wherewithal to follow a philosophical life of study. Hermetism, on the other hand, provided a more popular way to achieve the goals of the philosophers and existed in theosophic circles. Hermetism was the model for the pagan revival. Theurgy relied on the insights found in its predecessor. But it did not truly succeed in making itself a popular religion.

A second look at the *Hekhalot* literature suggests a similar function to that of Hermetism, the Mystery religions, and theurgy. The *Hekhaloth* literature demonstrates that the same kind of mystical ascent with the same small esoteric circles existed in Jewish culture, whether independently or part of the *Zeitgeist* ("Spirit of the Age") of late Antiquity. It may be that ascent theurgy was widely perceived as an antidote to the popularity of Christian ritual. Christianity ritualized the goals of immortal existence, bringing it to all, democratically through the sacraments. If paganism was going to compete with the popularity of Christianity, it was going to need the same appeal and it had to develop the same sacramental structure and martyrologies. This was provided by Iamblichus, who became, in effect, the intellectual theorist and architect of the pagan revival by justifying the necessity and efficaciousness of salvation, distinguishing it from simple and scurrilous magic.

But it was the Roman Emperor Julian who had the resources to put the theories of ascent and descent into wide practice. Julian the Apostate was the purveyor of this spiritual product as he himself was deeply involved in the discussions of late Neoplatonism and devoted to its promulgation. He was interested in these issues for their own sake but not just for his own intellectual development. He was personally averse to Christianity, and he was looking for a way to replace the hold that Christianity had achieved in the Roman Empire after Constantine. He wanted Iamblichus to design a religion that would substitute for Christianity and communicate the greater truths of Neoplatonism to the Empire.

To justify his return to paganism, Julian relied not merely on Plotinus but also on a number of Iamblichus' successors, including not only the famous Rhetor Libanius and the aging scholar Aedesius but also Maximus, who was forthrightly interested in developing a religious synthesis with Neoplatonism. Whatever Julian's personal dispositions religiously, he was an indefatigable worker for the Empire and its well-being. He lived an abstemious life and kept to a strict work regime, relieved mostly by soldierly training.

He must have realized that it was not enough merely to reinstate pagan sacrifices. Christianity was widespread within the Empire and had taught its inhabitants both the inefficacy of sacrifices and to expect transformative rites of personal salvation as one's spiritual fare. To compete with Christianity, paganism would need to reform itself into a similar religion. Julian practiced Christianity during his youth when he lived in the shadow of Constantine. But he was more taken by Neoplatonism. Julian himself apparently experienced the transformative rituals of Neoplatonism as he excelled in pagan sciences. With Maximus as his guide, he was anxious to make paganism more popular in his imperium. He did so by reforming paganism on a Christian model. As a result, he created a philosophical religion of the ascent of the soul.

Julian's early death campaigning against the Persians was met with unbridled rejoicing in the whole Christian community, the abandonment of Julian's scheme to rebuild the Jewish Temple (if it had not been abandoned earlier), the end of the pagan Neoplatonic revival, and the vilification of his person by a victorious and vengeful Church. The polemics of Christianity triumphant should not blind us to the sincerity of Julian's attempt to unify the Empire with a sophisticated religion forged out of Neoplatonism. He failed to do so, leaving the Christian religion as religious heir to his Empire, and positioning pagan magic everafter as the demonic, subversive underground to Christianity.

It is to the Church Fathers in the orthodox succession whom we must now turn to see the philosophical battle to unite resurrection with the immortality of the soul. If Christianity was to take hold in the intellectual corners of the Roman Empire, it was going to have to face the contradiction between the apocalyptic dispensation that Jesus brought within its Jewish context and the natural right of the philosophically defined soul to immortality.

13

The Church Fathers and
Their Opponents

THIS CHAPTER will be concerned mostly with the Apostolic Church Fathers, especially those of the second and third century of the Christian era. But, to understand them, we must look at their opponents, both within the church and without. The Church Fathers' writings overlap with the latest books of the New Testament and help us fill out the first few centuries of Christian life, already roughly sketched by reviewing popular apocryphal and pseudepigraphical religious literature. They also give us a clear example of how the New Testament was read by those leaders of the church who were responsible for forging what we now call the "orthodox" position.

The fathers would have maintained that their opinions were self-evident expressions of the tradition. But they are also significant and tendentious interpreters of the New Testament; in their comments, they reduce ambiguities and reformulate questions for ordinary Christians dealing with their Christian life. And they also produce a fascinating historical record of how Christianity fit its message to the Hellenistic world, while at the same time battling to retain the interpretation of its original *kerygma* or "proclamation." It is the Church Fathers who created the Christianity that we recognize. They, and not Paul, are the second founders of Christianity.

Although the Church Fathers offered us major innovations in Christian belief, they always presented it as the most primitive doctrine. We have already seen how the Gospel of John combats the equally ancient traditions in the *Gospel of Thomas*. The Church Fathers came to terms with resurrection because it stood at the center of their religious life but they did not seem overly concerned with defining resurrection at first. That is not to say that they are not concerned with resurrection; the mission of Christianity was very much helped by focusing on the afterlife in proselytizing.

It is significant that resurrection is the afterlife doctrine that needed to be explained in detail in the Hellenistic context. It is most puzzling and disquieting to the Hellenistic world. If we look at the *Letter of Barnabas,* for example, an early apostolic writing probably dating from the end of the first century, we see that the promises of Daniel 12, understood as resurrection of the flesh, is prominently displayed in his picture of the coming end, though the Jews are already disowned (e.g., *Let. Barn.* 4:1–15). The pagan world, on the other hand, was comfortable with immortality of the soul. Christians from that world carried this doctrine into Christianity and set up an opposition between immortality and resurrection inside Christianity. The more intellectual the Christian audience, the more immortality of the soul appealed.

The evidence from Barnabas suggests that the missionaries had to distinguish their message from that of the Jews, who were better known though not as emphatic proselytizers. Not many of the Jews living in diaspora were enthusiastic believers in resurrection. That was more characteristic of revolutionaries and millenarians living in the land of Israel and also of the Pharisees, who had not yet made major inroads in Diaspora Judaism. Instead, the Jews who spoke and thought in Greek were involved in a very significant hermeneutical process, a translation process that allowed them to understand afterlife as continuous with immortality of the soul, thus combining native Jewish ideas with Greek philosophical ones. Resurrection was the product the fathers offered as a prize for remedying sinful, pagan life. They had to explain the need for resurrection when immortality of the soul seemed both rational and satisfying as a universal human attainment. And then they had to distinguish it from Jewish views of resurrection.[1]

The continuous growth in interest in resurrection was due principally to three factors. The first was the centrality of the notion of resurrection in the preaching of the Christian faith. As Tertullian said: "The religion of Christianity is the faith in resurrection." Or again, "The resurrection of the dead is the Christian's confidence. By believing it we are what we claim to be" (*Res.,* 1). All Christians seemed to acknowledge that their faith depended upon the resurrection event in Jesus' life, however they judged that to have been possible or interpreted it to have happened.

The second factor is that the New Testament, for all its voices, is relatively unhelpful in explaining exactly what resurrection is. Where it does enter into description, it argues for a physical resurrection which conflicted with Paul, who was much more spiritual and equivocal on the subject. The naiveté of the New Testament narrative and the emphasis on resurrection may just have irritated ordinary gentiles, who quite innocently absorbed far more sophisticated, intellectual notions of the immortality of the soul. Eventually, the question of what exactly resurrection is would have to arise. At a second stage, the church would provide a cogent and comprehensible doctrine which made sense to a sophisticated, philosophical, pagan audience.

Lastly, as we saw in the last chapter, Christianity needed to explain resurrection in just the right way so as to allow for the delay of the parousia; it had to accomplish the explanation without diminishing the motivation for being Christian and firmly remaining within a moral universe in which virtue is rewarded while sin is punished. In Late Antiquity, the immortality of the soul, demonstrated to many philosophers' satisfaction by Plato, seemed, more and more, to be the self-evident end of earthly existence. Since it validated the life of the mind, it could almost be assumed among many philosophers. Even the Stoics took an interest in immortality, while it was the doctrine that the Cynics and Epicureans liked to dispute. Resurrection was a nonstarter; it was not even a worthy subject for discussion among the philosophers. They did not even understand it properly, thinking it more like resuscitation.

For their part, the Church Fathers took aim at immortality of the soul as the doctrine to defeat. They learned their task from the Stoics, Epicureans, and Cynics. Although the earliest fathers did not concentrate on the intellectual cogency of the resurrection, they did preach it steadfastly, fixing on immortality of the soul as a hostile doctrine because immortality of the soul vitiated the special salvation that the cross brought to the faithful alone. If immortality were a natural property of the soul, no one would need a Savior; one would need only an operational manual for the soul as an ethical guide, the right moral instructions to train the body to care properly for the soul.

Gospel of Peter

THE GOSPEL OF PETER offers an early reflection on the resurrection of Jesus. Actually it just supplies the scene that is missing in the Gospels, a description of the resurrection of Jesus.

Now in the night, when the Lord's day dawned, when the soldiers two by two in every watch, were keeping guard, there rang out a loud voice in the heaven, and they saw the heavens opened and two men come down from there in a great brightness and approach the sepulchre. That stone which had been laid against the entrance to the sepulchre started by itself to roll and gave way to the side, and the sepulchre was opened, and both the young men went in. When now those soldiers saw this, they awakened the centurion and the elders—for they also were there to assist at the watch. And whilst they were relating what they had seen, they saw again three men come out from the sepulchre, and two of them sustaining the other, and a cross following them, and the heads of the two reaching to heaven, but that of the one who being led by the hand reached beyond the heavens. And they heard a voice out of the heavens crying, "Thou hast preached to them that sleep," and from the cross there was heard the answer, "Yea." Those men therefore took counsel with one another to go and report this to Pilate. And whilst they were still deliberating, the heavens were again seen to open, and a man decended and entered into the sepulchre. (*Gos. Pet.* 10:35–43)[2]

This is a remarkably poignant and visually creative description of the resurrection. Although the exact moment of the resurrection is not described, the physical effects of the saving miracle are portrayed in one long, beautiful arc of motion, like a long camera pan: Jesus emerges from the tomb alive, regaining his exalted nature. Jesus looks as though he were recovering from a long, restful, deep sleep. The angels are depicted as huge in stature, a typical motif from Jewish mysticism and apocalypticism, where the immense size of God and his angels was an object of meditation. The portrayal synthesizes all the various accounts of the Gospels, since it witnesses to the arrival of the man who greets the women in the Gospel of Mark (Mark 16:5). It even attempts to suggest Jesus' recovery of his logos status, as the Prologue in John implies. Although the mystery is preserved, the narrative adds an enormous amount of information to the Christian master narrative, even while staying true to the Gospel accounts that no one actually saw the resurrection. One can see why this narrative needed to be written.

The cross itself speaks, explaining the ignorance of the world. Perhaps the personification of the cross is just a very vivid way to remove all the doubts that can be expressed about the ability of Jesus to save others when he had died in degradation, so ignominiously and painfully. That was what Paul found transforming and what the Gospels also emphasize. This Gospel wants to defuse the scandal of the cross within its message of exaltation and salvation. The ignorance of the world to the true nature of Christ's salvation bridges and explains the temporary degradation.

Before this description (*Gos. Pet.* 4–6), the gospel has already described the day of judgment prophetically, supplementing our knowledge of resurrection with knowledge of the final disposition of sinners and righteous. The resurrection is taken as a demonstration that the day of judgment will follow hard on Jesus' resurrection. It also demonstrates the importance of Gospel literature for the mission and expansion of Christianity.

In most Early Church writings, as Joanne Dewart shows, resurrection is central but not the focus of the fathers' discussion, rather assumed as the goal. It is the subject of the argument rather than the terms of it. Where it appears, it is usually ancillary to some other issue in Christian life—for instance, the rejection of docetism, or the coming end. On the other hand, it is like a snowball, gaining momentum as it moves until almost all the third- and fourth-century fathers write extensive separate tractates on the issue.[3] The reason for this is not hard to understand. As Christianity moved out of Judea and up the social ladder, Hellenistic philosophical and intellectual conflicts with pagan society became more and more important.

Resurrection started as a liability in the pagan world; the fathers turn it from an irritation to a pearl of theological reflection. Not everyone needs or wants philosophical coherence in religious belief; but those who want it tend to be extraordinarily interested in finding or creating coherence and intellectual adequacy, persevering until they can state it systematically.

In the early period, the eschaton is an important aspect of the church's proselytizing. The early fathers differed on the order of the events of the end of time. Will all the raised be judged (as *Polycarp, 2 Clement, Barnabas*) or will only those just who have successfully acquitted judgment be subsequently raised (as the *Didache, Papias,* and *Ignatius*)? This discussion evidently reflected not merely the continuous desire for more specificity in religious doctrine but also the community's lively interest in the coming end-time as well as the signs that should precede it. In the process of depicting the issues in more detail, an unmistakable trend toward a physical and bodily resurrection can be detected in the "orthodox" tradition. As would be expected, the Gospel writers were favored over Paul as sources for discussion in this regard. In the sectarian Christian position, there is just as strongly a trend away from bodily resurrection, with a characteristic emphasis on the Pauline corpus.[4] The nature of the resurrection is the bell-wether for the presence or absence of heresy. The use of passages from Paul or the Gospels is the wind that propels the boat.

Docetism and Gnosticism

APOSTOLIC CHRISTIANITY shows a distinct tendency towards an explicit description of bodily resurrection, which favors the Gospels' surety over Paul's ambiguity, the Gospels' vivid statements over Paul's dynamic, internal process of transformation. But most scholars of doctrine begin their histories with an intellectual challenge: the struggle against docetic Christology. Docetism, from the Greek word *dokeo*—"to appear to be" in the sense of "to seem to be," with the connotation of "(mistakenly) seeming to be human"—promulgated the notion that Jesus, being divine, only "seemed" to suffer and die. In reality, Christ's divine nature was never compromised. This is an obvious way out of a deep ambiguity about Jesus' nature. Docetism is a quick and dirty way to preserve Jesus' divinity at the moments when he "seems" most tragically human and lacking in divinity. This intellectual move was also characteristic of the "Gnostic" writers. The Gnostics and others suggested that Jesus only seemed to die, although the body was putrid and infected, so Jesus subsequently only seemed to be resurrected. His resurrection was merely the revelation of his true divinity.

As in the *Gospel of Thomas,* to the Gnostics, what was necessary was for the believer to come to the saving knowledge *(gnōsis)* that Jesus was divine and could return in his purified spirit *(pneuma)* to the abode of the divine above this corrupted and unsavable world. We have already discussed the physicality of the resurrection as not only characteristic of Jewish apocalyptic thinking, independent of any contact with Greek notions of the afterlife, and especially inimical to Platonism. Docetism and Gnosticism thus represent a first and most obvious way to connect the narration of Jesus' life, death, and resurrection with the Platonic thought-world of Greece. Mature, anti-Jewish Gnosticism also takes up a great many of the mythological themes of Genesis in the Bible.

"Orthodoxy" is "correct doctrine" but since it is the predominant position in the Church, it always means "the right doctrine" from the perspective of the winners. Though "orthodoxy" is always used by the church to indicate the truth, I mean by it only the position that predominated. The definition of "Gnosticism" has never been easy; at the current moment it is even harder to define than orthodoxy. "Gnostic" refers to someone who thinks that "knowledge" *(gnōsis)* rather than "faith" *(pistis)* is the way to salvation and indicates a second- through fourth-century heresy within Christianity, though we also know of pagan Gnostics. In the modern scholarly world, the word "Gnosticism" has evolved into a technical term in comparative religion, identifying a characteristic of any religion—like mysticism, ritual, or ethics—which leads to ambiguities when studying the ancient world.

Interest in Gnosticism has quickened considerably since the discovery in 1947 of the Nag Hammadi collection of thirteen mostly Coptic codices, evidently from a monastic library dating back to the first centuries of the Christian era in Egypt. It contains the *Gospel of Thomas* which has both "Gnostic" and "orthodox" characteristics. Some of the "Gnostic" texts, especially those having to do with Seth, seem to delight in revaluing the stories of the Bible, most particularly the primeval history, into mythological stories in which the God of the Old Testament figures as a demon, while the Gnostics themselves were those whom the Old Testament treats as enemies, like Cainites. Scholars call these documents Sethian Gnosticism.

This is to be contrasted with another form of Gnosticism—Valentianism, named after the churchman Valentinus. These Gnostic documents, also found within the Nag Hammadi Corpus, emanate from a relatively more moderate wing which existed within the church, asserting that its members were "elected" above ordinary Christians because they understood a higher, more elite revelation. Their Christian worship consisted of normal Christian practices augmented with secret rites. "Gnostic" became an umbrella term used by the "orthodox" to brand whole groups of Christians as heretics, even those who would not themselves have used the term "Gnostic," much less "heretic," to describe themselves. The *Gospel of Thomas* is a good example of this "name-calling" phenomenon because it has been branded as "Gnostic" but could just as arguably be seen as an unusual part of "orthodox" tradition. What is clear is that the Fathers opposed the Christianity we see in the *Gospel of Thomas*.

A group of scholars meeting at Messina in 1967 decided to call only full-blown, anti-cosmic dualism by the term "Gnosticism."[5] The religious phenomenon that existed previously in the first few centuries could either be called proto-gnosticism or pre-Gnosticism. Scholars disagreed about whether particular documents, like the Gospel of John, was pre-Gnostic or proto-Gnostic. Whatever clarity was gained in this discussion was vitiated by the lack of scholarly agreement about the differences between proto-Gnosticism and pre-Gnosticism. Was what preceded second century Gnosticism just an antecedent or already essentially Gnostic? To make matters worse, either of the antecedents to Gnosticism could be described by the term "Gnostic," making a muddle out of practically every article on the subject.

Hence, scholars have abandoned the attempt to define the term by common agreement. With this retreat from exactitude came the suspicion that the terminology does not always correspond to an actual phenomenon in the ancient world. Are scholars seeing Gnostics where none existed? We know that there were actually some people who called themselves Gnostics but the Church Fathers added wholesale to the characterization and the list. Instead, "Gnosticism" is now viewed more or less as a term of opprobrium in use among the Christian Fathers, as much as a phenomenon in and of itself. That is to say, we think they are Gnostics only because the Church Fathers call them Gnostics. It is probably just as well not to reify the term as a coherent and self-conscious movement; otherwise, we shall wind up taking sides in an ancient, almost forgotten debate instead of relating it.

The "Gnostic" interpretation of salvation can be characterized. It is the belief that there is a specific, divinely-revealed, saving knowledge *(gnōsis)*, which, when received and understood, sets the Gnostic above and in an elect position with regard to the rest of humanity. The "Gnostics" tended to depreciate life in this world as irredeemably corrupt. Matter itself was seen as feminine and not redeemable, in a manner quite similar to Plato and Philo. In Gnosticism the gendered coding of matter becomes part of a mythological pattern. Yet, some Gnostics may have regarded women as eligible for church positions. When the Church Fathers say that women achieved roles of leadership in Gnosticism they meant this report as a vilification of the movement, so one wonders how much they were exaggerating. The *Gospel of Thomas* allows for equality between women and men through women's transformation into men, viewed as the common gender. Yet the group that left us the Nag Hammadi corpus seems to be composed mostly of male monks living with little if any church structure, so it is hard to know whether women were actually in leadership positions.

If some "Gnostics" seemed to defame women and the Old Testament, so did the "orthodox" in a different way. Among the Church Fathers, death was explicitly connected with sin, particularly with Eve's sin rather than Adam's, functioning to define all future human existence without Christ. This interpretation, which is based on Genesis 2–3, as interpreted through a tendentious reading of Paul, especially in Romans 5:12–21 and 1 Corinthians 15:20–28, can be seen as early as the *Epistle of Barnabas* 12:5b[6] It is more characteristic of Latin than Greek fathers.

Vilifying Eve and women as the agents of "sin," at the same time, is parallel with or even dependent on a Jewish apocalyptic context in which the sinfulness of humanity is stressed. Even in Paul, the theme receives unusual emphasis (Romans 5:12–13). The interpretation that death is a punishment due to the sin of sexuality is massively developed in later church tradition, which we now associate preeminently with Augustine but was present already in the second century.[7] The progressive identification of sin with sexuality more and more came to define a state that humanity enters at birth and that can only be remedied through the sacraments of the church.

The "feminization of Original Sin" may be related to the equally polemical attempt to show that the Jewish religion has been entirely surpassed in the faith of Christianity. If Jews did not accept Jesus, they could be vilified as Satan's accomplices.[8] Thus, the Jews become the symbols for whatever the Gospel is not. Although the patriarchs might escape Original Sin, the Jews remain forever in sin and sexual lust; lack of Jewish interest in asceticism only furthered the stereotype. The need to reverse an Original Sin, so that without Jesus' sacrifice all humanity is condemned by Eve's sin, preserves the unique importance of the church's ritual and sacramental life for Christian life. Original Sin makes for very effective missionizing, especially as the fear of the end of days dissipate once the millenarian context of the Jesus movement and the Gospel period is vitiated. Original Sin replaced the coming eschaton as the guarantor of faith. Both created a world in which only Christians could achieve salvation; thus, all need the ritual sacramants of the church. Under these circumstances not to proselytize is a moral failing because it witholds the gift of salvation from those outside the church.

This development, which we have already seen in abundance in the Christian apocrypha, a result of the combination of notions of resurrection with the Platonic notion of the immortal soul, parallels the demotion of Mary Magdalene in the post-Gospel tradition. Mary Magdalene was already understood as a woman of low repute redeemed, due to her being (dubiously) equated with the woman taken in adultery (John 7:53–8:11). Peter is normally considered the head of the church not only because he was given the keys to the kingdom in Matthew but because he was the first apostle to view Jesus in the resurrection.[9] Yet, strictly speaking, it was Mary Magdalene (possibly together with Mary the mother of Jesus and other women of the movement) who first saw Jesus in his resurrection state.

The notion that Christianity was due to the theophanic visions of women was evidently too dangerous to be allowed to stand. Since men had the opportunity to build careers within the church, it was Peter rather than Mary who was given the right of priority. The apostolic succession was founded upon the list of early appearances of the resurrected Jesus, almost unconsciously honed down to the men who first saw the resurrected Jesus. Thus, the apostolic tradition is quintessentially a male tradition while there is good evidence that the religious experience on which the church was founded occurred quite frequently in women as well. One of the characteristics of the Gnostics is that they valued this experience more highly; some Gnostics raised women to the level of priests and even bishops.[10]

Bodily Resurrection, Asceticism, and Gender

THE GOSPELS needed to stress the physicality of the resurrection as a way of emphasizing Jesus' unique importance. This predisposition became a strong characteristic of the "orthodox" tradition. In popular thought anyone could become a spirit or ghost after death, and in Platonism everyone had an immortal soul by nature. To make Jesus unique in his postmortem state he needed to have a resurrected body. The church maintained the uniqueness of Jesus' sacrifice by claiming Jesus' bodily resurrection; all Christians (and only Christians) inherit their resurrection body by imitating him. But the very physicality of the resurrection might even prevent women from resurrection or from having a major role in transmitting tradition, since they are physically different from men.

For other Christians, Christian life was also an angelic life, transcending sexuality. This too became a major theme for many varieties of the Early Church.[11] For Paul, all genders were equal in the Christian life, just as there was no slave or free or Jew or gentile (Gal 3:28); but this liturgical confession and anticipation of the eschaton did not translate well into ordinary Christian life. For Paul, equality was true and accurate in baptism but would not become fully evident in life until the Parousia, which was to arrive momentarily. However well that may have worked in the baptismal ceremonies, the ordinary facts of Hellenistic life (Jewish life included) prevented the eschatological ideal from being translated effectively into action, except in the monastic movement, where celibacy did transcend gender, essentially by means of autonomy from expected gender-related roles within society. In ordinary life women were subservient to men; Jews and gentiles remained separate; slaves had to be returned to their masters. Baptism could symbolize the coming transformed state of humanity but it did not change the reality of everyday life.

But asceticism could. Asceticism derived originally from the training adopted by Greek athletes which included both athletics and diet regimens. Early Christian writing often actually compared martyrs and ascetics to athletes. Martyrs in the arena were described as entering an *agōn* or athletic contest, from which our word "agony" is derived.

Agōn could mean a number of different things in early Christianity, everything from dietary restrictions for health to fasting to celibacy and monastic life.[12] Asceticism could prepare a Christian for divine revelation, as in the *Gospel of Thomas*.[13] Asceticism was popular everywhere in Christianity, though to different degrees in different places. Its opposite was viewed as so terribly sinful that the "Gnostics" could be tarred with sexual libertinism and licentiousness, though all existing "Gnostic" documents eschew sexuality and embrace asceticism themselves. Indeed, the Nag Hammadi library seems to emanate from the monastic library of Pachomius; Pachomius is a founder of Egyptian Christian monasticism. Asceticism and monasticism were the only ways to manifest angelic life while on earth.[14] That made asceticism and monasticism the preferred Christian lifestyle in a great many Christian communities. Theresa Shaw points out a passage that sums up the issue at the beginning of her work on Christian fasting:

> Observe what fasting does: it heals diseases, dries up the bodily humors, casts out demons, chases away wicked thoughts, makes the mind clearer and the heart pure, sanctifies the body and places the person before the throne of God. . . . For fasting is the life of the angels, and the one who makes use of it has angelic rank.[15]

The benefits of asceticism, of which fasting is but one example, are ranked progressively from health to moral education to divine audience, which is clearly linked to visionary experience ("places the person before the throne of God") and is summarized by the attainment of angelic rank, which we have so often seen is the ultimate felicity of resurrection predicted by Daniel 12.

The Letters of Clement

CLEMENT OF ROME served as bishop at the end of the first century, according to church tradition. *First Clement*, a letter from Rome to Corinth weakly attributed to Clement, is usually listed with the Apostolic Fathers. It tries to settle the issue of the nature of resurrection by means of an ambiguous phrase, "immortal knowledge": "Through him the Master has willed that we should taste immmortal knowledge" (*1 Clem.* 36:1–2).[16] This terminology is a clever attempt to bridge the growing gap between religious experience and ecclesiastical authority. As an attempt to formulate the nature of Christ's immortality, the term "immortal knowledge" was shortly to become even more suspect than the problem it was designed to resolve. Here the immortal knowledge is specified as the apostolic tradition:

> The apostles have preached the gospel to us from the Lord Jesus Christ; Jesus Christ [has done so] from God. Christ therefore was sent forth by God, and the apostles by Christ. Both these appointments, then, were made in an orderly way, according to the will of God. Having therefore received their orders, and being fully assured by the resurrection of our Lord Jesus Christ, and established in the word of God, with full assurance of the Holy ghost, they went forth proclaiming that the kingdom of God was at hand. (*1 Clem.* 42)[17]

The resurrection guaranteed the truth of the apostolic tradition as much as the other way around. At the same time, *1 Clement* emphasizes the resurrection of believers.

First Clement does not describe the resurrection body; but *2 Clement* does:

> And let no one of you say that this very flesh shall not be judged nor rise again. Consider ye in what [state] ye were saved, in what ye received sight, if not while ye were in this flesh. We must therefore preserve the flesh as the temple of God. For, as ye were called in the flesh, ye shall also come [to be judged] in the flesh. As Christ, the Lord who saved us, though He was first a Spirit, became flesh, and thus called us, so shall we also receive the reward in this flesh. (*2 Clem.* 9)[18]

Unhappily, *2 Clement* is likely written by yet another writer, taking us rather far from the historical Clement. But the progression does clarify issues otherwise left ambiguous in *1 Clement*. Christians receive salvation in the flesh just as Christ himself was carnal and was himself resurrected in the flesh. It is therefore appropriate that the future reward shall also be in the flesh. Paul's pneumatology is combined with the notion of resurrection in such a way as to yield a justification for the continued importance of the church of the faithful and, indeed, the apostolic succession. It is not hard to perceive a real enemy behind this polemic. There were many in the Early Church who denied that the resurrection was fleshly or literal. Foremost among them were the "Gnostics," but also any other extreme interpreter of Paul, docetist or Platonist.

Ignatius

PHYSICAL RESURRECTION, martyrdom, angelic status, and heavenly exaltation continued to be seen together in orthodox Christian writings.[19] In a church that faced the terrible choice of martyrdom or apostasy, the encouragement to martyrdom shortly became an issue in and of itself.[20] To explain this crisis, the church could rely on Luke's tradition of the martyrdom of Stephen and his subsequent exaltation in Acts 7.

It is Stephen's role as the first church martyr that Ignatius emulates:

> Suffer me to become food for the wild beasts, through whose instrumentality it will be granted me to attain to God. I am the wheat of God, and let me be ground by the teeth of the wild beasts, that I may be found the pure bread of Christ. Rather entice the wild beasts, that they may become my tomb, and may leave nothing of my body; so that when I have fallen asleep [in death], I may be no trouble to any one. Then shall I truly be a disciple of Christ, when the world shall not see so much as my body. Entreat Christ for me that by these instruments, I may be found a sacrifice [to God.] (I. *Rom.* 4)[21]

The image of falling asleep, Luke's phrase used for Stephen's death, in order to become the true disciple of Christ is in both recensions of the letter. Ignatius is invoking the nascent martyr tradition. In some sense he offers himself as proof of the fleshly resurrection. His patient endurance is, first of all, proof of Christian faith. Next, he wants his body to be totally destroyed so the miracle of his resurrection will be the mightier. In destroying his body, Ignatius also affirms that his reward will be bodily. Like the martyrs in Maccabees, he expects a bodily resurrection, even if no part of his earthly body remains, making his physical disposal no trouble to anyone.

There is also an allusion to the Johannine use of heavenly bread, the bread of life, the basis of the Lord's Supper, and which specifies the literal flesh of Jesus (John 7) and figures strongly in the argument for Jesus' postresurrection materiality. Ignatius described the body being ground like flour and transformed into the host itself, made holy, so that it manifested the invisible and material body of Christ. The martyr becomes the host, to be consumed in the hour of his trial but promising salvation to others.

The example that Ignatius gives us was followed to some extent by all subsequent descriptions of martyrdoms. Although Ignatius follows the martyr tradition begun for Christian piety by the narrative of Stephen's martyrdom, he does not use the term "martyr" (witness) which had not yet become the standard title for the voluntary death of the faithful as an act of faith.[22] The specifically Christian interpretation of the tradition—using the metaphor of a legal trial—evolved slowly out of Christian experience. Even without the specific vocabulary of Christian martyrdom, Ignatius' description is deeply dependent on bodily resurrection. It is no surprise that when he outlines his creed to the Smyrneans, he outlines a very physical resurrection. After having outlined his creed which emphasized the physical pain of the crucifixion, Ignatius talks about the coming resurrection:

> Now, He suffered all these things for our sakes, that we might be saved. And He suffered truly, even as also he truly raised up himself, not, as certain unbelievers maintain, that He only seemed to suffer, as they themselves only seem to be [Christians]. And as they believe, so shall it happen unto them, when they shall be divested of their bodies, and be mere evil spirits.
>
> For I know that after His resurrection also he was still possessed of flesh, and I believe that He is so now. (I. *Smyrn.* 2 end and 3 beginning)[23]

Ignatius emphasizes the passion of Jesus, his physical suffering, and his physical death on the cross. He especially emphasizes that the resurrection was physical as well, and the resurrection of all believers will be physical and bodily. He then explicitly mentions that there are those who refuse to believe in the physical resurrection, hence will not get it (the Rabbinic notion as well), but that they will be forced to become evil spirits because they will be divested of their bodies.

This is a neat disposition for the Greek notion of the immortality of the soul, that had become known to Christianity by that time. Those who think like the Greeks will get the reward that immortality of the soul promises: they will become as the Greek gods themselves—in reality, nothing but evil spirits. The same is true for those Christians who preach that the resurrection with be spiritual. The true, final disposition is as fully physical bodies on a reconstituted earth. To the Ephesians, Ignatius even wrote that he hoped to be resurrected in his bonds so that he could be in the same lot with the Ephesians (*Ignatius to the Ephesians* 11.2), who were suffering persecution. There is no doubt that the physicality of the resurrection continues to cohere with issues of martyrdom, as we saw in the very beginning of the tradition in martyrdom.[24]

The Spirit and the Body: Valentinus

VALENTINUS (CA. 100–175 CE) shows us another side of the battle. He was an intellectual Christian leader, originally from the Egyptian Delta, who based his authority on the claim that he was a student of one of Paul's students.[25] Valentinus was educated in Alexandria, in the great school of Neoplatonism influenced by Philo, Clement, and later Origen. He was a student and colleague of the Hellenized Christian philosopher Basilides. Sometime between 136–140 CE Valentinus emigrated to Rome. By 180, Irenaeus was accusing him of Gnosticism, like others whom he met in both Alexandria and Rome.[26]

The writings of Valentinus exhibit a lot of Hellenistic and Gnostic characteristics: an interest in Platonic thought, mystic ascent, and narrative use of myth, in this case, often in place of philosophical discourse. But he does not reflect the entire Gnostic myth in its most obvious form. Rather he uses Christian imagery in a Gnostic way. He also wrote one of the earliest Christian mystical documents, the *Gospel of Truth*. He believed that salvation comes through *gnōsis,* a saving knowledge of the true purpose of the savior, which is not available through the flesh, since Jesus is not of the flesh. So *gnōsis* is achieved by spiritual meditation, which was taught in his movement, as it was in Platonism and as Paul can easily be interpreted.

Valentinus surely understood salvation to occur in the "spiritual body" of which Paul spoke, but interpreted so that it meant a spiritual existence, not a fleshly one at all. For Valentinus, the elect were those in the spiritual life, called the *pneumatikoi* (spiritually realized) by later Gnostics, explicitly referring to Paul's term *soma pneumatikon*. If Plato's word *psyche* (soul) is antithetical to Christianity, no one could criticize the word *pneuma* (spirit), the very word that Paul used so effectively. *Pneuma* could carry the whole significance of the Platonic soul yet also contain the added quantity of God's prophetic spirit. So it became a kind of augmented soul for Christians.

For Valentinus, no meaningful salvation could be gained through this fallen flesh, though he appears to admit that the lowest and most ignorant grades of Christians do preach this lesser enlightenment. If Irenaeus' tendentious description of Valentinus is factually correct, most of this is expressed through an elaborate cosmological myth, explaining how we came into this fallen state and therefore, by implication, how salvation can be gained. It was characteristic of Gnostic and Platonic writings to discuss cosmology in detail, from which soteriology could be implied.

> From the beginning, you (plural) have been immortal, and you are children of eternal life. And you wanted death to be allocated to yourselves so that you might spend it and use it up, and that death might die in you and through you. For when you nullify the world and are not yourselves annihilated, you are lord over creation and all corruption. (Frag. F)[27]

In his description of the beginning of the cosmos, we see the implicit soteriology, spelled out afterwards, of escaping from materiality to the immortal realm. Notice how he uses Biblical imagery and the language of Paul to express these truths. In a large sense, Valentinus can be seen as an extreme Hellenistic interpreter of Paul.[28] But, however it is derived, his resurrection conception is thoroughly spiritualized.

Martyrdom and Resurrection: Basilides

IN DIFFERENT ways, Elaine Pagels and William Frend have reported on the orthodox claim that the Gnostics and Docetists, who refuted the physical resurrection, reasoned out a refusal of martyrdom.[29] So far as the "orthodox" were concerned, the Gnostics did not see the point of sacrificing the material body in martyrdom and they did not care to be prominent in the ranks of the martyrs. The Gnostics further reject the whole theory of apostolic succession, which began in the narrative of resurrection appearances from Luke down to their own day. In some ways, the Gnostics parody it in their description of the evil archons, bishops in disguise. For the most part, the Gnostics suspect the literal view of the resurrection, some of them calling it "the faith of fools." [30] The "orthodox" fight this denigration of their faith with anything at their disposal and the language of the body is a primary code for conveying their distaste, not just their doctrine of resurrection.

So orthodox criticism of the Gnostics' reluctance to martyrdom is but one side of the battle. One can assume that the Gnostic and Docetic Christians underwent martyrdom and even sometimes sought it out, though the phenomenon was rare for both the Orthodox and Gnostics. It is rather the case that the orthodox were not willing to grant their opponents' asceticism true virtue nor their martyrdom true steadfastness. [31]

For the Gnostics, physical seeing (the disciples physically saw Christ) counted little; only symbolic spiritual vision (through visions brought on by ascetic practice) revealed the truth of his message. We have seen this attitude before in the *Gospel of Thomas*. The Gnostics observed that many who witnessed Jesus in his life remained totally blind to the significance of Jesus' mission, death, and resurrection. It was not those who literally carried on the written tradition that counted, but those who truly understood the meaning of the events, especially from visionary insight.

Ignatius of Antioch had already argued against his docetist opponents that one does not die for a ghost or phantom (*Ign. Smyrn.* 6) but rather for the right to be resurrected in the body and gain the full compensation for one's sacrifice. This understands resurrection in exactly the way that the Jewish sectarians who promulgated it had originally wanted. But it begins the characterization of Gnostics as those who would refuse to be martyred at all. But most people, both Orthodox and Gnostic, do not evince Ignatius' willingness to become a martyr, even ignoring chances to avoid martyrdom.

Basilides (fl. ca. 130–160 CE), a teacher, companion, and successor to Valentinus, illustrates the other side of the relationship between bodily resurrection and martyrdom. He explicitly used Platonism to interpret resurrection. For him salvation only belonged to the soul, not the body at all. As Frend says, "His is the earliest known attempt by a Christian to reconcile the Jewish requirement of righteous suffering as an atoning sacrifice with the Platonic view of providence." [32] The result is a major attack on the value of martyrdom. He believed that humanity was originally immortal, as did Valentinus. Death is the result of the demiurge who created the material world and imprisoned our immortal souls in matter.

The saving knowledge *(gnōsis)* of the redeemed is that humans are truly beyond the world, divorced from flesh, and free from its infection. Salvation was the abolition of death, not its acceptance through martyrdom. In his commentary on 1 Peter, Basilides states that all who suffer, suffer on account of sin, not merely those who committed grave offenses like adulterers and murderers. This did not mean that the sufferer led an evil life—that would be blaming the victim—rather that material life itself was an evil that needed atonement.

This is reminiscent of Plato's *Republic,* Book 2: "If our commonwealth is to be well-ordered, we must fight to the last against any member of it being suffered to speak of the divine, which is good, being responsible for evil." The true Gnostic then needs no martyrdom because the Gnostic has already triumphed over the devil in coming to the saving knowledge (the *gnōsis*).[33] The "orthodox" therefore used their greater willingness to be martyred as a proof of the truth of their doctrine while the other side used their understanding of the primacy of the human soul to justify their greater reticence to do so. Some of the orthodox, including Ignatius himself, seemed to welcome martyrdom, even where prudence would have dictated an honorable way to avoid it.[34] Some of the Gnostics were probably caught in unavoidable events and were martyred as well. But both sides adopted the characterization that they were defending or attacking the doctrine of bodily resurrection and lived by the consequences. The orthodox were training converts with high commitment and highly defined communal boundaries. The Gnostics, on the other hand, developed a tolerant sense of the common enterprise of all intellectual meditation. Though the orthodox may have been "universal" in their purview, the Gnostics were "culturally plural." There is nothing inevitable about this connection.

The Gnostics

THE GNOSTIC *Gospel of Mary* suggests that all the resurrection appearances were by means of visions, dreams, and ecstatic trance.[35] That is not to say that the Gnostics dismiss the dreams and ecstatic trance; rather the opposite, they value them the more highly. It is that they refuse to believe that Jesus continues to be physically present because the body is not destined for eternal life. Only the spirit has that privilege.

As Pagels points out, the *Letter of Peter to Philip,* discovered at Nag Hammadi, relates a different kind of appearance of Jesus:

A great light appeared, so that the mountain shone from the sight of him who had appeared. And a voice called out to them saying: "Listen . . . I am Jesus Christ, who is with you forever. (134.10–18)[36]

A voice comes out of the light, certainly not a physical body. In *The Wisdom of Jesus Christ* the disciples are gathered on a mountain after Jesus' death. Again, Jesus appears as a voice coming out of the light, this time as an invisible spirit who then appears as the great angel of light. Yet another passage appears in the *Gospel of Philip* where believers are warned against rising in the flesh and even from thinking that any one position is correct:

Certain persons are afraid that they may arise (from the dead) naked: therefore they want to arise in the flesh. And they do not know that those who wear the flesh are the ones who are naked. Those who [. . .] to divest themselves are not naked. Flesh [and blood will not] inherit the kingdom [of God]. What is this flesh that will not inherit it? The one that we are wearing. And what too is this flesh that will inherit it? It is Jesus' flesh along with his blood.

Therefore he said, "He who does not eat my flesh and drink my blood does not have life within him." What is meant by that? His "flesh" means the Word, and his "blood" means the Holy Spirit: whoever has received these has food, and has drink and clothing. For my part I condemn (also) those others who say that the flesh will not arise. Accordingly both positions are deficient. (56:20–57:10)[37]

Several interesting moves are made in this short passage. The *Gospel of Philip* argues against ordinary Christians, who believe in fleshly resurrection. It explicitly argues for a spiritual resurrection and offers an allegorical interpretation of the "flesh" and "blood" in the Eucharist. Then, he concludes that both fleshly and spiritual resurrection doctrines are deficient to those who have the full truth.

In like fashion, Jesus appears differently to different disciples. Jesus can appear in whatever form he likes but he is not a body or a physical presence in the ordinary way. He is rather spiritually present and the composition of the resurrection body is *adiaphora*, a matter of indifference:[38]

Jesus tricked everyone, for he did not appear as he was, but appeared in such a way that he could be seen. And he appeared to all of them—

he [appeared] to [the] great as someone great, he appeared to the small as someone small. He [appeared] [to the] angels as an angel and to human beings as a human being. For this reason he hid his discourse from everyone. Some saw him and thought they were seeing their own selves. But when he appeared to his disciples in glory upon the mountain, he was not small (for) he became great: or rather he made the disciples great so that they might be able to see that he was great. (*Gos. Phil.* 57:28–58:9)[39]

To those who have seen Christ and therefore seen themselves, these arguments are unnecessary. If one understands Jesus as a human being, one is merely underscoring one's humanity. But, it stands to reason that if one views Christ as an angel, one has been transformed into an angel. Thus, Gnosticism explicitly connects the nature of the savior with the transcendent value of the self. The way a person envisions the savior connotes the significance of a person's life. The point is to understand that the highest *gnōsis* is to get beyond the mere body to a higher conceptualization.

This connection has import not only for individuals but for communities. Mary Douglas has suggested that the body is particularly rich vehicle for expressing the implications of social and political life, the "body politic." Such is also the case with regard to the early Christians. The "orthodox" valorized martyrdom while the "Gnostics" eschewed it as unnecessary. The orthodox insisted on bodily presence but the "Gnostics" either did not or said it was of no ultimate importance. It is not a casual symbol but one that runs to the heart of their religious life.[40]

The *Testimony of Truth* suggests that the martyrs have misunderstood Christ's true nature:

The foolish think in their heart that if they confess, "We are Christians," in word only [but] not with power, while giving themselves over to ignorance, to a human death, not knowing where they are going, nor who Christ is, thinking that they will live, when they are (really) in error—hasten toward the principalities and authorities. They fall into their churches because of the ignorance that is in them. (31.22–32.8)[41]

The author ridicules the notion that martyrdom brings salvation. If that were true, everyone would be martyred, confessing, and being saved. The pretensions of the orthodox, no matter how affecting and brave, are merely illusions:

are [empty] martyrs, since they bear witness only [to] themselves . . .
When they are "perfected" with a (martyr's) death, this is what they
are thinking: "If we deliver ourselves over to death for the sake of the
name, we shall be saved." These matters are not settled in this way. . . .
They do not have the Word which gives [life.] (33.25–34.26)[42]

The stories of the orthodox martyrdoms are punctuated by complaints
from the heresiologists that the Gnostics show no willingness to undergo
martyrdom as do the orthodox, therefore their faith is weak. From a sociological perspective, nothing builds up commitment to a specific canon
of principles faster than persecution, torture, suffering, and death, provided that the community itself survives. The commitment of the orthodox to the canons of the faith must have been enormous. And so too were
the promises of restored bodily existence that awaited them.

The Spirit and Martyrdom

FOR THE GNOSTICS the converse must have been just as true. Anyone who
refused martyrdom by sacrificing to the emperor's genius would have had
to develop strong justifications for refusing this ultimate sacrifice. The notion that the body was unimportant, not the essential part of Christian
commitment, paralleled the Gnostic stance that martyrdom was not necessary. And so too were the promises of restored spiritual existence that
awaited them. The Gnostics likely did not build up the same kind of commitment to a single set of principles as communities suffering martyrdom.

If the body was to be left behind and the spirit *(pneuma)* was the carrier
of identity, why make such a pretense about acknowledging the Christian
commitment publicly? Could one not equally advance as far by acknowledging *gnōsis,* understanding the secret and hidden meaning in the Christian stories understood as allegories? The myths of other religions might
as easily contain the truths of Gnosticism. We find many allusions to other
religions—classical, mystery, Jewish, Zoroastrian—in the Nag Hammadi
library. Then who would need to die for one of them because they are
equally understandable in the stories of other religions as well?

Since truth could be found everywhere, Gnostic writers disliked the
way the orthodox clergy encouraged ordinary Christians to resign themselves to execution:

These are the ones who oppose their brothers, saying to them,
"Through this [martyrdom] our God shows mercy, since salvation

comes to us from this." They do not know the punishment of those who are gladdened by those who have done this deed to the little ones who have been sought out and imprisoned. (*Apos. Pet.* 79.11–21)[43]

There were also Gnostic martyrs, as there were Jewish and pagan martyrs, and there were some Gnostics, especially the Valentinians, who adopted the terminology of resurrection in their treatises but who believed in something rather closer to the immortality of the soul and called it resurrection.[44] The Valentinians in general took a more spiritual perspective on resurrection. The classic *Treatise on Resurrection* (also known as the *Epistle to Rheginus*), to cite but the most obvious text, neither accepts the notion that the spirit is capable of death nor that the material body is able to withstand the forces of decay in our life:

So then, as the apostle said of him, we have suffered with him, and arisen with him, and ascended with him.

Now, since we are manifestly present in this world, the world is what we wear (like a garment). From him (the savior) we radiate like rays, and being held fast by him until our sunset—that is, until our death in the present life—we are drawn upward by him as rays are drawn by the sun, restrained by nothing. This is resurrection of the spirit which "swallows" resurrection of the soul along with resurrection of the flesh. (*Treat. Res.* 45.23–46.1)[45]

Rheginus tried to get to a truth beyond antinomies of flesh and spirit, bodily and spiritual. One might think that he was on the way to the modern view that body and soul both speak to the same unity. But, in the end, Rheginus's perspective is an attempted synthesis of resurrection and immortality of the soul. He begins with the literal, saying that he has suffered and risen with Christ. But there are three stages of awareness, of which the resurrection of the flesh is the simplest and least interesting. Rheginus uses "resurrection" in a very allegorical way, seemingly to preserve the terminology of early Christianity but actually emphasizing the immortality of the soul or spirit. Resurrection of the soul is closer to the truth but the highest truth involves the resurrection of the spirit. Resurrection is really a symbolic process by which we ascend and, as much from the verb tenses, the ascension is coterminous with salvation in this life. At the end, we merely confirm the promise made in this life. Resurrection and salvation have already happened proleptically.

With this allegorical perspective, Gnostics could not have been uncritical Gospel readers. But even Paul was sometimes a difficulty for them. The famous passage in 1 Corinthians 15 allows for the interpretation that resurrection will be as "a life-giving spirit." Elaine Pagels has pointed out that in Valentinianism, the strategy was to attribute the different, seemingly conflicting passages in the New Testament to different groups of Christians, ascending in order of election, so that the most spiritual statements of resurrection also designated the most Gnostic Christians. They divided Christians into three types: The *hylics* (*hyle* means "matter" in Greek), those who are only material Christians, could be expected to understand flesh literally because that was their material *(hylic)* nature; it is no wonder they were often called the *sarkic* (from Greek *sarx* or flesh) or the fleshly race in other Gnostic documents. An intermediate group, the psychics (the *psychikoi,* "the ensouled" from *psyche,* the soul), have evidently understood more about the true nature of salvation but only the pneumatics (the *pneumatikoi,* the "spiritual" people from *pneuma* spirit) are fully aware of the real meaning of the Gospel. The pneumatics are in full possession of the *gnōsis* or saving knowledge.[46] Those who deny the fully spiritual interpretation of the Gospel are themselves denied the fullest rewards. The theme of the punishment fitting the crime runs throughout the arguments on resurrection. Whatever one believes, that is what one will get in the afterlife; for wrong believers, their beliefs will be the source of their punishment.

The exhortation to leave off the details for the sake of unity represents the most sophisticated Gnostic defense. It does not matter what the outward appearances are; it does not matter what the general church insists upon. These are only outward appearances; the *pneumatikoi* know better. They know that they are already resurrected and have arisen. They assent to every other belief merely for the sake of church unity. The Gnostics have a secret interpretation of the outward beliefs of Christianity. They neither accept nor reject ordinary church doctrine but transcend it in an allegory of higher salvation. This is as much a statement of intellectual superiority over the common folk in the church as a statement of the nature of the world. As such, it is also a statement of the superiority of an intellectual ("spiritual") approach to the Gospels as a fleshly one.

Such ideas, even mediated and compromised, as the Valentinian ones were, could not be expected to pass by the Church Fathers without notice. Polycarp, one of the most famous of the Early Church's martyrs, minces no words on this topic:

For whosoever does not confess that Jesus Christ has come in the flesh, is antichrist; and whosoever does not confess the testimony of the Cross is of the devil; and whosoever perverts the oracles of the Lord to his own lusts, and says there is neither a resurrection nor a judgment, he is the firstborn of Satan. (Pol. *Phil.* 7.1)[47]

Probably the Valentinians could confess to fleshly resurrection and attempt to avoid Polycarp's creedal test, retracting it by reinterpretation. So Polycarp's defense against this position is fruitless. So intense was the polemic that W. C. van Unnik declared that the second century was like no other, in the sharpness of its battles over the significance of the resurrection.[48]

The issue was not just the definition of resurrection, it was also symbolic of one's willingness to be martyred, to encourage others to martyrdom, or, conversely, to perform the acts of piety toward the civil cult. To one group, one could dissemble because it was all a matter of outward appearances, not a matter of inward *gnosis*. But to the "orthodox," the nature of the apostolic succession was at stake—whether church authority should be based on faith (the teaching of the apostles) or knowlege (the seeking of visions) and whether the church would adopt the Greek view of the natural immortality of the soul (at least to those who realized it) or retain the Jewish apocalyptic view of the resurrection of the flesh. All this was represented in the issue of the nature of the resurrection body. In spite of the protestations of "Gnostics" and "Docetists," the "orthodox" church insisted that that martyrdom was a great good to be encouraged and that the sacrificed and martyred flesh would be redeemed, not just the soul, at the final judgment.[49]

Gender and the Resurrection Body:
Mary Magdalene

JUST AS WE can see the important issue of martyrdom reflected in discourse about resurrection of the body, so the issue of gender also is prominently displayed in the discussion of resurrection. The *Gospel of Mary Magdalene,* which can be dated approximately to the second half of the second century, describes a discussion between Jesus and the apostles with a follow-up discussion among the apostles after Jesus has ascended to heaven.[50]

In the *Gospel of Mary Magdalene,* prophetic experience is the basis of spiritual authority. Mary saw Jesus in a vision and received instruction from him (*Gos. Mary Mag.* 7:1–2). This immediately raises the issue of a conflict with apostolic authority, which is based on faith and teaching rather than vision. Mary Magdalene, who is after all, among the first group of women to discover the resurrection of Jesus, plays a central role as visionary and spiritual guide for the other disciples. She replaces the Savior after his ascent, as the source of spiritual comfort and teaching:

> Then Mary stood up. She greeted them all and addressed her brothers: "Do not weep or be distressed nor let your hearts be irresolute. For his grace will be with you all and will shelter you. Rather we should praise his greatness, for he has joined us together and made us true human beings." When Mary said these things, she turned their minds [to]ward the Good, and they began to [as]k about the wor[d]s of the Savi[or]. (*Gos. Mary Mag.* 10:1–4)[51]

The "Good" appears to be both the Neoplatonic good and their internal spiritual nature. She urges them to find peace within themselves and work towards unity. Mary's special relationship with Jesus was already an issue when the present text was formulated because we have an apologetic included in the narration itself, significantly placed in the mouth of Peter: "Sister, we know that the Savior loved you more than any other woman. Tell us the words of the Savior that you know, but which we have not heard" (*Gos. Mary Mag.* 6:1–2). Apostolic succession and the authority of respected women were in conflict in this exchange, as was the case in Montanism and Gnosticism. In this case, Mary's authority comes not from visions but from her relationship with Jesus; probably disqualifying Montanism as a source because Montanism was an ecstatic, prophetic movement.

A problem arises, nonetheless, when Mary explains the "secret" teaching that Jesus has taught her:

> Andrew sai[d, "B]rothers, what is your opinion of what was just said? I for one do not believe that the S[a]vior said these things, be[cause] these opinions seem to be so different from h[is th]ought." After reflecting on these ma[tt]ers, [Peter said], "Has the sav[ior] spoken secretly to a wo[m]an and [not] openly so that [we] would all hear? Surely he did [not wish to indicate] that [she] is more worthy than we are?" (*Gos. Mary Mag.* 10:1–4)

The passage levels the playing field, suggesting that Mary was the equal but not superior to the other apostles, though her superiority is also implied in several places. The apostles challenge Mary's status but not her character or teaching. They were suspicious, perhaps, because "private, privileged" meetings would be morally as well as politically suspect. Levi, however, jumps to Mary's defense: "If the Savior considered her to be worthy, who are you to disregard her? For he knew her completely [and] loved her devotedly" (*Gos. Mary Mag.* 10:9–10).

Mary Magdalene is found to have an elevated status in other texts, such as the *Gospel of Philip,* the *Dialogue of the Savior,* the *Gospel of Peter,* and the *Pistis Sophia.* The *Gospel of Philip,* a Valentinian anthology dating from approximately 350 CE in its present form, describes Mary as one of three women who were companions of the Lord, in addition to his mother and sister. "Three women always used to walk with the Lord— Mary his mother, his sister, and the Magdalene, who is called his companion. For "Mary" is the name of his sister and his mother, and it is the name of his partner" (*Gos. Phil.* 59:6–10).[52] The word "partner" is particularly striking.

The following passage may clarify some of what is implied by the author:

> The companion of the [. . .] Mary Magdalene. The [. . . loved] her more than [all] the disciples, [and he used to] kiss her on her [. . . more] often than the rest of the [disciples] [. . .]. They said to him, "Why do you love her more than all of us?" The savior answered, saying to them, "Why do I not love you like her? If a blind person and one with sight are both in the darkness, they are not different from one another. When the light comes, then the person with sight will see the light, and the blind person the darkness. (*Gos. Phil.* 63:32–64:8)

Jesus used to kiss Mary on the mouth. The intimacy between Mary and Jesus in this passage is deliberatively provocative. It is parallel to the love shown between Jesus and Peter, as well as to "the Beloved Disciple" in the Gospel of John. The provocation of a male master showing favor to a female disciple risks implying a sexual relationship; it also clearly states that Jesus favored a woman's spiritual capabilities over that of a man. Having gotten the reader's attention, this Gnostic document wants to explain, polemicizing against a fleshly relation and arguing for the special, unique, spiritual acomplishments of Mary Magdalene.

In the *Dialogue of the Savior,* Jesus takes Judas, Mary, and Matthew to the ends of heaven and earth (*dial.* 17). On this journey the disciples gain a complete understanding of the savior's teachings (*dial.* 20). Jesus then commands the three disciples to teach what they have learned. "Mary said, 'Tell me, Lord, why have I come to this place—to gain or to lose?' " The Lord said, "[You have come] to reveal the greatness of the revealer" (*dial.* 24). As a result of this heavenly journey, Mary gained spiritual superiority and the authority to inform her fellow disciples of Christ's teachings.

The writer is sticking his thumb in the eye of the orthodox. The "Orthodox" church would have found these notions unacceptable. The writer means it to hurt because the purpose is important. The gender of the apostles is connected to the portrayal of the resurrection body. No one in the "orthodox" tradition (or probably anywhere else) would want to be resurrected in a female body at this time, which the culture had denigrated as an imperfect vessel for the intellect, being more easily perverted by lust. It is no surprise that the resurrection preached in these documents is less than full bodily resurrection because the female body was incomplete. Thus, a female can become a male in a material resurrection but not the other way around. Being male is important in a spiritual resurrection because the female gender is keyed to the inferior, material side of the dualist existence.

The spiritual body and immortality of the soul function to equalize the status of the afterlife, just as these documents argue for the equality of women as disciples of Jesus. The inferiority of women in this life was conceded but remedied in the next through various languages of transcendence of the feminine. In this respect, as Elaine Pagels showed in her *The Gnostic Gospels,* some Gnostics may have stressed the role of women in the church in a way that has not been equalled since.[53]

Gender and Resurrection: Perpetua

TERTULLIAN said: "The blood of the martyrs is the seed of the church." He meant that the martyr's example of courageous indifference to suffering and death in the arena served as the stimulus for further conversions to Christianity. The spread of Christianity through the reputation of the endurance of martyrs was forcefully defended by Frend in his important work on Christian martyrdom.[54] Whether or not it is entirely true that martyrdom furthered the cause of Christianity, accounts of martyrdom fueled conversions in at least two additional ways: They inspired later generations of the faithful to asceticism and motivated them to missionize foreign lands. If the martyrs had died for the faith in past generations, lay persons could win battles in ordinary life and the monks could conquer the world for Christianity.

For instance, the *Passio Perpetua,* also known as the *Martyrdom of Perpetua,* tells the events of the life of Saint Perpetua, who was martyred in the arena in Carthage on March 7, 203. If it is truly her account, and some of it seems safely beyond historical doubt, it is one of the earliest pieces of Christian writing produced by a woman. And she is universally praised as a woman of virtue and valor, who practiced ascetic modesty. Her asceticism transcends sexuality in order to defeat the devil in heavenly battle. Perpetua was a young married woman of about twenty from a well-off family who was arrested with two other prisoners, her brother, her baby, and her slave, Felicitas, who is pregnant. The prisoners were eventually transported to a prison where they awaited their fate—a spectacle with wild beasts. Perpetua and Felicitas were to battle with a mad cow rather than a lion or bear because, as the narrator explains, it corresponded to their feminine nature.

While Perpetua was in prison, she had three visions. The first was of the various beasts that she might meet in the arena. The second was of herself in battle against another warrior in the arena. She recalls, "I was stripped of my clothing, and suddenly I was a man. My assistants began to rub me with oil as was the custom before a contest." [55] Perpetua's identification as a male and participation like a male in the blood sport of the arena shows the effect of Hellenistic ideas of gender roles upon early Christianity.

Perpetua's vision is related to the famous Logion 114 of the *Gospel of Thomas,* where Jesus tells Mary that she must become a man to enter the kingdom of heaven. Mary's gender reversal serves as a key for interpreting Perpetua's *Imitation of Christ.* In this respect, Jesus' passion is viewed as the same kind of *agōn* (contest) which the martyr must endure in the arena. The purpose and reward of this ordeal is seen in the third vision, where Perpetua experiences a journey to heaven in which she and her companions are carried by four angels and stand before a heavenly throne. This prophetic dream foretells the heavenly reward of martyrs and, by extension, all the faithful. Perpetua's actual end is unknown, but the story is a great gift, a paradigm of Christian passion, and a martyr narrative for the future edification of the church. [56]

Besides the effect on spectators, the work has had an even greater effect on those who have read it. After martyrdom ceased to be a common experience in the church, it still retained its value to encourage faith, to garner conversions, to concentrate the will of the faithful, and to inspire missionizing. There is a definite relationship between stories of martyrdom and ascetic behavior. The "red" martyr was replaced by the "white" martyr, the person who sacrificed even ordinary pleasures like marriage and procreation to achieve the same immortal state that the martyrs achieved. Perpetua's example served as encouragement for missionizing as well. The monastics, unencumbered by family or relations, were important vectors in spreading the word of Christianity to new lands.

The Sethians: The Hypostasis of the Archons

THE HYPOSTASIS OF THE ARCHONS, otherwise translated as the *Reality of the Rulers,* is one of many Gnostic retellings of the creation story. It is from a school of Gnosticism called "Sethian" by scholars. The documents of this school consist of wildly mythological, sometimes dreamlike narratives, based on the Hebrew Bible. The Seth of the scholarly designation is the Biblical Seth, the surviving son of Adam, who carries *gnōsis* to the present, and not the Egyptian Seth. In this bizarre genre, the Bible's heroes are seen as villains, while some of the Biblical villains are seen as heroes. The text identifies those who transmitted the *gnōsis* to the present generations and Seth is a key link.

Gnōsis begins in the garden of Eden. The snake is a hero because it passes redeeming *gnōsis* to Adam and Eve. The God of the Old Testament is seen as an ignorant or evil *demiurge* (creator) because He thinks that He is the only God. He does not know that there is a God of salvation, who is above him. This is a polemical mythology, reflecting a Gnostic defense against Rabbinic and, especially, Christian opposition.[57] These texts reveal a radically anti-Jewish and anti-orthodox attitude.

The *Hypothesis of the Archons,* which will have to serve as a representative of a whole genre of Sethian texts found in the *Nag Hammadi Corpus,* discusses a conflict between the secondary authorities of the cosmos and the true reigning spirit of "Incorruptibility," who is gendered as a female power. The hierarchy of the evil ruling powers of the cosmos appears to be an ironic caricature of church hierarchy. We can characterize the *Hypostasis of the Archons* as a Sethian text, due to the portrayal of Eve and the serpent as salvific characters. Eating from the tree of knowledge is a positive act, which lifts the veil of ignorance deluding Adam and Eve. After the Female Spiritual Principle enters the serpent, it refutes the prohibition given to them by the god called "Samael,"[58] a depiction of the Hebrew God as an ignorant *demiurge.*

The serpent explains, "With death you shall not die; for it was out of envy that it said this to you. Rather, your eyes shall open and you shall come to be like gods, recognizing evil and good" (*Hyp. Arch.* 90:6–11). This is a perverse retelling of the text of Genesis 3:4–5: "But the serpent said to the woman, 'You will not die. For God knows that when you eat of it your eyes will be opened, and you will be like God, knowing good and evil.' " In this text the *gnōsis* that the snake gives to Adam and Eve is saving knowledge, while the God of the Old Testament is an evil demon.

So the *Hypostasis of the Archons* is using the text of the Old Testament turned around for the purposes of engaging in a mythological polemic. The saving *gnōsis* turns out to be that we are trapped in this irredeemable world and the Gnostics are the only ones who know it. Because they know it, they know that they must get out of it to communicate again with the God of salvation. Matter and materiality are evil; they prevent us from perceiving the truth.

The salvation *(gnōsis)* that these Gnostics seek is a variation on the immortality of the soul, which must free itself from the dirty, ignorant, irredeemable universe in which it is trapped. The cosmic conflict between the Archons (Rulers) and Incorruptibility expresses the "battle" between the body and soul (who are the Jews or the ordinary Christians as opposed to the saving remnant the Christians), the body of the church and its soul (the mass of the church as opposed to its Gnostic elite), and most emphatically, the "orthodox" Church Fathers and the "Gnostics." As myth does everywhere, the moral appears repeated on many levels simultaneously. The Archons are as much the evil rulers of the church as they are the evil rulers of the universe. This is a case of cosmology being used to define soteriology and hence, also, to define the transcendent part of the self.

The *Hypostasis of the Archons* can be divided into two sections: The first is the creation of the world as a result of the battle between the Archons and Incorruptibility, and the second, the attempted rape of Eve and Norea, resulting in Eleleth's revelation to Norea. The first section explains that the creation of the world was ascribed to Archons. One of these Archons is the god Ialdabaoth, also known as Samael, the creator god of Genesis. Man was also a creation of these lower powers, but his soul was either a divine spark or breath implanted in the mortal flesh by the Supreme God.

The Archons create Adam in an attempt to trap Incorruptibility, the Female Spiritual Principle. The Archons repeatedly attempt to rape the physical female characters in order to defile the spirit that they embody. The first instance of rape occurs directly after the creation of Eve.

Then the Archons (authorities) came up to their Adam. And when they saw his female counterpart speaking with him, they became agitated with great agitation; and they became enamored of her. They said to one another, "Come, let us sow our seed in her," and they pursued her. And she laughed at them for their folly and their blindness; and in their clutches she became a tree, and left before them a shadow of herself resembling herself; and they defiled [it] foully. (*Hyp. Arch.* 89:17–28)

Eve's transformation into the tree reflects her position as the embodiment of the Female Spiritual Principle—that is, Wisdom. The story itself is likely a borrowed trope from the story of Apollo and Daphne (Laurel), pulled into the narrative. In the original story, the gods turn Daphne into the beautiful plant to escape being raped by Apollo, so the story is very apt for the context. The implications are Biblical: She becomes the "Tree of Life" described in Genesis 2:9, which is specifically equated with Wisdom in the book of Proverbs, though the text itself has to be forced a bit to come up with the rape: "She is a tree of life to those who lay hold of her; those who hold her fast are happy" (Prov 3:18). This mixture of Hellenistic and Hebrew traditions, brought together in a completely new and polemical narrative, is typical of the Sethian tradition.

The second woman who the Archons attempt to rape in the text is Eve's daughter Norea. Norea is Seth's (otherwise unknown) sister, whom Eve bears after the death of Abel. Seth and Norea are conceived by divine providence. "Again Eve became pregnant, and she bore [Norea]. And she said, 'He has begotten on [me] a virgin as an assistance [for] many generations of humankind.' She is the virgin whom the powers did not defile" (*Hyp. Arch.* 91:34–92:2).

After a short but disagreeable interaction with Noah (now a villain), the remainder of the text describes Norea's confrontation with the Archons and her subsequent revelation of Eleleth (a Savior figure whose name appears to be a variation or garbling of a name of God in Hebrew) which reveals that she has the knowledge to save humanity. Seth and Norea are singled out as the progenitors of the Gnostic community due to their spiritual superiority. Norea's incorruptibility, in combination with her material presence, allows her to be the link between the cosmic Female Spiritual Principle and Eve's physical progeny. With Norea's help, humanity will eventually be saved. Pearson explains, "Just as the heavenly Eve functions in that text as an agent of salvation to Adam, so also does Norea function as an agent of salvation for Seth and the subsequent generations of the elect." [59]

As the Archons pursue Norea in an attempt to rape her, Eleleth comes down from the heavens and teaches Norea the truth about the powers of the world and promises salvation for her offspring. With the appearance of Eleleth there is a shift in the narrator's voice. The narrative is transformed from a dialogue to an eyewitness account by Norea. This personal account has been interpreted by some scholars as an inner psychological withdrawal.

Again, cosmology is being used to describe and define an ancient understanding of the self. This bizarre use of myth twice to split the saved personality from raped personality seems to many to indicate a "self" in great distress. In her essay, "The Book of Norea, Daughter of Eve," Karen King characterizes Norea's vision of Eleleth as a psychic dissociation.[60] King explains that Norea's reaction against her aggressors is a painful solution to her predicament. Her search for inner revelation splits the body and soul, therefore separating the body from the self and taking refuge in the spiritual soul. This is a very revealing detail that suggests a radical reaction to a terrible trauma. Severe disassociative responses to traumatic events, such as rape, not uncommonly produce the same reactions. Post-traumatic stress disorder (PTSD), for example, is a complex consequence of exposure to extreme events, which encompasses trauma-related symptoms, anxiety symptoms, and symptoms otherwise found in depressive disorders.

Perhaps behind these stories are real incidents of sexual abuse. PTSD is also thought to be the pathological outcome of many traumatic events.[61] Reexperiencing the traumatic event occurs spontaneously or in response to reminders that are linked to the traumatic event. A similar "rape trauma syndrome" exists that results in a form of psychological paralysis of the victims. Withdrawal is one psychological defense. Victims have described a sensation of leaving their bodies and looking down from above as their bodies are subjected to rape.[62] Norea's inner withdrawal, which resulted in her vision of Eleleth, could be an example of this type of stress-related disorder. If an abuse victim separates herself from her body, her true self emerges from the encounter unscathed.

In his dissertation, Lawrence P. Jones examines the *Hypostasis of the Archons* and suggests that it is a natural reflection of sexual abuse of slaves in the second and third centuries CE. Although society expected a master to be fair-minded and humane to his slaves, infidelity with servants was just as often overlooked because a master could misuse his slave in whatever ways he wished.[63] Jones suggests that slaves motivated by Christian or Jewish religious beliefs were most likely to refuse their masters' sexual advances, and therefore may have been more likely to be the victims of rape.[64]

For Jones, Norea's psychic withdrawal in reaction to her aggressors is an example of how a slave could have withdrawn psychologically into a spiritual world beyond the reach of abusive masters. Jones explains that she (Norea) took refuge in an experience of "gnosis," "knowledge" of her "true" identity, rooted in a "higher" reality, which she believed superior to the reality of the rulers." [65] It is doubtful that Jones' theory explains the origin of every Gnostic treatise or conversion, rather it supplies a social profile of one kind of person who would be attracted to Sethian Gnosticism and offers an insight into a completely different social reality from the Valentinian communities.

The ascent of the soul in these texts finds a renewed mythological relevance for Late Antiquity. These systems, with their mythologies and rapes, their overturning of the Biblical text and their subjection of the historical Christ to a subservient role amongst a host of redeemer figures, put the Church Fathers' on edge. But what really made their blood boil is that these texts suggest that faith is a low form of knowledge for those who have never seen the truths of these texts, as revealed in contemplation, meditation, and personal vision.

The Heresiologists

JUSTIN AND IRENAEUS

The Gnostics' spiritualization of the saving events of Christianity was a threat to the Church Fathers—for their myths of rape and deception and for their bowdlerization of Old Testament passages but especially because they spiritualized the resurrection. The defensive (apologetic) polemic against heresy started, naturally enough, with Justin, who was both martyr and disputant. His heresiological work is lost to us but is incorporated into Irenaeus' writings. Justin's *Dialogue with Trypho,* a fascinating work in itself, also contains a few interesting issues on this theme. Justin develops a very traditional association between resurrection and judgment. He believes that the Hebrews, at least those who do God's will before the coming of Christ, are to be saved. Resurrection will take place after Christ's thousand-year rule. For Justin, the superiority of resurrection is that it grants to each person exactly its due. He criticizes those who believe that the afterlife is only the immortality of the soul (*Dial.* 80).

Furthermore, Christianity is infinitely superior to pagan philosophers because they only have the vaguest notions about their future afterlife while Christians have sure knowledge that they will regain their bodies and be justly rewarded (*1 Apol.* 18). So for Justin, Christianity is superior to all because it, like all notions of resurrection before, grants exactly the right rewards and punishments to each and also contains the full truth of the future life. Docetists and Gnostics could hardly have missed the implications of this polemic against their spiritualizing of the Gospel. Though he is respectful of the righteous Jews of the past, he is less patient with his contemporary Jewish opponents. He mentions that the Jews say that the disciples stole the body of Christ from the tomb, the accusation that stimulates the development of the empty tomb tradition (*Dial.* 108). The story of the empty tomb not only raises these doubts, it also provides the readers with ready-made answers to the question.

Irenaeus follows Justin by two generations, with several intervening fathers to mediate the discussion. With Justin as a guide, he points out that both body and soul are necessary for complete human existence (*Adv. Haer.* 5.6.1). Irenaeus also brings in the Eucharist as an actual exemplar of the dual nature of Christ, as was implicit in the Gospel descriptions of the event. If it is not possible for God to save both the body and the soul, then he cannot transmit salvation through the Eucharist either (*Adv. Haer.* 5.2.2–3).[66] Irenaeus' opponents are basically the Gnostics, "falsely so-called," as he characterizes them, to refute their claim to "saving knowledge" *(gnōsis)*. He accuses them of denying God's power over creation when they deny resurrection:

They refuse to acknowledge the power of God . . . who dwell upon the weakness of the flesh but do not consider the power of him who raises it from the dead. For, if God does not give life to what is mortal and does not recall the corruptible to incorruptibility, then he is not powerful. But that he is powerful in all these matters, we ought to know from a consideration of our origins, because God took a lump of earth and formed man. For indeed how much more difficult and hard it is to believe that someone made out of previously non-existent bones and nerves and veins and all the other things which pertain to man something which is a living and rational man than that he reconstituted what was made and thereafter dissolved in the earth. (*Adv. Haer.* 5.3.2)

THEOPHILUS, ATHENAGORAS, AND TATIAN

All these fathers write at the end of the apostolic age, approximately 180–220 CE. Theophilus explains resurrection in the science of his time, as the remaking and perfecting of our earthly vessels. He takes Paul's metaphor that the seed seems to disappear before the plant appears, suggesting that resurrection is like the organic growth of a plant; it is making the body whole for the first time.[67]

Athenagoras' treatise *On the Resurrection* is the earliest surviving treatise specifically on the question, as Justin's is fragmentary and possibly inauthentic. As with the other early fathers who write on this subject, it is hard to discover its exact audience. The fact that neither Theophilus, nor Athenagoras, nor Tatian make any significant mention of the Christ in their tractates or involve Christology in their demonstrations of resurrection suggests that they were written for a gentile, non-Christian audience to convince them that resurrection per se was neither as unlikely nor as disgusting a possibility as pagans might otherwise have thought.[68]

Athenagoras' argument is straightforward: Christian teaching about the resurrection is worthy of belief. It is within God's power to raise the dead and it is appropriate that God should do so. Such an innocent-sounding and sensible stipulation actually involves a considerable contradiction with ordinary Platonism and Aristotelianism. God, in fact, would never know material things in these philosophies. For them, God knows the ideas but not the individual material events, which would entail God knowing change, which would, in turn, suggest that God is mutable. In Philo's discussion of God's immutability, he is willing to risk God's unity rather than give up his immutability. This was typical of the philosophical belief of the day. So Athenagoras actually propounds quite an exceptional view, one not likely to convince a serious Platonist of the day, a polemic rather than an argument. Ordinary people were likely to be the target audience. The argument does have a certain inexorable, pragmatic logic.

The resurrection body is produced by reconstructing the body from its constituent parts, which are reassembled for the purpose. A God who knows everything would know where the bodies of the dead are and, common sense tells us, that a God who knows everything is better than one who knows only some things.

Athenagoras argues that "reincarnating" the soul (clothing it in flesh again) will not wrong it as it did not wrong the soul to be "incarnated" in the first place. Certainly the pagans thought that clothing the soul with flesh was just, though it may not have been a pleasant status. After the body is decomposed, to put it back into an incorruptible body would commit no further harm (*Res.* 10.5), reasons Athenagoras. The incorruptible part of the equation is important to note because, otherwise, the body would eventually decompose again. It is the incorruptible, value-added quantity that transforms the resurrected believer into the resurrection body. It is the material reassembled that carries the identity. (This would not satisfy a modern philosopher but it does make the body the clear carrier of the self.)

Yet it would have seemed entirely wrong to Platonists. For them, the soul was the carrier both of life (sensation) and identity (memory and intelligence). They held the notion that souls were incarnated for remedial reasons, to make up for past infractions. But from Athenagoras' argument we learn that he had no difficulty using the pagan notion of an immortal soul to guarantee the identity between the dead person and his risen body, when necessary. He was speaking to a pagan audience where notions of soul were assumed.

His strongest argument is: Resurrection is, moreover and most important, the will of God:

We have put our confidence in an infallible security, that will of our Creator, according to which he made man of an immortal soul and a body and endowed him with intelligence and an innate law to safeguard and protect the things which he gave that are suitable for intelligent beings with a rational life. We full well know that he would not have formed such an animal and adorned him with all that contributes to permanence if he did not want this creature to be permanent. The creator of our universe made man that he might participate in rational life and, after contemplating God's majesty and universal contemplation, in accordance with the divine will and the nature alloted to him. The reason then for man's creation guarantees his eternal survival, and his survival guarantees his resurrection, without which he could not survive as man. (Res. 15.2–4)[69]

For Athenagoras, resurrection is the guarantee that we are what we seem to be—namely, human beings. To be perfected as humanity, we have to retain our bodily humanity; resurrection for him is the guarantee of that bodily perfection as humans. Death is but a temporary state for the faithful, a state in which their identity is temporarily dispersed. To survive forever merely as disembodied souls would be to survive at the expense of the essence of our humanity. The human being cannot be said to survive if the body has decomposed. It is not human survival unless the same body, newly perfected, is restored to the same soul (ch. 25).

The same seems to be true of Tatian, from what little we have of his writings. All that remains of Tatian's writings is some fragments and his *Oration for the Greeks,* which serves a quite similar purpose to Athenagoras' writings. But he argues quite differently to the same conclusions. Tatian, however, does not write systematically on this subject nor does he posit, as Athenagoras does, that we have an immortal soul. He seems to start from Biblical or Stoic rather than Platonic assumptions, believing that we come into existence out of nothing, with the creation of the body, explicitly saying that the soul is not in itself immortal. The soul is dissolved upon death, and so therefore the resurrection is a process of reconstituting both body and soul, as Athenagoras thought as well. Tatian rests with the confidence that no matter what happens to our bodies after death, God will restore the faithful to embodied existence, thus giving the lie to Irenaeus' contention that Tatian denied bodily resurrection.[70] What is striking about these writers is their attention not only to bodily resurrection but to fleshly resurrection.

TERTULLIAN

Tertullian continues the tradition, making fleshly resurrection yet more explicit:

> If God raises not men entire, He raises not the dead. For what dead man is entire. . . . What body is uninjured, when it is dead? . . . Thus our flesh shall remain even after the resurrection—so far indeed susceptible of suffering, as it is the flesh, and the same flesh too; but at the same time impassible, inasmuch as has been liberated by the Lord. (*Res.* 8)[71]

As Caroline Bynum reminds us, by the end of the second century the resurrection of the body had become a major topic of controversy among Christians, as well as for the pagan critics of Christianity. The body, and the fleshly body at that, was what guaranteed the Christians that they personally would be resurrected in the end-time. The opposition claimed that resurrection was not something to be desired because it was impure and not logically the continuation of the thinking mind. In some way then, the battle was not just about resurrection but about what kind of persons we essentially are. As a result, the argument necessarily also described the social position of the debaters, their attitudes toward philosophy and citizenship.

Tertullian is the first significant Church Father writing in Latin.[72] Although Justin and Irenaeus founded the patristic apologetic tradition, it was Tertullian who wrote a treatise directly discussing the resurrection of the flesh. Like Tatian, Tertullian wrote out of the Stoic philosophical tradition. Like Tatian, Tertullian's resurrection is a re-creation of body and soul with a reassembling of the physical parts, instead of a process of spiritual, dynamic development, as in Paul. Following the Stoics, Tertullian thought that even the soul has a material reality, being made up of very fine matter.

Tertullian wrote *On the Resurrection of the Flesh* at the beginning of the third century. His opponents were Gnostics and probably Valentinians. He criticized his opponents' notion that one receives *gnōsis* at baptism and hence can consider oneself resurrected and saved as well. Those who deny that the flesh is raised are also refusing to recognize that Christ lived in the flesh and that he was raised in the flesh (*Res.*, 2). Following Daniel 7:13, many fathers suggested that Christ had been taken bodily into heaven. Tertullian is cognizant of the conflict that this raises in Scripture. Paul's statement that "flesh and blood will not inherit the kingdom of God" in 1 Corinthians means for Tertullian not only that the spirit is necessary for humans to enter the kingdom (*Res.*, 50) but also that death will end because corruption cannot enter heaven (*Res.*, 51).

Needless to say, this is a tendentious interpretation of Paul. Tertullian compensates by describing the process of the self's perception through faith. He even envisions a flesh infused with spirit that is free of every malady, thus re-importing Paul's pneumatology. Tertullian was evidently aware of Rabbinic Midrash on this point and used it effectively to make his point. As does the Midrash, Tertullian argues that when the children of Israel wandered for forty years in the desert, neither their shoes nor their clothes wore out, neither their hair nor their fingernails grew.[73] This Jewish trope is used by Tertullian to demonstrate resurrection: If God could sustain the children of Israel in the desert miraculously, he can certainly preserve the body of the faithful for its future resurrection. So the saved rise with every infirmity, malady, and bodily handicap removed.

The resurrection body will contain all the same organs that we have but they may not all be used. We will have no need for organs of digestion or sex.[74] For flesh and spirit are as a bridegroom and a bride:

And so the flesh shall rise again, wholly in every man, in its own identity, in its absolute integrity. Wherever it may be, it is in safe keeping in God's presence, through that most faithful "Mediator between God and man [the man] Jesus Christ, who shall reconcile both God to man, and man to God; the spirit to the flesh and the flesh to the spirit. Both natures has He already united in His own self; He has fitted them together as bride and bridegroom in the reciprocal bond of wedded life. Now, if any should insist on making the soul the bride, then the flesh will follow the soul as her dowry. The soul shall never be an outcast, to be led home by the bridegroom bare and naked. She has her dower, her outfit, her fortune in the flesh, which shall accompany her with the love and fidelity of a foster sister. But suppose the flesh to be the bride, then in Christ Jesus she has in the contract of His blood received His spirit as her spouse. Now, what you take to be her extinction, you may be sure is only her temporary retirement. It is not the soul only which withdraws from view. The flesh, too, has her departures for a while— in waters, in fires, in birds, in beasts; she may seem to be dissolved into these but she is only poured into them, as into vessels. And should the vessels themselves afterwards fail to hold her, escaping from even these, and returning to her mother earth, she is absorbed once more, as it were, by its secret embraces, ultimately to stand forth to view, like Adam when summoned to hear from his Lord the Creator the words, "Behold, the man is become as one of us!" (*Res.*, 63)[75]

Tertullian is able to allegorize the preferred connection between flesh and soul. The bride is the flesh and the bridegroom is the soul, led together by the spirit. Note the gender identification of flesh and spirit; it is based on a social hierarchy of male and female, not the grammatical gender of the two words. The flesh can be summoned again, just as Adam was summoned by God at creation. The body will be complete and perfect, even containing the genitalia, which will have no possible purpose in the resurrection body. They were important for the purposes of excreting in this life, necessary for the health of the body. Same with the teeth, they were necessary in this life for eating and have no future purpose. But they will be retained in the future body, not because the reconstructed world will have sexuality or eating but because the body would look peculiar without them.[76] Thus, at the end of his life when Tertullian became a Montanist, an apocalyptic movement which expected the end of the world immediately, he took his notions of fleshly resurrection with him into apocalypticism. Indeed, anyone who starts from Stoic principles can end up in apocalypticism because Stoicism itself posited that the world would end in fire, an *ekpyrosis*. Certainly Tertullian would have interpreted Stoicism as most consonant with the Biblical tradition in this respect.

Tertullian decides that the resurrection body will be like the angels (*Res.*, 62). The importance of this statement is not in the identity between the two but in the immortalizing of the perfected believer. The emphasis on the fleshly nature of the resurrection is a mark of the importance of this early battle between Gnosticism and orthodoxy over the nature of the body. We have seen that this is just as certainly an argument over human identity, gender, and transcendent significance. Behind it, the nature of the believer's responsibility regarding martyrdom was being expressed as well.

THE ALEXANDRIAN SCHOOL

Clement of Alexandria and Origen, forming an Alexandrian school that was deeply influenced by Philo Judaeus and Hellenistic Jewish philosophy, attempt a very different kind of synthesis between the two cultures. Though Clement preceded Tertullian, it is more convenient to treat him together with Origen for that reason. It is the two seemingly mutually exclusive doctrines of immortality of the soul and resurrection of the body that are the most illuminating battlefield for the Alexandrian fathers. Clement's treatise on the resurrection is lost and was, no doubt, "heretical" from the perspective of more "orthodox" eyes. But we should see it as an attempt to combine the two doctrines in such a way as to build the truth of one upon the other, instead of seeing in them obvious clash and mutual disconfirmation. That is the dominant strategy of the Alexandrian writers from Philo forward.

Clement attempted to define the good Gnostic as the true Christian who is pious in every respect. The *Stromata* (carpets or miscellanies) has several depictions of the Christian who can resist pleasure and desire, grief and anger, and in general maintain complete composure through the strengths of the Christian life. Philosophy too purges the soul and prepares it for faith. In this, Clement attempted to reclaim the term *gnōsis* and "Gnostic" for Christianity—even using the term for saving knowledge to represent the center of the church's teaching: "For God created man for immortality, and made him an image of his own nature (Wis 2:22), according to which nature of [God] who knows all, he who is a Gnostic, and, righteous and holy with prudence, hastens to reach the measure of perfect manhood" (*Strom.* 6.12.97). It is not possible to take the full measure of Clement's thinking on the matter because of the missing document. But it does look as if Clement affirmed resurrection of the body in some form (*Strom.* 6.13.107.2). The nature of the resurrection body is, however, more ambiguous. He thought that sexual differentiation will disappear, that men and women will be human but they will cease reacting sexually.[77] In short, they will attain angelic status, as is implicit even in the New Testament.

The perfection of the knowledge of faith occupies Clement's attention, rather than bodily resurrection. It is the consummation of existence and the possession of eternal life: "For herein lies the perfection of the Gnostic soul, that having transcended all purifications and modes of ritual, it should be with the Lord where he is, in immediate subordination to him" (*Strom.* 7.10.56–57).[78]

ORIGEN

Origen brings this strand of thinking to perfection. He stakes out his territory between the extremes of the Gnostic and the pagan notions of afterlife and Jewish views of resurrection.[79] He and Augustine are clearly the most famous theologians of the ante-Nicene and post-Nicene periods respectively. He had help in the sense that he had to counter the anti-Christian polemic of Celsus. But his solution turns out to be too close to that of Celsus his opponent to be readily accepted by the "orthodox" tradition. Celsus apparently believed:

- The idea that God is going to destroy the world in a great fire that only Christians will survive is absurd.
- The idea that the dead will rise from the earth in the same bodies in which they were buried is a "hope for worms."
- The soul would not want a rotted body. Besides, there are even Christians who do not believe that the body is raised.
- Christians have no answer to the question: "With what sort of body will they return? They merely retreat behind the power of God the creator. But God cannot do what is shameful or contrary to nature.
- God can confer immortality on the soul. But to raise the flesh would be contrary to divine reason and character. Nothing could bring God to do something of that sort.[80]

This short summary makes clear the critical attack on Christianity which Celsus mounted based on the absurd Christian notion of resurrection. Like Galen, Celsus attacked the very fiber of Christianity from the unconquerable height of Greek philosophy, an intellectual discipline of impeccable prestige that included both critique and polemic, skills that demanded long training and an expensive higher education. By now, Christians could field their own intellectual debate team. Origen appears to have fully understood the threat that Christianity posed to pagan philosophy and have countered with a more systematic Hellenizing of the Christian position than any previous Father, creating a true *gnōsis* of Christianity in the same vein as Clement.

Origen essentially builds on the continuity between life and death. He stresses the spiritual nature of the resurrection body. He begins with the traditional notion that the flesh dies as result of Adam's sin whereas the soul dies as the result of personal sin. In the *Dialogue with Heraclides,* he addresses the issue of the immortality of the soul. He admits many different kinds of death and immortality. Because there are many kinds of death, from one point of view we are immortal, yet from others we are not. Certainly the soul that sins is giving up its immortal nature. So in this he differs radically from Platonic thinking and agrees with Philo.

As Origen shows in his *First Principles,* he goes considerably along the way towards the philosophers. Like the Platonists, he viewed material existence itself as a kind of punishment. Human souls descend into the human body from a preexistent purity (*Princ.* 1.4.1). When it comes to the issue of resurrection Origen returns to the Pauline idea of spiritual bodies. This allows him to avoid the issues associated with the resurrection of the flesh. He also states that there will be a continuum of resurrection bodies, each with a glory corresponding to its moral status, which echoes the Pauline formulation in 1 Corinthians 15. But the most important thing is that the resurrection body will not be ordinary flesh:

> Because if they believe the apostle [Paul], that a body which arises in glory, and power, and incorruptiblity, has already become spiritual, it appears and contrary to his meaning to say that it can again be entangled with the passions of flesh and blood, seeing that the apostle manifestly declares that "flesh and blood shall not inherit the kingdom of God, nor shall corruption inherit incorruption." But how do they understand the declaration of the apostle [Paul] "We shall be changed?" This transformation certainly is to be looked for, according to the order which we have taught above; and in it, undoubtedly it becomes us to hope for something worthy of divine grace; and this we believe will take place in the order in which the apostle describes the sowing of the ground of a "bare grain of corn, or of any other fruit," to which "God gives a body as it pleases Him," as soon as the grain of corn is dead. (*Princ.* 2.10.3) [81]

Origen claims that he is merely restating the Pauline concept of spiritual bodies. But he has traveled, in reality, a great distance from the apocalyptic mysticism of Paul. Origen's notion of a "spiritual body" has taken its lead from Paul but, like Valentinianism, the concept is the immortal soul of Platonism in disguise. He sees souls as the stuff of the stars and the perfected souls as the heavenly bodies.[82] Origen allows everything but the natural immortality of the soul. For him, it is the saving work of God which immortalizes the soul, just as it was for Philo. This is certainly a possible and consistent way for Christianity to have moved. As it turned out, it was rejected. However, it was taken up by Gnosticism and later by Manichaeanism.

Evidently one problem with his perception is that it threatened the personal identity of the believer: "Yet the form *(eidos)* of the earlier body will not be lost, even though a change to a more glorious condition takes place in it." For this Origen returns yet again to the Pauline term, "spiritual body" but he loads it this time with a different ammunition.[83] This time, he fills the term with the implications of the spermatic "Logos" of Stoicism. Thus, he forges yet one more link between Christianity and Greek philosophy. His notion of personal identity is the pagan notion of the soul.

We have come an enormous distance from the apocalypticism of the early Jesus movement, which claimed (as all movements of that type did) that they alone were faithful enough to merit God's future rewards. Origen's system is clearly the farthest that one can take the notion of resurrection into Greek philosophy. It represents the cynosure of coexistence or, more exactly, the subsumption of resurrection into the notion of the immortal soul of Plato. But it is a perfect harmonization that future fathers were to view as too radical. Origen was called "heretic" while Augustine's view returns to Tertullian's approach.[84]

Gregory of Nyssa and the Cappadocians

JAROSLAV PELIKAN wrote a magisterial study of the Cappadocian fathers, *Christianity and Classical Culture,* whose theology represents the high point of philosophical thinking after Origen and before Augustine.[85] As thinkers, the power of their arguments surpasses that of Augustine but does not have the same dogmatic authority. Pelikan sees the major enterprise of these fathers as attempting to resolve the differences between Greek natural philosophy and Christian revelatory explanations of life. This is entirely compatible with the approach I have been taking. So let me resume his development of the chapter on life after death among the Cappadocians—Basil of Caesarea, Gregory of Nyssa, Gregory Nazianzius, and Macrina, in many ways the most sophisticated teacher of them all, who was the older sister of Basil and Gregory of Nyssa.

Gregory of Nyssa made a significant contribution to the synthesis of the doctrines of resurrection of the body and the immortality of the soul.[86] It is unclear how much of his thinking is actually his and how much belongs to his extremely adept sister Macrina; in his most important treatise, *On the Soul and the Resurrection,* he gives her quite full credit for her sophisticated thinking and saintly life. Perhaps he should have ceded her authorship of the treatise. In lauding Gregory we may actually be praising his sister.

Gregory himself had considerable difficulty with the notion of resurrection and that difficulty is to be evidenced in his treatise *On the Dead.* There, with the Greeks, he argues that the soul is what constitutes the human person, that the body is an impediment to the realization of personhood, and that death is the fulfillment of this realization.

By the time of his great treatises, *On the Creation of Man* and *On the Soul and Resurrection,* Gregory's positions had matured considerably. In *On the Creation of Man,* written between 379 and 380, he presents several arguments for the reality of resurrection. The first is that good must triumph over evil so that we must expect an eventual return to the good of Eden that God made for us at the beginning (21.4). Resurrection itself may be best demonstrated from the miracles of Jesus in the Scripture but the final consummation cannot take place until "the . . . complement of human nature" has been filled.[87] Since these proofs are as much about revivifications as resurrections, Gregory's discussion risks describing the resurrection as the revivification of the material body. Hence, he goes out of his way to show that the resurrection bodies in the New Testament, including Jesus' own, had already corrupted, making the miracle of resurrection clear to all as a proof of the general resurrection to come:

And the disciples were led by the Lord to be initiated at Bethany in the preliminary mysteries of the general resurrection. Four days had already passed since the event; all due rites had been performed for the departed; the body was hidden in the tomb; it was probably already swollen and beginning to dissolve into corruption, as the body mouldered in the dank earth and necessarily decayed: the thing was one to turn from, as the dissolved body under the constraint of nature changed to offensiveness. At this point the doubted fact of the general resurrection is brought to proof by a more manifest miracle; for one is not raised from severe sickness, nor brought back to life when at the last breath—nor is a child just dead brought to life, nor a young man about to be conveyed to the tomb released from his bier; but a man past the prime of life, a corpse, decaying, swollen, yea already in a state of dissolution, so that even his own kinsfolk could not suffer that the Lord should draw near the tomb by reason of the offensiveness of the decayed body there enclosed, brought into life by a single call, confirms the proclamation of the resurrection, that is to say, that expectation of it as universal, which we learn by particular experience to entertain. (*On the Creation of Man* 25.11)[88]

It is the resurrection of Lazarus and the others, as much as Jesus', which shows us the truth of the general resurrection. And the contrast with his Origenism in previous writings could not be more complete.

Since then every prediction of the Lord is shown to be true by the testimony of events, and we have not only learned this by his words, but also received the proof of the promise in deed, from those very persons who returned to life by resurrection, what occasion is left to those who disbelieve? Shall we not bid farewell to those who pervert our simple faith by "philosophy and vain deceit," and hold fast to our confession in its purity, learning briefly through the prophet the mode of the grace, by his words, "Thou shalt take away their breath and they shall fail, and turn to their dust. Thou shalt send forth Thy Spirit and they shall be created, and Thou shalt renew the face of the earth" (LXX Ps 104:29–30); at which time also he says that the Lord rejoices in His works, sinners having perished from the earth: for how shall any one be called by the name of sin, when sin itself exists no longer? (*On the Creation of Man* 25.13)[89]

To Gregory, resurrection, though it may seem at first illogical, is demonstrated in nature too, just as the pagan natural philosophy is demonstrated in nature. He refers to the seed in the ground and the beginning of human life, finding that there is nothing in the doctrine which is beyond our experience. Resurrection is therefore a dynamic, natural process.

Having established the nature of the New Testament doctrine, Gregory begins a more significant attempt at synthesis. He uses the Platonic concept of *eidos* (form, idea) as the one element of the earthly body to be preserved for the resurrection. This was Origen's opinion as well; no doubt Gregory learned from him. Gregory explicitly uses this concept as the principle of identity, which allows for the reassembling of the body's atoms. Gregory uses the *eidos,* not as the form itself, but as a spiritual organ by which an individual's soul imprints the individual's identity on material (27.2–5). This is a complex and sophisticated attempt to combine immortality with resurrection, realized, transcendent humanity with personal identity.

Even Plato was of the opinion that the body affects the soul. Without demonstrating that it is the individual who is resurrected, Gregory had risked proving resurrection by losing the individuality of the resurrected person. This is quite similar to the philosophical problem involved in demonstrating that the soul that survives death is the same as the individual who lived. Is the soul personal enough to be the principle of identity for the living person or is the soul merely a general rational principle that is immortal? In the same way, by combining the soul with resurrection of the body, Gregory risks failing to demonstrate that the person resurrected is the same as the one that died.

This concretization of the *eidos* is Gregory's attempt to resolve that problem. In chapter 28, armed with this Origenist argument, Gregory refutes aspects of Origen's notion of reincarnation. Thus, though the ostensible subject of the treatise is the making of the human body, we find that Gregory uses it as a way to try to synthesize the primitive Christian notion of resurrection with a sophisticated, philosophical notion of the immortality of the soul.

Armed with these arguments, Gregory goes to the main event: His treatise *On the Soul and the Resurrection* is precisely what the title suggests. It is an attempt to reason with each concept to make a consistent description of the Christian message, both in terms of scriptural background and philosophical acumen. The problem, however, is not just academic. He and his sister Macrina are dealing with the overwhelming loss of their older brother Basil. At the beginning of the treatise, Gregory relates that he has gone to his sister in search of consolation but she brings him clarity on intellectual issues as well.[90] Gregory expresses his difficulty in demonstrating the immortality of the soul while Macrina explains the relation of the soul to the body and, in doing so, raises the issue of the resurrection of the body. And she immediately raises the issue of the identity of the raised individual:

One hears people . . . asking how, since the dissolution of the elements according to their kinds is incomplete, the element of heat [the soul] in a person, once it is mingled generally with its own kind, can be withdrawn again for the purpose of reforming a man. For, they would say, unless the very same element returns the result would be a similar being and not the individual himself, that is to say, another person would

577

come into being and such a process would not be a resurrection, but the creation of a new man. But, if the original is to be reconstituted, it is necessary for it to be entirely the same, taking up its original nature in all the parts of its elements. (*De Anima* 230)[91]

With this argument, one might easily turn to the resurrection of the body as the principle of identity, admitting that the soul is the life-force but not the individuality of the person. However, that would lead into its own difficulties about the condition of the resurrected:

> If our human bodies return to life in the same condition in which they left it, then man is looking forward to endless misfortune in the resurrection [old age, disease, infanticide] (*De Anima* 261)

Arguing in this way then leads to a different dilemma about the possibility of living eternally in a material body. So it is not to the body that Macrina turns to express the principle of identity, propounding, as Gregory did above, that the soul picks up and retains the individuality of a person's moral life (260). This is rather like the Philonic solution to the problem and, indeed, one is left with the feeling that the body is denigrated by means of Platonism so as to fit the New Testament's requirements. Gregory, too, admits Origen's notion that salvation will eventually be universal, after what punishments are meted out beyond the grave. The philosophical and logical necessity for the resurrection of the body at the final consummation will indeed fall to Augustine to express most fully, though he is even more negative about sexuality and the body's role in this life.

Augustine

THOUGH PERHAPS not the intellectual equal of the Cappadocians in philosophical discussion, Augustine was certainly the most influential Christian thinker in the West until Aquinas. He significantly transmuted Christian views of grace and law, determination and free will, love, charity, and sin and Original Sin by gathering them up into a huge synthesis. There is no way to do justice here to the huge corpus of writing left by this towering and maddening figure or the intellectual synthesis that he effected. We have already seen how Origen, in attempting to conquer philosophy, was himself conquered by it, in the opinion of his successors.

Seeking a true Christian *gnosis,* his successors judged him a Christian Gnostic, as Clement had argued, and condemned him for it as well.

For Augustine, the Christian notion of resurrection might be entirely subsumed into Greek categories but it would only remain resurrection if it was also material. It must be material because the sin of the first man was material. In a real sense, Augustine is returning to the Pauline observation that, "For as in Adam all die, so also in Christ shall all be made alive" (1 Cor 15:22). But, in doing so, he redesigns the notion of Original Sin so that it is a much stronger and foregrounded belief than in any other Church Father:

> The law of death is that by which it was said to the first man, "You are dust and unto dust you shall return," for we are all born of him in that state because we are dust and we shall return to dust as a punishment for the sin of the first man. (*Fort.,* 22)[92]

Augustine denies Origen's solution to the seeming contradiction between Hebrew and Greek thought, making a brave, seemingly backward move. He returns to the primacy of the body and insists that it is the seat of our fullest identity:

> "Spiritual body" does not mean "not a body" any more than "animated body" means "life." . . . "Spiritual body" means a body obeying the spirit. (*Serm.* 242.8.11)[93]

He returns on many occasions to the issues as Paul defined them. But, while Paul was an apocalypticist throughout his life, Augustine was only one at the beginning of his career. He moves more and more into the notion that humans are preempted from perfecting themselves without God's special grace. The body is only necessary to guarantee our identity. Therefore, it is to the body that humanity will return. Augustine's most extensive treatment of the resurrection before his *City of God* is in *Sermon 362,* dated to about 410. He tries to explain Paul's text "flesh and blood cannot inherit the kingdom of God":

> Your body does not possess anything, but your soul, through the body, possesses that which belongs to the body. If, therefore, the flesh resurrects in order not to possess but to be possessed, not to have but to be had, what wonder then if flesh and blood cannot possess the kingdom,

579

since they will certainly be possessed by another. . . . In so far as we will be resurrected, it is not we whom the flesh carries, it is we who will carry it. If we carry it, we will possess it; if we will possess it, we will not be possessed by it; for we are freed from the judgment of the demon; we are of the kingdom of God. In this sense, this flesh and blood do not possess the kingdom of God. (*Serm.* 362.33.14)[94]

For Augustine, the vocabulary has to agree with Paul, it is a "spiritual body." It further will all become clear at the end of history, at the eschaton, when the earthly realm will be perfected. Augustine describes the intermediary realm in which the faithful dead live. At the Second Coming, nature itself will change and be perfected. To have the form of a body, without the flesh of corruption, means for Augustine (as for Macrina before him), that none of the acts of the flesh (eating, drinking, begetting, etc.) will continue in heaven. Human beings will finally achieve the status of angels (stars) in the afterlife and this will become the model for a perfected earth in the eschaton:

[The heavenly body] will be called a body and it can be called a celestial body. The same thing is said by the Apostle when he distinguishes between bodies: "All flesh is not the same flesh: but one is the flesh of men, another of beasts, another of birds, another of fishes. And there are bodies celestial and bodies terrestrial" (1 Cor 15:39–40). However, he certainly would not say celestial flesh; although bodies may be said to be flesh but only earthly bodies. For all flesh is body; but not every body is flesh. (*Serm.* 362.18.21)[95]

Augustine must explain why, when souls can contemplate God in heaven, it should be necessary for them to have a body at all. For Augustine, the answer is more scriptural than philosophical. The purpose of having a spiritual body in heaven has to do with the identity of the believer and also with its purpose in heaven, to meditate upon God. The spiritual body is both infinitely superior to the soul and, at the same time, only complete when it has become a spiritual body. Augustine analogizes with the incarnation. If God can be incarnate, then the perfected soul can be embodied as a spiritual body.

This solves the question not by reason but by scriptural passage and analogy but it creates a whole slew of other questions. Augustine settles the issue with Scripture but, conveniently, he uses Paul's writing and not the Gospels to settle the question. He would have had a much harder time demonstrating how body and soul go together without Paul's notion of the "spiritual body." It would have been almost impossible to make his point from the Gospels alone. He more or less settles the issue of corporeality by using the word "body" to mean an intelligible rather than a material object, as he interprets Paul. So in some sense, his body is not really a body but rather a garment for the soul, simply an ornament for it.

Augustine does not here resolve all the issues satisfactorily for himself. But he relies on the experience of leaving the body in ecstasy as demonstration that the soul will achieve the intermediary state. He then says that even after we have reached the felicity of bodiless existence there is the further felicity of returning to a perfected body, so that wise and ascetic men in this world live as if they are already in the perfected world to come. It may be correct to say that humans may have the experience of leaving the body. It is a real and quite intense experience. But, it is another thing to say that this demonstrates the immortality of the soul (see ch. 8).

In his most extensive treatment of our final disposition, *The City of God*, Augustine locates the ultimate good in being reincorporated without the evils of corporeal life. But he also uses that peculiar future state to demonstrate that hellfire and punishment for the damned will be real. How else could the soul be punished except in a body (*Civ.* 19.1–17)? The saved have precisely the converse issue. They will be souls together in salvation, a community of those saved, just as the church creates a community on earth. They will need an incorruptible body for their reward:

So, in order to be happy, souls need not flee from every kind of body [as they taught], but must receive an incorruptible body. And in what incorruptible body will they more fittingly rejoice than in the one in which they groaned while it was corruptible. (*Civ.* 12.26)

Augustine is driven to the conclusion from which Paul started: the body that the faithful will enjoy eternally is like a fleshly body but it is not a fleshly body. It is not even a material body. It is perfected flesh:

We shall see the corporeal bodies of the new heaven and the new earth in such a way that, wherever we turn our eyes, we shall, through our bodies that we are wearing and plainly seeing, enjoy with perfect clarity the vision of the sight of God everywhere present and ruling all things, even material things. It will not be as it is now, when the invisible things of God are seen and understood through the things which have been made, in a mirror dimly and in part. . . . (*Civ.* 22.29)

Either, therefore, God will be seen by means of those eyes because they in their excellence will have something similar to a mind by which even an incorporeal nature is discerned—but that is difficult or impossible to illustrate by an example or testimony of the divine writings—or else, which is easier to understand, God will be so known by us and so present to our eyes that by means of the spirit he will be seen by each of us in each of us, seen by each in his neighbour and in himself, seen in the new heaven and the new earth and in every creature which will then exist. (*Civ.* 22.29)

For Augustine this means being subsumed into the body of Christ, who is the only member of the trinity to take on human form. Indeed for him, meditating on the trinity is a way to anticipate the last and final consummation, which in *The City of God* Augustine compares with the Sabbath:

There is no need here to speak in detail of each of these seven "days." Suffice it to say that this "seventh day" will be our Sabbath and that it will end in no evening but only in the Lord's day—that eighth and eternal day which dawned when Christ's resurrection heralded an eternal rest *both for the spirit and for the body* [emphasis added]. On that day we shall rest and see, see and love, love and praise—for this is to be the end without the end of all our living, that Kingdom without end, the real aim and goal of our present life. (*Civ.* 22, end)

In short, Augustine believes that saved Christians will enjoy eternity as a community of perfected beings, like angels. As opposed to Origen, Augustine sees the final disposition of the soul only at the Parousia, the Second Coming, when all the faithful are resurrected. The living will be transformed but the dead will find their souls reclothed. The soul, rather than hating the body as in Platonism, yearns for the body in order to complete its repentance, just as in late Neoplatonism. The difference, for Augustine, is that repentance must be done in a single lifetime and may only be accomplished by those who believe in the Christ. Augustine himself certainly had plenty of experience with repentance, having been a religious quester himself. Indeed, the interior life of the convert dominates his writings.

The Nicene Creed affirmed that Christians must firmly await the life of the *aeon* to come. For the Cappadocians, this meant affirming both the immortality of the soul and the resurrection of the dead, a formula which was by now the standard way of dealing with the opposing concepts of afterlife in Christian thought. There was certainly a difficulty in affirming both of them simultaneously. But for Augustine, both could be affirmed sequentially. Upon death, the correctly believing and acting soul could attain the immortality of the soul which had originally been the Greek notion. At the end of time, the soul would be returned to a body for the fulfillment that was contemplated by Daniel and the Jewish apocalypticists (of which Christianity was certainly the primary example): Immortality of the soul now; resurrection of the body at the last trumpet.

In Augustine, we find a philosophically sophisticated person who, after being a philosopher, is himself inimical to philosophy. Yet he sides with a doctrine of fallen human nature more than with Christianity's original apocalyptic past. Augustine uses dualism to balance millenarianism. Augustine had to avoid, to use Paula Fredriksen's words, "the Scylla of popular millenarianism" and "the Charybdis of Manichaean dualism," with the soul's escape from a depraved world.[96] As she says in another place:

> But Augustine's anthropology takes him even further beyond classical dualism. As he leaves man's freedom, the soul's integrity, and traditional education behind, he also leaves behind the cosmic architecture of the late Hellenistic universe and the resonances that culture had established between God's relation to the physical universe and the soul's relation to the body. No longer, for Augustine, is the human being a miniature map of the cosmos. That world, with its hairline fractures between orders of being and its twin fault lines dividing man, neatly, between soul and body, could not speak to the infinitely more complicated man of Augustinian anthropology—the man through whose soul ran the ancient fault line arising from the sin of Adam.[97]

With his doctrine of the embodied fulfillment of time, Augustine avoids the Greek philosophical notion that the soul merely discorporates and finds its final fulfillment. There is an immortal soul but it will be punished at death. Augustine never sees a return to the body as a return to bodily pleasures in the apocalyptic end, as would a Zoroastrian or a Jew (or a Muslim). All earthly pleasure is purged away. It is the body of an angel to which the faithful return, to contemplate God more completely.

The result is an interesting synthesis: The soul is immortal but only in the intermediate state. At the last judgment, it shall be judged again. Only the elect shall return to the perfected body at the end of time. There, it is most fully itself for the soul is not fully an individual. The synthesis is, in a way, a systematic description of the pictures of the last judgment in the

Christian apocrypha, combining a notion of a soul that survives death with a final judgment.

This synthesis may not be as satisfactory intellectually to us as is the synthesis of Gregory. (If the soul is not fully individual, then it is not fully the same as the original person on earth.) But we live in a different world than Augustine. Augustine represented the forceful partnership of the civil authority with the church and provided the synthesis most in line with the desired, new unification of the Christian Roman Empire. That is part of the importance of Augustine; the church seized upon his thought because it so thoroughly supported the orthodox position. The state seized upon his thought because it gave it the justification to demand higher allegiances from its inhabitants. But minority groups not part of the Christian synthesis, like the Jews, were forced into very subservient roles. Many were forced out, murdered, or converted and eventually left the territory controlled by Roman Christendom. Those who remained were constantly stripped of their rights as individuals and communities.

In her chapter entitled "The Politics of Paradise," Elaine Pagels summarizes Augustine's effect on church tradition by the articulation of a strong doctrine of Original Sin:

> Instead of the freedom of the will and humanity's original royal dignity, Augustine emphasizes humanity's enslavement to sin. Humanity is sick, suffering, and helpless, irreparably damaged by the fall, for that "Original Sin," Augustine insists, involved nothing else than Adam's prideful attempt to establish his own autonomous self-government. Astonishingly, Augustine's radical views prevailed, eclipsing for future generations of western Christians the consensus of more than three centuries of Christian tradition.[98]

Personally, Augustine gave up his longtime mistress, with whom he had fathered children; then he gave up a very promising Christian marriage with a socially prominent woman, who could have assured him a successful public career. It is easy for us to see the harm that this surely caused to his wives and children. What is harder to see is what was gained when either men or women adopted celibacy as a life-commitment. With it, they become autonomous individuals, freed from their roles as wives or husbands or tutors of the young or householders. Celibacy gave the ancients autonomy and freedom to travel, write, and even to rule ecclesiastically.[99]

Theologically, these life-changes also had consequences for Augustine. He gave up the positive and hopeful interpretation of the story of the garden of Eden. For him, the moral of the story of the first humans no longer represented the human achievement of enough wisdom to chose good over evil. Ever after it represented the story of our fall into slavery which had to be compensated by asceticism, self-mastery, and the sacraments of the church, available only to those who adhered to its civil and religious laws. The doctrine of Original Sin provided a justification for staying true to the church when the feeling that the end was near had abated; infant baptism both counteracted the notion and promulgated it. It is not hard to see behind this notion of human deficiency a new Christian justification for imperial and episcopal control of Christendom for the benefit of its adherents.

Augustine and Interior Experience

YET, THERE IS another side to Augustine as well. He was also a master at understanding the value and quality of human experience. He was able to relate internal experience to the doctrine of the soul in a way that has been fundamental to Western culture ever since. While his solution to these problems shows that he was a savvy reader of the social position of the church, his solution to the problem of the "self" shows him to be a very accomplished and sensitive philosopher.

Augustine had read the Neoplatonists, especially Plotinus, and was extremely impressed by the Neoplatonic attention to interior experience. Perhaps this was because his own internal experience, his own multiple conversions were such cruces in his life: Augustine went from conventional Christian to pagan orator and philosopher, from philosopher to Manichaean, from Manichaean to Christian, from Christian to priest, and finally from priest to Bishop of Hippo. Not only did Augustine travel a long and self-conscious spiritual odyssey, he wrote about each step and used his own interior feelings and experiences as a model for the progress of the soul towards redemption. He is exquisitely self-conscious of the values of each of these changes.

But Augustine's unique synthesis also derives from his education. He was taught in a center of Christian Neoplatonism by Ambrose who took Plotinus' spiritual inwardness seriously. Augustine took the interior consciousness of the Neoplatonists and turned it, even converted it, into a new Christian spiritual inwardness. In so doing, in Phillip Cary's estimation, he created the internal life of the soul with which we are so familiar today. Because Plotinus had described in detail the interior experiential process by which the intellect carries the soul upward to the divine, even in life, Augustine can take the attention to interiority into the meditations of the Christian life.[100]

At first, Augustine simply reproduced the Neoplatonic notion of the immortality of the soul. The soul was divine because it contained the "intelligible world," the world of the intellect, and thus could be nothing else than immortal itself. But, this argument becomes less possible for a Christian philosopher as time goes on. Augustine needs to deny the natural immortality of the soul when he takes on his role as church spokesperson.[101] Augustine does not avail himself of the Philonic argument that the soul is immortal but not indestructible, because he wants to emphasize the saving role of Christ and because it would never have led him to account for the resurrection of the body. So he needs to provide a real and palpable hell to punish sinners.

To be sure, the Platonists were religious, though they remained pagan. The greatest religious rewards came from the meditation and ascent of the soul to the divine realm. But for Augustine, who had tried the religious life of the Platonists, there were yet greater rewards to be had from being a Christian. Now no longer a pagan desiring to understand what seemed like a mechanistic universe, Augustine, the Christian Platonist and churchman, affirmed that the bond of love that the intellect discerns and that carries the soul upward to God is a personal love responding to the grace of God, who is Father, Christ, and Holy Spirit. This means that the soul and the divine are not the same thing. There is a separation between the two, a natural breach that can be healed by grace and the charity of God responding to the human will.

It is a personal relationship with the divinity, a mystical bond, not just an intellectual attempt to convey one's mind to the world soul. Augustine describes a God who became truly human and so is capable of supporting a human relationship. That relationship takes place totally on the intellectual level. Indeed, the trinitarian godhead itself, three persons in perfect intellectual love relationships with each other, gives the best example of how the soul yearns for its ascent for Augustine.

That very bond implies a separation between divinity and the human soul that needs to be overcome, not the identity of substance that Plotinus had outlined. Plotinus described a universe starting with the One which in turn is subsumed by the Divine Mind and so on outward and downward to the realm in which we live. The soul, however, is part of the same intelligible world and so is transparently part of the very center of the intellectual universe. For Neoplatonism, there was a mystical identity between the self and the universe. But for Augustine there was the separation of sin. The individual soul is essentially cut off from God and can only reach Him through an act of will. Because of this separation, the inner self, in a sense, becomes a private realm for us because it cannot be automatically subsumed within the intelligible world of the Platonic forms. So, because we are cut off from God, we become truly private human consciousnesses for the first time. At the same time, the soul becomes the place in which humans find God.

Memory played a crucial role in Plato's proof of the soul's immortality. With Augustine's *Confessions,* personal memory is the quality that accounts for the individuality of the person:

A great power is that of memory, something awesome, my God, a deep and infinite multiplicity. And this is what the mind is, and this is what I myself am. What then am I, my God—of what nature am I? A variegated and multifaceted life, and utterly immeasurable. Behold in my memory the fields and caves and caverns innumerable, and innumerably full of innumerable kinds of things. . . . I scamper and flit through them all, and poke this way and that as far as I am [quantum sum] and there is no end of it—so great is the power of life in a human being living mortally! (*Conf.* 10:26) [102]

The private space of the soul is made by roofing over our selves in our separation from God. But the house of the self is still furnished by memory. Augustine understood that the soul has to be a singular and newly created being for the ethical system outlined in the Bible to work fully. But at the same time Augustine used our ability to remember distant things in space and time as an example of the soul's power and divinity. For Augustine, this private space is the place where the battle of the will begins and in which one ascends from separateness to the beatific vision, which he identifies with the Christian God. It might be too much to say that Augustine invented the interior self but he certainly perfected the notion. The concept developed continuously throughout Platonic philosophy. But, for Augustine, philosophically definable individuals truly find God, for the first time, by looking within, as opposed to looking at the design in the universe. In a sense, Augustine breaks down the identity between intellectual cosmology and self which was created by Plato.

Augustine is the primary supporter and essayist of a new inner relationship between God and the soul. He even creates a series of writings, which he calls the *Soliloquies.* Some of them sound remarkably like the *Poimandres,* though they are more self-consciously an internal dialogue, and the narrator is not just a Platonist but also a Christian. Augustine professes ignorance about whether the dialogue is with his own self or with an outside voice. The dialogue of God and the soul is the basic internal dialogue over which the Christian life takes shape. Augustine's is a virtuoso synthesis; he powers his way through the various issues, protected by his powers as a bishop and the growing power of the church to enforce its dictates.

The Social Meaning of Resurrection, Martyrdom, and Asceticism

IMAGES OF THE afterlife—resurrection of the body and the immortality of the soul—had enormous consequences within the thought world of early Christianity. They began by defining pagan as against Christian. But they did so much more: Over time, the symbols mediate gender, identity and gender identity. They help distinguish between those who are willing to endure martyrdom and those who feel avoiding martyrdom is better. They help assess those loyal to establishment virtues and those who will rebel against them. They mediate asceticism of various kinds; if one factors in Judaism, they even mediate asceticism over against sexual fulfillment. They help discuss how much Christians have in common with the other humans on the planet.

Uncoding this language has been been going on for centuries but cracking the social message is largely due to scholarship in the last few decades, captained by such people as Elaine Pagels, John Gager, and Elizabeth Clark.[103] As Caroline Bynum characterizes the scholarship: "This interpretation recognizes that figures such as Augustine and Jerome were profoundly uneasy with the culture of upper-class pagans; nonetheless, it sees them rejecting and inverting worldly distinctions of class and gender only to inscribe another version in an ascetic or ecclesiastical hierarchy on earth that carries over, in its every detail, into heaven."[104]

The work of Caroline Bynum and Peter Brown, in some way, stands over against this synthesis, suggesting that the relationships are too complex for easy or predictable results. Bynum suggests, for example, that although Gregory's solution to the resurrection body problem may have been more satisfactory intellectually, the notion that the body was reassembled, which Augustine among others championed, actually helped the founding of the martyr cults, which were so important to the Middle Ages.[105] The proliferation of the cults depended on the theory that a piece of the martyr's body had the same efficacy as the whole body.

What we have seen throughout the history of the afterlife is that issues like the identity of the self in the afterlife may not be universal symbols but are historically significant because of the history of the terms and events in a specific culture. Once the code is established, social discourse develops. The symbols definitiely have consequences for how the self is construed within this life at a particular time and place. None of the formulations of self in the ancient world, including Jewish, Christian, or, pagan, or even the Church Father's extended discussion would pass modern philosophical criteria for cogency. The importance lies in the ways each of the formulations can be made to carry a social message, which the individual church father was promulgating. To study the conflict is to study a society in dialogue and polemic with itself.

Universalism and
Posthumous Baptism of the Dead

PAUL SAYS CLEARLY: "For we must all appear before the judgment seat of Christ, so that each one may receive good or evil, according to what he has done in the body" (2 Cor 5:10). Such a perception appears to preclude any generations previous to Jesus from achieving salvation. But does it absolutely prevent it?

At Corinth there was a peculiar practice in which people were baptized on behalf of the dead: "Otherwise, what do people mean by being baptized on behalf of the dead? If the dead are not raised at all, why are people baptized on their behalf?" (1 Cor 15:29) Paul mentions them to bolster his argument about resurrection but it is not clear whether he objects to the practice or approves of it. It may easily characterize those whom Paul was attempting to defeat.

This strange passage has been the source of an immense number of differing interpretations.[106] The interpretation that makes best sense of the context is to assume that Paul's statement refers to a vicarious baptism, effecting the salvation of people who died without its benefit while alive. But precisely what the ceremony was or how it was performed is obscure. Equally obscure is whether or not Paul himself was in favor of it. All we know for sure is that the disbelief of some of the Corinthians in the literal resurrection is inconsistent with the Corinthian practice of baptizing on behalf of the dead. The most obvious doctrine which the Corinthian schismatics could have believed in opposition to the resurrection of the dead would have been immortality of the soul. But there is not enough evidence to decide exactly what they believed.[107]

Jeffrey Trumbower has outlined a most interesting and important phenomenon in early Christianity.[108] Christianity, being born from sectarian Judaism, most often assumed that salvation was limited to the borders of its movement. There were three major exceptions to that rule: (1) occasional universalist tendencies, which are seen in Origen, and Gregory of Nyssa, for example, but also in Hosea Ballou, the nineteenth century founder of the Unitarian-Universalist church; (2) the later doctrine of the natural Christian, where some individuals live lives of such probity and sanctity that they are assumed to be naturally Christian and worthy of the rewards of a Christian; and (3) baptism for the dead, mostly those held dear to the first generation of Christian converts. Being the first Christian in the family, the new convert was often anxious to extend the benefits he had earned to his departed loved ones, who had not had the opportunity to assent to Christian conversions.

It is this last category that most interests Trumbower, as it was a major discussion in the Early Church. Although finally forbidden by Augustine, it has made two major contemporary appearances in American society. The first is in nineteenth-century Shaker communities, where members of the community were possessed by Native American spirits. Once summoned the spirits could be baptized and saved.

The second is in Mormonism. The Mormon Church today makes a maximal interpretation of Paul's words and does baptize on behalf of the dead. For instance, some 380,000 Holocaust victims have been baptized by the Mormon Church to save them posthumously with a living Latter Day Saint standing in as proxy, though in cases where family members object, the baptism is reversed. One can appreciate the honor offered but one must also appreciate the very unfriendly reaction of the Jewish Holocaust survivors and other relatives of the deceased.

Trumbower is more interested in the ancient phenomenon. Christian converts wanted naturally to save their departed parents and other relatives and so baptism for the dead became popular in the Early Church. To those familiar with the New Testament, the whole question seems out of place. The parable of the rich man and Lazarus seems to seal the fate of the unbaptized (Luke 16:19–31). This story is meant to illustrate the superior virtue of the poor over the rich, the believers over the Jews, and probably should not be used as an example of Christian views of the afterlife. But once life is over, so is all hope of repentance. It furthermore says that Jews can be expected to remain stubborn even in this life.

But the text of 1 Peter 3:16–4:7 describes a harrowing of hell in which

Christ is able to atone for the spirits, even those in hell. The Gospel was even preached in hell:[109]

> But they will give account to him who is ready to judge the living and the dead. For this is why the gospel was preached even to the dead, that though judged in the flesh like men, they might live in the spirit like God. The end of all things is at hand; therefore keep sane and sober for your prayers. (1 Pet 4:5–7)

This is a very problematic passage. Scholars would like to know who wrote it and what it means. The passage, though unlikely to have been written by Peter, surely gives witness to the notion that Christ can preach to the dead, evidently in the hope of saving them, though exactly which dead—whether the damned or those already saved who are rising to their beatified place at the end of time—is not entirely clear.

In two cases, stories illustrating the problem occur in Christian Apocrypha. In the *Passion of Perpetua and Felicitas,* a third-century Latin work, which we have already looked at briefly, Perpetua writes in her diary in prison of a vision of her brother Dinocrates who died at age seven of a facial tumor. He comes to her in a vision, begging relief from his discomfort, which has followed him into the tomb. Perpetua is able to help, as she later sees him playing, with the tumor gone and drinking comfortably again, which was not possible when he was sick.

So martyrs both reveal the truth of the faith and help the faithful perform the miracle of resurrection on others. Similarly the martyr Thecla was able to save the dead daughter of her recently acquired pagan friend Tryphaena. The resurrection of various sinners in the Christian Apocrypha affords them a further chance at salvation. For instance, Callimachus dies while defiling Drusiana's corpse, but, when raised up by John, he repents his error and becomes a Christian (*Acts John* 73–78).

In the *Ascension of Isaiah,* a Christian work based on an earlier Jewish apocryphon, Isaiah sees Abel, Enoch, and the righteous of previous generations. They are wearing their robes; but they may not sit on their thrones or don their crowns until the arrival of Christ.[110] These are narrative traditions, which aid in the acceptance of the notion that the dead are able to be saved.

But there are documents that explicitly offer salvation generally to the dead. These may include the *Gospel of Nicodemus* and the *Gospel of Peter,* especially 39–42. Origen and Gregory of Nyssa favored the notion that God could not leave any soul unsaved, allowing reincarnation for the purpose of further trial and improvement. Ambrose, Augustine's mentor, was at least expansive in his estimate of who was saved at Christ's descent. Ambrose also posited a "baptism of desire" for the deceased emperor Valentinian II, at his funeral oration in 392. Although Valentinian II had been assassinated (or committed suicide) while still a catechumen, Ambrose assured his funeral audience that his intention to be baptized was sufficient for his salvation.[111]

The doctrine is both attractive and dangerous. Many of the earliest descent traditions indicate that only the righteous of the Old Testament were rescued by Christ, so it is not a blanket offer of amnesty. Around the turn of the third century, for example, Hippolytus and Tertullian manifest the same idea: The purpose of the harrowing of hell was to "preach to the souls of the saints" (meaning "the Patriarchs," Hippolytus, *Antichr.* 26) or "for the purpose of informing the Patriarchs and prophets that he had appeared" (Tertullian, *An.* 55:2).

It was Augustine who finally settled the matter. Throughout his career, Augustine articulated a single view on the righteous before the coming of Christ: Their salvation is in accord with the opportunity of their respective eras. They were natural Christians before the incarnation and hence needed no posthumous salvation since they had lived properly during their lifetime.[112] But the events of Augustine's day made him more strict about the unbaptized, even unbaptized infants, after the incarnation. Aware of the views of Pelagius that unbaptized infants were entitled to some kind of eternal life, Augustine unequivocally declares that all without baptism were condemned as inheritors of Original Sin (*Pecc. Merit.* 1.60).[113]

For Augustine, the harrowing of hell was a fact recorded in Scripture. He interpreted that to be the liberation of the righteous from the bosom of Abraham because that is where the righteous dead, like Lazarus, would go. He also admits that Christ must have rescued some in their sorrows from hell. But he is totally pessimistic about the possibility of posthumous salvation from hell after those events. In the *Enchiridion,* his handbook of theology, Augustine says:

Now in the time intervening between a man's death and the final resurrection, the soul is held in a hidden retreat, enjoying rest or suffering hardship in accordance with what it merited during its life in the body. There is no gainsaying that the souls of the dead find solace from the piety of their friends who are alive, when the sacrifice of the Mediator is offered for the dead or alms are given in the Church. But these means are of profit for those who, when they lived, earned merit whereby such things could be of profit to them . . . It is here, then, that is won all merit or demerit whereby a man's state after this life can either be improved or worstened. But let no one hope to obtain, when he is dead, merit with God which he earlier neglected to acquire. (*Enchir.* 29)[114]

Even this does not stop entirely the practice of baptism for the dead. In the East, Orthodox bishops do not accept Augustine's conclusions. They tend to leave the matter up to God's mercy. In the West, there are some interesting intermediate cases. Gregory prayed for the soul of the Emperor Trajan and was able to get reassurance that his righteousness had been noted in heaven. Hadewijch of Brabant (fl. 1220–1240) may have claimed in her fifth vision that she saved four souls from hell. Catherine of Siena (1347–80) wished that she herself might be condemned to hell if it meant that all the sinners in it could be saved. Marguerite Porete (d. 1310) and Julian of Norwich (1343–ca.1416) each developed a theology that led to universal salvation.

Trumbower relates a story from the conquest of Friseland by Charles the Hammer in 692 from the *Rise of the Dutch Republic* by J. L. Motley. The defeated Frisian chief Radbod was about to accept baptism when he stopped and pondered:

"Where are my dead forefathers at present?" he said, turning suddenly upon Bishop Wolfran.

"In hell, with all other unbelievers," was the imprudent answer.

"Mighty well, replied Radbod, removing his leg [from the baptismal font], "Then will I rather feast with my ancestors in the halls of Woden than dwell with your little starving band of Christians in heaven."[115]

He remained a pagan until his death. A more prudent answer would have saved another soul. The new Catechism of the Catholic Church, Article 1257, provides a way out of Bishop Wolfran's dilemma when it states that: "God has bound salvation to the sacrament of baptism, but He himself is not bound by His sacraments." Furthermore, Article 1261 states:

As regards children who have died without baptism, the church can only entrust them to the mercy of God, as she does in her funeral rites for them. Indeed, the great mercy of God who desires that all men should be saved, and Jesus' tenderness toward children which caused him to say: "Let the children come to me, do not hinder them" (Mark 10:14; cf. 1 Tim 2:4), allow us to hope that there is a way of salvation for children who have died without Baptism. All the more urgent is the Church's call not to prevent little children coming to Christ through the gift of holy Baptism.

Summary

WITH THIS SHORT survey we must leave the fascinating and complicated world of the Church Fathers. The resurrection of the body functioned in the Early Church as it had in Judaism before it—as a consolation and solace to martyrs and their survivors and as the hope of those who remained true to their faith. Christianity differs from other varieties of Hellenistic Judaism at its origin in that it must radically deny immortality of the soul. This is because the immortality of the soul is universal grace, available to all, thus obviating the need of Jesus' suffering and death on the cross.

The *Gospel of Thomas* and Gnostic Christianity affirmed it anyway. In so doing, they were voting for the superiority of vision and *gnōsis* over creeds and statements of faith in the teachings of the apostolic tradition. A person who sought the presence of Jesus in ascetic preparations and visions had little need of the Gospel stories or creeds from the Church hierarchy for the person of Jesus was immediately available through visions. This differing view of the resurrection reflects the "Gnostic" realization that all can be saved provided they seek truth in the correct way, with or without the apostolic sacraments. For their part, "the orthodox" used martyrdom as a test and proof of the truth of their faith as everyone was impressed with the bravery and courage with which Christians went to their deaths.

Intermediary forms, such as Valentinianism, did not deny the authority of the other Christians, only denigrated them as incompletely aware of the power of the dispensation in which they lived. Thus, the Valentinian Christian Gnostics distinguished between levels of salvation. The truly elect realized that a number of issues that the "orthodox" obsessed over were truly *adiaphora,* of no real concern to the elect and enlightened. One could be ascetic or not ascetic; one could believe in the bodily resurrection or the spiritual resurrection; one could affirm or deny martyrdom. But the truly enlightened Christian knew that either way lay salvation if one had achieved *gnōsis.*

The Gnostics had more sophistication intellectually and arguably more universality and more of humanity than the "orthodox" but, by all accounts, the "orthodox" built a more committed populace, more willing to undergo death rather than recant. With it came the sectarian notion that salvation adhered only to the converted, not to anyone outside of the church. Such a notion became even more obvious when Augustine denied the practice of baptism on behalf of the dead. By then, Christianity had achieved a normative role and was no longer sectarian in outlook. It also had to face the issue that as an established religion it needed the respect, as well as the support, of the imperial rulers. To do so, it had to synthesize the pagan notion of the immortal soul with the apocalyptic notion of resurrection of the body. It was Augustine who wedded the two together and sealed both with political power. But before he did, the difference between resurrection and immortality had functioned to distinguish Christian from pagan, Jew from Christian, male from female, philosopher from ordinary Christian, and rich from poor.

14

The Early Rabbis

The Rabbis and Rabbinic Literature

WE TURN FROM the religious leaders who created Christianity to those who created contemporary Judaism. The Rabbinic movement had an entirely different function in Jewish society than the Church Fathers did in Christian society. They did not dispense sacraments nor lead services, they did not write intellectual tractates, they did not run dioceses. They did not even control synagogues. The Rabbis were legal specialists, religious lawyers, dispensers of wisdom, and judges, rather than priests or academic intellectuals. Their training prepared them to be judges; the Jewish legal system depends on panels of judges of various sizes, more like the Napoleonic Code than English common law. Rabbinic authority was based, first of all, on the respect in which they were held as judges—which is to say, on their ability to interpret the law.

The early Rabbis, the Tannaim, went through periods of Roman support and lack of support. Likewise, the progress of Rabbinic authority was slow within Jewish society, as the synagogue had its own local officers, who seem to be highly correlated with the wealth of the community. For instance, the synagogues of Galilee do not immediately seem to follow Rabbinic prescriptions for depicting human likenesses.[1] They often contained mosaic floors with zodiacs with the god Helios clearly depicted in the center, driving his quadriga with four galloping horses. The sun was a necessary part of the annual clock because it tells the zodiacal month, the constellation sign that governed that time period. Lunar months were easy to distinguish by the phase of the moon. But solar months were governed by signs of the zodiac and so the zodiac was just as much astronomy as an astrological system.

As time proceeded, there was a tendency to efface the depiction of Helios as a god and to replace it with another, less idolatrous symbol like a column or a sun with blazing rays.[2] By that time, aniconic Islam was already the government of the area. Exactly what to conclude from this evidence is hard to know. The Rabbis inexorably grew more respected within the Jewish community over the years, and it is reasonable to think that as they grew in power they would have gained some influence over the decoration of the synagogue, especially when renovations were attempted. As leaders of the community, they would have been circumspect about the desires of the land's overlords too.

Although the Rabbis were legal specialists, they had keen theological interests, which they evinced in their Scriptural exegesis and also in their legal opinions. They did not write theological treatises but incorporated ethical and theological issues into their legal writings. As a result, many readers mistake the nature of Rabbinic literature: They think Rabbinic literature has a very legalistic theology when they should be appreciating the amount of theological discourse that appears in Jewish law.

The Mishnah is a rational code, resembling Roman law. As the Jews moved out of the inhospitable Christian Roman Empire, they moved more and more into considerably more tolerant Zoroastrian Persia. There, they found a religion that was similarly attuned to ritual and which was similarly interested in the moral actions of its adherents. It is no surprise then that the religious literature of the period, the Gemarah, has many similarities to the *Videvdat* and other Zoroastrian legal commentaries.

The Difficulty in Isolating Rabbinic Theology

GIVEN THAT IT is a legal literature, organized on legal lines, it is very difficult to isolate issues like Rabbinic views of the afterlife. There are a number of modern anthologies of Rabbinic thought but to use them, one must understand the modern organizing principles of the editors. For instance, the very helpful anthology of Rabbinic thought translated into English, put together by C. G. Montefiore and H. Loewe, betrays the modern Jewish impatience with traditional Jewish notions of the afterlife:

> I propose now to close this anthology with some quotations concerning the Rabbinic views about the life beyond the grave. These extracts

will not be very numerous because the Rabbis knew no more about the future than we, they thought about it in terms and conceptions most which have become obsolete and remote for us today, and so their ideas are of small interest or profit.[3]

Inherent in this statement is a modern liberal Jewish notion that the Rabbis did not have much to say about the afterlife and that afterlife was not very central to their thinking; nor should it be to ours. Judaism in the modern period has naturally gravitated toward rational discourse over against Christianity's emphasis on mystery, this-worldly ethics over promises of salvation. Indeed, compared to Christianity, Montefiore and Loewe are right on the mark: In terms of the quantity of Rabbinic writings, very little of the explicitly legal material does deal with the afterlife. Why would it? There is no need to discuss law in the afterlife.

On top of that, unlike Christianity's interest in theological debate, the Rabbis do not write systematic philosophical discourse. Their method is to compare legal rulings to try to discover legal principles. Each Rabbi attempts to find the principle that best describes the body of tradition. Thus, the Midrashic or Rabbinic exegesis and lore contain a bewildering variety of different views. In like fashion, each Rabbi was free to use his imagination when it came to the afterlife and so we see short discussions of the afterlife within their exegeses of text, with little attempt to formulate a conceptually uniform perspective. This makes studying any theological idea in Rabbinic literature difficult, and partly explains the palpable apologetic tone to Montefiore and Loewe's essay on the subject. Nevertheless, their rather long anthology, as well as those equally long studies by Cohen and Urbach, are useful in finding one's bearings in this sea of interpretations.[4]

The collection shows us that Jewish notions of the afterlife were at the very least fitted to the period in which they were created and spoke to the interests of the people who listened to the Rabbis' interpretations and homilies. To understand how, one has to think of the religious crisis of first-century Judaism, following hard on the Roman pacification of Judea. The destruction of the Jewish homeland—the First Revolt resulting in the destruction of the Second Temple (70 CE) then the Second Revolt against Rome (135 CE) resulting in the complete economic destruction of the homeland—were also spiritual crises that demanded a theological answer.

The Rabbinic community's first reactions seem less satisfying: if, where, and how to blow the shofar after the demise of the Temple?[5] Since the shofar was originally blown from the walls of the Temple, inherent in this question is how Judaism should adapt to life without a Temple. These were not the grand questions that other Israelites, with access directly to divine revelation, faced. But they were questions that the Pharisees could answer authoritatively. From them came the precedents for Jewish self-government after the destruction of the state. In the process, the Pharisees were transformed into a new group, the Rabbinic class.

The Rabbis face theology obliquely. Their core beliefs are discoverable in their legal reasoning and in the immense body of folklore that they have recorded. We shall see that they believe in a world to come, resurrection of the dead, Messianic deliverance, divine recompense for corporate and individual deeds, the efficacy of repentance, all of which characterize the covenant between themselves and God.[6] But they designed new ways to express their doctrines, which were tailored to their political position and the social position of Jews in the wider world.

Consequently, the Rabbis have left us with an immense body of literature. Some is largely legal and even systematic, like the *Mishnah*. But most documents, like the commentary to the *Mishnah* called the *Gemarah*, which together with the *Mishnah* form the *Talmud*, are more freewheeling and discursive. Still other kinds of documents, like Midrash (a genre of verse-by-verse, Bible exegesis) are extraordinarily varied. We cannot fully explore all this literature, which comes from vastly different places and time periods, with few datable details. We shall take a close look at a few very important passages and take a brief, longer look at the vast variety of literature which surrounds it, together with at least a glance at liturgy (which was prepared by the Rabbis) and mystical literature.[7]

Rabbinic Humor

RABBINIC HUMOR is one of the most unexpected aspects of entering this strange world—so unexpected, in fact, that many people just miss it entirely. One joke that has to do with resurrection is hard to miss. It serves as a caveat against being too zealous in the commandment to celebrate the feast of Purim. There was also a custom of parodying Rabbinic exegesis on the holiday, which became known as "Purim Torah," Rabbinic satire.

Evidently, the Rabbis needed a special commandment to celebrate the holiday; the rule is to drink until one cannot tell the difference between "Blessed be Mordechai" and "Cursed be Haman." For the Rabbis, whose job it was to make very fine distinctions, this meant drinking quite a lot. The following story serves as a cautionary tale against too much celebration, through an early example of "Purim Torah":

Rabba and R. Zera joined together for a Purim feast. They became mellow and Rabba arose and cut R. Zera's throat. On the next day, he prayed on his behalf and revived him from the dead. Next year he said: "Will your honour come and we will have Purim feast together? He replied: "A miracle does not take place on every occasion." [In other words, "I respectfully decline your kind invitation. I can't count on a miracle happening every year."] (*b. Meg.* 7b)

Not only does this illustrate the Rabbinic *sang froid* in discussing resurrection, it illustrates some of the properties of humor that, unfortunately, we will need to analyze, which will spoil the humor. There are multiple ironies in this passage. The first irony is that intended by the teller of the joke itself: that the sadder but wiser Rabbi Zera refuses the invitation of Rabba because he fears for his life, despite Rabba's best intentions. The second irony is an inadvertent one, the euphemism "mellow" understood at the expense of the translator, whose work is evident. Nothing is so tedious as humor explained; unfortunately, in order to get at the Rabbinic notion of resurrection and life after death we will need to locate the source of subtle ironies, finding textual evidence for the intention of the Rabbis. This is not always easy. In this case, however, we can be sure that the original issue in the text is "drunkenness" not "mellowness." The Rabbis were not talking about marijuana intoxication. That was added by the translator inadvertently.

The Mishnah

THE EARLIEST identifiable book of Rabbinic Judaism is the Mishnah, a compendium of law largely from the enactments of a group of Rabbis we know as the Tannaim, whose activity ends at the beginning of the third century CE. It is a communal book of law, with multiple authorship, recording the many discussions of the earlier Rabbis, redacted by Judah the Prince around the year 220 CE, when the Tannaitic enterprise ends and a new age, the Amoraic or Talmudic period of commentary, begins. It is based on the Israelite law of the First Temple period 922–587 BCE and second Temple Period (515 BCE–70 CE) and includes many subsequent developments in legal discussion. Although it is a systematic legal code and legal commentary, tailored by the Patriarch Judah the Prince from a variety of earlier Mishnahs, individual traditions in them are notoriously difficult to date.

Rabbi (that is how Rabbi Judah the Prince is known in the Mishnah) kept careful control on what the Mishnah contains. He kept out all angelology, and most Messianism, and most discussion of resurrection and life after death (with one notable exception).[8] Since Rabbi Judah the Prince's Mishnah is the basis of the Talmud, and is a very rationally organized work of law with little attention to such issues as resurrection or life after death, the Talmuds are in turn mostly lacking a systematic theological discussion of the issue. It is easy to see how, in modern times, many Jews wrongly believe that afterlife issues are not properly part of Judaism. Even the magisterial compendium of Ephraim E. Urbach, *The Sages*,[9] contains no subject heading for resurrection or immortality of the soul, though the subject is touched on in the chapters on "Reward and Punishment" and "Redemption," which deal mostly with Messianism. Such is the Rabbinic ranking of these issues in the minds of modern experts.

Rabbi Judah the Prince's editing was the last systematic organization of Rabbinic material until the *"stam"* (the "just" or "only" or "nameless"), the unattributed voice who appears to organize the *Gemarahs,* more than four centuries later. In the meantime, the material had grown enormous by gloss and commentary so that all sorts of topics appear by association with topics where one would never expect them. The *Gemarah* to each *Mishnah,* the records of the commentary offered by the Palestinian and the Babylonian sages, was organized around the text of the Mishnah in a line-for-line commentary. Each of these became a *Talmud,* the Babylonian Talmud and the Palestinian Talmud. The former was the most authoritative because the Jews lived in greater security and affluence in Babylonia under Persian rule than in the intolerant Christian Roman Empire.

Two Talmuds exist because there was not enough central authority in Jewish life to unify the material into a single book like the *Mishnah.* There may not have been any desire to organize the Talmudic material either. Certainly, any editorial activity as stringent as Rabbi Judah the Prince's during the Amoraic period would have drastically reduced the creative energy inherent in the literature. As it is, part of the excitement of reading Talmud is to see the Rabbis grasping at legal analogies from other parts of the law and even analogizing from custom and ceremonies in the community to clarify a difficulty in legal interpretation. As a result, Jewish law and particularly Jewish lore contain a vast variety of sometimes seemingly contradictory material.[10]

Rabbinic tradition was written by the people the New Testament regarded as opponents. To read Rabbinic literature with any understanding, one has to be able to take the New Testament's judgment as a mark of the Pharisees' social and historical position, not as a judgment on their intentions. It will be useful to specify the kinds of issues the Rabbis usually deal with before getting into their discussion of life after death, which is an unusual subject for them to discuss in the abstract.

Here, for example, is a Tannaitic discussion of procedure at an execution, which touches on the issue of life after death:

> Mishnah: When he is about ten cubits away from the place of stoning, they say to him, "Confess," for such is the practice of all who are executed, that they [first] confess, for he who confesses has a portion in the world to come. . . .
>
> And if he knows not what to confess, they instruct him, say, "May my death be an expiation for all my sins." R. Judah said: if he knows that he is a victim of false evidence, he can say: "May my death be an expiation for all my sins but this." They [the sages] said to him: If so, everyone will speak likewise in order to clear himself. (M. *Sanh.* quoted from *b. Sanh.* 43b)

Here is an example of the Mishnah dealing with a more atypical subject. They are specifying how an execution should take place. They affirm that the confession of a person convicted of a capital crime is enough to assure his entrance into the life to come.

From a historical perspective, this scene is problematic. It is dubious that the Rabbis who produced the Mishnah in 220 CE had ever seen a Rabbinic execution or would ever get the chance to organize one, as the powers of the state had been firmly in the hands of the Romans for two centuries. This merely begs the question: From where do these traditions come? Did the Romans cede them power in religious cases, otherwise unattested? Are the Rabbis deliberating on traditions that have been passed down for two centuries, even though they have not been practiced? If so, and in spite of their very considerable powers of accurate transmission, do we have accurate information about Second Temple procedures for execution? If that is so, why do these traditions differ so much from stories in the New Testament, as in the martyrdom of Stephen?

We learn an important fact from this passage, one that certainly was important to the Tannaim after the destruction of the Temple—namely, that a person's own death can be thought of as expiation for sin. This is an especially important topic for the Rabbinate after the Second Temple's destruction. The Temple was the location of a sacrificial cult, one of whose purposes was to atone for the sins of the people with God, when adequate and just compensation had been made. After the destruction of the Temple, the Rabbis had to answer the question: "How may the sins of Israel be atoned, now that the Temple is in ruins?"

Many answers developed; one approach even comes from this passage concerning the final confession of a condemned criminal. If it is possible for sins to be forgiven in the case of a great sinner, the convicted perpetrator of a capital crime, should not an ordinary death with the correct and timely repentance itself be an expiation for each Israelite, whose sins are much less than a capital criminal? This logic only underlines the extent to which the concept of "vicarious atonement" was part of the thinking of the Jewish people while the Temple stood and sacrifices were offered daily.

Similar traditions also suggest that prayer, confession, and deeds of loving kindness have the same effect in atoning for Israel's collective sins. In the end, this notion will yield the multicultural assertion that we are all martyrs because we all die and the righteous of all nations will receive a place in the world to come. That notion can be seen developing in the Rabbinic texts.[11]

Mishnah Sanhedrin 10

THE TANNAITIC notion of life after death is discussed extensively only in Mishnah tractate Sanhedrin in chapter 10, where the Rabbis face directly the issue of what awaits after death. One should not expect the same kind of organized philosophical treatise as in the Church Fathers. The Mishnah is the result of a communal discussion about law and procedure, more a legal document than a theological one. It is a theoretical discussion taking place between Rabbis of different generations, whose opinions are compared one to another, in order to come up with a consistent practice. Here they seem to discuss both what will happen to individuals after death and to Israel at the end-time:

Mishnah 1: All Israelites have a share in the world to come, for it is written, "Thy people also shall be all righteous, they shall inherit the land for ever; the branch of my planting, the work of my hands that I may be glorified" (Isa 60:21). And these are they that have no share in the world to come: he that says that there is no resurrection of the dead prescribed in the Torah, and [he that says] that the Torah is not from Heaven, and an Epicurean. R. Akiba says: Also he that reads the books of the "outsiders," or that utters charms over a wound and says, *I will put none of the diseases upon thee which I have put upon the Egyptians; for I am the Lord that heals you.* (Exod 15:28) Abba Saul says: also he that pronounces the Name with it proper letters.

If the Tannaim counted the Pharisees as their forebears they still developed their own Rabbinic thought in amazingly different ways. For instance, Josephus recounts that the Pharisees thought that the souls of the good alone went to another body. This could be an explicit exegesis of Daniel 12: "And many of those who sleep in the dust of the earth shall awake, some to everlasting life, and some to shame and everlasting contempt" (Dan 12:2).

But not Sanhedrin 10 Mishnah 1. It is quite different. Rather it states that "all Israel will be righteous, they will have a share in the world to come, and they will all live in the land of Israel forever," not merely the members of the Pharisaic sect or the Tannaim. This is an important difference. Until now resurrection was a reward given only to the the members of the sect or the martyrs or the elected ones, which always followed some sectarian, denominational, or philosophical lines. Daniel only promised resurrection to "some" and suggested that most people will simply die.

The reward itself is not well described. All Israel will return to the land but is it an ideal land on this earth, or a reconstituted earth, or is it a heavenly Israel? Will death disappear? It is a Zionist hope but it is also idealized. Because the passage says "forever," one might assume that death will disappear. The subsequent discussion clarifies that the reconstituted Israel will include all those long dead, as it discusses a number of primeval personages including dead kings of Judah and Israel. It is certainly not like any of the visions of resurrection that we saw in the Jewish or Christian apocrypha or the apocalyptic literature.

This doctrine also differs from immortality of the soul. Immortality of the soul is available to all as a natural right, not a privilege for a few, no matter how widely defined. With immortality of the soul, one would not expect discussion of the land. Practically, the goals inherent in the immortality of the soul, that the soul has rest from earthly trouble, is available most easily to the philosophers, people who are able to pursue philosophical studies and cleanse their souls of material impurities. To do this, one needs a good education, which means ascetic living or inherited wealth. Immortality of the soul is an entitlement. In the philosophical schools, learning how to care for the soul is what ensured the soul's permanent felicity.

Neither Judaism nor Christianity wanted to promulgate that aristocratic view of salvation. In fact, we shall see that the Tannaitic conception is neither the one (resurrection of the body) nor the other (immortality of the soul) but an innovation that allows for Israel's ultimate felicity and good ethical practice on earth. Prophecy is cited but it is not the prophecy itself which is the basis of the doctrine. Rather, it is the way the prophecy is exegeted: What allows for Israel's felicity is the exegesis of Isaiah 60–66. It is part of the exegetical skills of the Rabbis that they can balance these new issues in the culture and yet derive it all from a credible and holy source so that it has cultural credibility.

Isaiah 60–66 has already surfaced in discussions of the afterlife but it has never been used in this way, without any reference to the evils which may befall those who are not included. Instead, the Rabbis envision a future that applies to everyone in Israel. This is also the reason that Daniel 12 is not quoted in the Mishnah; Daniel 12 is the only place where resurrection is clearly promised in the Hebrew Bible and it promises a very different, more sectarian kind of end-of-days, where only the members of the sect will receive resurrection, and maybe only some of them. So the Tannaim look for other proof-texts. Instead, they take Isaiah 60 as their primary text, which talks not about afterlife but about inheriting the land forever.

Even that was a wildly fantastic notion, given their current state. So they do not take the passage to refer to this world, rather the world to come, the 'olam haba' ('olām habbā'). They will reclaim their land forever. This may be an early Zionist sentiment. But it is not political Zionism. It is translated to the afterlife. Evidently, the Rabbis felt that all Israel would receive the gift of the land in the resurrection, in contradiction with the various sectarians traditions, which they must have known very well. There is no explanation for this new, more universal understanding of resurrection. Perhaps they felt that Israel had itself experienced a martyrdom in the tribulations it had undergone in the Roman Wars. Perhaps it was chauvinism, a privilege for its unique prophetic rank in the world. Perhaps it was merely a dream to recover the lost homeland. But, for whatever reason, they believed that the whole of Israel would receive the gift of the land of Israel in the resurrection. They claimed that the disasters that overtook Israel, in particular the destruction of the Second Temple, were due to "senseless hatreds." They were evidently setting out to make sure that no more senseless hatreds divide the nation further, bringing further catastophes upon them. They gave up the first century sectarian notion that divine justice adheres only to one's sectarian brothers and suggest that God's promises are now "catholic" for Israel.

Furthermore, the quotation from Isaiah 60:21, which surely was not about eternal life or resurrection in its original context, suggests that, for the purposes of this part of the Tannaitic discussion, "the world to come" may mean something as simple as all Israel, those alive and deceased, living eternally on this earth as masters of Israel's own land. The inflow of the exiles from all parts of the Roman Empire, whence they had been removed as slaves, was part of their idealized view of the future. The difference between this existence and the idealized one is that Israel will again be gathered together in its own land and master of its own territory.

Daniel 12 can be understood to mean that judgment will follow for some but not all humans who have ever lived. The specific identification of those groups occupies a significant part of the following Rabbinic discussion. In other words, in spite of the fact that they use a quotation from Isaiah 60, which expresses their particular view of what wholeness for the people Israel would entail, the entire organization of this discussion is based on categories of the afterlife which are implicit in Daniel 12, without actually quoting it. Everyone engaged in the discussion knows that the basic doctrine is outlined in Daniel 12 and the categories adduced—resurrected for reward, resurrected for punishment, and the great "in-between" those neither resurrected nor punished nor given further rewards. These are the logical categories derivable from Daniel 12 in Scripture and from nowhere else.

The Rabbis quickly turn to the legal connotations of the discussion, and not necessarily the most obvious one—namely, who is to be excluded from this promise? They indulge in what can only be their private ironic humor: "Those who do not believe in the world to come from the Torah are destined not to get it." This is not a surprise because a similar ruling has appeared in a number of communities. The Tannaim state that one must believe in the doctrine which they call, literally, the "vivication of the dead, tehiat ha-metim" and—this is the crucial issue to occupy the Amoraim commentators starting in 220 CE—that one must believe that the vivication of the dead is present in the Torah itself. By this, they mean that the doctrine must be derivable from the first five books of the Torah. But we know from long analysis that there are no very obvious demonstrations of beatific afterlife in Torah.

Even the phrase's literal meaning, the "vivication of the dead" (tehiat ha-metim), does not come from the first five books of Torah, and not from Daniel 12, but from the source of some of Daniel's images in Isaiah 26:19:

Thy dead shall live, their bodies [literally, corpses] shall rise.
O dwellers in the dust, awake and sing for joy!
For thy dew is a dew of light,
and on the land of the shades thou wilt let it fall.

We come suddenly on what will be the technical term for "resurrection" amongst the Rabbis from this passage in Isaiah. But note that Isaiah's description is not exactly the Rabbinic concept because the Rabbis deliberately pick the "vivication of the dead" *(teḥiat hametim)*, not the "raising of corpses" (a hypothetical *tequmat hanevelot*), just as explicitly mentioned in this very place in Isaiah 26:19. They ignore the term "corpses" and instead use the first clause, which contains much less definite terms. They are not actually interested in defining the afterlife with the notion of the resurrection of the fleshly body. Like their description of the "endtime," they would rather describe something a bit more ambiguously, not specifying exactly how God plans to bring the final consummation.

This observation helps resolve the paradox that we noted in the discussion of Josephus' description of the Pharisees in chapter 9, "Sectarian Life." If the Pharisees are best able to govern the remaining state of Judah after the war and share power before the war, then why should they believe in resurrection of the flesh, which is characteristic of the sectarian life of Judea? The answer to that vexing question is that they do not necessarily believe in resurrection of the dead corpses (with Isaiah), and certainly do not believe in anything like the Gospels' view of the matter. On the other hand, they cannot risk overtly contradicting Isaiah either, instead exegeting Isaiah in such a way that Isaiah seems to say what they have in mind. They build a paradise based on the land of Israel, which the living and dead share. They are content with an ambiguity whose resolution dominates Christian thinking for four centuries and maybe for all time. The contrast could not be more obvious.

The Rabbis certainly believe that God will do what He wills; but they are not tailoring their doctrine to explain martyrdom.[12] Rather they want a more general doctrine. To the Rabbis as to the Christians, human life is sacred. But Rabbinic policy is not to encourage martyrdom, indeed one might violate many commandments, including the food laws, to avoid martyrdom. The commandments one should not commit are murder, incest, adultery, blasphemy, apostasy, or idolatry (*b. Sanh.* 74a). According to this ruling, neither Eleazar, nor the woman and her seven sons, needed to endure martyrdom. But the issue is moot because they also judge that no law can be broken as a sign of apostasy. One is to undergo martyrdom rather than apostatize.

The general rule is: Breaking food laws is preferrable to martyrdom. But there are cases where martyrdom cannot be avoided. Death should be accepted as necessary and inevitable in that case. When necessary, one should die *'al qiddush ha-shem,* "for the sanctification of God's name," which is explicitly the technical Rabbinic vocabulary for martyrdom and refers to reciting the Shema (Deut 6:4) prayer at death. A person who does so is called a *Qadosh,* a "holy one," (even "a saint") just as the angels are called. Martyrdom was closely associated with human transmogrification into angels. But, to the Rabbis, martyrdom should be avoided, if possible.

The deliberate ambiguity in the definition of the afterlife and the lack of enthusiasm for martyrdom are connected. The Rabbis do not seem to care much whether resurrection is as literal, fleshly body, or as a perfected, spiritual body. Evidently, they believed that the nature of the resurrection was for God to define. Their job was to try to figure out his ethical will before that. While they concede the necessity of martyrdom, they do not see it as an earthly good, rather an ordeal that is sometimes unavoidable. The greater skepticism about resurrection and the lack of enthusiasm for martyrdom are structurally related.

This may explain why the most famous ex-Pharisee of the Western world—namely, Paul—did not believe in fleshly resurrection either. He believed that God would bring the consummation about as He wills and that the "resurrection body" is a "spiritual entity," a body but not a corruptible body. Perhaps Paul was again an accurate witness to the state of Rabbinic thinking in his own century.[13] We can translate *tehiat ha-metim* as "vivication of the dead," even "resurrection of the dead," but not "resurrection of the flesh."

This perception goes a long way towards answering our sociological quandary in reading Josephus: Why should the Pharisees, who sometimes share the reins of government, propound a doctrine that was characteristic of only the most extreme sectarians? The answer is that they do not; they do not tie themselves down to the specificity of the millenarian position. They pick a term and a pastoral vision of the end that is deliberately ambiguous. Like Paul, resurrection of the body for the Rabbis might not mean the fleshly body, at least in its corpselike form, but the "metamorphosis" or more properly a *"summorphosis"* of the corporeal body into a heavenly and spiritual body—like the angels, a sexually resolved and completed body. They do not pretend to know exactly what God has in mind for His faithful. It could be like the angelomorphism of the sectarians and Christians. But it was not necessarily a transformation of the martyr only. All Israel qualified for the reward. And, if necessary, it might be describable in a variety of other ways.

What Happened to the Villains of Yore?

WHAT OCCUPIES the Tannaim's attention next is the Biblical basis for the doctrine, not what the phrase means. They are expert exegetes, and they want to know what Scripture says. In the Mishnah—what is often quintessentially held up as a literature of casuistry, a literature that discusses subtly what right and wrong are and what the various punishments are for infractions against justice—there is no major discussion of which heinous crimes cause Israelites to be permanently stricken from the rolls of those who will be resurrected. A few general issues are mentioned: denying that the Torah is revelation from heaven, healing by incantation, pronouncing the name of God, becoming an Epicurean (a philosopher who denied divine providence), possibly reading heretical books (the Gospels?). The list is neither long nor involved. Instead, it looks like it was intended to be broadly inclusive and only later suffered a few last-minute qualifications.

Rather, the passage begins to describe those Biblical villains, Israelites or not (Balaam), who will not be resurrected or who will not be judged:

Mishnah 2: Three kings and four commoners have no share in the world to come. The three kings are Jeroboam and Ahab and Manasseh. R. Judah says: Manasseh has a share in the world to come, for it is written, *And he prayed unto him, and he was entreated of him and heard his supplication and brought him again to Jerusalem into his kingdom* (2 Chr 33:13). They said to him: He brought him again to his kindgom, but he did not bring him to the life of the world to come. The four commoners are Balaam and Doeg and Ahitophel and Gehazi.

The first question which appears to occupy the Mishnah is whether *all* Israelites are really entitled to life in the world to come. The Mishnah takes the position that *not quite all Israelites* will inherit the world to come. But it wants to know who will be left out. It picks what are clearly meant to be the most heinous of all Israelite sinners in the Bible and asks whether they have a share. The answer is "no"—except for Manasseh, about whom there is the slightest sliver of evidence that he repented: Second Chronicles is interpreted to mean that he prayed for forgiveness and so was forgiven, although the reading is certainly farfetched from our point of view. From this we learn two things: There *are* some Israelites who are so evil that they are denied a place in the world to come. Also we learn that "a moment's repentance can annul the decree," even for the most vicious of all sinners of all time. The presence of Balaam also implicitly raises the logical question that, although he is to be left out of the life to come because of his personal sins, perhaps the other gentiles can be saved. This topic is not systematically discussed here, though it will be later:

Mishnah 3: The generation of the Flood have no share in the world to come, nor shall they stand in the judgment, for it is written, *My spirit shall not judge with man for ever* (Gen 6:3). [Thus they have] neither judgment nor spirit. The generation of the dispersion have no share in the world to come, for it is written, *So the Lord scattered them abroad from thence upon the face of all the earth* (Gen 11:8); so the Lord scattered them abroad—in this world; *and the Lord then scattered them from thence*—in the world to come. The men of Sodom have no share in the world to come, for it is written, *Now the men of Sodom were wicked and sinners against the Lord exceedingly;* wicked in this world, *and sinners* in the world to come. But they shall stand in the judgment. R. Nehemiah says: Neither of them shall stand in the judgement, for it is written: *Therefore the wicked shall not stand in the judgment nor sinners in the congregation of the righteous* (Ps 1:8). *Therefore the wicked shall not stand in the judgment*—this is the generation of the flood; *nor sinners in the congregation of the righteous*—these are the men of Sodom. They said to him: They shall not stand in the congregation of the righteous, but they shall stand in the congregation of the ungodly. The spies have no share in the world to come, for it is written, *Even those men that did bring up an evil report of the land died by the plague before the Lord* (Num 14) *died*—in this world; *by the plague*—in the world to come. The generation of the wilderness have no share in the world to come nor shall they stand in the judgment, for it is written, *In this wilderness they shall be consumed and there they shall die* (Num 14:35). So R. Akiba. But R. Eliezer says: It says of them also, *Gather my saints together unto me, those that have made a covenant with me by sacrifice* (Ps. 50:5). The company of Korah shall not rise up again, for it is written, *And the earth closed upon them* in this world, *and they perished from among the assembly,* in the world to come. So R. Akiba. But R. Eliezer says: It says of them also, *The Lord kills and makes alive, he brings down to Sheol and brings up* (1 Sam 2:6). The

Ten Tribes shall not return again, for it is written, *And he cast them into another land like this day.* Like as this day goes and returns not, so do they go and return not. So R. Akiba. But R. Eliezer says: Like as the day grows dark and then grows light so also after darkness is fallen upon the Ten Tribes shall light hereafter shine upon them.

Readers who have never before encountered Rabbinic discussion may have trouble at first with the connections and the arguments among the discussants even in this basic Mishnaic passage. Various Tannaim often disagree with each other, and the disagreements are in some way created by the texts themselves, since the Rabbis may come from different places and different times. The Mishnah is organized on a principle of the subject matter of various laws, not as a commentary on the Bible. There are editorial principles and techniques of memorization operating behind the surface of the text. These principles are complex and have not been well defined yet but they are present, even in this rather simple text.

Mishnah, however, indulges in scriptural exegesis fast and furiously in this particular text. The Mishnah tries to define who will be raised and who not; who will be judged and who not. It discusses whether the "Ten Lost Tribes" are to be included in the ideal future. This is interesting because they are possibly understood as quasi-idolators. Possibly the Rabbis are recording a veiled discussion about very acculturated, "back-sliding" Jews in the diaspora.

But one sees that new categories are being adduced to judge these Biblical villains: "Will they stand in judgment?" and "Will they be resurrected?" The categories just appear, though Rabbi Nehemiah is named as someone who used them. But where do the categories come from? The categories come from Daniel 12. Daniel 12 defines both the resurrection and the judgment. Even though Daniel 12 is the backbone of the passage, it is not actually stated because it assumes a more sectarian position than the Rabbis want to propound.

As utilized here, the sectarian nature of the categories in Daniel 12 is actually deconstructed, removed from its sectarian context and placed in a new, more catholic Isaianic context. After receiving some examples of which Biblical personages are saved and which condemned, the reader learns something that is never stated—namely, that repentance annuls the heavenly decree against any person. That perception is never found in Daniel, where the saved and the damned are predestined to their deserts.

The topic of discussion switches to various Biblical non-Israelites and how they will fare in the last judgment. The precedents are not good.

Certainly the great sinners of the generation of the flood are lost, and they will not even be resurrected in time of judgment. (The discussion parallels the Church Fathers on the same issue, though Christ is sometimes seen to save some of the generation of the flood.) In this case, the well-documented sinning of the generation of the flood (ḥamas) condemns them.

Everyone taking part in the discussions already knows all the relevant Biblical quotations. So the Rabbis only need to discover the best arguments for discovering the truth. The repetitions in Scripture are used to show that they will neither live in this world nor be resurrected in the world to come. The principle that the Bible provides us with guidance is taken quite literally. All the precedents for the argument depend on Biblical quotations, interpreted by various Rabbis.

The Rabbis can disagree. For instance, with regard to the generation of Sodom, some Rabbis think that they will be resurrected for judgment but not attain the world to come. But R. Nehemiah finds the right combination of Scriptural passages to show that this is not possible. As with the previous question, the Rabbis are not just using their considerable expertise to answer questions about the final disposition of Biblical characters but are trying out some theories about how divine justice is dispensed. As with many Tannaitic discussions, and not a few Amoraic ones, the principles themselves are left wholly or partly unarticulated. They are left for the student of the literature to adduce from study.

The Rabbis are truly more generous to Israelite sinners than they are to the primeval ones. This is largely because their basic question is whether all Israelites will be saved. That is the basic sociological group to whom they must interpret the Bible. That the generation of the wilderness, who were Israelites, will not receive the benefits of the world to come is proposed. But R. Eliezer again finds a precedent for saying that even though they sinned, they will be part of the world to come, showing that God has mercy even on the stiff-necked and rebellious generation of Moses.

The same is true of the followers of Korah, who rebelled against Moses and were swallowed by the earth. There are certainly grounds for thinking them condemned. Yet again, the final word appears to be that God has spared them. The scriptural grounds for this conclusion may seem forced. And it is never wholly clear to modern readers whether the Rabbis are seriously discussing these issues or using them as examples for their very finely honed talents—tours de force for their own mutual appreciation and demonstration of their greatly rarefied talents. But, no matter how much legal virtuousity is contained in these writings, the conclusions are serious, because they demonstrate that God desires contrition; when He sees it, He forgives even heinous crimes. Yet a certain degree of freedom with the text is already evident, a freedom that undoes the original intention of the Biblical passages, which was certainly to report a terrible death by earthquake of the party of Koraḥ. One begins to appreciate the exegetical acumen of the Rabbis as much as their discussions. They are challenged to find Scriptural passages which will save ancient sinners from destruction. A certain suspense results from this process, once the reader figures out what is happening.

Another question, which might be answered here but apparently is not, is how punishment will be carried out in the world to come. There is no mention of hell for malefactors or permanent punishment of any sort. Indeed, Rabbinic Judaism is extremely reticent to discuss hell—as if the benevolence of the eternal God would not allow most souls to be permanently condemned. Only in later Jewish folklore do we find any concept of a hell.

Different approaches have been attempted to understand the relationship between the last judgment and individual reward and punishment. This section may be assuming that ordinary sins are punished in this world, as is certainly the case in the Hebrew Bible, and is frequently assumed in Rabbinic Judaism. At the very least, one might assume that a person's death would atone for sins.

The Gemarah's Commentary

THE RABBINIC discussion of the afterlife becomes even more interesting when the later Babylonian Gemarah (third to seventh century CE) is added to this interesting third-century Mishnah. This discussion largely takes place under the influence of Zoroastrianism and so a whole new, more literal notion of resurrection can be discussed without embarrassment. The same is just as true after the Arab conquest.[14] The Babylonian Talmud's discussion of this Mishnah begins on folio page 90a, with the quotation of the Mishnah.

The first question which the Gemarah asks is: "Why does the Mishnah rule with such severity?" As becomes clear, the first serious issue is the Tannaim's little ironic joke: "Those who deny that the vivification of the dead comes from the Torah will not get it." The Amoraim, the Rabbis in the Gemarah, ask why the Mishnah insists that the punishment for those denying life after death is not to receive it; it seems like such a great punishment for such a small infraction.

This first stubborn question, however, is quickly answered by reference to equity or "measure for measure," a well-known Rabbinic dictum explaining God's actions. The answer is explicitly that denying the world to come is the appropriate and equable punishment for someone who denies life after death, even though it seems harsh. Anyone who recants the "heresy" is admitted. It is interesting that the Rabbis are puzzled by a punishment that stands merely on a belief, not an action; while it is precisely belief that makes for salvation or damnation in Christianity, for instance. The question is more interesting and revealing than the answer, which satisfies the Rabbis.

What Is the Verse?

AFTER THIS, the Gemarah raises the issue that will dominate its discussion of life after death: How is resurrection derived from the Torah? Now, the Amoraim are expressly using the term "Torah" to refer only to the first five books of Moses, as is clear from the subsequent discussion. Since we know from historical analysis that the first sure reference to life after death is in the book of Daniel and that even the first hints of it are as late as the prophets, it seems a hopeless task to derive it from the the Mosaic Torah. But the issue is not history; it is hermeneutics. The Rabbis did not know of modern historical criticism; they wanted to see for themselves what could be said on the matter. They threw down a challenge to themselves, and they each tried to answer the challenge with the appropriate passage. The challenge creates the same kind of suspense that letting the previous Biblical generations off the hook did, except here they are trying to do the impossible.

Being absolute masters of the text of the Bible from their youths, they are clearly aware of the difficulty for their exegetical skills. The first candidate to answer the challenge is Numbers 18:28: "And you shall give the Lord's heave offering to Aaron the priest." Since Aaron died, this commandment now seems to to be falsified. But the Rabbis are pointing out that the commandment contains no time limitation so Aaron must be still "alive." From Aaron's resurrection we learn that we will be resurrected. But is it an adequate proof?

Immediately, the school of Rabbi Ishmael, who are credited with the rather modern notion that "the language of Torah is human language," suggest what most modern interpreters would think first: perhaps the "to Aaron," really means "to one like Aaron," namely, to Aaron's priestly descendants in the Aaronide line. The effect of this discussion was to bring the passage into question as the proof of life after death.

This is quite an astonishing moment. It is the first time within a community accepting resurrection as a religious doctrine that we actually see an argument about whether the belief in resurrection is true at all. To be sure it was debated within the Jewish community in the first century. And the Christians debated the nature of the resurrection. But, here, in the third century or later, the very scriptural demonstration of the belief was still under scrutiny. Such is characteristic of Rabbinic exegesis. The school of Rabbi Ishmael was not declared heretic and ostracized. Yet, no one would say that the Amoraic Rabbis denied the doctrine that Josephus claimed was central even to the Pharisees, predecessors to the Tannaim who themselves are the predecessors to the Amoraic Rabbis.

These Gemarah passages reflect very different historical times than the first century. The debates took place in relative freedom in the Parthian (Arsacid) and Sassanian Persian Empires. Even the most sacred assumptions were in principle subject to the same legal scrutiny as issues of marriage and divorce.

The issue of the scriptural basis for the doctrine of resurrection becomes a constant refrain, interrupted by intervening digressions. Passages that are presented as possibly demonstrating life after death follow:[15] Exodus 6:4*, Deuteronomy 31:16; Isaiah 26:19; Song 7:9; Deuteronomy 11:21*; Deuteronomy 4:4*; Numbers 15:31; Psalm 72; Isaiah 35; Isaiah 25:9; Isaiah 65:20; Deuteronomy 32:39*; Exodus 15:3*; Joshua 8:30*; Psalm 34:5; Isaiah 52:8*; Deuteronomy 33:6*; Daniel 12:2*; Daniel 12:13*; Ezekiel 37. Several of the passages are from later books of the Bible, adduced at first in conjunction with the first five books and then scrutinized themselves.

Many of the proofs are subjected to rigorous examination. For example:

> Sectarians asked Rabban Gamliel: Whence do we know that the Holy One, blessed be He, will resurrect the dead? He answered them from the Torah, the Prophets, and the Hagiographa, yet they did not accept it [as conclusive proof]: From the Torah, for it is written *And the Lord said unto Moses, Behold thou shalt sleep with thy fathers and rise up* [again]. But perhaps, said they to him [the verse reads] *and the people will rise up?*

The Rabbis assumed that everyone is familiar with the passage to know that the next word in the sentence after "rise up" is "the people." It happens that the two words occur in different verses in our Bible, so it is conventional to consider that there is a full stop between them, indicating that the sentence has ended. But the Rabbinic Torah originally had not yet received the standard punctuation. The issue, in effect, becomes one of punctuation. The word order of prose narrative Hebrew is exactly "Thou shalt sleep with thy fathers and rise up the people." Normally, we think Moses slept and the people arose. But, by reading across the two sentences, one can also compose the following sentence: "Thou shalt sleep with thy fathers and rise up. [Now] the people . . ." even though the normal expectation in Hebrew syntax would be that Moses died and the people rose up to go astray. The Rabbis' proof depends on moving the full stop one word into the next sentence. But they were not satisfied with this weak proof. Thus, the heretics were not satisfactorily answered, again raising the level of suspense. The Rabbis objected to a Rabbinic proof-text that was actually used to defend the faithful against the skepticism of heretics.

But Deuteronomy 11:21 or 4:4 is said to please them:

Thus he did not satisfy them until he quoted this verse, *which the Lord swore unto your fathers to give* . . . (Deut 11:21) to them; not to you, but *to them* is said: hence resurrection is derived from the Torah. Others say that he proved it from this verse. *But ye that did cleave unto the Lord your God are alive every one of you this day.* (Deut 4:4)

On the other hand, there are places where the great inventiveness of one Rabbi is immediately admired by his colleagues. One imagines that the Rabbis admire the argument, were amused by its virtuosity, even when they question it.

Our Rabbis taught: *I kill and I make alive* (Deut 32:39); I might interpret, I kill one person and give life to another, as the world goes on. Therefore the Bible says: *I wound and I heal.* Just as the wounding and healing refer to the same person, so putting to death and bringing to life refer to the same person. This refutes those who maintain that resurrection is not intimated in the Torah.

It has been taught: R Meir said, "Whence do we know resurrection from the Torah? From the verse, Then shall Moses and the children of Israel sing this song unto the Lord (Exod 15:1): not *sang* but *shall sing* is written: thus resurrection is taught in the Torah. Likewise you read, *Then shall Joshua build an altar unto the Lord God of Israel:* not *built,* but *shall build* is written: thus resurrection is intimated in the Torah. If so, then did Solomon build an high place for Chemosh the abomination of Moab? Does that too mean that he shall build? But there the writ regards him as though he had built. (*b. Sanh.* 91b)

Rabba said: Whence is resurrection derived from the Torah? From the verse, *Let Reuben live, and not die* (Deut 33:16). Rabina said, [it is derived] from this verse, *And many of them that sleep in the dust of the earth shall awake, some to everlasting life, and some to shame and everlasting contempt* (Dan 12:2–3).

These are exquisite arguments, if you like virtuoso performances and subtle rebuttals, and if you have a sense of humor. The first depends on the notion that one must be first wounded in order to then be healed. The Rabbis were clearly aware of the difficulty in demonstrating resurrection from the Torah. Since it is posited in the Mishnah, they take on the challenge very seriously and impress each other with their virtuosity. It looks as though besides some witty amusement, they got a great deal of serious fun out of the exercise.

The contrast with the New Testament could not be more obvious. Jesus was asked a similar question about basis for the belief in the afterlife. He offered a most interesting answer, very much in this Rabbinic genre: "When they rise from the dead, they neither marry nor are given in marriage but are like the angels in heaven" (e.g. Mark 12:25). This firmly states the Christian, sectarian notion that the believers should live with the knowledge that they will be angels. Then came the Rabbinic question: Then, how do we know that there is life after death? Jesus answered in the same way as the Rabbis would—that is, by adducing Scripture as a proof-text. In this case, he brought two different Scriptures and resolved the seeming contradiction between them. This too is very characteristic of Rabbinic discourse:

Jesus said to them, "Is not this why you are wrong, that you know neither the Scriptures nor the power of God? For when they rise from the dead, they neither marry nor are given in marriage, but are like angels in heaven. And as for the dead being raised, have you not read in the book of Moses, in the passage about the bush, how God said to him, '*I am the God of Abraham, and the God of Isaac, and the God of Jacob*'? He is not God of the dead, but *of the living;* you are quite wrong." (Mark 12:24–27) or its parallel in Matthew:

> And as for the resurrection of the dead, have you not read what was said to you by God, *'I am the God of Abraham, and the God of Isaac, and the God of Jacob'*? He is not God of the dead, but *of the living."* And when the crowd heard it, they were astonished at his teaching. (Matt 22:31–33)

The New Testament means these proofs to be taken seriously, just as the Rabbis did. They are, in fact, evidence that the kind of Midrash practiced by the Rabbis in the second and third centuries was already known and respected in the first.

But notice the enormous difference in the way the scriptural proofs are offered. In the New Testament, Jesus offered one proof, from a case taken from life. His opponents asked a hard question, intending to trip him up. Actually, he offered the same kind of virtuoso response as the Rabbis did, based on comparing two different scriptural passages: He points out that in Exodus, God reveals to Moses that He is "the God of Abraham, the God of Isaac, and the God of Jacob" (Exod 3:6). Jesus also points out that God is called the living God, quite cogently referring to where Deuteronomy describes this same scene at Mount Sinai in front of the burning bush, which in Greek comes out even more conveniently for his argument: "For who is there of all flesh, that has heard *the voice of the living God speaking out of the midst of fire,* as we have, and has still lived?" (Deut 5:26)

This is a beautifully crafted argument in the Rabbinic style, having even more elegance in expression than we usually see in the foreshortened Rabbinic texts. By a process of comparison, Jesus equated the designation "God of the Living" with "God of Abraham, God of Isaac, and God of Jacob." Abraham, Isaac, and Jacob must still be alive, even though we know that the Bible states that they died. From this Jesus concluded that they are still alive in the resurrection (although it had clearly not come to fruition yet on earth). Now this is a good type of Rabbinic argument, later called *Hekesh* (although the Rabbis doubt some applications of it), and is frequently used in later Rabbinic thought, though not this particular one in connection with this particular problem.

What is interesting is that Jesus offered a single Rabbinic proof, though a good one, and this settles the matter once and for all. In Rabbinic literature, each Rabbi contributed a proof, equally good, yet all of them are disputed by other Rabbis. That is their function, their acuity, and their great pleasure. This merely underlines what we already know: The New Testament was written to an entirely different audience than the Rabbinic literature. The Rabbis were indulging in a daring process of argumentation, a kind of serious play, which is then recorded in the Talmud. The New Testament is validating the charismatic leader and preaching Him as the Savior of the world. The Talmud is for exegetical study; the New Testament is for missionizing.

Liturgy

SYNAGOGUE LITURGY, a vast Midrashic literature, and Jewish mystical literature forcefully profess belief in vivification of the dead, with interesting, different, and even inconsistent characterizations about its meaning. Some may have had doubts about the Scripture on which resurrection depended, but they did not doubt the doctrine itself. The participants in the Talmudic discussions did not feel that they had to give up their critical scrutiny of Scripture because they had inherited a difficult-to-demonstrate doctrine from the Tannaim. After all, they did accept several passages as having demonstrated the vivification of the dead. In any event, they realized that doubt was a significant part of their religious affirmation.

On the other hand, we moderns can never completely overcome the suspicion that the objections are more taking than the proofs, especially when they are based on such clever but obvious misreadings. Some Rabbis may have at least partly understood the irony that we naturally feel in seeing these exegetical exercises. Such is the force of the Rabbinic method. Instead of promulgating divine truths, the text is available for discussion and debate. Once one learns to read the text critically from the paradigm of the Rabbis, one can even deny the doctrine which they seek to defend. The Rabbis were indulging in an early example of "deconstructionism." Because of the method of scrutinizing every doctrine in this way, modern Jews would certainly deny that Judaism depends on the notion of resurrection in any literal way. And they might even return to the following passage to show how all doctrine must be made subject to our own rational scrutiny.

This irony of deconstruction is peculiarly our own modern perspective, not theirs, for the Rabbis refused to take the method that far. In fact, a glance at the liturgy reveals that life after death is repeatedly valorized in daily prayers. For instance, we have these brave statements of the faith in human, eternal reward:

You are mighty, eternally, O Lord.
You bring the dead to life, mighty to save.
You sustain the living with loving kindness
With great mercy you bring the dead to life again.
You support the fallen, heal the sick, free the captives;
You keep faith with those who sleep in the dust.
Who can compare with Your might, O Lord and King?
You are Master of life, and death, and deliverance.

This passage is part of the great prayer, known simply as *Ha-tefilah*. The Prayer, which is said standing in every Jewish service, is known as the *Amidah*, the standing prayer. Since it has roughly 18 paragraphs, it is also known as the *Shmoneh 'Esre* ("Eighteen"), the eighteen-part prayer. The passage above is quoted from the weekday version and is known as the *Gevurot*, God's mightiness (plural of *gevurah*, might), after the first statement in the paragraph. It is one of the best-known prayers in Jewish liturgy.[16] It praises God for bringing the dead to life, without reference to ethnic identity.

The passage is attributed to various authors. One tradition holds it was composed by the *Anshe Knesset Hagedolah,* the men of the great assembly. A famous tradition in the Babylonian Talmud (*Meg.* 17b) says that the entire *Shmoneh 'Esre* was formulated by R. Shimon the Flaxworker at Yavneh in the presence of Rabban Gamaliel. That would date the prayer in our form at the end of the first century or the beginning of the second, since Rabban Gamaliel succeeded Rab Yohanan ben Zakkai, who received permission to leave the siege at Jerusalem with his scholars just before 70 CE. More likely, that tradition reflects not its original composition but an attempt by the Rabbinic movement to lay claim to the already traditional prayer, on the grounds that they corrected and standardized the liturgy. An earlier form of the prayer seems assured by the newly published writings from Qumran, which demonstrates that they too believed in resurrection and used a very closely related liturgical text to affirm it. So the Rabbinic enterprise was an attempt to impose a canonical form on the prayer.

In both the Rabbinic and Qumranic form, *Gevuroth* is largely a gloss on Psalm 146:5–8, which, however, has no reference to resurrection, concentrating as we would expect, given the topic, on theodicy and God's care of the poor, downtrodden and unfortunate. To this are added the phrases that God brings the dead to life and will keep faith with those who sleep in the dust. The first praises God for resurrecting the dead;

the second for remembering the plight of those who have died and are buried. It is but one of innumerable references to the resurrection which dot the prayerbook.

In the preparatory service for morning prayers, *The Birkhot Hashahar,* the liturgy also contains explicit discussions of the immortality of the soul. Taken from the text in *b. Talmud Berakhot* 60b, the prayer begins with the Biblical notion of soul but quickly dresses it in a more Greek garb:

> The *soul* which you, my God, have given me is pure. You created it, You formed it, You breathed it into me; *You keep body and soul together.* One day You will take my soul from me, *to restore it to me in life eternal.* So long as this soul is within me I acknowledge You, Lord my God, my ancestors' God, Master of all creation, sovereign of all souls. Praised are You, Lord who restores the soul to the lifeless, exhausted body. (*Siddur Sim Shalom* 9–10)

The prayer begins with a reference to the soul. The first line might be just a traditional Biblical understanding of soul. The last suggests that it means only to explain how a tired body is refreshed by a night of sleep. But in the middle is a statement that life consists of body and soul together. God takes the soul at death and will restore it in life eternal. The last phrase seems to suggest immortality of the soul, though there is a peculiar variation on it. The source of the identity and the soul are different. The paragraph actually seems to describe immortality of the soul returned to a recreated body (the "me"), very much what Augustine affirmed as well. But the phrasing leaves a lot of ambiguity unexplained.

The term *neshamah* (nĕšāmâ), translated as "soul" above, occurs in Scripture some dozen times. Probably the prayer is making direct reference to the creation story in Genesis 2: "And He breathed into his nostrils the breath of life and man became a living being."

The *Gevuroth* prayer is reflecting on the verbs of creation used in Genesis—"created" it, "formed" it, "breathed" it into me. However, in Genesis 2:7, *neshamah* means more literally "the breath of life" which effects Adam's change from dust of the earth to a "living being," *nefesh.* It is interesting that the prayer does not use *nefesh* itself to stand for "soul." But by the Rabbinic period, *neshamah* was probably a better translation for soul because *nefesh* can mean "a person," whereas *neshamah* is more technical in that it refers to a spiritually inbreathed presence. Perhaps, too, when this prayer was composed, *neshamah* had already received one of the several mystic meanings of "over-soul," which became an object of great speculation in later Jewish mysticism. This is a soul that can be separated from the body and which will return to God at death. It is one that goes back into a body, which must be reconstituted from dust. It is a soul in the Greek sense but it also includes resurrection, narratively like the Christian synthesis.

The prayer contains a suggestion for the way that the resurrection of the dead will take place. It compares the waking of the body after sleep directly with the resurrection of corpses. It does this because the prayer is said in the evening, before sleep. And it praises God for being the one who will return the souls to dead corpses just as he returns wakefulness to people after sleep. Beyond that, the mechanism has little interest to the Rabbis or their community.

The prayer for the dead contains scarcely more detail. This prayer itself is not the Kaddish prayer, the famous prayer said in memory of the dead, which is a doxology of God. The Jewish prayer for the dead, *El Malē Rahamim*, "God full of mercy . . ." is chanted at memorial services and at graveside, and it does prominently mention life after death:

> God, full of mercy, who dwells on high, let these holy and pure beings find perfect rest under the wings of your Shechinah in the heights, let them shine as the brightness of the heavens, the souls of all those dear ones who are remembered today for a blessing. Let the garden of Eden be their rest. O Master of Mercy, hide them in the hiding place of your wings forever. May their souls be bound up in the bond of life and let them rest in peace upon their biers. And let us say "Amen."

Some of the basic imagery is taken from 1 Samuel 25:29:

> If men rise up to pursue you and to seek your life, the life of my lord shall be bound in the bundle of the living in the care of the LORD your God; and the lives of your enemies he shall sling out as from the hollow of a sling.

This image of the providence of the Lord is taken from the wording of Abigail's blessing of David. She likens the way God guards the life of David to being bound in a bundle while the enemies of David are being cast out like stones in a sling. No one completely understands the metaphor. But in-gathering of the exiles is basic to the Rabbinic view of the afterlife.

The influence of Daniel 12 is also prominent in this very allusive passage from Jewish liturgy. The dead are to shine with the brightness of the heavens, just as Daniel 12 suggests. The garden of Eden has become the final resting place of the dead, as well as humanity's original home, just as it has appeared in one of the heavens in the apocalyptic literature. But, in spite of Rabbinic Judaism's eschewal of apocalyptic thinking, Daniel 12 continues to inform Rabbinic notions of the afterlife. In some way, the dead shine in the heavens, reside in Eden, yet their bodies find peace in the grave.

The World to Come

THERE ARE TWO other places where notions of the afterlife show up strongly in Jewish thought. The first is Midrash, that compendium of Biblical exegesis and homilies which glosses the Bible for use in study and in creating synagogue sermons, mostly for the feasts and holidays. There, we find a rich and completely free imaginative reconstruction of life after death. Each picture really depends on the imagination of individual Rabbis, who mirror the issues of different times and places as well as tell us of their own hopes. Because of the many treatments of this theme, there is no need to go into great detail about it.[17]

The dominant Rabbinic notion of life after death is 'Olam Ha-ba' ('olām habbā,' lit. "the coming world," or "the next world"), which is usually translated as "the world to come" and is contrasted with our present world, 'Olam Ha-ze ('olām hazzeh, lit. "this world"). Because Midrash is a communal literature, made up of the comments of many Rabbis over many centuries, one cannot expect a systematic or even a consistent treatment of "the world to come." While the terminology is standard, the conception varies, depending on the Midrash and the exegetical or rhetorical needs of the Rabbi. "Better is one hour of bliss in the world to come than the whole of life in this world," and yet we also hear at the same place: "Better is one hour of repentance and good works in this world than the whole life of the world to come." The moral point is made by contrast, yielding a deliberate paradox.

Both statements appear in the same Mishnah, Avot 4:17, showing that there was no real interest in logical consistency in this literature. Each Rabbi's exegetical statements and homilies were remembered and deliberately restated in such a way as to defy logic. This is due to the vision of the redactor. But each homily also contains its own deliberate literary technique, quite characteristic of the Rabbinic period in which it was written and continued into mystical literature.

Considering that the main Rabbinic interest was in resolving legal problems logically, this is especially striking and it is meant to be. Here, the interest of the Rabbis is in deliberately stating a paradox, challenging each reader to provide some kind of intellectual synthesis. Putting these two statements together yields a literature where the real interest of the Rabbis was conduct in this world, not the world to come explicitly, though many Rabbis might address it in their sermons and homilies.

The reticence of Rabbinic tradition to discuss the next life is summarized by the third-century Palestinian sage, Yoḥanan bar Nappaḥa: "All the prophets prophesied only about the days of the Messiah; but of the world to come, 'no eye has seen it.' (Isa 64:4)" (See *b. Sanh.* 99a, *Ber.* 34b). The effect of this statement is to dampen speculation on the pleasures of the afterlife. Perhaps it was meant to defend against particularly vivid depictions of heaven and hell in Christianity and Zoroastrianism, and later in Islam. But the Rabbis could not entirely resist imagining an afterlife as a life without some of the responsibilities of this world and with rewards impossible in this world. Rav Abba, a third-century Babylonian Amora describes a perfected world with restricted pleasures and difficulties:

> It was a favorite saying of Rab: "Not like this world is the world to come." In the world to come there is neither eating nor drinking, no procreation of children or business transactions, no envy or hatred or rivalry. But the righteous sit enthroned, their crowns on their heads, and enjoy the radiance of the *Shekhinah*. (*b. Ber.* 17a)

The passage seems to have behind it an interpretation of Exodus 24:10–11: "And they saw the God of Israel; and there was under his feet as it were a pavement of sapphire stone, like the very heaven for clearness. And he did not lay his hand on the chief men of the people of Israel; they beheld God, and ate and drank." The passage narrates the theophany between God, Moses, and the elders of the Children of Israel at Sinai. The life to come is taken on that model, with the inconveniences of life removed. Angelic life will remove eating and drinking, procreation or business and thus all envy hatred and rivalry will disappear. Sexuality disappears in this vision. In order to see these bodily processes as "inconveniences" one has to understand the Rabbinic love of study as a transcendent value, against which everything else is an interruption. We see here the Rabbinic penchant for exaggeration, possibly taken to a deliberately humorous, self-satirizing extreme.

In the idealized world, nothing will interfere with the righteous's contemplation of God. They will receive the crowns and probably the thrones reserved for the *maskilim* (those who make others wise) because they are an academic community. Indeed, they conceive of God's court no longer as a royal court, as in the Biblical traditions, but as a Rabbinic court where the righteous enjoy the ability to study Torah all day. They are a *"yeshivah shel maʿaleh"* (Rabbinic Academy on High). The equivalent Aramaic term is *metivta deraqiaʿ*. The Heavenly Yeshiva is meant to reward those who study in this life and promise the same reward to those without the ability or opportunity to study in earthly academies. All will have the pleasures of study in the coming life, when all will have the ability and time and opportunity to occupy themselves with Torah.

The Midrash *Eleh Ezkerah* ("Midrash 'Let Me Remember These'" and "The Legend of the Ten Martyrs") envisions the martyrs in the world to come. There, the purified souls of the righteous sit in the heavenly academy on golden thrones and to listen to Rabbi ʿAqiba (a martyr of the second century) discourse on Torah.[18] The rewards of the martyrs become the same as the rewards of everyone else. Everyone will have the ability to become a Rabbi and study the fine points of Torah in the heavenly academy.[19] This story is meant to underline and emphasize the study of Torah as the ultimate divine service, superseding the role of the angelic court in advising God (the Biblical portrait) and the angelic court's role in serving in the divine temple, where the service to God still continues.

The Academy on High is similar to the earthly academy. Scholars continue their studies and debates there. The death of a sage is expressed as a summons to the Academy on High to help settle an argument (Baba Metzia 86a). In a striking anthropomorphism, God himself participates in the debates and sometimes His authority is not accepted immediately. For example, one of His rulings is contested by all the other scholars, and a human, Rabbah b. Naḥmani, is especially summoned from earth (i.e., to die) for a final decision, which he gives before he dies. The potential theological issue of God's ultimate rightness is resolved when Rabbah b. Naḥmani's decision concurs with that of God.[20] This portrait is meant to further exalt as transcendent the legal discussions of the Rabbis. To do so, the Rabbis figure God as a Rabbi.

The theme of the angelic identity of those who make others wise is furthered in a new social context in this passage. The tradition of angelomorphism has been academically domesticated, though one can see its original form, complete with the notion that the ascetic on earth can approximate angelic states in heaven, indeed, even experience them proleptically by means of altered states of consciousness. But, if so, the Rabbis scarcely ever speak about it in classic Rabbinic literature. In this sense, it is like the prophetic notion of "The End of Days," rather than the apocalyptic eschaton. For the Rabbis, study and prayer is asceticism, as well as intellectual exercise.[21]

In the mishnayoth and gemaroth that we have so far seen, there is discussion of "the world to come" but there has been little actual description of it. The contents or nature of the "world to come" was not a central concern of the writers of Jewish legal documents. Instead, the descriptions are part of the Midrashic tradition. "The world to come" began its intellectual life parallel to apocalyptic notion, as a paradise on a reconstituted land of Israel, as the Mishnah's use of Isaiah 60 would suggest. More and more in Midrash, however, 'Olam Ha-Ba' does double duty as a postmortem realm.

Some Rabbis believed that the perfected days at the end of time would not contain any of the striving of this world. As one would expect, scenes of agricultural plenty predominate in Rabbinic descriptions:

> Not like this world will be the world to come. In this world, one has the trouble to harvest grapes and press them; but in the world to come a person will bring a single grape in a wagon or a ship, store it in the corner of his house, and draw from it enough wine to fill a large flagon. There will not be a grape which will not yield thirty measures of wine. (*Ketub.* 111b)

Wine was not a forbidden pleasure to the Rabbis or to Jews in general. But that is not the point. Visions like this appeal to an urban as well as an agricultural economy, lionize the land of Israel, and demonstrate exaggeration as the language of heaven, perhaps stimulated by periodic lack of provisions. They have a wonderful folkloric naive pastoralism, demonstrating how an apocalyptic vision can be domesticated into a normative society. There was no active apocalyptic hope in these communities but the eschatological hope of a better future in a reconstituted land of Israel served as a substitute for the view of heaven.

But it coexisted with a more explicit view of heaven with judgment coming right after death. "The world to come" can often be understood as "heaven," the abode of the souls, containing "the garden of Eden," another name for the place where souls go when they die. A very clear example of this is to be found in Tanḥuma, Vayikra 8, as translated by Simha Paull Raphael:

The sages have taught us that we human beings cannot appreciate the joys of the future age. Therefore, they called it "the coming world." ['olam ha-ba'], not because it does not yet exist, but because it is still in the future. "The World to Come" is the one waiting for man after this world. But there is no basis for the assumption that the world to come will only begin after the destruction of this world. What it does imply is that when the righteous leave this world, they ascend on high, as it is said: "How great is the goodness, O Lord, which you have in store for those who fear you, and which, toward those who take refuge in you, you show in the sight of men [Ps 31:20].

This passage demonstrates that the Midrashic literature is a product of individual talents anthologized. The writer of this homily is declaring himself against the common tradition to make a point to his hearers. The homily probably originated as a kind of sermon or Torah lesson. It also shows that the Rabbinic concepts were available to creative reinterpretation.

The Midrashist deliberately uses "'olam ha-ba'" as a substitute for heaven, together with an implied judgment upon death and the resultant ascent of the righteous. Many people have read the various opinions with great interest. But, the flexibility and playfulness of the tradition are most impressive.

For instance, the Rabbis almost always pin their hopes on a difficult turn of phrase in the Scripture, which they can then interpet in a comforting way by looking at the context:

God said to Moses, *"Behold thy days draw near to die"* (Deut 31:14). Samuel Bar Nahmani said: "Do days die?" But it means that at the death of the righteous, their days cease from the world, yet they themselves abide, as it says, *"In whose hand is the soul of all the living"* (Job 12:10). Can this mean that the living alone are in God's hand, and not the dead? No, it means that the righteous even after their death may be called living, whereas the wicked, both in life and in death, may be called dead. (*Tanh b., Ber.,* 28b end)

Samuel Bar Nahmani picks up the scriptural anomaly that the subject of the verb "die" is actually "days." Though it would be tempting just to say it was a Biblical idiom, he uses this interesting grammatical anomaly in the Bible to provide his homily. The Midrash is far more definite about the reward of the righteous than the punishment of the sinners and the truth of reward and punishment than any specific description of it. The notion that the wicked are dead in this life, the righteous alive in the next, has been sounded before.

On the other hand, there is the famous and very naive tradition, that the dead buried outside of the land of Israel will be provided with a subterranean path to Israel and they will roll there underground to be resurrected:

> R. Simai said: "The Holy One, blessed be He, will burrow the earth before them, and their bodies will roll through the excavation like bottles, and when they arrive at the land of Israel, their souls will be reunited with them. (*T. J. Ketub.* 12:3ff. see also *Ket.* 111a)

Perhaps it is the strangeness of the idea that impresses modern sensibilities but it does answer the question of the pious buried in Diaspora: How can even the dead participate in God's plan for the ingathering of the exiles? Are those buried in the diaspora left out of the privileges which those buried in Jerusalem obtain? In this case, Rabbi Simai even suggests that resurrection will include reclothing the soul with the body. The body makes its own way underground to Jerusalem where the soul meets it. This passage later states that the new body will be built from the single, root vertebra. Renewing the body from the bones is known in Zoroastrianism as well. If so, it has been subjugated to Zionistic longing. This is speculation, but it reflects the hunch that we do not entirely understand the context in which R. Simai is writing. We do not even know exactly who he was. In any event, both Zoroastrianism and Judaism as early as 2 *Maccabees* also affirm that God can reassemble the body from nothing.

The Rabbis aver that there are heretics who do not believe in life after death. When Moses and God are speaking at Sinai, Moses asks God: "Will the dead ever be restored to life?" God, in surprise, retorts, "Have you become a heretic, Moses, that you doubt the resurrection?" "If," said Moses, "the dead never awaken to life, then truly You are right to wreak vengeance upon Israel. But if the dead are to be restored to life hereafter, what will You say to the fathers of this nation, if they ask You what has become of the promise You have made to them?" [22] Here the issue is explicitly the justification of God's ways to man. Moses and God are depicted in a Rabbinic discussion where Moses' arguments overcomes God's objections.

The Targums

THE TARGUM, the translation of the Bible into Aramaic, served as Scripture for the Aramaic-speaking community, as the Septuagint did for the Greek-speaking community. Many targumim were written for use within the synagogue as Aramaic had largely replaced Hebrew in the Middle East by the third century BCE. Some of the targumim are quite ancient. They appear at Qumran, for instance, but the fragment found there do not correspond to the received texts later on. Although some targumim are indeed quite ancient, we may not have access to them.

The Targum is not just a translation of the Bible. It contains many additions and comments to the original text, which reveal the issues that occupied the ancient community. Targumim are as much Midrash as translation. As life after death is largely missing from the Hebrew Bible, the targumim take the opportunity to supply it. For instance, where the Hebrew Bible narrates the murder of Abel by Cain in Genesis 4:8, the Targum inserts a short Midrash in which they argue over resurrection, making it into the very subject of the first murder. The same is true of the argument between Jacob (Israel = the Jews) and Esau (Edom = Rome = Christianity). The same with the argument between the land and the sea as understood from "The Song At The Sea" in Exodus 15:12. Each of these Midrashim inserted into the Targum is also found in the Midrash.[23]

Interestingly, the figure of Lot's wife is also crux for the issue of resurrection. The targumim to Genesis 19:26 says that she shall remain a pillar until the resurrection, when she will live again. One can speculate what this means: The Biblical story becomes a crux for the doctrine of resurrection. Does Lot's wife not deserve the same treatment as the rest of humanity? This targum answers "yes." It is significant that Lot's wife receives resurrection although she is not an Israelite.[24]

Jewish Mysticism

THE SECOND place where the notion of an afterlife continues to have strong and important role was in Jewish mysticism.[25] On the surface, a great many Jewish mystical texts look like Midrash itself. But it is Midrash devoted to a very limited number of themes. The secret purposes of the various stories only emerge in the course of reading through a great many of them. The originally apocalyptic material—the *Kabod* imagery, Daniel 7:13–14, enthronement of God's principal angel in Exodus 24,

Ezekiel 1, and Psalm 110—continues to be a strong theme of Jewish mysticism, even into Kabbalah, where it is caught up in the complicated richness of speculation of the *sepheroth*. In mysticism, many different and somewhat conflicting notions of the soul are evidenced. Mysticism portrays themes of angelic doubles who serve as guardians, as well as human transformations into *sephirotic* powers, and a myriad of other conceptualizations, which we cannot describe in any detail.[26]

The specific connection between Psalm 110 and the visions of Daniel, which is crucial in Christianity, appears in the *Zohar* to similar effect, yet without any Christian coloring:

> The Holy One, blessed be He, said to Daniel, Thou shalt go towards the end, and will rest (Dan 12:13). Daniel asked: "Rest in this world or in the next world?" "Rest in the next world," was the answer (cf. "They will rest in their beds" Isa 57:2), "and thou shalt stand up to thy lot at the end of days." Daniel asked, "Shall I be among the resurrected or not?" God answered, "And thou wilt stand up." Daniel then said, "I know full well that the dead will rise up in various classes, some righteous and some wicked, but I do not know among whom I shall be found." God answered, "To thy lot." Daniel then said, "As there is a right end and a left end, I do not know whether I shall go to the right end *(l'qets hayamin)* or to the end of days *(l'qets hayamim)*." The answer was, "To the end of the right *(l'qets hayamin)*." Similarly, David said to the Holy One, blessed be He, "Make me to know my end," that is, he wished to know to which end he was allotted, and his mind was not at rest 'til the good tidings reached him, "Sit at my right hand" (Ps 110:1). (*Zohar Bereshith*, 1.63a)

The exegetical subject of this passage is Noah's flood. The Biblical phrase "the end of all things" summons up the final apocalypse. The *Zohar* then surveys other places where "the end" is mentioned, including the important passage in Daniel. It can interweave the two passages, gleaning what it can for its depiction of the end of days. It derives two choices—resurrection or not—and Daniel asks: "Will I arise?" The answer is "Yes."

The next question follows logically: What will his fate be in the resurrection? Two choices are again derived: "to the right," to a good end, or "to the end of days," for destruction. Daniel asks again what his final reward will be and is told that his end will be good. The passage depends on a pun between the word for "days" in Hebrew *(yamim)* and the word for "right" *(yamin)*. "Right" in this case refers to the direction right not vindication. But a good implication derives from the arrangement of the good *sepherot* (divine spheres) on the right. The categories of this passage are derived from Daniel 12:2, supplemented with the kabbalistic apparatus of the emanations of the *spheroth*.

Then a conversation between God and David is narrated. David essentially asks the same question, based on Psalm 39:5: "Lord, let me know my end, and what is the measure of my days; let me know how fleeting my life is!" (Ps 39:4; MT Ps 39:5). The answer, the kabbalist says, is to be found in Psalm 110, which narrates that David will be translated to heaven for his final reward, to be enthroned next to God, essentially what Daniel sees in 7:13–14.

The *Zohar* also equates the stars with the angels on the basis of Job 38:7, "The morning stars sang together and all the sons of God shouted for Joy," as well as Psalm 148:3, "Praise him, all ye stars of light." The praises that are sung are the same songs which Israel used in its liturgy, as Israel sings antiphonally with the angels in its services (see *Zohar Bereshit* I, 231b). The *Zohar* also mentions the image of the righteous (both *Ṣelem* [image] and *demut* [likeness] are used), which have a complicated and difficult relationship with the *neshamah*. Like the Rabbis, the *Zohar* describes dying as a kind of atoning sacrifice:

> The soul ascends to her place, and the body is given over to its place, in the same way as in an offering the devotion of him who offers ascends to one place, and the flesh to another. Hence, the righteous man is, of a truth, himself an offering of atonement. But he who is not righteous is disqualified as an offering, for the reason that he suffers from a blemish, and is therefore like the defective animals of which it is written, "They shall not be accepted for you" (Lev 22:25). Hence it is said, 'The righteous are an atonement and a sacrifice for the world.' (*Bereishit* I, 65b)

It was for the sake of the righteous that the world was created. The kabbalists considered themselves to be the enlightened of the prophecy in Daniel. This text forms the very basis of the introductory proem of the *Tiqqunei ha-Zohar,* as well as in many other places in the mystical corpus. The very title of the *Zohar,* the principal book of Kabbalah, is taken from Daniel 12:3. Like theurgic texts and hermetism, the texts tend to describe the process from the top down, as cosmology rather than as soteriology, but it is not hard to see that these cosmologies imply a corresponding and opposite journey upwards of the soul caught in earthly matter.

For the Kabbalists, all Israel (except for the most heinous and unrepentant sinners) will inherit the land of Israel, as among the Rabbis. But this particular kabbalistic plan for the end of days is found for both in Daniel 12 and associated passages. Both saw that some would be transformed into shining, angelic creatures; each thought it would be they—most dramatically in the case of the Zoharic masters. The *mekubalim,* the Kabbalists, thought themselves to be the *maskilim,* those who will lead many to knowledge and become shining stars prophesied in Daniel 12. This is but half a doctrine of salvation. The Kabbalists especially seemed willing to restrict membership of the saved to the members of Israel. But theirs was a consolation for very troubled times.

This consolation continued in the various medieval documents of heavenly ascent that are found in Rabbinic literature. Many of them can be conveniently read in Simcha Paull Raphael's book, *Jewish Views of the Afterlife.*[27] These stories serve, among other things, to confirm that the various rewards which the mystics seek are really to be found in heaven. Some seem stimulated by RASC and others seem merely to be imaginative narratives.

Elijah's Trip to Heaven in Rabbinic Literature

WE HAVE ALREADY seen in detail that only two figures in the Hebrew Bible are assumed into heaven while alive. The first is Enoch (Gen 5) and the second is Elijah (2 Kgs 2). While the apocalyptic and pseudepigraphical literature contains a vast romance about Enoch, Rabbinic Judaism was far more interested in Elijah. He is a tremendously popular figure in Jewish culture. Even today, at the *havdalah* service that begins every liturgical week, a hymn is sung to Elijah, who is viewed as the possible forerunner of the Messiah. This is due to the later prophecy of Elijah's return, which grants him the status of a Messianic figure by himself:

> "Behold, I will send you Elijah the prophet before the great and terrible day of the LORD comes. And he will turn the hearts of fathers to their children and the hearts of children to their fathers, lest I come and smite the land with a curse." (Mal 4:5–6)

For this reason alone, Elijah might have been invoked as present at the seder. But even earlier, Ben Sira (ca. 200 BCE) attributed the future restoration of the tribes of Jacob to him (Eccles 48:10). A cup of wine is set for him in the current seder. After dinner, most Jewish homes open the door to let him in to the seder to claim his cup of wine. What better place to insure that the hearts of children are turned to their fathers and vice versa than at a holy and joyful and very ample feast, whose venue is the home. One supposes that this both signals the possibility of the final consummation and avoids the curse of Malachi 4:6.

Perhaps the popularity of Elijah at the expense of Enoch in Rabbinic literature is due to the fact that Elijah was a Jewish prophet who battled for the Lord, while Enoch was a primeval hero. The Biblical text gives us many different miracles to add to his Midrashic repertoire of characteristics, including a battle against Ba'al, ending a drought, and the theophany where God appeared as "the still, small voice" (1 Kgs 19). More significantly, he raises the son of the widow of Zarephath from the dead (1 Kgs 17:17ff.). He ascends to heaven in a fiery chariot driven by fiery horses (2 Kgs 2:11). His mantle gave his successor Elisha magical power to continue his ministry. Elijah is praised while Enoch is criticized and remains a very ambiguous character in the Midrash.

Elijah is continually blessed as the bringer of good news in Jewish liturgy, preeminently in the grace after meals and the blessings over the Haftarah. He appears in other Jewish liturgy as well. The circumcision chair in a synagogue is known as the chair of Elijah. In the New Testament, Jesus is frequently compared with Elijah, where he is usually understood as a precursor, so as not to cast a shadow on Jesus' role, though the Hebrew Bible outlines an individual, eschatological role for Elijah. Jesus is acclaimed as Elijah (who is still alive because of his assumption alive into heaven preserved him from death) in Mark 8:27–33, Matthew 16:13–23, and Luke 9:18–22. Jesus also proclaimed John the Baptist as Elijah (Matt 11:10ff.; 17:10ff.; Mark 9:11ff.), so both prophetic figures in early Judaism were identified with this already legendary figure. Elijah was evidently a Messianic figure in his own right.

In the famous story of the oven of Akhnai (b. Mesi'a 59a), Elijah appears at the end to tell us that God is pleased with the ruling that we always incline towards the majority and do not heed miracles as legal proof.[28] In the equally famous story of Rabbi Shim'on bar Yohai living in a cave for ten years after the destruction of the Second Temple (Šabb. 33b), Elijah tells the great sage and mystic that he should leave the cave. Elijah reports in Midrash (Pirked Rabbi Eliezer 43, end) that the Messiah is to be found as a beggar at the gate of Rome, and he becomes the herald of the Messianic age (Sanh. 98a). Yet, he can also rescue people from danger, as he rescues Naḥum Ish Gamzu from the Romans (*Sanh.* 108b–109a; *Ta'an.* 21a). In the Midrash he announces that "the emperor" has died (*Šabb.* 33b), a very hopeful piece of news in a time of persecution.

Elijah's role was quite unlike the saints of the church and even unlike angelic presences elsewhere. He serves a basically Rabbinic function in these stories, demonstrating that Rabbinic *takkanot* ("corrections," really "innovations") are desired and wanted by God. In Rabbinic literature, angels do not, as a rule, serve as interpretive authorities, as they do in apocalyptic traditions. That job is squarely given to humans and to their exemplars, as Elijah surely serves here. Elijah has some of the formal characteristics of Hermes, in bringing messages back and forth between heaven and earth and also in occasionally leading souls to paradise, both in mystical ascent and after death, as in Baba Metzia 114a–b, where he leads Rabba bar Abuha to the garden of Eden, the standard Rabbinic word for the heaven of redeemed human souls.[29]

The most interesting of all the passages concerning Elijah for our purposes is one in which the secret of resurrection is revealed to human beings by Elijah, for which he is punished by means of sixty fiery lashes (Baba Metzia 85b). This punishment is otherwise known only as a punishment for angels, so Elijah is viewed as an angel in this legend. No mere human could have stood up to such a punishment. Since they viewed the doctrine as one of the most important in Rabbinic Judaism, they explained it as a heavenly secret that Elijah revealed, in much the same way that Prometheus was punished for his having stolen fire for humanity in the classical tradition. In this case, the punishment was not eternal; Elijah is always available as a savior figure and consoler, as well as a messenger between Israel and God.

Rabbinic Multi-culturalism as a Social Necessity on Earth

To SEE THE complete and more optimistic Rabbinic design, we must also look at the Rabbinic discussion for the final disposition of the gentiles. There is not a single answer to the question "What was the Rabbinic view of the place of the gentiles in God's scheme?"

Rabbinic writings debate the issue of the salvation of the gentiles, as they debate most every issue.

Rabbi Eliezer said: "All the nations will have no share in the world to come, even as it is said, 'the wicked shall go into Sheol, and all the nations that forget God' (Ps 9:17). The wicked shall go into Sheol—these are the wicked among Israel." Rabbi Joshua said to him: "If the verse had said, 'The wicked shall go into Sheol with all the nations,' and had stopped there, I should have agreed with you, but as it goes on to say 'who forget God,' it means there are righteous men among the nations who have a share in the world to come." (*t. Sanh.* 13:2)

Some Rabbis, represented by Rabbi Eliezer, said that only Israel will be saved. Others, represented by Rabbi Joshua, said that the righteous gentiles would be saved as well. The positions attributed to Rabbis Eliezer and Joshua b. Hananiah are typical of other remarks that Rabbinic literature has attributed to them. Rabbi Eliezer was a severe critic of gentiles. Rabbi Joshua b. Hananiah was more liberal. He removed all distinctions between Jew and gentile in attaining salvation through the doing of good deeds. He said: "Everyone who walks in blamelessness before his Creator in this world will escape the judgment of hell in the world to come." He even disagreed with Rabbi Gamaliel by maintaining that the blameless children of wicked heathen will also have a share in the world to come. Though Rabbi Joshua probably did not allow conversion without circumcision, he at least looked at the positive side of the issue, saying: "Baptism without circumcision makes one a *ger* (that is, "a proselyte," a person in the process of converting) (*b. Yebam.* 46a).

The status of the gentiles is discussed in later Rabbinic Judaism through at least two different rubrics—the resident alien and the doctrine of the "Noahide Commandments." These two legal constructions make different assumptions about the purpose of the gentiles and they sometimes imply conflicting approaches which need to be systematically worked out.

The issue of the resident alien derived from the Biblical rules incumbent upon "the stranger in your gates."[30] Resident aliens were obliged to abstain from offering sacrifices to strange gods (Lev 17:7–9), from eating blood in any form (Lev 17:10ff.), from incest (Lev 18:6–26), from work on the Sabbath (Exod 20:10ff.), and from eating leavened bread during the Passover (Exod 12:18ff.).[31]

Closely allied with this issue is the Rabbinic doctrine of the "Noahide Commandments." This Rabbinic doctrine is derived from a sophisticated and theological formulation that some legal enactments were given before Sinai, during the primeval history to all human beings. Furthermore, the sign of the Noahide covenant, the rainbow, is available to all humanity to symbolize God's promise of safety. And it was completely outside of the special covenant with Abraham and his descendants. The covenant with

Noah is expanded to the entire primeval period, encompassing all the revealed commandments preceding Sinai. The Noahide Commandments (e.g., *t. ʿAhed. Zar.* 8.4 and more fully in *b. Sanh.* 56b) function somewhat like a concept of "natural law," which any just person can be expected to follow by observation and reason.

In the Diaspora, Jews develop a proselytism and apologetic literature that is designed both to interest gentiles into joining the movement and to encourage Jews not to assimilate. It suggests that what Judaism has over even the greatest philosophers is moral superiority. The sins of the gentiles are always more or less equivalent to three: violence, sexual immorality, and idolatry—three of the sins which Jews must never do, not even to avoid martyrdom. These are three preeminent moral issues in which Jews knew better than their neighbors in Hellenistic literature. And they will be important for understanding how the Noahide Commandments developed.

Once the social significance of the different formulations is outlined, the reasons for the ambiguity become clear. The difference between the Noahide Commandments and the rules for the sojourner alien is clear from a social point of view. The resident alien must, because of his close association with Israelites, observe some of the laws of Judaism, while the Noahide Commandments refer to the ultimate disposition of gentiles and thus entirely to gentiles who were not observant. The resident sojourners may be ethical or not; the issue is irrelevant because the question was only how to keep them from somehow interfering with Jewish religious life. The law was there for the benefit of the Israelites who needed not to tolerate certain impieties within their own territory. With the Noahide Commandments the gentiles needed not to observe any Jewish law at all. The sole question is whether they could be righteous. They merely had to observe seven laws to prove worthy to inherit "the world to come." [32]

This corresponds to the two different but related social situations of Jews in the Roman Empire. The first, the resident alien, refers to a situation where Jews were in the majority and had political power. In that situation, they could maintain that gentiles ought to do a certain amount of Jewish ritual—such as circumcision, if they wanted to participate in the Passover sacrifice. This later became the legal basis for discussions of conversion in Judaism.

But more numerous even during the time of Jesus is the second situation, in which Jews were not the majority of the population and had very limited abilities to affect or control their neighbors. In such a situation, there was even a danger of gentile backlash in being too open to mission.

There is ample evidence of the concern of the pagan community that the Jews and Christians were stealing their children from them. This does not mean kidnapping but conversion, which was viewed as dividing the pagan family, driving a wedge between parents and children. In these situations, the concept of a righteous gentile, who eschewed sin but did not explicitly take up the special rules of Judaism, had a positive value because it relieved the community from the necessity of converting gentiles. We have ample evidence that Jews living in gentile areas understood very well that they depended on gentile toleration for their well-being and strove to live as good guests in the Diaspora.

Isaac in Synagogue Floors

THE ZODIAC was prominently displayed in the center of many Greco-Roman synagogue floors. Though one finds depictions of the zodiac in pagan art, one rarely sees it depicted in floors. The second panel of the synagogue floors was frequently a depiction of the Temple in Jerusalem. The two pillars in front, as well as the curtain of the ark are often depicted, along with the implements of Temple worship, and the familiar basilicate facade. The relationship between the Temple and the synagogue has been discussed many times. This depiction is easy to understand as a statement of the continuity of Israel's worship from Temple to synagogue. It is possible that the zodiac is itself a reference to the Temple, as one finds a zodiac on the base of the Temple menorah taken by Titus.

The third panel in a number of synagogues was the depiction of Genesis 22, the sacrifice of Isaac, yet another reference to the Temple. But it is also an important story within both later Judaism and Christianity. In Christianity it became a crucial typology and prophecy of the passion of Christ. First, and earliest in the tradition is the connection between the two fathers: Abraham and God are compared as being willing to give up their sons (e.g. John 3:16); amongst the Church Fathers the relationship between Isaac and Jesus as martyrs and sacrificial victims is often compared.

Why synagogue mosaic-floors so frequently depict the binding of Isaac (Genesis 22) is more ambiguous. The connection between the sacrifice of Isaac and Mount Moriah, already identified in Scripture as the Temple Mount, would have been clear to all. So the sacrifice of Isaac may be another symbol of the Temple sacrifice, now transferred to the prayers of the synagogue. That Isaac was not actually sacrificed might easily be seen as justification for the termination of sacrifice and its non-inclusion in the synagogue service.

Isaac was also viewed as actually sacrificed and resurrected in various places in Midrash.[33] This is likely to be the Jewish antidote to Christian notions of vicarious atonement, the symbol that could be turned to the Jewish equivalent of Christianity's cosmocrator crucifix. This possibility also raises the further serious and very strong pre-Christian tradition that Isaac stands with Abel within the martyr tradition. Too often in Late Antiquity and the Byzantine Period, Jews needed encouragement in their hour of trial, often when Christians were the persecutors. It was no wonder that they frequently welcomed the Arabs as liberators from the Christian Empire. But, as Isaac was not actually slaughtered, it is also possible that the symbol of Isaac stood for the Jewish notion that martyrdom should be avoided wherever possible, as well as encouraging martyrs in their unavoidable hour of trial. Isaac also stood for the synagogue's faith that, though Jews were constantly imperiled in the Christian empire, God would save them alive, not as martyrs, as he had saved Isaac and Daniel alive.

In a further development of the rescue motif, which began in the stories about Daniel and Isaac, the Jewish mystical tradition contains the folkloric story of Lupinus Caesar (otherwise unknown) and the martyrdom of Ḥananyah ben Teradion.[34] In the story, the emperor martyrs Ḥananyah, one of the mystic masters, but God substitutes one for the other and Lupinus, in fact, dies two deaths. The story shows that mystic knowledge helps the adept avoid martyrdom. Mystical traditions contain many rites and experiences of spiritual martyrdom—namely an ecstatic experience of martyrdom without any necessary, physical martyrdom. Not that it is a pretense. The mystic stands before God, handing his soul over to him *(mesirat nefesh)*. Lawrence Fine has called this "spiritual martyrdom" or "contemplative death." [35] Rather than use martyrdom to help propagate the faith, Rabbinic Judaism attempts to minimize the losses from martyrdom whenever it is avoidable.

15

Islam and the Afterlife

Muslim, Christian, and
Jewish Fundamentalism

Resurrection on the Day of Judgment
as the Primary Reward

IN VIEW OF THE martyrdom beliefs of the suicide attackers who brought
down the World Trade Center on September 11, 2001, the development
of the afterlife doctrine in Islam has become especially important to
Americans; but few have bothered to survey the Muslim tradition to get a
broader perspective on it. Though the attackers voiced visions of paradise
in their suicide notes, and thought of themselves as martyrs, not even their
intense faith can persuade Americans, or most Muslims, that their faith is
the norm for afterlife beliefs in Islam. Rather, they are eccentric and dangerous views, though they have something important to teach about afterlife beliefs and the production of martyrdom through fundamentalist
extremism in every religion.

Ordinary Islamic views of the afterlife are just as rich and manifold as
in Judaism or Christianity, but later in time than this book can study in
detail and different in some important ways from the religious ideas analyzed until now.[1] We cannot study the whole tradition. But we can learn
enough to know how to avoid the prejudices of seeing Islam from the perspective of its extremists. And we can also ask how the classic view of

Islam has been so liable to manipulation by contemporary Islamists (fundamentalist extremists).[2]

Coming after Judaism and Christianity and being cognizant of the previous revelations, Islam was built on the doctrines of both Judaism and Christianity but tailored them for its own needs and out of its own understanding of the meaning of Muḥammad's revelations. Unlike Christianity, Islam did not canonize the texts of its forebear religions; to the contrary, it posited that the traditions of the Old and New Testaments have been garbled where they disagree with the Quran. The watchword of Islam's faith is: "There is no god but God and Muḥammad is His apostle." With it, Islam claims its rank as the last and foremost of the Western monotheisms. It worships the same God as Judaism and Christianity. Its revelation is in the same tradition as Moses and Jesus, both of whom it acknowledges as true prophets.

Implicitly, in the next clause, Islam claims that the revelation given to Muḥammad is not just a special revelation for the Arabs but the fullest and most complete revelation for everyone. Muḥammad was the "seal of the prophets" *(khatam an-nabiyyin),* the last and most perfect prophet, hence revealer of the right path for the world at large. Islam in its classical form takes a freer view towards its predecessors than did Christianity and, at the same time, is even more organized than Christianity for missionizing the world. Functionally, this gives Islam an ever wider degree of freedom than Christianity has in reinterpreting its Jewish and Christian forebears.

Muḥammad's special title, *raṣul,* means "apostle" (Aramaic: *sheliḥa)* showing that, like Paul, Muḥammad's revelation contained the command to proselytize, conveying a specific message of salvation. The word already meant "apostle" in Muḥammad's own day. The Quran, however, uses this term especially for Muḥammad and uses other words for previous messengers.[3] Even more than Christianity, Islam is organized for mission and expansion. Its view of paradise is central to that purpose.

Muḥammad's revelations first came to him through the intermediation of the angel *Gibril* (English: Gabriel) at age 40 in the year 610 CE, while he was meditating in a cave near Mecca in what is today Saudi Arabia. The first revelation began with the word *'iqra,* "Recite!" from which the name *Al-Quran* ("The Recitation") is derived. Because books were in short supply, and reading itself was almost always done in public declamation, and because Arab culture had already developed extensive oral, public, poetic traditions (conventions which the Quran follows in its internal structure), the word "Recite!" also shares some implications of the word "Read!" or even "Read out publicly!" According to many Muslim traditions, Muḥammad was himself illiterate, a tradition that, among other things, augments the miraculous nature of his revelations. Whatever one may think of this legend, the fact is that Muḥammad's revelations were oral, and were preserved both orally and in written form throughout his career. Today, the word "'*iqra*" serves as the normal Arabic word for "Read!" (as does the same root in Hebrew). Today as well, though there is still a premium on memorization and recitation in Muslim piety; the place that most Muslims look for the revelation of their faith is in the book of revelations given to Muḥammad called the Quran.[4]

The revelations themselves vary from short ecstatic utterances to theological and ethical discourses on the importance of monotheism and moral behavior. The revelations pointed the way to a monotheistic system that Muḥammad was to bring to the originally polytheistic Arabs, although there were already groups of pre-Islamic Arab monotheists in the Hejaz, called by Muslim tradition the *ḥunafa* (sing. *ḥanif*), as well as some Arab Jewish and Christian tribes. Muḥammad's religious teachings soon brought him into conflict with the Jews and Christians, the other Arab tribes, and, indeed, even his own Quraysh tribe. Muḥammad exercised both religious and military leadership over his movement; there has never been a clear distinction between secular and religious power, between religious conversion and conquest in Islam. After many battles, his forces and his teachings gradually unified the whole Arabian peninsula, even making forays into the area of Syria. This unification of the Arabian peninsula was both difficult politically and important strategically because it melded together a new military force in a remote and forbidding peninsula from which neither the Byzantine Christians nor the Sasanian Persians expected any threat. When the Arabs exploded out of Arabia they conquered half the Mediterranean and more, making Islam a world religion as well as a universal one.

The Byzantine Empire in Anatolia and the Sasanian Empire in Iran had exhausted themselves in warring against each other.[5] After Muḥammad's death, Muslim armies took advantage of the power vacuum in the Eastern Mediterranean. Moving quickly out of Arabia, Islam and its armies captured Syria, Jerusalem, and the Levant, conquered large sections of North Africa and Asia, eventually reaching as far as Spain, with forays into France and Iran (eighth-century), and, by successive stages, even overran Anatolia, renaming Byzantium as Istambul in 1453 CE. By the sixteenth century, the Muslim armies of the Ottoman Sultan of Istambul were at the gates of Vienna. The result was that Europe was surrounded from east and west in a classic pincer movement. The speed of the Muslim conquest has itself been taken by Muslims as a demonstration of the truth of its doctrines, just as was the conversion of the Roman Empire by the Christians before them. There were setbacks as well but the first millennium of Muslim history was a record of constant and inexorable expansion. When it stopped Islam faced a crisis of confidence.

But the succession to Muḥammad's leadership proved problematic. None of Muḥammad's sons survived into adulthood to carry on his work. His successors (the *Khalifa,* the "Caliph") were the husbands of his daughters. In one of the greatest ironies of history, the family that eventually founded the first great Muslim Imperial Dynasty, the Umayyads, was also descended from the bitterest opponents of Muḥammad in his own Quraysh tribe. In spite of the enormous and complicated Muslim empires that quickly established themselves, the "ecclesiastical" organization of Islam itself has remained relatively informal. In contrast with to the very centralized, leadership of medieval Christianity, Islam seems almost bereft of a supervisory or episcopal structure, with administrative structures tending to be local and national rather than centralized, waxing and waning depending on the prestige of the various officials. There are no structures in Islam that are as universal as the hierarchy of the Roman Catholic church. In this respect, Islam resembles Judaism more than Christianity.

The religion of Islam is united not by clergy but by the revelation to the prophet. Muḥammad's utterances, as recorded in the Quran, concerned many things; on the subject of afterlife he spoke mightily about the resurrection and only hinted at any other forms of afterlife. The Day of Judgment *(Yawm al-Din)* or "the Hour" *(As-sa'ah)* is second only to the oneness of God in importance to Muslims. At the great Day of Judgment, there will be a reckoning *(Hisab)* for all who have breathed. Resurrection *(Qiyamah)* will be the blessing of the Day of Judgment for those who have faith and have acted justly: "Truly the Hour is coming—there is no doubt of it—when God will resurrect those who are in the graves" (Q 22:7). The Day of Judgment is featured in the famous *Fatihah,* now the opening *sura* (chapter) of the Quran itself: "In the name of God, the Merciful, the Compassionate, Praise belongs to God, the Lord of all Being, the All-merciful, the All-compassionate, the Master of the Day of Judgment. . . ."

This might argue for millennialist sentiments in the formation of the earliest Muslim community. But there have not been many studies of the earliest Islam which explore the few early, millennial notes.[6] Like Christianity, the millenarian *kernel,* if there was one, was soon integrated into more normative doctrines and institutions. But, as Islam was always a political as well as a religious power, the transformation must have been even quicker than in Christianity and therein lies its great interest. So, if millennialism was present, unlike Christianity, it was already rechanneled into the institutions of Islam before the major texts were promulgated.

Even though Muḥammad had already reached the age of forty when his revelations began, he had twenty years of contact with the community that he founded. This compares with the very short, probably one-year period of Jesus' entire ministry. Muḥammad's long and influential life, his continuing revelations, and his exercise of temporal and religious power, gave him the opportunity to build a movement that recognized the end but ruled for the present, an opportunity that was denied Jesus. In one sense, he serves as both "the Jesus" and "the Paul" of early Islam.

Muḥammad spoke often of the coming day of judgment but did not predict when it would arrive. The Quran gives no date for the "hour of doom" but does describe it in vivid and terrible images. It will devastate the earth and reverse all the natural processes that were established by Allah:

> When the sun shall be darkened, When the stars shall be
> thrown down,
> When the mountains shall be set moving, When the pregnant
> camels shall be neglected,
> When the savage beasts shall be mustered, When the seas shall
> be set boiling,
> When the souls shall be coupled, When the buried infant shall
> be asked for what sin she was slain,
> When the scrolls shall be unrolled, When heavens shall be
> stripped off,
> When hell shall be set blazing, When paradise shall be brought
> nigh,
> Then shall a soul know what it has produced. (Q 81:1–14)

The imagery itself is deeply involved in polemic and parenesis, showing Muḥammad's attention to the social evils of his day. The reference to the exposed baby girl reflects a practice which Muḥammad sought to end, explicitly building the inquiry for these secret sins into the vision of the end and thus to end all such practices. Paradise approaches and hell will be ignited. Judgment is at the end of time. Other, later descriptions go into great detail about hellfire and brimstone. This only makes more obvious that Islam was, from its inception, a religion of conversion. The images of the fate awaiting the damned is an argument to change one's life and join the early Islamic movement. Muḥammad was a preacher who challenged his hearers to convert because the soul will stand in judgment.

Indeed, it is arguable that the word "Islam" itself functionally means conversion (literally: "submission"), as well as becoming the proper name of the religion. That very well may make Islam the first great Western religion to develop its own name for itself, the others adapting names first used by others.[7] In any event, the close connection between the vision of the horrors awaiting sinners at the day of judgment and the necessity of conversion is at the base of Islam, and it is designed to convince its hearers to submit to the precepts of Islam, which is the only way for a pagan to avoid the coming eschatological disaster.

Neither Jews nor Christians would have found this message outlandish. They may have disagreed with it or with Muḥammad's sense of the coming end, but they would have agreed with the exhortation to a moral life and the revelation of the "Day of Judgment." The hostility to this part of the message came from the pagans around whom he lived. Muḥammad records in his revelations the hostile attitude of the Arabs to his message of a resurrection on the Day of Judgment. "They swear by God to the very limit of their oaths that God will not raise him who dies . . ." (Q 16:38) and "They say, 'Are we to be returned to our former state when we have become decayed bones?' They say, 'That would be a detrimental return!' " (Q 79:10–12). It is no surprise, then, that when Muḥammad reveals the doctrine of resurrection, it is in the context of missionizing an often quite hostile audience.

Here is the complete context, as revealed by the Quran:

O You people: If you are in doubt concerning the resurrection, know that We created you from dust, then from a sperm-drop, then from a blood-clot, then from an embryo partly formed and partly unformed, in order to make clear to you. We establish in the wombs whatever We wish for an appointed time, then We bring you out as an infant, then [sustain you] until you reach maturity. And among you are those who die and those who return to the infirmity of old age so that, after having been knowledgeable, they now have little understanding. You saw the earth lifeless, and then We poured down upon it water and it quivers and grows and sprouts forth all kinds of beautiful pairs. That is because God is the ultimately real [al-ḥaqq]. He is Who gives life to what is dead; He it is Who has power over all things. Truly the Hour is coming—there is no doubt of it—when God will resurrect those who lie in their graves. [Q 22:5–7].[8]

The dualist structure of these early Muslim ideas of the resurrection, its "two-way theology," its description of true, calm, peaceful life existing in the Islamic community, while death and suffering characterize all outside of it, served to further the mission of early Islam. The Fatiḥa, which functions like a creed for Islam, sums up the two-way theology: "Show us the straight path: the path of those whom You have favored; not [the path] of those who earn your anger nor of those who go astray" (Q 1:6–7). There is every reason to suppose that Muḥammad learned the value of missionary work from Jews and especially Christians active in the Arabian peninsula in his day. But his prophecy allowed him to hone it to new heights of effectiveness for his Arab audience. Islam downplayed the elaborate temple rituals of Arabia's polytheistic past, substituted simple daily devotions, and emphasized oral sermons (an art-form in the Hejaz), which both convinced hearers to convert, while continuously fostering and confirming the faith of those who had already entered the community.

So while the Quran is revelatory writing, it also reflects the traditions in use in the days of its composition and the use to which these utterances were put in the early days of Islam. One of the most obvious literary qualities of the Quran, besides its Arabic poetic couplet format, is its exhortatory tone. The *surahs* (chapters) and *ayyas* (verses) are mostly sermons, lectures, and exhortations, not narrative like the Hebrew and Christian Bible. The longest and most sustained narrative is the famous story of Yusuf (Joseph) in *Surat Yusuf,* Sura 12 of the Quran, which is used as a story illustrating the rewards of avoiding temptation, among other things. This only emphasizes the exhortatory core of the Quran's message.

Other than the obvious missionary zeal of early Islam, the social context and nature of the earliest community are hard to reconstruct. The difficulty may be partly due to the fact that, unlike Jesus, Muḥammad lived into his sixties and had ample chance to translate his visions into a social program. The relatively long life of the founder is itself an argument against seeing Muḥammad's mature view of Islam as a millennialist cult and raises the question of what Christianity would have become had its founder avoided martyrdom to missionize more.

We would like to understand the historical development of Muḥammad's message, but that is not easy to demonstrate. We may suspect that in the course of his relatively long life of sixty-two years, the emphasis of his message subtly changed, reformulating what had previously been tried and abandoned, perfecting what had been received and proven successful. We have but hints of what might have happened. One might hypothesize that the notion of the coming end, so important for conversion, was more and more supplemented by institution building. By the time of the Prophet's death, the Muslim community (the *Umma*) was firmly fixed and the principles of its piety were firmly in place.

The Prophet's message, even if it had a millennialist tone at the beginning, certainly became the basis of a movement more of purification and repentance, as it grew more successful. It demanded repentance and submission (*'Islam*) and joining the community of fellow believers. Jews, Christians, Sabeans (and eventually Zoroastrians) were allowed to remain in their own community, as "people of the book" (*'Ahl al-Kitab*), though they were subjected to taxation and social discrimination.

But it is arguable that, at its inception, the word *'islam* sometimes did not refer just to the explicit Arab community of the faithful (*ummah*), but "surrender to God" in general, as the word "God-fearer" could refer to anyone who accepted the One God in the Hellenistic world. Islam could tolerate Jews and Christians as actual believers: "Whoso desires to behave in any other way than surrendering [to God], it shall not be accepted of him [by God], who will punish the individual by making him among the losers in the world to come" (Q 3:83–84), which is often today understood to exclude all non-Muslims. But the understanding of *'aslama* as "surrendered, submitted" and not specifically "converted to Islam" is supported by the context of this prophecy, which suggests a far more tolerant interpretation:

> What do they desire another *din* (religion, way of conduct) than God's, and to Him has surrendered (*'aslama*) whoso is in the heaven and the earth, willingly or unwillingly, and to Him they shall be returned?
> Say: "We believe in God and that which has been sent down to us, and sent down on Abraham and Ishmael, Isaac and Jacob, and the Tribes, and in that which was given to Moses and Jesus, and the Prophets, of their Lord; we make no distinction between any of them, and to Him we surrender (*muslimun*)." (Q 3:83–84)[9]

Muḥammad may be understood as calling everyone to a moral life, respecting Judaism and Christianity, and using the Day of Judgment of those religions to extend the moral choice to the peoples of the Hejaz: "Believers are friends one to the other to the exclusion of outsiders. To the

Jew who follows us belong help and equality. He shall not be wronged nor shall his enemies be aided. The peace of believers is indivisible." [10] There were limits to his toleration (Muḥammad dealt harshly with those who opposed him militarily) but the pattern of his intentions is clear enough. Later tradition, though, usually interprets these passages to mean that neither Jews nor Christians will share the benefits of the resurrection, although they are to be tolerated. [11]

The Prophet spoke about and received good advice on how best to govern the growing *ummah* (community) of Islam. After the Prophet's death, it became more what we might recognize as a purification movement, in some ways like Judaism, except with fewer "special laws." Compared to Judaism and Christianity, the demands of Islam are elegant in their simplicity. [12]

Study of the Quran

SOME OF THE ambiguity about earliest Islam may be due to the way in which the Quran has come down to us. When Islam was first studied in the West, a number of scholars (and Ernest Renan perhaps foremost among them) pointed out that, unlike Judaism and Christianity, whose origins are lost in the darkness of time, the foundation of Islam took place "in the full light of history." [13] Hence, it ought to be easier to study. That first impression turns out to be mistaken. The most important reports about Muḥammad (ca. 570–632 CE) are all written long enough after the fact by people deeply impressed with the message of Islam so as to look suspicious to secular scholars. They are, essentially, as reliable as the early Christian writings or the writings in the Pentateuch and subject to the same kinds of historical constraints, although there are far more of them than exist for early Christianity. [14] Muḥammad personally touched far more lives than Jesus could in his short, earthly career. The modern, scholarly study of the Quran is, however, in its infancy.

The present Quran was compiled from separate prophecies ascribed to Muḥammad edited during the reign of 'Uthman (644–656 CE), the third *Khalifa* (Calif, literally: "successor"). All versions of the Quran which disagreed with his version were destroyed. 'Uthman was killed by the fourth Khalifa 'Ali, who in turn succumbed to the Umayyads by 661 when the Umayyad Dynasty was firmly founded. Under these circumstances, some scholars have rightly felt free to reconstrue the early history of Islam, trying to recapture the "original movement" free of 'Uthman's proto-orthodoxy.

'Uthman's redaction of the revelations of Muḥammad was not chrono-logical; he put the longest of Muḥammad's revelations first and the shorter ones later, exactly as the New Testament treats the letters of Paul. The overwhelming consensus of scholars today is that the shorter, more ec-static utterances are the earliest revelations which Muḥammad received, so the earliest prophecies are actually at the end of the book. Muḥammad eschewed any attempt to confuse his person with the message of Islam, and Muslims have, on the whole, avoided deifying the prophet, though a con-siderable hagiography has unavoidably grown up around him.

Rather, it is the volume of the Quran itself which is claimed to be divine in Islam, not the founding figure, as in Christianity. Indeed, the Quran was later claimed to be the Uncreated Word of God, actually an aspect of divinity in the way that Philo's *logos* is intradeical (part of God) and ex-tradeical (part of the world) at the same time. So instead of the divine *logos* being made flesh as in the Gospel of John, in Islam the divine *logos* is made "Recitation," Quran. Muḥammad is greatly venerated for being a pious man and the carrier of this revelation, perhaps in an analogous manner to the respect for Moses in Judaism. Even more than the pious bi-ographers of Muḥammad himself, 'Uthman's edition of the Quran, there-fore, is the arbiter of the divine and transcendent in Islam. It is partly for this reason that Muslims have resisted either translating the Quran or subjecting it to historical criticism.

Some scholars have gone so far as to suggest that early Islam was based on Judaism and originally indistinguishable from it. This movement, they call "Hagarism." [15] The term expresses the notion that Islam was formu-lated on the basis of Judaism and Christianity except that it was directed at Arabs and comprised of Arabs. But this portrait is drawn largely from the reports of Jews and Christians. To be sure, early Islamic practice was actually rather close to Judaism in some of its theology and organization, while its zeal for conversion resembled Christianity. It learned much from its older sibling religions. On the other hand, the more radical scholarly reconstructions of Islamic origins, like the Hagarism model, lack com-plete credibility because early Islam was hardly free from sectarian strife. One would have expected that such radically alternate tellings of the early story, had they existed, would have surfaced both before 'Uthman and af-terwards. It is one thing to critique the received story of Islam; it is an-other to critique it using only reports from outsiders who would naturally see it as a kind of Judaism. [16]

If Islam is the missionary religion par excellence, it has rarely been guilty of the crime for which it is always indicted in Western culture—

conversion by the sword. Islam's conversion strategy has often been caricatured by its most militant statement: "Convert or die!" Though there have been cases of forced conversion, the Quran is itself a powerful argument against it: "There is no compulsion in religion" is the firm conviction of the Quran right after the famous Throne Verse (*ayyat al-kursi*, Q 2:255–6). No one should be forced to convert. Islam rarely presented its subject populations with forced conversion by brutality. Rather it designed a system of subtle but effective persuasions.

The fact is that conversion to Islam did not follow immediately upon Muslim conquest. When one looks, for example, at the Islamization of Iran, after its conquest (646 CE), one sees that the movement of the populace to Islam began slowly and only reached rapid growth in 791–864 CE.[17] It is a full century and a half after the Muslim conquest. Likewise, as Islam conquered Anatolia in progressive stages, displacing the Byzantine Empire, Islamization followed slowly thereafter, with many interesting cultural combinations.[18]

Islam is, first and foremost, a code of living for a worldwide community. To say that it emphasized conversion should not imply that it neglects the daily needs of the believer, even at the beginning. Its call to prayer five times a day, its five pillars of pious deeds, its rites of passage, as well as its sophisticated theology mediate the lives of millions of Muslims and have done so since Muhammad instituted them. After the great period of conquest was over, Islam became primarily the religion of a very large, stable population. So it would not be fair to consider Islam only a religion of conversion. Like every successful world religion, it became the way millions of people understood their lives and purposes in the world, so much so that most Muslims would not even see directly how effective was the Muslim intuition on life for missionary purposes. Mostly at the edges of the Islamic world, and in its more sectarian forms, Islam continues its missionary activities. One might say the same for Christianity.

The Grave and the Barzakh

MUSLIM BURIAL customs generally parallel Jewish ones. The dead are buried as soon as possible and doing so is a good deed, in spite of the uncleanness associated with touching the dead. They are bathed, clothed simply, and put in a clean shroud, legendarily to allow the dead to visit each other in heaven. Coffins are unnecessary but simple ones may be used; excessive display at funerals is against the spirit of Islam, as it is in Judaism.

There are also unique aspects of the tradition: Because Muḥammad was buried at night, nighttime became opportune for a funeral but it is not a necessary aspect of the ceremony. Women are forbidden to attend funerals at all, presumably because of their unrestrained expressions of grief. In general, Muslim funeral rites attempt to correct the excesses of ancient Near Eastern mourning rituals, as do Jewish ones as well. We have seen evidence of the ancient elaborations of funerals in the myths of Babylon and Canaan. In Islam, the body's decomposition is often viewed as a sentient experience for the corpse, with the pain serving as penance for the sins of life.

At first, there is very little, either in the Quran or classical canonical Muslim texts, to explain what happens to the individual "in the grave" before the day of judgment. The seeds of the later teaching can be found in Q 23:100ff., a passage that discusses a *barzakh,* a barrier, separating the departed from this life. The Arabic term is a Persian loan word, *farsakh,* meaning "a physical barrier" or "hindrance" or "separation." It was used in Old Persian to designate a unit of measurement, which was also borrowed into Greek as the word *parasang.*[19] The original Quranic passage is, granted, somewhat ambiguous but the term *barzakh* eventually comes to extend to both the time every individual waits for the day of judgment (in the grave) and the habitation of the dead who are awaiting judgment.

The original Quranic idiom is used to express that those on earth have only one life to prove their worth, that the dead have no second chance. This is an important incentive to repentance and conversion, as well as a call to charitable works:

> When death comes to a wrongdoer, he will say: "Lord, let me go back, that I may do good works in the world I have left behind."
>
> Never! These are the very words which he will speak. Behind them there shall stand the barrier *(al-barzakh)* 'til the Day of Resurrection. And when the trumpet is sounded, on that day, their ties of kindred shall be broken, nor shall they ask help of one another. (Q 23:100–102)

The term appears in a sermon meant to convince the hearer of the necessity of submission to Islam by explaining that repentance and belated promises to do good will be of no avail after death. There is a barrier separating the dead from the living.

Although the exhortation to a moral life is conspicuous, the meaning of the term *barzakh* is not entirely clear to later tradition. Other occurrences of the term in Suras 25:55 and 55:60 do not mention the dead, rather talk about the insurmountable barrier that God has placed between the oceans. This may suggest that the original meaning had as much to do with the lack of communication between the living and the dead, a theme sounded at the end of the *ayya*. The dead are not able to contact the living hence no one is to be consulted in the grave because the dead cannot hear the living (Sura 35:19–22; 27:80). This is meant to arrest universally popular spiritualism. On the other hand, the living can visit the afterlife, both in dreams and visions, because that warns humans about what awaits believers and nonbelievers after death.

Earliest Islam essentially taught that only the good among the faithful could count on resurrection; the bad believers and infidels were punished by their inability to gain resurrection at the day of judgment. The development of a notion of an interim state develops in response to the perceived delay in the arrival of the "day of judgment," just as the notions of the immortality of the soul and Original Sin develop in Christianity in response to the delay of the parousia. Later Muslim tradition adds a hell to the story, *Jahannam* (cognate with the Hebrew *Gehinom*, "Gehenna," but also called *sijjin* or the *Wadi Barhut*), giving the imagination space to expatiate on the punishments that await sinners after the day of judgment. All of these notions have social benefits—they encourage the faithful and aid in missionary outreach to prospective converts, as they do in every religion. We have seen the phenomenon before in Christianity. Islam produces a unique but similar synthesis in which the dead retain a permanent identity in the interim period so that they can be rewarded and punished before the final consummation.

When the body, though dead, is conceived of as the residence of a sensate person in the grave until the bodily resurrection, there does not need to be much more philosophical reflection about an essence of the person's identity, because it adheres to the corpse. The carrier of identity can remain the body when the afterlife is thought of as resurrection of the body. But Arabic contains the equivalent terms to the other Semitic tongues we have studied: *nafs* for "soul" and *ruḥ* for "spirit." They appear in the Quran and early Muslim writings. Like the other Semitic tongues, Arabic imposes its own connotations on the terms. In Arabic, *nafs* generally means "self" in a reflexive, grammatical sense (as in "I myself") more than "soul" and the *ruḥ* means "spirit," which designates God's spirit imparted to humanity.

When the day of judgment does not arrive in Christianity and Judaism, attention turns to postmortem reward and punishment. Islam also readjusts its expectations and develops an intermediate sense of self. As Muslim tradition adumbrates, the *barzakh* period begins to be seen more and more as a separate place, like purgatory, in which the dead become penitents to work off their sins in contrition and punishment. Then, it becomes important to be able to account for how the person can be both a corpse in the grave and also have an identity somewhere else doing penance. When this happens there is a tendency to use the two terms, *nafs* and *ruḥ,* to carry the freight of a separate identity apart from the body. In this context, *nafs* and *ruḥ* are often synonymous.

In Quran 39:42 we find the difficult *ayya:*

God takes unto Himself the souls [*al-anfus,* plural of *nafs*] at their deaths, and that which has not died [He takes] in its sleep. He keeps that for which He has ordained death and sends the other to its appointed term. In that are signs for a thoughtful [person.]

In commenting on this verse, Muslim exegetes tried to determine the difference between the departure of souls at death and during sleep and the differences between the *nafs* and *ruḥ.* The *nafs al-ʿaql wa'l-tamyiz* ("the soul" possessing the rational faculties of intelligence and discrimination) is the part of the "self" that is taken by God during sleep while sometimes the *ruḥ* is viewed as another part of the "self," *nafs al-ḥayat wa'l ḥaraka* ("the soul" possessing life and movement), namely that by which God gives life. Again, the notion of "self" reaches a more distinct form when a community needs to define a person as different from the body, an identity that survives death—namely, the transcendent part of the personality, and to describe how the person continues into immortality.[20] In this case, however, the split is only temporary since in the final disposition persons will regain a renewed body on a reconstructed earth (or at least a new habitation in paradise). The bodily resurrection makes possible intensifications of earthly pleasures—like food and wine, shade and leisure, pleasant odors, tasty foods, and sexual congress.

Later Views of the Afterlife

AFTER ITS INITIAL statement, Islamic traditions of the afterlife proliferate in as many ways as do Jewish and Christian ones. People all over the world want more detail about what awaits them after death. Muslims narrate that the angel of death *(Izra'il)* comes to remove the soul, which happens painlessly as the soul travels upward in the company of angels. Time in *barzakh* is usually understood as a kind of purgatory in which the body can feel the excruciatingly painful effects of decomposition. The angels Munkar and Nakir question the deceased and supervise the punishment process in the grave, depending on the good deeds *(ʿibada)* of the deceased. The angel who blows the trumpet at the final judgment becomes Israfil, if it is not Gibril. This moment is the occasion of enormous elaboration in later Muslim tradition. People are reclothed in flesh and sit on the grave waiting for their verdict. This is followed by the great gathering *(al-Ḥashr)* and the standing *(al-Maʿamad)* when the pious and impious contemplate their lives on earth. The adumbrated story emphasizes contemplation of one's deeds so as to spur better behavior.

We cannot trace the entire history of Muslim afterlife. A sample will have to suffice. A famous and well-known fifteenth-century author, *al-Suyuti*, describes the blessed and the "heretical" or condemned *(kafirun)* in their abodes after the final judgment. *Al-Suyuti* believes that heaven and hell are part of the present cosmos, not created at the judgment; therefore, the faithful dead can travel about, even visiting the living through dreams and visions. Sometimes the faithful dead are winged creatures, like birds, visiting the various heavens. Martyrs are described as beautiful green (a lucky and prefered color) birds living in the highest heaven, enjoying its lush foliage and water features while the *kafirs* (heretics or non-muslims) are condemned to be devoured by huge black birds in hell *(sijjin* or the *Wadi Barhut)*.[21]

Islam rejects reincarnation because reincarnation encourages moral laxness: For a believer in platonic reincarnation any good deed missed or any bad deed perpetrated in this life can be fixed in the next. Reincarnation has been condemned in Judaism and Christianity as well, though the idea occurs more frequently in Jewish lore and sometimes sneaks in through the backdoor in mystical meditation or in the Church Fathers. It does the same in Islamic mysticism and various sectarian movements.

In general though, Muslim eschatology is geared towards conversion and then for enforcing correct, moral behavior: For an ordinary Muslim, there is only one chance to live morally; everything about one's destiny depends on doing good in this life, a single chance to earn one's immortality, making necessary continuous moral striving (literally: *jihad)*, and making Islam hard to synthesize with Neoplatonism.

Nevertheless, it did so, quite successfully, in exactly the same way that Judaism and Christianity did—by accepting the Neoplatonic cosmology with its view of revelation of the good through successive spheres and, at the same time, denying or deemphasizing reincarnation. As in Judaism and Christianity, Neoplatonism was an important stimulus to mysticism because it validated ecstatic states in which the good and the divine could be apprehended in meditation. Islamic mystical language particularly emphasized the subsumption of the soul entirely into the being of God in "extinction" *(fana')*, which sometimes becomes a description of the afterlife. Neoplatonism gave Islam its notion of an immortal soul also.

Mi'raj *and the Heavenly Journey of the Soul*

WHILE THE Quran itself says almost nothing about Muhammad's "Night Journey" (the *mi'raj*), it becomes the subject of a later tradition in which Muhammad leaves this earth from Jerusalem on his steed *al-Boraq* (from Lightning, *al-barq*). Although Jerusalem is not mentioned in the original quite brief report of the *mi'raj* in the Quran and, indeed, the Arabs did not conquer Jerusalem until after Muhammad's death, the adumbrated story certainly emphasizes the importance that Jerusalem quickly achieves in the Islamic world. The ascent tradition constructs a Quranic importance to the city, which is otherwise lacking. This seems to mirror the historical fact that Jerusalem became a Muslim pilgrimage site after its conquest, just as it had been a Jewish and Christian one before.

To give concrete expression to this triumph, Muslims quickly built on the Temple Mount in Jerusualem (691 or 692 CE), a new building called a *mikdasa* (a sanctuary, not a mosque), which explicitly mirrors a Hebrew designation for the Jewish Temple *(Beth Hamikdaš)*, destroying and replacing the church that the Byzantine Christians had constructed there. It is the oldest surviving Muslim building outside of Arabia. On the Dome of the Rock were placed inscriptions stating that God is single and unique, that He needs no help or partner, and that He neither begets nor is begotten: "Praise be to God, who begets no son, and has no partner;" "He is God, one, eternal;" "He does not beget, He is not begotten, and He has no peer" (Q 112).[22]

These brief statements certainly mean to contradict the main premise of Christianity, replacing it with a new dispensation, represented by the new, powerful, architectural statement (itself based on a Byzantine church). So Islam both inherited and emulated the importance that Jerusalem had achieved in Judaism and Christianity, which Islam acknowledges as its legitimate but incomplete predecessors.[23] At the same time as it incorporates themes from its predecessors, Islam always insists that its claims take precedence over the previous revelations.

According to the later tradition of the prophet's sayings (the *Hadith*), which is richly detailed, the soul, once separated from the body, goes on a journey similar to Muḥammad's *miʿraj,* leaving earth from Jerusalem. Muḥammad had already ascended to the heavens from there while alive and was able to look down into the recesses of hell. In later tradition, Muḥammad's body is specially prepared for the trip by the purification of his heart (from Q 94). The angel Gibril opens Muḥammad's chest and washes it clean of impurities in a golden basin before restoring it to him. Thus, Muḥammad was ritually cleansed of all doubt, idolatry, paganism, and heresy so he can visit the pure Temple precincts and then join the even purer, heavenly hosts in the celestial Temple.

Later tradition tells many more stories of Muḥammad's ascent. While in heaven, he meets all the prophets, including Moses, and the angels residing in the various heavens. He has an audience before the divine throne, during which the command for Muslims to pray fifty times a day is communicated. It is Moses who advises him to return to God's presence, again and again, to reduce the onerous prayer requirements. Islam eventually ordained that Muslims should pray in fixed fashion, five times a day, twice more than Jews, and equal in number to Zoroastrian daily prayers. The Quran itself specifies prayer only three times a day—morning, noon, and night—but this story makes the added requirements seem light.[24]

Besides legitimating an increase in the number of Islamic daily prayers, the "Night Journey" story also defends against some of the objections of Muḥammad's early Arabian detractors—namely, that Muḥammad was simply an ordinary person. Though he promulgated a revelation, he showed few of the conventional characteristics of ecstatic holy men and mantic prophets who practiced in the Arabian peninsula. The Quran preserves some of these objections: "What's with this 'messenger'? He eats food and walks about in the marketplace. Why hasn't an angel been sent down to him, to be a warner with him" (Q 25:7)?[25]

Quran sura 25:32 makes these objections painfully clear:

> We shall not believe in you until you cause a spring to burst
>> forth for us from the earth,
> Or until you have a garden of dates and grapes and cause
>> rivers to burst forth abundantly in their midst,
> Or until you cause the sky to fall upon us in pieces, as you
>> have pretended it will, or you bring God and the angels
>> before us,
> Or until you have a gilded house or you mount up into the sky.
>> And we will not believe in your mounting up until you
>> cause to come down upon us a book that we can read.

The expectation was that a holy man would mount to heaven and reveal a whole book, all at once, which Muḥammad did not do. In fact, later tradition sometimes suggests that the entire Quran was revealed in one "Night of Power." The Quran itself, however, advises that such complaints can be countered with simple statements of God's majesty: "Say, Glory to my Lord, am I anything but a mortal human being and a messenger" (Q 17:93)?

Ascension traditions are crucially important to the social process of confirming the picture of the universe and the ethical systems. They have been told about prophets and priests since the beginning of historical time. Already before Islam, the heavenly journey was a well understood religious mythologem of great antiquity which, like Jerusalem itself, had to be domesticated to the Islamic cause. In relating the tradition, one can see the drama of creative minds working out the most effective way to bend the ascent tradition to express best the revelation of Islam.

Muḥammad's journey, therefore, also forms the confirmation of the journey of the soul heavenward. The soul of the virtuous takes the same route: it slips easily and painlessly from the body, led by the angel of death, or the angel Gibril, through the seven heavens to a vision of God; then, it returns to the grave to await the resurrection. The wicked have a different experience: Their passing is painful, and their taste of the hereafter is fearful. They are foul-smelling and are not permitted to ascend to heaven. Instead, they have a vision of the hell that awaits them on the day of judgment, whereupon they return to the grave to await their punishment in dread.[26]

The story of the *mi'raj* also forms the basis of a number of important ecstatic and ascension traditions for the living, thus confirming the existence of the heavenly realm, as developed by Muslim tradition. One of the earliest accounts by Muḥammad's successors is found in "The Quest for God" *(Al-Qasd Ila Ilah)* attributed to Abu'l-Qasim al-Junayd, though it is most likely pseudonymous. The ninth chapter of this work contains the account of the *mi'raj* of Abu Yazid al-Bistami, a person whose ecstatic utterances are, in turn, discussed in "The Book of Flashes" *(kitab al-Luma')* of Abu Naṣr as-Sarraj (d. 988). To Bistami is attributed a number of ecstatic utterances *(shaṭḥiyat)*, like those of the prophet himself at the end of the Quran, but far more provocative. Among them is "Glory to me," which claims divine attributes for Bistami, probably within the transformation tradition, which we have traced in ancient Near Eastern religious life, as well as in Judaism and in Christianity. What justified the divine self-designation of Bistami may well be his heavenly journey, which is found in Pseudo-al-Junayd. A great journey to God is described in the *mir'aj* of Abu Yazid al-Bistami. In it he appears before the divine throne and is vouchsafed a vision of God and special status as a chosen one *(safi)*:

I continued to cross sea after sea until I ended up at the greatest sea on which was the royal throne *('arsh)* of the Compassionate. I continued to recite his praises until I saw that all that there was—from the throne to the earth, of Cherubim *(karubiyyin)*, angels, and the bearers of the royal throne and others created by All Most High and Glorious in the heavens and the earth—was smaller, from the perspective of the flight of the secret of my heart in quest for him, than a mustard seed between sky and earth. Then he continued to show me of the subtleties of his beneficence and the fullness of his power and the greatness of his sovereignty what would wear out the tongue to depict and describe. Through all that, I kept saying: O my dear one! My goal is other than that which you are showing me, and I did not turn toward it out of respect for his sanctity. And when Allah Most High and Glorious knew the sincerity of my will in quest for him, he called out "To me, to me!" and said, "O, my chosen one *(safi)*, come near to me and look upon the plains of my splendor and the domains of my brightness. Sit upon the carpet of my holiness until you see the subtleties of my artisanship I-ness. You are my chosen one, my beloved, and the best of my creatures."

Upon hearing that, it was as if I were melting like melting lead. Then he gave me a drink from the spring of graciousness *(lutf)* with the cup of intimacy. Then, he brought me to a state that I am unable to describe. Then, he brought me closer and closer to him until I was nearer to him than the spirit is to the body.

Then, the spirit of each prophet received me, saluted me, and glorified my situation. They spoke to me and I spoke to them. Then the spirit of Muḥammad, the blessings and peace of God be upon him, received me, saluted me, and said: O, Abu Yazid: Welcome! Welcome! Allah has preferred you over many of his creatures. When you return to earth, bear to my community my salutation and give them sincere advice as much as you can and call them to Allah, Most High and Glorious. I kept on in this way until I was like he was before creation and only the real remained *(baqiya)* without being or relation or place or position or quality. May his glory be glorified and his names held transcendent![27]

This is as complete a retelling of the ecstatic journey to heaven of Mesopotamian, Jewish, Christian, and Hellenistic cults as we are likely to find. And it seems to function in the same ways as its predecessors. The adept enters an ecstatic state, journeys to heaven, and is greeted in each heaven, verifying that each has all the things that the faithful are led to expect. Then, the adept is led into the presence of the saints and prophets and God himself, just as is narrated of Muḥammad himself. Ecstasy accompanies these miraculous events. The adept comes into the presence of God and is transformed into one of the immortal company, essentially becoming a saint or angel.[28] The metaphor for the transformation is of smelting metals together. As we have seen, there are physiological concomitants to these ascension traditions. The content is a mixture of physiological experience and cultural expectations.

The Martyr (Shahid)

IN QURAN Sura 29, "The Spider," Ayyas 57–58, we find the following stirring picture:

> Every soul must taste of death, then to Us you shall be brought back. And (as for) for those who believe and do good, We will certainly give them abode in the high places in gardens beneath which rivers flow, abiding therein; how good the reward of the workers.

This passage discusses the felicities awaiting all the faithful. But there are those who associate the verse with the word *shahid* of ayya 52. In any event, unlike the mass of humanity, "martyrs" (sing. *shahid*; pl. *shahada*) do not have to wait in their graves for the final consummation.

The word *shahid* is related to the Muslim affirmation of faith, the *shahada*. It means "witness" and appears to be a direct appropriation of the Syrian Christian term for "martyr," which, in turn, comes from the Greek Christian *martyr*. The watchword of Muslim faith can also be called "witnessing" because it is a kind of creed spoken publicly like an oath. It is always difficult to use the vocabulary of one religion to describe characteristics of another. But there is an added difficulty with the extension of the term to martyrdom. Because the Christian tradition of legal witnessing *(sacramentum)* is not present in Islam, there is a difficulty in the early Muslim tradition concerning exactly what "witness" means: for example, is the martyr the witness or does God witness the sacrifice?[29] This parallels the use of the term martyr in early Christianity, like the *pro-*

tomartyrium of Stephen.[30] It is quite probable that the vocabulary was borrowed from Christianity first, with its specific meaning in Islam developing subsequently.

From all that we know about martyrdom, we should expect a special reward between martyrdom and the afterlife, from everything we have come to understand about the two conceptions elsewhere in Western traditions. Islam adds an important new twist to the tradition: The martyrs await the day of judgment in a specially prepared pleasure-garden *(al-janna)*, which is elliptically described in several places in the Quran (see, e.g., Q 56:1–26). As in Rabbinic Judaism, this garden is the garden of Eden, where the original couple enacted their drama of disobedience. In Muslim tradition, Satan himself is present as Iblis (perhaps from Greek *diabolos*); he plays the role of the snake. He also sins against God by refusing a direct order to worship the newly created Adam (Q 2:29–30).

Not only is there a special heaven reserved for martyrs while they await the day of judgment, the same accommodations are available to the holy warriors (sing. *mujahid*; pl. *mujahidin*), who die in battle. These martyrs are those people who take on Jihad (from the root meaning "striving") as soldiers. The use of the term goes back to Muhammad, who spoke both of the striving to be moral in each person, the greater Jihad, and the lesser Jihad, a term usually translated "holy war." Most of the discussion of Jihad in the Quran, and for a considerable time afterwards, deals with "holy war" and not with personal striving. The term *mujahid*, striver, normally refers to the soldier-warriors of the "holy war."[31]

As a sacred duty, holy war is regulated by religious law. Over the centuries, many things about holy war are prescribed and proscribed in Muslim law. What we today call "terrorism"—that is, randomly killing civilians—is forbidden. So is suicide. Yet, in a "holy war," the *mujahidin* can attain the status of the *shahid*, the martyr. Not only that, the early *Hadith* literature encourages martyrdom. The person seeking martyrdom, the *talab al-shahada*, is to be exalted and emulated. This kind of martyrdom is earnestly prayed for and devoutly wished for. A merciful God would never deny the desire of a seeker of martyrdom: "One who prays for martyrdom sincerely: God will place him among the ranks of the martyrs, even if he dies in his bed."[32] The practice became associated with the Kharijite rebels and condemned.[33] Nevertheless, holy war and martyrdom are two tandem engines powering the early Islamic conquest of the Middle East, as well as large chunks of Europe and Asia.

According to Muslim tradition, Muhammad himself ruled that the soldier of Islam who died in attacking the infidel would go immediately to paradise. The tradition goes back to the battle of Badr, on March 15, 624, when Muhammad's greatly outnumbered band of Muslims faced the organized forces of his own tribe, the Quraysh. After spending hours in prayer, Muhammad told Abu Bakr that the angel Gibril himself, armed for war, and his entire angelic host would be fighting with them (Q 8:9). Muhammad announced to his troops that the soul of anyone killed that day while advancing against the enemy would be transported immediately to paradise. When a youth named Umayr heard the promise, he exclaimed: "Wonder of wonders! Is there nothing between me and my entry into paradise but that these men kill me?" Miraculously, the day was an enormous victory for Muhammad and the Muslim forces. Only fourteen Muslims died at the battle of Badr but among them was the fifteen-year-old Umayr.[34]

The rewards awaiting the *mujahidin* are similar to those of the faithful and righteous after the day of judgment but they are specially rewarded during the *barzakh* in Islamic imagination, with all the luxuries of the current life, including access to seventy-two wide-eyed beauties, the *hur* ("the pure," often called "Houris" in English), whose presence is inferred from the Quran itself:

> For them [i.e. God's sincere servants] is a known sustenance, Fruits, and they shall be highly honored. In gardens of pleasure, on thrones facing each other. A bowl shall be made to go around them from water running out of springs, white, delicious to those who drink. There shall be no trouble in it, nor shall they be exhausted therewith. And with them shall be those who restrain the eyes, having beautiful eyes; as if they were eggs carefully protected. (Q 37:41–49)

Since the word *hur* itself does not appear in the *Ayya*, the interpretation is somewhat obscure. "Those who restrain the eyes" *(Attaruf 'ayn)* can be interpreted in several ways. One key is to associate them with Quran 56:22, where the "pure of eye" *(hur 'ayn)* are described in a very similar description of paradise. Hence the women receive their name, the *hur*. In later tradition, they often are described as constantly repristinated virgins, possibly picking up on connotations of their designation as "pure." But a more cautious interpretation would be that they are wives *('Azw'aj)*, taking a clue from yet another, similar Quranic passage (36:56). In the original description, the *hur* are described as modest women. They restrain their glances and sex is never mentioned, though their glances may imply seductiveness. There are more than two *hur* but their number is not given.

Another opinion in later tradition, that *"ḥur"* is a specification of the fruit mentioned earlier in two locations, is unlikely grammatically and seems to be an apologetic against the later excessive sensuousness of this picture of paradise. But beautiful women who serve the needs of the men are a regular part of the folklore of the Hejaz. They are a conventional picture of the court and pleasure gardens of a wealthy, powerful *sheikh* (tribal chieftain) or an oriental potentate. Given the culture from which it arose, that the pleasures of kingship are used to describe Allah's special paradise reserved for His martyrs ought not to be surprising. The strict regulation of sexual access before marriage in this part of the world, a custom that preceded Islam and is by no means confined to it, accounts for the paradisal vision of the pleasures and wealth, as compensation for forgone youthful pleasures in this world.

This alluring portrait is part of Islam's efficient organization for conversion and conquest. Few have ever been convinced to fight to the death by a philosophical treatise. The *mujahidin's* attainment of a sheikh's harem is a more concrete and attractive reward. There is no corresponding reward for female martyrs.[35] But wine-drinking (forbidden to Muslims on earth), garden leisure, and other pleasures can be envisioned. Christians and Jews have tended to denigrate this description, especially in its most florid versions, because orgiastic sexual relations are implied in heaven. Neither Jews nor Zoroastrians should find the more temperate descriptions so jarring, as both religions affirm the benefit of sexual pleasures on earth and, sometimes, in heaven.

As for continued sexuality in paradise, Jews and Zoroastrians opine on both sides of the issue. For Islam, the imagery of the pleasure garden was also transformed by sophisticated theologians and mystics; but the pleasure garden remains a lively tradition with ordinary Muslims and is still especially relevant for those who seek martyrdom. Each tradition picks its own vocabulary to express the balance between pleasure and piety. In Islam, the words of the Prophet himself are a useful guide: *"la rahbaniyya fi al-Islam,"* he announced, "There is no monasticism in Islam." Neither is there in Judaism or Zoroastrianism. Modesty is a virtue but celibacy per se is not.

The concrete image encourages Muslims to greater bravery and piety. For intellectuals, for non-traditional Arabs, and for Muslims in non-Arab lands with very different notions of sexuality, Islam also contains a great many more sophisticated views of the afterlife, in which the nature and pleasures of postmortem identity are explored philosophically or mystically. But there is no doubt that the pleasure-garden motif is a strong characteristic of the traditional Muslim view of paradise. So characteristic is it of Muslim narratives of heaven that pleasures of this world and great works of art are regularly described as "the fragrance of paradise." [36]

The Early Extremist Shi'a Mystics

OTHER ENGINES of Muslim religious conquest are mystical Sufi orders, who often penetrated a new land before the armies of Islam reached it. A great many Islamic traditions pick up the mystical mythology of heavenly ascent. They seem deeply affected by the Merkabah and Gnostic traditions that preceded them, but the traditions also develop in purely Islamic directions.[37] Islam in its classical formulation disallows intercession. This powerful notion of improving one's passage to the hereafter (or, in contemporary Islamicist explanation, improving one's loved ones status) makes a strong comeback in Ṣufi and Marabout Islam, as well as in the description of the martyrs' rewards for extremist Islamic terrorism. Veneration of saints seems to be an almost universal phenomenon in human life and Islam contains its fair share of it.[38]

Jews and Muslims both emphasize their own strict monotheism in any polemic against Christianity and so tend to downplay these minority traditions of mediators. The issue of mediation is important in early Christianity and certainly continued in mystical Judaism. The *Kabod* figure, otherwise named Metatron by the Rabbis, and one of the bases of the conception of the risen Christ as a hypostasis of God, was occasionally reimagined in mystical Islam. In Islam it also designated the primary human representation of the divinity. For instance, we find a peculiar report in the Quran that the Jews compromise Biblical monotheism by worshiping Ezra: "The Jews say, "Ezra ('Uzair) is the Son of God'; the Christians say, 'The Messiah is the Son of God.' " This suggests that the prophet knew of these mystical traditions of mediation among Jews as well as among Christians.

Gordon Newby argues that 'Uzair is not actually the Biblical Ezra but should be equated with another familiar Biblical figure—namely, Enoch— who becomes the angel Metatron in *3 Enoch*.[39] All of these traditions seem to underlie the Quran's statements and to make them most fully intelligible. Steve Wasserstrom also suggests that the original name may be Azaz'el, from the term for the Biblical scapegoat (e.g., Lev 16:10) that eventually becomes the name for an angel (one of "the sons of God"), though a fallen one in the Enoch tradition.[40]

But, in spite of the warning, the same kind of doctrine shows up in Islam, in the *ghuluww* (the early extremist Gnostics and mystical Shi'a, a forerunner to Ṣufism which was often held heretical).[41] According to these doctrines, God himself did not create the universe, rather relegated *(fauwwida)* the act of Creation to a lesser divinity.[42] The clearest instance of this binitarianism is quite similar to the Jewish traditions about Metatron and can be found in the *'Umm al-Qitab,* a Persian Gnostic apocalypse of the eighth century. Salman al-Farisi, a human, becomes a demiurgic divine potency in the *'Umm al-Qitab.* But the demiurge is patterned on Metatron, as suggested by the phrase "lesser Salman," as in Metatron's "the lesser Lord."[43] Mas'udi in the tenth century, brings up the "Ashma'ath" (themselves categorized as a kind of Isra'iliyyun, "Judaizers"),[44] who adore a "little Lord," *(ar-rabb aṣ-ṣaghir).* The name itself is related to the Latin demon Asmodeus and may go back to Biblical traditions about the Samaritans, a mixed population of those Israelites left behind by the Assyrians and those whom the Assyrians brought in to resettle the land of Israel. Those who came from Hamath are said to have made Ashima their god (2 Kgs 17:31).

The transmitter of these traditions is likely to be Karaite Jews, not the Samaritans, who are too marginal to carry such a well-attested tradition. Maqdisi also mentions the Ashma'ath but says that most Jews follow the beliefs of Ashma'ath or 'Anan, the founder of Karaism, apparently assuming they are both founders of sects, if they are not meant to be the same. Ibn Ḥazm mentions the Ash'aniyya, whom he thinks are Rabbinic Jews. He criticizes them as worshipers of the Little Lord *(ar-rabb aṣ-ṣaghir).* Su'udi in the sixteenth century says that the Ashma'iyya assert that their creator has the form of an old man with white hair and a beard. They assert that He has a deputy in the third heaven whom they call the "Littler God" *(allah al-aṣghar):* they assert that He is the ruler (or organizer) of the world.[45] The *Gannat Bussame,* a Syriac compendium against heresy written about the year 1000 CE, suggests that the Jews worship a *Adonai Haqaton* (Hebrew for "the Little Lord" or "the Little YHWH"), General of *Adonai HaGadol* (Hebrew for "the Great Lord" or "the Great YHWH"), which it views as scandalous error. No doubt, this is a figuration of various Jewish mystical doctrines arising out of the Daniel 7:9–13 traditions, which somewhat conform to the ideas found in the Hekhaloth literature. Although the tradition is very ancient (it is, in a way, the basis of Christology in Christianity), it can also be seen throughout Muslim history, with outstanding examples even as late as the powerful Shi'ite cleric Muḥammad Baqir b. Taqi Al-majlisi of Isfahan (1628–99).[46]

To be sure, it is difficult to talk about "heresy" per se in Islam, where sects tend to delegitimize each other with epithets like "un-islamic" (*kafir,* "denier"). Nevertheless, we can talk about these struggles in a general way with the Christian conception of heresy. The differences in the way these sects are described suggest that the Muslim heresiologists are not just copying from each other but know the phenomenon personally, though they may not be familiar enough to describe it exactly. Under the circumstances, it remains all the more elusive to us.

Fana'

AS WE HAVE seen, the grave is the location for the Muslim masses to await the great day of judgment. Though no Muslim would formulate this as a rule, there are two great exceptions to the fate that awaits the dead in the grave until the day of judgment. The first and most important exception, as we have seen, is the martyr. But, in their own eyes, at least, mystics also are entitled to an exception to the rule that all have to meditate on their sins in the grave and be judged at the day of judgment. The exception evolved slowly. Early ascetics such as Ḥasan al-Baṣri (d. 728) stressed their fear of hell and their desire for paradise because they were overwhelmed with their own sinfulness. They sought the hereafter *(al-'aḥira)* because they rejected this world *(al-dunya)*. In Ḥasan's words, "Be with this world as if you had never been there, and with the other world as if you would never leave it." [47]

But ecstatic love of God soon took over from asceticism as the key element in Ṣufism and, as a result, new views of the otherworld began to appear. For the earliest Muslim love-mystic, the Arab poetess *Rabi'ah al-'Adawiyah* (d. 801), selfless love of God required the Ṣufi to be veiled from both this world and the other by visions of God. The Ṣufi must love God so much that even paradise and hell are forgotten. Ṣufis such as Yaḥya 'ibn Mu'adh ar-Razi (d. 871) replaced fear of punishment and hope of reward with complete trust in God's mercy. He found death beautiful because it joined friend with friend in God.

The Ṣufis, in particular, quite frequently articulate their goals after death and in life as pantheistic extinction *(fana')*, which may free them from what we might call in an extended sense the "purgatory" of the *barzakh* state or the grave. Their earthly asceticism and meditation effectively earn them an exemption from the grim job of the rest of us in atoning for our sins. Indeed, many Ṣufis like Yunus Emre of Turkey (d. approx. 1321 CE) simply ridiculed the Quranic notion of the afterlife as folklore for the naive masses.[48] His example has been followed by many modern, believing Muslims who look at the paradisal imagery of the Quran as appropriate more for the original Arab hearers of Islam than for mystics and moderns.

The goal of the Sufis became *fana'* or annihilation, which usually means the complete obliteration of the self in the personhood of God. This mystical state of oneness can be achieved either in this world or the world to come. In this world, *fana'* is the state of meditative absorption into the divinity, available to the greatest meditative masters, which is proleptically the state of the afterlife. It describes the pantheistic ecstasy and joy of the mystic absorbed into God on earth and, at the same time, it is the condition of the saved soul after death (and sometimes before birth as well). Thus, the mystic in the performance of his mystic meditation achieves a preview of the final consummation of the soul, perhaps even, by achieving the state on earth, insures his own final disposition after death. This search for ecstasy may function in many ways, not the least of which is that it claims that the joy which mystics achieve in meditation is proof of their own ultimate reward.

Aware of the arrogance of this position, some mystics suggest that the joys of *fana'* must themselves be given up so that one is absorbed into God with no ego left at all. This tradition therefore distinguishes between the *fana'* that is achievable by the mystic on earth and the final consummation. *Fana'* can also be expressed in a variety of other metaphors, like being in the light of the face of God or being subsumed into God. A famous Sufi statement of the subsumption of the individual in God is: "I was raw; I was cooked; I was eaten." The claim that the individual Sufi has achieved unity with God is a powerful claim to religious legitimacy and power, surpassing all other kinds of religious authority. We have already often seen this strategy of using direct contact with the divine to innovate and neutralize other forms of religious authority.

Although *fana'* sometimes also implies a previous ascent to God, and so can be identified with the heavenly journey of the soul as the Platonists understood it; it can also quite successfully be identified with the Aristotelian notion of intelligence. Al-Ghazzali, who was both a philosopher and and a Sufi, suggests that, as a soul ascends, its individuality fades away, which is considered "a second death." For a Sufi, however, this is how it should be: human intelligences, upon their death, are subsumed into God himself, who is quintessentially intelligence and love.

This synthesis of Neoplatonism and Aristotelianism carried over and developed in both Judaism and Christianity as well, which learned much of their Greek philosophy secondhand from the great Medieval Muslim philosophers. For Maimonides and some other medieval Jewish philosophers, this meant that the soul's afterlife was assured but that no convincing proof of a personal afterlife would come out of Aristotelian philosophy. Personal immortality was based on faith, guided by the knowledge that the soul's immortality could be proven. Maimonides developed this approach by personal study of Islamic philosophy—more exactly, by reading Arab philosophers like al-Farabi.[49]

Martyrdom in Shi'ite Islam

THE SHI'ITES are those Muslims who believe that Muḥammad's companion 'Ali b. Abi Ṭalib, the cousin and son-in-law of the Prophet, should be his immediate successor as the true Imam or prayer leader of the Muslim community. However, Abu Bakr, 'Umar, and then 'Uthman were appointed over 'Ali by the more powerful members of the Prophet's closest companions. Finally, 'Ali was appointed as the fourth Caliph but the dispute was exacerbated by 'Ali's refusal to punish the murderers of 'Uthman. This dispute continued for approximately 50 years after the death of the prophet, with considerable periods of antagonism between the various parties.

Shi'ite Islam as a formal movement began with the defeat, destruction, and deaths of the "party of the faithful" (Hizballah) at the battle of Karbala in Iraq on the Tenth of Muḥarram, 61 AH (680 CE), known in Arabic as "The 'Ashura," ("The Tenth"). The day is marked by most Muslims, but for the Shi'ites it is a very special and most holy day. For them, the battle signifies the formation of the denomination of Islam known officially as the Shi'at 'Ali, who hold 'Ali and his son Ḥussein (Muḥammad's grandson) legitimate successors (Caliphs) of the prophet.

In Shi'ite history, the defeat and death of Ḥussein are understood as a martyrdom in which the evil perpetrators of the murder were other, wrongly-guided Muslims. As a result, Shi'ite interpretation of the succession is quite different from the Sunni one; and Shi'ites also differ with each other about the order of the succession, spawning many messianic and mystical notions of the true Imam. Shi'ite religious piety differs significantly from Sunni practice even today. The most obvious difference is that the Shi'ites recite two added clauses about 'Ali's special status in their five-times-daily prayers. Shi'ites may also make a pilgrimage to Karbala as a mark of their religious devotion.

Shi'ite ritual and religious life contains a great many traditions that honor the memory of the early martyrs, giving the Shi'a an even richer martyrological tradition than the majority Sunna tradition. Some of the traditions feature flagellation and blood imagery prominently as signs of the remembrance of the martyrdom of Ḥussein.

Taʿziye

ONE INTERESTING Shiʿite folk tradition is the *Taʿziye,* a dramatic reenactment of the martyrdom of Ḥussein, the grandson of Muḥammad and and third Shiʿite Imam. This may be the only native Muslim dramatic form, which originated in rural Iran as well as now existing in Iranian cities in more refined form.[50] In the basic village format, traveling troupes perform the plays for the benefit of the villagers' religious devotion. Villagers become participants with the actors and so lose themselves in the tragic events of the play that some report they are transported to the original martyrdom. In this way, the play moves from commemoration to reenactment, becoming a truly religious ritual rather than theater.

The various cycles of *taʿziya* depict the entrapment and death of Ḥussein, his family, and followers. The play resembles medieval Christian Passion Plays in many respects. There are many obvious conventions that help the audience/participants interpret the action of this dramatic liturgy. For example, the good characters always wear colorful clothing and chant or sing their lines. The villains always wear black and always speak, never sing. Martyrs always don white clothing before their sacrificial act.

In one poignant cycle, the two young sons of a warrior named Muslim, a follower of Ḥussein, are tracked down relentlessly. They try to escape until they are found out and then vie with each other for the privilege of being martyred first. In recent years, the villains have often been costumed and figured as Jews or Israelis and, since the 1979 revolution, as Americans. The effect of this kind of religious drama is to divide the world dualistically into the Shiʿite Muslims, the only true Islam, and the rest of the world, who are not just neutral observers but active, demonic enemies of Islam. The Sunna and "The Great Satan" (the United States), are all equally enemies of Islam, while Israel is styled "the Little Satan." This justifies any Shiʿite attack against Sunnis, Jews, Americans, or non-Muslims as a defensive action. It is also a powerful religious encouragement to martyrdom, to say nothing of its depiction of the seemingly inevitable tragedy of life.

Salvation for the Crusaders

JIHAD IN THE sense of "holy war" has been part of Islam since its foundation. It has been used to conquer previously pagan lands as recently as 1896, when north-eastern Afghanistan was won for Islam through Jihad. Nevertheless, Jihad is normally understood as a defensive war, to protect the faithful from attack. But holy war was not a native or long-standing tradition in Christianity.[51] When Christianity sought to reclaim the Holy Land, it came up with the equivalent doctrine to Jihad and, to motivate its armies to fight the Muslims, a doctrine equivalent to *shahada*. A Christian religious war is a crusade and the religious instrument used to motivate soldiers for heavenly reward became the plenary indulgence, though it took several intermediary steps to get there.

Augustine himself outlined a theology of a "just war." While deploring the necessity of war, he maintained that even the righteous were compelled to fight wars to repress the sinfulness of the wicked. Thus, the church could endorse certain acts of violence as protection of the faithful. Daniel 2:21 allows that God both sets up and deposes kings, a verse that was soon interpreted to justify wars of the righteous against the wicked. John of Mantua suggested that even Jesus supported the use of religious violence. He based himself on Matthew 26:51–52, verses in which Jesus rejects violence at his arrest:

> And behold, one of those who were with Jesus stretched out his hand and drew his sword, and struck the slave of the high priest, and cut off his ear. Then Jesus said to him, "Put your sword back into its place; for all who take the sword will perish by the sword."

According to John of Mantua's interpretation, this verse allows for religious violence because Jesus asked the disciple to put his sword away instead of throwing it away. While this argument is a pretext for military action against Islam, it is also an insight into the violent age that produced it. It even became customary to bless the sword of a new knight in a religious ceremony.

Already in the ninth century, the Popes were promising that death in a war against infidels would bring salvation. Pope Leo IV (847) promised a heavenly reward for any warrior dying in battle for defense of the church. Pope Nicholas I (858) promised both an earthly and heavenly indulgence for those having violated canon law, if they took up arms against the infidels (which he called a "plenary indulgence"). Pope John VIII (872) extended this promise to mean that victims were as pure as martyrs for the cross and so received a remission of sins. Pope Alexander II (1061), promised the same indulgence for all those who fought for the cross in Spain, expelling the Moors from Christian lands (the *Reconquista*). Gregory VII became the first pope to call for a war of all Christendom against the infidels. All that remained was for his successor Pope Urban II to call for the First Crusade (1095), which resulted in the capture of Jerusalem in 1099 by soldiers of Christendom, who were told that if they died in battle, they would go directly to heaven, in spite of any previous sins.[52]

The history of the Crusades is riddled with terrors for Jews, Christians, and Muslims alike. Impatient to earn their salvation, the soldiers of Christ began by killing anyone not like them. In the Spring of 1096, when the Crusaders were passing through the Rhine Valley on their way to the Holy Land, they attacked the Jewish settlements, killing anyone they could catch—man, woman, or child. These tragedies formed the core of a medieval Jewish martyrological tradition, most fully attested in chronicles and poetry.[53] The Crusaders' capture of Jerusalem in 1099 inaugurated the short zenith of their military power. It was a disaster for Muslims, for Jews, and Eastern Christians as well.

The Muslim reconquest began in earnest when Reynald of Châtillon initiated raids and skirmishes from his fortress city of Kerak, south of Amman in Jordan, which harassed the local caravan and shipping routes. Saladin (Salah ad-Din) eventually called a *jihad* when Reynald's raids extended into Saudi Arabia and to the Red Sea. This brought the Crusader leader, Guy of Jerusalem, into the fray. The climactic battle took place at the Horns of Hattin (a topographic feature named for the god Baʿal) in the Galilee on July 4, 1187.

It was a total victory for the forces of Saladin. Reynald was captured and killed while King Guy of Jerusalem was captured and held for ransom. As a result, the Crusaders lost their Holy Land possessions, subsequently managing to burn Constantinople in their efforts to reclaim their possessions (1204). They also unknowingly killed thousands of Palestinian Christians throughout their rule, because they confused them with Muslims. They never regained Jerusalem again. For their part, Spanish Christians, after expelling the Muslims and Jews from Al-Andalus in 1492, turned to torturing and burning suspect converted Muslims and Jews, as an act of faith.

In spite of these grave injustices, many ordinary Christians learned altruism and piety from the stories of the early martyred saints. Just like medieval Christians, millions of ordinary Muslims have lived lives of religious striving and piety, gaining strength and motivation from the stories of Jihad, martyrdom, and suffering.[54] They are not particularly affected by the extremes of Islamic thought which have recently reached the attention of the West. They are quite commonplace spiritual meditations for ordinary people.

On the other hand, these ideas of martyrdom can be manipulated by unscrupulous political and religious leaders. It would be wrong to underestimate the force of these religious justifications for motivating soldiers of Christendom and Islam in the Middle Ages or even in our own day, whether the war be national or religious in nature. It is characteristic of our day that national and political conflicts are being reexpressed in religious terms.

Modern Islamic Views of the Afterlife

IF THE CLASSIC and medieval Islamic views of the afterlife are more complex than we can characterize in a few paragraphs, modern views are nearly impossible even to categorize in this chapter. It is, however, tentatively possible to divide modern Muslim views into ways similar to those of modern America. There is the traditional camp that views Quranic descriptions of bodily resurrection as still relevant today. This camp will include a number of ordinary pious Muslims for whom the language of the day of judgment and the *barzakh* remains especially meaningful, as well as the growing number of fundamentalists and the small but very dangerous group of fundamentalist extremists. These latter Muslims are very much more conscious of the value of conversion and mission in Muslim life and tend to favor the foundation of states based on Islamic law, the *shariyaᶜ*. Not only do heaven and hell retain a hold on their religious life, they are often quite elaborately described.

However, unacknowledged innovation abounds in these modern interpretations of tradition. The horrendous descriptions of the pain of dying for the sinful, and the pleasures which a *shahid* can bring for himself, his family, and friends are new ideas in Islam; many Muslims, with some justification, would judge these innovations as heretical. The people who promulgate them are in very many respects like modern Christian fundamentalists or Christian fundamentalist extremists, who innovate even while claiming they are returning to the ancient tradition.

On the other side, one sees another group of theologians who interpret Islam's traditional teachings much more broadly and attempt to see in Islam a justification for cultural pluralism and interreligious tolerance.

Though these writers are as yet only a small minority of Muslim writers, their existence is very significant. They tend to speak out of culturally plural situations, like India, or the Muslim Diaspora in Europe and the United States, and they try to demonstrate that Islam can coexist with other like-minded, tolerant religions.[55] But they do not come only from these places. And, indeed, some fundamentalist extremism was formed in Diaspora, European and American culture as well.

Osama bin Laden and Fundamentalism

FUNDAMENTALIST extremism is a phenomenon that exists in all religions, not just Islam. At the moment, Islam is numerically the largest sponsor of violent extremism. Since the events of September 11, 2001, Muslim extremist religious beliefs have been tragically emphasized for Americans, but Muslims have been very much aware of them for decades, while we have occasionally focused on our own brand of fundamentalist extremism.[56] It is crucial for Americans to realize that these movements are not normative for Islam, much less American Islam, but are sectarian movements of extraordinary intensity present in every religion. Islamic fundamentalist extremist sects have as much in common with sectarian, fundamentalist extremism throughout the religious world as they do with Islam in particular. We need to study them and their relationship to martyrdom and the afterlife.

The horrifying events of September 11, 2001 are instructive for our discussion of the role of the afterlife in motivating extremist actions. Some of the terrorists may have been agents of terrorist groups like *Hamas*,[57] *Hizballah*,[58] or *Al-Qaʿida*.[59] Whether or not Iraq has had a role in the World Trade Center attack (which has neither been proven nor disproven), Iran has certainly been bankrolling *Hamas* and *Hizballah* for decades while they engaged in terrorist acts against the United States and the West, as well as against Israel. Iraq, a ferocious secular despotism inspired by Nazi fascism, has been giving aid, support, and training to a variety of terrorist groups, without regard to the religious roots of their extremism. In the Middle East, the enemy of my enemy is my friend.[60]

Islamic extremism (or "Islamism") has been especially good at blaming the scandalous state of human rights in the Arab world on the existence of two mythologically evil opponents of Islam: Israel and the United States.[61] This is not predominantly a political statement although, obviously, there is some truth to the opposition of Israel and the United States to Islamicist goals. The United States has had a stake in supporting the governments of Egypt, Jordan, Turkey, and Saudi Arabia, as well as Israel, though it is hardly the reason why any particular regime has remained in power.

The United States, along with most of Europe, also supported the regime of the Shah, which was a very Western-oriented government, but did not prop it up when it was in danger of falling. In point of fact, the United States has stayed away from extreme forms of domestic interference since the embarrassments of CIA involvements in the 70s and 80s. It is also true that Israel has curtailed the rights of Palestinians in response to violence against its citizens. As a result, they have also strengthened the conditions of deprivation and hopelessness which underlie the production of martyrdom. To the dualist minds of Islamicists, this demonstrates the Israelis' satanic purposes.

If the West is not blameless, neither is the Arab world. In spite of attempts to help the Arab world develop, the economies of the Arab states are in shambles, because capital usable for development is siphoned away by the despotic and the wealthy. The entire Arab world ranks far below Israel in exports, goods, and services. Arguably anti-Western attitudes are part of the problem. The interference of the United States operates as much as an excuse as a real reason for the problems of the area. Certainly the Arab world has been no friend of American foreign policy in the modern period either. It gave significant aid and support to the Nazis during the Second World War and then to the Soviets in the Cold War. It consistently applauds the successes of terrorist actions against the United States and then irrationally blames the very same actions on Israelis or the CIA. It cannot find its way out of the quagmire of irrational hates. Favorable public opinion of the United States in the Arab world is steady at 4 percent. In spite of this, the American State Department continues to court both Arab governments and the people, both in the moderate and despotic states. In spite of considerable American aid to moderate states, Arabs judge the United States seemingly by one standard, its support of Israel, which has been positive but far more evenhanded than is ever admitted.

Islamicists merely provide one more excuse to ignore the real internal reasons blocking Arab development. By blaming the United States and Israel and characterizing them as Satan, they target them for destruction rather than try to understand how to use capitalism as a tool for economic development. Islamicists actually aid secular despotisms by ignoring the internal reasons for the current deprivations of the Arab world. They use the one positive symbol in these totalitarian states that has survived complete control of the despots, Islam itself. But they manipulate Islam so that it is often not recognizeable as a universal religion and they prevent Islam from becoming the engine for progress which it has often been.

"Everyone Who Disagrees with Us is Un-Islamic"

IN ISLAMIC extremism, the United States, as the greatest power, becomes the biggest enemy, the Great Satan. Anyone who supports the United States, including any Muslim who supports the United States, becomes an infidel. Since Satan is in constant battle with Islam, this attitude has already been responsible for enormous damage against the *Ummah*. This supernatural pretext essentially labels every violent act against non-Muslims as an act of self-defense, an answer for some previous offense against the faithful *Ummah*, and is used as an excuse to murder any non-Muslim or Muslim alike.

Any Muslim can be executed as a *kafr*, if he disagrees with Islamist interpretations of Islam, a theory that was promulgated by the outlawed Muslim Brotherhoods in Egypt but is traceable from the early heretical dissenters to 'Ali, the *Khawarij* (the "outsiders"). The outstanding founder of modern extremist thought is probably Ḥasan al-Banna, the founder of the Muslim brotherhood. He taught that those who oppose his interpretation of Islam were apostates and unbelievers. He emphasized *jihad* and preached seeking after martyrdom *(ṭalab al-shahada)*, like the early *kharijites*. In the end, he himself was assassinated in 1949.[62] His disciple Sayyid Quṭb was hanged in Egypt on August 29, 1966.[63] But other disciples and students like Mawlana Mawdudi (1903–79) of Pakistan and Ayatollah Ruhollah Khomeini (1902–89) of Iran, carried on his teaching.

This dangerous ideology is still vibrant in Islamism; it arguably became Iranian government policy after its Islamic revolution because the United States supported the outwardly moderate and secular regime of the Shah without too much attention to its sins of internal repression. Destructive dualism is characteristic of every fundamentalism, but it has been obvious since the revolutionary regime took power in Iran. The Iranian revolution of 1979, its very ease in defeating the Shah, seemed to many on the "Arab Street" to be the confirmation of the truth of Islamism. But, as is now evident to Iranian Muslims, even the overthrow of the Shah did not bring about a free or just society in Iran. It has not even brought about a just Islamic state. So far it has not brought significant actual reform; it merely substituted a more repressive religious elite for a repressive secular one. It is the very simplicity of Islamism's answer, with its underpinning of religious self-righteousness, which is so appealing at first. But, as more and more Iranians now see, the appealing answer was simply a wrongly guided, seductive dream.

Fundamentalism and millenarianism may be quite different. For one thing, fundamentalism is a broad intellectual movement that favors the limitation of knowledge to that part of modern science which serves religion. Fundamentalist extremism, however, is a violent form of fundamentalist sectarianism, usually promoted by a small political extremist cadre. Fundamentalist extremism and millenarianism are deeply intertwined; indeed, one could make the case that it is a modern variety of politically motivated millenarianism. At the same time, there are significant differences in how power is mediated in millenarianism and fundamentalism. In millenarian cults, normally, a charismatic leader is important, so the decrees of the leader can serve as absolute law. In a fundamentalist-extremist movement, the organization of the movement is usually more sophisticated. Besides the charismatic leader, other leadership roles are filled and supported by a class of people whose job it is to make absolute claims based on a scriptural tradition.[64] Usually this class of people claims clerical status, as in Iran and in American fundamentalism. But, they may not necessarily be trained as clergy in the standard, normative fashion. The effect in either case is that absolute and uncompromising claims are used to garner support for the political program of the "clergy." Simple truths are always easier to understand than more ambiguous complicated, relative ones.

Martyrdom as a Political Weapon?

THE MARTYRDOM beliefs of contemporary Muslim terrorists have much in common with the *Khawaraj*, as well as medieval Christian notions of crusaders dying for plenary indulgence, as they do with the preaching of Muḥammad. Their doctrine is also very much an innovation in Islamic thought and should be regarded as a combination of religious extremist fundamentalism redefined as a modern religio-political agenda. Indeed, since fundamentalism is a worldwide phenomenon, hardly confined to Islam, we will need to look at what forms it takes and how it sometimes becomes radical fundamentalist extremism. One key issue for us in post-9/11 analyses of fundamentalist Islamic terrorism is the relationship between fundamentalism, on the one hand, and millenarianism and martyrdom on the other. But the relationship between martyrdom, millennialism, and fundamentalism is neither simple nor one-sided.[65]

In its long history, Islam has fostered tolerance and understanding between faiths, particularly in Spain and Moghul India. It has also undergone intolerant revivals, just as have Christianity and Judaism. The intolerance of the Islamists of today represents a new and extremely worrisome development because of its use of martyrdom as an offensive weapon. These new Muslim martyrs are not the equivalent of Jewish, Christian, or Muslim martyrs of the historical past.

Focusing on the suicide or martyr terrorists of the World Trade Center and suicide bombings in Israel can help us understand some of the social conditions that produce this innovative doctrine of martyrdom as well as shed light on the birth of the notion of the resurrection of the dead in second century BCE Judaism. Suicidal martyrdom is a new idea for Americans (and the world) to comprehend, although the nineteenth-century colonial and imperialist powers certainly had to deal with native uprisings where the motivation to self-sacrifice was similarly religious.

In that century, the colonial powers simply understood their native opponents as religious fanatics. Just like suicide hijackers and bombers, who are fueled by notions of a paradisal afterlife, the ancient doctrine of resurrection arises directly out of situations of religious martyrdom—in this case, the execution of the pious by an oppressive political force. And the religious circumstances that produced the doctrine of resurrection were religious apocalyptic sectarianism.

What makes this new attack different is that the martyrs are essentially offensive soldiers who kill others, and the others are always civilians. Islam has had glorified soldiers who died in Jihad as martyrs. But it has never recommended suicide as a way of killing innocent civilians in Jihad. This is a total innovation and is strictly forbidden as murder and suicide in traditional Islam, both punishable by damnation. Nevertheless, there is an innovative religious message in their acts of terrorism. First, Islamism provides them with a rationale that they were attacked first; they are only striking back. Every single Western male, female, or child is demonic. Western culture is itself anti-Islamic and satanic in its orientation so its very existence is evil. Proof of this is that the West is responsible for every bad event that has happened in the Arab world. Willingness to undergo martyrdom emphasizes that the cause is so important that masses of Muslims are even willing to die for it.

But what gets public attention is the huge civilian toll of carnage. The very size of the reaction is part of the perceived victory of the policy. The suicide bombers believe they are also bringing the attack to the homelands of the perceived enemies of Islam. There is a further precedent of soldiers claiming the rewards of the righteous in medieval Christianity and Islam but even that is not a sufficient precedent to explain an event like 9/11/01.

A martyrdom in the ancient world was a way to take what looked like a defeat and turn it into a moral victory over the seemingly powerful. Islam saw soldiers who willingly gave their lives in battle as martyrs. Starting in the medieval world and into the present, soldiers have been given the afterlife reward of martyrs, both in Christianity and Islam. But, they rarely functioned like the kamikaze pilots whose intention was to sacrifice themselves for the Japanese homeland in World War II. For the kamikaze, self-sacrifice for the state was a religious as well as national duty. It too changed a looming defeat into a moral victory because it was performed as an act of desperation against a militarily superior force. So religion may be said to play its part in the production of martyrs, but one must also note the strong importance of political aims to which the religious idea is put. However the kamikaze only atacked military targets, while Islamists deliberately target civilians.

Behind this political agenda is the historical judgment that Ottoman Turkey's defeat in World War I and subsequent attempt to turn itself into a modern state was a terrible satanic mistake. The destruction of the Ottoman Empire was accomplished by Britain and France in the Sykes-Picot treaty of 1916, after Turkey's unwise entrance into the war. After its empire was taken away, Turkey repatterned itself as a modern European state, under the reforms of Mustafa Kemal Attaturk (1881–1938). In the Islamists' eyes, the secularization of Turkey must be undone because it is a temporary, damnable condition like the crusader kingdom. Then, Islam can return to its prior glory.

But in realistic politics, this judgment seems impractical in the extreme. However unwise the dismantling of the Ottoman Empire was, no practical, political analyst would believe that a single Muslim state (from North Africa to Indonesia) under a Caliph is plausible or desirable, much less a world Islamic empire, even less the conversion of all Christians to Islam. Nor will Israelis (or any other minority living in Muslim lands) give up their state or agree to live under traditional *dhimmi* ("protected") status. These apocalyptic aims make their appearance not only in *al-Qaʿida*'s charter but also in *Ḥizballah*'s and *Ḥamas*'s constitutions. Its implausibility is only underlined by the skepticism that it draws among ordinary Muslims. But poor, disadvantaged, and alienated youth, as well as educated youth with no employment, find the dream attractive because it fulfills their sense of the rightful moral leadership of Islam in the world.

The Religious Motivations of the Hijackers

IT IS VERY HARD to study the motivations of the 9/11 hijackers, though they left us notes professing their religious motivations. Their behavior seemed strange as well as horrifying at first because we know that in the days before their martyrdom, they went out to bars, sought out women for sex, and engaged in a variety of behaviors which would be considered un-Islamic. Perhaps, as their training manuals said, it was to allay any suspicions in the American public. Perhaps they were not as good Muslims as their handlers wanted us to believe. In any event, their suicide notes were full of the desire for martyrdom, leaving no doubt that they considered themselves to be Muslim *shahada,* even though their families often denied their adherence to fundamentalist Islam.

We have more information about the making of suicide bombers in Palestine. There, the dominant ideology is very favorable to the creation of martyrs. Palestine is dominated by Israelis, whom the Palestinians see as a hated, colonial oppressor. The success of *Al-Qaʿida* in bringing down the World Trade Center was itself encouragement. In response to Israeli domination, parents encourage martyrdom in their young children. This suggests a second necessary condition for martyrdom: Besides opposition (or some other deprivation), there must be a religious ideology. People must be willing to analyze the situation in such a way as to affirm that their personal death is meaningful and, indeed, that death is not the end of life. In the ancient world this was the general rule, but such notions are more open to doubt in the modern West. Usually, this means that the martyrs necessarily see their death in a transcendent context in which it is but a step to a higher reward on earth and in heaven. For our purposes, it is enough to say that anything functioning to give transcendent meaning to their sacrifice is operating as a religious motivator.

Closely associated with this disposition towards religious explanations, there must a public acceptance of the efficacity of the mission. The relationship between the public and the martyr is a social discourse of encouragement: The public reinforces the martyrdom, and the martyr reinforces the ideals of the public. Public acceptance, one might say, is necessary because it aids in creating the credibility structure that makes martyrdom seem natural and logical. For instance, in the occupied territories, after a suicide bomber is recruited and trained, his or her mission is often announced publicly. During that period, the *shahid* becomes a "living martyr" in which he (or rarely she) is publicly celebrated as a volunteer. He has a picture taken in a warlike or martyr's pose. In one example, the *shahid* was photographed holding his own head as an offering to God, using trick photography to depict his willingness to die. But all use photographic images, made into posters for the walls of Palestinian cities, to spread their fame in the community. Just as it takes a whole village to raise a child, it also takes a village to turn a child into a martyr.

We have already learned that martyrdom can be religious drama, a spectacle of transcendence staged around the death of a believer. In Iran, *Ta'ziye* is a ritual and a drama at the same time, though it is but a stage performance. But even real martyrdoms are played out as a religious, ritual, a socio-drama.[66] It always depicts the supreme confidence of the believer, showing that the martyr's religious beliefs are correct, thus the cause is just. All the statements are simple and absolute. The cause is so important that one can sacrifice one's life to it. The power structure, which appears to have the upper hand, is actually just one step from destruction. Martyrdom tends to confirm notions of life after death, which are the most obvious beliefs to be demonstrated by the death of the martyr. So it creates a new "master narrative" of revolution against the power structure, saying that the power is demonic and against divine wishes, and, at the same time, demonstrates that the religious belief of the martyr is true and manifest.

The 9/11 hijackers caused more than 2,800, unsuspecting, civilian deaths in one act of sabotage directed against entirely civilian targets. This act cannot be justified by any suffering in the Middle East; nor was it born out of the frustration of the Palestinian people. Indeed, Palestine was only a minor, supporting motivation in the act on bin Laden's bill of particulars. Bin Laden's major reason for the action is Jihad against the presence of infidel US soldiers in Saudi Arabia.

Few Muslims would join such an organization. Yet, young Palestinians and other Muslim youth, all over the Middle East, danced in the streets when the World Trade Center came down. Saudi, Egyptian, and Lebanese students, influenced by fundamentalist education, regularly justify the attack on the World Trade Center as repayment for various injustices—some real, some imagined—perpetrated entirely by the United States or Israel and in which the Arabs were portrayed as innocent victims without any defenses.

Conversely, educated people in the Western-leaning Arab countries simply denied that any Arabs would have done such a terrible deed. Rather, it was the work of the Israeli secret service, who even warned all the Jews to stay home on that morning. Both rationales are equally absurd. The story is still widely run in the Arab newspapers and on television stations. Egyptian television also recently ran a dramatization of the "Protocols of the Elders of Zion" in installments, though it is universally known as a cruel anti-semitic fraud.[67] Beyond the official statements of consolations, conveyed through diplomats, the two dominant Middle Eastern responses to 9/11 have been celebration and modern, anti-Semitic ideology used to foster denial.

This mythological anti-Semitism and anti-Americanism are being used in their classic scapegoating role towards the political aim of keeping the Arab "street" focused on mythical outside dangers rather than real, domestic injustices. So too is the United States targeted frequently, which is hardly responsible for the difficulties of Arab countries. With these grand, easy-to-understand, dualist simplifications, a great many, more complicated facts of life can be avoided. Anti-Semitism and anti-Americanism are being used to avoid facing any domestic responsibility for the horrific state of human rights and human development in Arab countries. Even secular despots see an advantage to fostering Islamism, as long as it is focused on outside enemies.

The Religious Motivations of Failed Suicide Bombers

INTERVIEWS WITH failed suicide bombers against Israel show that notions of the heavenly rewards for the martyrs are important motivators to violence. But they are not the only ones. Indeed, there are others that are just as significant, so much so that some scholars can credibly claim that religion is not important in the motivation of suicide bombers.[68] The agents of Ḥamas and Ḥizballah subtly change personal feelings of inadequacy into political motivations that the youth equally associate with Muslim martyrdom. The young, imprisoned, failed *mujahidin* do mention the dark-eyed maidens *(Ḥur)* as motivators (and they are mentioned in recruitment tapes too) but the potential martyrdom recruits noticeably warm to a modern addition to the tradition: The martyr's ability to get a special heavenly dispensation for family and friends is a much greater motivator in today's Palestine, though this is by no means a traditional reward to the martyrs, since Muḥammad explicitly ruled out intermediaries as affecting salvation. The potential martyr is attracted by the power he will gain in providing for his family in heaven, in contrast to the powerlessness to protect or earn for his family on earth.

Scott Atran has something important to add to this sketch. He denigrates educational or economic deprivation as explanations but stresses the fictive brotherhood created by the mostly unmarried men who become martyrs. While I think that many of the variables he discounts—deprivation, political organization of the sodalities, and religious faith—are critical for understanding the motivation of bombers, he still makes an important point about the way in which kinship responsibilities activate motivations for revenge in a society where notions of revenge play a dominant role in family pride.

Though it is not justified by the Quran, the *shahid* becomes a kind of intermediary between God and his family and friends. Lacking the ability to perform the traditional role of economic supporter, the young unemployed men substitute the notion of heavenly family provider for earthly self-sufficiency. The belief structure supplied by fundamentalist extremist Islam gives them the key ideology to equalize themselves in spiritual terms with their oppressors and even the economic score on a higher plane. Instead of losing their lives, they actually earn back their dignity in the heavenly sphere. There is a great relationship between this motivation and those we saw previously in ancient millennialist groups. But here the class of people who are affected by the motivation is much wider. Indeed, those who volunteer are apt to have achieved higher education than the norm, albeit in religiously sponsored schools. Their inability to find a position equal to their educational level is also a precipitating factor.

Thanks to the generosity of various foreign governments and charities, the martyrs do earn an earthly reward for their families. The actual monetary payment which the families of suicide bombers receive is also mentioned quite prominently in the interviews.[69] The sum itself varies, though $10,000 is often mentioned as the standard payment to the family of a suicide bomber. Payments totalling many thousand dollars have been received by the families of the Palestinian martyrs. A few, very public martyrs have received up to $35,000, as did the suicide bomber who killed four American soldiers during Operation Iraqi Freedom. A public square in Jenin was also named for him, showing Palestinian support for any action against the United States.

This is a significant sum for young Palestinians or Iraqis, many times higher than most could hope to earn in many a year. The payments come from Iran, from wealthy Saudi Arabians, and most recently also from Iraq—in short, from the sworn enemies of Israel and the United States. Within Palestine, teenagers are actively recruited by older young men who work for the much admired religious organizations of Ḥizballah and Ḥamas. Since these meetings are sometimes videotaped, a few have fallen into Israeli hands so we can actually see the dynamics at work with horrifying results.

The confirming society is not just the family. Family support is mirrored by national support. Newspapers and TV stations, which are usually instruments of state policy in Arab countries, have been equally passionate in their support of suicide bombers.[70] Together with the adulation that the volunteers receive before performing their act of self-immolation, the path to martyrdom has been hard to resist for young, unemployed, though often highly educated Palestinian Muslims. Though we do not know the personal histories of all the suicide terrorists who crashed into the World Trade Center, we can assume that they became fervent Muslims after suffering from the entire range of *anomie,* as well as social and economic dysfunction, which infects young Muslim men, both in Muslim countries and in the West. We can also suspect that their families were paid by persons anxious to hurt the United States.[71]

Fundamentalist Education Produces Fundamentalist Extremism

BUT NONE OF IT would be possible, were not religious extremist schooling the main source of education in these communities today. The secular schools in Palestine and many other Arab countries are in total shambles. Many have simply ceased to exist. Fundamentalist *madrassas* and colleges have filled in the gaps. They turn fundamentalism into fundamentalist extremism. There, the young learn unreformed Islam in which religious martyrdom and religious justification for *jihad* warfare are much praised, praised higher than finding an occupation and becoming a householder. When asked for help from the wealthy, Saudi Arabian donors are far more likely to donate a new mosque and *madrassa* than a vocational school or even give direct support for the needy. Secular schools are not even much in the interest of the secular dictators who rule many Arab countries, still less the religious leadership of the *'awqaf* (religious, charitable trusts, sing. *waqf*). Secular schools are expensive to maintain and they tend to teach democratic values. While Judaism, Christianity, and Islam do not produce the same fundamentalism, a strong fundamentalist education and atmosphere seem to be one of the indicators of the rise of extremist political radicalism and violence.

The relationship between fundamentalist and parochial education is strongest in Jihadi (extremist) Islam but it is true everywhere. Tariq 'Ali emphasizes that it is one of the strongest reasons why fundamentalism has flowered in Muslim countries. Here is his description of the fundamentalist *madrassas* in Pakistan and Afghanistan:

> Together with verses from the Koran (learned by rote) and the necessity to lead a devout life, these children were taught to banish all doubts. The only truth was divine truth, the only code of conduct was that written in Koran and the *Hadiths,* virtue lay in unthinking obedience. Anyone who rebelled against the *imam* rebelled against Allah. The aim was clear. These *madrassas* had a single function. They were indoctrination nurseries designed to produce fanatics. The primers, for example, stated that the Urdu letter *jeem* stood for *jihad; tay* for *tope* (cannon); *kaaf* for *kalashnikov* and *khay* for *khoon* (blood).
>
> As they grew older the pupils were instucted in the use of sophistcated hand weapons and taught how to make and plant bombs. ISI agents provided training and supervision. They could also observe the development of the more promising students or *Taliban,* who were later picked out and sent for more specialized training at secret army camps, the better to fight the "holy war" against the unbelievers in Afghanistan. . . .
>
> The dragon seeds sown in 2,500 *madrasas* produced a crop of 225,000 fanatics ready to kill and to die for their faith when ordered to do so by their religious leaders.[72]

The result of the upsurge in fundamentalist extremism has been a tragic polarization of public opinion in the democracies which have been targeted. Public opinion is one area in which terrorism has had a major and tragic effect. The majority of the Israeli electorate went from actively supporting the peace process (to the extent of trading back all the land) to desultory support for the continued occupation of Palestine simply because of the enormous upsurge in violence, starting with the second intifada (not a grassroots revolt) followed by waves of equally well-planned suicide bombing encouraged by the World Trade Center attack. The architects of this policy were the Palestinian radicals who did not support the existence of Israel in any form. And Israel got the message, perhaps too strongly, as did the United States when the Twin Towers fell, and as will any democracy that is attacked in this way. It will be a while before the folly of this policy is perceived on both sides.

One result is public justification in the US for a new crusade against the evildoers. To move from these responses to a true settlement of the issues—a just settlement of the Palestine issue and the establishment of economic and political progress in the Arab world—will take more than a change of public opinion in the United States and Israel. It will take a new voice in the Arab world as well, one that firmly rejects the absurd commitments of the fundamentalist extremists. Fouad Ajami sums up what is needed in his book *The Dream Palace of the Arabs:* "But there arises too the recognition that it is time for the imagination to steal away from Israel and to look at the Arab reality, to behold its own view of the kind of world the Arabs want for themselves."[73] He points out that the intellectual leadership of the Arabs has built a dream-palace and allowed itself to be seduced by hatred of Israel when it should just get on with the development of the Arab world.

The Original Fundamentalism: An American Phenomenon

FUNDAMENTALISM per se is not the same as millenialism or fundamentalist extremism. There are many perfectly law-abiding members of society everywhere who consider themselves fundamentalist.[74] Indeed, we as Americans are very familiar with fundamentalism. The term in its original usage was a self-designation of a conservative, American, Christian movement. Originally, it referred to a series of twelve volumes written by conservative theologians of the 1910s, all of whom espoused no compromise with a scientific worldview or any version of modern life that depended on it.[75] Actually, it demonstrated that the technology of science could be used to defeat any "demonic" scientific theory. It was not violent in its religious expression, though sporadic acts of intolerance (especially racist intolerance) were committed in its name. It had its own view of heaven and the apocalypse that involved heavy emphasis on "the tribulation" and the "rapture," two American concerns from earlier missionary and revivalist groups but that were clear innovations in Christian tradition, based on tendentious readings of Paul and Revelation. It is interesting that one of the characteristics of fundamentalist thinking is always that it innovates most just where it says it is returning to Scriptures to simplify and cleanse religious tradition of accretions.

The most important early victory of fundamentalist forces in the United States was the Scopes Trial of 1925. A young biology teacher, John T. Scopes, was put on trial in Tennessee because he used a text containing references to Darwin's work on the evolution of species. This was a violation of state law, enacted by fundamentalists, which prohibited the teaching of any theory that denied the divine creation of man. It did not matter that Darwin himself recognized the role of the creator in his writings or that neither the teacher nor his lawyer denied the divine creation of man, only the details of the creation account. The fact that the law of the country was seen to protect their religious premises was a clear example of how the technology of the state could be seen to defeat a scientific worldview.

Although the rest of the country roundly ridiculed these notions, the fundamentalists won the courtroom battle and that was the whole point for them. The ridicule of the sophisticated intellectuals made the courtroom victory even sweeter. From the perspective of northern intellectuals, "The Monkey Trial" became another small example of what made the South outdated and decadent. But that was its very importance for the fundamentalists, who saw it as a huge victory of their values against their patronizing superiors in the north. In some ways, The Monkey Trial represents the revenge of the believers against modernists, even southerners against northerners, because it simply prevents modern notions from having legal standing. Like Islamic fundamentalism, it is riddled with willful denial. As well, there is more than a whiff of American Civil War animosity behind the battle. It is the use of modern methods to defeat the modern powerstructure which most connects American fundamentalism with the postcolonial Muslim phenomenon.

Fundamentalism represents those in Christianity who intepret Scripture literally and, by so doing, turn back the clock to an idealized Christian community of the past, based on Scripture. At the same time, it has a political agenda to reclaim and retain power for those like-minded religious brethren who object to liberal northern patronization and exploitation. Nancy Ammerman says that in the 1970s and 1980s no two words better captured its reemerged fundamentalist image and agenda than the "moral majority." [76] One did not need to be a fundamentalist Christian to be a member of the moral majority in 1979, but the converse was surely true: Fundamentalists universally identified themselves as members of the moral majority. This means that they rejected the democratic northern federal government but, unlike millenarian movements, relied on their political clout to change it. It was an early expression of what has come to be known as "the southern strategy," the realization that the US population, hence political power, is shifting to the Sunbelt. But the demographics of power in the South are in the modern, urban, manufacturing and service sector, not in the farm belt. The genius of the "moral majority" is that it falsely suggests that these conservatives are moral, in the majority, and that they were heretofore silent. Actually statistics show that they are a very vocal minority and whether they are moral or not depends on one's religious assumptions. The new power of the South is not now primarily expressed as religion but in ordinary political terms.

Christian fundamentalists are largely Protestant; the clergy is not often in possession of the kinds of seminary education characteristic of the normative and mainline churches and certainly not characteristic of the long schooling that Catholic priests receive. The authority of the fundamentalist clergy tends to flow from a charismatic source. Some clergy receive their authority on the basis of their ability to receive spiritual gifts themselves (speaking in tongues, singing, dancing, etc.) and inspire others to receive them. These are characteristic of the pentecostal and charismatic churches, who are like fundamentalists in some ways but often in conflict with them as well.

Many kinds of charismatic or pentecostal Christianity are viewed with deep suspicion by fundamentalists, who trust no charismatic authority because it competes with their own. Far more characteristic of strictly defined fundamentalist clergymen, however, is their ability to speak and exegete the New Testament text. Their abilities are often ascribed to divine inspiration. Effective speaking and command of Scripture are themselves understood as divine gifts. Their authority essentially comes from their ability to gather crowds of followers, instead of from the church itself. So they are even freer to indulge in religious innovation, even while they claim that they are actually returning to the original message of Scripture.

The fact that Christian fundamentalists mostly work within the political system suggests an important distinction between American Christian fundamentalists and the word "fundamentalism" when used of Muslim extremists. In point of fact, few Arab countries contain any democratic mechanisms; so there is only limited fundamentalist access to political power, driving fundamentalists to extremism (violent actions to overthrow the political system). On the other hand, no dictatorship has been able totally to quell dissent in mosques, so that Islam represents a valued symbol system which still is able to express some political messages. In moderate Muslim countries like Egypt, the mosques become effective political forces. After prayer is over on Fridays, quite often the assembly is taken over by young, vociferous, political activists who attempt to convince the worshipers to stay for a more political message.

In some ways, the French word for Muslim fundamentalism, l'intégrisme, better suggests what Muslim and Christian fundamentalists have in common: the denial of the two spheres of secular and religious life and the total integration of religious values into every aspect of life. In the US, far more people have access to the political process than in Muslim countries, so fundamentalism can espouse the democratic values of the state and still make progress towards its religious agenda. The state for American fundamentalists need not be an evil in itself. But, by rejecting everything else but its own absolutes, Christian fundamentalism can also set the stage for violent extremism where access to political power is absent. And though it masquerades as a "majority," it is not by nature democratic and it is rarely a majority. Rather, it provides a supernatural justification for the work of militias in the US and for the work of the extremist Muslim brotherhoods and movements in the Arab world. The militancy of the position, however, in its opposition to modern life and its sometimes violent extremism is what characterizes the violent wing in all the various groups.[77] It turns political action into a religious crusade.

Jewish Fundamentalism

EXACTLY WHAT should be called Jewish fundamentalism has been debated strongly. More elastic Rabbinic traditions of scriptural interpretation make strict, univocal interpretation of Scripture a less obvious guide to Jewish fundamentalist community. Ian Lustick, for example, denies that ultra-orthodox *("Haredi")*[78] Judaism is fundamentalism at all because it has relatively elastic views of Scripture, allowing only that the extremist group, *Gush Emunim,* qualifies for the title of fundamentalism in Israel.[79] Many scholars follow Lustick in saying that even if there is a Jewish fundamentalism, it is so small a group that it has no effect on the political process anywhere else than Israel.[80]

This probably needs correction for the United States, especially the New York area, where relatively small groups of very religious Jews have occasionally been able to influence local religious life with their voting power.[81] And in Israel, Ḥaredi Jews have been able often to influence the course of elections and influence the civil life of the country in countless ways. It is also significant that the successful plot to assassinate Izḥak Rabin, as well as the unsuccessful plot to blow up the Dome of the Rock, came from conspirators in *ḥaredi* Yeshivas.[82] With these two significant exceptions, most Israeli fundamentalists prefer to work "from the bottom up," converting the mass of Jews to their form of Judaism, rather than "from the top down," in doing acts of terrorism designed to force their agenda on everyone else. On the other hand, they do sponsor the vast majority of the new settlements in the occupied areas.

But the privileging of early Rabbinic interpretations which one finds in most contemporary varieties of contemporary Ḥasidism and Ḥaredi Judaism has the same effect as scriptural fundamentalism in other religious communities. Or, to put it another way, Jewish fundamentalists do evince scripturalism because Rabbinic writings are part of Jewish Scripture in Jewish fundamentalist groups, as they are in all Rabbinic Judaism. Thus, with a wider view of Scripture, Ḥaredi Judaism can be seen as fundamentalist. The strict scripturalism in fundamentalist Judaism resides in its rigid interpretation of a certain few Rabbinic rulings, not Biblical writ itself, together with innovations in the tradition, which are then viewed as its original intent.

This, it shares with all the other forms of fundamentalism. One views the same characteristics of suspicion of the secular state and xenophobia in Ḥaredi Judaism that one sees in the other varieties of fundamentalism. In the Jewish case, fundamentalist ire is turned against gentiles, all viewed as potential or actual anti-Semites, all capable of another Holocaust, and the modern secular state of Israel, which has forgotten its religious constitution. This seems another variation on the theme of fundamentalist opposition to modern secular states, which is also strong in Islam and Christianity.[83] It is also a dualism that drives group definition and, sometimes, missionary activity to convert other Jews to their group.

One key that ultra-Orthodox Judaism in Israel is fundamentalist is that Ḥaredi Jews justify their opposition to the modern state and modern Zionism on religious rather than political grounds: The modern Israeli state was the result of a political action and not brought about by the coming of the Messiah.[84] Therefore, it is to be shunned, though one may accept all its social services. Like other fundamentalisms, there is no possible interim position. When forced by political life to barter, the ultra-Orthodox are willing to trade their support on virtually any issue for continued civil support for the laws of Judaism. So while they do not accept the validity of the state, they constantly pressure the state for more special rulings which agree with their interpretation of Rabbinic Judaism. The Jewish variety of fundamentalism relies on different justifications in history and Scripture than those of Christianity and Islam but the effect is pretty much the same. The ulta-Orthodox notions of the afterlife are suited for Talmud study. Traditionally the great scholars are those who are called to the heavenly Yeshivas, but even ordinary members of the movement are so rewarded when they die settling the Holy Land.

Both Christianity and Islam promote Scripture as their authority (just the plain meaning of Scripture). Both depend on tendentious univocal interpretations that come from their respective interpretive traditions rather than Scripture itself. So the big difference between Jewish fundamentalism and the other two is that the former can sometimes acknowledge that their beliefs are Rabbinic interpretations rather than Scripture itself because they also posit that that interpretation is part of the canon and divinely ordained. But this is not a complete contrast either because fundamentalist Islam makes frequent use of dubious *hadiths* (traditions from the prophet but not texted in the Quran), and fundamentalist Christianity quite often enshrines the Biblical exegesis of its founder figures and preachers.

The Bellwether Role of Women

FUNDAMENTALISM all over the world calls for a return to traditional roles for women. Perhaps this is partly because women often find work more easily than men in colonial states, usually in the service industry; this normally undercuts native notions of the value and dignity of men's work. The religious motivation provides a no-compromise way to deal with male feelings of inadequacy which come from an educated and competent group of women in the workforce.[85] And, as many perceptive scholars have shown, return to a traditional role for women is an aspect of fundamentalism throughout the world, though there is no exact analogy between fundamentalism in Christianity, where it was born, and associated notions of critiquing modern secularist Western society elsewhere in the world. From this one might easily reason that fundamentalism appeals to men specifically, who feel that their traditional role as head of household and breadwinner is endangered by modern, secular life. But women join fundamentalist groups as well, probably out of the converse argument that it validates their traditional roles in religious terms. As always, comparative study can give us helpful models but history itself provides each movement with its own special qualities and characteristics that affect its character and outcomes.

Al-Qaʿida

A GREAT MANY things need to happen before an extremist group arises out of a fundamentalist environment. Once it does arise, it has a number of interesting relationships to millenarian movements, which fundamentalism does not, even though the ideology may be a mixture of religion and politics and the group will by definition be activist rather than passive in regard to political and military actions. The shocking events of September 11 brought the phenomenon of the extremist Islamist movement to the forefront of American concerns. It was only the last in a series of terrorist assaults perpetrated by Osama bin Laden through his *Al-Qaʿida* network.

Al-Qaʿida was founded by Osama bin Laden, a modern, Western-educated, wealthy, Saudi-Yemeni businessman, who was, reportedly, often ridiculed by his brothers and more adroit partners in business. He has, however, become much more pious than they, doing an end-run around their critique of his financial abilities. *Al-Qaʿida* uses modern technology in partnership with extreme piety to try to defeat the modern Western world.

In some ways, Bin Laden's ideology is not only fundamentalist but apocalyptic because it seeks to foment a war of Islam against the West which will end in the total victory of Islam and the reestablishment of the true Caliphate, as a prelude eventually for "the day of judgment" *(Yawm al-Din)*. This is quite obviously an analogue to Messianism in Judaism and Christianity. His previous attacks on the United States had included the bombing of the Khobar Airbase and the US warship Cole, killing many soldiers, which belatedly alerted the world to his destructive potential.

But the fact that he has political targets does not mean that his efforts or motivations are wholly political. In his first post–9/11, well-publicized speech to the West, broadcast in its entirety by *al-Jazeera* News Service of Doha, Qatar, his powerful, religious oratory was much in evidence. Anyone who knows any Arabic knows the enormous, charismatic power of his Quranic syntax, calm delivery, and Saudi accent. His charisma is understandable in the exegetical tradition to which he belongs, though it may be totally alien to Western notions of political leadership. And, though it has political consequences, Bin Laden's message is distinctly religious: "The martyrs of the World Trade Center are among the stars on their way to paradise. . . . The Western nations will soon be expelled from the land of the two sanctuaries [Saudi Arabia]." He averred that his biggest worry was that the secret plan was in danger of being revealed inadvertently to the West by the enormous number of people who prophetically dreamt about it. But this destruction of the symbol of American commerce (far beyond his expectations) is the prelude to the coming worldwide Islamic revival. These are not political statements, though they may hope for the conquest of the West.

This hope has much in common with the earlier millenarian groups studied by anthropologists. The difference is that these Islamic groups are incredibly well financed and well armed by rich Saudi and other fundamentalist Muslims. Even so, they are not political movements, strictly speaking, though many nurse the notion that Osama bin Laden is the true

Caliph *(Khalifa)*. The dream of conquest is surely mistaken but the immediate effect of this rhetoric was not only to stir up fundamentalist sentiment in Islam but also the corresponding, opposing fundamentalist sentiment in Jews and Christians.[86] The danger in his deed is that it might turn his agenda into a self-fulfilling prophecy.

The murder of Daniel Pearl illustrates the extent to which these movements are fueled by Islamic fundamentalist extremism, which posits that every problem can be answered by casting out the mythic scapegoat, the Jew. Just as in Christianity, the Jew is an emblem for doubt because Jews are viewed as explicitly rejecting the message of Islam and of being agents for the Satanic Israel. By hating Jews, fundamentalists are exorcising doubt from within themselves as well. The unfortunate reporter for the *Wall Street Journal* had no direct contacts with Israel; he was, instead, offering his services to publicize the demands of the extremist group. Nevertheless, the group could not discern the political utility of giving the correspondent an interview and, instead, responded with murder, justified by mythologically-motivated religious hatred. It is another example of what Scott Atran calls a "counter-intuitive world" created by extremist commitments.[87]

The informative book by Gilles Kepel, recently translated from French as *Jihad: The Trail of Political Islam* makes a strong (and optimistic) case that the forces of Islamist terrorism are in retreat in all the major Islamic countries, not only because of their military defeat in Afghanistan but because many ordinary, rank-and-file Muslims recoil from this particular interpretation of Islam.[88] Let us hope that this assessment is correct; but it will depend on whether young, restless, educated Muslims can be given enough of a stake in a flourishing middle class in the Arab Middle East. So far, the situation does not look good. Nor is it yet clear how an unpopular American war in Iraq will improve the situation of the Arab world, even after it has succeeded in dislodging Saddam Hussein, who created one of the most reprehensible regimes in world history. One can hope that the sophisticated Iraqi people, with their taste of democracy in the twentieth century, will eventually manage on their own to recreate their nation in a very troubled and fractious neighborhood.

Martyrdom as Consolation

NORMALLY MARTYRDOM is not an offensive weapon but a defensive one protecting the worldview of a persecuted minority. As such, it is a consolation to the faithful. Sometimes offensive suicide martyrdom serves the same purpose. For instance, no one really knows why Baruch Goldstein killed so many people in the mosque in Hebron. Most Israelis are convinced that Baruch Goldstein suffered a psychotic break because they see the act as a senseless aggravator to an already tense situation. Most Israelis do not acknowledge martyrdom as religious motivation in their lives. Most do not accept the religious assumptions that appear to be part of Goldstein's and his fellow-settlers' worldview.

Within the settlers' community, a different motivation is expressed. Goldstein's actions are seen as grief and despair, due to his religious conviction that God favors his settlement activities, in danger of disconfirmation by the many casualties which the settlers have taken. While none of the settlers actually praise the murder of Arabs, many sympathetic reports excuse it as temporary derangement. They speak of his condition just before his actions, stressing his grief and despair over the recent deaths of neighboring settlers.

After he gunned down dozens of innocent worshipers and was himself killed, a small minority started a martyr's cult around his grave. While the rest of Israel was appalled at his behavior, and was even more scandalized by the few settlers' celebration of his terrible deeds, his supporters and sympathizers labeled his death as a martyrdom. Although ordinary Israelis can treat their victims of Arab terrorism as martyrs, they normally do not. They are normally seen as civilian casualities in a tragic war for the preservation of Israel. Furthermore, there is normally no incentive for suicidal bombing, especially if it includes killing innocent civilians, because those behaviors are contrary to the morals being affirmed in the formation of the Israeli state. In the minds of the vast majority of Israelis, there is no moral equivalency between the actions of suicide bombers and the Israeli army's occupation, even those who oppose the army's reoccupation of Palestinian territories.

In her interesting book on martyrdom, Elizabeth Castelli analyzes the deaths of early Christian martyrs Perpetua and Thecla and then compares them with the modern American martyr, Cassie Bernall, who died at the hands of two teenage misfits in Littleton, Colorado on April 20, 1999.[89] According to the popular memoir of the incident, *She Said "Yes,"* [90] Cassie was asked if she believed in God and, when she answered "Yes," she was killed. As a result, her parents and a large part of the evangelical world have proclaimed her a martyr because she died for her faith. This story, however, is factually inaccurate. Journalists interviewing several witnesses have demonstrated that it was another girl who made that remark and that she luckily survived the attack to confirm the story.

But the facts are not the only important aspect of the story. As Cassie Bernall was surely a tragic victim, grieving parents seek the religious solace of martyrdom as a way to understand the death of their daughter, taken from them by such horrible and senseless circumstances. In a way, it makes the claim that this tragically murdered youth is a kind of saint. Though the historian may critique the events, no one really blames the parents for seeking a solace in religious terminology when the martyr is truly a victim. Such is the power of martyrdom to inform our lives and help us come to terms with such terrifying intrusions of violence in our otherwise well-ordered society. But the religious motivation behind these sympathies can also be used to blind us to more practical ways of dealing with the violence: meaningful reform of gun-control laws, for instance, which has led to less violence in every modern country.

Very likely, the same sympathies are in the minds of the parents of Palestinian suicide bombers who praise their martyred children and profess no grief over their loss, though we might want to make a very large distinction between Cassie's victimhood and acts of war against civilians.

One might, in fact, want to point out the injustices done to to the teenage attackers of Columbine High School, Eric Harris and Dylan Klebold, who were clearly victimized by their own classmates. One might sympathize with the plight of intelligent, unathletic youth in an American high school where only athletics and popularity are valued. Similarly, one might sympathize with the terrible plight of the Palestinians in the political climate of the Middle East. Neither sympathy justifies deliberate killing of innocent civilians. The judgment seems simple enough, but it has never emerged publicly in Palestine and it does not seem clear to Americans opposed to gun control either. In fact, the closest Palestinian intellectuals have come to condemning suicide bombing is to say that it has not proven effective as a tactic. This only points out how these acts of carnage are never simply the acts of individuals; they are representations of the attitudes of the community. One might almost make the case that Palestinian national ideology is seeking to convince youngsters that they should seek to be transformed into popular Muslim saints. It is especially tragic when a viable Palestinian state seems possible now in a way that was never before true.

Cultural Pluralism and Religious Life

Islam has universalist and particularist voices, just like Judaism and Christianity. It is wrong to think that liberals in mainline religious institutions, those who eschew fundamentalist views of Scripture, are the only true cultural pluralists in a society. Liberal churches, synagogues, and Islamic communities have more at stake in promoting tolerance and even cultural pluralism, as their members normally also have a strong structure of interreligious interaction in their everyday life—including business and trade and sometimes even social relationships. But there are also many examples of conservative religious communities where tolerance and pluralism are valued.

Where the cultural conditions exist for these interactions, we can expect notions of toleration and even multiculturalism to emerge. For example, one thinks immediately of medieval Moorish Spain and Moghul India as two places where Islam was the protector of multicultural societies. It is important not to idealize these societies; they contained many episodes of intolerance and frequent patronization as well as very high degrees of toleration for the medieval period.

One thing they shared is lack of emphasis on traditional notions of conversion. We have already noted that religions which seek converts very often are quite articulate on the horrors awaiting sinners in the afterlife, as well as the pleasures awaiting the faithful. In both Moorish Spain and Moghul India, there was often a kind of moratorium on missionary activity. The conditions that produced the moratorium were partly similar and partly different. In both Moorish Spain and Moghul India, Muslim rulers found themselves ruling a large population of non-Muslims who had considerable relations with coreligionists in neighboring populations. Similarly the Moors had to rule amidst continuously changing political situations with large subject populations of Christians and Jews. The Moors were sometimes able to encounter Jews and Christians with significant degrees of sympathy and tolerance.

The notion of the afterlife adjusted to these social circumstances. In Muslim Spain, the high philosophical tradition covertly admitted that the universalists, the true philosophers of all religions, all had a place in eternity. Indeed Aristotelianism even banished personal afterlife as a logical possibility. It is hard not to think that the expression of these notions, if not their dominance in the society, was parallel to the toleration that sometimes developed in Moorish Spain.

In Moghul India, which had a different kind of problem because Hindus were not obviously categorizable to Islam as "a people of the book," notions of the afterlife began to fade in importance completely. For instance, Babur, founder of the Moghul Dynasty and legendarily the descendant of Tamerlane the Conqueror, wrote a Persian poetic couplet in which he stated that the faithful should enjoy the pleasures of this world for another world does not exist. Also Ṣufi mystics were active in the area, explicitly linking their mystic experience with that achieved by Hindus. This discussion of the afterlife fits a society that needs to develop toleration for its fellow members of different religions.

The Afterlife and Cultural Pluralism

THE VERY economic lack of development that causes Arabs to migrate to the West also contains some promising innovations. Islam is truly a world religion, fully as much as Christianity. It is the majority religion in the Arab world and its immediate neighbors but it is also a significant minority in India and a number of South Asian countries, as well as a growing vocal minority in Europe and the United states.[91] Styles of tolerant Islam have reemerged in some European countries, an Islam better equipped to deal with a more culturally plural world. Ṭariq Ramadan, for example, outlines new theological developments that emerge in Islam as it lives in Western countries.[92] A new book called *Taking Back Islam* asks why Islam is driven to these defensive postures when it can just as easily assert a moderate and more constructive voice. Many of the moderate voices are coming from Diaspora Islam.[93] These are promising developments for American Muslims as well as for Islam generally, and for non-Muslims.

This merely underlines the fact that religion can both shore up the ideology of states as well as undermine it. Where toleration is the goal, religion can help give that goal transcendent legitimacy, helping by redefining its afterlife to fit the society. This has the effect of making a tolerant model transcendent for the society. But of all the goals of states, toleration, and its rarer cousin cultural pluralism, are probably the most precious. They help foster religiously and ethnically complex democratic states like the United States or Canada, and some European states, in spite of the conservative and intolerant forces always arrayed against them.

The hallmark of cultural pluralism is the forthright admission that religious truths can be doubted. It seems an odd perception given the nature of religious life. But the most obvious distinction between fundamentalism and temperate religion in the West is the extent to which one allows doubt to enter one's religious consciousness. Fundamentalists have completely banished all doubt; every victory is really a victory of surety over doubt. Non-fundamentalists, by comparison, are willing to encounter the possibility that religious truths are relative and that others' truths may be equivalent in value and beauty. Without the presence of doubt, religious faith can justify any crime or violation of human rights. Religious faith, in short includes doubt while fundamentalism, insofar as it represses doubt, is merely fanaticism.

The majority of contemporary American culture has taken this to its logical extension. Most Americans are optimistic about life and grateful for the standard of living and political freedom and stability that have existed here. And so they have banished hell and given heaven to all as a kind of entitlement, regardless of religious allegiance. This suggests, perhaps, that whether the religion is liberal or conservative, the strategy that leads to cultural pluralism is two-fold: limiting conversion to members of one's own religion and imagining oneself globally as the member of a minority. The result of this revisioning should therefore yield a world in which everyone acknowledges each other's rights as a way of safeguarding one's own.

Afterword

Immortal Longings

Beyond Imagination

THE NOTION OF the afterlife only ramifies and grows more important in Judaism, in Christianity, and in Islam. Luckily, for those who want to continue the story, there are many more books already available to fill in the gap.[1] Not surprisingly, we have seen that every group in society normally searches for a transcendent justification for its religious position, lifestyle, and political position. Each group within the society develops an afterlife doctrine to parallel and legitimate its own position, taking the elements of its position from the historical past of the society and attempting to argue that its interpretation is the truest representation of it. This combination of functions and structures, we are used to calling religion.

Conversely, virtually every aspect of religion, politics, and society is involved in the doctrine of the afterlife. It is the afterlife that provides the answer to every unbalanced equation. Every injustice can be righted there, every disability can be made whole, every individual, rich or poor, can find solace from personal trials and tribulations. Because Christianity understood Jesus' death and resurrection as the central message of his life, it made otherworldly compensation the crucial aspect of the new faith.[2] But attention to afterlife also characterizes Judaism and Islam.[3] Even the notion that there is no afterlife is, in a sense, the justification for an earthly philosophical system for those who support it.

Why don't we believe we become butterflies when we die or, like the mermaids in Hans-Christian Anderson's fairy tales, turn into sea foam?

These are as sophisticated, beautiful and consoling beliefs as one might want personally. So why don't we in the West believe them? The question is facetious. We realize immediately that an individual fantasy, no matter how beautiful or moving, lacks the credibility structures that beliefs present in a society necessarily achieve. In fact, we are free to believe whatever we want. Imagination is not the point; social validity and confirmation are what is desired.[4] A purely personal view of heaven can never be an effective image for a society. The sureties provided by the afterlife normally demand that it be a socially shared phenomenon. That confirmation is normally provided by powerful, religious institutions in society.

To those who think the afterlife to be a simple delusion, the Western tradition offers an enormously complicated and socially determined answer to the question of what lies after death: It may be a delusion but there is nothing simple about it. Heaven is the best we can think of for ourselves at any historical time and hell is the worst we can imagine. They are all the rewards we want and punishments we fear (or the revenge we want our enemies to suffer) for the lives we lead. Imagining a heaven therefore also involves projecting our own hopes on heaven and then spending our lives trying to live up to them. But it is not only personal because Westerners have long-standing histories of what the afterlife is and how to attain a pleasurable one.

This book is a personal view. But it is not only a personal view; it is an attempt to deal with each culture of the West in a knowledgeable and respectful way, to sift through the myriad accounts that Western culture has to offer, and to look for enduring trends and similarities. The Western view of the afterlife is a complex of ideas and institutions that have had a long and very rich history. To understand the afterlife in the West, one must see beyond the explicit portraits and analyze how ideas functioned in the society of the living.

Review of the Previous Chapters

READING THE history of the afterlife is like reading through a great books course in the humanities. One needs to know not just the Bible but every important book in Western culture to understand why we envision our afterlife in heaven or on earth, as souls or as bodies, after death or at the end of time. One thing which becomes entirely clear is that the afterlife is not a single eternal truth that is an unchanging reward of the righteous or faithful. It is, instead, a mirror of the values of the society that produced it. Watching the afterlife change is watching a society's hopes and fears change, with the attendant change in social institutions and values.

Ideas about the afterlife do not exist in a vacuum; they have no life of their own. They do not spread out of inexorable logic or good sense or superior doctrine. All notions of the afterlife have benefited a particular social class and served to distinguish the purveyors of the idea from their social opponents. Their fortunes are closely tied to the fortunes of their earthly believers. The fact that it takes a close historical analysis of texts that are usually studied by religious specialists has kept the secret from us. Our notions of the afterlife are just as much a history of the constant civil war between religious factions in society as they are the record of the genius of our greatest literary masterpieces. Let us look at the story in the West in its broadest outlines.

EGYPT

Notions of afterlife are universal in human experience; indeed, they are older than human life, if Neanderthal grave sites are taken as evidence. The nations that surrounded Biblical Israel all investigated the notion of life after death. But no culture more spectacularly affirmed an afterlife than Egypt. The identity of the person was symbolized in the very image of the person, represented sometimes by the corpse itself, first perfected into an artful representation by mummification, then transformed into an eternal star to enjoy the breeze on a day of leisure in a perfected Nile valley. The corpse itself was preserved as a mummy in a pyramid or tomb for all times; when that was properly accomplished, any number of representations of the person, the *ba,* the *ka,* the *akh,* or some other metaphysical entities were set free to travel by day.

The lack of agreement about what carried the identity of the ancient Egyptian into the afterlife points out local differences. That they were never synthesized suggests that Egyptian religion did not need to develop an overriding notion of the self, if the ancestor showed up at all the different required ritual occasions. When the body of the Pharaoh, who was Horus on earth, was preserved by the priesthood of Osiris, his person was reunited with his divine father Osiris. The medium of preservation was the body itself, which could be preserved through the dry desert climate aided by the desiccant Natron. When the body was elaborately prepared and wrapped for its future life, the ancestor received all the proper spells and prayers for a successful journey to the afterlife. But that symbol came more and more to equal the other forms of postmortem life—the *ba,* the *ka,* and the *akh,* with the heart carrying the conscience and rationality.

Such a great advantage could not be available only to Pharaoh for long. More and more people were eventually included in his fortunate afterlife, but new, moral, entrance requirements were added. Only those who were deserving of the rewards of transformed existence by personal acts of piety to the gods and service to the state qualified. Unlike the Pharaoh, who answered for the government in this life, the newly privileged transformed souls had to answer for their behavior in an elaborate judgment of the dead, where the soul was judged against the feather of *Ma'at*, good order and justice.

The process of including more and more people in the afterlife was a gradual one. But, given a long enough duration (and Egypt had time to spare), changes are apparent in the notion of the afterlife. Ancient Egypt had stable government for over three thousand years. Because of archaeology and ancient historians, the history of ancient Egyptian is available at a glance, making correlations between religion and politics and sociology easier than it has been.

The relatively complete record of Egypt's history allows us to see that even their heaven was manipulated by their priests, kings, and writers. This is symptomatic of afterlife beliefs throughout the world. Over a generation or two, they appear stable and unchanging. But through the eyes of an ancient historian, the vast changes in their notion of the afterlife become entirely clear. This necessarily relativizes all views of the afterlife and points out how easily they are affected by social circumstances. Any intelligent understanding of the afterlife must eventually account for parallel development between the concept of the afterlife and the people's social world.

MESOPOTAMIA

In Mesopotamia the afterlife was less optimistic; it was a poor consolation compared to the Egyptian notion of immortality of the gods. If humans are lucky, we can achieve divine wisdom, but we never become immortal. Everyone must die. The fate of the dead is hardly pleasant in this culture, condemned to shadowy existence in the underworld. Gilgamesh tried for immortality but lost it. Utnapishtim, the only mortal who had escaped death, explains that no one else will ever be given this divine reward. Gilgamesh both realizes that immortality is impossible for humans and also becomes the king of the dead, which negates this clear-sighted realization.

Even the formidable goddess Inanna who, as the planet Venus, regularly descended beneath the horizon, could not herself escape the clutches of her sister Ereshkigal, the goddess of the underworld; her deliverance by means of Geshtinanna and Dumuzi had permanent climatological effects on the world but scarcely effected the fate of the departed. The situation is scarcely better in Canaanite culture. Access to the wisdom in the underworld was guarded by priests who upheld the traditions of the myths of the underworld. Funeral rites, however, celebrated the deeds of the ancestors and were the responsibility of the family to arrange. They were supplemented by regular, expensive rituals that commemorated the transformed ancestors as heroes.

FIRST TEMPLE ISRAELITE AND CANAANITE RELIGIONS

All this was rejected by the Biblical writers, though there are hints that Babylonian and Canaanite afterlife notions were very popular in Israel. If we had only the documents of the Bible, the First Temple period would have only had the most vague and unarticulated notion of the afterlife. This looks unique in human experience until we realize that we are looking at Israelite culture through the lens of editors who chose what would survive out of the ancient writings. They were not happy with Canaanite views of the afterlife, which were idolatrous and immoral. In the end, Israelite notions of the afterlife emphasize the same truth as the Mesopotamian and Canaanite ones: Like us, animals have earthly life; we have life and, if we act properly, we will gain wisdom; but only God has immortality.

SECOND TEMPLE JUDAISM

When the Jews came into contact with Greece and Persia, everything changed. By the time the Persians and the Greeks made contact with Jewish culture, both had developed significant myths that spoke of conquering death. The Jews listened to the Greek and Persians more attentively than they listened to the Canaanites. Though both Greece and Persia linked feasting with the dead in their ancient past, both imperial cultures also developed high philosophical understandings of the afterlife that avoided the sins the prophets decried.

Persia eventually influenced the invention of a beatific afterlife in Israel. The religion of the Persians left us uncertain evidence about influence during the time of Ezekiel (sixth-century BCE) when Zoroastrianism was growing important in Bactria in the East. But by the time the visions of the book of Daniel were written (168 BCE), Zoroastrianism was virtually the national religion of the elite Persian rulers and left us clear evidence of bodily resurrection and a beatific afterlife. These surely stimulated and encouraged similar notions in Jewish life, though we lack proof of how the transfer took place.

Unlike the Persians, the Greeks left footnotes when they influenced Hebrew thought. Greek culture contains a long meditation on the notion that the soul could separate from the body. Where the soul went was the major focus of Greek speculation. The early Greeks could envision a hero's choice of fame over immortality, the very choice which Odysseus makes at the beginning of the *Odyssey;* they could envision a ritual process of immortalization in the Eleusinian Mysteries, perhaps aided by drug-induced experience, making this mystery religion into a weekend "rave." Or they could believe the proofs of the immortality of the soul offered by Plato's Socrates.

All these notions were adopted into Israelite culture, after being retailored for adoption into a monotheistic scheme. The most long-lasting Greek contribution to Jewish culture was from the aristocratic, Platonist intellectual elite of Greek society that said that the soul was immortal. In return for a life of moderation and intellectual development, the soul went upward to receive its astral rewards.

The elaborate funeral rites of the Egyptians suggest that the method of body disposal had a great deal to do with how afterlife was interpreted, that the afterlife somehow begins as a meditation on the recognition that we die and the body dissolves in a culturally supervised way. In Egypt, where the body was preserved by mummification, the person after death was a living image. Afterlife was conceived of as bodily in roughly the same way as we inhabit this life, though the glorified spirit could take up residence in the stars at the same time. In Mesopotamia and Canaan, including ancient Israel, the body was buried, yielding notions of a pale underground exile for the dead spirit; its condition was somewhat alleviated by dramatic orgies. In ancient Greece, where the body was often burned, the soul could soar free to the heavens with the smoke of the funeral pyre. The Persians appear to have exposed their bodies to predation by vultures so reconstitution of the body appears to have been the preferred form of the afterlife. Their sky-burial can also be thought of as a variation on cremation.

Each culture also produces a carrier of personal identity, whether the true image was the mummified body, the *ba,* the *ka,* the *akh,* the heart, body, or soul, so that the dead did not have to live in exactly the fleshly body it had on earth. The nature of the afterlife self is significant because it also helps reify the concept of self in society. Every culture designs its own vision of a perfected life and expresses it in its notions of afterlife. From this vision that is often preserved in civic monuments and literature, what was important to the social class or cult or society emerges. The afterlife becomes a mirror to the deepest hopes of the society. But the symbols are not universal; they depend on specific cultural connections made between afterlife, the disposal of the body, and the nature of the self that survives death. The symbols of the afterlife are culturally specific.

Apocalyptic Israel seemed to envision a transformed body, though the martyrology of 2 Maccabees 6–8 shows that it could also be a literal reconstitution of the physical body, especially if the physical body had been cruelly tortured, destroyed and snatched away from proper burial by evil oppressors. It was this extreme form of persecution, preventing the righteous from receiving their Biblical reward of long life, that so captured the followers of Jesus when their leader was so unjustly martyred. Bodily resurrection was fit to make Christianity into a religion whose mission was the conversion of the world.

The preexilic Biblical tradition steadfastly maintains that what occurs after death is very unimportant: For instance, the book of Job teaches only that God is responsible and will answer for His seeming injustices, not that we will survive into another more beatific afterlife. Job testifies that God will appear to answer the charges; His appearance in theophanies is proof that His covenant is an equitable arrangement for both partners, though we cannot know why He seems to punish us innocently. Job is a heroic answer to the perennial question of theodicy. But Job did not satisfy everyone.

MARTYRDOM

The answer to Job, for example, is not sufficient for those brave young Jews who died at the hands of foreign oppressors, who taunt them with the public choice of apostasy or death. In the face of the torture and death at the hands of foreign oppressors, a new notion of afterlife was born— resurrection of the body. Under the pressure of martyrdom, the death of the faithful for their faith became a public drama that overcame the evil of the oppressor and testified to the truth of the faithful. It does not really matter whether the stories actually happened and, if they did, whether they happened in the way 2 Maccabees tells us. The stories themselves serve as the revelation of a new dispensation; they are the evidence that the inquiry took place in the face of this foreign oppression.

The effect of the new revelation in apocalyptic Judaism is clear: God will restore the bodies of the martyrs which the oppressors so cruelly destroyed. This is the belief of small groups of millennialists who receive apocalyptic prophecies saying so. Not everyone in Hebrew society valued these pronouncements or thought them authentic. The dreams and visions constituted a new answer to Job in the face of real torture ending in death, not the fabled suffering of Job, ending in restoration. They were based on the stories in Daniel in which the hero is rescued by God. In the visions of Daniel, the seer confirms that even those who were not rescued by God in this life will be rescued in the next. The new prophecy from God promises that the wicked will be punished, the martyrs will be restored to an ideal life, and the teacher-leaders of the sect will become angels (stars).

We see a community of angels and saints at Qumran. But the angels and the saints are the same, like the butterfly and the caterpillar. Possibly, the members attained angelic status in this life with their ascetic practices. At the very least, their strict purity made possible a partnership with the angels, who would defeat their enemies. This was the vision of the end envisioned by this small group of religious revolutionaries, not unlike the ones we have seen in our premillennial days.

IMMORTALITY OF THE SOUL

The second notion of afterlife to be adopted in Hellenistic Jewish culture was aristocratic, elitist, and available at first only to those few who could get a good Greek education— immortality of the soul. In its classic form, it seems also solipsistic because it depends entirely on thinking and meditation. But it depended heavily on having the right kind of individual tutoring and instruction, instruction only available to the very rich and those with leisure to study.

It was the new aristocracy, the client scribal and intellectual classes of the Hellenistic world, people like Philo and Josephus, who were afforded an expensive Greek education, who served the rulers and adopted the Platonic notion of the immortal soul. They built the notion of the immortal soul on the earlier and less comforting Semitic notion of the *nefesh*, but their philosophical education identified the Hebrew soul with the Greek *psyche*. Their perspective did not see the body as valuable, rather the opposite. Nor did it consider a large society as its purview. Immortality of the soul is, at first, an individual salvation or, at most, a camaraderie of but a few enlightened philosophers. It posits as immortal those aspects of consciousness which were deemed most valuable to an elite, intellectual class—its education *(paideia)*, knowledge *(gnōsis)*, in short, its memory *(anamnesis)*, a pious wish from a class of intellectuals totally subservient to their Hellenistic rulers except in the power of their minds.

These ideas of the soul's immortality are not entirely divorced from martyrdom; Socrates himself was a martyr. Cato the Younger got the courage to do away with himself after rereading the *Phaedo* several times. But the point of the Platonic synthesis, the immortality of the soul, was that immortality was a natural human endowment, part of the very predicament of being human. Salvation came from learning how to stop the cycle of rebirths and live in deathless perfection as a disembodied soul. Popular versions of the immortality of the soul began to be found in Hellenistic Jewish literature, mixed with other notions like martyrdom, in the century in which Jesus lived.

CHRISTIANITY

Apostolic Christianity at first wanted nothing to do with immortality of the soul. Christianity did not belong to that tiny, elite class of Jews who wanted to preserve their intellectual achievements after death; it would be at least a century, maybe two, before many Christians rose to the social level of a Philo or a Josephus. Christianity's beginnings were in the apocalyptic groups that believed in resurrection of the body. After all, the Jesus movement unexpectedly and tragically found itself faced with a martyred leader. It was natural, obvious in many ways, that a notion of resurrection would inform this group's continued narrative about its relationship to God; the surprise was that it believed Jesus to be *already* resurrected, which inevitably led both to the notion that he was divine and to the conclusion that the apocalyptic end-time had begun.

To produce this notion, Jesus had to be identified with a divine candidate. The crucifixion made sensible a Messianic claim for Jesus in the charge of the Romans: "Jesus of Nazareth, King of the Jews." The resurrection made divine (perhaps more correctly, angelic) status likely. Jesus' "divine" status was gained because he was higher than any other angel. It made him Son of God (Ps 110) and Son of Man (Dan 7:13). The risen Christ became both Messiah and LORD (YHWH).

Paul too was an apocalypticist but he was a powerful thinker in every area of life. For Paul, all were sinners and were redeemed by Jesus' death. The emphasis on sinfulness is typical of an apocalyptic missionary cult. Though Paul spoke for himself and for a small gentile minority, Paul's interpretation of these events gained a special cogency as gentiles more and more predominate in the church. But, Paul could not have known the success his "minority report" would gain; indeed, it was used to frame the triumph of the gentile church in a way that would certainly have saddened him.

What the Gospels narrate is not what actually happened; nor is it fraudulent. The evangelists naturally imported into the life of Jesus details and Bible texts that demonstrated their own faith in the crucified and risen Messiah. They naturally externalized the visionary truths of Paul's religious life; they may even have taken a polemical position against Paul's more "spiritual" position, that Christ's glorious body is the end point of our transformation in faith. Paul believed that believers shall become one with the body that Christ achieved in his resurrection.

COMPETING TRAJECTORIES OF THE
MEANING OF JESUS' LIFE

So did the evangelists. But for them, Christ's body was the earthly church, which they led and represented. The ritual of communion became incorporating the body and blood of Christ literally. When the evangelists told the narrative of Jesus' life, his resurrection naturally became more and more physical. Thus, the resurrection of believers also became a more and more material fact. The Gospels preach the literal, fleshly resurrection of Jesus and the subsequent literal, fleshly resurrection of all believers. Additionally, the state of sin was an apocalyptic characteristic, the necessary concomitant to the social necessity of conversion. Positing that humanity lacks something without Jesus is part of the uniquely suited missionary gospel of early Christianity. The remedy to the state of sin is a physical resurrection, a unique event in history. What demonstrated that Jesus' death was uniquely meaningful for human history was not the fact that he survived death but that he was physically resurrected, as the first sign that the general resurrection would soon be upon us.

One of the competing portraits of Jesus against which the Gospel of John polemicized, must surely be the Jesus of the *Gospel of Thomas*. By seeking a vision of him, like Paul's vision, the ascetics of the *Gospel of Thomas* learned the transformative RASC process which linked them with the direct knowledge *(gnōsis)* of Savior and hence with immortality of the soul. This was accomplished without the teaching of the apostles and indeed without the canonical Gospels but with the help of RASC, developed by reading their own Gospel while performing their ascetic discipline. This is what *gnōsis*, saving knowledge, meant—an actual religiously interpreted meditative state unique to the *Gospel of Thomas*.

In many ways, the central dramatic fights of early Chrisianity were caused by these differing sources of salvation. The early Christians believed that Jesus brought resurrection which could be communally experienced in ritual. The process was one of transformation but the issue was galvanized by an imaginative rendering of the end point, the body of Christ that was both the church and the goal of the believer.

The Synthesis of Immortality of the Soul with the Resurrection of the Body

As CHRISTIANITY moved slowly around the Roman Empire and slowly up the social ladder, it met a much more formidable form of the argument against the uniqueness of Jesus' postmortem existence: the immortality of the soul. The soul was immortal by nature in Platonic thought, not needing the redemptive sacrifice of Christ, and this was one of the dominant intellectual theories of the day. Perhaps it was *the* dominant, intellectual tradition of late Antiquity. The doctrine of the immortal soul was eventually adopted because it allowed Christianity to talk about an interim time when the good could be rewarded and the evil punished without waiting for the delayed, end-of-time. Without an imminent end-of-time, Christianity was in danger of losing its missionary edge. So it eventually articulated a doctrine of Original Sin, which built the apocalyptic notion of human sinfulness into the structure of the universe and made the sacraments of Christianity necessary to compensate for it.

THE RABBIS

In the Rabbinic community, there was a very different dynamic. The Rabbis did not need to define the nature of the resurrection body and they had no equivalent problem with the immortality of the soul; they quietly and quickly imcorporated both into their thinking of the afterlife, fudging the term *Teḥiat Hametim* (vivification of the dead) to mean whatever God had chosen to make it mean or whatever they needed it to mean at the moment. (For them it was the same thing.) There was, furthermore, no need to enforce intellectual orthodoxy. Each Rabbi might explain the afterlife as he wished, or indeed leave it to God to surprise us. Theirs was not the task of trying to define how God would bring about the fulfillment of His promises. Theirs was only the task of defining the human consequences of His covenant.

One can see their flexibility as a response to the changing location of Jewish life. Conceivably having its origin in Persian religion, the Rabbinic notion of resurrection could bend in the direction of Hellenistic philosophy, as the ex-Pharisees Paul and Josephus show. It could emphasize one kind of notion of resurrection in the presence of Christianity and another in the presence of Zoroastrianism. It could accommodate the philosophi-

707

cal speculations of Platonism or the literalism of early Islam. It needed to preserve that doctrinal flexibility to prevent religious intolerance from its host civilizations. The Gemara's discussion particularly demonstrates how at home Rabbinic notions could be under Zoroastrianism, with its notions of the resurrection of the perfected flesh. But it could also match Christianity as it slowly absorbed the Hellenistic notion of the immortality of the soul. It could accommodate Islam's early preference for resurrection of the flesh at the end-of-time. And it could even participate actively in Islam's flirtation with Aristotelianism in the tenth through thirteenth centuries, which necessitated an articulated doctrine of the immortality of the soul. It then passed that philosophical acumen to Christian Aristotelian philosophers like Aquinas who worked out their own synthesis. It could do all this because resurrection or immortality of the soul was not their central concern; not much about the social significance of the Rabbinic movement depended on it. Jews did not rely on the Rabbis to resolve theological problems for them; they relied on them to resolve legal issues.

ISLAM

Islam is even more clearly a missionary religion than Christianity. In forming itself to promulgate its revelations, it put the day of judgment foremost in its teaching, save only for the unity of God. Resurrection would follow and it would be literal and material, a pleasurable goal worth the efforts of being a good Muslim. It supplemented this with various promises of paradise and horrors of hell. It rarely had to force conversions; instead it put the choice of resurrection or not, of heaven and hell, in front of its hearers. Then, it outlined the many financial, economic, and social advantages to conversion to the Muslim *Ummah* and waited for the inevitable "bandwagon" effect. After a century, practically no one was able to resist conversion. Luckily, Judaism, Christianity, and Zoroastrianism were given reprieves because of their Scriptures: They were considered "People of the Book," though for their religious fortitude they endured many indignities and dangers as *Dhimmis* (protected ones). Thus, some Christians, Jews, and Zoroastrians managed to survive the inescapable advantages of submitting to the message of Muḥammad.

Muslim eschatology is fitted to conversion and mission, very much like Christianity's end-of-days. Both have in common the tendency to retreat into fundamentalism when challenged by new ideologies. Even Judaism develops fundamentalist sects when challenged in just the right way, as by the secular alternative of Zionism and the prospect of religious reform in

Reform, Conservative, and even modern Orthodoxy. But fundamentalism is a religious system that fosters highly motivated, yet parochial converts. It is a defensive strategy that can turn to extremism and violence for self-protection but it attacks enemies before it even makes them. One characteristic of this view is that it believes every inroad it makes on the others is God's providence but every in-road made against them is Satan's own imperialism. On the other hand, views of heaven which are culturally plural and nondenominational seem to predominate when all religions view themselves as minority religions and must share political powers with others. In that case, heaven develops a nondenominational character and adds to the culture's desire to remain tolerant.

Standing Back to Look for Patterns

WITH SUCH an enormous time span to look at, some interesting reassurances emerge. First, the basic questions of life four or five thousand years ago are still the questions of today but our answers are far more comforting to us: We see a refreshing trend to include more and more people within the rewards of the afterlife. In some ways, the history of Egyptian religion is emblematic of the history of the afterlife in the West in general. Over the millennia, Egyptian religion inexorably moved toward the inclusion of more and more people in the rewards of the afterlife. This "democratizing" movement was followed throughout the history of Western religion. Immortality of the soul accommodated more human hope than the Homeric achievement of fame in battle. It was available to all those who had the leisure to study and meditate, male and female.

The rewards of the martyrs in ancient Israel—resurrection and transformation—were also slowly expanded to the society as a whole and then, through Christianity and Islam, to the entire Western world and beyond. But it was not inevitable: Zoroastrian immortality was available earlier but it was not to be a world religion forever. Judaism was a missionary religion to an extent yet its truths were not adopted by many. One might, as a matter of choice, prefer true multiculturalism over universalism, which limits salvation to adopting a single religion viewed as the truth.

Rabbinic Judaism was forced to admit the multicultural prospect of God's plan, when meditating on its guest status in other cultures. Realizing that they needed tolerance to survive, they posited it as a value that all cultures should adopt. They unilaterally allowed that Christians and Muslims who were righteous were saved as well. By so doing, they hoped that Christians and Muslims would let them live amongst them in peace.

And they also downplayed the whole notion of afterlife to a much lower level than the typical missionary religion. This is parallel with their conclusion that missionizing would endanger their position as guests in a political world they could not control.

This merely underlines the contention that afterlife notions are mirrors of our cultural and social needs, available to development and manipulation, and that they tend to mirror our social goals. We need to ask ourselves if multiculturalism is what our society wants. Are we then saying that we need to set down rules as to how missionary religions—including Christianity, Islam, and Buddhism as a bare minimum—should behave with regard to each other? This immediately raises the question of the sense in which we can let toleration of opposing views of the universe into our lives without losing our basic direction. The answer is clear: We all need to behave as if we are minorities needing toleration.

This question is implicit in looking over the history of the afterlife. The first victim is the reassuring notion that the afterlife is part of unchanging, revealed truth. The notion of the afterlife changes just as surely and even more radically in Israelite culture than it did in Egypt, Mesopotamia, Persia, Greece, and Rome. The changes parallel the various uses of political power in the state. Sometimes the view of heaven dictates changes in the social circumstances; sometimes changes in the social circumstances dictate a necessary change in the notion of heaven. But there is always a tendency to bring the two realms into congruence. The notion of heaven and the afterlife always reflects what is most valuable to the culture. God may be sending revelations but we are talking to ourselves when we interpret our Scriptures. We are telling ourselves what the Scriptures must mean in the current circumstance; it is not God speaking to us directly. This is not comforting to the traditionally faithful. In fact, it is usually threatening. But it is just as true of fundamentalist doctrines as it is of liberal ones; both are innovations suited to the modern world. Neither is any better grounded in ancient Scripture.

Any simple determination of truth in matters of the afterlife becomes yet more elusive when one factors into the equation the differing and very contradictory beliefs of the religions of the rest of the world. Almost every view of the afterlife, worldwide, begins with an insight into what humans are, in and of themselves. Each has a deep perception of the nature of reality to tell us, to be respected, and understood. They cannot merely be ignored or dismissed. None lacks a belief in the continuance of life beyond the grave and none agrees in the slightest with any of the doctrines here described on the issue of the resurrection of the body. Some are flatly contradictory with each other as well.

This leaves a difficult and unattractive choice. Either we must view the beliefs selectively, taking seriously only the one that appeals most to us, convert, and become true believers of that religion—any religion—or we must face the surety that all are, at best, but approximations of what may await us. Or, maybe nothingness awaits all of us. Even if we remain within a canonical tradition, any canonical tradition, we must face the surety that it has changed radically over the centuries. Therefore someone in the canonical tradition must be wrong; even worse, we have no real ways of determining which one is right. From our inevitable social context within a specific culture, the best we can do is articulate what appeals to us most.

Looking in the Mirror of Our Souls, Do We Worship Ourselves?

HEAVEN IS the mirror of our souls and our souls are the creators of the landscapes of heaven. Yet another trap lies in either believing or disbelieving our own ecstatic experiences. Such experiences have always traditionally been self-justifying: People who have them find them so transforming that they cannot doubt the authenticity of their own experience. They are neither unusual nor insane in human experience. Humans have been traveling to heaven to see what was there before heaven was a place where the beatified and sanctified dead went. But that is no guarantee that they are true.

Religiously altered states of consciousness surely brought the notion of afterlife firmly into Jewish culture, from whence it spread out to Christianity and Islam, whose mystics and teachers continued to seek and receive visions of the afterlife. Those who have them are convinced that their experience is valid and true, whether they be theophanies or Near Death Experiences or moments of enlightenment or unitive mystical experiences. Rudolph Otto suggested that these experiences of the *numinous* are the core of religion; holiness is defined by the feeling of awe that is surely behind every religious experience.[5] Those who have never had them should stop reading about religion for they would surely never understand any analysis of religion. But can we really privilege our ecstatic experience in that particular way? Granting that seductive premise is essentially arrogating to ourselves the same legitimacy we want to deny Osama bin Laden.

Newberg and d'Aquili tell us that God will not go away because the human brain is "wired" to receive such experiences, even helping society find its direction. Yet the latter is not necessarily true. People who live in a scientific system do not need to interpret their ecstatic experiences as proof of divine providence. Thinking that humans will always find new and important revelations is no salvation; it does not distinguish between prophet and madman, between visions that take humanity in a good direction or a bad one.[6] To believe in the validity of all such experiences is surely dangerous. It can justify fanaticism and psychosis. Science should seek understanding, not infallibility.

This is exactly what Paul Tillich warned about half a century ago when he cautioned against the idolatry of divinizing the work of our hands. In fifty years, one more corollary must be added—namely, divinizing the thoughts of our minds or the revelations of our dreams and visions. Instead, Tillich advocated only the taking of universal, transcendent values as our ultimate concern.[7] To avoid idolatry, humanity, said Tillich, had to put its confidence only in transcendent values and, at the same time, to realize the importance of doubt to faith.

The Transcendent and Doubt

THE CONSENSUS of liberal theologians has for a long time been that the existence of God, hence the validity of religion, is not susceptible to ordinary scientific notions of confirmation and disconfirmation.[8] One person looks at a sunset and sees the handiwork of the creator; another sees merely the particles of pollution adding color to the sky. Neither can move the confidence of the other because neither perspective is subject to confirmation or disconfirmation. The perspective is, rather, something more fundamental about personal orientation to meaning in the universe. The existence of God is an aspect of our understanding of the meaning of existence—along with justice, love, beauty, and a host of other human values—not something that can be verified scientifically.

Life after death, at first, seems quite a different proposition. The major pictures of life after death in the world's cultures are propositions about objective places. They do not have the uniformity or cultural universality of the question of the existence or nonexistence of the transcendent. Yet, when subjected to historical analysis, which shows that the afterlife is constantly in flux and constantly being accommodated to social, political, and economic necessities in the society, the propositional value of any particular heaven grows much less important than the general claim that an afterlife exists at all.

So, in the end, the afterlife is another way to express the same transcendent, non-confirmable issue of God. The afterlife is particularly important to religions that organize themselves as missionary religions and not nearly as important to religions which do not. Instead, the very speculation that an afterlife exists seems like a human need and an ideal—again, like love, beauty, or justice—that exists in our minds rather than the world and gives a sense of meaning to our lives. Like beauty and justice, life after death is no less important for being unverifiable.

This is not a pleasant thought; nor is it a view that most people will appreciate easily. Most people will prefer to live within the system of beliefs that they inherit. The very variety and change of our notions about the afterlife speaks against any literal truth. The inherent implausibility of any one depiction of an afterlife based on the variety of contradictory notions has certainly brought naive notions of the afterlife into question. But implausibility alone does not actually reach the deep issue of the reality of personal afterlife or its potential meaning and significance in human existence. It has not even ended speculation of the soul's afterlife.

Physicians have placed word generators high up and facing the ceiling in operating rooms so that an out-of-body patient can read and report on them, thus confirming the actuality of the experience. To date none have. We may suspect that none ever will. For one thing, difficulties in confirmation occur because the EEG and other instruments used by doctors are not designed for the sensitivities that this research demands. The brain may be functioning deeply even when ordinary instruments can detect no activity. This conclusion is buttressed by the ability of various drugs to simulate out-of-body experiences, the bright light, the long tunnel, and the feelings of euphoria.[9]

All of these experiments show that concrete, material proof of immaterial hopes is not possible. The body does decompose and no one has convincingly demonstrated that it can recompose, or that even if it did, that it could be reanimated with the same consciousness, though many such miracles have been preached in the last two millennia. Furthermore, it seems unlikely that a reanimated and reassembled body would really be us, if our experience is as unique as we normally think it is. Proof of resurrection is never likely to be so easily demonstrable. Instead, perhaps we should take comfort that we have doubts. Doubts complete faith and keep it from becoming fanaticism.

The Soul and Afterlife

HEAVENLY JOURNEYS and NDEs have constantly reinforced notions of the immortality of the soul and testified to the reality of resurrection. But they cannot demonstrate them. Finally, in Neoplatonism and Augustine's thought, our very interior lives became the key to understanding how the material world and the intelligible world could affect each other. Though there is nothing inherently less plausible in the resurrection of the body at the end of time than in the immortality of the soul, it is the latter that has triumphed in Western philosophy in the last two hundred years. Again, social forces help explain this victory. It is the notion of immortality of the soul that fits most closely with our current experience of ourselves. The democratic West is based upon the internal experience of self-consciousness and the conviction that this individual self-reflection is the basis and definition of a unique, even a transcendent self. It valorizes that personal experience as transcendent, saying, in effect, the examined life transcends our short span of years.

In the eighteenth century, Moses Mendelssohn thought that immortality of the soul could be demonstrated rationally and did so in his essay *The Phaedon* (named for Plato's *Phaedo*) but he felt that resurrection was a religious doctrine that could only be accepted by faith. Most Americans are convinced of the same without relying on proof; it merely makes better sense of their individual experience.

In an earlier time, the Church Fathers stressed the exact converse: Only resurrection preserves the uniqueness of each life and the confidence of its historical purpose while the immortality of the soul ultimately implies survival only of the ideas themselves and trivializes the historical existence of the individual.

A relatively new American possibility is that we each get what we think we will get. It certainly is a frequent statement of American multicultural life. This new ideal has much affected the popular imagination; it was, for example, the premise of the film "What Dreams May Come." Even hell is nothing but the self-generated setting of the soul's despair. With appropriate "therapy" in the afterlife even suicides and sinners can be rehabilitated to partake of whatever heaven they best imagine. This was, in a way, the vision of Origen and Gregory of Nyssa.

They too lived in a culturally plural world. Regardless of where it came from, nothing could be more twenty-first century American. It reflects our American experience of living in fairly close contact with people whose most intimate religious beliefs and values differ significantly from our own. It offers the comfort that we all get what we want; therefore we are all correct, all validated, all justified. It further posits that even the dead need to work on self-realization, the idle dream of the Hollywood rich, who can finally finish their therapy in the next world.

Modern America, Christian or not, has ineluctably retreated to the position of the pagan philosophers of late antiquity: Our souls are immortal by nature; all will be saved, it just may take some souls longer to figure out that altruism and moral behavior are what guarantees salvation—or, alternatively, that it is really self-realization that guarantees our salvation. Either seems acceptable as a statement of the distinctively American hereafter because each validates quintessentially American values in this life.

Consciousness and Soul

CONSCIOUSNESS is the truly mysterious obsession of modern Western philosophical inquiry. Technical progress has not brought us much closer to understanding it, though research into the physical action of the brain has dethroned our surety of the self's importance. Although the history of philosophy for centuries has been devoted to a description of the soul and the self, both in the West and the East, it still remains the perennial subject of philosophy, religion, and poetry all over the world, with little hope of achieving a consensus soon. Nor have I proposed here to resolve any of the difficult problems on describing consciousness, much less defining it. But I am stating that the afterlife is a mirror for what each society feels is transcendent in its individuals' lives. In the modern period, the self has come more and more to be identified with the immortal soul. Personal consciousness is transcendent in our society because we value it as divine.

Afterlife as the Articulation of the Transcendent

THE NOTION OF the afterlife is an appropriate concern for faith and also for understanding society. Carol Zaleski, in her fascinating book, *Otherworld Journeys,* is critical of easy acceptance of any mind / body dualism or any easy demonstration of literal truth outside of socially promoted symbols.[10] Our religious truths come to us in a particular society, fitted to them and fitting for them. As we have seen together, ascension narratives are closely associated with conversion accounts because both are meant to serve as a guide for the pilgrimage of life. As Zaleski says as her conclusion:

Whatever the study of near-death visions might reveal about the experience of death, it teaches us just as much about ourselves as image-making and image-bound beings. To admit this is no concession to the debunkers; on the contrary, by recognizing the imaginative character of otherworld visions, we move beyond the merely defensive posture of arguing against reductionism. Within the limits here discussed we are able to grant the validity of near-death experience as one way in which the religious imagination mediates the search for ultimate truth.[11]

These are not easy sentences to come to terms with. I am, as well, particularly struck with the contribution that imagination makes to our religious life, the way in which our religious lives, our cultural lives, and our aesthetic lives interact. To explicate Zaleski's perceptions, I propose to turn Plato's thinking on its head. Instead of spending any more time analyzing Plato's argument that the soul was immortal, we should investigate the consequences: It was Plato's doctrine of the immortality of the soul that allowed us to focus on our conscious experiences, that valorized those experiences and eventually made the "self" the center of philosophical interest in the West, that made the "self" as well as God, a transcendent value in Western thought.

For the ancient Hebrew only God was immortal, but we think we share that immortality with God. Perhaps Plato's notion of the immortal soul did not do all these things single-handedly. But it certainly provided us with the necesssary focus to make all that possible. Samuel Johnson's famous quip that the prospect of death concentrates the mind is true in several ways at once. Death not only concentrates the mind, it concentrates us on our minds. It was the notion of the immortal soul that allowed us to focus on our own minds as transcendent objects, even if it no longer seems obvious that they will, indeed, survive death. Perhaps that is the force of the ancient Near Eastern notion that with mortality comes wisdom and wisdom is a divine gift.

Neither Plato nor the Greeks thought that consciousness per se was important—it was merely the experience of a soul caught in the prison-house of matter—but what Plato started was the valorization of the self because the experience of intellection was the key to demonstrating immortality of the soul. As we know Plato's argument for the immortality of the soul depended on *a priori* arguments about space, time, and relation which no longer impress the modern mind, with its increased knowledge of physiological and developmental psychology. It did manage to allow humans to focus on the transcendent importance of our intellectual powers for the first time. That perception led to the notion of a "self," eventually to a "transcendent self." If intellection was so valuable that it demonstrated our immortality (actually both Plato and Aristotle maintained this in different ways), it was worth paying attention to it, even grooming and developing it—even if it does not literally demonstrate our immortality.

The Greeks did not speculate on consciousness as much as we do or even in the terms that we do. But it was their symbolic representation of the soul that prepared the groundwork for our notions. In ordinary speech, we distinguish between two different aspects of consciousness. We can speak of consciousness as our basic monitoring that we are alive and experiencing. This is a primitive feeling that follows us when we are conscious: We are up rather than sleeping or unconscious; the mental machinery has been turned on. That is a minimum characterization of consciousness. But there is also another, more complicated aspect of consciousness, which happens when we are introspective in some way. Sometimes this is called self-consciousness, or even critical self-consciousness.

Physiological studies have now shown that critical self-consciousness is not actually one simple and uncomposed quality in itself. We think it is a single phenomenon because we experience our own consciousness as continuous monitoring of our waking lives. It actually contains a variety of different processes, each varying according to its own cycle and level of capability. We now know that no single organ in the brain provides us with consciousness; rather many different organs contribute to it. Since the brain has many organs in it that contribute to consciousness, not a single organ that provides it, the concept of self should be considered multiple, additive, and emergent. It arises from the combination of all the various contributions that the centers in the brain and the nervous system provide.

Ironically, this is not so different from the perspective of the very ancient Egyptians, Greeks, and Hebrews, though our notion of which organs provide these *qualia* of consciousness is very different from theirs. We no longer think that consciousness comes from the stomach or the blood or the heat of the body or the breath, though all of these are part of our normal proprioception. It was not that the primitive Greeks were wrong, it is just that they were not right enough. All those feelings are part of our consciousness but even more important to it are the monitoring functions of the various parts of our brain, a process that we do not fully understand, which still appears magical and enchanted.

Consciousness must also contain various aptitudes accessing motivations, emotions, memories, learned tasks, as well as dozens of reasoning abilities. It is hardly a *tabula rasa,* as Aristotle thought. It is not even a single *tabula.* Even what Kant called "the transcendental self" cannot be certified as unchangeable either in the history of culture.[12] In traditional religious parlance, notions of the transcendent self are not universal. In many kinds of Buddhism the concept of the "self" is itself a fundamental mistake; for many Buddhist intellectuals there is, in truth, no continuous self. Realizing that we are not ultimate is the better part of reaching enlightenment.

We might say that any concept of the self-conscious self is itself socially determined because it emerges from our most religious or philosophical, hence our social and cultural beliefs. In calling attention to memory for the purpose of demonstrating the immortality of the soul, Plato was calling for a kind of self-reflection, which we can call an introspective, critical self-consciousness. Plato did not invent self-conscious introspection; nor was he the first to have introspective moments. But Plato did instigate a particular style of introspection and imbued it with transcendental significance by valorizing introspection as part of the immortal aspect of human existence. Essentially he theorized the self as a transcendent being. Plato proposed a proof based on an aspect of experience—memory—that was significant enough to present introspection not just as a leisure activity but as a value beyond the individual and a comfort in the face of mortality.

Cultural Software

IT BEHOOVES US to try to understand why religious symbols are such poignant and important signifiers for us and speculate on how they can be compared adequately. An important perception comes from J. M. Balkin.[13] He compares the ideological content of culture to computer software. At first this may seem to compare the human brain with a computer and hence to replicate the mistakes of Cartesian dualism. But this is not so. Balkin suggests that ideology, even culture itself, is a kind of software or programming, not that the human mind is a computer. Individual minds are only secondarily involved since culture is not produced by individual minds at all; it is an intersubjective phenomenon. Furthermore, the term "cultural software" is not meant to suggest that ideology programs us to perform as machines, without having to make decisions. It merely suggests to us the terms by which we make our decisions, and those terms very often predispose our decisions. The terms suggest the dramas in which we play out our lives.

Religion is, in some sense, like the program "Windows," or any other graphically-based operating system. The program utilizes a simple metaphor: A personal computer can be managed like a desktop. Because of that visualization, any computer user can then perform important procedures—move, copy, store files, executing various useful operations. But a computer is in no literal sense a desktop. There is no literal analogy between the two. Religion is, likewise, a creative visualization that allows us to live our lives within a culture and society. Religion claims to point to transcendent values that go beyond the experience of any individual person believing in it. Some parts of the system may be confirmable and some are probably not, especially from within the system. So it is best to think of the terms that religion gives us as conventions, not truths.

Although we may have conventions and traditions for dealing with the world, in any given culture we have a group of different and sometimes contradictory ones and we differ in social class, in political and economic groupings, as well as in our personal abilities to adjudicate between them. Our culture does not force us to make decisions but predisposes us to see decisions in certain culturally approved terms. Furthermore, each of the "units" of this software, units Richard Dockins called *memes*—suggesting both the English "memory" (like the Greek *mimesis,* imitation) and the French *même* ("same")—changes over time, sometimes due to an individual talent but never only because of one person.[14] Balkin describes these units of cultural meaning as something:

1. that exists in each individual;
2. that shapes and enables individual understanding and cultural know-how;
3. that guarantees similarity of cultural understanding and know-how while permitting some variation, disagreement, and mistake among individuals within the same culture;
4. that changes and develops over time; and
5. that constitutes individuals as persons living in a particular culture at a particular point in history.[15]

Are *memes* real, actual, cultural basic units of transmission or just heuristic devices for understanding how cultural norms can be transmitted through culture and achieve stability over time? If *memes* need to be real, which part of a myth provides us with the basic unit? These are very hard questions to answer and must be left for other books. Nor is it entirely clear that culture provides the same evolutionary environment for the survival of "mutations" that nature does. *Memes* perceived to be helpful within one area—for instance, religion—may actually prevent progress in another area, like the economic or social sphere. There are no easy standards for what progress is. However one chooses to refer to culturally transmitted ideas, religion plays a significant role in the perpetuation of culture. It does so because it answers human needs, including the desire to survive over time. We have already seen how "martyrdom," which involves people giving up their individual lives, can be functional in establishing the perceived social truth of a minority position in society, as self-evidently as soldiers can be judged heroes for sacrificing their lives for country or companions. That we can understand such altruism as self-evidently heroic and honor it on monuments is part of what we call religion.[16]

One of the most interesting functions of memes has been articulated by John Gottsch.[17] Following Susan Blackmore, he suggests that one of religion's functions is to provide ways to deal with the fear of death.[18] Gottsch suggests that fear of death or death anxiety is a consequence of human self-consciousness and that the early ancient Near East provides us with many examples of myths designed to provide culturally plausible ways to reduce death anxiety.[19] Gottsch demonstrates that many of the religious doctrines of the ancient Hebrews are actually "fitness enhancing"—that is, they increase the chances of survival of the people—even though the ancient Hebrews have few specific memes relating to the afterlife. These would include their abhorrence of human sacrifice and ritual prostitution, on the one hand, and their civil code, on the other. In this regard Gottsch holds out that religion is, or can be, a positive and important fact in human evolution while Blackmore seems much more convinced of its virtually unique ability to delude us. Religion is not inevitably adaptive or non-adaptive in any evolutionary sense. However one chooses to treat "memes"—as real or heuristic—this perspective allows us to ask questions about the value of religious structures over considerable periods of time, not just in any snapshot of the culture.

In her book *Little Saint,* Hannah Green discusses the religious life of Conques, a small French village of the Languedoc.[20] Madame Benoit, a venerable Aquitainian, justifies a heretical practice, praying to St. Foy as to the Virgin Mary, by suggesting that the Conquois are rooting themselves to their place of origin. "Life is an envelope," she tells Hannah Green. "We come from the unknown and we are going toward we know not where in this envelope we call our life." Because St. Foy is the martyr closely associated with their pilgrimage town for so many centuries, the Conquois understand where they are in this void more completely by identifying the saint with the role that the Virgin has in wider Catholicism. St. Foy is both an historical datum and somehow an allegory for faith. Christian notions of the afterlife play significantly in this process of finding one's identity but they are only part of the process. Our modern theorizing is but an unpoetic way of describing this envelope which culture provides us as we go through life.

Transcendence Again and How We Express the Value of Our Lives

ONE OF BALKIN'S most interesting definitions, dependent on considerations such as this, is the existence of transcendent values in different societies. A transcendent value in his definition is one that can never be perfectly realized and against which all concrete articulations and exemplifications remain imperfect or incomplete. God's transcendence is what is enshrined in the famous Muslim motto *"Allahu Akbar"*—God is greater. The term "transcendence" starts as a theological term describing God's creation of, sovereignty over, and hence His "greaterness" than the universe. But it has developed other implications in philosophy and the attempt to provide a language for understanding and comparing the work that religions do.

The history of the term has been well discussed in Benson Saler's interesting monograph, *Conceptualizing Religion.*[21] From Saler's discussion, the importance of a notion of transcendence to many twentieth-century theorists of religion becomes entirely clear. But what is not entirely clear, either in the form Balkin discusses transcendence or the form that previous scholars like W. C. Smith or Karl Jaspers did, is whether the term "transcendence" can be adequately defined. It plays off of Platonic notions of the forms and also Christian theological descriptions of God, who must be greater than the universe and hence transcend it. Not all values are transcendent but some may be—values like truth or justice or, in religion, let us say, salvation (which receives a great deal of attention in Christianity) or justice (which receives more attention in Judaism) or submission to the will of God (which receives more attention in Islam). In

Balkin's terms, confidence in the existence of transcendent values is itself a transcendent value, as the confidence itself cannot ever be fully demonstrated. So transcendence is a kind of recursive variable.

In the West we tend to express transcendent values with the metaphor of divine agency. God defines justice through the *Torah* covenant for Jews; He makes salvation available to the faithful for Christians; He allows humanity to submit to His greatness and mercy in Islam. In the great Asian religions, transcendence is often signified by inscrutability: "the *Tao* (way) that can be uttered is not the real *Tao*," says the *Tao te Ching* in its first statement. Confucianism believes it cannot be fully understood by any one person or in any single instantiation. One cannot reach *Moksha* (liberation) merely by trying to understand it with the discursive mind but must meditate on it. By claiming that the mind cannot understand or comprehend a value, these systems are affirming transcendence in the values named as "inscrutable." All of these are ways of suggesting transcendence in traditional vocabularies. Yet, positing the existence of transcendence is itself a transcendent value, as we cannot be entirely sure that we have not just happened on a culturally important symbol that will lose its importance when translated into another culture or time. But they are functional to us as definitions even if they point only to the phenomenon in culture. And they are functional to us in society, if they do help us value and emulate some positive norm, even if we must always fall short of attaining it.

Most of our formulations of transcendence are combinations of high ideals with images that fail to express transcendence as time goes on. For example, the Grail legend encompassed a great many of the characteristics of transcendence. For the society that produced it, the Grail represented an ideal of courtly love, sexual innocence, religious fervor, endurance, and devotion, all represented narratively. Yet, today many would argue that its devaluation of women, sexuality, and ordinary existence could be seen as a real failure of human potential. Though we seem still to be able to appreciate some aspects of its symbolization, even when it is presented by, let us say, an intolerant, anti-Semitic man like Richard Wagner in his opera *Parzifal*, we certainly say that we only appreciate the artistic achievement in and of itself and decry the social context that we recognize is behind it.

In the same way, one might argue that the special laws of Judaism have outlived their usefulness. Some would contest Christian notions of salvation as fleeing the difficulties of this world instead of committing to resolving them. One might criticize Islam for claiming universalism while being intolerant of differences. In fact, one might criticize all of them for all the same reasons. And any of these values can be used to reduce the freedom or privilege the rights of one person over another, as we have seen in detail in the previous chapters. Nevertheless, by abstraction we can come to an appreciation of the admirable factors in many religious symbols while bracketing what seems no longer relevant. That is what allows us to continue to find values in religious symbols. But these are intellectual and aesthetic exercises and quite different from practicing a religion and assenting to it in a public communal context. This process of translating religious values into new contexts or finding new hermeneutics (translation principles) to instill them with new meaning is exactly what fundamentalism refuses to do. Or, more precisely, it substitutes its own innovative hermeneutics which claims to be the ancient meaning while actually representing a very modern, very conservative and eccentric one.

In its narrative context, resurrection points to the victory in martyrdom, even when it appears to be an outward failure, the sad end of one person's life, often in agony, but the valorization of the values for which the person died. The reward of immortality underlines and emphasizes the transcendent value, the victory inherent in what seems at first to be an abject failure. It says there is something transcendent present when the martyr elects to die rather than transgress what she or he thinks is a divine rule. The immortality of the soul outlines the victory that comes in valuing one's own thoughts, applying one's life to systematic, intellectual pursuits. The apocalyptic intuition about history affirms that history itself is important because it says that God will bring paradise about as a fulfillment of the historical process. The notion of our transformation into heavenly beings is also a symbol that our persons, represented by our bodies, have a transcendent meaning. These are concepts that we can personally affirm without necessarily affirming the specific claims and propositions of the apocalyptic and philosophical communities of Late Antiquity.

For those who have experienced a Near Death Experience or those who have complete and simple religious faith no further proof is necessary. Their job is to express to others how their doubt and disbelief disappeared.[22] After 9/11/01, the naiveté of this position no longer seems charming or innocent. People with naive faith are easily manipulated by political agents. But most of us are not in this category; we become skeptical even of arguments which seem reasonable. We do not have the gifts of previous generations; they could be confident that the dreams and visions proved resurrection or showed that the soul lived without the body. We can see that these were elaborately conceived overly-optimistic conclusions. And what is worse, it seems almost sure that the Near Death Experience is but another jump to an optimistic conclusion, based on physical processes which we do not understand.

Yet our knowledge of the function and relativity of our thoughts does not quench our immortal longings. The professorial community is renowned for its skepticism in matters of religion. In her recent Ingersoll Lectures at Harvard University, Carol Zaleski summarized the university's objections to immortality in the following succinct way: "Immortality is criticized on moral grounds as self-aggrandizing, on psychological grounds as self-deceiving, and on philosophical grounds as dualistic. Concern for the soul is faulted for making us disregard the body, neglect our responsibility on earth, and deny our kinship with other animals." From this fair assessment of academic skepticism, Zaleski begins an impassioned defense of the notion of the afterlife as wholesome, important, necessary, even real. Not only is religion still an important value in human life, it is everywhere resurgent; we ignore it at our peril. Zaleski's defense goes beyond the function of defining our ideals to recognizing religion as a necessary part of our self-understanding.

Since It Is Fiction, We May Safely Believe It: An Apology for Religion

EARLY IN HIS career, John Hick concentrated on issues that might confirm the truths of Christianity. He developed a model of "eschatological verification" in which one might verify the truths of Christianity by waking up in the afterlife. If you "wake up" from death and see Jesus on his heavenly throne, you know Christianity is right.[23] Most people—including him, apparently—were not convinced that this was actually confirmation in the scientific sense. After a time, he moved into a far more pluralistic mode, in which he accepted the truths of every religion as they oriented the believer towards reality. He further suggested that no religion was inherently superior to another but that all somehow were constructed manifestations of the real.[24] The history of the afterlife in the West tells that the "real" is itself defined by what cultures define as religious. There is no obvious way to unmediated reality, even if we suspect that religions give us a sense of order and greater clarity about life.

In short, history cannot tell us everything we want to know. Numerous historical questions are verifiable in principle but cannot be verified or falsified with our current knowledge and method. Then there are a number of questions which are not amenable to historical answers. Therefore, there are a number of questions which go beyond what a historian can tell us at all.

Most religious truths, I would put in this category. But that does not give us the freedom to believe anything we want. We cannot ignore what is demonstrable scientifically or historically; otherwise we are just operating irrationally. When Newton adduced his laws, it became clear that our understanding of our religious lives had to change. We now effortlessly appreciate a God of revelation in the Bible and Quran who works through the laws of the universe so that we but understand Him better when we study them. We must also understand that the same applies to the laws of society and the mind. If our notions of heaven are based on our understandings of the transcendent, that does not remove us from the religious universe, it merely clarifies that all religion is an act of the imagination. If we now understand that our religious experiences are triggered by the brain, that does not demonstrate that there is no God or transcendent process. It may mean that God works through these human neurological, psychological, social, and cultural laws as well as He works through history and the natural law. If we know that the brain produces religious experiences, we still may affirm that God made our brain so as better to communicate with us. But because we can see how much of religious vision is provided by culture, it does also mean that we now know we must be open to the truth that alternative visions of transcendence are just as valid interpretations of our neurological stimuli. It means that doubt must be part of our exact formulations of the afterlife. Above all, it means that a full description of our religious lives and our afterlives is an imaginative act with all the advantages and disadvantages of the imagination.

We can appreciate others' religion even if it is different and contradictory to our own, provided we know that they equally respect ours. We understand these issues better when they are expressed in fiction and presented to us through reading, as a private, asthetic experience. If religion is a way to look at ourselves and challenge ourselves, then religion is just as surely part of our creative life as is art. If what Christians, Jews, and Muslims of good faith are doing when they believe in their notions of the afterlife is not assenting to propositional truth but expressing a confidence in various transcendent values of human existence, then they are choosing to believe in something that is by nature not confirmable, neither true nor false of itself and not part of the discourse of propositions and syllogistic truths.

This is equally true when we consent to watch a play or read a novel.

We agree to treat a human confection as real for the purposes of enjoyment and edification. When the literal truth is not the point but the formulation of the truth is an expression of confidence in our ultimate significance, we seem to be able to understand other people's issues more clearly. In attending a play, we assume a certain number of things are true in order to watch the performance. Watching others leads directly to realizations about ourselves and our world, even if the writer creates a world quite different from our own. Our self-consciousness gives us the ability to appreciate our own lives as performances in which we are also the audience, even if we assume we are sharing our thoughts with God.

Shakespeare was enamored with his own powers as a poet and performer in his youthful conceit as a poet:

> Nor shall Death brag thou wander'st in his shade,
> When in eternal lines to time thou growest:
> So long as men can breath or eyes can see,
> So long lives this and this gives life to thee. (Sonnet 18)

The poet gives life to his beloved, making death itself envious of the immortalizing power of his verse. We cannot all be poets nor do many of us wish to brag so unmercifully. Nor can Shakespeare really grant his beloved immortality with his verse. But is not culture a kind of drama in which we play ourselves and give ourselves lines and then judge ourselves as the audience? So perhaps that is how, in the end, we must treat our religious values—as a script for the performance of a life—that is, as very important and meaningful lines to us because they are beautiful, true, and enduring in their own way, even if they are fiction. They point to what we feel are the transcendent values in our lives. Indeed, what we have seen is that our culture and religion itself tends to express itself in Scripture, which is a literature treated with transcendent importance.

We all know that history as well as religion tells lies but we can safely believe fiction because it makes only symbolic claims to truth, while we perhaps wrongly expect more from history and religion. Religion, by allowing us to believe our ecstatic experiences, allows us also to believe our own, most intimate dreams. As Gertrude exclaims when Hamlet begins talking to his invisible father: "This is the very coinage of your brain. This bodiless creation ecstasy is very cunning in" (Act 3, Scene 3, lines 136–7). That statement works on many levels at once. There is no one on stage with them but we know that what Hamlet sees is real. In art, we can handle the ambiguity that the invisible ghost is real to Hamlet and to us though invisible and false to another character. We know he has been seen and verified at the beginning of the play, though he might seem a delusion to his mother Gertrude. We can also appreciate that, really, there are no ghosts, so to us the entire presentation is a fiction, even if Hamlet's original audience thought otherwise. Such realizations, even when we do not spell them out explicitly, allow us to range through several different levels of significance simultaneously. Surely part of Shakespeare's genius is that he seems to be speaking to those different levels of signficance at the same time.

In *Antony and Cleopatra,* Shakespeare has given us a love story ending in death, somewhat like his more famous play, *Romeo and Juliet.* In both plays each lover gets to make a dying speech after the other's death, which is a very neat piece of plotting. In *Romeo and Juliet,* for example, the plot device that allows each to give a stirring speech over the body of the other is a miraculous drug that produces the symptoms of death. Everyone likes *Romeo and Juliet* because of its poetry and its story of young, tragic love. Fewer know the solaces which *Antony and Cleopatra* offers, with its story of mature love's martyrdom, all confused with imperial and dynastic ambitions. For some, *Romeo and Juliet* is all that needs be said, almost perfect in its poetic expression. But few of us would mistake it for history. On the other hand, in *Antony and Cleopatra,* Shakespeare gives us a more complicated story of passion where Cleopatra fakes her death to hurt Antony, to prove his love of her, not realizing it will cause his own suicide. (It also allows him to have each give a speech on the death of the other.) This is not history either but it comes closer to the historical reports we have in Plutarch (not history either), which Shakespeare knew. History is, in fact, a construction of our minds as redactors and editors of all the reports.

In *Antony and Cleopatra,* Shakespeare abandoned the earlier set speeches—poetic, purple passages that stop the action and show his poetic abilities in their best light, speeches we like so much in *Romeo and Juliet.* Shakespeare's *Romeo and Juliet* is poetry more than drama. But *Antony and Cleopatra* is drama more than poetry. Nor is it puppy love. Antony and Cleopatra are historical characters whose story is justly famous throughout Western history. Shakespeare portrays them as complex personalities, both decisive and indecisive, both heroic and cowardly, both industrious and lazy, with a myriad of complicated responsibilities that prevent any easy generalizations about their motivation.

At the end, when all political ambitions have been lost, when Antony is dead and Cleopatra is captured, she becomes noble in choosing death as the Egyptian Queen over life as a servant to a Roman conqueror: "Show me, my women, like a queen. Go fetch my best attires. I am again for Cydnus, to meet Mark Antony." She calls her servants to bring her royal trappings: "Give me my robe. Put on my crown. I have immortal longings in me. Now no more the juice of Egypt's grape shall moist this lip" (Act 5, Scene 2, lines 283–85).

She has determined to give up whatever pleasures life may yet hold and to die as a queen. She could have lived; she has been offered terms of surrender. But, as they turn out to be false terms, her death by her own hand is a victory and affirmation too—a martyrdom, though certainly not a simple act of following her departed beloved, whom she alternatively loves and deprecates. Her death is not a simple act of ending her defeated life. When she envisions the afterlife, we do not know whether to take her literally, either about her act of devotion or her heavenly ascent:

> Methinks I hear
> Antony call. I see him rouse himself
> to praise my noble act. I hear him mock
> The luck of Caesar, which the gods give men
> To excuse their after wrath. Husband, I come!
> Now to that name my courage prove my title!
> I am fire and air; my other elements
> I give to baser life. (lines 285–93)

An enormous ambiguity enters our minds with Cleopatra's "Methinks. . . ." Unlike Hamlet in Gertrude's bedroom, we do not know what she sees. Like us, she cannot be sure she sees the vision that promises a beatific heavenly abode reunited with her love. Yet she affirms it for his sake as well as hers: "Now to that name my courage prove my title!" Does she really see Antony or does she convince herself to act as if she does? But she does convince herself of her progressive immortality by ascent through the heavens. In a sense we too often convince ourselves of the literal truths of religion by an act of will when we know they are but metaphors.

The result is that she can speak of her own immortalization. She becomes the higher elements and rises, giving the lower elements of earth and water to baser life. She is apotheosized into a higher creature by her suicide and her martyrdom. It is an affirmation of life in a morally, existentially, and epistemologically ambiguous universe. Though Antony and Cleopatra are hardly the unblemished heroes that Shakespeare makes

Romeo and Juliet, Cleopatra is given the most self-conscious of all Shakespeare's affirmations of life beyond the grave.[25] But it is that ambiguity that makes her speech so powerful today when she sounds the major theme of all our doubts. She is the only one of the many characters in Shakespeare who truly tells us what lies in the "undiscover'd country" because she does so by a deliberate act of imagining, not by literal description. She resolves to be a wife at the same moment she succeeds at being a queen.

Of all Shakespeare's great tragic heroes, only Macbeth dies in total despair. When told of Lady Macbeth's death, he says:

> She should have died hereafter;
> There would have been a time for such a word.
> To-morrow, and to-morrow, and to-morrow
> Creeps in this petty pace from day to day
> To the last syllable of recorded time;
> and all our yesterdays have lighted fools
> The way to dusty death. Out, out brief candle!
> Life's but a walking shadow, a poor player,
> that struts and frets his hour upon the stage
> And then is heard no more. It is a tale
> Told by an idiot, full of sound and fury,
> Signifying nothing. (Act 5, Scene 5)

He begins as a good man, susceptible to his wife's ambitions, and ends as a villain. Shakespeare usually maintains a moral universe, even in the face of the moral challenges he constantly offers us. Does knowing that the religious belief system we often regard as true and enduring has changed, even changed radically and now seems relative rather than absolute over time, leave us with the despair of Macbeth? Do we live a life, "told by an idiot, full of sound and fury, signifying nothing?" Most of us do not, even when we know that the terms that we commonly use to signify our greatest aims must surely be false if taken literally. And, indeed, they can be true if taken imaginatively and metaphorically. But then we are acting first and, in our self-consciousness, judging our own performances as actors.

One could affirm our religious lives, even in the face of obvious and overwhelming doubt, as do the fundamentalists. That is a mark of fundamentalism; it is an affirmation of a logically disproved system. It can exist only by flying in the face of scientific knowledge consciously ignored.

That is why it thrives in courtroom trials and textbook controversies, demonstrating locally by majority numbers alone in little victories of ignorance what can never be demonstrated to the mind—that their most cherished ideas are literally right. That is why fundamentalists need Satan. They create him, a symbol of their own impulses and doubts which they can thereafter exorcise by orgies of hate. But we know that one cannot convince oneself of the truth of religion by winning victories in schoolboards or voting booths or even by killing vast numbers of a hated enemy.

People who live with faith today, whether in the majority or minority, are living in a world that does not need the hypotheses of religion to explain the universe. We can live perfectly complete lives without it if we want. But few do. All the polls show that while Americans are suspicious of religious surety, they still admire sincere faith. At least the case is no worse than it was when Newton came to his physical laws. If a God can coexist with a number of physical laws that seem unchangeable and unbridgeable, He can coexist with a number of complex social laws that seem equally unbridgeable. Human life may be possible without the images that give it purpose but most of us do not want that life.

Antony and Cleopatra, because of their longer lives and experience are privileged enough to "see through everything." They know the conventions of life and, by failing, come to know the price that conventions demand. But with failure comes the recognition of contigency, a "seeing through everything." Knowing that culture is but convention written large, we must also see "through" everything, see *by means of* everything. The symbols of culture point towards something ineffable. And that is what Cleopatra does at the end, using a vocabulary that she wills imaginatively to do the work she needs.

There are important moments in Shakespeare's plays when his characters speak both within and beyond their characters at once. Hamlet's famous soliloquy beginning, "To be or not to be," with which we began our journey through Western conceptions of the afterlife, is one. They are moments of transcendence, when we see beyond the play to a greater significance. There are moments when "this majestical roof fretted with golden fire" is both stage and universe. In Harold Bloom's words, these moments cannot be confined within the stage: "Hamlet's undiscovered country, his embassy of annihilation, voids the limits that ought to confine his drama to stage dimensions." [26]

Cleopatra gives us another. Shakespeare writes this speech because it perfectly fits Cleopatra's situation but he is writing it about all of us as well. We ascend, transcend, transform ourselves when we exceed our limitations through our use of intellect and imagination. Even a mind that knows the difference between a religious formulation and its truth, and that is keenly aware of its own limitations, can be guided by religious imagery.

Besides being intellectual adventurers, our ascending souls serving as symbols of our lives' journey, we are all also martyrs as mortality eventually defeats us. Shakespeare tells us what our religious imagery tells us: the victories of our life outlive its difficulties. The effort to transcend ourselves is all. "The rest is silence."

Religion's imagining of our hereafter also seems to say the same—our "immortal longings" are mirrors of what we find of value in our lives. They motivate our moral and artistic lives. Our longing itself deserves a robe and crown, nothing less. If humans can be, in Hamlet's words, "in apprehension like a god," do we not deserve his epitaph: "flights of angels sing us to our rest"?

NOTES

Introduction

1. The words of Robert J. Lifton, as reported in the *New York Times,* 14 January 2003, B: 2. One could certainly think of an exception or two.

2. Lisa Miller's cover-story in *Newsweek* of 12 August 2002, p. 44, investigated the bitter ironies of these conflicting religious motivations, pointing out that both the victims and the oppressors expect rewards in heaven for their efforts on behalf of their religion.

3. Walls, *Heaven,* p. 3

4. *De resurrectione carnis,* 1.

5. Since the US census is not allowed to ask questions about religion, George Gallup Jr.'s continuing interest in our religious life has provided researchers with major and significant measures of our religiosity. See Gallup and Castelli, *The People's Religion.*

6. Ibid.

7. See de Toqueville, *Democracy in America,* vol. 2, bk. 1, chs. 5–7: "How Religion in the United States Avails Itself of Democratic Tendencies," "The Progress of Roman Catholicism in the United States," and "What Causes Democratic Nations to Incline Toward Pantheism."

8. Lenski, *The Religious Factor.*

9. Gallup and Castelli, *The People's Religion,* p. 54.

10. Carter, *The Culture of Disbelief.*

11. Neimeyer and Van Brunt, "Death Anxiety," pp. 64–66.

12. See Greeley and Hout, "Americans Increasing Belief," p. 813.

13. The title is from Garrett, *The Demise of the Devil,* which is a very competent analysis of the meaning of magic in Luke-Acts. The title is quite relevant to the American context as well.

14. Gallup, *Adventures in Immortality,* pp. 55–66.

15. Pace Delbanco, *The Death of Satan.* Also see Walls, *Hell.* See *La Civilta Catholica* (Summer 1999), which endorsed the belief that hell is a place of psychological rather than physical torment; "The Emptiness of Hell," *Macleans* 8, September 1999, p. 35; and "Hell Hath No Fury," *U.S. News and World Report,* 31 January 2000, pp. 45–50.

16. Quoted from Walls, *Hell.,* p. 1.

17. L. Clark, *From Angels to Aliens,* pp. 24–45.

18. See the documentary "Hellhouse" directed and produced by George Ratliffe. For an account of the popularity of exorcism in American life, see Cuneo, *American Exorcism.*

19. Gallup and Castelli, *The Peoples Religion,* pp. 47–48.

20. We shall return to the meaning of transcendent in the last chapter. For now, it is enough to say that transcendent values are those values to which we give ultimate significance. The theological term originally described God—that he was necessarily greater than the universe, therefore transcending it. This protected us from thinking that God was the same as the universe. The converse term in traditional theology is God's immanence, His presence in all of our lives. Both were necessary to achieve even an outline of what Jews, Christians, and Muslims normally think of God.

21. See the interesting paper of L. Clark, "U.S. Adolescent Religious Identity."

22. See Moody, *Life After Life;* Morse, *Closer to the Light,* also *Transformed by the Light.*

23. The Tibetan Buddhist community in the United States has seen in them confirmation of the truth of a number of phenomena, described in their religious writings. In particular, the bright light is well documented in the *Bardol Thodol,* the so-called *Tibetan Book of the Dead.*

24. Gallup, *Adventures in Immortality,* pp. 1–54.

25. See Morse, *Closer to the Light.*

26. See, for example, Bloch and Parry, *Death and the Regeneration of Life.*

27. See Pearson, *The Archaeology of Death and Burial,* pp. 53, 147–151. This does not absolutely prove that they believed in life after death. They may just have been observing a taboo or a gift-giving rite. But chances are that some kind of continuity of personality on the other side of the grave was responsible for the inclusion of these grave goods.

28. *New York Times,* 24 December 2002, p. F2.

29. See Chidester, *Savage Systems.*

30. Cullmann et al., *Immortality and Resurrection.*

31. Kübler-Ross, *On Death and Dying.* There were many and important books which tried to counter society's "denial of death" with a more honest appraisal, constituting a kind of "death awareness" movement. See E. Becker, *The Denial of Death;* Ariès, *Western Attitudes Toward Death;* Wass and Neimeyer, *Dying: Facing the Facts.*

32. See "Expert on Death Faces Her Own Death: Kübler-Ross now questions her life's work," *The San Francisco Chronicle,* 31 May 1997. My thanks to several students who have investigated this story in the past few years, especially to Elise Cucchi of Williams College.

Chapter 1. Egypt

1. See Keel and Uehlinger, *Gods, Goddesses, and Images of God.*

2. J. Davies, "Death, Burial," p. 29.

3. See McDonald, *The Tomb of Nefertari,* p. 91.

4. John Wilson, "Egypt," p. 83.

5. Diodorus Siculus, *An Account of Egypt,* 1.70

6. J. Wilson, *The Culture of Ancient Egypt.*

7. For more detail, see Hornung, *Conceptions of God in Ancient Egypt.*

8. Quirke and Spencer, *The British Museum Book of Ancient Egypt,* pp. 36–37.

9. See Morenz, *Egyptian Religion,* p. 183.

10. See S. Walker, *Ancient Faces.*

11. J. Taylor, *Death and the Afterlife,* pp. 46–91.

12. A. B. Meiser, *Pyramid Texts* (New York: Longmans, Green, 1952),1.92, 1. 390a.

13. Ibid., I.234, 1473b–1474b.

14. Siliotti, *Dwellings in Eternity,* p. 87.

15. See Stilwell, "Conduct and Behavior," who summarizes where each major Egyptologist thinks the beginning of the democratizing process of immortalization, pp. 198–205.

16. Hornung, "Ancient Egyptian Religious Iconography," pp. 1722–23.

17. J. Davies, *Death, Burial, and Rebirth,* p. 32.

18. Meeks and Favard-Meeks, *Daily Life of the Egyptian Gods,* p. 142.

19. Other versions suggest that the penis was found and buried at Mendes. See Van Dijk, "Myth and Mythmaking," p. 1700.

20. Morenz, *Egyptian Religion,* p. 204–5.

21. See Assmann, *Aegypten,* pp. 151–57.

22. See Mettinger, "The Riddle of Resurrection," pp. 168–72 for a more complete description of these important rituals.

23. See Wilson, "Egypt," pp. 39–133; also *The Culture of Ancient Egypt.*

24. Quirke, *Ancient Egyptian Religion,* pp. 158–59.

25. See Forman and Quirke, *Hieroglyphs and the Afterlife,* p. 7.

26. The Canaanites turned *Mot* into a god who battled Baʿal for sovereignty. Because of Arab influence in Andalousia, the term enters Spanish even in the word *Matador,* the death-dealer, the executioner.

27. See the informative book by Hornung, *Ancient Egyptian Books of the Afterlife.*

28. *ANET,* pp. 33–34.

29. Forman and Quirke, *Hierglyphs,* p. 23.

30. *ANET,* p. 32.

31. *Pyramid Text* 302, north wall of the central chamber, quoted from Foreman and Quirke, p. 57.

32. See Brandon, *The Judgment of the Dead,* pp. 12–13.

33. His vital force, which dwells in him as a separate entity, and which he is supposed to retain in death. For further views as to the nature of the "ka" see CAH 1:334–37; *Proceedings of the Society of Biblical Archaeology* 38: 257–60.

34. Erman, *The Ancient Egyptians*, pp. 2–3.

35. Assmann, "Resurrection in Ancient Egypt," p. 130.

36. J. Taylor, *Death and the Afterlife in Ancient Egypt*, p. 162.

37. In fact, the bird-like qualities of the dead spirits is widespread, appearing in Mesopotamia as well as Israel. It also shows up in later Islam. It is difficult to know how to account for it.

38. J. Taylor, *Death and the Afterlife*, p. 20.

39. See Stilwell, "Conduct and Behavior," pp. 198ff. Stilwell makes his case that the judgment scene is early, perhaps even coterminous with the *ba*. This cannot be demonstrated from current evidence, though there are suggestions even in the texts so far quoted that the Pharaoh himself had to be judged righteous by standards appropriate to his functions and station. Note the very helpful compendium of Egyptian texts on the afterlife in the dissertation's appendices, as well as the annotated lists of the attributes of the Egyptians' souls.

40. Hornung, "Ancient Egyptian Religious Iconography," pp. 1718–23.

41. See Hornung, "Ancient Egyptian Religious Iconography," p. 1711; and *Agyptische Unterweltsbucher.*

42. Hodel-Hönes, *Life and Death in Ancient Egypt*, pp. 2f.

43. J. Taylor, *Death and the Afterlife*, p. 16.

44. See M. Fox, *Ancient Egyptian Love Songs*, pp. 20f; 53 n. 34.

45. Blackman, *Middle Egyptian Stories*, p. 37.

46. See the interesting article of Assmann, "A Dialogue Between Self and Soul.

47. Whitehead, *The Making of Religion*, p. 6.

48. Assmann, "A Dialogue Between Self and Soul," p. 403.

49. Assmann, *Ma'at*, pp. 123–153.

50. See also Assmann, "Confession in Ancient Egypt."

51. See Dorn, "The Beatific Vision," esp. pp. 37–44, which summarizes the doctrine of immortality in Egypt and other ancient cultures before moving on to its main purpose, an evaluation of the notion of a beatific afterlife in the biblical Psalms.

52. For more detail and for the relationship between the priesthood and the land exclusive of the cult of the dead, see Sauneron, *The Priests of Ancient Egypt.*

53. See Bonnet, "Sargtexte," pp. 669–70; *Attitude of the Ancient Egyptians;* see also Stilwell, *Conduct and Behavior,* for a short survey of the various Egyptologists' opinions.

54. Brandon, *The Judgment of the Dead*, pp. 21–48.

55. See Assmann, "Conversion, Piety, and Loyalism," p. 41. See also R. Meyer, "Magical Ascesis and Moral Purity."

56. Lichtheim, *Ancient Egyptian Autobiographies*, pp. 42–46.

57. Brandon, *The Judgment of the Dead*, p. 47.

58. Freed, Markowitz, and D'Auria, *Pharaohs of the Sun.*

59. Hornung, *Akhenaten and the Religion of Light*, pp. 95–104.

60. Ibid., pp. 95–96.

61. Brandon, *The Judgement of the Dead*, pp. 30–34.

62. In some simple sense, a tip is a payment to ensure that someone will do what they are supposed to do while a bribe is a payment to ensure that someone will do what they are not supposed to do. The Arabic word *bakshish* covers both cases.

63. Forman and Quirke, *Hieroglyphs*, pp. 153–54.

64. Bagnall, *Egypt in Late Antiquity*, esp. pp. 261–310.

65. See J. Davies, *Death, Burial, and Rebirth*, pp. 35–36. From Diodorus Siculus, *An Account of Egypt*, p. 209.

66. Forman and Quirke, *Hieroglyphics*, pp. 175–77.

67. See ibid., p. 178.

68. See Mazar, *Archeology*, p. 447.

69. See Mettinger, "The Riddle of Resurrection," esp. pp. 167–183.

70. The Israelites too felt that either one was resurrected or nothing happened, much as the Egyptians feared that sinners would be devoured on the way to their reward. However, there were some sinners who were so bad that they would be punished forever.

71. As we shall see, the elite teachers in Israel in the Hellenistic period sometimes received pre-eminence through astral immortality. That is where the first important connection is to be made.

72. Smolar, Aberbach and Curgin, *Studies in Targum Jonathan.*

73. Melzer, *Letters from Ancient Egypt*, p. 215, as quoted in Lesko, "Death and the Afterlife," p. 1765.

Chapter 2. Mesopotamia and Canaan

1. This chapter will not attempt a history of the Sumerians. See "Sumer" pp. 454–63 in *IDB*, vol. 4. See also *The Anchor Bible Dictionary.* This chapter will also ignore Hittite views, which are not important to the development of biblical notions of the afterlife. For a summary see, Dorn, "The Beatific Vision," pp. 46ff. For cuneiform, see Crystal, *Cambridge Encyclopedia of Language*, p. 200.

2. See Lambert, "Myth and Mythmaking."

3. See also Dalley, *Myths from Mesopotamia.* In many ways this is a more accurate translation but it lacks line numbers.

4. See Scurlock, "Death and the Afterlife." The bird-like qualities of the dead can be seen in the Egyptian *ba,* as well as in Canaan, Israelite, and in Islam.

5. See Lambert, "Myth and Mythmaking."

6. See Geller, "Some Sound and Word Plays." Geller shows that similar wordplays to those in Genesis [Adam (man) created from the Adamah

(ground), Isha (woman) from Ish (man)] are present in this Babylonian creation story. In the Atramḫasis myth, the *etemmum* (ghost) comes from *ṭemum* (wisdom, report, instruction, command), thus reprising the notion of wisdom inherent in knowing our mortality.

7. For a good description of the problem, see S. L. Sanders, "Writing Ritual and Apocalypse," pp. 22–54.

8. Ibid., p. 143.

9. See Ibid., p. 140.

10. Jacobsen, "Investiture and Anointing of Adapa."

11. See Izre'el, *Adapa and the South Wind*, p. 137.

12. Ibid.

13. Jacobsen, *The Sumerian King List*, pp. 80–81.

14. Oppenheim, "The Interpretation of Dreams," p. 259, see also pp. 267, 282, and 287. Also see Tabor, *Things Unutterable*, p. 102.

15. More exactly, Anu and Dingir were the same sign (and Anu was, of course, an astral god). Later, it became the sign for all gods. Thanks to Ben Sommer for this observation.

16. Keel, *Symbolism of the Biblical World*, p. 308; Moscati, *Face of the Ancient Orient*, p. 41.

17. See S. L. Sanders, "Writing Ritual and Apocalypse;" Dorn, "The Beatific Vision," pp. 78–103; Arbel, "Beholders of Divine Secrets."

18. *Koḥl*, collyrium, a blue eye-shadow, is cognate with the Arabic *Alkaḥool*, which is, in turn, evidently the source of our word "alcohol," perhaps from blue impurities that were part of its manufacture.

19. The Urnammu text demonstrates Dummuzi's return. In the text, after Urnammu, the founder of the Third Dynasty of Ur, dies, Inanna intervenes and complains to Enlil that she wants him back. This closely resembles her intervention for Dummuzi. See Mettinger, "The Riddle of Resurrection," p. 196.

20. A strong form of this observation, studied as "Dying and Rising Gods," has been recently revived by Mettinger, "The Riddle of Resurrection." He himself gives a very full account of the opposition to this position, starting with the "Covent Garden" school of myth interpretation (based on its use of agricultural metaphors to explain the myth), its dependence on Christian scholars looking for earlier patterns similar to Christianity, and the further helpfulness of the metaphor in the study of several pagan cults, particularly in Syria in the Hellenistic period. An impressive piece of scholarship, the book nevertheless does not completely establish the continued usefulness of the term, though in some "soft" form it does designate a series of possibly related myths, which report the death of the god. "Resurrection" when applied to an annually reviving god does not mean the same as the resurrection of historical humans in Judaism and Christianity, as we shall see in the following chapters.

21. See Garelli's review of "Cuneiform Texts from Cappadocian Tablets;" Hirsch, "Gott der Väter," pp. 56ff. For more information, see Cross, *Canaanite Myth and Hebrew Epic*, p. 10 n. 25.

22. Soden, "Zum Schlusstück von Ištars Unterweltsfahrt," p. 194, the quotation is from Sladek, "Inanna's Descent to the Netherworld," p. 262, quoted from Mettinger, "The Riddle of Resurrection," p. 193.

23. Mettinger, "The Riddle of Resurrection," p. 204.

24. See, for example, Kluger, *Archetypal Significance of Gilgamesh*. As the title suggests, she offers a Jungian interpretation of the myth.

25. Our use of the name Gilgamesh is conventional. The signs can be read in a number of ways—Izdubar, Bilgamesh, etc,—and the Sumerian stories used Sumerian names. Also the epic was assembled from separate stories, which appeared even in literary form as early as Sumer but also evidently orally before that. The story of the composition is fascinating, even confirming theories of biblical composition as well. See Tigay, *Evolution of the Gilgamesh Epic*.

26. See R. Harris, "Images of Women;" and especially Frymer-Kensky, "The Marginalization of the Goddess."

27. See also the language used of the friendship between David and Jonathan: e.g., 1 Sam 18:1, 3; 20:17; and especially 2 Sam 1:26.

28. T. Abusch, "Ishtar's Proposal and Gilgamesh's Refusal."

29. See T. Abusch, "The Epic of Gilgamesh;" "Ishtar's Proposal and Gilgamesh's Refusal."

30. See also *The Epic of Gilgamesh*, translated and edited by B. Foster.

31. See Dorn, "The Beatific Vision," p. 47.

32. Translation by Tigay, p. 168, taken from Gardner and Maier, *Gilgamesh Translated*, p. 214.

33. Ibid., p. 57.

34. Kübler-Ross, *On Death and Dying*. Also see Ray, "The Gilgamesh Epic."

35. See Tigay, *Evolution of the Gilgamesh Epic* and *Empirical Models for Biblical Criticism*.

36. Gadd, *RA*, pp. 126ff; for a new translation of this additional material, see George, *The Epic of Gilagmesh*, pp. 175–208.

37. George, *The Epic of Gilgamesh*, p. 177.

38. The primary translation is in French, Antoine Cavigneaux and Farouk N. H. Al-Rawi, *Gilgameš et la mort: Textes de Tell Haddad VI avec un appendice sur les textes funéraires sumériens*, Cuneiform Monographs (Gröningen: Styx, 2000). It has now also been translated into English, George, *The Epic of Gilgamesh*, pp. 195–208. George had access to further fragments from Nippur. There is no evidence that this was ever included in the so-called *Epic*.

39. For example, see Sommers, "Expulsion As Initiation," pp. 26–29 and notes.

40. The punishments essentially set up the marriage power arrangements of the Hebrew world and end the comic, "topsy-turvey" which had existed until that time: "To the woman he said, 'I will greatly multiply your pain in childbearing; / in pain you shall bring forth children, / yet your desire shall be for your husband, / and he shall rule over you.' And to Adam he said, 'Because you have listened to the voice of your wife, / and have eaten of the tree / of which I

commanded you, / "You shall not eat of it," / cursed is the ground because of you; / in toil you shall eat of it all the days of your life' " (Gen 3:16–17). See next chapter for more details.

41. There is some evidence, in fact, that the Akkadian Ishtar was originally a male deity who was subsumed to her closest correlative, the female Inanna.

42. From Livingstone, "Court Poetry and Literary Miscellanea," p. 71, as quoted in Scurlock, "Death and Afterlife," p. 1887.

43. Scurlock, "Death and the Afterlife."

44. See daSilva, "Offrandes allimentaires aux mortes en Mesopotamie."

45. M. Pope, "Cult of the Dead at Ugarit;" for Mesopotamia see J. S. Cooper, "The Fate of Mankind," pp. 19–33; Tsukimoto, *Untersuchungen zur Totenplege*; Bernstein, *The Formation of Hell*, p. 1–18.

46. See Shaffer, "The Sumerian Sources of Tablet 12 of the Gilgamesh Epic," (Ph.D. diss., University of Pennsylvania, 1963), pp. 116–119, as quoted in Scurlock, p. 1888.

47. See Abusch, "Ascent to the Stars," pp. 15–39; S. Sanders, "Writing Ritual and Apocalypse."

48. S. Sanders, "Writing Ritual and Apocalypse," p. 161.

49. Ibid., p. 158.

50. For the connection between Israelite Apocalyptic, Jewish mysticism, and shamanism, see Davila, "The Hekhalot Literature and Shamanism;" "The Dead Sea Scrolls and Merkavah Mysticism," pp. 249–64; "4QMess ar (4Q534) and Merkavah Mysticism."

51. See Cross, "Yahweh and 'El," in *Canaanite Myth and Hebrew Epic*, p. 45.

52. See Cross, "'El and the God of the Fathers," in *Canaanite Myth and Hebrew Epic*, p. 13.

53. Coogan, *Stories from Ancient Canaan*, pp. 86–115.

54. For a very full treatment of the correspondences and differences among the principal gods of the Middle East, see Mettinger, *The Riddle of Resurrection*. See especially his very intelligent discussion of Ugaritic Ba'al, Melqart-Heracles, Adonis, Eshmun-Asclepius, Dumuzi-Tammuz and the West Semitic gods.

55. The Hebrew root occurs in many ways—as *mawet* or *mavvet* (death), as well as the word *met* (dead).

56. See also Judg 6:25ff; 1 Kgs 15:13; 16:33; 81:19; 2 Kgs 13:6; 17:16; 18:4; 21:3–7; 23:4ff; 2 Chr 15:16.

57. See Pope's *Song of Songs*.

58. See Grey, *Near Eastern Mythology*, pp. 70–75.

59. The first captivity, including the exile of King Jehoiachin, begins in 597 BCE. The city of Jerusalem was destroyed in 587, starting the second and greater exile to Babylonia. The year 539 is the usual dating for Edict of Cyrus to return to the land of Israel.

60. Stager and Wolff, "Child Sacrifice at Carthage;" Stager, "Carthage."

61. See Mettinger, "The Riddle of Resurrection."

62. Ibid., p. 58. But see the connection with the destruction of the idols in Josiah's reign.

63. Grey, *Near Eastern Mythology*, p. 94.

64. See the interesting book by D. Wright, *Ritual in Narrative*, esp. pp. 100–22.

65. See, for example, Geertz, *The Interpretation of Cultures*, pp. 142–69; Bell, *Ritual Theory, Ritual Practice*, pp. 33–55; also see *Ritual: Perspectives and Dimensions*, pp. 115–20. Perhaps Peacock, *Rites of Modernization* can be seen to be relevant with allowances for the difficulty in applying the term "modernization" to this context. The epic story however does have implications for social and symbolic appreciation of the predicament of mortality.

66. D. Wright, *Ritual in Narrative*, pp. 118ff.

67. See Douglas, *Purity and Danger;* "The Contempt of Ritual;" "Deciphering a Meal."

68. The Passover seder, based as it is on a similar Greek drinking party called a "symposium," which implicitly has similar family functions, is a pale reflection in terms of the behaviors that were typical at these banquets.

69. See, for example, the three volume study of Psalms for the Anchor Bible by Mitchell Dahood, which claims that the Israelite notion of a beatific afterlife is based on Ugaritic parallels. There seems to be little or no beatific afterlife in Ugarit and, as we shall see, little that can be said about Hebrew views of the afterlife.

70. J. Z. Smith, "Dying and Rising Gods;" *Drudgery Divine*. Also see M. S. Smith, "Dying and Rising Gods."

71. See the different discussion of Mettinger, "The Riddle of Resurrection."

72. However, see McLaughlin, *Marzēaḥ in the Prophetic Literature*, who disputes Spronk's and Pope's interpretation of the texts, trying to disconnect the *marzeaḥ* practice from funerals and also disputing that the word *za'atar* refers to the herb in this context.

73. In this section, I am indebted, both for the translation and the organization of the material, to the fine work of Spronk, *Beatific Afterlife in Ancient Israel,* esp. pp. 145–202.

74. Hallote, *Death, Burial, and Aferlife*, pp. 12, 60.

75. For complete bibliography on the *marzeaḥ* or, more properly, the *marziḥ* in Ugaritic, see T. Lewis, *Cults of the Dead.*

76. An exhaustive study of the phenomenon can be found in Pope's commentary to Song of Songs. See esp. pp. 210–29. He does not discuss the origins—that is merely a logical inference—but it is supported by J. Armstrong, *Alcohol and Altered States.*

77. See Pardee, *Ritual and Cult at Ugarit*, pp. 192–210; it is the expanded and translated version of the book in the previous note.

78. Nut-tree gardens are Jewish symbols for mystical practices as well. As

difficult as it may be to believe at first, there is a historical relationship between these two phenomena through Song of Songs.

79. See Cross, "The Divine Warrior" in *Canaanite Myth and Hebrew Epic,* pp. 91–111, esp. p. 102.

80. Finkelstein and Silberman, *The Bible Unearthed.*

81. Lapp, "If a Man Die," p. 145.

Chapter 3. The First Temple Period in Israel

1. Damrosch, *The Narrative Covenant.*

2. Hallote, *Death, Burial, and Afterlife,* pp. 28–29; also see the expert opinion of Bloch-Smith *(Judahite Burial Practices).*

3. Bleiberg, *Jewish Life in Ancient Egypt,* pp. 14–20.

4. However, T. Lewis (*Cults of the Dead,* pp. 104–117), after reviewing all the *marzeah* texts of Ugarit, says that it is unlikely to be a *marzeah* and the fast which Saul was keeping beforehand is likely to be more meaningful. I think Lewis is right; the rite is meant to be a necromancy, not a wake.

5. *Pace* Schmidt. In spite of his learned and interesting book, *Israel's Beneficent Dead,* it seems much more likely to me from this evidence and more as well that these practices were early and not introduced in Israelite history first during Assyrian rule.

6. See M. S. Smith, *The Early History of God.*

7. Toorn, "Nature of the Biblical Teraphim;" also *Family Religion in Babylonia;* Brichto, *The Names of God.*

8. See A. Cooper and Goldstein, "The Cult of the Dead," p. 295.

9. The punctuation of v 20 has been altered for sense.

10. Douglas, *Leviticus as Literature,* p. 99.

11. Ibid., pp. 87–108.

12. See for example, A. Cooper and Goldstein, "At the Entrance to the Tent;" "The Cult of the Dead;" "Exodus and Maśśot."

13. Besides Amos 6:7, Barstad in "Religious Polemics of Amos Studies" has argued that two other passages in the book of Amos reflect the *marzeah* without actually using the term: Amos 2:8 and 6:4–6.

14. McLaughlin, *Marzēaḥ,* p. 83.

15. See Andersen, *Amos.*

16. McLaughlin, *Marzēaḥ,* pp. 185–95.

17. A. Cooper and Goldstein, "The Cult of the Dead."

18. See Aberbach and Smolar, "Aaron, Jeroboam, and the Golden Calves."

19. Finkelstein and Silberman, *The Bible Unearthed.*

20. See Hallote, *Death, Burial, and Afterlife,* p. 126. Hallote suggests that it might be translated as the Valley of the "Screaming Son."

21. See P. Johnston, *Shades of Sheol,* pp. 68–85; for notions of a threatening underworld, see pp. 86–124.

22. *IDB,* 1: 788 viz. "dead, the abode of."

23. The picture occurs in Ugarit (I *AB, i 1–3).

24. Dahood, *Psalms;* "The Ebla Tablets."

25. See P. Johnston, "The Pervasive Underworld?" in *Shades of Sheol,* pp. 98–124 for a good review of the evidence.

26. Italics mine and used to emphasize that the pronoun is not in keeping with our ordinary interpretation of the passage.

27. For an interesting treatment of the ancestor cult in ancient Israel, see Brichto, "Kin, Cult, Land, and Afterlife."

28. See Bailey, "Old Testament View of Life After Death."

29. Gen 25:8; 25:17; 35:29; 49:33. "He died" is omitted for Jacob, see also Gen 49:29. See P. Johnston, *Shades of Sheol,* p. 33.

30. See unpublished paper of Jonah Steinberg "Sheol: New Perspectives on the Netherworld in the Eschatological Ideologies of the Hebrew Bible." (Wächter, *TWNT,* 909.)

31. Bloch-Smith, *Judahite Burial Practices,* esp. pp. 133–47. Her book is a most responsible summary of the whole problem.

32. E. Meyers, "Secondary Burials in Palestine."

33. Heidel, *The Gilgamesh Epic.*

34. Alternatively, the phrase "gathered to one's ancestors" may witness to a common trait of oral cultures. People remember the names of their immediate forbears but gradually they are absorbed into the collective group of ancestors, with the exception of a few specially important ancestral heroes.

35. E. Meyers, *Jewish Ossuaries.*

36. This is particularly interesting because the Deuteronomic reforms of Josiah were key in breaking down the rampant cult of the dead around Jerusalem, which probably further served the unification of the Jerusalem priesthood as well.

37. See the previous chapter, on Mesopotamia and Canaan, n. 60. See also T. Lewis, *Cults of the Dead,* p. 144.

38. See the excellent book by Bloch-Smith, *Judahite Burial Practices,* pp. 132–51.)

39. Ibid., esp. pp. 133–51, which is used throughout this section.

40. Hallote, *Death, Burial, and Aferlife,* pp. 36–37.

41. Ibid., pp. 31–43.

42. J. Davies, *Death, Burial, and Rebirth,* pp. 71–83.

43. Barr, *The Garden of Eden;* J. W. Cooper, *Body, Soul, and Life Everlasting.*

44. Barr, *The Garden of Eden.*

45. See Eduard Löhse, "נפש/ψυχη in Hebrew Thought," in *TDNT.*

46. Lev 19:28 for "dead soul;" Num 6:6, where *"nefesh"* all by itself designates a corpse.

47. Bremmer, *Rise and Fall of the Afterlife,* pp. 11–40.

48. See ch. 8 under the topic of the Septuagint, for a fuller discussion of these passages.

49. Literally *their breath* or spirit, as below. The parallel is key, as it shows God's immortal breath in contrast to human breath, which fails.

50. Or *your breath*.

51. De Boer, *The Defeat of Death*, p. 43.

52. See, for example, Aufrecht's excellent book, *Studies in the Book of Job*, with excellent contributions by Ronald J. Williams, Peter C. Craigie, and Claude E. Cox.

53. J. Roberts, "Job's Summons to Yahweh."

54. See P. Johnston, *Shades of Sheol*, pp. 211–14, for a good review of the textual problems.

55. Possibly these are two different versions of the same Israelite tradition.

56. In the meantime, see Kvanwig, *Roots of Apocalyptic*; Vanderkam, *Enoch*; Boccaccini, *Beyond the Essene Hypothesis*.

57. Pope, *Song of Songs*.

58. See G. Wright, *Old Testament Against its Environment*.

59. A. Segal, *Rebecca's Children*.

60. Later in the story we find out that stars are angels but that is another issue entirely. In point of fact, the equation of the stars with the angels is much earlier than the Genesis ch. 1 creation story.

61. Childs, *Myth and Reality*.

62. See *ANET*, pp. 37–41 for the story of Enki and Ninhursag.

63. Alternatively, it may signify the Tigris or the Nile in an anachronistic way.

64. I know that many feminists want to see some justification for equality of the sexes in this passage. Our modern ethics are in need of no biblical justification.

Chapter 4. Iranian Views of the Afterlife and Ascent to the Heavens

1. See A. Segal, *Rebecca's Children*, pp. 13–37.

2. S. Cohen, *The Beginnings of Jewishness Boundaries*.

3. The best place to start one's study of Zoroastrianism in English is Oxtoby, "The Zoroastrian Tradition."

4. Mary Boyce, *A Persian Stronghold of Zoroastrianism*; *Zoroastrians*; *Study of Zoroastrianism*; J. R. Russell, *Zoroastrianism in Armenia*.

5. See Oxtoby, "The Zoroastrian Traditions," p. 159.

6. A good guess would be around 800–750 BCE, though no one really has convincingly dated Zarathustra's life.

7. Gnoli, "Zoroastrianism."

8. The other major possibility is that Zarathustra preached a more radical religion than was adopted in his name.

9. Zaehner, *Dawn and Twilight of Zoroastrianism*.

10. See also Zaehner, *The Teachings of the Magi; A Zoroastrian Dilemma*.

11. Gnoli, "Zoroastrianism."

12. See Gnoli, "Ateshgah."

13. See Oxtoby, "Interpretations of Iranian Dualism," pp. 62–63.

14. Boyce, *Zoroastrianism*, p. 73.

15. BeDuhn, *The Manichean Body*; Klimkeit, *Gnosis on the Silk Road*; Foltz, *Religions of the Silk Road*.

16. They may have been somehow alienated from their other Sanskritic language-speaking brethren because the word for *god* in Sanskrit is *deva*, *demon* is *asura*, while in the Avestan dialects, it is just the contrary: *daeva* means *demon* and *ahura* is *god*. Linguistic specialization alone might account for the variation between these cognate words in closely related languages. So attributing Iranian dualism to feelings of hostility against their neighbors is a lot to conclude from etymology alone. On the other hand, it is hard to believe that anyone in Zoroastrian Iran would have identified willingly with the *dregvans* and it is easy to understand how powerful a political belief dualism is for demonizing one's enemies.

17. See, for example, the thoughtful book by J. R. Russell, *Zoroastrianism in Armenia*.

18. Boyce, *Study of Zoroastrianism*.

19. See Hultgård, "Persian Apocalypticism," p. 67.

20. See Duchesne-Guillemin, *The Hymns of Zarathustra*, pp. 143–44; also *Symbols and Values in Zoroastrianism*.

21. For more detail, see Boyce, *Zoroastrians*, pp. 14–15.

22. See Kreyenbroek, *Sroaŝa in the Zoroastrian Tradition*.

23. See Kotwal and Boyd, *A Guide to the Zoroastrian Religion*, p. 78.

24. See Foltz, *Religions of the Silk Road*, pp. 28–29. His information, in turn, comes from Janos Harmatta, "Religions in the Kushan Empire," p. 315; and Trinkhaus, "Mortuary Ritual and Mortuary Remains," p. 677.

25. A year is often said to be the time that it takes for the bones to be purified of all the remaining flesh in Jewish as well as some Zoroastrian texts.

26. J. R. Russell, "Death in Persia."

27. Tibetan Buddhists also expose the dead to predation, and probably originally for similar purposes. In Tibet, the ground is too frozen to bury, and there is not enough wood to burn. In current Buddhism, "sky burial" serves to remind the faithful of the transitoriness of life. The Persian nomadic raiders probably did not want to bury their dead and leave them and yet did not want to burn them because that was against purity laws.

28. Any culture which participates in human history long enough will run into conflicting notions of burial and depiction of the posthumous self. It would be wrong to push the analogy too far, given the inventiveness of the human mind, but the correlation is hard to miss where it occurs.

29. J. Davies, *Death, Burial, and Rebirth*, p. 44, from Nigosian, *The Zoroastrian Faith*, p. 55.

30. See West, *Pahlavi Texts*.

31. See McDannell and Lang, *Heaven: A History*, pp. 111–44.

32. Colpe, "Syncretism;" also see *Die religionsgeschichtliche Schule*.

33. The rabbis also report that the capital punishment "burning" could be executed in Persian times by pouring molten metal into the victim.

34. Haoma is probably not the amanita mushroom—*pace* Allegro, *The Sacred Mushroom*; and Wasson, *The Road to Eleusis*—but henbane, a less dramatic psychotropic herb.

35. Shaked, "Quests and Visionary Journeys."

36. Ibid., p. 68. See B. T. Anklesaria, *Khurdah Avistābātarjamah-i Pahlavī-iān* (Shiraz: 1976), pp. 5–6, beginning 18–19.

37. See J. R. Russell, "Death in Persia," p. 8.

38. For the whole story in the *Dâstân-i Mēnōk-i Krat* see Zaehner, *The Dawn and Twilight of Zoroastrianism*, pp. 302–5.

39. See Bode, *Man, Soul, Immortality in Zoroastrianism*, pp. 107–8.

40. M. Smith, *Palestinian Parties and Politics*.

41. Is the last heir described as the suffering servant in Isa 53?

44. For the background to these notions, see Newman, *Paul's Glory Christology*.

42. D. Smith, *Religion of the Landless*, see esp. pp. 49–90.

Chapter 5. Greek and Classical Views of Life After Death

1. The bibliography is endless. As an introduction to the various aspects of the field, see Rhode, *Psyche*; Sourvinou-Inwood, *'Reading' Greek Death*; Garland, *The Greek Way of Death*. Also see Cullmann et al., *Immortality and Resurrection*; S. Johnston, *Hekate Soteira*; Bremmer, *Early Greek Concept of the Soul*; S. Johnston, *Restless Dead*; Guthrie, *Orpheus and Greek Religion*; Knight, *Ancient Greek and Roman Beliefs*; Riley, *Resurrection Reconsidered*; Bolt, "Life, Death, and the Afterlife in the Greco-Roman World;" N. Wright, "Shadows, Souls and Where They Go," in *Resurrection*, which, unfortunately, appeared after this chapter was written; Bernstein, *The Formation of Hell*, pp. 21–129.

2. See Ogden, "Greek Sorcerers."

3. Ibid., p. 14.

4. Lattimore, *The Iliad of Homer*.

5. See the discussion in Riley, *Resurrection Reconsidered*, pp. 26–27; also see Sourvinou-Inwood, *'Reading' Greek Death*, esp. pp. 17–140.

6. See Bremmer, *Early Greek Concept of the Soul*; also Riley, *Resurrection Reconsidered*, p. 31.

7. Snell, *Discovery of the Mind*, p. 8.

8. For example, *kradie, etor, ker,* which seem to be related to the heart, while *phrenes* is related to the lungs and *psyche* or *anemos* with the life force or breath. See Onians, *Origins of European Thought About the Body*; Snell, *The Discovery of the Mind*.

9. See C. Taylor, *Sources of the Self*, p. 120.

10. See again Garland, *The Greek Way of Death*; Toynbee, *Death and Burial in the Roman World*; Morris, *Death-Ritual and Social Structure*.

11. See S. Johnston, *Restless Dead*.

12. Garland, *The Greek Way of Death*, p. 21.

13. See Cancik-Lindemaier, "Roman Funerary Customs," p. 422.

14. On the history of the difficulty of deciphering this scene, see Brandon, *The Judgment of the Dead*, pp. 96–97; also see Stilwell, "Conduct and Behavior."

15. See Brandon, *The Judgment of the Dead*, esp. ch. 4.

16. Toynbee and Perkins, *Vatican Excavations*; Hopkins and Letts, "Death in Rome."

17. Garland, *The Greek Way of Death*, p. 60.

18. For another but closely related point of view, see T. Abusch, "Mourning the Death of a Friend."

19. DeConick, *Seek to See Him*.

20. Murray, *Homer: The Odyssey*, vol. 1, p. 421.

21. Foley, *Hymn to Demeter*, p. 25.

22. Ibid., pp. 80–82.

23. See Kerenyi, "Eleusis."

24. Many polemics against Canaanite child sacrifice can be found in Hebrew thought. And the famous story of the sacrifice of Isaac is deeply involved in the polemic. In the Hellenistic period, as we shall see, it became intimately connected with arguments about immortalization as well, when Christians and Jews argue over the most effective sacrifice, Isaac or Jesus, Isaac who was offered up for sacrifice or Jesus who was actually killed. Later still, the identity of the sacrificed offspring, Isaac or Ishmael, provides the Muslims with justification for saying that God's favor has passed to them.

25. Burkert, *Greek Religion*; and *Ancient Mystery Cults*.

26. Wasson and Ruck, *Persephone's Quest*; Wasson, Ruck, and Hofmann, *The Road to Eleusis*.

27. Frag. 15 = Synesius Dion 10, p. 48a.

28. See Foley, *Hymn to Demeter*, pp. 69–71.

29. Frag. 168 Sandbach = Stobaeus Anthologium 4.52.49. Burkert, *Ancient Mystery Cults*, pp. 91–92. Also see the passage inspired by the Mysteries at Plato, *Phaedrus*, 250bc.

30. Lord, "Withdrawal and Return," pp. 90–92 and 181–90.

31. See the *Golden Bough* which anthologizes myths of kingly succession and vegetation gods. Many historians of religion, influenced by this important work, came to the conclusion that all religion is conerned with this pattern, either in myth or in parallel ritual. Although these are certainly important motifs in religious life, that conclusion was overstated.

32. Euripides, *Suppliants* 533–34: "the spirit into the aether, but the body into the earth." See Riley, *Resurrection Reconsidered*, p. 30 n. 69.

33. Guthrie, *Orpheus and Greek Religion*.

34. Ibid.

35. Harrison, *Prolegomena to the Study of Greek Religion*, pp. 667–9. Cf. N. Turchi, *Fontes Historiae Mysteriorum Aevi Hellenistici* (Rome: 1923), p. 37; V. Macchioro, *Zagreus; studi intorno all'orfismo* (Florence: 1930), pp. 283–84; Guthrie, *Orpheus and Greek Religion*, pp. 173–75; Brandon, *The Judgment of the Dead*, pp. 91, 222 n. 89.

36. Epicurus, *Letter to Herodotus* in Diogenes Laertius 10.63.

37. Ibid., 10.139. Cf. also Lucretius 3.830: *nihil igitur mors est ad nos neque pertinet hilum.* Also see Cicero, *de finibus* 2.31.100; Sextus Empiricus, *Pyrrhonism* 3.229. See Riley, *Resurrection Reconsidered*, p. 37, esp. n. 90.

38. Also *non eram, eram, non sum, non curo.*

39. Cicero, *Tusculanae disputationes* 1.18.42–19.43. See Riley, *Resurrection Reconsidered*, p. 39 nn. 96, 97.

40. This translation is taken from *Plato's Phaedo,* trans. G. M. A. Grube (Indianapolis: Hackett, 1977).

41. Piaget, *Psychology of Intelligence; Moral Judgement of the Child; Adaptation and Intelligence.*

42. See Sorabji, *Aristotle on Memory,* p. 35 for this suggestion.

43. Ibid., pp. 37–46.

44. See Brandon, *The Judgment of the Dead,* p. 88.

45. See: Adam, *The Republic of Plato,* vol. 2, pp. 433ff. Also introduction, pp. Lff. for a good bibliography on the myth of Er. The translation is from Shorey, *The Republic,* vol. 2, pp. 488ff.

46. Translation from Sorabji, *Aristotle on Memory,* p. 53.

47. Ibid., p. 44–47.

48. Copleston, *A History of Philosophy.*

49. "The Dream of Scipio" from Cicero, *The Republic* 6.9–26.

50. Ovid, *Metamorphoses* 14, pp. 805–52, esp. 823–28.

51. See Temporini, *Die Frauen am Hofe Trajans,* pp. 245ff.

52. She cannot even claim as her victory what Shakespeare's Cleopatra does: "I am fire and air; my other elements I give to baser life" (*Antony and Cleopatra,* Act 5, scene 2, lines 201–2). We shall look at this scene again in the conclusion on this work.

53. See Festugière, *Personal Religion among the Greeks.*

54. Vergil, *Eclogue* 4. See Kraus, *Vergils vierte Ekloge*; Benko, *Vergil's Fourth Eclogue.*

55. See e.g., Pliny, *Naturalis historia* 2.8.68. He remains skeptical. But Seneca and Dio make references to a comet at the death of Augustus. See further.

56. Cumont, *Afterlife in Roman Paganism*; see also *Astrology and Religion; Lux Perpetua.*

57. Cassius Dio, *Roman History* 56.42.3.

58. See P. Fossing, *Catalogue of the Antique Engraved Gems and Cameos,* pp. 177n, 1199, also 1203ff.

59. O. M. Dalton, *Catalogue of Ivory Carvings of the Christian Era,* p. 1 and

plate 1. ("The Apotheosis of Romulus"). See the useful bibliography of Sr. Dominique Cuss, *Imperial Cults and Honorary Terms in the New Testament* (Freiburg: 1974), from whom I first heard of the triptych.

60. *Corpus inscriptionam latinarum* 6.29954.

61. N. Wright, *Resurrection of the Son of God*, p. 55.

62. Compare this with our current beliefs, reiterated at every planetarium show and astronomical TV program, namely that we are such stuff as stars are made of—because the higher elements are formed only deep inside stars.

63. Cassius Dio, *Roman History* 69.11; Pausanias, *Description of Greece* 8.9.7–8; Eusebius, *Historia ecclesiastica* 4.8.2; Justin, *1 Apology* 1.29; Clement of Alexandria, *Protrepticus* 4.

64. See Z. Smith, "Hellenistic Religions," in *The New Encyclopedia Britannica. Macropaedia* 8:749–51, 15th ed; Stendahl, *Immortality and Resurrection.* Also see Tabor, *Things Unutterable*, p. 63.

Chapter 6. Second Temple Judaism:
The Rise of a Beatific Afterlife in the Bible

1. The Hebrew is not so much ambiguous grammatically as ambiguous in context. The NRSV renders it as: "he will devise plans so as not to keep an outcast banished forever from his presence"; RSV: "but God will not take away the life of him who devises means not to keep his banished one an outcast"; both are attentive to the grammar but easy to interpret in a broader way. The LXX is not the source of the translation: "even as he devises to thrust his outcast from him." It is exactly the opposite of the English translations and, one supposes, takes the Hebrew subordinating conjunction "without" in a less negative sense. The source of the optimistic translation is the Vulgate: *nec vult perire Deus animam sed retractat cogitans ne penitus pereat qui abiectus est.*

2. Consequently, it has been dated in practically every century since the tenth century bce to the first century ce.

3. See, for example, Sperber, *Greek and Latin Legal Terms.*

4. Seow, *Ecclesiastes*, p. 22.

5. M. Smith, *Palestinian Parties and Politics.*

6. See the recent book by Bremmer for a convenient summary of these historiographical problems. Bremmer, *Rise and Fall of the Afterlife*, pp. 47–50.

7. Martin-Achard, *From Death to Life*, pp. 93–102. More recently, see Zimmerli, "Ezekiel 2," pp. 253–266.

8. Canannite roots have been suggested by van Baudissen, *Adonis and Esman*, pp. 403–6; Riesenfeld, *Repertorium lexicographicum graecum,* pp. 4–7; Robinson, *Job and His Friends;* Martin-Achard, *From Death to Life,* pp. 70–73; and Nikolainen, *Der Auferstehungsglauben*, pp. 50–60. Persian influence has been championed by Böklen, *Verwandtschaft der Jüdisch-Christlichen;* Causse, *Du Groupe Ethnique,* esp. pp. 24–30. See Cavallin, *Life after Death,* p. 25.

9. Perhaps better: "(as) a corpse they shall arise," a accusative of state, referring to the subject of the clause. See Schmitz, "Grammar of Resurrection in Isaiah 26: 19a–c." His conclusion that the resurrection is literal is more speculative, but his observation that the phrase refers to national regeneration correctly interprets the passage in context.

10. As a good example of a circumspect late dating of the text, see Kaiser, *Isaiah 13–39*. He understands the text to emanate from Maccabean times, like Daniel. He also gives a very full bibliography of the other commentators on this passage. As do the following good commentaries on the subject: Seitz, *Isaiah 1–39;* Wildberger, *Isaiah 13–27.*

11. The parallel has been noted often but none so articulately as Nickelsburg, *Resurrection, Immortality and Eternal Life,* p. 17; also see "Future Life in Intertestamental Literature."

12. See Isa 66:18–19.

13. Nickelsburg sees a relationship with the entire text of *3 Isaiah,* which is generally the case but the most succinct parallel with resurrection is in Isa 66:14.

14. See Cross, *Canaanite Myth and Hebrew Epic;* D. Freedman and Cross, *Studies in Ancient Yahwistic Poetry.*

15. See the studies compiled by van Henten, *Die Entstehung der jüdischen Martyrologie;* as well as van Henten and de Jonge, "Datierung und Herkunft des vierten Makkabaerbuches," pp. 136–49. Also see Weiner and Weiner, *The Martyr's Conviction.*

16. Doran, "The Martyr;" p. 201.

17. See the extremely interesting and subtle treatment of Christian martyrdom in Castelli, *Marytrdom and Memory.*

18. See also 2 Macc 7:9, 14; 12:38–46.

19. Sir 24:8 also suggests the same, but it is normally dated a bit later.

20. See Holleman, "Resurrection and Parousia," p. 144.

21. Boccaccini, *Beyond the Essene Hypothesis.* See the work of Elior, *The Three Temples.* It is less important to resolve these sectarian issues than to appreciate the sectarian nature of the afterlife notions in the Enoch literature.

22. The Enoch literature is possibly as old or older than the Daniel "son of man" traditions in which it participates. Knibb, *The Ethiopic Book of Enoch;* Black, *The Book of Enoch;* Boccaccini, *Beyond the Essene Hypothesis;* VanderKam, *Enoch;* J. Collins, *The Apocalyptic Imagination;* Kvanvig, *Roots of Apocalyptic.*

23. VanderKam, *Enoch,* p. 8.

24. See S. Talmon, "The Calendar Reckoning;" Elior, *The Three Temples;* Arbel, *Beholders of Divine Secrets.* Elior ingeniously argues that Qumran evidens a priestly form of Judaism and that the solar calendar of Qumran was the original solar calendar of the Temple.

25. Boccaccini, *Beyond the Essene Hypothesis.*

26. Black, *The Book of Enoch.*

27. Elior, *The Paradoxical Ascent to God; The Three Temples.*

28. See Hurtado, *One God, One Lord;* Newman, *Paul's Glory Christology;* Gieschen, *Angelomorphic Christology;* Dean-Otting, *Heavenly Journeys;* Crane, *The Languages of Criticism;* Fossum, *The Name of God;* VanderKam, *Enoch.*

29. See for example, J. W. Cooper, *Body, Soul, and Life Everlasting,* who does not know this particular passage but is very careful to present every passage he does know as positive examples of dualism, which he wants to valorize in the tradition. His is not truly disinterested scholarship but a systematic attempt to see our mature Western notion of apocalyptic end and intermediary state for souls in heaven as grounded in biblical tradition. Of course, since both an apocalyptic end and this kind of intermediary state for souls is present, one can say that he is right. But the problem is that the passage is not exegeted by our very loquacious narrator and remains for a later time to spell out.

Chapter 7. Apocalypticism and Millenarianism

1. Not every aspect of an apocalypse is concerned with the end. A number of scholars have isolated examples of non-eschatological apocalypses. See Front, *Old Testament Apocalyptic.*

2. See Charlesworth, *Pseudepigrapha in Modern Research;* Stone, *Scriptures, Sects, and Visions.*

3. See J. Collins and Nickelsburg, *Ideal Figures in Ancient Judaism.*

4. Goldstein, *1 and 2 Maccabees.*

5. Also see Sibylline Oracles 3:381–400; Goldstein, *1 and 2 Maccabees.*

6. See, e.g., Cross, *Canaanite Myth and Hebrew Epic.*

7. J. Collins, *Apocalyptic Vision of Daniel; The Apocalyptic Imagination;* "The Root of Immortality."

8. For a very full treatment of these passages, see J. Collins, *Apocalyptic Vision of Daniel,* pp. 166–79.

9. Gieschen, *Angelomorphic Christology.*

10. Plöger, *Theocracy and Eschatology.*

11. There is no relationship to the mystical group of the same name disciples of the Ba'al Shem Tov who trace their beginning to the eighteenth century and whose distinctive black or brown frock coats and caftans reflect their Polish ancestry.

12. See for example, the epochal writings of Foucault, *Language, Counter-Memory, Practice; Power/Knowledge.*

13. This is not the same thing as calling the group at Qumran "Sadducees." *Pace* Schiffman, *Sectarian Law in Dead Sea Scrolls.* Elior's *(Temples)* more recent reconstruction seems more suggestive and ingenious.

14. See Fletcher-Louis, *All the Glory of Adam,* p. 388.

15. DeConick, *Seek to See Him,* pp. 32–33.

16. Schiffman, *Sectarian Law in Dead Sea Scrolls.*

17. On August 30, 2000 The Israeli Supreme Court decided that Hershel

Shanks, editor of *Biblical Archeological Review,* a large-circulation journal that reports important archeological discoveries to the wider public, had violated a copyright in publishing the work of Elisha Qimron without permission. (See the *New York Times,* August 31, 2000, A:11.) Qimron's reconstruction was included in Shanks's *Facsimile Edition of the Dead Sea Scrolls,* a collection of 1700 photographs of scroll fragments, published in 1991. Other scholars, including Eisenman and Wise, published the remaining texts without permission, including their own commentaries and opinions about their meanings. While most scholars were happy to see the remaining texts, the rushed commentaries of "the scholars in revolt" contained several errors of haste and many immoderate, personal opinions, so that everyone still awaits with anticipation the considered commentary of Elisha Qimron. See also Eisenman, *Maccabees, Zadokites, Christians, and Qumran.*

18. Puech, *La Croyance des esséniens.*

19. Ibid., pp. 747, 748, 781, 795; and see 4Q 521.

20. For recent bibliography on the Essenes, see for example Boccaccini, *Beyond the Essene Hypothesis;* VanderKam, *Enoch.* See also Elior, *The Three Temples.*

21. See Nitzan, "Harmonic and Mystical Characteristics;" Elior, *The Three Temples;* Newsom, *Songs of the Sabbath Sacrifice;* "He Has Established for Himself Priests;" Schaefer, "New Testament and Hekhalot Literature;" "Engel und Menschen in der Hekhalot-Literatur;" *Hidden and Manifest God;* Schiffman, "Merkavah Speculation at Qumran;" Schuller, "Hymn from Cave Four *Hodayot* Manuscript."

22. See E. Wolfson's critique of Nitzan in "Mysticism and the Poetic-Liturgical Compositions."

23. Fletcher-Louis, *Luke–Acts,* pp. 184–98; *All the Glory of Adam.* The following paragraphs are heavily indebted to his work. He has been followed in part by Steinberg, "Angelic Israel." Steinberg advances the argument in several interesting ways. Also see Elior, *The Three Temples.*

24. See Newsom, *Songs of the Sabbath Sacrifice.*

25. Charlesworth, "Portrayal of the Righteous," p. 136.

26. Milik, " '4QVisions d'Amram,' " p. 94.

27. Noll, "Communion of Angels and Men."

28. M. Smith, "Two Ascended to Heaven;" "Deification in 4QMa;" A. Segal, "The Risen Christ," p. 308. Subsequently, M. Smith's interpretation was given support by the readings of Schuller, "Hymn from Cave Four *Hodayot* Manuscript."

29. Baumgarten, "Qumran-Essene Restraints on Marriage;" Qimron, "Celibacy in the Dead Sea Scrolls."

30. See Wimbush, *Ascetic Behavior in Greco-Roman Antiquity;* Vaage and Wimbush, *Asceticism and the New Testament.*

31. Edmunds, *The Shawnee Prophet.*

32. See Wallace, *Death and Rebirth of the Seneca.*

33. Wallace, "Revitalization Movements."

34. See Jarvie, *The Revolution in Anthropology*; Lantennari, *Religions of the Oppressed.*

35. On the Ghost Dance religion, see Barbar, "Acculturation and Messianic Movements," for an analysis of its sources and unhappy outcome. Mooney, in his classic report to the Bureau of American Ethnology, "Ghost Dance Religion," presented the first account of these events. See also, Overholt, "Ghost Dance of 1890."

36. Wallace, "Revitalization Movements."

37. For an exception, see Gager, *Kingdom and Community.*

38. On ancient Judaism and Christianity, see A. Segal *Rebecca's Children,* pp. 70–71.

39. The term "deprivation" was first used in connection with messianic movements by the anthropologist Phillip Nash. He borrowed the term from a more general usage by the political scientist Harold Lasswell.

40. Further general statements on the characteristics of leaders and messianic movements are: Tescher, "A Theory of Charismatic Leadership;" Worsley, *The Trumpet Shall Sound*; Burridge, *New Heaven, New Earth*; Jarvie, *The Revolution in Anthropology*; I. Lewis, *Religion in Context.*

41. S. Cook, *Prophecy and Apocalypticism.*

42. Ibid., p. 2.

43. Turner, *The Ritual Process; Dramas. Fields, and Metaphors.*

44. Gager, *Kingdom and Community*; Horsley, *Jesus and the Spiral of Violence*; Boswell, *Of the Christian Era.*

45. See Elior, *The Three Temples.*

46. In the last fifty years, sociologists, anthropologists, and historians have produced a whole literature on messianic movements. See, for example, Barbar, "Acculturation and Messianic Movements;" chapters by R. Linton, A. F. C. Wallace, W. W. Hill, J. S. Slotkin, C. S. Belshaw, D. F. A. Geertz, and C. Geertz on "Dynamics in Religion," in Lessa and Vogt, *Reader,* pp. 496–543; Y. Talmon in Lessa and Vogt, *Reader,* 2d ed., pp. 522–37; and Overholt, *Channels of Prophecy.*

Chapter 8. Religiously Interpreted States of Consciousness

1. Husser, *Dreams and Dream Narratives.*

2. The abbreviations are regularly used in psychological literature.

3. For a review of altered states of consciousness (ASC) and shamanism, see Winkelman, *Shamanism.*

4. See Aune's very informative study, *Prophecy in Early Christianity,* pp. 81–152.

5. E. Wolfson, *Through a Speculum That Shines,* pp. 108–9.

6. Dean-Otting, *Heavenly Journeys.*

7. Nicholas D. Kristof, "Alien Abduction? Science Calls It Sleep Paralysis," *New York Times,* July 6, 1999, F:1–2.

8. Austin, *Zen and the Brain,* p. 333; Tart, *Altered States of Consciousness,* pp. 73–113.

9. Merkur, *Gnosis,* pp. 44–54; "The Nature of the Hypnotic State," p. 345.

10. P. Miller, *Dreams in Late Antiquity,* esp. pp. 3–123.

11. See for example Ripinsky-Naxon, *The Nature of Shamanism;* Merkur, *Becoming Half Hidden;* Grim, *The Shaman,* for a review of research.

12. Eliade, *Le chamanisme et les techniques archaiques de l'extase* (Paris: Librairie Payot, 1951), translated into English as *Shamanism: Archaic Techniques of Ecstasy;* also *Yoga: Immortality and Freedom.*

13. See the newly published book by Davila, *Descenders to the Chariot,* which attempts to see Merkabah mysticism as a shamanistic phenomenon. See also Bourgignon, *Religion;* and I. M. Lewis *Religion in Context.*

14. Davila, *Descenders to the Chariot.*

15. Persinger, *Neuropsychological Bases of God Beliefs;* Cardeña, Lynn, and Krippner, *Varieties of Anomalous Experience;* Newberg, D'Aquili, and Rause, *Why God Won't Go Away;* Winkelman, *Shamanism.*

16. Newberg, D'Aquili, and Rause, *Why God Won't Go Away,* pp. 171–72.

17. Persinger, *Neuropsychological Bases of God Beliefs;* also see Cardeña, Lynn, and Krippner, *Varieties of Anomalous Experience,* esp. the chapter on "out-of-body" experiences.

18. Newberg, D'Aquili, and Rause, *Why God Won't Go Away,* p. 119.

19. Alverado, "Out-of-Body Experiences;" see M. Maddux, "Hallucinogenic Herb Attracts DEA Interest," *The Bergen Record,* July 6, 2003.

20. Here I am relying on interviews with them, made for the TV show, "Between Life and Death." Their findings are quite in consonance with the suggestions of Newberg, D'Aquili, and Rause. Since Ketamine is not licensed for human use in the US, all its users are technically abusers. But it has been used in various experimental settings to investigate its psychoactive properties. See Jansen, "Using Ketamine."

21. Alverado, "Out-of-Body Experiences."

22. See Atran, "Waves of Passion," pp. 174–96 in *In God We Trust,* for a cautionary note about how little of these processes we actually understand.

23. See A. Segal, "Taoist Ascent and Merkabah Mysticism."

24. See for example, the summary discussion in J. Collins, *Apocalyptic Vision of Daniel.*

25. Rowland, *The Open Heaven,* pp. 217ff.

26. Ibid., p. 218.

27. New confirmation of this point may be found in E. Wolfson, *Through a Speculum That Shines,* pp. 108–24, 383–92.

28. See Kilborne's article, "Dreams;" and Hanson, "Dreams and Visions." Also see P. Miller, *Dreams in Late Antiquity.*

29. See Saake, "Paulus als Ekstatiker;" Benz, *Paulus als Visionaer.*

30. Kim, "Origin of Paul's Gospel."

31. See A. Segal, "Heavenly Ascent in Hellenistic Judaism."

32. Rohde, *Psyche,* p. 364.

33. Flanagan and Block, *The Nature of Consciousness;* McGinn, *The Mysterious Flame;* Dennett, *Kinds of Minds, Consciousness Explained;* Searle, *The Mystery of Consciousness;* E. Walker, *The Physics of Consciousness;* Chalmers, *The Conscious Mind;* Churchland, *Matter and Consciousness;* Norretranders, *The User Illusion;* Hasker, *The Emergent Self.*

34. Povinelli and Povinelli, "Arboreal Clambering."

35. Gottsch, "Mutation, Selection, and Vertical Transmission."

36. Jaynes, *The Origin of Consciousness.*

37. One recent and useful language for dealing with these issues is that of "memes." See Dawkins, *The Selfish Gene; River Out of Eden;* Blackmore, *The Meme Machine.* Another fruitful language can be carried over from computer software. It is not that we are computers but that our culture operates as a kind of software that is shared and developed between people. The "memes," a Richard Dawkins neologism, therefore can be seen as a unit of cultural transmission or a software routine. But more on this at the end of the book.

38. Betz, *The Greek Magical Papyri,* pp. 48–49.

39. Copenhaver, *Hermetica,* p. 1.

40. S. Johnston, "Rising to the Occasion."

41. Luck, "Theurgy and Forms of Worship in Neoplatonism."

42. See M. Smith, *Observations on Hekhaloth Rabbati.* Also see Jamblique [Iamblichus], *Les Mystères d'Egypte; Oracles Chaldaiques.*

43. Proclus, *Theol. Plat.* I, 26.

44. G. Shaw, *Theurgy and the Soul;* "Apotheosis in Later Platonism," pp. 111–12, 119; Luck, "Theurgy and Forms of Worship in Neoplatonism."

45. See Stratton, "Naming the Witch."

46. Fowden, *The Egyptian Hermes,* pp. 126–31.

47. See the description of the rite in *PGM* I.1–42 and I.42–195. Compare it with the description of bringing down an angel in the *Sefer Harazim* and *Sefer Hekhalot* to swear him to accomplish one's bidding. Also see the description in Ciraolo's "Supernatural Assistants," pp. 285–86.

48. R. Gray, *Prophetic Figures,* pp. 63–64; also see Zeitlin, "Dreams and Their Interpretation," p. 12.

Chapter 9. Sectarian Life in New Testament Times

1. van der Horst, *Ancient Jewish Epitaphs.*

2. See J. Davies, *Death, Burial, and Rebirth,* p. 110.

3. Quotation from Longenecker, " 'Good Luck on your Resurrection.' "

4. See also 1QH 1.20–21; 2.20; 5:29–30, 34–39 as well as 1QH 6.29–35; 11.10–14.

5. See the recent article by Longenecker, " 'Good Luck on Your Resurrection.' " See also the important work of Puech, *La croyance des Esséniens.*

6. The Enoch literature is possibly as old or older than the Daniel "son of
man" traditions in which it participates. See Knibb, *The Ethiopic Book of
Enoch*; Black, *The Book of Enoch*; Boccaccini, *Beyond the Essene Hypothesis*;
VanderKam, *Enoch*; J. Collins, *The Apocalyptic Imagination*; Kvanvig, *Roots
of Apocalyptic.*

7. This is now reconfirmed by VanderKam, "Righteous One." Also see
Nickelsburg, "Salvation without and with a Messiah;" Kee, "Christology in
Mark's Gospel;" and Charlesworth, "From Jewish Messianology."

8. On the other hand, it may also be that the "parables" have a pre-
Christian or non-Christian origin, so far unattested, and this paragraph found
its way into Ethiopian Christianity with a minimum of alteration. In that case,
it has merely been subsumed within the Christian tradition because of its interpretation of the "son of man" which became such an important prophecy in the
New Testament.

9. Elior, *The Three Temples.*

10. Charlesworth has "bull," while Isaac, in *The Old Testament Pseudepigrapha*, vol. 1, p. 71 has "cow."

11. See Nickelsburg, *Resurrection, Immortality and Eternal Life*, pp. 123,
177–80, for a discussion of this passage. Nickelsburg justifiably criticizes Cullmann's strict distinctions between Greek and Hebrew modes of thinking; but
neither discusses adequately the fact that some Jews deliberately use the Greek
concepts for hermeneutical purposes and philosophical credentials. See below.

12. Ibid., p. 123; Cavalin, *Life After Death*, p. 48. See de Boer, *Defeat of
Death*, p. 57.

13. Aalen (" 'Reign' and 'House' " p. 10) tries to use this verse to demonstrate that faith in the resurrection was accepted virtually everywhere in the
land of Israel by the time of Jesus. Nothing could be further from the truth.

14. R. Scott, *Proverbs and Ecclesiastes*, p. 91; see Dahood, "Immortality."

15. See Cavallin, *Life After Death*, pp. 103–110 for more details.

16. See Birnbaum, *The Place of Judaism.*

17. Colson and Whitaker, *Philo.* Discussion is taken from Cavallin, *Life
After Death*, pp. 135–46.

18. Philo's text is Isa 54:1: "Sing, O barren one, who did not bear; / break
forth into singing and cry aloud, / you who have not been in travail! / For the
children of the desolate one will be more / than the children of her that is married, says the Lord."

19. *Pace* N. Wright, *Resurrection of the Son of God*, pp. 145, 421f, 492.

20. See for example, Baer, *Philo's Use of Male and Female*; also Sly, *Philo's
Perception of Women.*

21. Smallwood, *The Jews Under Roman Rule*; S. Cohen, *Maccabees to
Mishnah.*

22. See, for example, Bremmer, "Paradise."

23. See the work of Netzer and especially: *Hasmonean and Herodian Palaces;* "Tyros, the Floating Palace;" Burrell, Netzer, and Netzer, "Uncovering Herod's Seaside Palace."

24. They denied the aristocrats access unless they were just. But it is clear from the New Testament alone that most of the ordinary folk thought it was easier for a camel to go through the eye of a needle than for a rich person to enter the kingdom of heaven.

25. Mason, "Was Josephus a Pharisee?;" M. Smith, *Studies in the Cult of Yahweh.*

26. See Mason, *Flavius Josephus on the Pharisees.*

27. This, in fact, is what I will try to show later on, when we have had a chance to look at Paul and the rabbis' perspectives on resurrection. It may well be that this is also identical or close to the notions that we have seen briefly outlined in Enoch. It is certainly what Paul describes in far more detail in his letters, particularly 1 Cor 15, as we shall see. Thus, although we cannot be entirely sure about what the Pharisees actually believed, we also cannot blithely assume that they believed in exactly the same kind of resurrection that the Gospels describe, though they may have been, ironically, closer to the position of Paul. Paul, as we will see, had ideas that are at some odds with the Gospels and probably closer to what the Pharisees thought.

28. See Puech, *La Croyance des Esséniens.*

29. See Lachs, *A Rabbinic Commentary.*

30. *Pace* N. Wright, *Resurrection of the Son of God,* p. 172. At any rate, the point I make in this section is that Jewish eschatological notions are here figured in a very Hellenistic context in which immortality of the soul is prevalent. Any expressions of resurrection, if they exist, have been made secondary to the expression of a more Hellenistic notion of life after death, namely immortality of the soul. Both conceptions of the afterlife are present in Jewish society at this time.

31. This is counter to the argument of Holleman, *Resurrection and Parousia.*

32. For my views in more detail, see A. Segal, *Rebecca's Children,* esp. pp. 68–116; and *Paul the Convert;* also see Gager, *Kingdom and Community.*

33. Schweitzer, *Quest of the Historical Jesus.*

34. Archeology helps establish the context of the New Testament but it does not yet touch the basic religious claims of Christianity. What is obvious for the New Testament is true of the Old, by the way, and the archaeology, while plentiful, is still more difficult to evaluate.

35. See Gager, *Kingdom and Community,* esp. pp. 2–18.

36. Crossan, *The Historical Jesus.*

37. For a new discussion of the presence of Jesus in the life of the church, see Hurtado, *Lord Jesus Christ.*

38. For example, Crossan, *The Cross That Spoke; Who Killed Jesus?;* Barth, *The People of God.*

39. See Klawans, *Impurity and Sin.*

40. E. Sanders, *Jesus and Judaism; Paul and Palestinian Judaism.*

41. S. Davies, *Jesus the Healer;* Borg, *Meeting Jesus Again;* Witherington, *Jesus the Seer.*

42. Dahl, *The Crucified Messiah.*

Chapter 10. Paul's Vision of the Afterlife

1. For a detailed and most instructive treatment of what Paul's reports can tell us about Jesus, see Akenson, *Saint Saul.*

2. For the most recent treatment of the theme see McKnight, *Turning to Jesus.* Also see A. Segal, *Paul the Convert.*

3. Schweitzer, *Mysticism of Paul the Apostle.* Schweitzer was right about the mysticism but he misidentified the source of it because he did not know enough about Judaism in Jesus' day. The mysticism that best demonstrates his point is the Jewish mysticism later known as Merkabah Mysticism, which will be discussed in the pseudepigraphical literature.

4. Perkins, *Resurrection,* p. 197.

5. It is a similar question that appears to occasion the remarks of 1 Cor 15, concentrating so fully on resurrection. With Paul we can begin to discuss the effect of Jewish mystical and apocalyptic visions not just as a warning of the end of time and as vindication for those who stay faithful to the precepts of Judaism but as an important spiritual experience within the life of an individual (in this case a Christian, but Paul did not understand the difference between "Jew" and "Christian" in quite the way we do; he never uses the term Christian).

6. See, for example, the discussion of Lorenzen, *Resurrection and Discipleship,* pp. 127–146.

7. Paradise or the garden of Eden was often conceived as lying in one of the heavens, though the exact location differs from one apocalyptic work to another. See Himmelfarb, *Tours of Hell.* See *2 Enoch,* for an example that locates it in the third heaven. But *2 Enoch* may have been influenced by Paul's writings.

8. In different ways, the close relationship between mysticism and apocalypticism has been touched upon by several scholars of the last decade, myself included. See A. Segal, *Two Powers;* Gruenwald, *Apocalyptic and Merkabah Mysticism;* esp. Rowland, *The Open Heaven;* as well as Fossum, *The Name of God.*

9. Also see A. Segal, *Heavenly Ascent;* Dean-Otting, *Heavenly Journeys;* Culianu, *Psychanodia.* Culianu has also published a more general work, *Expériences de l'Extase.* The verb *harpazo* in Greek and its Latin equivalent *rapto* are sometimes shared with pagan ascensions (*sol me rapuit,* "the sun has 'abducted' me"), but also probably initially denotes both the rapture of vision and the specific heavenly journeys of Enoch (Hebrew: *laqah* = Greek: *metetheken*).

10. See Baird, "Visions, Revelation, and Ministry."

11. Encounters with the divine and heavenly journeys are fraught with dan-

ger. Jacob was wounded by his wrestling with the angel (Gen 32:25). Three of the four rabbis who entered paradise suffered injury (b. Hagigah 14b). See Baird, "Visions," p. 660 and Johann Maier, "Das Gefaehrdungsmotiv."

12. See the discussion between Goulder and A. Segal in "Transformation and Afterlife," and Goulder's response, pp. 137–152. See the chapter on Rabbinic Judaism in this book for further discussion of the limits of irony; and see Empson, *Seven Types of Ambiguity*.

13. Morray-Jones, "Paradise Revisited."

14. See Morray-Jones, *A Transparent Illusion*.

15. B. Taylor, "Recollection and Membership." Also see Beckford, "Accounting for Conversion;" Snow and Machalek, "The Sociology of Conversion."

16. See Tabor, *Things Unutterable*. See Kim, *The Origin of Paul's Gospel*, who suggests 2 Cor 12 is Paul's conversion experience; and his new book, *Paul and the New Perspective*, which argues strongly that it is. Scholarship is divided as to whether or not Gal 1 and 2 Cor 12 can be identified as the same experience and that it is to be identified with the Damascus Road experience. Baird ("Visions") reports that recently most scholars assume a distinction (p. 652 and n. 2). A good example of this position would be Dunn, *Spirit*, p. 103. The following earlier writers maintained the identification between the two experiences: Knox, "Fourteen Years Later" and "The Pauline Chronology." Yet, in a footnote to his *Chapters in a Life of Paul*, p. 78, he abandoned the notion. See Riddle, *Paul: Man of Conflict*, p. 63; Buck and Taylor, *Saint Paul*, pp. 220–26; Enslin *Reapproaching Paul*, pp. 53–55.

17. Hengel, *The Pre-Christian Paul*.

18. See Dunn, *Spirit*, for instance, pp. 107–9.

19. See Hekhaloth Rabbati 20 *Wertheimer*, I, pp. 98–99; Schaefer, *Synopse*, §§198–99; and Schiffman, "The Recall of Nehuniah ben Hakkanah;" also see Lieberman's corrections to Schiffman in Gruenwald, *Apocalyptic and Merkabah Mysticism*, p. 241. For the latest voices in the discussion, see Davila, *Descenders in the Chariot*; Morray-Jones, *A Transparent Illusion*; Wolfson, *Through a Speculum That Shines*.

20. Malherbe, *The Cynic Epistles; Moral Exhortation*; Engberg-Pedersen, *Paul and the Stoics*. See the interesting article by Lampe, "Paul's Concept of a Spiritual Body."

21. See the interesting theory of Mettinger, *The Dethronement of Sabaoth*, for the origin of the *kavod* idea and its original function in biblical literature.

22. See Halperin, *The Faces of the Chariot*.

23. Odeberg, *The Hebrew Book of Enoch*; Scholem, *Major Trends in Jewish Mysticism; Jewish Gnosticism*. Also see M. Smith, "Observations on *Hekhaloth Rabbati;*" Altmann, "Sacred Hymns in Hekhaloth Literature;" "Narboni's 'Epistle on *Shiur Koma*,' " p. 195.

24. A. Segal, *Two Powers*; Halperin, *The Merkabah in Rabbinic Literature*;

Gruenwald, *Apocalyptic and Merkabah Mysticism;* Dan, "The Concept of Knowledge;" *Ancient Jewish Mysticism;* Chernus, "Individual and Community;" "Visions of God;" *Mysticism in Rabbinic Judaism.*

25. Quispel, *Gnostic Studies;* Dahl, "History and Eschatology," in *Crucified Messiah,* Bowker, " 'Merkabah' Visions;" Schaefer, "New Testament and Hekhalot Literature." Betz, in *Galatians Hermeneia,* suggests several relationships between Jewish mysticism and Greco-Roman magic. Also see Rowland, *The Open Heaven.* See Stroumsa "Form(s) of God," who summarizes the basic ideas of the *Shiur Koma* and notes their relevance to early Christianity.

26. In Schaefer, *Synopse zur Hekhalot-Literatur.*

27. M. Cohen, *Shiur Komah;* Elior, *Hekhaloth Zutartey.* For the complete bibliography, see Halperin, *The Faces of the Chariot,* pp. 567–69.

28. For recent study of the material, see Fossum, *Image of the Invisible God;* Morray-Jones, *A Transparent Illusion;* Janowitz, *The Poetics of Ascent;* Davila, *Descenders of the Chariot;* Arbel, "Beholders of Divine Secrets;" Elior, *The Three Temples.* The issues are discussed in full in Giesehen, *Angelomorphic Christology.*

29. See Quispel, "Hermetism and the New Testament."

30. Strugnell, "The Angelic Liturgy at Qumran;" Newsom, *4Q Serek Shirot 'Olat Hassabbat; Songs of the Sabbath Sacrifice.*

31. See Steinberg, "Angelic Israel." The recent book of Fletcher-Louis, *All the Glory of Adam,* confirms these notions. In fact, the notion that liturgy provided the way in which eschatology was realized in early Christianity was presaged by Aune, *The Cultic Setting;* and Gleason, "Angels and the Eschatology."

32. Another unemphasized aspect of the journey motif is that it is a kind of travel narrative, purporting to be the actual experience of a trustworthy patriarch of the profoundly moral structure of the cosmos confirming the biblical account, which reassures the righteous of their final reward.

33. See Newman, *Paul's Glory Christology;* also see Capes, *Yahweh Text.*

34. See Knibb, "Date of the Parables of Enoch;" also see Milik and Black, *The Books of Enoch.* Though Milik and Black's dating of Hekhaloth literature has been criticized, the book does contain a good summary of the scholarship on the problem until their publication.

35. If that is so, ought we to count Wis 5:5–8 as a similar passage? In any event, Smith's translation parallels other hints of ascension in the Qumran texts. See, for example, 4QAgesCreat, 2; 4QpIsa 11:1–4; 1QSb C; 1QH 3:3, 3:19, 6:12, 7:22, 18:16, and frag. 2. These passages are discussed in Allan J. Pantuck's "Paul and the Dead Sea Scrolls: Ascent and Angelification in First Century Judaism," (unpublished).

36. Callan in "Prophecy and Ecstasy" shows how Paul wished to limit the term ecstasy. Prophecy for Paul was not ecstatic, in that it needed not be accompanied by trance. Therefore, our use of it, though proper, also remains an *etic* term.

37. Neher, "Le Voyage;" Séd, "Les Traditions." Also see Morray-Jones, *A Transparent Illusion.*

38. The most recent good analysis of pseudepigraphal writing is Meade, *Pseudonymity and Canon.* Mystical notions are not even mentioned.

39. Quispel, "Hermetism and the New Testament."

40. The use of the mirror here is also a magico-mystical theme, which can be traced to the word 'eyyin occuring in Ezekiel 1. Although it is sometimes translated otherwise, 'eyyin probably refers to a mirror even there, and possibly refers to some unexplained technique for achieving ecstasy. The mystic bowls of the magical papyri and Talmudic times were filled with water and oil to reflect light and stimulate trance. Paul's opponents looked into the mirror and saw only the text. But because Paul and those truly in Christ actually behold the glory of the Lord, they have clearer vision.

41. See Gaventa, *Darkness to Light,* pp. 45–48.

42. Dahl, *The Crucified Messiah;* Dunn, *Baptism in the Holy Spirit.*

43. Jonah Steinberg is finding evidence that the rabbis sought transformation too and thought of themselves as angels on earth.

44. See Bockmuehl, *Revelation and Mystery,* pp. 167–77.

45. Ibid., p. 158.

46. Ibid., p. 159.

47. Wedderburn, "Problem of the Denial."

48. Like me, Lampe suggests that Paul was arguing against Greek notions of immortality and replacing them with his own. See "Paul's Concept of a Spiritual Body."

49. Lorenzen, *Resurrection and Discipleship,* p. 158.

50. This has recently been reaffirmed by N. Wright, *Resurrection of the Son of God.*

51. This is, in fact, the position of B. Pearson, in *The Pneumatikos-Psychikos Terminology;* and Horsley in "Pneumatikos Vs. Psychikos." They maintain that Philonic exegesis, in fact, defines the background of the opponents of Paul at Corinth. They were people who knew Philo's exegesis of the two creation stories in Genesis as talking about two *anthropoi* to different "humanities," the spiritual (the idea of man) and earthly man (the mortal, embodied human). This, Paul defeats with this own exegesis. See de Boer, *The Defeat of Death,* p. 101.

52. See the summary article of M. Smith, "Ascent to the Heavens;" as well as the works of Odeberg, Meeks, and Dahl.

53. See A. Segal, *Two Powers,* pp. 205–19; also see Hurtado, *One God, One Lord.*

54. This was one of the consensual statements of the NEH conference on first-century Jewish messianism. The papers and agreements of the conference have been published in Charlesworth et al., *The Messiah.* This was the original perception of Dahl in the title essay in *The Crucified Messiah.*

55. See A. Segal, *Rebecca's Children*, pp. 60–67, 78–95 for a thumbnail sketch of this development.

56. The Hebrew makes clear that the two Lords refer to different personages, one God and the second the King. But the Greek uses *kyrios* to refer to both "Lords." Thus, it is easy to make both "Lords" into divine designations. See Bousset, *Kyrios Christos*.

57. See, e.g., *TDNT* 9, p. 661.

58. See Wink, *The Human Being*, pp. 207–211.

59. Other ancient authorities add "of God."

60. Hurtado, *Lord Jesus Christ*.

61. Ibid., p. 206

62. Dunn, *Jesus and the Spirit*, p. 327.

63. See Perkins, *Resurrection*, p. 293; W. Meeks, *The First Urban Christians*, p. 277.

Chapter 11. The Gospels in Contrast to Paul's Writings

1. McKnight, *Turning to Jesus*. McKnight wisely adopts the model of religious conversion developed by Lou Rambo in his book *Understanding Religious Conversion*.

2. Like every facet of the Christian Scriptures, the resurrection traditions have received a great deal of attention in modern scholarship. See C. F. Evans, *Resurrection and the New Testament*; Fuller, *Formation of the Resurrection Narratives*; Lake, *Historical Evidence for the Resurrection*; Gardner-Smith, *Narratives of the Resurrection*; R. Brown, *The Gospel According to John*, pp. 966–78; *The Death of the Messiah*; Marxsen, *The Resurrection of Jesus Christ*; Schillebeeckx, *Christ*, pp. 30–42; O'Collins, *Interpreting the Resurrection*; Osborne, *The Resurrection of Jesus*; Carnley, *The Structure of Resurrection Belief*; Perrin, *The Resurrection*; Benoit, *The Passion and Resurrection*; Riley, *Resurrection Reconsidered*; Davis, *Risen Indeed*; Davis, Kendall, and O'Collins, *The Resurrection*; Lüdemann, *Die Auferstehung Jesu*.

3. This is certainly the opinion of Lüdemann as well. See *What Really Happened to Jesus*, p. 18.

4. Some of the most ancient authorities bring the book to a close at the end of verse 8. One authority concludes the book with the shorter ending; others include the shorter ending and then continue with verses 9–20. In most authorities verses 9–20 follow immediately after verse 8, though in some of these authorities the passage is marked as being doubtful.

5. See Beare, *The Earliest Records of Jesus*.

6. Crossan, *The Cross That Spoke; Who Killed Jesus?*

7. See also Lüdemann, *What Really Happened to Jesus*, pp. 17–24.

8. This fact seems to me to pass the criterion of dissimilarity and argue strongly for the historicity of the person Jesus. No one would have made up a

story of a Savior who was resurrected and then neglected to narrate it. On the other hand, it does nothing for the historicity of the resurrection itself.

9. The attempt to link this figure with the man who ran away naked at the arrest of Jesus (Mark 14:51–52) is not convincing. That young man is fleeing, not sharing the death of Jesus. See Perkins, *Resurrection*, pp. 118–19.

10. That changes radically with the book of Revelation.

11. "Spirit" can be more or less equated with the English word "ghost" in this context.

12. I would argue that in the modern world doubt is important to keep faith from becoming fanaticism. One must face up to and include doubt within faith. But in the ancient world it was different.

13. Dahl, *The Crucified Messiah*.

14. Eskola, *Messiah and the Throne*, p. 352.

15. Pagels, *The Origin of Satan*.

16. Fossum, "Ascensio, Metamorphosis."

17. See Ulansey, "The Transfiguration;" "The Heavenly Veil Torn."

18. S. Davies suggests something like this in his book *Jesus the Healer*. He suggests that the vision is actually Jesus' shamanic trance. That seems hasty but it is not entirely different from saying that it is a model for that of the Early Church, reflecting some of the visions that were actually experienced by the early followers of Jesus.

19. See for example J. W. Cooper, *Body, Soul, and Life Everlasting*, pp. 127–29.

20. See Milikowsky, "Which Gehenna?" He argues that Luke has adapted immediate post-mortem punishment and immortality of the soul. For Muslim views of the afterlife, see ch. 15.

21. For a critical review of the Q-hypothesis, see Goodacre, *The Case Against Q;* for a positive evaluation of the hypothesis see Kloppenborg, *The Formation of Q*.

22. See Riley, *Resurrection Reconsidered*, pp. 127–75; and from another perspective DeConick, *Seek to See Him*. Also see Pagels, *Beyond Belief*.

23. DeConick, *Seek to See Him;* Patterson, *Gospel of Thomas and Jesus;* S. Davies, *The Gospel of Thomas;* Valantasis, *The Gospel of Thomas*.

24. Charlesworth, *The Pseudepigrapha and Modern Research; The Old Testament Pseudepigrapha*, pp. 725–71.

25. Dodd, *The Bible and the Greeks*.

26. Of course, there need be no actual relationship between the two groups. But the ascetic tendencies, the communal life, and the quest for a vision of God suggest that there is at least phenomenological similarity between them.

27. DeConick, *Seek to See Him*, pp. 3–42; *Voices of the Mystics*.

28. Fletcher-Louis, *All the Glory of Adam; Luke-Acts: Angels*.

29. The study of women in Late Antiquity, a much neglected topic, has expanded exponentially in the last few years. Besides the work noted previously,

for a start on the issue, as well as on the issues inherent in gender and asceticism, see Cameron and Kuhrt, *Images of Women in Antiquity;* Burrus, *Chastity As Autonomy;* Kraemer, *Maenads, Martyrs, Matrons, Monastics;* Elm, *'Virgins of God';* E. Clark, *Reading Renunciation;* Kraemer and D'Angelo, *Women and Christian Origins;* Castelli and Rodman, *Women, Gender, Religion.*

30. See Antti, *The Women Jesus Loved,* p. 49.

31. Buckley, *Female Fault and Fulfillment.*

32. P. Brown, *The Body and Society,* p. 114.

33. Ibid., p. 118.

34. Ibid., p. 116.

35. See Elizabeth Castelli's chapter in Kraemer and D'Angelo, *Women and Christian Origins,* p. 279.

36. Cary, *Augustine's Invention,* p. 42.

37. W. Meeks, "The Image of the Androgne," p. 166.

38. Buckley, *Female Fault and Fulfillment,* p. 125.

39. W. Meeks, "The Image of the Androgyne," p. 195.

40. Buckley, *Female Fault and Fulfillment,* p. 126.

41. Ibid., p. 127.

42. On the role of Scripture in asceticism, see E. Clark, *Reading Renunciation;* K. Cooper, *The Virgin and the Bride.*

43. Pagels, *The Gnostic Paul.*

Chapter 12. The Pseudepigraphic Literature

1. See Bowersock, *Martyrdom and Rome,* pp. 75–76.

2. Bowersock, *Martyrdom and Rome,* offers a handy place to find the classical antecedents to the martyrdom tradition, some of which have already been discussed in this work as well.

3. See A. Segal, " 'He Who Did Not Spare,' " reprinted with some minor improvements as "The Sacrifice of Isaac." I published some further reflections on the theme in "The Akedah."

4. See A. Collins, *Cosmology and Eschatology;* J. Collins, *Apocalyptic Imagination,* pp. 210–15; "Political Perspective Revelation to John;" and more generally, *Cosmology and Eschatology,* pp. 198–217.

5. See A. Collins, *Cosmology and Eschatology,* p. 201; A. Segal, *Rebecca's Children,* pp. 78–96 esp., p. 94.

6. See Wiley, *Original Sin,* though this conclusion is not found there.

7. Tertullian *Apol.* 39.2, cf. 32.1. See Gager, *Kingdom and Community,* pp. 44–45.

8. Bauckham, *The Fate of the Dead,* pp. 78–80.

9. An example of this process might be sought in the continuing interest in the painful final disposition of sinners in hell in all of the world's great religions—from Islam and Hinduism into Chinese and Tibetan Buddhisms, which favor greatly elaborated views of hell as well. On the other hand, in permissive

America, both Satan and hell have nearly fallen out of religious life, except in the fundamentalistic and evangelical communities where their reality, as well as the reality of the coming millennium, is still assumed and strongly emphasized.

10. Wiley, *Original Sin*, pp. 46–55.

11. See ch. 13.

12. *1 En* 51:1; *4 Ezra* 7:32; Rev 20:13; Pseudo-Philo, *L.A.B.* 3:10; 33:3; *2 Bar.* 21:23; *Apoc. Pet.* 4:3–4; 4:10–12; an apocryphal quotation in Tertullian, *Res.* 32.1; *2 Bar.* 42:8; 50:2; *4 Ezra* 4:41–43a; Pseudo-Philo, *Midrash on Ps.* 1:20; *Midrash Rabba on Cant.* 2:1:2; *Pirqe de R. Eliezer* 34; *Pesiqta Rabbati* 21:4; *b. Sanh* 92a; Bauckham, *The Fate of the Dead*, p. 271–74.

13. Stone, *Fourth Ezra*.

14. See Cavallin, *Life After Death*, pp. 80ff.

15. See Bergren, *Fifth Ezra;* "People Coming from the East;" "List of Leaders in 5 Ezra."

16. For more issues inherent in this passage, including the perplexing behavior of the Messiah, see Cavallin, *Life After Death*, p. 86 and literature mentioned there.

17. Translation by Klijn, in Charlesworth, *The Old Testament Pseudepigrapha*, vol. 1, p. 638.

18. See Cavallin, *Life After Death*, p. 89.

19. See also *2 En* 18; 31; *Gos. Bart.;* and Budge, *Book of the Cave of Treasures*, pp. 56ff. In any case, these stories are probably to be understood as originating in the story of the Fall of Ḥellal ben Shaḥar (Vg. Lucifer) in Isa 14, perhaps combined with Ezek 28.

20. Bauckham, *The Fate of the Dead*, p. 66; Himmelfarb, *Tours of Hell;* Ascent to Heaven.

21. See Klijn, p. 619, and Gaylord, p. 659, in Charlesworth, *The Old Testament Pseudepigrapha*, vol. 1.

22. See Tabor, *Things Unutterable*, pp. 84–85.

23. See de Boer, *Defeat of Death*, p. 67.

24. See Dean-Otting, *Heavenly Journeys*, p. 79.

25. See J. Becker, *Untersuchungen zur Enstehungsgeschichte*, pp. 353ff. and Cavallin, *Life After Death*, p. 54.

26. Nickelsburg, *Resurrection, Immortality and Eternal Life*, pp. 161, 165, 179; also see "Future Life in Intertestamental Literature."

27. Nickelsburg, *Resurrection, Immortality and Eternal Life;* "Future Life in Intertestamental Literature."

28. Tabor, *Things Unutterable*, pp. 85–86.

29. See E. Sanders, *The Testament of Abraham*.

30. Kraemer, *When Aseneth Met Joseph*. Kraemer opines that the book is most likely Christian and third century, at least in its current form.

31. It looks suspiciously like a sign of the cross is made over the bread.

32. Valantasis, *Spiritual Guides of the Third Century*.

33. Hick, *Arguments for the Existence of God*.

34. See on a related theme, Charlesworth, "The Jewish Roots of Christology."

35. Black, "The Throne-Theophany Prophetic Commission;" Rowland, "Vision of the Risen Christ;" Fossum, "Jewish Christian Christology and Jewish Mysticism."

36. Of course, *3 En* must be seen as a late document. See Hurtado, "Binitarian Shape of Christian Devotion," pp. 384–85; Horton, *The Melchizedek Tradition;* Kobelski, *Melchizedek and Melchiresa;* Noll, "Angelology in the Qumran Texts;" Quispel, "Gnosticism and the New Testament;" "Origins of the Gnostic Demiurge."

37. See A. Segal, *Two Powers in Heaven,* pp. 182–219; Schaefer, *Rivalitaet zwischen Engeln und Menschen,* pp. 9–74; Kuhn, "Angelology of the Non-Canonical Apocalypses;" Stier, *Gott und sein Engel.*

38. For the growing consensus that apocalypticism implies visionary or "mystical" experience as well as secret knowledge of the end of time, see Rowland, *The Open Heaven.* See Charlesworth, "Portrayal of the Righteous." See Idel, *Kabbalah,* who stresses the theme of transformation, but does not consider the Pauline corpus. This is a confirmation of the transformation vocabulary which we noted as important in the previous chapter.

39. Translated by M. Pravednoe in Charlesworth, *The Old Testament Pseudepigrapha,* vol. 1, p. 152.

40. J. Z. Smith, "The Prayer of Joseph." See Denis, *Fragmenta Pseudepigraphorum,* pp. 61–62.

41. Goodenough, *By Light, Light,* pp. 199–234; W. Meeks, *The Prophet-King;* "Divine Agent and His Counterfeit;" Holladay, *Theios Aner in Hellenistic Judaism,* pp. 103–69.

42. W. Meeks, "Divine Agent and His Counterfeit," p. 45; also see Hurtado, "Exalted Patriarchs," in *One God, One Lord.*

43. See Quispel, "Ezekiel 1:26 in Jewish Mysticism;" "Gnosis;" Quispel's review of *Hellenistische Erloesung in christlicher Deutung* by J. Frickel, in *VC* 39 (1985). Also see Holladay, "Portrait of Moses in Ezekiel;" Jacobson, "Mysticism and Apocalyptic;" van der Horst, "Moses' Throne Vision in Ezekiel;" and *"Exagoge* of Ezekiel."

44. See Jacobson, *The Exagoge of Ezekiel,* lines 68–89, pp. 54–55.

45. See A. Segal, *Two Powers in Heaven;* also see Dahl, "History and Eschatology," in *Crucified Messiah;* Quispel, "Origins of the Gnostic Demiurge." See esp. Fossum, *Image of the Invisible God,* p. 24 n. 30; and Hurtado, *One God, One Lord.*

46. See for example, *T. Sim* 5:4; *T. Levi* 10:5; 14:1; *T. Jud* 18:1; *T. Zeb* 3:4; *T. Dan* 5:6; *T. Naph* 4:1; *T. Ben* 9:1. See Hurtado, "Exalted Patriarchs," in *One God, One Lord.*

47. The term often used to describe Merkabah mystics, "the descenders into the chariot" *yordei merkabah,* seems to me best understood as referring to this position, (*Pace* Gruenwald, *Apocalyptic*).

48. See Lewin, *Otsar Ha-Geonim, Hagigah, Teshuvoth*, pp. 14–15.

49. Scholem, *Major Trends in Jewish Mysticism;* and M. Smith, "Observations on Hekhaloth Rabbati." Also see the Jewish-Christian evidence, for instance, *Ps.-Clem. Hom.* 17.16. See Fossum, *Image of the Invisible God,* pp. 13–39.

50. See the interesting theory of Mettinger, *The Dethronement of Sabaoth,* for the origin of the *Kabod* idea and its original function in biblical literature.

51. See Halperin, *The Faces of the Chariot.*

52. Odeberg, *The Hebrew Book of Enoch;* Scholem, *Major Trends in Jewish Mysticism; Jewish Gnosticism, Merkabah Mysticism.* Also see M. Smith, "Observations on *Hekhaloth Rabbati;*" Altmann, "Sacred Hymns in Hekhaloth Literature;" "Moses Narboni's 'Epistle on *Shiur Koma,*' " p. 195.

53. A. Segal, *Two Powers in Heaven;* Halperin, *The Merkabah in Rabbinic Literature;* Gruenwald, *Apocalyptic and Merkabah Mysticism;* Dan, "The Concept of Knowledge;" "Ancient Jewish Mysticism;" Chernus, "Individual and Community in Hekhaloth Literature;" "Visions of God in Merkabah Mysticism;" *Mysticism in Rabbinic Judaism.*

54. Quispel, *Gnostic Studies;* Dahl, "History and Eschatology," in *Crucified Messiah;* "Cosmic Dimensions and Religious Knowledge;" W. Meeks, *The Prophet King* Fossum, *Image of the Invisible God;* Rudolph, "Ein Grundtyp gnostischer Urmensch-Adam-Spekulation;" Tardieu, *Trois mythes gnostiques,* pp. 85–139; Bowker, " 'Merkabah' Visions;" Kee, "The Transfiguration in Mark;" Neher, "Le voyage mystique des quatre;" Sed, "Les traditions secrètes;" Schaefer, "New Testament and Hekhalot Literature;" "Engel und Menschen in der Hekhalot-Literatur;" Charlesworth, "Portrayal of the Righteous;" Hurtado, *One Lord, One God.* Betz, *Galatians Hermeneia,* suggests several relationships between Jewish mysticism and Greco-Roman magic. Also see Rowland, *The Open Heaven;* Stroumsa "Form(s) of God;" who summarizes the basic ideas of the *Shiur Koma* and notes their relevance to early Christianity.

55. In Schaefer, *Synopse zur Hekhalot-Literatur.*

56. M. Cohen, *Shiur Komah;* Elior, *Hekhaloth Zutartey.* For the complete bibliography, see Halperin, *The Faces of the Chariot,* pp. 567–69.

57. The ten volume compendium known in English as *The Theological Dictionary of the New Testament,* ed. by Kittel, has scarcely a dozen references to Ezekiel 1, although it is a crucial passage informing the christology of the New Testament, as Gilles Quispel has so cogently pointed out. See Quispel, "Hermetism and the New Testament."

58. See Saul Lieberman, "Metatron, the Meaning of His Name and His Functions," Appendix in Gruenwald's *Apocalyptic and Merkabah Mysticism,* pp. 235–41, esp. 237–39. *Pace* Stroumsa, "Form(s) of God."

59. See Morray-Jones, *A Transparent Illusion;* and Scholem, *Major Trends in Jewish Mysticism.*

60. L'Orange, *Apotheosis in Ancient Portraiture.*

61. Morray-Jones, *A Transparent Illusion.*

62. Virtually every scholar of these documents has offered a different entiology for "descenders" into the chariot. No crucial text has suggested itself to settle the issue. See Morray-Jones, *A Transparent Illusion;* and Davila, *Descenders in the Chariot.*

63. See A. Segal, *Two Powers in Heaven.*

64. Michael Swartz suggests that they are students who need divine help memorizing Torah from evidence in the *Sar Torah* sections of the documents. This is as good a guess as anyone has been able to make. It is also true that the texts become very popular in the late Middle Ages and early Renaissance with a group of Jewish mystics in Southern France known as the *Hasidei Ashkenaz.*

65. Lesses, *Ritual Practices to Gain Power,* pp. 279–367.

66. See ch. 5.

67. Griffiths, *Apuleius of Madauros,* p. 89.

68. See A. Segal, "Hellenistic Magic."

69. See Burkert, *Law and Science,* pp. 366ff.; Gottschalk, *Heraclides of Pontus,* 98ff; Ulansey, *Origins of the Mithraic Mysteries,* p. 86.

70. Love was a mysterious and magical power and hence even the implication of sexual congress might have been helpful in understanding the power which magicians had over their angelic helpers.

71. See the fine article by Ciraolo, "Supernatural Assistants."

72. The so-called *Mithras Liturgy* is one of the most controversial texts coming to us from antiquity. It can be isolated from lines 475–834 of the *Paris Magical Papyrus,* probably a third century Egyptian magician's *grimoire,* which was discovered early enough in this century to have impressed Karl Jung to the extent that it stimulated him to formulate the doctrine of the collective unconscious. Albrecht Dieterich suggested that it was a liturgy from the Mysteries of Mithras, a religion that was extremely popular in the Roman legions but has left us scarcely any literary remains. Others have felt that this is just a magical procedure. To me the value of this discussion rests with the scholarly uncertainty about just what magic is. In fact, magic itself becomes a kind of religion in late Antiquity. See A. Segal, "Hellenistic Magic."

73. This text is the very able translation of M. Meyer, quoted from his work, *The Ancient Mysteries,* pp. 213–21.

74. Fowden, *The Egyptian Hermes.*

75. Copenhaver, *Hermetica,* p. 6.

76. S. Johnston, *Hekate Soteira,* p. 88; *Restless Dead.*

77. For Porphyry and Julian's attitudes towards Christians, see Meredith, "Porphyry and Julian Against the Christians."

78. Searle, *The Mystery of Consciousness.*

79. Rappe, *Reading Neoplatonism,* pp. 88–89.

80. Ibid.; and "Self-Knowledge and Subjectivity;" also see O'Meara, *Plotinus: Introduction to the Enneads;* Miles, *Plotinus on Body and Beauty.*

81. My thanks to two of my students, Lock Reynolds of Williams College and Avigail Ziv of Barnard College who, in researching these topics for their own papers, helped me explore this fascinating and complicated subject.

82. Finamore, *Iamblichus*, p. 3.

83. See Ibid., pp. 33, 54 n.; Dodds, *Proclus*, p. 320; G. Shaw, *Theurgy and the Soul*.

84. See Finamore, *Iamblichus*, p. 51.

85. Ibid., p. 101.

86. MacMullen, *Christianity and Paganism*, p. 110; and *Christianizing the Roman Empire*.

Chapter 13. The Church Fathers and Their Opponents

1. There are many studies already available on individual fathers and many book length surveys as well. Dewart, *Death and Resurrection*; Perkins, *Resurrection*; Bynum, *The Resurrection of the Body*; Gatch, *Death, Meaning, and Mortality*; R. Brown, *Virginal Conception and Bodily Resurrection of Jesus*; Carnley, *The Structure of Resurrection Belief*; N. Wright, *Resurrection of the Son of God*.

2. See *Gos. of Pet.* 9–10, Hennecke-Schneemelcher, vol. 1, pp. 185ff.

3. Dewart, *Death and Resurrection*.

4. See Pagels, *The Gnostic Paul*.

5. Bianchi, *Le Origini dello Gnosticismo*; King, *What Is Gnosticism?*

6. See Dewart, *Death and Resurrection*, p. 36. Also see Pagels, *Adam, Eve, and the Serpent*. Nevertheless, *Gos. Barn.* 6 calls infants guiltless, which limits any notion of inherited sinfulness.

7. See Pagels, *Adam, Eve, and the Serpent*, throughout. Also see P. Brown, *The Body and Society*, throughout.

8. For more detail and a slightly different perspective on the growing difficulties between Judaism and Christianity, see Pagels, *The Origin of Satan*.

9. von Campenhausen, *Ecclesiastical Authority and Spiritual Power*, p. 17.

10. Pagels, *The Gnostic Gospels*.

11. See R. Fox, "Living like Angels." Pagels, *Adam, Eve, and the Serpent*.

12. See Vaage and Wimbush, *Asceticism and the New Testament*; T. Shaw, *The Burden of the Flesh*; Burrus, *Chastity As Autonomy*; Elm, *'Virgins of God'*; P. Brown, *The Body and Society*; E. Clark, "Ascetic Renunciation and Feminine Advancement;" *Jerome, Chrysostom and Friends*; "Theory and Practice in Late Ancient Asceticism;" *Reading Renunciation*; K. Cooper, *The Virgin and the Bride*; Kraemer, "The Conversion of Women;" Ruether, "Misogynism and Virginal Feminism;" Kraemer and D'Angelo, *Women and Christian Origins*.

13. For the later tradtion, see Stroumsa, "Madness and Divinization."

14. See Frank, *Angelikos Bios*, esp. 108–99.

15. Pseudo-Athanasius, *The Burden of the Flesh*, p. 1.

16. The quotation is from Grant and Graham, "1 Clement."

17. *1 Clem.* 42, Roberts, Donaldson and Crombie, p. 37. Also see Dewart, *Death and Resurrection,* here and throughout.

18. *2 Clem.* 9, Roberts, Donaldson, and Crombie, p. 61. See Perkins, *Resurrection;* and Dewart, *Death and Resurrection,* for more commentary on this interesting passage.

19. For a summary of the research done on angelomorphism, see Gieschen, *Angelomorphic Christology.* For martyrdom, see Straw, " 'A Very Special Death.' "

20. See van Hooff, *From Autothanasia to Suicide;* Droge and Tabor, *A Noble Death;* Seeley, *The Noble Death;* L. Smith, *Fools, Martyrs, and Traitors;* the classic: Frend, *Martyrdom and Persecution.* For a recent re-evaluation, see Bowersock, *Martyrdom and Rome.*

21. Ign. *Rom* 4, Roberts, Donaldson, and Crombie, p. 212.

22. Bowersock, *Martyrdom and Rome,* pp. 16–20.

23. Ign. *Symr.* 2 and 3, Roberts, Donaldson, and Crombie, pp. 241–42.

24. Frend, *Martyrdom and Persecution.*

25. Layton, *The Gnostic Gospels.*

26. See Layton, *The Gnostic Scriptures,* pp. 217–22.

27. See Ibid., p. 241.

28. See Pagels, *The Gnostic Paul.*

29. The earlier classic, Frend, *Martyrdom and Persecution,* has been supplemented by Pagels, *The Gnostic Gospels,* observation of the structural connection between resurrection notions and interest in marytrdom.

30. Origen, "Commentarium in 1 Corinthians," pp. 466–47). See Pagels, *Gnostic Gospels,* pp. 11 and n. 366, p. 158.

31. See, for example, Fredriksen, "Vile Bodies," pp. 73–85; "Beyond the Body/Soul Dichtonomy," pp. 87–114.

32. Frend, *Martyrdom and Persecution,* p. 245.

33. Ibid., p. 246.

34. See Droge and Tabor, *A Noble Death;* Bynum, *The Resurrection of the Body.*

35. Irenaeus, *Haer.* 1.30.13. See Pagels, *Gnostic Gospels,* p. 11 and n. 38, p. 158. I call this a modern perspective because this is the most often invoked explanation of the events in the modern period and it seems to me to be the most satisfactory explanation of the events.

36. *NHL,* p. 395.

37. Layton, *The Gnostic Scriptures,* p. 333.

38. See Pagels, *Gnostic Gospels,* p. 16.

39. Layton, *The Gnostic Scriptures,* p. 334.

40. Douglas, *Natural Symbols.*

41. *NHL,* p. 407.

42. *NHL* p. 408. This and the previous quotation are taken from Pagels, *Gnostic Gospels,* p. 92.

43. *NHL,* p. 342, from Pagels, *The Gnostic Gospels,* p. 93.

44. I will discontinue putting gnostic in quotation marks to indicate that they are "so-called" gnostics but I would still maintain the arbitrary nature of the term.

45. Layton, *The Gnostic Scriptures,* p. 321.

46. Pagels, "The Mystery of the Resurrection."

47. Pol. *Phil.* 7.1, Roberts, Donaldson, and Crombie, p. 73.

48. van Unnik, "The Newly Discovered Gnostic."

49. For more detail, see Dewart, *Death and Resurrection,* pp. 36–114.

50. For a recent feminist meditation on this fact, see Schaberg, *The Resurrection of Mary Magdalene.*

51. R. Miller, *The Complete Gospels.*

52. Layton, *The Gnostic Scriptures.*

53. Pagels, *The Gnostic Gospels.*

52. Frend, *Martyrdom and Persecution.*

54. Oden, *In Her Words,* p. 31; also see Castelli, *Martyrdom and Memory.*

55. It is what we expect at the end of life because of the heavenly journeyers—a long list of people that begins with Etana and Adapa and ends with some of those who claim to have been abducted by aliens.

56. See the very interesting treatment of this martyrology in Castelli, *Martyrdom and Memory.*

57. See A. Segal, *Two Powers in Heaven.*

58. "Samael" is Aramaic for the poison of 'El and is also a fairly common reference to Satan in rabbinic literature.

59. B. Pearson, "Revisiting Norea," p. 275.

60. Schüssler-Fiorenza, *Searching the Scriptures,* p. 71.

61. Shalev, "Post-Traumatic Stress Disorder." My thanks to Darcy Hirsh, a senior major in Religion at Barnard, with whom these interpretations were developed.

62. Jones, "A Case Study in 'Gnosticism,' " p. 206.

63. P. Brown, *The Body and Society,* p. 23.

64. Jones, "A Case Study in 'Gnosticism,' " p. 208.

65. Ibid., p. 216.

66. See Perkins, *Resurrection,* p. 363.

67. See Bynum, *The Resurrection of the Body,* pp. 30–32.

68. See Dewart, *Death and Resurrection,* p. 73.

69. As quoted in ibid., p. 77.

70. Ibid., p. 84.

71. Bynum, *The Resurrection of the Body,* p. 21.

72. See ibid., p. 37; E. Evans, *Tertullian's Treatise on the Resurrection,* pp. ix–xxxv; Cardman "Tertullian on the Resurrection."

73. Satran, "Fingernails and Hair."

74. Here Tertullian ignores a missionary advantage for resurrection that contemporary televangelists sometimes stress: resurrected flesh has more fun than resurrected souls.

75. Roberts, Donaldson, and Crombie, *Writings of the Apostolic Fathers*, vol. 15, p. 331.

76. See Bynum, *The Resurrection of the Body*, p. 37.

77. See Dewart, *Death and Resurrection*, p. 120.

78. See ibid., p. 122.

79. Bynum, *The Resurrection of the Body*, pp. 64–66.

80. Perkins, *Resurrection*, p. 375.

81. Roberts, Donaldson and Crombie, *Writings of the Apostolic Fathers*, vol. 10, p. 139.

82. A. Scott, *Origen and Life of Stars*.

83. See Dewart, *Death and Resurrection*, p. 135.

84. It was Methodius who most significantly captained the opposition to Origen's synthesis.

85. Pelikan, *Christianity and Classical Culture*.

86. Dennis, "Gregory on Resurrection of Body."

87. Quoted from Dewart, *Death and Resurrection*, p. 148.

88. From *A Select Library of Nicene and Post-Nice Fathers*, vol. 5, p. 416.

89. Ibid., p. 417.

90. See *On the Soul and the Resurrection;* Callahan, *Saint Gregory of Nyssa*, pp. 198–272.

91. Cf. Dennis, "Gregory on Resurrection of Body," p. 56.

92. See Dewart, *Death and Resurrection*, p. 164.

93. See Ibid., p. 174.

94. Quotations from this sermon are taken from Mourant, *Augustine on Immortality* and quoted from Dewart, *Death and Resurrection*, p. 175.

95. See Dewart, *Death and Resurrection*, p. 176.

96. Fredriksen, "Vile Bodies," pp. 84–85.

97. Fredriksen, "Beyond the Body/Soul Dichotomy," p. 250.

98. Pagels, *Adam, Eve, and the Serpent*, p. 99.

99. See, e.g., Burrus, *Chastity As Autonomy*.

100. See Cary, *Augustine's Invention of the Inner Self*.

101. See Ibid., pp. 112–13 and n. 48. According to Cary (p. 183), the first clear repudiation of the divinity of the soul in *On the Quantity of the Soul*, §§3 and 77, though this is tacked on to the beginning and the end of the treatise. In *On The Morals of the Catholic Church*, the fact that Christ is distinct from the soul is integral to the argument.

102. "Quantum sum" is one of the many verbal echoes of Augustine's *On the Quantity of the Soul*. See Cary, *Augustine's Invention*, p. 186. Passage is quoted, ibid., p. 126.

103. Pagels, *The Gnostics Gospels; Adam, Eve, and the Serpent;* Gager, "Body Symbols and Social Reality;" E. Clark, "New Perspectives on the Origenist Controversy," in *The Originist Controversey*.

104. Bynum, *The Resurrection of the Body*, p. 109.

105. Ibid., pp. 106–7.

106. Foschini amassed a collection of more than forty interpretations of this verse, which followed scholarship up until 1951 in a series of two review articles for the *CBQ*. By now there are evidently many more. My thanks to Yorgason for surveying these positions in his term paper "Paul, The Corinthians, and the Rite of Baptism for the Dead."

107. Perhaps it is as innocent as some of the Corinthian Christians waiting to be baptized until someone knowledgeable enough to perform it arrived. But before that could happen, some of the catechumens had died. This would certainly have occasioned the inquiries which Paul's letter answers. But it might be something far more interesting, a widespread early practice of baptizing the dead relatives of the new Corinthian Christians.

108. Trumbower, *Rescue for the Dead.*

109. See also Matt 12:40; Rom 10:7; Acts 2:24–31; Eph 4:8–10; see W. Harris, *The Descent of Christ.*

110. Trumbower, *Rescue for the Dead,* p. 165.

111. Ambrose, *On Valentinian,* 51; Trumbower, *Rescue for the Dead,* p. 179.

112. Ibid., p. 228.

113. Ibid., p. 229.

114. Ibid., p. 241.

115. Ibid., p. 260.

Chapter 14. The Early Rabbis

1. L. Levine, *The Ancient Synagogue.*

2. L. Levine, *Ancient Synagogues Revealed; The Ancient Synagogue.*

3. Montefiore and Loewe, *A Rabbinic Anthology,* p. 580.

4. See A. Cohen, *Everyman's Talmud;* Urbach, *The Sages: Their Concepts.*

5. See A. Segal, *The Other Judaisms,* esp. pp. 109–30.

6. See, for example, S. Cohen, *Maccabees to the Mishnah;* also A. Segal, *Rebecca's Children.*

7. Raphael, *Jewish Views of the Afterlife;* Elbogen, *Jewish Liturgy.*

8. Halivni, *Peshat and Derash.*

9. Urbach, *The Sages: Their Concepts.*

10. Neusner, *Judaism: Evidence of the Mishnah; Formative Judaism.*

11. Neusner, *First-Century Judaism in Crisis; The Rabbinic Traditions; Ancient Israel after Catastrophe; Judaism in the Beginning of Christianity.*

12. See Boyarin's provocative book, *Dying for God,* that should be read as a speculative theory; also see Stern and Mirsky, *Rabbinic Fantasies,* esp. "Midrash Elah Ezkerah," pp. 143–67, "Love in the Afterlife," pp. 249–63; Steinberg, "Angelic Israel."

13. This is a major theme of A. Segal, *Paul the Convert.*

14. The Talmud is comprised of the Mishnah plus a commentary, called the Gemara, from either Babylonia or Palestine. The Palestinian Gemara and the

Mishnah forms the Palestinian Talmud, which is shorter and less authoritative than the Babylonian Talmud, the standard compendium on law for classical Rabbinic Judaism. It is a composite document that stretches from the third to the seventh century. Both the Mishnah and the Gemarahs are divided into six orders and, in turn, into sixty-three tractates. The Mishnah is the size of a large desk dictionary. Each of the Talmuds, with its various commentaries as it is printed today, is the size of an ample, multivolume encyclopedia. Today's Talmud puts the Talmud text in the center, surrounded by even more commentaries endeavoring to reconcile even more contradictions.

15. The asterisk signifies that the passage is accepted as a proof.

16. It is even present in contemporary Reform Jewish liturgies. In the last century, the reference to resurrection was removed in many Reform prayer books. It is now sometimes being reinstated in Hebrew, although it is still often left out in English. Thus, the traditional form of the prayer remains intact but the congregation assents with its mind only to the censored form.

17. See, for example, Raphael, *Jewish Views of the Afterlife,* pp. 117–62; Moore, *Judaism in the First Centuries;* Urbach, "The Sages;" Bialik and Ravnitzky, "Sefer Ha-Aggadah;" Gillman, *The Death of Death;* Neusner, "Judaism;" Goldenberg, "Bound Up in the Bond of Life."

18. Stern, "Jewish Concepts."

19. See Urbach, *The Sages,* pp. 167, 308.

20. See H. Freedman, "Academy on High."

21. Steinberg, "Angelic Israel."

22. *Shemot Rabba* 443–49; *Midrash Shir.* 13b; *Debarim Rabba* 77.

23. See for example *Bereishit Rabba* 99.2 and *Shemoth Rabba* 263; also see Ginzberg, *The Legends of the Jews.*

24. See Sysling, *Teḥiyqat Ha-Metim.*

25. Smelik, "On the Mystical Transformation." He suggests that the Rabbis were reluctant to articulate these ancient Jewish traditions fully because they suggested that the righteous were gods. But they did not totally suppress the traditions either. See Steinberg, "Angelic Israel."

26. For more detail, see E. Wolfson, *Through a Speculum That Shines.*

27. Raphael, *Jewish Views of the Afterlife.*

28. See Rubenstein, *Talmudic Stories.*

29. For more information on these interesting legends, see Lindbeck, *Story and Theology;* older studies include Yassif, *The Sacrifice of Isaac;* Margaliot, *Elijah the Prophet.*

30. Here Novack, *The Image of the Non-Jew,* is right on the mark. But Christian scholarship has preceded him. For the history of scholarship on this point, see Dunn, *Jesus and the Spirit;* S. Wilson, *Gentiles and the Gentile Mission;* Richardson and Hurd, *From Jesus to Paul.*

31. See S. Wilson, *Gentiles and the Gentile Mission.* My interpretation depends heavily on Wilson's observations about the textual traditions though softens Wilson's arguments a bit.

32. See, for example, Waitz, "Das Problem des sog. Aposteldecrets."

33. Spiegel, *The Last Trial;* A. Segal, " 'He Who Did Not Spare His only Son,' " pp. 157–78 and reprinted as "The Sacrifice of Isaac;" "The Akedah;" Hengel, *The Atonement;* Levenson, *The Death and Resurrection.*

34. See "Hekhalot Rabbati" 113ff. and "Midrash Ezkerah" 3.40.38–42 in Schaefer, *Synopse zur Hekhalot-Literatur.* See particularly, R. Abusch, "The Marytrdom of Emperor Lupinus."

35. Fine, "Contemplative Death."

Chapter 15. Islam and the Afterlife

1. J. Smith and Haddad, *Islamic Understanding of Death and Resurrection;* also see Ayyub, "Islam;" Brockopp, "Islam," pp. 60–78; Chittick, "Your Sight Today Is Piercing."

2. Very helpful in this regard is the *Encyclopedia of Religion;* Martin, *Approaches to Islam in Religious Studies;* Oxtaby, *World Religions;* as well as the introductions to Islam of Esposito *(Islam)* and K. Armstrong *(Biography of the Prophet),* for example.

3. During Muḥammad's own day, his rival Musailimah (Thumamah ibn Kabir ibn Ḥabib) claimed the title. See the classic work of Widengren, *Muḥammad, the Apostle of God,* pp. 15ff. It is the second part of his monograph, *The Ascension of the Apostle.* This work is important even today, for its erudition and breadth of interest.

4. Peterson, "Muhammad," p. 502 n. 104.

5. Rodinson, *Muḥammed,* p. 34.

6. See, for example the dissertation of F. Denny, which observed as early as 1974 that there was inadequate study of the apocalyptic nature of early Islam. More recently, M. Cook has given the phenomenon of Islamic apocalyptic further study in his *Studies in Muslim Apocalyptic.*

7. W. Smith, *The Meaning and End of Religion.*

8. Quoted from Idleman and Smith, *The Islamic Understanding of Death,* p. 1.

9. See Sachedina, *Islamic Roots of Democratic Pluralism,* p. 39.

10. See Ishaq, *Life of Muhammad,* p. 232.

11. See, for example, M. R. Cohen, "The Legal Position of Jews."

12. See M. Cook, *Muhammad;* Crone and Cook, *Hagarism.*

13. Humphreys, *Islamic History—A Framework,* p. 69; Rippin, *Muslims,* p. ix, as cited in Warraq, below.

14. See Warraq, "Studies on Muhammad," esp. pp. 20–22.

15. Crone and Cook, *Hagarism;* Hawting, *The First Dynasty of Islam.*

16. Donner, *Narratives of Islamic Origins,* pp. 1–54; also Crone and Cook, *Hagarism.*

17. Bulliet, *Islam,* pp. 38–39.

18. DeWeese, *Islamization and Native Religion.*

19. B. Lewis, *What Went Wrong?* p. 120.

20. For this and further discussions on the relationship between the terms, see J. Smith and Haddad, *Islamic Understanding of Death and Resurrection,* pp. 18–21.

21. Ibid., pp. 54–55.

22. See B. Lewis, *The Crisis of Islam,* p. 44.

23. One exception to this reverence for Jerusalem are the followers of Ibn Wahhab (see below), who restrict their reverence to the sacred spaces in Saudi Arabia. This partly explains why Osama bin Laden is not as exercised by Israeli domination of Jerusalem as he is of the American presence in Saudi Arabia.

24. See Peterson, "Muhammad," p. 529, relying on Peters, *Muḥammad and the Origins of Islam,* pp. 144–47 and Widengren, *Muḥammad,* pp. 96–114.

25. See Peterson, "Muhammad," p. 526.

26. See Al-Ghazzali, *The Precious Pearl.*

27. Sells, *Early Islamic Mysticism,* pp. 248–49.

28. Muslims on the whole do not today identify the righteous dead with angels. Angels exist, of course. But they are the angels of Allah. (See for example, Cornell, "Fruit of Tree of Knowledge," p. 88). There is a lively Muslim tradition of the superiority of humanity over the angels, as there is in Rabbinic Judaism. Indeed, in private conversations with me, most young American Muslims note that Christians believe that the dead become angels but that Muslims feel this impinges on the unity of God. This is confirmed in the study of the effects on teens of religion in the media by L. Clark, *From Angels to Aliens,* pp. 152–54.

29. See Lewinstein, "Revaluation of Martyrdom in Early Islam;" also see Bowersock, *Martyrdom and Rome,* p. 19.

30. See Lewinstein, "Revaluation of Martyrdom," p. 86.

31. See Firestone, *Jihad.*

32. Malik *Muwaṭṭa',* 236 (no. 997) as quoted twice by Lewinstein, "Revaluation of Martyrdom in Early Islam," pp. 86, 90–91.

33. D. Brown, "Martyrdom in Sunni Revivalist Thought," p. 113.

34. Peterson, "Muhammad," pp. 547, 549.

35. There are certainly no equivalent rewards for women martyrs. Occasionally one even sees the notion that women are only accorded a place in heaven equal to the attainments of their husbands. But this is a minority opinion; see J. Smith and Haddad, *Islamic Understanding of Death and Resurrection,* pp. 157–82.

36. See Rustomji, "The Garden and the Fire."

37. Wasserstrom, *Between Muslim and Jew.* See especially "Origins and Angels: Popular and Esoteric Literature in Jewish-Muslim Symbiosis," pp. 167–205.

38. J. Smith and Haddad, *Islamic Understanding of Death and Resurrection,* pp. 183–92.

39. Newby, *History of the Jews of Arabia,* pp. 60–61

40. Wasserstrom cites Casanova, "Idris et 'Ouzair,' " and B. Lewis, *The Origins of Ismailism.*

41. See Halm, *Die islamische Gnosis;* Momen, *An Introductin to Shi'i Islam.*

42. Halm, *Die islamische Gnosis.*

43. This is like the polemical attacks on Jewish *mujassima* (anthropomorphizers) whom they accuse of worshiping a divine "chief agent."

44. The name "Ashma'ath" is possibly related to the Samaritan Ashima; see Fossum, *The Name of God.*

45. On all this, see Wasserstrom, *Between Muslim and Jew,* p. 185; also see A. Segal, "Ruler of the World," in *The Other Judaisms of Late Antiquity.*

46. See Halperin, "Hekhalot and Mir'aj."

47. See Waldman, "Eschatology in Islam," pp. 131ff.

48. See J. Smith and Haddad, *Islamic Understanding of Death and Resurrection,* pp. 104ff.; Waldman, "Eschatology in Islam," p. 132.

49. Maimonides, however, was forced to clarify his position and, especially in his *Treatise on the Resurrection,* he denied that Judaism preaches the extinction of the personal soul. It is hard to know how to put this together with the clear implications of the *Guide for the Perplexed.* The simplest synthesis is to assume that what Maimonides wrote in his *Guide* was only what could be proven by scientific and philosophical inquiry, but as a Jew he believed that a great deal more was revealed in Scripture. There are some who believe that Maimonides actually had an exoteric doctrine that approximated orthodox Jewish thinking and a more esoteric doctrine that correspondend to the beliefs of the philosophers. Some of the same kinds of ambiguity can be seen in Aquinas, who writes in full knowledge of Averroes and Maimonides. Aquinas's concept of the soul is the "form of the body," but his description of it owes as much to Aristotle as Plato. In contradistinction to the Ṣufis, Aquinas argues forthrightly for the soul's indestructibility (*Summa Theologica* 1 q 76, art. 6).

50. B. Lewis, *What Went Wrong?* p. 142, however, attributes the origins of this dramatic form to a Turkish adoptation of Italian *Commedia dell'arte* performances, which became very popular all over Turkey and was renamed *Orta Oyunu.* One hears about the form starting at the beginning of the nineteenth century.

51. See B. Lewis, *The Crisis in Islam,* p. 36.

52. See Runciman, *A History of the Crusades;* Schimmelpfening, *The Papacy;* and my thanks to Yehuda Kurtzer for his term paper on the subject.

53. See Einbinder, *Beautiful Death.*

54. See Quasem, *Salvation of the Soul.*

55. See Ramadan, *To Be a European Muslim; Islam, the West;* Mernissi, *Islam and Democracy;* Fadl, *The Place of Tolerance in Islam;* Kurzman, *Liberal Islam.*

56. See Juergensmeyer, *Terror in the Mind of God.*

57. Ḥamas means literally "fervor" in Arabic but it is, additionally, an

acronym for "the Movement for Muslim Resistance, a religiously-based "liberation" movement. Ironically, *Ḥamas* (with a *samekh*) means "violence" in Hebrew and is famously cited in Gen 6:11 and 13 as the condition which brought about the flood: "Now the earth was corrupt in God's sight and the earth was full of violence *(ḥamas)*." And, in verse 13, "God said to Noah, 'I have determined to make an end of all flesh for the earth is filled with violence *(ḥamas)* through them; behold, I will destroy them with the earth.' "

58. Literally, "the Party of God," the group is named after the founding events of Shiʿite Islam, which led inexorably to the martyrdom of Ḥuṣṣein. As a result, the very title of the group brings with it a rich tradition of martyrdom.

59. "The Base," but, in this case, probably more correctly translated as "The Database Network."

60. See Kepel, *The Revenge of God.*

61. Mylroie, *A Study of Revenge;* Emerson, *American Jihad.*

62. See D. Brown, "Martyrdom in Sunni Revivalist Thought," p. 113; also see Kepel, *Jihad,* pp. 23–42.

63. Paul Berman has written a feature article on Sayyid Quṭb for the *New York Times Sunday Magazine:* "The Philosopher of Islamic Terror," March 23, 2003.

64. This is exactly Paul Berman's description of the contribution of Sayyid Quṭb in his article.

65. Droge and Taylor, *A Noble Death;* Boyarin, *Dying for God.*

66. See, for example, Turner, *Dramas, Fields, and Metaphors.*

67. No proof is needed to counter this absurd allegation that Israel took down the World Trade Center, though the evidence is that approximately the same number of Jews died in the attack as there are in the general population of New York and New Jersey—roughly 15 percent. Besides, Friedman, *Longitudes and Attitudes;* also see Barbara Walters' 20/20 report of March 29, summarized as "Mosques and Malls: A Rare Look at Saudi Arabia," at http://more.abcnews.go.com/sections/2020/dailynews/2020_saudi_walters_020329.html for a summary of the program.

68. See Atran, *In Gods We Trust;* "Genesis of Suicide Terrorism."

69. See "MSNBC Investigates" episode called "Shahid: The Mind of a Suicide Bomber," broadcast in Winter 2002, which contains interviews with failed suicide bombers in Israeli jails.

70. Anyone who has watched Al-Jazeera can verify this information. Even the so-called independent Arab voice goes way beyond what could be called political support. See the new afterword in B. Lewis, *Semites and Anti-Semites,* written well before the recent post–9/11 spate of suicide bombers in Israel.

71. Goldberg, "In the Party of God." Nor are the activities of these extremist groups confined to the Middle East. The Islamists have formed international networks of economic support. They raise money by drug smuggling in Southeast Asia and cigarette smuggling in the United States, two skills which the usually unaffluent adherents may have perfected before their conversion to rad-

ical Islam. They also use criminal shakedowns to raise money from Arab shop-keepers throughout the world. The justification is that the money supports the widows and orphans of the suicide bombers. And some of it does, through payments to the families of the suicide bombers, though this is not continuing support and the families are not otherwise specially qualified for public assistance. But a great deal just goes into general funds or supports the ordinary nonsuicide soldiers. Another part of the money raised in these activities is then siphoned off into terrorist operations in non-Palestinian causes, like blowing up synagogues and Jewish civic institutions throughout the world, with prominent success in Argentina and Djerba.

72. 'Ali, *The Clash of Fundamentalisms*, pp. 196–197. 'Ali makes the important point that the US is also a bastion of fundamentalist education.

73. Ajami, *The Dream Palace of the Arabs*, p. 312.

74. Kepel, *The Revenge of God*.

75. A reissue of the text was edited with an introduction by Marsden, *The Fundamental*. See Barr, *Fundamentalism*.

76. See Ammerman, "North American Protestant Fundamentalism."

77. See Kepel, *The Revenge of God*, pp. 100–39.

78. Literally "tremblers," the Haredim are the self-styled, only true fearers of God. They take their self-description from Isa 66:2b: "But this is the man to whom I will look, he that is humble and contrite in spirit, and trembles at my word.

79. See, for example, Lustick, *For the Land the Lord;* a similar tack is taken by J. Harris in "Fundamentalism."

80. Lawrence, *Defenders of God*. Lawrence certainly deserves our thanks for early having pointed out the relationship between fundamentalism and the problematization of modern thought.

81. One thinks, for instance, of the Kiryas Yoel school district in Monsey and the deference shown to the Hasidic community in New York City. New York politics are, in general, more keyed to ethnicity than to political machines, at least in comparison with Chicago. See Fuchs, *Mayors and Money*.

82. Kepel, *The Revenge of God*, pp. 140–90.

83. See Shahak and Mezvinsky, *Jewish Fundamentalism in Israel*.

84. Careful thought would reveal that Messianism is not so much a Jewish Biblical belief as a postbiblical Jewish phenomenon, because the term "Messiah" always refers to the ruling king in the Bible and never to a future one. It is postbiblical thought and quintessentially Christianity that finds messianism to be fundamental to Biblical thought.

85. See K. Brown, "Fundamentalism and the Control of Women," in Hawley, *Fundamentalism and Gender*.

86. The greatest danger is not just from him but from the fact that his group is but one among many terrorist movements growing out of Islamic fundamentalism. The subsequent defeat of the Taliban, which deprived Osama bin Laden of his sanctuary in Afghanistan, is perhaps one sign that the tide may be turn-

ing in the fight against Islamist extremism. Obviously, there have been many terrorist acts on a smaller scale all over the world, both before and after the World Trade Center disaster. The terrible scourge of suicide bombing in Israel is obviously a result of the perceived success of bin Laden's operation. Under such circumstances, it will take years to root out the feeling that suicide bombing is an efficacious religious action, just as hard as rooting out the many different cells of terrorists around the world.

87. Atran, "Genesis of Suicide Terrorism."

88. Kepel, *Jihad.*

89. See the complete analysis of the events in ch. 6 of Castelli, *Martyrdom and Memory.*

90. Bernall, *She Said Yes.*

91. See, for example, Lawrence, *New Faiths, Old Fears.*

92. See Ramadan, *To Be a European Muslim; Muslims in France; Islam, the West.*

93. Wolfe, *Taking Back Islam;* Sachedina, *Islamic Roots of Democratic Pluralism;* Abou El Fadl, *The Place of Tolerance in Islam.*

Afterword: Immortal Longing

1. See, for example, McDannell and Lang, *Heaven;* Zaleski, *Otherworld Journeys; Near-Death Experience and Christian Hope;* Bynum, *The Resurrection of the Body;* Ariès, *The Hour of Our Death;* Zaleski and Zaleski, *The Book of Heaven.*

2. See for example the very full studies of Bynum, *The Resurrection of the Body;* and Zaleski, *Otherworld Journeys.*

3. See Gillman, *The Death of Death.*

4. L. Clark, in her study of teenage religion and the media, *From Angels to Aliens,* pp. 196–98, points out that many teenagers state that they "make up" their own religion. Clark shows that these created religions are mostly composed of bits and pieces of television shows and films. This public feature of the "creative religion" is important for its credibility.

5. Otto, *The Idea of the Holy.*

6. In his conclusion to *In Gods We Trust,* Atran asks whether religion is inherently either evolutionarily adaptive or maladaptive and decides that it is not essentially either one.

7. Tillich, *The Courage To Be; Systematic Theology; The Dynamics of Faith.*

8. See, for example, the helpful book of Diamond, *Contemporary Philosophy and Religious Thought.*

9. See, for example, Alvarado, "Out-of-Body Experiences."

10. Zaleski, *Otherworld Journeys,* pp. 184–205.

11. Ibid., p. 205.

12. Balkin, *Cultural Software,* pp. 13–14.

13. Ibid.

14. Dawkins, "Viruses of the Mind."

15. Balkin, *Cultural Software,* p. 13.

16. See Atran, "The Trouble With Memes," in *In Gods We Trust,* pp. 236–62, for a cogent argument analysis of the limitations of evolutionary models.

17. Gottsch, "Mutation, Selection, and Vertical Transmission."

18. See Blackmore, *The Meme Machine.*

19. For a review of this important concept see Neimeyer and Van Brunt, "Death Anxiety;" Neimeyer, *Death Anxiety Handbook.*

20. Green, *Little Saint;* see *New York Times Book Review* August 13, 2000, p. 4.

21. See Saler, *Conceptualizing Religion,* esp. pp. 50–69.

22. Greyson, "Reduced Death Threat." Greyson reports that people who have had a Near Death Experience have significantly less death anxiety than people who have had a brush with death and no NDE or people without any significant brush with death.

23. Hick, *Death and Eternal Life.*

24. See Walls, *Heaven,* pp. 75–79.

25. In a way it is the converse of Shakespeare's effective use of the notion of ghosts, abandoned in his own day, to serve the needs of his drama. For a more complete discussion of Shakespeare's notion of life after death, see Greenblatt, *Hamlet in Purgatory,* esp. pp. 151–204.

26. Bloom, *Hamlet,* p. 133.

Aalen, Svarre. " 'Reign' and 'House' in the Kingdom of God." *NTS* 8 (1962): 215–40.

Aberbach, Moshe, and Leivy Smolar. "Aaron, Jeroboam, and the Golden Calves." *JBL* 86 (1967): 129–40.

Abou El Fadl, Khaled. *The Place of Tolerance in Islam.* Ed. Joshua Cohen and Ian Lague. Boston: Beacon Press, 2002.

Abusch, Ra'anan. "The Martyrdom of Emperor Lupinus: Genre Inversion and Identity Inversion in *Hakhalot Rabbati.*" Annual Meeting of the Society of Biblical Literature. Toronto, Ontario, 2002.

Abusch, Tzvi. "Ishtar's Proposal and Gilgamesh's Refusal: An Interpretation of the Gilgamesh Epic, Tablet 6 Lines 1–7." *HR* 26 (1986): 143–87.

———. "Mourning the Death of a Friend: Some Assyriological Notes." Pages 101–21 in *The Frank Talmage Memorial.* Vol 1. Ed. Barry Walfish, 1993. Reprinted in John Maier, 1997.

———. "Ascent to the Stars in a Mesopotamian Ritual: Social Metaphor and Religious Experience." Pp. 15–39 in *Death, Ecstasy, and Other Worldly Journeys.* Ed. John J. Collins and Michael Fishbane. Albany: SUNY Press, 1995.

———. "The Development and Meaning of the Epic of Gilgamesh." *JAOS* 121 (2001): 614–22.

Adam, James, ed. *The Republic of Plato.* Cambridge: The University Press, 1963.

Ajami, Fouad. *The Dream Palace of the Arabs: A Generation's Odyssey.* New York: Random House, 1998.

Akenson, Donald H. *Saint Saul: A Skeleton Key to the Historical Jesus.* Oxford: Oxford University Press, 2000.

'Ali, Ṭariq. *The Clash of Fundamentalisms: Crusades, Jihads, and Modernity.* London: Verso, 2002.

Allegro, John. *The Sacred Mushroom and the Cross: A Study of the Nature and Origin of Christianity within the Fertility Cults of the Ancient Near East.* London: Hodder and Stoughton, 1970.

Altmann, A. "Sacred Hymns in Hekhaloth Literature." *Melilah* 2 (1946): 1–24.

———. "Moses Narboni's 'Epistle on *Shiur Koma.*' " *Biblical and Other Studies.* Cambridge: Harvard University Press, 1963.

Alvarado, Carlos. "Out-of-Body Experiences." Pp. 183–218 in *Varieties of*

Anomalous Experience: Examining the Scientific Evidence. Ed. Etzel Cardeña, Steven J. Lynn, and Stanley Krippner. Washington, DC: American Psychological Association, 2000.

Ammerman, Nancy T. "North American Protestant Fundamentalism." *Fundamentalisms Observed.* Ed. Martin E. Marty and R. Scott Appleby. Chicago: University of Chicago Press, 1992.

Andersen, Francis I. *Amos.* AB 24A. New York: Doubleday, 1989.

Antoun, Richard T. *Understanding Fundamentalism: Christian, Islamic, and Jewish Movements.* Lanham, NY: Altamira Press, 2001.

Antti, Marjanen. *The Women Jesus Loved: Mary Magdalene in the Nag Hammadi Library and Related Documents.* Leiden: Brill, 1996.

Arbel, Daphna Vita. *Beholders of Divine Secrets: Mysticism and Myth in Early Jewish Literature.* Ph.D. diss. Jerusalem: The Hebrew University, 1997 (Hebrew). Albany, NY: SUNY Press, 2003 (English).

Ariès, Phillip. *Western Attitudes Toward Death.* Baltimore: Johns Hopkins University Press, 1974.

———. *The Hour of Our Death.* New York: Knopf, 1981.

Armstrong, David E. *Alcohol and Altered States in Ancestor Veneration Rituals of Zhou Dynasty China and Iron Age Palestine.* Lewiston, NY: The Edwin Mellen Press, Ltd., 1998.

Armstrong, Karen. *A Biography of the Prophet.* San Francisco: Harper, 1992.

Assmann, Jan. *Ägypten—Thelogie und Frömigkeit einer Frühen Hochkultur.* Stuttgart: Taschenbücherei, 1984.

———. *Ma'at: Gerechtigkeit und Unsterblichkeit im Alten Ägypten.* München: Beck, 1990. 2d ed., 1995.

———. "A Dialogue Between Self and Soul: Papyrus Berlin 3024." Pp. 384–403 in *Self, Soul, and Body in Religious Experience.* Ed. A. I. Baumgarten, with J. Assmann and G. G. Stroumsa. Leiden: Brill, 1998.

———. "Confession in Ancient Egypt." Pp. 331–44 in *Transformations of the Inner Self in Ancient Religions.* Ed. Jan Assman and Guy G. Stroumsa. Leiden: Brill, 1999.

———. "Conversion, Piety, and Loyalism in Ancient Egypt." Pp. 31–44 in *Transformations of the Inner Self in Ancient Religions.* Ed. Jan Assman and Guy G. Stroumsa. Leiden: Brill, 1999.

———. "Resurrection in Ancient Egypt." *Resurrection: Theological and Scientific Assessments.* Ed. T. Peters, R. Russell, and M. Walker. Grand Rapids: Eerdmans, 2002.

Athanassiadi-Fowden. *Julian and Hellenism: An Intellectual Biography.* Oxford: Clarendon Press, 1981.

Atran, Scott. *In Gods We Trust: The Evolutionary Landscape of Religion.* New York: Oxford University Press, 2002.

———. "Genesis of Suicide Terrorism." *Science* 299 (2003): 1534–39.

Aufrecht, Walter E., ed. *Studies in the Book of Job.* Studies in Religion Sup. 16. Waterloo, ON: Wilfred Laurier University, 1985.

Aune, David. *The Cultic Setting of Realized Eschatology in Early Christianity.* Leiden: E. J. Brill, 1972.

———. *Prophecy in Early Christianity and the Ancient Mediterranean World.* Grand Rapids: Eerdmans, 1983.

Austin, James H. *Zen and the Brain: Toward an Understanding of Meditation and Consciousness.* Cambridge, MA: MIT Press, 1998.

Ayyub, Mahmoud. "Islam." *World Religions: Western Traditions.* 2d ed. New York and Toronto: Oxford University Press, 2001.

Baer, Richard. *Philo's Use of the Categories Male and Female.* Arbeiten Zur Literature und Geschichte Des Hellenistischen Judentums 3. Leiden: Brill, 1970.

Bagnall, Roger. *Egypt in Late Antiquity.* Princeton: Princeton University Press, 1993.

Bailey, L. R. "The Old Testament View of Life After Death." *Themelios* 11:2 (1986).

———. *Biblical Perspectives on Death.* Philadelphia: Fortress, 1979.

Baird, William. "Visions, Revelation, and Ministry: Relflections on 2 Cor. 12:1–5 and Gal. 1:11–17." *JBL* 104:4 (1985): 651–62.

Balkin, J. M. *Cultural Software: A Theory of Ideology.* New Haven: Yale University Press, 1998.

Barbar, Bernard. "Acculturation and Messianic Movements." *American Sociological Review* 6 (1941): 883–89.

Barr, James. *Fundamentalism.* London: SCM Press, 1977.

———. *The Garden of Eden and the Hope of Immortality.* Minneapolis: Fortress Press, 1993.

Barstad, Hans. "The Religious Polemics of Amos." VTSup 34 (1984): 285–303.

Barth, Markus. *The People of God.* Sheffield: JSNT Press, 1983.

Bauckham, Richard. *The Fate of the Dead: Studies on the Jewish and Christian Apocalypses.* Novum Testamentum. Leiden: Brill, 1998.

Baumgarten, Joseph. "The Qumran-Essene Restraints on Marriage." Pp. 13–24 in *Archeology and History in the Dead Sea Scrolls: The New York University Conference in Memory of Yigael Yadin.* Ed. Lawrence H. Schiffman. JSPSup 8. Sheffield: JSOT Press, 1990.

Beare, Frank W. *The Earliest Records of Jesus.* New York: Abingdon, 1962.

Becker, Ernest. *The Denial of Death.* New York: The Free Press, 1973.

Becker, J. *Untersuchungen Zur Enstehungsgeschichte der Testamente der Zwölf Patriarchen.* AGJU 8. Leiden, 1970.

Beckford, James A. "Accounting for Conversion." *British Journal of Sociology* 29:2 (1978): 249–62.

BeDuhn, Jason. *The Manichean Body: In Discipline and Ritual.* Baltimore: Johns Hopkins University Press, 1999.

Bell, Catherine. *Ritual Theory, Ritual Practice.* New York: Oxford University Press, 1992.

———. *Ritual: Perspectives and Dimensions.* New York: Oxford University Press, 1997.

Benoit, Pierre. *The Passion and Resurrection of Jesus Christ.* New York: Herder and Herder, 1969.

Benz, Ernst. *Paulus Als Visionaer.* Akademie der Wissenschaften und der Literatur. Weisbaden: Steiner, 1952.

Bergren, Theodore. "The 'People Coming From the East' in 5 Ezra 1:38." *JBL* 108 (1989): 675–83.

———. *Fifth Ezra: The Text, Origin and Early History.* SBLSCS 25. Atlanta: Scholars Press, 1990.

———. "The List of Leaders in 5 Ezra 1:39–40." *JBL* 120:2 (2001): 313–27.

Bernall, Misty. *She Said Yes: The Unlikely Martyrdom of Cassie Bernall.* Farmington, PA: Plough Publishing Company, 1999.

Bernstein, Alan. *The Formation of Hell: Death and Retribution in the Ancient and Early Christian Worlds.* Ithaca: Cornell University Press, 1993.

Betz, Hans Dieter. *Galatians Hermeneia.* Philadelphia: Fortress, 1979.

———. *The Greek Magical Papyri in Translation, Including the Demotic Spells.* Vol 1. Chicago: University of Chicago Press, 1986.

Bhabha, Homi K. *The Location of Culture.* London: Routledge and Kegan Paul, 1994.

Bialik and Ravnitzky, eds. *Sefer Ha-Aggadah.* Tel Aviv, 1936 (Hebrew). Tr. William Braude. New York: Schocken, 1992.

Bianchi, Ugo, ed. *Le origini dello gnosticismo.* Nunon Book Series 12. Leiden: Brill, 1967.

Birnbaum, Ellen. *The Place of Judaism in Philo's Thought: Israel, Jews, and Proselytes.* Atlanta: Scholars Press, 1996.

Black, Matthew. "The Throne-Theopany Prophetic Commission and the 'Son of Man:' A Study in Tradition-History." Pp. 57–73 in *Jews, Greeks, and Christians: Religious Cultures in Late Antiquity.* Ed. Robert Hamerton-Kelly and Robin Scroggs. Leiden: Brill, 1976.

———. *The Book of Enoch Or 1 Enoch: A New English Edition with Commentary and Textual Notes.* Studia in Veteris Testamenti pseudepigraphica 7. Leiden: Brill, 1985.

Blackman, A. M., ed. *Middle Egyptian Stories.* Bibl. Aeg. 2. Brussels, 1932.

Blackmore, Susan. *The Meme Machine.* New York: Oxford University Press, 1999.

Blair, Sheila S., and Jonah Bloom. *Images of Paradise in Islamic Art.* Hood Museum of Art of Dartmouth College; Austin: University of Texas Press, 1991.

Bleiberg, Edward. *Jewish Life in Ancient Egypt: A Family Archive from the Nile Valley.* New York: Brooklyn Museum of Art, 2002.

Bloch, Maurice, and Jonathan Parry, eds. *Death and Regeneration of Life.* London: Cambridge University Press, 1982.

Bloch-Smith, Elizabeth. *Judahite Burial Practices and Belief About the Dead.* *JSOT* Supplement Series 123. Sheffield: Sheffield Academic Press, 1992.

———. "The Cult of the Dead in Judah: Interpreting the Material Remains." *JBL* 111 (1992): 213–24.

Bloom, Harold. *Hamlet: Poem Unlimited*. New York: Riverhead Books, 2003.

Boccaccini, Gabriele. *Beyond the Essene Hypothesis: The Parting of the Ways between Qumran and Enochian Judaism*. Grand Rapids: Eerdmans, 1998.

Bockmuehl, Marcus. *Revelation and Mystery in Ancient Judaism and Pauline Christianity*. Grand Rapids: Eerdmans, 1990.

Bode, Dastur E. A. *Man, Soul, Immortality in Zoroastrianism*. Bombay, 1960.

Böklen, Ernst. *Verwandtschaft der jüdisch-Christlichen mit der parsischen Eschatologie*. Göttingen: Venderhoeck and Ruprecht, 1902.

Bolt, Peter G. "Life, Death, and the Afterlife in the Greco-Roman World." *Life in the Face of Death: The Resurrection Message of the New Testament*. Ed. Richard N. Longenecker. Grand Rapids: Eerdmans, 1991.

Bonnet, H. "Sargtexte." *Reallexicon der Ägyptischen Religionsgeschichte*. Ed. H. Bonnet. Berlin, 1952.

Borg, Marcus. *Meeting Jesus Again for the First Time: The Historical Jesus and the Heart of Contemporary Faith*. San Francisco: Harper, 1995.

Boswell, John. *Of the Christian Era to the Fourteenth Century*. Chicago: University of Chicago Press, 1980.

Bourguignon, Erika. *Religion, Altered States of Consciousness, and Social Change*. Columbus: The Ohio State University Press, 1973.

———. *Possession*. San Francisco: Chandler and Sharp, 1976.

Bousset, Wilhelm. *Kyrios Christos: A History of Belief in Christ from the Beginnings of Christianity to Irenaeus*. Trans. John E. Steely. Nashville: Abingdon Press, 1970.

Bowersock, G. W. *Julian the Apostate*. Cambridge: Harvard University Press, 1980.

———. *Martyrdom and Rome*. Cambridge: Cambridge University Press, 1995.

Bowker, J. W. " 'Merkabah' Visions and the Visions of Paul." *JSS* 16 (1971): 157–73.

Boyarin, Daniel. *Dying for God: Martyrdom and the Making of Judaism and Christianity*. Stanford: Stanford University Press, 1999.

Boyce, Mary. *A Persian Stronghold of Zoroastrianism*. Oxford: Clarendon Press, 1977.

———. *Zoroastrians: Their Religious Beliefs and Practices*. London: Routledge and Kegan Paul, 1979.

———, ed. and trans. *Textual Sources for the Study of Zoroastrianism*. Manchester: Manchester University Press, 1984.

———. *Zoroastrianism: Its Antiquity and Constant Vigor*. Columbia Lectures on Iranian Studies 7. Ed. Ehsan Yarshater. Costa Mesa and New York: Mazda Publishing, 1992.

Brandon, S. G. F. *The Judgment of the Dead: The Idea of Life After Death in the Major Religions*. New York: Charles Scribner's Sons, 1967.

Bremmer, Jan N. *The Early Greek Concept of the Soul.* Princeton: Princeton University Press, 1987.

———. "Paradise: From Persia, Via Greece, Into the Septuagint." Pp. 1–21 in *Paradise Interpreted: Representations of Biblical Paradise in Judaism and Christianity.* Ed. Gerard P. Luttikhuizen. Leiden, Boston, Köln: Brill, 1999.

———. *The Rise and Fall of the Afterlife.* London and New York: Routledge, 2002.

Brichto, Herbert Chanan. "Kin, Cult, Land, and Afterlife—A Biblical Complex." *HUCA* 44 (1973): 1–54.

———. *The Names of God: Poetic Readings in Biblical Beginnings.* New York: Oxford University Press, 1998.

Brockopp, Jonathan E. "Islam." Pp. 60–78 in *Death and the Afterlife.* Ed. Jacob Neusner. Cleveland, OH: Pilgrim Press, 2000.

Brown, Daniel. "Martyrdom in Sunni Revivalist Thought." Pp. 107–13 in *Sacrificing the Self: Perspectives on Martyrdom and Religion.* Ed. Margaret Cormack. New York: Oxford University Press, 2002.

Brown, Karen. "Fundamentalism and the Control of Women." *Fundamentalism and Gender.* Ed. John Stratton Hawley. Oxford: Oxford University Press, 1994.

Brown, Peter. *The Body and Society: Men, Women and Sexual Renunciation in Early Christianity.* Lectures on the History of Religions 13. New York: Columbia University Press, 1988.

Brown, Raymond E. *The Gospel According to John.* AB 29, 29A. Garden City, NY: Doubleday, 1970.

———. *The Virginal Conception and Bodily Resurrection of Jesus.* New York: Missionary Society of St. Paul the Apostle, 1973.

———. *The Death of the Messiah.* 2 vols. Garden City, NY: Doubleday, 1994.

Browning, Robert. *The Emperor Julian.* London: Weidenfeld and Nicolson, 1975.

Buccellati, G. "The Decent of Inanna as a Ritual Journey to Kutha?" *Syro-Mesopotamian Studies* 4 (1982): 3–7.

Buchanan, G. W. *Revelation and Redemption.* Dillsboro: Western North Carolina Press, 1978.

Buck, Charles, and Greer Taylor. *Saint Paul: A Study of the Development of His Thought.* New York: Charles Scribner's Sons, 1969.

Buckley, Jorunn Jacobsen. Female Fault and Fulfillment in Gnosticism. Chapel Hill: University of North Carolina Press, 1986.

Budge, A. A. W., ed. *Book of the Cave of Treasures.* London, 1927.

Bulliet, Richard W. *Islam: The View from the Edge.* New York: Columbia University Press, 1994.

Burkert, Walter. *Law and Science in Ancient Pythagoreanism.* Cambridge: Harvard University Press, 1972.

Burkert, Walter. *Greek Religion.* Trans. John Raffan. Cambridge: Harvard University Press, 1985.

———. *Ancient Mystery Cults.* Cambridge: Harvard University Press, 1987.

Burnet, Régis. "L'Aramnèse: Structure Fondelmentale de la Lettre Paulinienne." *NTS* 19:1 (2003): 57–69.

Burrell, Barbara, Kathryn Netzer, and Ehud Netzer. "Uncovering Herod's Seaside Palace." *Biblical Archaeology Review* 19 (1993): 50–57.

Burridge, Kenelm. *New Heaven, New Earth: A Study of Millenarian Activities.* New York: Schocken, 1969.

Burrus, Virginia. *Chastity As Autonomy: Women in the Stories of Apocryphal Acts.* Studies in Women and Religion 23. Lewiston, NY: Edwin Mellen Press, 1987.

Bynum, Caroline Walker. *The Resurrection of the Body in Western Christianity, 200–1336.* New York: Columbia University Press, 1995.

Callahan, V. W., trans. *Saint Gregory of Nyssa: Ascetical Works.* Washington, DC: Catholic University of America Press, 1967.

Callan, Terrance. "The Law and the Mediator: Gal. 3:19b–20." Ph.D. diss. New Haven: Yale University, 1976.

———. "Prophecy and Ecstacy in Greco-Roman Religion and in 1 Corinthians." *NovT* 27 (1985): 125–40.

Cameron, Averil, and Amélie Kuhrt. *Images of Women in Antiquity.* Detroit: Wayne State, 1983.

Cancik-Lindemaier, Hildegard. "Corpus: Some Philological and Anthropological Remarks Upon Roman Funerary Customs." Pp. 417–29 in *Self, Soul, and Body in Religious Experience.* Ed. Albert I. Baumgarten, with Jan Assman and Guy G. Stroumsa. Leiden: Brill, 1998.

Capes, David B. *Old Testament Yahweh Texts in Paul's Christology.* Untersuchungen zum Neuen Testament 2:47. Tübingen: Mohr (Siebeck), 1992.

Cardeña, Etzel, Steven Jay Lynn, and Stanley Krippner. *Varieties of Anomalous Experience: Examining the Scientific Evidence.* Washington, DC: American Psychological Association, 2000.

Cardman, Rancine. "Tertullian on the Resurrection." Ph.D. diss. Yale University, 1974.

Carnley, Peter. *The Structure of Resurrection Belief.* Oxford: Clarendon Press, 1987.

Carr, W. *Angels and Principalities: The Background, Meaning and Development of the Pauline Phrase: Hai Archai Kai Hai Exousiai.* Cambridge: Cambridge University Press, 1981.

Carter, Stephen L. *The Culture of Disbelief: How American Law and Politics Trivialize Religious Devotion.* New York: Baisic Books, 1993.

Cary, Phillip. *Augustine's Invention of the Inner Self: The Legacy of a Christian Platonist.* New York: Oxford University Press, 2000.

Casanova, Paul. "Idris et 'Ouzair.' " *Journal Asiatique* 205 (1924): 356–60.

Castelli, Elizabeth. *Martyrdom and Memory: Early Christian Culture-Making.* Forthcoming.

Castelli, Elizabeth, with Rosamond Rodman. *Women, Gender, Religion: A Reader.* New York: Palgrave, 1991.

Causse, Antonin. *Du Groupe ethnique à la communauté religieuse: le problème socologique de la réligion d'Israel.* Paris: Alcan, 1908.

Cavallin, H. C. C. *Life after Death: Paul's Argument for the Resurrection of the Dead in 1 Cor 15. Part I: An Enquiry Into the Jewish Background.* Coniectanea Biblica New Testament Series 7. Lund: CWK Gleerup, 1974.

Chalmers, David J. *The Conscious Mind: In Search of a Fundamental Theory.* New York: Oxford University Press, 1996.

Charlesworth, James, ed. *The Pseudepigrapha in Modern Research.* Missoula, MT: Scholars Press, 1976. Reprint with supplement, 1981.

———. "The Portrayal of the Righteous as an Angel." *Ideal Figures in Ancient Judaism: Profiles and Paradigms.* Vol. 136. Ed. G. W. E. Nickelsburg and J. D. Collins. SBLSCS 12. Chico, CA: Scholars Press, 1980.

———, ed. *The Old Testament Pseudepigrapha.* 2 vols. Garden City, NY: Doubleday, 1983.

———. "The Jewish Roots of Christology: The Discovery of the Hypostatic Voice." *Scottish Journal of Theology* 39 1986: 19–41.

———. "From Jewish Messianology to Christian Christology: Some Caveats and Perspectives." Pp. 225–64 in *Judaisms and Their Messiahs at the Turn of the Christian Era.* Ed. Jacob Neusner, William S. Green, and Ernest Frerichs. Cambridge: Cambridge University Press, 1987.

———. *Jesus Within Judaism: New Light from Exciting Archeological Discoveries.* New York: Doubleday, 1988.

Charlesworth, James, with James Brownson et al., eds. *The Messiah: Developments in Earliest Judaism and Christianity.* Minneapolis: Fortress, 1992.

Chernus, Ira. "Individual and Community in the Redaction of Hekhaloth Literature." *HUCA* 52 (1981): 253–74.

———. *Mysticism in Rabbinic Judaism: Studies in the History of Midrash.* Berlin: de Gruyter, 1982.

———. "Visions of God in Merkabah Mysticism." *JSJ* 13 (1983): 123–46.

Chidester, David. *Savage Systems: Colonialism and Comparative Religion in South Africa.* Charlottesville and London: University of Virginia Press, 1996.

Childs, Brevard S. "Myth and Reality in the Old Testament." Pp. 31–53 in *Studies in Biblical Theology* 27. Chatham, Eng.: W. J. Mackay, 1960.

Chittick, William C. " 'Your Sight Today is Piercing:' The Muslim Understanding of Death and Afterlife." *Death and the Afterlife: Perspectives of World Religions.* Ed. Hiroshi Obayashi. New York: Praeger, 1992.

Churchland, Paul M. *Matter and Consciousness: A Contemporary Introduction to the Philosophy of Mind.* Cambridge, MA: MIT Press, 1992.

Ciraolo, Leda Jean. "Supernatural Assistants in the Greek Magical Papyri." Pp. 279–96 in *Ancient Magic and Ritual Power.* Ed. Marvin Meyer and Paul

Mirecki. Religions in the Graeco-Roman World 129. Leiden and New York: Brill, 1995.

Clark, Elizabeth. *Jerome, Chrysostom and Friends: Essays and Translations.* Studies in Women and Religion 2. Lewiston, NY: Edwin Mellen Press, 1979.

————. "Ascetic Renunciation and Feminine Advancement: A Paradox of Late Ancient Christianity." *Anglican Theological Review* 63 (1981): 240–57.

————. "Theory and Practice in Late Ancient Asceticism: Jerome, Chrysostom, and Augustine." *Journal of Feminist Studies in Religion* 5 (Fall 1989): 25–46.

————. *The Originist Controversy: The Cultural Construction of an Early Christian Debate.* Princeton: Princeton University Press, 1992.

————. *Reading Renunciation: Asceticism and Scripture in Early Christianity.* Princeton: Princeton University Press, 1999.

Clark, Lynn Schofield. "U.S. Adolescent Religious Identity, the Media, and the 'Funky' Side of Religion." Center for Mass Media Research, University of Colorado at Boulder, 1997.

————. *From Angels to Aliens: Teenagers, the Media, and the Supernatural.* New York: Oxford University Press, 2003.

Cohen, Mark R. "The Legal Position of Jews in Islam. Pp. 52–76 in *Under Crescent and Cross: The Jews in the Middle Ages.* Princeton: Princeton University Press, 1994.

Cohen, Martin S., trans. *The Shiur Komah: Liturgy and Theology in Pre-Kabbalistic Jewish Mysticism.* Lantham, MD: University Press of America, 1984.

Cohen, Abraham. *Everyman's Talmud: The Major Teachings of the Rabbinic Sages.* London: J. M. Dent and Sons, 1934.

Cohen, Shaye J. D. *From the Maccabees to the Mishnah.* Philadelphia: Westminster, 1987.

————. *The Beginnings of Jewishness Boundaries, Varieties, Uncertainties.* Berkeley: University of California Press, 1999.

Collins, Adela. *Cosmology and Eschatology in Jewish and Christian Apocalypticism.* Leiden/New York: Brill, 1996.

Collins, John J. *The Apocalyptic Vision of the Book of Daniel.* Harvard Semitic Monographs 16. Missoula, MT: Scholars Press, 1977.

————. "The Root of Immortality: Death in the Context of Jewish Wisdom." *Harvard Theological Review* 71 (1981): 177–92.

————. *Cosmology and Eschatology in Jewish and Christian Apocalypticism.* Leiden: Brill, 1996.

————. *The Apocalyptic Imagination: An Introduction to the Jewish Matrix of Christianity.* New York: MacMillan, 1998.

Collins, John J., and Michael Fishbone, eds. *Death, Ecstasy, and Other Worldly Journeys.* New York: SUNY Press, 1995.

Collins, John J., and G. W. E. Nickelsburg. *Ideal Figures in Ancient Judaism: Profiles and Paradigms.* Chico, CA: Scholars Press, 1980.

791

Colpe, Carsten. *Die Religionsgeschichtliche Schule: Darstellung und Kritik Ihres Bildes Vom Gnostischen Erlösermythus.* Göttingen: Vandenhoeck and Ruprecht, 1961.

———. "Syncretism." *ER.*

Colson, F. H., and C. H. Whitaker, trans. *Philo.* 10 vols. The Loeb Classics Series. Cambridge: Harvard University Press, 1929.

Coogan, M. D. *Stories from Ancient Canaan.* Louisville, KY: Westminster, 1978.

Cook, David. *Studies in Muslim Apocalyptic.* Princeton: Darwin, 2002.

Cook, Michael. *Muhammad.* New York: Oxford University Press, 1983.

———. *Studies in Muslim Apocalyptic.* Princeton: Darwin, 2002.

Cook, Stephen L. *Prophecy and Apocalypticism: The Postexilic Social Setting.* Minneapolis: Fortress Press, 1995.

Cooper, Alan. "Ps 24:7–10: Mythology and Exegesis." *JBL* 102:1 (1983).

Cooper, Alan, and Bernard Goldstein. "Exodus and Maṡṡòt in History and Tradition." *Maarav* 8 (1992): 15–37.

———. "The Cult of the Dead and the Theme of Entry Into the Land." *Biblical Interpretation* 1:3 (1993): 285–303.

———. "At the Entrance to the Tent: More Cultic Resonances in Biblical Narrative." *JBL* 116:2 (1997): 201–15.

Cooper, Jerrold S. "The Fate of Mankind: Death and Afterlife in Ancient Mesopotamia." Pp. 19–33 in *Death and Afterlife: Perspectives of World Religions.* Ed. Hiroshi Obayashi. New York. Praeger, 1992.

———. "Canaanite Religion." *ER* 3.

Cooper, John W. *Body, Soul and Life Everlasting: Biblical Anthropology and the Monism-Dualism Debate.* Grand Rapids: Eerdmans, 1989.

Cooper, Kate. *The Virgin and the Bride: Idealized Womanhood in Late Antiquity.* Cambridge: Harvard University Press, 1996.

Copenhaver, Brian P., ed. *Hermetica: The Greek Corpus Hermeticum and the Latin Asclepius in a New English Translation with Notes and Introduction.* Cambridge: Cambridge University Press, 1992.

Copleston, Frederic. *A History of Philosophy.* Greece and Rome 1. Mahwah, NJ: Paulist Press, 1946.

Corbin, Henry. *Cyclical Time and Ismaili Gnosis.* London: Routledge and Kegan Paul International, 1957.

———. *Temple and Contemplation.* Trans. Institute of Ismaili Studies and Islamic Publications. London: Routledge and Kegan Paul International, 1986.

Cornell, Vincent. "Fruit of the Tree of Knowledge: The Relationship Between Faith and Practice in Islam." Pp. 63–106 in *The Oxford History of Islam.* Ed. John L. Esposito. New York: Oxford University Press, 1999.

Crane, R. S. *The Languages of Criticism and the Structure of Poetry.* Toronto: University of Toronto Press, 1953.

Crone, Patricia, and Michael Cook. *Hagarism: The Making of the Islamic World.* Cambridge: Cambridge University Press, 1977.

Cross, Frank M. *Canaanite Myth and Hebrew Epic: Essays in the History of the Religion of Israel.* Cambridge: Harvard University Press, 1973.

Crossan, John D. *The Cross That Spoke: The Origins of the Passion Narrative.* San Francisco: Harper and Row, 1988.

———. *The Historical Jesus: The Life of a Mediterranean Jewish Peasant.* San Francisco: Harpers, 1993.

———. *Who Killed Jesus?: Exposing the Roots of Anti-Semitism in the Gospel Story of the Death of Jesus.* San Francisco: HarperSanFrancisco, 1995.

Crowne, Douglas P., and Avid Marlowe. *The Approval Motive: Studies in Evaluative Dependence.* New York: John Wiley and Son, 1967.

Crystal, David. *The Cambridge Encyclopedia of Language.* 2d ed. New York: Cambridge University Press, 1997.

Culianu, Ioan Petru. *Psychanodia I: A Survey of the Evidence of the Ascension of the Soul and Its Relevance.* Leiden: Brill, 1983.

———. *Expériences de l'Extase: Extase, ascension et récit visionnaire de l'hellénisme au moyen âge.* Intro. Mircea Eliade. Paris: Payot, 1984.

Cullman, Oscar, Harry A. Wolfson, et al. *Immortality and Resurrection: Death in the Western World: Two Conflicting Currents of Thought.* Ed. with intro. Krister Stendahl. New York: MacMillan, 1965.

Cumont, F. *The Mysteries of Mithras.* Paris, 1903. Reprint. New York, 1956.

———. *Astrology and Religion among the Greeks and romans.* Paris, 1912. Reprint. New York, 1960.

———. *Afterlife in Roman Paganism.* New Haven, 1922.

———. *The Proceedings of the First International Congress of Mithraic Studies.* Ed. J. Hinnels. Manchester, 1975.

Cuneo, Michael. *American Exorcism: Expelling Demons in the Land of Plenty.* New York: Doubleday, 2001.

Dahl, Nils A. "Cosmic Dimensions and Religious Knowledge (Eph. 3:18)." Pp. 57–75 in *Jesus and Paulus.* Festschrift fuer W. G. Kuemmel. Ed. E. Earle Ellis and E. Graesser. Goettingen: Vandenhoeck and Ruprecht, 1967.

———. *The Crucified Messiah.* Minneapolis: Augsburg, 1974.

Dahood, Mitchell. "Immortality in Proverbs 12:28." Biblica 41 (1960): 176–81.

———. *Psalms.* AB 16, 17, 17A. New York: Anchor Doubleday, 1965.

———. "The Ebla Tablets and Old Testament Theology." *Theology Digest* 27 (1979): 303–11.

Dalley, Stephanie. *Myths from Mesopotamia: Creation, the Flood, Gilgamesh and Others.* Oxford: Oxford University Press, 1989.

Damrosch, David. *The Narrative Covenant.* San Francisco: Harper, 1988.

Dan, J. "The Concept of Knowledge in the Shiur Komah." *Studies in Jewish Intellectual History Presented to Alexander Altmann.* Ed. S. Stein and R. Loewe. Birmingham: University of Alabama Press, 1979.

———. *Three Types of Ancient Jewish Mysticism.* Cincinnati: Judaic Studies Program, 1984.

DaSilva, Aldina. "Offrandes Allimentaires aux Mortes en Mesopotamie." *Religiologiques* 17 (Printemps 1998): 9–7.

Davies, Jon. *Death, Burial, and Rebirth in the Religions of Antiquity*. Religions in the First Christian Centuries. London and New York: Routledge, 1999.

Davies, Stevan L. *The Gospel of Thomas and Christian Wisdom*. New York: Seabury Press, 1983.

———. *Jesus the Healer: Possession, Trance, and the Origin of Christianity*. New York: Continuum, 1995.

Davila, James R. "The Hekhalot Literature and Shamanism." Pp. 767–89 in *Society of Biblical Literature 1994 Seminar Papers*. Atlanta: Scholars Press, 1994.

———. "4QMess Ar (4Q534) and Merkavah Mysticism." *Dead Sea Discoveries* 5 (1998): 367–81.

———. *Descenders in the Chariot*. Leiden: Brill, 2001.

Davis, Stephen T. *Death and the Afterlife*. New York: St. Martin's Press, 1989.

———. *Risen Indeed: Making Sense of the Resurrection*. Grand Rapids: Eerdmans, 1995.

———. "Physicalism and Resurrection." *Soul, Body, and Survival: Essays on the Metaphysics of Human Persons*. Ed. Kevin Corcoran, Ithaca and London: Cornell University Press, 2001.

Davis, Stephen, Daniel Kendall. *The Resurrection*. Oxford: Oxford University Press, 1997.

Dawkins, Richard. *The Selfish Gene*. New York: Oxford University Press, 1989.

———. "Viruses of the Mind." Pp. 13–27 in *Dennett and His Critics*. Ed. Bo Halbom. Oxford: Blackwell, 1993.

———. *River Out of Eden: A Darwinian View of Life*. New York: Basic Books, 1995.

Dean-Otting, Mary. *Heavenly Journeys: A Study of the Motif in Hellenistic Jewish Literature*. Judentum und Umwelt 8. Frankfort, New York: Peter Lang, 1984.

de Boer, Martinus. *The Defeat of Death: Apocalyptic Eschatology in 1 Corinthians 15 and Romans 5*. JSNT Supplement Series 22. Sheffield, England: JSOT Press, 1988.

DeConick, April D. *Seek to See Him: Ascent and Vision Mysticism in the Gospel of Thomas*. Leiden: Brill, 1996.

———. *Voices of the Mystics: Early Christian Discourse in the Gospels of John and Thomas and Other Ancient Christian Literature*. Sheffield: Sheffield Academic Press, 2001.

Delbanco, Andrew. *The Death of Satan: How Americans Have Lost the Sense of Evil*. New York: Farrar, Strauss, 1995.

Delumeau, Jean. *Mille Ans de Bonheur*. Librairie Arthème Fayard, 1995.

———. *Que Reste-t-Il du Paradis?* Librairie Arthème Fayard, 2000.

Denis, A. M. *Fragmenta Pseudepigraphorm quae Supersunt Graeca Una Cum Historicum et Auctorum Judaeorum Hellenistarum Fragmentis.* Leiden: Brill, 1970.

Dennett, Daniel C. *Consciousness Explained.* Boston: Little Brown and Co., 1991.

———. *Kinds of Minds: Towards an Understanding of Consciousness.* New York: Basic Books, 1996.

Dennis, T. J. "Gregory on the Resurrection of the Body." Pp. 55–80 in *The Easter Sermons of Gregory of Nyssa: Translation and Commentary.* Ed. and trans. A. Spira and C. Klock. Cambridge: Philadelphia Patristic Foundation, 1981.

Denny, Frederick. "Community and Salvation: The Meaning of the Ummah in the Qur'an." Ph.D. diss. University of Chicago, 1974.

Desjardins, Michel. *Sin in Valentinianism.* Atlanta: Scholars Press, 1990.

des Places, É., ed. *Oracles Chaldaiques.* Paris, 1971.

de Toqueville, Alexis. *Democracy in America.*

Dewart, Joanne E. McWilliam. *Death and Resurrection.* Message of the Fathers of the Church 22. Wilmington, DE: M. Glazier, 1986.

DeWeese, Devin. *Islamization and Native Religion in the Golden Horde: Baba Tükles and Conversion to Islam in Historical and Epic Tradition.* University Park: The Pennsylvania State University, 1994.

Dey, Lala K. K. *The Intermediary World and Patterns of Perfection in Philo and Hebrews.* SBL Dissertation Series. Missoula, MT: Scholars Press, 1975.

Diamond, Malcolm L. *Contemporary Philosophy and Religious Thought: An Introduction to the Philosophy of Religion.* New York: McGraw Hill, 1974.

Dodd, C. H. *The Bible and the Greeks.* London, 1935.

Dodds, E. R. *The Greeks and the Irrational.* Berkeley, 1951.

———, ed. and trans. *Proclus The Elements of Theology.* Oxford: Oxford University Press, 1963.

Donaldson, Terence L. *Paul and the Gentiles: Remapping the Apostle's Convictional World.* Minneapolis: Fortress, 1997.

Donner, Fred M. *Narratives of Islamic Origins: The Beginnings of Islamic Historical Writing.* Princeton: The Darwin Press, 1998.

Doran, Robert. "The Martyr: A Synoptic View of the Mother and Her Seven Sons." Pp. 189–222 in *Ideal Figures in Ancient Judaism.* Ed. W. E. Nickelsburg and John J. Collins. Septuagint and Cognate Studies 12. Chico, CA: Scholars Press, 1980.

Dorn, Louis Otto. "The Beatific Vision in Certain Psalms: An Investigation of Mitchell Dahood's Hypothesis." Ph.D. diss. Lutheran School of Theology, 1980.

Douglas, Mary. *Purity and Danger: An Analysis of Concepts of Pollution and Tabboo.* New York: Praeger, 1966.

———. "The Contempt of Ritual." *New Blackfriars* 49 (1968): 475–82, 528–35.

———. *Natural Symbols: Explorations in Cosmology.* New York: Random House, Vintage, 1973.

———. "Deciphering a Meal." Pp. 249–75 in *Implicit Meanings: Essays in Anthropology.* London: Routledge and Kagan Paul, 1975.

———. *Leviticus as Literature.* Oxford: Oxford University Press, 1999.

Droge, Arthur J., and James D. Tabor. *A Noble Death: Suicide and Martyrdom among Christians and Jews in Antiquity.* San Francisco: Harper, 1992.

Duchesne-Guillemin, Jacques. *The Hymns of Zarathustra.* Boston: Beacon Press, 1952.

———. *Symbols and Values in Zoroastrianism, Their Survival and Renewal.* Religious Perspectives 15. New York: Harper and Row, 1966.

Dunn, James D. G. *Jesus and the Spirit: A Study of the Religious and Charismatic Experience of Jesus in the First Christians and Reflected in the New Testament.* Philadelphia: Westminster, 1970.

———. *Jesus and the Spirit: A Study of the Religions and Charismatic Experience of Jesus and the First Christians as Reflected in the New Testament.* Philadelphia: Fortress, 1975.

———. *Baptism in the Holy Spirit: A Re-Examination of the New Testament Teaching on the Gift of the Spirit in Relation to Pentacostalism Today.* Philadelphia: Westminster, 1977.

Edmunds, R. David. *The Shawnee Prophet.* Lincoln and London: University of Nebraska Press, 1983.

Einbinder, Susan L. *Beautiful Death: Jewish Poetry and Martyrdom in Medieval France.* Princeton: Princeton University Press, 2002.

Eisenman, Robert. *Maccabees, Zadokites, Christians and Qumran: A New Hypothesis of Qumran Origins.* Studia Post-biblica 34. Leiden: Brill, 1993.

Elbogen, Ismar. *Jewish Liturgy: A Comprehensive History.* Trans. Raymond Scheindlin. Philadelphia: JPS, 1993.

Eliade, Mircea. *Shamanism: Archaic Techniques of Ectasy.* Trans. Willard R. Trask. Princeton: Princeton University Press, 1958.

———. *Yoga: Immortality and Freedom.* Trans. Willard R. Trask. Princeton: Princeton University Press, 1958.

———. *Zalmoxis, the Vanishing God.* Chicago, 1972.

Elior, Rachel. *Hekhaloth Zutartey.* Jerusalem Studies in Jewish Thought. Jerusalem, 1982.

———. *The Paradoxical Ascent to God: The Kabbalistic Theosophy of Habad Hasidism.* Trans. Jeffrey M. Green. Albany: SUNY Press, 1993.

———. *The Three Temples.* Oxford: Littman Library, 2004.

Elm, Susanna. *'Virgins of God:' The Making of Asceticism in Late Antiquity.* Oxford: Clarendon Press, 1994.

El-Saleh, Soubhi. *La Vie Future Selon le Coran.* Ed. and trans. Étienne Gilson and Louis Gardet. Études Musulmanes. Paris: Librairie philosophique J. Vrin, 1986.

Emerson, Steve. *American Jihad: The Terrorists Living Among Us*. New York: Simon and Schuster, 2002.

Empson, William. *Seven Types of Ambiguity*. New York: New Directions, 1947.

Engberg-Pedersen, Troels. *Paul and the Stoics*. Edinburgh: T and T Clark, 2000.

Enslin, Morton S. *Reapproaching Paul*. Philadelphia: Westminster, 1972.

Erman, Adolf. A Handbook of Egyptian Religion. Trans. A. S. Griffith. London: Archibald Constable and Co., 1907.

———. *The Ancient Egyptians: A Sourcebook of Their Writings*. Trans. Aylward Blackman New York: Harper Torchbooks, 1966.

Eskola, Timo. *Messiah and the Throne: Jewish Merkabah Mysticism and Early Christian Exaltation Discourse*. WUNT 2:142. Ed. Jörg Frey, Martin Hengel, and Otfried Hofius. Göttingen: Mohr (Paul Siebeck), 2001.

Esposito, John. *Islam: The Straight Path*. New York: Oxford University Press, 1998.

Evans, C. A. "The Colossian Mystics." *Biblica* 63 (1982): 188–205.

Evans, C. F. *Resurrection and the New Testament*. London: SCM, 1968.

Evans, Ernest. *Tertullian's Treatise on the Resurrection*. London: SPCK, 1960.

Festugière, André Jean. *Personal Religion among the Greeks*. Berkeley: University of California Press, 1960.

Finamore, John F. *Iamblichus and the Theory of the Vehicle of the Soul*. American Philological Association American Classical Studies. Chico, CA: Scholars Press, 1985.

Fine, Lawrence. "Contemplative Death in the Jewish Mystical Tradition." Pp. 92–106 in *Sacrificing the Self: Perspectives on Martyrdom and Religion*. Ed. Margaret Cormack. New York: Oxford University Press, 2002.

Finkelstein, Israel, and Neil Asher Silberman. *The Bible Unearthed: Archeology's New Vision of Ancient Israel and the Origin of Its Sacred Texts*. New York: The Free Press, 2001.

Firestone, Reuben. *Jihad: The Origin of Holy War in Islam*. New York and Oxford: Oxford University Press, 1999.

Flanagan, Owen, Güven Güzeldere, and Ned Block. *The Nature of Consciousness: Philosophical Debates*. Cambridge, MA: MIT Press, 1998.

Fletcher-Louis, Crispin H. T. *Luke–Acts: Angels, Christology, and Soteriology*. Tübingen: Mohr (Paul Siebeck), 1997.

———. *All the Glory of Adam: Liturgical Anthropology in the Dead Sea Scrolls*. Leiden: Brill, 2002.

Florian, V., and S. Kravetz. "Fear of Personal Death: Attribution, Structure and Relation to Religious Belief." *Journal of Personality and Social Psychology* 44 (1983): 600–607.

Foley, H. P., ed. *The Homeric "Hymn to Demeter": Translation, Commentary, and Interpretive Essays.* Princeton: Princeton University Press, 1993.

Foltz, Richard C. *Religions of the Silk Road: Overland Trade and Cultural Exchange from Antiquity to the Fifteenth Century.* New York: St. Martin's Press, 1999.

Forbes, Christopher. "Comparison, Self Praise, and Irony: Paul's Boasting and the Conventions of Hellenistic Rhetoric." *NTS* 32 (1986): 1–30.

Forman, Werner, and Stephen Quirke. *Hieroglyphs and the Afterlife in Ancient Egypt.* Norman: University of Oklahoma Press, 1996.

Foschini, Bernard. "Those Who Are Baptized for the Dead, 1 Cor. 15:29." *CBQ* 12 (1950): 260–76, 379–88.

———. "Those Who Are Baptized for the Dead, 1 Cor. 15:29." *CBQ* 13 (1951): 46–78, 172–98, 276–83.

Fossing, P. *Catalogue of the Antique Engraved Gems and Cameos.* Copenhagen, 1929.

Fossum, Jarl. "Jewish Christian Christology and Jewish Mysticism." *VC* 37 (1983): 260–87.

———. *The Name of God and the Angel of the Lord: Samaritan and Jewish Concepts of Intermediation and the Origin of Gnosticism.* WUNT 1:36. Tübingen: Mohr (Paul Siebeck), 1985.

———. "Ascensio, Metamorphosis: The 'Transfiguration' of Jesus in the Synoptic Gospels." Pp. 71–94 in *The Image of the Invisible God: Essays on the Influence of Jewish Mysticism on Early Christology.* Novum Testamentum et Orbis Antiquus 30. Göttingen: Vandenhoeck and Ruprecht, 1995.

———. *The Image of the Invisible God: Essays on the Influence of Jewish Mysticism on Early Christology.* Göttingen: Vandenhoeck and Ruprecht, 1995.

Foster, Benjamin R., ed. and trans. *The Epic of Gilgamesh.* New York, Norton, 2001.

Foster, John L., trans. "The Hymn to Aten: Akhenaten Worships the Sole God." *Echoes of Egyptian Voices: An Anthology of Ancient Egyptian Poetry.* Norman: University of Oklahoma Press, 1992.

Foucault, Michel. *Language, Counter-Memory, Practice: Selected Essays and Interviews.* Ed. and trans. D. F. Bouchard. Ithaca: Cornell University Press, 1977.

———. *Power/Knowledge: Selected Interviews and Other Writings. 1972–1977.* Ed. and trans. Colin Gordon et al. New York: Pantheon, 1980.

Foulkes, David. *The Psychology of Sleep.* New York: Charles Scribner's Sons, 1966.

———. *In Search of Dreams: Results of Experimental Dream Research.* Albany: SUNY Press, 1996.

———. *Children's Dreaming and the Development of Consciousness.* Cambridge: Harvard University Press, 1999.

Fowden, Garth. *The Egyptian Hermes: A Historical Approach to the Late Pagan Mind.* Princeton: Princeton University Press, 1993.

Fox, Michael V. *The Song of Songs and the Ancient Egyptian Love Songs.* Madison: University of Wisconsin Press, 1985.

Fox, Robin Lane. "Living Like Angels." Pp. 336–74 in *Pagans and Christians.* New York: Alfred A. Knopf, 1987.

Francis, Fred O. "Humility and Angelic Worship in Col. 2:18." *Studia theologica* 16 (1962): 109–34.

Francis, Fred. O., and Wayne Meeks. "Conflict at Colossae: A Problem in the Interpretation of Early Christianity Illustrated by Selected Modern Studies." *Sources for Biblical Study.* Vol. 4. Missoula, MT: Scholars Press, 1975.

Frank, P. Suso. *Angelikos Bios: Begriffsanalytische und begriffsgeschichtliche Untersuchung zum 'engelgleichen Leben' im frühen Mönchstum.* Beiträge zur Geschichte des Alten Mönchtums und des Benediktinerordens 26. München: Aschendorff, 1964.

Fredriksen, Paula. "Beyond the Body/Soul Dichotomy: Augustine on Paul Against the Manichees and Pelagians." *Recherches Augustiniennes* 23 (1988): 87–114.

———. "Vile Bodies: Paul and Augustine on the Resurrection of the Flesh." Pp. 75–87 in *Biblical Hermeneutics in Historical Perspective Studies in Honor of Karlfried Froehlich on His Sixtieth Birthday.* Ed. Mark S. Burrows and Paul Rorem. Grand Rapids: Eerdmans, 1991.

Freed, Rita E., and Yvonne J. Markowitz. *Pharaohs of the Sun: Akehnaten, Nefertiti, Tutankhamen.* Boston: Museum of Fine Arts, 1999.

Freedman, D. N., and F. M. Cross. *Studies in Ancient Yahwistic Poetry.* Grand Rapids: Eerdmans, 1997.

Freedman, Harry. "Academy on High." EncJud 2.

Frend, W. H. C. *Martyrdom and Persecution in the Early Church: A Study of a Conflict from the Maccabees to Donatus.* Grand Rapids: Baker Books, 1981.

Frickel, J. "Gnosis." Pp. 413–35 in *Die Orientalischen Religionen im Roemerreich.* Ed. M. J. Vermaseren. Leiden: Brill, 1981.

Friedman, Thomas L. *Longitudes and Attitudes: Exploring the World after September 11.* New York: Farrar, Strauss, Geroux, 2002.

Frost, Stanley B. *Old Testament Apocalyptic.* London: Epworth Press, 1951.

Frymer-Kensky. "The Marginalization of the Goddess." Pp. 95–108 in *A Gilgamesh Reader.* Ed. John Maier. Wauconda, IL: Bolchazy-Carducci, 1977.

Fuchs, Ester. *Mayors and Money.* Chicago: University of Chicago Press, 1992.

Fuller, R. H. *The Formation of the Resurrection Narratives.* New York: Macmillan, 1971.

Gadd. *Revue d'assyriologie et d'archéologie orientale* 31. Paris, 1933.

Gager, John. *Kingdom and Community: The Social World of Early Christianity.* Englewood Cliffs, NJ: Prentice Hall, 1975.

———. "Body Symbols and Social Rality: Resurrection, Incarnation, and Asceticism in Early Christianity." *Religion* 12 (1982): 345–64.

———. *Reinventing Paul.* New York: Oxford University Press, 2000.

Gallup, George Jr., with William Proctor. *Adventures in Immortality.* New York: McGraw Hill, 1982.

Gallup, George Jr., and James Castelli. *The People's Religion: American Faith in the 90's.* New York: MacMillan, 1989.

Gardiner, A. H. *The Attitude of the Ancient Egyptians to Death and the Dead.* Cambridge, 1935.

Gardner, John, and John Maier, trans. *Gilgamesh Translated from the Sin Leqi Unninni Version.* New York: Vantage, 1984.

Gardner-Smith, P. *The Narratives of the Resurrection.* London: Methuen, 1926.

Garelli, P. "Cuneiform Texts from Cappadocian Tablets (CCT) V." *JSS* 3 (1958): 298–301.

Garland, Robert. *The Greek Way of Death.* Ithaca: Cornell University Press, 1985.

Garrett, Susan. *The Demise of the Devil.* Minneapolis: Fortress, 1989.

Gatch, Milton McCormick. *Death Meaning and Mortality in Christian Thought and Contemporary Culture.* New York: Seabury Press, 1969.

Gaventa, Beverly. *From Darkness to Light: Aspects of Conversion in the New Testament.* Philadelphia: Fortress, 1986.

Geertz, Clifford. *The Interpretation of Cultures.* New York: Basic Books, 1973.

Geller, Stephen A. "Some Sound and Word Plays in the First Tablet of the Old Babylonian *Atramhasis* Epic." Pp. 63–70 in *The Frank Talmage Memorial Volume.* Ed. Barry Walfish. Haifa: Haifa University Press and Boston: University Press of New England in Association with Brandeis University Press, 1993.

George, Andrew R. "Observations on a Passage in 'Inanna's Descent.' " *Journal of Cuneiform Studies* 37 (1985): 109–13.

———. *The Epic of Gilgamesh: A New Translation.* New York: Barnes and Noble, 1999.

Georgi, D. "Der Vorpaulinische Hymnus Phil. 2:6–11." Pp. 263–93 in *Zeit und Geschichte. Dankesgabe an Rudolf Bultmann.* Ed. E. Dinkler. Tuebingen: Mohr, 1964.

Al-Ghazzali. *The Precious Pearl.* Trans. Jane I. Smith. Missoula, MT: Scholars Press, 1979.

Gieschen, Charles. "Angelomorphic Christology: Antecedents and Early Evidence." Arbeiten zur Geschichte des Antiken Judenthums und des Urchristentums 42. Leiden: Brill, 1998.

Giller, Pinhas. *The Enlightened Will Shine: Symbolization and Theurgy in the Later Strata of the Zohar.* Albany: SUNY Press, 1993.

Gillman, Neil. *The Death of Death: Resurrection and Immortality in Jewish Thought.* Woodstock, VT: Jewish Lights, 1997.

Ginzberg, Louis. *The Legends of the Jews.* 7 vols. Philadelphia: Jewish Publication Society, 1922–1926.

Gleason, Randall C. "Angels and the Eschatology of Heb. 1–2." *NTS* 49:1 (2003): 90–107.

Gnoli, Gherardo. "Ateshgah." Trans. Roger DeGaris. *ER* 1.

———. "Zoroastrianism." *ER* 15.

Goldberg, Jeffrey. "In the Party of God." *The New Yorker,* 14 and 28 October 2002.

Goldenberg, Robert. "Bound Up in the Bond of Life: Death and Afterlife in the Jewish Tradition." Pp. 97–108 in *Death and Afterlife: Perspectives of World Religions.* New York: Praeger, 1992.

Goldstein, Jonathan. *1 and 2 Maccabees.* AB 41, 41A. New York: Doubleday, 1995.

Goodacre, Mark. *The Case Against Q: Studies in Marcan Priority and the Synoptic Problem.* Harrisburg, PA: Trinity Press, 2001.

Goodenough, Erwin R. *By Light, Light: The Mystical Gospel of Hellenistic Judaism.* New Haven: Yale University Press, 1935.

———. *Jewish Symbols in the Greco-Roman Period.* New York: Bollingen Foundation, 1964.

———. *An Introduction to Philo Judaeus.* Lanham, MD: University Press of America, 1986.

———. "Psychopomps." *Jewish Symbols in the Greco-Roman Period.* Ed. Jacob Neusner. Lawrencevill, NJ: Princeton University Press, 1987.

Goodman, Felicitas D. *Ecstasy, Ritual and Alternate Reality.* Bloomington: Indiana University Press, 1988.

Gottschalk, H. B. *Heraclides of Pontus.* New York: Oxford University Press, 1998.

Gottsch, John. "Mutation, Selection, and Vertical Transmission of Theistic Memes in Religious Canons." *Journal of Memetics: Evolutionary Models of Information Transmission* 5 (2001): 1–25. http://jomemit.cfpm.org/2001/vol5/gottsch-jd.html.

Goulder, Michael, and Alan F. Segal. "Transformation and Afterlife." Pp. 111–52 in *The Gospels According to Michael Goulder: A North American Response.* Ed. Christopher A. Rollston. Harrisburg, PA: Trinity Press International, 2002.

Grant, R. M., and H. H. Graham. "1 Clement." In *The Apostolic Fathers: A New Translation and Commentary.* Vol. 2. New York: Thomas Nelson and Sons, 1965.

Gray, Francine du Plessix. "The Work of Mourning." *The American Scholar,* Summer 2000.

Gray, Rebecca. *Prophetic Figures in Late Second Temple Jewish Palestine: The Evidence from Josephus.* New York: Oxford University Press, 1993.

Greely, Andrew M. *Religious Change in America.* Cambridge: Harvard University Press, 1989.

Greeley, Andrew M., and Michael Hout. "Americans Increasing Belief in Life After Death: Religious Competition and Acculturation." *American Sociological Review* 66 (1999).

Green, Hannah. *Little Saint.* New York: Random House, 2000.

Greenblatt, Stephen. *Hamlet in Purgatory.* Princeton: Princeton University Press, 2001.

Grey, John. *Near Eastern Mythology: Mesopotamia, Syria, Palestine.* London: Hamllyn, 1969.

Greyson, B. "Reduced Death Threat in Near-Death Experiences." *Death Studies* 16 (1992): 523–36.

Griffiths, J. Gwyn. *Apuleius of Madauros, The Isis-Book (Metamorphoses Book II).* EPRO 39. Leiden: Brill, 1975.

Grim, John. *The Shaman: Patterns of Siberian and Ojibway Healing.* Civilization of the American Indian Series 165. Norman: University of Oklahoma Press, 1983.

Gruenwald, Ithmar. *Apocalyptic and Merkabah Mysticism.* Leiden-Cologne: Brill, 1979.

Guthrie, W. K. C. *Orpheus and Greek Religion: A Study of the Orphic Movement.* New York: W. W. Norton and Company, 1966.

Halivni, David Weiss. *Peshat and Derash: Plain and Applied Meaning in Rabbinic Exegesis.* Oxford: Oxford University Press, 1991.

Hallo, William W. "Lamentations and Prayers in Sumer and Akkad." *CANE* 3: 1883–93.

Hallote, Rachel S. *Death, Burial, and Afterlife in the Biblical World.* Chicago: Ivan R. Dee, 2001.

Halm, Heinz. *Die islamische Gnosis: Die Extremische Schia und die Alawiten.* Zurich: Artemis, 1982.

Halperin, David. *The Merkabah in Rabbinic Literature.* New Haven: American Oriental Society, 1980.

———. *The Faces of the Chariot: Early Jewish Responses to Ezekiel's Vision.* Tuebingen: Mohr, 1988.

———. "Hekhalot and Mir'aj: Observations of the Heavenly Journey in Judaism and Islam." Pp. 265–84 in *Death, Ecstasy, and Other Worldly Journeys.* Ed. John J. Collins and Michael Fishbane. Albany: SUNY Press, 1995.

Hanson, John S. "Dreams and Visions in the Graeco-Roman World and Early Christianity." *ANRW* 2.23.2 (1980): 1395–427.

Harmatta, Janos. "Religions in the Kushan Empire." *History of the Civilizations of Central Asia*. Vol. 2. Paris: UNESCO, 1994.

Harris, Jay. " 'Fundamentalism: Objections from a Modern Jewish Historian." Pp. 137–74 in *Fundamentalism and Gender*. Ed. John Stratton Hawley. New York: Oxford University Press, 1994.

Harris, Rivkah. "Images of Women in the Gilgamesh Epic." Pp. 79–94 in *A Gilgamesh Reader*. Ed. John Maier. Wauconda, IL: Bolchazy-Carducci, 1997.

Harris, W. Hall III. *The Descent of Christ: Ephesians 4:7–11 and Traditional Hebrew Imagery*. Leiden: Brill, 1996.

Harrison, J. *Prolegomena to the Study of Greek Religion*. Trans. G. Murray. 3d ed. New York: Meridian Books, 1955.

Hartman, Lars. *Prophecy Interpreted: The Formation of Some Jewish Apocalyptic Texts and of the Eschatological Discourse Mark 13 Par*. Lund, 1966.

Hasker, William. *The Emergent Self*. Ithaca: Cornell University Press, 1999.

Hawting, Gerald. *The First Dynasty of Islam: The Umayyad Caliphate A.D. 661–750*. Carbondale and Edwardsville: Southern Illinois University Press, 1987.

Head, Constance. *The Emperor Julian*. Boston: Twayne Publishers, 1976.

Heidel, A. *The Gilgamesh Epic and Old Testament Parallels*. Chicago: University of Chicago Press, 1949.

Heinemann, Joseph, ed. *Literature of the Synagogue*. New York: Behrmann House, 1975.

Helck, Wolfgang. *Die Lehre für König Merikare*. Wiesbaden, 1977.

Hengel, Martin. "Hymn and Christology." Pp. 173–97 in *Studia Biblica*. Ed. E. A. Livingstone, 1972.

———. *The Atonement: The Origins of the Doctrine in the New Testament*. Trans. John Bowden. Philadelphia: Fortress, 1981.

———. *Judaism and Hellenism: Studies in Their Encounter in Palestine during the Early Hellenistic Period*. Philadelphia: Fortress, 1981.

———. *The Pre-Christian Paul*. Philadelphia: Trinity Press International, 1991.

Hennecke, Edgar. *New Testament Apocrypha*. Ed. Wilhelm Schneemelcher. Trans. R. McL. Wilson. 2 vols. London: Lutterworth Press, 1963.

Hick, John. *Arguments for the Existence of God*. Philosophy of Religion Series. New York: Seabury Press, 1971.

———. *Death and Eternal Life*. San Francisco: Harper and Row, 1980.

Himmelfarb, Martha. *Tours of Hell: An Apocalyptic Form in Jewish and Christian Literature*. Philadelphia: Fortress Press, 1985.

———. *Ascent to Heaven in Jewish and Christian Apocalypses*. New York: Oxford University Press, 1993.

Hirsch, H. "Gott der Väter." *Archiv für Orientforsehung* 21 (1966): 56–76.

Hodel-Hönes, Sigrid. *Life and Death in Ancient Egypt: Schenes from Private Tombs in New Kingdom Thebes*. Trans. David Warburton. Ithaca and London: Cornel University Press, 2000.

Hollady, Carl R. "The Portrait of Moses in Ezekiel the Tragedian." *SBL Seminar Papers.* Missoula: Scholars Press, 1976.

———. *Theios Aner in Hellenistic Judaism.* SBL Dissertation Series 40. Missoula, MT: Scholars Press, 1977.

Holleman, Joost. "Resurrection and Parousia: A Tradito-Historical Study of Paul's Eschatology in 1 Cor 15:20–23." Ph.D. Diss. Leiden, 1995.

Hopkins, Keith, and Melinda Letts. "Death in Rome." *Death and Renewal.* Cambridge: Cambridge University Press, 1983.

Hornung, Erik. *Conceptions of God in Ancient Egypt: The One and the Many.* Trans. John Baines. Ithaca: Cornell University Press, 1982.

———. *Agyptische Unterweltsbucher.* Ed. Eingel Ubers and Eric von Hornung. Zurich, Munchen: Artemis-Verlag, 1972. Reprint, 1994.

———. "Ancient Egyptian Religious Iconography." *CANE* 3: 1711–30.

———. *Akhenaten and the Religion of Light.* Trans. David Lorton. Ithaca: Cornell University Press, 1999.

———. *The Ancient Egyptian Books of the Afterlife.* Trans. David Lorton. Ithaca: Cornell University Press, 1999.

Horsley, Richard. "Pneumatikos Versus Psychikos: Distinctions of Spiritual Status Among the Corinthians." *HTR* 69 (1976): 269–88.

———. *Jesus and the Spiral of Violence:* Popular Jewish Resistance in Roman Palestine. San Francisco: Harper and Row, 1987.

Horton, F. J. *The Melchizedek Tradition: A Critical Examination of the Sources to the Fifth Century A.D. and in the Epistle to the Hebrews.* Cambridge: Cambridge University Press, 1976.

Hultgård, Anders. "Persian Apocalypticism." *The Encyclopedia of Apocalypticism.* Vol. 1: *The Origins of Apocalypticism in Judaism and Christianity.* Ed. John J. Collins. New York: Continuum, 1998.

Humphreys, R. S. *Islamic History—A Framework for Inquiry.* Princeton: Princeton University Press, 1991.

Hung, Luu, and Nguyen Trung Dung. "Other Journeys of the Dead." Pp. 198–215 in *Vietnam: Journeys of Body, Mind, and Spirit.* Ed. Nguyen Van Huy and Laurel Kendall. University of California Press, American Museum of Natural History, Vietnam Museum of Ethnology, 2003.

Hurtado, Larry. "The Binitarian Shape of Early Christian Devotion and Ancient Jewish Monotheism." Pp. 371–91 in *SBL 1985 Seminar Papers.* Atlanta: Scholars Press, 1985.

———. *One God, One Lord: Early Christian Devotion and Ancient Jewish Monotheism.* Philadelphia: Fortress, 1988.

———. *Lord Jesus Christ: Devotion to Jesus in Earliest Christianity.* Grand Rapids: Eerdmans, 2003.

Husser, Jean-Marie. *Dreams and Dream Narratives in the Biblical World.* Sheffield: Sheffield University Press, 1996.

Huy, Nguyen Van, and Nguyen Anh Ngoc. "The Village: God's Journey." Pp. 216–37 in *Vietnam: Journeys of Body, Mind, and Spirit.* Ed. Nguyen

Van Huy, and Laurel Kendall. Berkeley: University of California Press, American Museum of Natural History, Vietnam Museum of Ethnology, 2003.

Idel, Moshe. *Kabbalah: New Perspectives*. New Haven: Yale University Press, 1988.

Idleman, Jane, and Yvonne Yazbeck Haddad Smith. *The Islamic Understanding of Death and Resurrection*. Albany: SUNY Press, 1981.

Ishaq, Ibn. *Life of Muhammad*. Trans. A. Guillaume. New York: Oxford University Press, 1955.

Ismar, Elbogen. *Jewish Liturgy: A Comprehensive History*. Ed. Raymond P. Scheindlin. Philadelphia: Jewish Publication Society, 1993.

Izre'el, Shlomo. *Adapa and the South Wind: Language Has the Power of Life and Death*. Winona Lake, IN: Eisenbrauns, 2001.

Jacobsen, Thorkild. "The Investiture and Anointing of Adapa in Heaven." *American Journal of Semitic Languages and Literatures* 46 (1929–1930): 201–3.

———. *The Sumerian King List*. Chicago: University of Chicago Press, 1939.

———. "Mysticism and Apocalyptic in Ezekiel's Exagoge." *Illinois Classical Studies* 6 (1981): 272–93.

Jacobson, Howard, ed. *The Exagoge of Ezekiel*. Cambridge: Cambridge University Press, 1983.

Jamblique [Iamblichus]. *Les Mystères d'Egypte*. Ed. and trans. É. des Places. Paris, 1966.

———. *Oracles Chaldaiques*. Ed. and trans. É. des Places. Paris, 1971.

James, William. *The Varieties of Religious Experience: A Study in Human Nature*. New York: The Modern Library, 1922.

———. *The Varieties of Religious Experience*. New York: Collier Books, 1961.

Janowitz, Naomi. *The Poetics of Ascent: Theories of Language in a Rabbinic Text*. Albany: SUNY Press, 1989.

———. *Icons of Power*. Magic in History. University Park: The Pennsylvania State University Press, 2003.

Jansen, Karl L. R. "Using Ketamine to Induce the Near-Death Experience." *Yearbook for Ethnomedicine and the Study of Consciousness* 4 (1955): 55–81.

Jarvie, I. C. *The Revolution in Anthropology*. New York: Humanities Press, 1964.

Jaynes, Julian. *The Origin of Consciousness in the Breakdown of the Bicameral Mind*. Boston: Houghton-Mifflin, 1976.

Jervell, Jakob. *Imago Dei*. Göttingen: Vandenhöck and Ruprecht, 1960.

Jewett, Robert. *A Chronology of Paul's Life*. Philadelphia: Fortress Press, 1979.

Johnston, Philip S. *Shades of Sheol: Death and the Afterlife in the Old Testament*. Downers Grove, IL: InterVarsity Press, 2002.

Johnson, Sarah Iles. *Hekate Soteira: A Study of Hekate's Roles in the Chaldean*

Oracles and Related Literature. American Classical Studies 21. Atlanta: Scholars Press, 1990.

———. "Rising to the Occasion: Theurgic Ascent in Its Cultural Milieu." Pp. 165–94 in *Envisioning Magic: A Princeton Seminar and Symposium.* Ed. Peter Schaefer and Hans G. Kippenberg. HR 75. Leiden: Brill, 1997.

———. *Restless Dead: Encounters Between the Living and the Dead in Ancient Greece.* Berkeley: University of California Press, 1999.

Jones, Lawrence Patrick. "A Case Study in 'Gnosticism:' Religious Responses to Slavery in the Second Century CE." Ph.D. diss. New York: Columbia University, 1988.

Juergensmeyer, Mark. *Terror in the Mind of God: The Global Rise of Religious Violence.* Berkeley: University of California Press, 2000. 2d ed., 2001.

Kaiser, Otto, ed. "Isaiah 13–39." Pp. 173–233 in *The Old Testament Library.* Trans. R. A. Wilson. Philadelphia: Westminster, 1974.

Katz, Steven. *Mysticism and Philosophical Analysis.* New York: Oxford University Press, 1983.

Kee, Howard Clark. "The Transfiguration in Mark: Epiphany or Apocalyptic Vision?" *Understanding the Sacred Text.* Festschrift for Morton Enslin. Ed. John Reichman. Valley Forge, PA: Judson Press, 1972.

———. "Christology in Mark's Gospel." Pp. 187–208 in *Judaisms and Their Messiahs at the Turn of the Christian Era.* Ed. Jacob Neusner and William S. Green. Cambridge: Cambridge University Press, 1987.

Keel, Othmar. *The Symbolism of the Biblical World: Ancient Near Eastern Iconography and the Book of Psalms.* Trans. Timothy J. Hallett. New York: Seabury Press, 1978.

Keel, Othmar, and Christoph Uehlinger. *Gods, Goddesses, and Images of God in Ancient Israel.* Trans. Thomas H. Trapp. Minneapolis: Fortress, 1998.

Kennedy, Charles A. "Dead, Cult of the." *Anchor Bible Dictionary.* New York: Doubleday, 1992.

Kepel, Gilles. *The Revenge of God: The Resurgence of Islam, Christianity, and Judaism in the M odern World.* Trans. Alan Braley. University Park: Pennsylvania State University, 1994.

———. *Jihad: The Trail of Political Islam.* Cambridge: Harvard University Press, 2002.

Kerenyi, Carl. "Eleusis: Archetypal Image of Mother and Daughter." Bollingen Series 65:4. Trans. Ralph Manheim. Princeton: Princeton Universiy Press, 1967.

Kilborne, Benjamin. "Dreams." ER.

Kim, Seyoon. *The Origin of Paul's Gospel.* WUNT 2:4 (1981): Tübingen.

———. *Paul and the New Perspective: Second Thoughts on the Origin of Paul's Gospel.* Tübingen: Mohr (Paul Siebeck), 2002.

King, Karen L. *What Is Gnosticism?* Cambridge: Harvard University Press, 2003.

Kittel, G., ed. *The Theological Dictionary of the New Testament*. 10 vols. Grand Rapids: Eerdmans, 1976.

Klawans, Jonathan. *Impurity and Sin in Ancient Judaism*. New York: Oxford University Press, 2000.

Klimkeit, Hans Joachim. *Gnosis on the Silk Road: Gnostic Parables, Hymns, and Prayers from Central Asia*. New York: HarperCollins, 1993.

Kloppenborg, John S. *The Formation of Q: Trajectories in Ancient Wisdom Collections*. Philadelphia: Fortress Press, 1987.

Kluger, Sivkah Schärf. *The Archetypal Significance of Gilgamesh: A Modern Ancient Hero*. Eisiedeln, Switzer.: Daimon, 1991.

Knibb, M. A. *The Ethiopic Book of Enoch*. Oxford: Oxford University Press, 1978.

———. "The Date of the Parables of Enoch: A Critical Review." *NTS* 25 (1979): 345–59.

Knight, William Francis Jackson. *Elysion: On Ancient Greek and Roman Beliefs Concerning a Life After Death*. Intro. G. Wilson Knight. London: Rider, 1970.

Knox, John. " 'Fourteen Years Later:' A Note on the Pauline Chronology." *Journal of Religion* 16 (1936): 341–49.

———. "The Pauline Chronology." *JBL* 58 (1939): 15–29.

———. *Chapters in the Life of Paul*. New York and Nashville: Abingdon, 1950.

Kobelski, P. J. *Melchizedek and Melchiresa*. Washington, DC: Washington Biblical Association, 1981.

Kotwal, Firoze M., and James Boyd, eds. and trans. *A Guide to the Zoroastrian Religion*. Studies in World Religions 3. Chico, CA: Scholars Press, 1982.

Kraemer, Ross Shepard. "The Conversion of Women to Ascetic Forms of Christianity." *Signs* 6 (1980–1981): 298–307.

———, ed. *Maenads, Martyrs, Matrons, Monastics: A Sourcebook on Women's Religions in the Greco-Roman World*. Philadelphia: Fortress Press, 1988.

———. *When Aseneth Met Joseph: A Late Antique Tale of the Biblical Patriarch and His Egyptian Wife, Reconsidered*. New York: Oxford University Press, 1998.

Kraemer, Ross Shepard, and Mary Rose D'Angelo. *Women and Christian Origins*. New York: Oxford University Press, 1999.

Kraus, W. "Vergils Vierte Ekloge: Ein Kritisches Hypomnmea." *ANRW* 2.31.1 (1980): 604–45.

Kreyenbroek, G. *Sroaŝa in the Zoroatrian Tradition*. Leiden: Brill, 1985.

Kübler-Ross, Elisabeth. *On Death and Dying: What the Dying Have to Teach Doctors, Nurses, Clergy, and Their Own Families*. New York: Collier Macmillan, 1969.

Kuhn, H. B. "The Angelology of the Non-Canonical Apocalypses." *JBL* 67 (1948): 217–32.

Kurzman, Charles, ed. *Liberal Islam: A Sourcebook.* New York: Oxford University Press, 1998.

Kvanvig, Helge S. *Roots of Apocalyptic: The Mesopotamian Background of the Enoch Figure and the Son of Man.* Neukirchen-Vluyn: Neukirchener Verlag, 1988.

Lachs, Samuel. *A Rabbinic Commentary on the New Testament: The Gospels of Matthew, Mark, and Luke.* Hoboken, NJ: KTAV Publishing, 1987.

Lake, Kirsopp. *The Historical Evidence for the Resurrection of Jesus Christ.* London: Williams and Norgate, 1907.

Lambert, W. G. "Myth and Mythmaking in Sumer and Akkad." *CANE* 3: 1825–36.

Lampe, Peter. "Paul's Concept of a Spiritual Body." Pp. 103–14 in *Resurrection: Theological and Scientific Assessments.* Ed. Ted Peters, Robert John Russell, and Michael Welker. Grand Rapids, Eerdmans, 2002.

Lantennari, V. *Religions of the Oppressed: A Study of Messianic Cults.* New York: Knopf, 1963.

Lapp, Paul W. "If a Man Die, Shall He Live Again?" *Perspective* 9 (1968).

Lattimore, Richmond, trans. *The Iliad of Homer.* Chicago: University of Chicago Books, 1951.

Lawrence, Bruce. *Defenders of God: The Fundamentalist Revolt Against the Modern Age.* San Francisco: Harper and Row, 1989.

———. *New Faiths, Old Fears: Muslims and Other Asian Immigrants in American Religious Life.* New York: Columbia University Press, 2002.

Layton, Bentley. *The Gnostic Scriptures: Ancient Wisdom for the New Age.* 1987. Reprint. New York: Bantam Doubleday Dell Publishing, 1995.

Le Doux, Joseph. *Synaptic Self: How Our Brains Become Who We Are.* New York: Viking, 2002.

Leguff, Jacques. *The Birth of Purgatory.* Chicago: University of Chicago Press, 1984.

Lenski, Gerhard. *The Religious Factor: A Sociological Study of Religion's Impact on Politics, Economics, and Family Life.* Garden City, NY: Anchor, 1963.

Lesko, Leonard H. "Death and the Afterlife in Ancient Egyptian Thought." *CANE* 3: 1765–66.

Lessa, W. A., and E. Z. Vogt, eds. *Reader in Comparative Religion.* 2d ed. 1965. 3d ed. New York: Harper and Row, 1972.

Lesses, Rebecca. *Ritual Practices to Gain Power: Angels, Incantations and Revelations in Early Jewish Mysticism.* HTS 44. Harrisburg, PA: Trinity Press International, 1998.

Levenson, Jon. *The Death and Resurrection of the Beloved Son: The Transformation of Child Sacrifice in Judaism and Christianity.* New Haven: Yale University Press, 1993.

Levine, Baruch. "Dead Kings and Ephraim: The Patrons of the Ugaritic Dynasty." *JAOS* 104 (1984): 649–59.

Levine, Lee, ed. *Ancient Synagogues Revealed.* Jerusalem: Israel Exploration Society, 1981.

———. *The Ancient Synagogue: The First Thousand Years.* New Haven: Yale University Press, 2000.

Lewin, Benjamin. *Otzar Ha-Geonim.* Haifa, 1921.

Lewinstein, Keith. "The Revaluation of Martyrdom in Early Islam." Pp. 78–91 in *Sacrificing the Self: Perspectives on Martyrdom and Religion.* Ed. Margaret Cormack. New York: Oxford University Press, 2001.

Lewin, Benjamin, ed. *Otsar Ha-Geonim.* 13 vols. Jerusalem, 1928–1943.

Lewis, Bernard. *The Origins of Ismailism.* Cambridge, 1940.

———. *Semites and Anti-Semites: An Inquiry Into Conflict and Prejudice.* New York and London: W. W. Norton, 1999.

———. *What Went Wrong? Western Impact and Middle Eastern Response.* New York: Oxford University Press, 2002.

———. *The Crisis of Islam: Holy War and Unholy Terror.* New York: Modern Library, 2003.

Lewis, I. M. *Ecstatic Religion: An Anthropological Study of Spirit Possession and Shamanism.* Baltimore: Penguin, 1971.

———. *Religion in Context: Cults and Charisma.* Cambridge: Cambridge University Press, 1986.

Lewis, Theodore J. *Cults of the Dead in Ancient Israel and Ugarit.* Harvard Theological Monographs 39. Atlanta: Scholars Press, 1989.

Lichtheim, Miriam. *Ancient Egyptian Autobiographies, Chiefly of the Middle Kingdom.* Freiburg: Universitätverlag Freiburg Schweiz, 1988.

Lim, Timothy H., et al., eds. *The Dead Sea Scrolls in the Historical Context.* Edinburgh: T and T Clark, 2000.

Lindbeck, K. "Story and Theology: Elijah's Appearances in the Babylonian Talmud." Ph.D. diss. New York: Jewish Theological Seminary, 2001.

Livingstone, Alasdair. "Court Poetry and Literary Miscellanea." *State Archives of Assyria* 3:32 (1989).

Longenecker, Richard N. " 'Good Luck on Your Resurrection': Beth She'arim and Paul on the Resurrection of the Dead." Pp. 249–70 in *Text and Artifact in the Religions of Mediterranean Antiquity: Essays in Honor of Peter Richardson.* Ed. Stephen G. Wilson, and Michel Desjardins. Waterloo, ON: Wilfred University Press, 2000.

Lord, Mary Louise. "Withdrawal and Return: An Epic Story Pattern in the Homeric Hymn to Demeter and in the Homeric Poems." Pp. 79–178 in *The Homeric "Hymn to Demeter."* Ed. Helene P. Foley. Princeton: Princeton University Press, 1994.

L'Orange, H. P. *Apotheosis in Ancient Portraiture.* New Rochelle, NY: Caratzas, 1982.

Lorenzen, Thorwald. *Resurrection and Discipleship: Interpretive Models, Biblical Reflections, Theological Consequences.* Maryknoll, NY: Orbis Books, 1995.

Luck, Georg. "Theurgy and Forms of Worship in Neoplatonism." Pp. 185–225 in *Religion, Science, and Magic: In Concert and Conflict*. Ed. Ernest S. Frerichs, Jacob Neusner, and Paul Virgil. New York: Oxford University Press, 1989.

Lüdemann, Gerd. *Die Auferstehung Jesu: Historie, Erfahrung, Theologie*. Stüttgart: Radius, 1994.

———. *The Resurrection of Jesus: History, Experience, Theology*. Trans. John Bowden. Minneapolis: Fortress, 1994.

———. *Was mit Jesus Wirklich Geschah: Die Auferstehung Historisch Betrachtet*. Stuttgart: Radius-Verlag, 1995.

———. *What Really Happened to Jesus: A Historical Approach to the Resurrection*. Louisville: John Knox Westminster Press, 1995.

Lustick, Ian. *For the Land and the Lord: Jewish Fundamentalism in Israel*. New York: Council on Foreign Relations, 1988.

Macchioro, V. *Zagreus; Studi Intorno All'orfismo*. Florence, 1930.

Mach, Michael. "Entwicklungsstadien des Juedischen Engelglaubens in Vorrabbinischer Zeit." Texte und Studien zum Antiken Judentum. Tuebingen: Mohr (Paul Siebeck), 1992.

MacMullen, Ramsay. *Christianizing the Roman Empire*. New Haven: Yale University Press, 1984.

———. *Christianity and Paganism in the Fourth to Eighth Centuries*. New Haven: Yale University Press, 1997.

Maier, Johann. "Das Gefaehrdungsmotiv bei der Himmelsreise in der Juedischen Apokalyptic und 'Gnosis.' " *Kairós* 5 (1963): 18–40.

Maier, John. *Gilgamesh: A Reader*. Wauconda, IL: Bolchazy-Carducci Publishers, 1997.

Malarney, Shaun Kingsley. "Weddings and Funerals in Contemporary Vietnam." Pp. 172–95 in *Vietnam: Journeys of Body, Mind, and Spirit*. Ed. Nguyen Van Huy and Laurel Kendall. University of California Press, American Museum of Natural History, Vietnam Museum of Ethnology, 2003.

Malherbe, Abraham J. *The Cynic Epistles*. Atlanta: Scholars Press, 1977.

———. *Moral Exhortation, A Greco-Roman Sourcebook*. Philadelphia: Westminster Press, 1986.

Margaliot, E. *Elijah the Prophet in the Literature, Faith, and Spiritual Life of Israel*. Jerusalem: Kiryat Sefer, 1960. (Hebrew).

Marsden, George, ed. *The Fundamental: A Testimony to Truth*. New York: Garland, 1988.

Martin, Ralph P. *Carmen Christi: Philippians 2:5–11 in Recent Interpretation and in the Setting of Early Christian Worship Revised Edition*. Grand Rapids: Eerdmans, 1983.

Martin, Richard C. *Approaches to Islam in Religious Studies*. Oxford: One World, 1985.

Martin-Achard, Robert. *From Death to Life: A Study of the Development of the Doctrine of the Resurrection in the Old Testament.* Trans. John Penney Smith. London: Oliver and Boyd, 1960.

Marxsen, Willi. *The Resurrection of Jesus Christ.* Trans. Margaret Kohl. London: SCM, 1970.

Mason, Steve. "Was Josephus a Pharisee? A Re-Examination of the *Life* 10–12." *JJS* 40 (1989): 31–45.

———. *Flavius Josephus on the Pharisees.* Leiden: Brill, 1991.

Mathews, Thomas F. *The Clash of Gods: A Reinterpretation of Early Christian Art.* Princeton: Princeton University Press, 1993.

Mazar, Amiḥai. *Archaeology of the Land of the Bible 10,000–586 BCE.* New York: Doubleday, 1990.

McDannell, Colleen, and Bernhard Lang. *Heaven: A History.* New Haven: Yale University Press, 1988.

McDonald, John K. *The Tomb of Nefertari: House of Eternity.* Cairo: The American University of Cairo Press, 1996.

McGinn, Colin. *The Mysterious Flame: Conscious Minds in a Material World.* New York: Basic Books, 1999.

McKnight, Scott. *Turning to Jesus: The Sociology of Conversion in the Gospels.* Louisville: Westminster, 2002.

McLaughlin, John L. *The Marzēah in the Prophetic Literature: References and Allusions in Light of the Extra-Biblical Evidence.* Leiden: Brill, 2001.

Meade, David G. *Pseudonymity and Canon: An Investigation Into the Relationship of Authorship and Authority in Jewish and Earliest Christian Tradition.* Tuebingen: Mohr (Paul Siebeck), 1986.

Meeks, Dimitri, and Christine Favard-Meeks. *Daily Life of the Egyptian Gods.* Trans. G. M. Goshgarian. Ithaca: Cornell, 1996.

———. *The Prophet King.* Leiden: Brill, 1967.

———. "The Image of the Androgyne: Some Uses of a Symbol in Earliest Christianity." *HR* 13 (1974): 165–208.

Meeks, Wayne A. "The Divine Agent and His Counterfeit in Philo and the Fourth Gospel." Pp. 43–67 in *Aspects of Religious Propaganda in Judaism and Early Christianity.* Ed. E. S. Fiorenza. Notre Dame: Notre Dame University Press, 1976.

———. *The First Urban Christians: The Social World of the Apostle Paul.* New Haven: Yale University Press, 1983.

Meltzer, Edmund S., ed. *Letters from Ancient Egypt.* Trans. Edward F. Wente. Atlanta: Scholars Press, 1990.

Meredith, Anthony. "Porphyry and Julian Against the Christians." Pp. 1119–49 in *ANRW* 2:23:2. Ed. Wolfgang Haase. Berlin and New York: Walter de Gruyter, 1980.

Merkur, Daniel. "The Nature of the Hypnotic State: A Psychoanalytic Approach." *International Review Psycho-Analysis* 11 (1984), 345–54.

——. *Becoming Half Hidden: Shamanism and Initiation Among the Inuit.* Stockholm Studies in Comparative Religion. Stockholm: Almqvist and Wiksell International, 1985.

——. *Gnosis: An Esoteric Tradition of Mystical Visions and Unions.* SUNY Series in Western Esoteric Traditions. Albany: SUNY Press, 1993.

Mernissi, Fatema. *Islam and Democracy: Fear of the Modern World.* Cambridge, MA: Perseus, 1992.

——. *The Dethronement of Sabaoth: Studies in the Shem and Kabod Theologies.* Coniectanea Biblica Old Testament Series 18. Lund: C. W. K. Gleerup, 1982.

Mettinger, Trggve N. D. *The Riddle of Resurrection: 'Dying and Rising Gods' in the Ancient Near East.* Coniectanea Biblica Old Testament Series 50. Stolkholm: Almqvist and Wiksell, 2001.

Meyer, Marvin W. *The Ancient Mysteries: A Sourcebook Sacred Texts of the Mystery Religions of the Ancient Mediterranean World.* San Francisco: Harper, 1987.

Meyer, Robert. "Magical Ascesis and Moral Purity in Ancient Egypt." Pp. 45–64 in *Transformations of the Inner Self in Ancient Religions.* Ed. Jan Assmann and Guy G. Stroumsa. Leiden: Brill, 1999.

Meyers, Eric M. "Secondary Burials in Palestine." *Biblical Archeologist* 33 (1970): 2–29.

——. *Jewish Ossuaries: Reburial and Rebirth.* Biblica et orientalia 24. Rome, 1971.

Miles, Margaret R. *Plotinus on Body and Beauty: Society, Philosophy, and Religion in Third-Century Rome.* London: Blackwell, 1999.

Milik, J. T. " '4QVisions d'Amram' et une Citation d'Origène." *RB* 79 (1972): 77–97.

Milik, J. T., with M. Black. *The Books of Enoch: Aramaic Fragments of Qumran Cave 4.* Oxford: Oxford University Press, 1976.

Milikowsky, Chaim. "Which Gehenna? Retribution and Eschatology in the Synoptic Gospels and in Early Jewish Texts." *NTS* 34 (1988): 238–49.

Miller, Patricia Cox. *Dreams in Late Antiquity: Studies in the Imagination of a Culture.* Princeton: Princeton University Press, 1994.

Miller, Robert J. *The Complete Gospels: Annotated Scholars Version.* Sonoma: Polebridge Press, 1992.

Momen, Moojan. *An Introduction of Shiʿi Islam.* New Haven: Yale University Press, 1985.

Montefiore, C. G., and H. Loewe. *A Rabbinic Anthology.* Philadelphia: Jewish Publication Society, 1960.

Moody, Raymond A., with Elisabeth Kübler-Ross. *Life After Life: The Investigation of a Phenomenon—Survival of Bodily Death.* San Francisco: Harper, 2001.

Mooney, James. "The Ghost Dance Religion and the Sioux Outbreak of 1890." Washington, DC: US Government Printing Office, 1896.

Moore, George Foot. *Judaism in the First Centuries of the Christian Era.* Vol. 1. New York: Schocken, 1971.

Morenz, Siegfried. *Egyptian Religion.* Ithaca: Cornell University Press, 1970.

Morray-Jones, Christopher R. A. " 'Paradise Revisited' (2 Corinthians 12:1–12): The Jewish Mystical Background of Paul's Apostolate." *HTR* 86 (1993).

———. *A Transparent Illusion: The Dangerous Vision of Water in Hekhalot Mysticism.* Leiden: Brill, 2002.

Morris, Ian. *Death-Ritual and Social Structure in Classical Antiquity.* Cambridge: Cambridge University Press, 1992.

Morse, Melvin. *Closer to the Light: Learning from the Near-Death Experiences of Children.* New York: Ballantine Books, 1991.

———. *Transformed by the Light: The Powerful Effect of Near Death Experiences on People's Lives.* New York: Ballantine Books, 1992.

Moscati, Sabatino. *The Face of the Ancient Orient.* London: Routledge and Kegan Paul, 1960.

Mourant, J. A. *Augustine on Immortality.* Villanova: Augustinian Institute, 1969.

Mowinckel, Sigmund. "Die Sternnamen im Alten Testament." *Nederlands theologisch tijdschrift* 29 (1928): 65.

Murray, A. T. *Homer: The Odyssey.* 2 vols. Cambridge: Harvard University Press, 1984.

Mylroie, Laurie. *A Study of Revenge: Saddam Houssein's Unfinished War against America.* American Enterprise Institute, 2000.

Neher, Andre. "Le Voyage Mystique des Quatre." *RHR* 140 (1951): 59–82.

Neimeyer, Robert A. *Death Anxiety Handbook: Research, Instrumentation, and Application,* Washington, DC: Taylor and Francis, 1994.

Neimeyer, Robert A. and David Van Brunt. "Death Anxiety." Pp. 49–88 in *Dying: Facing the Fact.* Ed. Hannelore Wass and Robert A. Neimeyer. 3d ed. Bristol, PA: Taylor and Francis, 1995.

Netzer, Ehud. "Tyros, the 'Floating Palace.' " Pp. 340–53 in *Text and Artifact in the Religions of Mediterranean Antiquity: Essays in Honour of Peter Richardson.* Ed. Stephen G. Wilson, and Michel Desjardins. Studies in Christianity and Judaism 9. Waterloo, ON: Wilfred Laurier University, 2000.

———. *Hasmonean and Herodian Palaces at Jericho: Final Reports of the 1973–1987 Excavations.* Vol 1. Jerusalem: Israel Exploration Society, 2001.

Neusner, Jacob. *The Rabbinic Traditions about the Pharisees before 70.* 3 vols. Leiden: Brill, 1971.

———. *First-Century Judaism in Crisis: Yohanan Ben Zakkai and the Renaissance of Torah.* Nashville: Abingdon Press, 1975.

———. *Judaism: The Evidence of the Mishnah.* Chicago: University of Chicago Press, 1981.

———. *Ancient Israel after Catastrophe: The Religious World View of the Mishnah*. Charlottesville: University of Virginia Press, 1983.

———. *Formative Judaism: Religious, Historical and Literary Studies*. Chico, CA: Scholars Press, 1983.

———. *Judaism in the Beginning of Christianity*. Philadelphia: Fortress, 1984.

———. "Judaism." Pp. 30–60 in *Death and the Afterlife*. Ed. Jacob Neusner. Cleveland, OH: The Pilgram Press, 2000.

Newberg, Andrew, Eugene D'Aquili, and Vince Rause. *Why God Won't Go Away: Brain Science and the Biology of Belief*. New York: Ballantine Books, 2001.

Newby, Gordon. *History of the Jews of Arabia*. Columbia: University of South Carolina Press, 1988.

Newman, Carey. "Paul's Glory Christology: Tradition and Rhetoric." NovT Supplement 69. Leiden: Brill, 1992.

Newsom, Carol. "4Q Serek Shirot 'Olat Hassabbat (The Qumran Angelic Liturgy): Edition, Translation and Commentary." Ph.D. diss. Harvard University, 1982.

———. *Songs of the Sabbath Sacrifice: A Critical Edition*. Harvard Semitics Studies of the Harvard Semitic Museum 27. Ed. F. M. Cross. Atlanta: Scholars Press, 1985.

———. "He Has Established for Himself Priests: Human and Angelic Priesthood in the Qumran Sabbath Shirot." *Archaeology and History of the Dead Sea Scrolls: The New York University Conference in Memory of Yigael Yadin*. Ed. Lawrence Schiffman. Sheffield: JSOT Press, 1990.

Nickelsburg, George W. E. Jr. *Resurrection, Immortality and Eternal Life in Intertestamental Judaism*. HTS 26. Cambridge: Harvard University Press, 1972.

———. "Future Life in Intertestamental Literature." Pp. 384–51 in Interpreter's Dictionary of the Bible. Sup. vol. Nashville, 1976.

———. "Enoch, Levi, and Peter: Recipients of Revelation in Upper Galilee." *JBL* 100 (1981): 575–600.

———. "An Ektroma, Through Appointed from the Womb: Paul's Apostolic Self-Description in 1 Corinthians 15 and Galatians 1." *HTR* 79 (1986): 1–3, 198–205.

———. "Salvation without and with a Messiah: Developing Beliefs in Writings Ascribed to Enoch." Pp. 49–68 in *Judaisms and Their Messiahs at the Turn of the Christian Era*. Ed. Jacob Neusner and William S. Green. Cambridge: Cambridge University Press, 1987.

Nigosian, Sol A. *The Zororastrian Faith: Tradition and Modern Research*. Montreal and Kingston: McGill-Queens University Press, 1993.

Nikolainen, Aimo T. *Der Aufersthungsglauben in der Bible und Ihrer Umwelt*. 2 vols. Helsinki: Suomalainen Tiedeakatemia, 1992.

Nitzan, Bilḥah. "Harmonic and Mystical Characteristics in Poetic and Liturgical Writings From Qumran." *JQR* 85 (1994): 163–83.

Noll, S. F. "Angelology in the Qumran Texts." Ph.D. diss. Manchester, 1979.

———. "Communion of Angels and Men and 'Realized Eschatology' in the Dead Sea Scrolls." Pp. 91–97 in *Proceedings of the Eighth World Congress of Jewish Studies*. Jerusalem, 1982.

Norretranders, Tor. *The User Illusion: Cuttings Consciousness Down to Size*. New York: Viking, 1998.

Novak, David. *The Image of the Non-Jew in Judaism: An Historical and Constructive Study of the Noahide Laws*. Toronto Studies in Theology 14. Toronto: The Edwin Mellen Press, 1983.

O'Collins, Gerald. *Interpreting the Resurrection: Examining the Major Problems in the Stories of Jesus' Resurrection*. New York: Paulist Press, 1988.

O'Connor, J. Murphy. "Christological Anthropology in Phil. 2:6–11." *RB* 83 (1976): 25–50.

Odeberg, H. *The Hebrew Book of Enoch or Third Enoch*. 2d ed. New York: Ktav, 1973.

Oden, Amy. *In Her Words: Women's Writings in the History of Christian Thought*. Nashville: Abingdon, 1994.

Ogden, Daniel. "Greek Sorcerers." *Magic, Witchcraft, and Ghosts in the Greek and Roman Worlds: A Sourcebook*. Oxford: Oxford University Press, 2002.

O'Meara, Dominic J. *Plotinus: An Introduction to the Enneads*. Oxford: Clarendon Press, 1995.

Onians, R. B. *The Origins of European Thought about the Body, the Mind, the Soul, the World, Time, and Fate*. Cambridge: Cambridge University Press, 1951.

Oppenheim, A. Leo. "The Interpretation of Dreams in the Ancient Near East." American Philosophical Society 46 (1956).

Origen. "Commentarium in 1 Corinthians." *JTS* 10 (1909): 466–47.

Osborne, Kenan B. *The Resurrection of Jesus: New Considerations for Its Theological Interpretation*. New York: Paulist Press, 1997.

Otto, Rudolph. *The Idea of the Holy: An Inquiry Into the Non-Rational Factor in the Idea of the Divine and Its Relation to the Rational*. London: Oxford University Press, 1923.

Overholt, Thomas W. "The Ghost Dance of 1890 and the Nature of the Prophetic Process." *Ethnohistory* 21 (1974): 37–63.

———. *Channels of Prophecy: The Social Dynamics of Prophetic Activity*. Minneapolis: Fortress, 1989.

Overman, J. Andrew. "The Diaspora in the Modern Study of Ancient Judaism." Pp. 1–17 in *Diaspora Jews and Judaism: Essays in Honor of, and in Dialogue with, A. Thomas Kraabel*. Ed. J. Andrew Overman and Robert MacLennan. Minneapolis: Fortress, 1992.

———. "The Gospel of Matthew and Jewish–Christian Conflict." Pp. 38–61 in *Social History of the Matthean Community: Cross-Disciplinary Approaches*. Ed. David L. Balch. Minneapolis: Fortress, 1992.

Ovid. *Metamorphoses*. Ed. and trans. F. J. Meller. Loeb Series. Cambridge, Mass. and London, 1916.

Oxtoby, Willard G. "Interpretations of Iranian Dualism." Pp. 59–70 in *Iranian Civilization and Culture: Essays in Honour of the 2,500th Anniversary of the Founding of the Persian Empire*. Ed. Charles J. Adams. Montreal: McGill University Institute for Islamic Studies, 1972.

———, ed. *World Religions: Western Traditions*. 2d ed. Toronto: Oxford University Press, 2002.

Pagels, Elaine. "The Mystery of the Resurrection." *JBL* 93 (1974): 276–88.

———. *The Gnostic Paul: Gnostic Exegesis of the Pauline Letters*. Philadelphia: Fortress, 1975.

———. *The Gnostic Gospels*. New York: Random House, 1979.

———. *Adam, Eve, and the Serpent*. New York: Random House, 1988.

———. *The Origin of Satan*. New York: Random House, 1995.

———. *Beyond Belief: The Secret Gospel of Thomas*. New York: Random House, 2003.

Pardee, Dennis. *Ritual and Cult at Ugarit*. Atlanta: SBL Press, 2002.

Patterson, Stephen J. *The Gospel of Thomas and Jesus*. Sonoma: Polebridge, 1993.

Peacock, James. *Rites of Modernization: Symbolic and Social Aspects of Indonesian Proletarian Drama*. Chicago: University of Chicago Press, 1968.

Pearson, Birger. *The Pneumatikos-Psychikos Terminology in 1 Corinthians*. SBL Dissertation Series 12. Missoula, MT: Scholars Press, 1973.

———. "Revisiting Norea." Pp. 265–75 in *Images of the Feminine in Gnosticism*. Ed. Karen King. Philadelphia: Fortress Press, 1988.

Pearson, Mike Parker. *The Archaeology of Death and Burial*. 3d ed. College Station, TX: Texas A and M Press, 1999.

Pelikan, Jaroslav. *Christianity and Classical Culture: The Metamorphosis of Natural Theology in the Christian Encounter with Hellenism*. New Haven: Yale University Press, 1993.

Perkins, Pheme. *Resurrection: New Testament Witness and Contemporary Reflection*. New York: Anchor Doubleday, 1984.

Perrin, Norman. *The Resurrection According to Matthew, Mark and Luke*. Philadelphia: Fortress, 1977.

Persinger, Michael A. *Neuropsychological Bases of God Beliefs*. Westport, CT: Praeger, 1987.

Peters, F. E. *Muḥammad and the Origins of Islam*. Albany: SUNY Press, 1994.

Peterson, Daniel C. "Muhammad." Pp. 457–612 in *The Rivers of Paradise: Moses, Buddha, Confucius, Jesus, and Muhammad as Religious Founders*. Grand Rapids: Eerdmans, 2001.

Philo. *The Works of Philo: Complete and Unabridged*. Updated ed. with foreword by David M. Scholar. Grand Rapids: Hendrickson, 1993.

Piaget, Jean. *The Psychology of Intelligence*. Trans. Malcolm Piercy and D. E. Berlyne. London: Routledge and Kegan Paul, 1950.

————. *The Moral Judgement of the Child.* Trans. Marjorie Gabin. New York: Collier, 1962.

————. *Adaptation and Intelligence: Organic Selection and Phenocopy.* Trans. Stewart Eames. Foreword by Terrance A. Brown. Chicago: University of Chicago Press, 1980.

Plato. *The Republic.* Ed. and trans. Paul Shorey. London, 1888.

Plöger, Otto. *Theocracy and Eschatology.* Trans. S. Rudman. Richmond, VA: John Knox Press, 1968.

Pope, Marvin. *The Song of Songs.* AB 7C. Garden City, NY: Anchor Doubleday, 1977.

————. "The Cult of the Dead at Ugarit." *Ugarit in Retrospect.* Ed. G. D. Young. Winona Lake, IN: Eisenbrauns, 1981.

Povinelli, Daniel J., and John G. H. Cant. "Arboreal Clambering and the Evolution of Self-Conception." *The Quarterly Review of Biology* 70:4 (1995): 393–421.

Pritchard, James B. *Ancient Near Eastern Texts Relating to the Old Testament.* Princeton: Princeton University Press, 1969.

Proclus. *The Elements of Theology.* Ed. R. Dodds. Oxford, 1963.

Puech, Émile. *La Croyance des Esséniens en la Vie Future.* 2 vols. Paris: Gabalda, 1993.

————. "La croyance des Esséniens en la vie future: immortalité, résurection, vie éternelle?" Pp. 99–107 in *Vol. 1: La Résurrection des morts et le contexte scripturaire.* 2 vols. Paris: Gabalda, 1993.

Qimron, Elisha. "Celibacy in the Dead Sea Scrolls and the Two Kinds of Sectarians." *The Madrid Qumran Congress Proceedings of the International Congress on the Dead Sea Scrolls, Madrid, 18–21 March 1991.* 2 vols. Ed. J. Trebolle Borrera and L. Montaner. Leiden: Brill, 1992.

Quasem, Muhammad Abul. *Salvation of the Soul and Islamic Devotions.* London: Kegan Paul International, 1981.

Quirke, Stephen. *Ancient Egyptian Religion.* New York: Dover, 1992.

Quirke, Stephen, and Jeffrey Spencer, eds. *The British Museum Book of Ancient Egypt.* London and New York: Thames and Hudson, 1992.

Quispel, Gilles. "Gnosticism and the New Testament." Pp. 252–71 in *The Bible and Modern Scholarship.* Ed. J. P. Hyatt. Nashville, Abingdon, 1965.

————. "The Origins of the Gnostic Demiurge." Pp. 272–76 in *Kyriakon: Festschrift Johannes Quasten* 1. Ed. P. Granfield and J. A. Jungman. Muenster: Aschendorff, 1970.

————. *Gnostic Studies.* Istanbul: Netherlands Historisch-Archaeologisch Instituut in bet Nabije Osten, 1974.

————. "Ezekiel 1:26 in Jewish Mysticism and Gnosis." *VC* 34 (1980): 1–10.

————. "Gnosis." Pp. 413–35 in Die orientalischen Religionen im Roemerreich. Ed. M. J. Vermaseren. Leiden: Brill, 1981.

————. "Hermetism and the New Testament, Especially Paul." *ANRW* 2. 1998.

Qune, David Edward. *The Cultic Setting of Realized Eschatology in Early Christianity.* Leiden: Brill, 1972.

Ramadan, Tariq. *To Be a European Muslim: A Study of Islamic Sources in the European Context.* Leicester: The Islamic Foundation, 1999.

———. *Muslims in France: The Way of Co-Existence.* Leicester: The Islamic Foundation, 1999.

———. *Islam, the West, and the Challenges of Modernity.* Leicester: The Islamic Foundation, 2001.

Rambo, Lou. *Understanding Religious Conversion.* New Haven: Yale University Press, 1993.

Raphael, Simcha Paull. *Jewish Views of the Afterlife.* Northvale, NJ: J. Aronson, 1994.

Rappe, Sara. "Self-Knowledge and Subjectivity in the Enneads." Pp. 250–74 in *The Cambridge Companion to Plotinus.* Ed. Lloyd P. Gerson. Cambridge: Cambridge University Press, 1996.

———. *Reading Neoplatonism: Non-Discursive Thinking in the Texts of Plotinus, Proclus, and Damascius.* Cambridge: Cambridge University Press, 2000.

Ray, Benjamin Caleb. "The Gilgamesh Epic: Myth and Meaning." Pp. 300–326 in *Myth and Method.* Ed. Laurie Patton and Wendy Daniger. Charlottesville: University of Virginia Press, 1996.

Rhode, Erich. *Psyche: The Cult of Souls and Belief in Immortality Among the Greeks.* Trans. W. Hillis. 8th ed. London, 1925.

Riddle, Donald W. *Paul: Man of Conflict.* Nashville: Cokesbury, 1940.

Riesenfeld, H. *Repertorium lexicographicum graecum.* Stockholm: Almquist and Wiksell, 1948.

Riley, Gregory J. *Resurrection Reconsidered: Thomas and John in Controversy.* Minneapolis: Fortress Press, 1995.

———. *The River of God: A New History of Christian Origins.* San Francisco: Harper, 2001.

Ripinsky-Naxon, Michael. *The Nature of Shamanism: Substance and Function of a Religious Metaphor.* Albany: SUNY Press, 1993.

Rippin, Andrew. *Muslims: Their Religious Beliefs and Practices.* London: Routledge, 1990. 2d ed. 2001.

Roberts, Alexander, James Donaldson, and F. Crombie, eds. *The Writings of the Apostolic Fathers.* The Ante-Nicene Christian Library. Edinburgh: T. and T. Clark, 1867.

Roberts, J. J. M. "Job's Summons to Yahweh: The Exploitation of a Legal Metaphor." *Restoration Quarterly* 16 (1973): 159–63.

Robinson, J. A. T. "The Most Primitive Christology of All." Pp. 177–89 in *Twelve New Testament Studies,* 177–89. London: SCM Press, 1962. Reprinted from *JTS* 7 (1956).

Robinson, T. H. *Job and his Friends.* London: SCM Press, 1954.

Rodinson, Maxine. *Muhammed.* Trans. Anne Carter. Harmondsworth: Penguin Books, 1971.

Rohde, Erwin. "Psyche: The Cult of Souls and Belief in Immortality Among the Greeks." *International Library of Psychology, Philosophy, and Scientific Method*. London: K. Paul, Trench, Trubner, 1925.

Roster, Benjamin R. *The Epic of Gilgamesh*. New York: Norton, 2001.

Rowland, Christopher. "The Vision of the Risen Christ in Rev. 1:13ff.: The Debt of an Early Christology to an Aspect of Jewish Angelology." *JTS* 31 (1980): 1–11.

———. *The Open Heaven: A Study of Apocalyptic in Judaism and Early Christianity*. New York: Crossroads, 1982.

Royalty, Robert Jr. *The Streets of Heaven: The Ideology of Wealth in the Apocalypse of John*. Macon, GA: Mercer, 1997.

Rubenstein, Jeffrey. *Talmudic Stories: Narrative Art, Composition, and Culture*. Baltimore: Johns Hopkins University Press, 1999.

Rudolph, K. "Ein Grundtyp gnostischer Urmensch-Adam-Spekulation." *Zeitschrift für Religions und Geistesgeschichte* 9 (1957): 1–20.

Ruether, Rosemary Radford. "Misogynism and Virginal Feminism in the Fathers of the Church." Pp. 150–83 in *Religion and Sexism: Images of Women in the Jewish and Christian Traditions*. Ed. Rosmary Radford Ruether. New York: Simon and Schuster, 1974.

Runciman, Steven. *A History of the Crusades*. Cambridge: Cambridge University Press, 1951.

Russell, James R. *Zoroastrianism in Armenia*. Harvard Iranian Series 5. Ed. Richard N. Frye. Cambridge: Baikar Publications, 1987.

———. "Death in Persia." Paper delivered at conference: Last Things: Death and Immortality in the Ancient New World. New York University, 1997.

Russell, Jeffery Burton. *A History of Heaven: The Singing Silence*. Princeton: Princeton University Press, 1997.

Rustomji, Nerina. "The Garden and the Fire: Materials of Heaven and Hell in Medieval Islamic Culture." Ph.D. diss. New York: Columbia University, 2003.

Saake, Helmut. "Paulus als Ekstatiker: pneumatologische Beobachtung zu 2 Cor. 12 1–10." *NovT* 15 (1973): 152–60.

Sachedina, Abdulaziz. *The Islamic Roots of Democratic Pluralism*. New York: Oxford University Press, 2001.

Saldarini, Anthony. *The Fathers According to Rabbi Nathan*. Leiden: Brill, 1975.

Saler, Benson. *Conceptualizing Religion: Immanent Anthropologists, Transcendent Natives, and Unbounded Categories*. Studies in the History of Religion. Leiden: Brill, 1993.

Samellas, Antigone. *Death in the Eastern Mediterranean (50–600 A.D.)*. Studien und Textes zu Antike und Christentum. Tubingen: Mohr (Paul Siebeck), 2002.

Sanders, E. P. *Paul and Palestinian Judaism: A Comparison of Patterns of Religion*. Philadelphia: Fortress Press, 1977.

————. "Aspects of Judaism in the Greco-Roman World." *Jewish and Christian Self-Definition.* Philadelphia: Fortress Press, 1982.

————. "The Testament of Abraham." Pp. 871–89 in The Old Testament Pseudepigrapha. Vol 1. Ed. J. Charlesworth. Garden City, NY: Doubleday, 1983.

————. *Jesus and Judaism.* Philadelphia: Fortress Press, 1985.

Sanders, Seth L. "Writing Ritual and Apocalypse: Studies in the Theme of Ascent to Heaven in Ancient Mesopotamia and Second Temple Judaism/Israel." Ph.D. diss. Baltimore: Johns Hopkins University, 1999.

Satran, David. "Fingernails and Hair? Anatomy and Exegesis in Terullian." *JTS* new series 40 (1989): 116–20.

Sauneron, Serge. *The Priests of Ancient Egypt.* Trans. David Lorton. Ithaca: Cornell University Press, 2000.

Schaberg, Jane. *The Resurrection of Mary Magdalene: Legends, Apocrypha, and the Christian Testament.* New York: Continuum, 2002.

Schaefer, Peter. *Rivalitaet zwischen Engeln und Menschen: Untersuchungen zur rabbinischen Engelvorstellung.* Berlin/New York: De Gruyter, 1975.

————. "Engel und Menschen in der Hekhalot-Literatur." *Kairos* 22 (1980): 201–25.

————, ed. *Synopse zur Hekhalot-Literatur.* Tuebingen: Mohr, 1981.

————. "New Testament and Hekhalot Literature: The Journey Into Heaven in Paul and in Merkavah Mysticism." *JJS* 35 (1984): 19–35.

————. *The Hidden and Manifest God: Some Major Themes in Early Jewish Mysticism.* Albany: SUNY Press, 1998.

Schiffman, Lawrence. "The Recall of Nehunia Ben Hakkanah from Ecstacy." *Association for Jewish Studies Review* 1 (1976): 269–81.

————. "Merkavah Speculation at Qumran: The 4Q Serekh Shirot 'Olat Ha-Shabbat." Pp. 15–47 in *Mystics, Philosophers, and Politicians: Essays in Jewish Intellectual History in Honor of Alexander Altman.* Ed. Jehuda Reinhartz et al. Chapel Hill: University of North Carolina Press, 1982.

————. *Sectarian Law in the Dead Sea Scrolls: Courts, Testimony and the Penal Code.* Chico, CA: Scholar's Press, 1983.

Schillebeeckx, E. *Jesus: An Experiment in Christology.* New York: Seabury, 1979.

————. *Christ.* Trans. John Bowden. New York: Seabury, 1988.

Schimmelpfening, Bernard. *The Papacy.* New York: Columbia University Press, 1927.

Schmidt, Brian B. "Israel's Beneficent Dead: Ancestor Cult and Necromancy in Ancient Israelite Religion and Tradition." *Forschungen zum Alten Testament* 11. Tubingen: Mohr (Paul Siebeck), 1994.

Schmitz, Philip C. "The Grammar of Resurrection in Isaiah 2:19a–c." *JBL* 122:1 (2003): 145–49.

Schneider, C. *Die Erlebnisechtheit der Apokalypse des Johannes.* Leipzig, 1930.

Scholem, Gershom. *Major Trends in Jewish Mysticism.* New York: Schocken, 1961.

———. *Jewish Gnosticism, Merkabah Mysticism and Talmudic Tradition.* 2d ed. New York: Jewish Theological Seminary, 1965.

Scholer, David M., ed. *The Works of Philo: Complete and Unabridged.* Grand Rapids: Hendrickson, 1993.

Schuller, Eileen. "A Hymn from a Cave Four *Hodayot* Manuscript: 4Q427 i + ii." *JBL* 112 (1993): 605–28.

Schüssler-Fiorenza, Elisabeth. *Searching the Scriptures: A Feminist Commentary.* New York: Crossroad Publishing Company, 1994.

Schwartz, Stephen. *The Two Faces of Islam: The House of Saʿud from Tradition to Terror.* New York: Doubleday, 2002.

Schweitzer, Albert. *The Mysticism of Paul the Apostle.* Trans. William B. D. Montgomery. Preface by F. C. Burkitt. New York: Seabury Press, 1931. Reprint, 1968.

———. *The Quest of the Historical Jesus: A Critical Study of Its Progress from Reimarus to Wrede.* Ed. J. M. Robinson. Trans. W. B. D. Montgomery. New York: Macmillan, 1968.

Scott, Alan. *Origen and the Life of the Stars: A History of an Idea.* Oxford Early Christian Studies. Oxford: Clarendon Press, 1991.

Scott, R. B. Y. *Proverbs, Ecclesiastes.* AB 18. Garden City, NY: Doubleday, 1965.

Scroggs, Robin. *The Last Adam: A Study in Pauline Anthropology.* Philadelphia: Fortress, 1966.

Scurlock, Jo Ann. "Death and Afterlife in Ancient Mesopotamian Thought." *CANE* 3: 1883–94.

Searle, John R. *The Mystery of Consciousness.* New York: New York Review of Books Press, 1997.

Séd, Nicholas. "Les traditions secrètes et les disciples de Rabban Yohanan ben Zakkai." *RHR* 184 (1973): 49–66.

Seeley, David. *The Noble Death: Graeco-Roman Martyrology and Paul's Concept of Salvation.* JSNT Supplement 28. Worchester: Sheffield Academic Press, 1990.

Segal, Alan F. *Heavenly Ascent in Hellenistic Judaism, Early Christianity, and Their Environments.* ANRW 2:23:2. Berlin and New York: Walter DeGruyter, 1980.

———. "Hellenistic Magic: Some Questions of Definition." Pp. 349–75 in *Studies in Gnosticism and Hellenistic Religions: Presented to Gilles Quispel on the Occasion of His 65th Birthday.* Etudes préliminaires aux religions orientales dans l'empire romain 91. Leiden: Brill, 1982.

———. " 'He Who Did Not Spare His Only Son:' Jesus, Paul and the Sacrifice of Isaac." Pp. 169–84 in *From Jesus to Paul: Studies in Honour of F. W. Beare.* Ed. Peter Richardson and John C. Hurd. Waterloo ON: Wilfrid Laurier Press, 1984.

———. *Rebecca's Children: Judaism and Christianity in the Roman World.* Cambridge: Harvard University Press, 1986.

———. *The Other Judaisms of Late Antiquity.* BJS 127. Atlanta: Scholars Press, 1987.

———. "The Risen Christ and the Angelic Mediator Figures in Light of Qumran." *Jesus and the Dead Sea Scrolls.* Ed. James Charlesworth. New York: Doubleday, 1992.

———. "The Akedah: Some Reconsiderations." Pp. 99–118 in *Geschichte— Tradition—Reflexion: Festschrift für Martin Hengel zum 70. Geburtstag,* Vol. 1 Judentum. Ed. Hubert Cancik, Hermann Lichtenberger, and Peter Schäfer. Tübingen: Mohr (Paul Siebeck), 1996.

———. *Paul the Convert: The Apostasy and Apostolate of Saul the Pharisee.* New Haven: Yale University Press, 1997.

———. *Two Powers in Heaven: Rabbinic Reports About Christianity and Gnosticism.* Boston: Brill, 2002.

———. "Taoist Ascent and Merkabah Mysticism." *Memorial Volume for Julia Ching,* forthcoming.

Segal, Robert. *The Poimandres as Myth: Scholarly Theory and Gnostic Meaning.* Berlin and New York: De Gruyter, 1988.

Seim, Turid Karlsen. *The Double Message: Patterns of Gender in Luke–Acts.* Edinburgh: T. and T. Clark, 1994.

Seitz, Christopher. *Isaiah 1–39.* Interpretation: A Bible Commendary for Teaching and Preaching. Louisville: John Knox Press, 1989.

A Select Library of Nicene and Post-Nice Fathers of the Christian Church. Trans. Philip Schaff and Henry Wace. New York: The Christian Literature Company, 1893.

Sells, Michael, ed. Preface by Carl Ernst. *Early Islamic Mysticism: Sufi, Qur'an, Mi'raj, Poetic and Theological Writings.* New York and Mahwah, NJ: Paulist Press, 1996.

Selwyn, E. C. *The Christian Prophets and the Prophetic Apocalypse.* London, 1900.

Seow, Choon-Leong. *Ecclesiastes.* AB 18C. New York: Doubleday, 1997.

Shahak, Israel, and Norton Mezvinsky. *Jewish Fundamentalism in Israel.* London: Pluto Press, 1999.

Shaked, Shaul. "Quests and Visionary Journeys in Sasanian Iran." Pp. 65–86 in *Transformations of the Inner Self in Ancient Religions.* Ed. Jan Assmann and Guy G. Stroumsa. Leiden: Brill, 1999.

Shalev, A. Y. "Post-Traumatic Stress Disorder: Diagnosis, History and Life Course." Pp. 1–17 in *Post-Traumatic Stress Disorder: Diagnosis, Management, and Treatment.* Ed. D. Nutt, J. Davidson, and J. Zohar. London: Martin Dunitz, 2000.

Shaw, Gregory. "Apotheosis in Later Platonism: Salvation as Theurgic Embodiment." *SBL Annual Seminar Papers.* Ed. Kent Harold Richards. Atlanta: Scholars Press, 1987.

———. *Theurgy and the Soul: The Neoplatonism of Iamblichus.* University Park: Pennsylvania State University Press, 1995.

Shaw, Theresa M. *The Burden of the Flesh: Fasting and Sexuality in Early Christianity.* Minneapolis: Fortress, 1998.

Shipp, R. Mark. *Of Dead Kings and Dirges: Myth and Meaning in Isaiah 14:4b–2l.* Atlanta: SBL Academia Biblica, 2002.

Siculus, Diodorus. *An Account of Egypt.* Trans. W. G. Waddell. Cairo: University of Cairo Press, 1933.

Siliotti, Alberto. *Dwellings in Eternity.* Vercelli, Italy: White Star Books in association with Barnes and Noble, 2000.

Sladek, W. R. "Inanna's Descent to the Netherworld." Ph.D. diss. Baltimore: Johns Hopkins University, 1974.

Sly, Dorothy. *Philo's Perception of Women.* BJS 109. Atlanta: Scholars Press, 1990.

Smallwood, E. Mary. *The Jews Under Roman Rule: From Pompey to Diocletian.* Leiden: Brill.

Smelik, Willem F. "On the Mystical Transformation of the Righteous into Light in Judaism." *JSJ* 26:2 (1995): 122–44.

Smith, Daniel. *Religion of the Landless.* Foreword by Norman K. Gottwald. Bloomington, IN: Meyer Stone Books, 1989.

Smith, Huston. *Cleansing the Doors of Perception: The Religious Significance of Entheogenic Plants and Chemicals.* New York: Penguin Putnam, 2001.

Smith, Jane, and Yvonne Yazbeck Haddad. *The Islamic Understanding of Death and Resurrection.* Albany: SUNY Press, 1981.

Smith, Jonathan. "Hellenistic Religions." *The New Encyclopedia Britannica.*

———. *Drudgery Divine: On the Comparison of Early Christianities and the Religions of Late Antiquity.* Chicago: University of Chicago Press, 1990.

———. "Dying and Rising Gods." *ER* 4.

———. "The Prayer of Joseph." Pp. 253–94 in *Christianity, Judaism, and Other Greco-Roman Cults.* Ed. J. Neusner. Leiden: Brill, 1975.

Smith, Lacey Baldwin. *Fools, Martyrs, and Traitors: The Story of Martyrdom in the Western World.* New York: Knopf, 1997.

Smith, Mark S. *The Early History of God: Yahweh and the Other Deities in Ancient Israel.* San Francisco: Harper, 1990.

———. "The Death of 'Dying and Rising Gods' in the Biblical World: An Update, with Special Reference to Baal in the Baal Cycle." *Scandinavian Journal of the Old Testament* 12 (1998): 257–313.

Smith, Morton. "Observations on Hekhaloth Rabbati." *Studies and Texts.* Vol. 1. Ed. A. Altmann. Biblical and Other Studies. Cambridge: Harvard University Press, 1963.

———. *Clement of Alexandria and a Secret Gospel of Mark.* Cambridge: Harvard University Press, 1975.

———. *Jesus the Magician.* San Francisco: Harper and Row, 1978.

————. "Ascent to the Heavens and the Beginnings of Christianity." *Eranos Jahrbuch* 50 (1981): 403–29.

————. *Palestinian Parties and Politics That Shaped the Old Testament*. New York: Columbia University Press, 1971. Reprint. London: SCM, 1981.

————. "How Magic Was Changed by the Triumph of Christianity." Pp. 51–58 in *Graeco Arabica, Papers of the First International Congress on Greek and Arabic Studies*. Vol. 2. Ed. V. Christides and M. Papthomopolis. Athens, 1982.

————. "Ascent to the Heavens and Deification in 4QMa." Pp. 181–88 in *Archeology and History in the Dead Sea Scrolls: The New York University Conference in Memory of Yigael Yadin*. Ed. Lawrence H. Schiffman. JSPSup 8. Sheffield: JSOT Press, 1990.

————. "Two Ascended to Heaven—Jesus and the Author of 4Q491." Pp. 273–89 in *The Messiah: Developments in Earliest Judaism and Christianity*. Ed. James Charlesworth, with A. F. Segal, J. Brownson, M. T. Davis, and S. J. Kraftchick. Minneapolis: Fortress Press, 1992.

————. *Studies in the Cult of Yahweh*. Religions in the Graeco-Roman World 130. Ed. Shaye J. D. Cohen. New York: Brill, 1996.

Smith, Rowland. *Julian's Gods: Religion and Philosophy in the Thought and Action of Julian the Apostate*. London and New York: Routledge, 1995.

Smith, W. C. *The Meaning and End of Religion*. New York: Harper and Row, 1978.

Smolar, Leivy, Moses Aberbach, and Pinkhos Curgin. *Studies in Targum Jonathan to the Prophets*. New York: Ktav, 1981.

Snell, Bruno. *The Discovery of the Mind: The Greek Origins of European Thought*. 1953. Reprint. New York: Harper and Row, Harper Torchbooks/Academy Library, 1960.

Snow, David, and Richard Machalek. "The Sociology of Conversion." *Annual Review of Sociology* 10 (1984): 167–90.

Soden, W. von. "Zum Sclusstück von Ištars Unterweltsfahrt." *Zeitschrift für Assyiologie* 58 (1967): 192–95.

Sommers, Benjamin. "Expulsion as Initiation: Displacement, Divine Presence, and Divine Exile in the Torah." *Beginning Again: Towards a Hermeneutic of Jewish Texts*. Ed. Aryeh Cohen and Shaul Magid. New York: Seven Bridges Press, 2002.

Son, Ly Hanh. "The Yao Initiation Ceremony in the New Market Economy." Pp. 158–71 in *Vietnam: Journeys of Body, Mind, and Spirit*. Ed. Nguyen Van Huy and Laurel Kendall. University of California Press, American Museum of Natural History, Vietnam Museum of Ethnology, 2003.

Sorabji, Richard. *Aristotle on Memory*. Providence: Brown University Press, 1972.

Sourvinou-Inwood, Christiane. *'Reading' Greek Death to the End of the Classical Period*. Oxford: Clarendon Press, 1995.

Sperber, Daniel. *A Dictionary of Greek and Latin Legal Terms in Rabbinic Literature.* Ramat Gan: Bar Ilan, 1984.

Spiegel, Shalom. *The Last Trial.* Trans. Judah Goldin. New York, 1950. Reprint. New York: Random House, 1967.

Spong, John. *Resurrection: Myth or Reality?* San Francisco: Harper, 1994.

———. *Liberating the Gospels: Reading the Bible with Jewish Eyes.* San Francisco: Harper, 1996.

Spronk, Klaaus. *Beatific Afterlife in Ancient Israel and the Ancient Near East.* Vluyn: Verlag Butzon and Bercker Kevelaer, 1986.

Stager, Lawrence E. "Carthage: A View from the Tophet." Pp. 155–66 in *Phönizer im Westen.* Ed. Hans G. Niemeyer. Mainz-am-Rhein: Zabern, 1982.

Stager, Lawrence E., and Samuel R. Wolff. "Child Sacrifice at Carthage—Religious Rite or Population Control." *Biblical Archeological Review* 10:1 (February 1984): 31–51.

Steinberg, Jonah. "Angelic Israel: Self-Identification with Angels in Rabbinic Agadah and Its Jewish Antecedents." Ph.D. diss. New York: Columbia University, 2003.

———. "Sheol: New Perspectives on Netherworld in the Eschatological Ideologies of the Hebrew Bible." unpublished.

Stendahl, Krister, ed. *Immortality and Resurrection: Death in the Western World.* New York: Macmillan, 1965.

Stern, David. "Jewish Concepts." *ER* 1.

Stern, David, and Mark J. Mirsky. *Rabbinic Fantasies: Imaginative Narratives from Classical Hebrew Literature.* New Haven: Yale University Press, 1990.

Stier F. *Gott und Sein Engel im Alten Testament.* Muenster: Aschendorff, 1934.

Stilwell, Gary A. "Conduct and Behavior as Determinants for the Afterlife: A Comparison of the Judgments of the Dead in Ancient Egypt and Ancient Greece." Ph.D. diss. Tallahassee: Florida State University, 2000.

Stone, Michael Edward. "The Book of Enoch and Judaism in the Third Century, B.C.E." *CBQ* 40 (1978): 479–92.

———. *Scriptures, Sects, and Visions: A Profile of Judaism from Ezra to the Jewish Revolts.* Philadelphia: Fortress Press, 1980.

———. *Fourth Ezra.* Minneapolis: Fortress, 1990.

Stratton, Kim. "Naming the Witch: Power and Politics Behind Representations of Magic in Ancient Literature." Ph.D. diss. New York: Columbia University, 2002.

Straw, Carol. " 'A Very Special Death:' Christian Martyrdom in Its Classical Context." Pp. 39–57 in *Sacrificing the Self: Perspectives on Martyrdom and Religion.* Ed. Margaret Cormack. New York: Oxford University Press, 2001.

Stroumsa, Guy. "Form(s) of God: Some Notes on Metatron and Christ." *HTR* 76:3 (1985): 269–88.

———. "Madness and Divinization in Early Christian Monasticism." Pp. 73–88 in *Self and Self-Transformation in the History of Religions*. Ed. Guy G. Stroumsa and David Shulman. New York: Oxford University Press, 2002.

Strugnell, J. "The Angelic Liturgy at Qumran." VTSup 7. Leiden: Brill, 1960.

Sysling, Harry. *Teḥiyyat Ha-Metim: The Resurrection of the Dead in the Palestinian Targums of the Pentateuch and Parallel Traditions in Classical Rabbinic Literature*. Texte und Studien zum Antiken Judentum 57. Tübingen: Mohr (Paul Siebeck), 1996.

Tabor, James D. *Things Unutterable: Paul's Ascent to Paradise in Its Greco-Roman, Judaic, and Early Christian Contexts*. Lanham, MD: University Press of America, 1986.

Talmon, Shmaryahu. "The Calendar Reckoning of the Desert." Pp. 162–99 in *Aspects of the Dead Sea Scrolls*. Ed. C. Rabin and Y. Yadin. Scripta Hierosolymitana 4. Jerusalem: The Magnes Press, 1958.

Tannehill, Robert C. "Dying and Rising with Christ: A Study in Pauline Theology." Berlin: Toepelmann, 1967.

Taran, Leonardo, ed. and trans. *Parmenides: A Text with Translation, Commentary, and Critical Essay*. Princeton: Princeton University Press, 1965.

Tardieu, M. *Trois mythes gnostiques: Adam, Éros et les animaux d'Egypte dans un écrit de Nag Hammadi (II,5)*. Paris: Études Augustiniennes, 1974.

Tart, Charles T., ed. *Altered States of Consciousness: A Book of Readings*. New York: John Wiley and Son, 1969.

Taylor, Brian. "Recollection and Membership: Converts Talk and the Ratiocination of Commonality." *Sociology* 12 (1978): 316–23.

Taylor, Charles. *Sources of the Self: The Making of the Modern Identity*. Cambridge: Harvard University Press, 1989.

Taylor, John H. *Death and the Afterlife in Ancient Egypt*. Chicago: University of Chicago Press, 2001.

Temporini, H. *Die Frauen am Hofe Trajans*. Berlin, New York: de Gruyter, 1978.

Tescher, Robert C. "A Theory of Charismatic Leadership." *Daedalus: Journal of the American Academy of Arts and Sciences* (Summer 1968): 73–74.

Thinh, Ngo Duc. "Len Dong: Spirits' Journeys." Pp. 252–72 in *Vietnam: Journeys of Body, Mind, and Spirit*. Ed. Nguyen Van Huy and Laurel Kendall. University of California Press, American Museum of Natural History, Vietnam Museum of Ethnology, 2003.

Tigay, Jeffrey. *The Evolution of the Gilgamesh Epic*. Philadelphia: University of Pennsylvania Press, 1982.

———, ed. *Empirical Models for Biblical Criticism*. Philadelphia: University of Pennsylvania Press, 1985.

Tillich, Paul. *Systematic Theology*. 3 vols. Chicago: University of Chicago Press, 1951.

———. *The Courage to Be*. New Haven: Yale University Press. 1952. 2d ed. 2000.

———. *The Dynamics of Faith*. New York: Harper, 1958.

Tippet, Sarah. "Scientist Says Mind Continues after Brain Dies." *America Online*, 4 July 2001.

Toorn, Karel van der. "The Nature of the Biblical Traphim in the Light of the Cuneiform Evidence." *CBQ* 52 (1990): 203–22.

———. *Family Religion in Babylonia, Syria, and Israel: Continuity and Change in the Forms of Religious Life*. Leiden: Brill, 1996.

Toynbee, Jocelyn C. M. *Death and Burial in the Roman World*. Baltimore: Johns Hopkins University Press, 1971.

Toynbee, Joclyn C. M., and John Ward Perkins. *The Shrine of St. Peter and the Vatican Excavations*. London: Longmans, Green and Co., 1956.

Trinkhaus, K. Maurer. "Mortuary Ritual and Mortuary Remains." *Current Anthropology* 25.5 (1984).

Trumbower, J. A. *Rescue for the Dead: The Posthumous Salvation of Non-Christians in Early Christianity*. New York: Oxford University Press, 2001.

Tsukimoto, Akio. *Untersuchungen zur Totenplege (Kispum) in Alten Mesopotamien*. Neukirchen-Vluyn: Neukirchener, 1985.

Turner, Victor. *The Ritual Process: Structure and Anti-Structure*. Symbol, Myth, and Ritual Series. Ithaca: Cornell University Press, 1969.

———. *Dramas, Fields, and Metaphors: Symbolic Action in Human Society*. Symbol, Myth, and Ritual Series. Ithaca and London: Cornell University Press, 1974.

Ulansey, David. "The Heavenly Veil Torn: Mark's Cosmic 'Inclusio.' " *JBL* 110:1 (1991): 123–25.

———. "The Transfiguration, Cosmic Symbolism, and the Transformation of Consciousness in the Gospel of Mark." Paper presented at SBL meeting, 1996.

———. *The Origins of the Mithraic Mysteries: Cosmology and Salvation in the Ancient World*. New York: Oxford University Press, 1989.

Underhill, Evelyn. *Mysticism: A Study in the Nature and Development of Man's Spiritual Consciousness*. 1911. Reprint. New York: E. P. Dutton, 1961.

Urbach, Efraim Elimelech. *The Sages: Their Concepts and Beliefs*. 2 vols. Jerusalem: Magnes, 1972 (Hebrew). Trans. Israel Abrahams. Cambridge: Harvard University Press, 1975.

———. *The Sages: The World and Wisdom of the Rabbis of the Talmud*. Trans. Israel Abrahams. Cambridge: Harvard University Press, 1987.

———. "The Sages." *EJ* 14.

Vaage, Leif, and Vincent Wimbush. *Asceticism and the New Testament*. New York: Routledge, 1999.

827

Valantasis, Richard. *The Gospel of Thomas*. London and New York: Routledge, 1997.

———. *Spiritual Guides of the Third Century: A Semiotic Study of the Guide-Disciple Relationship in Christianity, Neoplatonism, Hermetism, and Gnosticism*. Harvard Dissertations in Religion. Minneapolis: Fortress Press, 1991.

van der Horst, P. W. "Moses' Throne Vision in Ezekiel the Dramatist." *JJS* 34 (1983): 21–29.

———. "Some Notes on the Exagoge of Ezekiel the Dramatist." *Mnemosyne* 37 (1984): 354–75.

———. *Ancient Jewish Epitaphs: An Introductory Survey of a Millennium of Jewish Funerary Epigrapy (330 BCE–700 CE)*. Kampen, Netherlands: Kok Pharos Publishing, 1991.

VanderKam, James C. "Righteous One, Messiah, Chosen One, and Son of Man in 1 Enoch 37–71." Pp. 169–91 in *The Messiah: Developments in Earliest Judaism and Christianity*. Ed. James Charlesworth, James Brownson, et al. Minneapolis: Augsburg-Fortress, 1992.

———. *Enoch: A Man for All Generations*. Columbia: University of South Carolina Press, 1995.

Van Dijk, Jacobus. "Myth and Mythmaking in Ancient Egypt." *CANE* 3.

van Henten, J. W. *Die Entstehung der jüdischen Martyrologie*. Leiden: Brill, 1989.

van Henten, J. W., and M. de Jonge. "Datierung und Herkunft des vierten Makkabaerbuches." *Tradition and Reinterpretation in Jewish and Early Christian Literature: Essays in Honor of J. C. H. Lebram*. Leiden: Brill, 1986.

van Hooff, A. *From Autothanasia to Suicide: Self Killing in Classical Antiquity*. London, 1990.

van Unnik, W. C. "The Newly Discovered Gnostic 'Epistle to Rheginos' on the Resurrection." *Journal of Ecclesiastic History* 15 (1964): 141–43, 153–55.

Vermaseren, M. J. *Mithras: The Secred God*. New York, 1963.

Viswanathan, Gauri. *Outside the Fold: Conversion, Modernity, and Belief*. Princeton: Princeton University Press, 1998.

Vogt, Karl. " 'Becoming Male:' A Gnostic and Early Christian Metaphor." Pp. 170–86 in *The Image of God: Gender Models in Judaeo-Christian Tradition*. Ed. Kari Elisabeth Børresen. Minneapolis: Fortress, 1995.

von Baudissen, Wolf W. G. *Adonis und Esmun: Eine Untersuchung zur Geschichte des Glaubens an Auferstehungsgötter und an Heilgötter*. Leipzig: J. C. Hinrich, 1911.

von Campenhausen, Hans. *Ecclesiastical Authority and Spiritual Power*. Trans. J. A. Baker. London, 1969.

Waitz, H. "Das Problem des Sog. Aposteldecrets." *Zeitschrift für Kirchengeschichte*, 1936.

Waldman, Marilyn. "Eschatology in Islam." *ER* 5.

Walker, Evan Harris. *The Physics of Consciousness: The Quantum Mind and the Meaning of Life*. New York: Perseus Books, 2000.

Walker, Susan, ed. *Ancient Faces: Mummy Portraits from Roman Egypt*. New York: Routledge and the Metropolitan Museum of Art, 2000.

Wallace, Anthony F. C. "Revitalization Movements." *American Anthropologist* 58 (1956): 264–81.

———. *The Death and Rebirth of the Seneca*. New York: Vantage Books, 1969.

Walls, Jerry L. *Hell: The Logic of Damnation*. Notre Dame: University of Notre Dame Press, 1992.

———. *Heaven: The Logic of Eternal Joy*. New York: Oxford University Press, 2002.

Warraq, Ibn. "Studies on Muhammad and the Rise of Islam: A Critical Survey." Pp. 15–88 in *The Quest for the Historical Muhammad*. Ed. and trans. Ibn Warraq. Amherst, NY: Prometheus Books, 2000.

Wass, Hannelore, and Robert A. Neimeyer, eds. *Dying: Facing the Facts*. New York: McGraw-Hill, 1979. 3d ed. Bristol, PA: Taylor and Francis, 1995.

Wasserstrom, Steven M. *Between Muslim and Jew: The Problem of Symbiosis Under Early Islam*. Princeton: Princeton University Press, 1995.

Wasson, R. Gordon, and Carl A. P. Ruck. *Persephone's Quest: Entheogens and Origins of Religion*. New Haven: Yale University Press, 1988.

Wasson, R. Gordon, Carl A. P. Ruck, and Albert Hofmann. *The Road to Eleusis: Unveiling the Secret of the Mysteries*. New York: Harcourt, Brace Jovanovich, 1978.

Webster, Jane S. *Ingesting Jesus: Eating and Drinking in the Gospel of John*. Atlanta: SBL, 2003.

Wedderburn, A. J. M. "The Problem of Denial of the Resurrection in 1 Corinthians 15." *Novum Testamentum* 23 (1981): 229–41.

Weinberg, J. P. "Bemerkungen zum Problem 'Der Vorhellenismus in Vorderen Orient." *Klio* 58 (1976).

Weiner, Eugene, and Anita Weiner. *The Martyr's Conviction*. BJS 203. Atlanta: Scholar's Press, 1990.

West, E. W., trans. "Pahlavi Texts." *Sacred Books of the East*. Vols. 5, 18. Ed. F. Max Mueller. New York: Charles Scribner's Sons, 1879–94.

Whitehead, A. N., The Making of Religion. Cambridge, 1927.

Widengren, G. *The Ascension of the Apostle and the Heavenly Book*. Uppsala and Wiesbaden: A.-B. Lundequistska Bokhandeln and Otto Harrassowitz, 1950.

———. *Muhammad, the Apostle of God, and His Ascension*. Uppsala and Wiesbaden: A.-B. Lundequistska Bokhandeln and Otto Harrassowitz, 1955.

———. *Religionsphänomenologie*. Berlin: Walter de Gruyter, 1969.

Wildberger, Hans, ed. *Isaiah 13–27*. Trans. Thomas H. Trapp. A Continental Commentary. Minneapolis: Fortress Press, 1997.

Wiley, Tatha. *Original Sin: Origins, Developments, Contemporary Meanings.* Mahwah, NJ: Paulist Press, 2002.

Wilson, John A. "Egypt." *Before Philosophy: The Intellectual Adventure of Ancient Man An Edday on Speculative Though in the Ancient Near East.* Ed. H. Grankfort, H. A. Grankfort, et al. Baltimore: Penguin Books, 1946.

———. *The Culture of Ancient Egypt.* Chicago: University of Chicago Press, 1951.

Wilson, Steven. *The Gentiles and the Gentile Mission.* Cambridge: Cambridge University Press, 1974.

Wimbush, Vincent L., ed. *Ascetic Behavior in Greco-Roman Antiquity.* Minneapolis: Fortress, 1990.

Wink, Walter. *The Human Being: Jesus and the Enigma of the Son of Man.* Minneapolis: Fortress Press, 2002.

Winkelman, Michael. *Shamanism: The Neural Ecology of Consciousness and Healing.* Westport, CT: Bergin and Garvey, 2000.

Witherington, Ben III. *Jesus the Seer: The Progress of Prophecy.* Peabody, MA: Hendrickson, 1999.

Wolfe, Michael, and the producers of Beliefnet, eds. *Taking Back Islam: American Muslims Reclaim Their Faith.* Rodale, 2002. Distributed by St. Martin's Press, New York.

Wolfson, Elliot R. "Mysticism and the Poetic-Liturgical Compositions from Qumran: A Response to Bilhah Nitzan." *JQR 85* (1994): 185–202.

———. *Through a Speculum That Shines: Vision and Imagination in Medieval Jewish Mysticism.* Princeton: Princeton University Press, 1995.

Wolfson, Harry Austryn. *Philo: Foundations of Religious Philosophy in Judaism, Christianity, and Islam.* Cambridge: Harvard University Press, 1968.

Worsley, Peter. *The Trumpet Shall Sound: A Study of "Cargo Cults" in Melanesia.* New York: Schocken, 1968.

Wright, David P. *Ritual in Narrative: The Dynamics of Feasting, Mourning, and Retalliation Rites in the Ugaritic Tale of Aqhat.* Winona Lake, IN: Eisenbrauns, 2001.

Wright, G. Ernest. *The Old Testament Against Its Environment.* London: SCM Press, 1950.

Wright, N. T. *The Resurrection of the Son of God.* Minneapolis: Fortress, 2003.

Xella, Paolo. "Death and the Afterlife in Canaanite and Hebrew Thought." *CANE* 3: 2063.

Y, La Cong. "The Perilous Journey of the *Then* Spirit Army: A Shamanic Ritual of the Tay People." Pp. 238–51 in *Vietnam: Journeys of Body, Mind, and Spirit.* Ed. Nguyen Van Huy and Laurel Kendall. University of California Press, American Museum of Natural History, Vietnam Museum of Ethnology, 2003.

Yassif, Eli. *The Sacrifice of Isaac: Studies in the Development of a Literary Tradition.* Jerusalem: Makor, 1978 (Hebrew).

Zaehner, Robert Charles. *Zurvan: A Zoroastrian Dilemma.* Oxford: Clarendon Press, 1956. Reprint, with intro. by A. F. Segal. New York: Biblo and Tannen, 1972.

———. *The Dawn and Twilight of Zoroastrianism.* The Putnam History of Religion. New York: Putnam, 1961.

———. *Hinduism and Muslim Mysticism.* New York: Schocken, 1969.

———. *The Teachings of the Magi: A Compendium of Zoroastrian Reliefs.* New York: Oxford University Press, 1976.

Zaleski, Carol. *Otherworld Journeys: Accounts of Near-Death Experience in Medieval and Modern Times.* New York: Oxford University Press, 1987.

———. *Near-Death Experience and Christian Hope: The Life of the World to Come.* New York: Oxford University Press, 1996.

Zaleski, Carol, and Philip Zaleski. *The Book of Heaven: An Anthology of Writings from Ancient to Modern Times.* New York: Oxford University Press, 2000.

Zehnle, Richard. *Peter's Pentecost Discourse.* Nashville: Abingdon Press, 1971.

Zeitlin, Solomon. "Dreams and Their Interpretation from the Biblical Period to the Tannaitic Time: A Historical Study." *JQR* 66 (1975–76): 1–18.

Zimmerli, Walther. "Ezekiel 2: A Commentary on the Book of the Prophet Ezekiel Chapters 25–48." *A Critical and Historical Commentary on the Bible.* Trans. James D. Martin Hermeneia. Philadelphia: Fortress, 1984.

F

127, 159–60, 169, 662; Zoroastrian
    dualism, 178–80
Montanism, 556, 570
Montefiore, C. G., 597–98
Moorish Spain, 669, 675, 693
moral function of afterlife: Adam and
    Even story and knowledge of good
    and evil, 168; Christianity, 529;
    Classical world, 235, 247 529;
    covenant between God and Israelites,
    169–70; Egypt, 60–62; Enoch
    literature, 280; *Isaiah, Ascension of,*
    503; Islam, 653; late antique tours of
    hell, 488; Philo Judaeus, 372–73;
    Plato, 235; Zoroastrianism, 186
"moral majority," 684–85
Morenz, Siegfried, 41
Mormonism, 590
mortality. *see* death and mortality
mortuary cults and funerary practices,
    702 (*see also* grave goods; offerings to
    the dead); Canaan, 98, 111, 112,
    115–18; Classical world, 209–10;
    direction taken after death, burial
    practices paralleling, 188; Egypt, 39,
    40, 42–49, 54, 57–58; First Temple
    Judaism, 129, 131–34, 141–42,
    743n.36; Islam, 649–52; Jews can be
    buried everywhere, 491; *masteba*
    tombs, 36–37; Mesopotamia, 75,
    80–81, 91, 96, 97–98; New England
    cemeteries, 44, 351–52; New
    Testament period, 351–53; pyramids,
    27–28, 37–39, 65; tombstones and
    epitaphs, 210, 352–53;
    Zoroastrianism, 187–89
Moses: apocalypticism and
    millenarianism, 305; First Temple
    Judaism, 134; Gospels, 463–64;
    Islam, 640, 648, 655; Jubilees, Book
    of, 353; Paul, 406, 417;
    pseudepigraphic literature, 487–88,
    505, 508, 510–11; Rabbinic Judaism,
    612, 616, 618, 624, 628; Second
    Temple Judaism, 262; Septuagint, 364
Moses (Ezekiel the Tragedian), 510–11
Moses, Testament of, 490–91, 510
Mot, 107, 109, 110, 114, 258, 735n.26
Motley, J. L., 593
Mousterian culture, 15
MT (Masoretic Text), 286, 363–64,
    366, 631
Muhammad (prophet): burial of, 650;
    deification, avoidance of, 648;
    martyrs and holy warriors, 659–60;
    night journey *(mi'raj)* and heavenly

journey of soul, 652–58; revelations
    and development of Islam, 639–47
mujahidin (holy warriors), 659–60, 679
multiculturalism and acculturation,
    709–10, 714–15; American
    multicultural life, 714–15; conversion,
    695; gnosticism, 549; Islam, 670–71,
    692–95; Judaic influences, 174–75,
    280–81, 368, 394; Judaic prohibition
    of idolatry, 124, 127, 169, 257,
    280–81; Philo Judaeus, 369–70;
    Rabbinic Judaism, 198, 603, 634–37,
    709–10; Zoroastrian orthodoxy of
    Sasanian period, 192–94
multiverse *vs.* universe, 122, 160
mummies and embalming, 36–39, 43,
    46, 54, 66
Munkar, 653
Murray-Jones, Christopher, 408–9
Muslim Brotherhood, 673
Muslims. *see* Islam
mut, 45
Mycenaean tombs, 210
mystery religions: Eleusinian mysteries,
    81, 214–18, 221, 519; Hellenistic
    world, 218, 436; Isis cult, 519–20,
    521; journeys to heaven/underworld,
    521–22; late antiquity, 519–22, 529;
    Mithras cult, 520–21; Nag Hammadi
    texts, 552; Paul, 436
mysticism (*see also* Hekhaloth
    Literature; Merkabah mysticism):
    American religious belief, 14;
    apocalypticism and millenarianism,
    296, 298, 304, 410–12, 507; defined,
    507; Egypt, 27, 64, 67–68; Fana,
    664–66; Hellenistic world, 221; Islam,
    653–54, 662–66; Kabbalah, 266, 410,
    415, 507, 514; Mesopotamia and
    Canaan, 103, 118; neurology and,
    333–36; New Testament period,
    358–60, 370, 372, 392; Paul, 405,
    407–16, 421, 431, 511; Peter, Gospel
    of, 535; Rabbinic Judaism, 470, 472,
    473, 475, 619, 622, 629–32, 638;
    RISCs, 332, 333–36, 339, 345, 349;
    Second Temple Judaism, 266, 274;
    Shi'a mystics, 662–64; *Therapeutai*
    (Healers), 296; Thomas, Gospel of,
    470, 472, 473, 475, 476; Valentinus'
    interest in, 546; "white martyrs" in
    Islam, mystics as, 638, 664
mythology: Canaan, 106–9; Egypt, 29,
    33–36, 39–43; Judaism and Bible's
    lack of, 121–23, 158; Mesopotamia,
    72–74, 79–82

853

Resurrection of the body (*cont.*)
flesh and spirit, 569–70; Valentinian
gnosticism, 553; Zoroastrianism,
184–85
*Reuyoth Yehezkel (The Visions of
Ezekiel)*, 413
Revelations (Apocalypse of John),
189, 191, 467, 481–86, 494, 518,
683
revitalization movements, 309, 311–12
revivification/resuscitation: First Temple
Judaism, 145–46; Isaac, sacrifice of,
637–38; Odysseus' journey to Hades,
212; Rabbinic Judaism, 606–7, 619;
Septuagint, 364
reward and punishment: Baruch
literature, 496–97; delay of *parousia*,
490, 651; Hekhaloth literature,
516–17; *Isaiah, Ascension of*, 502–3;
Islam, 651–52, 664; late antique tours
of hell, 487–89; Rabbinic Judaism,
601, 609–14, 628, 631
Rhadamanthys, 206, 210, 244
Rheginus, Epistle to, 553
RISCs. *see* religiously interpreted/altered
states of consciousness (RISCs and
RASCs)
ritual prostitution, 84, 92, 108, 118,
280
Roberts, J. J. M., 148
Rohde, Eric, 208, 340–41
Romans, 240–47 (*see also* Hellenistic
world; New Testament period);
animus (soul), 208; Antiochus IV
Epiphanes, 288; burial practices, 210;
Christianization of empire, 177, 525;
Egypt, 63–65; Epicureans, 221–23,
224, 368, 378, 385–86, 609; Esau as
type for, 629; Essenes tortured by,
303, 382; First Jewish Revolt against
Rome, 383, 486, 493, 605; gardens
and gardening, 377–78; Josephus,
298–301, 375, 380; multiculturalism
and religious diversity, 192; pagan
revival, 525–27, 529–31; patriotism
and the state, 240–42; Plutarch, 39,
217, 245–47; political/economic
deprivation and resistance to, 317,
362–63; Qumran community, end of,
320–21; Revelations, 484; rulers,
divinity of, 219, 240–42, 245–47;
Second Jewish Revolt (Bar Kokhba
Revolt) against Rome, 196, 491, 605;
Second Temple destroyed by, 276;
Stoicism, 223, 224, 249, 368, 372,
378, 385–86, 568, 570–71, 574; :The

Ten Martyrs" and Bar Kokhba revolt,
196; Vergil, 242–45
Romans, Paul's letter to, 403, 405, 416,
420, 421, 431, 434–35, 436, 438, 540
romantic love. *see* love
Romeo and Juliet (Shakespeare), 727,
729
Romulus, 241–42
Rosh Hashanah, 262
Rowland, Christopher, 338
ruaḥ, ruḥ, 113, 116, 117, 142–45, 156,
651–52
rulers, divinity of, 219, 240–42, 245–47

S

Sabeans as "people of the book," 646
sacredness of afterlife concepts, 19–21
Sadducees, 253, 281, 298–300, 317,
367, 376–79, 384, 478
saints (*see also* names of individual
saints): Crusades, 669; Elijah
compared, 634; theurgist
counterclaims, 529
Saladin, 669
Saler, Benson, 721
Samael, 179, 497, 560, 561
Samaria and Samaritans, 105, 355, 413,
510, 512, 663
1 Samuel, 102, 125, 144, 145, 363, 364,
611, 622
2 Samuel, 162, 207, 248, 363
Samuel the prophet, 211 (*see also* Saul
and the witch of Endor)
Sanders, Seth, 101
Sanhedrin, 326
Sanskrit, 176, 178, 187, 745n.16
Sar Torah, 349
sarcophagi, 141, 190, 210
Sasanian period, 177, 192–94, 198, 615,
641
Satan. *see* Devil and hell
satire, 408, 599
Saudi Arabia, 640, 669, 672, 678, 680,
681, 689
Saul, 504
Saul and the witch of Endor, 124–26;
ancestor cults and divine beings,
130–31; Deuteronomic
pronouncements against necromancy
and conjuring, 125, 126–30; *Maqlu*
ritual, 102; *marzeaḥ* feasts, 131, 133;
Sheol, root meaning of, 135–36
Schaefer, Peter, 413, 513
Schechem, 500–501
Scholem, Gershom, 413, 512–14